✛ Our Sunday Visitor's ✛

ENCYCLOPEDIA
OF
CATHOLIC HISTORY

Matthew Bunson

Illustrated by Margaret Bunson
Foreword by
Archbishop Oscar H. Lipscomb

Our Sunday Visitor Publishing Division
Our Sunday Visitor, Inc.
Huntington, Indiana 46750

*This book is dedicated to
His Excellency, Bishop John J. Scanlan,
retired Bishop of Honolulu.*

The eternal Shepherd and Guardian of our souls, in order to make lasting the saving work of redemption, chose to establish his Holy Church so that in it, as in the house of the living God, all of the faithful might be held together by the bond of one faith and one love. For this reason, before he was glorified, he prayed to the Father not for the Apostles only, but for those also who would believe in him on their testimony, that all might be one as he, the Son, and the Father are one.

Vatican Council I, *First Dogmatic Constitution on the Church of Christ* (July 18, 1870)

The Catholic Church has been established by Jesus Christ as Mother and Teacher of all nations, so that all who in the course of centuries come to her loving embrace, may find salvation as well as the fullness of a more excellent life. To this Church, "the pillar and mainstay of truth," her most holy Founder has entrusted the double task of begetting sons unto herself and of educating and governing those whom she begets, guiding with maternal providence the life both of individuals and of people.

Pope John XXIII, *Mater et Magistra* (May 15, 1961)

TABLE OF CONTENTS

Foreword

"If it is true that history turns our gaze towards the past, it is equally true that history . . . reveals the present more than the past; it shows us what has been, in order to enable us to foresee what must and will come to pass in the future; it confidently projects the life of the Church into the future" (*Paul VI: The First Modern Pope*, by Peter Hebblethwaite). These words from a lecture on Church history given by the future Pope Paul VI in 1951 give a broad context for the publication of *Our Sunday Visitor's Encyclopedia of Catholic History*.

This single volume has been crafted to give easy and instant access to a wide range of material encompassing two millennia of faith voyaging, and faith voyagers, to our own time on the journey. For Catholics it offers a sense of connectedness with the events, persons, and ideas that will help them to a greater understanding of their own identity. For others such specifics are here available to shed light on a religious phenomenon whose influence has deeply touched, and often defined, our common history for twenty centuries.

Designed for the average reader who has a particular need or general interest in Catholic history, the *Encyclopedia* undertakes to present historical and theological issues, even the more complex, in a way that satisfies initial inquiry and invites further study. The brief chronology makes it possible for a user to situate subjects within the flow of time, which necessarily conditions their comprehension. Of special advantage are the appendices, notable among them, the "Documents of Vatican Council II" and the "Writings of Pope John Paul II." The Catholic Church in the present age cannot be studied in a serious and effective fashion without access to such sources.

Our Sunday Visitor has done a considerable service to the quality of life in Catholic households in this user-friendly resource. Libraries, offices, and schools, any information source serving the public, will find the *Encyclopedia* to be an asset in the task of offering clear, concise, accurate, and current data on Catholic history. Its compact format should make the work an easy and appropriate acquisition for every Catholic classroom at the middle and high school level — as essential a tool for young learners as the dictionary.

In its own way, the *Encyclopedia* fulfills a role in Catholic history analogous to that of the dictionary in the use of language. Just as is true of words and their usage, so the facts, faces, and events of history must be seen in relationship and juxtaposed to each other to express that meaning which conveys the reality of the past in a way that does it justice. Those who seek to know the past by less complete or accurate means do an injustice to the present and imperil the future.

As Monsignor Montini observed in mid-century, Catholic history "reveals the present more than the past." In so doing, history serves us in ways that are unique to the human condition. But, as the future pope went on to note, history enables us "to foresee what must and will come to pass in the future." Projection into the future does not necessarily imply determination, but it is in keeping with the specific endowments of intellect and will that have entrusted the future to our care. This *Encyclopedia* offers the reassurance from the past that in such a task we are by no means alone.

OSCAR H. LIPSCOMB
ARCHBISHOP OF MOBILE
January 30, 1995

Editorial Consultant's Remarks

"Those who know nothing about what happened before they were born will always remain a baby." It sounds better in the original Latin, but Cicero's famous dictum is forever true. Pope John XXIII called history "the great teacher," realizing that the most effective way of surveying the present and looking into the future is on the shoulders of the past.

A knowledge of history is important for any person concerned about the political, social, and cultural perplexities of life. Only those ignorant of history, for instance, would be surprised by the present tragic tension in the Balkans or the Middle East. However, for a believer, a Christian, a Catholic, history takes on an even more critical importance, for we belong to a Church that sees nothing less than the hand of God in two millennia of popes and prayers, councils and needs, missionaries and martyrs, preachers and persecutions, crusades and cardinals, sacraments and saints, all and more making up the most colorful history around that of the Catholic Church. As Lord Macaulay, hardly a defender of things Catholic, said of the Church, "There is not and there never was on this earth a work of human policy so well deserving of examination. . . ."

Anyone so desirous of improving one's knowledge and appreciation of the Church's history will join me in welcoming this useful, compact yet thorough encyclopedia by Matthew Bunson. From St. Peter to Karl Rahner, from Pentecost to Vatican Council II, it's all here.

Those who just enjoy browsing and picking out certain entries, or those who need helpful explanations of terms or names, will find this book most enlightening. And those who spend time over these pages will receive, not just data and information, but an added bonus: a sense of serenity when contemplating the myriad of problems of the present; for, simply put, the Church has been through it all before.

As the late John Tracy Ellis cautioned those who ignored Church history: "They will lose a firm foundation on which to rest their confidence that the encircling gloom of the present hour will in due time lift, as it has so many times before, and there will open upon them a bright ray of hope that will help carry them through their present unease."

Rev. Msgr. Timothy M. Dolan, Ph.D.
Rector, Pontifical North American College, Rome

Introduction

Our Sunday Visitor's Encyclopedia of Catholic History is intended to offer for the first time a comprehensive, single-volume "A to Z" compendium on the vast panorama of the Church's past, from the Pentecost to the reign of Pope John Paul II. While the book has been researched utilizing the enormous body of historical writings and studies available to the modern writer, it is offered first and foremost for the use of the general reader and with the objective of presenting the often complex and intricately interwoven issues and events that have occurred in the historical life of the faith in a style that is accessible, easily consulted, and, hopefully, interesting. In the several thousand entries within this work, the reader will find all of the important, significant, and memorable topics, issues, and crises that have confronted the Church, as well as the saints, pontiffs, theologians, philosophers, kings, queens, political and literary figures, and the social, economic, intellectual, and spiritual movements that have influenced and shaped the Church throughout its rise to prominence within the Roman Empire, its role in forging the Christian civilization of the West, and its ongoing mission of bringing the light of salvation to all the corners of the world. Above all, this book has been written in the spirit of Pope Paul VI's words that "The Church is an offering of truth, placating and saving. It is the road sign in the history of mankind, it is the outstretched hand of redemption and happiness"; and the declaration of St. Irenaeus that "Just as God's creation, the sun, is one and the same the world over, so too does the Church's preaching shine everywhere to enlighten all who wish to come to a knowledge of the truth."

In the preparation of this encyclopedia literally hundreds of different sources were consulted, ranging from encyclopedias and dictionaries, to atlases, histories, studies, periodicals, journals, and collections, not to mention the staggering corpus of writings encompassing the entire literary, theological, and philosophical legacy of the Church. Especially valuable were the collections of writings and decrees promulgated by the popes, councils, synods, saints, and theologians, and the interpretational and analytical studies on the writings themselves. A small number of the more valuable sources used includes: the *Enchiridion Symbolorum*; the *Patrologia Latina*; the *Liber Pontificalis*; *The Papal Encyclicals* by Claudia Carlen, I.H.M.; *The Catechism of the Catholic Church*; *Our Sunday Visitor's Catholic Encyclopedia* and *Dictionary*; *The Catholic Encyclopedia* by Robert C. Broderick; *The Atlas of the Christian World*; *The Catholic Encyclopedia*; the *New Catholic Encyclopedia*; *The Cambridge Ancient History*; *The Cambridge Medieval History*; *The Oxford Dictionary of the Christian Church*; *The Cambridge Modern History*; *The Dictionary of Christian Biography*; and *The Oxford*

Classical Dictionary. Two other important sources are mentioned on the copyright page of this work.

As this book covers a time period stretching across some two thousand years of human history, it naturally is concerned with varying epochs and wide-ranging cultural environments. Concomitant with these concerns are the multiplicities of dates and names that will be encountered throughout the text. Whenever possible, the dates of events have been based upon the most reliable scholarship available, but many periods, such as the earliest time of the formative Church, have dates that remain uncertain or subject to speculation and even disagreement among sources and experts. It is therefore likely that readers who go on to other readings or who already are familiar with the eras in question will find alternative or more approximate dates in other sources. Spellings, likewise, have been based on the most commonly accepted ones by scholars or on those that appear most often in popular usage. In this case, the use of the index and the cross-referencing throughout the book may prove beneficial when searching for a particular individual or subject. While unusual for an encyclopedia, an index has also been included in order to facilitate ease of consultation and to provide swift access to broad subjects with a host of related entries.

Finally, there are a great many persons to whom a special debt of gratitude is owed for their kind assistance during the writing of this book: Msgr. Paul Lenz, head of the American Bureau of Catholic Indians, for his support of the project; Msgr. Timothy Dolan, currently rector of the North American College, for very kindly taking the time from his busy schedule to serve as editorial consultant; Bob Lockwood (OSV's president and publisher), Greg Erlandson (editor in chief), and the board of directors of Our Sunday Visitor for their confidence and faith that this project would meet all of their hopes and expectations; Jackie Lindsey (acquisitions editor), for her vision, trust, and encouragement; Henry O'Brien (managing editor of religious books) and his staff for their tireless work in editing, copy-editing, and bringing to published life a manuscript of nearly three thousand pages, and most of all for their patience; Margaret Bunson for the magnificent illustrations; Stephen Bunson for his help throughout; and the staffs of several libraries, in particular the staff of Sahara West Library.

MATTHEW BUNSON

Chronology

c. 33 The Pentecost; death of St. Stephen.

c. 34 Conversion of Paul of Tarsus.

c. 49 Council of Jerusalem.

64 Persecution of Christians in Rome under Emperor Nero.

64 or 67 Martyrdom of St. Peter.

70 Destruction of the Great Temple of Jerusalem by Titus.

88-97 Pontificate of St. Clement I.

95 Persecution of Christians in Rome under Emperor Domitian.

c. 100 Death of St. John; end of the Apostolic Age.

c. 107 Martyrdom of St. Ignatius of Antioch.

c. 117-138 Persecutions under Emperor Hadrian.

c. 144 Excommunication of Marcion.

202 Persecution under Emperor Septimius Severus.

249-251 Persecutions under Emperor Trajanus Decius.

c. 254 Death of Origen.

257 Persecutions under Emperor Valerian.

284-305 Reign of Emperor Diocletian.

311 Edict of Toleration.

313 Edict of Milan.

314 Council of Arles.

325 Council of Nicaea.

337 Death of Constantine the Great.

361-363 Reign of Emperor Julian the Apostate.

381 First Council of Constantinople.

410 Sack of Rome by the Visigoths.

430 Death of St. Augustine.

431 Council of Ephesus.

449 Robber Council of Ephesus (Latrocinium).

451 Council of Chalcedon.

452 Invasion of the West by the Huns under Attila the Hun; Rome is spared through Pope St. Leo I.

455 Sack of Rome by the Vandals.

476 End of the Roman Empire in the West.

496 Conversion of Clovis, king of the Franks.

553 Second Council of Constantinople.

589 Third Council of Toledo.

590-604 Pontificate of St. Gregory I the Great.

622 The *Hegira* of Muhammad from Mecca to Medina.

664 Synod of Whitby.

680-681 Third Council of Constantinople.

692 Trullan Synod.

711 Conquest of Spain by the Muslims.

726 Beginning of the Iconoclast Controversy.

787 Second Council of Nicaea.

800 Crowning of Charlemagne by Pope Leo III.

843 Treaty of Verdun brings the division of the Frankish Empire.

846 Pillage of St. Peter's and St. Paul's in Rome by the Saracens.

869-870 Fourth Council of Constantinople.

910 Founding of Cluny.

962 Coronation of Emperor Otto I the Great.

997 St. Stephen becomes king of Hungary.

1009 Rupture between the Eastern and Western Churches.

1054 Final rupture of the Eastern and Western Churches.

1066 Norman conquest of England.

1073-1085 Pontificate of St. Gregory VII.

1095 Call for the First Crusade by Pope Urban II.

1099 Capture of Jerusalem by the Crusaders.

1115 Founding of Clairvaux.

1122 Concordat of Worms.

1123 First Lateran Council.

1139 Second Lateran Council.

1170 Murder of St. Thomas Becket in Canterbury Cathedral.

1198-1216 Pontificate of Innocent III.

1204 Fourth Crusade; capture of Constantinople by the crusaders.

1209 Approval given for the Franciscan order.

1216 Approval given for the Dominican order.

1231 Founding of the Inquisition.

1274 Second Council of Lyons; brief reunion of the Eastern and Western Churches.

1291 Fall of Acre to the Mamelukes; end of the Crusader States in the Holy Land.

1309-1377 Avignon papacy.

1337 Start of the Hundred Years' War; it will end in 1453.

1347-1350 The Black Death ravages Europe.

1377 Return of the popes to Avignon.

1378 Start of the Great Schism; it will end in 1417.

1409 Council of Pisa.

1414-1418 Council of Constance; end of the Great Schism with the election of Pope Martin V.

1431 Execution of St. Joan of Arc.

1431-1445 Council of Ferrara-Florence.

1453 Fall of Constantinople; end of the Byzantine Empire.

1492 Conquest of Granada and end of the *Reconquista* in Spain; Columbus reaches the New World.

1512-1517 Fourth Lateran Council.

1517 Posting of the ninety-five theses by Martin Luther; beginning of the Protestant Reformation.

1530 Issue of the Augsburg Confession.

1533 Excommunication of King Henry VIII of England.

1540 Approval of the Society of Jesus (Jesuits).

1545-1563 The Council of Trent.

1558-1603 Reign of Queen Elizabeth I of England.

1570 Excommunication of Queen Elizabeth.

1571 Battle of Lepanto.

1582 Issue of the Gregorian calendar.

1588 Defeat of the Spanish Armada.

1605 Gunpowder Plot in England.

1613 Catholics are banned from Scandinavia.

1618-1648 Thirty Years' War.

1648 Treaty of Westphalia ends the Thirty Years' War.

1653 Condemnation of Jansenism by Pope Innocent X.

1678 Popish Plot in England.

1682 Issue of the Gallican Articles in France.

1689 Issue of the Toleration Act.

1732 Founding of the Redemptorists.

1773 Suppression of the Jesuits by Pope Clement XIV.

1775 Start of the American Revolution; it will end in 1783.

1789 Start of the French Revolution.

1798 Seizure of Pope Pius VI by the French.

1800-1823 Pontificate of Pope Pius VII.

1801 Concordat with Napoleon Bonaparte.

1804 Crowning of Napoleon as emperor of France.

1808-1809 Annexation of the Papal States and seizure of Pius VII; he will remain a prisoner until 1813.

1814 Restoration of the Society of Jesus.

1815 Final defeat of Napoleon at Waterloo.

1833 Beginnings of the Oxford movement in England.

1846-1878 Pontificate of Pius IX.

1848 Year of revolutions in Europe. Revolution in Rome and flight of Pope Pius IX to Gaeta; he will return in 1850.

1850 Restoration of the hierarchy in England.

1860 Loss of the Papal States.

1864 Issue of the Syllabus of Errors.

1869-1870 First Vatican Council.

1870 End of the temporal power of the papacy with the loss of Rome; end of the *Risorgimento*.

1878-1903 Pontificate of Leo XIII.

1903-1914 Pontificate of St. Pius X.

1914-1918 World War I.

1917 Appearance of Our Lady at Fátima.

1922-1939 Pontificate of Pius XI.

1929 Lateran Treaty settles the Roman Question.

1933 Adolf Hitler becomes chancellor of Germany.

1936-1939 Spanish Civil War.

1937 Issue of the encyclical *Mit brennender Sorge*.

1939-1945 World War II.

1939-1958 Pontificate of Pius XII.

1962-1965 Second Vatican Council.

1963-1978 Pontificate of Paul VI.

1978 Election of Pope John Paul II.

1983 Issue of the Revised Code of Canon Law.

1985 Signing of a new concordat between Italy and the Holy See.

1989-1991 Collapse of Communism and the Soviet Empire in Eastern Europe.

1991 Gulf War.

1994 Formal relations established between the Holy See and Israel.

Abbreviations

AAS: Acta Apostolicae Sedis (Latin for "Acts of the Apostolic See").

A.D.: Anno Domini (Latin for "the Year of Our Lord").

b.: Born.

B.C.: Before Christ.

Bl.: Blessed.

BVM: Blessed Virgin Mary.

c.: Circa.

CCD: Confraternity of Christian Doctrine.

cf.: Confer (Latin for "compare").

ch.: Chapter.

C of E: Church of England.

d.: Died.

d. c.: Died circa.

e.g.: Exempli gratia (Latin for "for example").

fl.: Flourished.

i.e.: Id est (Latin for "that is").

IOR: Instituto per le Opere di Religione (Italian for "Institute for Religious Works").

M.P.: Member of Parliament.

n.d.: No date.

NT: New Testament.

OT: Old Testament.

Ph.D.: Philosophiae doctor (Latin for "doctor of philosophy").

r.: Reigned (or ruled).

Rev.: Reverend.

St. (also S., Sta., Ste.): Saint.

Sts.: Saints.

U.S.: United States.

v.: Verse.

vv.: Verses.

Ven.: Venerable.

vol.: Volume.

vols.: Volumes.

Key to Abbreviations of Biblical Books (In Alphabetical Order)

Old Testament Books

Am — Amos

Bar — Baruch

1 Chr — 1 Chronicles

2 Chr — 2 Chronicles

Dn — Daniel

Dt — Deuteronomy

Eccl — Ecclesiastes

Est — Esther

Ex — Exodus

Ez — Ezekiel

1 Kgs — 1 Kings
2 Kgs — 2 Kings
Lam — Lamentations
Lv — Leviticus
Mal — Malachi
Ezr — Ezra
Gn — Genesis
Hb — Habakkuk
Hg — Haggai
Hos — Hosea
Is — Isaiah
Jer — Jeremiah
Jb — Job
Jdt — Judith
Jgs — Judges
Jl — Joel
Jon — Jonah
Jos — Joshua

1 Mc — 1 Maccabees
2 Mc — 2 Maccabees
Mi — Micah
Na — Nahum
Neh — Nehemiah
Nm — Numbers
Ob — Obadiah
Prv — Proverbs
Ps — Psalms
Ru — Ruth
Sg — Song of Solomon
Sir — Sirach
1 Sm — 1 Samuel
2 Sm — 2 Samuel
Tb — Tobit
Wis — Wisdom
Zec — Zechariah
Zep — Zephaniah

New Testament Books

Acts — Acts of the Apostles
Col — Colossians
1 Cor — 1 Corinthians
2 Cor — 2 Corinthians
Eph — Ephesians
Gal — Galatians
Heb — Hebrews
Jas — James
Jn — John
1 Jn — 1 John
2 Jn — 2 John
3 Jn — 3 John
Jude — Jude
Lk — Luke

Mk — Mark
Mt — Matthew
Phil — Philippians
Phlm — Philemon
1 Pt — 1 Peter
2 Pt — 2 Peter
Rom — Romans
Rv — Revelation
1 Thes — 1 Thessalonians
2 Thes — 2 Thessalonians
Ti — Titus
1 Tm — 1 Timothy
2 Tm — 2 Timothy

A

Abarca, Pedro (1619-1693) ● Spanish Jesuit theologian who taught at the University of Salamanca. Joining the Jesuits (or Society of Jesus) in 1641, he subsequently taught for his remaining years, writing a number of theological treatises and historical works, including the *Annals* of the kings of Aragon.

Abbo, St. (c. 945-1004) ● Also Abbo of Fleury or Abbon, abbot of Fleury. An avid supporter of the Cluniac Reform, he was born near Orléans, eventually entering the Benedictine monastery of Fleury before studying at Paris, Reims, and elsewhere. He assumed control of monastic instruction at the school of Ramsey in 985, a post he held until 987. The following year, he was elected abbot of Fleury. As abbot, Abbo promoted both the Cluniac Reform and the authority of the papacy. Aside from his valued correspondences, Abbo wrote on canon law, mathematics, astronomy, the lives of the popes, and was the author of *Quaestiones Grammaticales* (*Grammatical Questions*). He was killed, probably by accident, while attempting to suppress a riot by monks at La Reole in Gascony, dying in the arms of his disciple Aimoin.

Abelard, Peter (1079-1142 or -1144) ● Controversial philosopher and theologian whose views earned his condemnation by the Church. Born in La Pallet, Brittany, he studied at Tours, Paris, and Laon under some of the foremost intellectuals of the era including Roscelin of Compiègne, William of Champeaux, and Anselm of Tours. While a

brilliant student, he disagreed sharply with many of the views of his instructors, especially William. Abelard brilliantly refuted his ideas on realism. He lectured in theology and philosophy at Paris, gaining such fame that Canon Fulbert of Notre Dame cathedral school asked him to serve as tutor to his niece, Heloise. The two, master and student, soon fell in love and entered into a forbidden affair that resulted in their secret, tragic marriage, the birth of a son (Astrolabe), and Abelard's castration by Heloise's outraged uncle. She fled to Arenteuil, and he went to St.-Denis where he continued to study, authoring his first *Theologia* and *Sic et Non* (*Yes and No*). The views contained in *Theologia* concerning the Trinity were considered so unorthodox that it was probably burned and Abelard condemned without petition at the Council of Soissons (1121). In *Sic et Non*, he further appalled Church officials by collecting various inconsistencies (according to him) in Church teaching. After a brief period of incarceration at St.-Medard, he returned to St.-Denis but soon fled after insulting the monks by questioning the historical validity of the tradition concerning the patron saint. He traveled to Champagne, taught from 1122-1125, and was elected (1125) abbot of St.-Gildas-de-Rhuys in Britanny. Soon, he was forced to leave the monastery owing to a disagreement with the community; he subsequently assisted Heloise in founding a new order of nuns at Quincey, near Troyes, called the Paraclete. Back in Paris by 1136, he resumed teaching, claiming among his pupils John of Salisbury and Arnold of

Brescia. He authored another *Theologia, Scito te ipsum* (*Know Thyself*, or *Ethica*), and *Dialogus inter philosophum, Judaeum, et Christianum* (*Dialogue between a Philosopher, a Jew, and a Christian*). His teachings, while those of a genius, were much opposed by philosophers and orthodox theologians, particularly St. Bernard of Clairvaux, William of St. Thierry, and Hugh of St. Victor. Several propositions were condemned in 1140 at the Council of Sens, and Bernard — who had spearheaded the condemnation — secured its ratification by Pope Innocent II. Peter returned to the sanctuary of Cluny where Peter the Venerable gave him shelter and assistance in being reconciled with the Church. He died at Cluny but was later buried at Pere-Lachaise cemetery, Paris, next to Heloise. His own difficult life was written in the autobiographical *Historia Calamitatum* (*History of My Calamities*).

Abelites ● Also Abelonians, a minor heretical sect in Africa, centered around the diocese of Hippo. They derived their name from Abel, second son of Adam and Eve, placing much importance on marriage. By the time of St. Augustine in the late fourth century, the Abelites had declined considerably and would otherwise be unknown except through St. Augustine's writings.

Abercromby, Robert (1532-1613) ● Also called Robertson, he was a Scottish Jesuit who labored in his homeland during the period of severe Catholic persecutions. He earned considerable notoriety in his day by successfully converting Queen Anne of Denmark, wife of King James VI and the future King James I of England. First introduced into the palace by the broad-minded James, Abercromby received the queen into the Church (c. 1600). In the ardently Protestant kingdom, Abercromby celebrated Mass in secret in the palace and was made more secure by the king by being granted the post of superintendent of the Royal Falconry. His position changed, however, when James became king of England. Abercromby was eventually forced to flee the British Isles, after the Jesuits were supposedly implicated in the Gunpowder Plot. He died in Prussia.

Aberle, Maritz von ● See **Von Aberle, Maritz**.

Abgar, The Legend of ● Tradition, firmly believed by the historian Eusebius, that King Abgar V of Edessa exchanged letters with Christ. While generally rejected in the West, the legend gained immense popularity in the East and has long been accepted as authentic by many. According to tradition, King Abgar fell ill and wrote to Christ asking him to come to Edessa and heal him. The Lord, refusing, nevertheless told him that after his ascension, he would send one of his disciples to bring relief to the king and to preach the Gospel. According to Eusebius, Thaddaeus was subsequently sent by St. Thomas to Edessa. He healed the king and converted many people in the city. Another story, preserved in the *Pilgrimage of Etheria*, says that the letter from Christ, written in Syriac, was preserved at Edessa, and that the reputed copies have powerful, miraculous effects. Later additions told that Christ also sent his own portrait, miraculously imprinted on a canvas. Another variation on the story was recounted in the *Doctrine of Addai*.

Abortion ● Considered in Catholic morality to be direct and indirect expulsion of a human fetus. It is one of the most severe moral issues facing the Church in the twentieth century and one in which its teaching — especially as emphasized by Vatican Council II — has been remarkably consistent from the earliest days in condemning "abortion and infanticide" as "unspeakable crimes" (*Gaudium et Spes*, No. 51). Two kinds of abortion are recognized.

Indirect abortion is the morally permissible evacuation of a fetus that cannot survive outside of the womb or as part of a morally permissible and entirely legitimate medical procedure, the side effect or regrettable result of which is to render the fetus inviable. Direct abortion is the intended destruction of a fetus, viewed as an end in itself or as a means to an end. The direct abortion, regardless of method (spuriously described as anesthetic, or painless), is always a grave medical evil with no possible justification; its sinfulness is compounded by the fact that the unborn child is utterly defenseless and completely innocent, entirely dependent upon the mother who is bearing it and the father who helped conceive it. Beyond even this terrible murdering of the fetus, abortion's malign influence can be seen in the women who had the procedure performed, as is clear in the medical effects that range from sterility, hemorrhaging, and infection to lasting and permanent emotional and psychological damage.

There is a vast and entirely consistent body of teachings throughout Church history on the question of abortion, never changing in its moral certitude that it is a grave sin and that there is an important interconnectedness between abortion, contraception, and sterilization. Abortion is the murder of innocent life, contraception is the willingness to participate in the creation of an atmosphere leading to murder, and sterilization is the deliberate denial of the potentiality of life. The *Didache* (i.e., *The Teaching of the Twelve Apostles*), dating to the first century, stated clearly, "You shall not procure an abortion. You shall not destroy a newborn." Numbers of Church Fathers, saints, and theologians from that time have only served to reinforce that declaration, making their appeals and exhortation within the structure of their eras and in the face of the specific theological or moral needs of the location. A few of the early writers were Athenagoras, Clement of Alexandria, Epiphanius of Salamis, John Chrysostom, Augustine, and Cyril of Alexandria. The first formal laws with defined punishments were passed in 572 at the Council of Braga (Canon 77) under St. Martin of Braga.

The modern popes have been outspoken in their opposition to the entire abortion culture. Pope Pius XI (r. 1922-1939), in the encyclical *Casti Connubii*, extended the moral argument beyond the person who procures an abortion to those who are accomplices in the procedure, noting with accuracy that there would be those "who would ask that public authorities provide aid for these death-dealing operations." Pope John XXIII (r. 1958-1963) proclaimed in *Mater et Magistra*, "By violating his (God's) laws, the divine majesty is offended, the individual and humanity are degraded, and the bonds . . . of society are disunited and enervated." Pope Paul VI (r. 1963-1978), in the *Declaration on Procured Abortion*, was quite specific: "Respect for human life is called for from the time that the process of generation begins, from the time that the ovum is fertilized, which is neither that of the father nor of the mother. It is rather the life of a new human being with its own growth. It would never be made human if it were not human already." Pope John Paul II (r. 1978-) has been particularly active around the world in speaking out on abortion, birth control, and sterilization, perceiving the inevitable effect upon the wider population and in eroding the value of all human life. Under his leadership, the Church has been ever vigilant in studying latest trends or developments in the field of abortion. Thus, in response to the creation of new abortifacient drugs (e.g., RU-486), the Pontifical Commission for the Authentic Interpretation of the Code of Canon Law extended the official definition of abortion to include the deliberate eradication of an immature fetus, a step approved by John Paul on May 23, 1988.

Abrabanel, Isaac (1437-1508) ● Also Isaac Abravanel. A noted Jewish theologian and philosopher, he became in 1471 the head of the treasury under King Alfonso V of Portugal, the post that had been held by his father. After the death of the king, he was forced to flee to Spain (1483), as he was wrongly implicated in a plot to overthrow the royal house. Abrabanel was soon granted a post by King Ferdinand and Queen Isabella, also working to overcome the country's persecution of the Jews. Exiled with all other Jews in 1492, he eventually settled in Venice where he carried out several missions for the Venetians. He composed works on biblical exegesis (i.e., critical analysis of the texts found in the Bible) that were respected by both Jews and Christians.

Absalon of Lund (c. 1128-1201) ● Also known as Axel. Archbishop of Lund, adviser to Danish kings, and a formidable political figure in the land of the Danes, he was a half-brother of King Waldemar I, proving instrumental in his succession and acquiring much influence at court. Named bishop of Roskilde in 1158, he helped convince his brother to side with Holy Roman Emperor Frederick I Barbarossa against Pope Alexander III, until, at last, an accommodation was reached with the pontiff. In 1169, the prelate defeated the Wends (or Slavs) and attached large portions of their territory to his diocese and hence to Denmark. Elected archbishop in 1177, he served as adviser to King Canute VI and continued to campaign militarily, adding Pomerania and Mecklenburg to the Danish realm. As archbishop, he introduced the first ecclesiastical laws to Denmark. He was a patron of the writer Saxo-Grammaticus. (See also **Denmark**.)

Acacian Schism ● Schism between the Holy See and the East, specifically the patriarchate of Constantinople. It lasted from 482 or 484 until 519. The name was derived from the patriarch of Constantinople, Acacius, and the cause was a decree, or edict, issued by the patriarch and the Byzantine emperor Zeno in 382. The edict, called the *Henotikon*, was promulgated to bring about the union of the Orthodox Church and the Monophysites. It was written with the aim of reconciling the Monophysites and thus omitted references to the two natures of Christ. As this was in contradiction to the Council of Chalcedon (451), the Holy Father, Felix III, demanded an explanation. One from Acacius was not forthcoming, and in 484 Felix excommunicated him, thus starting the schism. A reconciliation would not be made until 518 with the accession of Justin as Byzantine emperor. (See also **Monophysitism**.) The Acacian Schism was significant in establishing the first theological rupture between the Eastern and Western Churches, a break that would become permanent in 1054.

Acacians ● See **Acacius of Caesarea**, following entry.

Acacius of Caesarea (d. 366) ● Bishop of Caesarea, successor, disciple, and biographer of Eusebius of Caesarea, and an ardent Arian theologian. Acacius succeeded Eusebius to the see of Acacius in 340, becoming a leading spokesman for the cause of Arianism in the Roman Empire. In 343, he was deposed by the anti-Arian Council of Sardica, subsequently serving as the head of a smaller Arian party known as Homoeans, who repudiated both parties of the opposing Homoeasions and Homoiousions (related to the definitions of the nature of Christ). Acacius offered a Homoean Creed at the Council of Seleucia in 359 and, at the Homoean Synod of Constantinople in 360, he authored the acts of the synod, now lost. In 365, he was deposed again by the Synod of Lampsacus, disappearing from history. His death was placed at 366 by the historian

Baronius. His followers in the Homoean cause were also called Acacians in his honor.

Acacius of Constantinople (d. 489) ● Patriarch of Constantinople (471-489) and main leader in causing the Acacian Schism, a breach between the Eastern and Western Churches that would last from 482 or 484 until 519. Appointed papal legate by Pope Simplicius, Acacius distinguished himself as a vocal defender of orthodoxy, having repudiated the Monophysite doctrines of Emperor Basiliscus. As patriarch, Acacius labored to promote the see of Constantinople as the center for Eastern Christian Church. Toward that end, he hoped to unite all Byzantine Christians, including the Monophysites, by promulgating, with Emperor Zeno, the *Henotikon*, an edict that attempted to reconcile the Monophysites with the Orthodox Church. Since the *Henotikon* failed to include declarations of the two natures of Christ as decreed by the Council of Chalcedon, Acacius earned the displeasure of Rome and ultimately excommunication by Pope Felix II. The excommunication precipitated the so-called Acacian Schism, and Acacius died unreconciled with the papacy. While the schism was finally ended in 519, Acacius was responsible in part for beginning the ultimately permanent split of the Churches.

Academies, Pontifical ● See **Pontifical Institutes of Higher Learning** in TABLE 11.

Acclamatio ● Rare but still valid form of papal election in which a candidate is proclaimed pontiff by the unanimous acclamation of the cardinals of the conclave. This method precludes the casting of any votes and must be done without prior consultation among any of the cardinals. This last stipulation is the reason for the other name for this electoral process — "quasi-inspirational," meaning that the declaration must come from some spiritual inspiration, that is, the Holy Spirit. There have been several elections by *acclamatio*, including Clement X (r. 1670-1676) and Innocent XI (r. 1676-1689), who was said to have been surrounded by the cardinals in the conclave chapel and acclaimed pope, each cardinal kissing his hand. (See also **Papal Elections**.)

Acosta, José de (1540-1600) ● Jesuit who became provincial of the order in Peru in 1576. Born at Medina del Campo, he joined the Society of Jesus in 1553, serving as a lecturer in theology in Spain before being sent to Peru in 1569 where the society had been established only the year before. Filling a chair of theology at Lima, Acosta was instrumental in founding a number of universities throughout New Spain, including colleges at La Paz and Panama, after his election as provincial. He later taught theology at the Roman College in 1594. Acosta was well respected as a teacher, writer, and as an expert on the flora of whole parts of South America. He also made a study of Mexico and its natural inhabitants during a three-year period (1585-1588).

Acquaviva, Claudius (1543-1615) ● Fifth superior general of the Society of Jesus from 1581. He was largely responsible for strengthening the order and guiding it through a period of considerable upheaval both in Europe and within the order itself. The son of Prince Giovanni Antonio Acquaviva, duke of Atri, Claudius studied canon and civil law at Perugia before joining the Jesuits in 1567. He subsequently served as provincial in Naples and then Rome. Elected general, he headed an order that was expelled from Venice, suffered intense persecutions in Elizabethan England, and was faced with an internal schism in Spain, organized by Gabriel Vázquez and supported by both the pope and King Philip II. While attacked in Rome, Acquaviva succeeded in winning the backing of the pope both in the matter of the schism and later when the Inquisition demanded the right to examine the constitution of the Jesuits. Pope Sixtus V, successor of Gregory XIII, decided to make extensive changes in the order but died before he had a chance to implement his plans. Aside from these temporal difficulties, Acquaviva was successful in drawing up the *Ratio Studiorum*, promoting the inner life of the order, and developing extensively the order's missionary activities.

Acre ● Also Akko or Akka. Seaport and major fortress on the Palestinian coast, along the Bay of Haifa. The castle of Acre was captured in 1104 by King Baldwin I of Jerusalem but fell to a Muslim army under the great general Saladin in 1187. The next years witnessed a bloody and wasteful siege, in which a crusader army besieged the city from August 1189 until July 1191. Some historians put the number of crusaders killed during the siege at one hundred thousand. Captured by Richard the Lionhearted, Acre was given to the Knights Hospitallers, who controlled it until 1291 and made it the base of their operations in the region.

Acta Apostolicae Sedis ● Latin for *Acts of the Apostolic See*, the official journal of the Vatican that serves as the standard record of the Holy See. It was established by Pope Pius X in the decree *Promulgandi Pontificios Constitutionis*, promulgated on September 29, 1908. The first issue was published on January 1, 1909. The *Acta Apostolicae Sedis* (abbreviated as AAS), contains the texts of encyclicals, apostolic constitutions, papal and curial audiences, and releases from the various dicasteries of the Roman Curia. Its other major function is to issue canon law, as decreed by Canon 8, such new decrees becoming effective three months from the date of their promulgation. The AAS is published as often as considered necessary, the actual publishing being done by the

Libreria Editrice Vaticana, and is available by subscription.

Acta Pilati ● See *Acts of Pilate* under **Pilate, Pontius**.

Acta Sanctae Sedis ● Predecessor publication to the *Acta Apostolicae Sedis* and served as the principal source of the published public documents of the Holy See. Meaning *Acts of the Holy See*, it was made official on May 23, 1904, and declared an organ of the papacy. Begun in 1895, it had previously been an unofficial journal. It was superseded in 1909 by the AAS.

Acta Sanctorum <1> ● Very popular and well-known series of saints' lives first collected by the Bollandists, a small group of Jesuit editors in the 1600s. The *Acta Sanctorum* (*Acts of the Saints*) were arranged in the order of the individual feast days of the saints, according to the ecclesiastical calendar. The idea was first conceived by H. Rossweyde, who died in 1629 before any major part of the work was completed. Many years passed before any large parts of the *Acta* were compiled and only in 1773, when the Society of Jesus was suppressed, had fifty volumes been published, up to October 7 on the calendar. Revisions have been made over the years and the *Acta* are now available in numerous languages. Other names for the *Acta* are *Legends of the Saints* and the *Golden Legend*.

Acta Sanctorum <2> ● In full, *Acta Sanctorum Ordinis Sancti Benedicti*. The first volume of this history of the saints of the Benedictine order was published in 1668 by the Maurist scholar Jean Mabillon.

Acta Sanctorum Hiberniae ● Well-known collection of lives of the Irish saints, compiled by the Franciscan John Colgan. The first volume of the work presented saints' lives for the months of January, February, and March and was printed at Louvain in 1645.

Action Française ● French sociopolitical movement first established in 1898 by Henri Vougeois and Maurice Pujo but which soon became associated closely with the atheist intellectual Charles Maurras. Finding considerable support in the country, Maurras established in 1899 the fortnightly review *L'Action Française*, with Leon Doudet as editor. From 1908 onward, the newspaper was published on a daily basis. *Action Française* promoted a strong nationalistic policy, disdaining democracy, particularly as exemplified by the French Third Republic, and calling for a monarchist revolution. Although Maurras was a foe of religion, the movement both attracted and manipulated many Catholics who were conservative royalists. Members of the French hierarchy allowed the Church to become identified politically with the movement, and the condemnation of the social Catholics, Le Sillon especially, by Pope Pius X (1903-1914), was greeted by *Action Française* as a great victory.

Soon, however, the violence and hatred espoused by the movement earned calls for the papacy to take steps against it, but the popularity of the cause, especially during World War I, compelled the Holy See to stay its hand. Finally, in 1926, Pope Pius XI condemned it and placed the newspaper on the Index of Forbidden Books. The ban was lifted only in 1939 after the leadership apologized. Under the Vichy government, 1940-1944, *Action Française* once more prospered, only to face criticism with the fall of the Third Reich. Maurras was put on trial and imprisoned; he died in 1952, and the movement has been in decline ever since. Some of the elements of *Action Française* are said to be apparent in the writings of the late Archbishop Marcel Lefebvre.

Acton, John (1834-1902) ● In full, John Emerich Edward Dalberg Acton, first Baron Acton, English historian and a prominent Catholic liberal. Acton was the son of Catholic émigrés, born at Naples and educated in Paris and Munich. In the latter place he became a friend of Johann Döllinger, the Bavarian Church historian. He was unable to attend Cambridge because of his Catholic faith; but in 1859 he was elected a member of Parliament (M.P.) for Carlow as a Liberal. That same year, he took over editorship of the Catholic newspaper *Rambler* from John Henry Newman, renaming it *Home and Foreign Review* in 1862, and suspending it in 1864 because of a possible veto from the Holy See over his opposition to Ultramontanism. Acton was an outspoken figure for anti-Ultramontanism, was a critic of the *Syllabus Errorum* (1864; *Syllabus of Errors*), and journeyed to Rome to fight the idea of papal infallibility at Vatican Council I (1869-1870), supplying support and material to Döllinger when he was writing the famous "Quirinus" letters. In his later years, Acton promoted modern historical study, delivering a famous lecture on the study of history and writing the introductory chapter to the *Cambridge Modern History* (1901-1911) that he helped plan.

Act of Settlement <1> ● So-called Irish Act of Settlement. Law passed in 1662 by the Irish Parliament that attempted to restore to Protestants and Catholics properties that had been confiscated during the preceding years of severe religious strife. By the terms of the law, the lands that had been confiscated in Leinster, Connaught, and Munster were returned to Protestant victims and any Catholics who could prove their innocence in the affair. The result of the act was the return of the Anglican Church to Ireland by regaining its estates and reestablishing its hierarchy. The Irish Parliament was under the majority of Puritans and soldiers from the time of Cromwell's ruthless campaigns in

Ireland and thus was naturally favorably disposed to reaching an accommodation that benefited the Protestants. (See also **Ireland** and **Cromwell, Oliver.**)

Act of Settlement <2> ● Also the English Act of Settlement. Bill passed by the English Parliament in 1701 that to this day requires the ruler of England to be a member of the Church of England. The law further stipulates that should the monarch wish to convert to another religion, particularly Catholicism, he or she must abdicate.

Act of Toleration ● Act passed by the English Parliament in 1689 granting freedom of religion and religious practices to all creeds except Catholics and those denying the Trinity. Passed during the reign of William and Mary, the act was later replaced by more broad-minded legislation. (See also **England.**)

Acts of the Apostles ● Fifth book of the NT. Long accepted as having been authored by St. Luke, the Acts of the Apostles is a continuation of the narrative of Luke's Gospel, presenting the progress of the Church from the ascension of Our Lord to the period when St. Paul preached in Rome. It has as its purpose to proclaim the divine institution of the Church and to describe the spread of the Good News by the intervention of the Holy Spirit across much of the Roman world: from Jerusalem to Samaria and then into Syria, Cyprus, Asia Minor, Europe, and finally the Eternal City itself. It is possible to divide Acts into two broad parts, the first (1:4—20:30) covering the Church in Jerusalem and the second (13:1—28:31) Paul's missions. The narrative can be further divided: Introduction (1:1-3); the Church in Jerusalem (1:4—8:3), including the preaching of St. Peter and the martyrdom of St. Stephen; the spread of the Church (8:4—12:25) across Judaea and Samaria, with the conversion of Saul (9:1—19); Paul's

mission to the Gentiles (13:1—21:16), including the Council of Jerusalem; Paul's return to Jerusalem and his trial (21:17—26:32); and Paul's journey to Rome and the establishing of the Church there (27:1—28:31).

Throughout the work, the author makes prominent mention of the important role of the Holy Spirit in guiding the ministry of the Apostles and the rise of the Church (2:1-13; 5:12-16; and 8:26-40). Further, it is clear from the account that the Christian faith was, from the foundation of Christ, separate and distinguishable from Judaism, tracing the events that led to the decision of the Council of Jerusalem to make possible the conversion of Gentiles without adherence to some Mosaic laws. Paul's mission to the Gentiles is detailed, with special emphasis on the process by which the faith entered the Hellenistic world and became a universal religion.

The authorship of Luke is generally not disputed and has been attested by many Christian writers, including Tertullian, Clement of Alexandria, and the Muratorian Canon. The date of its composition, however, is open to some question. The Anti-Marcionite Prologue to Luke, written in the late second century, declares Acts to have been composed by Luke in Achaia (Achaea), after Paul's martyrdom. The earliest possible date would be 60, the year of Paul's arrest by the Romans; the latest date would be between 75 and 80. Beyond its profound spiritual content, the Acts of the Apostles is a major historical source on the rise of the early Church, its leadership, and the fascinating intellectual process involved in its evolution. Luke adds considerably to the account by interweaving so many points of interest on contemporary society, daily life, and wider events of the time.

Acts of the Martyrs ● Name given to a large body of writings presenting accounts of the martyrdoms of numerous saints of the early Church. The accounts are of varying authenticity and the writings have been grouped into different types — trial accounts, personal or narrated versions of trials and executions, and descriptions written after, perhaps long after, the events actually took place. The most reliable of these are the official Roman court records of trials. The best of these unfortunately few reports is the *Acta Proconsularia* of St. Cyprian, highly respected because of the excellent specimen of the record that survived. Another type of act is the legend — one of the definitions being a famous story created entirely out of imagination. The earliest of the martyrologies date, according to some scholars, to the time of the martyrdom of St. Justin and his six brothers in 165. The first collection was probably authored by Eusebius of Caesarea, including a now lost but reportedly large collection of the Acts of the Martyrs. The Bollandist scholar Hippolyte Delehaye (d. 1941) is credited with categorizing the various types of martyrdoms.

Acts of Sts. Paul and Thecla ● Work generally considered to be apocryphal describing the travels of St. Paul and St. Thecla (an early Christian virgin). The book is part of the larger apocryphal work, the *Acts of St. Paul*, which also included the *Martyrdom of St. Paul*. It was immensely popular in the early Church and was found not only in Greek but in Armenian, Syriac, and assorted Latin versions. The *Acts* tells of how St. Paul delivered a sermon on celibacy in the house of Onesiphorus while visiting the city of Iconium. He was so persuasive that young Thecla refused to wed Thamyris, to whom she had been betrothed. Paul was charged and beaten by the civil authorities while Thecla was condemned to death. Her execution was unsuccessful, as she was miraculously saved. Other adventures are recounted, ending with Thecla's death in Seleucia.

Acts of St. Peter ● Apocryphal work dated to around A.D. 150-200, written in Greek in Asia Minor. It is preserved in several Greek versions, and is also found complete in a Latin version in a Vercelli manuscript. Included as part of the *Acts* is the *Martyrdom of St. Peter*. This contains two of the most celebrated stories related to St. Peter — the *Quo Vadis?* event and the crucifixion of Peter upside down.

Acts of the Saints ● See **Acta Sanctorum <1>**.

Adalbert, St. (d. 997) ● Apostle of the Slavs. Worked to establish Christianity in Slavic lands, particularly Russia. A native of Lorraine, Adalbert was a monk before being consecrated a bishop and sent to Russia in 961. He was the choice of Emperor Otto I the Great after the ruler received a request for missionaries from the Russian princess Olga. On his way to the East with several assistants, Adalbert was waylaid, barely escaping with his life. His assistants, however, were all killed. Returning home, he became abbot of Weissenburg and later bishop of Magdeburg. His mission as prelate was to launch the evangelization of the Slavs, and the see soon acquired much power and prestige. Adalbert was also named metropolitan of the Slavs, establishing several sees, including Posen, Brandenburg, and Meissen. Feast day: April 23.

Adalbert of Bremen (c. 1000-1072) ● Archbishop of Bremen and Hamburg from 1043 (or 1045) until 1072 and a patron of the evangelization of Scandinavia. He was the son of Count Frederick von Goseck, serving as subdeacon to the archbishop of Hamburg (1032), provost of the Halberstadt Cathedral, and then archbishop. His appointment as prelate came with extensive powers over parts of Scandinavia, the territories of the Wends, and the regions beyond the Elbe. Adalbert was also made papal legate to the north in 1053, allowing him to focus even further on missionary efforts. These, however, were only partially successful. Adalbert's ecclesiastical powers were matched by his political influence, since he enjoyed the favor of Emperor Henry III (who offered him the papacy in 1046) and was a tutor and royal adviser to Emperor Henry IV. He thus earned the jealousy of the nobles at court, and they secured his banishment until a reconciliation was achieved with Henry IV. He was thereafter a fixture at court. It is believed that the destruction of Hamburg by the Slavs in 1071-1072 broke his heart and probably hastened his death.

Adalbert of Mainz ● See **Adalbert of Bremen**, preceding entry.

Adalbert of Prague ● Apostle of Prussia, bishop of Prague from 982-988 and again from 992-994, the first Czech to hold the episcopal see in Prague. Appointed bishop in 982, he was a supporter of Boleslav II, prince of Bohemia, as it was Adalbert's hope that the ruler might aid him in promoting the Christian cause in the region. Failing to make any appreciable headway and facing much opposition from antireformist forces in the diocese, Adalbert stepped down in 988. Recalled by popular demand in 992, he worked to Christianize the Hungarians, possibly baptizing the future Stephen I of Hungary. Expelled once again by his own followers in 994, Adalbert took to extensive missionary work journeying into the aforementioned Hungary, into Poland, and among the dangerous tribes of Prussia. While he had some success, Adalbert was martyred by a group of pagans who were unwilling to destroy their idols. His body was supposedly bought by Boleslav for its weight in gold.

Adam of Bremen (c. 1040-c. 1076) ● German canon and historian, the author of the important chronicle *Gesta Hammaburgensis ecclesias pontificum*

(*History of the Bishops of Hamburg*). Little is known about Adam's life, although he was certainly a teacher in the cathedral school of Bremen and traveled to Denmark. He possibly came to Bremen at the invitation of Archbishop Adalbert of Bremen in 1068, and was buried, by tradition, in the convent of Ramesloh, in a grove he had devoted to the institution. His history, dated around 1075, was written in four books, with its focus on the efforts of missionaries. Composed with accuracy and excellent organization, the work is important in preserving details about the Church and secular events in northern Europe during the tenth century and part of the eleventh.

Adam of Fulda (d. after 1537) ● Monk of Franconia and one of the foremost musicians of the late 1400s and early 1500s. He was the author of a well-known musical treatise, written in 1490 and printed in the *Scriptores eccles. de Mus. Sacra* (*Writings on Sacred Church Music*) by Herbert von Hornan. Adam called himself *musicus ducalis* (duke of music), so it has been surmised that he was in the service of some nobleman or prelate, perhaps the bishop of Würzburg.

Adam of Marsh (d. c. 1258) ● Also called Adam of Marisco, a noted Franciscan theologian in England and France. Educated at Oxford, he joined the Franciscan order probably in or around 1230. Subsequently, he was the head of the Franciscans at Oxford, declining the offer of the Franciscan chair at the University of Paris. Adam also served as an adviser to Simon de Montfort and King Henry III of England.

Adam of St. Victor (c. 1110-c. 1180) ● Composer of hymns in Latin and canon at the Abbey of St. Victor in the area around Paris. Adam was born in England or perhaps Brittany, since he was known to his contemporaries as the Briton, or Breton. Other sources suggest he may have been born in Paris. He entered St. Victor around 1130, working prodigiously on hymns and sequences (hymns sung after the Alleluia during the liturgy on special feasts), proving one of the most prolific and brilliant hymn writers of the era; his sequences were noted for their theological depth. He may also have written an encyclopedia on biblical terms.

Adam, John (1608-1684) ● Member of the Jesuits in France and ardent opponent of the French Calvinists and the Jansenists. A native of Limoges, he entered the Society of Jesus in 1622. In a number of works, including "Calvin Defeated by Himself" and "The Tomb of Jansenism," Adam attacked both Calvinism and Jansenist thinking. He was later assailed by Cardinal Henry Noris in *Vindicae Augustinianae* (*Vindication of St. Augustine*) for his controversial writings on St. Augustine.

Adam, Karl (1876-1966) ● Catholic theologian and priest from Bavaria who was ordained in 1900, later teaching at the University of Munich. Appointed professor at the University of Strasbourg in 1918, he moved a year later to Tübingen. He taught there until 1949. Adam was highly influential with the Catholic public through such works as *Christus unser Bruder* (1926; *Christ Our Brother*), and *Das Wesen des Katholizismus* (1924; *The Essence of Catholicism*), and is generally held to have anticipated the ecumenical movement of the later twentieth century.

Adamantius ● Fourth-century Greek writer against Gnosticism. He was the author of a dialogue, *De recta in Deum fide*, in five books, that presented a debate between himself and, first, two disciples of the heretic Marcion and then supporters of the heretics Bardesanes and Valentinus. At the conclusion of the disputation, the pagan Eutropius, who had served as arbiter, declared Adamantius the victor. Adamantius

was incorrectly identified as Origen by both St. Gregory of Nazianzus and St. Basil the Great. (See also **Origen**.)

Adamites ● Obscure Christian sect of the second century first mentioned by St. Augustine and St. Epiphanius. They earned the name from their sincere desire to emulate or recapture the primeval innocence of Paradise by wandering about completely naked and condemning marriage as foreign to the Garden of Eden. Some have identified them with the Carpocration Gnostics, perhaps as an offshoot; the community described St. Clement of Alexandria as engaging in communal marriages and extreme sensuality. Similar groups appeared during the Middle Ages: the Beghards and the Brothers and Sisters of the Free Spirit, for example. The last appearance of the Adamite sect was in the 1400s under a Frenchman named Picard, who declared himself the reincarnation of Adam.

Adamnan, St. (c. 624-704) ● Also Adamnon, abbot of Iona and one of the major monastic figures to come out of Iona, the island monastery of the Inner Hebrides. He was elected abbot there in 679, working over the next years in Ireland and Scotland to bring about the ecclesiastical supremacy of the Roman observance over Celtic models, including the acceptance of the Roman date for Easter. The "Canon of Adamnon" was also adopted in Ireland, prohibiting women and children from being seized in war. The abbot was a remarkable scholar and writer, authoring a life of Columba, an invaluable survey of early monasticism in Celtic lands, and the attributed *De locis sanctis*, a listing of holy places. Feast day: September 23.

Ad Apostolicae Dignatalis Apicem ● Apostolic letter issued by Pope Innocent IV (r. 1243-1254) against Emperor Frederick II on July 17, 1245, during the Council of Lyons. The letter was a formal attempt to bring about the deposition of the ruler by declaring him unfit to rule because of the many crimes and sins of which Frederick was responsible. Because of his guilt, including not paying tribute to Sicily (a patrimony of St. Peter), incurring the suspicion of heresy, breaking terms of a treaty with the papacy, and murdering bishops, the pope declared Frederick's subjects free of their duty to obey him as their monarch. The letter was a provocative and decidedly hostile act in the long and bitter struggle between the papacy and the emperor.

Adelard of Bath ● Twelfth-century philosopher, scholar, and one of the foremost travelers of his age. Few details about his life have survived, although it is known that Adelard journeyed to North Africa, Asia Minor, Greece, and throughout Europe. During his travels he became familiar with the writings of Islamic scientists and later made translations of Arabic scientific treatises, manuals, and studies, including the *Almagest* of Ptolemy. Adelard also authored *De Eodem et Diverso* (*On the Identical and the Diverse*), a dialogue on the liberal arts and the philosophies of Plato and Aristotle, from around 1105-1110; he also produced *Quaestiones Naturales* (*Natural Questions*). These works and especially the translations were to be used in later years by Christian scholars studying Aristotle and the writings of the Arab scientists.

Adeodatus I ● See **Deusdedit, St**.

Adeodatus II ● Pope from 672-676. Also called Deusdedit II. Originally a Benedictine from the Roman cloister of St. Erasmus, he was elected on April 11, 672, and was the first pontiff to date his own reign's events. Aside from supporting several monasteries, most notably the Abbey of St. Peter in Canterbury, and rebuilding many churches that had fallen into disrepair, his period on the papal throne was generally uneventful.

Ad Extirpanda ● Bull issued in 1252 by Pope Innocent IV detailing the activities that were to be allowed by the Inquisition in compelling a possibly guilty person to confess. The bull specifically prescribed torture as a legitimate method of extracting a confession.

Ad Gentes ● Vatican Council II decree, promulgated on December 7, 1965. Known in full as *Ad Gentes Divinitus*, its English title is the "Decree on the Church's Missionary Activity." *Ad Gentes* was a reaffirmation of the important missionary nature of the Catholic Church, founded on the biblical idea of the people of God. The decree, in six chapters with an introduction, examined specifically the doctrine of the Church's activities in missions, the nature of the work, the need for new churches, the role of missionaries, the organization of missionary planning, and the utilization of Church resources in missionary work. The decree also called for a thorough reappraisal and reform of so-called Christian or Catholic imperialism, the teaching of Christianity in a purely Western (or Eurocentric) fashion, thus theoretically alienating many in the native African or Asian communities. Pope Paul VI issued *Ecclesia Sancta III* on August 16, 1966, to establish the means of actually implementing *Ad Gentes*.

Adhémar of Monteil (d. 1098) ● Also called Adhémar de Puy, he was bishop of Puy, papal legate, and an important figure in the organization of the First Crusade that was to recapture Jerusalem from Muslim control. Made a bishop by 1080, he was the first Christian to pledge to embark on the crusade that had been called by Pope Urban II in 1095 at the Council of Clermont. On November 28 of that year, Adhémar was named by Urban to be papal legate, with the task of serving as supreme chaplain to the crusader armies. In the succeeding years, he was to prove instrumental in creating relations between the Latin crusaders and their Byzantine hosts at Constantinople, particularly the leaders of the Eastern Church, who had misgivings about dealing with Western Churchmen. He also prevented serious quarrels from erupting within the crusader ranks, aided the poor wherever crusader armies visited, and worked to establish a Christian presence in the Holy Land once more. When plague broke out in Antioch in 1098, Adhémar died on August 1; his death was a bitter blow to Christian unity.

Ado, Martyrology of ● Martyrology compiled by the Benedictine monk Ado (later archbishop of Vienne). The influential work was supposedly based on a Roman martyrology, the *Martyrologium Romanum Parvum*, that Ado had found at Ravenna. As his martyrology is inconsistent and error-filled, scholars generally believe that Ado's sources were either wholly unreliable or that he himself fabricated the entire work. It was nevertheless the model and inspiration for such subsequent efforts as the Martyrology of Usuard. (See also **Martyrology**.)

Adoptionism ● Heresy originating in Spain during the eighth century. It proclaimed that Christ was the Son of God but only in the sense that he had been adopted. While he was the natural Son of God, Christ, as man, was merely adopted. Originating in earlier heresies such as Monarchianism and especially Nestorianism, Adoptionism probably developed out of the writings of the otherwise unknown Migetius, who rejected the concept of a separation or delineation of the Incarnation of Christ and the Second Person of the Holy Trinity. Elipandus, archbishop of Toledo, took exception to these and declared that there was in Christ a clear distinction between the human and the divine. He was given support in his day by Felix, bishop of Urgel. The controversy over Adoptionist theories soon

spread, particularly as it resembled Nestorianism, and Felix went before Charlemagne at Ratisbon in 792. He was forced to recant, however, and the Spanish bishops failed once more at Frankfurt in 794 to secure the orthodox blessings of the Church. Returning to Urgel, Felix wrote to Alcuin for support. In response, Alcuin authored the seven-volume attack *Contra Felicem* (*Against Felix*) in 799. That same year Felix recanted after being anathematized by Pope Leo III. After Elipandus's death in 802, the heresy was wiped out. In the twelfth century, it reappeared in a modified version, in the writings of Peter Abelard and Gilbert de la Porrée, and later in the interpretations of doctrine by John Duns Scotus and Durandus of St.-Pourçain.

Adrian I ● Pope from 772-795. Also called Hadrian I, he was a Roman by birth, who proved a remarkably effective pontiff. The successor to Stephen III (IV) he continued the policies of his predecessor in maintaining good relations with the Franks, especially Charlemagne (742-814). These efforts thus made possible Adrian's success in convincing the emperor to invade Italy, defeat the Lombards, and ultimately depose King Desiderius in 774. With Charlemagne's seizure of the iron crown of the Lombards, Rome and the papacy were freed from the chronic threat of Lombard invasion, although Charlemagne gained considerable political prestige from his conquest. Adrian was forced to acknowledge Charlemagne's influence even in Church matters, but relations between the leaders remained generally amicable; Adrian had the emperor's support in the suppression of Adoptionism, but they disagreed over the Iconoclastic Controversy. The pope was an able administrator, working to rebuild churches and to restore the walls of Rome.

Adrian II ● Pope from 867-872. A relative of two previous popes, Stephen IV (V) and

Sergius II, he was married prior to his ordination and was made a cardinal in 842 by Pope Gregory IV. He was so highly regarded in Rome that twice, in 855 and 858, he was elected pope, declining both times; finally, on December 14, 867, Adrian accepted, succeeding Nicholas I as a compromise candidate. His reign began with much bloodshed, for the troops of Duke Lambert of Spoleto sacked Rome for some unspecified reason, and his daughter by his previously mentioned marriage was raped and murdered. Adrian was the inheritor of a powerful papal office, but he had an overly conciliatory nature, in part because of his personal weakness and advanced age. While he sponsored the missions of Cyril and Methodius and allowed the use of the Slavonic language in the liturgy, his pontificate also witnessed the loss of Roman influence in the Balkans, as Boris I, king of the Bulgars, invited Ignatius, patriarch of Constantinople, to send missionaries to Bulgaria from the Eastern Christian Church.

Adrian III, St. ● Pope from 884-885. The successor to Marinus I on May 17, 884, his brief reign is largely obscure. He adopted a more conciliatory policy toward the Eastern Church and was conspicuous for the aid he gave the Romans during a famine. Adrian died in September 885 while journeying to Worms to meet Emperor Charles III the Fat. It is possible that his death was not by natural causes. Buried at the Abbey of Nomantula, he soon attracted a cultus and was revered locally for centuries until finally recognized as a saint by Pope Leo XIII in 1891.

Adrian IV ● Pope from 1154-1159. The only Englishman elected to the Holy See, Nicholas Breakspear was born around 1100 near St. Alban's, the son of a lowly royal clerk. He studied in France and entered the Augustinian monastery of St. Rufus at Avignon where he was named abbot in 1137. Around 1144, he was named cardinal bishop of Aldano by Pope Eugenius, ironically in part because relations with the monks in the monastery had been strained. Named a papal legate a short time later, he was given the task of reorganizing the Church in Scandinavia. This undertaking he accomplished with such brilliant success that on December 4, 1154, he was unanimously elected successor to Anastasius IV. As pope he was a firm

Pope Adrian IV

defender of papal rights. One of his first acts was to place Rome under interdiction after riots and bloodshed had occurred. Adrian crowned Frederick I Barbarossa on June 18, 1155, but only after exacting a pledge of full homage. Relations between them were never cordial and Adrian's insistence that the imperial crown was a *beneficium* (i.e., a gift of the papacy) caused a conflict that would continue long after Adrian's pontificate. He also intervened in France and granted to Henry II of England overlordship of Ireland. This came supposedly at the behest of John of Salisbury, but the authenticity of the bull *Laudabiliter* has long been questioned by scholars. Adrian died quite suddenly on September 1, 1159.

Adrian V ● Pope from July 4 to August 18, 1276. Ottobono Fieschi, born around 1205 in Genoa, was a member of the noble family of Lavagna and a nephew of Pope Innocent IV, who named him a cardinal in 1251. Sent as a legate to England in 1265 by Clement IV, he was responsible for making peace between King Henry and his barons. His election as successor to Innocent V came only after a lengthy conclave that had grown so deliberative that the overseer Charles of Anjou cut down on their rations and did nothing to alleviate the oppressive Roman heat. Adrian's only act was to promise a new decree concerning conclaves. He died at Viterbo without being ordained, crowned, or consecrated. Dante placed Adrian in purgatory for suspected avarice.

Adrian VI ● Pope from 1522-1523. The only pope in modern times to retain his baptismal name (with the exception of Marcellus II in 1555), he was also the last non-Italian pope until the election in 1978 of Karol Wojtyla as Pope John Paul II. A native of Utrecht, he studied under the Brethren of the Common Life before entering Louvain University. Known as Adrian Florensz Pedal, he became a professor of theology in 1492 and chancellor in 1497. In 1507, Emperor Maximilian I made him tutor to his grandson, the future Charles V. He served as regent with Cardinal Francisco Ximénez de Cisneros for Charles as ruler of Spain from 1516-1517, wielding virtually supreme power in the country. After serving as bishop of Tortosa and inquisitor of Aragon, Navarre, Castile, and León, he became cardinal of Utrecht in 1517. On January 9, 1522, he was unanimously elected successor to Leo X, retaining his baptismal name. A devout and ascetic person, he launched a thorough reform of the papacy and the Roman Curia and desired to repulse the spread of Protestantism while uniting the Christian princes against the Ottoman Turks and Suleiman I the Magnificent. From the start, however, he was disliked by the Romans, who resented a "barbarian" northerner as pope and dreaded an inquisitor as their pontiff. Many in the Sacred College of Cardinals resisted his efforts at reform; Rhodes fell in October 1522 to the Turks, and the fires sparked by Martin Luther continued to spread. Adrian VI died on September 14, 1523, from exhaustion and sadness, his good intentions proving insufficient to the crises at hand. After his death, the cynical Romans sent flowers and good wishes to the doctor who had treated him. His successor was Clement VII.

Aduarte, Diego (1566-1635) ● Spanish Dominican missionary, historian, and author of a well-known history of the Dominicans in the Philippines. Aduarte was born in Saragossa, receiving his education at the University of Alcalá before joining the Dominicans. In 1594, he sailed to the Philippines where he worked as a highly successful missionary, eventually being chosen to launch an evangelizing effort onto the Asian mainland. He subsequently served as prior of the Dominicans and rector of the College of Santo Tomás (1595) and procurator of the order back in Spain (c. 1608). It was while back at home that he began his history, preserving considerable detail on the nature of civil and religious government, especially exposing the corrupt and often ruthless style of rule in the islands.

Aegidius of Viterbo (d. 1532) ● Cardinal and theologian, best known in Church history for his brilliant oratory delivered in 1512 at the Fifth Lateran Council. A native of Viterbo, he entered the Augustinian order, ultimately becoming its general. Pope Leo X appointed him cardinal, giving him the post of legate. Aegidius participated in a number of important papal missions, receiving in 1532 the title of Latin patriarch of Constantinople. He also authored a number of works, including an unpublished history of philosophy, a commentary on the *Sentences* of Peter Lombard, and his correspondence.

Aelfric (d. c. 1020) ● Known as "The Grammarian," abbot of Eynsham, a noted prose writer in Anglo-Saxon England, and an important figure in the history of English monasticism. Aelfric was educated at the Benedictine Abbey of Winchester, studying under Ethelwold, bishop of Winchester, and proving himself a brilliant monk and scholar. In 987, he went to Cerne Abbey in Dorset to serve as abbot. While there, he issued two homilies concerned with the liturgical year and other historical subjects. In 1005, he was named abbot of the newly established monastery at Eynsham in Oxfordshire. Aelfric was the author of numerous works, including a life of Ethelwold; a Latin grammar in English for students; a glossary with a reader; translations of parts of the OT; a collection of homilies; and a lives of the saints in English alliterative prose. Aelfric theologically denied the Immaculate Conception and supported Ratramnus's opposition to transubstantiation. Rediscovered by theologians in the 1500s, Aelfric was very popular during the Reformation.

Aelia Capitolina ● See **Jerusalem**.

Aelred of Rievaulx ● Also Ailred, a Cistercian abbot and historian who distinguished himself as a major figure in both English and medieval monasticism. He was born in Hexham, Northumberland, and spent much time at the court of King David I of Scotland. Joining the Cistercian order around 1134, Aelred became the abbot of Revesby in 1143 and abbot of Rievaulx in 1147. As abbot, he earned much acclaim for personal sanctity and skill in organizing the monastic life. He traveled extensively throughout Scotland, England, and France, promoting the monastic life with such vigor and success that he earned the name

"Bernard of the North," a reference to Bernard of Clairvaux. Among his writings were *De spirituali amicitia* (*On Spiritual Friendship*); *De Jesu duodenui* (*On Jesus at Twelve Years Old*); *Vita S. Eduardi Confessoris* (*Life of Edward the Confessor*); *Genealogia Regnum Anglorum* (*Genealogy of the English Kings*); and *Speculum Caritatis* (*Mirror of Charity*).

Aeneas of Gaza ● Sixth-century philosopher who studied under Hierocles at Alexandria, focusing on Neoplatonism. He later wrote on various aspects of Platonism, although he rejected those elements that were in contradiction to Orthodox Christianity, as demonstrated by his dialogue "Theophrastus" in which he defended the resurrection of the body and the eternal nature of the soul. He was a member of the so-called "Gaza Triad" with Procopius of Gaza and Zacharius Scholasticus.

Aeterni Patris <1> ● Apostolic letter issued by Pope Pius IX on June 29, 1868. Through it, the Vatican Council (First Vatican Council) was convened. While it begins with the same words as the encyclical *Aeterni Patris* by Pope Leo XIII, and is quoted in that work, its purpose was fundamentally different. (See **Vatican Council I**.)

Aeterni Patris <2> ● Well-known encyclical issued on August 4, 1879, by Pope Leo XIII. The purpose of the encyclical was to promote the revival, already under way, of Scholastic philosophy with special interest placed on the value, importance, and significance of St. Thomas Aquinas. *Aeterni Patris* was highly influential in spurring so-called Neo-Scholasticism and Neo-Thomism both within the Church and throughout academic centers. Pope Leo wrote that "Thomas has reigned supreme, and the minds of all, teachers as well as taught, rested in wonderful harmony under the shield and authority of the Angelic Doctor."

Aetius of Antioch (d. c. 370) ● Christian physician, grammarian, and sophist who became an influential spokesman for the ideas of extreme Arianism. He journeyed to Alexandria, mastered the philosophy of Aristotle, and was later consecrated a bishop by the Arians, although without a fixed see. Condemned by the Third Synod of Sirmium, Aetius was known to Orthodox Christian critics as "the godless one," a play in Greek on his name. A major point of theological contention was the idea he supported that the Son was unlike the Father. His followers were called Anomoeans or Aetians. (See also **Eunomianism**.)

Africa ● Continent where the Christian Church dates to apostolic times and has survived various vicissitudes over the centuries to enjoy an eruption of growth and conversions in the modern era. It is unclear exactly when Christianity reached Africa. According to tradition, it first arrived in Alexandria with St. Mark the Evangelist, founder of the Church in Alexandria, which would produce such brilliant figures as Origen, Cyril, Athanasius, and Clement. The faith then spread into Egypt and into Nubia and Ethiopia to the south and across North Africa. This part of Africa would become a strong Christian center; it would claim such theologians as Augustine, Tertullian, and Cyprian. By the third century, in fact, the Church in Africa was highly developed, with more than a hundred bishops under the overall authority of Carthage. The heart of the leadership was in the Roman provinces of Numidia and Africa Proconsularis, although the faith was also to spread to other regions. Persecutions of the Christian community were often severe, especially under Emperor Trajanus Decius around 250. Aside from the suffering and dislocation they caused, persecutions also brought controversy over, for instance, the readmission of lapsed Christians (the *lapsi*) and a schism by the Novatianists. More persecutions occurred

under Emperor Valerian in 258 and Emperor Diocletian in the late third century and early fourth. This last persecution brought the rise of Donatism. Further heresies would plague the African Church, despite the best efforts of St. Augustine and others to prevent their proliferation and to defeat their errors in doctrine. The chief heresies were Pelagianism (opposed vigorously by Augustine), Manichaeanism, Arianism, and Monophysitism. Arianism was advanced by the Vandals, who carved a kingdom for themselves in North Africa from 429-534. During this long period, the Orthodox Christians were frequently oppressed, although at times toleration was the adopted policy. Orthodoxy was formally reestablished by the Byzantines under General Belisarius. That the Church was vital in this last pre-Islamic period is seen in the work of converting the tribes of North Africa (the Berbers), and the opposition of the local hierarchy to Monothelitism. The Arabic conquest of the late seventh century virtually extirpated the African Church, as the Christian communities were cut off from the rest of the Church. (See **Alexandria** and **Ethiopia**.)

While some small Christian communities were established along the African coast during the crusades, the faith was not brought back to Africa in any appreciable sense until the 1500s, starting with the erection in 1514 of an archdiocese on the Madeira Islands by the Portuguese, a see that had as its jurisdiction the entire west coast of Africa. Subsequently, East Africa was placed under the authority of the hierarchy in Goa, India. In 1612, the prelature nullius of Mozambique was removed from the authorities in Goa — a mark of the growing Church in that part of Africa. Another notable missionary endeavor in the seventeenth century was undertaken by the Jesuits to Ethiopia. They enjoyed some success and were able, albeit temporarily, to restore the kingdom to union with Rome.

The 1700s brought American Catholic missionaries, including an organization devoted to assisting liberated slaves in their hope of creating a homeland. The result would be Monrovia (named in honor of President James Monroe), which later became the capital of Liberia. In the mid-nineteenth century, further progress in missionary activity was made possible by the recently founded Society for the Propagation of the Faith and the energetic Holy Ghost Fathers. The later decades of the 1800s would witness the flourishing of the Society of Missions for Africa, the White Fathers, founded in 1868 by Charles Lavigerie, later a cardinal. This period also saw numerous martyrdoms among the White Fathers, most notably in Uganda in 1879.

By 1939, the Catholic Church was sufficiently organized to warrant the consecration of the first bishops below the Sahara Desert by Pope Pius XII. After the war, bishops were appointed in South Africa and elsewhere, culminating in 1960 with the elevation of Bishop Laurean Rugambwa of Tanganyika as the first black cardinal. Despite restrictions in some countries, such as South Africa and Ethiopia, the Church grew in the next years. Today, the faith is found everywhere on the continent and is one of the most important sources for education, medical care, and food in many countries long torn by civil war, famine, and political instability. The continent remains, despite democratic advances in some regions, a dangerous and troubled place for missionaries and the established Church. Nowhere has that been more clear in recent years than in Rwanda where the civil war there has claimed thousands of Catholic lives and has been the source of sorrow and prayers from members of the Church everywhere in the world. Among those killed in the vicious fighting was the archbishop of Kigali, massacred with his bishops. Entering the next millennium, however, the Church can be optimistic about the faith in Africa,

despite the dangers, challenges, and obstacles.

"Against the Christians" ● Work by the gifted pagan intellectual Porphyry (d. c. 305) in which he sharply criticized and vilified the tenets of Christianity. The work was to serve as a philosophical foundation for the severe persecutions of the Church in the late third century, particularly under Emperor Diocletian. In "Against the Christians," Porphyry poked fun at the Scriptures and the Eucharist, and dismissed Christ as a feeble, weak, and pitiful figure.

Agapetus I ● Pope from 535-536. A briefly reigning pontiff (only ten months), he nevertheless proved himself an ardent defender of Christian orthodoxy. His main achievement was the deposition of Anthemius, patriarch of Constantinople, for being a Monophysite, despite the opposition of Emperor Justinian I. He was also called Agapitus I.

Agapetus II ● Pope from 946-955. Also called Agapitus, he was dominated throughout his reign by the powerful duke of Spoleto, Alberic II (d. 954), the virtual ruler of Rome from 932-954. Alberic had control of the papal government and was able to ensure that Agapetus would be succeeded by his own son, Octavian — the infamous John XII. Agapetus issued a bull in 948 that placed all of Christianized Denmark under the jurisdiction of the metropolitan see of Hamburg and surrendered to Emperor Otto I administrative authority over the bishops of Germany.

Agatha, St. ● Fifth-century virgin martyr who is the patron saint of the city of Catania and of bell-founders. She was traditionally said to have been martyred at Catania, Sicily, and was much revered in later centuries, although most of the legend is spurious. She supposedly had her breasts cut off at her execution and so is seen carrying them in a dish. Their similarity to bells, according to one story, is generally considered the source for her patronage of bell-founders. Feast day: February 5.

Agatho, St. ● Pope from 678-681. He was active in combating the heresy of Monothelitism with a council in Rome in 680 that would produce a formula to be used later that year against the Monothelite supporters at the Sixth General Council (Third Council of Constantinople). Agatho also worked to further the use of the Roman liturgy in England and supported the cause of Wilfrid, archbishop of York, in his dispute with Theodore of Tarsus, archbishop of Canterbury, over the division of the former's see in 678. He was probably from Sicily. Feast day: January 10.

Agde, Council of ● Council held at Agde in Languedoc, France, in 506 that was attended by thirty-five bishops under the presidency of St. Caesarius of Arles. It produced forty-seven canons, primarily concerned with clerical discipline, including celibacy, obligations of the faithful, and the canonical age for ordination. The canons provide scholars with valuable details about the life of the Church in southern France in the early sixth century.

Age of Reason ● See **Enlightenment**.

Aggiornamento ● Italian for "updating" or "renewal" that was used and popularized by Pope John XXIII in his effort to modernize and revitalize the Catholic Church through the Second Vatican Council (1962-1965). *Aggiornamento* was intended to signify a new way of presenting the faith to the world so that it can be understood and accepted more readily and has become the central word for the spirit to be found in the actual implementation of the decrees and documents of the Church.

Aglipay Schism ● Schism that erupted in the Philippines at the start of the twentieth century and named after its founder, Father Gregorio Aglipay. It began as the result of the departure in large numbers of Spanish clergy in the Philippines first during the revolution in 1896 and then again when the United States assumed control in 1898. Aglipay, sensing that a vacuum of authority had developed, declared himself the head of the Church in the Philippines in 1902. He soon attracted over a million followers, and the schismatics seized extensive Church properties. These possessions were restored by American courts in 1906. Aglipay was also later reconciled to the Catholic faith and, after his death in 1941, the schism declined rapidly.

Agnellus, Andreas ● See **Agnellus of Ravenna**.

Agnellus of Pisa, Bl. (c. 1195-1236) ● Important Franciscan figure during the 1200s and founder of the Franciscan province in England. Agnellus was accepted into the order by St. Francis himself, who sent him to Paris to establish a monastery there. He later returned to Italy, but in 1224 he was instructed to go to England. On September 10, 1224, he landed at Dover with eight friars, beginning immediately to introduce the order to the English. Friaries were created in Canterbury and Oxford, and Robert Grosseteste was brought in to teach at the latter house, helping to make Oxford a major center of learning in England. (See also **Adam of Marsh**.) Agnellus is especially revered by Franciscans.

Agnellus of Ravenna (805-c. 850) ● In full, Andreas Agnellus, a cleric (with the title of abbot) and a historian who authored a history of the see of Ravenna, *Liber Pontificalis Ecclesiae Ravennatis*. Written as a defense of the see's claims against Rome and full of errors, the work preserves valuable information on the city from the fourth to the eighth centuries. Agnellus referred to the realm of Charlemagne as the Roman Empire and opposed clerical marriage.

Agnes, St. ● Also Agnes of Rome, one of the most venerated of all Roman martyrs, who was executed perhaps in 304, almost certainly in the early fourth century. It is unfortunate that little is known about her with any certainty beyond the facts that she was martyred in Rome and buried in the cemetery on the Via Nomentana. A church was later built (c. 350) on the site of the cemetery. According to generally accepted tradition, she was a young woman, perhaps twelve or thirteen, who chose to adopt a celibate life. When persecutions broke out, she offered herself as a martyr and was executed by being stabbed in the throat. Feast day: January 21.

Agnosticism ● Philosophical theory that states it is not possible to know whether God exists, since the human mind is incapable of comprehending such knowledge that is within the realm of the supernatural or that pertains to the Divine Being. The term was apparently coined by Thomas Henry Huxley (d. 1895) in 1869. The basic concept of agnosticism differs profoundly from the teaching of the Church that the human mind is capable of reaching beyond material phenomena and comprehending basic truths, including the existence of God. Agnosticism has also been used to mean all forms of skepticism toward religion or knowledge of the spiritual.

Agobard (769-840) ● Archbishop of Lyons and a somewhat controversial theologian. Ordained in 804, he was made coadjutor to the see of Lyons in 813, succeeding Leidrad of Lyons in 816. He was deposed and exiled by the Council of Thionville in 835 because of his opposition to various plans or schemes of Empress Judith, traveling to Italy where he was under the protection of Lothair I, the German king, until 838 when he was allowed to return home. As a scholar, Agobard attacked Adoptionism, folklore, the veneration of images, paganism, and Jews, but his books were placed on the list of prohibited writings as the result of some of his theological views. (See also **Adoptionism**.)

Aguirre, Joseph de (1630-1699) ● Cardinal, theologian, and head of the Holy Office in Spain. He entered the Benedictine monastery of Monte Cassino and then was director of studies at the monastery of St. Vincent of Salamanca for many years before becoming abbot. Later secretary to the Holy Office, he was made president of the congregation's province in Spain. In his capacity as watchdog for dogmatic theology, he labored against the Declaration of the Gallican Clergy of 1682, an act that won him the cardinalate from Pope Innocent XI (see **Gallicanism**). Aguirre authored numerous works on philosophy and theology, including a defense of St. Thomas Aquinas and Aristotle, a commentary on Aristotle's *Ethics*, a treatise on angels, and commentaries on the theology of St. Anselm. He died suddenly of apoplexy and was buried in Rome, his heart sent to Monte Cassino as per his long-standing wish.

Aidan, St. (d. 651) ● English monk and bishop of Iona who founded the major monastic community of Lindisfarne. Originally a monk at Iona, Aidan was consecrated a bishop in 635 and sent to Northumbria to revive missionary work in the region. He established himself at Lindisfarne Island, using it as his base for travels, the site emerging as a profound religious center. Aidan's journeys took him far and wide across Northumbria, with highly successful missionary efforts. In the process, Aidan became a close friend of Oswald and Oswiu, kings of Northumberland. When Oswiu died in 651, Aidan had a hut built against the west wall of the church in Bamborough, capital of the Northumbrian kingdom. He died there, traditionally of a broken heart, but he had trained twelve young Englishmen to become the ecclesiastical leaders of the nation.

Aikenhead, Mary (1787-1858) ● Founder of the Irish Sisters of Charity. Born in Cork, Ireland, she was raised in the Church of England, but became a Catholic following the deathbed example of her father who, as his last act, accepted the Catholic faith. Desirous of joining a religious order devoted to charity work, she was unable to find one, and instead was chosen, against her will, by Archbishop Murray of Dublin to establish a new congregation, the Sisters of Charity in Ireland. Toward that end, she made a novitiate of three years (1812-1815), adopting there the religious name Sister Mary Augustine. On September 1, 1815, the first members of the congregation took their vows, with Aikenhead as their superior general. Over the next years, the order spread, distinguishing itself during the terrible years of the plague in Ireland in 1832. By the time of her death, Aikenhead was presiding over a congregation with numerous institutions in Ireland, France, and Australia.

St. Aidan

Ailred ● See **Aelred of Rievaulx**.

Alain of Lille ● See **Alan of Lille**.

Alais, Treaty of ● Peace treaty orchestrated by Cardinal Armand Jean du Plessis Richelieu and signed on June 28, 1629, that brought a settlement to the struggle between French royal forces and the Huguenots. The treaty reaffirmed the points of the Edict of Nantes (1598), but it ended the military position and political threat of the Huguenots toward the French crown. They did retain their religious and civil liberties. (See also **Huguenots**.)

Alan of Lille (c. 1128-1202) ● Also Alanus de Insulis, a French theologian, mystic, and respected intellectual, given the title *Doctor Universalis* (the Universal Doctor). He was born in Lille, studying at Paris or Chartres under the renowned theologian Gilbert de la Porrée. After teaching at Paris, he lived for many years in Montpellier and finally joined the Cistercians. A gifted theological writer, he wrote numerous treatises including *Theologiae regulae*, establishing rules for theology, and an untitled *summa theologica*. He also authored *De planctu naturae* (*On the Lamentation of Nature*) and *Anticlaudianus*.

Alan of Tewkesbury (d. 1202) ● Benedictine abbot, ardent supporter of St. Thomas Becket, and author of a biography on the saint. Probably of English blood, Alan spent some time in Benevento, Italy, before entering the Benedictine house at Canterbury. He became prior there in 1179. Alan emerged as an outspoken adherent of Thomas's cause against King Henry II in the struggle over the English clergy, a dispute that ended with Becket's murder in 1170. In order to reduce his vocal complaints about Henry's rapacious treatment of the Church, Alan was removed from Canterbury to Tewkesbury. The main source of information on Alan is the chronicler Gervase of Canterbury.

Alaric (c. 370-410) ● See **Arianism, Rome,** and **Visigoths**.

Alban, St. ● Called *Protomartyr Anglorum,* Latin for "the first English [or British] martyr." According to tradition, he was originally a pagan at Verulamium (modern St. Alban's) in Roman Britain, who was converted to Christianity by a priest to whom he gave shelter during the Roman persecutions (probably under Emperor Septimius Severus around 209, although other stories put the persecutions at the time of Diocletian in the late third century). When Roman troops searched his house, Alban dressed as the priest and was captured and sentenced to death. The priest was himself killed a short time later. Honored as an early martyr, he was mentioned favorably by Venantius Fortunatus around 580. He was also noted by the Venerable Bede in his *Ecclesiastical History.* His shrine is still in the Abbey of St. Alban's. Feast day: June 20, observed locally; his feast day of June 22 was dropped from the Roman calendar in 1969.

Albergati, Nicolo, Bl. (1357-1443) ● Bishop of Bologna and cardinal who proved very useful to several popes in fulfilling demanding or diplomatically sensitive missions. A native of Bologna, Albergati entered the Carthusians in 1394 serving as prior in various monasteries before being compelled to accept the episcopal see of Bologna in 1417. Despite being bishop, he adhered to the rule of the order, and distinguished himself as a reformer. He was also a patron of learning, showing favor to Aeneas Sylvius, the future Pius II. Popes Martin V and Eugenius IV sent him on missions to France and Lombardy. In 1426, Albergati became a cardinal and was a participant at the Council of Basel (1432, 1434, and 1436) and the Council of Ferrara (the reconvened and moved Council of Basel, 1438, also called the Council of Ferrara-Florence, 1438-1445), holding at several sessions the rank of papal legate from Pope Eugenius IV. He helped lay the foundation work for the formal but ultimately unsuccessful union of the Eastern and Western Churches at the Council of Florence.

Albert of Aachen (fl. mid-1100s) ● Also Albert Aguensis, a chronicler of the First Crusade (1095-1099), who was also probably canon of Aachen (French name: Aix-la-Chapelle), although some less reliable sources declared him canon at a church in Aix-en-Provence. His chronicle — *Chronicon Hierosolymitanum de bello sacro,* written in twelve books — is full of historical, narrative, and chronological errors, but it is nevertheless useful in presenting a clear portrait of the social and religious fervor generated by the launching of the crusades. He himself was of the view that the knights setting off for the Holy Land were bringing Christian salvation to the territories long under the sway of the infidel. The history was also influential in his era in attracting soldiers to the crusader cause.

Albert of Brandenburg (1490-1545) ● Cardinal archbishop and elector of Mainz and elector of the Holy Roman Empire. He studied originally at Frankfurt-on-Oder and as early as 1509 he was given the post of prebendary of Mainz. His advance was subsequently swift: archbishop of Magdeburg and administrator in 1513, archbishop of Mainz (making him an imperial elector) in 1514, and cardinal priest from 1518. Albert was entrusted in 1517 with an indulgence of St. Peter's (an indulgence intended to help pay for a new St. Peter's Basilica in Rome) for Brandenburg and Saxony. To head the acquisition of funds, Albert procured the services of the notorious Dominican preacher Johann Tetzel. Tetzel's corrupt and irregular methods prompted the growing ire of Martin Luther who believed that in Albert he had an ally in spreading the call for Church reform. Albert was considered liberal, a patron of humanists, and an early supporter of the Reformation. His patronage of the humanist Ulrich von Hutten was particularly reprehensible to the pope and earned Albert an admonition. After vacillating again about the Reformation during the Peasants' War (1524-1525), he finally threw himself firmly into the Church cause at the meeting of Dessau in 1525. Henceforth, he was a staunch defender of Catholicism, particularly at the Nuremburg Meeting (1538), which marked opposition to the League of Schmalkalden. He also gave his warmest support to Peter Faber and the new Jesuit order, keeping Faber in the diocese from 1542-1543. Albert died a defender of the Church in all German lands.

Albert of Castile (1460-1522) ● Historian and member of the Dominican order. He joined the Dominicans while still young at the Convent of Sts. John and Paul at Venice, distinguishing himself over the next years by his remarkable gifts as a historian. Aside from his work as an editor, including a defense of the Order of Friars Preachers, Albert authored numerous histories, most notably *Chronica brevis ab initio ordinis usque ad praesens tempus* (1504), an account of the popes, the generals of the order, and notable members throughout its past until his own era. Its primary source was the writings of the Dominican Giacomo de Luzato.

Albert of Mainz ● See **Albert of Brandenburg**.

Albert of Prussia (1490-1560) ● Last grand master of the Teutonic Knights and the first duke of Prussia. Albert is most remembered for bringing an end to the mastery of the Teutonic Order in East Prussia and for becoming a Protestant. The son of Frederick Hohenzollern, margrave of Ansbach-Bayreuth, he was named grand master of the order and embarked upon a destructive war in East Prussia from 1519-1521. As the political and military position of the knights was continuing to deteriorate, Albert was convinced by Martin Luther to switch in 1523 to the Protestant cause and dissolve the order, thereby transforming these holdings into a personal, hereditary dukedom under the suzerainty of the Polish crown. Content to be rid of the knights, King Sigismund I accepted his plan in 1525 thereby ending the domination of the Teutonic Order over East Prussia. Albert was soon ordered by the Holy Roman Emperor Charles V to return all lands to the order, but Albert refused, joining the anti-imperial coalitions. By the time of his death, the secular dukedom was fully established as a Protestant stronghold and the knights had been dealt a blow from which they would never recover.

Alberti, Leandro (1479-1552) ● Dominican historian. He served as secretary to the master general of the order, Francisco Ferraris, until the latter's death in 1527, by which time Alberti had established himself as a respected writer and historian. In 1517, he published a survey on the notable friars of the order that enjoyed wide readership and was later extensively translated. He also authored *Descrizione d'Italia* (1550), an archaeological and topographical survey of Italy; wrote a chronicle of Italian history from 1499-1552; and compiled biographical sketches of famous Venetians.

Alberti, Leon Battista (1404-1472) ●

Italian architect and humanist who spent many years in the service of the papacy as an adviser on the construction and restoration of churches. He was originally from Genoa, the illegitimate son of an exiled Florentine banker. Raised in Venice, he was educated in Bologna and Padua and ultimately was given the post of secretary in the papal chancery (Curia) in Rome. When a long-standing ban on the family was finally lifted, Alberti visited Florence in 1432, returning two years later with Pope Eugenius IV. While there, he first met with such luminaries of the period as Bracciolini, Lorenzo Ghiberti, and Donatello. His next years were spent fulfilling his duties to the popes, but he authored a number of treatises, including *Della pittura* and *Della statura*, on painting and sculpture, and his *magnum opus*, *De re aedificatoria*, on architecture (dedicated to Pope Nicholas V in 1452), which was not published until 1485. Alberti also wrote several humanist works: *Della famiglia* (*On the Family*), *De iciarchia* (*On the Head of His Family*), and poetry. He died in Rome.

Albertini, Nicolo (c. 1250-1321) ●

Cardinal, papal legate, procurator-general of the Dominicans, and a highly successful diplomat on behalf of the papacy. An Italian from Prato, he joined the Dominicans in 1266, studying at Florence and then Paris around the time that Albert the Great and Thomas Aquinas were at the height of their fame in the order. After successfully preaching in Florence and Paris, Albertini was named head of several houses and then procurator-general of the Dominicans by Nicolo Boccassini, the master general. Pope

Boniface VIII made him bishop of Spoleto in 1299, soon using him as a reliable representative (papal legate). Albertini achieved considerable notoriety for his surprising success in bringing King Philip IV of France and King Edward I of England into peaceful discussions — a task that had seemed virtually impossible. As a reward, Boniface made him cardinal vicar of Rome, and Benedict XI elevated him to cardinal bishop of Ostia and dean of the College of Cardinals. He later tried to end the incessant wars and civil strife in Italy between the cities and among the embittered Guelph and Ghibelline factions, meeting with only limited success — Florence had to be placed under interdict because of its citizens' unwillingness to end the bloodshed.

Albertus Magnus, St. (c. 1200- or 1206-1280) ●

Also Albert the Great or Albert of Cologne, a Doctor of the Church, called *Doctor Universalis*, one of the most intellectual figures of the Middle Ages and an important leader of Scholasticism within the Church. Albertus was born in Lauingen, on the Danube in southern Germany. The son of a wealthy nobleman, he attended the University of Padua where he was drawn to the Dominican order in 1223, under the influence of Bl. Jordan of Saxony (d. 1237), the second master of the order. He then studied further at Padua and in Germany before receiving a position as teacher in Cologne. In 1245, he went to Paris where he earned his doctorate and where he began to encounter the writings of the philosopher Aristotle that were just becoming available. While in Paris he also met his future pupil and friend Thomas Aquinas.

Returning to Germany in 1248, Albertus established a house of studies (*studium generale*) at Cologne, serving as master of the university until 1254. That year he was elected prior general of the Dominicans for Germany. He was aided in Cologne by the brilliant Thomas Aquinas, working with the

Albertus magnus cum discipulis suie.

St. Albert the Great

1263-1264. After this he was allowed to retire to Cologne as *lector emeritus*. In his remaining years, he would travel from Cologne only twice, in 1274 and 1277, when he went to Paris to defend Thomas Aquinas and his teachings and the rightful place of Aristotle in Christian thought. He died at Cologne.

Called the "Great" even in his own lifetime, Albertus was the author of a large body of works, on theology, logic, philosophy, ethics, and metaphysics. He also wrote commentaries on Aristotle, the Scriptures, and the *Sentences* of Peter Lombard. While not as vast and systematic as his friend Thomas, Albertus is considered by many scholars to be more accessible and less imposing. Described by Roger Bacon as the most famous of the Christian scholars, Albertus was important in advancing the important cause of uniting reason and faith, a labor that would find its fullest expression in St. Thomas Aquinas. Credited with making Aristotle "intelligible to the Latins," he was honored by the Church in 1931 when Pope Pius XI canonized him and declared him a Doctor of the Church. Feast day: November 15.

young theologian and others from the mendicant orders, such as St. Bonaventure, to defend the place of the friars in the Church and the universities.

His successful participation in the defeat of those who opposed mendicant orders came to the attention of the Holy See. Thus, after lecturing for several years in Germany again (1257-1260), he was appointed bishop of Regensburg by Pope Alexander IV, despite his own misgivings and the protests of his Dominican superiors. He held the see from 1260-1261. Pope Urban IV then commissioned him to preach another crusade throughout German lands, from

Albigensian Movement ● Known during the Middle Ages as the Albigenses, a famous heretical sect of the twelfth and thirteenth centuries, spreading throughout southern France and centered in the city of Albi from which it took its name. The heresy found much support across Europe, its adherents elsewhere acquiring assorted names such as the Cathari, or Cathars. The Albigensians adhered to a belief in a sort of Manichaean dualism between the forces of good and evil.

In their thinking, all matter — especially the body — was created by evil, while the spirit was created by Goodness. In order to demonstrate the validity of their theological arguments, they attempted to use the Scriptures, particularly the NT, to

Albi Cathedral

show that Christ's death and resurrection were only allegorical, and he was actually an angel. As an extension of their logic, the Christian Church, with its powerful place on the earth and its propagation of the belief of the incarnation of Christ, was adding to the evil in the world and was thus inherently corrupt.

Many Albigensians practiced a form of rigorous austerity, including starvation and frequent suicide. These followers of the creed were called "perfects," while regular members led more average lives and were known as "believers." Some believers, eager to assist the perfects into the world of the spirit, where they themselves hoped to journey before long, would murder them. Despite such extremes, the movement became a genuine political force, securing the patronage of Peter II of Aragon and Raymond VI of Toulouse.

The Church was understandably concerned about the heresy, using various synods and councils to condemn it. Pope Innocent II also attempted to send missionaries to the Albigensians, including a number of Cistercians and St. Dominic as his main spokesmen. These efforts proved ultimately futile, and the hostility of the sect toward the Church finally erupted in violence when, in 1209, the papal legate Peter of Castelnau was murdered. Direct action was launched in the form of the so-called Albigensian Crusade, an extremely bloody and ruthless campaign of extirpation. Overall command of the crusade was given to Simon de Montfort. In 1209, for example, the city of Beziers was captured and its Albigensian population was massacred and the papal legate Arnaud Amoury supposedly (but erroneously) was heard to say: "Kill them all; let God sort out the good ones." With the Battle of Muret in 1213, Peter of Aragon was defeated by de Montfort, an event that signaled the rapid eradication of the sect. Pope Gregory IX commanded the Dominicans to use the Inquisition to destroy whatever was left of the heresy, a task they fulfilled with such vigor that by the end of the century the Albigensians had all but ceased to exist. (See also **Cathari, Heresy,** and **Waldenses.**)

Albornoz, Gil Álvarez Carillo de (c. 1310-1367) ● Powerful cardinal and statesman. Born at Cuenca, New Castile, in Spain, he was a descendant of both royal houses of León and Aragon, studying law at Toulouse and receiving swift ecclesiastical promotion: royal almoner, archdeacon of Calatrava, and in 1338 archbishop of Toledo. Two years later, he took part in the campaign of King Alfonso XI against the Moors, saving the king's life at the Battle of Rio Salado on October 30, 1340. Meanwhile, as archbishop he convened two synods to introduce and advance reform, in 1339 and 1347. In 1350, he was forced to flee Spain on the accession of King Pedro the Cruel, who had a deep hatred for Albornoz owing to the prelate's harsh criticisms of his brutality and immorality. Albornoz fled to Avignon where he was received by Pope Clement VI, who created him cardinal in December 1350. He resigned as archbishop of Toledo and in 1352 was charged with the difficult task of restoring papal authority and some semblance of order in the Papal States. By virtue of the bull issued on June 30, 1353, he possessed extraordinary powers. On March 10, 1354, he defeated Giovanni di Vico, prefect of Rome and lord of Viterbo, who had seized part of the papal lands, forcing upon him a treaty of submission. Albornoz also appointed Cola di Rienzi senator of Rome in the hopes that the popular adventurer and onetime tribune might establish sound government in Rome. Rienzi, however, proved a harsh master of the city, and his oppressive taxes and irrational administration hastened his fall and murder by a mob on October 8, 1354.

Albornoz entered Rome and suppressed the anarchy that had plagued the city for years. He then continued to reduce opposition to papal control in the region. With the help of the commander Ridolfo da Varano, Albornoz defeated a number of ambitious noble houses such as the Malatesta and the Manfredi. By 1356, virtually all of the Papal States had been restored, and Albornoz asked to be recalled to Avignon. On October 23, 1357, he arrived at Avignon and was honored by Innocent with the title *Pater Ecclesiae.* His successor in Italy, Androin de la Roche, abbot of Cluny, proved unequal to the demands of dealing with the intrigues of the Italian nobles, and Innocent ordered Albornoz back to Rome. More fighting followed, ended only in 1364 by a treaty signed with Bernabo Visconti of Milan. The treaty was highly favorable to Bernabo owing to the desire of the new pontiff, Urban V (1362-1370), to devote his full attention to a crusade against the Turks. A gifted general, statesman, and administrator, Albornoz was largely responsible for the military and political recovery of the papal position in Italy that would make the return of the popes to Rome in 1377 a possibility. He was also the founder (through his will) of the Spanish College of St. Clement at Bologna.

Alchemy ● Ancient mystical science, defined in its strictest sense as the transmuting of base metals into gold; it is considered a predecessor of chemistry. Alchemy is a truly old field of study, found among the Egyptians, Chinese, Greeks, and Indians, transmitted by tradition and often secret writings to the Arabs, Byzantines, and Europeans. It was called during the Middle Ages the "Great Work" or the "Art," and its study entailed complex experimentation with large numbers of compounds, elixirs, and elements. The aim was to find the elixir that could add to the life-span — perhaps even obtain immortality — through the *elixir vitae,* the Philosopher's Stone that could transmute metals into gold. While the Church condemned false alchemists, especially those who preyed upon the gullible, a number of major Church figures either examined alchemy or were reputed alchemists themselves. St. Thomas Aquinas discussed it in his *Summa Theologiae* and was the reputed author of several alchemy treatises. So too were St. Albertus Magnus (with the dubious work *De Alchimia*), Roger Bacon, Arnold of Villanova, Vincent of Beauvais, and Pope John XXII. That pontiff issued the bull *Spondent quas non exhibent* in 1317 against dishonest alchemists.

Alcuin (c. 735-804) ● Also known as Alcuin of York, Flaccus, and Albinus, a central figure in the so-called Carolingian Renaissance of the eighth century in which learning and the arts were promoted by the court of Charlemagne. Alcuin was a native of Northumbria, in England, receiving his education in York, at the cathedral school. By 766 he was a teacher there and by 768 headmaster. While on a visit to the Continent in 781, he met Charlemagne and was offered by that mighty ruler the position of head instructor in the palace of Aachen; he was soon also a prominent adviser. From this position, Alcuin helped guide, influence, and shape the rebirth of learning in the Carolingian Empire. He penned manuals of education, devised a course of study (stressing the dialogue, the *trivium* and elements of the *quadrivium*, with readings from Boethius and Augustine), and attracted to Aachen the finest minds of the day, including Peter of Pisa and Paul the Deacon. Alcuin himself taught Amalarius of Metz and Rabanus Maurus, all of whom would be prominent Churchmen or theologians. He also advised Charlemagne on important theological matters, most notably during the Adoptionist Controversy. In 796, Alcuin became spiritual guide to the monks of St. Martin in Tours, dying there in 804.

Aldhelm, St. (d. 709) ● Bishop of Sherborne and an important figure in the English ecclesiastical reform movement. A Saxon, Aldhelm was a relative of King Ine of Wessex, although other details of his life are sketchy. In 675, he became abbot of Malmesbury, but he also spent much time at Canterbury. There he studied under the many scholars who had been attracted to Canterbury by Archbishop Theodore of Tarsus. It was said that Aldhelm had a particularly difficult time with mathematics, especially fractions. Bishop of Sherborne in 705, he became an adherent of the reform movement sponsored by Theodore, writing against the Celtic Church in favor of the Roman Church, establishing several monasteries and churches, and calling for a Christian community that was unified. While a writer of little style or grace, Aldhelm composed poetry (now lost) that was said to have been much enjoyed by Alfred the Great. Two main sources for his life are William of Malmesbury and Faricius of Abingdon. Feast day: May 25.

Alexander I, St. ● Pope of the first century, reigning as the fifth successor to St. Peter from approximately 105-115 or 109-119. Alexander followed St. Evaristus and was most likely martyred by decapitation during the reign of Trajan or Hadrian. Alexander is credited with introducing holy water and the mixing of sacramental wine and water. Feast day: May 3.

Alexander II ● Pope from 1061-1073. Originally known as Anselm of Lucca, he studied under Lanfranc of Bec and was an ardent supporter of reform in the Church, preaching against simony and for the celibacy of the clergy. The archbishop of Milan found him so troublesome that he sent Anselm on a mission to Emperor Henry III. Bishop of Lucca in 1057, he was elected as Pope Alexander II in 1061, mainly through the support of Hildebrand (later Gregory VII). Enthroned without the blessing of Emperor Henry IV, Alexander found the election of an antipope (Honorius II, who died in 1072) sponsored by the emperor, although imperial backing for the antipope essentially ended after 1062. As pope, Alexander focused on reform in the Church, using papal legates to enforce his views on simony and celibacy. He also gave his blessing to William of Normandy in his invasion of England in 1066.

Alexander III ● Pope from 1159-1181. Originally from Siena, Orlando Bandinelli, as he was called, became one of the most respected canonical legalists of his era, teaching at the University of Bologna (a leading center of canon law) and working in the Roman Curia as an adviser to Pope Adrian IV, whom he succeeded. Appointed a cardinal, he worked within the Curia to oppose wherever possible the increasing ambitions of Holy Roman Emperor Frederick I Barbarossa, a struggle that would continue long after the election of Bandinelli to the Holy See in 1159. Frederick secured the election of an antipope, Victor IV, to challenge Alexander, a schism ended only in 1177. In the meantime, Alexander was forced to flee Italy and go to France in 1162, returning in 1165, although he departed again in 1166. As part of his conflict with Frederick, the pope helped organize the Lombard League in Italy, which delivered a crushing blow to Frederick's ambitions at the Battle of Legnano in 1176. The following year, a peace was arranged with the signing of the Treaty of Venice. While in exile in France, Alexander involved himself in the dispute between Thomas Becket, archbishop of Canterbury, and King Henry II of England. Not an enthusiastic admirer of Becket, Alexander nevertheless inflicted a severe penance for Becket's murder in 1170. Alexander also had a lasting influence upon the papacy by forcing the adoption of rules that called for the acceptance of a new pope by a vote of two-thirds of the cardinals in conclave.

Alexander IV ● Pope from 1254-1261. Born Rinaldo, count of Segni, he was the nephew of Pope Gregory IX, who elevated him to cardinal deacon in 1227 and then to the powerful cardinalate of Ostia in 1231. Elected in 1254, he continued the work of the Inquisition in France, promoted a crusade against the Tatar menace in the East, and sided with the mendicant friars in their struggle with the secular masters of the University of Paris, support that had far-reaching consequences for the presence of the mendicants, especially the Dominicans, in the universities of the West. He called St. Thomas Aquinas away from the University of Paris in 1259 and gave him a post in the Curia as adviser, preacher, and lecturer. Alexander also worked unsuccessfully for the reunification of the Eastern and Western Churches and struggled against the Italian ambitions of Manfred, illegitimate son of Emperor Frederick II.

Alexander V ● Pope from 1409-1410, although considered by some historians to be an antipope. Originally Pietro di Candia, he was a member of the Franciscan order and a noted theologian. Archbishop of Milan in 1402, he became a cardinal in 1405 and was subsequently a papal legate to Lombardy. Elected pope in 1409 at the age of seventy by the Council of Pisa, it was hoped that he would bring an end to the Great Schism (1378-1417), but the other rival popes, Gregory XII and the antipope Benedict XIII, refused to step down, so the schism continued. Alexander reigned only ten months, dying mysteriously on May 3, 1410, at Bologna. It has been argued that he was probably poisoned by his successor, the antipope John XXIII. His lectures as Pietro di Candia at the Franciscan convent of St. Mary Magdalene, especially on the *Sentences* of Peter Lombard, are much praised by medieval scholars.

Alexander VI ● Pope from 1492-1503. One of the most infamous of all pontiffs who neglected the spiritual good of the Church in order to assist in the aggrandizement of his family — the Borgias — especially the two notorious children Cesare and Lucrezia Borgia. Originally Rodrigo Borgia (in full Spanish, Rodrigo de Borja y Doms), he was born in Jativa, Spain. He was named head of the papal administration by his uncle, Pope Callistus III. Serving from 1457-1492, Rodgrigo was the most powerful official in the Vatican, patronizing the arts and amassing for himself and his family a huge fortune. He secured the election of Sixtus IV in 1471 and used massive bribes in 1492 to have himself elected pope. The reign of Alexander is considered a dark period in papal history, for the power of the Holy See was used to aid the Borgias in their wars of supremacy in Italy. Thus, a jubilee had most of its money diverted to Cesare, and Alexander's reprehensible conduct helped set the stage for the Reformation later in the century. He did try unsuccessfully to reform himself after the murder (of which Cesare was probably an accomplice) of his eldest and favorite son in 1497. Alexander also helped propagate a papal bull in 1493-1494, dividing the New World between Spain and Portugal and

ensured the death of Savonarola. His rebuilding of Castel Sant' Angelo would prove significant in 1527 when Austrian mercenaries pillaged the city and the Vatican.

Alexander VII ● Pope from 1655-1667. Originally Fabio Chighi, he distinguished himself more before becoming pope than after. Born and educated in Siena, he studied theology, law, and philosophy. Grandnephew of Pope St. Pius V, he entered the service of the Church in 1626, holding the post of inquisitor of Malta and then papal nuncio at Cologne from 1639-1651. He thus was a participant in the negotiations that would lead to the eventual end of the Thirty Years' War by the Treaty of Westphalia (1648). He called upon the Catholic princes not to deal with heretics, especially protesting several clauses of the treaty. The princes, weary of the war, proceeded nevertheless. Made cardinal in 1652, he became papal secretary of state and was elected pope a few years later. As pope, Alexander vigorously opposed Jansenism, receiving support from King Louis XIV of France, although the two later had a parting of the ways over a dispute concerning the French ambassador. A patron of the Society of Jesus, he succeeded in gaining the readmission of the order into Venice. (See also **Bernini, Giovanni Lorenzo**.)

Alexander VIII ● Pope from 1689-1691. Originally Pietro Ottoboni, he was a member of a noble Venetian house. After studying at Padua, he became a doctor of canon and civil law in 1627. Made a cardinal by Pope Innocent X in 1652, he was appointed bishop of Brescia in 1654. As pope, he was successful in bringing about a reconciliation with King Louis XIV of France, securing the return of Avignon and Venaissin that the king had seized during the reign of Alexander VII (1655-1667) in a dispute. Alexander also condemned the Four Gallican Propositions of

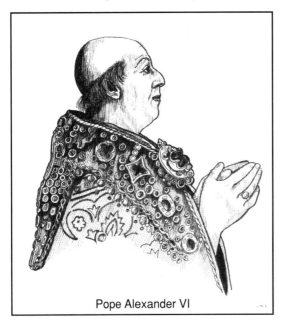

Pope Alexander VI

1682 and the proposition of Cornelius Jansen (or Jansenius). He aided Venice against the Ottoman Turks, enriched the Vatican Library, and strove to improve social conditions in the States of the Church.

Alexander of Abonateichos (fl. second century) ●

Notorious impostor of oracles who was especially successful in his native Paphlagonia (a Roman province in ancient Asia Minor) and promoted the persecution of Christians. He delivered cleverly phrased oracles to his highly gullible audience, enriching himself and proclaiming that his god would show displeasure upon Paphlagonia if the Christians were not stoned and persecuted — particularly as it was the Christian leaders who attacked his ridiculous proclamations. He eventually earned the contempt of the populace when none of his prophecies came true; he died, according to Lucian of Antioch, of a loathsome disease.

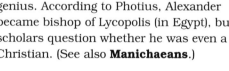
Pope Alexander VII

Alexander of Hales (c. 1180-1245) ●

Franciscan theologian, the so-called *Doctor Irrefragabilis* (the Irrefutable Doctor). He was born in Hales, or Halesowen, in Worcestershire, England, studying at Paris where he would later teach and serve as master of theology from 1220 until his death. In 1236, however, he joined the Franciscans, nevertheless retaining his chair at the University of Paris, a chair henceforth held by the Franciscan order. One of the great early Franciscan theologians, Alexander authored highly influential glosses on the *Sentences* of Peter Lombard, helping to make the work one of the main sources of theological training. He also wrote *Quaestiones* on theology and a *summa theologica* (first published in 1475), compiled with the help of other Franciscans, including William of Melitona and John de la Rochelle, who continued the work he had begun.

Alexander of Lycopolis (fl. third century) ●

Probably a pagan who may never have embraced Christianity but known for his treatise against the Manichaeans. He attacked the doctrines of Manichaeism as illogical, contrasting it with the much more favorable simplicity of Christianity. His treatise, written in twenty-six short chapters, has been much valued as a source of information on Manichaeism and as a spirited defense of Christian theology through Greek analytical genius. According to Photius, Alexander became bishop of Lycopolis (in Egypt), but scholars question whether he was even a Christian. (See also **Manichaeans**.)

Alexander Sauli, St. (1533-1592) ●

So-called Apostle of Corsica who reinvigorated the Church on the island. A member of a respected Lombard family, Alexander joined the Congregation of the Barnabites and later served as a teacher of theology and philosophy at the University of Pavia. In 1565, he became superior general of the congregation. Six years later, in 1571, he was sent to Corsica with the task of reviving the Church there, for it had declined severely over the previous years and the populace and clergy were generally ignorant of the faith.

Alexander rebuilt churches, established seminaries and colleges, and taught the inhabitants how to be full members of the Church body. In 1591, his work completed, he became bishop of Pavia.

Alexandria ● Once mighty city in Egypt, situated on the Lower Nile, near the mouth of the Nile. Known in Arabic as *Al Iskandariya* and flanked by the sea and Lake Mareotis, it was one of the most important cities anywhere during the early Church. Founded in 331 B.C. by Alexander the Great, Alexandria was the second most important metropolis in the Roman Empire because of its place as the port for the vital Egyptian grain that fed Rome, the residence of the prefect of Egypt, and its traditional status as a major trading center in the Mediterranean and the East. It was inevitable then that Christianity should spread there in the first century A.D., especially given the fact that Alexandria also had the largest Jewish community anywhere in the classical, or ancient, world. Surprisingly, Paul did not preach there, but the Church was probably founded by St. Mark. Christianity soon spread, and by the second century the well-established body of believers was noted for its writers and its mystics. Throughout the second and third centuries, the Alexandrian Christians were best known for their catechetical school under Clement and Origen. Further fame was acquired under the patriarchates of Athanasius and Cyril in the fourth and fifth centuries.

Because of its respected past, Alexandria was honored by the formative Church as the second city of Christianity, ranking behind only Rome. When the system of patriarchates was established, that of Alexandria was not merely considered second only to Rome, but enjoyed ecclesiastical supremacy over the East, including Antioch, a status affirmed by the Council of Nicaea in 325.

The rise of Constantinople, however, caused a decline in power so that at the Councils of Constantinople (381) and Chalcedon (451) the patriarch of Constantinople was made superior over all the East, including Alexandria. The city's ecclesiastical unity was also damaged by a number of heresies, most notably Arianism and Monophysitism. The latter heresy caused the Alexandrian Church to reject the Council of Chalcedon and remain in schism until 616 when Egypt passed under the domination of the Persians; later that century the Islamic conquest of Egypt further isolated the Church there even further. With the division of Christendom into East and West, Alexandria was nominally in the Eastern Church, although the Greek patriarchate had little authority. A Latin patriarch, purely titular, was installed in the 1200s. Recently, however, the centuries of schism ended, since the Coptic Christian Church of Alexandria was recognized as a patriarchate of the East. (See also **Coptic Church** and **Monophysitism**.)

Pope Alexander VIII

Alexandrian Rite ● Liturgy used throughout the patriarchate of Alexandria, Egypt, found in the Eastern Church. Its creation has been generally attributed to St. Mark, although it was most likely established out of the Antiochene rite and was certified by St. Cyril of Alexandria in the fifth century. The Greek liturgy of St. Mark is no longer used, as it was replaced by its Melchite practitioners with the Byzantine rite. The Coptic liturgies were adapted from it and modified into the Coptic language, as was the Ethiopian (or Abyssinian) Church. The current Catholic patriarch of Alexandria uses the Coptic rite. The present Churches of this rite are the Coptic, with jurisdiction under the patriarch of Alexandria, and the Ethiopian, with jurisdiction under its metropolitan.

Alexis Falconieri, St. (1200-1310?) ● Founder of the Holy Order of Servites. The son of Bernard Falconieri, a powerful merchant in Florence and a leader of the Guelph party in the city, Alexis was said to have evidenced extreme humility even at a young age. He joined the *Laudesi*, a confraternity devoted to the Virgin Mary and, on August 15, 1233, was given an apparition of the BVM, as were the six companions whom he had met in the *Laudesi*. (They were eventually known as the Seven Founders.) Alexis subsequently adopted the life of a mendicant, working to bring assistance to the communities that he helped establish. Throughout his life, however, he refused to be ordained into the priesthood, since he felt himself unworthy. St. Juliana Falconieri was his niece.

Alfonso of Burgos (d. 1489) ● Notable Spanish Dominican who was also an influential figure in the court of Ferdinand and Isabella of Spain and was instrumental in securing the funds of discovery for Christopher Columbus. From a noble family of Burgos, Alfonso entered the Dominicans at a young age. His preaching in Spain was of such brilliance that he attracted the favor of their Catholic Majesties, Ferdinand and

Isabella; they made him royal confessor, and provided successful recommendations that he be made bishop of Cordoba by Sixtus IV in 1477. He subsequently held several successive sees, and while at the court he was made the grand chaplain, counselor of the king, and president of the council of Castile, the Curia Regis. As president, he was able to supply grants of money to Christopher Columbus, funds absolutely vital to the success of his mission of exploration that would bring about the discovery of the New World in 1492. Alfonso was also pivotal in completing the Dominican College — the Collegium Sancti Gregorii — at Valladolid.

Alfred the Great (849-899) ● King of Wessex, in England, from 871-899, known as the Great because of his achievements as a warrior and enlightened ruler. The fifth son of Ethelwulf (or Aethelwulf) of Wessex, he was far from being considered a possibility for the throne, chosen by his father probably to enter the clergy. He traveled to Rome with Ethelwulf in 853 and was accepted as a godson to Pope Leo IV. He later went to the Carolingian court of Charles the Bald. His father died in 858, and Alfred assisted his brother Ethelred I against a Danish army that was threatening Mercia. Ethelred, however, died in 871 and, despite the presence of Ethelred's sons, Alfred was made king of Wessex. Years of bitter conflict followed, but in 878 Alfred defeated the Danes at the Battle of Edington, bringing about peace for a number of years. Further campaigns would prove necessary to resist Danish advances, but by 896 Alfred had routed them and was ruler of all England not under control of the Danes. His heirs — recipients of a strong, centralized kingdom — would conquer the Danish territories (the Danelaw).

Alfred cultivated a rule of artistic, legal, and intellectual achievement. With the scholar Asser (author of a biography on Alfred), he translated numerous books into

English, including the works of Gregory I, the Venerable Bede, Augustine, and Boethius. Scholars were attracted to his court, and the *Anglo-Saxon Chronicle* (or *Old English Annals*) was begun during this period. He also collected the codes of earlier rulers such as Offa of Mercia and Ine of Wessex and used them to organize a legal system for his subjects. His reign became almost mythical and he was long considered the epitome of the Christian monarch. In his translation of Boethius's *Consolation of Philosophy*, he wrote: "I may say that it has always been my wish to live honorably, and, after death, to leave to those who come after, a memory of my good works."

Alfred the Great

Allatius, Leo (1587- or 1588-1669) ●

Custodian of the Vatican Library and a learned Greek Roman Catholic theologian. Also known as Leo Allacci, he was a native of Chios, an island east of Greece. In 1600, he entered the Greek College in Rome, spent some time in Lucania, and then returned to Chios where he served as an assistant to the Latin bishop there, Bernard Giustiniani. He was later a *scriptor* (clerk) in the Vatican Library and for two years taught as a professor of rhetoric in the Greek College. In 1622, Pope Gregory XV sent him to Germany to bring to Rome the Palatinate Library, which had been given to the pope by

Emperor Maximilian. Spending the next years doing research on the Palatinate Library, Allatius was named custodian of the Vatican Library in 1661 by Pope Alexander VII, a post he held until his death. Allatius worked aggressively to promote the union of the Eastern and Western Churches, authoring *De Ecclesiae Occidentalis atque Orientalis perpetua consensione* (1648), a work that stressed the similarities of the two Churches.

Allen, John (1476-1534) ●

Archbishop of Dublin and chancellor of Ireland. Educated at Oxford and Cambridge, he was ordained in 1499 and served in assorted posts until 1522 when he attracted the notice of Cardinal Thomas Wolsey, the immensely powerful English prelate. The cardinal found Allen useful in the suppression of minor monasteries, an act that earned Allen condemnations of such volume that they reached King Henry VIII. Nevertheless, Allen continued to receive preferment from Wolsey, assisting the cardinal in his efforts to secure the divorce of the king from Catherine of Aragon and accompanying him on his trip to France in 1528. That same year, Allen was made archbishop of Dublin and chancellor of Ireland. The following year, Wolsey fell from power, and in 1531 Allen, like the other members of the clergy, had to pay a stiff fine for violating the Statute of Provisors. Three years later, he was murdered near Dublin by assassins from the Irish house of Kildare — the Fitzgeralds — in revenge for what they thought had been the execution of their lord, the ninth earl, in the Tower of London by order of the king. The earl had been imprisoned by his political enemy, Cardinal Wolsey, once before. Allen was to be the last of the so-called Catholic archbishops of Dublin; his successor, George Browne, would be the first Anglican (i.e., Protestant) prelate in Ireland.

Allen, William (1532-1594) ● English cardinal who spent most of his later years working for the conversion of England back to the Catholic faith. The third son of John Allen of Rossall, Allen studied at Oxford and became a fellow at Oriel College, Oxford. After the accession of Elizabeth I in 1558 as successor to Mary and the return of England to Protestantism, Allen chose to remain staunchly Catholic. He left England in 1561 for Louvain, returning home the next year. In 1565, he was forced to depart again, working thereafter to bring about England's conversion. Allen was firmly convinced that the English people actually remained Catholic in heart and that the Protestant Church there could not endure. To further missions to England, he founded several colleges in Douai (1568), Rome (1575-1583), and Valladolid (1589). The Douai Bible was produced through his influence. Allen earned considerable hostility in England for his ill-timed support of the attempted invasion of England by the Spanish under King Philip II in 1588. A cardinal in 1587, he was nominated two years later to be archbishop of Malines but was never confirmed. His last days were spent at the English College in Rome. (See also **Appellant Controversy**.)

Allies, Thomas (1813-1903) ● English writer and theologian. He studied at Eton and Oxford and was a fellow at Wadham College, Oxford, from 1833-1841. In 1842, he became vicar of Launton, subsequently becoming involved with the so-called Oxford movement. Increasingly disenchanted with Anglicanism, his doubts were confirmed while traveling abroad in 1845 and 1847. After the Gorham Case in 1847 (a controversy in the Anglican Church), he joined the Catholic Church. Allies became a prominent apologist for Catholicism in his later years, and he was named by Pope Leo XIII a Knight Commander of St. Gregory in 1885; the pope conferred upon him a gold medal of merit in 1893. He was also the last survivor of the Oxford movement.

Almeida, John (1571-1653) ● English Jesuit missionary, originally known as John Meade, who distinguished himself in Brazil. Born in London, he was taken to Portugal at a young age and from there to Brazil. There, at the age of twenty-one, he joined the Jesuits, becoming a disciple of the famous missionary Joseph Anchieta. Ordained in 1602, Almeida spent years wandering across Brazil, aiding the missions, and developing close relations with numerous native communities. A severe ascetic, he practiced extreme forms of self-mortification, including wearing chains and hair shirts. His death was the cause of great sorrow in Rio de Janeiro.

Aloysius Gonzaga, St. (1568-1591) ● Patron saint of Catholic youth, he was born at Castiglione of noble descent, spending some time in Florence at the court of Francesco de' Medici. Going to Brescia, he came under the guidance of St. Charles Borromeo from whom he received First Communion. In 1581, he and his family went to Spain where he and his brother became pages to James, son of King Philip II. Already increasingly determined to join a religious order, Aloysius finally chose the Society of Jesus. Returning to Italy in 1584, he faced intense opposition to his vocation, but his perseverance and the intensity of his desire won permission from his father. In 1585, he renounced his inheritance and, securing the permission of the emperor, joined the Jesuits. As a novice, he came to the attention of Claudius Acquaviva, fifth superior general of the order. Taking his vows in 1587, he died at the age of twenty-three while caring for the stricken in Rome during an outbreak of plague. He was beatified in 1621 and canonized in 1726. Feast day: June 21.

Alphege, St. (954-1012) ●

Also called Elphege or Aelfheah, archbishop of Canterbury and celebrated martyr. Of noble birth, he joined the Benedictine Abbey of Deerhurst in Gloucestershire. He later became an anchorite (hermit) at Bath but was named abbot there by his followers and in 984 became bishop of Winchester, thanks to his friend Archbishop St. Dunstan of Canterbury. King Ethelred II the Unready used him as an ambassador to King Olaf I Trygvasson of Norway whom he supposedly confirmed and talked into refraining from invading England again. Alphege next became archbishop of Canterbury (1005), holding the Council of Enham (1009?) where he tried to institute several canons of disciplines. In 1011, a host of Danes ransacked Canterbury, and Alphege was taken captive. Held for many months, he was finally murdered when he refused to ransom himself by using the tax money of the poor. By tradition, he was first stoned with ox

St. Aloysius Gonzaga

bones left over from a feast and then killed. Feast day: April 19.

Alphonsus Liguori, St. (1696-1787) ●

Properly Alfonso Maria dei Liguori. A moral theologian and founder of the Redemptorists, Alphonsus was born near Naples, Italy, and was the son of Giuseppe dei Liguori, a Neapolitan noble. A brilliant student, he received a doctorate of law at the age of sixteen and was an eminently successful lawyer for eight years. In 1723, however, he lost a very important case and abandoned the law. Entering the religious life, he joined a group of preachers and was ordained in 1726. He worked as a highly successful preacher around Naples, eventually (1729) taking up residence in the missionary college in the city. While there he met and was influenced by Tomaso Falcoia (d. 1743) who, in 1730, became bishop of Castellamare. Falcoia had organized a community of women in Scala, and in 1731 Alphonsus undertook their reorganization, marking the beginnings of the Redemptorists. The following year, in Scala, Alphonsus formed a group of men into a society devoted to preaching and missionary work among the poor in rural districts. From this small group would come the Redemptorists, or Congregation of the Most Holy Redeemer, although Alphonsus was not actually elected superior general until after Bishop Falcoia's death in 1743. The society was also troubled by bitter internal dissensions. Approval was given, however, for the rule in 1749 by Pope Benedict XIV;

approval was given for women in 1750. Meanwhile, in 1745, Alphonsus wrote his first devotional works and in 1748 published the first edition of his guide to moral theology.

In 1762, the future saint was named bishop and reluctantly accepted the see of Sant' Agata dei Goti, a small but needy diocese. He was a devoted bishop and preacher but found time to continue his literary productions. In 1775, he was permitted to resign his see owing to poor health, retiring to Nocera, only to be confronted by new crises and controversies within the Redemptorists. He was eventually pushed out of the very congregation he had founded and spent a long part of his last years in spiritual torment. Peace was achieved through prayer, and Alphonsus died in quiet retirement in Nocera.

Alphonsus is ranked as one of the greatest moral theologians in the history of the Church. He labored to bring the Gospel to simple people through straightforward preaching, once declaring that he had never given a sermon that could not be appreciated by the most humble old woman in the crowd. At the same time, he developed a moral system of rich beauty and subtlety. In moral theology, Alphonsus sought to reverse the dangerous trend of the period that had been promoted by the Jansenists, namely excessive rigorism, which frequently discouraged Catholics from repentance because of its harshness and spread of fear. His system, first presented in 1748, found greater development in the *Theologia Moralis* (2 vols., 1753 and 1755), which was reprinted in numerous editions in his life and became a major work in the teaching of moral theology. In the field, he is considered the principal proponent of equiprobabilism.

Alphonsus also wrote on papal infallibility, prayer, and topics of dogma. His devotional works became enormously popular in Europe and beyond and were translated in the centuries after his death into some sixty languages. Among the best known of these books are *Visits to the Blessed Sacrament, The True Spouse of Jesus Christ, The Glories of Mary,* and *The Way of Salvation.* Pope Gregory XVI canonized him in 1839, and Pope Pius IX named him a Doctor of the Church in 1871. In 1950, Pope Pius XII declared him the patron of confessors and moralists. Feast day: August 1.

Alphonsus Rodríguez, St. (1532-1617) ● Special patron of Majorca and a member of the Jesuits. A native of Segovia, Alphonsus married at the age of twenty-six, but by thirty-one he was widowed with one surviving child (of three). The death of his third child freed him to pursue a life in some religious order. Lack of any substantial education did not permit his entry into the Jesuits, but he was allowed to become a lay brother in 1571. Sent eventually to Majorca, he served for over forty years as a humble porter (or door opener) in the college there, distinguishing himself for his deep spirituality; he influenced St. Peter Claver. Declared venerable in 1626, he was canonized in 1887. He should not be confused with two Jesuit contemporaries of the same name, one a martyr in Paraguay, the other a writer of religious works. Feast day: October 30.

Álvarez, Baltasar (1533-1580) ● Spanish mystic and the spiritual director for St. Teresa of Ávila. Of noble descent, he studied at the University of Alcalá and in 1555 entered the Society of Jesus. Further study at Alcalá and Ávila followed under the tutorship of the Dominicans, since there were as yet no theologians among the Jesuits. Ordained in 1558, he was appointed spiritual director of Teresa, at that time a member of the Order of Carmel but who was soon to establish the Discalced Carmelites. His influence was considerable, particularly in the forming of the rules of the new order. He also defended Teresa from critics. In 1574, he became rector of Salamanca and in 1579 was supposed to be sent to Peru as provincial, but the mission was never confirmed. St. Teresa was said to have received a vision of his glory in heaven after his death.

Álvarez de Paz, Diego (1560-1620) ● Noted mystic of the Society of Jesus and provincial of Peru. Born at Toledo, he joined the Jesuits in 1578, subsequently serving in the New World. He taught at Lima and was later provincial. His abiding mysticism was well-known throughout Spanish domains in South America; upon his death at Potosi on January 17, 1620, the entire city went into mourning, including the workers in the silver mines who stopped their labors to join in prayer.

Amalarius of Metz (c. 780-850 or -851) ● Possibly bishop of Trier, liturgist, and a prominent figure in the Carolingian Renaissance. A student and admirer of Alcuin, he was named bishop of Trier, perhaps in 811. Charlemagne (d. 814) sent him as a trusted representative to Constantinople in 813. Some years later, in 853, Louis the Pious appointed him bishop of Lyons as a replacement for the exiled prelate Abogard. Amalarius also authored the four-volume treatise *De ecclesiasticis officiis*, examining the liturgies of the Gallican and Roman rites. While his writings were attacked at the Synod of Quiercy in 838 as being partly heretical, the work was notable for preserving elements of medieval liturgy.

Amalric (d. c. 1207) ● Scholastic philosopher also known as Amalric of Bena, a native of Chartres. Amalric studied and taught at Paris, authoring extremely controversial ideas about the nature of God. He believed that God was the universe and that all things in the universe took their form from God. Further, a sincere and pure love of God made a person incapable of sin, a concept that allowed Amalric to reject the transubstantiation and the belief in the division of good and evil. Amalric found a

number of supporters who gathered around him and took the name Amalricians. They furthered and promoted his ideas in Paris and elsewhere. Both Amalric and the Amalricians were condemned at the Council of Paris in 1210 and at the Fourth Lateran Council in 1215. (See also **David of Dinant**.)

Amandus (d. c. 675) ● So-called Apostle of Flanders. A Merovingian ascetic who labored as a missionary in Flanders and Carinthia, he was taught by St. Austregesilus in Bourges and, through the influence of King Clotaire, was named a bishop with no fixed see in 628 to facilitate his missionary work. In 635, he established two monasteries in Ghent, and later founded a monastery at Elnon, near Tournai, serving as abbot there in later years. It was later called St. Amand. Much information about him, including his supposed writings, is dubious.

Ambrose, St. (c. 340-397) ● Bishop of Milan and, with Sts. Augustine, Jerome, and Pope Gregory I the Great, one of the four great Fathers of the Latin Church. Also ranked among the Doctors of the Church, he was perhaps the most active opponent of Arianism. Born in Trier, he was the son of the Praetorian prefect of Gaul. After studying law, he began practicing in the Roman courts until 370 when he was named governor of Aemilia-Liguria with his capital at Milan. In 374, at the death of Auxentius, Arian bishop of Milan, Ambrose was chosen by the Catholics of the city to succeed him. While respected deeply by the people, Ambrose was at first unwilling to accept owing to the fact that he was only a catechumen and was not yet baptized. Finally agreeing, he was baptized and then ordained, continuing, however, to study orthodox theology under his onetime tutor Simplicianus. As bishop, Ambrose was forced to involve himself in numerous political affairs, particularly as Milan in this period had become the main city of the Western Roman Empire. He thus had dealings with both the Eastern and Western emperors, exercising enormous influence at the imperial courts and within the government. Officially the imperial chaplain, he was also a formidable adviser. In 382, he convinced Emperor Gratian to remove from the senate the pagan altar of victory, subsequently opposing the efforts of the influential senator Symmachus to have it restored. In 390, he spoke out against Emperor Theodosius I and demanded public penance after the ruler grew angry with rioters in Thessalonika and ordered his troops to massacre seven thousand people. Theodosius accepted Ambrose's demands and made a public atonement for his brutal act. Ambrose also successfully resisted the efforts of Empress Justina to give a church to the Arians. He and his followers seized the church, holding it until Justina relented. The bishop, however, was ever careful not to abuse his power and used his authority not for his own good but for the good of the Church.

As a theologian, Ambrose was steadfastly orthodox. He devoted much effort to the extermination of paganism and to resisting Arianism. At the Council of Aquileia (381) he succeeded in having the Arian bishops removed, and he wrote several treatises defending orthodox doctrines against the Arians. His writings included: *De Sacramentis* (a treatise on the sacraments); *De Officiis Ministrorum* (a treatise on Christian ethics); sermons; doctrinal works on faith and the Holy Spirit; and letters. He promoted monasticism in Italy, introducing many Eastern elements into the liturgy (see **Ambrosian Rite**), and used hymns extensively as a means of giving praise. Numerous hymns have been attributed to him, although recent scholarship has determined the *Te Deum* not to be his; he possibly wrote the Athanasian Creed. A supporter of virginity and devoted to the Virgin Mary, he wrote several treatises on the subject of Christian virginity, such as "On

Virginity," "On Widows," and "To Sister Marcellina on Virginity." Perhaps his greatest act was to bring about the conversion of St. Augustine in 386 whom he baptized and launched on his great career. Feast day: December 7.

Ambrose of Camaldoli ● See **Traversari, Ambrogio**.

Ambrose of Siena (1220-1268) ● Schoolmate of St. Thomas Aquinas, student of Albertus Magnus, and an active figure in the Dominican order and Italian political life. A member of the noble family Sansedoni, Ambrose entered the Dominicans of Siena in 1237, studying at Paris under Albertus. While there he came to know Thomas Aquinas and in 1248 journeyed with him to Cologne where he taught in the Dominican College there. In 1260, he took part in the missionary effort into Hungary. By 1266, Ambrose was back in Italy, answering a petition from Siena to act as its representative to the pope. The pontiff had put the city under interdict because of its support for the imperial cause. Ambrose proved successful in having the ban lifted, returning again before the pope when the Sienese cast off their papal loyalty a second time. Once more, Ambrose was successful. He later effected a reconciliation between Pope Clement IV and Emperor Conrad, preached a crusade, and helped have the studies at the Dominican convent in Rome reinstated after years of suspended activity because of civil and military upheaval. According to tradition, Ambrose was noted for his love of the sick, pilgrims, and prisoners; he was said to have been born with a congenital deformity but was cured in the Dominican Church of St. Mary Magdalene in Siena.

Ambrosian Chant ● Type of chant in iambic dimeter that was composed by St. Ambrose and his students and followers for use in the Ambrosian rite. Originally the chant was a simple rhythm, written in syllabic form, meaning that there is a single note to each syllable of text. It also possessed certain Eastern characteristics and was a distinct forerunner of the better known religious music of the Gregorian chant.

Ambrosian Rite ● Rite used in the early archiepiscopal province of Milan, named after St. Ambrose of Milan, although he did not probably have any role in its creation. The Ambrosian rite has survived over the centuries, one of the few non-Roman rites to endure in Western Christendom. Theories have been proposed concerning its origins. These include the ideas that it developed out of the Roman rite; that it was an older rite in the West that has endured only in Milan; or that it was originally an Oriental rite brought to Milan by the Arian bishop Auxentius and was subsequently cleansed by Ambrose of its heretical elements. Scholars today believe that it is of an entirely Western descent. The present Ambrosian rite is very similar to the Roman rite save for several differences: there is a procession before the Offertory, a litany is chanted by a deacon, and the creed is read after the Offertory. The rite also includes baptism. While used in Milan, it is not found in every church in that archdiocese.

Ambrosians ● Properly the Order of St. Ambrose. Two religious orders founded in the 1300s and 1400s, both were established in the area around Milan and took St. Ambrose as their patron. The first, for men, had its origins in the woods just outside Milan where three Milanese nobles (Alexander Grivelli, Antonio Petrasancta, and Albert Besuzzi) took up a solitary life and received from Pope Gregory XI (r. 1370-1378) the Rule of St. Augustine. Joined by other men, including several priests, they organized themselves into a community of religious, followed the Ambrosian rite in their liturgy, and took the

name *Fratres Sancti Ambrosii ad Nemus.* Several monasteries were begun along similar lines, and Pope Eugenius IV in 1441 united them into one single congregation under the name *Congregatio Sancti Ambrosii ad Nemus.* A reform was launched by St. Charles Borromeo in 1579. A decade later, in 1589, Pope Sixtus V combined them with several other monasteries belonging to the Brothers of the Apostles of the Poor Life, the so-called *Apostolici* or Brothers of St. Barnabas; for obvious reasons, the Ambrosians added Barnabas to their title in 1606. Pope Innocent X dissolved the order in 1650. The second order, the Ambrosian Sisters (or Nuns) of St. Ambrose, received papal approval in 1474 from Pope Sixtus IV. The order was founded by Bl. Catarina Morigia of Palanza.

Americanism ● A tendency of thought found among some Church leaders in the United States of America in the latter decades of the nineteen century. It proposed that Catholicism should be adapted as much as externally possible to the modern cultural ideas and values of America. It stressed receptivity to the social movements of the time as well as the sociopolitical virtues in the country, such as democracy, humanitarian works, and the separation of Church and State. Also proposed was the relaxing of the stringent requirements for converts so as to make the Church less singular in its dealing with the numerous faiths of America. Americanism was led by several prelates, including Archbishop John Ireland of St. Paul, Bishop John Keane of Richmond, and Monsignor Dennis J. O'Connell, the rector of the North American College in Rome. Many of the ideas of Americanism earned condemnation by conservative elements in the Church, but other European intellectuals considered it an ideal basis for an aggressive renewal of the Church, particularly in France. Pope Leo XIII (r. 1878-1903) was initially responsive to the movement. When, however, a biography of Isaac Hecker, founder of the Paulists, was published in which he was ranked as a patron saint of Americanism, the pope reconsidered his position, particularly since the work caused a stir in France. As a consequence, Leo sent to Cardinal James Gibbons of Baltimore a letter for the entire American hierarchy. The letter, *Testem Benevolentiae*, stated in courteous but very clear terms that Americanism as described above was to be condemned; at the same time, however, it lauded the status and arrangement of the Church in the United States. The movement quickly disappeared as a meaningful force in the U.S.

Amiot, Joseph (1718-1793) ● Jesuit missionary to China and a native of Toulon. He joined the Society of Jesus in 1737 and was sent to China in 1740. Aside from his work as a missionary, Amiot distinguished himself as a scholar of some note, studying many facets of Chinese life, customs, and language. He mastered the extremely difficult Chinese tongue and also made a study of Chinese music. His correspondence provided his superiors with much badly needed information on China and Asia as well as the culture of the Manchus. Amiot became especially familiar with the Manchu court at Beijing, as the Chinese emperor placed much confidence in him. He died in Beijing.

Ammon, St. (d. c. 350) ● Also known as Amun, an Egyptian hermit who was mentioned by St. Athanasius in his *Vita Antonii* (*Life of St. Antony*). Ammon was supposedly forced into marriage at the age of twenty-two, persuading his wife on their wedding night that they should live a henceforth celibate existence. This they did for some eighteen years. Ammon then became a celebrated hermit in the desert of Nitria while his wife founded a house of religious women. He was visited by many anchorites (hermits) who came to live near

him, including St. Antony, who encouraged Ammon to bring together the scattered hermitic communities into monasteries. Antony was said to have seen Ammon's soul enter heaven upon the latter's death. Feast day: October 4.

Amort, Eusebius (1692-1775) ● Philosopher and theologian who was a prominent figure among German theologians, particularly as a guiding influence of young students of the natural sciences. A Bavarian by birth, he was educated by the Jesuits and then joined the canons regular in their convent in Polling where he would spend most of his remaining years teaching and studying. He counted among his friends and correspondents St. Alphonsus Liguori, Pope Benedict XIII, and Cardinals Leccari and Galli. His literary output was generally prolific, as he authored some seventy volumes, including *Philosophia Pollingana* (1730), *Theologica eclectica, moralis et scholastica* (1752), and *Ethica Christiana* (1758). The academy he established at Polling was the basis for the well-known Academy of Sciences in Munich.

Anabaptism ● Heresy of the 1500s that rejected certain Church teachings concerning baptism, particularly infant baptism. The Anabaptists were established in several similar communities in Europe, including the Zwickau Prophets in Wittenberg in 1521; the Melchiorites or Hoffmanites under Melchior Hoffman (d. 1543) in the Low Countries and parts of Germany; the Mennonites in Friesland and Holland who spread to other European countries and eventually journeyed to America; and the Swiss Brethren in Zurich in 1525. In general terms, the Anabaptists also stressed a simple lifestyle, sometimes community ownership of property, and a precise separation of Church and State. While derived in part from the teachings of Martin Luther and other Reformation leaders, Anabaptism was denounced by Luther,

Zwingli, and Calvin. The Catholic Church also condemned the heresy. Both Catholic and Protestant officials persecuted the Anabaptists, putting many to death.

Anacletus Reiffenstuel ● See **Reiffenstuel, Johann Georg**.

Anacletus I, St. ● Also Cletus or Anencletus, the second pope (Bishop of Rome), from 76-88 or 79-91. Anacletus was the successor to St. Linus, who succeeded St. Peter as the head of the Christian community of Rome. Very little is known about him, although tradition states that he established the division of Rome into twenty-five parishes. He was martyred, probably during the reign of Emperor Diocletian. Feast day: April 26.

Anacletus II (d. 1138) ● Antipope from 1130-1138, although some scholars still hold that his claims to the papacy against Pope Innocent II are legitimate. His reign was part of a serious schism in the Church. Originally called Pietro Pierleone, he was a native of Rome studying at Paris before becoming a monk at Cluny. He was made a cardinal in 1116. The conclave to select a successor to Honorius elected Pietro by a majority as Anacletus II in 1130. A minority, however, chose Cardinal Gregorio Papareschi as Innocent II, precipitating a schism. Anacletus was supported by the powerful family of Frangipani and most Romans, but Innocent received the backing of St. Bernard of Clairvaux, the Holy Roman emperor Lothair

II, and the Byzantine emperor John II Comnenus. Years of struggle ensued, ending only in 1138 with Anacletus's death. The following year, Innocent called the Second Lateran Council to end formally the schism.

Anagni ● Town in central Italy, on a hill above the Sacco Valley, in the region of Latrium (Lazio). Anagni was the birthplace of four popes: Innocent III, Gregory IX, Alexander IV, and Boniface VIII. Pope Alexander IV (r. 1254-1261) chose to reside in Anagni instead of Rome not only because it was his birthplace but also because of the undesirability of a Roman residence at the time. Moreover, Anagni was the site of one of the blackest episodes in papal history. In 1303, Pope Boniface VIII was held prisoner there by French troops under Guillaume de Nogaret, who had been dispatched by King Philip IV of France, with whom Boniface was engaged in a political struggle. While the pope's imprisonment lasted only three days, the cruel treatment he received from Nogaret and the mercenaries shattered his health. Rescued by Italian forces and the populace, he returned to Rome and died a month later. His seizure and subsequent death were severe blows to the prestige of the medieval papacy.

Pope St. Anacletus

Anastasia, St. (fl. early fourth century) ● Martyr who perhaps died in 304 at Sirmium. Little is known about her, although later, unreliable sources declared that she was a Roman noblewoman, a disciple of St.

John Chrysostom, and was martyred on the island of Palmaria. Other traditions place her death at Sremska Mitrovica in Yugoslavia (Sirmium in Pannonia at the time). Her relics were translated by St. Gennadius to Constantinople in the late fifth century and placed in the Church of Anastasia. Byzantine clerics then spread her cult throughout the Roman world. Feast day: December 23, until 1969; December 22 in the East.

Anastasius I, St. ● Pope from 399-401. The successor to Pope Siricius and a Roman by birth, Anastasius was best known for his condemnation of various writings by the influential early Christian theologian Origen. He was praised by St. Augustine, St. Jerome, and St. Paulinus of Nola.

Anastasius II ● Pope from 496-498. His main contribution was attempting a reconciliation between the Eastern and Western Churches, as both had been in a state of schism since the reign of Pope Felix III, who in 484 had excommunicated Acacius, patriarch of Constantinople, starting the Acacian Schism. Anastasius received the deacon Photinus, a supporter of Acacius, and thus set off a firestorm of controversy as Western theologians charged the pontiff with allowing Photinus to lead him into heretical views concerning Christ's divinity. Anastasius died before any progress could be made in resolving the disputes. Dante, in the *Divine Comedy*, placed Anastasius in hell.

Anastasius III ● Pope from 911-913. He reigned during the time that Rome was under the complete control of the House of Theophylact; Anastasius had virtually no authority.

Anastasius IV ● Pope from 1153-1154. Originally known as Corrado di Suburra, he reigned specifically from July 1153 to December 1154. He is noted principally for

reconciling Emperor Frederick I Barbarossa with the see of Magdeburg.

Anastasius Bibliothecarus (c. 810-c. 878) ● Theologian and the most respected Greek scholar of his age, known as "The Librarian" (*Bibliothecarus*). He was educated by Greek monks, emerging as one of the foremost scholars of the ninth century. In 855, he allowed himself to be made an antipope by the enemies of Pope Benedict III. He soon lost political support, however, because of his lack of discipline and was reconciled to the Church. His great reputation convinced several popes to give him appointments. Pope Nicholas I made him abbot of S. Maria in Trastevere, and Anastasius was later made papal librarian, thus earning him his name. He remained librarian throughout the reigns of Adrian II and John VIII. He also authored a history of the Byzantine Empire from the sixth to the ninth centuries and a work on theology.

Anathema ● Type of severe excommunication of a person by the Church for an act of sin, heresy, or apostasy. In the OT, the term implied something that must be set aside or removed because it was inherently evil. Generally, the most severe of all actions that could earn a ban was human sacrifice to some god or God himself. St. Paul, in the NT, later used the word as a type of punishment in which a person is excluded utterly from the kingdom of God for such sins as the teaching of a false gospel or for neglecting to love the Lord. By the tenets of canon law, particularly as expressed by the brilliant canonist Gratian, anathema could be differentiated from excommunication, as the former was an absolute separation from the Church and faith while the latter was separation from the sacraments. By custom, the anathema was delivered by a bishop vested in a purple cope. He was joined by twelve priests bearing candles. As the pronouncement was made, the candles were thrown to the ground and put out. Vatican Council II abolished the use of anathema.

Anchorite ● More precisely anchorite (male) or anchoress (female), a Greek term for a person who withdraws from the world to adhere to a life of prayer and humility. The anchorites developed in the early Church as hermitlike individuals who would depart the world and retreat into a private life of solitude. Early anchorite living, however, was never formal and individuals were free to depart their hermit abode. In later years, the Church established rules to govern their behavior and activities, and the nearby bishop would enclose anchorites or anchoresses in their cell, the place where they would be confined forever after. The favorite abode for the first anchorites was the Egyptian desert. They were the precursors of the monastic life and institutions that would spread throughout all of Christianity. (See also **Antony, St**.)

Ancyra ● Modern Ankara, a town in Asia Minor (modern Turkey) where several important synods of the early Church were held. The council of 314, attended by a number of bishops from Syria and across Asia Minor, was concerned with the so-called *lapsi*, those individuals who denied the Christian faith during times of persecution. By the terms of the canons, definite ecclesiastical punishments or penalties were placed upon the *lapsi*, but the council made clear that all such persons

should eventually return to the faith. The council of 358 was attended by Semi-Arians under the leadership of Basil of Ancyra. The council rejected the Nicene formula of *homoousios* (Greek for "of the same substance") and all extreme Arian teachings.

Andrew, St. ● Apostle, brother of St. Peter, Andrew was a fisherman from Bethsaida in Galilee. The first-called of the Apostles, he brought forward his brother Simon (renamed Peter by Jesus). The Gospels mention Andrew several times (Jn 1:35-42; Mt 4:18-20; Jn 6:8; and elsewhere). The stories of his later activities are generally unreliable. According to them, he journeyed to Scythia and Epirus and was martyred by crucifixion at Patras, in Achaia, sometime around A.D. 60. The tradition that he died on a crucifix shaped as an "X" (called a saltire) most likely began in the 1200s. Andrew has been the patron saint of Scotland since the eighth century. Feast day: November 30.

St. Andrew

Andrew, Acts of ● Apocryphal work. Dated to the early third century, it presented the imprisonment and persecution at Patras of St. Andrew. The book was held in high repute among the Gnostic heretics and an epitome of it was given by Gregory of Tours. While it has not survived in its original form, a fragment is contained in several papyri.

Andrew of Crete, St. (c. 660-740) ● Archbishop of Gortyna in Crete and a hymn writer. Originally from Damascus, he served as a deacon at Constantinople in the Church of Hagia Sophia before being appointed archbishop in 692. A participant in the Synod of Constantinople in 712, he apparently professed adherence to Monothelitism but recanted the following year. As a composer of hymns, he was perhaps the composer of a new kind of canon or hymnography. He also authored the Great Canon, used today in the Greek Church. In the Eastern Church his feast day is October 20.

Andrew of Longjumeau (fl. mid-1200s) ● Also Andrew of Longjumel, a Dominican friar, an ambassador of King Louis IX (St. Louis), and traveler. Andrew first served as an ambassador for King Louis on a mission to Constantinople in 1238. He brought back via Venice the famous relic of what is supposedly Christ's crown of thorns. King Louis built St.-Chapelle in Paris as a fitting receptacle for this holy relic. Andrew next took part in an expedition sponsored by Pope Innocent IV to the Mongol Empire, especially to the Mongols in Armenia. Louis sent Andrew on another mission in 1249 to follow up on negotiating with the Khanate of the Mongols an alliance against Islam. He went to Karakorum and hoped to meet with the khan Guyuk. The khan had just died, however, and Andrew was sent home with a sneering letter from the regent. The Franciscan friar William of Rubriquis noted in his writings that Andrew's account of his journey was quite accurate.

Andrew of Rhodes (d. 1440) ● Dominican theologian who labored to bring about a union of the Eastern and Western Churches. A Greek by birth, Andrew was raised in the Greek Church. Having studied the theology and traditions of both the Latin and the Greek Churches, he abandoned the Eastern Church and ultimately entered the Dominicans. In 1413, he became the

archbishop of Rhodes, later participating perhaps in the Council of Constance, the Council of Basel, and the Council of Ferrara-Florence. He was one of the six theologians named by the papal legate Cardinal Julian to draft a reply to the objections of the Greeks at Ferrara-Florence. Pope Eugenius IV also sent him to Cyprus where he brought an end to the violence that erupted between the Greeks and the Latins on the island.

Andrew of St. Victor (d. 1175) Biblical scholar and author of exegetical works, including commentaries on the Prophets, Proverbs, and other books. He served as canon of St. Victor at Paris but around 1147 became abbot of the Victorine Abbey of Wigmore in Herefordshire, England. As a result of poor relations with the monks, he departed Wigmore and returned to St. Victor. In the year 1171, however, he went back to Wigmore and spent his final days there.

Angela Merici, St. (1474-1540) ● Foundress of the Ursulines, Angela spent her early years as a Franciscan tertiary, working for some time to care for the sick women of Brescia and to educate young girls. In 1524-1525, she went on a pilgrimage to the Holy Land but while there was stricken temporarily with blindness. As a consequence of this illness and of visions, she founded in 1535, in Brescia, the Order of the Ursulines, what was to become the oldest teaching order of women in the Church. The Ursulines were approved by Pope Paul III in 1544. Angela became superior of the order in 1537 and was canonized in 1807. Feast day: January 27.

Angela of Foligno, Bl. (c. 1248-1309) ● Mystic from Umbria, Italy, who spent most of her life in the town of Foligno. A member of a wealthy family, she adopted a severe life of austerity following the death of her husband. Later, she became a Franciscan tertiary and received a number of visions, particularly of the Lord's passion. The account of the visions, dictated by Angela's confessor, Brother Arnold, was published under the title *Liber Visionum et Instructionum*, earning notoriety as a profound expression of Franciscan spirituality. (See also **Franciscans**.)

Angeli, Girolamo (1567-1625) ● Jesuit missionary to Japan. A Sicilian by birth, he entered the Society of Jesus in 1585. In 1602, he arrived in Japan and would spend the next twenty-one years there, working ceaselessly to convert the inhabitants. His missionary endeavors were conducted in the face of considerable hostilities from Japanese officials; twenty-six converts were crucified at Nagasaki in 1597. Unable to accept the continuing persecution of his flock, Angeli surrendered himself in late 1623 and was martyred by fire on December 4.

Angelico, Fra ● See **Angelico, Bl.**, following entry.

Angelico, Bl. (c. 1395- or 1400-1455) ● Great painter of the Middle Ages and an important figure in the birth of Florentine Renaissance art. Born Guido de Piero near Florence, he probably studied under Battista di Bagio Sanguigni. He entered the Dominicans sometime between 1418 and

Angel, by Fra Angelico

1421 at the house of S. Dominico of Fiesole, taking the name Fra Giovanni da Fiesole. The name that came to be used for him, however, was Fra Angelico because of the reputation he acquired for the depiction of saintliness in his art. Fra Angelico was responsible for a large body of endeavors, never ceasing to work as a Dominican. It was written that he had no equal. Some of his greatest works are the frescoes in the Chapel of Sacraments at the Vatican and in the private chapel of Pope Nicholas V with scenes from the lives of Sts. Lawrence and Stephen. By tradition, he was offered but declined the archbishopric of Florence; he did accept the post of prior of Fiesole from 1449-1452.

Angelus Silesius (1624-1677) ● Originally Johannes Scheffler, a mystical poet. The son of a Lutheran nobleman of Poland, Angelus initially studied medicine and served (1649-c. 1653) as court physician to the duke of Oels in Silesia. In 1653, however, he became a Catholic and was ordained a priest in 1661. From the time of his conversion, he devoted himself principally to writing; he authored, among other works, *Heilige Seelenlust* (1657) and a series of fifty-five controversial tracts (begun in 1663) attacking assorted Christian sects. He also wrote *Der Cherubinische Wandersmann* (1657; *The Cherubic Wanderer or Pilgrim*). Thirty-nine of his chosen tracts were published in 1677 in two folio volumes under the title *Ecclesiologia.*

Angilbert (c. 750-814) ● Carolingian poet and court official. Educated at Aachen as part of the so-called Carolingian Renaissance, he studied in the palace school headed by Alcuin. This great teacher would call Angilbert "Homer" for his poetry; his compositions ranged from contemporary events to the family of Charlemagne to monastic life. Angilbert accompanied Charlemagne to Rome in 800, the fateful journey ending with his master being crowned emperor on Christmas Day by Pope Leo III. He also witnessed Charlemagne's will and fathered two illegitimate children by Bertha, Charlemagne's daughter. From 781, he served as abbot of Riquier (Centula).

Anglican Orders ● Holy orders of the Anglican Church (the Church of England). From the time of the separation of the English Church from the Catholic Church in the sixteenth century, it was a matter of some debate among many Catholic theologians and hierarchy whether the Anglican orders had any validity in the eyes of the Church. The matter remained unresolved until the time of Pope Leo XIII (r. 1878-1903). That pontiff issued on September 13, 1896, his pronouncement *Apostolicae Curae* declaring that the Anglican orders were "absolutely null and utterly void" because of the defect in the intention of the ordaining prelate or bishop and especially because of the severe defect in the form used for the Rite of Ordination.

Anglican-Roman Catholic International Commission ● Joint commission established by the terms of the Common Declaration of Pope Paul VI and Archbishop Arthur Ramsey of Canterbury of 1966 and the Report of the Joint Preparatory Commission of the two Churches, which met in Malta in 1968, that brought together nine representatives each of the Anglican and Catholic Churches. Part of the ongoing effort to increase the dialogue between the faiths, the commission released the results of the discussions in a series of documents following the meetings (or "Conversations") at various locations. These were: "An Agreed Statement on Eucharistic Doctrine" (Windsor, 1971); "Ministry and Ordination, An Agreed Statement on the Doctrine of the Ministry" (Canterbury, 1975); "Authority in the Church" (Venice, 1976); "Elucidations" (Salisbury, 1979); and the "Final Report" (Windsor, 1981), which included the four previous reports, along with an "Introduction on the Church," another "Agreed Statement on Authority," and a further "Elucidation." An official response was made by the Vatican to the "Final Report" on December 5, 1991. Drafted by the Congregation for the Doctrine of the Faith and the Pontifical Council for Promoting Christian Unity, it declared that the report "constitutes a significant milestone not only in relations between the Catholic Church and the Anglican Communion but in the ecumenical movement as a whole." Nevertheless, the Vatican officials noted a number of topics where considerable disagreement remains over "essential matters of Catholic doctrine." These include: the Eucharist, Ordination, Church Authority, Infallibility, the Immaculate Conception, and Apostolic Succession. (See also **Ecumenism** and **Great Britain**.)

Anglicanism ● See **England**; see also **Anglicanism** and **Church of England** in the GLOSSARY.

Anglo-Catholicism ● Movement within the Anglican community of the Church of England that sought to emphasize the Catholic heritage of Anglicanism over Protestantism. Anglo-Catholicism began in the nineteenth century (c. 1838) as an outgrowth of the Oxford movement, the term itself being first used in some writings of the intellectual leaders of the Oxford movement. Much importance has been placed by them on Catholic practice and the sense of continuity of dogma and the sacraments, historical continuity dating back to the Middle Ages. While they have traditionally been opposed by the so-called Anglican Evangelicals (of the Low Church), the Anglo-Catholics remain a legitimate presence in the Anglican Church. (See also **Oxford Movement**.)

Anglo-Saxon Church ● Term used by historians of the Church to denote the Christian Church in England as it existed and functioned from the sixth century until the Norman Conquest of 1066. (See also **Celtic Church** and **England**.)

Anicetus, St. ● Pope from c. 155-c. 166. Successor to Pope St. Pius I, he focused on combating several heresies, especially those of Marcion and the Gnostics. Anicetus also met with St. Polycarp of Smyrna and conferred with him about the then considerable controversy in the Church concerning the proper date of Easter. It is doubtful that he was martyred.

Animoeans ● See **Eunomianism**.

Ankara ● See **Ancyra**.

Annat, François (1590-1670) ● French Jesuit and an ardent opponent of Jansenism. He joined the Society of Jesus in 1607, subsequently serving as professor of philosophy and then theology at the Jesuit College at Toulouse; he was later rector. After holding the post of assistant to the general of the order in Rome and then to the provincial in Paris, Annat became confessor to King Louis XIV. He later resigned as confessor because of the king's illicit affair with the duchess de la Valliere. In defense of Jesuit and orthodox doctrine, he authored several works, particularly attacking Jansenism. His

complete writings appeared in the three-volume *Opuscula Theologica* (1666) in Paris.

Annibaldi, Annibale d' (d. 1271) ● Dominican theologian and good friend of St. Thomas Aquinas. A member of a noble senatorial family, Annibaldi entered the Dominicans while still young, studying at Paris to complete his education. While there, he developed a close friendship with Thomas, later succeeding him as regent of studies at the convent of St. Jacques in Paris. He taught in Paris for many years before being summoned to Rome by Pope Innocent IV to serve as his master of the sacred palace (i.e., papal theologian); he held the post under Alexander IV and Urban IV. Urban made him a cardinal in 1262. Annibaldi played a prominent part in the papacy's dealing with Charles of Anjou, investing him in Rome as king of Sicily. St. Thomas dedicated to him the *Catena Aurea*.

Anno, St. (d. 1075) ● Archbishop of Cologne from 1055 who possessed much influence in the political affairs of the Holy Roman Empire. His uncle was the canon of Bamberg, and Anno entered the Church under his guidance. Recognizing his remarkable learning, Emperor Henry III summoned him to court. In 1055, he became archbishop of Cologne, although with considerable reluctance. After the death of Henry, Empress Agnes made Anno regent, with the task of educating the prince Henry IV. Stripped of the regency by ambitious ministers at court, he returned to the post in 1072. Anno was a supporter of Hildebrand (the future Pope Gregory VII) and St. Peter Damian, in their efforts at bringing reform to the Church, and Anno backed the legitimate pontiff, Alexander II, at an assembly in Augsburg in 1062, when Alexander was challenged by the antipope Cadalus, bishop of Parma.

Annuario Pontificio ● Pontifical directory or yearbook of the Catholic Church published by the Vatican Publishing House (or Libreria Editrice Vaticana), printed by the Vatican Polyglot Press, and compiled by the Central Statistics Office of the Church. The *Annuario* presents a massive up-to-date listing of the major and useful statistics and biographies of all relevant individuals and offices of the Church.

There are details on the dicasteries of the Roman Curia and the diplomatic corps, as well as biographical details on all the members of the College of Cardinals, bishops, and the superiors of the major religious orders. The section on episcopal biographies is particularly valuable, including addresses and telephone numbers. There is also a listing of the officially declared true popes. By custom, a special white leatherbound volume is presented annually to the reigning pontiff.

The *Annuario* had its origins in the *Notizie*, which was first published by the Holy See in 1716. It was given the title *Annuario Pontificio* in 1860, which was changed to the *Catholic Hierarchy* in 1872. The title was restored to *Annuario Pontificio* in 1912, and the publication, which was declared to be official in 1885, was stated to be no longer "officially" official in 1924, although its enormous value and "unofficially" official status make the book indispensable. The book is published in Italian, with some portions in Latin.

Anointing of the Sick ● Sacrament of the new law instituted by Christ to give spiritual comfort to the sick and dying, to bring the remission of sins, and to make known the concern and prayers of the Mystical Body of Christ, the Church. Also known as extreme unction, it consists of the anointing of a sick or infirm person's forehead and hands with olive oil that has normally been blessed by a bishop; in emergency situations, however, any vegetable oil may be used. The scriptural basis for the sacrament, as noted in conciliar documents and papal pronouncements, is found in the NT. First, in Mark (6:13) — after Christ sent out the disciples "two by two, and gave them authority over the unclean spirits" (6:7) — ". . . they cast out many demons, and anointed with oil many that were sick and healed them." The Church recognizes that this does not specifically state the anointing of the sick; but, according to the Doctrine on the Sacrament of Extreme Unction of the Council of Trent, the sacrament is "implied."

As developed in the Latin (Roman) rite, the anointing was originally administered by a priest to the eyes, ears, lips, head, and feet of the sick person. Until the twelfth century, it was common practice to give the sacrament to those who were actually sick (and not necessarily in terminal or gravely ill condition). In examining anointing in terms of its spiritual effect, many theologians came to the conclusion that it ought not be administered to the sick but rather to the dying, as the sick (those who might recover) had recourse to other sacraments, namely baptism and penance. Anointing, therefore, was better suited as a sacrament administered to the dying, as the means of remitting sins just before death. This understanding found wide acceptance until the time of the Council of Trent (1545-1563) when a reappraisal was undertaken and it stated that "anointing very fittingly represents the grace of the Holy Spirit, anointing the soul of a sick person in an invisible manner." Further long-term study found final fruition with the Second Vatican Council and the "Constitution on the Sacred Liturgy" (*Sacrosanctum Concilium*), which changed the name from extreme unction to anointing of the sick, adding that "as soon as any of the faithful begins to be in danger of death from sickness or old age, the appropriate time for him to receive this sacrament has certainly already arrived" (No. 73).

In 1974, Pope Paul VI implemented the directives of the council with the apostolic constitution *Sacram Unctionem Infirmorum*.

Specific guidelines were laid down in the Rite of Anointing and Pastoral Care of the Sick.

Anse, Councils of ● Several councils held during the Middle Ages in the French town of Anse, near Lyons. They were in 954, 1025, 1076, 1100, and 1112.

Anselm of Canterbury (c. 1033-1109) ● A leading mind in the Scholastic movement and a defender of Church rights in England, Anselm was the son of a Lombard family in Aosta, Lombardy. In 1059, he entered the famed monastery of Bec in Normandy, then under the leadership of Lanfranc of Pavia. Under Lanfranc's influence, he took monastic vows in 1060 and three years later succeeded him as prior. In 1078, he became abbot, upon the demise of Abbot Herluin.

St. Anselm of Canterbury

Increasingly respected because of his spirituality, his reputation as a teacher, and his writings, Anselm was the choice of the English clergy to become archbishop of Canterbury in 1089 upon Lanfranc's death, but several disputes with King William II

Rufus of England delayed his consecration until 1093. Anselm would spend the next years in constant strife with William and Henry I over the rights of the Church, particularly investiture. Twice he was faced with exile (1097 and 1103), although a compromise was reached in 1107 at the Synod of Westminster. As a theologian, Anselm was a formidable spokesman for the Scholastic movement, creating an ontological argument for God, using a simple notion that the existence of the Creator proves his being. He coined the term *"Credo ut intelligam"* ("I believe in order to understand"), thereby anticipating such philosophical innovations as those of Thomas Aquinas, René Descartes, and Karl Barth. Among his notable writings were *Monologum* (*Monologue*), *Cur Deus Homo?* (*Why Did God Become Man?*), and *Proslogium* (*Addition*). He was probably never officially canonized, but Pope Clement XI declared him a Doctor of the Church in 1720. Feast day: April 21.

Anselm of Laon (d. 1117) ● French theologian and a distinguished member of the Scholastic movement. Also known as Ansellus of Laon, he may not have been educated under Anselm of Canterbury as is traditionally believed. He did teach at Paris, however, and established a cathedral school at Laon (c. 1100) where he was assisted by his brother Ralph. The school at Laon was to become a very influential institution, claiming such students as Peter Abelard, William of Champeaux, and Gilbert de la Porrée. Anselm authored commentaries on the Gospel of St. John, the Pauline Epistles, and the Psalter; he also gave lectures on the Bible.

Anselm of Lucca, St. (d. 1086) ● Bishop of Lucca from 1071. He should not be confused with his uncle, Anselm of Lucca (the Elder), who became Pope Alexander II in 1061. Anselm was nominated to the see of Lucca in 1071 by his uncle and reluctantly accepted the investiture by Emperor Henry IV. He soon regretted this, however, resigned from his office, and retired to the monastery of Cluniac reform at Polirone, near Mantua. Nevertheless, Pope Gregory VII ordered him to return to his see. While he obeyed, he thereafter led the life of a simple monk while vigorously enforcing the Gregorian Reform on the clergy begun by the pope. These actions caused Henry and the antipope Guibert to expel him around 1080. Anselm fled to the sanctuary of Matilda of Tuscany, whose spiritual director he became. Later, he served as papal legate to Lombardy. Anselm authored a treatise against lay investiture, *Contra Guibertum et Sequaces ejus*, and made a collection of canons later incorporated into the *Decretum* of Gratian. Feast day: March 18.

Anskar, St. (801-865) ● So-called Apostle of the North, missionary, and the first archbishop of Bremen. Also called Ansgar, he was originally from Picardy in France. After becoming a monk at Corbie (near Amiens), he journeyed to Westphalia, visiting also Denmark whose king had just been converted to Christianity. Anskar established a school at Schleswig, but he was forced to leave because of violent opposition from the local pagans. In 828, he returned to Frankish lands, receiving, however, a request from the Swedes to visit their country. Journeying to Sweden he founded the first Christian church there. Pope Gregory IV named him bishop of Hamburg around 832, and he became archbishop of Bremen on or about 848. His last years were devoted to continuing missionary work in Denmark and Sweden, laboring especially to end the slave trade. After his death, the regions he had visited lapsed into paganism once more. Despite this setback, Anskar is known as the patron saint of Scandinavia. Feast day: February 3.

Anterus, St. ● Also Anteros and Antherus. Pope for only a few weeks in late 235 and early 236. He was elected after St. Pontianus, his predecessor, had been sent to a terrible fate in the mines of Sardinia. He himself was soon sentenced to death by Roman imperial officials. According to the *Liber Pontificalis*, Anterus earned martyrdom by having collected the acts of the martyrs and ordering them added to the young Church's activities. His burial site in the catacombs was discovered in 1854 by the archaeologist Giovanni Battista de Rossi. Feast day: January 3.

Anthony ● See under **Antony**.

Anticlericalism ● Popular movement that spread from Europe to Central and South America. It was strongly hostile to clergy in general and most forms of Christianity, targeting particularly the Catholic Church. While anticlericalism was found in Europe as early as the 1100s and 1200s with the heresy of Catharism, it found its fullest expression in the late 1700s with the French Revolution. The leaders of the revolution were opposed to the place of the Church in sociopolitical life in France and so, in 1792-1793, the adherents of Catholicism were overthrown save for those clergy who were willing to submit to the decrees and commands of the State, who were left unharmed. By the terms of the Concordat of 1801 signed by the Church with Napoleon Bonaparte, full rights were to be restored, although this did not happen until 1815 and the return of the monarchy. Anticlericalism remained strong in France into the twentieth century. Elsewhere, it appeared to vary in degrees of hostility in Belgium, Italy, Spain, Portugal, and the recently established independent countries of Central and South America of the twentieth century. The movement was, in the 1800s, closely associated with liberalism and has come to mean a virulent opposition to any ecclesiastical influence in public life.

Anti-Catholicism ● See GLOSSARY.

Antinomians ● Name used for those individuals who believed Christians were set free from any adherence to moral law, especially Mosaic law or even the Ten Commandments, by virtue of their received grace. As the name would suggest (*antinomos* — Greek for "against the law"), the Antinomians based their belief on a very extreme interpretation of St. Paul, who attacked Mosaic law in favor of the so-called "new covenant" established by Christ. It was used against Paul by his opponents (Rom 3). While he strenuously opposed the view, it was applicable to many sects of Gnosticism. During the Reformation, Antinomianism was revived by some Protestants (the Anabaptists, for example), who adhered to the concept of "purification by faith." Both Martin Luther and the Council of Trent repudiated such a view. Antinomians surfaced yet again during the English Commonwealth (mid-1600s) and in New England.

Antioch ● City in modern Syria that was, for centuries, an important center for the early Church. At the time of the foundation of Christianity, Antioch was one of the chief cities of the Roman province of Syria, and a major metropolis of the empire. The Acts of the Apostles mentions Antioch as the place of an early Christian community and where the Apostles first were known as "Christians" (11:26). It was natural that the first Christians should journey to Antioch, as it had a large Jewish population. After the martyrdom of Stephen in Jerusalem, many Christian fled there, working at first to convert the Jewish residents; in time, however, Gentiles joined. The local community emerged as a strong supporter of Paul in his first missionary efforts and backed his policy of anti-Judaizing the sect. Peter is held to be the first bishop of the city, and Antioch is thus counted as one of the early Church's original apostolic sees. By the second century, under St. Ignatius, the community was fully established, and by the fourth century it ranked only after Rome and Alexandria in ecclesiastical importance. As Constantinople's patriarch, and later Jerusalem's patriarch as well, increased in prestige and power, Antioch declined, a deterioration hastened by the city's involvement in the Nestorian and Monophysite heresies. In 1100, the patriarch and, by then, the orthodox prelate, departed for Constantinople as the crusaders installed a Latin patriarch. From the fourteenth century, the patriarchate has been titular and the patriarch actually resides in Damascus. The Antiochene rite was used by the early Christians of Antioch and subsequently spread to Jerusalem and was translated into both Greek and Aramaic. It is preserved in Book 8 of the Apostolic Constitutions, a fourth-century Syrian work, and exerted considerable influence on the Byzantine rite. Its influence elsewhere is seen in the Malankar and Malabar rites in India and the Liturgy of St. James of Christians in Syria and Iraq. The Liturgy of Antioch is also sometimes called the West Syrian rite. This evolved after the condemnation of Nestorianism in 431. In the original form of the rite, it differed from that of the West by deleting the Our Father and the names of the saints. The Council of Antioch (341), called the "Dedication Council," was held to consecrate the Golden Church of Constantine at Antioch. At the council, there were efforts made to replace the Nicene Creed with other less orthodox versions.

Antipope ● Name given a rival claimant to the papacy. An antipope can be a person who is elected, appointed, or who assumed the title of pope illegally or in direct opposition to the legitimate holder of the Holy See. While there were antipopes in the early Church, they were most common during the Middle Ages when the Christian Church was beset with secular challenges (particularly from

Holy Roman Emperors), doctrinal disputes, and double or doubted elections. The Great Schism of 1378-1415 was also a cause. Scholars have long been confronted with a difficult time in compiling lists of antipopes, as there are questions of legitimacy on the part of some popes, inadequate historical or documentary details on several elections, and unclear reasons or causes of an antipope's election. In all, there have been thirty-nine known antipopes from Hippolytus (r. 217-235) to Felix V (r. 1439-1449).

They include: Hippolytus (217-235); Novatian (251); Felix II (355-365); Ursinus (366-367); Eulalius (418-419); Lawrence (498-505); Dioscorus (530); Theodore (687); Paschal (687); Constantine II (767-768); Philip (768); John (844); Anastasius (855); Christopher (903-904); Boniface VII (974, 984-985); John XVI (997-998); Gregory VI (1012); Benedict X (1058-1059); Honorius II (1061-1072); Clement III (1080, 1084-1100); Theodoric (1100); Albert (1102); Sylvester IV (1105-1111); Gregory VIII (1118-1121); Celestine II (1124); Anacletus II (1130-1138); Victor IV (1138); Victor IV (1159-1164; not to be confused with the previous Victor IV); Paschal III (1164-1168); Callistus III (1168-1178); Innocent III (1179-1180); Nicholas V (1328-1330); Clement VII (1378-1394); Benedict XIII (1394-1423); Alexander V (1409-1410); John XXIII (1410-1415); Clement VIII (1423-1429); Benedict XIV (1425-1430); and Felix V (1439-1449).

Anti-Semitism ● See GLOSSARY; see also **Jews and Judaism**.

Antonelli, Giacomo (1806-1876) ● Cardinal secretary of state and formidable Vatican figure who earned the nickname "Red Pope" during the long reign of Pope Pius IX (r. 1846-1878). He was born in Sonnine in the Papal States to a family later ennobled by Pope Gregory XVI. After studying at a Roman seminary, he took up law at Sapienza and

there obtained a doctorate. Appointed to the diplomatic service of the Holy See, he held various posts under Gregory, including assessor of the criminal tribunal, canon of St. Peter's (deacon in 1840), and treasurer of the Apostolic Camera (1845). On the accession of Pope Pius IX in 1846, Antonelli was made cardinal deacon (1847), one of the few cardinals of modern times who was not advanced beyond the diaconate. In 1848, after holding several offices, he helped arrange the flight of the pope to Gaeta where Antonelli was made secretary of state. Returning to Rome in 1850 with Pio Nono (as Pius was called), he retained his post until his death, wielding immense power. He guided Pius's ultramontane policies, opposed Vatican Council I, and struggled to defend the papacy against the Risorgimento in Italy. While his admirers defend and praise his gifted labors for the Holy See, his enemies charge that he was the virtual ruler of Rome until 1870 and was too much a devious statesman than prelate.

Antonians ● Name of several communities whose members claimed descent from or the patronage of St. Antony of Egypt. The oldest communities were the original followers of Antony in the Egyptian desert. Other groups included: a congregation established in 1095 by Gaston de Dauphine that flourished in France, Italy, and Spain, lasting until the French Revolution — their name was the Hospital Brothers of St. Antony; a community founded in 1615 in Flanders; and an Antonian sect in Switzerland at the start of the 1800s.

Antoninus, St. (1389-1459) ● Archbishop of Florence, a noted Dominican, and a founder of the concept of moral theology. He entered the Dominicans in 1403, making his novitiate with the likes of Fra Bartolomeo and Fra Angelico. Eventually, he became the head of the convents in Rome, Naples, Siena, Fiesole, and elsewhere; in 1436, he laid the foundation for the Florentine convent of San Marco, and, with the financial help of Cosimo de' Medici, built an adjoining church. Made archbishop in 1446 by Eugenius IV, he was also appointed counselor of the popes. Antoninus authored a *Summa theologica moralis* and a world history as well as some works on the Christian life. His charity, care for the sick, and miracles were legendary. Feast day: May 10.

Antony, St. (251-356) ● Famed hermit. Called St. Antony of Egypt, he was considered the patriarch of all monks and the founder of Christian monasticism. Born near Memphis, in Upper Egypt, he was the son of Christians. Drawn to austerity, he gave away all of his possessions around 269, including a sizable inheritance, and retired to a life of strict asceticism, eating only bread and water and living for a time in a cemetery tomb near his native village. During this period, while praying and meditating, he was said to have been severely tested by the devil and his demons, who appeared in the disguise of wild animals.

Around 285, desiring even greater solitude, he moved to a mountaintop. This lifestyle soon attracted followers, however,

St. Antony

and Antony came out of the desert in 305 to organize a community of ascetics near Faiyum under a rule. While this was a major development and the group of monks are generally held to have formed the first Christian monastery, the community had little similarity to later monastic or religious orders. In 311, Antony went to Alexandria where he gave moral support to the Christians there who were suffering under the persecutions of the Roman government. He then returned to the desert, settling on Mt. Kolzim, near the Red Sea, with his well-known disciple Macarius. Later, around 355, he traveled once more to speak out against Arianism, giving needed aid to his friend St. Athanasius. Going back to Mt. Kozim, he continued to give advice and counsel to all who asked, his fame and influence only increasing as the numbers of adherents of the rigorous ascetic life multiplied. The chief source for details on his remarkable life was *Vita Antonii* by Athanasius; its authenticity is today accepted. Feast day: January 17.

Antony of Padua, St. (1195-1251) ● Also Anthony of Padua, Franciscan friar and Doctor of the Church. Born Ferdinand to a noble family in Lisbon, he was educated in the cathedral school, joining the Augustinian Canons in 1210. In 1212, with the permission of his superiors, he went to the convent of Santa Croce in Coimbra to devote himself to a life of prayer and study. In 1220, however, he saw the relics of the first Franciscan martyrs (who had died in Morocco the same year) carried into the Church of Santa Croce. Resolving to join the Franciscans, he wanted to go on a missionary journey to Africa where he might also suffer martyrdom. He entered the Franciscans a short time later, setting off for Morocco. Illness soon caused him to cut short his trip and to return home. The ship in which he was traveling was caught in a storm, taking forced refuge in Sicily where Antony (the name he had taken upon entering the Franciscans) recovered his health. While in the company of the Italian Franciscans Antony was discovered by accident to be not only theologically profound but a brilliant preacher. He was put to work teaching theology in the schools of Bologna, Montpelier, and Toulouse, especially acquiring a great reputation for his sermons throughout Italy and France. He also held the posts of guardian of Le Puy (1224), custodian of Limousin (1226), and provincial of Emilia (1227). This last office he resigned in 1230 to devote himself to preaching. He concentrated himself in the area around Padua, routinely attracting enormous crowds of faithful who would come eagerly to hear his words. While at Padua, he reportedly performed the miracle of the restoration of the severed foot. Retiring to Camposanpiere, near Padua, he fell ill in 1231, dying at Vercelli on June 13. He was canonized the next year and declared to be a Doctor of the Church in 1946 by Pope Pius XII. A great patron of the poor, he is also invoked as protection for travelers and pregnant women, and lost property. Feast day: June 13.

Antony of Siena (d. 1585) ● Dominican theologian. Also called Lusitanus, he was

St. Antony of Padua

popularly known as Antony of Siena because of his great devotion to St. Catherine of Siena. After studying at Lisbon, Coimbra, and Louvain, he taught at the latter institution and was made a doctor of theology there in 1571; three years later, in 1574, he became head of the Dominican College. Antony is best known for his work as an editor in preparing the Roman edition of many of the writings of St. Thomas Aquinas, including the *Summa Theologica* and the *Quaestiones Disputatae*.

Apocrypha ● Properly Apocrypha of Christian Origin, to distinguish it from Apocrypha of Jewish Origin. Writings that originally were supposed to have been of divine inspiration but were said to have been long hidden and later formed a body of literature that had aspirations toward canonical authenticity. The term "apocrypha" was derived from the Greek *apokryphos* (hidden) and found expression in the Latin as *apocryphus* (apocryphal or uncanonical) as a means of delineating those writings that imitated the books of the NT. They were largely composed by both Christians and heretics, mostly members of the pervasive sects of Gnosticism, and are dated to the first centuries of the Church. Various types of apocryphal literature existed. Old Testament apocryphal writings included such forms as didactic, apocalyptic, and historical. New Testament apocryphal writings were found in the forms of gospels, acts, epistles, and apocalypses.

Apocryphal New Testament ● Name given to a number of early Christian works that were not included in the Canon of the NT. The use of the term "apocryphal," however, is generally not meant in this title to imply that these books are inaccurate or of an unorthodox nature. They are customarily divided into gospels, acts, and epistles. Among the numerous apocryphal gospels are several of some genuine historical or oral-tradition value, such as the Gospel of Peter or the Gospel According to the Egyptians. Others range from the Gospels of Marcion or Thomas, to the frequently unreliable or scandalous History of Joseph the Carpenter or the Departure of Mary. Among the apocryphal acts, the most notable were those dated to the second century, such as the Acts of Peter, John, Paul, Andrew, and Thomas. Collectively, they were called the Leucian Acts, since they were supposedly written by Leucian Charinus, as noted by Photius. The Church has long had the view that these are heretical in nature to some degree, with the exception of the Acts of Paul. The epistles include those of Barnabas and the spurious Epistles of Paul to the Corinthians.

Apollinarianism ● Fourth-century heresy proposing that Christ possessed a human body and soul but not a human spirit; instead, his spirit was replaced by the *Logos*. Advanced by Apollinarius, bishop of Laodicea (d. c. 390), the heresy taught that Christ did not possess complete or full manhood in an

effort to argue that the Savior had only one nature, not two. The position was very similar to that of the Arians insofar as it questioned the possibility of two distinct natures in one person. Considered the first of many so-called Christological controversies, Apollinarianism was vigorously opposed by the Orthodox Church, which rejected it by pointing out that by denying the complete human nature in Christ the Apollinarianists render impossible his redemption of humanity. The heresy was condemned at the Synod of Rome (374-380) and the Council of Constantinople (381). Apollinarius left the Church and his teachings were forbidden.

Apollinaris, St. ● First bishop of Ravenna. Long revered as the first and only martyr there, although there is virtually no historical information on him and even his martyrdom is doubtful, his name is known from the famous Church of Sant' Apollinare near Ravenna, at Classe. Feast day: July 23.

Apollinarius, Claudius (fl. mid-second century) ● Early Christian apologist and the bishop of Hierapolis. He authored several works in defense of Christianity, the most notable being his *Defense of the Faith*, presented to Emperor Marcus Aurelius around 172. His writings are lost save for a few fragments.

Apologetics ● Defense of the faith through intellectual proofs or reasoning undertaken by trained theologians. Apologists (propounders of apologetics) endeavor to provide explanations of Christian principles so that those persons opposed to Christianity or who had heard only misinformation will be informed fully of the faith's doctrine and will come away with an understanding, perhaps even acceptance, of all the Church has to offer. The earliest of the apologetics drew their inspiration from the brilliant sermons of St. Paul and first appeared in the second century with the so-called apologists, Church Fathers such as Justin Martyr, Theophilus, and Tertullian. Initially, apologetics were concerned with presenting the reasonableness of the faith to non-Christians; but later, they became useful in offering vigorous defenses against unorthodox or heretical teachings. They have been found subsequently throughout Church history, including St. Augustine's *City of God*, Thomas Aquinas's *Summa Contra Gentiles*, and the writings of John Henry Newman. While Vatican Council II de-emphasized the importance of apologetics, ongoing and ever-increasing anti-Catholicism and anti-Christian activities have prompted a resurgence of the discipline. (See also **Apologists**, following entry.)

Apologists ● Name used for those Christian writers who author often spirited, reasoned, and intellectual defenses of Christian doctrine in the face of anti-Christian writings or an anti-Christian atmosphere. The apologists are best known from the second century during the time of severe persecution of the Church by the Roman Empire; the name "apologist" itself, derived from the Greek, was bestowed upon these authors as a title of honor for one well-qualified to defend the faith. Among the most notable early apologists were Tertullian, Justin Martyr, Aristides, Tatian, Minucius Felix, and Theophilus.

Apostasy ● Term used for the total abandonment of the Church or faith. In the early Church, apostasy was ranked as one of the most heinous of all crimes, placed with fornication and murder as a sin for which no pardon was initially attainable if the person was baptized; later, pardon was possible through public penance. The basis for apostasy was the Old and New Testaments, particularly Acts 21:21, in which Paul is accused of the sin because of his rejection of Moses. Subsequently, canon law defined apostasy as the total rejection or repudiation

of the Christian faith by someone who had been baptized or received into the Church. Apostasy warrants immediate excommunication. Another form is the desertion or departure from the Church of a religious who has taken vows. Among the most famous of all apostates were Emperor Julian (d. 363), Martin Luther (d. 1546), and King Henry VIII of England (d. 1547).

Apostles ● See under the individual Apostles.

Apostles of Places and Peoples ● See TABLE 1.

Apostleship of Prayer ● Catholic pious movement that promotes devotion to the Sacred Heart of Jesus. It was founded in 1844 at Vals, France, by the French Jesuit François Xavier Gautrelet. It received formal papal statutes in 1879 (revised in 1896). The apostleship has three degrees of membership and is publicized through the *Messenger of the Sacred Heart* and the *Monthly Leaflet*.

Apostolic Church Orders, The ● Document from the early Christian Church, probably composed in Egypt in the early fourth century. It provides information on ecclesiastical practices and moral regulations. Originally written in Greek, it was translated into Latin, Arabic, Coptic, Ethiopian, and Syriac. The name is derived from the fact that it was supposedly based on the words of the Apostles spoken at a council reputedly attended by Mary and Martha.

Apostolic Canons ● Set, or series, of eighty-five canons, originally attributed to the Apostles, forming the seventh book of the fourth-century work Apostolic Constitutions. They were probably compiled by the same authors of the Constitutions. The canons were concerned mainly with clerical conduct, including ordination; a few canons dealt with the responsibilities of all Christians. While the apostolic attribution is today not substantiated, the canons did have a considerable influence on Church law. The first fifty were translated into Latin in the sixth century by Dionysius Exiguus, making them part of the Western Church; in the East, they were accepted by the Trullan Council of 692. They were also called Canons of the Apostles.

Apostolic Constitutions, The ● Set of ecclesiastical laws dated to the late fourth century and probably composed in Syria. The author may have been an Arian. Known in full as *Ordinances of the Holy Apostles through Clement*, the compilation was organized into seven chapters. The seventh and final chapter was comprised of the Apostolic Canons, although these were added at a later date. (See also **Didache**.)

Apostolic Delegate ● See **Papal Legate**.

Apostolic Fathers ● Name given to those important members of the early Church who immediately succeeded the Apostles and thus learned from them. These Fathers were responsible for many important writings, works that have survived completely or in part and that had been long held in great esteem. Some of the Apostolic Fathers are Clement of Rome (Pope Clement I), Papias, Hermas, Polycarp of Smyrna, and Ignatius of Antioch. The term Apostolic Fathers has been used since the 1600s. (See also **Fathers of the Church**.)

Apostolic See ● See **Holy See**.

Apostolic Signatura ● Known today in full as the Supreme Tribunal of the Apostolic Signature, this is the supreme court of the Church. Dating to the thirteenth century, the Signatura serves as a court of appeal from those decisions made by the Roman Rota, particularly examining cases appealed to it

because of what may be considered defective juridical procedure. There are also provisions for hearing appeals of clergy against decisions by superiors. By custom, the Signatura is organized into a body of six cardinals under a cardinal prefect. In practice, however, the day-to-day affairs are administered by the cardinal prefect with the assistance of the secretary (an archbishop) and a staff.

Apostolic Succession ● Name given to the long sequence, or succession, of validly ordained bishops to the Apostles. It is based on the tradition that Christ entrusted into the hands of his Apostles the continuation of his ministry. The Apostles then became the leaders of the first Christian communities whose members, in turn, were given authority to teach, minister, and guide the growing Church. The chief figures delegated to conduct these ministries were chosen by the Apostles; they subsequently received the title of bishop. These bishops then selected other bishops, thereby ensuring the link directly to Christ himself. This line of succession was very important in the early Church, as it allowed the orthodox membership to stand in strong defense against heretical sects, especially the Gnostics, who claimed to be the bearers of a message of salvation that bypassed or ignored the successors of the Apostles. Pope St. Clement I in the first century stressed the importance of a succession from the successors to the Apostles and hence to Christ, a tradition from then on recognized as a fundamental historical Church reality.

Apostolicae Curae ● Title of the papal encyclical, or brief, issued on September 13, 1896, by Pope Leo XIII (1878-1903). It declared "absolutely null and utterly void" the Anglican orders because of defect of both form and intention. The following year, the Anglican archbishops of York and

Canterbury issued a *responsio*. (For further details, see **Anglican Orders**.)

Apostolicae Servitutis ● Bull issued on February 23, 1741, by Pope Benedict XIV (1740-1758) that placed strong prohibitions against secular pursuits by the clergy. It was declared as the result of the increasing activities of a worldly nature by many clerics. The bull went so far as to prohibit and condemn secular involvements by priests who tried to avoid punishment by using the name of a layperson.

Apostolicam Actuositatem ● Decree issued on November 18, 1965, by the Second Vatican Council defining the mission to which all laity (or laypeople) are called, by virtue of their baptism into the faith. Known in English as the "Decree on the Apostolate of the Laity," it promotes the right of the laity to establish and participate in associations that help carry out the lay apostolate, encouraging and charging the hierarchy to provide spiritual assistance and guidance to ensure the common good and to preserve doctrinal purity.

Apostolicam Pascendi Munus ● Bull issued on January 12, 1765, by Pope Clement XIII (1758-1769), vigorously defending the Jesuits in the face of recent and severe criticisms that had been made upon the order in numerous countries. The bull confirmed papal confidence in the Society of Jesus, restated its purpose, and approved both its aims and methods used to attain them.

Apostolici ● Latin for "Apostolics" that was used to refer to the various sects of a heretical nature. It was first used in the second to fourth centuries in the early Church to signify several branches of the Gnostic heresy. Members preached an extreme form of poverty and claimed to be emulating the Apostles. Other *apostolici* were found during the Middle Ages. One group, condemned by St. Bernard of Clairvaux, was located in Pèrigreux, France, and around Cologne. They rejected marriage and meat. Another sect was in Parma, established by Gerard Segarelli. Despite claiming to be based on Franciscan teaching, the group was condemned at Rome in 1286 and 1291. Segarelli was burned to death at Parma in 1300. Fra Dolcino, however, revived the sect soon after, although he too was burned, in 1307.

Appellant Controversy ● Dispute that arose in England following the death in 1594 of Cardinal William Allen concerning the direction and position of the Church in the country. The name was derived from the title used for the thirty-one Catholics who made an appeal to Rome under the leadership of William Bishop. In the time following the demise of Cardinal Allen the Catholic population had broken into two increasingly hostile camps — those who wished to see the destruction of Queen Elizabeth I, led by Roger Parsons (d. 1610) and fellow Jesuits, and the many Catholics who, while faithful to the Church, expressed loyalty to the queen. The appointment in 1598 of George Blackwell (d. 1613) as archpriest of the Catholic mission in England brought matters to a head, since he promoted continued hostility and had what many considered to be pro-Jesuit sympathies. An appeal was then made in 1599 by Bishop and the Appellants. Initially rebuffed, they tried again in 1601 and 1602, finally gaining the support of the French ambassador. Blackwell was ultimately reprimanded and, on January 31, 1603, Bishop and twelve other priests accepted the "Protestation of Allegiance" by which they swore political fealty to Elizabeth and condemned all forms of violence to return England to the Church. Blackwell himself ended the controversy in 1608 by taking the Oath of Allegiance to King James I. (See also **Great Britain**.)

Appellants ● Name used by several members of the French clergy, under the direction of Cardinal L. A. de Noailles and four bishops, who appealed in 1713 to an ecumenical council against a papal condemnation of Jansenist writings. Archbishop of Paris, de Noailles opposed the papal bull *Unigenitus* of Pope Clement XI that condemned one hundred one propositions of the French Jansenist Pasquier Quesnel (d. 1719). He and the Appellants first used pamphlets to change the papal decree but finally took the decisive step of appealing to an ecumenical council. In 1718, the Appellants were condemned and excommunicated by the bull *Pastoralis Officii*; de Noailles recanted in 1728, crippling the movement, which soon disintegrated.

Aquarians ● Known as the Aquarii, a minor sect in the early Church, also called in the Greek the Hydroprastate, which means "those who offer water." They were called the Aquarii because of their habit of substituting water for wine in the Eucharist, as the use of wine was considered sinful. The sect flourished in the second century but then quietly disappeared.

Aquileian Rite ● Early rite in the Christian Church that was used in Aquileia, a city on the Adriatic and, at the time, an important center in the Roman Empire. Aquileia was also the seat for centuries of a Western patriarchate. The rite of Aquileia is largely unknown in any detail because of the absence of any surviving information. It was also used, however, in surrounding areas, including Verona, Pola, and Trent. During the Carolingian period of the ninth century, the rite was superseded by a version of the Roman rite. Finally, in 1597, it was suppressed.

Archaeology, Commission of Sacred ● Commission on archaeology that was established in 1852 by Pope Pius IX. Its purpose was to study, explore, and excavate ancient Christian monuments, particularly the Roman catacombs and the rich excavations in the Vatican as well as tombs, mosaics, sculptures, inscriptions, and paintings. The commission also has the responsibility of caring for the vast museums of the State of Vatican City. The most famous of all excavations by the commission took place beneath St. Peter's Basilica (1939-1949). The excavations led to the discovery of an entire metropolis dating to the early Christian and pagan era; found there was the generally accepted burial place of St. Peter. (See also **Peter, Tomb of**.)

Archange de Lyon (1736-1822) ● Preacher of the Capuchin order, originally known as Michael Desgranges. He entered the Capuchins in 1751, subsequently serving as a lecturer of theology until 1799 when, having antagonized the government, he was forced to flee the country. He returned to Lyons in 1796 in disguise, becoming curé of the local Carthusian parish. In 1818, he returned to his monastic habit and thereafter played a role in restoring the Carthusian order in France following the Revolution and the Napoleonic Wars.

Argentina ● South American country with a largely Catholic population. The faith first arrived in the region with several priests who sailed with Magellan on his explorations. Although a Mass was celebrated there on April 1, 1519, actual missionary work did not begin until 1530, coinciding with the efforts of Spanish officials to establish colonial domination. Buenos Aires was founded in 1536 by Pedro de Mendoza but was soon abandoned owing to the attacks of the local inhabitants. The Church, meanwhile, began to lay the groundwork for diocesan organization in the 1540s, and, at the request of the local governor, the Jesuits were asked to preach among the Indians. The first Jesuit missionaries landed in 1586.

After establishing a college in Córdoba, they set out and within a few years they gathered together over a hundred thousand natives into various townships. These growing communities proved exceedingly prosperous, so much so that they contributed to the decision of the Spanish to expel them in 1767.

Buenos Aires was reestablished in 1580, although it did not become the capital of the Spanish viceroy until 1776. In 1816, after a six-year war, Argentina won its independence from Spain. The next decades brought frequent troubles from dictatorships and civil wars, and the Church suffered from repressive regimes and the anticlerical policies of liberal governments. Nevertheless, Argentina grew into a prosperous nation from the latter part of the 1800s. Under Juan Perón, dictator from 1946, many in the Church gave support to his policies, especially the efforts of his wife to promote the Catholic faith. Harsh military rule from 1976-1983 brought severe repression, human rights violations, and the disappearance of thousands, most of whom were brutally murdered. The defeat of Argentina in the Falklands War with Great Britain hastened the fall of the junta, which was replaced in December 1983. Earlier that year, the Argentine conference of bishops released a compilation of its communiques sent to the government in protesting its grave violations of human rights. Two notable Argentine churchmen of recent years are Cardinal Juan Carlos Aramburu (b. 1912), former archbishop of Buenos Aires, and Cardinal Eduardo Pironio (b. 1920), currently president of the Pontifical Council for the Laity, who reportedly was the target of death squads in the 1970s.

Arianism ● Major heresy that confronted the Christian Church in the fourth century. Arianism took its name from Arius (260-336), the heretical priest of Alexandria who formulated its principles and doctrines. According to the Arians, Christ was not truly divine but was created by the Father to serve as the fulcrum for his divine plan; he was like the Father, but, as a created being, Christ was temporal and changeable rather than divine and eternal.

Arius was commanded not to advance this theory by his superior, Bishop Alexander of Alexandria. When he refused, he was condemned and excommunicated by a synod at Alexandria around 320. Despite his condemnation, however, the heresy continued to spread, ultimately becoming a crisis of such proportions that Emperor Constantine the Great felt compelled to intervene and attempt to find a resolution. He thus convened the Council of Nicaea (325) where the anti-Arian party, under the guidance of Athanasius, then a deacon of Alexandria, secured an orthodox definition of the faith and the use of the term *homoousios* (consubstantial; i.e., of the same substance) in describing Christ's nature; Arian prelates, such as Eusebius of Nicomedia, were banished.

While not an Arian, Constantine gradually relaxed his anti-Arian position under the influence of his sister, who had certain Arian sympathies. Eusebius and others were allowed to return and soon began working for the defeat of the Nicene cause. At the behest of Eusebius of Nicomedia, Constantine attempted to bring Arius back to Constantinople (334-335) and restore him to orthodox favor, but he died while en route in 336. Meanwhile, the Arian party was slowly gaining the upper hand, securing the exile of Athanasius, now bishop of Alexandria, and Eustathius of Antioch. Further progress was made under Constantine's successor in the East, Constantius II (r. 337-361), who declared his support for Arianism. In 341, a council was held in Antioch where a majority of Eastern bishops, headed by Eusebius of Nicomedia, accepted several heretical statements on Christ's nature. Opposition was such in the West that both Constantius II and his colleague in the Western Empire,

Constans (r. 340-350), convened the Council of Sardica in 343. Fearing defeat, the Arians withdrew from the assembly, although the non-Arians managed to have the oft-banished Athanasius restored to Alexandria and several Arians deposed from their sees.

Constans died in 350 and Constantius became sole emperor, an event that heralded a new outbreak of Arianism and severe persecutions of Catholics in the empire. During this period, the Arian party broke apart into three main groups: (1) the Anomoeans, the most radical, who had favored a sharp difference between the Father and the Son; (2) the moderate party, the Homoians (from *homoios*, or "similar"), who advocated a theological ambiguity; and (3) the so-called Semi-Arians, the Homoiousians, who favored the theological term *homoiousios* (that Jesus is "like the Father") and stressed the similarities and differences between the Son and Father. In 359, the Arians were able to unite and, at the councils held at Seleucia and Ariminum, they won their greatest doctrinal triumph, of which St. Jerome wrote that it made the "world groan and wonder to find itself Arian."

The tide finally turned against Arianism from this point. Constantius died in 361, depriving Arianism of its greatest patron. Further, the Semi-Arians, alarmed by the hard-line Arian views of their fellow partisans, began leaning toward a compromise. Under Emperor Valentinian (r. 364-375), Orthodox Christianity was reestablished in the West and in the East, and the magnificent examples of orthodoxy provided by the Cappadocian Fathers (Sts. Basil, Gregory of Nyssa, and Gregory of Nazianzus) laid the groundwork for the final defeat of the Arians at the Council of Constantinople in 381. The heresy would not die out for several centuries, finding fertile ground among the Germanic tribes. St. Ulfilas, for example, preached Arianism to the Goths. The Goths then brought Arianism back to the Roman Empire in the fifth century with their invasion of the West. The Arian Vandals often persecuted Catholics in North Africa and Spain. An influential event was the conversion of the Franks under Clovis in 496 to Orthodox Christianity. Arianism, for all practical purposes, died out by the sixth century. (See also **Ambrose, St**.)

Ariminium and Seleucia, Synods of ● Two synods that were held in 359 by the convening of Emperor Constantius, who summoned the bishops of the Eastern and Western Empires to Ariminium and Seleucia respectively in the hopes of ending the Arian dispute within the Christian Church. The Synod of Ariminium (Rimine) was heavily attended by orthodox and hence anti-Arian prelates who, not surprisingly, passed a stern anti-Arian edict. The emperor, however, was advised by two Arian supporters, Valens and Ursacius, who managed to undo the efforts of the orthodox prelates. Soon, under pressure from the imperial court, the bishops at Ariminium, who had not dispersed, were forced to recant. A new, Arian creed was then drawn up and accepted at Nice, in Thrace. The Synod of Seleucia, with fewer bishops in attendance but firm in Arian sympathizers, also accepted the Creed of Nice. St. Jerome remarked that the terrible year of 359 made the "world groan and wonder to find itself Arian." (See also **Arianism**.)

Aristotle (384-322 B.C.) ● One of the most important and influential of all philosophers. The son of a court physician, he was born in Stagirus, on Chalcidice, and in 367 journeyed to Athens where he studied under Plato (427-347 B.C.) from 366-347. Aristotle was later a tutor to Alexander the Great (343-336) and founded the so-called Peripatetic School, from the fact that his lessons were taught while in a covered portico (*peripatos*). It would be impossible in this limited space to examine fully the entire Aristotelian philosophical system, but in broad terms Aristotle agreed with Plato about the universe as an ideal world, differing with him on the relation of form and matter. Aristotle argued that these were inseparable. He proposed that the union of matter and form became the principle by which growth could be explained in terms of motion; motion and change, he declared, are the realization of form in matter. In explaining this movement, he was led to a theory of causation, developing the Final Cause, finding the final, efficient, and formal causes in God, called by Aristotle the Unmoved Mover. These theories, along with his creation of the science of logic and his *Ethics* — governed by the principle of the ideal life being one of adherence to the golden mean — made him enormously influential in the development of philosophy in the succeeding centuries.

In the early period of the Church, however, Aristotelian ideas were examined with a certain skepticism by theologians who feared that the system might lead to excessive materialism. The view was in large part the result of the pervasive influence of Plato, who stood as the exact opposite in such fundamental questions as form and matter and the good. As the foremost theologian of the era, St. Augustine (354-430) was very expressive of Platonism, so it was not surprising that Aristotle should be eclipsed by Plato, who was more widely regarded by Church Fathers. He would remain generally neglected for centuries in the West with the exception of the sixth-century philosopher Boethius. In the East, his writings were still preserved, among the scholars and intellectuals of the Arab world, and translated from Greek into Arabic.

In the Middle Ages, thanks to trade and the crusades, manuscripts by Aristotle began making their way into Europe. These were translated by scholars, most notably Jews, from the Arabic into Latin. (See also **William of Moerbeke**.) These rediscovered works, with commentaries by such Arab philosophers as Averroës and Avicenna, soon created a major stir among Christian philosophers and theologians. While viewed at first with serious apprehension by Church officials, the Philosopher — as Aristotle was called — soon found acceptance in Scholastic circles, and Aristotelianism was energetically adapted to Christian thought by such towering figures as St. Albertus Magnus and St. Thomas Aquinas. Despite resistance from Augustinianists in the thirteenth and fourteenth centuries, Christianized Aristotelianism became the basis of much in Christian theology. (See also **Scholasticism**.)

Arles, Synods of ● A number of synods or councils held in the town of Arles, located in southern France, near Marseilles, from the fourth to the thirteenth centuries. In all, there were some fifteen synods, concerned with a variety of topics or issues. The first, in 314, was convened by Emperor Constantine the Great to discuss the schism of Donatism. Another council, in 353, promoted Arianism, and one in 1234 condemned Albigensianism. The synod of 1263 condemned the teachings of Joachim of Fiore. The last synod (1275), in comparison with the aforementioned, was uneventful.

Armagh, Book of ● Also called by some scholars the *Codex Dublinensis*, an important collection of documents on vellum dating to the eighth and ninth centuries. The work is useful in shedding light on certain aspects of Irish history, comprising two lives of St. Patrick, a life of St. Martin of Tours (by Sulpicius Severus), and a Latin (non-Vulgate) translation of the text of the NT. It has been attributed to Ferdomnach of Armagh (d. 846), and is presently located in Trinity College, Dublin (MS No. 52), hence its name *Codex Dublinensis*.

Armenia ● Onetime republic of the former Soviet Union located in Asia Minor. Armenia has a long connection with the Church, claiming the distinction of being the first nation to accept Christianity officially. An ancient land, it was traditionally said to have been founded by a descendant of Noah. Owing to its strategic location, it was the battleground of numerous ancient empires, including the Assyrians, Medes, Persians, and the Macedonians under Alexander the Great. The kingdom of Armenia (189-69 B.C.) was conquered by the Romans, who established useful satellite kingdoms and used the region in its military and diplomatic struggles with the Parthians and then the Persians. Its long subsequent history was one of domination by the Byzantines, Seljuk Turks, Ottoman Turks, and Russians. Turkish rule was especially harsh, with bloody massacres of the population occurring from 1894-1915.

Christianity was brought to Armenia in the third century by Gregory the Illuminator, who baptized King Tiridates III (238-314). Tiridates declared Armenia a Christian state, and Gregory made his seat of authority in Etchmiadzin, near Mt. Ararat. His position as primate (*Catholicos*) became hereditary, although the Church was under the jurisdiction of the metropolitan of Caesarea. A break with Caesarea occurred in 374, and in the fifth century an extensive reform was introduced by St. Isaac the Great and St. Mesrob. The Bible and liturgy were translated into Armenian.

The Church and its people suffered under the persecutions of the Persians and then the Arabs, although autonomy was achieved from 885-1046 under the native Bagratids. They were conquered by the Byzantines who were ejected by the Seljuk Turks. An Armenian dynastic group, pushed westward by the Turks, founded the kingdom of Little Armenia in Cilicia, thereby creating two areas, Greater and Little Armenia. The latter survived until 1375 during which the Armenians were able to enter into communion with Rome. This development, coupled with the crusades, brought various Western influences from the Western Church. Armenians took part in the Council of Florence (1438-1439) where a decree of reunion was effected, although subsequent religious and political events, most notably the fall of Constantinople to the Ottoman Turks in 1453, rendered the agreement impractical.

As noted, persecutions have been severe in Armenia, by the Turks, the Russians, and then by the Soviet Communist government after the declaration of a Soviet republic in 1920 and the institution of an atheistic regime. The Armenian Catholic rite is today found wherever Armenian faithful fled or were exiled. The Armenian rite has jurisdictions in Iraq, Egypt, Syria, Romania, Lebanon, Argentina, Mexico, France, Greece, and the United States. Diplomatic relations were initiated between the Armenian government and the Holy See in May 1992.

Arnauld, Antoine (1612-1694) ● Known as the "Great Arnauld," he was a French theologian, philosopher, and major supporter of Jansenism. Born in Paris, he studied at the Sorbonne and became a familiar figure in French intellectual circles. After receiving the subdiaconate in 1638, however, he was closely associated with the convent of Port-Royal where he retired in 1641 after ordination. Two years later, he caused a major controversy with the publication of his work *De la frequente communion* (*On Frequent Communion*), which postulated many Jansenist ideas. So heated was the Jesuit response that Arnauld withdrew from public activity. Nevertheless, in 1644, he had published anonymously *Apologie de M. Jansenius*, a defense of Jansenism. The apology elevated Arnauld to the position of theological leader of the Jansenists. By January 1656, opposition was such that he was censured by the Sorbonne and soon demoted. He remained in retirement until 1668 and the Peace of the Church. The following year, he was restored to Doctor of the Sorbonne and was received by King Louis XIV. In 1679, he left France when a Jansenist revival began, living and writing in the Netherlands until his death. He was joined there by Pasquier Quesnel. His sister, Jacqueline Marie Angélique Arnauld (1591-1661), became abbess of the convent of Port-Royal and was known as Mère Angélique.

Arnobius (d. c. 330) ● Christian apologist who was active during the reign of Emperor Diocletian (284-305). According to St. Jerome, Arnobius had served as a rhetorician at Sicca in Africa before his conversion, traditionally through the influence of a dream. He wrote his famous apology, *Adversus Nationes* (called *Adversus Gentes* by St. Jerome), as a means of proving his sincerity to a skeptical local bishop. The work, in seven books, is a vigorous defense of Christianity, filled with curious information from highly reliable sources of Roman imperial literature. It is thus also prized by Latin philologists. Lactantius was a pupil of his.

Arnold of Brescia (c. 1100-1155) ● Also Arnaldus, an ecclesiastical reformer and a supporter theologically of Peter Abelard. He was most likely from Brescia and studied at Paris, perhaps under Abelard himself. Returning to Brescia, he became a canon regular of the local monastery and by 1137 was its prior. He soon earned increasing notoriety by attacking the worldliness of the Church, calling for a radical reform of its institutions and decrying the corruption of the clergy. Because of his involvement in local political disputes, Arnold returned to France in 1139, actively backing Peter Abelard in his squabbles with Church officials. Both Arnold and Abelard were condemned in 1140 by the Council of Sens. By 1145, he was in Rome, leading the verbal attack on the papacy and aiding the Roman party in its struggle with the pontiff. Pope

Eugenius III excommunicated him in 1148, and Arnold responded by calling him a "man of blood." Pope Adrian I took a more direct approach. Arnold was seized by soldiers executing a papal interdiction in Rome. As Frederick I Barbarossa was in Rome at the time (1152) for his coronation as emperor, Arnold was put on trial. An ecclesiastical court condemned him, and Arnold was hanged, burned, and his ashes thrown in the Tiber. No one, including St. Bernard of Clairvaux, a dedicated enemy of his, could dispute the moral uprightness of his life.

Arnolfo di Cambio (c. 1232-1302) ● Italian architect and sculptor who worked mostly in Florence, serving as a leading influence in the evolution of Italian Gothic architecture. He was possibly an assistant to the sculptor Nicola Pisano from 1265-1268 in Siena. In 1277, he went to Rome where he may have created the monument to Cardinal Annibaldi in St. John Lateran and the tomb of Pope Adrian V of Viterbo. Other labors for the Church included a monument to Cardinal de Braye and the altar canopies for S. Paolo Fuori le Mura (1285) and St. Cecilia in Trastevere (1293). By far his greatest commission was the design for the Cathedral, or Duomo, of Florence. (See **Ferrara-Florence, Council of.**)

Arnulf, St. (d. 641) ● Bishop of Metz and one of the founders of the Carolingian dynasty of rulers. A member of a Frankish noble family, he secured a prominent position in the court of King Theudebert II of Austrasia (r. 595-612) and then King Clotaire of Neustria. In 611 or 612, he was named bishop of Metz, playing a major role in the royal government of King Dagobert of Austrasia with the mayor of the palace, Pepin, from around 622 until his retirement in 627. After resigning his see, he took up residence near Remiremont and devoted himself to prayer. Arnulf's son by his marriage to the daughter of Bologna before his consecration as bishop was the father of Pepin II of Heristal, the great-grandfather of Charlemagne, greatest of the Carolingians. Feast day: August 19.

Arnulf of Lisieux (d. 1184) ● Bishop of Lisieux, brother of the bishop of Seez (Sagi). Arnulf studied canon law in Rome, authoring a vigorous attack on Gerard, bishop of Angoulême, in the defense of Pope Innocent II, who was troubled by the antipope Anacletus II. Made a bishop in 1141, he took part in a crusade with King Louis VII in 1147 and was noted for his fidelity to Pope Alexander III during the schism that occurred in his pontificate. While he defended Church rights in England against the inroads of King Henry II, Arnulf supported the king in the affair of Thomas Becket; after Thomas's murder in 1170, he even made an appeal for Henry before the pope.

Arsenius, St. (354-c. 450 or later) ● Monk and a brief court figure during the reign of Emperor Theodosius I the Great (374-395). Arsenius was probably born in Rome, serving first as a deacon and then tutor to the sons of Emperor Theodosius at Constantinople. The opulence of his lifestyle at the imperial court proved too much for him, however, and after hearing a voice tell him that he should flee the company of men to find salvation, he departed Constantinople to the deserts of Egypt. Around 400, he joined the monks at Wadi Natrum (Scetis) and then at Canopus and Troe. There, he

St. Arsenius

was the humblest of the monks and the most reclusive. He is the author of some forty-four written maxims, being especially known for the saying "I have often been sorry for speaking, but never for having held my tongue." He is also said by biographers to have had the gift of tears, crying with tears of devotion at the slightest or most trifling event. He died in Troe. Feast day: July 19.

Asaph, St. (fl. mid-sixth century) ● Welsh saint, probably student of St. Kentigern and the founder of the Church of Llanasa in Flintshire. Few details of any reliability have survived, although it is believed that he became the first Welsh bishop of the see of Llanelwy (later called St. Asaph) in Wales, established in Norman times out of the monastery at Llanelwy. Feast day: May 1.

Asia ● See **China, India,** and **Japan**.

Assemblies of French Clergy ● Known in the French as *Assemblées du Clergé de France*, the quinquennial gathering of the representatives of the French Church that lasted as a genuine institution from the 1500s until the time of the French Revolution (1789). The assemblies discussed ecclesiastical matters, but they were principally concerned with financing the massive outlays of money that had been placed upon the Church by the French kings. Over time, the clergy were able to wield considerable financial power. By accepting in 1682 and approving the Golden Articles of King Louis XIV, the assemblies earned the censure of Pope Innocent XI. (See also **France, Gallican Articles,** and **Gallicanism**.)

Assisi ● Italian city in the Umbrian hills, best known as the birthplace of St. Francis in 1182. In the early 1100s, Assisi became an independent commune, becoming embroiled in several wars and skirmishes with nearby Perugia, conflicts that were to help shape the life and spiritual development of Francis. Eventually passing into the Papal States, Assisi was added to the kingdom of Italy in 1860. The city is today the repository for numerous important shrines and structures. These are the three-storied Basilica of San Francisco (1228-1253) where Francis' remains are venerated; a basilica to St. Clare where her remains are located; San Damiano, the chapel and thirteenth-century convent where Clare lived; and the nearby Basilica of Santa Maria degli Angeli in which is sheltered the Portiuncula, the tiny shrine that was the starting point for the Franciscan order.

Assize of Clarendon ● See **Clarendon, Constitutions of**.

Association, Law of ● One of the anticlerical decrees passed by the French government on July 1, 1901, declaring that no new religious congregations could be formed in the country without the recognition and authorization of the state. The restriction applied to both orders of men and women, although those congregations that had been recognized previously were allowed to continue. Such congregations, however, were forced to submit annual reports of their financial status, membership, and property holdings, and the acceptability of any congregation remained in the hands of the Council of Ministers, which could rescind authorization. Further, new congregations had to be approved by the Council of State and any previously unauthorized orders were declared immediately dissolved. The next years witnessed even more harsh regulations, such as forbidding the orders from teaching, culminating in 1905 with the formal rupture of the Church and State in France. (See also **France**.)

Assumptionists ● Religious congregation, known formally as the Augustinians of the Assumption. They were formed at Nîmes in 1843, receiving approval from Pope Pius IX in 1864. The Assumptionists are devoted to hard religious labor, working throughout the world in missions, running schools, and caring for the sick, particularly the mentally ill. Members follow a modified version of the Augustinian rule. The original order was liquidated in France in 1900 by a decree of the French government, in a precursor of the Law of Association.

Astrology ● Type of divinatory practice based on the ancient belief that human destiny and actions are influenced by the stars and planets. Practiced with considerable skill in the ancient world, astrology was condemned by the early Church, an opposition that has remained constant over the centuries. St. Augustine in the *City of God* (vv. 1-8) expressed his severe disapproval of the practice, and the Church from the fourth century equated it with the wholly unacceptable pagan practices left over from the pre-Christian period of Roman culture when divination and augury played an important role in virtually every aspect of life and religion. As astrology was part of such popular cults as Mithraism, it became common among the soldiers in the legions and the common citizens and was thus hard to suppress. Under the influence of Church leaders, however, the imperial government took steps to curb the practice; Emperor Constantius II in 357 finally proclaimed divination to be a crime punishable by death. Practiced clandestinely in the West, astrology declined in interest during the so-called Dark Ages, emerging out of apparent obscurity in the 1200s with the influx of books and ideas from the East through trade and the crusades. In medieval Europe, astrology was one of the great occult arts, practiced by initiates who often knew alchemy and were even said to be masters of sorcery. While still opposed by the Church, astronomy once more found a widespread following, its adherents only growing during the sixteenth century when the Reformation caused many to turn away from traditional religion to the alluring arcanum of supposedly mystical and ancient beliefs. Astrology once more declined during the Age of Reason (1700s) but increased in the public mind in the twentieth century. Today, it is a firmly entrenched part of the broad New Age movement (with crystals, incense, yoga, pop psychology, and pseudo-mystical teachers, and a wide variety of divinational practices). The Church's position on astrology is that it is harmful because of its basic denial of the providence and sovereignty of God. Trust is not placed in God but in his creation, and the practitioner presumptuously assumes that the events are rightly known only by God.

St. Athanasius

Astronomy ● See under the following: **Copernicus, Nicolaus; Galileo;** and **Vatican Observatory**.

Asylum, Right of ● See **Sanctuary, Right of**.

Athanasian Creed ● Profession of faith approved and used in the West, although it is generally not recognized in the East, despite its appearance in the Greek liturgical book *Herologion* and in the service books of the Russian Church from the seventeenth century. The creed probably dates to the fourth or fifth century. Its attribution to St. Athanasius is no longer considered credible and authorship is placed by scholars to southern Gaul (France), perhaps written by St. Ambrose. In content, it is divided approximately into two halves, dealing with the doctrines of the Trinity and the Incarnation, with other references to assorted dogmas. It also begins and ends with the declaration that belief in the truth is essential for salvation.

Athanasius, St. <1> (296-373) ● Bishop of Alexandria, theologian, and a firm adherent of Christian orthodoxy in the fourth century. Athanasius was a native of Alexandria, serving as a deacon and then secretary to Alexander, bishop of Alexandria. He went with the prelate to the Council of Nicaea (325) and three years later succeeded him as bishop. Over the next decades he emerged as a controversial figure by vigorously opposing Arianism, particularly antagonizing the Arian party in the Eastern Empire. The Arians secured his deposition and exile to Trier in 336, although he returned following the death of Emperor Constantine the Great in 337. Two years later, he was once again expelled and forced to flee to Rome. Supported in the Western Church, Athanasius was restored in 346 through the assistance of Emperor Constans. As the Eastern emperor Constantius did not agree, Athanasius was driven out once more in 356. In hiding near Alexandria, he returned briefly in 361 but was exiled in 362 by Emperor Julian. The next year, he went again to Alexandria, this time remaining, with the exception of a brief exile in 365-366. His efforts at defeating Arianism helped lay the groundwork for the triumph of Orthodox Christianity at the Council of Constantinople in 381, years after Athanasius' death. Athanasius authored numerous works, including defenses of orthodox doctrine and treatises, particularly *De Incarnatione*. Feast day: May 2. (See also **Arianism**.)

Athanasius, St. <2> (c. 920-1003) ● Byzantine monk and founder of the famed monastic settlements of Mt. Athos. He was originally from the Greek Empire of Trebizond, joining a Byzantine monastery before establishing himself on Mt. Athos. His monastery, the Laura, was founded in 961, becoming the first such colony of anchorites on the mountain, although there were individual ascetics already there who opposed his fledgling institution. He also encountered hostility from the entrenched ecclesiastical parties in Constantinople and their political allies. Nevertheless, Athanasius secured the imperial patronage of Emperors Nicephorus II Phokas and John I Tzimiskes. John gave him a charter in 971-972, and Athanasius eventually became abbot general of Mt. Athos, overseeing some fifty-eight monasteries. He died from injuries sustained when a building he was dedicating collapsed. Athanasius is revered as a major figure in Byzantine monasticism. He is also known as Athanasius the Athonite. (See also **Athos, Mt.**)

Athicus (d. 425) ● Patriarch of Constantinople and a major opponent of St. John Chrysostom. Athicus was a native of Armenia, spending many years as a follower of the Pneumatomachian heresy. After moving to Constantinople, however, he was converted to Orthodox Christianity. As he rose through the ranks of the Church in the city, he became a bitter foe of Chrysostom. In 405, he succeeded Arsacius as patriarch of Constantinople, making some concessions to

the supporters of Chrysostom after the latter's exile and later death in 407. As patriarch, Athicus worked to enlarge his power and ecclesiastical prestige.

Athos, Mt. ● Called the "Holy Mountain," a mountain on the Aegean Sea, along the Macedonian coast that has, for centuries, served as a monastic center for the Eastern Orthodox Church. Mt. Athos was established as a monastic site by St. Athanasius the Athonite with his founding in 961 of the Laura, a community of anchorites, although the mountain and the adjoining peninsula had long been a gathering place for hermits and ascetics. These original but unorganized residents opposed unsuccessfully the actual creation of monasteries. St. Athanasius received imperial patronage, including a charter in 971-972, and was later made abbot general of the fifty-eight monasteries on the mountain. Since that time, Mt. Athos has never ceased to be the property of the Eastern Orthodox Church's monastic institutions. Currently, they are approximately twenty monasteries, visited by many tourists. Of note, however, women — even female animals — are not allowed to set foot on the peninsula, as it is held that they would be disruptive to the atmosphere of the monks. The law dates to 1060.

Attila the Hun (d. 453) ● Infamous ruler of the Huns from 434-453, known to the West as the "Scourge of God" because of his appalling cruelty. The son of King Mandiuch, Attila shared control of the Huns with his brother, Bleda, until 444 when he had him murdered, claiming sole kingship thereafter. At the head of his dreadful armies, he launched attacks along the Danube frontier and then threatened Constantinople in 447. A treaty was arranged, however, with the Eastern Empire that pacified his ambitions toward the East and made his invasion of the West inevitable. Starting in 448, Attila rode into Gaul (Roman France). He was defeated but not destroyed at the Battle of the Catalaunian Plain, allowing him to regroup and head into Italy. Aquileia was stormed and Rome threatened. In a famous episode, Pope St. Leo I convinced him through prayer and spiritual intimidation not to sack the Eternal City. Rome was thus saved and, within a year, Attila died from a burst artery on his wedding night. The Huns never recovered, although Attila had earned an eternal

Attila the Hun

reputation for cruelty. His title *Flagellum Dei* (Scourge of God) became a fixture in Christian legend.

Atto of Vercelli (d. 961) ● Bishop of Vercelli and a gifted theologian and canonist. The son of the viscount Aldegarius, Atto became a bishop in 924, a post he would hold until his death. His main distinction was based on his learning, particularly expressed in his writings. He authored sermons, letters, a collection of ecclesiastical canons, and a commentary on the Pauline Epistles.

Auctorum Fidei ● Bull issued on August 28, 1794, by Pope Pius VI condemning eighty-five articles of the Synod of Pistoia (1786). The synod had approved articles that were both pro-Jansenist and pro-Gallican in nature, declaring, for example, that ecclesiastical authority came from the Church at large, and the pope was head of the Church only in a ministerial sense; bishops are not required to take an oath of obedience to the pope; only one Mass should be celebrated on Sundays; and the religious

orders should live under the same rule and wear the same habit.

Augsburg, Diet of ● Important assembly held in the Bavarian city of Augsburg in 1530 during which Emperor Charles V heard a petition from the supporters of Martin Luther that they be granted an equal legal recognition to that of Catholics. The petition that was presented to the emperor was called the Augsburg Confession. It was written by the ardent Protestant Reformer Philipp Melanchthon (d. 1560) and was presented in the most inoffensive terms possible to the Catholics. Theologians examined the petition at the behest of the emperor and accepted without reservation nine of the articles; six more were approved with reservation, and the remaining thirteen were rejected. The Lutheran party responded with a defense of the confession, but the emperor refused to accept it. Melanchthon then wrote him the "Apology of the Confession" in much more strident and controversial language.

The Confession of Augsburg and the "Apology" remain authoritative Lutheran documents and were important in revised or modified form in influencing the so-called Reformed or Calvinist Churches in parts of Germany. In Augsburg, however, where pro-Lutheran sentiment ran high, Catholic worship was forbidden in 1537 and several wars erupted. These inconclusive Schmalkaldic Wars resulted in the Diet of Augsburg of 1555 and the signing of the Peace of Augsburg (1555).

Augsburg, Interim of ● Formula accepted in 1548 as a provisional means of achieving religious settlement between Catholics and Protestants in Germany. The interim was the result of the failure of a joint Catholic-Protestant commission assembled in 1548 by Emperor Charles V to find sufficient common ground for a settlement. The emperor thus appointed several prominent ecclesiastical figures, including Julius von Pflug, bishop of Naumburg, and Johann Agricola, to draw up a formula. The result was a document with twenty-six articles that was intended to serve as a provisional compromise until the more final settlement that was expected from the Council of Trent. Accepted at the Diet of Augsburg in 1548, it was enforced throughout parts of Germany while in bastions of Protestantism, a less Catholic document called the "Leipzig Interim" was accepted.

Augsburg, Peace of ● Political settlement between the Catholics and the Lutherans within the German Empire that was signed on September 25, 1555. It was accepted by Emperor Ferdinand I and the electors at Augsburg. By the terms of the treaty, both Catholicism and Lutheranism were recognized in Germany, although only those Protestants who had signed the Augsburg Confession were accepted. Calvinists were thus not included. An essentially territorial agreement, it was decided that the subjects in each land should follow the religion of their ruler, a formula expressed by the term *cuius regio, eius religio.* Those inhabitants who found this settlement unacceptable were allowed to emigrate from their homes after disposing of or selling their property. In imperial cities, however, members of both communions were to exist side by side, both receiving full recognition. The Peace of Augsburg remained the basis for religious settlement in the empire until the Treaty of Westphalia in 1648, which would bring the bloody Thirty Years' War (1618-1648) to an end.

Augustine of Canterbury, St. (d. 604 or 605) ● Apostle of England, first archbishop of Canterbury, and the missionary most responsible for bringing Christianity to southern England. Augustine was a Roman by birth, serving in the Church at Rome as a prior in the monastery at St. Andrew's until 596 when Pope Gregory the Great selected him to lead a missionary effort to England. Christianity had to be reintroduced into the isles, since the faith had suffered grievous setbacks in the previous generations as Roman Britons faced invasions from Anglo-Saxons, Jutes, Picts, and others, essentially extirpating the old order. Augustine set out with a group of monks but turned back somewhere in Gaul. Encouraged by Gregory, however, they resumed their journey, reaching Kent in 597. Well received by King Ethelbert of Kent, Augustine met with great success, converting many in the kingdom, including Ethelbert. He then went to Arles where St. Virgilius consecrated him bishop of the English, with his see at Canterbury. In 601, he was made metropolitan, establishing before his death the episcopal sees of London and Rochester. In 603, he also attempted to unite the Celtic Church with Rome but without success. However, Augustine made Canterbury the ecclesiastical center of England, and his use of the Roman rite and calendar would eventually be accepted universally in England. Feast day: May 27.

Augustine of Hippo, St. (354-430) ● Bishop of Hippo, the greatest of the Fathers of the Western Church who exercised an enormous influence on the formation of Christian theology and Western civilization.

Life: Augustine was born on November 13, 354, in the town of Tagaste, North Africa. His father, Patricius, was a landholder and local political leader; he was also a pagan for most

St. Augustine of Hippo

of his life. Augustine's mother was St. Monica, a devoted Christian who labored to impress the faith on her son. He studied at Tagaste and then at the nearby town of Madauros where he was to focus on Latin grammar and rhetoric. He abandoned a possible career in law for literary interests, but he also led a rather dissolute existence so eloquently expressed with regret in the *Confessions*. Taking a mistress, he fathered an illegitimate son, Adeodatus, and remained devoted to the boy's mother for many years. In 373, he read Cicero's *Hortensius* (now lost) and developed an interest in philosophy. Abandoning his sensual pursuits, he became a student of the Manichaeans, but his associations with them ended in 383. Always possessing doubts about the sect, he became entirely disenchanted when his questions for the noted Manichaean teacher Faustus produced unsatisfactory answers.

In 383, Augustine journeyed to Rome where he stayed for several months before settling in Milan as a teacher of rhetoric. His philosophical studies led him to Neoplatonism, but in Milan, he also came under the influence of the formidable St. Ambrose, archbishop of Milan. (See

Neoplatonism in the GLOSSARY.) That great Churchman answered all of Augustine's questions and doubts, and after several months of retreat at Cassiciacum, Augustine was baptized on Holy Saturday of 387. He returned to Africa the next year, forming a kind of monastic community at Tagaste. His notoriety soon spread to surrounding towns, and in 391, while visiting Hippo Regius (a city in North Africa), he was seized by a crowd, carried to the aged bishop, Valerius, and ordained a priest. Four years later, he was appointed coadjutor to the diocese of Hippo and soon succeeded Valerius as bishop.

Augustine would remain bishop of Hippo from around 395 until his death. The intervening years were filled with constant writing and the need to confront numerous crises caused by the heresies of the time: the Donatists, Pelagians and Semi-Pelagians, and the Manichaeans. For his defense of Church doctrine concerning grace against the Pelagians, he is known also as the Doctor of Grace. From 426, he entered into semiretirement, surrendering most of his duties as bishop to concentrate on his writings. His final days were spent in depression as the Vandals (Germanic Arians) stormed across Africa. Augustine died on August 28, 430, as the Vandals were laying siege to Hippo.

Writings: Augustine was a voluminous writer, authoring one hundred thirteen books, two hundred eighteen letters, and some five hundred sermons. His literary output covers the entire sphere of human thought and ranges from the psychological complexity of the *Confessions*, to the political insights of the *City of God*, to the stridently polemical. He was especially concerned with the combating of the three great heresies of the time: Pelagianism, Donatism, and Manichaeism. His writings, however, are distinguished by their eloquence, superb Latinity, and the degree, born out of the necessity of the crisis of the moment, to which he examined and elucidated vital points of Christianity.

His earliest writings were the *Dialogues*, composed before his baptism and representing the consideration of a convert to Christianity in the traditions of Platonic philosophy. This was followed by a vast corpus of controversial and noncontroversial works. His controversial writings were centered in refuting the prevailing heresies. Against the Manichaeans he wrote: *Acts of the Dispute with Fortunatus the Manichaean* (392); *Acts of the Conference with Felix* (404); *Against Faustus* (c. 400); *Against Secundinus* (405). Against the Donatists: *Psalmus contra partem Donati* (c. 395); *De Baptismo contra Donatistas* (c. 400); *Contra epistolam Parmeniani* (400); *De peccatorum meritis et remissione* (412; *On the Merit and Forgiveness of Sins*); *De spiritu et littera* (412; *On the Spirit and Letter*); *De Gestis Pelagii* (reproducing the acts of the Council of Diospolis, 417); *De Gratia Christi et de peccato originali* (418; *On the Grace of Christ and on Original Sin*). Against the Semi-Pelagians: *De praedestinatione Sanctorum* (428; *On the Predestination of the Saints*); and *De Dono perseverantiae* (429; *On the Gift of Perseverance*); Against the Arians: *Contra sermonem Ariarnorum* (418; *Against the Sermons of the Arians*).

On theology, Augustine wrote: *De Trinitate* (*On the Trinity*), writing the work from 400-416, considered his most theologically deep treatise; *Enchiridion* (421), a handbook on faith, hope, and love, written at the request of a Roman named Laurentius; assorted treatises on marriage, widows, prayer for the dead, continence, and lying. In matters of exegesis can be included *De doctrina Christiana* (begun in 397 and finished in 426), considered the first formal treatise on exegesis, as the literary production of St. Jerome was often of a more controversial nature, and treatises on the Epistle of St. John, Epistle to the Galatians, the Sermon on the Mount, and *De Consensus Evangelistarum* (400; *Harmony of the Gospels*).

Aside from the apologetics *De vera religione* (389-391), letters to Consentius, and *De utilitate credindi*, his chief apology, and arguably his most famous book (with the exception of the *Confessions*), was *De Civitate Dei* (*The City of God*), begun in 413 and written in response to the attacks made by pagans that the fall of Rome in 410 to the Visigoths was the fault of the Christians, who were wrecking the civilization of the Roman Empire. Augustine argues instead that all of the virtues of the past — of the Romans, Greeks, and Hebrews — find fulfillment in Christ and possess virtue only in direct relation to the degree that they offer prayer and worship to God. He expresses as well a philosophy of history, noting that only Christianity embraces a history to the beginning of time and a future until the end of time. For Augustine, the City of God is a city insofar as it can be considered a heavenly society, in sharp contrast to the City of the World.

Finally, in the *Confessions*, Augustine gives not a confession in the common understanding but an account in which the soul is praised that it admires the procession of God within itself. The *Confessions* provides a penetrating glimpse into the human soul. The first nine chapters recounted Augustine's life up to the time of his conversion; the tenth covers the life until the time of the writing of the work (c. 397-400). Entirely revealing in its presentation of his sins and failings, it is more concerned with the operation of God's grace and with trumpeting to all people the glory of God and his creation.

Influence and Thought: Augustine's position in the history of the Church is unquestioned. His enormous contributions to Christian theology would be preeminent until the 1200s and would surrender their virtual monopoly on theological thought only to another towering figure, St. Thomas Aquinas (d. 1274). His extensive system — including such doctrines as grace, original sin, and the Fall — would serve as the impetus for a host of theologians and interpreters, the so-called Augustinians or adherents of Augustinianism.

Augustine is considered a pivotal figure in the history of Christian thought chiefly for his immense role in reconciling Platonism with Christianity. His philosophical outlook is thus essentially Platonic. He advances the notion of eternal truths that correspond to Plato's subsistent ideas, but for Augustine, since truth subsists in the intellect, therefore, eternal truths must subsist in the intellect of God. The pursuit of these truths is the ultimate pursuit of the person; the central motivation, though, is not reason but love. Love forms the central basis of life. The influence of the late classical philosophers is obvious in this — with their desire to find the happy life — only Augustine put as his object of desire the blessed life of the Christian in finding God. Philosophy to Augustine is insufficient in itself in discovering this blessed life. It does, however, offer to the Christian a means to improve the understanding of the faith and hence is a positive asset in the rational approach to the love of God. The place of rationalism is clear in the famous maxim *"Credo ut intelligam"* ("I believe in order to understand"), an expression of the preeminence given by Augustine to faith over reason.

Augustinian Canons ● Also called the "Black Friars," Black Canons, or Regular Canons, the first religious order in the Church to adhere to the common life for canons, meaning that the canons of a particular diocese — the staff of a cathedral — followed the Rule of St. Augustine with its call for poverty, celibacy, obedience, and strict monastic life. The Augustinian Canons probably originated among the communities of clerks in Italy and parts of France sometime in the eleventh century, although the idea of establishing a common life had existed for centuries. The orders received

sanctions from the Church at the Lateran Councils of 1059 and 1063, subsequently becoming very popular. By the 1100s, most canons of the Church belonged to the Augustinians and were called Regular Canons or Black Canons. Toward the end of the Middle Ages, however, the Augustinian Rule had been diluted and the ideals of service were often forgotten in the wake of struggles and disorders in the 1400s and 1500s. The Canons suffered considerably during the Reformation and many houses were suppressed. Some of the congregations continue today. (See also **Premonstratensian Canons** and **Victorines**.)

Augustinian Hermits ● One of the foremost mendicant orders of the medieval Church, known officially as the Order of the Hermit Friars of St. Augustine or, more commonly, as the Augustinian Friars. The order evolved out of widely separated communities of hermits, who all adhered strenuously to the Rule of St. Augustine. For purposes of organization and to ensure adherence to doctrinal orthodoxy, these communities were brought together in 1256 by Pope Alexander IV, who chose as their model the Dominican order. They thus ceased being secluded hermits and became preachers and active religious in cities and towns. They eventually spread throughout Western Europe, joined toward the end of the Middle Ages by less severe congregations. Martin Luther belonged to one of these, the German Reformed Congregation. Devastated by the effects of the Reformation, the Hermits survived nevertheless and are still found in parts of Europe, America, and elsewhere under the title Augustinians (O.S.A.). The more severe Augustinian Recollects (O.A.R.) were founded in 1588.

Augustinianism ● Also Augustinism, the extensive body of thought formulated by St. Augustine that found wide acceptance in the theology of the Church from the fifth century and preeminent until the thirteenth century and the rise of Thomism. Augustinianism was characterized by adherence to Augustine's doctrines on grace, original sin, the Fall, and predestination. It should be noted that in speaking of a specific school of thought, such as Augustinism, one should refer to the doctrines as they were elucidated by experts and theologians; the corpus of his teachings was adopted as entirely official Catholic dogma. Augustinianism in that sense would not be significantly challenged until the time of St. Thomas Aquinas (d. 1274). At the heart of the difference between the two schools is the divergence of the original philosophical foundation of the movements: Platonism and Aristotelianism; Augustine Christianized Platonism and Thomas Aquinas Christianized Aristotelianism.

Augustinian, Rule of ● In Latin, *Regula Sancti Augustini*, the rule or body of laws traditionally established by St. Augustine and subsequently used by a number of monastic bodies, particularly the Augustinian Canons. There is considerable debate and discussion among scholars concerning the origins of the rule. It was most likely drawn up during St. Augustine's lifetime by a devoted disciple and, with his blessing, it was used by the communities of men and women in the early fifth century, although details of this remain a source of some dispute in scholarly circles. All but forgotten over the succeeding years, it was revived in the eleventh century by the Augustinian Canons and later adapted to the needs of such orders as the Dominicans, Ursulines, and Augustinian Hermits. The rule was, from the sixth century, preserved in two parts: a prologue establishing definite monastic observances (the *Regula Secunda*) and a general consideration of the common life (the *Regula ad servos Dei*). In broad terms, the rules call for poverty, obedience, celibacy, and a monastic life.

Ausculta Fili ● Letter addressed on December 5, 1301, by Pope Boniface VIII to King Philip IV the Fair of France. In it, the pontiff expressed his genuine dismay over the king's interference with the rights of the Church, particularly his appointing bishops to sees, conferring benefices, and expelling those bishops loyal to the papacy. As the letter went unheeded, Boniface issued his celebrated bull, *Unam Sanctam*, on November 18, 1302. The words *Ausculta Fili*, meaning "Listen, my son" in Latin, were also used to open the Rule of St. Benedict.

Ausonius (d. c. 395) ● In full, Decimus Magnus Ausonius, poet, governor of Gaul (France), and a prominent figure in the fourth century. A native of Burdigala (Bordeaux), he studied rhetoric and grammar, earning such prominence that Emperor Valentinian I appointed him tutor to his son, the future ruler Gratian. Ausonius later served as adviser to Gratian, ultimately returning to Burdigala. He was probably a Christian, although his poems, while ostensibly sympathetic and properly Christian, do not reveal any particular zeal; his friend Paulinus of Nola was able to convince him not to give up his wealth and become a monk. Among his many poems, several were clearly Christian, most notably *Versus paschales pro Augusto* and *Oratio Matutina*. Ausonius is an excellent example of the gradual conversion of the intellectual and learned segments of Roman imperial society to Christianity.

Australia ● Island continent situated between the Pacific and Indian Oceans; the Church had a difficult early history in the region but today claims that more than a quarter of the populace is Catholic. Australia as an English possession had its origins in the explorations of Captain Cook (1728-1779), who claimed the east coast for England in 1770.

The entire continent was claimed by the English in 1829, by which time it was already in long use as a penal colony. The infamous penal colony was begun in 1785 when New South Wales was declared a prison colony. The first shipload of prisoners arrived in 1788. Over the next decade, the population swelled, thanks to the practice of sending Catholic "criminals" from Ireland to the colony, normally innocent Catholics who were deported without trial or who resisted the numerous laws then in place in Ireland. The convict system would endure until the middle of the 1800s when it was finally abolished through the work of numerous individuals of conscience, including William Ullathorne (1806-1889), later bishop of Birmingham.

Priests in the colonies were forbidden from exercising their ministry for many years. The first Mass was celebrated in May 1803 by a Father Dixon who had to use a chalice of tin made by a prisoner. A long era of persecution was gradually lessened in the early 1800s. A major breakthrough came in 1821 when two priests were placed on the government payroll as chaplains. In 1834, Australia, Tasmania, New Zealand, and the surrounding islands were formed into an apostolic vicariate; its first bishop was John Bede Polding, O.S.B. Dioceses were established soon after, in Adelaide (1843), Perth (1845), and Melbourne, Maitland, and Port Victoria (1848). Sydney also became an archiepiscopal see. Mission status was formally ended in 1876. Currently there are four archdioceses and twenty-four dioceses.

Auxiliary Saints ● Name traditionally given to a group of fourteen saints who are revered for their supposed willingness to assist, through their prayers, all persons who have need. Also called the Fourteen Holy Helpers, they are termed Auxiliary Saints from the Latin *auxilium*, or assistance. They are: Catherine of Alexandria, Christopher, Barbara, Giles, Margaret, George, Pantaleon, Vitus, Erasmus, Blaise, Eustace, Acacius, Denys, and Cyriacus.

Avancini, Nikola (1612-1686) ● Jesuit ascetical writer, theologian, and author of *Vita et Doctrina Jesu Christi ex Quattuor Evangelistis Collecta* (1665; *Meditations on the Life and Doctrine of Jesus Christ*). Avancini was born near Trent, at Bretz, entering the Society of Jesus in 1627. He then taught at Trieste, Laibach, and Vienna, serving later as the rector of the colleges of Passau, Vienna, and Graz. Appointed visitor of Bohemia in 1675, he was subsequently provincial of the Austrian province (1676) and assistant for the German province (1682). While these duties required much travel and labor, Avancini also authored numerous works on theology, philosophy, and sacred literature, one of which — *Vita et Doctrina Jesu Christi* — was certainly the most famous. This collection of meditations became a classic of devotional literature and was translated into a host of languages.

Avenpace ● See **Ibn Baddja**.

Averroës (1126-1198) ● Important figure in the history of Islamic intellectual and religious philosophy, who also influenced Western philosophy and Christian theology by inspiring the thirteenth-century movement called Averroism. Known in full as Abu al-Walid Muhammad ibn Ahmed ibn Muhammad ibn Rushid, Averroës (also Averrois) served as a judge (or *qadi*) in Córdoba, being appointed as the personal physician to two Spanish-Islamic caliphs, although he later fell out of favor and was exiled in 1195, returning just before his death. Aside from his medical writings, Averroës was best known for his extensive works on philosophy, especially his commentaries on Aristotle's writings (from 1162-1195) and on Plato's *Republic*, for which he earned the nickname among Westerners as "The Commentator." An ardent Aristotelian but influenced by Neoplatonism, he accepted the monopsychism of the intellect and the idea of one intellect; however, he did not believe in immortality of a personal nature. His commentaries and other writings were discovered by Western theologians in the early 1200s and quickly became both popular and controversial. (See **Averroism** [following entry] for other details.)

Averroism ● Popular philosophical movement in the thirteenth century and beyond that took its name and inspiration from the twelfth-century Islamic writer Averroës (1126-1198). The main impetus for Averroism was the discovery in the early 1200s of Averroës's commentaries on Aristotle, writings that quickly became popular in the centers of learning in Europe. In 1255, it was openly supported by the faculty of arts at the University of Paris and strenuously defended by Siger of Brabant, John of Jandun, and Taddeo of Parma as well as other so-called Averroists. Averroism argued that reason was superior over faith and that, among other things, there existed one intellect for all mankind, thereby negating the vital doctrinal concepts of immortality and the potentiality of the person. Thomas Aquinas disagreed vociferously with the Averroists, attacking their views in his treatise *De Unitate intellectus contra Averroistas* (1270; *On the Unity of the Intellect Against the Averroists*) and helping to secure their condemnation at the Council of Paris in 1270. They would be condemned again by the Church, but Averroists continued to persist until the Renaissance.

Avicebron ● See **Ibn Gabirol**.

Avicenna (980-1037) ● Islamic philosopher and doctor who was a considerable influence on philosophers of the 1100s and 1200s, particularly the Schoolmen, or members of the Scholastic movement. Known in full as Abu al-Husayn ibn Abd Allah ibn Sina, he was born in Bukhara, Persia (present-day Iran), studied medicine and philosophy, and became court physician to the Persian rulers, the Samanids. His two main medical works were *The Book of Healing* and the *Canon of Medicine*; the *Canon* would serve as the standard medical text throughout the Middle Ages until the sixteenth century. Avicenna was known in the West not only for his medical writings but also for his philosophical teachings. A devoted Aristotelian, he was, like the even more influential Averroës, deep in Neoplatonic ideas. Schoolmen found him a major inspiration in their study of Aristotle, but the wide adoption of his Neoplatonism required much doctrinal and theological correction in the 1200s. (See also **Aristotle**.)

Avignon ● City in southern France that served for a time during the Middle Ages as the home of the popes during the so-called Avignon Papacy or the Babylonian Captivity from 1309 until 1377. Avignon was generally unimportant until the late twelfth century when the Albigensians seized it, requiring the destruction of most of the city's walls in 1226, during the Albigensian Crusade. A vassalage to the papacy in 1309, it was chosen by Clement V as his residence when the popes departed Italy. It did not become papal property until 1348 when Pope Clement VI purchased it from Joanna I, queen of Naples. While the "captivity" ended in 1377, during the Great Schism (1378-1417) Avignon was the residence of two antipopes, Clement VII and Benedict XIII. Avignon during this long period in the 1300s became the gathering place for some of the worst members of medieval society and was called a sewer by Petrarch because of its filth, disease, and prostitutes.

Avignon Papacy ● See **Babylonian Captivity** and **Schism, Great**; see also **Avignon** (preceding entry) and **Petrarch**.

Avitus, St. (d. 518) ● Bishop of Vienne and a notable Church leader in early France (Gaul) during the final era of the Roman Empire in the West. A member of a Roman senatorial family, Avitus, like his father, Isychius, entered the Church and, upon Isychius's death (c. 490), succeeded him as bishop. The post brought him into contact with the Germanic and often pro-Arian tribes who were then infesting the onetime Roman province of Gaul (or Gallia). Through his sermons, for example, Avitus converted Sigismund, king of the Burgundians, away from Arian Christianity to orthodoxy. He also greatly impressed Clovis, king of the Franks, and was the author of poems and epistles. Feast day: February 5.

The papal residence at Avignon

Babylonian Captivity ● Name used by Petrarch and subsequent writers to describe the period from 1309-1377 when the papacy was situated at Avignon, France. Also known as the Avignon Papacy, the period was noted for the loss of considerable prestige by the popes, who were dominated by the French. The initial move to Avignon, which was made by Pope Clement V, and the foul reputation of the city prompted Petrarch and others to compare the exile of the popes from Italy to the captivity of the Jews in Babylonia. The popes at Avignon were Clement V (1305-1314), John XXII (1316-1334), Benedict XII (1334-1342), Clement VI (1342-1352), Innocent VI (1352-1362), Urban V (1362-1370), and Gregory XI (1370-1378). The "Captivity" ended in 1377 when Gregory moved back to Rome at the behest of St. Catherine of Siena. Upon his return, however, the Great Schism proved inevitable.

Bacon, Roger (c. 1214-1292) ● English Franciscan, philosopher, teacher, and scientist of high repute in the Middle Ages. Born in Ilchester in Somerset (or possibly Bisley), he studied at Oxford before traveling to Paris where for a number of years he taught and lectured on Aristotle. In 1247, he resigned, however, to focus on scientific experiments, returning home to Oxford in 1250 or 1251. Around 1251, Bacon joined the Franciscans, continuing to conduct scientific experiments and studying astronomy, alchemy, optics, languages, and mathematics. He was much influenced by the brilliant Robert Grosseteste, although the complexity and number of Bacon's experimental ideas aroused the suspicions of the Franciscans. Troubling questions about his orthodoxy prompted Bacon to petition Pope Clement IV for aid. Bacon sent the pontiff (c. 1268) his *Opus Majus* (*Great Work*) and other writings in the hopes Clement would give his approval for Bacon to continue his labors. Clement died in 1268, and Bacon was condemned and possibly imprisoned in 1277; he wrote of his troubles in the *Opus Tertium* (*Third Work*). A figure of much legend, Bacon was almost certainly ahead of his time in many scientific endeavors, supposedly inventing an early telescope, a flying machine, gunpowder, and spectacles. He also authored works on mathematics, philosophy, theology (unfinished), alchemy, and a Greek and Hebrew grammar. While stories that he was a sorcerer were untrue, he did have the title *Doctor Mirabilis* (the Amazing Doctor).

Bainbridge, Christopher (c. 1464-1514) ● Cardinal and archbishop of York who was a trusted emissary of both King Henry VIII and Pope Julius II. He was born at Hilton, near Appleby, studying at Queen's College, Oxford. After serving as provost of the college in 1496 and dean of Windsor (1505), he was consecrated bishop of Durham in 1507; the next year he moved to York. Sent to Rome by Henry VIII, Bainbridge earned the confidence of Julius II, who made him a cardinal in 1511 and then employed him as a commander of a military expedition against the Ferrara. He also served as messenger from Henry to the pontiff, informing Julius of Henry's joining the Holy League. Bainbridge was poisoned, probably by one of his chaplains.

Baius, Michel (1513-1584) ● Flemish theologian and author of a theological system known as Baianism. Educated at Louvain University, he studied philosophy and theology. Shortly after 1550 he proposed with John Hessels (d. 1566) several controversial theological positions on grace and sin; these were met with much disapproval from the chancellor of the Louvain and the archbishop of Malines and in 1560 eighteen propositions were censured by the Sorbonne. Nevertheless, in 1563, both Baius and Hessels attended the Council of Trent. Baius's continued writings, however, particularly his numerous short treatises, brought new censure from ecclesiastical authorities. Pope Pius V in 1567 condemned seventy-nine propositions in the bull *Ex Omnibus Afflictionibus*. Baius was reconciled, but later statements brought new condemnations in 1579, in the bull *Provisionis Nostrae*. Baius then formally recanted, although his later writings continued to demonstrate independence of thought. His system taught that innocence was, in a primitive state, a necessary complement of human nature and not a gift from God to man and that redemption allows individuals to recover the original innocence. He was much concerned with the Fall and the loss of innocence by Adam and Eve. His views both anticipated and influenced the development of Cornelius Jansen and Jansenism.

Baker, Augustine (1575-1641) ● English Benedictine monk and a writer on ascetic and mystical theology. Born at Abergavenny, Monmouthshire, he was educated at Broadgate's Hall (modern Pembroke College), Oxford. A convert to Catholicism, he entered the Benedictines at Padua in 1605 and was ordained a priest around 1615. Baker subsequently served in Cambrai and Douai,

and was a chaplain in England. It was after his appointment in 1624 as spiritual director for the English nuns at Cambrai that Baker wrote his ascetical treatises. His most famous work, however, was the *Sancta Sophia (Holy Wisdom)*, published posthumously in two volumes in 1657, in which he covered the spectrum of mystical theology. He also conducted extensive research into the origins of the Benedictine order in England, published in *Apostolatus Benedictinorum in Anglia* (1626). Baker died of the plague in London.

Baldwin (d. 1190) ● Also known as Baldwin of Canterbury, archbishop of Canterbury, who had a contentious reign, particularly in his dealings with the monks of Christ Church. A native of Exeter, he was ordained a priest by Bartholomew, bishop of Exeter, and subsequently became a Cistercian monk at the Abbey of Ford. Within a year he was abbot there, and in 1180 he was made bishop of Worcester. In 1184, Baldwin became archbishop of Canterbury, but the election was contested by the monks at Christ Church, who disagreed with his promotion of austerity. The troubles with the Canterbury monks continued, requiring the intervention of both King Richard the Lionhearted (r. 1189-1199) and the Holy See. The monks did finally submit. Starting in 1188, Baldwin also began preaching a crusade to recover Jerusalem, setting out in 1190. He died in the Holy Land, during the siege of Acre, his death probably hastened by the wanton cruelty and immorality of the crusaders. The chronicler Giraldus Cambrensis described him as gentle, religious, and kindly.

Ball, John (d. 1381) ● Onetime English priest who was the leader of the Peasants' Revolt in England in 1381. Ball had served as a priest in York and Colchester, but in 1366 he had been excommunicated for his sermons calling for the abolition of the classes and his controversial criticism of the established Church. Stripped of his title, he continued nevertheless to preach to crowds at marketplaces or wherever anyone would listen. After 1376, he was imprisoned frequently and in 1381, at the outbreak of the Peasants' Revolt, he was rescued from the prison at Maidstone and taken by enthusiastic supporters to Canterbury. Going to London, he called for a revolution and was present at the meeting between Wat Tyler and the king at Smithfield. Captured at Canterbury, Ball was condemned and hanged at St. Alban's. The chronicler Jean Froissart called him a mad priest.

Ballerini, Pietro (1698-1769) ● Noted theologian and patristic scholar. His brother was Girolamo Ballerini, also a scholar, and their father was a distinguished surgeon in Verona. Educated by the Jesuits, Pietro was ordained a priest in 1722, becoming principal of a classical school in Verona. His writings soon became controversial and he was engaged in lively disputes over such issues as the methods of study used by St. Augustine and usury. His views on usury were condemned in 1745 by Pope Benedict XIV in his bull *Vix pervenit*. Three years later, however, Ballerini represented Venice in Rome as a canon, arguing the city's case in a dispute with the patriarchate of Aquileia. The remarkable talent demonstrated on the mission earned the attention of Pope Benedict, who commissioned him to prepare a new edition of the works of St. Leo the Great, to replace that of Pasquier Quesnel which had been written in part to promote Gallicanism. The resulting work, published in three volumes (1753-1757), remained the standard text on Leo. Pietro also authored numerous works with his brother Girolamo and by himself.

Balsamon, Theodore (d. c. 1195) ● Patriarch of Antioch and an important Byzantine scholar and canonist, Balsamon was born at Constantinople. Promoted to several ecclesiastical positions, he became patriarch of Antioch sometime before 1191 but was prevented from taking up his duties because the crusaders installed a Latin patriarch. Balsamon thus resided at Constantinople, serving as chancellor of law to the patriarch of Constantinople. His principal literary work is the *Scholia*, a commentary on the *Nomocanon*, the collection of laws and decrees of the Eastern Church.

Baltimore, Councils of ● Series of ecclesiastical councils that were held throughout the nineteenth century to discuss and deal with the many pastoral questions facing the Church in the United States. There were seven provincial councils (1829, 1833, 1837, 1840, 1843, 1846, and 1849), and three plenary councils (1852, 1866, and 1884). The presiding prelate over the councils was the archbishop of Baltimore, as that was the premier see, but true inspiration and leadership were provided by John England, bishop of Charleston, who proclaimed the need for unity and harmony among the hierarchy of the Church in America.

Among the various topics covered by the councils were Catholic education, organization of new sees, vocations, opposition to and careful watch of anti-Catholicism, and the safeguarding of family life. The Second Plenary Council, convened from October 7-21, 1866, under Archbishop Martin Spalding, condemned doctrinal errors and established norms for diocesan organization and the conduct of clergy. The Third Plenary Council, convened from November 9-December 7, 1884, by Archbishop John Gibbons, was the most important and far-reaching. It approved the establishment of The Catholic University of America, mandated parochial schools, and supported the so-called Baltimore Catechism, which became the main source of religious instruction in the country. Following the

Third Plenary Council, the archbishops of the country began to meet annually to consider questions of Church policy.

Baluze, Étienne (1630-1718) ● French ecclesiastical historian and scholar. Baluze was born at Tulle, studying at the Jesuit College there and at Toulouse. In 1656, he became secretary to Peter de Marca, archbishop of Toulouse, himself a noted historian. Just before de Marca's death in 1662, he gave Baluze the task of publishing all of his papers. In 1667, after serving as secretary to the bishop of Auch, Baluze became librarian to Jean-Baptiste Colbert, the future minister to King Louis XIV. He would remain at this post some thirty years and also would be appointed professor of canon law at the Collège Royal; in 1707, he became director of the college. After the 1708 publication of his *Histoire généalogique de la maison d'Auvergne* (*Genealogical History of the House of Auvergne*), Baluze was stripped of his offices and banished for a number of years from Paris. He also authored *Capitularia regum Francorum* (1677), *Miscellanea* (1678-1683), *Vitae Paparum Avenionensium* (1693), and *Historia Tutelensis* (1717; written while in exile and providing a history of Tulle).

Báñez, Dominic (1528-1604) ● Dominican theologian and Thomistic scholar. Also known as Domingo Báñez (or Váñez), he was born at Medina del Campo in Old Castile, Spain, entering the Dominicans in 1547. Having studied philosophy at Salamanca, Báñez was given theological training by the Dominicans, studying under Melchior Cano, Diego de Chaves, and Pedro Sotomayor. He soon began to teach and continued to learn under Dominic Soto. From 1561-1566, he taught at the Dominican University at Ávila and from 1573-1577 he was regent of St. Gregory's Dominican College at Valladolid. Báñez was also first chair of theology at Salamanca from 1580. So great was his reputation for learning that he had the nickname "The Brightest Light" in Spain. Báñez was a great proponent of Scholasticism and was a renowned exponent of Thomism. He was also the spiritual director and confessor of St. Teresa of Ávila.

Banneux, Apparitions of ● Name given to the eight appearances of the Blessed Virgin at Banneux, a village near Liège, Belgium. The BVM appeared to a twelve-year-old girl, Mariette Beco, in the family garden between January 15 and March 2, 1933. She was described as dressed in white with a blue sash, with a rosary draped over her right arm; she identified herself as the "Virgin of the Poor," promising to relieve the sickness of the poor in the world. Approval was given in 1942 by the Holy See for public devotion to Our Lady of Banneux. In 1949, the bishop of Liège authorized devotion to "Our Lady of the Poor, the Sick, and the Indifferent." There are currently over one hundred shrines dedicated to Our Lady of Banneux and millions are devoted to her through visits to the shrine at Liège or by membership in the International Union of Prayer.

Baptism ● Sacrament of rebirth. It is a ceremony of initiation by which one becomes a member of Christ's Mystical Body (the Church), is cleansed of original and actual sin, and is infused with sanctifying grace; the baptized person is allowed to partake of the other sacraments and receives the theological virtues of faith, hope, and charity as well as the gifts of the Holy Spirit. Normally, baptism is conferred by the pouring of water on the head (or by immersion) while the minister pronounces the words "I baptize you in the name of the Father, and the Son, and the Holy Spirit." The ordinary minister of a solemn baptism is a bishop, a priest, or a deacon. The Church, however, recognizes as valid an emergency baptism, even one administered by a non-Catholic.

In instituting the sacrament of baptism,

Christ was adopting a powerful symbolic act used by other religions, but he gave it supernatural effects and very special meaning, the fulfillment of the call of St. John the Baptist for all men to repent when he administered the baptism of penance. Through Christ, baptism became the consecration to the Holy Spirit, spiritual rebirth, purification, the cleansing of sin, and union with Christ. It is the marking of the soul with an indelible character and the infusion of grace, the theological virtues, and the gifts of the Holy Spirit. All of these elements are attested to in a host of NT writings, receiving affirmation, elaboration, and development through the Church Fathers.

As noted by Matthew, baptism was conferred by water, with the use of the names of the members of the Trinity. The *Didache* reiterates this formula in the late first century: "Baptize in the name of the Father, the Son, and the Holy Spirit." It also instructs baptisms to be done in running water; if none is available then baptize in standing water (cold is preferred; if not, then warm); but if neither is available, simply pour water on the head and recite the formula. The earliest practice was probably immersion, but the custom of pouring water was present early on, as is seen in the *Didache*. The baptizing of children, more specifically infants, dates to apostolic times. Its scriptural origin is considered by some to be inferred in Christ's command: "Let the children come to me, do not hinder them; for to such belongs the kingdom of God" (Mk 10:14). Additional weight was added by the understanding of the sacrament as the Christian circumcision: "In him also you were circumcised with a circumcision made without hands, by putting off the body of flesh in the circumcision of Christ; and you were buried with him in baptism, in which you were also raised with him through faith in the working of God, who raised him from the dead" (Col 2:11-12; cf. Rom 4:11).

A number of changes were made in the administration of the sacrament by Vatican Council II, although the Council Fathers were careful to note that ritual alterations in no way affected the character of baptism and the faith that is expressed. The council, however, introduced a number of innovations such as a new rite that could be used in mission lands in those cases where there was a shortage of priests or deacons, or an absence of them entirely. Most importantly, reform was introduced into the entire process of catechetical training. It reinstituted the catechumenate so as to improve the introduction of the faith to converts and to ensure that they were fully prepared, both in the mind and heart, to become full members of the Church.

Barbara, St. ● Early Christian martyr, listed among the Auxiliary Saints. An account of her martyrdom, providing probably elements of validity, was preserved in the *Golden Legend*. Barbara was supposedly a beautiful maiden of great virtue living in Nicomedia whose father first locked

St. Barbara

her up to prevent the attentions of unwanted suitors and then tried to murder her upon learning that she had become a Christian. Denounced to Roman officials, Barbara was condemned and her father ordered to execute her. This he did, and he was immediately struck by lightning — all that remained were ashes. The legend, first appearing in the seventh century, was probably fictitious, but her cultus was widespread. She is the patroness of artillerymen and firemen and is invoked against storms and lightning. Feast day: December 4 (suppressed in the Roman calendar in 1969).

Bardesanes (154-c. 222) ● More properly Bar-Daisan, an early Christian heretic, considered the foremost figure in Syrian Gnosticism. He was probably a native of Edessa and a convert to Christianity around 174. He spent some years engaged in missionary work in Syria but was later excommunicated because of his ideas, fleeing to Armenia sometime around 216. Bardesanes probably mingled Christian and Gnostic teaching, arguing that Christ's body was a phantasm, rejecting the Resurrection and denying the creation of the world and of Satan by a Supreme Being, favoring instead a hierarchy of beings. He was not, however, a Gnostic dualist as has been traditionally supposed. His writings and hymns, often composed with the help of his son Harmonius, are considered the oldest works of Syriac literature and hymnology. Chief among his writings is *The Dialogue of Destiny, or the Book of the Laws of the Countries*, recorded by Philip, a disciple. Fragments of this were preserved by Eusebius and other Christian Fathers. The cult of Bardesanes existed for several centuries before finally dying out.

Barefoot Friars ● Name customarily used for Discalced Monks.

Bar-Hebraeus, Gregorius (1226-1286) ● Syrian bishop, scholar, and philosopher. Known originally as Abu al-Faraj and called by the common name Bar-Hebraeus, he was the son of a Jewish physician who had converted to Christianity. A student of medicine in Tripoli and Antioch, Bar-Hebraeus was made a bishop at the age of twenty. Six years later, he was promoted to archbishop, and in 1264 he became primate of the East for the Eastern Jacobite Church. His residence was at Mar Mattai near Mosul. Of a scholarly nature, he used his extensive travels throughout Syria and Armenia to collect works from numerous libraries on a wide variety of subjects. His writings reflected his erudition and included astronomy, theology, and classical learning; his major works were a *Chronicle*, a Middle Eastern history; *Granary of Mysteries*, an analysis of the Bible; and *He' wath hekkmtha* (*Butter of Science*), a huge encyclopedia of knowledge. His works were originally composed in Syriac but were translated into Arabic.

Barlaam and Josafat ● Popular anonymous collection of romances that was found in a number of countries and languages during the Middle Ages in Europe. The earliest known version dates to the seventh century and was in Greek; the first Latin version was probably available in the 1100s. Barlaam and Josafat (or Barlaam and Josaph) was a Christianized retelling of the Buddha story, in which a prince of India is locked away to prevent a prophecy that he would become a Christian from coming true. Naturally, he escapes and is converted by the Christian hermit Barlaam.

Barnabas, St. ● First-century Christian in Jerusalem, described in the Acts of the Apostles as "a good man, full of the Holy Spirit and of faith" (11:24). Also known as an "apostle," Barnabas was originally a Jew from Cyprus, although he was not an original

Apostle of Jesus. Called at first Joseph, he was given the name Barnabas by the Apostles, a name said by St. Luke to mean "son of consolation." It was Barnabas who introduced St. Paul to the Apostles after his conversion, vouched for Paul to the Christians of Jerusalem, and was sent to Antioch to look into the affairs of the growing Church there. He later fetched Paul from Tarsus and, with him, he embarked on the first missionary journey, starting with Cyprus. Barnabas is thus considered the founder of the Cypriot Church. At the Council of Jerusalem, he defended the membership of Gentile Christians but later split with Paul over the issue of John Mark (see **Mark, St. <1>**). Barnabas probably continued his travels and was martyred, according to legend, in 61 at Salamis, although nothing of this is recorded in the NT. The work called Epistle of Barnabas was not written by him. Feast day: June 11.

Barnabites ● Religious order established in 1530 by St. Antonia Maria Zaccaria at Milan, known officially as the Clerks Regular of St. Paul but deriving the name Barnabites from the Church of St. Barnabas at Milan. The order stresses educational, parochial, and missionary work, with much emphasis placed on Paul's Epistles. The order was begun in the United States in 1952.

Baronius, Cesare (1538-1607) ● Cardinal and ecclesiastical historian, author of the important *Annales Ecclesiastici.* Baronius was born in Sora, near Rome, joining the Oratorians under St. Philip Neri in 1557. He became superior in 1593. Three years later, Pope Clement VIII made him a cardinal and the following year (1597) appointed him librarian of the Vatican. Aside from the two corrected versions of the Roman Martyrology, Baronius was best known for his *Annales Ecclesiastici,* a history of the Church, originally published in twelve folio volumes from 1588-1607. A Catholic response to the

Historia Ecclesiae Christi by the rabid Protestant authors, the Centuriators of Magdeburg, the *Annales* were completed by Baronius only to the year 1198, and efforts by the Oratorians to continue were unsuccessful. Interestingly, the defense of the papal claims to Sicily against Spain in Volume 11 (later published separately as a treatise) so angered the Spanish that they connived to deny Baronius possible election to the Holy See in 1607.

Bartholomaeus Anglicus (fl. early 1200s) ● Franciscan encyclopedist and onetime professor at the University of Paris. Bartholomaeus, English by birth, taught theology at Paris until 1224 or 1225 when he joined the recently founded Franciscan order along with his fellow professor Haymo of Faversham. He continued to teach at the Franciscan school in Paris, but in 1231 the order sent him to Magdeburg. His successor at Paris, Alexander of Hales, would elevate the Franciscans to a place of considerable repute in Paris. Bartholomaeus died sometime after 1231. His main work, *De proprietatibus rerum* — an encyclopedic survey of the sciences, including theology, philosophy, astronomy, botany, and zoology — is remarkable as one of, if not, the first major encyclopedia of the Middle Ages and an early notable work using the writings of the recently translated (into Latin) Arab, Greek, and Jewish naturalists, as well as medical experts. The book was immensely popular.

Bartholomew, St. ● One of the Twelve Apostles, mentioned in the Synoptic Gospels as sixth (Mt 10:3; Mk 3:18; Lk 6:14) and in the Acts of the Apostles (1:13) as seventh. His name meant "son of Talmai," an ancient Hebrew name that has been taken to mean that he was of Hebrew descent, although it could also denote merely that he was the son of Talmai. Other than the aforementioned references, Bartholomew is unknown, although some scholars identify him with

Nathaniel (Jn 1:45-51; 21:2). By tradition, Batholomew journeyed to India where he preached and spread the word. He was supposedly flayed alive and beheaded at Albanopolis, in Armenia. The historian Eusebius wrote that when Pantaenus reached India (c. 150-200) he found there the Gospel according to Matthew, in Hebrew, that had been left behind by Bartholomew centuries before. Feast day: August 24.

St. Bartholomew

Bartholomew of Lucca (1227-c. 1327) ●
Also Tolomeo, Dominican historian and a friend of Thomas Aquinas. Born at Lucca, in Tuscany, Italy, he entered the Dominicans at an early age, distinguishing himself in the order for his studious nature and devotion to his teacher Thomas. Batholomew served as his confessor and in 1272 accompanied him to Naples where they labored to establish the new Dominican house of studies there. He was still at Naples when word arrived that Thomas had died on March 7, 1274, at Fossanova. Elected prior of the Naples convent in 1288, he took part in the 1294 demonstration at Naples to prevent the resignation of Pope Celestine V. He was later prior of the Santa Maria Novella in Florence (1301), chaplain to Cardinals Patrasso and William of Bayonne, and friend and confessor of Pope John XXII. It was John who named him bishop of Torcello in 1318. A dispute with the patriarch of Grado led to his excommunication and exile in 1321, but he was reconciled in 1323 and died, still at his see, around 1327. He was the author of a number of books, including *Annales*, a history of events from 1061-1303; *Historia*

Ecclesiastica Nova, a history of the Church until 1294; and *De Regimine Principum*, a work begun by Thomas, which he finished.

Bartholomew of the Martyrs, Ven. (1514-1590) ●
Portuguese Dominican theologian, born Bartholomew Fernandez but known as *A Martyribus* because of the church in which he was baptized. He entered the Dominicans at Lisbon in 1527, subsequently holding a number of teaching posts in theology and philosophy until his elevation as bishop of Braga in 1548. Bartholomew took a prominent role in the Council of Trent, playing a significant role in drafting the decrees concerning reform of the clergy. He was subsequently noted for his enthusiasm in implementing the Tridentine reforms of the Church.

Bartholomew of Pisa (d. 1347) ●
Dominican theologian and chronicler. Also known as Bartholomew of San Concordio, he was often confused with Bartholomew Albisi of Pisa, who lived there at the same time. Albisi was the author of *De Conformitate Vitae B. P. Francisci ad Vitam Domini Nostri Jesu Christi*, a very popular history paralleling the lives of St. Francis and Christ. Bartholomew of San Concordio entered the Dominicans in 1277, studying at Bologna and Pisa before assuming various teaching posts in Dominican houses. He is best known for his work *Summa de Casibus Conscientiae*, an alphabetically arranged work on law, also known as the *Summa Pisana, Summa Bartholomaea*, and *Summa*

Pisanella. It was immensely popular in the 1300s and 1400s.

Bartholomew's Day Massacre ● See **St. Bartholomew's Day Massacre**.

Barton, Elizabeth (1506-1534) ● English nun, called the "Maid of Kent" and the "Nun of Kent." Barton was a young serving girl in Kent who began making prophecies in 1525 after suffering an illness. These prophecies were investigated by a committee of the Benedictines from Canterbury the following year, who found no complaint and endorsed her entry as a nun into St. Sepulchre's Convent in Canterbury. She soon proved a source of considerable irritation to King Henry VIII for her outspoken opposition to his divorce. In 1533, therefore, Henry's principal adviser, Thomas Cromwell, had her placed in the Tower of London. A confession, extorted through torture, was obtained by Archbishop Cranmer that her prophecies were false. She was then executed at Tyburn on April 20, 1534. A source of contention between Catholics and Protestants, Barton remained a mystery as to whether or not she was a legitimate prophet.

Basil of Ancyra ● Fourth-century Arian bishop who participated in many of the councils and synods concerning the Arian dispute in the middle of the century. Basil was elected to the see and Ancyra (now called Ankara) in 336, as the successor of Marcellus. Deposed because of his moderate Arian views at the Council of Sardica in 343, he was reinstated in 348 by the Arian sympathizer Emperor Constantius. He subsequently attended the so-called Arianizing Synods of Sirmium (351), Ancyra (358), and Seleucia (359). The following year, after Seleucia, however, Basil was deposed and banished to Illyria because his Arianism was too moderate for the tastes of the extreme Arians. He died in exile. Basil authored a short dogmatic treatise, with George of Laodicea, that was preserved by Epiphamus. (See **Arianism**.)

St. Basil the Great

Basil the Great, St. (c. 329-379) ● Bishop of Caesarea and one of the foremost Doctors of the Church who was noted, with St. Athanasius, as a great defender of Christian orthodoxy against Arianism. With his brother St. Gregory of Nyssa, and St. Gregory of Nazianzus, Basil is one of "The Three Cappadocians" who distinguished themselves in Church history. Basil was the son of St. Basil the Elder and Emmelia, the daughter of a martyr, and was one of ten children, three of whom — Basil, Gregory, and Macrina — would become saints. Largely raised by his grandmother, he studied at Caesarea, his native town, and at Constantinople, where he developed his long friendship with Gregory of Nazianzus. Having obtained a superb education, he returned to Caesarea as a teacher. He soon also underwent a profound spiritual transformation, embarking on a journey in 357 to the monasteries of Egypt, Palestine, and Mesopotamia. Returning, he founded a monastic community near Annesi where his sister Macrina had already established a religious house. Basil's innovations within the monastic community, especially his rule, earned him the title Father of Eastern (or Oriental) Monasticism. The Rule of St. Basil is still followed by the members of the religious life in the lands of the Orthodox Churches.

In 360, he was finally convinced to depart his hermitage and take part in a council at Constantinople. Subsequently ordained with great reluctance, he played a major role in the administration of the diocese of Caesarea under Bishop Eusebius, so much so that the two entered into a dispute. Basil withdrew to his monastic community but was recalled in 365 at the insistence of Gregory of Nazianzus. In 370, he was chosen to succeed to the see of Caesarea that had by now acquired the status of metropolitan. His appointment was a great pleasure to St. Athanasius but was greeted with suspicion by the ardent Arian Emperor Valens. Over the next nine years he was conspicuous for his care of the poor, his efforts at the defense of ecclesiastical rights, and most of all, for his steadfast opposition to heresy, especially Arianism. When defending himself before Valens, Basil was so fiery that a courtier questioned his nerve, to which the saint gave his famous reply: "Perhaps you are not familiar with a proper bishop." Owing to the controversy over Melitius, bishop of Antioch, and the efforts of Valens to reduce Basil's power, his friendship with Gregory was severely strained. He died on January 1, 379, at a time of terrible upheaval in the Roman Empire both politically (because of the Goths) and religiously (because of the Arians). Because he was so beloved, his funeral was attended by a large, weeping crowd, including Christians, Jews, and pagans.

Basil is ranked as a truly great Church figure owing to his spiritual achievements and his vast contributions to Christianity in the fourth century. His letters reveal a remarkably holy and eloquent person, who, while never strong physically, was utterly fearless in defense of orthodoxy or in the face of imperial threats and pressures to conform to the doctrinal trends of the day. Some three hundred sixty-six letters are extant, most from after his elevation to the episcopacy. His other writings included: a treatise, *On the Holy Spirit*; three books against Enomius, an outspoken Arian bishop of Cyzicus; a compilation with Gregory of Nazianzus from the works of Origen in the Philocalia. He is also the ascribed formulator of the Liturgy of St. Basil, still used on certain days in the liturgy of the Greek Orthodox Church. Feast day: January 2.

Basilians ● Name given to the members of a number of monastic communities who took their name from St. Basil the Great and were part of the non-Latin rite of the Catholic Church. Basilians are found in the Byzantine rite and among the Melkite Catholics.

Basilica ● Type of architectural structure of Roman origin that came to be used by the Church in the centuries following the recognition of the Christian faith throughout the Roman Empire. In its original sense, the basilica was a large public building holding courts, markets, or commercial exchanges, and records centers. Varying in size and layout, the basilica often had side aisles running down its rectangular length, with high ceilings, rows of pillars, and an apse at one end. This type was largely adopted by Church officials from the reign of Constantine the Great after formal recognition in 313. It is believed that the organization of the basilica appealed to Christians because it was similar to the halls in the homes of wealthy Christians where ceremonies were often held during the eras of persecutions. Impetus was given for the acceptance of the architectural design by Constantine himself, who built three basilicas in Rome: S. Giovanni in Laterano, St. Peter's, and S. Paolo Fuori le Mure; these also introduced the innovation of a transept, meaning a lateral aisle that cut across the nave before the apse, thereby creating an interesting cross effect that would be duplicated throughout the churches of Western Christendom. The simple design made the exterior quite plain, but the interior offered enormous opportunity for sumptuous decoration, such as seen today in St. Peter's Basilica or the Lateran Basilica.

In ecclesiastical terminology, the term basilica is understood to be a canonical title of honor, bestowed upon certain churches in recognition of their historical value or their importance as a center of worship. The 1917 Code of Canon Law declared that no church might be called a basilica unless it received designation as such by the Holy See or was known as a basilica in ancient custom. There are currently two types of basilicas, the major and minor. Major, or patriarchal, basilicas are the churches most often understood by the term; these include the great basilicas of Christendom, such as the four major basilicas of Rome: St. Peter's at the Vatican, St. John Lateran (the pope's own church as Bishop of Rome), St. Paul-Outside-the-Walls, and St. Mary Major. Each of these has an altar used only by the pope. Minor basilicas are other churches in Rome or around the world granted this honor. With the title come certain privileges such as indulgences and the bearing of the *ombrellino*, an umbrella emblem in stripes of yellow and red to represent the colors of the papacy and the senate. In earlier times, the *ombrellino* was carried over the pope when he visited the basilica. Other designative insignia include the papal coat of arms, placed in the sanctuary or above the door, and a staff with a bell. (See also **Cathedral**.)

Basilides (fl. second century) ● Syrian theologian who became the founder of the Alexandrian school of Gnosticism. He taught at Alexandria probably in the second quarter of the second century, during the reigns of the Roman emperors Hadrian and Antoninus Pius. His writings are preserved only in fragments, but these include psalms, odes, an otherwise unknown work entitled "the Gospel," and a biblical commentary, in twenty-four books, called the *Exegetica*. The doctrine he apparently espoused was a combining of Neoplatonism, Gnostic teachings, Persian dualism, and traditions derived from the supposed teachings of Sts. Peter and Matthias. (See also **Basilidians**, following entry.)

Basilidians ● Name given to the followers of the second-century Gnostic theologian Basilides. They were essentially religious dualists who accepted the idea that spirit was good, matter was bad, and that salvation was possible through the discovery of secret knowledge, or *gnosis*. These secret tenets were, of course, carefully guarded from the uninitiated and taught only to devoted members of the sect. Later Basilidians adhered to the notion that the universe had not been created but had formed through a series of emanations. They also denied the corporeal nature of Christ, thus doubting the Crucifixion because of his incorporeal state, thereby arguing that true Gnostics are impervious to the powers of the earth because of their spiritual nature. (See also **Gnosticism**.)

Basel, Council of ● General council of the Church, sitting from 1431-1449, convened at Basel (also spelled Basle) to discuss and settle such vexing problems as the Hussite heresy and papal supremacy, particularly the ongoing conflict within the Church over the conciliar theory advanced by the Council of Constance (1414-1418) that ultimate authority rested with the councils and not the popes. The council promulgated the Compactata of Prague to end the Hussite War, but the conciliar problem proved more troublesome. An antipapal declaration (1437) was denounced by Eugenius IV (who had confirmed the council) in the bull *Doctoris gentium*, demanding that the council move to Ferrara, Italy. Those delegates who refused to go were excommunicated. They then elected as antipope Amadeus VIII, duke of Savoy, under the name Felix V, declaring Eugenius to be deposed. A decade of bickering followed, ending only in 1449 with Felix's abdication in favor of Eugenius's successor, Nicholas V, and the final dissolution of the council. While theologians and scholars have debated the legitimacy of the council, there is no question that conciliarism suffered a mortal blow when the council was dissolved in 1449. Intended to bring reform to a troubled Church, the council was a failure, particularly as it was plagued throughout by poor attendance and allowed many princes to tighten control over the Church in their territories in the absence of strong Church leadership. The Council of Basel is also considered the first of the three councils comprising the Council of Florence. (See also **Ferrara-Florence, Council of**.)

Beaton, David (c. 1494-1546) ● Also David Bethune, a cardinal, statesman, and formidable figure in Scotland who worked vigorously against the Scottish Reformation and promoted a close alliance between France and Scotland. Beaton became abbot of Arbroath in 1523 and was soon used as a trusted emissary by King James V. Keeper of the privy seal in 1528, he became bishop in 1537, cardinal in 1538, and archbishop of St. Andrew's in 1539. Beaton wielded much influence at the court of King James, convincing the king not to pursue a reformist policy such as that then being undertaken by Henry VIII of England. He also arranged two of James's marriages to French noblewomen and, after the ruler's death in 1542, opposed the pro-English policies of the regent of young Mary Stuart, James Hamilton, second earl of Arran; Beaton was briefly imprisoned in 1543. From December 1543, Beaton was virtual ruler of Scotland, serving as chancellor. He persecuted the Protestants of the realm, defeated the proposed marriage of Mary to the future King Edward VI of England (thereby causing the English invasion of 1544), and burned at the stake the reformer George Wishart on March 1, 1546. In retribution for the execution, a group of Protestant nobles murdered Beaton in St. Andrew's Castle on May 29. While he kept Scotland in the Church for many years after the start of the Reformation, his oppressive measures alienated many in the nobility and hastened the Scottish embrace of Protestantism after his death. (See **Scotland**.)

Beauduin, Lambert (1873-1960) ● Belgian liturgist and founder of the Benedictine community at Chevetogne in Belgium. Beauduin was ordained in 1897, entering in 1906 the Benedictine Abbey of Mont-César in Louvain. He helped to establish the periodical *La Vie Liturgique* (*The Liturgical Life*; after 1911, *Les Questions Liturgiques*, or *Liturgical Questions*) and authored the work *La Piété de l'Église* (*The Piety of the Church*) that helped make Mont-César one of the most important Benedictine houses in the liturgical movement, with Maredsous, Solesmes, and Maria Laach. In 1925, Beauduin founded the future monastery of Chevetogne at Amay-sur-Meuse in response to a call by Pope Pius XI that the Benedictines should pray for Christian unity (1924; *Equidem verba*). Attending the Malines Conversations between Catholic and Anglican theologians, he caused a storm of criticism, when in a report to Cardinal Mercier, he suggested that the Anglican Church should be united to Rome, not absorbed (*unie non absorbée*). In 1928, he was forced to leave Amay and in

1930 he was condemned by a tribunal in Rome; in 1950, he returned to the community, now settled at Chevetogne. Pope John XXIII recognized the validity of his proposed method of Anglican reunion.

Beaufort, Henry (c. 1373-1447) ● English cardinal, bishop of Lincoln and Winchester, and chancellor of England who was one of the most important political figures in England for much of the first half of the 1400s. Beaufort was the son of John of Gaunt, duke of Lancaster and son of King Edward III, and Catherine Swynford. Educated at Cambridge, Oxford, and Aachen, he became the chancellor of Oxford University in 1397 and bishop of Lincoln in 1398. In 1403, he was named chancellor of England by King Henry IV, his half brother, and then bishop of Winchester in 1404. He soon resigned his chancellorship to lead the opposition on the royal council against Archbishop Arundel of Canterbury in favor of the political advance of his own nephew, the prince of Wales (the future King Henry V). When Henry became king of England in 1413, Beaufort was made chancellor once more, until 1417. Beaufort then assisted Oddo Colonna in becoming Pope Martin V, who made him a cardinal and papal legate; Henry forced him to resign these offices, however, so as to prevent him from acquiring even more power. Chancellor once more from 1424 to 1426 and a guardian of Henry VI, Beaufort practically ruled the kingdom until accepting the cardinalate in 1426 because of attacks from Humphrey, duke of Gloucester. As cardinal he led an unsuccessful attack on the Hussites. Returning to England, he once more was a major royal adviser, from 1435-1443 when he retired, dying at Wolvesey Palace on Palm Sunday, 1447. While of dubious spirituality and religious devotion (he was present at Joan of Arc's trial in 1431), he was a remarkable statesman and financier.

Beaulieu, Abbey of ● Important Cistercian abbey in Hampshire first established in 1204 by King John of England. It was intended to be used by some thirty monks from Cîteaux and was dedicated in 1246. Its main historical significance was its value as a sanctuary, an exemption given by Pope Innocent III. A number of notable individuals sought sanctuary there, including Ann Neville and Perkin Warbeck. Portions of the original abbey (suppressed in 1539) include the refectory and the cloister house.

Beauraing Apparitions ● Name given to the thirty-three apparitions of the Virgin Mary in Beauraing, Belgium, between November 29, 1932, and January 3, 1933. The visions of the BVM were beheld by five children in the garden of the convent school of Beauraing; the children were Andrée and Gilberte Degeimbre and Fernande, Albert, and Gilberte Voisin. Mary, seen dressed in white and wearing a crown of golden rays, her golden heart exposed in her breast, told the children to pray and make sacrifice for sinners. After a ten-year investigation by the Church, reserved approval was given on February 2, 1943. Formal approval by Bishop Charles of Namur came on July 2, 1949. A shrine, built on the spot of the apparition, was the site of reported miracles and became a popular place of pilgrimage.

Bec ● Famous Benedictine monastery near Rouen, in Normandy, that was founded in 1041 by Abbot Herluin. Rebuilt and enlarged in 1061 or (1060), it was destroyed by a fire in 1263. The rebuilt abbey passed in 1626 to the Maurists, who held it until the French Revolution brought its suppression in 1790. The largely ruined structures were reinhabited by the Olivetan Congregation in 1948, marking the return of the Benedictines to Bec. (See **Benedictines**.)

Bede the Venerable, St. (673-735) ● Known popularly as the Venerable Bede, he was an Anglo-Saxon historian, biblical scholar, and one of the greatest of all chroniclers of the Middle Ages. Most of what is known about his life comes to us from Bede himself, writing in the last chapter of the *Historia Ecclesiastica*. He was born in Northumberland and at the age of seven was sent into the care of St. Benedict Biscop, abbot of Wearmouth. He was transferred (c. 681) to the monastery of St. Paul in Jarrow, being ordained a deacon at nineteen and a priest at thirty. He rarely traveled outside of Northumbria, with the exception of a trip to Lindisfarne and one to York. He died on May 25, 735, at Jarrow and was buried there; in the eleventh century he was moved to Durham Cathedral. He was canonized by Pope Leo XIII in 1899.

Called the Father of English History, Bede authored numerous important works on grammar, history, and the Scriptures. His commentaries on the Bible included the Gospels, Acts of the Apostles, and elements of the Old and New Testaments as well as a scientific study based on Pliny the Younger and Suetonius, two influential Roman writers. There were also grammars; two treatises on chronology, *De temporibus* (*On Time*) and *De temporibus ratione* (*On the Reckoning of Time*); a life of St. Cuthbert; and the *Historia Abbotum* (a history on the lives of the abbots of Wearmouth and Jarrow). His chief work was the *Historia Ecclesiastica*, examining English history from 55 B.C. to A.D. 597. It was written with considerable skill and scholarship, with particular care to the proper and judicious use of sources. While often preoccupied

St. Bede the Venerable

with some questionable miraculous events, it remains an absolutely invaluable record of Christianity in early Anglo-Saxon England. Of Bede, the disciple Cuthbert declared: "I can truly declare that I never beheld with my eyes or heard with my ears anyone return

thanks so unceasingly to the living God."
Feast day: May 27.

Bedini, Cajetan (1806-1864) ● Cardinal
and a notable papal diplomat. Appointed to
the commissary extraordinary to Bologna by
Pope Pius IX, he helped oversee the
maintenance of the papal territory, which at
the time was held only by force in the Papal
States by troops from Austria. In 1853, he
was named apostolic nuncio to Brazil and
was ordered by Pius to visit the United States
to examine and report back on the
ecclesiastical state of affairs there. Bedini
arrived at Washington in June 1853 and
soon met with President Franklin Pierce.
Their meeting sparked numerous
anti-Catholic demonstrations and an
ill-planned and abortive assassination
attempt on the nuncio. Nevertheless, Bedini
visited Pittsburgh, Louisville, and Cincinnati,
becoming so concerned about possible
assassination attempts that he departed New
York in secret and was taken by tug to his
steamer. After his return to Rome he was
elevated to the rank of cardinal. (See also
United States of America.)

Beghards ● Semireligious organization
that first appeared in 1220 at Louvain, in the
Netherlands. They derived their name from
the preacher Lambert le Begue (d. 1177) and
were the male equivalent of the female sect of
the Beguines. They practiced severe austerity
but were allowed to marry and made no
lasting obligations or commitments. The
focus of their lives was to care for the sick
and the poor, and the Beghards became very
popular in the Low Countries, France, Italy,
and Germany. The Council of Vienne
condemned both the Beghards and Beguines
in 1312 as heretics, although Pope John XXII
permitted a reformed version of Beghards to
continue after 1321. They endured until the
French Revolution. (See also **Beguines**,
following entry.)

Beguines ● Female equivalent of the
Beghards, a quasi-religious sisterhood that
was established in the late 1100s in the
Netherlands. Like the Beghards, the
Beguines lived in an austere fashion and
spent much time in prayer. There were no
specific rules, however, and any Beguine
could marry or leave. Their main work was
with the sick and poor. Beguinages (or
communities), as they were called, flourished
in the Netherlands, France, and Germany;
however, after their condemnation in 1312 as
heretical, they declined throughout the 1200s
and 1300s. There are several Beguinages still
in existence. (See also **Beghards**, preceding
entry.)

Belgium ● European country, a
constitutional monarchy dating as a
sovereign state only from 1831; the Church
has wielded considerable influence
throughout its history. The name is derived
from the Gallic tribe of the Belgae, who were
conquered by the Romans and ultimately
absorbed into the empire. Christianity was
introduced into the area early in the fourth
century and its power was cemented through
the founding of the Carolingian Empire and
the flowering of the Carolingian Renaissance
in the eighth century. After centuries of
various noble rulers, the region had passed
to the dukes of Burgundy by the fifteenth
century; it came under Habsburg (or
Hapsburg) control from 1482. The
Reformation gained some favor among the
people, but the strength of the Church, with
the Spanish Habsburg monarchy, allowed a
restoration of Catholic supremacy. The
Church suffered in the 1600s from
Jansenism and in the 1700s from
Josephinism, which was introduced by
Austrian authorities. The French annexed the
area in 1797, marking the beginning of a
period of severe persecution under Napoleon.
His oppression was replaced in 1815 by that
of William I of Holland (r. 1813-1844), who
permitted the Calvinist minority in Belgium

to enforce hard measures against Catholics. In 1830, a revolution was launched by the Catholics and Liberals. Belgian independence was declared and the next year King Leopold I was chosen king. Cooperation between Catholics and Liberals lasted until 1847. The Liberals then pursued a sharp anti-Catholic program. From 1880-1884, there were no relations between the Holy See and the Belgian government. In 1884, elections removed the Liberals and replaced them with a more cooperative and pro-Catholic administration. In World War I, much damage was done to churches and convents; in World War II, the occupation by the Nazis brought a wave of terror.

Bellarmine, Robert, St. (1542-1621) ●
Originally Roberto Francesco Remolo Bellarmino, a cardinal, theologian, and remarkable controversialist who opposed the Protestant Reformation and became one the Church's greatest defenders. Born at Monte Pulciano, in Tuscany, he joined the Society of Jesus in 1560, and was ordained in 1570 at Louvain where he served as a professor of theology. Because of the prevailing Protestant thinking in the region, Bellarmine was forced to become absolutely learned in theology and doctrine, departing the north in 1576 for Rome. His aversion to the cold weather also affected his decision. In Rome he became a professor in the newly established Jesuit institution of the Collegium Romanum where he lectured on a host of controversial subjects. Made a cardinal in 1599 by Pope Clement VIII, Bellarmine became archbishop of Capua in 1602. A highly regarded theologian, he was consulted by the Holy Office on the writings of Galileo. He urged that the Copernican theory, supported by Galileo, be declared "false and erroneous," and urged the astronomer not to defend the theory so as to head off any further controversy with the Protestants over the matter. He also supported Paul V in his struggle against Venice. While he attacked a

book by William Barclay (d. 1608), Bellarmine did adhere to the idea that pontiffs exercised only an indirect kind of authority, a view that caused a sharp disagreement with Sixtus IV. Bellarmine provided a definition for the Catholic Church when he wrote: "The one and true Church is the assembly of men, bound together by the profession of the same Christian faith, and by the commission of the same sacraments, under the rule of legitimate pastors, and in particular the one Vicar of Christ on earth, the Roman Pontiff."

Bellarmine was the author of numerous and highly influential works, the most important being a series of lectures published under the title *Disputationes de controversiis Christianae fidei adversus huius temporis haereticos* (1586-1593; *Lectures Concerning the Controversies of the Christian Faith Against the Heretics of This Time*). His reply to Barclay was *De Potestate Summi Pontificis in Rebus Temporalibus* (1610; *Concerning the Powers of the Supreme Pontiff in Temporal Matters*). He also participated in the Clementine edition of the Vulgate, known as the Sixto-Clementine (1592), which corrected the inaccuracy of the edition produced under Sixtus V. His autobiography appeared first in 1675. Bellarmine died a pauper, having spent many years working to relieve the poor. He was revered as the foremost saintly figure of the late Counter-Reformation and was noted for his impartial treatment of Protestant writings and ideas. Made venerable in 1627, he was canonized in 1930 by Pope Pius XI and declared a Doctor of the Church in 1931. Feast day: September 17 (formerly May 13).

Belloc, Joseph-Pierre Hilaire (1870-1953) ● Catholic historian, poet, essayist. He was born at La Celle-St.-Cloud, near Versailles, and was educated at the Oratory School in Birmingham, studying under John Henry Newman. After serving briefly in the French artillery, he entered

Balliol College, Oxford, in 1892. Elected a Liberal M.P. in 1906, he subsequently joined G. K. Chesterton and his brother Cecil Chesterton in a number of political attacks, known as Chesterbellocs. An ardent Catholic, his abiding faith was visible in his historical writings, particularly *Europe and the Faith* (1920), *History of England* (4 vols., 1925-1931), and a series of biographies, including James II (1928), Joan of Arc (1929), Richelieu (1930), Wolsey (1930), Napoleon (1932), Charles I (1933), Cromwell (1934), and Milton (1935). While Belloc was best known for his light verse and essays, he also authored the popular travel book *The Path to Rome* (1902). He was married in 1896 to Elodie Hogan (d. 1914) of Napa, California.

Benedict, St. ● See under **Benedict of Aniane, St.** and **Benedict of Nursia, St.**

Benedict I ● Pope from 575-579. A little-known pontiff, he was elected to succeed John II, although he was not consecrated until June 575, leaving an absence of a pope for some eleven months after the July 574 death of John. Benedict's reign coincided with the terrible social and economic times in Italy, with famines and invasions rife. He died during a Lombard siege of Rome but did manage to consecrate some twenty-one bishops before his demise.

Benedict II, St. ● Pope from 684-685. The successor to Pope Leo II, he was elected in 683 but was not consecrated until June 26, 684, owing to the need to have the election approved by Emperor Constantine IV Pogonatos at Constantinople; as a result, the papacy was vacant for a year. His reign was notable for two main achievements: he restored a number of churches in Rome; and he secured from Emperor Constantine the decree that in the future there should be no need for a newly elected pontiff to secure the approval of the Byzantine emperor before beginning his reign. Nevertheless, imperial

approbation continued to be sought. Feast day: May 8.

Benedict III ● Pope from 855-858. The successor to Leo IV, elected in July 855, Benedict was unable to secure the approval for his election by Holy Roman Emperor Louis II the Bavarian, and Louis established as antipope Anastasius the Librarian. Imprisoned for a time, he was released in October and was recognized by Louis as the legitimate pontiff. He repaired churches in Rome that had been damaged by the raids of the Saracens.

Benedict IV ● Pope from 900-903. Reigned during a very dark period in papal history. He is little known, although he did excommunicate Baldwin II, count of Flanders, for the murder of Fulk, archbishop of Reims, in 900. He also crowned Henry the Blind as Holy Roman Emperor in 901. He succeeded John IX.

Benedict V ● Pope from 964-966. The successor to John XII, he is considered by some lists as an antipope. Known originally as Grammaticus (a nickname because of his learning), he was elected pope by the Romans in late May 964, an act of defiance of Emperor Otto I, who had already deposed John and appointed Leo VIII as his replacement. The emperor stormed Rome, deposed Benedict on June 23, and moved him to Hamburg. Leo was initiated once more as Otto's choice for pope.

Benedict VI ● Pope from 973-974. Succeeded John XIII. His consecration was delayed after his election in 972 until early 973 because of the need to secure the approval of Holy Roman Emperor Otto I. Benedict's reign was short and unhappy owing to the domination of Rome by the Crescentii family. The pope was imprisoned in 974, replaced by the antipope Boniface VII, and eventually strangled.

Benedict VII ● Pope from 974-983. Successor to Benedict VI who had been strangled by order of the Crescentii family and their antipope Boniface VII. His election was made possible through the patronage of Emperor Otto II whose agent, Count Sicco, expelled Boniface VII and tamed, temporarily, the Crescentii. Benedict promoted monasticism and issued an encyclical in 981 against simony. He also terminated the post of bishop of Merseburg, thereby depriving the north of Europe of a vital outpost of Christianity and a means of converting the Slavs.

Benedict VIII ● Pope from 1012-1024. Reign marked the resurgence of papal authority in the political affairs of Rome and Italy. A member of the formidable Tusculani family, he profited by the rise of his house at the expense of the Crescentii family, who had dominated the papacy in the tenth century. Eager to restore papal power, Benedict defeated the choice of the Crescentii for the throne of Peter and then solidified his position by having his brother, Romanus, named civil ruler of Rome; Romanus would succeed him as John XIX. Aside from promoting ecclesiastical reform and clerical celibacy, Benedict was a remarkable warrior pope. He defeated the Saracens in their raids on northern Italy (1016-1017), restored papal control of Campagna and Roman Tuscany, and allied himself with the Normans, at the expense of the Byzantines.

Benedict IX ● Pope from 1032-1044, again in 1045, and finally once more from 1047-1048. A member of the Tusculani family, Benedict was a rather notorious figure, particularly for selling the papacy to his godfather and then surviving attempts at deposing him by using the power of his family. He was the son of Count Alberic of Tusculum, and the nephew of two popes, Benedict VIII and John XIX. Elected at the instigation of the Tusculani, he so enraged

the Romans that by 1045 they tried to remove him by electing John of Sabina as Sylvester III. Benedict soon ejected Sylvester and returned to his office, whereupon he sold the Holy See to his godfather, the priest Giovanni Graziano, who became Gregory VI. Regretting his decision, Benedict reappeared in Rome in 1046, challenging both Gregory and Sylvester as he decided to reclaim the throne. The Council of Sutri (1046), convened by Henry III of Germany, rejected all three popes and named Suidger of Bamberg to be Clement II. When he died, Benedict installed himself once more, in 1047, only to be deposed in 1048 by order of Emperor Henry. He died around 1055 at a monastery at Grottaferratta. Benedict was the last pope from the Tusculani.

Benedict X ● Antipope from April 1058 to January 1059. Known originally as John Mincius, he served as bishop of Velletri, near Rome, and was picked to be pope by the Tusculani family. Placed upon the papal throne upon the death of Pope Stephen IX (X), he was soon removed as part of the papal reforms of Hildebrand (the future Gregory VII) and declared an antipope. He died around 1080, a prisoner in the monastery at Sant' Agnese. His brief reign helped lead to the creation of the College of Cardinals in the election of popes.

Benedict XI ● Pope from 1303-1304. Born Niccolo Boccasini, he entered the Dominicans in 1254 and became the master general of the order in May 1296. A cardinal in 1298, he was noted for remaining at the side of Boniface VIII in 1303 during the time that Boniface's struggle with King Philip IV of France climaxed with the pope's seizure at Anagni by Philip's troops. The pope was released through the efforts of the local populace but died a short time later. Boccasini was elected his successor unanimously on October 22, 1303, inheriting Boniface's troubles, especially in dealing with

Philip's determination to tax the clergy of France. His reign proved too brief to produce any meaningful accomplishments. He was beatified by Clement XII in 1736.

Benedict XII ● Pope from 1334-1342. Third of the Avignon popes. Born Jacques Fournier, he was a respected Cistercian theologian, abbot of Fontfroide in 1311, and bishop of Pamiers in 1317. Named a cardinal in 1327, he was elected as the successor to John XXII in 1334. An active pontiff, he initiated both extensive ecclesiastical reforms and a series of ultimately unsuccessful diplomatic efforts. His reforms of the clergy, especially the religious orders, were adopted to some degree by the Council of Trent, but others were rescinded by his successors. He settled the dispute over the question of the deposition of the beatific vision that had been preached by John; he argued that the vision would only be granted after the day of judgment. Benedict issued the bull *Benedictus Deus* (1336) in which he stated the deserving perceived the vision upon death instead of after the day of judgment. Benedict failed to prevent or to stop the Hundred Years' War (which actually lasted from 1337-1453), to launch another crusade, and to improve relations with the Holy Roman Empire, because of the constant interference of King Philip IV of France. While he did not return to Rome as was hoped by the Romans, he did send money to repair the churches of the city and to aid its suffering inhabitants. Benedict also constructed a lavish papal palace. (See also **Babylonian Captivity**.)

Benedict XIII <1> ● Antipope at Avignon from 1394-1417 or 1423. Born Pedro de Luna, he was a professor of canon law, who became a cardinal in 1375 through Gregory XI. Originally a supporter of Gregory's successor, Urban VI, he became instead an ardent adherent of the antipope Clement VII. Upon Clement's death in 1394, he was elected as Pope Benedict XIII at Avignon, promising to end the Great Schism even if it meant his abdication. He soon refused to step down, participating in a siege of the papal castle at Avignon. The Council of Pisa deposed him in 1409, and negotiations with the Roman popes Boniface IX, Innocent VII, and Gregory XII all failed to resolve the crisis. Benedict was able to cling to his post through the support of Scotland and various states in Spain until 1417, when his deposition was upheld by the Council of Constance. Refusing to abdicate, he took up residence in Peniscola, declaring his legitimacy even as he lay dying in 1423.

Pope Benedict XIII

Benedict XIII <2> ● Pope from 1724-1730. He was noted for his efforts at reforming the extravagant lifestyles of his cardinals and the simplicity of his reign, although his pontificate was marred by the unpopular Cardinal Niccolo Coscia, who managed Benedict's affairs of state. Born Pierfrancesco Orsini, he entered the Dominicans in 1667, becoming a cardinal in 1672. After serving as archbishop of Manfredonia (1675), Cesena (1680), and Benevento (1686), he was finally elected pope in 1724; in his time, he attended five conclaves. As pope, he continued the papal opposition to Jansenism, although he gave the Dominicans permission to preach the Augustinian doctrine of grace.

Benedict XIV <1> ●
The name given to two so-called counter-antipopes, meaning that they were antipopes chosen in opposition to another antipope, a highly irregular and rare event in Church history. The first Benedict was Bernard Garnier, a fanatical supporter of Antipope Benedict XIII, who was elected on November 12, 1425, in opposition to Clement VIII, an antipope to Pope Martin V. Garnier was given protection by the count of Armagnac and was so invisible in his affairs that he earned the nickname the "Hidden Pope." Benedict ended his "reign" in 1430 after Clement abdicated. The second Benedict XIV was another follower of Benedict XIII, Jean Carrier, dying as a prisoner "pope" in the castle of Foix. The two Benedicts, the only two such antipopes in Church records, are considered the last gasp of the Great Schism (1378-1417).

Benedict XIV <2> ● Pope from 1740-1758. Known for his remarkable intelligence and moderation, his reign came at a time when Europe was in the midst of the Enlightenment and when the Church was being challenged by the absolute monarchs of the time. Born Prospero Lambertini, he was elected to succeed

Pope Benedict XV

Clement XII on August 17, 1740. His moderate nature prompted him to instruct the organizers of the Index of Forbidden Books to use restraint, to make concessions to the kings of Spain, Sardinia, Naples, and Portugal in secular matters, and to reduce taxation on the Papal States. He did, however, use the bulls *Ex quo singulare* (1742) and *Omnium sollicitudinum* (1744), in which certain traditional practices by converts in India and China that were permitted by the Jesuits were strictly curtailed. The bulls cut down severely on conversions and were partly modified in 1939. A learned and much respected figure, Benedict corresponded with many great intellectuals in Europe, including Voltaire. He also helped establish the groundwork for the Vatican Museum.

Benedict XV ● Pope from 1914-1922. His reign was overshadowed by World War I (1914-1918). Born Giacomo della Chiesa, he entered the priesthood after graduating from the University of Genoa, serving in the Vatican diplomatic corps and in the Secretariat of State. Made archbishop of Bologna in 1907, he became cardinal in 1914 through St. Pius X, and was elected his successor only a month after the eruption of the Great War. As pope, he adopted a policy of impartiality, working to mediate a peace, bringing aid to the millions who were suffering, and refusing to condemn any of the belligerents. His hopes of a negotiated peace were aborted by the entry of the United States into the war in 1917. Because of the neutral stand of the Holy See, Benedict was punished by the victorious powers through exclusion from the peace negotiations and at Versailles. The latter part of his reign, however, brought renewed relations with France and the establishment of a representative from Great Britain accredited to the Vatican for the first time in some three centuries. Benedict was also responsible for publishing the Code of Canon Law that went into effect in 1918, after being officially released on May 27, 1917.

Benedict Biscop, St. (d. 689 or 690) ●
Originally known as Biscop Baducing, he was a monk, abbot, and a major figure in the rise of Benedictine monasticism in England. Benedict was a Northumbrian who lived for many years at the court of King Oswiu of Northumbria. In 653, he gave up material interests and made the first of his trips to Rome, with St. Wilfrid. In 666, he journeyed to Rome again and soon after became a monk at Lerins. He was, for some time, a companion of Theodore of Tarsus, archbishop of Canterbury, and in 669 was named abbot of the monastery of Sts. Peter and Paul (later St. Augustine's), at Canterbury. He later established the monasteries of St. Peter at Wearmouth (674) and St. Paul in Jarrow (682). A respected and learned figure, he left a large collection of relics, paintings, and manuscripts that were an inspiration to the Benedictines for centuries to come. The Venerable Bede wrote of his life in *Historia Abbotum* (*History of the Abbots* of Wearmouth and Jarrow). (See also **Benedictines**.) He is also credited with the introduction of glass windows and churches made of stone to England. Feast day: January 12.

Benedict of Aniane, St. (c. 750-821) ●
Abbot of Aniane and a leading monastic reformer in France. He served under both Pepin II the Short and his son Charlemagne before becoming a monk at St.-Seine, near Dijon, in 773. Six years later, he used his

own property at Aniane to establish his own monastic institution, aiming at reforming French monasticism. At the Synod of Aachen (817) his systematization of the Benedict Rule was granted official approval as the *Capitulare Monasticum*; he also organized a collection of known monastic rules. His work thus became official royal policy and his reforms were introduced for all monasteries. Feast day: February 11.

Benedict of Nursia, St. (c. 480-c. 550) ●
Founder of the monastery of Monte Cassino and the revered patriarch of Western Monasticism. Also called simply St. Benedict, he was born in Nursia and educated at Rome. He departed the city, however,

St. Benedict of Nursia

because of its notorious vice and corruption, settling instead in a cave at Subiaco around 500. Here he rejected the world, living a highly ascetic life and attracting followers drawn by his example. There soon developed around this small community a dozen other monastic institutions, headed by abbotlike leaders each appointed by Benedict. Around

525, Benedict left Subiaco with a small band of adherents because of local difficulties, setting off for Monte Cassino, between Rome and Naples. Here he spent the rest of his days composing his famed rule and planning to reform monastic institutions in Christendom.

Benedict never intended to create orders of religious; however, through his sanctity and example, he inspired not only the Benedictines but had a major impact on Christianity itself. His rule formed the basis of the Benedictine order and was the guiding light of monasticism in the West, even though he was never ordained. He was buried in Monte Cassino in the same grave as his sister, St. Scholastica. The only major source on Benedict was the *Dialogue of St. Gregory*, specifically Book Two. Feast day: July 11. (See also **Benedictines** and **Monasticism**.)

Benedict, Rule of ● Monastic regulations established by Benedict of Nursia in the middle of the sixth century to guide the monastic organization at Monte Cassino. It was largely derived from the earlier rules of innovators, including John Cassian, Basil, Augustine, Caesarius of Arles, and the Fathers of the Desert. The Rule of Benedict was intended to serve as an inspiration for living a religious life of moderation while adhering to vows of chastity, community, and obedience in the following of Christ. Within a community it was to be safeguarded by the abbot, who applied it for the good of all. As it was enlightened, compassionate, flexible, and not an unbending set of strict codes, the rule was adopted throughout much of Western monasticism. (See also **Benedictines**, following entry.)

Benedictines ● Order of St. Benedict (O.S.B.), meaning those men and women religious who follow the Rule of St. Benedict. One of the greatest monastic orders, the Benedictines were established in the sixth century in an effort to continue the highly influential example of monastic life set by St. Benedict of Nursia (c. 480-c. 550), creator of the famed rule and the founder of the monastery of Monte Cassino. He did not found an actual order, however, and the communities that were begun under the Benedictine Rule enjoyed autonomy, in a system still largely in place today. The early history of what would be called the Benedictine order was characterized by the spread of the rule and hence the development of monasticism throughout Europe. A major impetus for this was given by Pope St. Gregory I the Great (r. 590-604), himself a Benedictine, who sent out missionaries, most notably St. Augustine of Canterbury. Augustine brought the rule to England where it gradually replaced the more austere Rule of St. Columbanus and then returned to the Continent with the significant missionary St. Boniface (680-754), the Apostle of Germany.

Monasteries soon grew all over Western Europe — in France, England, Spain, Italy, and elsewhere; but the irregularity of their organization prompted Emperor Louis in 817 to decree that some kind of uniformity should be implemented. He thus commanded that the Benedictine Rule be adopted by monastic communities within the empire. While such a reform proved difficult owing to the independence claimed by the houses, most of the communities took to calling themselves Benedictines, although more often than not, they were known to the faithful simply as "monks." Reforms were undertaken in the ninth century to restore austerity to the monasteries; the chief figure in this was St. Benedict of Aniane (d. 821). A much more enduring reform came in the tenth century with the founding of the Abbey of Cluny by William of Aquitaine, an event that signaled the rise of other orders in the eleventh century (Carthusians, Cistercians, and Camaldolese) and a trend toward centralized monastic government, a much more severe rule than that of the Benedictines, and a general revival of monasticism in the West.

They resisted institutional centralization, despite the efforts of the Fourth Lateran Council (1215) and the bull *Benedictina* (1336) of Pope Benedict XII. Instead, the order adopted the system of congregations as a means of reform and revitalization. These national and even international unions of houses brought improved organization while permitting the retention of self-determination and identity. Among the more memorable congregations begun from the 1400s to the 1600s were those of St. Justina of Padua, Bursfeld in Germany, St. Vanne in Lorraine, and, most famous of all, the Congregation of St. Maur, the Maurists, started in 1621.

These reforms, of course, did not prevent the decline of monasticism that commenced toward the end of the Middle Ages and which would be hastened by the Renaissance and the events of the Reformation. Throughout the medieval era, however, the Benedictines had been a major influence in the preservation and then the advancement of learning in Christian Europe. The tradition of erudition and scholarship would never be lost. They were instrumental in preserving the flicker of culture and civilization in the West during the Dark Ages, and were, for centuries, virtually the sole possessors of learning and classical thought. The Benedictines suffered terribly in the Reformation and beyond. In England under King Henry VIII (r. 1509-1547), their monasteries were ruthlessly suppressed; the same was done in Germany and Scandinavia. In France, the Benedictines were crushed by the Revolution starting in 1789, oppression that would continue throughout the Napoleonic Wars, ending finally in 1815. The nineteenth century witnessed a revival, with new houses instituted in France (such as Solesmes, begun in 1833 by Prosper Guéranger) and England (at Downside and Ampleforth). The first Benedictine house was opened in the United States in Latrobe, Pennsylvania, in 1846. There are currently some ten thousand Benedictines worldwide, organized into a number of congregations, including the American, Cassinese, South American, English Benedictine, Camaldolese, Sylvestrine, Subiaco, and Olivetan. The Benedictine nuns (Benedictine Sisters of Pontifical Jurisdiction, O.S.B.), were founded in 529 by Benedict's sister, St. Scholastica. Their habit, like that of the monks, is black. They are organized into three federations: St. Scholastica, St. Gertrude the Great, and St. Benedict. The Benedictines have produced some twenty-three popes, including St. Gregory I the Great, St. Gregory VII (r. 1073-1085), and Pius VII (r. 1800-1823). (See also **Mabillon, Jean**.)

Benno, St. (c. 1010-c. 1106) ● Bishop of Meissen, the patron saint of Munich, and a largely legendary figure of whom little is known with any certainty. Born perhaps in Hildesheim, he served for a time as a canon in Goslar, becoming a bishop in 1066. He was imprisoned by Emperor Henry IV for remaining loyal to the papacy during the imperial-papal struggle of the time, and in 1085 he was deposed by the Synod of Mainz. After the death of Pope Gregory VII, however, Benno submitted and, through the intercession of the antipope Clement III, was restored to his see. Feast day: June 16.

Berengarius of Tours (c. 999-1088) ● Scholastic theologian and participant in the Eucharist Controversy in the eleventh century. Berengarius was a student of Fulbert of Chartres before becoming a canon of the cathedral school at St. Martin's in Tours around 1030, with whom his family was associated. In 1040, he was made archdeacon of Angers and then held various posts, including treasurer of Angers (1047) and so-called master of the schools (c. 1070). It was around 1040, however, that Berengarius began teaching ideas on the

Eucharist that ran counter to Church doctrine. For example, he opposed the model of transubstantiation of Paschasius Radbertus that the bread and wine actually became Christ at Mass, adopting instead the theory of Ratramnus of Corbie that the Real Presence of Christ was symbolic rather than literal. After a letter of his concerning this was read by Lanfranc at the Council of Rome in 1050, Berengarius was excommunicated. He recanted in 1054 (and again in 1059), but he apparently deserted this position, for several more trials and synods took place from 1076-1080. Around 1080, he retired to an island hermitage near Tours.

Bernadette Soubirous, St. (1844-1879) ●
In full, Marie Bernarde Soubirous, a French peasant girl who was granted a series of visions by the Blessed Virgin at Lourdes. Born to a poor family in Lourdes, France, she was named Bernadette as a child. Her early years were remarkably difficult owing to her poor health and the abject poverty of the household. She was considered to be a pleasant and innocent person but also backward and uneducated. On February 11, 1858, however, while she was gathering firewood on the banks of the Gave River, near her town, she beheld the BVM in a cave. Informing others, she was greeted with severe skepticism and much derision, but she followed Our Lady's instructions, faithfully appearing daily to receive visions. Local authorities treated her harshly. On February 25, a spring was caused to flow where previously there had been none, and on March 25, the vision proclaimed that she was the BVM, under the title "Immaculate Conception." After eighteen visitations, the phenomenon stopped and Bernadette was forced to endure the rigorous examination of the Church and the even more difficult scrutiny and insensitivity of the public. In 1866, she entered the Sisters of Notre Dame at Nevers. Her health, always weak, soon deteriorated, and she died after terrible suffering on April 16, 1879. Lourdes, meanwhile, emerged as one of the foremost pilgrim sites in Christendom, a development that took place entirely without impetus from Bernadette. Her canonization, in fact, by Pope Pius XI in 1933 was not for her visions at Lourdes (although the apparitions were fully approved) but for her remarkable life of humility and devotion. Feast day: April 16. (See also **Lourdes, Apparitions of**.)

Bernal, Agostino (1587-1642) ● Spanish Jesuit theologian. A native of Magallon in Spain, he entered the Society of Jesus in 1603. He thereafter devoted his life to two main endeavors: prayer and study. His reputation was of great standing at Saragossa where he taught philosophy and theology and was ranked the most learned man of his age.

Bernard of Chartres (1090-1153) ●
French Scholastic philosopher and humanist, the older brother of Thierry of Chartres. Bernard taught at Chartres from 1114, serving as chancellor there in 1119. Around 1124, he taught at Paris and had the distinction of teaching John of Salisbury. A brilliant Platonist, Bernard was a crucial figure in the establishing of the Platonic tradition at Chartres, authoring a study on Plato and Aristotle and treatises on the fourth-century Neoplatonist Porphyry. In his work *Metalogicon*, John of Salisbury called him "the perfect Platonist."

Bernard of Clairvaux, St. (1090-1153) ●
Abbot of Clairvaux, mystic, and an important figure in the history of the medieval Church. Bernard was born to a noble family in Fontaine, near Dijon, France. One of many children, he was chosen by his mother, Aleth, to enter the Church; her death influenced him deeply so that around the age of seventeen he left the school of Châtillon-sur-Seine and in 1113 entered the monastery of Cîteaux. Joining him at Cîteaux

were several brothers and many other young men eager for the monastic life. Bernard threw himself into the rigorous austerity of the community, declaring that "he was conscious of the need of my weak nature for strong medicine." His devotion to mortification, however, caused severe problems of health, especially as he had a weak constitution. Illness, aggravated by stern ascetic practices, would plague him for the rest if his life.

At Cîteaux, Bernard came under the instruction of the remarkable Abbot Stephen Harding, who in 1115 chose him to go forth and select a site for a new monastery. He chose Clairvaux, which was granted a charter by Pope Callistus II in 1119. It became a center for the Cistercian order and gained for Bernard widespread fame as a brilliant abbot and deeply respected mystic whose guidance was sought by many in the Church and secular governments. His influence was only heightened over the next years, as in 1128 he was secretary to the Synod of Troyes; in 1130, he assisted Pope Innocent II in overcoming the threat of Antipope Anicletus; and he preached tirelessly against heresies and to gather support for the Second Crusade. In defending Church orthodoxy, he spoke out against the onetime monk Henry of Lausanne and, most notably, against Peter Abelard, whose condemnation he secured in 1140 at the Council of Sens. In 1148, he condemned the writings of the theologian Gilbert de la Porrée. His last years were marked by severe disappointment over the failure of the crusade he had labored to mount. He died at Clairvaux.

One of the most powerful and influential leaders of the Middle Ages, Bernard's enormous authority stemmed not from his office but from his indomitable will, his active saintliness, and the example he provided to all who knew him. When Bernardo Pignatelli, abbot of the Cistercian house of Sts. Vincenzo and Anastasio, was elected as Pope Eugenius III (r. 1145-1153), Bernard sent him a treatise (*De consideratione*) on the proper duties of the pontiff and the problems facing him in the papal government. He wrote more than three hundred letters and sermons and other mystical treatises such as *De Diligendo Deo* (*On the Diligence of God*). Particularly beautiful was his sermon "On the Song of Songs." Criticized by some, including William of Champeaux, for extreme asceticism (it was said that he took to living away from the main community at Clairvaux because the other monks could not bear to look at his emaciated face and body), his devotion and mysticism, as expressed in his writings, are still held by many to be profound examples of how one individual could touch the lives of so many. He was unflinching in taking positions others deemed unpopular or unrelated to daily life — the call for prayer and the denunciation of the persecution of the Jews — characteristics that caused some to call him willful and hard. Canonized in 1174, he was given the title *Doctor Mellifluus* (the Honeysweet Doctor); Pope Pius VIII in 1830 named him a Doctor of the Church. Feast day: August 20.

Bernard of Cluny ● Twelfth-century Benedictine monk, also known as Bernard of Morval or Morlaix. He was a member of the famed monastery of Cluny during the time of the eighth abbot, Peter the Venerable. Aside from his devotional poem to the BVM and his sermons, Bernard was best known for his three-thousand-line poem *De Contempu Mundi* (*On Condemning the World*), composed around 1140. In the popular work, he attacked the immorality of the times and the evil of the material world, stressing the need for Christians to remember the transitory nature of their lives. His rather vivid ending, with a description of hell, may have influenced Dante in the writing of the *Divine Comedy.*

Bernard of Manthon, St. (d. 1081) ● Patron saint of mountain climbers who gave his name to the Great and Little St. Bernard Passes in the Alps. Originally a Savoyard cleric in the diocese of Aosta, Italy, he became archdeacon and worked thereafter to continue the advance of Christianity in the mountainous regions of Italy and Switzerland. He is best known for founding two hospices in the passes of Switzerland and Italy, places of refuge for travelers. These were so successful that the passes were named for him. He also gave his name to the St. Bernard rescue dog. Pope Pius XI named him patron saint of mountain climbers in 1923. Feast day: May 28.

Bernard of Pavia (d. 1213) ● Canonist and author of the *Breviarium Extravagantium*, a continuation of the *Decretum* by the brilliant canonist Gratian. Bernard served as the provost of the cathedral chapter of Pavia and in 1190 was named bishop of Faenza. In 1198, he was made bishop of Pavia. His *Breviarium* was completed around 1190. Intended to complete and update the *Decretum Gratiani*, the work was a massive compilation of decrees and important matters of ecclesiastical and judicial law. It was divided into five books, with one hundred fifty-two titles and nine hundred twelve chapters. Among the books' subjects are ecclesiastical jurisdiction, civil judicial processes, laws pertaining to clerics, matrimony, and ecclesiastical crimes. The *Breviarium* was very popular at the University of Bologna and was called the *Compilatio prima*, the first collection of law, after Gratian. (See also **Canon Law**.)

Bernardino of Siena, St. (1380-1444) ● Prominent Franciscan theologian and reformer, he was called the "Apostle of the Holy Name." Joining the Franciscans around 1402, he became a member of the Observants, those Franciscans who adhered devotely to the Rule of St. Francis. He began preaching in 1417, largely because he

desired to curb, if possible, the severe moral decline he saw around him in Italy. Within a short period, Bernardino was a major figure in social and religious reform. Pope Pius II declared that men and women listened to him as they would to St. Paul. Bernardino also promoted devotion to the Holy Name of Jesus and attended in 1439 the Council of Florence, with its furthering of the short-lived union of the Roman and Greek Churches. (See also **Franciscans**.)

Bernini, Giovanni Lorenzo (1598-1680) ● Italian baroque sculptor and architect. A native of Naples, Bernini studied sculpture with his father, soon attracting the attention and patronage of the Borghese family. His work for them, including "Apollo and Daphne" (1623-1624) and "David" (1623-1624), was to be highly influential in the development of baroque sculpture. Increasing notoriety brought him the patronage of Pope Urban VIII, for whom he produced the Baldacchino (1624-1633), the tomb of Urban (1628-1647), and the statue of "St. Longinus" (1629-1638), all in St. Peter's Basilica. His other great works in the Vatican are the "Cathedra Petri" (1657-1666; "The Chair of Peter") and, of course, the famed Bernini colonnade, enclosing the piazza of St. Peter's (1656-1667). The tomb of Alexander VII (1671-1678), in St. Peter's, was one of his last works. He also designed the royal staircase in the Vatican. Pope Urban, the former Maffeo Barberini, once reputedly remarked to the gifted artisan: "It is your great fortune, O Cavalier, to see Cardinal Barberini pope, but much greater is our own that the Cavalier Bernini lives during our pontificate." Despite being Urban's close friend, Bernini fell out of favor after bungling the construction of the towers planned for atop St. Peter's. (See also **St. Peter's Basilica**.)

Bernward, St. (d. 1022) ● Bishop of Hildesheim who helped promote cultural development in his German diocese. Bernward was a member of a powerful Saxon family in Germany, the grandson of Athelbero, count Palatine of Saxony. Educated at the cathedral school of Heidelberg, he became noted for his proficiency in mathematics, architecture, painting, and the mechanical arts. Ordained at Mainz, he was named in 987 chaplain to the imperial court and tutor to the future Emperor Otto III. In 993, he was elected bishop of Hildesheim. Under his episcopal leadership, Hildesheim received numerous churches and fortifications against the Normans (Norsemen), who were still plaguing parts of Germany and the North Sea. Bernward is also credited with designing the famed "Bernward Cross," the Bernward column — with reliefs depicting the life of Christ — and two bronze doors of the Cathedral of Hildesheim. Just before his death, he was invested with the Benedictine habit. Feast day: November 20.

Berthold (d. 1198) ● So-called Apostle of the Livonians who attempted to convert the devotedly pagan people of Livonia. The abbot of a Cistercian monastery at Lockum, in Hanover, Berthold was named around 1196 to be the successor of Meinhard, the recently deceased bishop of Livonia, in the ecclesiastical province of Bremen. Berthold adopted the same initial policy as his predecessor, using kindness in the hopes of converting the Livonians. This proved a failure, especially when Berthold attempted to bless the Christian cemetery of Holm. The Livonians erupted in full fury, and Berthold barely escaped to Lübeck with his life. He returned in 1198 with an army of crusading knights that had received the support of Pope Celestine III and then Innocent III. In the ensuing battles, Berthold was killed, traditionally said to have been killed by a lance thrust into his back. The Livonians, however, soon regretted their actions and many were converted by Berthold's

successor, Bishop Albert of Apeldern. Albert was assisted by the newly founded military order of the Brethren of the Sword.

Berthold of Henneberg (1441-1504) ● Archbishop and elector of Mainz, also known as Berthold of Mainz. A formidable reformer, he sought to bring both political and ecclesiastical changes to the Holy Roman Empire but was naturally opposed by the emperor. Educated at the University of Erfurt, he became canon of the Cathedral of Cologne in 1464 and archbishop of Mainz in 1484. Berthold, who was appointed chancellor of the Holy Roman Empire in 1493, proposed radical changes in the power structure of the empire by creating a seventeen-member council (Reichsrath), chosen by the electors and the estate, and a permanent high court. If adopted, the reforms would have reduced the emperor to a mere figurehead. Presented to Emperor Maximilian by the nobles at the Diet of Worms in 1495, the plan was rejected. Later accepted under threat of financial penalties, Maximilian connived to ensure that no court or council members were paid, and soon both bodies ceased to convene and so disappeared as effective bodies of reform. Berthold's ecclesiastical reforms were urged upon the clergy and religious orders.

Berthold of Ratisbon (1210-1272) ● Franciscan monk who became one of the most powerful speakers for reform in the 1200s. A native of Ratisbon, Berthold was probably a member of a reasonably well-off family, entering the Franciscans at a mature age. In 1246, he was named, along with David of Augsburg, an inspector of the convent of Niedermunster. By 1250, he had earned a good reputation in Bavaria for his sermons, broadening his preaching over the next years throughout the Rhine Valley, Alsace, and into Switzerland. He later preached in Austria and Silesia and in 1263 was named by Pope Urban IV to preach a crusade. Albert the Great was his assistant. Called by contemporaries "the teacher of nations" and "sweet Brother Berthold," Brother Berthold and his sermons were largely forgotten in succeeding centuries. In his time, however, his eloquence spoke to people of all classes, calling them to true repentance, a salvation that must come from the heart to be sincere and of which pilgrimages and absolutions were mere outward symbols.

Bérulle, Pierre de (1575-1629) ● French cardinal and statesman, founder of the Oratory, and an important figure in the reform and revival of the Church in the seventeenth century in France. Born at Sérilly, near Troyes, he was ordained in 1599 and thereafter labored to convert Protestants in France to the Church and to bring about genuine reform of the clergy. Inspired by his cousin, the mystic Madame Acarie, he journeyed to Spain in 1604 and returned with seven nuns who were to establish, with his help, the Order of the Discalced Carmelites in France. In 1611, Bérulle himself founded the Oratory and received papal approval under the name Oratoire de Jesus-Christ in 1613. The Oratory was a congregation of priests that was intended to improve the standing of the clergy among the public. New seminaries were created, theology promoted, and teaching and sermons improved. The Oratory would serve as a model for other congregations — Lazarists, Eudists, and Sulpicians — just as it was inspired by the Oratory of St. Philip Neri that had been founded in 1564. Bérulle worked with Cardinal Richelieu in the suppression of the Protestants of La Rochelle (1627-1628) but broke with him over Richelieu's policy toward Spain and support of Protestants in Germany because they desired to curb the power of the Habsburgs, something Richelieu was also eager to effect. Made a cardinal in 1627, Bérulle spent most of his last years out of favor at the court of King Louis XIII.

Bessarion, John (c. 1395-1472) ● Greek scholar, cardinal, and statesman. One of the foremost figures in the rise of the intellectual Renaissance in the 1400s, Bessarion was born at Trebizond and educated at Constantinople. Becoming a Basilian monk in 1423, he studied under Georgius Plethon (c. 1431-1436), the famed Renaissance scholar, and attempted to unite two systems of Platonism and Aristotelianism. In 1437, Emperor John VIII Palaeologus made him archbishop of Nicaea. He subsequently accompanied the emperor to Italy where he participated in the Councils of Ferrara and Florence in 1439 that were intended to unite the Eastern and Western Churches. At the councils, and because of his reputation for learning, Bessarion was made a cardinal in 1439. He settled in Italy where he was nearly elected pope and labored ceaselessly to revive classical learning and promote Greek studies. With the fall of Constantinople in 1453, scholars from the Byzantine Empire flocked to his patronage. He also served as governor of Bologna (1450-1455) and was papal ambassador to several courts, including France. His collection of eight hundred manuscripts, most in Greek, was given to the senate of Venice in 1468; it was the basis of the *Bibliotheca Marciana*. In his time, Bessarion was the most respected Greek scholar in the West.

Bethlehemites ● Name given to several orders that did not survive into the twentieth century. The first was apparently founded in England during the 1200s. Located at Cambridge, it was devoted to military service in the name of Our Lady of Bethlehem. Its existence was noted by the chronicler Matthew Paris. Another military order was established during the reign of Pope Pius II (1458-1464) devoted to the BVM of Bethlehem. It was intended to defend the area of the Aegean against the Ottoman Turks after the fall of Constantinople in 1453.

Bethune, David ● See **Beaton, David**.

Bible ● Collection of books accepted by the Christian Church as bearing witness to God's plan for human salvation and as a record of the revelation made by God to humanity. The Bible is divided into two large sections: the OT, assembled by the Hebrews; and the NT, collected by the members of the Christian faith after Christ had walked upon the earth. The name Bible is derived from the Greek *biblia* (plural for a collection of books; singular: *byblos*, or papyrus) and the Latin *biblia* (book). Testament is from the Latin *testamentum* (testament or covenant). It is also called Sacred Scripture; in Catholic teaching, Sacred Scripture is united with Sacred Tradition as the expression of the revelation of God's will and person.

The OT was composed between the twelfth and second centuries B.C., and is an amalgamation of historical, legal, poetic, prophetic, and cultic literature. It was written mainly in Hebrew and Greek, with portions of some books in Aramaic (e.g., Jer 10-11; Ezr 4:8—6:18, 7:26; Dn 2:4—7:8). Christian interpretation of the OT declares that the rich accounts it offers of the struggles, triumphs, obedience, and journeys of the Jewish people provide a foreshadowing of the mission and revelation brought by Christ. The NT was written completely in Greek. From the earliest days of the Church, however, the question arose as to what books could be considered authentic sources of divine revelation and which ones could be set aside as lacking in divine inspiration.

The Canon of the Bible: The Church teaches that certain books are to be considered canonical, meaning that they are recognized as divinely inspired. It was first used as a term by Origen in the third century when referring to the Sacred Scriptures, finding affirmation in the writings of St.

Athanasius (d. 373), who gave the term common currency among subsequent writers. Early Christians differentiated canonical and noncanonical books of the Bible, describing them as *homologoumenoi* (accepted) and *antilegomenoi* (contested or questioned). In the 1500s, it became common practice to call these classifications protocanonical and deuterocanonical respectively. The deuterocanonical books (and certain fragments) of the OT are: Judith, Tobias, Sirach, Wisdom, 1 and 2 Machabees, and Baruch; also Daniel 3:24-90; 13; 14; and Esther 10:4-16; 24. The NT books or fragments are: Epistle to the Hebrews; Epistle of James; Epistle of Jude; 2 Peter; 2 and 3 John; Revelation; and Mark 16:9-20; also Luke 22:43; and John 5:4; 8:1-11. Customarily, the Protestants consider these to be apocryphal works; the Church, however, views them to be divinely inspired.

At the council in 1546, the Council Fathers gave formal definition of the Canon of the Bible (while declaring the Vulgate to be authentic), promulgating a list of the books accepted as entirely canonical in the decree *Sacrosancta*: in the OT there are forty-five books; the NT has twenty-seven books. The complete list as declared by the Council of Trent follows.

Old Testament: Genesis, Exodus, Leviticus, Numbers, Deuteronomy, Joshua, Judges, Ruth, 1, 2, 3, and 4 Kings, 1 and 2 Paralipomenon, 1 and 2 Esdras (also Nehemiah), Tobias, Esther, Job, Psalms, Proverbs, Ecclesiastes, Canticle of Canticles, Wisdom, Ecclesiasticus (Sirach), Isaias, Jeremiah, Lamentations, Baruch, Ezechiel, Daniel, Osee, Joel, Amos, Abdia, Jona, Micheas, Nahum, Habacuc, Sophonias, Aggeus, Zacharias, Malachias, 1 and 2 Machabees.

New Testament: The four Gospels — Matthew, Mark, Luke, and John; Acts of the Apostles; Epistles of Paul, which are Romans, 1 and 2 Corinthians, Galatians, Ephesians, Philippians, Colossians, 1 and 2

Thessalonians, 1 and 2 Timothy, Titus, Philemon, and Hebrews; 1 and 2 Peter; 1, 2, and 3 John, James; Jude, and Revelation.

In issuing the decree, the Fathers added: "The council follows the example of the orthodox Fathers and with the same sense of devotion and reverence with which it accepts and venerates all the books of both of the Old and New Testaments, since one God is the author of both; it also accepts and venerates traditions concerned with faith and morals as having been received orally from Christ or inspired by the Holy Spirit and continuously preserved in the Catholic Church."

In the early Church, there was no list of books accepted as canonical. Christ and then the Apostles did not provide any kind of authoritative statement as to what books might be consulted, but throughout the NT there are some three hundred quotations from the OT writings, in cooperation or agreement with the Septuagint. The choice of citations and allusions to deuterocanonical books is taken by scholars to imply that Christian writers of the apostolic era were moving away from the Jewish community and were adopting the Septuagint (or the LXX), which would be translated from the Greek into the Latin by St. Jerome (d. 420). The Christian thus chose not to embrace the Canon of the Jewish OT; this Palestinian canon would be formalized in the year 90 by the rabbinical synod at Jamnia, which included twenty-four books. Despite the lists formulated by Origen and others, the Septuagint canon was used by Augustine; he thus influenced the Councils of Hippo (393) and Carthage (397 and 416). This Greek canon was translated by Jerome and was approved by Pope St. Innocent I (r. 401-417). Further affirmation was given over

Bible illustration

succeeding centuries, culminating with the official decree of the Council of Trent.

The Canon of the NT developed slowly and was a complex literary and historical process. The books of the NT were written by the Apostles or their disciples after the crucifixion of Christ and his subsequent resurrection and ascension. They are testaments to the life and soteriological undertaking of Christ and to the spread of the Church that he established on earth. Completed before the death of the Apostle John in 100, they are divided into accounts of Christ's life and the birth of the Church, epistles or letters (separated into the Pauline and Pastoral Letters), and an enigmatic set of prophecies (Revelation). The formation of recognized and accepted canonical writings by the Church was hindered by a number of factors, including the sheer size of the Roman Empire with its attendant communication problems, the lack of cohesion among the early churches, the difficulties of copying the books and epistles, and the rise of heretical or unorthodox sects each often producing bodies of apocryphal literature. Church leadership, however, was able to determine within a short time what was divinely inspired, and discussions came to center on those books of a deuterocanonical nature. These were adopted and it is possible to see in the lists from the fourth century a near universal agreement on the canon.

The first lists of the NT canon appear during the time of Marcion, the second-century heretical leader. He rejected the OT and approved only of portions of the NT writings; the others he would not tolerate because of their Jewishness. He was opposed by St. Irenaeus (d. 200) and others. Various lists appeared in succeeding years, but, as noted, uniformity was well in place by 350, receiving impetus for the NT canon from the aforementioned Councils of Hippo and Carthage and from St. Augustine. St. Jerome translated all twenty-seven books as part of the Vulgate. In the East, meanwhile, there was doubt as to the canonicity of the following: 2 Peter, 2 and 3 John, Jude, and Revelation. These doubts led the Syrian Churches to adopt a canon of only twenty-two books.

Versions of the Bible: As one of the most important books in the history of the world (with respect to the non-Judaeo-Christian faiths), the Bible has been translated into a staggering number of languages. As has been pointed out, the OT was composed in Hebrew, Greek, and partly in Aramaic, while the NT was written entirely in Greek. The current extant Hebrew manuscripts of the OT dating to the pre-Christian period are preserved with the Dead Sea Scrolls (recently made available for the first time for display in the Vatican). The two most notable early translations of the OT Bible were into Greek and Latin, the Septuagint and Vulgate respectively.

Within the Jewish community following the exile of the Jews (580 B.C.), Hebrew ceased to be the common tongue. It was replaced by Aramaic and then, during the ascendancy in the Mediterranean world in the fourth century of Hellenic culture, by Greek. For Aramaic speakers, translations were made normally after readings in the synagogue. These translations were named Targums (or Targumic literature) and varied from careful following of original texts to slight differences in readings. More influential was the translation of the Hebrew OT into Greek, the Septuagint (or LXX), named after the seventy (thus LXX) scholars who worked on it. (For details, see **Septuagint**.)

Unfortunately, the first texts, called autographs, of the writers of the NT are not extant and so experts are forced to use the earliest surviving manuscripts and other sources (such as quotations or citations in early writings by Church Fathers) to determine the original content of the first works. The earliest NT manuscripts are papyri, such as the Chester Beatty collection, preserved in the British Museum. With the rise of the Christian Church as a recognized, legitimate institution, it was feasible (both in terms of time and cost) to authorize copies not just of the NT but the entire Greek Bible. These were no longer on papyrus but on parchment, and the most famous were *Codex Alexandrinus, Codex Sinaiticus,* and the *Codex Vaticanus.* (See also **Codex**.)

It was inevitable that the Bible should be translated into Latin in a world essentially ruled by the Roman Empire and in whose Latin culture the Church was flourishing. Vernacular (Latin) translations began appearing almost coincidentally with the penetration of the faith into provinces where Greek was not commonly spoken or where

Latin customs predominated. Interestingly, Greek remained the language of the Church in Rome as late as the third century, a fact attested by the preponderance of Greek-named pontiffs, or Bishops of Rome (for example, Telesphorus, Soter, and Eleutherius). The Latin versions are found in parts of Gaul and North Africa in the second century, and others soon followed. There were considerable differences in editions, and the variety of the manuscripts were a source of frustration to biblical scholars in the Church, including St. Jerome. He was asked by Pope Damasus in 382 to undertake a revision of the Gospels, which he completed by 384. Jerome then launched into a massive translation of the Bible from Greek and Hebrew into Latin, working from around 390-405. His monumental work was called the Vulgate, from the Latin *vulgus* (people) or *vulgaris* (coarse or common), a reference to the fact that it would be read by the common people, who did not speak or read Greek, the language of the learned. The Vulgate was adopted as the recognized and official text of Sacred Scripture for the Christian Church and was so proclaimed by the Council of Trent on April 8, 1546. This was reaffirmed by Pope Pius XII in 1943 in the encyclical *Divino afflante Spiritu*. It was first printed in 1456 with the so-called Gutenberg or Mazarin Bible.

The Bible today is found in a host of English versions, from the translations of the Jerusalem Bible, to the Douai-Reims Bible (still very popular), to the King James Version, to the Reader's Digest Bible (abridged version), to the Gideon Bible. The earliest surviving translation of parts of the Bible into formative English was done supposedly by Caedmon who, in the late seventh century, attempted to paraphrase passages of the Scriptures. Other work included the Lindisfarne Gospels, the translations of part of the Gospel of John by the Venerable Bede, and the Paris Psalter with its translations of parts of the Psalms.

The language used by the Anglo-Saxons would be virtually unrecognizable today, save by those with training in old English. After the Norman Conquest of England in 1066, the dominant language of translation was French (from the 1100s to the 1300s), becoming the so-called Anglo-Norman dialect during the fourteenth century. Important work was carried out in the late 1300s by the followers of John Wycliffe (d. 1384) within the Lollard movement, but scholars do not accept the traditional or popular belief that Wycliffe was the first person to translate the entire Bible into English.

Numerous English versions were translated and printed during the Reformation, and such works were an important activity of the Reformation in England under King Henry VIII (r. 1509-1547) and his ministers. Subsequent versions would include the so-called Authorized Version (called also the King James Version), launched by King James of England in 1611. Notable Catholic vernacular Bibles, based on the Vulgate, are the Douai-Reims, Challoner Revision, and Knox Bible. Two editions approved for the liturgy are the New American Bible and the New Revised Standard Version.

Biblical Commission ● See **Pontifical Biblical Commission**.

Biblioteca Apostolica Vaticana ● See **Vatican Library**.

Bickell, Gustav (1838-1906) ● Austrian patristic scholar. Converted to Catholicism in 1865, Bickell was ordained in 1867 and elected to professorships in Innsbruck (1874) and Vienna (1892). His chief writings were on Isaac of Antioch (1873-1877) and editions of St. Ephraem's *Carmina Nisibena* (1866).

Biel, Gabriel (c. 1420-1495) ● Philosopher, scholar, and theologian, called *Ultimus Scholasticorum* (Last of the

Scholastics) because he was one of the final scholastic intellectuals of the Middle Ages. Biel was educated at Heidelburg and Erfurt, serving around 1460 as vicar of Mainz. In 1468, he joined the Brethren of the Common Life at Butzbäch; he was prior there in 1470 and at Urach in 1479. He was then instrumental in the founding of the University of Tübingen, with the help of Count Eberhard of Württemberg, and served there as professor of theology. A devoted adherent of William of Occam, Biel earned such respect from Occamists at Erfurt and Wittenberg that they called themselves Gabrielistae. His writings included the *Collectorum circa IV Libros Sententiarum*, a commentary on the *Sentences* of Peter Lombard.

Biondo, Flavio (1392-1463) ● Known in the Latin as Flavius Biondus, an influential Italian humanist, historian, and archaeologist, the first writer to recognize the Middle Ages as the intervening period between classical times and the Renaissance. Born at Forli, he received an excellent education at Cremona but spent years in exile for various offenses in Imola, Ferrara, and Venice. In 1433, however, he moved to Rome and was named secretary to the Roman Curia. He was later a papal diplomat to Venice and Francesco Sforza. His two most important works are: *Italia illustrata* (1448-c. 1460) examining Italian history and geography from classical Rome to contemporary events; and the forty-two-volume *Historiarum*, examining European history from the sack of Rome in 410 to around 1442. Known in full as the *Historiarum ab inclinatione Romane imperii decades* (1439-1463; *Decades of History from the Deterioration of the Roman Empire*), his work laid the basis for the term Middle Ages and made Biondo a founder of modern historiography. Both writings preserved useful materials on the history and figures of Church history.

Birth Control ● Euphemism used to describe the process of contraception by which conception and/or birth are deliberately prevented by a variety of means. Also known as onanism, from the sin of Onan (Gn 38:8-10), birth control can involve sterilization, abortion, or one or a combination of contraceptive methods. Actual methods can vary from simple withdrawal to the adoption of the most up-to-date medical techniques and inventions such as the implant or the RU-486 drug. Condoms, contraceptive pills, and numerous devices are the most common methods today in most of the developed countries; in those areas of Eastern Europe where prophylactics are either unobtainable or far too expensive, abortion is a regular form of birth control, with some women having over a dozen abortions.

From its earliest days, the Church has been adamant in its teachings against abortion and birth control. The unaltered and uncompromising position of the Church has been based on the important purpose of contraception — namely to prevent conception or birth, thereby rendering sexual intercourse merely an act of lust, destroying the sacred, God-given act of procreation within the natural boundary of marriage, and creating the atmosphere in which abortion becomes increasingly likely when contraception fails. Birth control implies a lack of trust in God, who made all humanity and granted the gift of human life as the result of the natural procreative act between married persons who desire children. The Church teaches that each sexual act must be open to the creation of new life. Couples should thus be aware that contraception violates this necessity by making impossible the very purpose of the marriage act.

The Church was faced in the first century with a Roman culture that considered contraception, abortion, and even infanticide to be normal and commonly used methods of family planning (in a primitive sense). Roman law, for example, permitted exposing babies or young children to the elements (infanticide), an act considered utterly abhorrent to the members of the Christian community, who recognized the essential need for the reverencing of human life. The early teaching guide of the *Didache* included the specific stricture "You shall not use magic (a term for contraception). You shall not destroy a newborn child." This was soon joined by other exhortations, such as the treatise *Paidagogos* by St. Clement of Alexandria, which observed that to engage in sexual intercourse without intending children is an outrage to nature, from which we ought to take instruction. The subsequent years brought condemnation from Origen, Ambrose, Jerome, and especially Augustine, all of whom gave further body to the principles underlying Church teaching.

In the modern era, with the proliferation of contraceptive methods and a sociopolitical culture that often encourages promiscuity and an abortion-birth control mind-set, the Church has been severely challenged in presenting its unchanging teaching in the face of louder and more ubiquitous media outlets. As Pope Paul VI (r. 1963-1978) noted, however, "How many times have we trembled before the alternatives of an easy condescension to current opinions?" Pope Pius XI (r. 1922-1939) wrote in his encyclical *Casti connubii* (1930) that "any use of marriage, whatever, in the exercise of which the act is deprived through human industry of its natural power of procreating life, violates the law of God and nature. . . ." On July 29, 1968, Pope Paul VI issued the famous encyclical *Humanae vitae*, reiterating Church teaching and proclaiming all forms of contraception to be condemned, adding, "Similarly included is every action that, in anticipation of the conjugal act, or in its accomplishment, or in the development of its natural consequences, purposes, whether as an end or as a means, to render procreation impossible." Pope John Paul II has been even

more vocal in arguing against birth control, condemning it not only on its own merits but as part of a broader philosophical question of respect for human life and the need for all individuals to recognize the inherent worth, value, and sacredness of each person.

Bishop ● See GLOSSARY.

Bishop, Edmund (1846-1917) ● English historian and liturgist, noted for his contribution to the study of the history of the Roman rite and liturgy. Educated at Exeter and in Belgium, Bishop served for a time as the secretary to the Scottish historian and essayist Thomas Carlyle and worked in the government from 1864-1885. In 1867, he became a convert to Catholicism, expressing a desire to join a monastery, at Downside Abbey, after his government service ended in 1885; ill health prevented him from actually joining, however. Through his association with Downside, he came to know and befriend Cardinal Francis Gasquet. With Gasquet, he published *Edward VI and the Book of Common Prayer* in 1890. This was followed by a study of early English calendars (1908) and assorted liturgical studies (1909). He also authored a paper, delivered in May 1899, to the Historical Research Society on "The Genius of the Roman Rite," and conducted remarkable researches into the Roman liturgy, particularly the history of the Gregorian Sacramentary.

Bishop of Rome ● One of the titles of the pope and an important element in his primacy over the universal Church. The conclave that assembles to elect a new pope is, in fact, choosing a new bishop of Rome, the successor to St. Peter in that episcopal see. Peter established the see of Rome in A.D. 42 and, as he had been the recipient of the "keys of the kingdom of heaven" (Mt 16:19) from Christ, and was declared the rock on which Our Lord would build his Church, the successor to Peter would receive that divinely appointed power and authority. The Bishop of Rome thus possessed primacy over the Church and is the undisputed head of the College of Bishops. Beyond this broad undeniable position of the pontiff is the more local authority of the pope, namely that of Bishop of Rome. As head of the Church in the Eternal City, the pope has responsibility over the parishes of Rome and, regardless of nationality, is viewed as a kind of revered possession of the Romans. The diocesan Church of Rome is the Lateran Basilica, the Basilica San Giovanni Laterano. (See also **Primacy of the Pope**.)

Bishop, William ● See **Appellant Controversy**.

Black Canons ● Term used to designate members of the Augustinian Canons. It was also applied during the Middle Ages to describe the Benedictine monks, although the more common term for them was Black Monks.

Black Friars ● Term used, especially during the Middle Ages, to describe the members of the Dominican order (The Order of the Friars Preachers). It was derived from the fact that the friars wear a black cape, or *cappa*, and a black cowl over their white, or off-white, tunic when in choir or in public.

Black Monks ● Name used during the Middle Ages for the members of the Benedictine order (O.S.B.), derived from their black religious habit. (See also **Grey Friars, Grey Nuns,** and **White Friars**.)

Blackwell, George ● See **Appellant Controversy**.

Blondel, Maurice (1861-1947) ● In full, Maurice Edward Blondel, a French philosopher who formulated the so-called "philosophy of action" that attempted to integrate Neoplatonism and modern pragmatism in the broader context of Christian doctrine. Blondel was a native of Dijon. Educated at the École Normale, he served as a professor of philosophy at Montaubon, Lille, and Aix-Marseille. His principal writings were *L'action* (1893), *La Pensée* (2 vols., 1934; *Thought*), *Histoire et Dogme* (1904; *History and Dogma*), *Le Probleme de la philosophie catholique* (1932; *The Problem of the Catholic Philosophy*), and *Exigences philosophiques de Christianisme* (1950; *The Philosophical Demands of Christianity*). He was of considerable influence in Modernism and modern philosophy.

Boethius (c. 480-c. 524) ● Roman philosopher, statesman, and theologian, one of the last great philosophers of the Roman tradition who made contributions to the preservation of classical knowledge and learning. Known in full as Anicius Manlius Torquatus Severinus Boethius, he was a member of the ancient Roman family of the Anicii, receiving a thorough education at Athens and Alexandria. Named in 510 as consul under the Ostrogothic king Theodoric, he became *magister officiorum* (master of the offices) by 520, a post of immense political power. He soon fell out of favor, however, most likely because of his strongly orthodox views on Christianity, thus placing him in opposition with Theodoric. When Boethius defended the ex-consul Albinus on the charge of treason, Theodoric had him imprisoned, condemned, and executed. While in prison, Boethius wrote his most famous work, *De Consolatione Philosophiae* (*The Consolation of Philosophy*). In it, he argued that knowledge of virtue and God were attainable by the study of philosophy. The work was to be very popular in succeeding years and made him a major figure in the development of medieval philosophy. Questions as to whether Boethius was really a Christian were answered by Boethius's own treatises on the

Trinity (*De Sancti Trinitate*) and a biography by Cassiodorus. He also wrote translations of Aristotle, *Isagoge* by Porphyry, and a commentary on the *Topics* of Cicero. He has been considered a martyr for the Catholic faith.

Bogomils ● Name given to a heretical sect that first appeared in Bulgaria during the tenth century, surviving in some parts of the Balkans until the 1400s. The Bogomils were founded by Bogomile, a name probably derived from a Bulgarian translation of Theophilus, or "Beloved of God." Bogomile lived in the first half of the tenth century, giving his name to the subsequent movement. The Bogomils preached a version of neo-Manichaeism, holding that the material world was created by the devil and the spiritual by God. Based on this, they condemned numerous Christian doctrines, including baptism, the Eucharist, marriage, and especially the Incarnation. Churches and clergy were especially attacked. The sect became widely popular by 1100 and was particularly large in the Byzantine Empire, most notably in Constantinople. Such were their numbers, in fact, that Emperor Alexius I Comnenus ordered a pogrom. Their leader, Basil, was burned to death, many others executed, and still more imprisoned. The sect soon prospered elsewhere, in Bosnia where, from the 1100s to the 1400s, it became a national movement, being curbed only by a decree by the Bosnian state in 1450 enforcing Christian orthodoxy. When the Ottoman Turks conquered the Balkans in the second half of the fifteenth century, many Bogomils were converted to Islam. The Bogomils were influential in the evolution of a number of heretical sects in the Middle Ages, including the Cathars and Albigensians. (See also **Heresy**.)

Bohemia ● See **Czechoslovakia**.

Bohemian Brethren ● Also later known as the *Unitas Fratrum* and the Moravian Brethren, a splinter group of the Utraquists of Bohemia who broke from that radical religious body and established themselves as an independent sect in 1467. Their break came under the leadership of one "Brother Gregory," who espoused a desire for all brethren to adhere to the teachings of Peter Chelcicky (d. 1460). They stressed strict asceticism, a simple form of Christian worship, and rejected living in towns and ownership of private property. Under the guidance of Lukas of Prague, the Bohemian Brethren were reorganized as a formal Church, the previous writings of Chelcicky and Lukas condemned by the Synod of Rychnov. The Brethren spread successfully under Lukas, although their efforts to become joined with the Lutherans were not possible until 1542, after Lukas's death in 1528. Oppressed by Emperor Ferdinand, they settled in large numbers in Poland where they united with the Calvinists at the Synod of Kozminek in 1555. Those who remained in Bohemia were granted their religious freedom in 1575; in 1609, Rudolf I gave them the University of Prague. Many of them, however, had migrated to Moravia where they became known as the Moravian Brethren. Caught up in the religious strife of the Thirty Years' War (1618-1648), they were exiled with their bishop in 1620 following the Battle of White Mountain. The Brethren endured for another century and were ultimately amalgamated with the founder of the Herrnhuter, Nikolaus Ludwig von Zinzendorf.

Bollandists ● Name given to the Dutch Jesuit editors of the *Acta Sanctorum* (or *Acts of the Saints*), named after the founder and first editor of the work, Rev. John Bolland (1596-1665). The Bollandists had their origins in the efforts of Heribert Rosweyde (d. 1629) to organize a mammoth and critical version of the lives of the saints. He did not survive to see any of the work actually published, but Bolland continued his great labors. Bolland was assisted after 1635 by his famous pupil Godefroid Henschenius, and much progress was made in organizing and editing the huge collection of materials. The archives, libraries, and collections of religious houses were visited and carefully studied for all information and useful sources they might provide. Finally, in 1643, the first of the volumes was published to great acclaim. Work continued after Bolland's death in 1665 and received much support from a number of popes, most notably Alexander VII (r. 1655-1667) and Benedict XIV (r. 1740-1758). A museum was also established in Antwerp to house the material that had been gathered for the *Acts*. The work of the Bollandists was suspended when the Jesuits were suppressed in Belgium in 1773, but work began again in 1837 or 1840. The Bollandists continue to work on the *Acts*. A supplement, the *Analecta Bollandiana*, has been published since 1882.

Bologna, Concordat of ● Agreement signed in 1516 between Pope Leo X and King Francis I of France that effectively ended the Pragmatic Sanction of Bourges (originally issued in 1438). By the terms of the concordat, the French king received extensive control over Church appointments in France. He was able to nominate candidates to cathedral and metropolitan churches, abbeys, and other posts. Papal confirmation was not to be refused so long as the king took pains to adhere to the specific rules of nomination. In cases, however, where two invalid nominations were made for a post, the right of appointment to that office passed to the pope. The concordat remained in effect until 1790 and the difficult time of the French Revolution.

Bolsec, Hieronymus (d. 1584) ● Reformation theologian who waged a bitter feud with John Calvin at Geneva. Also known as Jerome-Hermes Bolsec, he was originally a Carmelite friar at Paris. Accepting many Protestant doctrines, he was forced to flee to Italy, where he worked as a physician and received the protection of the duchess of Ferrara. Moving to Chablais, he came to know John Calvin and was soon studying his Reformist teachings. Bolsec, however, disagreed vehemently with Calvin over predestination. He journeyed to Geneva in October 1551 and publicly challenged Calvin. Arrested and imprisoned, Bolsec received surprising support from the Swiss Churches of Basel, Zurich, and Berne, but Calvin's position was such that on December 22, 1551, Bolsec was banished for life from Geneva. Bolsec then launched a highly personal and vicious series of attacks on Calvin, authoring the hostile biography of Calvin (1577). He eventually returned to the Church shortly before his death.

Bolshevism ● See under **Communism** and **Soviet Union**.

Bonald, Louis Jacques Maurice de (1787-1870) ● French cardinal who was a distinguished member of the French Church in the nineteenth century. The fourth son of the statesman and philosopher Vicomte de Bonald, he was ordained in 1811 and attached to the imperial chapel. Following the Restoration of the King (Louis XVIII) in 1815, he served as secretary to Archbishop de Presigny, Louis's representative to Rome in negotiating a new concordat with the Holy See. In 1823, Bonald was made the first bishop of the reestablished see of Puy. Here he labored for sixteen years until his promotion to the primatial see of Lyons (1839). In 1842, he was made a cardinal by Pope Gregory XVI. As a prelate, he worked to destroy the last vestiges of Jansenism and Gallicanism, convened a provincial synod in 1850 to examine Church government, and promoted discipline among the clergy. He was also one of the first bishops in France to speak out in favor of the Revolution of 1848 because of its declaration of *Liberté, Egalité, et Fraternité.* Throughout, however, Bonald was a stern defender of Church rights and the papacy.

Bonaventure, St. (1221-1274) ●

Franciscan theologian, cardinal, and Doctor of the Church. Bonaventure is also called the second founder of the Franciscan order. He was born Giovanni di Fidanza near Viterbo, Italy, joining the Franciscans in 1238 or 1243. Studying at the University of Paris, he claimed as one of his instructors Alexander of Hales. In 1248, he began teaching in Paris, his studies continuing for a number of years during which time he demonstrated himself to be a great preacher and a profound theologian, one of the foremost in Christendom; he was ranked with the renowned Dominican St. Thomas Aquinas, who was to become a good friend. His advancement to the degree of doctor of theology was delayed for several years owing to the severe disagreement that took place at the University of Paris between the secular professors and the mendicant orders. Finally, in October 1257, he was granted his doctorate; he received the degree on the same day as Thomas Aquinas. That same year, he was elected minister-general of the order.

Bonaventure proved a brilliant general, working tirelessly to restore the Franciscans to a united, dynamic order, by ending the factious controversies among members caused by the desires of some to adhere to strict poverty in keeping with the example of St. Francis and the call by others for less stringent standards. His labors were codified in 1260 and proved so remarkable that he was given the title Second Founder. In 1263, he wrote a new life of St. Francis. This became the approved, official biography of the great saint and was declared in 1266 to replace all previous biographies. A highly respected and influential Church figure, he declined the archiepiscopal see of York in

1265 but was instrumental in securing the election of Tedaldo Visconti to the papal dignity as Pope Gregory X (r. 1271-1276), thereby ending an interregnum of three years. Gregory made Bonaventure a cardinal in 1273, sending several legates to him with the red hat. When they arrived with the symbol of great honor, they found him washing dishes. He asked them to hang the red hat on a nearby tree, since his hands were wet and dirty. The hat subsequently became his symbol. Summoned to the Council of Lyons in 1274, he took an active part in the negotiations with the Eastern Church on reunion. He died during the proceedings.

A gifted theologian and philosopher, he was the author of numerous works including *Itinerarium mentis ad Deum* (*Journey of the Mind to God*), *De Reductione Artium ad Theologiam* (*On the Reduction of the Arts to Theology*), and *Breviloquium* (*A Short Treatise*); he also wrote various religious works and a commentary on the *Sentences* of Peter Lombard. Bonaventure was a dedicated adherent of Augustinianism, rejecting many of the elements of Aristotelian thought that played such an important role in the body of writings developed by St. Thomas Aquinas. He believed that philosophy in the advanced form of metaphysics is not possible without the supernatural light of faith. He thus felt that pagan philosophers, unexposed to faith, were not reliable sources for the study of metaphysics. While, as a good Augustinian, he was willing to accept a number of Platonic principles, he found Aristotle to be ill-suited for metaphysical study. He thus came into conflict with Thomas Aquinas, although he acknowledged some Aristotelian points, and his relationship with Thomas remained cordial. Canonized in 1482 by Sixtus IV, he was made a Doctor of the Church in 1588 by Sixtus V. Feast day: July 15.

Bonet, Nicholas (d. 1360) ● Friar Minor,

theologian, and a noted traveler to the court

of the Mongol ruler Kublai Khan. Bonet was probably French by birth. He taught at the University of Paris with such distinction in theology that he was given the name *Doctor Pacificus* (the Peaceful Doctor), the result of his tranquil and ever measured style of lecturing. He participated in the controversy of the time concerning the beatific vision that was then raging during the pontificate of John XXII, a matter settled by the decree *Benedictus Deus*, promulgated by John's successor Benedict XII. It was Benedict who chose Bonet as a member of the papal embassy to be sent to Kublai Khan, master of the Mongol Empire and grandson of Genghis Khan, to follow up on the progress made by John of Monte Corvino and Giovanni Pianô Carpini (or John da Pian del Carpine). The delegation departed Avignon in 1338, ultimately reaching Beijing in 1342. After four years of visiting various Christian settlements in the domain of the Mongols, the papal representatives headed home in 1346. They arrived at Avignon in 1354. Shortly after his return, Bonet was made titular bishop of Mileve, in recognition of his long journeying for the Church. He was also author of several theological treatises, including a commentary on the *Sentences*.

Boniface, St. (680-754) ● Apostle of Germany, an English missionary who was responsible for the evangelization of much of Northern Europe. Originally known as Winfrid or Wynfrith, Boniface was a native of Devon, England, probably born in Crediton. Seized by the missionary spirit, Boniface set out on his first Christianizing effort in 716, journeying to Frisia. Unable to convert many of the inhabitants, he returned home and in 718 went to Rome to seek approval from Pope Gregory II for his work. This he received and in 719 Boniface set out once more. His efforts were far more successful this time, since many in Hesse, Thuringia, and Bavaria were converted. As word of his achievements reached Rome, Pope Gregory summoned

Boniface, made him a missionary bishop, gave him a collection of canons, and encouraged him with vocal papal support. By custom, Boniface first used that name on the feast of St. Boniface, but it is probable that he was already known as Boniface among the Germans and did not change from Winfrid at Rome. Back among the Germans, he smashed pagan institutions whenever possible, dealing a major blow to paganism in the region by cutting down the Sacred Oak of Thor at Geismar. Germany was henceforth placed under ecclesiastical organization: churches were founded and monasteries established with the aid of the Benedictine. As a part of his civilizing effort, Boniface also brought parts of Germany and Bavaria into the Carolingian Empire. This association led to Boniface being granted by the sons of Charles Martel (d. 741) — Carloman and Pepin — the authority to reform the entire Frankish clergy. He used five synods to bring this about. Made archbishop of Mainz around 747, he resigned his see a few years later to return to his mission in Frisia. There he was martyred, traditionally on Pentecost Sunday in 754. He was buried at Fulda Abbey, which he had established in 743. Feast day: June 5.

Boniface I, St. ● Pope from 418-422. Boniface, whose reign was much troubled by the rival candidacy of Eulalius, served as a presbyter in Rome before his election. He was supposedly ordained by Pope St. Damasus I, and was an assistant to Pope St. Innocent I at Constantinople. He was chosen the successor to Pope Zosimus on December 26, 418, but on the same day, Eulalius was also elected by a rival faction in Rome; both were consecrated on the same day, December 29. There resulted much upheaval in Rome in the months that followed, and the matter was not settled until April 419 when Emperor Honorius at Ravenna decided in Boniface's favor, in part because Eulalius would not depart Rome while the emperor made up his mind. Once established, Boniface proved a strong, competent pope. He condemned Pelagianism, enthusiastically supported St. Augustine, and secured jurisdiction of the prefecture of Illyricum at a time when Emperor Theodosius was planning on transferring it to the control of the patriarch of Constantinople. Feast day: September 4.

Boniface II ● Pope from 530-532. First German pontiff. Named by Felix IV to be his successor, Boniface was considered unacceptable to the Romans because of his Gothic origins. They thus elected instead the deacon Dioscorus of Alexandria, thereby creating a schism that lasted until October 530, when Dioscorus died. As pope, he convened three Roman synods and endorsed the conciliar decrees of the second Council of Orange, which condemned Semi-Pelagianism.

Boniface III ● Pope from February 19 to November 12, 607. He had served previously as a legate to Constantinople from Pope Gregory the Great in 603. Elected as successor to Sabinianus, Boniface was able to secure the recognition of the Byzantine emperor Phocas that the see of Rome was head of all the Churches.

Boniface IV, St. ● Pope from 608-615. His pontificate was much troubled by heresy, most notably Monophysitism. His main achievement as pope was the conversion of the Pantheon in Rome into a church — Our Lady of the Rotunda — in 609, marking the first transformation of an old pagan structure into a site of Christian worship. Boniface died in monastic retirement and was buried in St. Peter's. Feast day: May 8.

Boniface V ● Pope from 619-625. He is best known for his ardent support of the evangelization of England. He also established the right of asylum. His election as successor to Pope St. Deusdedit ended an interregnum that had lasted for more than a year.

Boniface VI ● Pope for around fifteen days in 896. Successor to Formosus during a particularly bleak period in papal history, Boniface was elected on April 4, but soon died, either from illness (possibly gout) or murder. If it was the latter, the likely assassins were members of the so-called Spoleto Party, who desired the election of Stephen VI (VII). Stephen was elected and would go on to convene the infamous Cadaver Synod of January 897. Boniface was denounced in 898 by the council in Rome held by John IX.

Boniface VII ● Antipope. Reigned from June to July 974 and again from 984-985. A supporter and vassal of the powerful Roman family of the Crescentii, Boniface was serving as a cardinal deacon in 974 when he connived to have Pope Benedict VI strangled. Made pope by the influence of the Crescentii, his brief first reign was ended when Emperor Otto II had him exiled. He fled to Constantinople but returned in 984 under the protection of the Crescentii. He soon had Pope John XIV murdered and once again claimed the papacy. Unable to bear his corruption, however, he was deposed by the Romans and put to death.

Boniface VIII ● Pope from 1294-1303. His reign was dominated by his often bitter struggles with King Philip IV of France. Born Benedict (Benedetto) Gaetani at Anagni, he studied at Todi, Spoleto, and Bologna, later serving in the retinues of papal legates to Spain and France from around 1265-1268. Named a consistorial advocate in 1276 and then apostolic notary, he was made a cardinal deacon in 1281 by Pope Martin IV (r. 1281-1285) and cardinal priest by Pope Nicholas IV (r. 1288-1292) in 1291. After proving his diplomatic skills as a legate to France (1290-1291), he emerged as a major figure in the unfortunate reign of Celestine V (July-December 1294), advising the pontiff on matters of canon law during Celestine's tumultuous abdication. A prominent cardinal, Gaetani was elected to succeed Celestine on December 24, 1294.

As pope, Boniface was convinced of the need to restore the papacy to its position of supremacy in Christendom. Despite his many talents and a forceful personality, he could not overcome the deteriorated influence of the popes and was thus destined for disappointment. This was particularly true in his protracted disagreements with King Philip. This crisis began with Boniface's effort to end the inveterate hostilities between England and France by banning the taxation of the clergy to pay for wars. In his bull *Clericos Laicos* (February 25, 1296), Boniface declared such taxes to be needed. Philip responded by prohibiting exports and expelling foreign merchants, a move that placed Boniface in an awkward position owing to the needs of the Papal States for French commerce. He backed down, permitting in July 1297 the taxation of the clergy in times of national emergency or for defense. Conflict began once more in 1301 with Philip's trial of the papal legate, Bernard de Saisset. Recognizing the threat such an act implied, the pontiff issued the bull *Ausculta fili* on December 5, 1301, followed by the convoking of a synod in Rome in November 1302 that was attended by a number of French prelates. Emboldened, Boniface issued the famous bull *Unam Sanctam* on November 18, 1302, stressing the superior position of spiritual power over temporal rulers and concluding with the well-known assertion that for salvation, "every human creature be subject to the authority of the Roman pontiff." Philip remained firm, however, and launched a harsh denunciation of Boniface through his councillor Guillaume de Nogaret. On September 7, 1303, Nogaret — with the help of Boniface's vicious enemies, the Colonna family — seized the pope at Anagni, a day before the pope had planned to publish his excommunication of Philip. Probably abused, the pope was finally freed after several days by some outraged citizens of the city. With the help and protection of the Orsini family, Boniface returned to Rome but died on October 12, never having recovered from the shock and disappointment of the humiliation to his person and office.

While his reign has been overshadowed by the disastrous policy with France and a focus on Boniface's rather intemperate nature, he was responsible for a number of important contributions to the Church. He proclaimed 1300 to be a jubilee, the first Holy Year (in celebration of his triumph over the Colonna), cataloged the papal library, and launched a careful reorganization of the Vatican Archives. Most notably, he published in 1298 the *Liber Sextus*, a major part of the *Corpus Juris Canonici*.

Boniface IX ● Pope from 1389-1404. Second pontiff to reign in Rome during the Great Schism (1378-1417). Born Pietro Tomacelli, he was elected to succeed Pope

Pope Boniface VIII

137

Urban VI, the pope whose election in 1378 had caused the eruption of the schism in the West. His reign was marked by his efforts to secure allies against the Avignon antipopes, Clement VII and Benedict XIII. He excommunicated Clement and earned considerable ill will for his often unscrupulous methods of raising money. (See **Schism, Great**.)

Bonner, Edmund (d. 1569) ● Last bishop of London before the English Reformation. He remained a staunch supporter of the Catholic Church during the reigns of Henry VIII (1509-1547) and Elizabeth I (1558-1603). A native of Potter's Henley, Worcestershire, England, he was the son of Edmund Bonner and Elizabeth Frodsham. Educated at Pembroke College, Oxford, he was ordained in 1519. Appointed chaplain to Cardinal Wolsey sometime a little after 1525, Bonner gained the notice of the king and was able to keep Henry's favor even while staying devotedly loyal to Wolsey right up until the cardinal's death in disgrace in 1530. Thereafter, Henry used Bonner on a number of diplomatic missions, including a year in Rome from 1532-1533 when he acted as the king's agent concerning the question of the divorce. Promoted steadily by the English ruler, he was elected in 1538 to the see of Hereford and the following year was translated to London. In the next years, while remaining carefully faithful to Catholic doctrine, he supported the king's divorce, the suppression of the monasteries and churches, and the Oath of Supremacy that was to cost Thomas More and John Fisher their lives. His acceptance may have stemmed from personal devotion to Henry, for after the king's death in 1547 Bonner was adamant in his opposition to the changes that were occurring in the English religion. Punished under King Edward VI, he was restored by the Catholic queen Mary, playing an important role in returning England, albeit briefly, to the Church. He was given

the unpleasant task of degrading Thomas Cranmer at Oxford in February 1556 and earned the enmity of the English Reformers for his persecution of recalcitrant Protestants. When Elizabeth became queen in 1558, Bonner's days were numbered. He refused to take the oath under the Act of Supremacy of 1559, was arrested, and died in Marshalsea Prison on September 5, 1569. He was the last bishop of London to die in communion with the papacy.

Bordeaux Pilgrim, The ● Name given to the earliest known pilgrim of the Christian faith to travel to the Holy Land. The accepted date of his pilgrimage is 333-334, the account of his trip preserved in the *Itinerarium Burdigalense*, a listing of his stopping points with a few descriptions of Palestine. He apparently began in Bordeaux (Roman Burdigala), journeyed to Constantinople, the Holy Land, and then reached Milan where he finished the pilgrimage. (See **Pilgrimage**.)

Borgia, House of ● The famous and often notorious family of the Italian Renaissance. The Borgias were of Spanish-Italian descent and, although best known for their roles in the early Renaissance period, they actually came to prominence during the terminal era of the Middle Ages. The house involved itself with the Church in several ways. The first great Borgia, Alfonso (1378-1458), became Pope Callistus III in 1455, reigning for three years. Through his patronage, he secured the advance of his nephew Rodrigo, who became a cardinal while still in his twenties. Rodrigo was himself elected pope, as Alexander VI in 1492, reigning until 1503. He is still considered one of the most corrupt of all pontiffs, earning notoriety as well through the misdeeds of his two children, Cesare and Lucrezia Borgia. Cesare was made a cardinal by his father but received dispensation in 1499 so that he could marry Charlotte d' Albret, sister of the king of Navarre.

Appointed captain general of the Church, he waged violent wars to recover lost papal provinces that had tried to withdraw from the Holy See. Cesare did not take part in the conclaves to elect the successors to Alexander — Pius III and Julius II. Pope Julius was an implacable enemy of the Borgias, so Cesare fled Rome upon Julius's election in 1503. He would later die in a siege of the castle of Viana in 1507. The corrupt and cruel family did produce a saint — Francis Borgia (1510-1572). (See also **Alexander VI, Callistus III <2>**, and **Francis Borgia** for other details.)

Borgongini-Duca, Francesco (1884-1954) ● Italian cardinal, best known for his skillful authorship of the Lateran Treaty. A native of Rome, he was ordained in 1906, serving from 1907-1921 as professor of theology at the Urban College of Propaganda, Rome. A member of the faculty of the North American College in Rome, he instructed numerous seminarians, including the future cardinal Francis Spellman. In 1929, Borgongini-Duca helped negotiate with the Fascist government of Benito Mussolini an agreement that resulted in the Lateran Treaty, establishing the independence of the Holy See from Italy and its sovereignty in international relations. As assistant to Vatican Secretary of State Cardinal Pietro Gasparri, he wrote the treaty and signed as secretary of the Congregation

Cesare Borgia

for Extraordinary Ecclesiastical Affairs. After the Lateran Treaty went into effect, he became the first papal nuncio to Italy. Made archbishop in 1929, he was named cardinal in 1952 by Pope Pius XII. Cardinal Spellman translated his book of meditations, *The Word of God*, into English in 1921. (See also **Lateran Treaty** for other details.)

Bosio, Antonio (d. 1629) ● Italian archaeologist responsible for important excavations and study of the catacombs of Rome. Born in Malta, he studied in Rome, focusing originally on philosophy and law but later devoting himself to archaeology. Perceiving the possible ramifications of his accidental discovery of the underground passageways on the Via Salaria in Rome (May 13, 1578), Bosio undertook an investigation in December 1593 on his own into the as yet unnamed catacombs of Domitilla on the Via Argentina. Becoming lost in the twisting labyrinthine passages, he barely found his way out, teaching himself an invaluable lesson about the subterranean burial grounds. He spent the next years investigating the catacombs thoroughly, compiling his findings in the work *Roma sotterranea* (1620; *Subterranean Rome*, although not published until "1632," actually 1634, due to printing delays). The book was of immense value to succeeding researchers until the time of Giovanni de Rossi. That great archaeologist called Bosio the "Columbus of the Catacombs." (See also **Catacombs**.)

Bossuet, Jacques (1627-1704) ● Bishop of Meaux, French preacher, and an eloquent spokesman for the French Church. Ranked as one of the greatest preachers of all time, Bossuet was the fifth son of a judge in the Parlement of Dijon. In 1642, he journeyed to Paris where he entered the Collège de Navarre to prepare for the priesthood. Seven years later, he was ordained a deacon; in 1652, after receiving preparation from St. Vincent de Paul, he was ordained at Metz. The next years found Bossuet serving as a deacon in Metz where he continued studying, entered into a controversy with the Protestants, and began acquiring a considerable reputation for his preaching skills. In 1659, he went to Paris where his preaching was in much demand, especially after 1660. His sermons included appearances before the court and especially brilliant funeral orations, including the three classic orations for Henrietta Maria (1669), Henrietta Anne d' Angleterre (1670), and the prince of Condé (1687).

Bossuet was largely responsible for the conversion of Marshal Turenne from Protestantism in 1668. The next year he was appointed bishop of Condom and subsequently served for eleven years as tutor to the dauphin (1670-1681). Translated to Meaux in 1681, he grew in prominence in French ecclesiastical affairs. He authored the four Gallican Articles (1682), supported the revocation of the Edict of Nantes (1685), and attacked quietism. While he hoped for an eventual peaceful reunion with the Protestants, Bossuet was a vociferous defender of the Catholic faith, authoring many works against Protestant doctrine. He also authored a number of treatises, including *Histoire des variations des Églises protestantes* (2 vols., 1688; *History of the Various French Churches*), *Discours sur*

l'histoire universelle (1681; *Discourse on Universal History*), and *Élévations sur les mystères* (1727; *Elevation of the Mysteries*), which remains a classic of French devotional literature. Bossuet is counted as one of the Church's foremost preachers, his eloquence matched by his passion and strict adherence to doctrine.

Botulph, St. ● Also known as Botolph, a seventh-century saint mentioned in the Anglo-Saxon Chronicle as the founder of a monastery at Icanhoe in 654. Immensely popular in medieval England, Botulph is otherwise little known, as few details about him are clear. By tradition, he became a monk, with his brother St. Adulf, and later established Icanhoe (or Icanhoh), often identified with Boston (or Botulph's Stone) in Lincolnshire. Much revered in England he had some seventy churches dedicated to him and was especially honored in East Anglia. St. Ceolfrid supposedly journeyed all the way from Wearmouth to meet Botulph. Feast day: June 17.

Bourdaloue, Louis (1632-1704) ● French Jesuit preacher, renowned for his brilliant sermons before the French royal court. He entered the Society of Jesus in 1648, serving over the next years as a teacher of humanities in various provincial Jesuit houses. While in the provinces, he began preaching (1665 or 1666) and was sent to Paris where he preached in the Church of St.-Louis. Attracting the attention of King Louis XIV, Bourdaloue preached before the French court from 1670, delivering sermons in Advent and Lent. King Louis was so delighted with his sermons that it was said the king preferred to hear an old topic covered by Bourdaloue than a new one presented by someone else. Bourdaloue was called "the king of preachers and the preacher of kings."

Bourne, Francis (1861-1935) ● Cardinal archbishop of Westminster who helped guide the Church in England during World War I, distinguishing himself for his defense of Catholic rights and his patriotism. Born in Chapham, Bourne was educated at St. Sulpice in Paris and the Louvain before receiving holy orders in 1884. In 1889, he became rector of St. John's Seminary in Surrey, was made a monsignor in 1895, and in 1896 became coadjutor bishop of Southwark. In 1905, he was made archbishop of Westminster, becoming a cardinal in 1911. As archbishop he earned considerable notoriety for partially defying a ban on a procession through the streets with the Blessed Sacrament in 1908 by having the benediction given from the *loggia* of Westminster Cathedral. Noted for his patriotic views during the war, he also spoke out against violence in Ireland and in defense of the rights of Arabs in Palestine. He had reservations about the Malines Conversations (1921-1925) that brought together Catholic and Anglican theologians. Bourne also consecrated Westminster Cathedral in 1910.

Boy Bishop ● A custom that was widespread during the Middle Ages, especially in England, in which a young boy was elected or chosen to act as a kind of bishop for a specific period of time, fulfilling various episcopal duties save that of saying the Mass. Found most often in country parishes and monasteries, the custom, while highly irregular, was intended to express the great reverence for children shown in the Gospels. The boy was usually elected on December 6, the feast of St. Nicholas, patron of children, executing his duties until December 28, Feast of the Holy Innocents. More common in England than on the Continent, the practice was condemned by a number of ecclesiastical councils, most notably the Council of Basel in 1431, but its popularity made curtailing or abolishing it difficult. King Henry VIII (r. 1509-1547)

attempted to suppress it in England, although Queen Mary briefly revived it, before Queen Elizabeth I finally ended it. An analogous custom was found in Germany where a schoolboy was elected bishop to honor St. Gregory the Great on March 12. It endured into the 1800s.

Boys' Town ● Internationally renowned boys' home established in 1917 in Omaha, Nebraska, by Father Edward Flanagan. The institute, begun officially on December 10, 1917, was founded under the title "Father Flanagan's Boys' Home." It was intended to care for the needs of abandoned, orphaned, and underprivileged boys, and was started by Father Flanagan with five boys and eighty-nine dollars. Since that time, Boys' Town has grown into a self-sufficient, incorporated city, now situated some ten miles west of Omaha. With facilities for up to a thousand boys, the institution teaches grades five through high school, with full academic studies, music, athletics, drama, and the manual arts, including electronics, baking, computer science, and painting. There is also an affiliated center to promote the study of adolescent psychology at The Catholic University of America. Young girls have been accepted at the school since the 1960s. The town is supported by voluntary donations and covers some fifteen hundred acres with over fifty-five buildings.

Bracton, Henry de (d. 1268) ● English priest and one of the leading medieval legalists in England. Known also as Henry de Bratton or Bretton, he was, like many other lawyers in England at the time, a priest; he later served as chancellor of Exeter Cathedral (from 1264). Bracton's importance was based on his *De legibus et consuetudinibus angeliae* (*On the Laws and Customs of England*), a systematic corpus on English law, the first of its kind for common law. Begun probably no later than the 1250s, the work was left unfinished at the time of Bracton's death. He served as a justice to King Henry III and was a judge from 1247-1257 at the King's Court.

Bradwardine, Thomas (d. 1349) ●
Archbishop of Canterbury who earned the title *Doctor Profundus* (the Profound Doctor) for his theological writings, particularly his main work *De Causa Dei contra Pelagium*. Bradwardine was born at Chichester, serving as a fellow at Balliol College and then Merton College, Oxford. Chaplain in 1335 to Richard of Bury, bishop of Durham, he became chancellor of St. Paul's Cathedral in 1337. After serving as confessor to King Edward III, he was consecrated archbishop of Canterbury in 1349 at Avignon. His time as archbishop was brief, however, for he died of the plague soon after returning to England. A gifted theologian and mathematician, Bradwardine made contributions to the study of physics and mathematics, particularly geometry. His attack on Pelagianism in *Contra Pelagium* secured his title *Doctor Profundus*. Bradwardine attempted unsuccessfully in 1346 to bring about a negotiated peace between England and France in the Hundred Years' War that had begun a few years before. He was also noted for his care of soldiers during the conflict.

Braga, Council of ● Council held in Braga, Portugal, in 572. It was notable for its declaration against contraception, the first such Church legislation. (See **Birth Control**.)

Braga, Rite of ● Form of the Latin, or Roman, rite used in the Cathedral of Braga, Portugal. The rite may have been compiled by St. Giraldus at the start of the twelfth century, and it is known to have been in existence in the fourteenth century. Differing only slightly from the Roman rite, it was confirmed for the archdiocese of Braga by Pope Pius XI (1922-1939).

Bramante, Donato (1444-1514) ●
Important High Renaissance architect, best known in Church history for his work on St. Peter's Basilica for Pope Julius II (r. 1503-1513). He was probably born in Fermignano, Italy, although his early life is rather obscure. He worked in Milan from around 1480, laboring often for the powerful Milanese family of the Sforzas and sometimes collaborating with Leonardo da Vinci. Following the termination of Sforza supremacy in Milan by the French in 1449, Bramante journeyed to Rome. There he gained the patronage of Pope Alexander VI, the Borgia pope, receiving, as well, commissions from Cardinal Oliviero Carafa of Naples. His most ambitious patron, however, was Julius II, who made Bramante his principal architect and planner in the anticipated rebuilding of Rome. Bramante was chief architect from 1506, serving as one of the planners of that great church. He would be succeeded by such notables as Michelangelo, Maderno, and Bernini. He also designed the Belvedere Court in the Vatican (begun around 1505), part of his extensive Vatican legacy. (See also **St. Peter's Basilica** and **Vatican**.)

Branch Theory ● Also Branch Theory of the Church, the theory or opinion mainly supported by the Anglican Church that the one, true Church of Jesus Christ is comprised of the three distinct Churches: Anglican, Roman Catholic, and Eastern Orthodox. It functions on the idea that while the Church of Jesus Christ may have passed into schism, with various provinces or elements out of communion with each other, each may still be considered a "branch" of the Church so long as they adhere to the faith of the original Church and maintain apostolic succession. The Branch Theory was first developed in the 1800s, receiving inspiration from the Oxford movement. It is in opposition to the oneness of the true Church and has lost much credibility by the declaration of Pope Leo XIII in his 1896 decree *Apostolicae Curae* that Anglican ordinations are not valid.

Brazil ● South American country, one of the largest Catholic nations in the world. Brazil was first visited by Europeans in 1500 with the arrival of the Portuguese Admiral Pedro Álvares Cabral, who was accompanied by seven Franciscan missionaries. A priest said the first Mass in the country on April 26, 1500; thereafter, missionary activity established the Church, keeping pace with colonial and military settlements. On February 25, 1551, the first bishop was named, Dom Pedro Fernandes Sardinha, to the see of São Salvador da Bahia. Particularly important missionary work was carried out from 1553 by the so-called Apostle of Brazil, Padre José de Anchieta. Further activity was undertaken by various religious orders, such as the Carmelites, Capuchins, Maurists, and Vincentians. Of these orders, however, the most successful were the Jesuits. The conversion of the local native population, especially the Amazonian Indians of the interior, was hampered by the brutal treatment given them by the colonial authorities, who regularly exploited them and sold many into slavery. Nevertheless, evangelization was remarkably successful between 1680 and 1750. The Jesuits earned the enmity of local officials and in 1759 were suppressed, although other orders continued their work. The period between the suppression of the Jesuits and declaration of Brazilian independence from Portugal in 1822 was a tragic one. Vocations declined. Liberalism poisoned both the atmosphere of the Church-State relations and the Catholic outlook of much of the population. The independent Brazilian government further tightened its control over the Church, refusing to recognize its rights. By the terms of an agreement with the Holy See, the Brazilian royal house was obligated to finance the Church in Brazil, an opportunity used by Dom Pedro II (crowned in 1841) to prevent reform and to act as temporal head of the Brazilian Church. He was long opposed by many clergy, who disliked his style of government. Dom Pedro II was overthrown by an army coup. The republic that was created restored many rights to the Church, but it also separated Church and State through the Constitution of 1891. Further lessening of Church influence was achieved in the early to mid-1900s by additional constitutional measures. The Catholic faith in the second half of the century has been faced with an ongoing series of crises: quasi-Catholic sects such as Umbanda, abject poverty that fosters the popularity of liberation theology, and the activities of bishops, priests, and nuns in programs of radical reform. A notable reform movement was led by Dom Helder Camara, archbishop of Olinda and Recife. A demonstration of the increasing economic and other tensions in the country was provided by the temporary kidnapping in 1994 of Cardinal Aloisio Lorscheider, O.F.M., archbishop of Fortaleza, by convicts in a prison where he was visiting.

Breakspear, Nicholas ● See **Adrian IV**.

Breastplate of St. Patrick ● Ancient Irish hymn that has generally been attributed to St. Patrick, although his direct authorship is probably unlikely. The *Breastplate* probably began as the *Canticum Scotticum* mentioned in the Book of Armagh. It is one of the most popular of all Irish hymns or prayers.

Bremond, Henri (1865-1933) ● French writer on spirituality. Entering the Jesuits in 1882, Bremond was ordained in 1892, after spending his novitiate in England. In 1899, he became editor of the Jesuit periodical *Études*, but, in 1904, left the order to focus on purely literary pursuits. His writings soon attracted much controversy, especially his essay on John Henry Newman (1906). A life of St. Jane Frances de Chantal (1912) was placed on the Index of Forbidden Books. He also authored *Prière et poesie* (1926; *Prayer and Poetry*), *Histoire littéraire du sentiment religieux en France* (11 vols., 1915-1932; *Literary History of Religious Sentiment in France*).

Brendan, St. (d. 578) ● Also Brendan the Voyager, a renowned Celtic abbot, founder of monasteries, and a legendary voyager. Brendan was traditionally said to have been born in Tralee, County Kerry, Ireland. Educated at a school run for boys by Abbess St. Ita in County Limerick, he later studied under Abbot St. Jarlath of Tuam, in County Galway. Becoming a monk and priest, Brendan was made abbot of Ardfert Abbey, in County Kerry. He also worked to establish monasteries in Scotland and Ireland. A constant traveler, one of the foremost journeyers of his era, Brendan visited the Hebrides, parts of Scotland, Wales, Britanny, and elsewhere. He was subsequently immortalized in the tenth-century Irish epic the *Navigatio Brendani* (*Voyage of Brendan*), in which he becomes a hero of legendary Christian tales. In the *Navigatio* (preserved in over a hundred manuscripts), Brendan sails throughout the Atlantic, and makes a daring voyage with other monks to the so-called "Promised Land of Saints," possibly to be identified with the Canary Islands. He may have well founded the monastery of *Cluain Fearta* (Clonfert, in County Galway). Feast day: May 16.

Brest-Livotsk, Union of ● Agreement, or union, signed in 1596 between the Catholics and so-called Ruthenian Churches. By its terms, several million Ukrainian and Belorussian Orthodox Christians, residing in Lithuania under Polish rule, joined the Roman Catholic Church. Included in the union were the metropolitan of Kiev and the bishops of Ruthenia. The union was the result of the expressed desire of Michael Ragoza, metropolitan of Kiev, and his leading bishops, to be united with the Catholic instead of the Orthodox Church. The Catholic king of Poland, Sigismund III, naturally encouraged the development as a means of solidifying Catholic culture in the lands under his rule and to check Russian religious influences in the region. He promised the Ruthenians that they could continue the traditional Eastern rite, and they would have the same rights and privileges enjoyed by those Catholics of the Latin rite. At a synod in Brest, the terms of the agreement were accepted by the Ruthenian bishops, Pope Clement VIII's approbation was given, and a union proclaimed. The union, however, was immediately challenged by the Ruthenians, who feared the inevitable Latinization of their liturgy and customs. Russia also opposed the agreement, exerting much pressure on the Ukrainians and Belorussians to return to the Orthodox Church. Little help was given by Polish religious leaders, who looked down on the Ruthenians. The result was that within a few years, many Ruthenians had returned to the Orthodox Churches after often violent confrontations. (See also **Russia** and **Poland**.)

Briçonnet, Guillaume <1> (1445-1514) ● French cardinal. A onetime counselor for King Charles VIII of France, Briçonnet became a priest following the death of his wife. He was subsequently archbishop of St.-Malo, archbishop of Reims, archbishop of Narbonne, and finally a cardinal. His position as a major prelate and former royal adviser gave him considerable political influence. His son, Guillaume Briçonnet (see next entry), also became a bishop.

Briçonnet, Guillaume <2> (d. 1534) ● French prelate who was also leader of the so-called Meaux evangelicals. The son of the royal counselor and future cardinal Guillaume Briçonnet (see preceding entry), he became bishop of Lodève (1489), abbot of St.-Germain-des-Prés (1507), and finally bishop of Meaux in 1516. As bishop of Meaux, he promoted extensive reforms and eagerly encouraged devotion to the Virgin Mary and the Blessed Sacrament. He was also the head of the evangelicals at Meaux, who fostered a teaching based on the Bible, particularly the writings of St. Paul, with humanism. Because of the similarity of the group's ideas with those of Martin Luther, Briçonnet, who condemned Lutheranism in 1523, was forced to appear twice before the Paris Parlement on charges of heresy.

Bride, St. ● See **Brigid of Ireland, St**.

Bridget of Sweden, St. (c. 1303-1373) ● Also Birgitta and Birgida, a mystic, founder of the Brigittine order, and the patron saint of Sweden. Bridget was the daughter of Birger Persson, a governor of Uppland, and the wife of Ulf Gudmarsson with whom she had eight children, including the future St. Catherine of Sweden. From 1341-1343, she and Ulf journeyed to Compostela on a pilgrimage. On their return, Ulf entered a Cistercian monastery where he died in 1344. Freed from earthly connections, Bridget chose to enter a religious life near the Cistercian monastery of Alvastra, on Lake Netter, where Ulf had died. There she dictated her numerous visions and divine messages to Peter Olafsson, who translated them into Latin. One of the commands that she received was to found a new religious order, the Brigittines, which she did in 1346. In 1350, she journeyed to Rome for the Holy Year to urge the pope to accept her order. Papal confirmation of the order came in 1370. She remained in the Eternal City for most of her remaining years, aided always by Catherine, with the exception of several pilgrimages, including one to the Holy Land in 1372. Bridget worked tirelessly for the poor of the city; she also tried to secure the return of the papacy to Rome from Avignon. She died in Rome shortly after her return from the Holy Land. Canonized by Pope Boniface on October 7, 1391, her famous visions were first published in 1492. Feast day: July 23. (See also **Brigittine Order**.)

Brigid of Ireland, St. (d. 528) ● Also Bridget and Bride of Ireland, one of the foremost saints of Ireland, abbess of Kildare, and the "Mary of the Gael." While much revered among the Irish, she is known to have accomplished great works and to have established a mighty legacy, but the details of her life are little known, obscured by legend and lore. By tradition, Bridget was born in County Louth, the daughter of a slave mother and a nobleman; both parents were supposedly baptized by St. Patrick. Much respected even in her youth for her saintliness, she was placed under the spiritual direction of Bishop St. Mel, or perhaps St. Machalleus. The king of Leinster was so impressed with her that he gave her a parcel of land in Kildare. There she established Ireland's first convent, at Cill-Dara (Church of the Oak). It eventually became a monastery as well. The early Irish Church was greatly aided by her prayers and efforts, including miracles, and she is ranked, with St. Patrick, as a patron saint of Ireland. Much discussed in Irish literature and legend, she has also inspired many generations of Irish nuns and has given her name (or variations of it) to countless Irish children. Feast day: February 1.

Brigittine Order ● Order of the Most Holy Savior (*Ordo Sanctissimi Salvatoris*, O.SS.S.), the women's religious order founded in Vadstena, Sweden, by St. Bridget in 1344. The Brigittines were originally founded as a double monastery, meaning both men and women, although the separation was virtually complete, only the confessor having access to the nuns. The community was under the authority of an abbess, the first one being Katherine (or Catherine), daughter of Bridget. As the order was intended principally to be one for women, the government was in the power of the abbess, called "Sovereign," the monks being so intended to supply spiritual assistance. The constitutions of the Brigittines were first approved by Pope Urban V (r. 1362-1370), receiving formal approbation from Pope Martin V (r. 1417-1431). The Brigittines spread during the late 1300s to France, Germany, Italy, Spain, and elsewhere, including the famous Syon House founded in England by King Henry V in 1415. In the 1500s, largely owing to the Reformation, the majority of double houses were ended and many others were suppressed altogether. The Brigittines of the Recollection were begun in Valladolid, Spain, in the seventeenth century by the Ven. Marina de Escobar, who modified the rule to fit Spanish culture. The constitution was approved by Pope Urban VIII (r. 1623-1644). The Brigittine Sisters arrived in the United States in 1957.

Brother Lawrence (c. 1605-1691) ● Known in full as Brother Lawrence of the Resurrection, a Carmelite mystic. Born Nicholas Herman, he served for a time as a soldier but, rejecting the world, became a hermit before entering the Carmelite monastery of Paris in 1649. There he worked as a brother in the kitchen, pursuing a life of near total recollection. His writings reveal a highly elevated prayer life, encouraging the practice of the presence of God. Abbé de Beaufort edited his writings in two volumes, *Maximes spirituelles* (1692; *Spiritual Maxims*) and *Moeurs et entretiens du F. Laurent* (1694; *Morals and Discussions of Brother Lawrence*).

Brothers of the Sword, Order of ● See under Livonian Knights in **Military Orders**.

Bruno, St. (d. 1101) ● Founder of the Carthusian order. He was educated at Cologne and Reims, becoming a canon at Cologne and appointed head of the cathedral school at Reims around 1057. Among his students was Odo of Lagery, the future Pope

Urban II (r. 1088-1099). Named chancellor for the diocese of Reims in 1075, Bruno soon entered into severe disagreements with the archbishop, Manasses de Gournai, over the prelate's corruption. In 1076, Bruno was forced to flee, returning, however, in 1080 after Manasses was dismissed. Offered the post of archbishop, Bruno refused and instead set out to adopt a purely ascetical life. After spending some time under the direction of Robert of Cîteaux, he made his way to a mountain retreat near Grenoble and there, with the help of St. Hugh of Chateauneuf and six companions, he established the Carthusians in 1084. Pope Urban, his old student, summoned him to Rome in 1090 and offered him the archbishopric of Reggio. Bruno again refused and this time retired to a desolate area in Calabria. There, at the monastery of La Terre, he spent his remaining days. While never officially canonized, Bruno was honored by his own festival, which the order secured permission from the papacy in 1514 to celebrate. In 1623, his feast day was imposed on the Western Church. His order, which practices a rigorous lifestyle of community and solitude, attracted many recruits during Bruno's lifetime and grew quickly in the years after his death. Bruno himself was especially touched by the beauty of nature and the hermitage, writing to a friend, "Only those who have experienced it can know the benefit and delight to be gained from the quiet and solitude of the hermitage." Feast day: October 6. (See also **Carthusian Order** and **Chartreuse, La Grande**.)

Bruno of Querfurt, St. (d. 1009) ● Missionary to the Prussians and martyr. Bruno was born at Querfurt to the noble family of the counts of Querfurt. He was educated at the cathedral school of Magdeburg and in 997 journeyed to Rome with Emperor Otto III. There he came under the influence of St. Romuald, entering the monastery of Sts. Bonifazio and Alessio and taking the name Boniface. He is thus also known as St. Boniface of Querfurt. For Romuald and Bruno, Otto established a monastery at Preum near Ravenna in 1001. Inspired by the recently martyred Adalbert of Prague, Bruno hoped to use the monastery as the launching point for a continued evangelization of Prussia. Consecrated an archbishop by Pope Sylvester II and given papal blessing to work as a missionary, Bruno set out around 1004 for Germany to enlist the aid of King Henry II of Ratisbon. As Henry was engaged at the time in a war with Poland, he was not in favor of the mission and so Bruno journeyed to Hungary. There, with the aid of Stephen, king of Hungary, he preached among the Magyars and then among the Petchenegs of Ukraine. He was unsuccessful in ending the war between Poland and Henry, but, supported by Boleslav I, king of Poland, he embarked upon his Prussian effort. The Prussians were quite unwilling to be converted, however, and Bruno, with eighteen companions, was soon murdered. Bruno authored during his time in Hungary a remarkable and extant biography of St. Adalbert. Feast day: June 19.

Bruno the Great, St. (925-965) ● Also Bruno of Cologne, archbishop of Cologne, and a prominent figure in the Holy Roman Empire. Bruno was the youngest son of King Henry I the Fowler of Germany and St. Matilda; his brother was Emperor Otto I the Great. He received his education at the cathedral school of Utrecht and in the court school of Otto, serving from 940 as Otto's chancellor. Appointed abbot of Lorsch and Corvei (modern Höxter, Germany), he worked to reform the monasteries, enforce monastic observance, and improve learning. In 953, he was elected archbishop of Cologne and was soon named duke of Lorraine by his brother, a title that gave Bruno considerable political power beyond his formidable ecclesiastical position. Bruno, however, proved both a gifted duke and a remarkable pastor. Peace

was brought to Lorraine, and the see of Cologne was transformed into one of the most respected in Germany. Bruno continued to promote learning and established the monastery of St. Pantaleon. During the time that Otto spent in Italy in 962 for his coronation, Bruno acted as coregent of the government, sharing also the care of Otto II. Feast day: October 11.

Bruno, Giordano (1548-1600) ● Italian philosopher, mathematician, astronomer, and heretic. Born at Nola, near Naples, he studied at Naples before joining the Dominicans in 1562. He soon earned censure from his superiors and in 1576 fled to Rome to avoid excommunication for heresy. Wandering frequently over the next years, he journeyed to Geneva (1578) where he became a Calvinist, but his views again earned condemnation, this time from the Calvinists. He escaped to Paris in 1581 and then went to London (1583) where he gave a series of controversial lectures in favor of the theories of Nicolas Copernicus. Back in Paris, in 1585, Bruno attacked the Aristotelians of the city and was forced to flee. Excommunicated by the Lutherans in 1589 he nevertheless continued to lecture on mathematics and occult matters until 1592 when he was seized in Venice by the Inquisition, imprisoned at Rome in 1593, and finally burned at the stake on February 17, 1600. Bruno espoused a strong pantheistic philosophy in which God was the beginning, middle, and end, the universe being one and the same. In his later years, his name was used by Italian members of the nationalistic anticlerical party in the 1800s, who erected his statue in the Campo dei Fiori in Rome.

Bull ● Name used for certain types of papal letters, derived from the Latin *bulla* (seal), the lead or waxen seal shaped like a disk that is attached to the document. The *bulla* was initially a type of round or disk-shaped plate, coming to be applied to the metal seals that accompanied certain papal or royal documents. Sometime around the thirteenth century, it began to signify not just the seal but the document itself. From then until the fifteenth century, the bull was a broad term for most papal documents. A change, apparently long in coming, began around the start of the pontificate of Pope Eugenius IV in 1431. Already there was a delineation of papal documents, so that in 1265, for example, Pope Clement IV wrote to a nephew and used not a bull but a seal of wax bearing the impression of the ring of the fisherman. Eugenius effected administrative changes to remove the cumbersome system of bulls, replacing it with a variety of documents, most notably the apostolic brief. Bulls were still used, however, at times in conjunction with briefs; such was the case under Pope Julius II (r. 1503-1513), who first granted a brief granting a dispensation to King Henry (VIII) of England to marry Catherine of Aragon and then a formal bull. By custom, the bull has a superscription in which the pope uses the title *Episcopus, Servus Servorum Dei*. (See **Servus Servorum Dei**.) This title was probably adopted by Pope St. Gregory I (r. 590-604), since he had chosen *Servus Servorum Dei* as a protest against the patriarch of Constantinople, John the Faster, who styled himself "Ecumenical Patriarch." It came into popular usage in the 1800s. A collection of bulls is called a *bullarium*. (See also **Papal Letters**.)

Bulla Coenae ● Name given to comprehensive listings promulgated by popes containing the excommunications that were then in force. The name *coenae* was derived from the fact that listings were read in the presence of the pontiff and cardinals on Holy Thursday. The *bulla coenae* began sometime in the 1300s; it was given official form by Pope Urban VIII in 1627, continuing in practice until 1770, when Pope Clement XIV ceased the ceremonial readings on Holy Thursday. The punishment of excommunication, while left unread, remained in full force, however. From time to time, the popes ordered that the *bulla coenae* be issued in various nations, normally to stress papal censure of specific heresies, or errors, but there were calls to make the promulgation universal. St. Charles Borromeo, for example, wished it to be posted in each confessional for its reading by the penitent. Pope Pius IX (r. 1846-1878) abrogated the *bulla coenae* as part of his extensive reforms of Church law in 1869.

Bulla Cruciata ● Name given to the collection of papal favors and dispensations first granted to the Christians of Spain in 1063 to aid them in their crusade to free Spanish lands from Islamic domination, the *Reconquista*. The privileges bestowed by the papacy included dispensation from fasting and abstinence (except for few specific days) and a special plenary indulgence given to all Spanish subjects during the time that the *Reconquista* was being waged. These favors were made permanent in 1492 with the final defeat of the remnant Moorish kingdoms. Interestingly, the *bulla cruciata* has not been rescinded and thus the privileges are still applicable to all persons on Spanish territory or under the political control of Spain, regardless of nationality. Further, those places, such as the countries of Central America and areas of South America that were once part of the Spanish Empire, also receive the favors. (See also **Spain**.)

Bullarium ● Collection of papal bulls or similar documents, customarily arranged in chronological order. The term *bullarium* was probably first coined by the gifted canonist Laertius Cherubini (d. 1626), who also possessed one of the best known of all *bullaria*. There are numerous such collections extant, most being in the possession of private collectors, or major institutions such as Catholic universities and libraries. Smaller *bullaria* may cover the reign of one pope, while major collections may cover many reigns. Among the greatest and best known *bullaria* are the *Regesta Pontificum Romanum*, the *Magnum Bullarium*, the *Bullaria Romana* (or the *Bullarium Romanum*), the Turin *Bullarium*, and the Luxembourg *Bullarium* that was supposedly printed in Geneva in the eighteenth century. (See also **Bull**.)

Buonaroti, Michelangelo ● See **Michelangelo**.

Burchard (d. 1025) ● Bishop of Worms and a remarkable canon legalist. Appointed bishop in 1000, he worked strenuously to improve the social and political standing of the see, bringing reforms to the clergy, and insisting on extensive powers in secular affairs. Burchard is also well-known in the history of canon law for the extensive compilation of his *Decretum* (c. 1008-1012), a collection of canon law that was highly influential until the time of Hildebrand, the future Pope Gregory VII (r. 1073-1085). (See also **Canon Law**.)

Burchard, John (d. 1506) ● Also John Burckard, a noted papal master of ceremonies who made important contributions to pontifical ceremonial organization. Originally from the area around Strasbourg, Burchard served as canon of Strasbourg from around 1477 until about 1481 when he journeyed to Rome. There, after practicing as an advocate, he was named master of ceremonies in 1483 by Pope Sixtus IV. Aiding his predecessor, Agostino Patrizzi, Burchard helped organize a revision of the *Pontificale Romanum* in 1485 and the creation of the new *Ceremoniale Romanum* in 1488 (published in 1515). He was especially important in the collection of the *Ordo servandus per sacerdotem in celebratione Missae* (1502), a compilation of rubrics on the celebration of the Mass. It was used as a major source in the putting together of the *Ritus celebrandi* during the reign of Pope Pius IV (1559-1565). In 1503, Burchard was made bishop of Orte and Civita Castellana and became a cardinal the same year. His diary has also been an extremely critical primary source for the history of the popes during his era, known in full as the *Diarium sive Rerum Urbanerum Commentarii* (1483-1506).

Buridan, Jean (1300-1358) ● Prominent French Scholastic philosopher and a leading Aristotelian in his era, also known as John Buridanus. He studied at the University of Paris and was a student of William of Occam. In 1328, he became rector at Paris, a post he was still holding in 1358. His writings, in sharp opposition to those of Occam with whom he disagreed, were placed on the Index of Forbidden Books from 1474-1481. Buridan was a nominalist, adhering to causality. He proposed a version of determinism that mankind possesses the free will to choose good but also the free will to delay such a decision. The created moral dilemma of suspending moral deliberations was examined in the famous allegory of "Buridan's Ass," falsely attributed to Buridan. By its terms, an ass, placed between two perfectly equal piles of hay, will have no motive to choose between them and so will starve to death. The animal Buridan used in his analysis of Aristotle's *De caelo* (*On the Heavens*) was a dog. Buridan also revised Aristotle's theory of motion, authored numerous commentaries on Aristotle's writings, and studied optics. (See also **William of Occam**.)

Busch, Jan ● See under **Common Life, Brethren of the**.

Butler, Alban (1710-1773) ● Priest and author of the renowned collection *The Lives of the Saints*. Butler was born in Northampton, England, receiving his education at the English College in Douai,

France. Ordained in 1734, he subsequently held the chairs of philosophy and divinity; he was also later president of the English College at St.-Omer. His monumental achievement was *The Lives of the Fathers, Martyrs, and other principal Saints, compiled from original Monuments, and other authentic records, illustrated with remarks of judicious modern critics and historians*, published in 1756-1759 and known commonly today as *The Lives of the Saints*, or *Butler's Lives of the Saints*. The some sixteen hundred lives are a mine of hagiographical material and, while intended to edify the reader and not always discerning of fact and legend, the biographies are still of much interest to the historian, particularly given Butler's wide-ranging research. A revised edition, *Butler's Lives of the Saints*, was published in 1956.

Byrd, William (1543-1623) ● Generally considered the foremost English composer of the Shakespearean era, he was called the Parent of British Music and made important contributions to Church music in England, despite his adherence to the Catholic faith. Byrd was probably a native of Lincolnshire, serving as organist at Lincoln Cathedral from 1563-1572. In 1572, he was appointed a gentleman of the Chapel Royal, serving with his famous teacher, Sir Thomas Tallis, himself a brilliant composer. Byrd departed London in 1577, settling in Middlesex and Essex. He composed both secular and religious works, creating a staggering number of compositions for virtually every medium, including the keyboard, choral music (secular and religious), and string music, save perhaps for the lute. Frequently accused of recusancy, he nevertheless fulfilled his duties as a member of the Chapel Royal with much distinction. Queen Elizabeth was evidently willing to overlook the fact that he was a devout Catholic because of the magnificence of his music. He composed three Masses, two complete

services, sacred songs, and set to music Latin motets, preces (prayers), and responses as well as a litany of the English liturgy. His published works included *Psalms, Sonnets, and Songs* (two books, in 1588 and 1611), *Cantiones Sacrae* (three books, in 1575, 1589, and 1591), and *Songs of Sundry Natures* (1589).

Byzantine Empire ● Also called the Eastern Empire or the Eastern Roman Empire, the successor state to the Roman Empire that survived from the late fourth century until 1453 and the fall of Constantinople to the Ottoman Turks. The empire was effectively born in 395 with the division of the Roman world into two spheres, the East and the West. Centered in Constantinople and relying upon the stable and developing provinces of Asia Minor, the Eastern Empire was able to avoid the bloody and destructive Germanic invasions that characterized the final era of the Western Empire in the fifth century. Although the Eastern Empire claimed succession to the entire Roman world after the fall of the last Western ruler, Romulus Augustulus, to the barbarians of the chieftain Odoacer in 476, the heart of their realm remained Constantinople and their territories in the southern Balkans and Asia Minor. The name Byzantine was derived from the ancient city of Byzantium, over which Constantinople was built. The culture that developed, flourished, and then declined over the period of a millennium was highly structured, remarkably rich in artistic and intellectual achievements, and deeply religious.

The Christian Church as it emerged in the lands of the Eastern realm was to wield enormous influence in social and political affairs. The closely interwoven relationship between the Church and the imperial government was characterized by the religio-political system of Caesaropapism by which the emperor was able to interfere in the administrative and doctrinal life of the creed. At the same time, this close association would allow the empire to be plagued by religious crises that would have both theological and political ramifications. Chief among these were Arianism, Nestorianism, Monophysitism, Monothelitism, and the Iconoclastic Controversy. Beyond these internal developments were the long-term and complex dealings between the Byzantines and the Western Church and the gradual gulf that widened into schism between the Churches of East and West (for this breach, see under **Schism, Eastern**).

The Eastern Empire underwent its first great revival under Emperor Justinian I (r. 527-565), who oversaw the construction of the Hagia Sophia and the restoration of Africa and Italy to Byzantine control. The presence of the Byzantine exarchate in Italy permitted the emperors in Constantinople to influence the papacy, demanding, for example, the right of granting approval to the election of a new pontiff. This power was abused at times, as in 545 when Justinian arrested Pope Vigilius (r. 537-555) and imprisoned him over the Three Chapters Controversy. Over the next years, however, the Byzantines lost their holdings in Egypt, Africa, Sicily, Palestine, and Syria to the Arabs and much of Italy to the Lombards. The rise of the Lombards and the decline of the Byzantine authority prompted Pope Stephen II (III) (r. 752-757) to request the

Empress Theodora

help of King Pepin III of the Franks (r. 751-768). His intervention ended the dependency of the popes on the Byzantine Empire, launched their close ties with the Frankish-Carolingian Empire, and made possible the founding of the Papal States. Charlemagne (r. 768-814) cultivated his relationship with the popes (see also **Leo III, St.**) so as to acquire prestige and legitimize his vast empire, which was held in scorn by the Byzantines.

The very difficult situation between the Eastern and Western Churches (already exacerbated by several minor schisms and disagreements) continued to deteriorate over the next centuries, culminating in the schism of 1054, which was never healed. Byzantine missionaries, meanwhile, found fertile ground in Slavic lands, converting large parts of the Bulgars, the Slavs, and the Russians. Their success is attested to by the lasting Byzantine influence in Slavic — especially Russian — art, architecture, and religion. This evangelization coincided with the revival of the empire under the Macedonian Dynasty of Emperors (867-1025), which brought a flourishing of art, increased centralization, several victories over the Muslims, and a heightened acceptance of Orthodox Christianity. The demise of the dynasty signaled the empire's collapse in Asia Minor before the onslaught of the Seljuk Turks and, despite the schism of 1054, Emperor Alexius I Comnenus asked for help from the West. Pope Urban II (r. 1088-1099) called for a crusade, receiving an enthusiastic response.

The crusades brought unwanted Latin interference in Byzantine affairs and the creation of Christian states in the Holy Land with the concomitant preaching of Western clergy. So weakened were the Byzantines by 1204 that the conditions were ripe for the toppling of the entire government. This took place with the Fourth Crusade. The empire was replaced by the so-called Latin Empire of Constantinople. Various Byzantine claimants survived until 1261 when Michael IV Palaeologus overthrew the Latin Empire and returned to Constantinople. The Byzantines never fully recovered, slowly and unavoidably losing territory to the Ottoman Turks. The last period, from around 1261-1453, did produce an intellectual renaissance and a last-ditch effort to rally Western support.

Emperor John VIII Palaeologus attended the Council of Florence in 1439 and agreed to acknowledge the supremacy of the Roman Church. This was never popular with the people of Constantinople and was repudiated when the West failed to repel the Turks. The last emperor was Constantine IX Palaeologus (1449-1453), who died defending the walls of his city. Constantinople fell on May 29, 1453, to the Ottoman Turks under Sultan Mehmet II the Conqueror. The death of the empire is seen by many scholars as the end of the medieval epoch and the start of the modern era.

Byzantine Rite ● See under the following: **Eastern Catholic Churches** and **Orthodox Eastern Churches**. See also **Byzantine Empire** (preceding entry), **Constantinople**, and **Schism, Eastern**.

Cabasilas, Nicholas (c. 1320-1371 or -1390) ● Byzantine mystical writer and theologian. He is best known for his works, in Greek, *Commentary on the Divine Liturgy* and *Life of Christ*. Both books were important theological sources, preserving in extensive detail Byzantine religious thought. Cabasilas should not be confused with Nilus Cabasilas, a contemporary who became archbishop of Thessalonica (c. 1355).

Cabrini, Frances Xavier, St. (1850-1917) ● Italian foundress and the first American citizen to be canonized. Mother Cabrini was born in Sant' Angelo Lodigiano, Italy, one of thirteen children of Stella and Agostino Cabrini, a farmer. After studying with the Daughters of the Sacred Heart at Arluno, she hoped to join that order and then the Canossians of Crema but was turned down by both, perhaps because of questions about her health (she had been stricken in 1872 with smallpox). Taking up the post of teacher in Vidardo, she taught for two years and then received encouragement from the local pastor to become head of an orphanage in the town of Codogno. She attempted to form the group of women who gathered about her in the orphanage into a kind of community for the religious life. In 1880, they were formally founded as the Missionary Sisters of the Sacred Heart, moving into an abandoned Franciscan friary in Codogno after the orphanage closed (1880). Additional convents opened in northern Italy, but Mother Cabrini hoped to go to China to devote herself to missionary work. Pope Leo XIII, however, had a different idea. He suggested that she go to America to care for Italian immigrants. With six sisters, Cabrini arrived in New York on March 31, 1889, following Leo's saying: "Do not go to the East, but to the West."

St. Frances Xavier Cabrini

Initially given a lukewarm greeting by Church officials — some even suggested that she go home — Mother Cabrini embarked upon the care of Italian immigrants. Her work took her to slums, hospitals, and prisons, and she established schools, orphanages, and care centers. While sailing back and forth across the ocean to Europe some thirty times, Cabrini and her sisters labored throughout the United States (and then South America and Europe) including New York, Denver, Los Angeles, Chicago, Philadelphia, and Seattle. It was in New York City that she established Columbus Hospital, the first of a number of others. Her prodigious travels were made even more remarkable by the fact that she had a terrible fear of water owing to a childhood accident. She became a naturalized American citizen in 1909 and died in Chicago in 1917. Canonized in 1946 by Pope Pius XII, she was named in 1950 the patroness of all emigrants. She was the first American citizen to be canonized. Feast day: November 13.

Cadaver Synod ● See **Formosus** and **Stephen VI**.

Caedmon (d. c. 680) ● First English Christian poet. Virtually all that is known about Caedmon comes from the Venerable Bede's *Ecclesiastical History*. This source presents Caedmon as a laborer at the monastery of Whitby. Unable to sing or compose verse, Caedmon was supposedly so ashamed of this failing that he would hide anytime there was a musical performance. One night, however, God granted him the gift of being able to turn Scripture into verse. He thus became a monk with the blessing of the abbess Hilda. He emerged as the earliest Anglo-Saxon composer of popular vernacular poetry. A fragment of a poem he was given in a dream was recorded by Bede. It is preserved in an eighth-century blank leaf in the Moore manuscript of Bede. Other poems are attributed to him, often with no justification.

Caeremoniale Episcoporum ● Liturgical work meaning "Ceremonial of Bishops" that contains the various rubrics and directives governing the ceremonies, rites, and dress to be followed by bishops of the Roman (or Latin) rite. An edition was published in 1587 under the title *De Caeremoniis cardinalium et episcoporum in eorem diocesibus* that was revised in 1600 by the order of Pope Clement VIII. In the ensuing centuries, a number of revisions have taken place, leading to the current Latin version promulgated in 1984 under the auspices of Pope John Paul II. The *Caeremoniale* covers such topics as the

consecration of bishops, funerals for bishops, the blessing of abbots, and proper dress for all possible occasions. There are also nonepiscopal ceremonial matters such as cathedral activities that may be celebrated during a period in which the bishop is absent. It also presents the order of rank or precedence to be followed when organizing a procession of clergy and laypersons.

Caeremoniale Romanum ● Title of two works of note in Church history. The first was a service compiled during the pontificate of Gregory X around 1275. It was intended to be used at the investiture of the newly elected pope. It was not formally published until 1689 by the Maurist scholar Jean Mabillon under the title *Ordo Romanum XIII*, part of Mabillon's *Mussaeum Italicum*. The second was a treatise on the ceremonial of the Papal (or Roman) Curia. Also known as the *Caeremoniale Capellae Pontificae*, it was organized by P. Piccolomini, bishop of Pienza from 1483-1496, and was published in 1516 by Christophorus Marcellus, archbishop of Corcyra.

Caesarius, St. (d. 542) ● Gifted preacher and archbishop of Arles who was successful in establishing the claim of primacy for the see in Gaul (France). Caesarius entered the monastery of Lérins in 489, being appointed archbishop in 502. He was active in organizing the Church in southern Gaul and used excellent relations with Theodoric the Great, ruler of the Ostrogoths, to make Arles the primatial see. He also succeeded in having the heresy of Semi-Pelagianism condemned in 529 at the Council of Orange. The *Statuta Ecclesiae Antiqua*, a collection of canons, has been attributed to him, although opinion is divided among scholars as to whether he was in fact the compiler. He did author a directory for monks and a rule for the women's monastery of St. John's (later St. Caesarius), which Caesarius had established and where he had appointed his sister St. Caesaria as abbess. The name of the rule was *Regula ad virgines*. Feast day: August 27.

Caesarius of Heisterbach (c. 1180-1240) ● German preacher and ecclesiastical writer who was one of the most popular authors of his era in Germany. Born in Cologne, he was educated at the school of St. Andrew in Cologne. Entering the Cistercians in 1199, he resided at the monastery of Heisterbach where he became prior in 1228. Caesarius authored a number of important works, the most popular being *Dialogus Miraculorum* (c. 1223; *Dialogue on Miracles*), a collection of edifying narratives for novices that was also a useful source on German history in the 1200s. He also wrote eight books on miracles, a biographical compilation of the archbishops of Cologne from the late first century to 1238, a life of St. Engelbert, and a life of St. Elizabeth of Hungary.

Caesaropapism ● Religio-political theory advancing the idea that a secular ruler should also have authority over the Church within his realm. Such power, according to this theory, should not be limited to ecclesiastical appointments but ought to extend to matters of doctrine. The emergence of Caesaropapism was an inevitable by-product of the socioreligious and political system created to govern the Roman Empire by Constantine the Great (r. 306-337), especially after the completion of Constantinople and its rise as the first city of the empire. The emperor exercised enormous influence upon the Church, enjoying the privileges of summoning synods and councils, of appointing and removing patriarchs, and of having a major role in theological deliberations. The degree to which Caesaropapism had became a very real part of imperial life was made manifest in the mid-fourth century with the Arian controversy. The tendency of Byzantine emperors to influence Church affairs continued over the next centuries, finally encountering opposition from the Holy See as the successors of Peter increased their ecclesiastical and political authority in the years following the demise of the Roman Empire in the West in 476. Other variations in Caesaropapism developed in France (Gallicanism), Germany (Febronianism), and the Holy Roman Empire (Josephinism).

Caius, St. ● Pope from 283-296, of whom virtually nothing is known. Elected in December 283, he was the successor of Eutychianus, reigning during a time of relative freedom for the Church between the outbreaks of persecutions throughout the Roman Empire. He died on April 22, 296. Caius was mentioned in the fourth-century *Depositio Episcoporum* and by Eusebius who mistakenly assigned him a fifteen-year reign.

Cajetan, St. (1480-1547) ● Also Cajetan of Thiene and Gaetano da Thiene, a priest and a co-founder of the Theatine order. A native of Vicenza, Italy, he was educated at Padua, receiving a doctorate in civil and canon law in 1504. Two years later, Pope Julius II appointed him protonotary of the Roman Curia. Ordained a priest in 1516, he continued the charitable works of the Oratory of Divine Love with which he had become associated a few years before. He was responsible for the revitalization of the oratories of Vicenza (1518), Verona (1519), and Venice (1520). Back in Rome in 1523, he met Archbishop Pietro Caraffa (the future Pope Paul IV) and established with him the Congregation of the Clerics Regular, the Theatines, in 1524, to promote a new spirit of devotion among the clergy, particularly those living in common and bound by vows who were actively involved in pastoral work. Cajetan and Caraffa fled Rome in 1527 when troops of Emperor Charles V sacked the Eternal City, going to Venice. Cajetan later went to Naples where he opened the Church of St. Paul Major in 1538 and where he labored to bring about Catholic reform, becoming a leading figure in the Catholic Reformation. Beatified in 1627, he was canonized in 1671 by Pope Clement X. Feast day: August 8. (See also **Theatines**.)

Cajetan, Thomas de Vio (1469-1534) ● Also called Cajetanus and Gaetano, a prominent theologian and a major member of the Thomistic school. Called Cajetan (or Gaetano) from his place of birth, Gaeta, he entered the Dominicans in 1484, studying in Bologna and Padua. He later taught at Padua, Pavia, and Rome, devoting much of his time while in Rome (1501-1508) to his remarkable commentary on Thomas Aquinas's *Summa Theologiae*. Appointed master general of the Dominican order, Cajetan promoted the ideals of the Dominicans, particularly poverty and theological study. He also investigated the cult of Girolamo Savonarola, supported the papacy at the Council of Pisa (1511) and the Fifth Lateran Council (1512-1517), and worked to bring about reform in the Church. Made a cardinal in 1517, he journeyed to Germany to examine Martin Luther. The two had an amicable meeting at Augsburg, but their doctrinal disagreements were irreconcilable. In 1520, he helped draft the bull *Exsurge Domine* that condemned Luther. Bishop of Gaeta in 1519, he helped secure the election of the reforming pope Adrian VI, later dedicating to him the commentary on the third part of the *Summa*. He was later legate to Hungary, Poland, and Bohemia (1523-1524), and opposed the planned divorce of King Henry VIII of England. He retired to Gaeta in 1527. His commentary on the *Summa* is still ranked as one of the classics of Scholasticism and marked the extensive revival of Thomism in the 1500s. He also authored commentaries on Aristotle and was a vigorous opponent of the doctrines of John Duns Scotus.

Calatrava, Knights of ● See under **Military Orders**.

Callistus I, St. ● Also Calixtus I, pope from around 217-222. His reign was marked by schism of the antipope St. Hippolytus, although details about his life were preserved in the *Philosophumena* by Hippolytus, a work that was partly an attack on him. According to Hippolytus, Callistus was originally a slave who had been denounced as a Christian and sent to the mines of Sardinia for involvement in bank fraud. His release was secured by Marcia, mistress of Emperor Commodus. Granted a pension by Victor I, he was ordained a deacon by Zephyrinus in 216, served as his chief councillor, and succeeded him as Bishop of Rome in 217. He was challenged by his rival Hippolytus, who attacked him for favoring Sabellianism and for being lax in enforcing discipline, particularly in readmitting those who had engaged in adultery and fornication. Callistus, however, did condemn Sabellius, author of Sabellianism, and the charges of Hippolytus are known largely from Hippolytus's own biased writings. He also transferred the Roman Christian burial ground from the Via Salaria to the Via Appia. It was later called the "Cemetery of San Callisto." He himself was buried in the Via Aurelia. Feast day: October 14.

Callistus II ● Pope from 1119-1124. Born Guido di Borgogne (Guido of Burgundy) he was the son of Count William I of Burgundy, being named in 1088 archbishop of Vienne, France, by Pope Urban II. Papal legate in France (1106), he participated in the Lateran Council of 1112, which proclaimed the rights of investiture that Emperor Henry V had forced Pope Paschal II to pronounce to be null and void. That same year, he presided over the Council of Vienne that declared lay investiture to be a heresy. In 1119, at Cluny, he was elected the successor of Pope Gelasius II, holding a Council at Reims

(1119) where he excommunicated Henry and the antipope Gregory VIII. The following year, he celebrated a triumph in Rome, and the German princes, anxious to bring about a peaceful settlement between pope and emperor, compelled a reconciliation upon Henry. The result was the Concordat of Worms (1122) that ended the long and bitter investiture controversy. The Lateran Council of 1123 ratified the concordat and promulgated a series of decrees on simony, priestly marriage, and the election of high-ranking churchmen. In 1120, Callistus also issued the bull *Etsi Judaeis*, which granted some degree of protection to the Jews of Rome.

Callistus III <1> ● Also Calixtus III, an antipope from 1168-1178 in opposition to Pope Alexander III. Elected through the wishes of the Holy Roman Emperor Frederick I Barbarossa, Giovanni di Strumi was, as Callistus III, the successor of the antipope Paschal III. He remained loyal to Frederick until the time of the signing of the Treaty of Anagni in 1176, which terminated the schism in the Church then raging in the favor of Alexander. Callistus was to be granted an abbacy, but he refused to step down and remained firm in his claims to the papacy until 1178. In August of that year, he finally submitted to Alexander after receiving a promise from the pope of generous and courteous treatment. (See also **Antipope**.)

Callistus III <2> ● Also Calixtus III, pope from 1455-1458. The first of the Borgia popes, Alfonso de Borgia was originally from Valencia. A jurist, he was a noted figure at the court of King Alfonso V of Aragon and Sicily, reconciling the ruler with Pope Martin V. Although he initially supported the claims of the antipope Benedict XIII, his successful efforts at convincing Martin's successor, Clement VIII, to step down secured his own appointment in 1429 as bishop of Valencia by Martin. Created a cardinal in 1444 by Pope Eugenius IV, he was elected as Callistus III on April 8, 1455, as a compromise candidate between the powerful families of the Colonna and the Orsini, largely because he was not expected to live long. His reign is most known for his efforts at organizing a crusade against the Ottoman Turks who, in 1453, had captured Constantinople and brought an end to the Byzantine Empire. He met with little success in this effort, although the fleet that he raised did relieve some islands in the Aegean; moreover, Belgrade was captured in 1456 by St. Giovanni Capistrano (see **John Capistran, St.**). In commemoration, Callistus instituted the Feast of the Transfiguration in 1457. He also revised the trial of Joan of Arc by declaring her to be innocent of all charges. While he led a personally blameless life, Callistus did practice a certain amount of nepotism by advancing several relatives, most notably Rodrigo Borgia, his nephew, whom he made a cardinal and who later became Pope Alexander VI.

Calmet, Dom Augustine (1672-1757) ● Well-known scholar responsible for inaugurating a new method of biblical exegesis. A native of Lorraine, he was educated at the Benedictine priory of Breuil. Ordained in 1696, he taught theology and philosophy at the Abbey of Moyen-Moutier and was later (1704) made sub-prior and professor of exegesis at Münster, in Alsace. He spent a number of years gathering material for his ambitious commentary on the Bible. The first volume appeared in 1707 under the title *Commentaire littéral sur tous les livres de l'Ancien et du Nouveau Testament* (*Literal Commentary on All the Books of the Old and New Testament*).

Subsequent volumes appeared over the next decade, and a second edition of twenty-six volumes was issued in the years 1714-1720. More editions followed, as the work was highly esteemed and quite popular. The commentary was particularly notable for

Calmet's focusing on literal interpretation of the Scriptures rather than focusing on moral and allegorical interpretations. It thus marked a new style of biblical exegesis. Calmet authored a number of other works, including a civil and ecclesiastical history of Lorraine.

Calvin, John (1509-1564) ● French theologian and an important figure in the Protestant Reformation. Born in Noyon, in Picardy, France, Calvin was intended by his family for a career in the Church, early receiving a benefice and tonsure. Studying at Paris from 1523-1528, he increasingly faced a crisis of faith and severe doubts about his vocation. His concerns only mounted at Orléans from 1528 while studying law as he became part of a group of Protestant intellectuals. In 1533, he experienced a sudden conversion that left him convinced that his mission was to reform the Church. The next year he resigned his benefices and was forced to flee from France to Basel in the face of persecution under King Francis I of France. Initially planning to devote himself to study, he authored the first edition of the *Institutes* (*Christianae Religionis Institutio*), a defense of Protestant principles, which was published in Latin in 1536. That same year, while visiting Geneva, he agreed to assist local Protestants in establishing the Reformation there, being appointed professor of theology and preacher. By 1538, an oath was extracted from all residents of Geneva, but Calvin's extremism, especially his introduction of excommunication, caused his expulsion from the city. He then preached in Basel and Strasbourg and took part in the Conference of Frankfurt (1539), the Conference of Hagenau (1540), the Disputation of Worms (1540-1541), and the Diet of Ratisbon (1541).

Calvin returned to Geneva in 1541 and was able to see installed a theocratic regime governing the city through a sweeping and harsh set of ordinances that inflicted severe punishments for pleasures such as dancing, laughing, and games. There were numerous religious offenses that could be committed, and Calvin ruthlessly extirpated the local opposition, torturing and executing the resistance, most notably the physician Michael Servetus (1511-1553), who was burned. From 1555-1564, Calvin ruled Geneva as undisputed master, wielding control over virtually every aspect of life and earning the resentment of many Protestants in the city and elsewhere. A more gifted organizer than Luther, Calvin was to give encouragement and support to other Protestant groups, especially the French Protestants (the Huguenots), who would be a major presence in French sociopolitical affairs, and English Protestants, many of whom fled to Geneva during the reign of Queen Mary (1553-1558).

Calvin's *Institutes* was one of the most influential of all Protestant works. In it he set forth his doctrines: he rejected papal authority, systematized the doctrine of predestination, and believed in justification by faith alone. The Bible, he declared, was the sole source of God's laws, and he used it to form the foundation of his theocracy. His other writings included NT commentaries, *Articuli de Regimine Ecclesiae* (1536), and a treatise on predestination. Through the tenets of what came to be called Calvinism, he was able to shape to a profound degree the direction of Protestantism, the ideas set forth in the *Institutes* finding expression among the Huguenots of France, the Puritans of England and America, and the Covenantors of Scotland. (See also **Calvinism** in the GLOSSARY.)

Calvinism ● See **Calvin, John**, preceding entry; see also in the GLOSSARY.

Camaldolese ● Known in full as the Congregation of the Monk Hermits of Camaldoli, a religious order founded in 1012 at Camaldoli, near Arezzo, Italy, by St.

Romuald. It was part of the monastic reform that prevailed during the era. It promoted a very austere form of common life with severe hermetical asceticism, with newer members residing in a stern monastic setting and the more advanced living in the associated hermitage, at the discretion of the abbot or abbess. As St. Romuald did not leave a written rule, individual foundations of the Camaldolese differed in organization and type. For example, the monastery at Fontebuono (founded in 1102) was along regular cenobitic lines, meaning that the religious lived in a community rather than as hermits. In 1523, a reform group of the Camaldolese was founded under the name Congregation of Monte Corona.

Camerlengo ● Also, in Latin, *camerarius*, the chamberlain of the papal court who is always a cardinal. Historically, the camerlengo was a powerful figure, as the office included administration of the properties and revenues of the Holy See during a pontificate and of the entire Church during the *sede vacante* (i.e., the interregnum, or vacancy) between the popes. Today, the camerlengo's power has been reduced primarily to the administration of the Holy See from the death of the pontiff to election of a successor. The duties include making certain that the pope is truly dead (by tapping the deceased pontiff three times on the head with a hammer and calling out his pre-pontifical name), destroying the pope's ring and seals, and closing the papal apartments. The camerlengo also helps organize the dead pope's funeral, summons the College of Cardinals to Rome, informs the world of the sad event of a pontiff's demise, and, especially, convenes the conclave to elect a new successor to Peter. The camerlengo can be reappointed at the new pope's discretion, but it is absolutely necessary that the new Holy Father name a camerlengo immediately, since the Holy See should not go a minute without the chamberlain. The last camerlengo to convene a conclave was Cardinal Jean Villot, who did so twice in 1978, after the deaths of Pope Paul VI and Pope John Paul I. (See also **Conclave**.)

Campeggio, Lorenzo (1472-1539) ●
Archbishop of Bologna, Italian cardinal, and humanist. Campeggio entered the service of the Church after the death of his wife (by whom he had five children), was ordained in 1510, promoted to the see of Feltre in 1512, and named papal nuncio (representative) to the court of Emperor Maximilian from 1513 to 1517. A trusted representative of the papacy, he was a legate to the Diets of Regensburg (1524) and Augsburg (1530), and was sent to England in 1518 by Pope Leo X to try to enlist the aid of King Henry VIII for a crusade against the Ottoman Turks. While he failed in this mission, he was nevertheless made protector of England within the Roman Curia, being appointed bishop of Salisbury in 1524 through King Henry; the year before, he was made archbishop of Bologna. In 1528, Campeggio returned to England as co-legate with Cardinal Wolsey to look into the projected divorce of Henry from Lady Catherine of Aragon. Pope Clement VII, however, had already pledged him to refer the matter to the pontiff and so he was unable to satisfy Henry's desire to settle the divorce in England. In 1535, Henry had him deprived of the see of Salisbury by Act of Parliament. Made a cardinal in 1535, he took part in the preparatory commissions of the Council of Trent before his death.

Campion, Edmund, St. (1540-1581) ●
Most famous of the Jesuit martyrs of England, one of the Forty Martyrs canonized in 1970. Campion, the son of a London bookseller, was educated through the Grocer's Guild, studying at Christ's Hospital and St. John's College, Oxford. In 1557, he became a junior fellow at St. John's and was teaching at Oxford when he was ordained a

deacon in the Anglican Church. Increasingly, however, he suffered a crisis of faith and reached the decision to enter the Church. In 1571, he departed England in disguise and joined William Allen at Douai where he was welcomed into the Catholic faith. From there, he journeyed to Rome as a pilgrim, entering the Society of Jesus in 1573 and receiving holy orders in 1578. After teaching in Prague for a time, he joined the first Jesuit mission sent in 1580 to England, a hazardous undertaking, as Catholics were forbidden to practice their religion. He preached quite successfully in secret assemblies in Berkshire, Oxfordshire, London, and Lincolnshire, and created a sensation by having four hundred copies of his book *Decem rationes* (*Ten Reasons*) distributed before a service in St. Mary's, Oxford, in June 1581. Arrested in July as a spy at Lyford, Berkshire, the authorities offered him his life if he would return to the Church of England. Refusing, he was convicted of treason (charged with conspiring against the queen) and executed at Tyburn on December 1, 1581. Beatified in 1886, he was canonized by Pope Paul VI. (See also **Forty Martyrs**.)

Canada ● The history of the Church in Canada traditionally dates to July 7, 1534, when a priest in the exploration force under Jacques Cartier said Mass on the Gaspé Peninsula. From this humble beginning, there followed some sixty years of relative inactivity, with no formal colonization commencing until 1603 when Champlain sailed up the St. Lawrence and established the first French settlement in North America at Port Royal in Nova Scotia. In 1608, Quebec was begun and henceforth two objectives would be the focus of the French: the fur trade and the planting of the Catholic faith among the native inhabitants. The first missionaries, the Franciscan Recollects (*Recollets*) who had accompanied Champlain, arrived in 1615. They were succeeded in 1625 by the Jesuits, launching a period of

genuinely heroic missionary activity as these priests, called the Black Robes by the Indians, set out for the interior and preached among such tribes as the Huron, Algonquins, and Iroquois (see also **Tekakwitha, Kateri, Bl.**). The first two Jesuits, Jean de Brébeuf and Gabriel Lalemant, were both martyred; they would be joined in death by others. Eight missionaries put to death in the period were canonized in 1930 (see **North American Martyrs**).

As the value of Canada to France increased, Cardinal Richelieu encouraged more missionaries, including more Jesuits. There came as well the remarkable women Marie de l'Incarnation of the Ursulines in 1836 and Marguerite Bourgeoys, foundress of the Congregation of Notre Dame, in 1653. The Sulpicians arrived in 1657. The next year, Canada was officially made a vicariate apostolic under Bishop François de Laval-Montmorency; he would become the first bishop of Quebec in 1674. Under his leadership and especially that of the Jesuits, New France (as Canada was called) became a strong Catholic colony and its treatment of the natives was in sharp contrast to the English colonies and especially the Spanish possessions in Central and South America. French Canada would survive repeated attacks by the British, but the colony would finally fall in 1759 with the capture of Quebec in the Seven Years' War (1756-1763). By the terms of the Treaty of Paris (1763), New France was ceded to Britain.

Catholics in the former French colony were understandably concerned about falling under the British, who had already forcibly deported the French Catholics from Nova Scotia, the Acadians, in 1755. By the Quebec Act of 1774, however, Catholics were allowed to practice their religion, although the hierarchy was not recognized, and in 1774 the Jesuits and Recollects were dispossessed. Additional pressures were brought to bear with the establishing of the Church of England, followed by Protestant denominations. In 1793, priests who had been exiled from France during the French Revolution were allowed into the country. This influx improved the state of Catholic affairs, and by the early 1800s the Church was again on the move. In 1819, the British government permitted Bishop Octave Plessis to become archbishop of Quebec. Other sees followed and, under Lord Elgin, governor-general from 1847-1854, the Acts of 1851 confirmed religious freedom and opened the way for new religious communities. The see of Montreal was begun in 1836, Toronto in 1841, and Ottawa in 1847. In western Canada, the vicariate apostolic was created in 1844. Three years later, Modeste Demers became bishop of Vancouver Island. The Confederation of Canada was born in 1867 with the British North American Act. Currently there are nearly twelve million Catholics in nineteen archdioceses.

Cano, Melchior (1509-1560) ● Spanish Dominican theologian. A native of Tarancón, Spain, he entered the Dominicans in 1523 at Salamanca. There he studied under the famed theologian Francisco de Vitoria (d. 1546). Starting around 1533, Cano taught in Valladolid, was named the first theological professor at Álcalá, and in 1546 was chosen the successor to de Vitoria at Salamanca. Emperor Charles V sent him to the Council of Trent (1551-1552) where he took part in the debates on the Eucharist and penance. Back in Spain, he developed ties with King Philip II, defending his antipapal policies, particularly through his *Consultatio theologica* (1556). These activities earned the displeasure of Pope Paul IV (r. 1555-1559), who refused to confirm the election of Cano in 1557 as provincial of the Dominican order and delayed confirmation of his reelection in 1559. Cano's main theological work was his posthumous *De locis theologicis* (1563), analyzing the scientific value of the theological statements and promoting a

controversial theory on the sacrament of matrimony.

Canon Law ● Body of laws used to govern the Catholic Church. The name is derived from the Greek word *kanon* (rule, i.e., rule of practical direction), which, from the fourth century, was used to denote the ordinances and regulations promulgated by the various Church councils that were convened to discuss problems or important topics. The actual term "canon law" (*ius canonicum*) came into use in the 1100s and was intended to differentiate ecclesiastical law from civil law (*ius civile*); still later the *Corpus Juris Canonici* came into being.

In a practical sense, the laws and regulations began to take shape as early as apostolic times and were evident in their nascent form in the *Didache*. Owing to the persecution of the Church, however, there was little effort to gather laws together, and certainly less time was devoted to systematizing them.

The fourth century brought freedom of the Church from persecution and the resulting rapid growth in membership that was a concomitant of the favors bestowed upon by the rulers of the Roman Empire. New laws were naturally needed and desired. Local regulations were soon established through the decrees of the councils, although these most often had only a local authority and adherence. The general (or ecumenical) councils made laws for the whole Church, and the custom developed of carrying on the decrees of previous assemblies by having them read before the start of a new council. Collections of these laws or canons were then undertaken, but these did not bear the weight of being an official code or they were gathered under private authority.

The earliest efforts at collecting Church laws were centered around the private compilation of the decrees of the Eastern councils to which were added those of the Western Church. The councils of the African

Church also made lasting contributions, the most significant coming out of the Seventeenth Council of Carthage (419), which accepted the book of canons later adopted into the canon law of both the Eastern and Western Churches. An official Code of Canon Law was recognized in the seventh century under the Isidorian Collection. Other important influences were in the writings drawn up by the monks in England and Ireland of sins and various offenses by confessors who then applied the proper fines or penances. The resulting books were called Penitentials, and they offer scholars an invaluable glimpse into the state of Church law in early medieval England and the development of moral theology.

The Carolingian Reforms of the Church under Charlemagne facilitated the enactment of much legislation that was beneficial to the faith, but it also signaled a long period of secular interference in ecclesiastical affairs. Two by-products of this lay intrusion were the creation of the forged but interesting False Decretals (collections of false canons and decrees of the popes used to falsify the Church's position) and the application of legal arguments by Churchmen that could protect the Church from abuse. Efforts at revitalization would become heightened under the Gregorian Reform, in particular with the reign of Pope St. Gregory VII (1073-1085). From that time, throughout the Middle Ages, laws from the Church would be centered in and produced by the papacy, assisted in running the administration of the Church by the Roman Curia.

Gradually, legal experts collected the decrees of popes, enactments of councils, and sources of older, ancient canons. To these were added glosses, or commentaries, to assist in the teaching of the details of the subject. Still, the study of canon law was severely handicapped by the sheer number of collections, the contradiction between many points of law, and the inability to find specific laws because of the chronological arrangements of the material. Thus can be seen the major significance of the *Decretum* of Gratian, published around 1148 in Bologna. Compiled by the legal expert Gratian, the *Decretum* (in full, *Concordantia discordantum canonum*) was not a formal collection of canons but sought to provide a juridical system for its readers. Toward this end, though, Gratian examined (and excerpted) virtually every canon ever published. The *Decretum* was quickly adopted as the textbook of canon law, despite the fact that it was a private collection and not codified.

Over the next centuries, the popes would add to the body of laws by giving rulings to those questions posed to them by bishops from around the Church. These decretal letters were then brought together and, for purposes of comprehensiveness, added to the *Decretum Gratiani*. The most important of these was the *Liber extra*, the collection made by St. Raymond Peñafort for Pope Gregory IX. This received official approval and was to be a vital source for the *Corpus Juris Canonici*. Other remarkable contributors to canon law in the late Middle Ages were Zenzelinus de Cassanis, Jean Chappuis, Guido de Baysio, John the Teuton (or Joannes Teutonicus), Stephen of Tournai, and most of all, Joannes Andreae (d. 1348).

Considerable activity was initiated by the Council of Trent (1545-1563), which sought to reform and reinvigorate the Church in the wake of the Protestant Reformation. The same century brought the formation in 1588 of the Sacred Congregation of the Curia by Pope Sixtus V (r. 1585-1590), which became the main means of implementing new laws and examining facets of established ones.

The final decision to codify the laws of the Church was made by Pope St. Pius X who, in 1903, issued *Arduum*, the *motu proprio* ordering the complete reform and codification of all canon law. It would be completed in 1917 as the *Corpus Juris Canonici*, the first official guide to the laws of the Catholic

Church. A new Code of Canon Law was issued by Pope John Paul II in 1983, the final result of a call for a new code dating back to Pope John XXIII (r. 1958-1963) and continued by Pope Paul VI (r. 1963-1978).

Canonization ● See GLOSSARY.

Canon of St. Augustine ● See **Augustinian Canons**.

Canon of Muratori ● See **Muratorian Fragment**.

Canoness ● Most commonly, a woman who lives as a religious in a community adhering to a rule similar to that followed by the canons regular, normally the Rule of St. Augustine. The name canoness was first applied in the fourth century to a woman who performed certain functions in a church. During the Carolingian period, the canoness (or canonica) meant a woman who resided in a community of religious, took vows of celibacy and obedience but not a vow of poverty, meaning that she could hold property. It could also mean a woman who followed a devout life without vows.

Canons of the Apostles ● See **Apostolic Canons**.

Canterbury illustration, from the Utrecht Psalter

Canon Regular ● See GLOSSARY.

Canons, Chapter of ● See GLOSSARY.

Canterbury ● Cathedral city in Kent, England, the site of the important see of Canterbury, long serving as the primal see of the kingdom until its loss in the English Reformation. Canterbury has traditionally been the spiritual center of the island and was at the height of its power and influence during the Middle Ages. According to legend, Canterbury was first founded by the British king Lud-Hudibras (c. 900 B.C.), but archaeologists have dated the earliest known community to approximately 200 B.C. It had a Roman population after the invasion of A.D. 43; it later had the name Durovernum. The name Canterbury was from the tribe known as the Cantii and was called Cantwaraburh (town of the Kents), serving as the capital city of Ethelbert, king of Kent. The ruler married a Frankish princess named Bertha, who was able to bring into the region a bishop, Liuthard. He took up residence at St. Martin at Canterbury and was followed by the renowned St. Augustine of Canterbury, who had been sent in 597 by Pope St. Gregory I the Great to bring the Christian faith to the inhabitants of England. He converted Ethelbert, founded a Benedictine monastery, and built the Cathedral of Christ Church at Canterbury. From that time, Canterbury was considered the primal see of England and through the work of Augustine's successors, such as Theodore of Tarsus (archbishop from 668), most of England was brought under their jurisdiction.

The first Norman archbishop of Canterbury was Lanfranc, appointed in 1070 by King William I the Conqueror, who introduced a host of reforms to the English Church. He was followed by Anselm (1093-1109), who had been a monk at Bec and emerged as a leading spokesman against lay investiture, coming into conflict with Kings William II and Henry I. Even greater struggles would fill the time of St. Thomas Becket (1162-1170). His contentious disagreements with King Henry II ended with his murder in Canterbury Cathedral. King Henry later performed penance at Thomas's tomb and was flogged by several monks. During the later Middle Ages, the archbishops were frequently very powerful politically, wielding extensive influence in royal affairs. Among the notable archbishops of this period were Hubert Walter (1193-1205), Stephen Langton (1207-1228), Robert Kilwardby (1273-1280), Simon Islip (1349-1366), Simon of Sudbury (1375-1381), Thomas Arundel (1396-1397, 1399-1414), John Kempe (1452-1454), Thomas Bourchier (1454-1486), and William Warham (1504-1532). Warham would be the last archbishop before the reign of Thomas Cranmer (1533-1556), who would preside over the separation of the English Church from Rome. The see of Canterbury subsequently became the primal see of the Church of England. When the hierarchy was reconstituted in England in 1850 by Pope Pius IX (r. 1846-1878), it was clear that a Catholic archbishop of Canterbury could not be appointed. Instead, Pius named Nicholas Wiseman (1802-1865) the first archbishop of Westminster.

Cappadocian Fathers, The ● Name given to the three leading fourth-century Christian theologians Basil the Great, Gregory of Nazianzus, and Gregory of Nyssa. The name was derived from the fact that all three were from Cappadocia.

Capreolus, John (c. 1380-1444) ● Also Jean Capreolus, a Dominican theologian who earned the title *Thomistarum Princeps* (Prince of the Thomists) for his energetic and brilliant defense of Thomistic thought. Born at Rodez, in modern Aveyron, France, Capreolus joined the Dominicans in Rodez and later lectured on the *Sentences* at the University of Paris where he later received degrees in theology in 1411 and 1415. He was then regent of studies at Toulouse before returning to Rodez. His principal achievement was his defense of the teachings of St. Thomas Aquinas in the *Four Books of Defenses of the Theology of St. Thomas Aquinas* (1409-1433), commonly called the *Defensiones*. The work was a leading cause for the revival of Thomism in the 1400s. (See also **Thomism**.)

Capuchins ● Properly, in Latin, the *Ordo Fratrum Minorum S. Francisci Capucinorum*, the Order of the Friars Minor Capuchin (O.F.M. Cap.), a branch of the Franciscan order that was established as a separate jurisdiction in 1528 by the Observant friar (a friar who belonged to the Observantines) Matteo di Bassi Urbino (d. 1552). It was di Bassi's hope to promote within the order a return to the simple, or primitive, rule of the original Franciscans. A rule was written in 1529 that called for members to adhere to strict austerity while enforcing very firmly the traditional idea of poverty. Owing to the earlier difficulties encountered by the order with the Fraticelli (Spiritual Franciscans) in the 1200s and 1300s, there was, not surprisingly, considerable opposition to the Capuchins from many other Franciscans. Coupled with the doubts and concern was the severe blow that struck in 1541 when the third general, Bernardino Ochino, became a Protestant. Surviving this unfortunate episode — including the near suppression of the entire branch — the Capuchins began to flourish in the Catholic Reformation and emerged as a powerful voice of reform within the Church. The Capuchins are known around the world for their work as missionaries, preachers, and confessors. Their rule, while eased in some ways from the original, is still noted for its call for austerity, and the Capuchins are still the most rigorous of the three autonomous branches of the Franciscans. Members wear a white pointed cowl (*capuche*), with the option of sandals and a beard.

Cardinal ● See GLOSSARY.

Cardinal Protector ● Title used in prior years for those cardinals who were appointed by the pope or one of the dicasteries of the Roman Curia with the task of giving his protection and patronage to a specific order, congregation, or institute. Protection might also extend to pious associations of laypeople. The cardinal gave these organizations his advice and concern in a variety of matters, but his practical role was to take up their cause in important matters or business they might have before the pope or with the Curia. Cardinal protectors were also appointed to the national colleges at Rome from the time of the Council of Trent in the sixteenth century. Cardinal protectors are now virtually extinct because of extensive improvements in the bureaucracy of the Curia, who act on their behalf. The Franciscan order was long the recipient of protection from a cardinal; Cardinal Ugolino Conti (the future Pope Gregory IX) was appointed by Innocent III, and again by Honorius III, traditionally at the request

initially of St. Francis himself. As a sign of intense papal favor, both Alexander IV and Nicholas III retained for themselves the post of protector of the Franciscans. The Franciscans, in fact, were the only order with a cardinal protector until the late 1300s when the office was extended. Pope Innocent XII (r. 1691-1700) was responsible for creating the final regulations, protocol, and the rights of the office. (See also **Curia, Roman**.)

Cardinals, College of ● Properly the Sacred College of Cardinals, the collective name given to the body of bishops chosen by the pope to provide their advice and to gather together after the death of a pontiff to elect a successor. These bishops bear the title of cardinal, an office that developed gradually over the history of the Church. The name cardinal is derived from the Latin *cardo* (hinge) and was probably first used as a colloquial term to describe certain advisers considered essential to the governing of the Church, "hinge" men. By custom, the college is divided into three categories, bishops, priests, and deacons: cardinal bishops are titular bishops of the suburbicarian (or suffragan) sees of Rome; cardinal priests are titular heads of the presbyterial churches in the diocese of Rome; and the cardinal deacons are titulars of the diaconal churches of Rome.

Cardinal bishops originated out of the actual bishops of the suffragan dioceses surrounding Rome, the suburbicarian sees. They were routinely called upon by the early popes for advice and had a share in the administration of the Church. From the twelfth century, there were seven dioceses headed by cardinal bishops: Ostia, Sabina, and Poggio; Mirteto; Albano; Palestrina; Velletri; Frascati; and Porto and Santa Rufino. Actually there were only six cardinal bishops because the senior cardinal was the bishop of Ostia as well as bishop of his own diocese, a post of considerable power and prestige. In 1962, Pope John XXIII declared that the cardinal bishops should bear the title only in an honorary capacity. The suburbicarian would be administered by noncardinal bishops and the titular cardinal bishops would devote their efforts to the assistance of the Holy See. Cardinal priests were originally pastors of the dioceses of Rome, and the cardinal deacons were at first officials in Rome charged with various tasks, receiving a church that would serve his center of activity. While originally used to describe the actual sacred order of the cardinal in question, this ceased at an early time so that cardinal priests and cardinal deacons could be bishops; cardinal bishops were always bishops.

The College of Cardinals did not exist in the early Church, but it came into existence over time as is seen with the suburbicarian bishops. It is possible that cardinal priests and deacons existed before the cardinal bishops, as they are mentioned in surviving documents from the sixth century; the term cardinal bishop is found in the eighth century. The college itself began taking definite shape in the 1100s, receiving formal recognition in 1150. In 1179, Pope Alexander III (r. 1159-1181) decreed that only a pope could select the cardinals. The size of the college has varied widely over the years. Pope Sixtus V decreed that there should be only seventy members, a number that remained constant until 1958. In that year, Pope John XXIII increased the number to seventy-five. Further additions followed under Popes Paul VI and John Paul II. Currently, there are 148 cardinals from all over the world, the most international distribution in the history of the Church. Only one hundred twenty are allowed to take part in papal elections, as cardinals over eighty years old are ineligible to vote and are required to retire from any offices or curial positions.

Cardinals are chosen by the pope and are introduced into the college at a consistory, a ceremony of considerable pomp and

significance in the constant reinvigorating of the Church. The title of cardinal was made specific to the members of the college in 1567. By the Code of Canon Law of 1917 (which became effective in 1918), it was decreed that all cardinals must be priests. The last nonordained cardinal was the great statesman Giacomo Antonelli (1806-1876), secretary of state to Pope Pius IX. John XXIII ordered in the decree *Cum Gravissima* that all cardinals should be invested with episcopal dignity. Cardinals and all regulations pertaining to them are covered in the Code of Canon Law (Canons 349-359). Considered the most powerful prelates of the Church, cardinals are distinguished by their widened field of authority, their distinctive vestments, and numerous rights and privileges, in keeping with the added responsibilities they bear in the service of the supreme pontiff, the Holy Father. Cardinals carry the high honorific title of "Prince of the Church" and are addressed as "Eminence."

Carmel, Mt. ● Known in the Hebrew as *Ha-Karmel* or *Har Karmel*, a mountain in northwestern Israel that is above the port of Haifa and that divides the central plain of Israel between the plain of Esdraelon and Galilee from the coastal plain of Sharon. From the earliest times, Mt. Carmel was revered as a holy place, being mentioned by the Egyptians in records dating to the sixteenth century B.C. It was the site of Elijah's confrontation with the false prophets of Baal (1 Kgs 18:19-46; also 2 Kgs 2:25 and 4:25) and was an important habitation site for early Christians. Hermits resided there from around the sixth century, and from then on Carmel was especially associated with the veneration of Mary. Greek monks established a church and a monastery about 500. The Carmelite order was founded on Mt. Carmel around 1154. (See also **Carmelite Order**, following entry.)

Carmelite Order ● One of the great mendicant orders, known in full as the Order of Our Lady of Mt. Carmel (O. Carm.). The Carmelites were founded around 1154 by St. Berthold (d. c. 1195) when, according to tradition, he established a community on Mt. Carmel in Palestine comprised of former crusaders, hermits, and pilgrims who had taken up residence there; there was already a long-standing tradition of hermits on the mountain, claiming descent from Elijah. A rule was handed down for the community around 1209 by Albert de Vercelli, Latin patriarch of Jerusalem. It called for strict adherence to a regimen of self-mortification, abstinence, and poverty. Owing to the thirteenth-century collapse of the Crusader States in the Holy Land, most of the Carmelites were forced to leave the Middle East, assembling in 1247 in England for their first general assembly under the leadership of St. Simon Stock. The remaining Carmelites in Palestine were martyred in 1291. St. Simon, elected prior general of the order at the first chapter (at Aylesford, Kent), was the principal architect of the rise of the order in Europe. He adapted the rule to the needs of life in the West, designed the brown scapular (after a vision of the Blessed Virgin), and encouraged the Carmelites to enter university life. Under him, the order was transferred into a mendicant organization, spreading all over Christendom and then into the New World. The friars were joined in 1452 by the second order, the Carmelite nuns, founded by Bl. John Soreth (1405-1471) and living in the cloister.

By the 1500s, the Carmelites, both nuns and friars, were in need of a general reform, which was accomplished by two truly remarkable saints, Teresa of Ávila (1515-1582) and John of the Cross (1542-1591). Teresa launched her reforms in 1562 by restoring the so-called Primitive Rule among many Carmelite cloisters, while promoting the contemplative life. John of the Cross brought similar reforms to the friars.

They were opposed by a number of members who preferred retention of the less severe Mitigated Rule. Their resistance led in 1593 to the separation of the Carmelites into two congregations, the Discalced Carmelites (O.C.D.) following the Primitive Rule and the Calced Carmelites (O. Carm.) adhering to the Mitigated Rule.

Dedicated to Mary, the order has its main activities in theology, missionary work, and especially contemplation. The Carmelite Nuns are dedicated to prayer, penance, and intercessions, most notably for priests. The habit consists of a brown tunic, brown *capuche* (hood), brown scapular, and black belt. On solemn occasions, they might wear a white cloak and white *capuche*. There is also a third order composed of laypeople, begun by Bl. John Soreth. (See also **Salmanticenses**.)

Caroline Books, The ● So-called *Libri Carolini*, a treatise written from around 790-792 that attacked the Iconoclastic Council of 754 and the Second Council of Nicaea in 787 for their views on Iconoclasm, the controversy in the Byzantine Empire concerning the veneration of icons. *The Caroline Books* was supposedly written by Charlemagne, but it was certainly composed by a trained theologian; scholars thought for a long time that the author was Alcuin, although recent scholarship favors Theodulf of Orléans. Its purpose was to ridicule the Byzantine empress Irene, who was a source of some irritation to Charlemagne, and to increase the validity of Charlemagne's assumption of the imperial title, a coronation vigorously opposed by the Byzantines.

Carolingian Schools ● Institutes of learning established during and after the reign of Charlemagne (r. 768-814), an important part of the so-called Carolingian Renaissance of the ninth century in which the ruler and his immediate heirs sponsored the creation of schools, supported teachers, and promoted literacy among the Frankish clergy. Charlemagne was the principal sponsor in the rise of the Carolingian schools, particularly through the support he gave such advisers as Alcuin and Theodulf of Orléans. The groundwork for the schools was laid 787 in the capitulary (or enactment) that Charlemagne sent to Bangulf, abbot of Fulda, instructing him to establish places in monasteries and bishops' houses where teaching could take place, declaring to the abbot and bishops that "care should be taken that there should not only be a regular manner of life, but also the study of letters, each to teach and learn them according to his ability and the Divine assistance." Known as the "charter of modern education," the capitulary was followed by several others that both confirmed and added to the framework of education. Especially influential was the Palace School under Alcuin of York whose reforms in learning were passed on to the Church-sponsored and state-supported schools throughout the Carolingian Empire. While primitive by the standards of later medieval universities, the Carolingian schools were a bold and innovative institution. The seven liberal arts were taught, along with basic theology, and there resulted as well the evolution of the Vulgate Bible and extensive revisions of the liturgy. Latin was restored as the language of education for the first time since the fall of the Roman Empire in the fifth century, and an education was available to both the nobles and the members of the lay plebeian class. Aside from the Palace School, the chief learning places were associated with cathedrals and monasteries; many of these emerged as the leading educational centers of Europe. While the quality of the education at the schools could not endure the decline of the Carolingian Dynasty, they nevertheless were crucial in establishing the education system that would endure throughout the Middle Ages and the Renaissance and played a major role in associating the Church with the highest levels of learning and intellectual achievement throughout the epoch. (See also **Cathedral Schools** and **Universities**.)

Carroll, John (1735-1815) ● Archbishop of Baltimore, the first prelate of the hierarchy in the United States, and a member of that remarkable American Catholic family of the Carrolls; his cousin was the brilliant patriot Charles Carroll (1737-1832), the last surviving signer of the Declaration of Independence and the only Catholic to sign that famous document. John Carroll was born in Upper Marlborough, Maryland, and was educated at St. Omer's in Flanders. Joining the Society of Jesus in 1753, he was ordained in 1769. He subsequently taught at Liège and St. Omer's, returning to America in 1774 after the 1773 suppression of the Jesuits. From that time, Carroll was active as a missionary and was an ardent patriot in the drive for American independence from England. A good friend of Benjamin Franklin, he participated in Franklin's ill-fated embassy to Canada in 1776. Franklin was also helpful in having Carroll appointed superior of the missions in the United States by Pope Pius VI in 1784, an important development, as it made the U.S. Church independent of the vicars apostolic in England. Five years later, Carroll was appointed the first American bishop, being consecrated at the chapel of Lulworth Castle, Dorset, as bishop of Baltimore. When, in 1808, his huge diocese was divided into four sees, he became archbishop of Baltimore. Carroll was one of the most important of the American Catholics during the era of the Revolutionary War and the founding of the United States. He helped assure a legitimate and lasting place for the Church in American life and was highly successful in securing a certain degree of toleration of Catholics in the fledgling republic. In responding to the anti-Catholic attack concerning the war, Carroll wrote that Catholic blood "flowed as freely [as others'] to cement the fabric of independence as that of their fellow citizens. They concurred with perhaps greater unanimity than any other body of men in recommending and promoting that government from whose influence America anticipates all the blessings of justice, peace, plenty, good order, and civil and religious liberty."

Carta Caritatis ● See **Charter of Love**.

Carthage, Councils of ● Series of ecclesiastical synods that were held at Carthage between the third and sixth centuries. The first councils were held under St. Cyprian in 251, 252, 254, 255, and 256. They were first concerned with the reconciliation of so-called lapsed Christians, those believers who had wavered from the faith during the persecutions of Emperor Trajanus Decius (r. 249-251). Later councils examined the rebaptism of heretics, a matter of some dispute with Rome. The councils held under Gratus (c. 348) and under Genethlius (350) are notable because their extant canons are the earliest surviving ones from the African councils. The councils held under Bishop Aurelius extended from 395-424, the most famous being those of 412 and 419; at the former council Pelagianism was condemned and at the latter, in May 419, the claims of the see of Rome to jurisdiction over Africa were challenged. The council is also known for the collection of canons called the *Codex Canonum Ecclesiae Africanae*, mostly compiled from earlier councils. The last Councils of Carthage were held in 525 and 534, although only canons from the latter council are extant.

Carthusian Order ● Contemplative order founded in 1084 by St. Bruno (d. 1101). Its name is taken from the Grande Chartreuse, a valley near Grenoble, France. As first established by Bruno, the Carthusians did not have a formal rule; rather, the members tried to adhere in spirit and by custom to the example of the founder. Over time, a rule became necessary and one was finally compiled by Gigues de Chatel (or Guigo), the fifth prior of Grande Chartreuse, in 1127. It was not written with any kind of formal authority, but it was given approval in 1133 by Pope Innocent II. A new edition was issued in 1258, called the *Statuta Antiqua*; the *Statuta Nova* appeared in 1368. A collection of the various ordinances of the chapter and a synopsis of the statutes was issued under the title *Tertia Compilatio* (1509). The next year the rule was printed for the first time at Basel by Johann Amorbach, and the *Nova Collectio Statutorum* was published in 1581.

From its inception, the Carthusian order was one of the strictest and most contemplative in the entire Church. Its monks were to be removed from the world, and the initial regulations laid down by Bruno included silence, personal isolation, and many hours of prayer. The monks ate, prayed, and labored alone, coming together into community only at morning Mass, Vespers, and for the evening Office; meals were eaten together only on feast days. Owing to the removed and deeply contemplative nature of the order, the Carthusians were largely unaffected by the upheavals of the Middle Ages. Under King Henry VIII of England (r. 1509-1547), several were put to death. Later suffering was caused by the French Revolution. The order in France had to endure hardships owing to the anticlerical legislation of the government during the 1800s and early 1900s. The Carthusians were always popular in Spain, Italy, and elsewhere. Carthusian nuns were established in 1245 but were never numerous. (See also **Hugh of Lincoln, St.**)

Cashel, Synod of ● Synod held in Cashel in County Tipperary, Ireland, in 1171 or 1172. It was convened by order of King Henry II after his invasion of the island with the aim of completing the reorganization of the Irish Church along the lines of the Western rite.

The meeting thus marked the last period of the usage of the Celtic Church. (See also **Celtic Church** and **Ireland**.)

Casimir, St. (1458-1484) ● Patron saint of Poland. Casimir was the second son of King Casimir of Poland and grandson of King Wladislaus II Jagiello of Poland, who was responsible for introducing Christianity into Lithuania. The early education of Prince Casimir was entrusted to two notable instructors, Father John Dlugosz and Filipo Buonaccorsi, known as Callimachus. Dlugosz, a patriot and devout historian, was especially important in fostering the prince's religious development, already much pronounced in his youth. In 1471, the prince was offered the throne of Hungary by a political faction of that kingdom, but his less than wholehearted efforts at securing the crown proved unsuccessful. Returning home, Casimir was again placed under the instruction of Father Dlugosz until 1475 at a castle near Cracow. In 1479, when his father went to Lithuania, Casimir was named viceroy of Poland, but his focus was now on religious devotion. He rejected a proposed marriage to a daughter of Emperor Frederick III in 1483 because of his personal oath of celibacy. Owing in part to self-mortification and a natural physical weakness, Casimir fell ill with lung trouble, dying at Grodno. He was interred in the chapel of the Blessed Virgin in the Cathedral of Vilna, and miracles were soon reported at his tomb. Canonized by Pope Adrian VI in 1522, he was named patron saint of Poland by Pope Clement VIII in 1602. Feast day: March 4.

Cassander, George (1513-1566) ● Flemish theologian and humanist. Born at Pitthem in West Flanders, he was educated at Louvain and was appointed a professor at Bruges in 1541. He resigned in 1543 to devote himself to travel so as to receive instruction and in part because of the controversy he caused by expressing certain pre-Reformation viewpoints. After visiting Rome, he stopped at Cologne and finally settled there in 1549. From that time, he ceased his work on the classics and devoted himself to biblical and ecclesiastical study. He worked to promote peace between the Catholics and Protestants, authoring at the request of the jurist Francis Baldwin the work *De officio pii viri in hoc religionis dissidio* (1561). In the book he argued through the Scriptures and the writings of the Fathers that abuses in the Church should not cause a person to abandon the faith, although he disagreed with many claims of papal supremacy. When presented at the Colloquy of Poissy in 1561, both sides took offense. For Ferdinand I (but addressed to Emperor Maximilian II), Cassander wrote *Consultatio de Articulis Religionis inter Catholicos at Protestantes Controversis* (published posthumously in 1577), hoping that it would be useful in advancing Ferdinand's efforts at a reunion. Once again, Cassander provoked both sides. He also wrote *Hymni Ecclesiastici* (1536), *Liturgica de ritu et ordine Dominicae coenae* (1588) — both were placed on the Index of Forbidden Books, *Ordo Romanus* (1558), *De Baptisme Infantium* (1539), and *De Sacra Communione Christiani Populi in utraque Panis et Specii* (1564).

Cassian, John, St. (360-435) ● Also Eremita, Johannes Cassianus, and Johannes Massiliensis, monk and ascetic writer, generally considered the first monk to introduce the Eastern styles of monasticism into the West. He was born possibly in the region that is now Romania; the ecclesiastical historian Gennadius of Marseilles wrote that Cassian was *"natione Scythia."* While still a young man, he entered a monastery in Bethlehem, but soon he departed for Egypt where he received eremitic training (i.e., training to be a hermit) from Egyptian ascetics of the deserts. By 399, he was at Constantinople where he served as a disciple of the patriarch St. John

Chrysostom. When Chrysostom was deposed illegally by Theophilus, patriarch of Alexandria, and exiled by Empress Eudoxia, Cassian was sent to Rome by partisans of Chrysostom to make an appeal before Pope St. Innocent I. During this Roman period, Cassian was ordained in 405, receiving the strong support of the pope. In 413, he founded at Marseilles the monastery of St. Victor, where he was abbot until his death, and a nunnery. While at St. Victor (c. 420-429), he authored two important works, *Institutes* and *Conferences*. The *Institutes* (in full, *Institutes of the Monastic Life*) presented basic rules for monastic life and was an important source for St. Benedict in the creation of his rule; the *Conferences* (in full, *Conferences of the Egyptian Monks or Collations of the Fathers*) presented conversations of the foremost figures of Eastern monasticism, the Fathers of the Desert. Around 430, he also authored *De Incarnatione Domini*, against the heresiarch Nestorius, for Pope Leo I the Great. He was also a leading exponent of Semi-Pelagianism and is considered its founder. Revered as a saint in the Eastern Church, he was never canonized in the West, although his feast is kept in southern France, particularly in Marseilles, on July 23. (See **Benedict, Rule of** and **Monasticism**.)

Cassiodorus (c. 485-c. 580) ● In full, Flavius Magnus Aurelius Cassiodorus, a Roman senator and monk who was an important figure in preserving Roman literature and culture during the chaotic sixth century. He was a member of an ancient Roman noble family, but, as with many other Romans, he served in the government of the Ostrogothic kings of Italy. Cassiodorus was a quaestor (507-511), consul (514), and at the time of the death of King Theodoric the Great, the powerful *magister officiorum* (master of the offices, 526). He was subsequently praetorian prefect (533), finally retiring from public life in 540.

Cassiodorus had been able to use his influence on Theodoric to convince the ruler to forsake Arianism, all the while attempting wherever possible to preserve Roman culture. After his retirement, he became a monk, establishing at Vivarium two monasteries on Benedictine lines. A prolific writer, he authored a number of influential books: *De artibus ac disciplinis liberalium litterarum; De Orthographia*, a compilation of classical grammar; *De anima*, on the soul; a chronicle, from Adam to 519; the *Historia Ecclesiastica Tripartita*, a Church history; *Institutiones divinarum et seculae litterarum*, a study of religious and secular thought written in two parts, the first for monks, examining Scripture, and the second a manual on the seven liberal arts; and the lost *Historia Gothica*, a history of the Goths in twelve volumes that was later abridged by the historian Jordanes. Cassiodorus's efforts to preserve both pagan and Christian learning were pivotal in forging the monasteries into repositories of classical knowledge during the eras of barbarian supremacy in Europe and as vital centers for learning during the entire medieval era. (See also **Monasticism**.)

Castel Gandolfo ● Small town situated in the Alban hills, on the edge of Lago (or Lake) Albano, approximately eighteen miles to the south of Rome. It is best known today as the summer residence of the popes. Castel Gandolfo derived its name from the castle of the House of Gandalfi, whose members resided there in the twelfth century. In 1608, it came into the possession of the Holy See under Pope Paul V. The current papal or apostolic palace was begun by Pope Urban VIII (the former Maffeo Barberini, r. 1623-1644) in 1629. This onetime villa was enlarged during the reigns of Alexander VII (r. 1655-1667), Clement XIII (r. 1758-1769), and Pius IX (r. 1846-1878). By the terms of the Lateran Treaty of 1929, Castel Gandolfo is considered an extraterritorial domain of the Holy See. The villa has also since housed the

Vatican Observatory (the Specola Vaticana), first established by Pope Gregory XIII (r. 1572-1585). It was frequently visited in the early part of his reign by Pope Paul VI. He would later die at Castel Gandolfo on August 6, 1978. Pope John Paul II (r. 1978-) had a swimming pool constructed at the residence, part of his long-standing pursuit of physical exercise.

Castel Sant' Angelo ● Also nicknamed Hadrian's Mole, and also called the Mausoleum of Hadrian or the *Sepulcrum Antoninorum*, the original mausoleum of Emperor Hadrian, constructed from A.D. 135-139, and subsequently holding the remains of the Roman emperors until the time of Caracalla (d. 217). In the fourth century it was turned into a fortress with a circular design and containing apartments, chapels, and prison cells. Throughout its long history it was most frequently a prison. The current name was first used after the famous incident of 590. In that year, Pope Gregory I the Great led a penitential procession to pray for relief from a city-wide plague. While walking, he looked upon the mausoleum and beheld a vision of the archangel Michael sheathing his sword over the fortress. The name of the structure and the marble statue of the archangel that rests atop it were both in commemoration of the event. On a number of occasions, Castel Sant' Angelo became a refuge for popes who were forced to flee marauders. The most famous of these events came in 1527 when Pope Clement VII barely escaped to the castle as Rome was captured by the troops of the Emperor Charles V. As Clement sat a virtual prisoner, Austrian mercenaries stabled their horses in St. Peter's. The safety of the fort was usually reached via a loggia from the Vatican Palace. Today, the loggia has fallen into disrepair. It was traditionally called the *Passetto*.

Castillo Interior, El ● See under **Teresa of Ávila, St**.

Casuistry ● See GLOSSARY.

Catacombs ● Subterranean burial places used by Christians during the first centuries of the Church to escape persecution by the Roman imperial government. The term catacomb probably came from the Latin *catacomba*, meaning "vault," coming into popular usage through the term *ad catacombas* — "to the vaults" — for the cemetery of St. Sebastian in Rome, a reference to the location of the burial site on the Appian Way. The catacombs were characterized by a series of galleries connected by chambers. The walls of the galleries were used as niches, carved out of the rock or earth, in which were placed several bodies, sometimes two or three, and then sealed off by a stone slab. For those individuals of note or prominence, a special niche was made, called the *arcosolia*; better designed, this spot could hold a sarcophagus. Early on, it became popular for the Christians who buried their brethren in the catacombs to cover the walls with art. These stucco paintings are considered the earliest form of Christian art.

Catacombs were found throughout much of the Roman world, including Malta, Sicily, Asia Minor, North Africa, and some places in Western Europe. The best known and most elaborate, however, were in Rome, where the soft tufa stone could be evacuated with great ease. Christians took to burying their dead in the catacombs for a number of reasons. First of all, they could be reasonably certain that imperial authorities would not molest them, as Roman law and custom prohibited violation of burial sites — the places of the dead were sacred. Secondly, the catacombs provided the means to bury poorer members at a reasonably low cost, in a cemetery clearly set aside for Christian burials. Finally, the vaults were often established as

Catacomb

and shafts were dug, called *luminaris*, to improve light and ventilation. Over time, however, the relics of martyrs and saints were moved from these sites to the churches that had been erected by the increasingly prosperous Christians of the empire.

In the wake of the Germanic incursions and then throughout the Middle Ages, the catacombs were almost completely forgotten. Then on May 31, 1578, the catacombs on the Via Solaria were accidentally discovered, causing a major stirring of public interest. The first serious study of the underground sites was conducted by Antonio Bosio (d. 1627), called the "Columbus of the Catacombs." His work on the subject, *Roma sotteranea* (1632), was the standard book used by students until Giovanni Battista de Rossi (1822-1894) made his immense contributions in the late 1800s, particularly through his masterwork, *Roma sotteranea christiana* (3 vols., 1864-1877). The most important of the catacombs are found on the Via Appia (those of Sts. Praetextatus, Sebastian, and Callistus); the Via Nomentana (of St. Agnes), and the Via Ardeatina (of St. Domitilla).

a result of donations by wealthy Christians, who perhaps already had underground chambers on or near their property to house deceased members of the family. The Christian authorities simply added new chambers.

While catacombs were also used by non-Christians, such as the Jewish community of Rome, most were the property of the Church.

Popular legend depicts Christians residing in these subterranean cemeteries during severe persecutions, but in truth they were not popular places of refuge, and scholars point out that the catacombs underwent their greatest development in the fourth century, after the recognition and acceptance of the Church by the Roman Empire. With the official toleration of Christianity achieved, Church officials were able to increase the size and complexity of the underground chambers, especially to improve those areas where martyrs' remains were kept. For a long time, the Eucharistic celebration was held in the catacombs on the anniversaries of various martyrs. Later, when many people began attending, wider areas were dug around tombs to allow crowds of the faithful,

Catechetical School of Alexandria ●
Important Christian center of learning in Alexandria that was established in the later second century. Its main purpose was to promote Christian learning among the educated classes, particularly those who had already been trained in the Greek methods of education, called the *paideia*. Eventually the school emerged as a great influence upon theological development in the Church, attracting students from the growing Christian communities in the Roman Empire and serving as the basis for other catechetical schools and for later Christian educational institutions. Its first known teacher was the late second-century figure Pantaenus (d. c. 190), receiving vigorous development under Clement of Alexandria (d. c. 215) and Origen (d. c. 254). Other heads of

the school were Heraclas, St. Dionysus, Theognostus, Peter, and Didymus the Blind. (See also **Alexandria**.)

Cathari ● Name used for a number of heretical sects found in Europe during the 1100s and 1200s. The name, derived from the Greek for "pure," was initially applied in the early Church by a number of Greek Fathers, such as St. Epiphanius, to several heretical sects, Novatianists and certain Manichaeans. Its widest application, however, came during the Middle Ages when the Cathari (or Cathars) were both popular and, in some regions, a definite threat to the Church. They were largely adherents of Manichaean dualism, preaching for severe asceticism and attacking the Church, particularly the clergy, as corrupt and evil. They were probably much influenced by the Bogomils and spread throughout Germany and Italy. Members of the sect in France became known under the title Albigensians (see **Albigensian Movement** for details), causing the Albigensian Crusade to be launched against them in the thirteenth century. As a result of the crusade as well as assorted pogroms and especially the work of the Inquisition, the Cathari declined rapidly. (See also **Heresy**.)

Cathedral ● Official church of a bishop and the central church of a diocese. Derived from the Latin term *cathedra* (seat), the cathedral is customarily the site of the bishop's throne, wherein the bishop fulfills many of his episcopal functions, such as consecrating holy oils and the conferring of sacraments (confirmation and holy orders) when they are not administered in parishes. The bishop is also normally ordained and enthroned (or installed) upon the *cathedra*, which then becomes the symbol of his authority over the diocese and which thus cannot be used by any other cleric without the bishop's express permission, not even a higher ranked prelate from another diocese.

Cathedrals are also used for diocesan synods and the promulgation of new regulations. By tradition, it must be situated in the city where the bishop exercises his duties; only cathedrals named for diocesan patrons may be termed such, otherwise they are called pro-cathedrals.

In the early history of the Church, the seats of local bishops were not particularly grand, being known as cathedral churches to denote the presence of the *cathedra*. The great churches of the time were located in Rome, especially from the fourth century and the granting of freedom to the faith. These, however, were not cathedrals but basilicas, in keeping with the Roman custom (see **Basilica** and **St. Peter's Basilica**). As the Church increased in size and temporal influence, as bishops came to wield considerable sociopolitical as well as religious power, the cathedral churches began to increase in size and grandeur. Cathedrals became more ornate and began to reflect both the contemporary trends in architecture and the local or regional innovations and tastes. There was no rule to be followed in cathedral building save that it should be the embodiment of faith and the result of genuine pride and concern by the city over which it would normally tower.

Cathedral building became one of the great achievements in the whole history of the Middle Ages, epitomizing the pervasive influence of the Church in the lives of the people, the degree, financial, political, and social authority it wielded, and the depth of the belief of the people who were willing to sacrifice perhaps as much as a century's labor to complete an edifice of stone and glass. The cathedrals give profound testimony to the name bestowed upon the Middle Ages — the Age of Faith. At the same time, however, cathedrals also represented an economic stake on the part of civil and even royal government for those churches that might be crowned the greatest of the time or house important relics that could attract pilgrims from all over Christendom as well as merchants and tradesman. Cathedral towns thus served as vital commercial centers, sources of power for the entire community, only enhancing the position of the local bishop and clergy, who also profited from the attention.

The clergy of the cathedrals of the Middle Ages and beyond should not be overlooked, since the cathedral itself was not owned by the bishop or any other members of the clergy.

According to Church law, the church was run by a chapter (or capitulum) of clerics, known as canons. They were given a place of preeminence among diocesan clerics with the right to elect their own dean and to assist the bishop in his diocesan administration. They were eventually allowed to own property and came to possess the cathedrals with the full task of making repairs and maintaining the upkeep. When a new cathedral was to be built, they would enter into a corporate relationship with the bishops, a union that would last at times for generations of priests and prelates.

The first notable period for cathedral building was part of the wider Romanesque, which lasted roughly until 1200 and took as its main inspiration the long-faded art of classical Rome. Among the best known examples of this art form are Pisa in Italy, Tournai and Angloulême in France, Worms and Aachen in Germany, and Durham in England. The golden age of cathedrals was the next major art period, the Gothic, whose ascendancy is said by scholars to have begun with the restoration of the Church of St. Denis (c. 1140) by the famed abbot Suger and to have been furthered by St. Bernard of Clairvaux. Gothic cathedrals were

St. Sernin Cathedral, Toulouse

characterized by open skeletons of stone to support vaulting while diagonal ribs gave added strength to the groined vaults. These made possible the attaining of enormous height in the characteristic pointed arches. Flying buttresses (arches of masonry on the outside of the walls) dispersed the weight of the vaults and added stability. Gothic is divided into three main eras — Early, High, and Late, with fascinating variations being developed throughout Europe. A partial list of the magnificent cathedrals of the period would include Notre Dame de Paris, Laon, Chartres, Bourges, Amiens, Beauvais (which was never completed because of the collapse of its vaults), and Ste.-Chapelle in Paris (built by King St. Louis IX, r. 1226-1270), which was considered a masterpiece of the Rayonnant (or radiant) style. (See also **Stained Glass**.) Also notable were the English cathedrals of Canterbury, Lincoln, Wells, and York, and, of course Westminster Abbey (c. 1500-1512), begun under King Henry VII; elsewhere could be found sumptuous cathedrals in Vienna, Milan, Cologne, Venice, and Assisi.

Cathedral building did not end with the onset of the Renaissance, but the tastes and styles of the architects were adapted to meet current trends and the aesthetic wishes of their patrons and employers. The first cathedral in the United States was the Basilica of the Assumption, which was designated the cathedral of the premier see of Baltimore around 1815; the current cathedral is that of Mary, Our Queen, an excellent example of modernized Gothic. Other remarkable American cathedrals are Immaculate Conception in Denver, Immaculate Conception in Kansas City, St. Patrick's in New York, Sts. Peter and Paul in Philadelphia, and St. Matthew's in Washington, D.C. (See **Notre Dame de Paris** and **Santiago de Compostela**; see also **Pilgrimage** and **Relics**.)

Cathedral Schools ● Institutions of learning established during the Middle Ages and run by members of the cathedral clergy. The cathedral schools were originally created to serve as places of instruction for the choirboys and then priests. Because of the superior nature of the educational system to be found in the schools, as compared to other training then available, they eventually opened their doors to lay students, especially the sons of nobles or high-ranking officials. Such students were prepared for careers in government, commerce, or, more commonly, the Church. The schools received money for their services and provided initial training in the seven liberal arts and rudimentary coverage of theology. Much influenced by the Carolingian Renaissance and the schools of the Carolingians under the guidance of Alcuin, the cathedral schools spread across Europe and soon most cathedrals had their own learning centers. Among the chief schools in the eighth and ninth centuries were those of Reims, Orléans, and York (supposedly the earliest of all schools, founded in the seventh century), while important later schools were found in Reims, Paris, and elsewhere. These schools were important foundations for the universities of the West. (See also **Carolingian Schools** and **Universities**.)

Catherine de' Medici (1519-1584) ● Also Catherine de Médicis, queen consort of King Henry II of France, daughter of Lorenzo de' Medici, regent to her son King Charles IX of France, and one of the most powerful figures in the French kingdom during the latter part of the 1500s. Catherine married Henry, duke of Orléans, in 1533, a union that was of much assistance to Pope Clement VII; as she was a relative of the pope, the marriage gave immediate French support to the papacy, allowing Clement to break free from the constant threat and influence of Emperor Charles V, whose troops had already stormed the Vatican in 1527. Henry succeeded

Charles in 1547, ruling until 1559. Catherine wielded little political clout during the reign, but in 1560 she became regent to her son Charles IX, assuming virtual control of the country. Her preeminence continued during the reign of her other son, Henry III (r. 1574-1589). Catherine initially embarked upon a policy of conciliation and toleration in France between the Catholics and Protestants, hoping both to bring an end to the bloody religious wars that had raged for some time and to curb the political ambition of the Catholic party in government. The Protestants, however, were never given any authority, and Catherine eventually changed her policies, siding with Catholic extremists. She embarked on violent anti-Protestant measures and was largely responsible for the St. Bartholomew's Day Massacre in which French Protestants (Huguenots) were killed in the thousands. (See **St. Bartholomew's Day Massacre**.)

Catherine de' Medici

Challenged by a group of fifty philosophers, she destroyed their arguments in favor of paganism, causing them all to be burned alive for their failure. The emperor then demanded that she deny her faith and wed him. When she refused, the emperor had her tortured and placed on a spiked wheel. The wheel immediately fell apart, and two hundred soldiers were converted by her remarkable faith. They were beheaded. Maxentius had Catherine beheaded, but instead of blood flowing from her wound, it was milk. Her body was carried by angels to Mt. Sinai where it was discovered around 800. St. Catherine's Monastery near the site is named after her. It dates to 527, a time before Catherine was known. Her symbol is the spiked wheel, and she is the patron saint of scholars, attorneys, and young women, remaining one of the most beloved woman saints. Feast day: February 25, suppressed in 1969. She is also one of the Auxiliary Saints.

Catherine of Alexandria, St. (d. early fourth century) ● Very popular martyr who was especially revered during the Middle Ages, particularly in France during the crusades. Virtually all that is known about her comes from legend, and she is unknown prior to the eighth century. She is not mentioned in any of the early martyrologies, although she has, at times, been identified with a woman mentioned by Eusebius in his *Ecclesiastical History*, an association without foundation. According to tradition, Catherine, a noble maiden in Alexandria and a devout Christian, protested the persecution of Christians by Emperor Maxentius.

Catherine of Aragon ● See under **Henry VIII**.

Catherine of Bologna, St. (1413-1463) ● Poor Clare abbess, born Catherine Vigri. Belonging to a noble family, she served as a maid of honor at the court of Nicholas III d'Este at Ferrara, receiving an education there. In 1453, she joined the Poor Clares (initially a group of Franciscan tertiaries), establishing in 1456 a convent of Poor Clares. She served as abbess until her death. The recipient throughout her life of numerous visions and revelations, she judged some of them to be evil temptations and others to be of a pure origin. Her spiritual writings were very popular in Italy into the 1700s, and a breviary that she wrote and decorated with her remarkable calligraphic and artistic skills is still in the possession of her convent in Bologna. She was canonized in 1712 by Pope Clement XI. Feast day: March 9.

Catherine of Genoa, St. (1447-1510) ●

Italian mystic. Born Caterina (or Caterinetta) Fieschi, she was a member of a noble family, receiving an excellent education. While she desired to become a nun, she was compelled by her relatives to marry, at the age of sixteen, Giuliano Adorno. Over the next ten difficult years she found her husband to be quick-tempered, pleasure-loving, and unfaithful. Her efforts to seek comfort in the social life of Genoa proved fruitless and she sank even further into misery. In 1473, however, she was suddenly converted by a mystical experience. From that time, she devoted herself to the spiritual life, ultimately converting her husband. Together they worked for some twenty years in caring for the sick in the Pammatone Hospital; she was matron there from 1490 to 1496. Her husband, Giuliano, who became a Franciscan tertiary, died in 1497. She survived him for thirteen years, suffering in her final days from an agonizing disease. A profound mystic, she took Communion every day from 1473, an extremely rare practice for laypeople during the Middle Ages but one that allowed her to make long fasts while continuing her labors for the sick. Her mystical doctrine was published in the 1551 book *Vita e dottrina*, presenting the source for her *Dialogo* (*Dialogue*) and *Trattato del Purgatorio* (*Treatise on Purgatory*). She personally did not write these works, but they certainly contained the heart of her spiritual thought and conviction. Pope Benedict XIV declared her a saint in 1737 and placed her name on the Roman Martyrology. Pope Pius XII declared her

patroness of the hospitals in Italy in 1944. She was the subject of a study in *The Mystical Element of Religion as studied in St. Catherine of Genoa and her Friends* (1908), by Baron Friedrich von Hügel, in which it was proposed that her two mystical works did not take shape until a much later date. This contention was much criticized by Umile Bonzi da Genova, O.F.M. Cap., who argued that large parts of the treatises were written by Catherine herself.

Catherine of Ricci, St. (1522-1590) ●

Italian visionary also known as Catherine dei Ricci. Born at Florence, she entered the Dominicans in Prato in 1535 where she was professed the following year, spending the rest of her life in the convent at Prato in Tuscany and becoming widely known for her profound religious experiences. Once a week, from noon on Thursday until 4:00 P.M. on Friday, she would lapse into ecstasy, reliving the passion of Christ. This took place, with regularity, for twelve years. She was also concerned with reforming the Church, writing letters to many notable reformers of her era, including St. Charles Borromeo, St. Philip Neri, and St. Pope Pius V, and revering the memory of Savonarola, who had opposed the corruption of Pope Alexander VI and hanged in 1498. Pilgrims by the hundreds routinely visited Prato to meet her. Beatified in 1732, she was canonized in 1746 by Pope Benedict XIV. Feast day: February 13.

Catherine of Siena, St. (1347-1380) ●

Great medieval mystic and patron saint of Italy. Born Caterina Benincasa in Siena, she was one of the numerous children of a Sienese dyer. Receiving mystical experiences and visions in her youth, she refused her parent's desire for her to marry, instead joining the Sisters of Penitence of St. Dominic in Siena in 1367, the Third Order of the Dominicans, meaning that it was open to laypersons. Catherine devoted herself to the care of the poor and sick and to prayer. Word of her devout nature soon spread, and she gathered about her a remarkable group of disciples and followers, who came to be called Caterinati, friends who traveled with her on her many journeys. Chief among the Caterinati was the Augustinian friar William Flete. In 1375, she resolved to do what she could to settle the struggle between Florence and the Avignon pope Gregory XI. She traveled to Avignon where, before the pope, she spoke on behalf of the Florentines and, even more importantly, begged Gregory to return to Rome, thereby bolstering the pontiff's resolve to leave France. Gregory made a triumphal entry into the city on January 17, 1377, but died the next year and was succeeded by the erratic Urban VI. Catherine, meanwhile, had gone back to Siena but was drawn once more into Church affairs by the eruption of the Great Schism a short time after Urban's election. She gave herself entirely to his cause, working to restore unity to Christendom. Letters were dictated — she could not write — and sent to rulers, cardinals, and people of influence to give their backing to Urban. The pope had much trust in her views, but his peculiar behavior and the widespread confusion proved difficult for Catherine to overcome. She died in Rome.

A profound mystic, Catherine was the recipient of numerous spiritual experiences and the stigmata. In her case, the stigmata was invisible. Nevertheless, her suffering from the mystical wounds was considerable. Her place in Church history is often said by scholars to be based on her spirituality and sanctity rather than her legitimate contributions in resolving the Avignon Papacy and in attempting to end the Great Schism. Her letters reveal a formidable personal will and determination. The *Dialogo* by her is ranked as a classic of spirituality, composed in four treatises and examining the religious challenges and obligations faced by mankind. Canonized by Pope Pius II in 1461, she was declared a Doctor of the Church by

Pope Paul VI on October 4, 1970, the second woman, after St. Teresa of Ávila, to be honored. Feast day: April 29.

Catherine of Sweden, St. (1331-1381) ● Known in full as Katarine Ulfsdotter, the daughter of St. Bridget of Sweden. Always very close to her mother and early demonstrating personal sanctity, Catherine departed Sweden in 1350 to join her mother in Rome; her husband, Egard Lydersson, died a short time after her departure. Long a companion of Bridget, she succeeded her in 1374 as head of the Order of St. Savior, the Brigittines. She spent the next years promoting the organization of the order, working for the canonization of her mother and supporting Pope Urban in his struggles with the antipope Clement VII during the Great Schism. She died in retirement in Vadstena where she had served as abbess. While never formally canonized, she is venerated as a saint. Feast day: March 24.

Catholic Action ● Often misunderstood term used for the apostolate of laity that is organized under the leadership and with the mandate of the hierarchy of the Church and that participates in various religious activities under its guidance. Pope Pius XI defined Catholic Action as "the participation of Catholic laity in the apostolate of the hierarchy," implying his understanding of it to mean the cooperation or action of the laity in a social sense, under the control of a bishop on a local level or the Holy See on an international level, to promote or achieve a spiritual or cultural result, particularly the salvation of souls and the sanctification of society at large. While mentioned by Pope St. Pius X (r. 1903-1914), Catholic Action was given needed organization and direction by Pope Pius XI, who published the encyclical *Ubi Arcano* (December 23, 1922), which gave encouragement to the formation of various lay organizations that could function in close cooperation and under the authority of the clergy. Catholic Action subsequently developed in Western Europe, especially France and Belgium. In the United States, there was such an enthusiastic response that American bishops found it necessary in 1935 to clarify the specific terms of Catholic Action and to remind the laypeople of the requirement that Catholic Action cannot function unless or until it has received a commission from the episcopacy or a universal commission from the pope to the bishops. Catholic Action continued to receive the support of the papacy under Pope Pius XII (r. 1939-1958), but under John XXIII (r. 1958-1963) there was an increasing move away from formal bodies to a wider concept of the lay apostolate dedicated to working on behalf of the Church. In the deliberation of Vatican Council II, the evolution of lay activity was recognized and addressed and the term Catholic Action ceased to be used in a sanctioned manner, although it was mentioned in both *Apostolicam Actuositatem* ("Decree on the Apostolate of the Laity," No. 20) and *Christus Dominus* ("Decree on the Bishops' Pastoral Office in the Church," No. 17). As was noted in *Apostolicam Actuositatem*, "All associations of the apostolate must be given due appreciation. Those, however, which the hierarchy has praised or recommended as responsive to the needs of time and place, or has directed to be established as particularly urgent, must be held in the highest esteem by priests, religious, and laity and promoted according to each one's ability" (No. 21). A demonstration of the view of the Church toward the lay apostolate was provided by the Synod of Bishops in 1987 with its "Message to the People of God." Pope John Paul II responded to it with his apostolic exhortation of January 30, 1989, *Christifideles laici* ("The Christian Faithful Laity"). While the name Catholic Action is not used, its spirit and inspiration continue to influence the nature of the work undertaken by the lay apostolate in promoting the

teaching and doctrine of the faith. (See also **Grail Movement** and **Jocists**.)

Catholic Emancipation Acts ● See **Relief Acts, Catholic**.

Catholic Patriotic Church ● See **Patriotic Association of Chinese Catholics**; see also **China**.

Catholic Worker Movement ● Movement founded in 1933 by Dorothy Day (1897-1980) and Peter Maurin (1877-1949) that strove to heighten the awareness of Catholics and others concerning the terrible plight of the poor in the United States and to identify closely in spirit with all who were in poverty or suffering oppression. The first major effort of the Catholic Worker movement was the opening of the House of Hospitality in the Bowery, New York, by Day in 1933. There anyone who might be unemployed, hungry, or desperate could receive shelter. The house soon inspired other such refuges around the country, and the movement attracted many young idealistic Catholics, who willingly embraced personal poverty and lived in small groups of workers devoted to caring for the sick and poor while leading active lives of prayer and frequent reception of the sacraments. Maurin and Day promoted their philosophy of life through numerous meetings and their paper the *Catholic Worker*; the paper quickly reached a circulation of over one hundred thousand, espousing the cause of labor. They believed that the social teachings of the Church should be actually applied to better society, rejecting much of modern culture as impersonal and dehumanizing, while openly criticizing America for its capitalist system, racism, and bellicose imperialism. They especially called for a society based on faith and grace with the use of Scripture to solve contemporary problems. Although the movement began in opposition to Communism, the Catholic Worker adherents were sharply criticized for their reliance upon idealized applications of Marxist theory ("from each according to his abilities and to each according to his needs"), their belief in commune-like farming, and their denunciation of the United States' social and economic systems. Much support was lost for the movement when Day and Maurin opposed the entry of the United States into World War II, but the Catholic Workers continued to serve the needs of the poor around the country. Worker houses are still functioning today. The movement itself was an important foundation for many of the pre- and especially post-Vatican Council II efforts among lay Catholics to involve themselves directly in social action and reconstruction.

Cavour, Camillo ● See **Italy**.

Cecilia, St. ● Highly venerated Roman martyr, patron saint of Church music. The exact time of her death is unknown, and many details about her life and martyrdom are wanting, as the acts about her that were written are considered apocryphal, dating to around the latter part of the fifth century. Nevertheless, by the sixth century she was considered a saint and ranked as a beloved Roman martyr. According to the traditional story about her, she was a young Christian girl of a patrician (or noble) family who was betrothed to a young pagan, Valerian. On their wedding day, she told him that she had taken an oath of virginity to God. Instead of calling off their marriage, however, Valerian accepted Christianity, as did his brother Tiburtius. Soon arrested, they were executed along with a third Christian named Maximus. Cecilia herself was then executed. Buried in the catacomb of St. Callistus, her relics were found in the catacomb of Praetextatus by Pope Paschal I (r. 817-824) and were moved to the Church of St. Cecilia in the Trastevere quarter of Rome. When repairs were done on the church in 1599, her body was said to have been discovered in a completely uncorrupted state. As patroness of Church music (from the 1500s), her symbol is the organ. Feast day: November 22.

Cedd, St. (d. 664) ● Brother of St. Chad and bishop of the East Saxons in England. He was raised with his brother at the famous missionary center of Lindisfarne under St. Aidan. In 653, he was sent as part of a group of missionaries to Oswiu, king of Northumbria, to help convert the Middle Angles. He next undertook a mission to Essex and in 654 was consecrated bishop of the East Saxons. Cedd is best known for the many churches he established, including monasteries on Bradwell-on-Sea and Tilbury. He also founded Lastingham Abbey in North Yorkshire where he became the first abbot. He died of the plague at Lastingham in 664. Feast day: January 7.

Celestine I, St. ● Pope from 422-432. He was traditionally held to have come from Campania and was a deacon at the time of his election on September 10, 422, to succeed Boniface I. He soon undertook to continue the efforts of his predecessor in combating the various heresies that were plaguing the Church. Pelagianism was attacked by sending St. Germanus of Auxerre to Britain in 429 to counter the teachings of Pelagius in the isles and by writing letters condemning the Semi-Pelagianism being propagated by John Cassian in southern France (Gaul). Celestine launched a campaign against Nestorianism by condemning its author, Nestorius, at a Roman synod in August 430. St. Cyril of Alexandria was then ordered to excommunicate and depose the troublesome patriarch of Constantinople, Nestorius, if he did not submit. Nestorius refused, and, on December 7, 430, the sentence by Cyril was delivered to Constantinople in a set of twelve anathemas. Celestine also consecrated St. Palladius at Rome in 431 and ordered him on his short-lived mission as bishop of the Christians of Ireland. Feast day: July 27.

Celestine II ● Pope from 1143-1144. Born in Tuscany, he was originally named Guido di Città del Castello. Of noble birth, he was a longtime friend of Peter Abelard, remaining personally loyal to him even after the philosopher's condemnation by the Council of Sens in 1140. Elected on September 26, 1143, to succeed Innocent II, his main act as pontiff was to end Innocent's interdict on King Louis VII of France. He died on the eve of a very serious conflict with Roger II, the Norman king of Sicily.

Celestine III ● Pope from 1191-1198. Born Giacinto Bobo, he was the first pontiff to come from the House of Orsini and had a very long career before his election as successor to Clement III. Bobo (or Bobone) had been a friend and student of Peter Abelard, defending him at the Council of Sens in 1140-1141. He was also a friend of Thomas Becket and served as a cardinal deacon for forty-seven years before coming to the papacy in his eighty-fifth year. On the night before his consecration, Celestine was ordained a priest. His pontificate was noted for its conciliatory position toward Emperor Henry VI; he did nothing to curb Henry's aggressive imperial ambitions in Italy and Sicily or his imprisonment of King Richard the Lionhearted of England. Celestine instead accepted Henry's assurance that he would agree to a call for a crusade. Not surprisingly, the emperor never embarked for the Holy Land. Scholars have long been divided on possible reasons for Celestine's inactivity, some arguing pontifical patience, others proposing age and senility. He did, however, approve the Military Orders of the Templars, Knights Hospitallers, and Teutonic Knights.

Celestine IV ● Pope from October 25 to November 10, 1241. A native of Milan, he was the nephew of Urban III. Already old and seriously ill when elected to succeed Gregory IX, Celestine lived for only a few days, dying with the papacy embroiled in its struggle with Emperor Frederick II. His successor was the energetic Innocent IV.

Celestine V, St. ● Pope from July 5 to December 13, 1294. The first holder of the Holy See to abdicate, he was also the founder of the Celestine order. Born Pietro da Morrone, he entered the Benedictines at the age of seventeen, but, drawn to an even more ascetic life, he withdrew to Monte Morrone in Abruzzi where he adopted a hermit's life. There, with a group of supporters, he established what was to become the Celestine order. Renowned for his remarkable asceticism, he was elected pope at the age of eighty in order to end a gridlock in the conclave and to fill the papacy after a vacancy of some two years. When informed of his election, he expressed amazement and considerable reluctance. Convinced to accept, however, he was consecrated at Aquila with the name Celestine. Untrained to be pontiff and ill-suited for the office, Celestine proved a disaster. He was completely ignorant of his duties, committing numerous gaffes and errors and, more importantly, falling under the manipulative control of King Charles V of Naples. Aware of the damage he was doing to the Church, Celestine resigned before a consistory of cardinals at Naples. A few days later, Boniface VIII was elected. The shrewd, hard, new pontiff ordered Celestine to be taken into custody to prevent his misuse by scheming opponents. The onetime Vicar of Christ was imprisoned at the castle of Fumone, near Anagni, where he died on May 19, 1296. When taken to his cell, he reportedly commented: "I have wanted nothing in my life but a cell, and a cell they have given me." Celestine was canonized by Clement V in 1313. Dante placed Celestine at the entrance to hell in the *Divine Comedy*, referring to him with the line ". . . him who made, through cowardice, the great refusal." (See also **Celestine Order** [following entry] and **Spiritual Franciscans**.)

Celestine Order ● Branch of the Benedictine order (O.S.B.). First established in 1250 by Pietro Morrone (the future Pope St. Celestine V) on Monte Morrone. Papal approval was given in 1264 by Pope Urban IV. The Celestines, deriving their name from their founder's pontifical name, grew quickly in popularity. They followed the strict asceticism of Celestine and briefly had their constitutions imposed on the motherhouse of the Benedictines at Monte Cassino. Despite the abdication of Celestine in December 1294, the Celestine order continued to flourish over the next years. In the succeeding centuries, however, the congregation declined steadily until, in 1785, the last remaining house was closed.

Celestius ● Fifth-century English heretic, an important disciple of Pelagius, and a spokesman for the heresy of Pelagianism. Celestius first met Pelagius at Rome where both were practicing law. Pelagius convinced him to give up a secular life and devote himself to helping to bring about reform in society in response to the immorality of the times. Around 409, they left Rome to escape the approaching menace of the Goths, journeying to Sicily and then Africa. When Pelagius went to Palestine in 411, Celestius remained behind and soon his teachings created trouble with the local Catholic communities. Celestius taught that all people had a direct responsibility for their actions, a doctrine of free will that negated the idea of grace; further he denied that original sin ever existed and the teaching that baptism brought the remission of sins. The Council of Carthage (412) condemned and excommunicated him. Celestius departed for Ephesus, but the act of the Council of Carthage was reaffirmed by the Council of

Diospolis (415) and two additional African councils (416). Pope Innocent I upheld the excommunication, but his successor, Zosimus, took a more moderating position. Zosimus rescinded Innocent's decree, only to retract his own decision when a riotous outbreak of violence by Pelagians prompted Emperor Honorius to condemn Pelagianism and exile Celestius from Rome and Italy. Zosimus excommunicated Celestine and condemned Pelagianism. The Council of Ephesus added further censures. Celestine and Pelagius were especially opposed by St. Augustine and St. Jerome. (See also **Pelagianism**.)

Celibacy ● State of perfect continence that is practiced and maintained by priests and bishops and those members of the permanent diaconate who have never married or are widowed. Laypersons have also practiced celibacy in keeping with the long-standing tradition of the Church as expressed by St. Paul (see 1 Cor 7:32, 34). Ecclesiastical celibacy is the age-old tradition of the Latin Church, the rule taking as one of its spiritual foundations Christ's exhortation in Matthew (19:10-12). In reaffirming the requirement of celibacy, the Second Vatican Council declared that "the whole priestly mission is dedicated to that new humanity which Christ, the conqueror of death, raises up in the world through His Spirit. This humanity takes its origin 'not of blood, nor of the will of the flesh, nor of the will of man, but of God' (Jn. 1:13). Through virginity or celibacy observed for the sake of the kingdom of heaven, priests are consecrated in a new and distinguished way. They more easily hold fast to Him with undivided heart. They more freely devote themselves in Him and through Him to the service of God and men" (*Presbyterorum Ordines*, No. 16). In the early Church, celibacy was not a general rule. It came to be increasingly practiced by those persons who entered into an exclusively religious life, particularly among hermits and the members of the foundational monastic communities established by St. Pachomius (d. 346). The important declaration by Church authorities in favor of celibacy was made first by the Council of Elvira in 305 in Spain. This was followed by the Councils of Galatia and Cappadocia in 315, and the highly influential First Council of Nicaea (325) at which it was decided to accept the prohibition of marriage after ordination. While affirmed by the Roman council in 386 and in other assemblies, celibacy was not universally recognized in the West until the eleventh century and the Gregorian Reform. At the Synod of Sutri (1074) convened by Pope Gregory VII (r. 1073-1085), priests were not allow to marry and married men were declared ineligible for ordination. From the time following Gregory's pontificate, the Church remained absolutely firm on the rule, despite secular pressure to relax it and the demands of the leaders of the Reformation that clergy should be permitted to wed. Confronted by the challenge of the Reformation, the Council of Trent (1545-1563) was abundantly clear that celibacy was mandatory and that anyone who taught otherwise should be anathematized. Vatican Council II, as noted, upheld the tradition, but it also recognized the need to create a body of individuals who might be married and still assist the Church through a ministry. The permanent diaconate was thus authorized, although it had the provision that married men might be ordained but cannot marry again if widowed. The rule of celibacy remains firm in the modern Church, part of the recognition of its value to the priestly life and its enhancement of the sacred ministry. In the Eastern Churches, celibacy is required of bishops and unmarried priests and deacons after ordination; married men are permitted into the ranks of the clergy. A recent development has confronted the Church as a result of the desire of increasing numbers of Anglican priests to enter the Catholic communion.

Rather than turn them away, the Church has permitted these clerics, married prior to reception, to remain so and still enter the Church and be ordained priests.

Celsus ● Second-century pagan philosopher and Platonist, the earliest known literary critic of Christianity. Celsus lived either in Rome or Alexandria, authoring the Greek work *True Discourse*. In it he attacked Christian doctrines through a series of questions and answers, such as why should God come to earth, or why should he visit the earth in the shape of Jesus, and why in Palestine? He rejected the exclusive nature of Christian teachings, dismissed Christ as the illegitimate son of Mary and a Roman soldier, took special exception to the Incarnation and Crucifixion, and complained about the Christian unwillingness to conform to the laws of the Roman state. The actual work by Celsus is lost, but it is known almost in its entirety through the reply written by Origen (246-248) in his *Contra Celsum*. Over the next years, a number of Neoplatonists would utilize Celsus' writings as a source in composing their own polemics against the Church. (See also **Paganism** in the GLOSSARY.)

Celtic Church ● Name given to the Church in the British Isles from around the second century until the sixth century and the arrival of St. Augustine at Canterbury; the name Celtic Church is also used to describe the Church in the isles until, and even beyond, the invasion of England in 1066 by the Normans under William the Conqueror. The Celtic Church was probably established by early Christian missionaries from Rome or Gaul who helped lay the groundwork for the increased organization throughout the fourth century. Christianity soon spread beyond the limits of the Roman holdings of Britannia (Britain), but it seems clear that the faith was largely confined to poorer elements in Celtic society, rather than

Roman colonial communities. Nevertheless, the Church was associated with the Christian community on the Continent, as evidenced by the participation of bishops from Britain at the Synods of Arles (314) and the Council of Ariminum (359), and the arrival in 429 and 447 of St. Germanus of Auxerre to check the possible growth of the heresy of Pelagianism.

In the fifth century, however, the Church in the isles endured the often bloody invasions of the Saxons, an event that severely isolated the Christian community from the rest of Europe. The number of Celtic conversions was important in ensuring the survival of the faith, since it was part of the indigenous culture that remained in the isles after the departure of the Romans in the early to mid-400s. Nevertheless, such isolation prevented the Celts from remaining aware of and integrated with the developing Roman Church. Not surprisingly, when St. Augustine arrived around 603, he was opposed by many in the Church who were reluctant to accept the supremacy and Roman usages. The Synod of Whitby in 664 ostensibly ended the independence of the Celtic Church, although Celtic Christianity would endure for centuries in parts of the isles, most notably in Ireland where Celtic images were finally curtailed only by the Synod of Cashel in 1171 or 1172 with its reorganization of the Irish Church. (See also **England, Anglo-Saxon Church,** and **Monasticism.**)

Censure, Ecclesiastical ● See GLOSSARY.

Center Party, German ● See **Germany**.

Centesimus Annus ● Encyclical dated May 1, 1991, and issued by Pope John Paul II. Translated as "The 100th Year," the encyclical commemorates the one hundredth anniversary of Pope Leo XIII's encyclical *Rerum novarum*, called the charter of Catholic social doctrine. John Paul reiterated

many of the central points of Leo's encyclical declaring, "What was essential to the encyclical was precisely its proclamation of the fundamental conditions for justice in the economic and social situation of the time. . . . We need to repeat that there can be no genuine solution of the 'social question' apart from the Gospel, and that the 'new things' can find in the Gospel the context of their correct understanding and the proper moral perspective for judgment on them."

The pontiff reaffirmed the principle laid down by Leo, such as the ownership of private property, the formation of private associations, just wages, religious freedom, and other basic rights. After citing the main threads of Leo's work, John Paul examined current trends in the "new things." He discussed the fall of oppressive regimes all over the world, their demise hastened by a "spiritual void brought about by atheism," and then examined in great detail the prevailing economic order: material goods, free markets, profit, consumerism, ecology, abortion, capitalism, authentic democracy, and the welfare state.

Central America ● Region situated from Mexico to Panama, comprising the nations of Mexico, Guatemala, Honduras, Belize, Costa Rica, Panama, El Salvador, and Nicaragua. The Church first arrived in the New World with the vessels of exploration launched by Spain. Clergy were present on these ships from the time of Columbus's second voyage, thereafter participating in all of the major voyages. The first friars were generally very learned and had both a sincere missionary zeal and a willingness to endure considerable hardships for the evangelization of the recently discovered lands. The native inhabitants they found were highly varied and developed, including the Aztecs, Maya, Zapotecs, and others. These states were unfortunately virtually obliterated by the Spanish conquistadors and the indigenous peoples were severely reduced through disease, starvation, migrations, slavery, and war.

To their credit, many Churchmen voiced opposition to this destructive program, and efforts were undertaken to learn the native languages for purposes of missionary work. A number of scholars preserved the linguistic traditions, customs, and history of the natives, an invaluable preservation endeavor. These researches were supplemented by assorted grammars and dictionaries, and some original writings (such as Aztec codices) were sent back to Spain along with the vast treasures plundered from the Aztec cities. Familiarity with the language aided greatly to the conversion of the Indians. In Mexico alone, for example, the Franciscan friars were able to claim over a million converts by the early 1530s.

Regrettably, the Church in the New World, in close cooperation with Spanish colonial authorities, proved frequently willing to go beyond persuasion and use such methods as violence, torture, and murder. As a consequence, many conversions were insincere and the converts lapsed from the faith a short time later. Further difficulties for the natives were created starting in 1569 when King Philip II of Spain approved the formation of tribunals of Inquisition (under the Holy Office) in Mexico (and Lima in Peru). The Indians were at first placed under its jurisdiction, but authorities later ended their merciless examinations of Indians when they decided to classify the natives as savages of limited responsibility in matters of faith.

It is more than unfortunate that Churchmen supported and participated in the extirpation of wholesale parts of the vibrant cultures of Mesoamerica (as pre-Columbian America is called). Some consideration should be taken of the mind-set of many Church leaders in the New World. They genuinely considered themselves to be superior to the Indians and looked upon the extermination of "heathen" writings in Central America (there was no written language in South America) to be both necessary and desirable for the conversion of the surviving Mesoamerican peoples and the establishment of the Church on sure footing in the Americas.

As most of the indigenous states were theocratic in outlook and organization, Church leaders determined the destruction of their religious states to be paramount. Regardless of the historical environment or milieu and orientation of the Churchmen in colonial Spain, the loss in terms of lives and culture was catastrophic, and the willingness of many in the clergy to take part left a shadow over much of the early period of the faith in the region.

Given its ties with the Spanish authorities (King Ferdinand had secured in 1508 full power to nominate all clergy for the New World from Pope Julius II), the early Church was quite successful in creating missions and an organized presence in Central America. Missions were launched in Panama (1514), Guatemala (1524), Nicaragua (1524), and Mexico (1530). The captain general was able to form a diocese for all of the region in 1534. In Mexico, meanwhile, a major boost to conversions and the flourishing of Catholic devotion was given by the appearance of Our Lady at Guadalupe in December 1531 to the native Juan Diego. As the dioceses became fully instituted, conflicts erupted between the religious orders and the secular clergy, a dispute settled in 1583 by the royal decree stating that in all appointments the secular clergy were to receive preference over the regular clergy.

Over the next centuries, the Church in colonial Latin America grew extremely wealthy and profited enormously from patronage and gifts from the ruling Spanish elite. The hierarchy, and most of the clergy, became closely identified with the Spanish colonials, a connection that tended to create a gulf between the Church and the population at large. Corruption and assorted abuses were also common among many of the clergy. In marked contrast to this, however, was the example set by the Franciscans who traveled throughout Central America and into Spanish territories in North America, including California and New Mexico. The missions they founded in both territories as well as Texas and elsewhere were testaments to the deep planting of the Catholic faith by the friars and other missionaries and a positive legacy of the Spanish Empire.

Spain's colonial possessions would endure for some three hundred years in Latin America. Its rule, long deteriorating, came officially to an end in 1821 when independence was declared for the region at Guatemala City, with the full approval of El Salvador, Costa Rica, Honduras, and Nicaragua. A Central American republic was proclaimed in 1823 by a congress convened at Guatemala City. This federation survived only until 1838 when member states began breaking away. Since that time, the history of Latin America has been one of countries struggling to maintain political stability and to promote economic growth for the traditionally poor inhabitants.

The Church long suffered from the handicap of its historical association with Spain and was criticized in the recent past for identifying its interests with the assorted oppressive regimes that emerged in the nineteenth and twentieth centuries. Today, the charge that the Church is in collusion with ruling classes or with dictatorial regimes is generally without foundation. In the past decades, the hierarchy of Latin America has consistently denounced oppression, exploitation, and the presence of death squads as a form of political control and repression. The courage of many of the prelates fighting against dictatorship cannot be contested and was epitomized by the assassination of Archbishop Oscar Romero of El Salvador while saying Mass on March 24, 1980.

It has been argued that the principal crisis now facing the Church in Central America (and in South America) is the close identification of many priests and nuns with potentially destabilizing elements calling for radical, even violent, removal of the prevailing economic and political systems that are struggling to introduce democracy and true economic change.

The chief mode of socioeconomic and political reform for these groups is the highly controversial system of liberation theology. This trend was noted by Pope John Paul II in the Puebla Conference in 1978 and has come to represent one of the gravest difficulties facing the Church as it heads into the next millennium. (See also **Mexico, South America,** and **West Indies**.)

Centuriators of Magdeburg ● The name of a group of Lutheran scholars who gathered at Magdeburg to write a Church history from its beginnings to the year 1400. Their name was devised from the fact they divided their work into centuries (century by century) and wrote the first five volumes at Magdeburg. The other volumes were written at Wismar or elsewhere. Published in Latin at Basel from 1559-1574, the so-called *Historia Ecclesiae* was the inspiration of the rabid anti-Roman Matthias Vlachich, known as Matthias Flacius Illyricus, and was dominated by severe Lutheran ideas. It stated that the original Church was not "popish," but from the death of the last of the Apostles it had gone astray, led into corruption and sin by the Roman Antichrist of the papacy. However, it went on to claim, Luther had restored the true religion. The history was the first modern effort to examine ecclesiastical history in a scholarly and critical fashion and thus it marked an epoch. In its execution, the work was virulent in its anti-Catholic and antipapal statements, abusing legitimate historical facts and documents to make a harsh, intolerant, even hysterical attack on the occupants of the Chair of Peter. It was thus easy prey for gifted Catholic historians, most notably Cesare Baronius in his *Annales Ecclesiasticae* (1588-1607). (See also **Luther, Martin**.)

Cerinthus (fl. c. 100) ● Christian heretic of Gnostic sympathies. Cerinthus, probably an Egyptian Jew, taught that the world had not been created by the supreme God — who transcended utterly the universe — but by some other powerful being or, perhaps, the angels. He accepted only the Gospel of Matthew and held that Jesus, the human offspring of Mary and Joseph, had received the "Christ," at his baptism, a kind of divine power that revealed God and that departed from his body at the time of the Crucifixion. Followers of Cerinthus formed a very brief sect of Jewish Christians with Gnostic principles, but he was rejected strongly by the rest of the Christian Church. Polycarp, for example, learned that Cerinthus was in the same bathhouse as he in Ephesus and so fled for his life out of fear that the building might collapse on such a terrible enemy of the truth; according to Irenaeus in his *Adversus omnes Haereses*, St. John authored his Gospel to refute the numerous errors espoused by Cerinthus. (See also **Gnosticism**.)

Cesarini, Giuliano (1348-1444) ● Also Julian Cesarini, a gifted cardinal and reformer of the Church following the end of the Great Schism (1378-1417) in the West. Cesarini was a member of a noble family of Rome, receiving an education at Perugia and Padua; he was a noted expert on Roman law and was later considered a remarkable scholar and humanist. Nicholas of Cusa was one of his pupils. Around 1417, he entered the service of the Curia and became a useful assistant to Cardinal Branda. In 1419, he accompanied Branda on a mission to Germany and Bohemia where they attempted to end the troubles bring caused by the Hussites. Cesarini was then sent on missions to France and England before being created a

cardinal by Pope Martin V. In 1431, the pope sent him as a legate to Germany to preach a crusade against the Hussites. That same year he was appointed president of the Council of Basel, resisting successfully Pope Eugenius IV's efforts to dissolve it; but then, in 1437, he grew concerned by the council's efforts to debilitate the pontiff rather than bring about true reform. At the transferred Council of Ferrara-Florence, he took a leading part in bringing the Hussites back to the Church and participated in the negotiations with the Greek Church on possible reunion with Rome. In 1442, Cesarini went to Hungary as a legate, this time to preach a crusade against the Turks. By his diplomatic insistence, King Ladislaus of Hungary broke the Peace of Szegedin (1444) with the Turks and renewed the war. The result was the disastrous Battle of Varna on November 10, 1444, in which the Christian army was wiped out. Cesarini was killed in the flight from the field.

Chad, St. (d. 672) ● First bishop of Lichfield, monastic founder, and brother of St. Cedd. Born in Northumbria, he was educated with his brother at the great center of learning, Lindisfarne, studying under St. Egbert at the monastery of Rathmelsigi in Ireland. Cedd recalled him to England to assist in the foundation of the monastery of Lastingham in Yorkshire, and Chad succeeded his brother as abbot there in 664. Around the same time, he was made bishop of the Northumbrians by King Oswiu in irregular fashion because the person originally chosen for the see, St. Wilfrid, had traveled to France for consecration and was a very long time in returning. Archbishop St. Theodore of Canterbury in 669 resolved the resulting dispute by finding in Wilfrid's favor. Chad obediently accepted and retired to Lastingham. He was soon summoned from the abbey and made bishop of Lichfield, an important appointment, as the new diocese permitted him to serve as bishop of the

Mercians. The following years found him working ceaselessly to spread the faith in Mercia, founding several monasteries including that of Barrow. The main source on his life is the Venerable Bede's *Ecclesiastical History*. Feast day: March 2.

Chalcedon, Council of ● Fourth ecumenical council held from October 8 to November 1, 451, in the town of Chalcedon, in Asia Minor, just outside of Constantinople. A major council in the history of Christology, it asserted once and for all the orthodox doctrine concerning the nature of Christ, namely that he is one Person with two distinct natures, divine and human; it brought to an end furious theological debate and controversy that had raged for much of the fifth century. In specific terms, the Council of Chalcedon was convened by Emperor Marcian to deal with the pressing crisis of the Eutychian heresy which argued that Christ had two natures but that these were so intimately connected that they became one, thereby resulting in the human nature being absorbed by the divine. The chief spokesman for this was Eutyches, the archimandrite of a monastery just outside of Constantinople. He was soon opposed by orthodox theologians, and there ensued a bitter controversy, exacerbated by the Second Council of Ephesus (449), the Latrocinium (or Robber) Council, which was manipulated by Dioscorus, patriarch of Alexandria, who restored Eutyches, deposing Flavian, the patriarch of Constantinople, and refusing to allow the reading of the *Epistola Dogmatica* by Pope St. Leo I, the so-called *Tome* of Leo, elucidating the orthodox doctrine on the Incarnation. While condemned by the pope and opposed by most of the Church, the work of the Latrocinium stood unrepealed as long as Theodosius II, a patron of Eutyches, sat on the imperial throne. His sudden death in July 450, however, changed the complexion of the situation, as his sister Pulcheria succeeded him, marrying Marcian

(r. 450-457); both were enemies of Eutyches and Dioscorus and thus sent to Pope Leo their approval for a new council to address the heresy.

The council opened at Chalcedon on October 8. In attendance were around 600 bishops (Pope Leo wrote that there were 600, other sources say 520 or even 630). All were from the East save for two who had come from Africa and the two papal legates, Boniface and Paschasinus, bishop of Lilybaeum (who also presided). The sessions were held in the Church of St. Euphemia, Martyr, directly opposite Constantinople. The work of the council was clear from the start and resulted in a complete triumph for the orthodox position. The decrees of the Latrocinium were annulled, Eutyches was condemned, Dioscorus deposed, and the *Tome* of Leo given full approval; the council delegates said of the epistle: "This is the faith of the Fathers and of the Apostles. This we all believe. Peter has spoken through Leo . . . anathema to him who teaches otherwise. . . ." In the fifth session (October 22), a formula or definition was written to make absolutely clear in a statement of faith the dogma of the Church: "One and the same Christ, Son, Lord, Only-begotten, known in two natures, without confusion, without change, without division, without separation." All of the canons were acceptable to the pope except for Canon 28, which proclaimed the see of Constantinople to be a patriarchate second only to Rome. Initially opposed by papal legates, the canon was rejected by Leo on the grounds that it was an insult to the older patriarchates; there were also political considerations involved, as the see of Constantinople had long harbored ambitions of eventual equal status with Rome.

Chaldean Rite ● Also Chaldaean rite, the broad term designating those Catholics who are members of the Chaldean rite as listed by the Congregation for the Oriental Churches. The Chaldeans are descendants of the ancient Nestorian Churches. These communities, long separated from Rome and existing in Turkey and Persia, were first contacted by missionaries and representatives of the Roman Church in the 1200s. The process of reunification soon began, culminating in 1692 with the return of the Chaldeans into communion with Rome under Pope Innocent XII. The rite is derived from the Antiochene rite and is divided into two main groups, the Chaldean and the Syro-Malabar. The Chaldean rite is found in Turkey, Syria, Lebanon, Egypt, Iraq, Iran, and the United States. They are under the patriarch of Babylonia with twenty-one archdioceses and dioceses, and use Syriac and Arabic for the liturgical languages. The Syro-Malabar rite is located in India, in two archdioceses and nineteen dioceses. They claim descent from the Christians who were converted by St. Thomas in India and use as their liturgical languages Syriac and Malayalam. (See also **Eastern Catholic Churches** and **Malabar Rite**.)

Challoner, Richard (1691-1781) ● English Catholic leader and author of *The Garden of the Soul.* Challoner was born at Lewes, in Sussex, of Presbyterian parents, but while still young he became a Catholic. In 1705, he was sent to Douai where he studied at the English College and was ordained in 1716; he was appointed vice-president and professor of theology at the college in 1720. Finally, in 1730, Challoner returned to England to improve the lives of the much oppressed Catholic community there. He was compelled to leave briefly in 1738, due to a sharp counterreaction to his efforts, but by 1741 he was back, being consecrated titular bishop of Debra. In 1758, he was named vicar apostolic of the London district. He established the Benevolent Society for the Relief of the Aged and Infirm Poor and was remarkably successful in attracting converts to the faith. Challoner was responsible for

several devotional works, including *The Garden of the Soul* (1740), a prayer book for laypeople that was very popular among English Catholics, and *Meditations for Every Day of the Year* (1753). He also authored *Britannia Sancta* (1745; *Lives of the British Saints*), *British Martyrology* (1760), and made a translation of the Latin Vulgate that was to become the authorized Bible for the Catholics of England.

Chardinism ● See **Teilhard de Chardin, Pierre**.

Chardon, Louis (c. 1596-1651) ● French Dominican mystical author, best known for his work *La Croix de Jésus* (1647; *The Cross of Jesus*). He entered the Dominicans in 1618 at Paris in the Convent S. Annuntiationis, spending most of the remainder of his life there. *La Croix de Jésus* was a remarkable manual on the mystical life, presenting the action of sanctifying grace in the soul and the presence of the Three Divine Persons within it. It was much influenced by Thomas Aquinas, Pseudo-Dionysius, and Johannes Tauler. His other writings included *Raccourci de l'art de mediter* (1649; *Recourse on the Art of Meditation*) and *Méditations sur la passion de Jésus-Christ* (1650; *Meditations on the Passion of Jesus Christ*).

Charlemagne (742-814) ● King of the Franks from 768-814, and emperor from 800, the first Holy Roman Emperor. Charlemagne, or Charles the Great, was given the title *Rex Pater Europa* (King Father of Europe) for his achievements in establishing long-lasting political and social institutions. The son of Pepin III the Short, he grew up with his brother Carloman in the household that watched Pepin rise from mayor of the palace (*major domus*) to ruler of the Franks after the deposition of the Merovingian king in 751. Charlemagne was deeply influenced by the papal blessing of this dynastic change and by the arrival of Pope Stephen II in France in 753-754. Charlemagne would ever after maintain close and cordial relations with both the Church and the papacy.

In 768, Pepin died and Charlemagne came to the throne, sharing power with his brother because of the Frankish custom of dividing possessions among the surviving children of a warrior. The two were soon embroiled in a heated rivalry that ended abruptly in 771 when Carloman died suddenly. He seized control over all of Frankish territory and, after solidifying his authority, Charlemagne embarked upon an ambitious series of campaigns to create a vast Christian empire. In 773, he stormed into Italy and crushed the Lombards, taking the iron crown of the Lombard kingdom for himself; the destruction of the Lombards was of considerable help to the Holy See, which was constantly threatened, and Pope Adrian I rewarded him with the title Patricius. He then turned to the Saxons, launching a massive campaign starting in 775 with the aim of subduing and Christianizing them. Numerous campaigns proved necessary, culminating in the final surrender of the Saxons and the long-term integration of Saxon lands into the Carolingian Empire. By the time of his death, Charlemagne's empire stretched from the Pyrenees and the so-called Spanish March, through France, Italy, and Switzerland, into Germany, Bavaria, and even into the Balkans.

Crowning of Charlemagne

Charlemagne chose as his residence from 794 the town of Aachen, picked supposedly because of its hot springs. He presided from there over the intellectual, political, and cultural reinvigoration of Europe. Under such gifted intellectuals as Einhard, Alcuin, Peter of Pisa, and others, there took place the Carolingian Renaissance, spearheaded by Charlemagne himself. The ruler was well read in theology, spoke several languages including Latin, and was versed in mathematics and astronomy. He also established laws and an extensive machinery of state that was generally feudal in nature.

While famous for his leniency, especially toward illegitimate children, Charlemagne was a devoted patron of the Church, recognizing early on the need and desirability of having the support of the popes for his regime, particularly as it gave him legitimacy and the ability to proclaim his empire at the political expense of the Byzantine Empire that had, since the fifth century, been the only universal empire in the West. The popes found Charlemagne a powerful protector, first against the Lombards and then against the dangerous Roman nobles who drove Pope Leo III out of the Eternal City in 799. Charlemagne restored him and in November 800 journeyed himself to Rome. There, on Christmas Day, Leo III crowned him Roman Emperor, an act that was displeasing to the ruler according to the chronicler Einhard, since it implied a reception of the crown at the pleasure of the pontiff; for Leo it gave a powerful symbol of the final independence of the papacy from the Byzantines and the heightened temporal authority of the Holy See in Italy and throughout Western Christendom. Charlemagne refused to remain the apparent vassal of the pope, announcing his independence by having his son, Louis the Pious, crowned as his successor in 813 at Aachen and not in Rome. The emperor died at Aachen on January 28, 814; in a testament to his personal greatness, his empire disintegrated swiftly after his death and his reign became virtually legendary, described by chroniclers as a golden age.

Charles V (1500-1558) ● Powerful king of Spain and Holy Roman Emperor from 1519-1556, considered the greatest Habsburg emperor on whose vast domain it was said "the sun never set." Charles was the son of Philip I and Joanna of Castile and was the grandson of their Catholic Majesties, Ferdinand and Isabella of Spain on one side and Emperor Maximilian I and Mary of Burgundy on the other. Charles became king of Spain in 1506 (but did not rule there until 1516) and emperor-elect of the Holy Roman Empire in 1519. He thus inherited the enormous Habsburg holdings in Spain, the Spanish Empire in the Americas, Naples, Sicily, the Netherlands, and territories in Austria — a realm that would involve him in most of the political and religious affairs of the time. In 1521, Charles rejected Luther at the Diet of Worms, thereby declaring war on Protestantism. The wars ended in Germany in 1555 with the Peace of

Emperor Charles V

Augsburg and his departure from German lands, having accepted the pragmatic political maxim of *"Cuius regio, eius religio"* ("In a prince's country, a prince's religion"). While he promoted reform in the Church, his relations with Catholic France and the papacy were often poor. In 1526, Pope Clement VII formed the League of Cognac with France against him under the influence of King Francis I of France. Charles invaded Italy, capturing and sacking Rome in May 1527. Clement was essentially imprisoned in Castel Sant' Angelo, and Charles's Austrian mercenaries stabled their horses in the Basilica of St. Peter. The emperor later defeated a French army in Italy in 1529, thereby ensuring that King Henry VIII of England could not receive an annulment of his marriage to Catherine of Aragon, the aunt of Emperor Charles. The refusal of Clement to grant the divorce (under threat of imperial troops) precipitated the eventual split of Henry from the Church. Charles's interference also delayed and prevented any meaningful response from Clement to the growing fire of Reformation that was engulfing parts of Germany, flames caused to spread only by the indecisive nature of the pope. Charles retired in 1556 with much of the empire shattered by war and upheaval the emperor himself had caused. He died at the monastery of Yuste in Estremadura. (See also **Germany, Holy Roman Empire,** and **Reformation, Catholic [and Protestant].**)

Charles Borromeo, St. (1538-1584) ● Archbishop of Milan and a major figure in the Counter-Reformation in Italy. Charles, born to a noble family at Arona, Italy, was educated at the University of Paris where he received a doctorate in civil and canon law in 1559. That same year, he was summoned to Rome by his uncle, Pope Pius IV, and in 1561 was named cardinal and archbishop of Milan. He was soon an important adviser to Pius, who employed him extensively in the organization and direction in the third convocation of the Council of Trent (1562-1563). Borromeo was particularly instrumental in drafting the catechism that came out of the council and was issued in 1566, the *Catechismus ex Decreto Concilii Tridentini*, the so-called Roman Catechism. The same year of the catechism, he worked to bring the Protestants of Switzerland to the faith and then participated in a conclave that elected a successor to Pope Pius IV.

As archbishop of Milan, Borromeo was responsible for a diocese that stretched from Venice to Geneva, with six hundred thousand laypeople and three thousand clergy. He implemented aggressively the reform of the Church under his jurisdiction by fostering administrative improvements, greater education of his priests, and heightened moral education for his one thousand parishes. Seminaries were established and lay students were entrusted to the care of the Jesuits, who received much support from the cardinal. Borromeo did encounter some difficulties from the so-called Humiliati, one of whom, Girolamo Donato Farina, attempted to assassinate him in 1569. Despite Borromeo's pleas for leniency, Farina and several others were tortured and executed. Upon recovering from the wounds of the

St. Charles Borromeo

would-be assassin, Borromeo rededicated himself to reform and care for the poor and sick. He traveled constantly throughout his diocese, identifying himself with the poorest of his flock. During the terrible famine of 1570, he earned wide acclaim for managing to find food for thousands of suffering people, but even greater renown came during the plague of 1576-1578 when he refused to leave the disease-stricken city. Upon his death in 1584 in the arms of his Welsh confessor, he was heard to exclaim, "Behold I come. Your will be done." Canonized in 1610 by Pope Pius V, his influence was far-reaching throughout the Church. Feast day: November 4.

Charles Martel ● See **Tours, Battle of**.

Charron, Pierre (1541-1603) ● French theologian, philosopher, and preacher. Born in Paris, he studied law at Orléans and Bourges and became a renowned preacher to Margaret of France, queen of Navarre. He was later (1594) vicar-general of Cahors and then canon of Condom. Charron authored several important works, including *Les Trois Vérités* (1593; *The Three Truths*), an ardent defense of the Church, against the Reformation, particularly the reformed theology of Calvinism; and *De la sagesse* (3 vols., 1601; *On Wisdom*), which was much inspired by the French essayist Michel de Montaigne and examined the possible attainment of knowledge other than via revealed truth. He points to three forms of wisdom: the evil wisdom of the world, the wisdom attained through grace, and human wisdom, which exists between the two. The work was attacked by many as being irreligious, but it would prove influential in the rise of ethics as a secular discipline. Charron, like Montaigne, has been the figure of much debate and scholars over the precise meaning and intent of his writings.

Charroux, Council of ● See under **Peace of God**.

Charter of Love ● In Latin, *Carta Caritatis*, the name given to the constitution of the Cistercian order that was presented in 1119 by St. Stephen Harding to Pope Callistus II. It was given papal approbation and took a final form around 1155. The charter called for asceticism, manual labor for all monks, and a simplified liturgy. By its terms, the Cistercians created a system of autonomous houses that had much independence in settling their own affairs but in accordance with the terms established by the annual general chapter at Cîteaux. There was to be an annual visit from the abbot of its founding abbeys, and there were general guidelines for the election of abbots and the maintenance of discipline. The Charter of Love would be highly influential in shaping other monastic institutions. (See also **Cistercians** and **Monasticism**.)

Chartreuse, La Grande ● In English, "the Great Chartreuse" (or Great Charterhouse), it was the motherhouse of the Carthusian order, located to the north of Grenoble in the Dauphine Alps of France. This original foundation of the Carthusians was established in 1084 by St. Bruno, apparently on the remains of an early monastic community. The present monastery was constructed in 1676. It was converted from a monastic purpose in 1904 in the wake of the Association Law (1901) that caused the monks to be dispelled, but the Carthusians returned in 1940. The popular liqueur called Chartreuse originated at La Grande Chartreuse and was made by the monks.

During the time of exile, the Carthusians made the liqueur in Tarragona, Spain.

Chaucer, Geoffrey (c. 1340-1400) ● English poet and one of the foremost writers of the Middle Ages. Chaucer was the son of a London merchant, serving as a page from 1357-1358 in the household of Prince Lionel. He then took part in the campaign of King Edward III in France but was captured during the siege of Reims in 1359; he was ransomed the next year. Admitted into the royal household in 1367, he held a variety of posts and ultimately received gifts and pensions from Edward III, Richard II, and Henry IV. He was buried in Westminster Abbey in 1400 where he had retired, taking a lease on a house in the garden of the abbey.

A genuinely talented and highly influential writer, Chaucer is best known for the *Canterbury Tales*, a collection of stories told by a group of pilgrims journeying from London to Canterbury who are staying at the Tabard Inn. After a charming general prologue introducing each pilgrim, the various characters (such as a knight, miller, reeve [a local official], cook, lawyer, friar, clerk, merchant, squire, physician, and prioress) give their own tales. The *Canterbury Tales* preserved vital elements of fourteenth-century English thought and society. Of particular interest are the tales of the friar and prioress, earning Chaucer the long reputation of being anticlerical in disposition. This view has been revised in recent years by experts who prefer the position that Chaucer was merely attempting to provide his readers with as authentic a depiction of the era as possible. He also translated *De Consolatio Philosophiae* by Boethius and composed *The Book of the Duchess* (1369) and *Troilus and Criseyde* (c. 1385-1386).

Chester Plays ● Cycle of twenty-five religious plays that date to the 1300s, so named because they were performed traditionally in the city of Chester, England. The plays were presented during the summer feast day of Corpus Christi and took three days to complete. Plays 1-9 were performed on the first day, presenting the fall of Lucifer, with notable episodes from the OT, leading to the birth of Our Lord and the presentation of the Magi; Plays 10-18 covered the life of Christ, including his crucifixion and descent into hell; Plays 19-25 offered Jesus' resurrection, ascension, and the last judgment. The text of the Chester Plays has survived in a number of manuscripts. (See also **Plays**.)

Chesterton, G. K. (1874-1936) ● English essayist, author, and a prominent convert to Catholicism. Gilbert Keith Chesterton was born in London, studying at St. Paul's School, the London Slade School of Art, and University College, London. A brilliant writer of social criticism, literary criticism, and theology, he was converted in 1922 from the Church of England and was henceforth an active apologist for the Catholic Church. Some notable works after his reception into the Church were *The Catholic Church and Conversion* (1926), *The Everlasting Man* (1925), *Avowals and Denials* (1934), and remarkable biographies of St. Francis of Assisi (1923) and St. Thomas Aquinas (1933). Chesterton also authored the beloved detective series featuring Father Brown, the priest-sleuth who debuted in *The Innocence of Father Brown* in 1911. Chesterton's *Autobiography* (1936) is much regarded by literary and social critics. His writings, particularly *The Catholic Church and Conversion*, are highly recommended for anyone interested in the intellectual process involved in embracing the Catholic faith. In 1936, Pope Pius XI granted him the remarkable title of "Defender of the Catholic Faith."

Chevetogne ● Well-known Benedictine monastery at Chevetogne, Belgium. In 1925,

Dom Lambert Beauduin responded to the call of Pope Pius XI to the Benedictines that they should pray for Christian unity (*Equidem Verba*, March 1924), by establishing at Amay-sur-Meuse a monastery of Union. The community moved in 1939 to its present location at Chevetogne. There the Benedictines pray for improved relations between the Catholic Church and other Christian faiths, particularly those of the Orthodox.

Children's Crusade ● See under **Crusades**.

Chile ● South American republic. The Church first came to the region with the Spanish conquistadors in 1535, the earliest of whom was Almagro. He launched an expedition from Peru but was defeated by the difficult elements and the fierce native Indians. Gradual Spanish presence was introduced over the following years, bringing with it the opportunity for missionary activity. The first parish was established in 1547 and evangelization was undertaken by the Franciscans and the Jesuits. The first bishopric was begun in 1561, followed by a formal Church organization in succeeding years. The conversion of the native inhabitants proved difficult because of the terrain and the Indians' determination to resist Spanish influence. Progress was hampered by the long struggle for independence (1810-1818) led by Bernardo O'Higgins, Juan Martínez de Rosas, and José Miguel Carrera. Final independence was won at the Battle of Maipu by José de San Martín. The Church in this period continued to enjoy state subsidies, but much of the clergy was discredited because of its close association with the Spanish. Over the next years, government interference manifested itself in Church affairs and the Church also suffered from an acute shortage of native clergy, especially in work among the native inhabitants. A formal separation of Church and State was effected in 1925 in the Chilean constitution. Relations deteriorated during the rule of the Marxist regime of Salvador Allende Gossens (1970-1973). He was overthrown in a coup and reportedly killed himself in May 1973. There was little improvement in both the dealings of the Church with the junta and the violations of human rights. The bishops of Chile protested vehemently during the dictatorship, issuing numerous statements that were critical of the regime. Prospects improved considerably with democratic elections in 1990.

China ● According to legend, the Christian faith was first brought to China by the Apostle St. Thomas as part of his missionary endeavors in the Far East. As there is no evidence to support this, historians generally credit the introduction of the faith to the Nestorians in the sixth century. They would flourish in succeeding years and then decline in the ninth century, rising again in the eleventh century and surviving until the fourteenth. Christianity from the West came in two waves. The first came under the renowned traveler John of Monte Corvino, who began a Franciscan mission in 1294 and became an archbishop in 1307. More missionaries arrived, but this promising campaign was ended in 1368 with the rise of the Ming Dynasty. The second wave began in 1582 when the Jesuits Matteo Ricci and Michele Ruggieri arrived. Shrewdly, they became superbly well-informed about Chinese culture and society and used their knowledge of science and astronomy to win the trust of high government officials and influential scholars. Further, they allowed converts to keep elements of Chinese custom and religious ceremony, an innovation that led to a Chinese community of some three hundred thousand by the start of the 1700s. These so-called Chinese rites were also the cause of much controversy and were ultimately forbidden by order of the papacy, starting with Clement XI (r. 1700-1721). The

Jesuits had been opposed in the use of the Chinese rites by other missionary orders (Dominicans and Franciscans especially), but the ban on their use brought a drop in converts and offended Chinese officials, who disliked foreign interference. As hostility had already been growing against foreigners, persecutions were launched, only increasing with the changes of dynasties and concomitant sociopolitical instability. Most of the missionaries left the country in the eighteenth century.

As the Western powers pried open China to their commercial and political interests in the 1800s, missionaries of both Catholic and Protestant denominations seized the opportunity, particularly after the West compelled the Chinese by force to allow missions to be developed. Starting out from the so-called treaty ports, the Western missionaries established missions all over China. By the start of the twentieth century there were some half a million Chinese Catholics. The Boxer Rebellion brought the deaths of many thousands of Chinese Christians and missionaries, but it would prove only a forerunner of the terrible wars and revolution that would plague China in the coming decades. Despite the civil wars, the fall of the Manchu Dynasty in 1911, and the chronic anti-Christian purges launched by warlords, the Church prospered, permitting the consecration of several Chinese bishops in 1926.

The Communists then came to power in the years after World War II, declaring a republic in 1949. Brutal anti-Catholic persecutions followed, including the deportation of over five thousand foreign clergy, the closing of schools, orphanages, and hospitals, and the imprisonment, harassment, and murder of native priests, nuns, and laypeople. To secure control over the remnants, the Chinese government launched the Patriotic Association of Chinese Catholics in 1957, which was condemned the following year by Pope Pius XII. The most famous American missionary during this period was Bishop James Walsh, M.M. (d. 1981), who was arrested and sentenced to twenty years in prison in 1960; he was released in 1970 and thrown out of the country. After a long period of cold diplomatic contact, the last few years have witnesses a slight improvement in relations between the Holy See and the Beijing regime, despite ongoing repression.

Chi-Rho

with Benedict XIV's reaffirmation of *Ex illa die*. While unpopular with the missionaries and Chinese Catholics, the ban long remained into the pontificate of Pope Pius XII (1939-1958). He stated that the practice might be reconsidered, but by then China was sinking into Communist oppression and the question of the rites was obviated by other concerns. (See also **China**, preceding entry.)

Chinese Rites ●
Those practices performed by early Chinese Christians of an ancient or traditionally Chinese nature that were permitted by Christian missionaries so as to attract new converts, increase their gradual assimilation into the faith, and make them more comfortable in the practice of their creed. Among the "Chinese rites" (as they were called) were the adherence to certain forms of Confucianism, ancient names for God, and especially ancestor worship. There was understandable question about the orthodoxy or regularity of such rites and an investigation was launched in 1693 to determine their compatibility with the doctrines of the Church. The matter was finally resolved in 1715 when Pope Clement XI issued the apostolic constitution *Ex illa die*; the practices were rejected and missionaries were directed to convince their converts to discontinue them. Years of discussion ensued, however, culminating

Chi-Rho ● Monogram for the name Christ composed from the Greek letters *Chi* and *Rho*, the first letters in the Greek name *Christos*. They appear in the form of an X and a P, and are normally depicted superimposed, the X placed on the stem of the P. The Chi-Rho was one of the most common symbols for Christ within the Roman Empire, frequently decorating the banners (the *labara*) of the imperial legions from the time of Emperor Constantine the Great (d. 337).

Christian Brothers ● Known in full as the Brothers of the Christian Schools (F.S.C.), a men's religious institute founded around 1680 at Reims, France, by St. Jean Baptiste de la Salle. Its primary purpose is to promote the Christian education of youth. The Christian Brothers first arrived in the United States in 1819; their first permanent American institution was Colbert Hall

College, Baltimore, Maryland, in 1845. Edmund Ignatius Rice founded the Irish Christian Brothers in 1803 in Waterford, Ireland. These brothers reached the United States in 1906 and are today found in numerous American dioceses.

Christ, Supreme Order of ● See Knighthood under **Papal Decorations**.

Christian Democrats ● Members of the political philosophy or movement known as Christian Democracy, which adheres to the concepts of religious freedom, the rights of workers, full participation in the democratic form of government, a vital and strong family unit, and the creation of a sociopolitical environment in which a person is able to take part in the important affairs of the country while remaining fully in tune with Christian principles. The Christian Democrats advocate government involvement in programs for social welfare, but they do not agree with any extreme forms of socialism and are especially opposed to Communism and the state takeover of private property. At the same time, they do not accept unrestricted capitalism. Christian Democracy was extremely successful in the post-World War II environment of Western Europe, and the Christian Democratic parties won majorities in a number of traditionally Catholic countries — France, Belgium, and Italy, for example — as well as in Germany. The two main forms of Christian Democracy are the more radical party of strong republican leanings and the more moderate party that tolerates monarchical government with full democratic control over the functioning of the executive, legislative, and judicial systems.

Christina, Queen (1626-1689) ● Queen of Sweden from 1632-1654 who abdicated the throne and was converted to the Catholic faith in 1655. Christina was the only surviving child of the Swedish king Gustavus Adolphus, succeeding to the throne in 1632 after the death of her father at the Battle of Lützen during the Thirty Years' War (1618-1648). The government was under the direction of a council of regents until 1644 when, on her eighteenth birthday, Christina assumed control of Swedish affairs. She devoted herself strenuously to bringing about an end to the Thirty Years' War and was responsible to some degree for the Treaty of Westphalia (1648) that finally ended the destructive struggle. Her reign was plagued by constant calls from her advisers that she should marry and that her growing interest in Catholicism was inappropriate; she refused to wed and antagonized the Swedish Protestant leaders by her expressed desire to formulate controversial alliances with such countries as Spain. Criticized for ruling irresponsibly, erratically, and extravagantly, she began mentioning abdication as early as 1651. Finally, after once more declining to get married, she abdicated formally on June 6, 1654, in favor of her cousin Charles X. In November 1655, she was formally received into the Catholic Church at Innsbruck by the Vatican librarian Lucas Holste. Settling at Rome (in the Palazzo Farnese and then at the Palazzo Riario), she tried twice to regain the Swedish throne and was unsuccessful in becoming the ruler of Naples and Poland. Christina had received a remarkable education in her youth, studying philosophy, languages, and politics. Her court in Sweden was noted for its encouragement of learning; she opened schools and colleges and attracted foreign scholars, including René Descartes. In Rome, where she died, she was the main leader of the intellectual group known as the Arcadia Academy. Her own writings were much praised by Descartes. (See also **Sweden**.)

Christopher, St. ● Patron saint of travelers and one of the most popular of all saints. According to the Roman Martyrology, Christopher (whose name means "one who bore Christ") was a third-century Christian who died in the Roman province of Lydia during the persecution under Emperor Trajanus Decius, around 250. He was the subject of numerous legends, some presenting him as a giant who, after his conversion, devoted himself to carrying travelers across a river. One day a child asked to be taken across; Christopher obliged, but in midstream the weight of the child grew enormous. Bent under the load, Christopher was told that the child was Christ and the burden was the entire world. Recently, Christopher has become the patron of motorists. His feast day, July 25, was dropped from the Roman calendar in 1969 because of the almost completely legendary accounts of his life. He was included in the list of Auxiliary Saints.

Christophers ●

Movement begun in 1946 by Father James Keller, M.M., to promote positive action and to stimulate personal constructive initiative. With the motto "It is better to light one candle than to curse the darkness," the Christophers reach millions through their radio and television programs, the free publication *Christopher News Notes* (published ten times a year), the newspapers, and the individual efforts of its members. The movement is deliberately structured in a loose organization, with no meetings and no membership fees or dues, but the success it has enjoyed over the years in assisting so many in need attests to the effectiveness of those who belong and the vision of the movement's founder. Its headquarters are located in New York. The Christophers also give annual awards to writers, producers, and directors for excellence in books, films, and television.

St. Christopher

Christus Dominus ●

One of the documents of Vatican Council II (promulgated on October 25, 1965, and given the English title "Decree on the Bishops' Pastoral Office in the Church"), it discusses the numerous roles of bishops in the Church, in their own dioceses, and in cooperation with each other. *Christus Dominus* placed special emphasis on the collegiality of the bishops. The decree tells us: "As lawful successors of the apostles and as members of the episcopal college, bishops should always realize that they are linked one to the other, and should show concern for all the churches. . . . They should be especially concerned about those parts of the world where the Word of God has not yet been proclaimed or where, . . . the faithful are in danger of departing from the precepts of the Christian life, and even of losing the faith itself"; in light of this, it exhorts bishops to "make every effort to have the faithful actively support and promote works of evangelization and the apostolate" (No. 6).

Chrodegang, St. (d. 766) ● Also Chrodegang of Metz, Chrodegand, and Gundigran, the bishop of Metz and noted ecclesiastical reformer. A member of a noble Frankish family, he was a relative of the Frankish king Pepin and held several offices under Charles Martel. Bishop of Metz in 742, he was a keen supporter of reform and a promoter of monasticism in his diocese. Feast day: March 6.

Chronicles ● Type of historical writing in which political or religious events are presented, without comment or excessive interpretation, in a strictly chronological order. Chronicles were thus different from annuals or histories, and early chronicles of the Middle Ages were much influenced by the writings of Eusebius of Caesarea, Sulpicius Severus, and Orisius. While many chronicles have a universal nature, covering events from the creation of the world to present times, there developed a trend from around the eleventh century for the works to be concerned more and more with local history, be it of a city, a group of people, or a monastery. Examples of localized chronicles are the *Anglo-Saxon Chronicle* and the *History of Thietmar*. Monks were the main writers of chronicles in the early Middle Ages, mainly because they were the best educated, had access to extensive (for the time) libraries, and possessed familiarity with current events. Among the most notable chroniclers were Ordericus Vitalis, Ranulf Higden, and Matthew Paris.

St. Chrodegang of Metz

Chronographer of A.D. 354 ● Unknown compiler of an almanac that was used by the Christians of Rome in the fourth century; the name was first used by the great Roman historian Theodore Mommsen, who called him the *Chronographen vom Jahre 354*. The surviving elements of the document provide invaluable insights on early life in the Church, with details of the calendar of Roman holidays; a listing of Roman consuls until the year 354; an Easter table; a listing of the prefects of the City of Rome from 254-354; a *Depositio Episcoporum*, a compilation of the dates of death of the Bishops of Rome from 255-352; an early martyrology of Rome; a listing of the Bishops of Rome down to Liberius; a general history of Rome down to the early fourth century; and a survey of the fourteen regions, or districts, of Rome.

Church in the U.S.A. ● See **United States of America**.

Cibot, Pierre-Martial (1732-1780) ● Jesuit missionary to China. A native of Limoges, France, he joined the Society of Jesus in 1743. He was sent to China in 1758 at his own request, reaching Macao the following year and Beijing in 1760. Cibot then joined the Jesuits who were part of the court of the emperor, spending the rest of his life in missionary activities and various historical and scientific researches. His sixteen-volume survey of the history and literature of China (published in Paris, 1776-1787) was the main source of information in Europe regarding the Chinese people and their intricate and fascinating culture.

Circumcision Controversy ● Controversy that erupted in the early Church concerning whether Gentile converts should be required to undergo circumcision. The debate was the result of misgivings among Jewish Christians that recent converts from among the Gentiles were not adhering to Jewish law nor were they being circumcised. The more traditional Jewish Christians — followers of the Jewish law who largely continued to see the sect in terms of its native Jewish culture and character — understandably feared that the large influx of Gentiles would endanger the faith and introduce ideas and customs foreign to their way of life. In a broader sense, the controversy was an important point of decision for the early Church whether it was going to remain a Jewish body or reach out and become a universal faith. The central figure in the debate was St. Paul, the individual who had done so much to bring the Gospels to the Gentiles. He looked upon the issues of circumcision as determining the very nature of the Church, for to him required adherence to Jewish law would lead to the inevitable declaration that faith in Christ in itself was not enough for salvation. For Paul, Christ had signaled an end to the law in the traditional understanding (cf. Phil 3:8-9).

The situation only increased in tension as the relationship between Gentile and Jewish Christians deteriorated, reaching a crisis point when the two parties essentially ceased joining together to share the Eucharistic meal. Recognizing the need to resolve the situation, Peter, after a verbal lashing from Paul, agreed to summon a council at Jerusalem in 49. The deliberations were no doubt intense, but in the end Peter sided with the Gentiles, pronouncing, "Now therefore why do you make trial of God by putting a yoke upon the neck of the disciples which neither our fathers nor we have been able to bear? But we believe that we shall be saved through the grace of the Lord Jesus, just as they will" (Acts 15:10-11). To give some satisfaction to traditional Jewish Christians, it was decided that Gentiles should be required to adhere to some Jewish laws, such as certain dietary restrictions. The council, however, signaled a major departure for the Church as it now reached out to the entire world, an effort spearheaded by Paul. Henceforth, the Church would be universal.

Cistercian Order ● Monastic order founded by St. Robert of Molesme in 1098, named after its motherhouse at Cîteaux, in Burgundy. The Order of Cistercians (O. Cist.) was born out of St. Robert's unhappiness with the lax attitude that pervaded his own monastery at Molesme. He departed the community with a group of fellow monks and established himself at Cîteaux where he instituted a far more austere program of life, in keeping with traditional Benedictine ideals. Robert was succeeded as abbot by St. Alberic and then the truly remarkable St. Stephen Harding, abbot from 1109-1133. Called the second founder of the Cistercians, Harding wrote in 1119 the Charter of Love, the constitution of the order (approved by Pope Callistus II), which called for manual labor, a simplified liturgy, and strict asceticism (see **Charter of Love**). During Harding's time as abbot, there arrived in 1112 the foremost member of the Cistercians, St. Bernard of Clairvaux. He founded the Abbey of Clairvaux and, through the fame and brilliance of his work, the order spread across Europe. The monks adhered to a rigorous life of work and prayer, prizing labor and distinguishing themselves by their advances in agriculture and stock-breeding. According to the order's laws, each house was to be plain and primitive, with control over its own affairs, although it was to adhere faithfully to the regulations passed by the annual general chapter, an important gathering that helped the monks to maintain discipline and introduce new or needed reforms and innovations.

The Cistercians enjoyed wide prominence during the 1100s and 1200s, deeply influencing the monasticism of the times. The White Monks, as they were called, had over five hundred abbeys at the start of the thirteenth century, including houses in Scotland and Scandinavia, and the famed house of Rievaulx. The order gradually lost its preeminence from that time and subsequently suffered from the vicissitudes of the late Middle Ages, Renaissance, and Reformation. A reform movement began in the 1600s that called for the return to a more precise adherence to the rule. The members, known as the Strict Observance, found support among many in the French houses, so that a division grew in France between those of the Strict Observance and the Common Observance. The French Revolution had a terrible impact upon the Common Observance, but the order recovered.

Meanwhile, the Cistercians of the Strict Observance became centered around the monastery of La Trappe in France whose members were expelled by the Revolution but returned in 1817. Under their abbot, Augustine Lestrange, their austere rule was revitalized and found appeal among the houses that were reestablished throughout the country. They took their work into other countries and the name Trappists became popularly used for those of the Strict Observance. When, in 1898, Cîteaux was restored to the order, its community chose to join the Strict Observance. Its abbot is the

general of the Cistercians of the Strict Observance (O.C.S.O.), which is today a separate body from the Order of Cistercians (O. Cist.). The name Trappists is still used for the monks of the Strict Observance. Trappists wear a white habit with a black scapular. There are currently over twenty-five hundred Trappists worldwide and nearly fifteen hundred Cistercians. In this century, the best known Trappist was Thomas Merton. There are also Cistercian Nuns (O. Cist.) and the Order of Cistercian Nuns of the Strict Observance (O.C.S.O.).

Cîteaux ● Famous motherhouse of the Cistercian order situated to the south of Dijon, France. Known in the Latin as *Cistercium* (hence the name of the order), Cîteaux was founded in 1098 by St. Robert, abbot of Molesme, with a group of Benedictine monks. He named it Novum Monasterium (or New Monastery) to distinguish it from Molesme and received considerable charity from Eudes II, duke of Burgundy, who assumed all of the institution's expenses. Robert was abbot of Cîteaux, but he was soon called away and replaced by St. Alberic, who gave the monks their distinctive white habits and placed the monastery under the care of the Holy See. Further development came under St. Stephen Harding (d. 1134) during whose time as abbot the order began establishing other houses and St. Bernard of Clairvaux first rose to prominence. The abbot of Cîteaux came to wield considerable power in the Church and France and was the superior general (or abbot of abbots) for the entire order. Today the abbot is still the head of the Cistercians, residing in Rome but administering Cîteaux through his auxiliary. In 1791, the abbey was taken by the French Revolutionary government and sold, beginning a one-hundred-seven-year period of interruption that was ended on October 2, 1898, with the return of the monks under

Dom Sebastian Wyart, who became the sixty-third abbot.

City of God, The ● See under **Augustine of Hippo, St**.

Civil Constitution of the Clergy ● Known in the French as the *Constitution Civile du Clerge*, the legislative enactments by the French Revolutionary government, signed on July 12, 1790, that attempted to reorganize the Church along national lines, imposing upon it a structure that caused a schism among the French clergy. The constitution came about as a result of the already implemented "reforms" of the French Church by the National Assembly, most notably the abolition of tithe collection, the seizure of Church properties, and the termination of civil sanction of religious vows. Going even further in promoting the Gallicanist nationalization of the Church, the constitution ordered the restructuring of the dioceses so that they corresponded to the *départemente* system of territorial administration. The number of dioceses was reduced from 135 to 83. Enfranchised citizens elected their bishops and clergy, bishops were stripped of most of their power, and the state paid all wages to ensure that the clergy were always aware of their position as servants of the government. The popes were to be recognized as the heads of the Church and could be followed in doctrinal matters, but they were to have no temporal influence and could not even confirm episcopal appointments. Formally sanctioned by King Louis XVI, against his will, on August 24, the measures soon provoked a considerable backlash by Catholics. The National Assembly responded by declaring that the clergy must take an oath of loyalty to the new constitution. A mere handful of the bishops and some of the priests took the oath, causing a split in the clergy between those who accepted the constitution (jurors) and those who refused (nonjuring priests,

called *refractaires*). The refractory clergy were deprived of their offices and treated harshly. Attacked by French bishops as schismatic, the measures were officially condemned by Pope Pius VI in the brief *Caritas* on April 13, 1791. The schism was brought to an end under Napoleon Bonaparte with the Concordat of 1801. (See also **France** and **Gallicanism**.)

Civiltà Cattolica, La ● Twice-monthly periodical published by the members of the Jesuits in Italy. During the reign of Pope Pius IX (r. 1846-1878) and especially around the time of the First Vatican Council (1869-1870), *La Civiltà Cattolica* was an outspoken opponent of liberalism in the Church and a supporter of papal infallibility. Attacked by liberals as a mouthpiece for the Holy See, the paper provoked a major liberal reaction to its article denouncing Catholic liberalism in France and extolling the *Syllabus Errorum* (1864), particularly from Johannes Döllinger.

Clairvaux ● Famous Cistercian abbey in northeastern France, to the southwest of the city of Troyes. Clairvaux was first established in 1115 as the fourth house of the Cistercian order by St. Bernard of Clairvaux. The land where the monastery rested was built on part of the feudal holdings of Hugues (Hugo) I, count of Troyes, and was known as the *Vallée d'Absinthe* (Valley of Bitterness); the nobleman donated it to the Cistercians, who called it *Clara Vallis*, or Clairvaux. Receiving its official charter in 1116, the abbey developed swiftly under Bernard and would, over ensuing centuries, produce one pope (Eugenius III), fifteen cardinals, and numerous other prelates. In 1143, Alfonso of Portugal proclaimed his kingdom a vassal of Clairvaux, thereby committing his successors to pay a certain amount of money each year to the monks. The monastery suffered from a period of decadence, but in 1614 it became one of the first centers of reform when Abbot

Denis Largentier reinstituted stern practices of abstinence, fasts, and monastic regularity. In 1790, however, the monastery was seized by the French government. In 1824, Dom Louis-Marie Rocourt, the fifty-first and last abbot, died. During the 1800s, the buildings were converted into a prison. (See also **Cistercian Order**.)

Clare, St. (1194-1253) ● Abbess and foundress of the Poor Clares. Greatly influenced by St. Francis of Assisi, Clare refused to accept a marriage that was ardently desired by her family and in 1212 gave up all her possessions to join Francis at Portiuncula, near Assisi. Francis initially placed her in a Benedictine convent, but as Clare was soon joined by many other women, including her sisters Agnes and Beatrice and eventually her own widowed mother, Ortolana, she moved to the convent and Church of San Damiano. Here, from 1215, she performed the duties of abbess. Through her work was established the Second Order of St. Francis. Her principal concern was the creation of a rule for her community that was far more strict and austere than that of the Benedictines, a rule in the spirit of Francis. Pope Innocent IV approved the final version of her rule two days before her death. Canonized in 1255 by Pope Alexander IV, she was declared in 1958 by Pope Pius XII the patroness of television because she was allowed miraculously to see and hear the Christmas Mass in the basilica on the opposite side of Assisi. Feast day: August 11.

Clarendon, Constitutions of ● Set of sixteen articles issued by King Henry II of England in January 1164 that sought to define the relations of Church and State in the kingdom. The constitutions were intended to restore the balance between religious and ecclesiastical affairs in the area of law that had been upset during the troubled reign of King Stephen (1135-1154). During that time the Church had superseded many rights. While the measures by King Henry were supposed to reinstate a harmony, they actually went far beyond a return to the status quo. Henry's reforms put restrictions on excommunications, placed secular courts in a position of superiority to ecclesiastical courts, required permission from the crown for clerics to travel out of England or make appeals to Rome, and, most importantly, declared that any cleric charged with a felonious crime was to be within the jurisdiction of a lay court. Presented at the Council of Clarendon, the articles were initially accepted by Thomas Becket, archbishop of Canterbury, but within a year Thomas had rejected them, especially the clause concerning clerical subordination to civil courts. After Becket's murder in 1170, Henry moderated his efforts at control over the Church, but the constitutions were never rescinded.

Claudel, Paul (1868-1955) ● French poet, playwright, and essayist. Claudel was born at Villeneuve-sur-Fin in Champagne and was the son of a farming family. In 1890, he began a diplomatic career that would eventually take him to Tokyo, Washington, and Brussels as French ambassador. His fame, however, rests as a poet and author. His plays, of a symbolist and Christian theme, included *La Ville* (1893), *Repos des septieme jour* (1896), and *L'Annonce faite à Marie* (1912). Other notable works included *Le Soulier de satin* (1924), *L'Otage* (1911), and *Le Père humilié* (1916). A devoted Catholic, Claudel tried unsuccessfully to join the Benedictine order in 1900.

Claudianus Mamertus (d. c. 437) ● Christian theologian and philosopher of Gaul (France), the brother of St. Mamertus, bishop of Vienne. Born to a prominent Gallo-Roman family, he gave up a promising career as a rhetorician and his possessions to enter the monastic life, most likely near Lyons. Ordained a presbyter by his brother,

Claudianus assisted him in various capacities, also aiding the great Roman orator Sidonius Apollinaris. He was a vigorous opponent of Semi-Pelagianism and authored the treatise *De Statu Animae* (*On the State of the Soul*), written between 468 and 472 and addressing the point of the corporeity of the soul. In rejecting the ideas of Faustus, bishop of Riez, Claudianus relied upon Plato, Plotinus, and St. Augustine, arguing against the corporeal nature of the soul. Claudianus also wrote letters to the rhetorician Sapaudus and Sidonius Apollinaris.

Clement I, St. ● Also called Clement of Rome, the third successor to St. Peter as Bishop of Rome, serving as pope from around 88-97. In official lists, Clement is the successor to St. Anacletus (r. 76-88), although according to both Tertullian and St. Jerome, he was the immediate follower of St. Peter, and was consecrated by him. He was possibly a onetime slave in the household of Titus Flavius Clemens, the cousin of Emperor Domitian. Origen and others, meanwhile, identified him with the Clement mentioned by St. Paul: ". . . they have labored side by side with me in the gospel together with Clement and the rest of my fellow workers, whose names are in the book of life" (Phil 4:3). Other stories such as his banishment to Crimea and martyrdom by having an anchor

Pope Clement IV

tied around his neck and then thrown into the sea are probably unreliable. He was the subject of numerous legends and the reputed author of a considerable body of generally suspect writings, the so-called Clementine Literature, an apocryphal body of works including the Second Epistle of Clement, Apostolic Constitutions, Homilies, Recognitions, the Apocalypse of Clement, and two Epistles to Virgins. He was most likely the author of the very notable First Epistle of Clement, considered the most important Church document, outside of the NT and the *Didache*, of the first century.

Written around 96, the epistle was addressed to the Christians of Corinth where there had been severe strife in the community and several presbyters had been deposed. Clement calls upon the Corinthians to repent, to reinstate the presbyters, and to accept their commands, emphasizing that the Apostles were the ones who established the order of succession in the Church by appointing bishops and deacons. He then stresses the role of these clergy in the offering of gifts — meaning the Eucharist. Much read and deeply respected in the early Church, the First Epistle of Clement was publicly proclaimed at Corinth, with the Scriptures and was even combined with or added to the NT. It provides to historians an excellent picture of the conditions in the Church in the era, especially in Rome. Feast day:

November 23 in the West, November 24 or 25 in the East.

Clement II ● Pope from 1046-1047. Originally known as Suidger, he was of Saxon noble birth, serving as imperial chaplain and bishop of Bamburg (1040-1046). In 1046, he accompanied the German king Henry II on his trip to Italy. Henry subsequently deposed the three rival popes then each claiming to be the legitimate pontiff: Sylvester III, Gregory VI, and Benedict IX. Suidger was then named pope, taking the name Clement II. The following year, he crowned Henry Holy Roman Emperor and convened the Council of Rome to begin reforms of the Church, particularly to curb simony. Clement died suddenly on October 9, 1047; he was possibly poisoned, as Benedict returned to Rome a short time later.

Clement III ● Pope from 1187-1191. Known originally as Paolo Scolari, he was elected to succeed Gregory VIII on December 19, 1187. His principal effort as pope was to organize the Third Crusade (1189-1191) to recapture Jerusalem after its loss in 1187 to the armies of the great Muslim general Saladin. While he had the support of such rulers as Richard the Lionhearted of England, Philip II Augustus of France, and Frederick I Barbarossa, the crusade was ultimately a failure. Clement also attempted to curb the ambitions of Henry VI, Frederick's successor, in southern Italy, a region that would be the source of much conflict between popes and emperors.

Pope Clement V

Clement IV ● Pope from 1265-1268. Born Guido Fulcodi, he was a well-known French lawyer in the service of King Louis IX of France. After the death of his wife in 1256, he was ordained, and the following year he became bishop of Le Puy and then archbishop of Narbonne in 1259. Made a cardinal in 1261 by Pope Urban IV, he was on a diplomatic mission for the papacy when news reached him that Urban had died and that he should proceed immediately to Perugia. Reaching the city, he was informed that the cardinals had unanimously elected him pope. He accepted reluctantly, took the name Clement to honor the saint of his birthday, and was noted throughout the pontificate for his asceticism. His main achievement was to bring an end to the long and bitter struggle with the Hohenstaufen rulers of the Holy Roman Empire by managing to liquidate the last of the dynasty's rulers in Italy. Clement crowned Charles of Anjou king of Naples and Sicily in 1266, and this formidable client defeated the two Hohenstaufens, Manfred and Conradin of Swabia; both were dead by 1268, and Clement died in November of the same year, having strengthened the papacy.

Clement V ● Pope from 1305-1314. A Frenchman, he was the first pontiff to reside at Avignon, France, thus beginning the Avignon Papacy that would last until 1377. Born Bertrand de Got, he was a French lawyer, becoming bishop of Comminges in 1295 and archbishop of Bordeaux in 1299. His election as successor to Benedict XI came after a conclave of some eleven months and was secured through the influence of King Philip IV of France. Refusing the pleas of the cardinals to go to Rome for his coronation, he ordered them to Lyons where he was crowned on November 14, 1305. He then chose to remain in France and soon began appointing French cardinals to reduce the Italian influence in the Sacred College. The result was French control over the papacy for years to come, a reality certified by Clement's decision to reside at Avignon from 1309. His pontificate was dominated by King Philip for whom he ordered the extirpation of the Knights Templars in 1312 and whom he absolved of any wrongdoing in the king's dealings with Boniface VIII, Clement's predecessor. Clement did help found the Universities of Orléans (1306) and Perugia (1308) but was charged with nepotism and some financial misconduct.

Clement VI ● Pope from 1342-1352. Another French pope, he continued the so-called Avignon Papacy, in which the pope displayed pro-French sympathies. Born Pierre Roger, he joined the Benedictine order at the age of ten and was an abbot by 1326. Named bishop of Arros in 1328, he became archbishop of Sens the following year, archbishop of Rouen in 1330, and a cardinal in 1338. Elected as successor to Benedict XII, he was consecrated on May 19, 1342. As pope, Clement was a firm supporter of a crusade against the Turks, but, as a large-scale struggle was not possible, he helped organize naval campaigns against

them. Clement also opposed Emperor Louis IV of Bavaria, secured the reconciliation of the extreme Franciscans with the papacy (c. 1347), and purchased outright the city of Avignon for the papacy from Joanna I, queen of Naples.

Clement VII ● Pope from 1523-1534. The reign of this Medici pope was overshadowed by the rise of the Protestant Reformation, the sack of Rome in 1527, and the divorce of King Henry VIII. Born at Florence, Giulio de' Medici was the illegitimate son of Giuliano de' Medici but was raised by his renowned grandfather Lorenzo the Magnificent. Made archbishop of Florence and created a cardinal in 1513 by his cousin, Pope Leo X, he wielded considerable influence at the papal court and was noted for his patronage of the arts, especially Michelangelo's work. Elected to succeed Adrian VI, he soon acquired the historical reputation for being a Renaissance pontiff, spending much time enjoying art and culture and involving himself in political affairs. While a sincere and goodly individual, he was at times overwhelmed by current events, vacillating between the political camps of Emperor Charles V and Francis I of France. Clement first joined with Francis in the League of Cognac (1526), but Charles responded by invading Italy and brutally sacking Rome and the Vatican in May 1527. Clement sat as a prisoner in castle Sant' Angelo for some time, crippling the papacy at a decisive moment when the Protestant Reformation was growing in

Pope Clement VII

strength in Germany and needed an aggressive, competent response. Clement unfortunately provided neither and by the time he realized the threat, Germany was aflame with Luther's movement of destructive reform. Clement was faced with a difficult situation in Henry VIII's desire to divorce his wife, Catherine of Aragon. He was forced to render a decision heavily influenced by the fact that the Emperor Charles, Catherine's nephew, was in a position of supremacy in Italy. With little choice in the matter, Clement proclaimed in 1533 that Henry could not remarry as his marriage to Catherine was valid. Henry responded with the Act of Supremacy (1534), and England was lost to the Church.

Pope Clement IX

Clement VII ● Antipope from 1378-1394. (For details, see **Schism, Great.**)

Clement VIII ● Pope from 1592-1605. He is ranked as the last pope of the Catholic Reformation and was known for his purity and charity. Born Ippolito Aldobrandini, he was the son of a renowned Italian lawyer. Appointed cardinal by Pope Sixtus V in 1538, he was elected to succeed Innocent IX on January 30, 1592. His reign was partly devoted to reducing the influence of Spain on the papacy, working to limit the number of Spanish cardinals in the Sacred College and taking the major step of abandoning the long-standing papal-Spanish alliance in favor of excellent relations with King Henry IV of France. Henry proved a reliable promoter of the Catholic Reformation. Clement gave backing to the reform efforts of St. Francis de Sales, approved the Vulgate, and established a commission to look into the controversy between the Jesuits and Dominicans on grace. He also added the duchy of Ferrara to the Papal States, thereby increasing considerably papal revenues.

Clement IX ● Pope from 1667-1669. Born Giulio Rospigliosi, he served a number of popes as a diplomat to Spain and was cardinal secretary of state under Pope Alexander VII whom he succeeded on June 10, 1667. Noted for his charitable nature and his literary talents, Clement was forced to spend most of his pontificate dealing with the intransigent king Louis XIV of France, who curtailed papal power in France through the revival of Gallicanism. Clement reached a compromise with Louis on the troublesome subject of Jansenism in the Peace of Clement IX, signed in April 1669. He was also deeply concerned with the defense of Crete by the Venetians against the Ottoman Turks, but he could not convince any Christian power to aid the island and so it fell in September 1669. Clement died in Rome on December 9, 1669, while mourning the Christians who were killed during the siege of Candia on Crete.

Clement X ● Pope from 1670-1676. Known originally as Emilio Altieri, he was a Roman by birth. His long career in the service of the papacy included diplomatic work in Poland from 1623-1627 and ambassador to Naples. Made a cardinal in 1669 by Pope Clement IX, he was elected his successor on April 29, 1670, after a long and difficult conclave. His main concerns were in attempting to organize resistance to the Ottoman Turkish threat to Europe and dealing with the troublesome King Louis XIV of France, both problems inherited from Clement IX. He also canonized Francis Borgia (1671), Rose of Lima (1671), and Cajetan (1671).

Clement XI ● Pope from 1700-1721. A brilliant pontiff known for his vast learning, Clement was confronted during his reign with severe political troubles and the difficult heresy of Jansenism in France. A member of the Roman nobility, Giovanni Francesco Albani was reputed to be one of the best educated men of his time prior to his appointment as cardinal in 1690 by Pope Alexander VIII. Elected on November 23, 1700, to succeed Innocent XII, he was unavoidably drawn into the bitter conflict between the Habsburg and Bourbon claimants for the throne of Spain, a struggle that erupted into the War of the Spanish Succession (1701-1714). The Papal States were invaded in May 1708 and the treaties of Utrecht and Rastatt (1713-1714) ending the war were political defeats for the papacy. Clement attempted to curb Jansenism by issuing the bull *Unigenitus* on September 8, 1713, a decree that agitated the Gallican views of several French bishops who were subsequently excommunicated in August 1718. Clement also issued the bull *Ex illa die* in 1715, reaffirming his decrees of 1704 that prohibited the use of the so-called Chinese rites by Chinese converts.

Clement XII ● Pope from 1730-1740. Clement was largely devoted to strengthening the papacy when its influence was declining in the face of political absolutism and intellectual upheaval. Born Lorenzo Corsini, he was a member of the Florentine house of Corsini, serving as papal ambassador to Vienna in 1691. Made a cardinal in 1706 by Clement XI, he succeeded Benedict XIII on

July 12, 1730. Clement continued to condemn Jansenism, reaffirming Clement's *Unigenitus* (1713). He also continued Clement XI's bull *Ex illa die* (1713) on Chinese rites but promoted missionary activity, most notably Franciscan efforts in Ethiopia. In the bull *In Eminenti*, he condemned Freemasonry. From 1732, Clement suffered from blindness and poor health.

Clement XIII ● Pope from 1758-1769. Clement's pontificate was darkened by the ruthless eradication of the Society of Jesus throughout much of Europe, a destruction he tried in vain to prevent. Born Carlo della Torre Rezzonico, he was a native of Venice. After holding a number of offices, he was made cardinal by Pope Clement XII in 1737 and was elected successor to Benedict XIV on July 6, 1758. The terrible problems of the Jesuits would trouble both Clement and his successor Clement XIV. Having studied with them at Bologna, Clement was willing to go to great lengths to protect them, but his efforts would prove fruitless as one by one the kingdoms of Europe took steps to crush the Jesuits. The first realm was Portugal (1759), followed by France (1761) where the Parlement (parliament) demanded massive changes in the constitution of the society. Clement responded with his famous declaration *"Sint ut sunt aut non sint"* ("Let them be as they are or not at all"). The papal bull *Apostolicum pascendi munus* (January 9, 1765) praising the Jesuits could not prevent continued liquidations in Spain (1769) and the kingdom of Naples and Sicily and the duchy of Parma (1768). Finally, in 1769, delegations from Spain, France, and Naples demanded that the Jesuits be suppressed everywhere. This Clement would not do, dying a short time later from a stroke.

Clement XIV ● Pope from 1769-1774. Clement inherited the difficult problem of the Jesuits from his predecessor Clement XIII; it would be resolved during his pontificate.

Born Giovanni Vincenzo Antonio Ganganelli, he was a native of Rimini and received his early education from the Jesuits. Entering the Franciscans in 1723, he was appointed consultor of the Holy Office by Pope Benedict XIV and a cardinal by Clement XIII in 1759, mainly because he was reputed to be a friend and supporter of the much beleaguered Jesuits. Elected on May 18, 1769, he was faced right from the start with the need to end the crisis surrounding the Society of Jesus. He was reluctant, at first, to take a decisive step, but mounting pressures and hostilities, particularly from France and Spain, compelled him to issue the brief *Dominus ac Redemptor* on July 21, 1773, officially dissolving the Jesuits. The suppression of the order lasted until 1814 during the reign of Pius VII. Clement suffered in his final years from a series of maladies, exacerbated by feelings of personal remorse over the Jesuits. He lived in terror of assassination and died from what was rumored to be poison. An autopsy proved, however, that death resulted from natural causes.

Clement of Alexandria, St. (c. 150-c. 215) ● Theologian, apologist, and second known head of the Catechetical School of Alexandria. A native of Athens, Clement was probably converted to Christianity and given instruction by Pantaenus, the first head of the school of Alexandria whom he succeeded in 190. He was forced to flee Alexandria in 201-202 as a result of the persecutions of Emperor Septimius Severus, fleeing to Jerusalem where he was given help and sanctuary by Alexander, bishop of Jerusalem, a former pupil. There he remained until his death. Clement's main extant works are the *Protreptikos* (*Exhortation to the Greeks*), *Paidagogos* (*The Instructor*), and *Stromateis* (*Miscellanies*). Listed in earlier martyrologies, as suffering martyrdom on December 4, Clement was excised from the list during the reign of Clement VIII (r.

1536-1605), as some of his writings were considered unorthodox.

Clement of Rome ● See under **Clement I, St**.

Clementines ● Term used for a collection of decretals issued on March 21, 1314, by Pope Clement V. Also called the *Liber Septimus*, the Clementines compiled the Decretals of Clement himself and two immediate predecessors, Boniface VIII (r. 1294-1303) and Benedict XI (r. 1303-1304); they were promulgated with decrees of the Council of Vienne (1311). As Clement died before the general acceptance of the collection, his successor Pope John XXII issued it again, on October 25, 1317.

Clericis Laicos ● See under **Boniface VIII**.

Clermont, Council of ● Important council convened in November 1095 by Pope Urban II; out of it came the call for the first of numerous crusades to free the Holy Land from Muslim domination. Clermont began as a council of reform and was attended by more than two hundred bishops as well as many members of the European feudal nobility. Among its many enactments were a confirmation of the Truce of God and thirty-two canons on secular and ecclesiastical behavior, including bans on lay investiture, prohibitions on eating meat between Ash Wednesday and Easter, prohibitions on payments for burials, and the declaration that a pilgrimage to Jerusalem had greater weight than any other form of penance. Most importantly, Urban called for a holy crusade against the Muslim world to recover Palestine in response to urgent pleas for help from Emperor Alexius I Comnenus, ruler of the Byzantine Empire. The council was thus notable for beginning the crusade movement, with all its ramifications, that would last for the next centuries; it also gave birth to the famous cry *"Deus vult!"* ("God wills!"), the motto of the First Crusade.

Clitherow, Margaret, St. (1556-1586) ● English martyr, called the Martyr of York. The daughter of the sheriff of York, she was wed in 1571 to John Clitherow, a butcher and widower twice her age. Although raised an Anglican, in 1574 she embraced Catholicism, working to care for the much oppressed Catholics in England. She refused to attend Anglican services and was thus charged with recusancy in 1576 and imprisoned from August 1577 to June 1578. Imprisoned frequently from then on, she routinely allowed Masses to be said in her home and gave clandestine shelter to priests. Arrested once more in 1586, she was this time charged with harboring Catholic priests, a crime punishable by death. She refused to plead on the charges, however, to spare her children having to testify against her and with the statement that only God had the right to judge her. The court ordered her crushed beneath a huge weight. Beatified by Pope Pius XI in 1929, she was canonized by Pope Paul VI in 1970 as one of the forty English martyrs (see **Forty Martyrs**). Feast day: March 23.

Cloister ● See GLOSSARY.

Clovis (466-511) ● Ruler of the Franks from 481-511, generally held to be the first founder of the French monarchy, a brilliant king, and, from 497 a patron of the Church in his lands. Clovis was the son of Childeric I, becoming king of the Salian Franks in 481. Initially weak politically, he managed over the next years to unify the Franks, extend Frankish domination over most of Gaul (France), and stabilize the royal line through his marriage to the Burgundian princess Clotilde around 493. Under Clotilde's influence (she was an ardent Christian), Clovis was slowly converted to Christianity. During his campaign against the neighboring Alamanni (c. 496), Clovis took a vow to receive baptism if he should prove victorious. Good to his word, Clovis was baptized at Reims with thousands of his soldiers, following his victory over the Alamanni at Tolbiac (Zülpich). Henceforth, Clovis was a leading patron and champion of Orthodox Christianity. He supported monastic development, gave the Church grants of land, summoned the Council of Orléans in 511, and condemned Arianism.

Clovesho, Councils of ● Series of synods held in England throughout the eighth and ninth centuries that examined issues of critical importance at the time to the Anglo-Saxon Church. While the location of Clovesho has never been verified, the acts of the councils are accepted historical fact. Inspired by Archbishop Theodore of Tarsus (d. 690), the Councils of Clovesho were intended by him to be held every August. The synods of known historical authenticity were those of 742, 747, 794, 798, 803, 824, and 825. The two most important of these were 747 and 803. The council of 747 was concerned with ecclesiastical discipline and the organization of the liturgy, placing much stress on the careful adherence to the Roman rite; the council of 803 returned the see of Mercia to the ecclesiastical province of Canterbury. All of the councils were distinguished by the fact that customarily in attendance were not only bishops and abbots but the king of Mercia and all important leaders of the Mercian kingdom. The king and the nobles gave their approval to the spiritual acts of the bishops and abbots, but they could not veto or revise any pronouncements of the Church.

Cluny, Order of ● Monastic foundation based in the monastery of Cluny in south-central France. Cluny became the heart of a major reform movement, the so-called Cluny (or Cluniac) Reform, that spread across Western Christendom. Cluny

Cluniac monastery, Paray-le-Monial, France

was first established in 910 by William the Pious, duke of Aquitaine, who immediately granted the abbey complete independence. Under its first abbot, Berno of Baume (910-927), the atmosphere of monastic life that was to prove so attractive to other institutions was given its initial shape. A revival of the Benedictine Rule served as the foundation of the abbey, with a reduction in manual labor to accommodate greater stress on prayer and worship, especially the choir office. Leadership flowed directly from the abbot, and Cluny was blessed with several truly remarkable ones. St. Odo of Cluny (927-942) helped to extend the authority of the abbey to other houses as the fame of the reform gained the attention of those monasteries that were themselves seeking to change discipline and improve organization.

Monasteries throughout France and then Italy requested to join the Cluniac Reform, placing themselves under the jurisdiction of the abbot of Cluny, joining in certain common observances, or even asking for direct control or dependence. The exact terms of association might vary, but the reforms and revitalization were strikingly successful. Receiving formal papal approval, Cluny extended itself even further, into Spain, Germany, and England. Members of the order also acquired great reputations as theologians and advisers, serving numerous popes and kings. Cluny, moreover, was a voice against such contemporary evils as lay investiture, simony, and clerical incontinence. By the twelfth century, however, the influence of Cluny had begun to decline, in large part because of the changing social and political climate, the average quality of the formidably empowered abbots, and the new innovations of reform launched elsewhere in the Church, such as Cîteaux. The abbots increasingly were from the leading families of France so that the concerns and interests of the French nobility and crown began to intrude upon the wider objectives of reform. At the height of its glory, there were over a thousand Cluniac institutions. Cluny survived until 1790 and the era of the French Revolution.

Cluny Reform ● See under **Cluny, Order of** (preceding entry); see also **Monasticism**.

Cochlaeus, Johannes (1479-1552) ● Controversialist, originally or properly Johann Dobeneck. Cochlaeus studied at Nuremburg (c. 1500) before pursuing additional educational opportunities from 1504 in Cologne. There he became a dedicated humanist and a supporter of revived classical learning through the Renaissance. While he disliked traditional Scholasticism, Cochlaeus was nevertheless a devoted Catholic. He spent much time after 1521 trying to reconcile Martin Luther to the Church, but he also authored a number of highly critical polemical treatises on various aspects of Luther's theses. These were so harsh, however, that neither side was willing to listen to Cochlaeus or to view him with much favor. He served as a canon several times: at Mainz (c. 1526), Meissen (c. 1534), and Breslau (1539). His most famous work, *Commentaria de Actis et Scriptis M. Luther* (1549; *Commentaries on the Acts and Writings of Martin Luther*), became one of the most useful polemics used by Catholic controversialists against Lutheranism.

Code of Canon Law ● See **Canon Law**.

Codex ● Term used for a manuscript containing a copy of the Sacred Scriptures, vitally important documents because of their preservation of some of the earliest materials and copies of the sacred writings, particularly the NT. Customarily each codex (plural: codices) is said to be pure or mixed. The classification is based on whether the codex contains exclusively Greek texts (pure) or texts and commentaries in Greek, Latin, and Syriac (mixed). The oldest and most important codices are: *Codex Vaticanus* (fourth century), containing the Bible from Genesis 46:28 to Hebrews 9:14 and was most likely of Egyptian origin; *Codex Alexandrinus* (early fifth century), probably from Egypt and containing a remarkable extant text of the Book of Revelation; *Codex Sinaiticus* (fourth century), a well-known manuscript of the Greek Bible, discovered in the monastery of St. Catherine on Mt. Sinai and now in the British Museum; *Codex Bezae* (fifth century), a Graeco-Latin manuscript of the Gospels, presenting them in the order of Matthew, John, Luke, and Mark, with the Acts and a fragment of 3 John, currently owned by Cambridge University; *Codex Ephraimi* (fifth century), a Greek manuscript that, in extant form, contains every book of the NT save for 2 Thessalonians and 2 John, deriving its name from St. Ephraim Syrus, who converted it into a palimpsest in the twelfth century, and currently in the possession of the Bibliotheque National in Paris.

Codex Amiatinus ● Oldest surviving manuscript of the Latin Vulgate. It is one of the three Bibles written either at Jarrow or at Wearmouth under the direction of Abbot Ceofirth in the late seventh century. It was intended as a gift for Pope Gregory II, to be presented to him by Ceofirth while the abbot was on a visit to Rome; Ceofirth died on the way, however, and the Bible passed into the possession of the monastery of Monte Amiata (ninth century) from where its name is derived. In 1782, it was taken to the Laurentian Museum in Florence.

Codex Ephraimi ● See under **Codex**.

Codex Iuris Canonici ● Term for the canon law presently followed in the Church. The Western Church has had two codes this century, the *Codex Iuris Canonici* of 1917 promulgated under Pope Benedict XV and the *Codex Iuris Canonici* of 1983 under Pope John Paul II. In 1990, a *Codex Iuris Canonici Orientalis* was issued covering canon law for the Eastern Churches. (See under **Canon Law** for other details.)

Codex Sinaiticus ● See under **Codex**.

Codex Vaticanus ● See under **Codex**.

Codex, Canonical ● See **Canon Law** and **Codex Iuris Canonici**.

Colettines ● Branch of the Poor Clares, founded by St. Collette (1381-1447). The Colettines are today found mostly in France.

Collegiality ● Term used to signify the authority that is collectively exercised by the College of Bishops. The bishops possess their power under the pope, who has supreme, universal authority and, while in union with the episcopal college, is fully empowered to exercise his authority with complete independence. When exercised in union with the pope, the bishops of the Church have supreme teaching and pastoral authority over the entire Church and the authority of the office of bishop for their individual dioceses. This is exercised in the ecumenical council and in other ways, so long as such collegiate action is undertaken at the call and with the approval of the head of the college.

The theological basis of collegiality is rooted in the foundation by Christ of the community of pope and bishops and the bishops among themselves. The Second Vatican Council examined collegiality in its deliberations, proposing in the "Dogmatic Constitution on the Church" (*Lumen Gentium*) that "Just as, by the Lord's will, St. Peter and the other apostles constituted one apostolic college, so in a similar way the Roman Pontiff as the successor of Peter, and the bishops as the successors of the apostles are joined together" (No. 22). Aside from exercising in a collegial fashion when gathered in an ecumenical council and in union with the pope, bishops also exercise collegiality in their own diocese as noted above. In this sense, they are the representatives of Christ rather than as representatives or vicars of the supreme pontiff.

Collyridians ● Fourth-century heretical sect known through the writings of St. Epiphanius. The group apparently originated in Thrace and was devoted to sacrificial veneration of the BVM. Comprised mostly of women, they sacrificed bread to her in the shape of rolls, hence the name Collyridians, which is derived from the Greek for "roll of bread." The sect may have been influenced by the pagan Roman custom of offering cakes to the goddess Ceres. (See also **Heresy**.)

Colman of Lindisfarne, St. (d. 676) ● One of the founders of monasticism in Ireland and the spiritual head of the Celtic Church in England. A native of Ireland, Colman entered the monastery of Iona and in 661 was elected successor to St. Finian as bishop of Lindisfarne. As bishop, he worked aggressively in defense of the Celtic Church and was opposed to the implementation of the Roman rite over the Church in England. He thus attended the crucial Synod of Whitby in 664 as the main spokesman for Celtic customs, but the so-called Romanizing party, led by St. Wilfrid, bishop of York, convinced King Oswiu of Northumbria to accept the Roman customs instead. Colman refused to accept the results of the synod. He resigned his see and sailed to Ireland with a group of followers. There he founded monasteries at Inishhofen and Mayo, serving as abbot of both. The Venerable Bede's *Ecclesiastical History* is the best source on Colman's life; Bede held him in high regard, although he did not approve of the Celtic customs. Feast day: February 18.

Colombini, Giovanni ● See **Gesuati**.

Colosseum ● Amphitheater of the Flavians, a huge stadium in Rome, between the Caelian and Equiline Hills that was erected between A.D. 71 or 75 and 81 by the Flavian emperors Vespasian, Titus, and Domitian. Called the Colosseum from the colossal statue of Nero that once stood nearby, it remains one of the world's greatest architectural feats. Not completed until 81 but officially opened in 80, the amphitheater could seat between forty-five thousand and fifty-five thousand people and was the site of some genuinely spectacular games and events, especially the animal shows and the supposedly awe-inspiring sea battles, complete with ships, that were possible through an ingenious system of drains. The Colosseum was also probably the place of numerous martyrdoms in the years of harsh Roman persecution in the Eternal City. While the Colosseum has traditionally been venerated as a place of martyrs, there remains some question as to the accuracy of the claim. Some Catholic scholars have disputed the possibility, most notably the Bollandist Hippolyte Delehaye (d. 1941). Nevertheless, such is the power of the traditional belief that Pope Benedict XIV (r. 1740-1758) gave instructions that no more stones should be removed from the Colosseum (it had served for centuries as a kind of quarry), thereby also ensuring its survival. The cross, placed in the center of the arena to commemorate the martyrs, was removed in 1874 after the fall of the Papal States (1870) but was replaced in 1927. The Venerable Bede preserved the famous Roman motto *"Quandus stabit coliseus, stabit et*

Roma; quando cadit coliseus, cadet et Roma; quando cadet Roma, cadet et mundus" ("While the Colosseum stands, Rome shall stand; when the Colosseum falls, Rome shall fall; when Rome falls, so falls the world").

Colossians, Epistles to the ● Letter written by Paul to the small town of Colossa in the province of Phrygia in Asia Minor (near Ephesus) while he was in prison. Dated to the early 60s and Paul's house arrest in Rome, it was composed around the same time as his Epistle to the Ephesians and was brought to the Colossians by Tychicus, "a beloved brother and faithful minister and fellow servant in the Lord" (4:7), who was also responsible for carrying the letter to Philemon of Colossae. The town first received the Gospel from Epaphras, a Colossian, who had been sent there by Paul (1:7; 4:12). The great Apostle, however, had learned of false teachings that had infested the community, making "a prey of you by philosophy and empty deceit, according to human tradition, according to the elemental spirits of the universe, and not according to Christ" (2:8). The epistle is divided into two parts, a doctrinal portion (1:13—2:3) and a series of exhortations against false teachers and on ethics and morality (2:3—4:1). Paul tells his readers: "Put on then, as God's chosen ones, holy and beloved, compassion, kindness, lowliness, meekness, and patience, forebearing one another, . . . forgiving each other. . . . And above all these put on love, which binds everything together in perfect harmony" (3:12-14). Current opinion favors the view that Paul was indeed the author of this letter, a position in keeping with the traditional acceptance of genuine Pauline authorship.

Columba, St. (c. 521-597) ● Beloved Irish missionary and abbot of Iona. A member of an Irish noble family, he entered the monastic school of Neville and studied under St. Finian. Later, he joined the monastery of

Clonard, receiving instruction from Finian of Clonard (not the saint of Columba's early years) and others. In 551, he was ordained a priest by Bishop Etchen of Clonfad. Columba subsequently founded a number of churches in Ireland, but around 563 he departed the island to undertake work as a missionary. He settled on the island of Iona with a group of followers, founding a church and monastery to serve as a base for evangelization of Scotland and the surrounding islands. Columba labored for the next thirty-four years to bring Christ to Scotland, gaining a wide reputation for saintliness. Iona also became during this period a major ecclesiastical center. The main source for his life is St. Adamnan. Among the many stories about his travels was one concerning his driving away with the Sign of the Cross a sea serpent — in Loch Ness. Adamnan described Columba as "happy-faced, rejoicing in his inmost heart with the Joy of the Holy Spirit."

Columbanus, St. (c. 550-615) ● Also Columban, a famed abbot who promoted monasticism throughout much of Western Europe. Columbanus was born in Ireland, probably in Leinster province. Educated at the monastery of Bangor, County Down, he left Ireland around 590 for the Continent, passing through England on the way. Reaching Gaul (France) he began to establish monasteries at Luxeuil and Annegray in the mountains of Vosges. In 603, however, he was forced to defend himself at a synod on various charges, largely based on his adherence to the Celtic customs that he had brought with him from Ireland. Seven years later, he was expelled from Burgundy because of the condemnations he had hurled at the immoral Burgundian court. Traveling to Switzerland, he began preaching to the Alamanni but was soon forced to move on (c. 612) when the Burgundians came to dominate the region. Fleeing to Italy, he founded the monastery of Bobbio (c. 612). Columbanus was much revered during his lifetime as a miracle worker; he was also familiar with classical literature as seen in his sermons, poems, and letters. Columbanus's rule was known for its strict authority and severity, but it spread quickly throughout France, Germany, and elsewhere until replaced by the Rule of St. Benedict. Feast day: November 23.

Commodian (fl. mid-third century) ● Christian Latin poet and a fanatical adherent of the faith. He probably resided in Africa and may originally have come from Gaza in Palestine. Two poems by Commodian are extant: *Instructiones* (known in full as *Instructiones adversus Gentium Deos pro Christiana Disciplina*), a partly satirical exhortation on the faith, with passages against Jews and pagans; and *Carmen Apologeticum* (or *Carmen Apologeticum adversus Judaeos et Gentes*), a defense of the faith, divided into four parts — a preamble, a résumé of the doctrine of God and Christ, a demonstration of the need for faith to attain salvation, and a vivid description of the end of the world. Some scholars put Commodian at a later date, at the start of the fourth century or even in the fifth century.

Common Life, Brethren of the ● Influential religious community first established in the 1300s by Gerhard Groote (d. 1384). Known in the Latin as the *Fratres Communis Vitae*, the Brethren (and Sisters) of the Common Life were devoted to accomplishing good works, furthering the devotion of the people, and improving the Christian life. They were established by Groote during the period of his wanderings through the Netherlands, during which he called on all people to repent. The association grew quickly in size because it struck a harmonious balance between the promotion of spiritual development and the continuation of a person's vocation, either as a layperson or a cleric. Much importance was placed on teaching, and the Brethren founded many schools. After Groote's death, the chief organizer of the community was Florentius Radewyns. Achieving their greatest influence in the 1400s, they were ultimately eclipsed in the 1600s by the rise of diocesan seminaries and universities that claimed students who would have otherwise entered an institution run by the Brethren. Among the notable people educated or influenced by the association were Pope Adrian VI, Nicholas of Cusa, Thomas à Kempis, Martin Luther, and Erasmus.

Communism ● Radical form of socialism articulated by Karl Marx in which the property of all citizens in a state is held in common and private property is largely forbidden in terms of the means of production and real property. Communists believe in the inevitable process of the class struggle that will lead to the foundation of worldwide classless society in which workers control the means of production and a collective state administers all institutions and holdings. While "communism" in a broad and pre-Marxian sense was found in a variety of settings and was even discussed in Plato's *Republic* (outlining a basic communal social system), the intellectual basis of Marxism was British empiricism, French socialism, and German idealism, especially among the philosophers Ludwig Feuerbach (1804-1872), Pierre Joseph Proudhon (1809-1865), and Claude Henri de Rouvroy St.-Simon (1760-1825); Marx also was influenced by Georg Wilhelm Friedrich Hegel (1770-1831). As Marx noted, however, he stood Hegel's system of the dialectic on its head, substituting the German philosopher's historical law of the dialectic with his own materialistic dialectic of the struggle between classes. Such dialectical materialism is utterly contrary to religion, denying the existence and the need for God. The Marxian version of Communism, as developed by Karl Marx (1818-1883) and Friedrich Engels (1820-1895), spread as a political idea

throughout Europe after the founding of the International Workingmen's Association, called the First International in 1864, which had as its purpose uniting all workers under the Communist Manifesto (1848). There followed a Second International, dissolved as a result of World War I and the Third International, known as the Comintern, which was launched in Moscow through the Bolshevik Revolution in Russia in 1917. The Communist state as realized in the Soviet Union created a theoretically classless society, but it also proved one of the most oppressive, monolithic, and ineffective systems of life in history, ultimately falling from a combination of external pressure and internal decay. Today, with a few increasingly archaic strongholds, Communism is essentially discredited.

The Catholic Church recognized and rejected Communism from the theory's earliest inception. From the time of Pope Pius IX (r. 1846-1878), theologians and philosophers of the Church examined Communism and rejected it as antithetical to all of Christian thought, especially its claims that the only reality is matter and not the spirit of God. Most of the popes of the modern era have condemned Communism in various ways, starting with Pius IX in 1846. Leo XIII (1878-1903) critiqued the theory in two encyclicals, *Quod Apostolici muneris* (1878) and *Rerum novarum* (1891). Having seen the effects of the Communist state on the human spirit and its oppression of the Church, Pius XI (r. 1922-1939) wrote the encyclicals *Quadragesimo anno* (1931) and *Divini Redemptoris* (1937); in the latter work, Pius was explicit in his condemnation, calling on Catholics to refuse any association with the Communists and their political aspirations. Even more hostile was Pope Pius XII (r. 1939-1958), who had faced with unbending resolve the rise of the Soviet Union in the postwar era and the spread of Communism in Eastern Europe. Pius resisted Communist parties wherever possible, once opening the cloisters of Italy to do what he could to secure their defeat in Italian elections. His successor, John XXIII (r. 1958-1963), softened Pius's policy and took the first steps toward opening a dialogue with Communists, a program much promoted by Pope Paul VI (r. 1963-1978), most notably under the auspices of *Ostpolitik*. In 1978, Cardinal Karol Wojtyla was elected Pope John Paul II, bringing a brilliant theologian and philosopher to the throne of St. Peter as well as a Polish prelate who had long experience with the Communist system. His pontificate has witnessed the virtual death of Communism in its traditional understanding in Europe and the discrediting of worldwide socialism, an event considered unthinkable at the time of his election.

Communion ● See **Eucharist**.

Compostela, Pilgrimage of ● See **Santiago de Compostela**.

Conciliarism ● Also the conciliar movement or conciliar theory, an idea that flourished in the Middle Ages that a general council of the Church possessed greater authority than the pope and thus could depose him. Conciliarism arose in the twelfth and thirteenth centuries among theologians and scholars who were attempting to systematize and delineate the powers of the papacy. The concept received further development throughout the 1300s through the writings and theories of such notable intellectuals as Marsilius of Padua and William of Occam. In its advanced form it declared that the entire Christian community was responsible for preventing errors of the faith; no one person, even the pope, should be allowed to make such decisions. John of Paris (d. 1306) argued in his treatise *De Potestate Regia et Papali* (1302) that the pontiff was the steward of God in spiritual and temporal matters, but he could be

removed by those who elected him, as they were the representatives of the wider body of the faithful. Marsilius of Padua, in *Defensor Pacis* (1324), proposed that the state should be supreme not merely in temporal matters but in spiritual ones as well.

Conciliarism grew in popularity during the fourteenth century because of the chaos caused in the Church by the Great Schism, particularly when, early in the fifteenth century, the crisis was left unresolved by three competing popes in Avignon, Rome, and Pisa. The Council of Constance (1414-1418) was able to end the schism, marking the high point of the conciliar movement. It deposed or compelled to resign all three popes, including the legitimate pontiff, Gregory XII (r. 1406-1415), electing Martin V as the only recognized successor to the Holy See. Further acts by the council to make conciliarism a formal element in the Church's order were never totally approved and the strife-filled Council of Basel (1431-1449) signaled the decline of the movement, particularly after its attempt to overthrow Pope Eugenius IV. Its continued deterioration was confirmed in 1460 by Pope Pius II in his bull *Exsecrabilis*. The First Vatican Council (1869-1870) condemned conciliarism, but Vatican Council II (1962-1965) affirmed the collegial or corporate nature of the episcopate while stressing that such collegiality was not over or superior to the powers of the papacy. The 1983 Code of Canon Law makes punishable by censure any attempt to make appeal to an ecumenical council an act or declaration by the pope.

Conclave ● Name used for both the canonical assembly of cardinals whose duty it is to elect a new pope, and the site chosen for the purposes of holding the election. It is derived from the Latin *con* (with) and *clavis* (key), and implies the fact that the cardinals are locked together in a room until a new pontiff has been chosen. This form of papal election began in 1274 and is considered the third period in the historical evolution of choosing the successor to St. Peter.

In the early Church, new Bishops of Rome were chosen in the manner customarily used in the other dioceses, that is, the clergy, with the people of the diocese, elected or chose the new bishop in the presence of the other bishops in the province. This was a simple method, but it became impractical as the Christian population grew in size and there arose rival claimants and a certain hostility between the upper classes (the patricians) and the lower classes (the plebeians), each of whom had their own candidates. This situation created considerable upheaval in Rome as demonstrated by the riots accompanying the contested elections of Pope St. Damasus I (366-384) and the antipope Ursinus in 366. Such was the violence that the prefect of the city was called in to restore order.

On the basis of these disturbances, the Roman emperors began to involve themselves in the elections by guaranteeing proper procedure and ensuring free voting by the clergy in cases where two claimants had emerged. This intervention launched a long period of secular interference that would continue, to various degrees, until 1903. The so-called barbarian kings often supervised elections until the sixth century when the Byzantines reconquered Italy. The emperors not only demanded tribute from the popes but also retained the right of confirmation, a practice that routinely created long delays, as word would have to be sent to Constantinople (later Ravenna) to request approval. The last pope to seek confirmation from imperial authorities was Gregory III in 731. After this time, the popes sought the protection of the Franks, and in 769, Pope Stephen III convened a synod at Rome that confirmed the decree of 502 (under Symmachus) that laypeople should no longer vote for the popes and that only higher clerics should be considered eligible.

While making elections more efficient, the decrees did not remove the troublesome Roman nobility and their ambitions toward the papacy from 843 and the decline of the Frankish Empire. The next centuries saw such ruthless families as the Crescentii and Tusculani scheme to have their candidates elected, freely murdering those popes who displeased them and deposing others. A major reform was achieved in 1059 when Pope Nicholas II decreed that the cardinal bishops should choose the popes, a procedure modified by the Third Lateran Council (1179), which declared an end to distinctions among the three orders of cardinals in terms of voting, and requiring that a candidate receive a two-thirds majority.

The new need of a majority complicated many elections as a two-thirds plurality would often be quite difficult to reach owing to competing international interests among the cardinals. Vacancies were prolonged by squabbles, and sickly candidates were picked as compromises while negotiations would take place among the factions. After the death of Pope Clement IV in 1268, for example, three years passed until the eighteen cardinals gathered at Viterbo could agree on Pope Gregory X (r. 1271-1276), and this only after the citizens of the city reduced them to bread and water and tore the roof off the palace in which they were residing. Gregory introduced changes through the Second Council of Lyons (1272) to speed up elections, inaugurating the system of the conclave. It remained essentially unchanged until 1975. In that year, Pope Paul VI issued the apostolic constitution *Romano Pontifici Eligendo* (October 1) which stipulated: only cardinals may be electors; their number is limited to one hundred twenty, with each cardinal allowed to bring two or three assistants; while not essential for validity, it is the recognized form of election; three forms are acceptable — acclamation (see **Acclamatio**), compromise (by which certain cardinals are named delegates and are given power to act on behalf of the others), and balloting; if the person chosen is not a bishop, he is to be ordained to the episcopacy immediately (if a bishop, he is pope at once); secrecy is to be carefully observed; all ecumenical councils are immediately adjourned; and, if no one is elected after three days, one day is to be spent in prayer and meditation.

The last election not held in the Vatican (the Sistine Chapel) was in 1846 (Pius IX), which took place at the Quirinal Palace. The last pope not a cardinal at the time of his election was Urban VI (1378-1389); the last by compromise was John XXII (r. 1316-1334); and the last by acclamation was Gregory XV (1621-1623). The procedure of election is always said to be guided by the Holy Spirit; the entire process — from the death of the pope, through the election, and up to the announcement to the expectant millions "*Habemus papam!*" — is governed carefully and is one of the most riveting of events for Catholics and non-Catholics all over the world.

Concord, Formula of ● Formula of the Lutheran faith that was drafted in March 1577 to present a clear, concise statement of Lutheran orthodoxy in the same spirit as those drawn at the Council of Trent for the Catholic Church. Crafted by several theologians, including Martin Chemnitz (1522-1586), Jakob Andreae (1528-1590), and Nikolaus Selnicker (1530-1592), the formula strove to strike a middle ground between the Catholic and Calvinist positions on the major doctrinal issues of the time, such as sin, human freedom and divine foreknowledge, justification, predestination, salvation, and the relation between the divine and human natures of Christ. Its positive dimensions were intended to mirror the doctrinal precision of confessional pronouncements.

In 1580, the Formula of Concord was published in Dresden, in German, as the *Book of Concord* (*Konkordienbuch*). The work included also the Apostles', Nicene, and Athanasian Creeds, the Augsburg Confession and Apology, the Schmalkaldic Articles (1537), and two catechisms of Luther (with three drafts on which they were based). The *Book of Concord*, however, was never popular outside of Germany, encountering much opposition and rejection. It never attained the authority of the Augsburg Confession (1530). A Latin edition appeared in 1584. (See **Lutheranism** in the GLOSSARY.)

Concordat ● Treaty or agreement drawn up between the Holy See and the civil government of a nation or empire. In a broad sense, a concordat is concerned with those matters of vital importance to both parties, ecclesiastical and secular, but in specific terms it was intended to protect or even enhance the spiritual welfare (and at times the temporal welfare) of the Church within the country or territories with whom the concordat is signed, with special concern for those Catholics who may reside in such places. The first formal concordat was signed in 1122 between Pope Callistus II and Emperor Henry V. It would be followed by some one hundred fifty other agreements over the succeeding centuries. A few of the more notable concordats are the Concordat of 1801, the Lateran Treaty of 1929, and the concordat reached between Pope Pius XI and Nazi Germany in 1933. (See also TABLE 2.)

Concordat of 1801 ● Agreement signed on July 16, 1802, between Napoleon Bonaparte and Pope Pius VII that officially reestablished the Church in France. Part of Napoleon's efforts as first consul to unify the people of France to ensure long-term political and social stability, the concordat provided for recognition by the French government that Catholicism was the religion of the majority of the people in the country. Further, new dioceses were to be formulated, the state was granted the right to nominate new bishops, and properties were to be given to the bishops and priests to compensate for the properties seized and hence alienated by the Revolutionary government. The more beneficial aspects of the concordat were largely reduced or nullified by the attached Organic Articles (1802).

Confession ● See **Penance**.

Confessions of St. Augustine, The ● See under **Augustine of Hippo, St**.

Confirmation ● Sacrament by which the full maturity of the Christian life is conferred upon a baptized Christian, thereby making him or her a soldier and a witness of Christ to the world. Along with baptism and the Eucharist, it is considered one of the three "sacraments of initiation." Confirmation was instituted by Christ in his promise to send the Holy Spirit (Jn 14:15-21). It found fulfillment in the Pentecost ("And there appeared to them tongues as of fire, distributed and resting on each one of them. And they were all filled with the Holy Spirit and began to speak in other tongues, as the Spirit gave them utterance," Acts 2:3-4) and the words of Peter afterward to the people who asked, "Brethren, what shall we do?" ("Repent, and be baptized every one of you in the name of Jesus Christ for the forgiveness of your sins; and you shall receive the gift of the Holy Spirit," Acts 2:38). The Apostles were transformed by the Holy Spirit, receiving the powers of public speaking (Acts 4:33), performing miracles (2:43), and demonstrating the personal holiness of the Christian life (2:42-47; 4:32-35). This testimony culminated with the conferring of the Holy Spirit upon others by Peter and John in Samaria: "Now when the apostles at Jerusalem heard that Samaria had received the word of God, they sent to them Peter and John, who came down and prayed for them that they might receive the Holy Spirit; for it had not yet fallen on any of them, but they had only been baptized in the name of the Lord Jesus. Then they laid their hands on them and they received the Holy Spirit" (8:14-17).

In the early Church, the sacrament underwent a process of development in terms of the rites involved, subsequently changing in the East and the West, although the essential element of the conferring of the Holy Spirit has always been preserved. Confirmation in early periods was often quite indistinguishable from other forms of initiation (baptism and the Eucharist), largely because they were administered by a bishop to catechumens on Holy Saturday as a continuous rite. Further, actual practices differed from place to place. It was increasingly a separate rite from the second century, although it was not known under the name confirmation. Its status was acknowledged by Pope Cornelius (r. 251-253), and by the next century it was a recognized rite in its own sense, despite the continued practice of slight differences in the actual conferring. From that time, there was a clearer delineation in the sacramental roles of priests and bishops, a necessity born out of the increased Christian population and the heightened responsibilities of the bishop from the time of the granting of freedom and imperial favor to the Church from the reign of Constantine the Great (d. 337). The bishop could no longer baptize and confirm all Christians, so the task of baptism fell to the priest and confirmation (anointing) was retained by the bishop. In the East, it was decided that the more primitive custom should be followed. This meant that baptism and anointing were conferred at the same time by the priest, who used oil (chrism) that had been consecrated by a bishop. It became common practice as well to give Holy Communion, thereby giving the recipient (normally infants, from the fourth and fifth centuries) all three sacraments. This custom was not used in the West. Instead, the bishop continued to confer the sacrament of confirmation and it was not given at baptism but was deferred until a later date when the bishop might make a pastoral visit or when a candidate could be presented.

Owing to the duties of the bishops during the Middle Ages and the nature of society, travel, and communications, confirmation was not a regular event in the activities of a diocese. The medieval ceremony had some interesting points such as the custom of tapping or slapping the cheek of the recipient. This came from the idea advanced by theologians of the time that the sacrament gave strength and fortitude to fight for the faith, and the bishop thus reminded the candidate that he was a soldier of Christ, ready to die for the Church. Until the twentieth century, the ritual remained essentially unchanged. Some revisions were gradually introduced, most notably the use of priests as ministers of the sacrament under certain circumstances, leading the extensive reforms launched by Vatican Council II and Pope Paul VI. The pope, in his apostolic constitution on the sacrament of confirmation (1971), changed the formula used for the conferring to one derived from the Byzantine rite: "Receive the seal of the Gift of the Holy Spirit." This is declared by the minister with the action of anointing with holy chrism. Modern theologians, in reflecting the spirit and intention of the council and Pope Paul, consider confirmation to be the strengthening of the baptized by the Holy Spirit, a completion of baptism that they may be able to profess the faith steadfastly and to give witness to the faith in a mature way. The age of the conferral of the sacrament remains a point debated still by bishops and theologians.

Confraternity of Christian Doctrine (CCD) ● Confraternity devoted to providing religious education and instruction for converts and young people who do not have the opportunity to attend parochial schools. The CCD was first established in the 1500s as a result of the reforms of the Church through the Council of Trent (1545-1563). It was intended to improve and offer religious education for young people and adults in Milan who, for various reasons were unable to receive proper catechetical instruction. Much encouragement and leadership for the CCD was provided by some of the greatest figures of the era, including Sts. Charles Borromeo, Peter Canisius, Francis de Sales, and Robert Bellarmine. It was also supported by the popes, starting with Pope St. Pius V, who approved the new catechism in 1566.

The modern history of the confraternity dates from 1905 and the reign of Pope St. Pius X (1903-1914). He expanded and renewed its activities, publishing some twenty-one documents on catechesis, although the most important was the encyclical letter *Acerbo Nimis* (1905). He ordered that the program of instruction be established in every parish, including the directive in the Code of Canon Law of 1917. Its work was affirmed yet again in *Christus Dominus*, "Decree on the Bishops' Pastoral Office in the Church" (October 28, 1965), issued by the Second Vatican Council. The confraternity originates from the various Roman curial congregations concerned with Catholic education, direction passing to the various organs of the Church on a national level. In the United States, national authority is in the hands of the Division of Catechesis/Religious Education in the Department of Education of the United States Catholic Conference. The program then passes to the diocesan level where, ideally, education is headed by a diocesan director. In the parish, a local director, who is supposed to be well-trained in catechetical instruction, administers a program customarily developed by a parish commission or board.

Congé d'Élire ● Royal permission granted in medieval England to the dean and chapter of a cathedral to elect a bishop to a vacant see. Derived from the French for "permission to elect," it was based on the custom, dating from long-standing English practices, that the crown had the right to nominate bishops. The procedure for such nominations was defined in the Constitutions of Clarendon (1164). King John, however, in 1214, accepted the election of a bishop by the dean and chapter of the cathedral of the see but retained the royal rights to grant permission to proceed with the election (*congé d'élire*) and to confirm the bishop so chosen. This arrangement would remain in effect until the time of Henry VIII, who promulgated a number of measures to strengthen the royal position even further. (See also **Praemunire**.)

Congregatio de Auxiliis ● Commission established in 1598 by order of Pope Clement VIII to look into the major theological controversy over grace that was then raging between the Dominicans and the Jesuits. The commission was convened on January 2, 1598, under the presidency of Cardinals Madrucci and Arrigone. After passing judgments against writings of the Jesuit Luis de Molina on March 19, the commission was ordered back to work by Clement, as the pope was dissatisfied that an important issue should be decided so hurriedly. The commission rendered a second condemnation of Molina in November, whereupon Clement ordered Jesuit and Dominican theologians to appear before the cardinals and reconcile their differences. Debates would continue before the commission for the next several years.

Conon ● Pope from 686-687. Probably the son of a Thracian soldier, he was ordained a priest at Rome and elected to succeed John V as a compromise candidate. Already very old and in poor health, Conon died after a pontificate of only eleven months. He is buried in St. Peter's.

Conrad of Gelnhausen (d. 1390) ● German theologian and supporter of conciliarism. Conrad taught at Paris, was chancellor of the University of Heidelberg, and was also provost of Worms. An ardent adherent of the conciliar movement, he believed that the only solution to the Great Schism (1378-1417) was the general council possessing the authority to depose the illegitimate popes and elect a new one. Such would take place with the Council of Constance. His ideas were much influenced by Marsilius of Padua and William of Occam and presented in his work *Epistola Concordiae* (1380). (See also **Conciliarism**.)

Conrad of Marburg ● Properly Conrad von Marburg (1180-1233), confessor to St. Elizabeth of Hungary and a powerful papal inquisitor. A native of Marburg, Conrad studied at Paris and Bologna and was called by his contemporaries *magister* (master), a title taken to mean that he had completed his studies in the university system. He first gained notoriety around 1203 when he preached for the crusade that had been called for by Pope Innocent III, a venture that would become the infamous Fourth Crusade. Appointed in 1231 to the post of the first papal inquisitor to Germany by Pope Gregory IX, Conrad distinguished himself by his personal asceticism and his absolute ruthlessness in extirpating heresies, including the Cathari and Waldenses. After charging Henry II, count of Sayn, with heresy in 1233, Conrad was denounced at Mainz by a court of bishops. Departing Mainz, he was on his way to Marburg when he and his traveling companions were murdered on July 30, 1233. (See also **Inquisition**.)

Consalvi, Ercole (1757-1824) ● Italian cardinal and a gifted secretary of state under Pope Pius VII (r. 1800-1823) during the very difficult period of the Napoleonic Wars. A Roman by birth, Consalvi belonged to a noble family from Pisa. He studied at Urbino (1766-1771), the seminary of Frascati (1771-1776), and the Academy of Noble

Ecclesiastics (1776-1782), and in 1788 was appointed private chamberlain by Pope Pius VI (r. 1775-1799). His rise in the papal government was swift, especially distinguishing himself in 1796 as assessor of the military commission that had been formed to prevent any outbreaks of revolutionary fever in the Papal States and potential intervention by the French. His tact and skill, however, could not prevent the French occupation of Rome under General Berthier (later Napoleon's chief of staff) in February 1798. Consalvi was arrested and finally ended up in Venice, via Naples and Florence. In Venice for the conclave to choose Pius VI's successor in 1800, Consalvi was unanimously picked to serve as secretary, working for the election of his friend Cardinal Chiaramonti. Chiaramonti was elected as Pius VII and Consalvi was soon named pro-secretary of state. On August 11, 1800, he was granted the red hat and appointed secretary of state.

Consalvi first concerned himself with the condition of the Papal States, introducing a series of reforms with the full approval of Pius. Rome was much improved, free trade was introduced, and a number of laymen were brought into the administration of the states. In foreign affairs, Consalvi was principally concerned with Napoleon Bonaparte, then first consul of the French Republic. After long and difficult negotiations, a concordat was reached with France in 1801, an agreement quickly breached by Napoleon with the Organic Articles, which were condemned by Pius and Consalvi. The cardinal urged Pius to accept Napoleon's invitation to come to France and

Cardinal Ercole Consalvi

crown him emperor in 1804, but he also strongly advised the pope against recognizing himself as a vassal to the new imperial master of the French. Ranked as one of the major enemies of Napoleon, Consalvi came under intense pressure from the French to resign or be removed, finally receiving permission from Pius to step down in June 1806; he remained an important adviser and in 1810 was deported from Rome to Paris by Napoleon's order, the French, having annexed the Papal States in 1809, now being in control of the Eternal City. Consalvi lived in semiretirement for a short time, but after refusing, with twelve other cardinals, to endorse Napoleon's second marriage — to Marie-Louise of Austria — Consalvi and the others were ordered to be shot by the irate emperor, a sentence modified to deprivation of property and suppression of their privileges and dignities as cardinals. Consalvi thus became the most prominent of the so-called Black Cardinals, who were dispersed to various French cities and forbidden from wearing any garments denoting the rank of cardinal. Sent to Reims, Consalvi was finally freed on January 26, 1813. Resuming his duties at the side of Pius in May 1814, he took part in the Congress of Vienna (1814-1815), winning the restoration of all lost papal lands before the French Revolution, with a some exceptions, such as Avignon. Once back in Rome, he embarked again upon reforming the administration of the Papal States, his work encountering much opposition from conservative elements in the Curia. He also negotiated new concordats with several European powers, including France and Prussia. After Pius's death and the election of Pope Leo XII (r. 1823-1829), Consalvi's influence was much reduced owing to the rise of the so-called *zelanti*, conservative curial cardinals who disliked his reforms and of whom the new pope approved. Consalvi was replaced as secretary of state and soon went into retirement. He died on January 24, 1824. A statesman of the first order, he helped the papacy survive a potentially disastrous period under Napoleon, and his reforms in the Papal States anticipated but could not prevent the severe sociopolitical upheaval that would characterize the 1800s.

Constance, Council of ● Sixteenth ecumenical council, held in forty-five sessions from 1414-1418, ending the Great Schism that had divided the Church since 1378. Convened by the antipope John XXIII at the insistence of Emperor Sigismund, the council marked the high point of the conciliar movement (see **Conciliarism**) and has been the subject of intense discussion concerning its legality and activities. The main purpose of the council was to bring about a solution to the division of the papacy into three camps, representing three papal claimants: Antipope John XXIII in Pisa, Antipope Benedict XIII in Avignon, and Pope Gregory XII in Rome. After a dispute arose over the procedures to be used for voting, a compromise was worked out by the cardinals by which one vote was given to the delegations from Italy, England, France, Germany, and eventually Spain, while one vote was given to those cardinals acting together as a group. As deliberations proceeded, John, who had hoped to come out of the council as the only pontiff, grew increasingly concerned by the apparent willingness to remove all three popes and elect a new one for the entire Church. Scheming to force a legal end to the proceedings, John fled, but the council continued, urged on by Sigismund. John was

deposed in May 1415, Gregory was convinced in July to resign, and, finally, in July 1417, Benedict was removed after months of diplomatic and political haggling. Oddone Colonna was then elected Pope Martin V in November thereby ending the Great Schism.

Under the influence of Sigismund, the council issued the decree *Sacrosancta*, asserting the authority of the general council over the entire Church, including the papacy. The decree *Frequens* was passed to make frequent councils desirable by declaring that they were crucial for the good of the Church. Both decrees were hotly debated in the succeeding centuries and would prove ineffectual as the spirit and influence of conciliarism declined. The council also tried, convicted, and executed Jan Hus for heresy, condemned John Wycliffe, and attempted to institute other reforms. (See also **Schism, Great**.)

Constantine ● Pope from 708-715. A Syrian, he succeeded Sisinnius. His main achievement was asserting papal authority over the see of Ravenna. He also journeyed to Constantinople in 741 and was received by the Byzantine emperor Justinian II.

Constantine the Great (d. 337) ● Roman emperor (sole ruler from 324) who gave the Church the full protection of Roman law and during whose long reign the Roman world was gradually but irreversibly Christianized. The son of Emperor Constantius I Chlorus and St. Helena, he was born around 285 at Naissus in Upper Dacia, part of the Roman lands along the Danube. He was given an excellent education and served in the court of Emperor Diocletian from around 293 when his father was named Caesar (or junior emperor); he then took part in military campaigns against the Persians and was a hostage to the suspicious other junior emperor, Galerius, until 305 when Constantius became senior emperor. The next year, Constantine journeyed to Britain to join his father, who died in July. The troops in Britain then hailed Constantine emperor, a development accepted by Galerius, although he would agree only to Constantine serving as junior emperor. That same year, however, the system of imperial rule established by Diocletian — that of the tetrarchy, comprising two senior and two junior emperors — fell apart with the usurpation of Maxentius, son of Emperor Maximian. There followed several years of civil and

Constantine the Great

political struggle, finding resolution in two phases. The first came in 312 with the defeat of Maxentius at the Battle of the Milvian Bridge and the second in 324 when Constantine crushed his fellow emperor Licinius Licinianus at Adrianople, making him sole master of the Roman Empire.

Constantine brought about extensive reforms in the military, political, and economic life of the empire that were to transform the Roman world and permit it to survive in the West for another century and in the East for over a millennium. His governmental reforms were characterized by a continuation of the process of centralization that had been started under Diocletian. The central imperial administration grew more efficient, but its heightened authority also represented and epitomized Constantine's firm belief in the unity of the state with society. This policy was clearly displayed with Christianity.

Constantine's first important association with Christianity came just before the Battle of the Milvian Bridge when he reputedly received the vision of the Cross, placing the Christian symbol on his standards and triumphing over Maxentius. He then agreed with Licinius to cease the persecution of the Christian faith (see **Milan, Edict of**), working to secure a favored position for the creed. As its foremost patron, he was able to make himself an active participant in its affairs, starting the long-enduring imperial policy of Caesaropapism, by which rulers involved themselves in the temporal and ecclesiastical concerns of the Christian Church. He thus influenced the Council of Arles (314) and the Council of Nicaea (325), even though he was not a baptized Christian. He supported orthodoxy in doctrinal matters against the Arians and Donatists, but he also banished some orthodox leaders such as St. Athanasius in 336. Great churches were constructed in Rome, and the major imperial city of Constantinople (built by Constantine from 324-330) was a Christian center, its dimensions supposedly laid out by Constantine, who walked its measurements with the so-called Lance of Longinus, his steps purportedly guided by the "Hand of God." While, according to legend, he was baptized in the Lateran by Pope Sylvester, in fact, he received baptism from Bishop Eusebius of Nicomedia only a few days before his death, on May 22, 337. (See also **Roman Empire**.)

Constantinople ● Capital of the Byzantine Empire from 330-1453; at its height it was one of the most magnificent cities in the world and long a center for art, culture, and commerce. It was also the seat of the patriarchate of Constantinople (still held in the Orthodox Church), which long struggled with Rome for a preeminent position in Christendom. Called New Rome and the Queen of Cities, it was long a masterpiece of art and architecture, preserving the Greek and Roman heritage upon which it was founded and the Christian faith through which it endured.

Constantinople was built on the site of Byzantium, a small city located on the European side of the Bosporus, on the edge of land called the Golden Horn. With its proximity to East and West, the site was ideally suited strategically and symbolically to the desire of Emperor Constantine the Great to create a Christian capital for the Roman Empire. According to tradition, he walked off the dimensions of the seven-hilled city by allowing God to guide his footsteps while he wielded the Lance of Longinus, which had supposedly pierced the side of Christ. Named after him, the New Rome was much like Old Rome, with seven hills and fourteen districts. Construction took six years (324-330), although the city never stopped growing or undergoing sumptuous improvements. There developed a mixture of Roman law and government and Oriental culture and art. The population spoke Greek and, over time, the Oriental flavor of life came to dominate, widening throughout the Middle Ages the cultural gulf that opened up between the Byzantine Empire and the West.

From the start, Constantinople was a Christian center. Byzantium had possessed a community of Christians as early as the second century, and Constantinople was intended to be an expression of Constantine's esteem for the Church only recently freed from persecution by the Roman Empire. The lives of the city's inhabitants were thus closely tied to the Church, and the bishop of Constantinople came to wield immense sociopolitical power. In the early period, the local bishop was under the authority of the see of Heracles. Gradually, with the status of Constantinople as the capital of the Eastern Empire from 395, the bishop of Constantinople grew in stature to rival the other major Eastern prelates of Alexandria and Antioch. At the Council of Constantinople (381) the see was made second only to Rome. Further aggrandizement came in 451 at the Council of Chalcedon when the bishop received patriarchal status, an act strenuously opposed by Pope St. Leo I the Great. The efforts of the patriarchs of Constantinople to win an equal or even superior status with Rome exacerbated the differences between the Eastern and Western Churches that led to schism in 1054.

The transformation of Constantinople into a Byzantine metropolis came about with the adoption of Greek and Oriental customs. Its zenith was under Emperor Justinian I (r. 527-565) when the Hagia Sophia was built. Forever after, it shared in the triumphs and numerous troubles endured by the empire, finally constituting the entire empire after the loss of all Byzantine territories outside its walls in the 1400s. From the time of the Nika Revolt in 532 (when Justinian massacred thirty-three thousand rebels) until the final capture on May 29, 1453, by the Ottoman Turks, the city suffered plagues, sieges, and the inevitable pressure of crowded urban life. Especially hard and humiliating was the overthrow of the Byzantine Empire in 1204 by the members of the Fourth Crusade. The resulting Latin Empire of Constantinople was itself destroyed in 1261 by Emperor Michael VIII Palaeologus, who restored the empire, although the city never again regained its beauty, wealth, or vitality. Entire portions of the city fell into ruins in the years preceding the final siege in 1453. Under the Turks, most of the churches, especially the Hagia Sophia, were turned into mosques. The name Constantinople was officially changed in 1930 to Istanbul.

Constantinople, Councils of ● Four ecumenical councils that were held at various times in Constantinople between the late fourth and ninth centuries. The Catholic Church recognizes all four, but the Eastern Orthodox Church accepts only the first three. The councils were:

Constantinople I (381): Convened by Emperor Theodosius I, this council sought to bring a sense of unity back to the Eastern Church after the divisiveness of the Arian Controversy. It was attended by one hundred fifty bishops under the presidency of Melitius, bishop of Antioch. It ratified the work of the Council of Nicaea (325) concerning the Nicene Creed and the doctrine of Christ, condemned Apollinarianism, and granted to Constantinople precedence over all churches save Rome. It is counted as the second ecumenical council.

Constantinople II (553): Summoned by Emperor Justinian I, it was attended by one hundred sixty-five bishops under the presidency of Eutychius, patriarch of Constantinople. The council condemned Nestorianism; it also condemned the Three Chapters and anathematized their authors (see **Three Chapters**), and, because of Justinian's poor treatment of Pope Vigilius, it was not immediately recognized as an ecumenical council in the West. It is now counted as the fifth ecumenical council.

Constantinople III (680-681): Convoked by Emperor Constantine IV Pogonatos, it was intended to settle the Monothelite controversy in the Eastern Church. Attended by some one hundred sixty bishops, the council condemned Monothelitism, anathematized its leaders, and issued a dogmatic decree on the subject, essentially a reaffirmation of the declarations of the Council of Chalcedon (451) concerning the two natures of Christ. (See also **Monothelitism**.) It is counted as the sixth ecumenical council.

Constantinople IV (869-870): A council not recognized by the Eastern Church, convened by Emperor Basil I and attended by over a hundred bishops. The council excommunicated Photius, patriarch of Constantinople, and restored St. Ignatius as the legal patriarch. The event was an important episode in the widening gulf between the Eastern and Western Churches. The Eastern Orthodox Church recognizes instead the council of 880 that supported Photius in his claims. Constantinople IV is counted as the eighth ecumenical council. (See also **Photius**.)

Constantinople, Patriarch of ● See **Patriarch**.

Constitutional Church ● Name given to the schismatic Church that existed in France from 1791-1801. Established as a result of the Civil Constitution of the Clergy that was passed by

Emperor Basil I

228

the National Assembly of the French Revolutionary government on July 12, 1790, the Constitutional Church was the state-dependent religious body as opposed to the legitimate Church of France, which was comprised of those clergy who refused to take the constitutional oath. Thus those members of the Constitutional Church who took the oath were called juring priests while those priests and bishops who would not take it were called nonjuring. Nonjuring clergy were much persecuted in the country, but they were supported by most French laypeople because the Constitutional Church quickly began to allow irregularities in discipline — priests and bishops married, divorces were permitted, and the cruelties of the state condoned. The Constitutional Church, however, was itself soon oppressed by the Jacobins under Maximilien Robespierre, who came to power in June 1793, initiating the Reign of Terror. After Robespierre's fall on July 17, 1794, a more tolerant atmosphere prevailed. As a result of the Concordat of 1801, Napoleon undertook to abolish the Constitutional Church, with the full approval and at the urging of Pope Pius VII.

Nicolaus Copernicus

Contarini, Gasparo (1483-1542) ● Humanist, theologian, and cardinal. Born at Venice, he was a member of a noble Venetian family, receiving his education at the University of Padua. He later served as Venetian ambassador to several courts, including those of Emperor Charles V, England, and the papacy. A noted theologian, he attacked Martin Luther in the work (c. 1530) *Confutatio Articulorum seu Questionum Lutheri* (*Confutation of the Articles and Questions of Martin Luther*). He was made a cardinal in 1535 by Pope Paul III and was appointed to a commission charged with preparing for the council intended to reform the Church (see **Trent, Council of**). Contarini adopted a conciliatory tone with Luther, hoping at the Colloquy of Ratisbon (1541) to effect a reunion of Luther with the Church. Toward that end, he authored his *Epistola de Justificatione* (1541; *Letter on Justification*), an attempt to find common ground with the Lutherans on the theology of salvation. His profession of faith was attacked by Counter-Reformers for compromising the faith.

Conventuals ● See **Franciscans**.

Copernicus, Nicolaus (1473-1543) ● Polish astronomer and founder of the Copernican system, the basis of modern astronomy. Born in Torun, Poland, he was educated at the University of Cracow (studying mathematics, philosophy, and medicine) and at Bologna (studying law). Returning to Poland in 1503, he took up residence at Frauenburg where he had been elected canon in 1497, remaining there from 1512. Having rejected the Ptolemaic system of the universe in which the sun and stars orbited the earth, he set out to devise a new system; the result was a new view that the earth, with the other planets, revolved around the sun. Copernicus's theories were circulated in summary form first in the manuscript *Commentariolus*, and the complete treatise (*De revolutionibus orbium coelestium*) was not published until 1543; he supposedly received a copy on the last day of his life. Pope Clement VII gave his initial approval to *Commentariolus* around 1531 at the time of its publication, but the Copernican system would become a central element in the Galileo Controversy in the first half of the 1600s. The treatise *De revolutionibus* was placed on the Index of Forbidden Books in 1616; it would be removed in 1757. (See also **Astronomy** and **Galileo**.)

Coptic Church ● Name given to the Egyptian Christian Church, today applying to two ecclesiastical entities, the Uniate Coptic Church and the Coptic (Orthodox) Church. According to tradition, the Church in Egypt was founded by St. Mark the Evangelist, the see of Alexandria emerging as one of the great centers of the early Church, with Antioch and Rome. Alexandria came to be an often bitter opponent of the see of Constantinople after the rise of that city in the Eastern Empire. The rivalry between the patriarchs of the two sees would influence the theological debates of the fourth and fifth centuries. Many Egyptians were staunchly orthodox in their outlook, vigorously opposing Arianism (see **Athanasius, St. <1>**), but the patriarch of Alexandria, Dioscorus, gave his support to Eutychianism, presided over the Latrocinium (Robber Council of Ephesus) in 449, and was deposed, excommunicated, and exiled by the Council of Chalcedon in 451.

The excommunication of Dioscorus caused a split within the Egyptian Church. Those who chose loyalty to the Council of Chalcedon were called Melkites ("King's Men") while the supporters of those who advocated Monophysitism were the Copts (from the Greek *Aigyptos*, later Arabic *qubt*, hence Copt). The Church of Egypt, under the Copts, adopted the doctrines of Monophysitism, drawing increasingly away from the Christian Church. They came into conflict with the Melkites and with Byzantine authorities, and efforts to restore the Copts

to unity with the Church proved fruitless. The Melkites subsequently adopted the Byzantine rite while the Copts would formulate what became the Coptic rite.

The Copts welcomed the invasion of Egypt by the Arabs in the seventh century, since they saw it as a means to free themselves from Byzantine influence. Under the Muslims, the Coptic Church was given permission to continue generally unharassed for many years. The Copts were respected by their Muslim overlords because of their long disagreement with the Byzantine Empire and their high degree of learning. They were given posts in the government and were eventually the backbone of the bureaucracy. Nevertheless, purges and pogroms were launched, most notably under Caliph el Hakim (r. 996-1021) and several sultans of the Mamelukes (1350-1517). The Mamelukes, however, discovered that ejecting the Copts from the administration of the state caused the government to grind virtually to a halt, and they were forced to reinstate the Copts. Muslim rule over the Copts would last until 1882 and the seizure of Egypt by the English through the Battle of Tel-el-Kebir. From that time, the Copts enjoyed freedom of worship. In modern times, they have endured local persecutions in Egypt, particularly in Upper Egypt where radical Islamic groups have conducted terrorist acts upon Coptic churches and members.

The Coptic (Orthodox) Church is under the leadership of a patriarch. To use the term Monophysites to describe the current Coptic Church is inaccurate, given the declarations of several popes in working to improve relations between Catholics and Orthodox communities. In the encyclical *Sempiternus Rex* (1951) Pope Pius XII stated that the differences are in the terminology, "when they expound the doctrine of the Incarnation of the Lord"; Pope Paul VI also signed positive statements concerning the similarities of doctrine (see also **Orthodox Eastern**

Churches). The Catholic or Uniate Coptic Church was established in 1741 when Bishop Athanasius of Jerusalem, a Monophysite Copt, entered into communion with Rome. He was named head of all Catholics throughout Egypt, although he did not return to Egypt out of fear of imprisonment. Vicars apostolic were later appointed to help the Catholics. In 1824, Maximos Joed was consecrated bishop, the year in which Pope Leo XII erected a Coptic patriarchate. The patriarch did not function fully until 1899 when Pope Leo XIII made Cyril Makarios the first formal Coptic patriarch. After his resignation in 1908, an apostolic administrator governed the Coptic Church until 1947 when Patriarch Mark II Khouzam took over. The Catholic Coptic Church uses the Alexandrian rite; its liturgical languages are Arabic and Coptic, a Hamio-Semitic tongue, and a Bahairic dialect of Alexandria. There are around one hundred eighty thousand Catholic Copts, situated mostly in Egypt.

Coptic Rite ● See **Coptic Church**, preceding entry; see also **Egypt**.

Cordeliers ● Name used in France, particularly during the Middle Ages, for Franciscan Observantines, derived from the French for "tying a knot," an allusion to the knotted cord or rope worn by the Franciscans. The term is also used for those individuals who assist the sick at the shrine of Our Lady of Lourdes.

Corinthians, First Epistle to the ● Letter from St. Paul to the Christian community of Corinth, an important city in the province of Achaia (Achaea) in Greece. Known customarily as 1 Corinthians, it is one of the two surviving letters from Paul to the Church that had been established around 50-51. The letter was written while the Apostle was in Ephesus with "our brother Sosthenes" (1:1) and "Stephanas and Fortunatus and

Achaicus" (16:17-18), who were from Corinth. As is clear from the message, Paul cared deeply for the Church of Corinth, which he had established, writing in the hopes of resolving various matters that were troubling the community. He had heard from "Chloe's people that there is quarreling among you. . . . What I mean is that each of you says, 'I belong to Paul,' or 'I belong to Apollos,' or 'I belong to Cephas,' or 'I belong to Christ.' Is Christ divided?" (1:11-13). He then responds to their recent dispute (1:10—4:21) before exhorting his readers against immorality: "Shun immorality. Every other sin which man commits is outside the body; but the immoral man sins against his own body. Do you not know that your body is a temple of the Holy Spirit within you, which you have from God?" (6:18-19). The bulk of the remaining text is devoted to answering questions sent by the members of the community. These include the matters of marriage, conjugal relations, and divorce (ch. 7); food offered to idols (8:1—11:1); the proper practice of worship, such as whether men and women should wear a covering of the head, and the speaking in tongues (11:2—14:40); the resurrection of the dead (ch. 15); and financial obligations of members of the community (16:1-4). Beyond the brilliance of its theology, the epistle is also an invaluable document on the conditions in the early Church, particularly in Corinth in the first century.

Corinthians, Second Epistle to the ● Second surviving letter of Paul to the Church in Corinth (see **Corinthians, First Epistle to the**, preceding entry), dated to sometime after the first, perhaps around 55. While it is generally accepted by experts that its Pauline authenticity cannot be disputed, there are questions as to whether the two very different parts of the letter were not individual epistles combined together; the second section, being of such shortness and so different from the first, may be a fragment of another letter.

Chapters 1-9 are concerned with Paul's own relationship with the community of Corinth. It is made clear by Paul that his relations with the Corinthians had become strained in the period following the writing of 1 Corinthians. He mentions that he "refrained from coming to Corinth" (1:23) and instead "wrote you out of much affliction and anguish of heart and with many tears, not to cause you pain but to let you know the abundant love that I have for you" (2:4). He makes clear his authority as an Apostle and the abiding affection that he has for all Corinthians (1:12—7:16). At the same time, he gives encouragement to them to continue their work of penance and reunion in the difficulties that had divided the Church there. Chapters 8-9 ask for donations for the Church in Jerusalem, calling upon them to be generous.

The mood changes dramatically in Chapter 10, for Paul vigorously defends himself against the charges of enemies who questioned his authority. He cites his qualifications by noting the suffering he had undergone for Christ: "Five times I have received at the hands of the Jews the forty lashes less one. Three times I have been beaten with rods; once I was stoned. Three times I have been shipwrecked; a night and a day I have been adrift at sea; on frequent journeys, in danger from rivers, danger from robbers, danger from my own people, danger from Gentiles, danger in the city, danger in the wilderness, danger at sea, danger from false brethren. . ." (11:24-26). He concludes by exhorting the Corinthians: "Examine yourselves, to see whether you are holding to your faith. Test yourselves. Do you not realize that Jesus Christ is in you? — unless indeed you fail to meet the test!" (13:5).

Cornelius, St. ● Pope from 251-253. He was elected as the successor to the martyred St. Fabian during a lull in the intense persecutions of the emperor Decius, ending the vacancy of the Holy See that had lasted for some fourteen months. His pontificate was noted for the controversy over the Church's position toward the *lapsi*, those who had lapsed from the faith during the persecutions. Novatian, leader of the rigorist party in the Church, took his followers to schism to protest what they felt was Cornelius's lax attitude. The pope was supported, however, by synods at Rome and Carthage, and by bishops in the East; a major support came from St. Cyprian of Carthage. Several letters from Cornelius to Cyprian have survived. When the Christian persecutions under Gallus resumed in 252, Cornelius was exiled, traditionally dying as a martyr at Centumcellae (modern Civitavecchia). He was buried at Rome, in the crypt of Lucina; his tomb contains the inscription "Cornelius Martyr." Feast day: September 16.

Cornelius à Lapide (1567-1637) ● Properly Cornelis Cornelissen van den Steen, a Flemish Jesuit exegete, the author of the celebrated series of commentaries on the entire Canon of Scripture, with the only exception being Job and the Psalms. Born at Bocholt, near Liège, he was educated at the Jesuit colleges of Maastricht and Cologne and elsewhere, and entered the Society of Jesus in June 1592. In 1596, he was appointed professor of exegesis at Louvain, and in 1616 was summoned to Rome. There he continued to teach and completed his commentaries except for the two aforementioned books. His commentaries, which were immensely popular, were printed in numerous editions and were even praised by Protestant theologians and exegetes.

Coronation of the Pope ● See **Papal Coronation**.

Corpus Iuris Canonici ● See **Canon Law**.

Cosmas Indicopleustes (fl. mid-sixth century) ● Greek traveler, geographer, and monk, his name means Cosmas the Indian Voyager (or Navigator). A native of Alexandria, he spent a number of years as a merchant, traveling extensively in the region. He was personally familiar with the Mediterranean, the Red Sea, and the Persian Gulf, and acquired much information on the Far East; he probably did not visit India. In his later years, Cosmas entered a monastery on the Sinai Peninsula. While there he wrote his famous work, *Christian Topography*, preserved in two manuscripts, one in the Laurentian Library in Florence, the other in the Vatican. Written around 547, the book attempted to harmonize astronomy and natural phenomena with a literal interpretation of the Bible. Its principal value was its compilation of geographical information, particularly Book 9 (of the twelve) on Ceylon, and its testimony to the spread of Christianity. Cosmas was held in much repute among medieval geographers. Aside from some fragments on the Psalms and Gospels, *Christian Topography* is the only work of his to survive of the several geographical treatises he authored.

Councils ● Formal assemblies of cardinals, bishops, theologians, and heads of religious orders as well as other Church representatives who have been convened to examine or discuss matters of religious or doctrinal importance or to formulate regulations on Church teaching or discipline. Councils have varied throughout history in size and importance. For example, there are so-called local councils that bring together the religious leadership of a region — province, exarchate, or patriarchate — that have only limited authority, with jurisdiction extending to clearly defined boundaries. The most important of councils are the general, or ecumenical, councils of the Church, bringing together the bishops and representatives from the entire world. An often monumental assembly, these ecumenical councils act with the highest of all possible authority and thus must be summoned by the pope and its acts approved by him. There have been twenty-one general councils in history; the last was Vatican Council II (1962-1965). By custom, the first council was described in Acts (15:6) when "The apostles and the elders were gathered together" at Jerusalem. (See also **Ecumenical Councils**.)

Counter-Reformation ● See **Reformation, Catholic**.

Coustant, Pierre (1654-1721) ● French Benedictine patristic scholar. Born at Compiègne, he studied at the Jesuit College there and then entered the Benedictine monastery at St.-Rémè, Reims, at the age of seventeen; he took his vows to belong to the Benedictine Maurist Congregation on August 12, 1672. Sent to the Abbey of St.-Germain-des-Prés in Paris (1681) to assist his confrére Thomas Blambin with the editing of an edition of the works of St. Augustine, he was particularly useful in separating the legitimate and suspicious writings of the great Doctor of the Church. His main work was in organizing a new edition of the writings of St. Hilary (1693), a compilation that remains one of the finest efforts ever produced by the Maurists. Coustant also spent some twenty years collecting and editing the papal letters from St. Clement of Rome to Innocent III (first century A.D.-1216). The first volume appeared in 1271, covering the years 67-440, under the title *Epistolae Romanorum Pontificum*. His death cut short the continuation of the collection. He was noted for his incredible capacity for work, remaining devoted, all the while, to rigorous spiritual and meditative devotion. Coustant also served a three-year term as prior at Nogent-sous-Courcy.

Cranmer, Thomas (1489-1556) ● Archbishop of Canterbury, a loyal adherent of King Henry VIII (1509-1547), and a central figure in the English Reformation. Born in Nottinghamshire, he studied at Cambridge, was ordained in 1523, and emerged as one of the kingdom's foremost theologians. In 1529, he wrote a defense of the king's right to divorce Catherine of Aragon. Sent by Henry as a representative to Emperor Charles V, Cranmer married in secret in 1532 Margaret Osiander, daughter of the reformer Andreas Osiander (1498-1552). Cranmer was soon appointed archbishop of Canterbury, giving full support to the Reformation in England and energetically working to establish royal supremacy over the Church in the kingdom. He annulled Henry's marriage to Catherine in 1533, subsequently presiding over the royal divorces of Anne Boleyn, Catherine Howard, Anne of Cleves, and Catherine Parr. Cranmer also helped organize the Bible into the vernacular. After Henry's death in 1547, he served as a leading adviser in the court of young King Edward VI, guiding the Church of England more and more away from its ties to the Catholic Church in doctrine and ceremony. With the death of Edward (1553), Cranmer gave hesitant recognition to Lady Jane Grey (d. 1554), the doomed claimant to the throne. Arrested and condemned for treason under Queen Mary Tudor (r. 1553-1558), he was initially spared but was soon imprisoned by those elements anxious to punish him for his work on behalf of Protestantism. Degraded from his episcopal rank, he recanted his views on the papacy and the Eucharist, declaring these later, however, to be mere lapses forced upon him. On March 21, 1556, he was burned at the

Archbishop Thomas Cranmer

stake as a heretic. Held by the Anglican Church to be a martyr, Cranmer made a lasting contribution to the development of the Church of England with his promotion of the Bible into English and his extensive work on the Book of Common Prayer.

Cromwell, Oliver (1599-1658) ● Lord protector of England, Scotland, and Ireland from 1653-1658. He was born at Huntingdonshire, England, studying at Sidney Sussex College, Cambridge. In 1620, he married Elizabeth Bourchier and eight years later was elected to Parliament for Huntingdon. Elected in 1640 to the Short Parliament for Cambridge, he emerged as one of the leaders of the Puritans in Parliament, promoting Puritan religious views and supporting the actions of the House of Commons against King Charles I in 1641. When the civil war broke out the next year, Cromwell entered into the conflict with deep religious fervor. After fighting at the Battle of Edgehill (1642), he helped organize the formidable force called the New Model army, a superbly trained corps of which Cromwell was second in command. He played a major role in the defeat of the Royalists at Marston Moor (1644) and Naseby (1645), and at the siege of Oxford (1646). He was a guiding hand in bringing about the execution of Charles, his name being quite prominent on the death warrant for the king in 1648. Cromwell was next the first head of the Council of State for England, ruthlessly and mercilessly using the army to crush any opposition or social unrest. His most bloody campaigns were in Scotland and Ireland. The Scots were defeated at Dunbar (1650) and Worcester (1651) thereby aborting their hopes of independence. In Ireland, however, Cromwell's hatred of the Catholic Church was revealed as he exterminated an Irish rebellion. The uprising that lasted from 1641-1651 ended with some six hundred thousand dead and a terrible massacre at Drogheda. Churches were burned and women and children put to death. Cromwell also continued the policy of English immigration to the country. Unhappy with Parliament, he dissolved it on April 20, 1653; on December 16, 1653, he was named lord protector, ruling over England through a series of unsuccessful constitutional innovations. Declining the throne in 1656, he nevertheless added to his broad powers through the new constitution of 1657. He instituted regulations on public morals and enforced many elements of Puritanism on the Church of England. Abroad, he supported the Protestant cause on the Continent, but his policy was tempered by a recognition of the need for trade with the major European powers of the era. While he generally favored religious toleration, he placed limits on it so that it extended only to specific Protestant groups (non-Anglicans, for example) and Jews. Nor was Cromwell ever particularly well-liked; his dour Puritanism and hard style of government found little favor with the people. He died on September 3, 1658, and the protectorate would not long survive him under his son, Richard (1626-1712).

Oliver Cromwell

Cromwell, Thomas (d. 1540) ● Earl of Essex and one of the most ruthless servants of King Henry VIII (r. 1509-1547). Born at Putney, London, he was the son of a merchant, spending a number of years on the Continent before returning to England after serving in the French army during its campaigns in Italy. While working as a merchant of cloth like his father, Cromwell studied law, eventually being appointed solicitor to Cardinal Wolsey in 1520. The cardinal found him useful in a number of affairs, including the suppression of several minor monasteries. Cromwell, however, was able to distance himself from the cardinal when Wolsey failed to secure for Henry a divorce from Catherine of Aragon. He thus survived the fall of Wolsey in 1529 and entered into the service of the king. Cromwell soon emerged as one of Henry's most influential advisers in the reorganization of the English Church and the launching of the Reformation; he created the plan for the seizure by the state of supremacy in matters of religion and was instrumental in securing the passage of the Act of Supremacy (1534). In 1535, he was named vicar-general with the important position of leading the dissolution of the monasteries (1536-1539) and the confiscation of the vast monastic properties in 1540. As a reward, the king created him earl of Essex (April 1540) and granted to him various estates that had been seized. Cromwell urged Henry to enter into an alliance with the Protestant princes of Germany, advocating the marriage to Anne of Cleves to his master. This proved a disappointment to Henry, who blamed his minister. Arrested on June 10, 1540, Cromwell was charged with treason and beheaded on July 28, his value to the king having been exhausted.

Crown, Franciscan ● Also known as the Seraphic Rosary, a rosary introduced in 1422. It contains seven decades instead of the regular fifteen, recited in honor of the seven joys of the Blessed Mother: the Annunciation, the Visitation, the Birth of the Lord, the Adoration of the Magi, the Finding in the Temple, the Resurrection, and the Assumption-Coronation. The Franciscan cross had its origins in the Franciscan tradition that the BVM appeared to a novice of that order and taught him to say the crown. (See also **Rosary**.)

Crown of Thorns ● Thorny branches that were placed upon the head of Jesus as part of the humiliation suffered by him at the hands of his jailers. The episode is mentioned by Matthew (27:29), Mark (15:17), and John (19:2). Mark wrote: "And they clothed him in a purple cloak, and plaiting a crown of thorns they put it on him." The crown was probably made out of the plant *Poterium spinosum*, which was quite common around the region of Jerusalem; it was frequently used for firewood and had a slender, sharp spike. There is some question as to whether the crown was shaped like a helmet (as seen in the catacomb of Praetextatus from the second century), or a rounded wreath as traditionally depicted in art. The earliest mention of the crown of thorns was in the fifth century. St. Paulinus of Nola wrote in 409 of "the thorns with which Our Savior was crowned." Cassiodorus in the sixth century called it one of the glories of earthy Jerusalem: "We may behold the thorny crown." This relic was later supposedly taken to Constantinople sometime around 1063. Some of the individual thorns were said to have been

given to various rulers in previous centuries. In 1238, in an attempt to secure aid for the much troubled Latin Empire of Constantinople, Emperor Baldwin offered the crown to King Louis IX of France. It was then taken to the French ruler by the famed traveler Andrew of Longjumeau. Louis built St.-Chapelle in Paris (completed in 1248) to house it. (See also **Relics**.)

Crown, Papal ● See **Papal Coronation** and **Tiara**.

Crusades ● Collective name given the various holy wars that were launched during the Middle Ages with the aim of recovering the Holy Land from Islamic domination or to defend Christendom from attack, both internal and external. The most famous of the crusades were those undertaken from 1095-1271 to free the sacred places of the Middle East, but other crusades were proclaimed, such as the Albigensian Crusade in southern France, the campaigns of the Teutonic Knights in the Baltic and in parts of Eastern Europe, and the *Reconquista* in Spain, which had as its ultimate aim the expulsion of all Islamic presence from the Iberian Peninsula. By far, however, the crusades to the Holy Land most captured the public's imagination and had the most significant long-term historical consequences.

The crusades against the Muslims were an important demonstration of the deeply pervasive nature of the faith within medieval society and of the enormous sway that was held by the popes in the period. The crusades were largely encouraged, organized, and given spiritual leadership by the papacy. The popes were able to attract segments of every class of medieval life with an authority that was greater than any in the West and with a message that appealed to the most sincerely felt religious devotion of simple serfs, knights, and kings. The demise of the crusader spirit in the 1200s coincided with the gradual deterioration of the papal position as the pontiffs struggled with rising national interests and the resistance of Christian rulers to embark upon military adventures they had little hope of winning, regardless of the potential spiritual gains offered to them and the financial or political riches that had been acquired in the past.

Central to the cause of the crusades was the genuinely devout religious nature of medieval society. Thousands of pilgrims every year traveled to Palestine to visit the holy places of Jerusalem, a movement of worship that had long been permitted by the Islamic Fatimid caliphate, which controlled the cities of the Holy Land because of the generally tolerant nature of the government and the money that pilgrims brought into their domains. The normal pilgrim trails extended across Europe into the Balkans, through the Byzantine Empire, over Asia Minor, and into Palestine.

This activity, despite the longtime antipathy of Christians and Muslims, had continued for centuries when, suddenly, in the eleventh century, a major event took place that threatened not only the pilgrimages but the very survival of the Byzantine Empire. This was the arrival of the Seljuk Turks as a potent military force. The Turks swept into Asia Minor and, at the Battle of Manzikert in 1071, smashed the Byzantines and seized whole stretches of Anatolia. Devout Muslims, they were opposed to pilgrims wandering over their land and so launched a program of harassment. Word spread of deaths and oppression, reaching Europe over the next years. Antagonism toward the Muslims grew in the West so that when the Byzantine Emperor Alexius I Comnenus sent an appeal for aid to Pope Urban II, the pontiff found all of Christendom willing to listen. In 1095, at the Council of Clermont, he called upon all Christians to take up arms and to go on a crusade. The objective, he said, was the capture of Jerusalem, and the rewards were spiritual blessings from God; the cry of the age as expressed by Pope Urban was *"Deus vult!"* ("God wills!"). The response was overwhelming as the common folk willingly pledged themselves with the knights and other soldiers. The nobility and royalty of much of Europe also took up the flag of crusade, sensing that there might be rich treasure and enormous financial opportunities awaiting them in the Levant. In all there would be eight

Crusader fortress of Aleppo

major crusades, with two tragic minor ones, the People's Crusade and the Children's Crusade.

People's Crusade (1096): Before the armies of the First Crusade reached Asia Minor, there had occurred what came to be called the People's Crusade. All across Europe, simple people, their enthusiasm and zeal set afire by the call for a march to the East, had gathered together into often unruly, poorly armed, and highly disorganized bands whose only clear goal was to reach and free Jerusalem. When these mobs reached Constantinople they were told by Emperor Alexios that they would be wiser to await the crusader forces who were already en route to the Byzantine capital. The crowds, however, became so unmanageable and increasingly dangerous that the imperial authorities gave them leave to set out, having a difficult time as it was restraining them from rushing out toward the Turks. The two leaders of the People's Crusade, Walter the Penniless and Peter the Hermit, took their followers across Asia Minor. Thousands soon died of starvation and thirst, and Peter turned around to seek help from the Byzantines. The Greeks were far from disposed to give aid, and the main crowd of weakened, reduced, and poorly armed pilgrims were cut to pieces by the Turks near Cibotus or massacred at various sites in Anatolia.

First Crusade (1096-1099): The First Crusade is considered the most successful of all the campaigns into the Holy Land, as it brought not only the capture of Jerusalem but the birth of the Crusader States, the Latin States, some of which would survive until 1291. Among the leaders of the crusade were Bohemond of Taranto, Count Raymond of Toulouse, and Godfrey of Bouillon. Their various armies assembled at Constantinople and an agreement was signed with Emperor Alexios by which the Byzantines promised to provide support for the soldiers in return for the loyalty of the crusader leaders and the return of all lands that had been lost to the Turks.

The crusader host moved out of Constantinople and on June 19, 1097, captured Nicaea, followed by Antioch on June 3, 1098. After defeating a Turkish force just outside of the city at the so-called Battle of the Lance (supposedly with the help of the Holy Lance, or Lance of Longinus), the Christian force set out for Jerusalem. The holy city finally fell on July 18, 1099. A massacre ensued as the Muslim and Jewish populations were put to the sword. The campaign ended with a triumph by Godfrey of Bouillon over an Islamic relief force from Egypt. Having conquered Jerusalem, many knights went home, but others remained and over the next years the Crusader States were formed, including the principality of Antioch, the county of Edessa, and, most importantly, the kingdom of Jerusalem.

Second Crusade (1147-1149): This crusade was mounted in response to the threat to the Crusader States that had materialized in the wake of the capture of Edessa in 1144 by Imad ed-Din Zengi, atabeg (or governor) of Mosul. Its leaders were King Louis VII and Emperor Conrad III of Germany. This campaign was an absolute disaster, as Conrad was virtually destroyed by the Turks at the Battle of Dorylaeum. Louis then decided to besiege Damascus, only to be forced to withdraw by the approach of Imad's son, the dangerous Nur ed-Din Zengi. The fiasco was the source of severe demoralization on the part of the entire crusading movement and gave needed encouragement to the Muslims in Palestine.

Third Crusade (1189-1192): The Third Crusade was necessitated by the successes of the great Islamic general Saladin (d. 1193) whose rise as a major figure in the Islamic world was certified by his stunning capture of Jerusalem on October 2, 1187. In response, three of the most powerful figures in all of Christendom agreed to embark for the Middle East: Emperor Frederick I

Barbarossa, King Richard the Lionhearted of England, and King Philip II Augustus of France. Frederick died while en route in Cilicia, falling into a river and drowning, his armor preventing him from rising. Of his large force, only a thousand desperate men arrived at the crusader lines, which had surrounded the besieged fortress of Acre. Richard, after conquering Cyprus, arrived at Acre where he was awaited by Philip. After two bloody years of fighting, Acre finally fell on July 12, 1191. Philip then withdrew as a result of a squabble with the English king, and Richard was forced to contend with Saladin alone. The king defeated Saladin at Arsuf on September 7, 1191, but he realized that Jerusalem was beyond his resources. Instead, a treaty was signed with Saladin that permitted pilgrims to enter Jerusalem. One of the most ambitious of undertakings, the crusade had ended only in a partial victory, and the recovery of the holy city seemed farther away than ever.

Fourth Crusade (1202-1204): Back in Europe, meanwhile, the Holy See continued to round up support for another effort. Leading the cause was Pope Innocent III (r. 1198-1216). He won the promise of several promising leaders such as Baldwin of Flanders, Boniface of Montferrat, and Geoffrey of Villehardouin. The plan was to

King Richard the Lionhearted

sail to Egypt and push across to Jerusalem. Transportation was to be provided by the Venetians under their doge, Enrico Dandolo.

From the start, things went badly as the anticipated numbers of soldiers failed to arrive at Venice and the those who did could not pay the fare for transport. Dandolo then cunningly suggested that they might earn the fare by assisting in the seizure of the Hungarian dependency of Zara, a Christian community that Venice wished to add to its holdings. The crusaders obliged over the protests of the pope, and, while at Zara, were offered money to overthrow the imperial government at Constantinople on behalf of the son of the deposed emperor Isaac II Angelos. On June 23, 1203, the crusaders arrived at Constantinople and in July removed Emperor Alexios III in favor of the young Alexios and his father. These two proved weak, however, and on April 13, 1204, the city was taken over by the crusaders. The Latin Empire of Constantinople was founded, lasting from 1204-1261. During that time, the Latin (Roman) rite would be forced upon the Byzantine population and the regime would earn the undying hatred of the Greeks. (For further details, see **Byzantine Empire** and **Constantinople**.)

Children's Crusade (1212): After the appalling events of the Fourth Crusade, calls for another crusade were greeted with cynicism or indifference by various monarchs and influential nobles, but the crusading spirit was, surprisingly, far from dead. The call began among children to march to Jerusalem and reclaim it in God's name. A foolish enterprise, it was supported by youths from all over Western Europe. In 1212, they set out, much like the People's Crusade before them, and soon found the road filled with misery and death. The children died from disease, slaughter, and starvation, most of the survivors sold into slavery by their Turkish captors. The chief rulers of Christendom were shamed.

Fifth Crusade (1218-1221): Pope Innocent IV called for another crusade in 1215 but did not live to see it come to fruition; that would be left to his successor, Honorius III (r. 1216-1227). This enterprise chose as its target Egypt and claimed the promise of troops from Frederick II. He never showed, and the forces of John of Brienne, king of Jerusalem, supported by a small papal army and the newly constituted Teutonic Knights under Hermann von Salza, were forced to handle most of the fighting. In overall command was Cardinal Pelagius, the papal legate, who insisted on controlling the entire campaign in the belief that he represented the higher authority of the pope. The crusaders besieged the city of Damietta, capturing it in November 1219. The still-anticipated forces of Frederick failed to show, and by the time Pelagius ordered an advance on Cairo, the Christians had to contend with the Nile floods, the oppressive heat, and stout Muslim resistance. With their numbers dwindling, the crusaders entered into negotiations and withdrew, accepting for the loss of thousands of men an eight-year truce and a few relics.

Sixth Crusade (1228-1229): Having incurred enormous displeasure from the popes for his inactivity in the Fifth Crusade, Emperor Frederick II decided that the time had come at last to fulfill his pledge and sail to the Holy Land. He embarked in 1227, only

to have a fever break out on his ships. Fearing it might spread, he returned to Sicily. Upon hearing of yet further delay, an irate Pope Gregory IX excommunicated the emperor. Choosing to ignore the papal pronouncement, Frederick set sail in 1228; Gregory, taking the failure of the emperor to respond to his excommunication as a direct snub of papal rights, renewed the ban. Thus, upon reaching Palestine, Frederick found the Latin States there unwilling to offer any assistance. Undaunted, he opened negotiations with the Muslims and through some excellent discussions secured for the Christians control of Jerusalem, Bethlehem, and Nazareth. Incredibly, Gregory spurned the good news, refusing to accept the treaty. Frederick was forced to crown himself king of Jerusalem on February 18, 1229, with only his own men and the Teutonic Knights in attendance. After his departure, various political factions sprang up vying for control of Jerusalem. The city, poorly defended and weakened by internecine squabbling, fell to the Muslims in 1244. It would never again be taken.

Seventh Crusade (1248-1254): The first of two crusades headed by King St. Louis IX of France (the second being the Eighth Crusade), this was inspired by the pleas of Pope Innocent IV (r. 1243-1254), who was sick at heart about the fall of Jerusalem in 1244 to the Turks and their allies. King Louis decided to concentrate on Egypt, as had several earlier crusader efforts. He captured Damietta in June 1249, choosing to wait until autumn and cooler weather to make his attack against Cairo. He made his initial advance in November, but the going was slow and on February 8, 1250, he fought the Battle of Mansura. Seemingly in full control, he was, to his own disbelief, forced to retreat and narrowly avoided capture after his brother, Robert of Artois, made a highly ill-advised charge against what he thought was a beaten Islamic enemy. On April 6, 1250, Louis was taken by the Egyptians and was forced to pay a large ransom to secure his freedom. He spent the next four years trying fruitlessly to buy the aid of the Mongols.

Eighth Crusade (1270): This would prove to be the last of the major efforts to save the Christian presence in Palestine. In 1260, the Mongols, long hoped for by the crusaders to destroy the Islamic states, were defeated at the Battle of Ain-Jalut by the Mamelukes, an energetic dynasty based in Egypt under the control of the talented general, the sultan Baybars. He embarked on a systematic campaign against the lingering Christian regimes, taking Antioch in 1268. This development so alarmed King Louis IX of France that he made preparations for one more martial enterprise. Instead of Egypt, he chose Tunis at the urging of the local ruler, the bey, who feigned a desire to become a Christian. These promises were quickly proven false and Louis, with his son and Charles of Anjou, laid siege to Tunis. With his son, he died from the plague when an epidemic ravaged his camp. Charles of Anjou took command, retreated with the army, and sailed home. Virtually unchallenged by the Christians, the Mamelukes reduced the last crusader strongholds from 1271-1291. The last to fall was Acre.

Over the next centuries, a number of popes would beseech the Christian powers of Europe to try again to rescue Jerusalem or, more common, to band together to stop the advance of the Ottoman Turks. They would be met most often with a lack of enthusiasm. On several occasions the popes were able to put together alliances. One ended in total disaster at the Battle of Varna in 1444 and another proved a mighty triumph, the naval battle at Lepanto in 1571.

The crusades had been near total failures in the military sense throughout the two centuries in which they were waged. Their importance, though, lay not in the abysmal campaigns of conquest but in the opportunities they presented in terms of commerce, trade, and culture. For the Church, they offered the means to introduce to the Holy Land the first representatives of the papacy in centuries and to make contact with Christians long cut off from the Western Church, such as the Maronites of Lebanon. The campaigns also made possible the accelerated process of bringing translations of long-lost writings by Aristotle to the West, a development that had the most far-reaching consequences for the future of Christian thought. These positive gains were offset in part by the ill feeling that was engendered by the Fourth Crusade and the forcing of the Latin rite upon the Byzantines, their hostility only clouding further the stormy relationship between the Eastern and Western Churches and contributing to the blasé attitude of the West in 1453 toward the imminent demise of the Byzantine Empire and the fall of Constantinople to the Turks. (See also **Acre, Albigensian Movement, Islam, Jews and Judaism, Military Orders, Patriarch**, and **Turkey**.)

Crutched Friars ● Also Crossed Friars. In Latin, *Fratres Cruciferi*, an order of mendicant friars deriving their name from their custom of carrying a cross in their hand (or surmounted on a wooden stick) and having a cross sewn on the front of their habit. A somewhat obscure community, their origins are uncertain. They claim to have been founded in the East, by St. Cletus in the first century, and to have been reconstituted by St. Cyriacus in the fourth century as patriarch of Jerusalem. They eventually reached Italy and were given a constitution and rule (Augustinian) by Pope Alexander III. Pope Pius II prescribed for them a blue habit, substituting a silver cross for the wooden one. Houses of the friars quickly spread, but, because of corruption and irregularities, they were suppressed by Alexander VII in 1656. Other orders of Crutched Friars came from Bohemia and Poland, and another, more successful one was established around 1210 in Flanders by Theodore of Celles (d. 1236). It would have houses in England, France, Germany, and Holland. The order survived into the twentieth century and continues to operate houses around the world.

Cuba ● Island nation situated in the Caribbean Sea, approximately ninety miles from Florida. Cuba was first visited by Europeans in 1492 and was then explored by the Spanish. By 1511, a colony had been established, and Cuba emerged as a major base for the military exploits of the Conquistadors. Known as "the Pearl of the Antilles," it was a clearinghouse for the Spanish treasure ships carrying back the gold and other valuables looted from the New World. The Church was active on the isle from around 1514. Cuba was a strong source of vocations among Spanish colonial possessions, particularly during the eighteenth century, but the decline in the new clergy coincided with the deterioration of Spain's overseas empire. While other colonies won their independence in the early nineteenth century, Cuba remained part of the empire. The Spanish-American War (1898) ended Spanish control and in 1902 the island gained its independence. The Platt Amendment gave the United States a right to intervene until 1934, when a new relationship was established under President Franklin Roosevelt. From 1935, Fulgencio Batista dominated the country until overthrown in 1959 by Fidel Castro. Castro's Communist dictatorship brought the oppression of the Church: Catholic schools were nationalized, priests were expelled, social activities severely curtailed, and Catholic activists desiring political reform were arrested. While a new constitution in 1976 supposedly granted freedom of conscience, it placed severe restrictions on its exercise, so that any so-called reforms were rendered meaningless. Despite the continued anti-Catholic policies of the Castro regime, Catholic charities provide badly needed assistance to the island's children, mentally ill, and infirm, who are victims of Cuba's collapsing economy and backward economic policies. In 1993, for example, the archdiocese of Boston donated half a million dollars' worth of medical supplies.

Cum Occasione ● Constitution promulgated on May 31, 1653, by Pope Innocent X in which he condemned five propositions that were to embody the theological heart of Jansenism. The proclamation had been the result of a thorough examination of Jansenism by a papal commission at the request of the French bishops.

Cuius Regio, Eius Religio ● Term translated as essentially "In a prince's country, a prince's religion." It was a religio-political formula that came out of the Religious Peace of Augsburg (1555) and meant that whatever the religion of the ruling prince of a territory might be, that would be the religion of the territory itself. It was a compromise solution that tried to settle the difficult question of where throughout Germany and the lands of the Holy Roman Empire either Lutheranism or Catholicism should prevail. (See **Augsburg, Peace of**.)

Cuncolim, Martyrs of ● Five members of the Jesuits who were murdered by a mob of Hindus on July 25, 1583, in the village of Cuncolim in the territory of Goa, India. The martyrs were Rudolph Acquaviva, Alphonsus Pacheco, Peter Berno, Anthony Francis, and the lay brother Francis Aranha. They were set upon as they were looking for a suitable spot to build a church. Each was murdered brutally and their bodies were thrown into a well. The water from this well soon acquired a reputation for having miraculous properties. The martyrs were beatified in 1693 by Pope Innocent XII.

Curé d'Ars ● See **Vianney, John, St**.

Curia, Roman ● Central administrative departments or ministries, known as dicasteries, that assist the pope in the enormous task of governing the Roman Catholic Church. The Curia exists in every sense at the will of the supreme pontiff, deriving its authority, prerogatives, and activities at his behest and with his approval. The name *curia* is from the Latin for "court" and in its current sense is applied to the congregations, tribunals, offices, and commissions that collectively comprise the central government of the Church. The Curia also includes the Secretariat of State, the Apostolic Camera, Prefecture of the Papal Household, and Administration of the Patrimony of the Holy See. The Curia is thus an important aspect of the understanding of the Holy See.

The Curia Romana has its origins in the earliest period of the papacy when various pontiffs found it expedient to delegate authority to assistants. This was most true as the size of the papal administration grew in the fourth century and beyond with the Christianization of the Roman Empire. The first office to handle administrative matters was the Apostolic Chancery, dating to the fourth century. From that time, popes appointed various commissions and agencies to give assistance in matters that might arise. Around the pope grew a court of advisers, secretaries, notaries, and other officials that included, over time, cardinals, bishops, priests, and others. This bureaucratic system would endure throughout the Middle Ages and the Renaissance, but the growth of the Church throughout the world and the need for improved efficiency convinced Pope Sixtus V (r. 1585-1590) to introduce extensive reforms. The Roman Curia was formally organized in 1588 with the creation of permanent congregations with official designations and specific duties. The initial congregations were concerned not only with affairs of the Church but the temporal holdings of the Holy See, the States of the Church. The congregations consisted of, or were involved, in the following: the Holy Inquisition; the Signature of Grace; the erection of churches; the papal territories; the sacred rites and ceremonies; the papal navy; the Index of Forbidden Books; interpreting and advancing the decrees of the Council of Trent; aiding and relieving the ills of the States of the Church; religious orders; bishops; the maintenance of roads, bridges, and waterways; the printing press of the Vatican; and the regulation of the affairs of the temporal dominions of the Church.

It is no doubt obvious that many of these departments have long ceased to function, replaced over the centuries by other dicasteries or simply abolished. Three significant reforms have been made since the time of Sixtus (with numerous minor changes by various popes). These were under St. Pius X (1908), Paul VI (1967), and John Paul II (1989). Paul launched a four-year reorganization in 1963, and in 1967 issued the constitution *Regimini Ecclesiae Universae* (August 18), which took effect in March 1968. Pope John Paul continued Paul's overall plan, reconstituting the dicasteries through the constitution *Pastor Bonus* (June 28, 1988), becoming effective on March 1, 1989. The current Curia has the Secretariat of State, nine congregations, twelve councils, and three offices as well as other agencies and commissions and committees. (See also **Cardinals, College of; Holy See**; and APPENDIX 2.)

Cursillo ● See GLOSSARY.

Cuthbert, St. (d. 687) ● Bishop of Lindisfarne and an immensely popular saint in medieval England, Cuthbert was originally a shepherd, but, receiving a vision, he entered the monastery of Melrose in Northumbria in 651. He became prior at the monastery in 661 after an outbreak of the plague; during the epidemic, he reportedly performed miracles. Three years later, he and the abbot of Melrose, Eata, attended the Synod of Whitby. There, despite his Celtic background, he agreed to the adoption of the Roman rite, abandoning Celtic customs. Soon thereafter, both Cuthbert and Eata were transferred to Lindisfarne. Cuthbert, however, retired in 676 to an ascetical life, from which he was called by King Ecgfrith of Northumbria, who made him bishop of Hexham (684). He became bishop of Lindisfarne the next year. Cuthbert spent his brief episcopate in missionary activities. Buried initially at Lindisfarne, he was later translated to Durham, a site much visited by pilgrims of the Middle Ages. The Venerable Bede authored his biography, but there was also a life written by an anonymous monk at Lindisfarne.

Cynewulf ● Early ninth-century monk, the author of four poems in Old English. While there is no evidence to connect him with the bishop of Lindisfarne in the eighth century, he is virtually unknown. His name is derived from epilogues for the poems containing runes which spell out CYNWULF or CYNEWULF. The poems were written from Old English and Germanic epic traditions and displayed a deep sense of devotion. They were: *Eleni* (1,321 lines), on the finding of the True Cross by St. Helena; *The Fates of the Apostles* (122 lines), on the legends

St. Cuthbert's Cross

concerning the deaths of the Apostles; *Juliana* (731 lines), on the martyrdom of Juliana; and *The Ascension*, a lyrical rendering of the homily by Gregory the Great — it was part of a trilogy, *The Christ*. The poems are preserved in two tenth-century manuscripts, the Vercelli Books (*Eleni* and the *Fates of the Apostles*) and the Exeter Book (*Ascension* and *Juliana*).

Cyprian, St. ● Late third-century convert at Antioch. According to a story already known in the fourth century, Cyprian was a sorcerer of some power who attempted to use arts to ensnare the favor of a Christian maiden, Justina. When his efforts failed, he grew despondent and converted to her faith. Baptized, he became a bishop and Justina the head of a convent. Both were martyred at Nicomedia and their feast days were placed together on September 26; the feasts were dropped in 1969.

Cyprian of Carthage, St. (d. 258) ● Bishop of Carthage and an important early Christian theologian. Born at Tunisia, Thrascius (in full, Thrascius Caecilius Cyprianus) studied law and was a pagan rhetorician prior to his conversion to Christianity on or about 246. Elected bishop of Carthage around 248, he was soon forced to flee in 249 when the persecutions of Emperor Trajanus Decius began. Cyprian remained in communication with his flock by letter and, upon his return in 251 to Carthage, he was reestablished as bishop.

He then faced a controversy that would trouble the Church for years to come: many Christians had lapsed from the faith or had purchased *libelli pacis* certificates stating that they had made sacrifices to the Roman gods when in fact they had not, and now were being welcomed back into the flock with no consequences. Cyprian opposed such lax discipline, allowing the so-called *lapsi* to return to the Church after suitable penance; he did not support the Novatianists, who refused the idea of rebaptism, giving aid to Pope Cornelius (r. 251-253) in his struggle against Novatian. His stand later put him at odds with Pope Stephen I, since the Bishop of Rome held that both schismatics and heretics could administer valid baptisms. Cyprian was supported by the African bishops, but the controversy was cut short by the persecution by Emperor Valerian during which Cyprian was martyred at Carthage on September 14, 258. A theologian of deep learning, he authored numerous letters and treatises. His correspondences, providing a clear picture of the times and the horrors of the persecutions, consists of eighty-one items, sixty-five from Cyprian and sixteen in response to him from others. The treatises included: *De Catholicae Ecclesiae Unitate* (or simply *De Unitate*), discussing the nature of unity in the Church and the ideal of equality among the bishops; *De Lapsis*, detailing the conditions by which the lapsed could be readmitted into the Church; and *Ad Quirinam* (or *Testimonia*), a compilation of biblical proof texts. He was much influenced by Tertullian and coined a number of remarkable statements such as "You cannot have God for your Father, if you cannot have the Church for your mother."

Cyril of Alexandria, St. (d. 444) ● Bishop of Alexandria from 412, a Doctor of the Church, and an influential theologian, one of the most forceful figures in the Church during the fifth century. Born in Egypt, he was the nephew of Bishop Theophilus of Alexandria, succeeding him to the see in 412. A devoted Orthodox Christian, Cyril spoke out against lingering elements of paganism in the city and heresy. His role in the brutal death of the Neoplatonic philosopher Hypatia in 415 (she was flayed alive with a whip made from abalone shells) is still questioned by scholars, and he helped expel the Jews from Alexandria after Christians were attacked by members of the Jewish community. Cyril's principal focus, however, was against Nestorius, bishop of Constantinople and founder of the heresy of Nestorianism. Cyril represented the Alexandrian theological position, arguing for the unity of two natures in Christ against Nestorius's theory that Christ had two separate persons, divine and human. Cyril entered into the severe conflict with Nestorius specifically over the former's adherence that the Blessed Virgin be honored with the title *Theotokos* (Greek for "bearer of God"), a name opposed by Nestorius. Beyond the theological dispute — itself enough to alarm Alexandrian theologians — the dispute had religio-political ramifications, since it represented the potential rise of Constantinople as one of the most important sees in all of Christendom, a development that threatened and was much opposed by the Alexandrians. Both sides attempted to gather supporters, political maneuvering that culminated with the Council of Ephesus in 431.

Wielding the firm approval of Pope St. Celestine I (r. 422-432), Cyril served as president of the council, securing the condemnation of Nestorius, moving so precipitately that he did not wait for the arrival of a number of bishops from the East. As most of these prelates were allies or supporters of Nestorius, they convened on their own and condemned Cyril. While Nestorius was exiled, a breach had opened between Cyril and the see of Antioch, a disagreement resolved only in 433 with a compromise declaration on the nature of Christ. Cyril remained bishop until his death. He made important contributions to Christian theology, especially the Trinity and the nature of Christ. His brilliant writings included letters and anathemas, and a refutation of the work *Against the Galileans* by Emperor Julian the Apostate (r. 361-363); this defense of Christianity is the last of the great apologies for the faith in the Roman era. Long honored as a saint and profound theologian, he was declared a Doctor of the Church in 1882 by Pope Leo XIII (r. 1878-1903). Feast day: June 27 in the West; June 9 in the East.

Cyril of Jerusalem, St. (c. 315-386) ●
Bishop of Jerusalem during the troubled era of the Arian Controversy who helped establish Jerusalem as a major site of pilgrimages. A native of Jerusalem, Cyril became bishop in Jerusalem around 349 or 350, succeeding Maximus. He was exiled in 357 from his post by the Arians because of his opposition to their cause, the first of three separate periods of exile; of the thirty-five years he spent as bishop, Cyril was in exile for sixteen of them. The last period was from 367-378 when he was banished by the Emperor Valens. He returned to Jerusalem in 378 after Valens's defeat and death at the terrible Battle of Adrianople (378). Jerusalem was in a state of severe moral decay and was plagued by spiritual and social disorder. Cyril thus spent his last year bringing reforms and revitalization. Possibly suspected himself of heresy (he did not like the term *homoousios* — concerning the nature of Christ — because it was man-made), he went to the Council of Constantinople in 381 and recited the creed used at Jerusalem, which contained *homoousios*. He survived the reign of Julian the Apostate without banishment. Cyril's primary surviving work is the *Catecheses*, eighteen instructional addresses for baptismal candidates during Lent and five for the newly baptized after Easter. The last five are known as the *Mystagogic*, as they are concerned with mysteries. He was declared a Doctor of the Church by Pope Leo XIII in 1883. Feast day: March 18.

Cyril and Methodius, Sts. ● Called the Apostles of the Slavs (or Slovakia), they were two brothers who brought the Christian faith to Slavic lands and were also remarkable linguists and scholars. Cyril (c. 827-869) and Methodius (c. 825-884) were born to a noble family of Thessalonika (Thessalonica), working together around 860 to convert the Khazars along the Black Sea. Two years later, they were sent to Moravia by Emperor Michael III in response to a plea for missionary assistance from the local ruler there. Using their linguistic skill, the brothers taught in the Slavic vernacular, using the language in the liturgy and translating the Scriptures into the Slavonic tongue. To make the reading of Scripture even easier, Cyril invented an alphabet — the Glagolithic — that was based on Greek letters. This would serve as the basis of Cyrillic, the language used in Russia and throughout the Slavic world. They soon encountered opposition from several German prelates, most notably the archbishop of Salzburg, who desired ecclesiastical control over Slavic territory and the use of an exclusively Latin liturgy. Reaching Rome in 868, they won approval from Pope Adrian II (r. 867-872) to use the Slavic liturgy. Cyril died at Rome and Methodius was dispatched to Moravia as a papal legate and archbishop of Sirmium. Further troubles with the Germans ensued, and Methodius was seized, brutalized, and imprisoned for three years until he was finally freed through the urging of Pope John VIII (r. 872-882). He won approval once more to use the Slavic, but peace was never fully enjoyed owing to Germanic interference and the machinations of his own suffragan, Wicking. Methodius died in 885 and Pope Stephen V placed a ban on the use of the Slavic tongue. The loyal followers of Cyril and Methodius were exiled, fleeing to Bulgaria. Revered by the Eastern Church as saints, Cyril and Methodius were also recognized by the Western Church. On December 31, 1980, Pope John Paul II named them, with St. Benedict, patron saints of Europe. Feast day: February 14.

Czechoslovakia ● Collective name given the Czech and Slovak regions of Central Europe that became separate republics in 1993 and where the Church has long been an active and important part of the lives of the people. Historically, the area that became Czechoslovakia is divided onto three broad territories: Bohemia (to the west, near Germany), Moravia (between Poland and Austria), and Slovakia (south of the Carpathians). Early states developed in the regions, coming into contact with the Franks, the Byzantines, and, later, the Holy Roman Empire. Christianity was first introduced among the Slavs by the Frankish missionaries in the eighth century; they were joined by other clerics from Germany and Ireland. The most important development in the early life of the Church was the request in 863 of the local ruler Ratislav for Sts. Cyril and Methodius to preach to his people. They proclaimed Christ to the inhabitants in the Slavs' own language, introducing Old Slovak into the liturgy and earning the title Apostles of Slovakia (see **Cyril and Methodius, Sts.** for other details). The first church to be consecrated was at Nitra in the early ninth century; it became a diocese in 880 and, with the exception of a period from around 924-1024, it remained in continuous existence.

The Church in Bohemia, based in the city of Prague, a diocese since 973, came to exercise considerable influence over the rise of Christianity in the neighboring lands. Missionaries set out from Bohemia to convert Poland, and the famed St. Adalbert (martyred in Prussia in 997) was at one time bishop of Prague. In the city was also found the great university, founded in 1348 by King Charles IV (r. 1346-1378). This center of intellectual activity emerged in the 1400s as the heart of the radical reform movement launched by Jan Hus (d. 1415), who was rector of Prague University and a vocal advocate of the doctrines of John Wycliffe. His execution at the stake in 1415 sparked the long and bitter Hussite Wars that devastated Czechoslovakia from 1419-1434 and left the kingdom of Bohemia bitterly divided between lingering Hussite factions and Catholics. Further strife was to be caused by the accession of a Catholic Habsburg to the Bohemian throne in 1526, bringing Bohemia into the Holy Roman Empire, a development opposed by the Czech nobility.

The Reformation was to become quite popular in Bohemia, as it permitted the nobles to strike against the Habsburgs. Their ambitions at independence found fulfillment in 1618 in their uprising against their Catholic Habsburg masters. Catholic victory was won in 1620 at the Battle of White Mountain, but in the long years that would follow in the Thirty Years' War (1618-1648) all of Central Europe would suffer, and massive depopulation would make possible the Germanization of Bohemia by immigrants. The Slovaks further to the East resisted the loss of culture, especially to the Hungarians from the south, by using their Catholic faith to preserve language and custom.

The republic of Czecho-Slovakia was created only in 1919. Two years later, the so-called Czechoslovak Church was formally constituted as a religious body. A schismatic church, it attracted a small minority of Catholics, preaching such doctrines as an end to celibacy and a denial of apostolic succession. Tensions between the Czech and Slovak populations would plague the republic right up to the humiliating dismemberment of the country in 1938 when the Western powers "gave" Adolf Hitler the Sudetenland.

In 1939, Bohemia and Moravia were seized and a puppet state created for Slovakia. The Church suffered severely in the Nazi occupation, the repression epitomized by the total liquidation of the population of the town of Lidice in 1942 as retaliation for the assassination of the feared SS official Reinhard Heydrich who had served as *reichsprotector* of Bohemia.

After the war, the reinstated Czech Republic was undermined by the Communists and finally overthrown in 1948 with Soviet assistance. The Communists had already been working against the Church in Slovakia since 1944. By 1945, the Catholic press was shut down, Church schools nationalized, and various other institutions closed or suppressed. The degree of the repression was made clear in April 1947, with the execution of Monsignor Josef Tiso, president of the Slovak Republic. In Czech regions, the same pattern of persecution was undertaken, with the nationalization of property and the arrest of Josef Beran, archbishop of Prague. He was later allowed to leave the country and died a cardinal in Rome in 1969. Diplomatic relations were ended in 1950 between Czechoslovakia and the Holy See. All religious houses were seized in 1950-1951 and thousands of priests were thrown into prison. To take even greater control of the Church, the government promoted the so-called "peace protests," although the majority of the clergy refused to join. A brief improvement came in 1968 during the so-called Prague Spring, but the flicker of democracy was stamped out by Soviet troops and the restrictions on priests and nuns were reinstated. A gradual thaw in relations took place in the early 1980s. In 1983, the Prague foreign minister visited the Vatican; the next year, Vatican representatives visited Czechoslovakia. The Communists finally fell in 1989 in the Velvet Revolution, permitting the Holy See to fill all vacant sees throughout the country. Formal diplomatic ties were reestablished and John Paul II visited the now democratic country. Currently, the two countries of Slovakia and the Czech Republic both have ambassadors to the Holy See; almost half of the Czech Republic and nearly three-quarters of Slovakia is Catholic.

Damasus, St. ● Pope from 366-384. His pontificate began with much violence in Rome, but he proved subsequently a strong, active, and capable pontiff. Born at Rome around 304, he served as a deacon during the reign of his predecessor, Pope Liberius, accompanying him into exile when Emperor Constantius banished Liberius for his anti-Arian beliefs. Chosen to succeed Liberius in October 366, he was opposed immediately by a party supporting and electing Ursinus. The result was the eruption of violence in the streets of Rome during which one hundred thirty-seven people were killed, according to the historian Ammianus Marcellinus. Emperor Valentinian banished Ursinus, but Damasus was not free from internal dissent until around 381. Damasus attempted vigorously to suppress heresy. He used synods and the patronage of the imperial government to combat Luciferians as well as the followers of Arianism, Mecedonianism, and Donatism. The first pope to make reference to Rome as the Apostolic See, he secured the pronouncement during a synod at Rome in 382 that the see was primatial, a move intended to counter the growing influence and strength of the see of Constantinople. During the synod, Damasus came to know St. Jerome, who remained in Rome serving as Damasus' secretary; at Damasus' request he began his revision of the Latin translation of the Bible that was to become the Vulgate. Damasus also rebuilt old churches and built new ones; in addition, he introduced Latin as the language of the Mass. Feast day: December 11.

Damasus II ● Pope for a brief period in 1048. Originally named Poppo, he came from Bavaria and was serving as bishop of Brixen (modern Bressanone, Italy) when, in December 1047, Emperor Henry II nominated him to succeed Pope Clement II. The Holy See, however, had already been seized by the candidate supported by the Roman family of the Tusculani, Benedict IX, who had been pope twice, from 1032-1044 and again in 1045. Benedict was soon deposed by order of Henry and Poppo was installed as Damasus II. The new pope survived only twenty-three days, dying from malaria.

D'Amboise, George (1460-1510) ● French cardinal and archbishop. Notable figure in the French Renaissance. Born at Charmont-sur-Loire, he was nominated bishop of Montauban at the age of fourteen, but he did not assume his duties until he was twenty-four. He became archbishop of Rouen in 1493 and was subsequently a supporter of the duke of Orléans in domestic French political affairs. When, in 1498, the duke became King Louis XII, d'Amboise was appointed his prime minister; Pope Alexander made him a cardinal the same year. As prime minister, he guided Louis's foreign policy by promoting his conquest of Milan and at home introduced reforms to law and finance. He was eager, however, to become pope, using the prestige of King Louis toward that end. His ambitions were unfulfilled.

Damien de Veuster, Bl. (1840-1889) ● In full, Joseph Damien de Veuster, a priest of the Sacred Hearts Congregation (S.S.C.C.)

who devoted his life to the care of the lepers on the island of Molokai in Hawaii. Born in Tremeloo, Belgium, Joseph (as he was known to his family) chose at an early age to follow his brother Pamphile into the Sacred Hearts. A strong, muscular, and seemingly slow person, he was not considered ideal ecclesiastical material by other members of the congregation, but with his brother's help he mastered Latin and was accepted into the priesthood. Prior to his ordination, however, Damien volunteered for the missions in Hawaii and was eventually ordained in Honolulu, Hawaii. Sent to the island of Hawaii, called the Big Island, he administered a missionary area of some two thousand square miles. After working there for some time, he volunteered for service in 1873 on Molokai, at the small community of Kalaupapa, where local authorities had sent the victims of leprosy (as Hansen's disease was called). At first sent as part of a temporary assignment, Damien impressed his superior, Bishop Louis Maigret, with his zeal, and the bishop, in his speech to the lepers at Kalaupapa, intimated that Damien would be there permanently.

Bl. Damien de Veuster

Conditions at the colony were so absolutely appalling that the hopelessness of the residents was summed up in a sign that read: *Aole Kanawai me Keia Wahi* (Here we have no law). Using an ever-lit pipe to mask the odor of rotting corpses and the stench of the suffering, Damien set to work. He built some two thousand coffins, gathered the children together to keep them safe, and, to the best of his ability cared for the patients — amputating arms and legs, bandaging the open wounds, and repairing or building new huts and shelters. Starting in 1877, he began receiving help from the Hawaiian Board of Health. In 1881, he was given the Order of Knight Commander of the Royal Order of Kalakaua from Queen Liliuokalani in recognition of his work. He was also assisted by the Civil War veteran Brother Joseph Dutton (1843-1931) and especially by a group of Franciscan Sisters of Syracuse under the guidance of their onetime mother-general, Marianne Kope, whose cause is now open. By 1885, Damien knew for certain what he had suspected for several years: he had contracted leprosy, announcing the fact to the residents by beginning his sermon one day not with the customary "My dear brethren" but by saying "We lepers. . . ." He continued working right up until he was finally incapacitated by the disease, dying on April 15, 1889. His example of love and absolute sacrifice has served as encouragement to those who care for lepers around the world, most notably a group called the Damiens who provide assistance to lepers in India. In 1936, his body was taken from Molokai and returned to Belgium. Plans for his beatification in May 1994 were cut short by the hip injury to Pope John Paul II.

Daniel, St. (d. 493) ● Also Daniel the Stylite, a most famous disciple of St. Simeon Stylites. A native of Maratha, near Samosata, he lived as a monk for some time near his home before moving to a hermitage near Constantinople. A visitor from time to time of St. Simeon on his pillar at Telanissus, Daniel decided to move himself to the top of the pillar after Simeon's death in 459. His place of seclusion was a platform shelter resting on two pillars. Ordained a priest, he soon attracted many people who flocked to him for advice, including the Byzantine emperors Leo I and Zeno. He came down only once in thirty-three years, in 476, to rebuke Emperor Basiliscus for his support of Monophysitism. Feast day: December 11.

Daniel of Kiev (d. 1122) ● Also Daniel the Pilgrim or Daniel Palomik, a Russian abbot, traveler, and monk. He is best known for his extant account of a journey to the Holy Land in 1106-1107. The narrative covers his travels from Constantinople through Asia Minor, to Cyprus, and finally Jerusalem itself, where he spent a year. His description of the Easter liturgical services there is very useful to scholars and historians.

Dante (1265-1321) ● In full, Dante Alighieri. An Italian poet, he was considered the Father of Italian Poetry. He was the son of Alighiero d'Alighiero, a Florentine nobleman, and a strong supporter of the Guelph cause. Studying in Florence, he was heavily influenced by Brunetto Latini and Guido Cavalcanti, his respect for Cavalcanti being preserved in a sonnet that was later used in *La Vita Nuova* (*The New Life*), a work dedicated to his onetime friend. Dante was also inspired by Beatrice Portinari (d. 1290), who would reappear in both the *Vita* and, of course, in the *Divine Comedy*. After his father's death in 1283, Dante married Gemma di Manetto Donati and embarked on a political life. He served as a member of the Guild of Doctors and Pharmacists, the Council of the Hundred, and one of the six priors of the guilds of Florence (1300).

Dante

The city at the time was divided politically into two main factions. While still Guelph in disposition, there were two opposing parties — the White and the Black. As a White Guelph, Dante embarked on a delegation to Pope Boniface VIII in the hopes of negotiating a settlement to restore unity to Florence. In his absence, however, the Black Guelphs gained political control, and Dante's name headed their list of exiles. He never returned home, wandering across Italy, frequently the guest of powerful local magnates. He died at Ravenna after a bout of malaria.

One of the great figures in literature, Dante was the author of a massive treasury of works. *La Vita Nuova* (1283-1291) was a collection of thirty-one lyric poems, centering on his idealistic love for Beatrice. He also wrote epistles in Latin; poems, including *Canzoniere*; the unfinished *Convivio* (1304-1308; *Banquet*) and *De vulgari eloquenti* (c. 1304; *On Eloquence in the Vulgar Tongue*); and *Monarchia*, in which he proposed a world government, centered in the city of Rome. Above all these, however, was the *Divine Comedy* (*Comedia*), an epic allegorical poem describing the journey of the soul toward salvation. Dante began the *Divine Comedy* in 1306 or 1308, taking as his model Virgil's *Aeneid* and drawing much inspiration from Scripture. It was ultimately finished in *cantiche*, or three parts: *Inferno*, *Purgatorio*, and *Paradiso*. *Inferno* was finished by 1312, *Purgatorio* by 1315, and *Paradiso* after 1316 but before 1321.

Darboy, George (1813-1871) ● Cardinal and archbishop of Paris from 1863-1871, during the terminal period of the reign of Napoleon III. He was born at Fayl-Billot, Haute-Marne, and was ordained a priest in 1836. Appointed bishop of Nancy in 1859 and archbishop of Paris in 1863, Darboy became an important figure in the French imperial government; Napoleon III made him chief almoner, and he later served as a senator. A supporter of the Gallican tradition in France, he came into conflict with Pope Pius IX for stressing episcopal independence, and — both before and after the First Vatican Council — he expressed opposition to papal infallibility. He eventually subscribed to it, however. During the Franco-Prussian War (1870-1871), he labored tirelessly to help the wounded and starving, especially during the siege of Paris by the Prussians. Arrested on April 4 by members of the Commune who had seized the government, Darboy was shot in prison on May 24, 1871, the third bishop of Paris to be killed between 1848 and 1871. He blessed his executioners. Darboy also authored a life of Thomas Becket (1858) and consecrated the newly restored Notre-Dame in 1863.

D'Arcy, Martin (1888-1976) ● Jesuit philosopher and theologian. Ordained a priest in 1921, he was educated at Oxford and the Gregorian University in Rome. Master of Campion Hall at Oxford from 1933-1945, he headed the English province of the Society of Jesus from 1945-1950. His theological and philosophical writings included: *St. Thomas Aquinas* (1930); *Nature of Belief* (1931), an analysis of faith; *Mirage and Truth* (1935); *The Pain of this World and the Providence of God* (1935); and *The Mind and Heart of Love* (1945).

Davenport, Christopher ● See **Francisco à Sancta Clara**.

David, St. (d. c. 601) ● Patron saint of Wales, known largely through legend with little corroborative evidence, although he has long been one of the most popular of all saints in England. According to an early life on him (c. 1095) by the Welsh scholar and bishop Rhygyfarch, David (more properly Dewi) was the son of a chieftain. Educated at Henfynyw, he established around twelve monasteries, went on a pilgrimage to Jerusalem (where he was consecrated a bishop), and then had prominent roles in two councils, at Brefi and Caerleon in which the heresy of Pelagianism was condemned. After being named primate of Wales, he moved his see to Mynyw (or Menevia, or St. David's), where he died. His traditional canonization by Pope Callistus II around 1120 is unproven. Feast day: March 1.

David of Augsburg (1200-1272) ● German mystic and preacher of the Franciscan order, he was the author of a number of Latin and German works on the spiritual and contemplative life. Born at

St. David of Wales

Augsburg, he entered the Franciscans, became a novice-master, and in 1243 was transferred to the recently established convent at Augsburg under his friend Berthold of Regensburg. Among his Latin writings are *De Compositiones Hominis Exterioris* (*On the Composition of the Exterior Man*) and *De Inquisitione Haereticorum* (*On the Inquisition of Heretics*), although the authenticity of the last work is questioned. A popular writer, his works were much read in the late medieval period. He was also the earliest author to produce spiritual books in German. His writings have, at times, been falsely attributed to St. Bonaventure and St. Bernard of Clairvaux.

David of Dinant (fl. early 1200s) ● Scholastic philosopher whose writings were burned at Paris in 1210. He was probably born in Dinant, Belgium, and apparently lived in Paris and later at the court of Pope Innocent III. It is possible that he taught at Paris, for it was there that his works on matter were condemned. A kind of materialistic pantheist, he adhered to the view that all things — material, intellectual, and spiritual — consisted of the same essence as "first matter." This was bitterly opposed by Albertus Magnus and, at the order of the Council of the Province of Sens, his writings on the subject, his *Quaternuli* (or *Notebooks*), were burned. They are known only in fragments through the criticisms of Albert and Thomas Aquinas. According to the *Compilatio de Novo Spiritu* (which is housed in the Munich Library), contributed by St. Albert, David fled France to avoid punishment for his views; he supposedly traveled for a number of years and died in 1215.

Decius, Trajanus (201-251) ● Roman Emperor from 249-251 who was responsible for the first systematic persecutions within the Roman Empire. A senator and onetime consul, Gaius Messius Quintus Trajanus

Decius was appointed to a command over the Danube legions around 245. Proving successful against the Goths on the frontier, he then won the confidence of his troops, was proclaimed emperor by them in 249, and was accepted by the senate after the defeat and death of Philip the Arab, the man who had initially named him to the Danubian frontier. Aside from his ultimately disastrous campaign against the Goths, Decius' reign was distinguished by the empire-wide persecution of Christians, starting with the execution of Fabian, the Bishop of Rome, in January 250. The emperor then decreed that all citizens must perform a religious sacrifice to the emperor in the presence of government commissioners and present certificates of proof of having done so. Many Christians, later called *lapsi*, took the oath, while others, the *libellatici*, purchased through bribes certificates (*libelli pacis*) that they had performed the sacrifice.

Most Christians refused to make the sacrificial oath, and Decius' officials put to death many Church leaders and faithful. Rather than discouraging the faith, however, the repression increased Christian devotion and swung popular sentiment in favor of the courageous adherents of the Creed. The persecutions were already on the decline when Decius was wiped out with his son and part of the army by the Goths at the Battle of Abrittus, near Dobriya in June 251. The Decian persecution caused considerable upheaval in the Church, as the *lapsi* became the source of debate as to whether they should be allowed back into the Church, and, if so, under what terms. (See **Cyprian of Carthage, St.** and **Novatian**; see also **Roman Empire**.)

Declaration of the Sovereign ● Also called the Royal Declaration, the oath or declaration taken by William III and Mary in which they repudiated the Catholic faith as a requirement for receiving the English throne. Imposed on them by Parliament in 1689, the oath included a repudiation of Catholic doctrine such as the invocation of saints and also involved the so-called Declaration Against Transubstantiation (denying the transubstantiation). The declaration was changed in 1910 to make it less anti-Catholic while it still affirmed the Protestant devotion of the sovereign. All rulers of Britain have taken the oath since William and Mary.

Decorations, Pontifical ● See **Papal Decorations**.

Decretals ● Term for papal letters written in response to a question. The first known decretal was the one sent by Pope Siricius to Himerius, bishop of Tarragona. Since that time, decretals have been gathered into collections for purposes of preservation. The earliest such collection was the one organized by Dionysius Exiguus around 520. Later collections, such as those of Popes Gregory IX (1234), Boniface VIII (1298), and Clement V (1317) were given the force of law. One of the most famous of all collections is the so-called False Decretals that first appeared around 850. The study of decretals remains an important aspect of canon law. (See **Decretist, Decretum Gelasianum**, and **Decretum Gratiani**, following entries.)

Decretist ● Name given to scholars of canon law who have studied the work of the twelfth-century master of canon law Gratian, the *Decretum Gratiani* (*Decree of Gratian*). The decretists generally authored a commentary called the *Decretum Gratiani*, providing opinions on various parts of the large work. The writings of the decretists are much used by students and experts of modern canon law. (See also **Canon Law**.)

Decretum Gelasianum ● Early Latin Church document containing various materials on the Scriptures, councils, and apocryphal writings. Traditionally placed under the name of Pope Gelasius (r.

492-496), the *Decretum* was also found in some manuscripts under the names of Damasus (r. 366-384) or Hormisdas (r. 514-523). The work concerned itself with Christ and the Holy Spirit, the canonical Scriptures, the Roman Church, the Orthodox councils, and various biblical and patristic apocryphal writings.

Decretum Gratiani ● See under **Gratian**.

Defender of the Faith ● Known in the Latin as *Fidei Defensor*, a title given at his own request to King Henry VIII of England by Pope Leo X in 1521 as a reward for Henry's pamphlet *Assertio septem sacramentorum adversus Martinum Lutherum*, a defense of the seven sacraments against Martin Luther, written with the help of St. John Fisher. The title was similar to the names *Catholicus* (Catholic) for the rulers of Spain and *Christanissimus* (most Christian) for the rulers of France. When Henry broke with Rome, he was stripped of the honor by Pope Paul III, but Parliament restored it to him and recognized it as an official title of the English monarchy. It has been borne by the British monarchs since then; King George I (1714-1727) placed the letters FD (for *Fidei Defensor*) on his coinage. Pope Paul III also bestowed it upon King James V of Scotland, and G. K. Chesterton was given the honorary name "Defender of the Catholic Faith" by Pope Pius XI in 1936.

Defense of the Seven Sacraments ● See under **Henry VIII**; see also **Defender of the Faith**, preceding entry.

Defensor Ecclesiae ● "Defender of the Church," the title borne by the individual in previous eras who was given the task of administering the temporal affairs and holdings of the Church in a given region. By custom, the *Defensor ecclesiae* was appointed by the ruler of a territory or country in which such temporal goods or concerns were located. Another name was *Advocatus ecclesiae*. The defender was specifically charged with representing a particular church or monastery in civil courts, defending such institutions from attacks both physical and legal, and leading a force of knights and soldiers into battle in the name of the church or monastery. In return, the protector received revenues, usually in the form of services or supplies as well as definite spiritual benefices. Such defenders were found in Europe as early as the fifth century when the Council of Carthage (410) decreed that the emperor in conjunction with the bishops should provide certain *defensores* for churches. The position during the Middle Ages was quite prestigious, but by the 1100s definite rules and decrees were issued by Rome to curtail abuses on the part of various protectors.

De Groot, Hugo ● See **Groote, Gerhard**.

De Haeretico Comburendo ● Act taken by Parliament in 1401 that began the direct persecution of the Lollards in England. By the statute, all heretics were to be arrested and tried under canon law; if convicted, they would be handed over to secular court and burned at the stake. (See **Lollardy** and **Wycliffe, John**.)

Deiniol, St. (d. c. 584) ● Abbot, bishop, and Welsh saint, Deiniol was said to have come from Strathclyde, although few details about his life are known with certainty. Probably consecrated by St. Dubricius as the first bishop of Bangor, he was called "of the Bangors" for his founding of the monasteries of Bangor Fawr and Bangor Iscoed (the monks there were massacred in 615 by the troops of King Ethelfrith of Northumbria). Numerous Welsh churches are dedicated to him, including the Cathedral of Bangor. He is buried on Bardsey. Feast day: September 11.

Dei Verbum ● Vatican Council II document promulgated on November 18, 1965, and known in English as the "Dogmatic Constitution on Divine Revelation." Its focus is on the nature of divine revelation, its transmission, inspiration, and interpretation, and the place of Scripture in the life of the Church. *Dei Verbum* is generally considered to be a successor or complimentary document to the "Dogmatic Constitution on Catholic Faith," *Dei Filius*, that had been issued by Vatican Council I (1869-1870). It is divided into the following related categories: Revelation, Transmission or Revelation, Inspiration and Interpretation, the OT, the NT, and Scripture in Church Life.

God chose to give to humanity a fundamental revelation of himself and to make known to us the hidden purpose of his will (or the mystery of his will).

In examining the transmission of revelation, *Dei Verbum* observes that "Christ the Lord, in whom the full revelation of the supreme God is brought to completion. . . , commissioned the apostles to preach to all men that gospel which is the source of all saving truth and moral teaching, . . . But in order to keep the gospel forever whole and alive within the Church, the apostles left bishops as their successors, 'handing over their own teaching role' to them. This sacred tradition, therefore, and sacred Scripture of both the Old and New Testament are like a mirror in which the pilgrim Church on earth looks at God" (No. 7).

The "Dogmatic Constitution on Divine Revelation" (Nos. 9, 10) then traces the development of doctrine, elaborating upon the "close connection and communication between sacred tradition and sacred Scripture," which "form one sacred deposit of the word of God, which is committed to the Church." It adds, however, the important element of the magisterium, the teaching authority of the Church, declaring that all three — sacred Scripture, sacred tradition, and the magisterium — "are so linked and joined together that one cannot stand without the others, and that all together and each in its own way under the action of the one Holy Spirit contribute effectively to the salvation of souls."

In examining both inspiration and interpretation, *Dei Verbum* states that "Holy Mother Church, relying on the belief of the apostles, holds that the books of both the Old and New Testament in their entirety, with all their parts, are sacred and canonical because, having been written under the inspiration of the Holy Spirit . . . they have God as their author and have been handed on as such to the Church herself" (No. 11). It then studies the questions of inerrancy, literary forms, and the analogy of faith.

Both the Old and New Testaments are given their place in the "planning and preparing the salvation of the whole human race" (No. 14). The OT is described as having as its primary purpose "to prepare for the coming both of Christ, the universal Redeemer, and of the messianic kingdom, . . . the books of the Old Testament with all their parts, caught up into the proclamation of the gospel, acquire and show forth their full meaning in the New Testament" (Nos. 15, 16). The NT, written under the inspiration of the Holy Spirit, gives confirmation of "those matters which concern Christ the Lord" and "His true teaching is more and more fully stated, the saving power of the divine work of Christ is preached, the story is told of the beginnings of the Church and her marvelous growth, and her glorious fulfillment is foretold" (No. 20). Finally, the role of Scripture in Church life is emphasized, exhorting that ease of "access to sacred Scripture should be provided for all the Christian faithful" and calling for biblical studies to progress "under the watchful care of the sacred teaching office of the Church," adding that the careful study of Sacred Scripture is "the soul of sacred theology" (Nos. 22-24).

Deism ● Type of natural religion that was developed in the late 1600s and became highly popular among philosophers, especially in France, during the Enlightenment. Originally considered synonymous with theism (meaning a philosophical system that accepts a transcendent God), Deism became much more highly defined and came to embrace a belief that while God does exist and did create the world and establish the laws of nature that govern his creation, he refrains from any kind of active interference or direct participation, allowing his creations of the world and humanity to proceed according to the previously organized set of laws. The philosophy, which removes any rationale for a personal religion or an active, concerned God, was developed out of the ideas of such intellectuals as Lord Herbert of Cherbury (1583-1648), Pierre Charron (1541-1603), and John Locke (1632-1704), especially his treatise *Reasonableness of Christianity* (1695). A formal presentation of Deist concepts was made by the onetime Irish Catholic John Toland (1670-1722) in his *Christianity not Mysterious* (1696) in which he argued against the notion that God and his revelation were beyond human reason and that supernatural elements from paganism should not be allowed to intrude upon Christianity. While the work was condemned and burned by the Irish Parliament (1697), Toland gave much inspiration to other Deists such as Anthony Collins (1676-1729) and Matthew Tindal (1655-1733).

Deism had many critics, especially in England, but it soon found a wide following among French rationalists, notably Voltaire, Rousseau, and the Encyclopedists. Deist ideas also spread to Germany — where it influenced Immanuel Kant (1724-1804) — and even America where certain Deist elements can be found in the works of Ben Franklin and Thomas Jefferson. Given its rejection of formal religion and especially any kind of supernatural revelation, Deism was naturally opposed by religious leaders, theologians, and intellectuals, especially in England where the Anglican establishment, typified by Joseph Butler, bishop of Durham (1692-1752) and his *Analogy of Religion*, inhibited and opposed the Deists wherever possible.

De la Taille, Maurice (1872-1933) ● French theologian, author of the controversial work *Mysterium Fidei* (1921). De la Taille was born at Semblancay and studied at St. Mary's College, Canterbury. Entering the Jesuits in 1890, he taught theology at the Catholic University of Angers from 1905-1916. After service in the war as a chaplain in the Canadian army (1916-1918), he became an instructor of dogmatic theology at the Gregorian University in Rome. He is best known for *Mysterium Fidei*, a treatise on the Mass, divided into three parts: the Sacrifice offered by Christ himself, the Mass as a sacrifice of the Church itself, and the Eucharist as a sacrament.

Delehaye, Hippolyte (1859-1941) ● Member of the Bollandists. A native of Antwerp, Delehaye joined the Society of Jesus in 1879 and studied philosophy at Louvain from 1879-1882 and theology at Innsbruck from 1886-1887; in between he taught mathematics at the Collège St. Barbe at Ghent (1882-1886). Ordained in 1890, he joined the Bollandists the following year and henceforth worked on hagiographical writings, making enormous contributions, from 1894 on, to the *Acta Sanctorum* and the *Analecta Bollandiana*. He was elected in 1912 to the post of president of the Bollandists. (See **Acta Sanctorum <1>** and **Bollandists**.)

De Lisle, Ambrose Lisle March Phillipps (1809-1878) ● English Catholic who worked for many years to promote the conversion of England and for Christian unity. The son of Anglican parents (his mother was of Huguenot descent), he was raised an Anglican, meeting an actual Catholic only around 1820 when he encountered the French émigré priest Abbé Giraud. Increasingly drawn toward the Church, he was finally converted in 1824. His university career was cut short at Cambridge because of illness, and he journeyed to Italy to recover, meeting the Italian philosopher Antonio Rosmini-Serbato during the winter of 1830-1831. Marrying in 1833, he received one of his family's estates, donating in 1835 some two hundred thirty acres of Charwood Forest to the Trappists for the building of the monastery of Mt. St. Bernard. In 1838, he founded the Association for Promoting the Unity of Christendom (A.P.U.C.), which he left upon its condemnation by Pope Pius IX in 1864. A friend of many members of the Oxford movement, he was a gifted and gentle proponent for Catholicism in England. He signed his name "de Lisle" starting in 1862; prior to that he signed it "Ambrose Lisle Phillipps."

De Lubac, Henri (1896-1984) ● Influential French theologian and cardinal. A native of Cambrai, he entered the Society of Jesus in 1913. He was drafted into the French army in 1915, saw action in World War I, and was eventually wounded. After studying philosophy and theology in England and France in several Jesuit houses, he was ordained a priest in 1927. Two years later, he was named a professor of theology at the University of Lyons. At the Second Vatican Council, de Lubac served as a *peritus* (expert) and was subsequently appointed to the International Theological Commission. The author of a vast body of writings, de Lubac won the Catholic Grand Prix of Literature in 1968. His writings include *The Mystery of the Supernatural*, *The Drama of Atheistic Humanism*, *The Christian Faith*, *The Splendor of the Church*, and *Motherhood of the Church*. In 1941, he co-edited the massive collection of patristic texts, *Sources chrétiennes*. He was deeply influenced by the Fathers of the Church and the work of St. Thomas Aquinas. In *The Mystery of the Supernatural*, he vindicates the teaching of Aquinas that man's intellect has a natural desire to seek God and states that there is a unity of nature and grace. The desire of the intellect, however, finds fulfillment only through the free gift of grace from God. Shortly before his death, de Lubac was created a cardinal by Pope John Paul II in recognition of his contributions to contemporary theology.

Demetrius, St. (d. c. 231) ● Bishop of Alexandria from 188 or 189 until his death, the first prelate of Alexandria about whom anything is known with certainty, and a much revered saint in the Coptic Church. According to Julius Africanus, Demetrius was the eleventh bishop of the see, having been appointed in the tenth year of the reign of Commodus. When Clement retired as head of the Catechetical School of Alexandria, Demetrius named Origen as his successor around 203-204. He gave Origen much support and encouragement in their early years of cooperation, but, when, in 215-216, Origen fled the city during the bloody visit by Emperor Caracalla and went to Caesarea, the two had a falling out. The cause was Origen's accepting an invitation from the bishops of Jerusalem and Caesarea to preach, an act that Demetrius felt was presumptuous for a layman. He recalled Origen in 216 and censured him. This was followed by formal condemnation and banishment in 231 after Origen's irregular ordination at Caesarea. His successor, Heracles, allowed Origen to return to Alexandria. Feast day: October 9 (in the East, October 26).

Demiurge ● See **Gnosticism**.

Denifle, Heinrich (1844-1905) ● Dominican Church historian. Born Joseph Seuse Denifle, he was a native of the Tyrol in Austria, the son of a village schoolmaster and

church organist. After studying at the episcopal school of Brixen, he was received into the Dominicans in 1861, taking the name Heinrich. He studied Aristotle and St. Thomas Aquinas at Graz, Rome, and Marseilles, teaching philosophy and theology for ten years (1870-1880) at Graz. In 1880, he was summoned to Rome where he served as an associate to the general of the Dominican order. His main task was to carry out an extensive search of libraries all over Europe for manuscripts by Thomas Aquinas as part of Pope Leo XIII's directive to organize a new edition of the works of the Angelic Doctor. Impressed with his work, Leo appointed Denifle sub-archivist of the Vatican in December 1883. Two years later, he founded with the medievalist Franz Ehrle the *Archiv für Litteratur und Kirchengeschichte des Mittelalters* (*Archive for Medieval Literature and Church History*). Among his remarkable writings were the enormous four-volume *Chartularium Universitatis Parisiensis* (1884-1897, a collection of the records of the University of Paris organized with Emile Chatelain), several studies of German mystics (Meister Eckhart, Henry Suso, and Johannes Tauler), and an unfinished study on Luther and Lutheranism.

Denmark ● European country with currently a very small Catholic community; it is almost entirely Lutheran. According to tradition, the first attempt at converting the wild pagan Danish warriors was made by St. Willibrord (d. 739), although there is no reliable evidence for his work. Another effort, that of Archbishop Ebbo of Reims in 823 to Jutland was also a failure. Real progress was not realized until later in the ninth century when the chief Harold visited King Louis the Pious of France and accepted baptism. On his return, he took with him St. Anskar (801-865), the Apostle of the North, who later converted King Erik of Jutland. The Church in Denmark was placed under the jurisdiction of the see of Hamburg-Bremen and, during the reigns of Sven I (985-1014) and especially Cnut the Great (1014-1035), it spread rapidly. Bishoprics were established and early monasticism began to flourish. In 1104, the Danish sees were removed from the authority of Bremen-Hamburg and placed under the archiepiscopal see of Lund. Henceforth, the bishops enjoyed increasing sociopolitical power and influence; chief among them was Absalon, archbishop of Lund (d. 1201). The secular involvement of the prelates, particularly in the dynastic affairs of the kingdom and the struggles between the kings and the nobles (among whom they were counted), contributed to the appeal of the Reformation in the sixteenth century. It was partly his desire to free himself of the bishops that King Christian II in 1520 invited the Reformer preacher Martin Reinhard into the country. This early effort came to nothing initially, but it marked only the beginning of a process of reform that ended with the loss of Denmark to the faith and the adoption of Lutheranism. Initial laws against Catholics were less severe than in other Protestant lands but became more severe in the seventeenth century; in 1624, priests caught performing their rituals were put to death and, in 1683, converts to the Catholic Church were declared in forfeit of their lands. Religious freedom was officially granted only in 1849. There is only one diocese in modern Denmark.

De Noailles, Louis Antoine (1651-1729) ● Cardinal and archbishop of Paris who promoted reforms in the French clergy but also had sympathies toward Jansenism. He was born at Château de Teyssiere in the Auvergne, received his education at the Collège des Plesses, Paris, and in 1679 was consecrated bishop of Cohors. Sent to Châlons-sur-Marne in 1680, he became archbishop of Paris in 1695. Pope Innocent XII made him a cardinal in 1700; in 1720, he was appointed head of the Sorbonne. De

Noailles worked hard to promote reform, particularly in clerical discipline and learning. He called for residence in seminary before ordination and insisted on theological training. This work was overshadowed, however, by his support of the *Réflexions morales* in 1693 by Pasquier Quesnel, which, combined with his rejection of probabilism, caused many to suspect him of Jansenist leanings. While he condemned certain Jansenist doctrines in 1698, he opposed the condemnatory bull *Unigenitus* (1713), appealed against it in 1718, but finally submitted in 1728. On his deathbed he recanted his submission. He authored several works, including a number of pastoral guides or instructions.

De Nobili, Robert (1577-1656) ● Jesuit missionary in India, responsible for converting as many as one hundred thousand Indians to the faith. De Nobili joined the Society of Jesus in 1597. He was sent in 1604 to the mission in India where he adopted a unique method for attracting converts: he assumed the lifestyle of an Indian *fakir*, or ascetic, indoctrinating himself thoroughly with Indian social life and culture, particularly the caste system. He refused to associate with the lowest class of untouchables and thereby won the confidence of many others, most notably the brahmins, who were very influential in society. The irregularity of his methods soon earned censure from other missionaries, but, after defending himself before the archbishop of Goa, he was granted permission from Rome to continue. He proposed to have separate missionary efforts to the different classes, a move that helped remove many barriers to social interaction between Catholics and Hindus. De Nobili mastered Sanskrit, Tamil, and Telugu, authoring some twenty books in these three languages. (See also **Malabar Rite**.)

Denys the Carthusian (1402-1471) ●
Also Dionysius the Carthusian, Denys van
Leeuwen, and Denys Rychel, a Belgian
theologian and mystic. He was born at
Rychel, in modern Belgium, hence the name
Denys Rychel, given him by writers.
Educated at Cologne, he entered the
charterhouse of Roermund in 1423. In 1451,
he traveled to Germany with Cardinal
Nicholas of Cusa to preach a crusade against
the Turks and to promote reform in the
Church. A mystic of much repute, he earned
the title *Doctor Ecstaticus* (the Ecstatic
Doctor) and drew many visitors to his cell as
they sought his advice. In between his very
active prayer life and duties as a Carthusian,
Denys undertook numerous writing efforts,
coupling a series of commentaries on the Old
and New Testaments, and editing a
commentary on the works of Peter Lombard,
Boethius, and John Climachus. He was
much influenced by Dionysius the Areopagite.

Denzinger, Heinrich (1819-1883) ●
Leading theologian in Germany and a
promoter of positive theology. He was born at
Liège, the son of a professor at Liège
University. Receiving a doctorate in
philosophy from the University of Würzburg,
he entered the Würzburg seminary in 1838,
attended the German College in Rome, and
was ordained in 1844. In 1848, he became
professor of dogmatic theology at Würzburg,
remaining at the university until his death. A
pioneer of the German school of the exact
investigation of the historical development of
theology, Denzinger authored the *Enchiridion
Symbolorum et Definitionum* (1854), a
handbook on the decrees and enactments of
the councils (including the earliest forms of
the Apostolic Creed) and those propositions
that were condemned. He also wrote a
number of works on medieval theology.
Scholars and others have found the
Enchiridion to be an enormously useful
source. The 1963 revision, the thirty-second
edition and some eighty years after

Denzinger's death, was edited by Adolphus
Schönmetzer.

Deposition, Bull of ● See **Regnans in
Excelsis**.

De Rossi, Giovanni Battista (1828-1894)
● Christian archaeologist especially noted for
his work on the Roman catacombs. A native
of Rome, he studied philosophy at the
Collegio Romano from 1838-1840 and
jurisprudence from 1840-1844 at the Roman
University (Sapienza). He was appointed a
scriptor at the Vatican Library in 1844, a post
he proudly held for the rest of his life.
Fascinated by the catacombs (he had read
Antonio Bosio's *La Roma Sotteranea* when he
was eleven), De Rossi met Giuseppe Marchi,
S.J., in 1841, who convinced him to study
the catacombs; his subsequent excavations
and researches marked a major advance in
knowledge of the catacombs, particularly as
De Rossi utilized extensive knowledge of
Christian literature and historical sources to
assist in the interpretation of archaeological
data. The author of innumerable works on
the catacombs and early Christian
inscriptions, his writings included:
*Inscriptiones Christianae Urbis Romae
septimo saeculo antiquiores* (2 vols.,
1861-1868); *La Roma Sotteranea Christiana*
(3 vols., 1864-1877); *Sur les Catacombes de
Rome* (1867); and *Inscriptiones Urbis Romae
Latinae* (1876); he also edited for thirty years
the *Bulletino di Archeologia Christiana* (1863),
which he founded. De Rossi was friends with
or an associate of a huge number of
important personages and scholars, such as
Pope Leo XIII, Theodor Mommsen, Franz
Xaver Kraus, and Johannes Döllinger. (See
also **Catacombs**.)

De Sacramentis ● Liturgical treatise on
the sacraments generally held by scholars to
have been written by St. Ambrose (d. 397).
While some historians propose that the
author might have been Maximus of Turin,

most believe that he was, indeed, Ambrose. Addressed to the newly baptized during Easter week, the work was concerned with the Eucharist, confirmation, and baptism, and is an important early account of the Roman Canon of the Mass.

Descartes, René (1596-1650) ● French philosopher and scientist who made lasting contributions to philosophy through his teachings, called Cartesianism (from his Latin name Renatus Cartesius). Descartes was born to a noble family in La Haye, studying at the Jesuit College of La Flèche. In 1613, he journeyed to Paris and in 1619 was in Neuberg on the Danube when he received certain dreams that seemed to give a sign that he should devote himself to finding a doubt-proof system of science based on mathematical principles. He returned to Paris in 1625 and found encouragement from Cardinal Pierre de Bérulle (1575-1629). Paris, however, provided little opportunity for study, so he moved to Holland in 1629 where he conducted most of his researches. In 1649, at the invitation of Queen Christina, he traveled to Sweden. There he died of pneumonia.

Aside from contributions to mathematics (including the foundation of analytic geometry), he formulated a philosophical system that attempted to apply mathematical methods to philosophy. Using the idea of universal doubt, he reduced knowledge to that which could not be doubted, doubt itself. This self-consciousness permitted him to express the action of the mind in the maxim *"Cogito ergo sum"* ("I think, therefore I am"). He argued that whatever can be conceived of in logic must be true, proclaiming that the idea first conceived outside the ego is God, an idea that is unaccountable save that God exists. In arguing for the existence of God, he relied upon modifications of Scholastic thought including causation and ontologism, seeing God as the link between the rational world of the mind and the mechanical world of the intellect. The mind and the body, he felt, were two different entities. He was, despite his failings, a major figure in examining questions concerning the validity of knowledge, the so-called epistemological problem. His insights, the originality of his method, and the excellent degree of his ordered mind all made him a profoundly influential philosopher. While his writings were placed on the Index of Forbidden Books, he found wide support from among the French clergy. His chief works were *Discourse de la methode* (*Discourse on the Method*), *Méditations metaphysique* (from the Latin *Meditationes de prima philosophia*, or *Meditations on First Philosophy*), *Principia philosophia* (*Principles of Philosophy*), and *Regulae ad directionem ingenii* (*Rules for the Direction of the Mind*).

René Descartes

Deusdedit, St. ● Pope from 615-618. Also called Adeodedit I or Deusdedit I (see **Adeodatus II**), he was the successor of Boniface IV. The main event of his pontificate was the support he gave the Byzantines in their war with the Lombards over control of Italy. He also gave aid to the poor, and those inspired or left homeless by an earthquake in the area around Rome. His reign marked the first time that leaden seals (*bullae*) were used on pontifical documents. Feast day: November 8.

Deutschen Orden ● See Teutonic Knights under **Military Orders**.

De Veuster, Joseph ● See **Damien de Veuster, Bl**.

Diaspora ● See under **Jews and Judaism**.

Dictatus Papae ● Collection of twenty-seven declarations of papal power and authority, issued probably during the reign of Pope Gregory VII in 1075. The collection was intended to support the position of the papacy in temporal and spiritual affairs, especially during the often bitter struggles with the Holy Roman Emperors. By the terms of the statements, the pope was declared superior to all other members of the clergy, above kings, and even emperors: "the pope cannot be judged by anyone . . . the pope alone is able to depose and restore bishops . . . he alone can call general councils and authorize canon law . . . a duly ordained pope is undoubtedly made a saint by the merits of St. Peter." Finally, and most significantly, the pontiff had the authority to depose any king or emperor, but no temporal rules could remove him. (See also **Gregory VII**.)

Didache ● Earliest known Christian writing aside from the NT that presents, in sixteen chapters, a kind of summary (or abstract) of Christian moral teaching. Known in the original Greek as the *Didache ton Dodeka Apostolon* (or *Teaching of the Twelve Apostles*), it was written in Syria almost certainly in the first century, dated variously by experts to around 60 or even later. The anonymous author used Jewish sources and was clearly familiar with several of the Gospels, especially Matthew and Luke. The work's chapters can be divided into four parts: Chapters 1-6 deal with the two ways — the Way of Life and the Way of Death; Chapters 7-10 are concerned with liturgical matters, namely baptism, fasts, prayer, and the Eucharist; Chapters 11-15 cover matters of discipline, such as obligations to teachers, the welcoming of apostles, details of false and true prophets, proper keeping of the Lord's own day, the election of bishops and deacons, and correct behavior within the community; and Chapter 16 presents an epilogue prophesying the return of Our Lord, who will come with all the saints and "the world shall behold the Lord riding upon the clouds of the sky." The *Didache* was well-known in the early Church and it exercised great influence; St. Athanasius encouraged its use by catechumens and it can be seen in the Apostolic Constitutions. Modern familiarity with it dates from 1873 when the complete text was discovered in a monastery in Constantinople. The text, dating to 1056, was found by Philotheus Bryennios, metropolitan of Nicomedia. It is of immense interest to scholars given its preservation of details of early liturgical development, including two Eucharistic prayers. Also of interest is the first formal condemnation by the Church of abortion, with the command "do not kill a fetus by abortion, or commit infanticide."

Didascalia Apostolorum ● "Teaching of the Apostles," a work traditionally ascribed to the Apostles, although it was actually written by a physician convert from Judaism in the third century. Composed in Syria, it was originally in Greek and took as one of its models the *Didache*. The *Didascalia*, however, is not as well-organized or methodical as the *Didache*. It is concerned with such topics as fasting; the duties of bishops, deacons, presbyters, husbands, wives, and widows; the liturgy; and penance. The *Didascalia* takes a much more lenient position with respect to penitents than do other similar works. The author is also much concerned with those Christians who continued to adhere to the view that Jewish law was still in force.

Didymus the Blind (310- or 313-395 or -398) ● Theologian from Alexandria, so-called because he lost his sight at the age of four; nevertheless, he was one of the most learned men of his time. His immense knowledge was not gained by reading, as this was impossible, but by listening to readers for days at a time. Appointed by St. Athanasius to head up the Catechetical School of Alexandria, he claimed as some of his pupils Jerome, Rufinus, and Gregory of Nazianzus. Jerome, however, later retracted the statement that Didymus was his master when Didymus became embroiled in the controversy of Origen and Origenism. At the Council of Constantinople in 553, Didymus's works were condemned but not Didymus himself. As a result, he fell into obscurity during the Middle Ages and his works were not copied. Many were long lost, but some were known, including his writings *On the Holy Spirit*, *Against the Manichaeans*, and *On the Trinity*. The discovery in 1941 of several papyri dated to the sixth and seventh centuries near Toura, to the south of Cairo, provided details on his commentaries on Zechariah, Job, Genesis, Ecclesiastes, and parts of the Psalms. He was also an opponent of Arianism.

Dietrich of Nieheim (d. 1418) ● Member of the papal government who nevertheless joined the conciliar movement. He attended the Council of Constance (1414-1418) in the hopes of ending the Great Schism that had plagued the Church since 1378 and was especially pointed in attacking the antipope John XXIII. His writings were generally biased toward conciliarism but provided useful details on the events of his time; these included *De Schismate* (1410) and *Avisamenta edita on Concilio Constanciensi*, a defense of the powers of the general assembly

in deposing a pope. In 1395, he had been appointed bishop of Verden by Pope Boniface IX but was not consecrated and was removed around 1400. (See also **Conciliarism**.)

Dignitatis Humanae ● "Declaration on Religious Freedom," issued by Vatican Council II on December 7, 1965. A powerful statement on the fundamental rights of all persons to enjoy freedom of worship, a right to be guaranteed and reaffirmed by civil law, the Vatican decree was the result of extensive deliberation both on the nature of religious freedom and the way it should be defined. In the end, the declaration proclaimed: "This Vatican Synod declares that the human person has a right to religious freedom. This freedom means that all men are to be immune from coercion on the part of individuals or of social groups and of any human power, in such wise that in matters religious no one is to be forced to act in a manner contrary to his own beliefs. Nor is anyone to be restrained from acting in accordance with his own beliefs, whether privately or publicly, whether alone or in association with others, within limits" (No. 2). The basis of this right is the inherent dignity of the human person, as an individual and as a social being. This reality is revealed by the Word of God and also by reason.

The declaration also examines the rights of the family, especially in choosing schools, noting that many states violate "the rights of parents" (No. 5) when they compel children to attend a single system of education. Further, there are recognized certain limits on freedom, when the need for public order and morality require it, but "the freedom of man [must] be respected as far as possible, and curtailed only when and in so far as necessary" (No. 7). In its conclusion, *Dignitatis Humanae* observed that many constitutions of government throughout the world contain specific rights of religious freedom, but there are other governments that do not; the Council "greets with joy the first of these two facts, as among the signs of the times. With sorrow, however, it denounces the other fact, as only to be deplored" (No. 15). (See also **Pacem in Terris** and **Social Encyclicals**.)

Diocletian (d. 316) ● Roman Emperor from 284-305. Known in full as Gaius Aurelius Valerius Dioclecianus, he was born to a poor family of Dalmatia (Illyricum) under the name Diocles. After entering the armed forces, he was promoted swiftly, reaching the post of commander of the elite bodyguard called the *protectores domestici* under Emperor Numerian in 284. When the emperor died under suspicious circumstances, Diocletian, at the behest of the troops, put to death Prefect of the Guard Arrius Aper, who was believed to be guilty of poisoning Numerian. Diocletian was then proclaimed emperor, marching west from Nicomedia to crush Numerian's brother Carinus in 285. As emperor, he launched an ambitious and far-reaching reform of the entire imperial government. The administration was centralized, the frontiers were stabilized, and the important system of the tetrarchy introduced. By this reform, the empire was to be ruled by two emperors, co-rulers called Augusti (singular: Augustus), who would each be assisted by a junior emperor, called a Caesar. Diocletian named Maximian his co-emperor, and the Caesars were Galerius (the infamous hater of Christians) and Constantius I Chlorus (father of Constantine the Great). While this type of government would prove ultimately a failure, it worked for a number of years and contributed to a general revival throughout much of the Roman world.

Diocletian is known in Christian history for the support he gave Galerius in the severe persecution of the Church. At Galerius's prompting, Diocletian launched in 303 the last great Christian persecution. Churches were burned, gatherings for worship forbidden, the Scriptures were pitched into the flames, and later public sacrifices to the imperial cult (the Roman state religion) were made mandatory for all. The suffering caused by the pogrom was considerable, but it soon proved fruitless, and the failure against the now widespread faith contributed to Diocletian's retirement in 305. His later years were filled with much disappointment for him as the tetrarchy fell apart and the empire sank into civil war. He died in 316, having been unable to prevent the Edict of Milan (312) granting full toleration of Christianity and an end to hundreds of years of open hostility to the Church by the Roman Empire.

Diodore (d. c. 390) ● Bishop of Tarsus and a theologian of the Antiochene school. A native of Antioch, he studied at Athens before becoming the head of a monastery just outside of Antioch. He was compelled to depart the monastic setting of Antioch to fight Arianism and was later banished to Armenia in 372. Returning eventually, he was appointed bishop of Tarsus in 378. The author of numerous commentaries on the Bible and other writings, Diodore is known today largely in fragmentary form because of the destruction of many of his works by the Arians and the suppression of others due to his possible sympathies with his condemned pupil Theodore of Mopsuestia. Another student was St. John Chrysostom.

Dionysius, St. ● Pope from 259-268. The pontificate of Dionysius was marked by a strengthening of the papacy in matters of faith, mainly the result of settling the controversy of tritheism involving St. Dionysius of Alexandria. Probably a Greek by birth, Dionysius served as a presbyter under Pope Stephen I (r. 254-257) and was elected on July 22, 259, to succeed St. Sixtus II after a vacancy of the Holy See of almost a year. Dionysius found the Church much troubled because of the persecutions of Emperor Valens; Sixtus, in fact, had been martyred.

The pope in 260 convened a synod in Rome to deal with the charges made against Dionysius of Alexandria that he adhered to tritheism (a belief that the members of the Trinity were three distinct deities). The synod, which came to be called the "the affair of the two Dionysii," cleared the Alexandrian prelate through his *Refutation and Apology* and, significantly, his acceptance of the pope's authority over such matters. According to Basil of Caesarea, he sent aid to the Church of Caesarea around 290 when the city was invaded by the Persians.

Dionysius Exiguus (d. c. 560) ● Scythian monk, astronomer, canonist, and the founder of the Christian calendar. He was reputedly very humble, adopting the name Dionyius Exiguus (Denis the Little), according to the sixth-century historian Cassiodorus. Entering the service of the popes in 496, he worked in the papal archives and in 525 began an organization of Christian chronology. By using the Roman calendar, he calculated the birth of Christ to be 754 after the founding of Rome; by this model, Christ was born in the Roman year 753. This system was subsequently adopted by the Synod of Whitby in 664 and then was generally accepted by the rest of the Church. Dionysius translated the Greek patristic writings into Latin (including a life of St. Pachomius) and authored the so-called *Dionysiana Collectio*, a compilation of the canons of the Councils of Sardinia, Constantinople, and Chalcedon, the Apostolic Canons, and papal decretals from the late fourth to the late fifth centuries. An important early corpus of canon law, it was accepted by the Frankish Church at Aachen in 802.

Dionysius of Paris, St. (c. 250) ● Also St. Denys, a patron saint of France. According to St. Gregory of Tours in the sixth century, Dionysius was one of seven "bishops" sent to convert the people of Gaul around 250. He was soon martyred in Paris at the site now called Montmarte (or Martyr Hill), decapitated along with Rusticus, a priest, and Eleutherius, a deacon. He was subsequently attached to various legends. In the eighth century, it was widely acclaimed that he had been sent to Gaul by Pope St. Clement of Rome in the first century; Hilduin, abbot of St. Denis in the ninth century, identified him with Dionysius the Areopagite. He was also ranked as one of the *cephalophore* (head-carriers), martyrs who supposedly carried their severed heads to their places of interment.

Dionysius the Areopagite ● First-century convert to Christianity, brought into the Church by St. Paul at Athens, as recorded in Acts (17:34): "But some men joined him and believed, among them Dionysius the Areopagite and a woman named Damaris and others with them." According to Dionysius of Corinth, he became the first bishop of the Christian community of Athens. He was later identified in the ninth century with Dionysius of Paris and his name attached to the theological writings of Pseudo-Dionysius (Dionysius the Pseudo-Areopagite).

Dionysius the Carthusian ● See **Denys the Carthusian**.

Dionysius the Great (d. c. 264) ● Bishop of Alexandria and leading opponent of the heresy of Sabellianism. Dionysius was a native of Alexandria and a pupil of Origen, whom he succeeded as head of the Catechetical School of Alexandria from around 233. Bishop of Alexandria in 247, he was forced to flee the city in 251 during the persecutions of Emperor Trajanus Decius, going to the Libyan Desert. Another period of exile lasted from 257-260 during the persecutions by Emperor Valerian. Back at Alexandria, he faced plague, civil unrest, and famine as well as the controversy over the rebaptizing of lapsed Christians — he did not demand harsh penalties for apostates, favoring readmission for all penitent Christians. His dispute with the Sabellians, who taught that the Trinity was indivisible, caused him to be accused of tritheism (the Trinity as three distinct deities), a dispute eventually brought before Pope Dionysius in a Roman synod, the so-called "affair of the two Dionysii." In his *Refutation and Apology*, Dionysius of Alexandria secured formal vindication, and the entire incident set the stage for the Council of Nicaea in 325. While much respected for his writings, especially by the theologians of the Byzantine Church, his writings are preserved mostly in fragments or extracts by Eusebius of Caesarea, St. Athanasius, and other ecclesiastical writers. Dionysius also denied that St. John the Evangelist was the author of both the Fourth Gospel and the Book of Revelation.

Dionysius the Pseudo-Areopagite ● See **Pseudo-Dionysius the Areopagite**.

Dioscorus ● Patriarch of Alexandria who was a central figure in the bitter struggle over the nature of Christ that took place in the mid-fifth century. A native of Alexandria, he was an archdeacon at Alexandria when, in 444, he was named successor of St. Cyril of Alexandria as patriarch. Starting around 448, Dioscorus gave his support to the monk of Constantinople, Eutyches, who formulated the controversial theological doctrine of Eutychianism (in which it was declared that Christ had only one nature) and was condemned at Constantinople. The following year (449), Dioscorus presided over the so-called Robber Synod (Latrocinium) of Ephesus where Eutyches was reinstated, Pope St. Leo I the Great was excommunicated, and St. Flavian of Constantinople was deposed as patriarch. When, however, Dioscorus's patron, Emperor Theodosius II, died in 450, a swift change in theological policy took place. The Council of Chalcedon condemned Eutychianism,

deposed Dioscorus, excommunicated him, and exiled him to Gangra in Paphlagonia. He is revered as a saint in the Monophysite Churches. His defeat at Chalcedon was the occasion of a considerable triumph for Pope Leo.

Discalced ● Term meaning barefoot or unshod. It is used to describe the members of those religious congregations whose rule requires the wearing of sandals rather than shoes. The discalced lifestyle was begun by St. Francis of Assisi and St. Clare of Assisi and is today followed by such communities as the Clerks of the Holy Cross and the Augustinians. It is also used to distinguish between the two divisions of the Carmelite order.

Disciplina Arcani ● Latin for "discipline of the secret," it was the practice found among the early Christians of revealing only gradually the tenets and sacramental instruction of the faith to catechumens. Found during periods of persecution throughout the Roman Empire, the *disciplina* entailed a reluctance on the part of Christians, especially instructors of Christian doctrine, to speak openly about details of the faith. Such particulars were revealed only over a period of time as the catechumen displayed more knowledge and steadfastness in studies. The practice, which withheld the most important of mysteries (especially the Eucharist) until the candidate approached baptism, was a means of safeguarding the creed from blasphemy or betrayal. The *disciplina* had all but disappeared by the sixth century, by which time Christianity was widespread in Europe and elsewhere. Among the symbols used to give secret representation of the faith was the fish — meaning Christ — and the Chi-rho. (See also **Roman Empire**.) Scholars have long discussed the possible origins of the *disciplina*; they have theorized that they may have come from certain pagan practices or, most likely, from a desire to withhold the most vital elements of the faith from those not initiated. Mention was made of the practice by a number of early Christian writers including St. Cyprian, Origen, St. Cyril of Jerusalem, St. John Chrysostom, St. Ambrose, and St. Augustine.

Dissidio ● Italian for "division," which described the separation between the Holy See and the Italian government that lasted from 1870 to 1929. The *dissidio* began with the seizure of the Papal States by the unified Italian kingdom through the Risorgimento. As this deprived Pope Pius IX (r. 1846-1878) of the temporal holdings of the papacy, he declared himself a "prisoner of the Vatican," remaining in the one-hundred-eight-acre Vatican City that had been established by the Law of Guarantees of 1871. Pius therefore warned and instructed all loyal Catholics in Italy to have nothing to do with the Italian state, a declaration that created the *dissidio*. It remained in effect for many years, until Pope Pius X (1903-1914) urged Catholics to perform their civil duties, a tacit recognition of the ineffectual nature of the *dissidio* and the political realities of the Church's position in Italy. The *dissidio* was formally ended by the signing of the Lateran Treaty in 1929 between Benito Mussolini and Pope Pius XI.

Dissolution of the Monasteries ● Harsh and often brutal liquidation of the monasteries of England under King Henry VIII (r. 1509-1547), a particularly dark episode in the English Reformation. While the monasteries of England had been targets of complaints in the later Middle Ages for their laxity and corruption, no extensive programs of reform had been introduced. As a result, by the era of the Tudors, a small number had become quite infamous for abuses and a few were suppressed. No action on a grand scale was contemplated during the reign of Henry VII (r. 1485-1509) and in the early period of Henry VIII. This situation changed, however,

as a result of two circumstances: Henry's desire to advance his claims of supremacy over the Church of England (C of E) and his dire need of money to bolster his depleted treasury. The monasteries, generally staunch supporters of the papacy and often very well-off because of the treasures and gifts, proved a tempting target.

With the help of the able but unscrupulous minister Thomas Cromwell, Henry secured a report that, not surprisingly, found the monasteries to be hives of corruption; in fact, only a tiny number of houses were actually visited and abuses were minimal. On the basis of this false report, the Act for the Dissolution of Smaller Monasteries was passed in 1536, terminating those houses with an annual value below £250. An uprising soon began (October 1536) to protest this measure, called the Pilgrimage of Grace, that was swiftly put down. Having seized the goods of some two hundred fifty monasteries, Henry and his agents passed the Act for the Dissolution of Greater Monasteries in 1539. In early 1540, the last houses had been suppressed and the treasury considerably enhanced. The dissolution had caused the dislocation of a large body of clergy. Most of the priests were either pensioned or compelled to enter the ranks of the clergy of the C of E. Nuns spent years in disrepute and received pitiful pensions. The monks, who had been the focus of Henry's program, were the most harshly treated. Aside from this tragedy, there was the catastrophic loss of valuable manuscripts, works of art, treasure, and buildings — seized, looted, or destroyed by Henry's officials. Moreover, England lost a tradition of learning that dated back over a millennium.

Divine Comedy, The ● See under **Dante**.

Divino Afflante Spiritu ● Encyclical issued on September 30, 1943, by Pope Pius XII to encourage and give guidance to biblical scholars in their scientific study of the Bible. Taking its title from the first three Latin words of the document, it was published on the fiftieth anniversary of the encyclical *Providentissimus Deus* by Pope Leo XIII in 1893, which was called the Magna Carta of Biblical Studies. Both encyclicals were commemorated by Pope John Paul II in April 1993 at which the pontiff observed that while both were concerned with problems in their own era, they nevertheless possessed a validity for continuing studies and translations of Scripture.

Divino afflante Spiritu recognized the more open and flexible environment that prevailed in the field of biblical study, especially when compared with the era of Leo XIII. Nevertheless, Pius was aware of the dangers of abuse and speculation without proper analysis and the need for a clear sense of direction from the Church for those involved in such scientific endeavors. The encyclical sanctions the careful study of Oriental languages so as to promote proficiency in the language originally used in the writing of the Scriptures. This process of study would thus promote and permit the scientific application of textual criticism, which would lead to the determination of those extant manuscripts that are the closest to the first or earliest writings that have not survived the passage of time. At the same time, Pius warned against the excessive use of scientific examination to the detriment of doctrine. In other words, scholars should not arbitrarily apply their preliminary findings to the questioning or even rejection of essential elements of Church teaching. Rather, such study should be thorough, painstaking, corroborated, and ultimately weighed against not just one specific aspect of Scripture but the entire body of sacred writings as well as all of Tradition.

Doctor Authenticus ● "The Authentic Doctor," the name given to Gregory of Rimini (d. 1358), the general of the Augustinian Hermits. He has also been called *Doctor Acutus*, or "the Acute Doctor."

Doctor Angelicus ● "The Angelic Doctor," the name given to St. Thomas Aquinas (1224- or 1225-1274).

Doctor Christianissimus ● "The Most Christian Doctor," a name given to the French spiritual writer Jean Gerson (1363-1429).

Doctor Communis ● "The Common Doctor," a title given to St. Thomas Aquinas (1224- or 1225-1274) to denote his universality and timelessness to all who study the teachings of the Church.

Doctor Ecstaticus ● "The Ecstatic Doctor," the title given to Jan van Ruysbrock (1293-1381), the Flemish mystic. It was also bestowed upon Denys the Carthusian (1402-1471).

Doctor Gratiae ● "The Doctor of Grace," a name given to St. Augustine of Hippo (354-430) to honor his profound teachings on the theology of grace.

Doctor Invincibilis ● "The Invincible Doctor," the title granted to William of Occam (c. 1285-1347), the English philosopher and theologian. He is also called *Doctor Singularis*.

Doctor Irrefragibilis ● "The Irrefutable Doctor," the name given to Alexander of Hales (c. 1186-1245).

Doctor Marianus ● "The Marian Doctor," the title conferred upon St. Anselm of Canterbury (1033-1109) as the result of his writings on the important role and privileges of the Blessed Virgin, particularly *Cur Deus Homo?* and *De Conceptu Virginali*. St. Anselm is also called the Father of Scholasticism. The title *Doctor Marianus* is also used for John Duns Scotus.

Doctor Mellifluus ● "The Honeysweet Doctor," the title given to St. Bernard of Clairvaux (1090-1153), considered the last Father of the Church.

Doctor Mirabilis ● "The Amazing Doctor," the title bestowed upon Roger Bacon (c. 1214-1293) in recognition of his works in science and partly because of the reputation he acquired for "amazing" deeds such as alchemy and sorcery.

Doctor Profundus ● "The Profound Doctor," the title granted to Thomas Bradwardine (c. 1290-1349), the archbishop of Canterbury and a respected figure in theology and mathematics. It was also used for Jacobus de Esculo.

Doctor Seraphicus ● "The Seraphic Doctor," a title given to St. Bonaventure (1231-1274) in recognition of his many spiritual and theological writings. It is derived from the tradition that St. Francis had received his stigmata during a vision of a crucified Christ being borne aloft by Seraphim. In the Franciscan order, Bonaventure is called the Seraphic Father. He is also called *Doctor Devotus* (the Devoted Doctor).

Doctor Solidus ● "The Solid Doctor," a name used for Richard of Middleton (b. c. 1249), the Franciscan theologian and philosopher.

Doctor Subtilus ● "The Subtle Doctor," a title given to John Duns Scotus (c. 1265-1308), the much respected Franciscan philosopher. He is also called *Doctor Marianus.*

Doctor Universalis ● "The Universal Doctor," the high honorific title granted to St. Albert the Great (Albertus Magnus, 1206-1280) in recognition of his vast knowledge of theology and philosophy. He is

also known as *Doctor Venerabilis* (the Venerable Doctor) or *Doctor Expertus* (the Expert Doctor).

Doctors of the Church ● See TABLE 3.

Döllinger, Johannes (1799-1890) ● In full, Johannes Joseph Ignaz von Döllinger, Church historian, theologian, and one of the most famous opponents of the doctrine of infallibility. Born in Bamberg, Bavaria, he studied theology at the University of Würzburg and was ordained on April 22, 1822. From 1823-1826, he taught canon law at Aschaffenburg, near Frankfurt. In 1926, he was appointed a professor at Munich, retaining this post until 1873. He was also provost of the Royal Chapel and in 1848 served in the National Parliament of Frankfurt. While in the Parliament, he was against an agreement between the state and the Holy See to regulate Church affairs. Originally a supporter of Ultramontanism, his researches and association with various leading intellectuals drew him away from this position and toward a general favoring of independence for the Church in Germany and its theologians from Rome. This view would harden over succeeding years so that in 1854 he expressed regret over Pope Pius IX's decision to issue a definition of the Immaculate Conception, and in 1861 published two letters attacking the temporal power of the papacy and the mismanagement of the Papal States. Two years later, he participated in the Munich Conference defending Catholic liberalism and demanding greater freedom in the field of theology.

In response to the First Vatican Council (1869-1870), Döllinger (who was naturally not invited) gave vocal denunciation to both its doctrine of infallibility and its assault on liberalism. In anticipation of the council, he wrote, with others such as Johannes Friedrich (1836-1917), a series of pseudonymous articles called the Letters of Janus. Published in the *Allgemeine Zeitung* of

Augsburg in the early part of 1869, the articles decried the *Syllabus of Errors*, the Jesuits, and the Roman Curia. These were followed by the famous Letters of Quirinus, also published in the *Allgemeine Zeitung* and comprising sixty-nine letters assailing the majority party at the council. They were composed largely with information supplied by allies in attendance at Rome, including Lord Acton, and are, despite their virulent orientation against the proceedings, a major source on the events of the council.

Döllinger refused to accept the decision of the Council Fathers and was excommunicated in 1871 by the archbishop of Munich. Many of his adherents would join the Old Catholic Church with which Döllinger had sympathies, although he never actually became a member. In 1873, he was made president of the Bavarian Royal Academy of Sciences. He died unreconciled to the Church. The Letters of Quirinus and Döllinger's break with Rome overshadowed a brilliant mind and a large body of writings on Church history, including: *Reformation* (3 vols., 1845-1848); *Hippolytus und Callistus* (1853); *Christentum und Kirche* (1860); and *Die Papstfabeln des Mittelalters* (1863), a survey of fables about the medieval popes. He died in Munich on January 10, 1890.

Domesday Book ● Name given to the two-volume manuscript containing the important survey that was conducted throughout England in 1087 at the command of King William I the Conqueror. Known originally as the "description of England," it was later called Domesday, for from its directives there was no appeal. The book remains one of the most remarkable administrative feats in medieval history, for through its massive compilation Norman feudalism was imprinted on Saxon England, thereby allowing William and his successors to claim all of the country as theirs, granting territorial holdings with feudal titles to loyal barons who, in turn, provided political

St. Dominic

stability and taxes. Domesday is a valuable source of information concerning the state of the Church of England in the latter half of the eleventh century. By its accounting, Church lands were truly enormous: the possession represented some twenty-five percent of the assessed country in 1066 and twenty-six-and-a-half percent in 1086. The lands were rather unevenly distributed, however, with the bulk of the Church properties found in southern England.

Dominic, St. (c. 1170-1221) ● Founder of the Order of the Friars Preachers, the Dominicans, and one of the most important leaders of the medieval mendicant movement. Born at Calaruega, Old Castile, in Spain, Domingo de Guzman was the son of a noble family. After studying at Palencia, he entered around 1196 the Canons of Osma, in his native diocese. He became subprior in 1201 and was highly respected by the local bishops. In 1203, Bishop Diego was appointed to head a papal delegation to preach to the Albigensian heretics in southern France. He chose Dominic as his companion. By 1206, Dominic was actively preaching against Albigensianism, journeying among the heretics and meeting with them on their ground. He won over many converts through his austerity, sincerity, and goodness; with Bishop Diego he founded a house for women converts. The next year Bishop Diego died and a crisis erupted with the murder of Peter of Castelnau, the papal legate. The so-called Albigensian Crusade was soon launched at the command of Pope Innocent II, a campaign marked by its savagery and bloodshed. Dominic labored throughout to win over the Albigensians but with little success and at constant threat to his own life. A number of individuals joined him in his travels, and Dominic was greatly encouraged from 1214 when Simon de Montfort gave him use of the castle of Casseneuil. Dominic used the fortress near Toulouse as the headquarters for what he hoped would be a religious order devoted to the conversion of heretics. Local approval was given in 1215 by the bishop of Toulouse, but the papal response was for members to adopt a conventional monastic life. Dominic and the bishop went to Rome in 1216 where he presented the results of the *capitulum fundationis* (chapter foundation), which had been held earlier that year in Toulouse and at which the members had chosen the Augustinian Rule, with other regulations. Pope Honorius III gave his approbation and the *Ordo Praedicatorum* was born.

Dominic spent the rest of his life traveling, preaching, and promoting the spread of the order. Friars were sent throughout France, Italy, and Spain, and houses were established in Bologna and Paris; ultimately the friars would become attached to the universities with momentous consequences for the intellectual vitality of Europe and the Church. In 1220, he attended the first general chapter, held in Bologna. The next

year he set out to preach to the pagans of Hungary. He fell ill on the way, returned to Bologna, and died there on August 6, 1221. A great figure in the history of the Church, Dominic has long been somewhat overshadowed by his friend and giant contemporary St. Francis of Assisi. He made lasting contributions to the revitalization of the faith through his vision, innovative solutions to the needs of the time, and of course, through his foundation of the Order of Preachers, a religious body that would produce a host of theologians and philosophers, including Thomas Aquinas and Albertus Magnus. Pope Gregory IX canonized him in 1234. Feast day: August 8.

Dominican Order ● Properly the Order of the Friars Preacher (*Ordo Praedicatorum*, or O.P.), the mendicant order established in 1215 by St. Dominic; they have been called also the Black Friars in England and Jacobins in France (from their first house in Paris dedicated to St. James). The Dominicans were born out of the efforts of St. Dominic to convert the Albigensian heretics of southern France. Its first members were from all walks of life joining with Dominic to wander the countryside and preach to heretics in the hopes of winning them back to the faith at a time when authorities were massacring the Albigensians. After giving it an initial organization, Dominic received approval in 1215 from the local bishop for his fledgling community. Formal approval was won on December 22, 1216, from Pope Honorius III. The pontiff gave his blessing to the name *Ordo Praedicatorum* (Order of Friars Preacher) and its preaching mission in January 1217. That same year, at a chapter foundation (or *capitulum fundationis*) at Toulouse, the order took on the Augustinian Rule and other monastic guidelines. Dominic then wandered and sent members throughout France, Italy, and Spain with the aim of attracting new candidates and creating houses. An early house was begun at Paris, inaugurating the close association of the friars with the universities of Christendom. In 1220 and 1221, two general chapters were held at Bologna, drafting further measures for the order's government. Special emphasis was placed on corporate and individual poverty.

The Dominicans, while following many monastic rules of life and adhering to prayer and devotion to the liturgy, were remarkably innovative and did much to advance the bold new religious movement of the mendicants. They did not reside in monasteries away from the world but used preaching among all people; where other institutes often adhered to manual labor as their main temporal activity, the Dominicans placed primary importance on the intellect. They focused on education, affiliating themselves with universities and, after a period of struggle, secured for themselves an honored place in the schools of higher learning in the West. Dominican theologians would be renowned for their erudition and their fidelity to orthodoxy, earning the title *Domini Canes* (Watchdogs of the Lord) and being chosen by the Church to administer the early Inquisition.

Dominicans obtained two chairs in theology at the University of Paris. From this first house at Paris would follow new ones at Oxford, Montpellier, Cologne, and Bologna in 1248. In 1259, the order's own curriculum was completed, providing for the extensive education of members, from the priory schools to the superb general houses of study in Paris and elsewhere. By this time, there were over thirteen thousand friars, and the Dominicans would soon claim some of the greatest intellectual figures in the history of the entire Church: Sts. Albertus Magnus (d. 1280) and Thomas Aquinas (d. 1274). Throughout the 1200s, the friars not only were in the forefront of harmonizing Aristotle with Christianity, they, with the other important mendicant order, the Franciscans, won the right to exist equally in the Church and to have a meaningful role in its life. They faced opposition in the universities from secular professors and other religious and in many communities from the Churchmen who questioned their right to preach and perform such functions as hear confessions. This latter controversy would continue until the time of the Council of Trent (1545-1563). Meanwhile, the order, like the Franciscans, was sending forth missionaries to Africa, the Middle East, northern Europe, and the Far East.

From around 1290, a period of decline began as the order encountered difficulties from its rule of poverty. It was further troubled by the command of Pope Boniface VIII in 1303 restricting some of its privileges. An important impetus in the revival of its fortunes came in 1475 with the revocation by Pope Sixtus IV of its law of corporate poverty. A general renewal of discipline and studies occurred in the 1500s, with new houses of study being opened in Spain, Rome, and overseas, such as Santo Tomás in Manila. These new houses would help give even more vigor to Thomism under such gifted theologians as Cajetan (or Tommaso de Vio; 1469-1534), Dominic Soto (1494-1560), Dominic Báñez (1528-1604), and John of St. Thomas (1589-1644).

The order suffered terribly during the Reformation and the French Revolution, being singled out for attack because of its traditional excellence in learning and loyalty to the Holy See. A recovery was launched in the nineteenth century, most notably in France under Jean Baptiste Henri Lacordaire and in the United States. Today, there are some sixty-five hundred Dominicans worldwide. The second order, dating to the community of women religious begun in 1206 by St. Dominic at Prouille, France, also is found all over the world, involved in perpetual adoration, education, hospital work, and the perpetual rosary. The Dominican habit consists of a white robe with a leather belt from which hangs a rosary; they also have a scapular, a white mantle, a black cowl, and a black cappa, or cape. (See also **Catherine of Siena, St.; Inquisition; Neo-Scholasticism; Scholasticism; Thomism;** and **Universities**.)

Dominici, Giovanni, Bl. (1356-1420) ● Cardinal and statesman who participated in the negotiations that brought an end to the Great Schism. Born at Florence, he was a member of the Florentine House of Banchini, entering the Dominicans at Santa Maria Novella in 1572 but only after being cured of a speech impediment by St. Catherine of Siena. After studying at Paris, he taught for twelve years in Venice and then, with the blessing of the master general Bl. Raymond of Capua, he established convents for the Strict Observance in Venice (1391), Fiesole (1406), and a convent for nuns at Venice. An envoy of the order at the conclave that elected Pope Gregory XII in 1406 at Venice, he became the new pontiff's confessor and was appointed bishop of Ragusa and then cardinal in 1408. Dominici influenced Pope Gregory in his decision to resign as pope in the hopes of ending the Great Schism. Pope Martin V appointed him legate to Bohemia, but he had little success with the Hussites whose leader, Jan Hus, had been burned by the Council of Constance that Dominici had attended.

Dominus Ac Redemptor ● Brief issued reluctantly by Pope Clement XIV on July 21, 1773, ordering the suppression of the Society of Jesus. Promulgated under pressure from the Spanish ambassador, the decree placed the task of suppression in the hands of all local bishops. The liquidation of the Jesuits was thus irregularly implemented with severe repression in some areas and only slight measures in others.

Domitilla, Flavia, St. (d. c. 95) ● Granddaughter of Emperor Vespasian and niece of Emperor Domitian who became famous for her conversion to Christianity. In 95, she, her husband (Flavius Clemens), and a number of their friends were arrested and tried by Domitian on charges of impiety and favoring Christians and Christian and Jewish festivals. This is generally taken to mean they had converted to Christianity. To an ardent Roman such as Domitian this was unacceptable, particularly as Domitilla and her husband were both part of the imperial family. Clemens was executed and Domitilla was exiled to the tiny island of Pandateria; her two sons, designated heirs to the throne, had their names changed to Vespasian and Domitian. The Coemeterium Domitillae, on the Via Ardeatina outside Rome, became a place of Christian burial. It had been her property.

Domus ● Also Donus and Dommus. Pope from 676-678. The successor of Adeodatus II, he is best known for his efforts to rebuild and restore the churches of Rome and surrounding areas. He also defeated the attempt by Archbishop Maurus of Ravenna to make the see of Ravenna independent from Rome, the cause of a brief schism.

Donation of Constantine ● Name given to a forged document that had supposedly been issued by Constantine the Great to Pope Sylvester in the fourth century. It was said to have granted to the popes spiritual authority over all Christendom and temporal power over all of Rome and the Western Roman Empire. The document, now accepted as a fabrication, was probably written in the fifth century. Nevertheless, it was used throughout the Middle Ages to support the political position of the papacy, its usefulness being particularly broad because of its wide acceptance of its authority by both popes and their allies and enemies alike. The original purpose of the creation was most likely to strengthen the popes against the Byzantine Empire in Italy. Only in the 1400s was it considered a forgery, although scholars continued to debate it for many years.

Donation of Pepin ● Grant of territory in Italy, made by Pepin III the Short, founder of the Carolingian Dynasty and father of Charlemagne, in 756 to Pope Stephen II. Pepin's donation had its origins in the promise first made in 754 that he would donate territory in Italy to the pontiff in return for papal approval of the deposition of the last Merovingian king of the Franks and recognition of the Carolingian Dynasty. The actual grant itself was comprised of Rome and the surrounding territories that had been former holdings of the Byzantines in Italy. While such territories were dependent upon the Franks for protection, they helped lay the foundation for the Papal States.

Donatism ● Schismatic sect that originated in North Africa during the early fourth century; the Donatists derived their name from Donatus, the second schismatic bishop of Carthage. The members of the Donatist sect originated out of the rigorists within the African Christian community, who were vehemently opposed to the so-called traditors (or traitors), those Christians who had handed over the Scriptures to Roman officials during the terrible persecutions under Emperor Diocletian. Their focus became centered on Caecilian, bishop of Carthage, who was consecrated in 311 by Felix of Aptunga. The rigorists refused to accept Caecilian on the grounds that Felix had been a traditor, thereby making him no longer able to administer the sacraments validly. In support of this position, Numidian bishops consecrated Majorinus, thus setting him up as a rival bishop for the Carthaginian see. Majorinus was soon succeeded (in 313) by Donatus, who emerged as the leader of the movement. An appeal was made to Pope St. Melchiades in 313, but the commission looking into the matter found against the Donatists, whereupon they turned to the

Council of Arles (314) and then to Emperor Constantine the Great (316). Both appeals were unsuccessful, although the sect continued to grow. It found fertile ground among African Christians who resented the interference of the Roman Church in what they felt was an internal matter of the independent African Church.

Efforts to convince the Donatists to return to the Church on the part of Constantine were made from 316 to 321 but were abandoned in the face of rigorist recalcitrance. Many Donatists, however, turned to violence, forming roving bands of raiders known as Circumcelliones. The imperial government responded by launching an intervention in 347. The repression continued for some years, ceasing under Emperor Julian (r. 361-363). Within the Church, opposition to the Donatists was spearheaded by St. Augustine, who elucidated the important doctrinal truth concerning the sacraments: the true minister of the sacraments is Christ and thus the unworthiness of any other minister does not in any way affect the efficacy of a sacrament. Further repression began in 405, leading to a formal declaration against the schism in 411 at a conference at Carthage. The subsequent persecution weakened the movement, but it survived in North Africa until the extirpation of much of the Church in Africa by the Muslims in the eighth century.

Don Bosco ● See **John Bosco, St**.

Dorothy, St. ● Probably an early fourth-century virgin and martyr, also known as Dorothea. She was first mentioned in the *Hieronymian Martyrology* (mid-fifth century), where her name appears with Theophilus; in the later legendary *Acta Sanctorum*, she was said to have come from Caesarea in Cappadocia, but her name is not known on any calendars in the East. Her emblem is a basket of apples and roses. Feast day: February 6.

Douai ● Town in modern France, situated to the southwest of the Belgian border, that was the onetime site of several educational centers teaching English Roman Catholics during the reign of Queen Elizabeth I of England (r. 1558-1603). The most prominent of the colleges is the one established by William Allen (1532-1594). It was originally intended to train priests in anticipation of England's return to the Church. When, however, this proved increasingly unlikely, Douai was modified as a seminary to train priests for missionary work in Elizabethan England. All graduates were aware of the inherent dangers faced by missionaries to the isle, and many Douai priests were tortured and executed by the royal government. Members of the English College also produced the Douai-Reims Bible. The college was suppressed during the French Revolution, moving to England where it was reestablished at Crook Hall, near Ushaw, and at St. Edmund's Old Hall, Ware. (See **Douai-Reims Bible**.)

Douai-Reims Bible ● Also spelled Douay-Rheims. An English-version Bible produced by members of the English College at Douai for use among English Catholics. The name was derived from the fact that work was begun at Douai and completed at Reims; the NT was published at Reims in 1582 and the OT at Douai only in 1609. The principal work on translating from the Latin Vulgate was accomplished by several former Oxford students: William Allen, Gregory Martin, Richard Bristowe, and Thomas Worthington. The Bible was used for hundreds of years and influenced even the Authorized Version (or King James Version in the U.S.). Richard Challoner (1691-1781) was responsible for an important revision of the Douai-Reims Bible, on which most modern editions are based.

Drexel, Katherine, Bl. (1858-1955) ● Heiress and foundress who devoted her fortune to the care and education of Native Americans and blacks. Born in Philadelphia, she was the second daughter of Francis Drexel and Hanna Jane Langstroth. Her mother died shortly after Katherine's death and her father was subsequently remarried, to Emma Bouvier, who was well-known for her charitable works. Katherine and her sisters inherited a vast estate in 1885 after the deaths of both Emma (1883) and Francis (1885). They decided to use the money to assist Native Americans and blacks, requesting Pope Leo XIII (r. 1878-1903) to send missionaries to America. The pope responded by challenging Katherine to become a missionary herself. She accepted his call and, after studying with the Sisters of Mercy in Pittsburgh, Pennsylvania, she was professed in 1891 in the religious order she had founded, the Sisters of the Blessed Sacrament for Indians and Colored People. Under Katherine's leadership, the sisters established St. Catherine's School for Pueblo Indians (in Santa Fe, New Mexico, in 1894), followed by other schools and missions. In 1915, she and the order launched Xavier University in New Orleans, at the time the only such institution in the United States devoted to the education of African-Americans. She remained head of the order until 1937. Her cause was opened in 1964; Pope John Paul II beatified her in 1988. Feast day: March 3.

Droste zu Vischering, Clemens August von (1773-1845) ● Archbishop of Cologne who was imprisoned by the Prussian government. Born at Münster, Germany, to a noble Westphalian family, he studied at the University of Münster and included among his teachers the famed historian Johann Theodor Hermann Katerkamp. Ordained in 1798 by his brother, Caspar Maximilian, auxiliary bishop of Münster, Clemens was swiftly promoted, but after the fall of Napoleon in 1813 he was considered unacceptable to the extremist Prussians, withdrawing into seclusion where he studied and continued his works of charity. He remained out of public life even after consecration in 1827 as auxiliary bishop of Münster. To the surprise of most Catholic observers, the Prussian government expressed its desire in 1835 that Droste should succeed to the see of Cologne, a move interpreted as one of conciliating the Catholic noble families of Westphalia and parts of Prussia. His election by the cathedral chapter was confirmed in 1836 by Pope Gregory XVI (r. 1831-1846).

Droste soon came into conflict with the Prussian authorities, first by aggressively supporting the pope in the condemnation of Hermesianism (the teachings of Georg Hermes, a professor of theology at Münster) and then vociferously refusing to abide by Prussian laws concerning mixed marriages. Frederick Wilhelm III, the Prussian king, at the advice of Minister Christian Bunsen, ordered the arrest of the archbishop. This was carried out on November 20, 1837, and Droste was taken to the fortress of Minden. Instead of demoralizing the Catholic population, the arrest had exactly the opposite effect. Catholic Germans, long thought to be unenthusiastic at best, were polarized, their outrage further fueled by the vocal protests of German bishops and Pope Gregory. In an attempt to assuage public opinion, the government had published the *Darlegung* (*Statement*) in which it accused the archbishop of treason. A response was made by Joseph Görres in the well-known apology *Athanasius*. Admitting its mistake, the Prussian government released Droste on April 22, 1839. He was permitted to retain the title archbishop of Cologne, but his coadjutor ran the affairs of the see. In 1844, on a visit to Rome, he was offered the red hat but declined, returning to Münster where he died the next year on October 19. (See also **Germany**.)

Dubois, Jean-Antoine (1765-1848) ● French missionary in India. Born at St.-Remèze, he was ordained in 1792, sailing to India during the French Revolution as a member of the Missions Étrangères (Foreign Missions). He remained some thirty-two years in India, trying but failing to convert the natives. Finally giving up, he returned to France in 1823, convinced that the conversion of the Hindus was impossible, an opinion much attacked in England. Dubois became head of the Missions Étrangères, serving as supervisor from 1836-1839. Among his writings were the highly regarded *Description of the Character, Manners, and Customs of the People of India, and their Institutions, religious and civil* (1817), and the translation of the *Panchatantra* into French (1826).

Ducaeus, Fronto (1558-1624) ● French patristic scholar and Jesuit. He entered the Society of Jesus in 1577, serving as the librarian at the College of Clermont at Paris from 1604. His best known works were edited versions of the writings of St. John Chrysostom, St. Gregory of Nyssa, and St. Basil the Great.

Du Cange, Charles Du Fresne (1610-1685) ● French historian and philologist, one of the foremost scholars of his era. A native of Amiens, he was educated at the Jesuit College of Amiens, studying law at the University of Orléans. After a brief legal practice in Paris, he returned to Amiens and succeeded his father-in-law as the treasurer of France, serving from 1645-1668. He left Amiens in 1668 because of a plague and settled in Paris where he lived for his remaining years. A passion for languages, history, law, and geography allowed Dubois to amass vast amounts of information on all of these subjects and to author several important dictionaries on Medieval Latin and Greek: the *Glossarium ad Scriptores Mediae et Infimae Latinitatus* (1678; *Glossary for*

Writers of Middle and Low Latin) and *Glossarium ad Scriptores ad Mediae et Infimae Graecitatus* (1688; *Glossary for Writers of Middle and Low Greek*). He also wrote works on French and Byzantine history.

Duchesne, Louis (1843-1922) ● French Church historian who helped inspire the revival of Catholic learning in the late nineteenth and early twentieth centuries. Born at St.-Servan, he was ordained a priest in 1867, subsequently studying in Rome and Paris. Appointed professor at the Institut Catholique in 1877, he founded in 1881 the *Bulletin Critique de Literature, d'Histoire et de Theologie* (*Critical Bulletin of Literature, on History, and Theology*). He resigned his professorship temporarily in 1885 over criticism that had been made about his lectures on the history of doctrine. From 1885, he served as director of the French school at Rome (École Française de Rome), where he worked until his death. In 1910, he was elected to the Academie Française. Duchesne was an important figure in promoting the critical study of Church history, particularly in the fields of Christian archaeology and events in the early Church. He compiled an edition of the *Liber Pontificalis* (2 vols., 1886-1892), and authored *Origines du cult chrétien* (1889; *Origins of the Christian Cult*) and *L'Histoire ancienne de l'Eglise chrétienne* (3 vols., 1906-1910; placed on the Index of Forbidden Books in 1912).

Dunstan, St. (d. 988) ● Also St. Dunstan of Canterbury. Abbot of Glastonbury, archbishop of Canterbury, and an important figure in the revival of monasticism in England. Dunstan was born to a noble family near Glastonbury around 909, receiving an education at the monastery there before entering into the service of his uncle Athelm, archbishop of Canterbury. After securing a post at the court of King Athelstan, he made several enemies and was removed on false

charges of black magic. He fled to Aelfheah, bishop of Winchester, where he became a monk and then a hermit at Glastonbury. Around 939, however, he was suddenly recalled by King Edmund I. Overcoming more attacks by courtiers in 943, Dunstan was made abbot of Glastonbury, instituting and promoting the Benedictine Rule. He acted as a counselor and treasurer to Edmund's brother Edred but was expelled around 955 by Edwy the Fair. He traveled to the Continent and observed monasticism at the Abbey of Blandinium, returning to England in 957 at the behest of Edgar the Peaceful, who made him bishop of Worcester and then bishop of London. In 959, he was appointed archbishop of Canterbury. With Edgar, Dunstan labored to bring reform to the Church in England, using Benedictine monasticism as his model. His views on monastic life were compiled in the *Regularis Concordia*. His influence was considerable during the reign of Edgar, ensuring the succession of Edward the Martyr in 975. Dunstan retired to Canterbury to teach at the cathedral school. Feast day: May 19.

Dupanloup, Félix Antoine Philibert (1802-1878) ● Bishop of Orléans, promoter of Catholic education in France, and one of the Church's most liberal spokesmen at Vatican Council I. Dupanloup was born at St.-Felix and ordained in 1825. After ordination, he was appointed *vicaire* of the catechetical classes at the Church of the Madeleine in Paris, being transferred to St.-Roch in 1834. During this period, Dupanloup became one of the foremost educators in France, especially through his foundation of the educational system called the "Catechism of St. Sulpice." From 1837-1843, he was director of the junior seminary of St.-Nicholas-du-Chardonnet, attracting numerous students. Consecrated bishop of Orléans in 1849, he fought for the instructional freedom of the Church in France and was a major architect of the *Loi*

Falloux (1850; *Falloux Law*), which granted legal status to the independent secondary schools. As a liberal, Dupanloup helped establish the liberal Catholic journal *Le Correspondent*, called Pope Pius IX's *Syllabus of Errors* (1864) thesis and hypothesis, and advised the minority at Vatican Council I to abstain from voting and to withdraw from assembly; when, however, the council was concluded, he accepted its decrees. He also authored *La Haute Éducation intellectuelle* (1850) and *La Femme studieuses* (1869).

Duperron, Jacques (1565-1618) ●
French cardinal most remembered for his participation in the conversion of King Henry IV of France. A native of Bern, he was the son of a Huguenot refugee and was raised a Protestant. Returning to France in 1576, he was soon drawn to the Church, was baptized, and received holy orders. A loyal servant of King Henry III, he nevertheless acquired a reputation as a gifted spokesman for the Catholic faith. After the succession of King Henry IV in 1589, Duperron gave instructions to the monarch in the Catholic doctrine, serving as bishop of Evreux from 1591. In 1594, he went to Rome as Henry's representative to Pope Clement VIII to secure the pontiff's formal absolution. Made a cardinal in 1609, he was a prominent figure in the reign of Marie de' Medici after Henry's death in 1610. He was much influenced by St. Robert Bellarmine.

Durandus of St.-Pourçain (c. 1270-1334)
● Scholastic philosopher, theologian, and an opponent of St. Thomas Aquinas. After entering the Dominicans and studying at Paris, he received his doctorate in 1311 and then lectured on the *Sentences* of Peter Lombard. Summoned to Avignon by Pope Clement V, he taught theology and was subsequently appointed bishop of Limoux (1317), Le Puy-en-Velay (1318), and Meaux (1326). He was an adherent of nominalism and thus entered into opposition with Thomas Aquinas, holding steadfastly to a sharp contrast between faith and reason, a view that contradicted completely the Angelic Doctor's beliefs. His views earned considerable criticism within the order and Durandus modified some of his passages, but after being appointed bishop he was free from Dominican jurisdiction. Among his many writings were a *Commentary on the Sentences* and *De Origine Potestatum et Jursidictionum* (1329; *On the Origins of Power and Jurisdiction*). He has been called *Doctor Modernus* and *Doctor Resolutissimus*.

Durandus of Troarn (d. 1088) ● Abbot of Troarn in Normandy, author of *Liber de Corpore et Sanguine Domini* (*Book on the Body and Blood of Christ*). In his work, he examined the Eucharist, disagreeing strenuously with Berengarius of Tours and his idea that the presence of Christ in the Eucharist was a figurative one. (See **Eucharist**.)

Durrow, Book of ● Earliest of the illuminated Gospel books, dated to the years 675-680 and drawing its title from the monastery of Durrow, Ireland. A magnificent example of the Hiberno-Saxon style, it was kept at Durrow until 1661 when it was moved to Trinity College Library, in Dublin. (See also **Manuscript Illumination**.)

Easter Controversy ● Also called the Paschal Controversy, a dispute that occurred several times in the history of the Church concerning the date of Easter. The earliest of the controversies occurred in the second century between the Christians of Rome and a minority group of Christians in Asia Minor who chose to adhere to Jewish custom on the accepted day of the Jewish Passover, meaning that their Easter fell on the fourteenth day of the month of Nisan, regardless of the day of the week rather than on Sunday, the day accepted by the Church. Known as a result as the Quartodecimans (or followers of Quartodecimanism), these Christians took the custom from their belief that it was taken from St. John. They were opposed by Rome, especially under Pope Victor I (r. 189-198), who excommunicated the Quartodeciman leader Polycrates, bishop of Ephesus. The Quartodecimans were never fully suppressed, ultimately departing the Church to form one of their own, surviving for several centuries.

A second disagreement was caused by divergent opinions on the use of calendars for the calculation of Easter, some favoring the traditional lunar calendar (namely the Antiochenes), others preferring the solar calendar (the Alexandrians). This argument was largely the result of the adoption by most of the Christian community of the solar-based Julian calendar of Rome, which was at variance with the Jewish calendar. The competing schemes were debated at both the Council of Arles (314) and the Council of Nicaea (325). At the latter, it was decided to adopt the observance of Easter on the first Sunday following the first full moon after the vernal equinox. There remained some discrepancy between the Alexandrian method of calculation and that of Rome, but by the fifth century this was slowly resolved in favor of the Alexandrian method, receiving formal adoption by the influential monk Dionysius Exiguus around 525.

Another controversy, arguably the most famous, took place in the British isles. There the members of the Celtic Church used the Celtic calendar for Easter. This was in sharp disagreement with the Roman calendar used by the Christian missionaries on the Continent who had come to Britain under St. Augustine of Canterbury in the late sixth century. The matter was finally settled at the Synod of Whitby (664) where the Roman custom prevailed. Despite the protests of the Irish monks and others who preferred the Celtic calendar, St. Theodore of Tarsus, archbishop of Canterbury, imposed the Roman custom on the entire English Church in 669.

Eastern Catholic Churches ● Those Christian Churches whose members follow the Eastern rite and are in communion with Rome. (Also simply Eastern Catholic Church and similar variants.) The Eastern Catholic Churches, like their Orthodox counterparts, trace their origins to the four great patriarchates in the East: Alexandria, Antioch, Jerusalem, and Constantinople. The fifth, and supreme, patriarchate was, of course, Rome, in the West. These so-called Mother Churches were the bases of the various rites to which the Eastern Christians belong: the Alexandrian, Antiochene, Armenian, Byzantine, and Chaldean. They differ from each other through their liturgies, traditions, histories, theology, hierarchy, and language. Eastern Catholic Churches are distinguished from the Orthodox Churches by their acceptance of the supreme pontiff; most, at one time, were not in communion with Rome. The jurisdictions of these Churches are as follows: Antiochene — Syrian, Malankar, and Maronite; Armenian; Chaldean (or Chaldaean) — Chaldean and Malabar (or Syro-Malabar); and Byzantine — Albanian, Belorussian, Bulgarian, Croatian, Greek, Hungarian, Italo-Albanian, Melkite, Romanian, Russian, Carpatho-Russian (or Ruthenian), Slovak, and Ukrainian. Also called the Galician-Ruthenian, the Ukrainian Catholic Church has recently experienced an explosion in membership in Ukraine owing to recently established freedom of worship, the high degree of respect Ukrainian Catholic clergy earned during the long years of Soviet oppression, and the widespread disaffection with the Orthodox Church owing to its ties to the discredited Communist regime. As in other parts of Eastern Europe, the newfound freedoms enjoyed by the Catholic Church have created friction with the Orthodox communities over such matters as property, jurisdiction, and the right to proselytize. These are part of ongoing negotiations between the Holy See and the Orthodox hierarchy.

Vatican Council II made special mention of the rich and important heritage and contributions of the Eastern Catholics, proclaiming their vital role in the life of the entire Church in the "Decree on Eastern Catholic Churches," *Orientalium Ecclesiarum.* (See the individual Rites; see also **Orthodox Eastern Churches** and **Schism, Eastern.**)

Ebbo (c. 775-851) ● Also Ebbo of Reims, archbishop of Reims and a missionary to Denmark. Ordained a priest at the Carolingian Court, Ebbo became a friend and counselor of Louis I the Pious, successor to Charlemagne. Louis made him the head of the imperial library at Aachen and archbishop of Reims in 816. As archbishop, Ebbo promoted monastic reform, undertook an ambitious building program of churches, and fostered continued development of manuscript production, work that helped produce the Ebbo Gospels (*Evangelarium*). In 822, Pope Paschal I appointed him apostolic delegate (or legate), giving him a mission to Denmark (822-823). Ebbo journeyed north and there met with some success in making converts and establishing a cloister in Holstein. Real progress, however, was made by Ebbo's representative to the Danes, St. Anskar. Ebbo later became deeply embroiled in the dynastic politics of the Carolingians, supporting the illegal deposition of Louis. Defeated, he fled to Rome and was eventually stripped of his ecclesiastical offices and defrocked by Pope Sergius II. Louis the German, however, made him archbishop of Hildesheim.

Ecclesiam Suam ● Encyclical, the title of which means "His Church," issued on August 6, 1964, by Pope Paul VI, the first of his pontificate. *Ecclesiam Suam* was published during the proceedings of the Second Vatican Council and was intended in no way to obstruct the work of the council. Rather, it was a firm declaration of Paul's hopes and desires for the ongoing process or renewal for the Church that had begun under his predecessor, Pope John XXIII. The encyclical was centered on three main points: the nature of the Church; the nature of reforms then being undertaken; and the role of the Church in the modern world. In the first concern, Paul emphasized the foundation of the Church and the mission for it that was intended by Christ. The Church, Paul wrote, should ever project an "ideal image of the Church just as Christ sees it, wills it, and loves it. . . ." In the second matter, he calls upon the bishops of the council to enact those reforms and then implement them that will correct the defects of the members of the Church and guide them to a greater ideal of perfection. Finally, he reminded the Church of its need to have a dialogue with the modern world. The Gospels must be presented in new ways so as to overcome the reality that the modern world has "come to the point of separating and detaching itself from the Christian foundation of its culture."

Eck, Johann (1486-1543) ● Also Johann Maier von Eck, a German theologian and ardent defender of the Church in the early years of the Reformation. Born at Eck (or Egg, Swabia), he served from 1510 as a professor of theology at Ingolstadt. A humanist, he was, for some years, on good terms with Luther; he soon split with Luther, however, when the controversy of indulgences began. Henceforth, he opposed Luther and the other reformers, debating Luther and his allies in a number of public debates — particularly the one held in Leipzig in 1519 with Martin Luther and Andreas Karlstadt. Eck was then influential in securing Luther's excommunication in 1520 by Pope Leo X in the bull *Exsurge Domine.* The same year he wrote *De primatu Petri adv. Ludderum Libri III* (published at Paris, in 1521; *On the Primacy of Peter against Luther*), a vigorous defense of papal authority. He then spent the remaining years of his life traveling through Europe organizing Catholic opposition to the Reformation. Eck also drafted an attack on the Augsburg Confession (1530) and published a German-dialect version of the Bible for Catholic use (1537).

Eckhart, Meister (c.1260-c.1328) ● Medieval German mystic and Dominican theologian, also called Eckehart. Born to a noble family at Hochheim, Thuringia, he entered the Dominicans at Cologne around 1280, completing his studies at Paris where he began lecturing around 1293. Named prior of the Dominicans at Erfurt in 1294, he was soon appointed head of the Dominican vicariate in Thuringia. He later served as provincial for Saxony in 1303 and vicar-general of Bohemia (1307). Highly respected as one of the order's greatest theologians and intellectuals, he was given the title *magister sacrae theologiae* (master of sacred theology) from which his name, Meister, was derived and twice received a professor's chair at Paris. His writings, however, particularly his speculative theology, made him the first Dominican to be accused of heresy. He was charged and tried before the archbishop of Cologne, dying while making an appeal to Pope John XXII (r. 1316-1334). The pontiff found against the late Eckhart, condemning twenty-eight sentences as dangerous or heretical. This censure hurt his reputation, causing considerable difficulties for subsequent theologians and writers in assessing his views and tendencies. Eckhart seems to have leaned toward a kind of pantheism, calling for personal prayer and *Gottesgeburt in der Seele* (or the *birth of God in the soul*), bringing with it the overcoming of temporal concerns and the reflecting of the divine light of God. He authored fifty-nine known sermons (he was a brilliant preacher) and numerous works in German: *Buch der göttlichen Trösting* (*Book of Divine Consolation*); *Von Aberscheidenheit* (*On Emptiness*); *Reden der Unterscheidung* (*Talks of Instruction*); and *Rechtfertigungschrift* (*Letter of Justification*), a defense of his own works. His Latin writings included a commentary on the *Sentences* of Peter Lombard and a compendium of theology, only a part of which is extant, the mostly complete *Opus expositionum.* Eckhart influenced such notable figures as Henry Suso, Johannes Tauler, Nicholas of Cusa, Jakob Böhme, Martin Luther, and Georg Hegel.

Ecumenical Councils ● See TABLE 4; see also **Councils**.

Ecumenism ● Modern movement described by Vatican Council II as "Promoting the restoration of unity among all Christians" (*Unitatis Redintegratio*, No. 1). The ecumenical movement has its furthest origins in the calls for unity in the Church dating to the era of the NT and was based on the fact of Christ's foundation of his Church and his intention that it remain one until the end of time (Jn 17:21, Mt 16:18). Nevertheless, from the early periods of Church history, individuals and groups chose to separate themselves from the body of the faithful (see **Heresy**). Christian cohesion was further broken by schism with the Eastern Church from 1054 and further strained by the Great Schism (1378-1417). By far the most severe blow was, of course, the Reformation, which brought the loss of whole parts of Europe to the Catholic faith. Since the onset of the Protestant Reformation, there have been efforts to restore Christian unity, but it has only been in the twentieth century that the movement has found its fullest and most successful expression.

The Protestant foundation of ecumenism dates to the Edinburgh World Missionary Conference (1910), which led to the International Missionary Council, the Universal Christian Conference on Life and Work (1925), and the World Conference on Faith and Order (1927). These efforts culminated with the final formation of the World Council of Churches in 1948.

The response of the Catholic Church to the ecumenical movement in its early stages was to strive ever for a restoration of Christian unity, but, as expressed by Pope Benedict XV (r. 1914-1922), the Church should not surrender its fundamental position as the universal Church of Christ, the instrument of his mission in the world. From the time of Pope Leo XIII (r.

1878-1903), however, many individuals, such as Cardinal Désiré Joseph Mercier and Abbé Paul Couturier, worked to promote ecumenism in the Church and, prior to Vatican Council II, certain encouragements were given by the Holy See; Pope John XXIII (1958-1963), for example, received Archbishop Geoffrey Fisher of Canterbury in 1960. The magna carta of Catholic ecumenism, however, came with Vatican II in a number of documents: *Unitatis Redintegratio* ("Decree on Ecumenism"), *Orientalium Ecclesiarum* ("Decree on Eastern Catholic Churches"), and *Lumen Gentium* ("Dogmatic Constitution on the Church"). The main principles of the movement are: recognition that Christ established the Church on the Apostles and their successors, whose head was Peter and his successor, the Bishop of Rome; divisions in the Church have existed since early times, but these "separated brethren" are Christians and thus possess to a varying degree the fullness of grace available to the Catholic Church; and Catholics should take part in and promote the ecumenical developments in fostering Christian unity.

Since the Second Vatican Council, the Church, under the leadership of Popes Paul VI and John Paul II, has been very heavily involved in ecumenism on a number of national and international levels. The chief forms of participation include the Pontifical Council for Promoting Christian Unity (begun in 1960 as a preparatory secretariat for the council and made a pontifical council in 1988) under Cardinal Edward Cassidy, and the U.S. Bishops' Committee for Ecumenical and Interreligious Affairs (initiated in 1964). The remarkable progress of the interfaith dialogues is attested by the high number of declarations, statements, and reports issued over the last few decades. Among the most notable are the Anglican-Roman Catholic International Commission, the International Theological Colloquium between Baptists and Catholics, the Evangelical-Roman Catholic

Dialogue on Mission, the Reformed-Roman Catholic Conversations, the International Catholic-Orthodox Theological Commission, and the Joint Lutheran-Roman Catholic Study Commission. In 1993, Pope John Paul II approved the new Directory for the Application of the Principles and Norms of Ecumenism.

Edmund of Abingdon, St. (d. 1240) ● Also Edmund Rich, archbishop of Canterbury and a gifted scholar and preacher. He was educated at Oxford and Paris, and later taught at both universities, acquiring a reputation for holiness and austerity. Made a canon of Salisbury Cathedral in 1222, he preached the Sixth Crusade in England in 1227. In 1233, he became archbishop of Canterbury. Edmund spent many years of his reign in sharp disagreement with King Henry III concerning the monarch's affairs in Sicily and his favoritism toward foreign advisers. Henry countered Edmund's political influence by securing from the pope a papal legate, Cardinal Otto, who helped to undercut the ecclesiastical supremacy of Canterbury. Edmund responded by leaving England for the Cistercian monastery of Pontigny. He died the same year. Renowned for his saintliness, he was canonized in 1247 by Pope Innocent IV. His devotional treatise *Speculum ecclesie* was highly influential in shaping subsequent devotional literature. Feast day: November 16.

Edmund Rich ● See **Edmund of Abingdon, St.**, preceding entry.

Edward the Martyr, St. (d. 978) ● King of England from 975-978. The son of King Edgar (r. 959-975) and brother of King Ethelred II the Unready, Edward was elected king in 975. Three years later, however, he was assassinated, perhaps as a result of the antimonastic movement, although William of Malmesbury wrote that he was killed near Corfe at the instigation of Elfrida, his stepmother. There has been some question as to Ethelred's complicity. He was buried in the Church of Wareham but was translated to Shaftesbury in 980. Miracles were soon reported, and Edward was considered a saint and martyr. He was much influenced by St. Dunstan. Feast day: March 18.

Egbert (d. 766) ● Also Ecgbert, archbishop of York, who brought reform to the English kingdom of Northumbria. Egbert was a member of the royal House of Northumbria. He was ordained a deacon at Rome and appointed bishop of York around 732. On the advice of the Venerable Bede, he asked and received the pallium from Pope Gregory III; the letter from Bede to him is extant. He was aided as archbishop from 738 by the accession to the Northumbrian throne of his brother, a political union that allowed him to introduce numerous reforms to the Northumbrian church. Egbert also established the renowned cathedral school of York, counting as one of his most famous pupils Alcuin. Among Egbert's writings were: *Dialogus Ecclesiasticae Institutionis*, a treatise on Church discipline; the *Pontificale*, providing details on the English liturgy; and *Excerptiones Egberti* (or *Excerptiones e dictis et canonibus SS. Patrum*), a compilation of canons.

Eger, Golden Bull of ● See under **Golden Bull**.

Egypt ● See under the following: **Coptic Church**; see also **Africa; Antony, St.; Arianism; Athanasius, St. <1>; Catechetical School of Alexandria; Clement of Alexandria, St.; Crusades; Dioscorus; Eastern Catholic Churches; Mark, St. <1>; Melchite Rite; Monophysitism; Nestorianism; Origen;** and **Patriarch**.

Eight Saints, War of the ● Conflict fought from 1375-1378 between Pope Gregory XI and a Florentine coalition. It was caused by the opposition of the city leadership of Florence to the political authority being wielded by the papal legates in Italy, who represented the papacy in its Italian temporal affairs while the pontiff remained in Avignon. Gregory sent Cardinal Robert of Geneva to Italy and excommunicated the Florentines. The war was concluded by the Treaty of Tivoli (1378), but the mounting political instability in Italy and the dangers to Rome contributed to Gregory's decision to move the papacy from Avignon, thereby ending seventy years of papal residence in France. The name Eight Saints was derived from the council of war in Florentine, the Eight of War (*Otto della Guerra*), euphemistically called the saints.

Einhard (c. 770-840) ● Also Eginhard, a famous Frankish scholar, the author of the important work on Charlemagne, the *Vita Caroli Magni*. Einhard was probably a native of Franconia and was educated at the monastery of Fulda. Around 791, he was appointed to the royal court of Aachen, largely through the recommendation of the abbot of Fulda. He soon became an adviser to Charlemagne and was employed by him as a teacher, architect, and poet, acquiring a reputation for his learning. As an architect, he helped design the basilica and palace of Aachen. After the death of Charlemagne in 814, he remained a major figure in the Carolingian government, particularly helping Louis the Pious. In recognition of Einhard's help in securing the Carolingian throne, Louis gave him several abbeys and, later, a land grant at Mühlheim. Einhard retired to Mühlheim in 830 with his wife, Imma; he died there as a monk. Aside

from several Latin religious works, he is best remembered for the *Vita Caroli Magni* (830-833), a biography much influenced by classical historians such as Livy, Suetonius, and Tacitus. Despite its errors, the work remains a useful source on Charlemagne and the early Carolingian period.

Einsiedeln ● Also spelled Einsedeln, a Benedictine abbey located in central Switzerland, first established in 934. According to tradition, Einsiedeln was built on the site of Meinrad's cell, the place of residence of the hermit Meinrad, who had been murdered in 861. The monastery was favored by the Ottonian kings of Germany, receiving the rank of principality in the Holy Roman Empire in 1274; it was later granted protection by the Counts of Rapperswil and then the Laufenberg Habsburgs. In 1350, it was declared a national sanctuary of the Swiss Confederation and in 1386 it was officially transferred to the Swiss Canton of Schwyz. The abbey was a noted pilgrim center because of the presence of the "Black Madonna," a statue of the Virgin Mary that had been brought there by Meinrad, so-called because of its discoloration from smoke. The present abbey at Einsiedeln has a library that houses a large collection of manuscripts. It has long enjoyed a reputation for promoting learning.

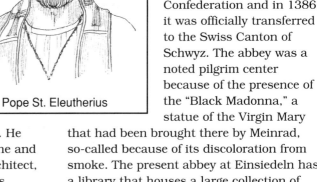

Pope St. Eleutherius

Election, Papal ● See **Conclave**.

Eleutherius, St. ● Pope from around 175-189. A native of Nicopolis, Greece, he was forced to spend much of his pontificate dealing with the heresy of Montanism. According to St. Hegesippus, Eleutherius was a deacon under Pope St. Anicetus (r. c. 154-c. 166). Elected to succeed Pope St. Soter, he was confronted immediately by the Montanists, receiving a (now lost) letter from the Christians around Lyons imploring him not to compromise but at the same time not to be unyieldingly harsh. He died on May 24, 189, and was buried on the Vatican Hill (in Latin, *Mons Vaticanus*), near St. Peter. Feast day: May 24.

Elias of Cortona (d. 1253) ● Twice vicar-general of the Franciscan order and a companion of St. Francis of Assisi. A native of Assisi, Elias became a respected member of the newly founded Franciscans, journeying to the Holy Land in 1217 where, in 1219, he was appointed provincial of Syria. He returned to Italy with Francis in 1220 and the following year was made vicar of the Franciscan order. This office he held until 1227 when John Parenti was named his successor. Five years later (1232), Elias was reelected, but his second term was marked by severe upheaval, as many members of the order took exception to Elias's dictatorial methods of rule and what appeared to be his grand and opulent lifestyle. As tensions increased, Pope Gregory IX took the step of deposing Elias as a means of restoring order and unity. Elias responded by joining Emperor Frederick II in his antipapal policy, for which Elias was expelled from the Franciscans and excommunicated. He returned to Cortona with a small group of friars, establishing a monastery in honor of St. Francis. Just before his death, he was reconciled with the papacy. Elias was also a guiding force behind the erection of the Basilica of Assisi. (See also **Franciscans**.)

Elipandus of Toledo ● See under **Adoptionism**.

Elizabeth I, Queen of England (1533-1603) ● Queen of England from 1558-1603. The daughter of King Henry VIII

(1509-1547) and Anne Boleyn, the princess Elizabeth was declared illegitimate as a result of her mother's execution in 1536 for adultery and treason. Despite the impediments caused by the invalidation of the royal marriage, she was declared by Parliament to be established in the succession in 1644 behind Edward (VI) and Mary Tudor. Her early years, while troubled, were marked by her receiving an excellent education at Hatfield House, with Edward. After Edward's accession, she was placed in the care of Henry's last wife, Catherine Parr; Elizabeth became involved during this period in the well-known affair involving Catherine's fourth husband, Lord Seymour. While raised outside of the Church, she conformed to Catholicism during the reign of Queen Mary (1553-1558) but was imprisoned on suspicion of involvement in a Protestant plot and as a symbol for discontented Protestants. She ultimately cleared herself, returned to court, and then lived largely in retirement at Hatfield until Mary's death.

Her reign, one of the longest in history, would witness truly momentous events. Upon coming to the throne, she was confronted by the serious question of chronic religious strife as well as the failure of England in its war with France and a large debt. In matters of religion, she adopted a pragmatic position, seeking to implement many Protestant measures to strengthen her position as head of the Church of England and to placate the troublesome Calvinists while retaining many Catholic elements in the liturgy and ecclesiastical organization, a recognition of the reality that the population was still Catholic in much of its outlook, as was the parish clergy. The members of the episcopate were also still unwilling to embrace her, as seen at her coronation (which numerous bishops would not attend), and by their refusal to take the Oath of Allegiance. Elizabeth hoped to instill some semblance of national religious unity through the appointment of Matthew Parker (1504-1575) as archbishop of Canterbury in 1559. Under his guidance were passed the Thirty-Nine Articles (1563) defining the doctrines of the Church of England and the Advertisements (1566), which ordered the use of the surplice in place of vestments and forbade the Sign of the Cross in baptism. Elizabeth herself struck out Article 29 ("Of the Wicked which eat not the Body of Christ") and added Article 20, which gave the crown authority over ceremonies and rites. She thus laid the foundation of the Church of England cautiously, plotting that the wholesale acceptance of the new religious system would come after long-term worship according to the new rites laid down by the state church. This entire enterprise came to be called the Elizabethan Settlement, the collective name given to the formulation of monarchical or state authority over the religion of the kingdom and its liturgy, creed, and hierarchy.

As England drifted toward a more Protestant religious outlook, relations with her English Catholic subjects deteriorated, ending her generally conciliatory attitude toward them. The first main cause was the Northern Rebellion (1569-1570) in which a group of Catholic nobles tried to force Elizabeth to name Mary, Queen of Scots, to be her heir and remove some of her councilors. Even more provocative was the decree of Pope St. Pius V (r. 1566-1572) by which she was proclaimed excommunicated and by which her subjects were released from their obedience to her. The result was the implementation of Article 29, the outlawing of the Catholic Mass, and the creation of a gradually harsher program of anti-Catholic legislation and oppression. Between 1571 and 1593, laws were passed against recusancy, and other activities were declared illegal; the attending of a Mass, for example, was made punishable by death. A cunning and well-organized spy network kept

Queen Elizabeth I

watch on known Catholics and hunted down priests, particularly Jesuits, who secretly entered the country. The concerns of Elizabeth and her ministers about Queen Mary of Scotland (her prisoner since 1568) led to the Scottish Queen's execution in 1587, as the war with Spain was imminent; Elizabeth was anxious to prevent Mary from becoming a rallying point for Catholics. The defeat of the Spanish Armada (1588) not only dealt a crippling blow to the Spanish Empire, but it gave Elizabethan England enormous prestige, catapulting the island to first place among the Protestant powers. She was succeeded by James VI of Scotland, Protestant son of Mary of Scotland who became James I of England. Elizabeth's reign, one of the most significant in the history of Europe, witnessed the irremediable separation of England from the Roman Catholic Church and launched a long and very difficult period for the Church in the isles. (See also **England**.)

Elizabeth of Hungary, St. (1207-1231) ● Also Elizabeth of Thuringia, the daughter of King Andrew II of Hungary, renowned for her spirituality and her charity. She was betrothed at the age of four to the eventual Louis IV of Thuringia, marrying him in 1221 upon his succession as landgrave of Thuringia. Always deeply concerned with the plight of the poor, she worked ceaselessly to provide them with bread and comfort, her labors confounding her husband because of the expense involved. When he protested, however, a basket of roses was miraculously transformed into a basket of bread. He ceased all complaints and thereafter assisted her charity, kept vigils with her, and held her hand during prayer. Louis died in 1227, and Elizabeth came under the control of her brother-in-law Henry Raspe; he exiled her on the complaint that he could not pay for her good deeds. Elizabeth fled to her uncle, the bishop of Eckbert. She became a member of the Third Order of St. Francis, settling at Marburg and coming under the influence of Conrad of Marburg (c. 1228). His harsh demands on her were found to be such that she was removed from his supervision of her ascetic life. She continued, however, to care for the poor of Marburg, funding the construction of a hospital there. Elizabeth is always portrayed with roses. She was canonized by Pope Gregory IX in 1235. Feast day: November 19.

Elizabethan Settlement ● See under **Elizabeth I, Queen of England**.

Elmo, St. ● See **Peter Gonzalez, St.**

Elne, Council of ● See **Peace of God**.

Elvira, Council of ● Earliest Church council in Spain for which records have survived. It was held around 306, attended by nineteen bishops, and headed by Bishop Hosius of Córdoba, who would preside over the Council of Nicaea (325). The council was convened toward the end of the Roman Empire's severe persecutions and was deeply concerned with discipline among the clergy and the faithful. It enacted some eighty-three canons, with penalties for apostasy; celibacy was confirmed for priests under penalty of excommunication (Canon 33), the earliest canonical enactment on clerical continence. Other canons included the empowerment of bishops to direct the duties of priests and deacons and to be the sole ministers of confirmation. Fourteen canons were retained by the Council of Nicaea. The date of the council has been much debated among scholars, with alternative dates given as 305, 309, 313, and 324.

Emanationism ● See **Gnosticism**.

Emblems of the Saints ● See TABLE 5.

Ems, Congress of ● Meeting held in August 1786 at Bad Ems, in Hesse-Nassau, near Cologne, by the representatives of the archbishops of Mainz, Cologne, Trier, and Salzburg. It sought to advance the tenets of Febronianism within the German Church — opposing the temporal authority of the papacy in Germany, reducing the pontiff to a purely spiritual figure. The congress issued the *Emser Punktation* (German for Draft Agreement of Ems) on August 25, 1786, which proposed to the German bishops that all papal bulls or official declarations should not be in force in Germany until accepted by the German episcopate, that all future appeals to the pope be curtailed or severely limited, and that the right of matrimonial dispensations be removed from the control of Rome and granted to the bishops. The archbishops soon encountered opposition to their declarations from Pope Pius VI (1775-1799) and from the German bishops who feared that the archbishops were scheming to seize vast powers in the German Church. On February 20, 1790, Archbishop Wenceslaus of Trier withdrew from the *Punktation*, partly from papal pressure but largely because he had serious misgivings and had been compelled to join the congress by his fellow prelates. The wars in Europe caused by the French Revolution soon rendered the *Punktation* meaningless.

Emser, Hieronymous (1478-1527) ●
Theologian, editor, and controversialist, best known for his long dispute with Martin Luther. Emser, born at Ulm, studied at Tübingen University and the University of Basel. He lectured at Erfurt on the classics in 1504 and in the same year became secretary to Duke George of Saxony. Ordained a priest in 1512, he at first supported the Reformers but did not seek wholesale doctrinal changes; rather, he hoped simply for a reformation of the clergy. The radical opinions of Martin Luther thus drove Emser to oppose the Reformers, culminating in a bitter controversy between the two that started in 1519; it would continue until Emser's death. In 1520-1521, Emser authored eight polemic works against Luther, and in 1527 published a counter-edition to Luther's December Bible (1522), essentially a revision of Luther's own translation. The German translation of the NT from the Vulgate by Emser proved immensely popular and went into more than one hundred editions over the succeeding centuries. Emser also worked to bring reform to Catholic Germany as a means of countering Luther's activities.

Encyclical ● Name given to an important papal document that may consider any broad topic or issue but which is normally concerned with the welfare of the Church. It is customarily addressed to bishops all over the world, although it may also be addressed to all the faithful. There are technically two kinds of encyclicals: the letter and the epistle. The letter is ranked as more formal and has a broader audience. The epistle is sent by the pope often to the bishops and faithful of a region, area, or specific country and may cover some pressing moral or doctrinal crisis, examine prevailing conditions, or commemorate a historical event. Encyclicals bear full authority regardless of whether they are letters or epistles. While an encyclical is not considered an infallible pronouncement by the supreme pontiff, it should always be remembered (as noted by Pope Pius XII in the 1950 encyclical *Humani generis*) that it does belong to the ordinary teaching authority of the Church, the magisterium, and therefore merits the respect and interior assent of all Catholics. Encyclicals have been one of the main methods of presenting papal teaching and thought since the 1700s and have contained some of the most important pronouncements in the modern history of the Church. The title is taken from the first words or opening expression of the document. For the list of the most important encyclicals since the time of Pope Pius IX (r. 1846-1878), please see TABLE 6.

Encyclopedists ● Also Encyclopaedists, the name given to the approximately sixty contributors to the famous *Encyclopédie ou Dictionnaire raisonné des sciences, des arts, et des métiers* (*The Encyclopedia or Explanatory Dictionary of the Sciences, Arts, and Occupations*), published between 1751 and 1780 in fifty-five volumes. Edited by Denis Diderot (d. 1784), the *Encyclopédie* was intended to be a compendium of all human knowledge and was the chief expression of those intellectuals of the Enlightenment who supported rationalism, Deism, and natural religion. It was thus opposed by most traditional institutions, particularly the monarchy and the Church and was the cause of censorship by French Jesuits and government officials and much controversy over its political and religious topics. Among the most notable of the Encyclopedists were Jean Jacques Rousseau, François Marie Arouet (better known as Voltaire), Jacques Necker, and Paul Heinrich Dietrich Holbach (also known as Paul Thiry, Baron d'Holbach). Their ideas, extremely radical in the 1700s, helped to form the intellectual base of the French Revolution and foreshadowed the secularization of European culture. Many articles in the *Encyclopédie* promoted anti-Catholicism in subtle and supposedly rational terms. The Encyclopedists opposed the pontificate of Pope Clement XIII (r. 1753-1764), denied the divinity of Christ and Church teaching on original sin, and promoted the scientific method and the individuality of a person's relationship to God.

England ● Britain (known to the Romans as Britannia) was the object of Rome's attention from the time of the ultimately unsuccessful invasion by Julius Caesar (d. 44 B.C.). It was finally conquered by the legions in the first century A.D. under Emperor Claudius (r. 41-54), and the Roman presence would remain until the fifth century. During that long and important period of Roman occupation, Christianity came to the island, although the specific dates of its arrival and first development are generally lost to history. It is known that by the third century there was a Christian community in the colony, and a well-organized British Church can be

King St. Edward the Confessor

deduced by the attendance of British bishops at the Council of Arles (314).

In the early fifth century (c. 410), Roman rule was brought to an end by the massive invasion of the isles by the Jutes, Saxons, and Angles. The effect of this on the British Church was to drive the Christians away from the eastern coast to the western regions. This effectively isolated the Church of the Celtic-Roman population from the rest of the Church on the Continent. The barbarian invaders, meanwhile, settled throughout much of Britain and established various kingdoms. Christianity slowly began to penetrate among the mostly pagan warriors through the work of missionaries from Celtic Ireland, Scotland, and the Continent; chief among the latter missionaries was St. Augustine of Canterbury, who in 597 was sent to the tribes by Pope St. Gregory I the Great (r. 590-604). The evangelization was remarkably successful throughout the seventh century, but the members of the Celtic Church refused to associate with the recent converts among the Germanic or Teutonic communities. An increasingly sharp separation thus developed between the Celtic Church, which adhered to the early customs of the first Christians in Britain, and the Church founded in close cooperation with Rome, which followed the Roman customs in liturgical matters, such as the date of Easter.

A resolution of this situation was finally found in 664 at the Synod of Whitby. There

King Oswiu (Oswy) of Northumbria made the decision to adopt Roman customs in the matter of the date of Easter, signaling the effective end of the division of the Church; the Celtic Church would continue to have its supporters, but henceforth the faith in the isles would have a Roman disposition. Heightened organization was laid down by Theodore of Tarsus (d. 690), who had been sent to England as archbishop of Canterbury. He unified the English Church, made conciliatory gestures to the Celtic remnant, and promoted Canterbury as both the heart of ecclesiastical authority and of learning.

The next years would witness the flowering of the faith, in large part because of the influential work of the Benedictines, called the Black Monks by the English, who founded monasteries and promoted education and many arts. This bright period of Anglo-Saxon culture would produce such scholars as the Venerable Bede (d. 735), author of the *Ecclesiastical History of the English People*, and great missionaries, including St. Boniface, who were so influential in converting the German tribes of northern Europe. This bright era began to darken in the eighth century with the first raids of the Norsemen. The cry heard in the monasteries, churches, and towns would be noted in the *Anglo-Saxon Chronicle*, which declared: "Never before has a terror such as this descended on the isle." The Danes brought wholesale carnage and destruction, offset by the temporary rebirth of Christian culture under King Alfred the Great (849-899). Lasting reforms were also carried out under St. Dunstan (d. 988), archbishop of Canterbury.

Anglo-Saxon culture was slowly supplanted by Norman influences, partly introduced by King Edward the Confessor (d. 1066), the last Saxon ruler of England. In the year of his death, arguably the most famous in the history of England, William the Conqueror sailed across the Channel and defeated his rival, Harold Godwinson, at the Battle of Hastings, thereby winning the English crown and implanting Norman rule over the land. The Norman conquest had momentous consequences for the English Church. As seen with the Domesday Book, Church possessions throughout England were considerable, and William recognized the essentiality of forging religious, social, and political unity with the close cooperation of ecclesiastical authorities. Extensive reorganization of the Church was thus undertaken by Lanfranc, archbishop of Canterbury (d. 1089), who became archbishop in 1070 and was assisted by numerous bishops and abbots, most of whom were Norman. New dioceses were created, ambitious programs of church construction were launched, and the influence and rights of the pope extended.

Owing to the efforts of local Church leaders and the broader policies of the papacy to reduce the temporal control over Church affairs, relations gradually deteriorated with the English crown. Chief among the topics was the Investiture Controversy, which would embroil St. Anselm of Canterbury (d. 1109) and Kings William II and Henry I. The long and bitter struggle between St. Thomas Becket and King Henry II, culminating with Becket's murder in 1170 in Canterbury Cathedral, epitomized the degrees of difference between Church and State. A resolution was found in part in 1215 with the Magna Carta signed by King John, guaranteeing assorted feudal rights and confirming the freedom to be enjoyed by the Church in its appointments.

The 1200s saw the widening of papal influence in English ecclesiastical government, the result of the decline of royal strength, the intense piety of King Henry III (r. 1216-1272), and the adoption of the reforms launched by Pope Innocent III (r. 1198-1216) and the Fourth Lateran Council (1215). A royal recovery began with the accession of the formidable King Edward I

(1272-1307). To help finance his continuous programs, especially his wars, Edward summoned the Model Parliament, an assembly with long-term historical implications and the foundation of the principle of "no taxation without representation." Taxation soon became a vexing problem between the crown and the English Church.

Concurrent with these events was the important role played in English society by the monastic and then mendicant orders. As seen, the Benedictines had contributed considerably to early medieval England; the work of the monks only continued through the Cistercians and the Augustinians. In the thirteenth century, they were joined by the new mendicant orders, the Franciscans (Greyfriars), Carmelites (Whitefriars), and particularly the Dominicans (Blackfriars). The English branches of the orders were to produce such significant figures as St. Simon Stock (d. 1265) for the Carmelites, and William of Occam, John Duns Scotus, and Roger Bacon for the Franciscans.

The decline of the papacy in the 1300s through the Avignon period (the so-called Babylonian Captivity, from 1309-1377) and then the Great Schism (1378-1417) brought with it a rise in popular resentment against the pope among the English and a gradual disposition toward independence by the English bishops. Antipapal feeling was fueled by the taxes imposed by the papacy on the Church in England, the appointment of foreign prelates, and the frequent diversion of revenues to purposes other than the perceived good of the Church in general. An even more devastating blow to religious sentiment in the broadest sense was the Black Death, the devastating plague that reached England in the mid-fourteenth century, wiping out nearly a third of the population and leaving entire parishes depopulated and without any clerical or religious presence at all. Not surprisingly, the nationalist sentiment engendered by the Hundred Years' War (1337-1453) fostered antipapal legislation aimed at curbing papal influence, namely the Statute of Provisors and the Statute of Praemunire, both having their start in the mid-fourteenth century.

Crises continued to beset the Church in the fifteenth century, such as the dynastic conflagration known as the War of the Roses (1455-1485) in which the two great Houses of Lancaster and York vied for the throne. As many bishops and abbots had ties to both families or owed their benefices to one or the other, the hierarchy of the English Church was forced to vacillate between the combatants. Other complaints expressed by the common people and members of the universities were centered on the great wealth and corruption of the bishops. Unrest was exacerbated by the heresies of the era, the most widespread of which was launched by John Wycliffe (d. 1382) whose supporters were called Lollards. Persecuted by Church and civil authorities, the Lollards nevertheless endured until the 1500s and provided much encouragement to the Hussites in Bohemia and to advocates of radical reform in England. Beyond all these developments was the widespread discontent concerning the Church that simmered among the intellectuals and humanists of England.

Such was the sociopolitical situation in the isle when, in 1485, the Tudors under King Henry VII (r. 1485-1509) ended the dynastic wars and took the throne. Under the Tudors, a policy of centralism and absolutism was pursued; their efforts against the papacy, building on the mounting social and intellectual foment, found a warm reception. King Henry VIII (r. 1509-1547) was not at first desirous of abolishing papal rights in England, receiving, in fact, the title Defender of the Faith from Pope Leo X for his writings against Martin Luther. There was, however, growing alarm on the part of the king that an heir had not been produced through his marriage with Catherine Aragon. The momentous event, then, that sparked the separation of England from the Church was Henry's unsuccessful effort to secure a divorce, the papacy refusing to assent to his wishes. Having long prepared the episcopate and other ruling elements in England, Henry took the step of breaking with Rome, using Parliament to make the separation legal. The Church in England was placed under royal control, the king receiving the title "head of the Church of England" through the Act of Supremacy (1534). The clergy were compelled to repudiate their obedience to the pope, a measure acceptable to most of the antipapal clergy but resisted by others, the most famous being St. John Fisher, bishop of Rochester. The other famed martyr of the reign of Henry was St. Thomas More, onetime chancellor of England who, like Fisher, was beheaded in 1535.

It was not Henry's intention to preside over the transformation of the English Church to Protestantism. He would not permit wholesale doctrinal change, even though Lutheran ideas found their way into the country and Henry presided over the complete dissolution of the monasteries and the cruel destruction of shrines. The reign of his successor, Edward VI (r. 1547-1553), brought with it the steady advance of Protestantism as Catholic teachings were gradually replaced by Protestant practices. A major event of the period was the introduction of the Book of Common Prayer in 1549 and 1552, crafted by Archbishop Thomas Cranmer.

Catholicism was briefly restored upon the accession of Mary Tudor after Edward's death in 1553. Mary (r. 1553-1558) brought a reunion with Rome, but she lost favor with the English people and outraged the establishment with her severe persecution of Protestants (including the execution by the stake of Cranmer in 1556) and her marriage to King Philip II of Spain. At her death the crown came to Elizabeth I. One of the foremost monarchs in the history of England, Elizabeth (r. 1558-1603) ended relations with the Holy See and implemented the so-called Elizabethan Settlement by which she strove to create a national church with the help of

Bayeux Tapestry

Matthew Parker (1504-1575), archbishop of Canterbury. She was opposed in this by the Puritans and by the Catholics. Both groups would be persecuted, following the formal excommunication of Elizabeth that was proclaimed by Pope St. Pius V (r. 1566-1572) in the bull *Regnans in excelsis*. As the pontiff had declared Elizabeth deposed, Catholics were abused as traitors and laws were passed to force all citizens to attend the services of the C of E; those who refused were charged with recusancy and were subject to imprisonment and death.

The Catholic community in England declined as many fled to the Continent. Some remained, despite the oppression, aided by courageous missionaries, particularly Jesuits, who entered the islands in secret and were ruthlessly hunted by royal spies and secret police. The advocating of Elizabeth's death by some in the Catholic groups caused a rift that was resolved by the Appellant Controversy. Catholics became even more unpopular after 1588 with the defeat of the Spanish Armada whose arrival members of the Catholic Church had anticipated with glee. (See also **Allen, William** and **Douai**.)

Upon the death of the heirless Elizabeth in 1603, the throne came to King James VI of Scotland, the Protestant son of Mary, Queen of Scots. He reigned as James I of England from 1603-1623. Despite the eruption of anti-Catholic and antipapal fervor as a result of the ill-fated and highly dubious attempt by Catholic conspirators (including the well-known Guy Fawkes) to blow up Parliament and the king and to replace them with a Catholic regime, Catholic repression was generally eased, as the laws were not as vigorously enforced. Many Catholic nobles paid assorted fines for the practice of their religion, but Catholics elsewhere were handicapped by laws and the shortage of priests and proper Church organization.

Under James and then his successor Charles I (1625-1649), the country was much troubled by political upheaval as Parliament resisted the absolutist tendencies of the kings and the Puritans pushed for a wider Protestant outlook in religious life. The final result of these squabbles was the Civil War that began in 1642 and ended finally in 1649 with the beheading of King Charles and the institution of the Commonwealth or Protectorate. The chief figure of the era was Oliver Cromwell, who favored a general toleration of religion in the country but brought savage oppression of the Church in Ireland. Cromwell died in 1658 and the

English, tired of Puritanism, restored the monarchy. King Charles II (r. 1660-1685), son of Charles I, restored the C of E as the religion of state. He did marry a Catholic and was a convert to Catholicism on his deathbed. This was not a signal of favor toward Catholics, since acts of conformity were passed against Catholics and Puritans and the Test Act (1673) placed prohibitions against Catholics holding any public office.

Charles was followed by his brother, James II (r. 1685-1688). A Catholic, he proclaimed toleration for Catholics and ended the restrictions on Catholics holding public positions. As James fathered a son (meaning a Catholic heir to the throne) and as fears of popery spread among the social classes, calls mounted for the king to be overthrown. The Glorious Revolution by which James was removed and replaced by Protestant William and Mary occurred in 1688.

Having aborted the return of England to Catholicism, the new regime installed regulations against Catholics: crushing land taxes were imposed, they were not permitted to sit on the throne, and all government officials were to deny the jurisdiction of the popes and the doctrine of transubstantiation. The Catholic community was hard hit as ecclesiastical organization was upset and many upper-class Catholics gave up their faith to avoid financial ruin. The period from the Glorious Revolution until the Catholic Emancipation of 1829 has been known as the Penal Period.

The 1700s brought an easing of intolerance, largely the result of other events in the country, such as economic expansion and the Enlightenment, rather than any conscious effort at religious liberality. Further progress was made as a result of the need for more troops against the American Revolution. King George III issued the Catholic Emancipation Act of 1778, followed by another one in 1791 that permitted the Mass. The process of reform was hastened by the French Revolution, which produced a wave of refugees from Frances and the relations between England and the Holy See during the Napoleonic Wars. Finally, in 1829, thanks to the leadership of the duke of Wellington, the long-standing restrictions were lifted and Catholics were able to take their rightful place in the life of the country.

The 1800s marked the rebirth of English Catholicism, with extensive conversions, the most renowned coming from within the Oxford movement — John Henry Newman, later a cardinal. By 1850, Pope Pius IX (r. 1846-1878) determined that the time had come to reestablish the hierarchy in England and Wales. He appointed Nicholas Wiseman the first archbishop of Westminster. Anti-Catholic outbursts accompanied his arrival, but Catholic life continued to flourish. Under Herbert Vaughan, archbishop of Westminster (1892-1903), the Catholic schools were promoted and Catholics were granted permission to enroll in Oxford and Cambridge. Formal diplomatic relations were established between England and the Holy See in 1916. While currently less than ten percent of the English population, the Catholic Church in England has recognized the promise of the next years, as Anglicans have been returning to the faith owing to the splintering of the C of E over the ordination of women and the decline of attendance in the churches of England. Among the recent converts have been Anglican priests and bishops and the duchess of Kent. (See also **Ireland, Scotland**, and **Wales**.)

English Martyrs ● Large body of some six hundred martyrs in England and Wales who gave their lives as a result of their refusal to deny the Catholic faith during the years of the English Reformation and beyond (1534-1685), specifically during the reigns of Henry VIII (r. 1509-1547), Elizabeth I (r. 1558-1603), James I (r. 1603-1625), Charles I (r. 1625-1649), and Charles II (r. 1660-1685). Generally they were executed (hanged, drawn, and quartered) for treason or died in prison (especially the Tower of London); their principal crime was refusing to accept the enactments of the English Reformation, particularly that the monarch was head of the Church and the suppression of the Catholic Mass. The first recognition of the martyrs came in 1583 by Pope Gregory XIII when he gave permission for paintings depicting some of the martyrs to be placed on the wall of the church in the English College in Rome. Since that time, there have been several canonizations (St. Thomas More and St. John Fisher by Pope Pius XI in 1935), numerous beatifications (in groups by Pope Leo XIII in 1886 and 1895, Pope Pius XI in 1929, and Pope John Paul II in 1987); the remainder are venerable, or *dilati*, persons whose causes have been delayed seeking verification of their martyrdom. The feast for the English martyrs is celebrated on May 4. (See also **Forty Martyrs**.)

Enlightenment ● Also called the Age of Reason, the name given to the eighteenth century in Europe during which there were major trends of thought in humanism, science, rationalism, and philosophy that were at major variance with Christian ideals and important Catholic doctrines. Known originally in the German as the *Aufklarung*, the Enlightenment had its origins in the scientific revolution and advances of the seventeenth century and in the theories of Isaac Newton (1642), René Descartes (1596-1650), John Locke (1632-1704), and Thomas Hobbes (1588-1679). The proponents of the Enlightenment held that the most reliable basis of knowledge was that which was obtained through observation, experiment, and reason; they held in suspicion the traditions of the Church, considering the long-held teaching that faith and authority should be used for the reaching of truth to be anachronistic and inhibiting to intellectual freedom and the unrestricted application of human reason. While the movement fostered the development of a variety of scientists and philosophers (Voltaire, Rousseau, Adam Smith, David Hume, and Charles Louis Joseph de Secondat, Baron de la Bride et Montesquieu), they were united by a firm commitment to reason and social improvement. Many advocates of the Enlightenment were ardent enemies of the Church. Through rationalism they rejected faith in favor of reason; in religious freedom, especially as expressed by Diderot, the Encyclopedist, they condemned the Church for forcing the faith upon people; and in Deism they questioned whether revealed religion was in fact even feasible.

At the heart of the Age of Reason was the desire to apply to the entire sphere of intellectual life the same exactness that was then being used in the natural sciences where, thanks to scientific experimentation and observation, certain natural laws were discerned. Once the same process of scientific inquiry was adopted for the examination of religion, ethics, and natural law, it became inevitable that the process would lead to secularism and the declaration that revelation could be doubted because of its lack of observable or verifiable characteristics. Once reason became transcendent in the question of religion, doubt replaced faith and atheism or Deism displaced revelation and the profound teaching of the Church. Many modern Church scholars look to the Enlightenment as one of the most significant contributing factors to the crises faced by Christian culture in the nineteenth and twentieth centuries.

Ennodius, St. (473-521) ● In full, Magnus Felix Ennodius, poet, rhetorician, and bishop of Pavia. Ennodius was born at Arles to a noble Roman family (the Anicii) and was probably raised at Pavia. Ordained a deacon around 483 under St. Epiphanius, bishop of Pavia, he taught for a number of years, probably in Milan. He was made

bishop of Pavia in 513, serving twice as a representative of Pope Hormisdas to Constantinople in an ultimately unsuccessful effort to reconcile the differences between the Eastern and Western Churches. Ennodius was also considered a friend to Theodoric, king of the Ostrogoths. A gifted writer, he was one of the last to combine Roman tradition with Christian belief and writings. While often lacking in style, he has preserved important details of the era. His works include a panegyric on Theodoric, poems, a collection of hymns, a biography of Epiphanius, and *Eucharisticon de vita sua*, an account of his personal religious experiences.

Eparch ● See GLOSSARY.

Ephesians, Epistle to the ● Letter written by St. Paul while he was a prisoner. It is considered one of his finest and contains so many similar phrases to the ones present in his Epistle to the Colossians that scholars believe it to have been written around the same time. Scholars also have postulated that the epistle was intended as a kind of encyclical or general circular letter for the entire Church rather than to a specific place or community. This theory is based on the fact that there is no reference to Ephesus (in 1:1) and Paul gives no specific greeting or salutation. Reference is made by the heretic Marcion (d. c. 160) to this letter under the name "to the Laodiceans," and it is only from the time of St. Irenaeus in the late second century that the earliest manuscript calling it "to the Ephesians" dates. Therefore, it is speculated that copies were sent to various cities; when Paul's writings were collected, the one from Ephesus was chosen; this may have been because Ephesus was the capital of the Roman province of Asia, a part of the region to which the communication was universally addressed.

In his epistle, Paul is chiefly motivated by a desire to remind his fellow Christians of the divine plan of salvation that was ordained by God "even as he chose us in him before the foundation of the world. . ." (1:4). "For he has made known to us in all wisdom and insight the mystery of his will, according to his purpose which he set forth in Christ as a plan for the fullness of time, to unite all things in him, things in heaven and things on earth" (1:9-10). Broadly, Paul divides his message into two parts, a theological and doctrinal presentation of salvation (Chapters 1-3) and a practical series of exhortations on the leading of "a life worthy of the calling to which you have been called" (Chapters 4-6).

Ephesus, Council of ● Third ecumenical council, held at Ephesus in 431 with the aim of bringing an end to the crises caused by Nestorianism. The specific cause for the need of the council had been the power granted St. Cyril of Alexandria in August 430 by Pope St. Celestine I to excommunicate Nestorius, bishop of Constantinople, should he not recant his heretical position that there were two separate Persons in Christ, the divine and the human. Using his influence to prevent his immediate condemnation, Nestorius convinced Emperor Theodosius II to summon a general council. Organized with the full approval of the pope and under the presidency of Cyril, the council convened on June 22, 431, at Ephesus. In attendance were some two hundred bishops. Celestine was to be represented by two legates, Bishops Projectus and Arcadius, and the Roman priest Philip; but Cyril did not wait for their arrival before beginning the proceedings, nor did he delay for very long while awaiting the Syrian bishops under John, patriarch of Antioch, whom Cyril knew to be favorably disposed to Nestorius. Acting with the full authority as president and "as filling the place of the most holy blessed archbishop of the Roman Church, Celestine," Cyril maneuvered the majority of bishops into condemning Nestorius. The heresiarch was excommunicated and deposed, his

doctrines formally condemned, and the Nicene Creed upheld.

The Eastern bishops, who had arrived and were immediately at odds with the council, were soon joined by a number of prelates, such as Theodoret, bishop of Cyrrhus, also unhappy with Cyril's driving the deliberations to such a precipitate conclusion. The rival bishops haled their own council at which Cyril was excommunicated. Protracted negotiations followed, resulting in a compromise in 433 that brought a reconciliation between Cyril and John. Ephesus, however, had been a triumph for Orthodox Christianity. Through its seven sessions, Nestorianism had been clearly defeated in favor of Alexandrian theology, especially with the definition of the hypostatic union and the endorsement of the Marian title *Theotokos*, or Bearer of God.

Ephesus, Robber Council of ● See **Latrocinium**.

Ephraem, St. (d. 373) ● Also Ephraem Syrus or Ephraem the Syrian, a Syrian theologian, poet, biblical exegete, and Doctor of the Church. According to the fifth-century Byzantine historian Sozomen, Ephraem authored more than a thousand separate works. He was probably the son of a pagan priest at Nisibis, although many scholars reject these Syriac sources and prefer the theory that his parents were both Christian. Ordained a deacon at Nisibis by St. James of Nisibis, he most likely did not travel with him to the Council of Edessa in 325 but was credited with securing the deliverance of Nisibis from the Persians by prayer in 328. When the town was ceded to the Persians in 363, however, he journeyed to Edessa and there taught theology. He declined any advancement in the Church and supposedly prevented his being made bishop by feigning madness. Nevertheless, he was renowned for his saintliness, austerity, and his intellect.

Ephraem preferred to write in verse,

composing an enormous body of writings, including dogmatic, exegetical, and ascetical subjects. His biblical commentaries were on the OT books of Genesis and Exodus, and he annotated the Syriac-Greek version (second century) of the NT, the Diatessaron. Hymns ranged from the great feasts of the Church to refutations of the heresies of the times (especially Marcion and Bardesanes) to theology, such as faith, the superior nature of the virgin state, and the existence of the Church as a continuation of Christ on earth. His hymns were much respected by his contemporaries, although the style is quite difficult for modern readers. Ephraem promoted special devotion to the saints and particularly revered the Virgin Mary for her sinless state. A description he wrote of heaven and hell was an inspiration to Dante in the writing of the *Divine Comedy*, and his hymns influenced the development of both Syriac and Greek hymnography. Ranked traditionally as a great teacher in the Syrian Churches, his works were translated into Greek, Latin, and Armenian. Pope Benedict XV declared him a Doctor of the Church in 1920. Feast day: June 29.

Epistolae Obscurorum Virorum ● See under **Reuchlin, Johannes**.

Erasmus, Desiderius (c. 1466-1536) ● Dutch humanist and one of the greatest scholars of Europe in the first half of the 1500s. Born in the Low Countries, he was probably the illegitimate son of one Rogerius Gerardus. Educated at Gouda and then at Deventer under the Brethren of the Common Life, he entered the Augustinian Canons in 1486 and

Erasmus

was ordained in 1492. Studying at Paris from 1495, he began to develop a distaste for Scholasticism and was encouraged in this by John Colet when Erasmus visited England (1499-1500) for the first time. Colet also urged him to study the Bible. Returning to Paris, he undertook an exhaustive program of Greek. After another journey to England (1505-1506), he went to Italy for three years, going to England again in 1509 at the accession of King Henry VIII (r. 1509-1547). Here he became a friend and intellectual associate of Sts. Thomas More and John Fisher. He remained there until 1514, lecturing in Greek and theology. After serving as a councillor to the future Emperor Charles V (1516), he settled at Basel, subsequently declining numerous invitations from such august personages as King Henry of England and Francis I of France. Erasmus fled from Basel in 1535 to Freiburg after the arrival of the Reformation; he died at Basel, however, having gone there to oversee the printing of one of his books.

While a harsh critic and satirist of the Church and Scholasticism, Erasmus's peaceful nature would not allow his joining the Protestant cause, and he eventually came to look upon the Church as necessary for the maintenance of an ordered society. Such were his writings that both Protestants and Catholics ultimately condemned them. Pope Paul IV (r. 1555-1559), the hard leader of the Catholic Reformation, placed a prohibition on his works. This was eased slightly by the Council of Trent, but Sixtus V (r. 1585-1590) condemned all of his writings in 1590. His chief works were the extremely influential translations of the

Greek NT into Latin and versions of the Fathers of the Church, including St. Jerome (9 vols., 1516), St. Ambrose (1527), St. Augustine (1528-1529), and St. Basil (1532). He also wrote criticisms of the Church, such as its corruption and the state of monasticism, also penning a refutation of Luther's doctrine on free will, prompting Luther to respond with *De Servo Arbitio* (1525) to which Erasmus replied with *Hyperaspistes* (1526). His two famous satires were *The Praise of Folly* (1509) and *The Education of a Christian Prince* (1515).

Erastianism ● See under **Erastus**, following entry.

Erastus (1524-1583) ● Swiss theologian, originator of Erastianism, which came to denote a theory of the subordination of the Church to the State. Erastus was born Thomas Lieber (or Liebler), adopting a Latinized form of his name, Erastus, for his writings. A native of Baden, he studied at Basel, entering the university there in 1542. After surviving an outbreak of the plague, he went to Bologna to study philosophy and medicine, spending some time also at the University of Padua. In 1553, he was granted the post of court physician to the prince of Hennenberg, in Germany. Five years later, he was named court physician to the elector Palatine Otto (Otho) and received the chair of medicine in the University of Heidelberg. As his main interest, however, was in matters of theology, Erastus, an adherent of Huldrych Zwingli, worked against the Lutherans, authoring several defenses of Zwingli and numerous theological studies. Among his chief concerns was the process that he termed excommunication among the Protestants, actually the equivalent of interdict in Catholic law. He died at Basel on December 31, 1583; on his tomb was inscribed "an acute philosopher, a clever physician, and a sincere theologian."

Erastianism, as it is understood today or as it developed, was not the main preoccupation of Erastus's writings. He considered the issue of supremacy of the State over the Church to be secondary or subsidiary to other theological matters. He based his argument on the necessity of civil authorities in a state with only one religion to have jurisdiction in all affairs, both civil and ecclesiastical for the good of society and to maintain discipline and punish violations of law. His book, *Explicatio Gravissimae Quaestionis*, was published in English in 1659, although its main principles became popular in the years following his death, especially in Germany and England. Erastianism was naturally opposed by the Church and was rejected by the First Vatican Council (1869-1870) in the definition it issued on papal supremacy.

Escrivá de Balaguer y Allia, Josemaría ● See **Opus Dei**.

Eskil of Lund (1100-1181) ● Archbishop of Lund and a brilliant leader of the Church in Scandinavia, particularly in defending its rights against the Danish rulers and the archbishop of Hamburg-Bremen. The son of noble parents and related to several royal lines, Eskil entered the cathedral school of Hildesheim at the age of twelve. There he had a vision of the Virgin Mary. In 1134, he became bishop of Roskilde, succeeding his uncle Asser as archbishop of Lund upon the latter's death in 1139. Eskil proved successful in defending his see against the claims of the archbishop of Hamburg-Bremen, securing the rescinding of a papal bull of 1133 that had affirmed Hamburg-Bremen's superiority over the see of Lund. At the provincial synod at Lund in 1139, Cardinal Theodignus, papal legate of Pope Innocent II, gave the pallium to him. Eskil completed the new cathedral, which he consecrated in 1145, and introduced extensive reforms to the Scandinavian Church. With Absalon of Lund, he promulgated a code of canon law. He also promoted the work of French monks in the region and, following the model of St. Bernard of Clairvaux, called for a crusade against the Wends, the pagan tribes of the area. His efforts at establishing ecclesiastical independence brought him into conflict with King Waldemar I of Denmark. From 1159-1168, Eskil was in exile as the result of the king's support of Antipope Victor IV against Pope Alexander III. Eskil retired in 1177 after naming Absalon bishop of Roskilde as his successor. He spent his last days at Clairvaux.

Estates General ● Also States General. The French representative body before the Revolution that was comprised of three main estates, or social orders of the realm: the clergy, the nobility, and people. It was summoned generally to deal with matters of importance in the running of the state, most often to be asked by the king for taxes. After the fifteenth century it was to be called upon at the succession of a new king, to give advice, to assist in the regency, and to give approval to taxation. The Estates General originated in the reign of King Philip IV the Fair (r. 1285-1314), during his struggle with Pope Boniface VIII. Called in April 1302, the first meeting as well as the early sessions was essentially a gathering of the *curia regis*, the royal council. During the Hundred Years' War, however, when the kings were in dire need of money, the Estates General seized control of the taxes it was approving and, under the leadership of the populist leader Étienne Marcel, it insisted not only on the right to vote new taxes but also demanded a heightened place in the government and the removal of unpopular ministers. Marcel was assassinated and the attempt to institute a constitutional government was aborted. Thereafter the Estates General had a reduced place in the government, particularly after 1500 and because of the *taille* (or direct tax) levied by the king. The body was convened

only in times of crisis and at those times the members did gather, the deliberations were often hampered or wrecked entirely by the disagreements between the Estates General, most notably the nobility and the third estate. The last meeting was held in 1789 when King Louis XVI, desperate to prevent social, political, and financial disaster, agreed to call it. The third estate, however, soon formed the National Assembly on June 17, 1789, thereby launching the French Revolution.

Eternal City ● See **Rome**.

Ethelbert, St. (d. 616) ● King of Kent from 560-616, the first Anglo-Saxon ruler to be converted to Christianity. Said by the Venerable Bede to be the ruler of the region south of the Humber in England, Ethelbert (also Aethelbert) was probably influenced toward the faith by his wife, Bertha, daughter of Charibert, king of Paris. Ethelbert promoted Christianity throughout the kingdom, promulgated laws establishing a system of penalties for crime against the crown and the clergy (thereby laying the groundwork for royal patronage of the Church in Anglo-Saxon England), and welcomed St. Augustine of Canterbury in 597. Feast day: February 25.

Ethelbert of York (d. 781 or 782) ● Also Adalbehrt, Aelberht, and Eadelberht, archbishop of York and a friend and teacher of Alcuin. A student of the cathedral school of York, Ethelbert was ordained and placed in charge of the school by his predecessor Archbishop Egbert, brother of the king of Northumbria. Described by Alcuin as a master of erudition who was severe to the stubborn and gentle to the docile, and ever caring and nurturing toward scholars, his intense interest in books and the promoting of learning spurred him to amass a large library, considered perhaps the largest outside of Rome at the time. He journeyed far and wide (even to Rome) to find more books for his school, acquiring an immense reputation for learning all over England. Thus, in 766, when Egbert died, Ethelbert was unanimously elected to succeed him. Consecrated in April of 767, he received the pallium from Pope Adrian I. The main source on his life is Alcuin's poem on the saints and prelates of York, *"De Sanctis et Pontificibus Ecclesiae Eboracensis."*

Ethelreda, St. (d. 679) ● Daughter of the king of East Angles (East Anglia) and the founder of the double monastery of Ely. Marked at an early age for her spirituality and prayer life, she was nevertheless convinced by her family to marry Egfrid, the eventual king of Northumbria. The marriage, however, was never consummated and, after twelve years, she was granted permission by Egfrid to become a nun. Around 672, she was formally made a nun by St. Wilfrid at Coldingham where her aunt, Ebbe, was abbess. Soon after, she laid the foundation for Ely, where she served as abbess until her death. Traditionally called St. Audrey, she was the basis of the word "tawdry" as a result of the cheap finery sold at the St. Audrey's fair. It is generally accepted that prior to her marriage to Egfrid, Ethelreda had wed the prince of Gyrwe (Gyrvii), receiving from him as a wedding gift the lands that were to form the basis of Ely. This marriage was also never consummated and, after her first husband's death, she spent several years on the Isle of Ely in seclusion. Feast day: June 23.

Ethelhard (d. 805) ● Fourteenth archbishop of Canterbury. His early life prior to his becoming archbishop is quite obscure, and William of Malmesbury was almost certainly incorrect in identifying him with Ethelhard, bishop of Winchester. While Symeon of Durham describes him as an abbot it is not known to which monastery he was referring; speculation has placed it in Lincolnshire, in Kent, or at Malmesbury. It is theorized, however, that Ethelhard was a Mercian abbot, since his election as archbishop came about in large part through the intervention of the formidable Offa, king of Mercia, who had already been working to weaken the see of Canterbury by securing the pallium for the archiepiscopal see of Lichfield in Mercia, at the expense of Canterbury, which was in Kent, a neighboring and rival province. Ethelhard was elected in 791, but his consecration did not take place until 793, probably because of the opposition of the Kentish clergy. Kentish resentment erupted into violence in 796 with the rebellion of the cleric Eadbert Praen and the nobles of Kent. Despite Alcuin's plea to hold his ground, Ethelhard was forced to flee, recovering his see only in 798 with Eadbert's capture. Ethelhard from then on labored to have restored to Canterbury those rights that had been lost to Lichfield. In 802, after securing a favorable verdict from Pope Leo III while on a visit to Rome, Ethelhard won recognition of the papal decision from the Council of Clovesho (803). Higbert, archbishop of Lichfield, was deprived of the pallium, an important moment in the movement of the English Church toward national unity, particularly as records from the time of Ethelhard's reign show professions of faith and obedience made to him by English bishops-elect. (See also **Canterbury**.)

Ethiopia ● Also called at one time Abyssinia, the northeastern African country with a long Christian tradition. The faith first came to the region in the fourth century under Edesius of Tyre and especially St. Frumentius (d. c. 380), the so-called Apostle of Abyssinia. He and Edesius were brought to Ethiopia (or Abyssinia) as prisoners and were dragged before the local ruler at Axum. They so impressed the king, however, that they were set free. Frumentius was subsequently consecrated by St. Athanasius and returned

Ethiopian St. George

with the Abyssinians and to restore them to communion with Rome. The success of the program proved short-lived and cost the lives of many missionaries. Pope Julius III (1550-1555) tried again, sending Jesuits to the kingdom. They achieved remarkable progress, and in 1614 the Monophysites were officially renounced, as orthodoxy was imposed under pain of death by the ruler. A Catholic patriarch journeyed to Rome in 1625 and the next year Catholicism was proclaimed the religion of state. This was ended in 1632 when the new ruler expelled the Jesuits and reinstituted Monophysitism. From then until the 1800s, there was little contact with the Roman Church.

Missionary activity began once more in 1839, increasing into the twentieth century with the military adventures of the Italians. A vicar apostolic was appointed in 1839 under Bl. Giustino de Jacobis. He converted the Ethiopian monk Bl. Ghebré Michael, who died in 1855, the first martyr of the native clergy. An apostolic delegate was named in 1937. Currently the Catholic population in the country numbers around three hundred sixty thousand, only a fraction of the fifty-three million inhabitants; most reside in the area of Eritrea, the onetime Italian colony that became an independent state in 1993. The population is mostly Muslim or of the Ethiopian Church, which is of the Alexandrian rite, its liturgical language being Geez. In 1985, Archbishop Paulos Tzadua was named the first cardinal from Ethiopia by Pope John Paul II.

to Abyssinia to promote the conversion of the inhabitants around 340. After his death, Frumentius was called Abuna (Our Father), the title later adopted by the primate of the Ethiopian Church. Christianity apparently prospered over the next centuries, but in the sixth century the members of the Church, under the influence of the authorities in Egypt, were drawn into Monophysitism; from the seventh century they followed the patriarch of Alexandria and thus were under the ecclesiastical authority of the Coptic Church. This situation would remain essentially unaltered as Abyssinia became isolated, thanks to the Islamic invasion of North Africa and the conquest of Egypt in 639-640.

During the Middle Ages, efforts were made by several popes, including Innocent IV, Urban IV, and Clement V to open a dialogue

Eucharist ● Greek for "thanksgiving." Used to denote the sacrament of the Real Presence of Christ under the consecrated species of bread and wine offering himself in the sacrifice of the Mass. The Eucharist is given to the faithful as spiritual food during Holy Communion. The Eucharist is thus understood in any of these three senses: the Real Presence, the sacrifice of the Mass, and Communion.

The Eucharist was established by Christ at the Last Supper as attested by the Synoptic Gospels (Mt 26:26-28; Mk 14:22-24; Lk 22:17-20) and 1 Corinthians (11:23-25). The sacrificial nature of the sacrament was fully accepted in the early Church. The *Didache*, for example, speaks of the Eucharist in sacrificial terms. Further testimony was given in the second and third centuries by Sts. Justin Martyr and Irenaeus, and especially St. Cyprian, one of whose epistles (No. 63) was the first theological document prior to the Council of Nicaea in 325 to examine in exclusive detail the nature of sacrifice in the Mass. This truth was given additional affirmation in the councils of the Church in the succeeding centuries, although a formal definition of the sacrifice of the Mass was undertaken by the Council of Trent (1545-1563) so as to provide a response to the views being expounded by the Protestants. Pope Pius XII in the encyclical *Mediator Dei* (November 20, 1947) proclaimed that the Mass is a true sacrifice in which Christ offers himself as he died on the Cross at Calvary — but in an unbloody immolation.

The Real Presence is equally supported by the testimony of the early Church, such as St. Ignatius of Antioch, who wrote to the Philadelphians (4): "Take care, then, to partake of one Eucharist; for one is the Flesh of Our Lord Jesus Christ, and one the cup to unite us with His Blood. . . ." Ignatius, however, noted that there were those who denied the Real Presence (in a letter to the Smyrnaeans) and in the ninth century a genuine controversy erupted over the doctrine because of the writings of Ratramnus (d. 868). He favored a symbolic understanding of the Eucharist rather than an actual corporeal presence. While condemned, his ideas were supported by Berengarius of Tours who, in 1079, was compelled to recant and accept a declaration of faith at the insistence of Pope St. Gregory VII (r. 1073-1085).

The Protestant Reformation spread the denial of the Real Presence. The leaders of this movement were John Calvin and Huldrych Zwingli but not Martin Luther, as he did not deny this teaching. In response to them, the Council of Trent again gave solemn definition that the whole Christ was truly present under both species, bread and wine. Meaning is given to the doctrine by transubstantiation, the changing of the substance of bread and wine into the body and blood of Christ. This is attested to by St. Cyril of Jerusalem in his lecture to newly baptized Christians, "On the Mysteries," and has been developed and reaffirmed throughout the whole history of the Church.

Eudists ● See under **John Eudes, St.**

Eugene ● See **Eugenius**, following entries.

Eugenius I, St. ● Pope from 654-657. He was the successor to Martin I, who had been deposed by the Byzantine Emperor Constance II and sent into exile. Eugenius received from Martin, however, a letter in September 655 declaring recognition of his legitimacy. Most of his pontificate was taken up by the heresy of Monothelitism, which had cost Martin his throne because the old pontiff would not submit to the dictates of the Byzantines. If the Greeks had accepted the election of Eugenius in the hopes that he would submit, they were mistaken, for the pontiff steadfastly refused to recognize Peter as patriarch of Constantinople because he was a Monothelite. According to contemporary sources, Eugenius was a kindly, gentle, and saintly person. He was buried in St. Peter's. Feast day: June 2.

Eugenius II ● Pope from 824-827. The successor to St. Paschal I, Eugenius was elected on June 6, 824, as the result of the success of the nobles of Rome, in conjunction with their Frankish patrons, to secure a candidate who would reverse the policies of his predecessor. Eugenius thus allowed the nobles who had been exiled by Paschal to return home. He was also forced to greet the co-ruler of the Holy Roman Empire, Lothair I, and to accept the *Constitutio Romana* that acknowledged the supremacy of the emperors in Rome. By its terms, the pope was to be elected by the clergy and nobles of Rome, but approval was left to the emperor; Eugenius gave Lothair his oath of fealty. The pope fought against the doctrine of Iconoclasm, especially in the Byzantine Empire.

Eugenius III ● Pope from 1145-1153. Born Bernardo Pignatelli (or Bernard of Pisa), he was a Cistercian and a student of Bernard of Clairvaux at Clairvaux, making him the first Cistercian pope. He served as abbot of Sts. Vincent and Anastasius in Rome and was elected by unanimous vote to succeed Pope Lucius II. His enthronement as Eugenius III was performed quite hastily, as the Sacred College of Cardinals was deeply concerned about the hostile ambitions of the Roman mob to make the pope subordinate to the wishes of the Roman senate. Nevertheless, shortly after his election, Eugenius was forced to flee Rome because of civil unrest. He journeyed to France in 1147 and there promoted the Second Crusade in response to the fall of Edessa in the Holy Land. Bernard was appointed preacher of the cause, and King Louis VII was called upon to give his full support. In 1148, Eugenius returned to Italy. There he excommunicated the rebellious Roman leader Arnold of Brescia, who called him "a man of blood." Numerous councils were held from 1147-1148 to combat heresy and to bring reform and strengthen doctrine. The Treaty of Constance (1153) with Emperor Frederick I

Pope Eugenius III

Barbarossa attempted to fix the rights of the Church and the conditions of Frederick's coronation, but Eugenius died before the ruler could enter Italy. The pontiff died near Rome on July 8, 1153. He was greatly respected by his contemporaries and had encouraged Gratian in his enormous task of organizing the decretals. In 1872, Pope Pius IX approved his cult. Feast day: July 8.

Eugenius IV ● Pope from 1431-1447. His pontificate would witness the decline of conciliarism within the Church and the all-too-brief reunion of Christianity in the East and West. A Venetian by birth, Gabriello Condulmaro was a nephew of Pope Gregory XII. Inheriting a vast fortune, he gave it all to the poor and entered the Augustinian Canons. In 1408, he became cardinal of San Clemente. Elected as the successor to Martin V on March 4, 1431, he took the name Eugenius, perhaps anticipating a stormy pontificate such as was endured by Eugenius III. If that was his belief, he was proven utterly correct, for his reign was filled with turbulence, most notably caused by the

Council of Basel (1431-1449). As the council put forth the conciliar view that had so dominated the Council of Constance, Eugenius felt obligated to oppose it. He tried unsuccessfully to dissolve it in 1433, and by 1439 the succeeding Council of Ferrara-Florence (1438-1439) declared him deposed, electing in his place Felix V (Amadeus VII, duke of Savoy), in response to Eugenius's excommunication of its founding members. His ultimate triumph signaled the defeat of conciliarism and the restoration of papal authority over the Church. During Ferrara-Florence, Eugenius was able to negotiate the short-lived reunion of the Eastern and Western Churches, but the return to a unified Christendom would prove brief, as the Byzantines themselves rejected the Roman Church and, in so doing, doomed the city of Constantinople to capture by the Turks, a cataclysmic event, in 1453. Eugenius had organized an ill-fated crusade against the Turks, but this had ended with the annihilation of a Christian host at the Battle of Varna in 1444. The other major setback of his reign was the issuing in 1438 of the Pragmatic Sanction of Bourges by King Charles VII of France limiting papal authority in France.

Eunomianism ● Extreme system of Arian thought named after Eunomius, bishop of Cyzicus (d. 394). He was originally from Cappadocia, going to Alexandria where he studied under the Arian Sophist Aetius. With Aetius he attended the Arian synod of Antioch, becoming an ally of Eudoxius, who later became bishop of Constantinople (360), appointing Eunomius to the see of Cyzicus. He resigned a short time later in the face of chronic opposition from the Orthodox clergy. Over the next years, he would be banished and recalled by various emperors, finally exiled once more by Emperor Theodosius I. He died in exile and his writings were burned around 399.

Eunomianism (also termed Anomeanism),

characterized by the complete rejection of any generation within God, claims that the Son was not generated within the Father; rather, he was created, receiving all powers from God the Father, a gift that enabled Christ to create in turn the Holy Spirit. The Trinity was thus presented as three entirely different or exclusive Substances and thus the Son was not, indeed could not be, God. Eunomianism is largely known today through the writings of the Cappadocian Fathers St. Basil and St. Gregory of Nyssa, the latter authoring *Contra Eunomium* and the *Refutatio Confessionis Eunomii*. Other references were made to it by Socrates, Photius, and Philostorgius. (See also **Arianism**.)

Eusebians ● See **Eusebius of Nicomedia**.

Eusebius, St. ● Pope from April 18 to August 17, 309 (or 310), according to the Liberian Catalogue. The main source of information on his pontificate is from an epitaph for his tomb that was ordered by Pope St. Damasus I. It survived through ancient transcripts; fragments of the original, with a sixth-century marble copy that had been ordered to replace the original, were found by the archaeologist Giovanni Battista de Rossi in the crypt of Eusebius, in the catacomb of Callistus. The epitaph tells of a severe dispute that occurred in Rome as a result of apostates (*lapsi*), individuals who renounced the faith during the persecutions of Diocletian, being allowed to return to the fold with only light penance, or none at all. The group that disagreed with Eusebius and desired full readmission with no penance was probably headed by Heraclius. Both Eusebius and Heraclius were exiled by Emperor Maxentius. Eusebius was sent to Sicily where he died soon after and was succeeded by Pope St. Melchiades, who brought his predecessor's body back to Rome. Placed in the catacomb of Callistus (as reported by the fourth-century *Depositio*

Episcoporum in the Chronographer of 354), Eusebius was revered as a martyr. Feast day: August 17.

Eusebius of Caesarea (c. 260-340) ●
So-called Father of Church History, one of the most important of all Church historians and bishop of Caesarea. Eusebius was born in Palestine. He studied in Caesarea under the notable scholar Pamphilius, who died in 310 during the severe persecution of the Church. Eusebius fled, first to Tyre and then to Egypt where he spent some time in prison. Returning to Caesarea, he became bishop around 315. In the ensuing Arian controversy that confronted the Church, Eusebius struck a moderate position. He at first gave some support to Arius but, after his efforts at organizing a compromise failed, he accepted the Nicene Creed at the Council of Nicaea (325) and attended the Council of Tyre (335) with its condemnation of Arianism. A friend of Emperor Constantine the Great, he delivered an honorific speech to the ruler in 335 and composed a panegyric at his death in 337, the *Vita Constantini* (*Life of Constantine*).

A prolific writer, Eusebius was the author of the *Praeparatio Evangelica* (*Preparation for the Gospel*); *Demonstratio Evangelica* (*Demonstration of the Gospel*); *Against Hieracles*; *Chronicle* (covering from Abraham to Eusebius's own era, translated by St. Jerome from the Greek); *Theophany*, on the Incarnation; and *De Solemnitate Paschali*, a treatise on Easter. His most famous work was the *Historia Ecclesiastica* (*Ecclesiastical History*). Covering the events of the Church from its origins to 324, the history was a perfect demonstration of Eusebius's own view of the faith as the inevitable creed of the Roman Empire. While poorly written, it relied upon a host of valuable sources, including the Acts of the Apostles and Josephus and remains the most important source for the history of the Church from its beginnings until the fourth century. It was written in ten

Books, the last three focusing on Eusebius's own era. It was first translated from the Greek into Latin by Rufinus of Aquileia (d. 410) the scholar and monk who also extended the coverage to 395.

Eusebius of Dorylaeum ● Fifth-century bishop of Dorylaeum who was an ardent opponent of heresy, particularly Nestorianism. Eusebius first achieved notoriety while still a layman, speaking publicly in 429 against the teachings of Nestorius. His attack was addressed to the clergy of Constantinople in a *Contestatio*. In it he called for the people of Constantinople to rise up and defeat Nestorianism, a plea that led to the condemnation of Nestorius by the Council of Ephesus (431). By 448, Eusebius had become the bishop of Dorylaeum and in that year he charged his onetime friend Eutyches with heresy at the so-called Home Synod of Constantinople. Thus Eusebius was the first leader of the Church to oppose Monothelitism and his efforts secured Eutyches's deposition. The next year, however, he was himself deposed and exiled by the Latrocinium (the Robber Council of Ephesus). He appealed to Rome and was given refuge by Pope Leo I the Great. In 451, he was reinstated by the Council of Chalcedon at which he played a prominent role in drafting the Definition of Faith that delineated the accepted doctrine on the Person and natures of Christ. (See **Chalcedon, Council of**.)

Eusebius of Emesa (d. c. 359) ● Bishop of Emesa, described by St. Jerome as "a standard bearer of the Arian cause." A native of Edessa, Eusebius was probably a student of Eusebius of Caesarea, emerging as a biblical exegete and an influential writer on the doctrines of the Semi-Arians. As a friend of the Emperor Constantius II, Eusebius was offered, but refused, the see of Alexandria in 339 when Athanasius was deposed for his opposition to Arianism. A short time later, however, Eusebius accepted the see of Emesa. He was driven from the city by his own flock because of his unorthodoxy but was reinstated through the influence of George, bishop of Laodicea. The writings of Eusebius were long known in fragmentary form, largely in the works of the fifth-century historians Sozomen and Socrates. Recently, however, a collection of some seventeen homilies have been ascribed to his pen by the Benedictine patristic scholar André Wilmart (1876-1941).

Eusebius of Nicomedia (d. c. 342) ● Leading figure in the fourth-century Arian movement, whose followers took the name Eusebians in his honor. Eusebius was probably a fellow pupil of Arius (the founder of Arianism) under the instruction of the martyr St. Lucian of Antioch. He served as bishop of Berytus and then Nicomedia (c. 318). When, around 323, Arius was deposed by Alexander, the patriarch of Alexandria, Eusebius responded to his old fellow pupil's call for aid by granting him sanctuary and convening a synod in Bithynia (October 323), which attempted to nullify Arius's excommunication. Influential within the royal court and family (he baptized Constantine on his deathbed in 337), Eusebius succeeded in elevating the Arian controversy into an empire-wide dispute. His connections with the imperial family assisted him in his labors against Athanasius and his supporters, but, at the Council of Nicaea (325), he signed the Creed. Eusebius refused, however, to sign the anathema condemning the Arians. In the subsequent years, he continued to promote Arian doctrines, securing the deposition and exile of St. Athanasius of Alexandria. In 339, he was moved from Nicomedia to the see of Constantinople by order of Emperor Constantius II. (See **Arianism**.)

Eusebius of Samosata, St. (d. c. 380) ● Bishop of Samosata, martyr, and an outspoken opponent of Arianism. Appointed in 361, he was faced with the constant threat of deposition by the Arians in the Eastern Church and was in fact exiled in 374 to Thrace by the Arian Emperor Valens. During Valens's persecution of Orthodox Christians, Eusebius journeyed through Syria and Palestine restoring those priests and bishops who had been removed by Valens. Restored to his see in 378 after Valens's death at the Battle of Adrianople, Eusebius was murdered by an Arian woman while visiting Dolikha to consecrate a bishop. Eusebius carried on an extensive correspondence with St. Basel of Caesarea and St. Gregory of Nazianzus. Feast day: June 21 in the West, June 22 in the East.

Eusebius of Vercelli, St. (d. 371) ● First bishop of Vercelli, Italy, a supporter of Orthodox Christianity during the Arian controversy. Born in Sardinia, he was named bishop in 340 or 345, taking the then unique step of residing with his priests in a monasticlike community, marking the innovation in the West of combining community life with active ministry. At the behest of Pope Liberius, he journeyed with St. Lucifer of Cagliari as a papal representative to Emperor Constantius, who was a pro-Arian; at the subsequent Council of Milan (355), Eusebius refused to sign the condemnation of St. Athanasius of Alexandria and was exiled to the East. He would not return until receiving a pardon from Emperor Julian the Apostate in 362. At the Council of Alexandria (362) he helped secure the restoration of orthodoxy to the Church, fighting against Arianism in the succeeding years. Three of his lectures are extant, and he made a (now lost) Latin translation of Eusebius of Caesarea's *Commentary on the Psalms*. Other works attributed to him include the Old Latin Gospel Index in the Cathedral Library of Vercelli (improbable), the Athanasian Creed (no proof), and the first seven books of *De Trinitate* (possibly). Feast day: December 16.

Eustathius of Antioch, St. (d. c. 337) ● Also called Eustathius the Great, bishop of Antioch from 324 and an opponent of Eusebius of Caesarea. A native of Side, in Pamphylia, Eustathius was appointed bishop of Beroea (c. 320) and several years later was translated to Antioch. After the Council of Nicaea (325) he pursued the removal of Arians with much vigor, eventually entering into conflict with Eusebius of Caesarea. Through the machinations of the pro-Arian bishop of Caesarea, Eustathius was deposed by the Synod of Antioch and exiled to Thrace by Emperor Constantius the Great. There he died, but his supporters at Antioch, who called themselves Eustathians, formed the basis for the Melitian Schism. The author of numerous works, Eustathius' writings are known today only in fragmentary form, with the exception of the *De Engastrimutho*, an attack on Origen. Feast day: July 16 in the West, February 21 in the East.

Eustathius of Sebaste, St. (d. c. 377) ● Bishop of Sebaste in Pontus who influenced the development of monasticism despite his often heterodox views. Born the son of a bishop, Eustathius studied at Alexandria under Arius. It was there that he was introduced to the heretical doctrines of Arianism, propositions about which he would vacillate throughout much of his life. While condemned in 343 by the Council of Gangra, he nevertheless accepted the Nicene Creed and was on good terms with Pope Liberius (r. 352-366). In 357, despite his checkered theological past, Eustathius was made bishop of Sebaste. In his earlier years, he had focused extensively on monasticism, adhering to a very severe idea of asceticism. His student, St. Basil the Great, was almost certainly much influenced by him, although ultimately the two had a parting of the ways over Eustathius' adoption of Semi-Arian

teachings that took shape in the so-called Macedonian heresy.

Eustochium, Julia ● See **Paula, St**.

Eutyches (c. 378-c. 451) ● Famed heresiarch, founder of Eutychianism, an extreme heretical sect that supported an ultra-Monophysite position by stressing the virtual exclusive divinity of Christ. Eutyches was the archimandrite (an Eastern type of abbot or monastic superior) of a monastery at Constantinople. Educated under the influence of Cyril of Alexandria (d. 444), he vigorously opposed the doctrines of Nestorianism, particularly as embodied by Nestorius, the patriarch of Constantinople from 428. This disagreement led in 448 to an accusation by Eusebius of Dorylaeum that Eutyches held the heretical positions of confusing the natures of Christ. He was summoned before Flavian, by then patriarch, and the Synod of Constantinople. There he declared the maxim "two natures before, one after the Incarnation," expressing the Monophysite idea that Christ's human nature was subsumed by the divine one into a single essence. Deposed by Flavian, Eutyches nevertheless used friends at the imperial court to secure a new trial. At the Latrocinium (the Robber Council of Ephesus), in 449, he was acquitted; in 451, at the Council of Chalcedon, however, he was once more condemned and was exiled. After his exile, Eutyches disappeared from prominence. His followers remained as adherents of Eutychianism, and he is ranked as one of the most important figures in the rise of Monophysitism.

Eutychianism ● See **Eutyches** (preceding entry) and **Monophysitism**.

Eutychianus, St. ● Also Eutychianos. Pope from 275-283. Virtually nothing is known about him, and he most likely did not die a martyr, as the Roman Empire was generally free of persecution during his pontificate. For example, he was listed in the fourth-century *Depositio Episcoporum* but not in the list of martyrs. Fragments of his epitaph in Greek — *Eutychianos epis (kopos)* — were discovered in the crypt of Eutychianus in the catacomb of Callistus. He was the successor of St. Felix I. Feast day: December 8.

Evagrius Ponticus (346-399) ● One of the more important ascetical writers of his time, called Ponticus after Pontus, the place of his birth. Ordained a deacon by St. Gregory of Nazianzus, he emerged as a preacher of high repute in Constantinople. He accompanied Gregory to the Second Council of Constantinople (381) but ultimately departed the city and went first to Jerusalem and then to the Nitrian Desert. There he devoted himself to an ascetical life, studying under the monks there. He refused a bishopric that was offered to him by Theophylus of Alexandria and became famous for his ascetical writings. His writings, however, were attacked by Jerome as suffering from Origenism; they were later condemned by the sixth, seventh, and eighth ecumenical councils. Translations into Latin were done by Rufinus and Gennadius.

Evaristus, St. ● Pope from around 98 or 99 to 106 or 107. Ranked as the fifth Bishop of Rome, he was the successor to St. Clement I. His pontificate fell during the reign of

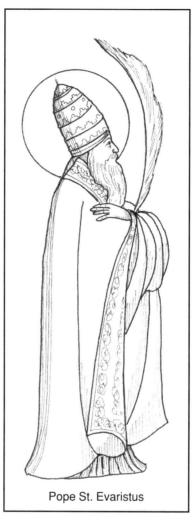

Pope St. Evaristus

Emperor Trajan. According to the *Liber Pontificalis*, he was the son of a Bethlehem Jew and was buried on the Vatican Hill (*Mons Vaticanus*) near the tomb of Peter. His martyrdom is not historically verified. Feast day: October 26.

Exarch ● See GLOSSARY.

Excommunication ● See GLOSSARY.

Exemption ● See GLOSSARY.

Exequetur ● Latin for "he may perform." Denotes the right of a country or government to prevent or delay a decreed enactment by the Holy See from taking immediate effect within the territory under its control. Also called *regium placet* (it pleases the ruler), the practice was developed in Europe, particularly under the influence of Gallicanism in the 1600s and Jansenism in the 1700s in France. It found particular expression in the work *De Promulgatione Legum Ecclesiasticorum* (1712), by Zeger Bernhard Van Espen (1646-1728). Pope Pius IX vigorously opposed *exequetur*, attacking it in his *Syllabus of Errors* (1864).

Exorcism ● See GLOSSARY.

Exsecrabilis ● Bull issued by Pope Pius II in 1460 in which he condemned any appeal from the pope to a council. The bull was intended to eradicate conciliarism, but it was opposed by many Churchmen in France and Germany who adhered to the idea of a council's supremacy over the pontiff. Nevertheless, the bull pointed to the inevitable decline of the Conciliar Theory in the Church.

Exsurge Domine ● Bull issued on June 15, 1520, by Pope Leo X excommunicating Martin Luther. The document lists forty-one condemned propositions that had been declared by Luther, stating that these were "heretical, scandalous, false, or offensive to pious ears, or seductive to those of simple minds. . . ." Its promulgation, entrusted to the unpopular Johann Eck, sparked a firestorm of controversy in Germany, culminating in Luther's burning of the bull in Wittenberg on December 10, 1520. (See also **Reformation, Catholic [and Protestant]**.)

Faber, Frederick William (1814-1863) ●
Hymnist, theologian, oratorian, and a notable
English convert to Catholicism. Faber was
born at Calverly, Yorkshire, and raised a
Calvinist. Educated at Shrewsbury and
Harrow and at Balliol and University College,
Oxford, he was elected a fellow of University
College, in 1837. While at Oxford, he came
under the influence of John Henry Newman.
Ordained in 1839, he was appointed rector in
1842 of Elton (in modern Huntingdon and
Petersborough). Already leaning toward
Catholicism, Faber caused a sensation with
his *Life of St. Wilfrid* (1844), which was full of
Catholic opinion and sympathies. On
November 17, 1845, he took the decisive step
of entering the Church, largely through the
help and guidance of Newman. Soon after, he
established with other converts the
Wilfridians (or Brothers of the Will of God) at
Birmingham. This was later merged with the
Oratory of St. Philip Neri, which had recently
been brought to England by Newman. In
1849, a branch was founded in London with
Faber at its head. He was ordained a priest in
1847. Among his writings are *The Foot of the
Cross* (1858), *The Creator and the Creature*
(1858), and *Notes on Doctrinal Subjects* (2
vols., 1866). His hymns include "Sweet
Saviour, bless us ere we go," "My God, how
wonderful Thou art," and "Hark, hark, my
soul!"

Faber, Johannes (1478-1541) ● German
theologian who ultimately rejected the
Reformation and became an ardent defender
of the Church. Faber was born at Leutkirch,
Württemberg, studying at Tübingen and
Freiburg Universities. Made bishop of Vienna
in 1520, he initially gave his support to the
Reformers, particularly Philipp Melanchthon,
but when the Reformation took the sharp
and bitter turn toward the tearing apart of
Christendom, Faber became staunchly
orthodox. His polemic and controversial
writings on behalf of the faith, such as his
Malleus in Haeresim Lutheranam (1524;
Hammer of the Heresies of Luther), earned
him the title "Hammer of the Heretics."

Fabian, St. ● Pope from 236-250. The
successor of St. Anterus as Bishop of Rome,
Fabian is credited with dividing the city of
Rome into seven ecclesiastical regions, each
under the authority of a deacon. He also
established churches in France and
continued to promote the recording of the
deeds of martyrs for the faith. His lengthy
pontificate was ended on January 20, 250,
when Emperor Decius began his
persecutions, starting with Fabian, the first
of the martyrs of the new oppression. Fabian
was initially buried in the catacomb of
Callistus, but his body was later moved to
the Church of San Sebastiano where it was
found in 1915. Feast day: January 20.

Fabiola, St. (d. 399) ● Famous Roman
Christian noblewoman. According to
tradition, Fabiola was the founder of the first
public hospital in the West, the result of her
desire to do penance for her divorce and
improper second marriage. She adopted an
austere life and distributed her vast wealth;
her charitable works included funding a
hospice for pilgrims, supporting various

monasteries, and establishing her hospital. Much influenced by St. Jerome, she journeyed in 395 to Bethlehem, following Jerome to the Holy Land. There she lived for a time with Sts. Paula and Eustochium. Fabiola returned to Rome in 396, in large measure because of the imminent invasion of Palestine by the Huns and in part because of her personal difficulties with the severe asceticism of the community in Bethlehem. Back in Rome, she resumed her charitable efforts. Feast day: December 27.

Facundus ● Sixth-century bishop of Hermiane in Africa who is best known for his spirited defense of the so-called Three Chapters. Little is known about him prior to around 547-548; however, at that time he journeyed to Constantinople to voice his severe disapproval of the condemnation of the three theologians (Theodore of Mopsuestia, Ibas of Edessa, and Theodoret of Cyr) who authored the Three Chapters. Facundus declared that Justinian's censure was unjust because of the orthodoxy of the writers and that it rejected the Christological doctrine of the Council of Chalcedon (451). His arguments were presented in the treatise *Pro Defensione Trium Capitulorum*. The Three Chapters were anathematized nevertheless, and Facundus and his supporters were briefly excommunicated by Pope Vigilius. During the period of schism with the Holy See, Facundus authored two works at the request of his fellow African bishops, both around 571, *Contra Mocianum Scholasticum* and *Epistola Fidei Catholicae in defensione trium capitulorum*. (See also **Monophysitism** and **Three Chapters**.)

False Decretals ● Apocryphal papal letters. Also called the Decretals of the Pseudo-Isidore that were purported to be a collection of canon laws attributed to St. Isidore of Seville (d. 636). The decretals were almost certainly compiled in the mid-ninth century in France by a very talented forger

known by the pseudonym Isidore Mercator. While the actual name False Decretals refers to the papal letters forged by Isidore (and comprising part of the collection), the title was also applied to the entire compilation, which contains a number of authentic documents.

The False Decretals were apparently written to promote the idea of papal authority and to present the rights of bishops against their metropolitan. The collection can be divided into three main parts: a treatise on the early Church and the Council of Nicaea, with the canons of some fifty councils, almost all of which are genuine; letters from thirty-three popes, from Sylvester I (r. 314-335) to Gregory II (r. 715-731), some considered authentic, others ranked as forgeries; and sixty apocryphal decrees from the time of Clement I (r. 88-97) to Melchiades (r. 311-314) — of the sixty letters, fifty-eight are forgeries. First appearing in the ninth century, the False Decretals were accepted as entirely authentic during the Middle Ages, doubts initially commencing in the Renaissance when the Cardinals Juan de Torquemada and Nicholas of Cusa determined much of the collection to be fraudulent. Despite increasing doubts among canonists, many scholars in the 1500s continued to utilize the writings, such as St. Thomas More and St. John Fisher, who were wholly unaware of the dubious nature of the work upon which they relied. Further attacks were made by the Centuriators of Magdeburg in 1558, but some Catholic academics remained firm in accepting the authenticity of the decretals because of the vicious anti-Catholic mind-set of the Centuriators. The decisive determination was made by the Protestant David Blondel (1590-1655) in his 1628 study *Pseudo-Isidorus et Turrianus vapulantes*. The False Decretals, a cunning and masterful forgery, enjoyed for many centuries a place of high regard among canonists, influencing Gratian in the organization of the *Decretum*.

Fathers of Mercy ● Congregation of missionary priests that was first established in Lyons, France, in 1808 by Father Jean Baptiste Rauzan (1757-1847). Rauzan taught theology and was chosen vicar-general of Bordeaux before embarking on a missionary effort to revive the vitality of the Church in France. In 1808, he was invited by Cardinal Joseph Fesch of Lyons to come to the city and there gather together preachers who might then go out throughout the country. These missionaries of France were at first supported by Napoleon, but, after the emperor's split with Pope Pius VII, the priests were suppressed. In 1814, Rauzan reestablished the congregation at Paris. The work of the priests proved immensely successful and was financed by the restored royal family until the revolution of 1830 when the Fathers were again dispersed, their house in Paris utterly sacked. Rauzan went to Rome where he was given the patronage of Pope Gregory XVI. This pontiff proposed a new congregation, the Fathers of Mercy, granting formal approval on February 18, 1834. The Fathers of Mercy arrived in the United States in 1839 at the suggestion of Bishop John Hughes of New York. They continue to engage in missionary work today.

Fathers of the Church ● Collective name given to the renowned figures of the early Church who had a monumental role in the defense, elucidation, and propagation of the faith; these ecclesiastical writers are the authors of an extensive corpus of doctrinal works given heightened authority by the Church. The study of their writings, called patrology (or patristics), is heavily encouraged for all desirous of learning the faith. They are recognized as Fathers as a result of the holiness of their lives, the orthodoxy of their teachings, the antiquity of their eras, and the recognition of their merits by the Church. The term Father is not explicitly bestowed by the Church; rather it is a traditional title unlike Doctor of the Church, which is formally conferred by the Church in recognition of merit and sanctity.

The term first appeared in the NT and was used in the early Church for bishops. It was restricted in use to bishops who were revered as witnesses of the faith. From the fourth century, it was broadened to include those exceptional ecclesiastical authors who made lasting contributions to the faith and whose writings wielded much authority in matters of doctrine. Such individuals did not have to be bishops. It is customary to consider the so-called Age of the Fathers as enduring for specific periods in the West and the East. In the West, it dates from the first days of the Church to the passing of St. Isidore of Seville in 636. St. Isidore is thus considered the last of the Western Fathers. In the East, the age covers until the death of St. John Damascene in 749. He is the last of the Eastern Fathers.

It is possible to divide the Age of Fathers into various periods: broadly, the pre-Nicene (to 325) and the post-Nicene (from 325). Within the pre-Nicene period can be seen the era of the Apostolic Fathers and that of the apologists. The name Apostolic Fathers (used since the 1600s) is applied to those major writers who labored in the years just after NT times. They either knew or were directly influenced by the Apostles. Among them are Pope St. Clement I of Rome, St. Ignatius of Antioch, and Hermas. The apologists flourished in the second and third centuries and defended the faith from intellectual attack and persecution, writing with the intention of reaching out to non-Christians, as most of them were themselves at one time. (See **Apologists**; see also TABLE 7 for the **Fathers of the Church**.)

Fátima ● Site just north of Lisbon, Portugal, where the Blessed Mary Virgin appeared six times between May 13 and October 13, 1917. Our Lady appeared before three children, Lucia dos Santos and her cousins Francisco Marto and Jacinta in a field near Fátima known as Cova da Iria.

During the apparitions, Mary instructed the children to undertake processions in honor of the Immaculate Conception and to promote frequent recitation of the Rosary. Our Lady also requested that the faithful do penance, pray for the conversion of Russia, that a Communion of reparation be made on the first Saturday of each month, and that a church be built in her honor. During her last appearance, on October 13, she revealed herself as Our Lady of the Rosary; before a crowd of between fifty thousand to seventy thousand people, a miracle that she had promised took place, a solar phenomenon described as a spinning sun. Our Lady promised that should her requests be followed, Russia would be converted, a terrible war would be avoided, many souls would be saved, and world peace would be achieved. Francisco died in 1919, followed by Jacinta in 1920. Lucia, who later became a Carmelite nun, received a seventh apparition on June 18, 1921.

In 1930, the bishops of Portugal declared the apparitions to be authentic after a seven-year investigation. Approval was given for the devotion to Our Lady of Fátima under the title of Our Lady of the Rosary. Pope Pius XII in 1942 consecrated the world to Mary under the title of her Immaculate Heart, and ten years later fulfilled the request to consecrate the people of Russia to her by issuing an apostolic letter addressed to the Russians. Pope Paul VI in 1967 visited Fátima to worship at the shrine on the fiftieth anniversary of Our Lady's appearance. In 1982, Pope John Paul II went to Fátima to give thanks for surviving the attempt on his life by Mehmet Ali Agca on May 13, 1981, and, on March 25, 1984, on the Feast of the Annunciation and in front of St. Peter's Basilica, he formally consecrated Russia to the Immaculate Heart. Fátima is one of the most popular of all Marian shrines in the world. Much speculation has surrounded the prophecies made at Fátima, especially the third and last secret of Fátima,

which has never been revealed. It is thought to be kept today in the Vatican's secret archives and can be read only by His Holiness the pope.

Faulhaber, Michael von (1869-1952) ●
German cardinal and archbishop of Munich who was an outspoken critic and opponent of the Nazi regime. Born at Heidenfeld, he was educated at Rome and ordained in 1892. After teaching at the University of Würzburg (1899-1903) and Strasbourg (1903-1910), he was appointed bishop of Speyer (1910-1917). In 1917, he became archbishop of Munich and was elevated to the cardinalate in 1921. This office he would hold until his death, throughout the rise of Nazi Germany, World War II, and its aftermath. In the face of severe government threats, Faulhaber was an unceasing enemy of the Nazi Party. He worked to defeat Hitler's *putsch* in Munich in 1923, called for a recognition of the need by Germans for the retaining of fundamental Christian values, and in a series of brilliant sermons, showed that Christianity owed much to Judaism. Twice he was nearly assassinated and, after the war, was given the Grand Cross of the Order of Merit by the West German Republic. Faulhaber also authored several works in the field of patristics.

Faustus of Riez (c. 408-c. 490) ●
Important supporter and defender of Semi-Pelagianism and bishop of Riez. Faustus was probably from Roman Britain, entering the monastery of Lérins on the Îsle de Lérins (off the southeastern coast of France). There he became abbot around 433 and was made bishop of Riez about 459. He was forced briefly from his see by King Euric of the Visigoths for opposing his efforts at Arianizing (i.e., introducing Arianism to) the territories under Visigothic control. Faustus supported the tenets of Semi-Pelagianism, insisting on the inability of God to interfere with human freedom and the necessity for

human cooperation with divine grace. His ideas, which went beyond even the Pelagian teachings of John Cassian, were accepted by the Council of Arles in 472 or 473 but were later rejected by the Council of Orange in 529. Faustus is considered a saint in southern France, with his feast day on September 28; the universal Church does not recognize him because of his theologically irregular teachings. He authored the work *De Gratia* (*On Grace*), one of the most important writings in the formation of Semi-Pelagianism.

Fawkes, Guy (1570-1606) ● One of the main figures in the Gunpowder Plot of 1605, an attempt to blow up the House of Parliament and, hopefully, permit Catholics to take over the government. Fawkes was born in Yorkshire to a Protestant family. He soon abandoned both Protestantism and England, becoming a fervent Catholic and joining the Spanish army in 1593, serving in the Netherlands. During his time in the armed forces of Spain, Fawkes acquired the reputation for courage and bravery. This led to his being recruited by the members of the Gunpowder Plot, particularly Robert Catesby, the originator of the conspiracy. Fawkes returned to England in 1604 and was given the task of igniting the barrels of gunpowder that were hidden near the Parliament. Arrested on November 5, 1605, he was tortured and finally revealed the names of fellow plot members. He was executed on January 31, 1606, and is remembered through the celebration every November 5 of Guy Fawkes Day, the source of much merriment and perpetuation of anti-Catholicism throughout England in previous years.

Feast of Asses ● In Latin, *Festum asinorum*. Customarily held during the Middle Ages in a number of French towns on January 14 or, more often, at Christmas. The feast was characterized by the staging of plays depicting the Flight of the Holy Family

into Egypt or the prophecy of Balaam's Ass. It should not be confused with the Feast of Fools, although that celebration has also been called the Feast of Asses.

Feast of Fools ● Celebration customarily held on January 1 (the Feast of the Circumcision) that was known for its wild behavior and drunken revelry by members of the lower clergy in the churches of France and in various parts of England as well as in Germany. The feast probably originated during the twelfth century when there began a period of merrymaking around New Year during which lower-ranking clerics, such as subdeacons, elected their own bishops, archbishops, and even a grand pope of fools for several days. Ultimately, the buffoonery went beyond the accepted limits of the Church, and the feast was condemned by such reformers as Robert Grosseteste, bishop of Lincoln. The Council of Basel deemed it utterly unacceptable, imposing stiff fines and penalties in order to suppress it. By the 1500s, the Feast of Fools had all but died out. Among the blasphemous activities that were part of the festivities were gambling on the altar and singing raunchy or bawdy songs in churches.

Febronianism ● Movement in the German Church during the late eighteenth century that challenged the authority of the pope in both temporal and ecclesiastical affairs and argued that the state — with the general, or ecumenical, council — should have supervisorial powers over the Church. Febronianism was first outlined by Johann Nikolaus von Hontheim, auxiliary bishop of Trier, who, at the behest of the German archbishop-electors, presented their complaints against the papacy and developed a religio-political system by which the Holy See would be sufficiently reduced in influence to facilitate a possible reunion with the Protestants. Hontheim presented his theories, a radical form of Gallicanism, in the

1763 work *Justini Febronii Juris consulti de statu ecclesiae et legitima potestate Romani Pontificis*, written under the pseudonym Justinus Febronius.

Febronianism argues that Christ entrusted the care of the Church — the power of the keys — to the whole body of the faith, which exercises its authority through bishops. The pope is first among prelates but is subordinate to the Church on the whole. Further, the concept of primacy is acknowledged, but the Roman see does not derive its primacy from Christ but from Peter, thereby permitting the Church to move such power to another see if so desired. The pope remains the center of Christian unity; only his authority is of an administrative nature, unifying the Church rather than ruling over it in a monarchical fashion. The basis in history for this contention is the nature of the papacy until the eighth century when only inherent rights were exercised. After that time, through especially the False Decretals, the popes were able to usurp greater power. Further, the infallibility of the pontiff and his jurisdiction in matters of heresies and discipline were denied.

Condemned immediately in 1764 by Pope Clement XIII (r. 1758-1769), the book was placed on the Index of Forbidden Books. The archbishop-electors, however, gave their backing to Febronianist ideas in 1769, the book having become extremely successful and undergoing numerous editions and translations. Pope Pius VI (r. 1775-1799) condemned Hontheim in 1778 when it was made clear that the bishop's retraction was far from sincere. The movement, however, had come to the attention of many governments and monarchs of the period desirous of forming state-nominated national Churches. Notable among these royal adherents was the Holy Roman Emperor Joseph II (r. 1765-1790), who established the deleterious ecclesiastical reforms known under the title Josephinism. Febronianism declined sharply in Germany because of opposition from German bishops and the severe upheaval caused in Europe by the eruption of the French Revolution in 1789. Efforts to apply Febronianism elsewhere, such as in Italy under Scipione de'Ricci, failed. Vatican Council I (1869-1870) condemned all such theories as Febronianism, Josephinism, or Gallicanism.

Felix I, St. ● Pope from 269-274. The successor to St. Dionysius, he was elected on January 5, 269. The main achievement of his pontificate was his authoring of a letter probably sent to the bishops of the East that delineated the doctrine concerning the Trinity. He was buried in the catacomb of St. Callistus and was mentioned in the *Liber Pontificalis* as a martyr. This was an error, as he was not martyred and was listed in the *Depositio Episcoporum* and not in the collection of martyrs (the *Depositio Martyrum*). Feast day: May 30.

Felix II ● Antipope from 355-358. At the time of Pope Liberius's banishment to Thrace by Emperor Constantius because of the pontiff's refusal to submit to the emperor's Arian tendencies, Felix was serving as an archdeacon in Rome. Summoned to Milan in 355 by the emperor, Felix was convinced to accept appointment as successor to Liberius. Consecrated by Acacius of Caesarea and two other Arian bishops, Felix was given recognition by most of the Roman clergy, but the laypeople steadfastly opposed him. Thus, in May 357, the laity called upon the visiting Constantius to recall Liberius from Greece. The pope did soon return and was greeted with wild enthusiasm by the Romans. Felix, however, was finally driven from the city and exiled by the Roman senate. He retired to Porto, dying there in 365. Felix had been listed at times as a martyr or saint but is officially considered an antipope by the *Annuario Pontificio*.

Felix III, St. ● Pope from 483-492. The successor to St. Simplicius, he was elected on March 13. He is most remembered for excommunicating Acacius, patriarch of Constantinople, in 484, for supporting the cause of Monophysitism. The excommunication helped cause the so-called Acacian Schism that divided the Eastern and Western Churches for nearly thirty-five years. Felix was a member of a Roman senatorial family and an ancestor of Pope St. Gregory the Great. Feast day: March 1 (kept in Rome).

Felix IV, St. ● Pope from 526-530. Felix was elected to succeed John I (who had died in prison in Ravenna) largely through the influence of Theodoric, king of the Ostrogoths. The new pontiff was generally accepted by the Romans out of respect and fear of the ruler of the Ostrogoths. He was responsible for bringing an end to the controversy within the Church concerning the role of grace by convening the Second Council of Orange in 529; he condemned Pelagianism, and gave full approval to the teachings of St. Augustine concerning original sin and God's grace. To provide for an orderly succession, he stated his desire that the archdeacon Boniface (see **Boniface II**) should follow him, going so far as to place the pallium upon Boniface's shoulders. Felix died a short time later, but his wishes were not followed and Dioscorus was elected by the Romans, causing a schism. Feast day: September 22.

Felix V ● Antipope from 1439-1449. Actually Amadeus VIII, duke of Savoy. The

Pope Felix IV

ruler of Savoy from 1391-1451 (although he abdicated in name only in favor of his son Louis in 1434), he was made a duke by Emperor Sigismund in 1416, adding a number of territories to the already vast holdings of Savoy. In 1439, he was elected antipope by the rump Council of Constance that was feuding with Pope Eugenius IV. He accepted on January 5, 1440, and was consecrated on July 24. He never gained significant support in Christendom but retained his title of pope until 1449 when he surrendered to Pope Nicholas V. His last two years were spent as a cardinal, having been appointed by Nicholas.

Felix of Urgel (d. 818) ● Bishop of Urgel in Spain who, with Elipandus, bishop of Toledo, was a leader of the heretical movement of Adoptionism. At the Council of Ratisbon (792) he accepted that Adoptionist views were heretical, formally recanting before Pope Adrian I. He soon returned to the heresy, however, and was accused by the Councils of Frankfurt (794) and Aachen (798). Finally convinced by Alcuin of his errors, Felix recanted yet again but spent the rest of his life under the careful supervision of the Church.

Fénelon, François (1651-1715) ● In full, François de Salignac de la Mothe-Fénelon, archbishop of Cambrai and author of the highly controversial book *Explication des maximes des saints*. Born at Périgord in the Château de Fénelon to a noble but poor family, Fénelon studied at the University of Cahors, the Collège des Plessis, and the seminary of St.-Sulpice, Paris. Ordained around 1675, he was appointed in 1678 to the post of director of the Nouvelles-Catholiques, a house established in 1634 for Protestant women who were entering the Church or converts in need of fortifying their faith. Having had extensive experience in dealing with former Protestants, Fénelon in 1685 was chosen, with five companions, to undertake a mission to the Huguenots in Saintonge. There he worked to convert the Protestants, his methods differing completely from the harsh treatment meted out to Huguenots under the so-called *dragonnades*, who forced conversion to Catholicism upon the inhabitants. His work coincided with the revoking in 1685 of the Edict of Nantes by King Louis XIV, an act that launched severe intolerance of Protestantism. While he disagreed with the Protestants, Fénelon did not accept the idea of forced conversion and promoted instead a peaceful process of convincing his hearers of the rightness of the Catholic faith. His first important writing, *Traité de l'éducation des filles* (*Treatise on the Education of Girls*), a remarkably innovative study on education based on his experience in the Nouvelles-Catholiques, was published in 1687. Two years later, he was named tutor to Louis, duke of Burgundy, grandson of King Louis XIV. For his student, Fénelon authored several educational tales, including *Fables* and *Les Dialogues des morts* (1690; *The Dialogue of the Dead*). Best known was *Les Aventures de Télémaque* (1699), a novel describing the search of Telemachus for his father, Ulysses, in which

Cardinal François Fénelon

Fénelon expressed such political thoughts as the need for moral considerations in the law and economic reform, and the undesirability of absolutism. In 1695, he was made archbishop of Cambrai.

Drawn increasingly to the mystical, Fénelon first met Jeanne Marie Bouvier de la Mothe Guyon, the leading proponent of quietism, in the autumn of 1688. He seems to have been much impressed with many quietist tenets and went to some lengths to defend Madame Guyon in 1691 when she was first censured. In 1696, however, he signed the thirty-four Articles of Issy condemning quietism. In response to Jacques Bossuet's continued attacks on Guyon, he wrote the *Explication des maximes des saints sur la vie intérieure* (1697; *Explanation of the Sayings of the Saints on the Interior Life*). Bossuet replied with a protracted and public assault on Fénelon. A controversy followed and the archbishop was expelled from the court. At Louis's urging, Pope Innocent XII issued a brief on March 12, 1699, condemning twenty-three propositions in the *Maximes des saints*. He submitted and was outspoken against Jansenism in the next years, remaining in his diocese where he wrote the *Traité sur l'existence de Dieu* (1712, in part; 1731, complete; *Treatise on the Existence of God*).

Ferdinand II, Emperor (1578-1637) ●
Holy Roman Emperor from 1619, king of Bohemia and Hungary, archduke of Austria, and one of the most staunch defenders of the Counter-Reformation. The eldest son of Archduke Charles of Austria, he was educated by the Jesuits at the University of

Ingolstadt and thus was anxious to reduce Protestantism in any lands over which he might rule. In 1617, he succeeded his cousin as king of Bohemia (and Hungary from 1618), using a secret treaty with the Spanish Habsburgs to secure his elevation to emperor in 1619. Unacceptable to the largely Protestant diet of Bohemia, he was deposed by them as king and replaced by Frederick V. This move essentially launched the Thirty Years' War (1618-1648). In fighting the Protestant cause, Ferdinand used his remarkable generals Johann Tilly and Albrecht von Wallenstein, defeating Frederick in 1620 and achieving so many victories that he forced the recalcitrant Protestant princes to accept the Treaty of Lübeck in 1629. Emboldened by his triumphs, he issued the Edict of Restitution (1629) by which he compelled the Protestants to return all property that had been seized from the Church. This act precipitated a new series of bloody campaigns, during which the emperor's armies faced the rebel German princes as well as the forces of Sweden and France and were possibly spared ultimate defeat by the fortuitous death of the brilliant general (and king of Sweden) Gustavus II Adolphus at the Battle of Lützen in November 1632. Ferdinand defeated the Swedes in 1634 and negotiated the Treaty of Prague (1635). He almost certainly connived the murder of Wallenstein in 1634. Before his death, he secured the naming of his son Ferdinand (III) as his heir. (See also **Holy Roman Empire** and **Thirty Years' War**.)

Ferrara-Florence, Council of ●

Seventeenth general (or ecumenical) council of the Church, held at Ferrara and Florence, and also at Rome, from 1438-1445. Aside from the discussion of important doctrinal matters, the council had as its principal aim the possible reunion of the Eastern and Western Churches. While technically a continuation of the Council of Basel (convened in 1431) and held supposedly under the influence of conciliar ideas, Ferrara-Florence proved a major triumph for the papacy against the conciliar movement. The impetus for the discussions of reunion was given by the need on the part of the Byzantines for assistance from the West for aid against the Ottoman Turks, who were menacing Constantinople. In order to accommodate the large delegation (including Emperor John VIII Palaeologus, the patriarch of Constantinople, Joseph, and some seven hundred other Greek theologians and prelates), Pope Eugenius IV ordered the members of the Council of Basel to travel to Ferrara. Only those adherents of the pope agreed to go, but the council opened on January 8, 1438, with Eugenius in attendance, along with such notables as Cardinals Giuliano Cesarini and John Bessarion. Plague broke out in the city and, with the Florentines agreeing to pay the cost of the proceedings, Eugenius moved the council to Florence on January 10, 1439.

Long, protracted negotiations followed, resulting in July 1439 in an agreement by which a reunion was at last reached. The Eastern Church agreed to the basic tenets of Western doctrine, most importantly the *Filioque,* as well as the theological points of purgatory and the Eucharist. Further, Eugenius won recognition of papal primacy and was thus able to issue the bull *Laetentur Coeli,* which was signed on July 5, 1439, with only one Eastern prelate, Mark Eugenicus, metropolitan of Ephesus, dissenting. After the Greeks returned home, the council stayed in session to work toward reunion with the other schismatic Churches of the East and to resolve the schism that had erupted over the rump Council of Basel. Reunion was achieved with the Armenians and the Copts, and a little later with the Syrians and Chaldaeans. The recalcitrant members of the Council of Basel were excommunicated and in the bull *Etsi non dubitemus* (April 20, 1441), Eugenius proclaimed his authority over the general council. From 1443, the council convened at Rome. Quite unpopular with the people of Constantinople, the reunion was soon repudiated by many of the Eastern bishops, dissatisfaction with the agreement only increasing as it became clear that no aid from the West was forthcoming. In 1453, Constantinople fell to the Turks, effectively ending the unity of Christendom.

Fesch, Joseph (1763-1839) ● French cardinal and uncle of Napoleon Bonaparte. Like his nephew, Fesch was born at Ajaccio, Corsica. He studied at Aix and then was appointed archdeacon at Ajaccio sometime before 1789. In 1790, with the passage of the Civil Constitution of the Clergy, Fesch swore the oath of allegiance and was promoted to episcopal vicar. However, owing to the opposition of the Bonapartes to the Corsican revolution and the Corsican general Pasquale Paoli, Fesch departed Corsica for Toulouse, France, in 1793. He then left the Church and worked for a time in the commissariat department of the army; while Napoleon served as commander in Italy, Fesch was his supply master from 1794-1797. Reentering the Church in 1800, he was named canon of Bastia and then archbishop of Lyons in 1802; Pope Pius VII elevated him to cardinal in 1803. Fesch had assisted in the negotiations that led to the Concordat of 1801 between Napoleon and Pius. The master of France, his nephew, appointed him on April 4, 1803, to be ambassador to Rome. He convinced Pius to travel to Paris to crown Napoleon emperor but from then on grew increasingly disenchanted with his relative's harsh treatment of the Church in general and Pius in particular. The offer of the archiepiscopal see of Paris was refused by him to protest against Napoleon's virtual imprisonment of the pope in 1809. Two years later, he made a clear pronouncement of loyalty to Pius at a Gallican council and was forced to retire. After the fall of Napoleon and the restoration of the Bourbons, Fesch

moved to Rome. There he remained, but the pontiff refused to remove him as archbishop of Lyons; until his death, the see was run by an administrator. He also gave encouragement to Jean Baptiste Rauzan in founding the Missionaries of France, later called the Fathers of Mercy.

Feuillants ● Name given to those members of the reformed Abbey of Le Feuillant, who were the basis of the Order of Feuillants. Le Feuillant was established by Abbot Jean de la Barrière (d. 1600). Appalled by the laxity of the house, he introduced a series of reforms, expelling those members who would not submit. A new and even more strict rule was then adopted, receiving approval from Pope Gregory XIII in 1581. In 1589, Barrière was granted permission to found the Feuillants as a separate order by Pope Sixtus V. The Feuillantines were founded in 1588, a similar order for women. The orders did not survive the Napoleonic Wars (1796-1815).

Fides Hieronymi ● One of the earlier versions of the Apostles' Creed, dated to around the late fourth century and traditionally ascribed to St. Jerome, hence the title, *Fides Hieronymi* (*Faith of Jerome*). It is especially notable for its inclusion of the phrase "communion of saints" (*sanctorum communionem*).

Fifth Lateran Council ● See under **Lateran Councils**.

Filioque ● Latin for "and from the Son." It became one of the central causes of the schism in 1054 between the Eastern and Western Churches and has remained a source of division ever since. *Filioque* in theology means that the Third Person of the Holy Trinity, the Holy Spirit, proceeds from the Father and the Son (*filioque* in Latin). This phrase was added to the Nicene Creed as an interpolation in 589 at the Third

Council of Toledo. It was not part of the original creed and its insertion was met with objections by theologians of the Eastern Church. At the Synod of Friuli (796), Paulinus of Aquileia defended its use and thereafter it was adopted throughout the lands of the Carolingian (or Frankish) Empire. Impetus was given by Charlemagne who, in the *Libri Carolini* (c. 790), condemned the Byzantines for their opposition to it. Both Popes Adrian I (r. 772-795) and Leo III (r. 795-816) preferred the Eastern position with regard to the formula, but they defended the doctrine itself. Usage continued, however, in the West, and by the start of the eleventh century it was given formal acceptance at Rome. Tensions only increased between the churches, culminating with the break in 1054 in Constantinople. In all subsequent efforts to reunite the Churches and end the schism, the *Filioque* was one of the key doctrinal points of discussion. The West, at the so-called unionist Councils of Lyons (1274) and Ferrara-Florence (1438-1445) made acceptance of it an absolute requisite for unification — although the Greeks were not, in the interests of compromise, required to insert the phrase into the Nicene Creed. Such unions proved very brief, however, and after each rupture, Orthodox assemblies rescinded adoption of the doctrine. The final breach that ensued from the fall of Constantinople in 1453 caused centuries of disagreement. In the twentieth century, however — with the recognition by both Churches that the Third Person proceeds from the First and the Second Persons of the Trinity, coupled with the extensive researches conducted by theologians from both sides on the underlying points of the controversy — the long dispute has been rendered more of historical interest than ongoing dogmatic dispute, although it continues to serve as a major obstacle to unity.

Finland ● Scandinavian republic with a tiny Catholic population; it is almost entirely Lutheran. It is unclear precisely when Christianity entered Finland. The monastery of Valamo claimed to have been established in the late tenth century, but verifiable evidence indicates that the faith began penetrating the country in earnest during the twelfth century. the Christian advance came from two sides, Sweden and Russia. King Erik of Sweden invaded in 1157, bringing with him Henry (Henrik), bishop of Uppsala. The bishop attempted to preach among the pagans and was murdered in 1158, as was his successor Rodulfus. Meanwhile, the grand duke of Novgorod sent Russian missionaries to eastern Finland, the start of a Russian religious presence that would last until modern times. The Church gradually took root and an independent Finnish Church was attained under Bishop Thomas (d. 1248) around 1220. His see was located at Räntemäkai; it would later be moved to Abo. Two notable bishops of Abo were Magnus Tavast (1412-1450), who went on a pilgrimage to the Holy Land, and Olaus Magnus (1450-1460), who had been twice rector of the Sorbonne. The last Catholic bishop of Finland was Ericus Svenonis, who resigned his see, as his election was not given confirmation from Rome. The king, Gustavus I Vasa, then picked his personal favorite, a Dominican, Martin Skytte, who energetically promoted Lutheranism. The two leading figures of the Reformation in Finland were Peter Särkilax (d. 1530) and Michael Olavi Agricola (d. 1557). By the end of the 1500s, the Church in Finland had been violently and mercilessly extirpated. In eastern Finland the Orthodox Finns endured persecutions until 1809 when Finland fell under the rule of Russia. Catholicism was officially tolerated as laws were passed in 1869 and 1889. A vicariate apostolic was created in 1920, converted to the lone Finnish diocese in 1955. The current Catholic population is around five thousand.

Fioretti di S. Francesco ● See **Little Flowers of St. Francis**.

Firmicus Maternus, Julius ● Late fourth-century Christian rhetorician, the author of *De errore profanorum religionum* (*On the Errors of the Pagan Religion*). Little is known about him save that he was from Sicily and that his conversion was in adulthood. By this time, he had probably written the *Mathesis* (in eight books around 337), a large compendium on astrology. His main work, however, was *De Errore*, written around 347, that was an appeal to Emperors Constantius II and Constans I to extirpate all paganism and pagan idols. Its value to historians is in preserving excellent details concerning the state of Roman pagan and Christian culture in the fourth century.

Fisher, John, St. (1469-1535) ● Bishop of Rochester, humanist, and martyr. He was born at Beverley, the son of a mercer from Yorkshire. After studying at Michaelhouse, Cambridge, he was appointed there as master in 1496; in 1501, he became vice-chancellor and in 1504 chancellor. Chaplain to Lady Margaret Beaufort, he was able to undertake, with her considerable help, the improvement of the university, including endowments for Greek and Hebrew and the encouragement of the work of Desiderius Erasmus (d. 1536). Named in 1502 the first Lady Margaret professor of divinity, two years later he was promoted to the post of chancellor and bishop of Rochester. As bishop he distinguished himself by his concern for his diocese and his excellent preaching; such was his

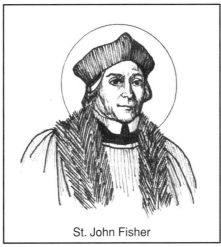

St. John Fisher

reputation that he delivered funeral orations for King Henry VII and Lady Margaret Beaufort, both of whom died in 1509. While aware of the need for Church reform, he was opposed steadfastly to the spread of Protestantism, authoring a defense of the Real Presence in *De Veritate Corporis et Sanguinis Christi in Eucharisti* (1527). He was also the reputed author of the *Assertio Septem Sacramentorum* (1521) of Henry VIII, although he himself denied it; he did write *Defensio Regiae Assertionis* (1525) and probably assisted in the king's work.

Fisher fell out of royal favor starting in 1527 because of his adamant refusal to approve of Henry's efforts to divorce Catherine of Aragon whom Fisher served as confessor. He refused to take the oath that was attached to the Act of Succession in 1534 and, having already lost his property because of supposed involvement in the Elizabeth Barton affair, he was arrested and placed in the Tower of London. The king tried — but failed — to win Fisher's acceptance of the oath and was infuriated by the decision of Pope Paul III in May 1535 to declare Fisher a cardinal. Placed on trial at Westminster Hall on the charge of treason, he was not surprisingly found guilty. Such was his poor state of health from imprisonment that he had to be carried in a chair to his execution. He was beheaded on June 22, 1535.

One of the foremost scholars of his day, Fisher was also an influential theologian whose writings were to be used by the Church in the Catholic Reformation and at the Council of Trent (1545-1563). With his good friend St. Thomas More, he was the most prominent victim of Henry's break with the Church. Pope Pius XI canonized him in 1935. Feast day: June 22, with Thomas More.

Fisher the Jesuit (1569-1641) ● Also John Fisher, an English Jesuit missionary to his homeland. Born John Percy, in County Durham, he was raised a Protestant but entered the Church while still a young man. He departed England, studied on the Continent, and joined the Society of Jesus in 1594. Returning home, he spent many years trying to convert the English; his most notable success was the duchess of Buckingham. Fisher also engaged in controversies and disputations with such prominent Anglicans as King James I and William Land, archbishop of Canterbury.

Fitzralph, Richard (c. 1295-1360) ● Archbishop of Armagh. A native of Dundalk, Ireland, he studied at Oxford where he served as a teacher, became a doctor of theology (before 1333), dean of Lichfield (1337), and then archbishop of Armagh (1347). In 1350, he visited Avignon and there presented a memorial on behalf of the English clergy in which the secular priests complained about the special rights of the mendicant orders. Fitzralph served on a commission established by Pope Clement VI to look into the matter, authoring subsequently a treatise, *De Pauperie Salvatoris*, discussing evangelical poverty, particularly the questions then being raised over dominion, possession, and use, and their reaction to the state of grace in humans. The work later influenced John Wycliffe. Fitzralph also took part in a controversy with the representatives of the Armenian Church, attacking the Armenian and Greeks heresies in *Quaestionibus Armenorum* (1357; *Summa on the Armenian Questions*). He returned to Avignon in 1357 on the matter of the mendicant orders; his views on the orders (such as voluntary begging being contrary to the teachings of Christ) were rejected, but he was never condemned, dying at Avignon in good

standing on December 16, 1360. Fitzralph had a reputation for being a remarkable preacher and truly gifted biblical scholar.

Five Ways of Thomas Aquinas ● See **Quinque Viae**.

Flagellants ● Name used for groups of extreme religious fanatics who beat themselves with whips, sticks, and rods in order to do penance for the sins of the world. The flagellants first became common in the 1200s and were especially prevalent during the 1300s until finally being condemned by the Church. The causes of the movement have been traced to the social, economic, and political upheaval found during the period: the Hundred Years' War (1337-1453), the bitter struggles in Italy, constant famines, the apocalyptic predictions of Joachim of Fiore, and, most importantly, the Black Death, which convinced many of the survivors that the world was being punished by God and would soon end. As they felt no relief from the Church, the extremists took to wandering the countryside in packs of suffering souls. Men scourged themselves in public exhibitions that were usually accompanied by spiritual readings and exhortations for their listeners to repent. Women beat themselves in private. The Church inevitably found it necessary to take steps to curb the flagellants, especially in Germany where they had become quite well-organized. First censured in 1261, they were finally condemned in 1349 by Pope Clement VI. The Inquisition then pursued the movement's extirpation.

Flavian, St. (d. 449) ● Patriarch of Constantinople, best known for his excommunication of Eutyches in 448 and his involvement in the Monophysite controversy. Chosen as a successor of St. Proclus as patriarch in 446, he was immediately confronted with the difficulties created by the archimandrite Eutyches and his ideas on the nature of Christ (see **Eutyches** for details). At the Council of Constantinople (448) Flavian attempted to deal with Eutyches moderately, but Eutyches's staunch refusal to take an oath of orthodoxy compelled Flavian to pronounce a ban of excommunication. In this act he was fully supported by Pope Leo I. The following year, however, the Latrocinium (the Robber Council of Ephesus) reversed this decision, reinstated Eutyches, and deposed Flavian. He died several days later from his mistreatment at the council and while on his way to his place of exile in Lydia. His body was brought back to Constantinople by Empress Pulcheria, and he was listed in the Roman Martyrology.

Fléchier, Esprit (1632-1710) ● French bishop, preacher, and a member of the French Academy. He was born at Pernes, studying at Tarascon. After entering the congregation headed by his uncle in Tarascon, he departed and went to Paris in 1660 where he secured favor at the court of King Louis XIV through a Latin poem in honor of the king; he was soon the tutor of the dauphin. Fléchier was especially praised as a preacher, achieving the same reputation as François Fénelon, Jules Mascaron, and Jacques Bossuet. Like Bossuet, he excelled at funerary orations, including memorable oratorical presentations at the funerals of Marie Theresa and Turenne. He has been criticized for being highly pretentious in his oratory. Admitted to the French Academy in 1673, he became bishop of Louvain in 1685 and bishop of Nîmes in 1687. There he distinguished himself for his charity and zeal in converting many Huguenots to the faith and for easing the upheaval caused by the revocation of the Edict of Nantes (1685).

Fleury, André Hercule de (1653-1743) ● French cardinal and minister who controlled the government of King Louis XV. It was said by one writer of the three cardinals, who were masters of France, that "Richelieu bled France, Mazarin purged it, and Fleury put it on a diet." Fleury was born at Lodève, the son of a collector of ecclesiastical revenue. After ordination, he was appointed in 1679 to be a chaplain to Marie-Therese, wife of Louis XIV, and then to the king himself in 1683. Appointed bishop of Frejus in 1698, he resigned the see in 1715 when he was given the Abbey of Tournus and was appointed the tutor of Louis XV by the dying Louis XIV. For the next years he guided the education of the new king, remaining largely in the background but growing in the trust and esteem of the young Louis. When in 1723, the duke of Bourbon connived to reduce the ascendancy of Fleury, the latter seemed to accept defeat, returning to Issy. By 1726, Louis had banished the duke of Bourbon from court, replacing him with Fleury. While he never assumed the title *premier ministre* (first minister), Fleury was nevertheless the chief minister of state. From 1726-1743, Fleury was the heart of the government, bringing extensive reform to help France recover from the costly wars of Louis XIV. He presided over the last period of prosperity and sound government before the onset of the political and economic crises that led to the French Revolution. Fleury was a gifted minister but never achieved the notoriety of Richelieu and Mazarin. Louis appointed him cardinal in 1726 to ensure his preeminent position in the royal court.

Fleury, Claude (1640-1725) ● French Cistercian abbot and ecclesiastical historian. Born at Paris, he was educated under the Jesuits at the Collège de Clermont and was called to the bar in 1658. During his years as an attorney, he became an acquaintance of such notables as Jacques Bossuet and Louis Bourdaloue. His increasingly religious nature and the influence of Bourdaloue led to his entering the priesthood in 1672. That year he was appointed by King Louis XIV to be tutor to the princes of Conti; he later tutored the count of Vermandois. In token of his appreciation, Louis made him abbot of the Cistercian monastery of Loc-Dieu. He preached extensively — and worked with Fénelon — to convert the Huguenots. In 1689, he was made tutor to the grandsons of Louis, the young dukes of Burgundy, Berry, and Anjou. He held this post for sixteen years. He was elected to the French Academy in 1696 and was made prior of Notre Dame-d'Argenteuil, near Paris, in 1706. After the death of Louis, Fleury was named (1715) to the post of confessor to Louis XV because he was "neither Jansenist, nor Molinist, not Ultramontanist, but Catholic." A prolific writer, he authored such works as *Histoire du droit français* (1674; *History of the French Right*), *Les moeurs des chrétiens* (1682; *Christian Morals*). His most famous work was *Histoire ecclesiastique* (20 vols., 1691-1720; *Ecclesiastical History*), the first ambitious history of the Church, brought down to 1414. The *Histoire* and several works were placed on the Index of Forbidden Books because of their Gallican views.

Florence, Council of ● See **Ferrara-Florence, Council of**.

Florentius Radewyns (1350-1400) ● Also Florentius Radwijns, the successor of Gerhard Groote (d. 1384) as the leader of the Brethren of the Common Life. One of the earliest members of the society, he was responsible for establishing the first house at Deventer, Holland. (See **Common Life, Brethren of the**.)

Florus (d. c. 860) ● Deacon of Lyons who authored works on theology, canon law, poetry, and the liturgy. Nothing is known about his family or birthplace, although it is generally agreed that he came from the area around Lyons. He served as a deacon to the archbishops of Lyons, Agobard, Amolo, and Remius; he was also a canon of the cathedral church. Much respected for his knowledge of theology, he was often consulted as the

expert in the Frankish Church on important ecclesiastical matters. He wrote extensively on canon law, including *De electionibus episcoporum* (*On the Elections of Bishops*), and liturgy, especially his attacks on Amalarius of Metz for his liturgical changes, and was a specialist on patristic writings. Florus also participated in the predestination controversy; he opposed John Scotus Erigena and defended the ideas of Gottschalk of Fulda. He also wrote poems and an exposition on the Pauline Epistles.

Fonte-Avellana ● Suppressed order of hermits, known for the location of their first hermitage, a valley in the Apennines called Fonte-Avellana after a spring among the pine trees. The order was founded in 977 by Ludolf (d. 1047), a member of a German family that had settled in Gubbio. He took to the life of a hermit and soon attracted followers. By 989, the numbers had grown sufficiently to warrant a rule; this was granted to them by St. Romuald. The rule followed by the hermits was remarkably severe, with the members eating small amounts of bread and water on four days a week, engaging in prayer and manual labor, practicing self-mortification (including self-inflicted scourging), and wearing chains. Known at first as the Congregation of the Dove, they were eventually called the Hermits of Fonte-Avellana (c. 1000). The hermits soon grew prominently, securing the patronage of several popes, including Gregory VII, Boniface VIII, and John XXII. After 1393, however, it entered into a state of decline and was absorbed into the Camaldolese on January 6, 1570. The two famous members of the order were St. Peter Damian and St. Dominic Loricatus.

Fontevrault, Order of ● Also Fontevrand, an order or double order of monks and nuns that was founded in 1099 at the Abbey of Fontevrault in western France near the Vienne and Loire rivers by Robert d'Arbissel

(d. 1177). The monastery was under the Benedictine Rule and was governed by an abbess. As a double order, the monastery had separate area for nuns and monks; it was also characterized by a number of severe additions to the Benedictine Rule. The first abbess was Petronilla, who received a constitution around 1115. Over the next years, dependent houses were established throughout France and in parts of England and Spain. The communities were quite poor until the fourteenth century. Various reforms were instituted between 1475 and 1502, and the order was able to survive the French Revolution. An order for women was revived in 1806 by Madame Rosa. The monastery of Fontevrault was famous in France, especially as the final resting place of King Henry II of England, Eleanor of Aquitaine, and Richard the Lionhearted.

Formosus ● Pope from 891-896 whose posthumous trial by his successor Stephen VI (VII) was one of the darkest moments in papal history. Formosus was made Cardinal of Porto in 864 by Nicholas I. He was utilized subsequently by Nicholas and Adrian I on several diplomatic missions, and was sent to aid in the conversion of Bulgaria. Pope John VIII so feared Formosus that he drove him into exile. Returning to the papal court in 883 under Marinus I, he was elected as successor to Stephen V (VI) in 891. The two main events of his pontificate were his harsh dealings with the Eastern Church and his crowning of King Arnulf as emperor in 896 in an attempt to smash the power of the Italian nobleman Guy of Spoleto. The result was the so-called Cadaver Synod in which Pope Stephen VI (VII) presided over the trial of the deceased pontiff. Formosus was exhumed, placed in a chair, and was charged with various crimes. The decaying corpse had a deacon respond on its behalf. Convicted, his corpse was violated and the acts of his pontificate declared illegal. Succeeding popes repudiated the synod and reinstated Formosus in papal records.

Fortunatus, Venantius (c. 540-c. 600) ● In full, Venantius Honorius Clementianus Fortunatus. Last Gallic poet whose compositions are held to mark the transitional period between ancient and medieval writing. Born in Treviso, near Venice, he was educated at Ravenna. Setting out on a pilgrimage in 565 to give thanks to St. Martin of Tours for healing some ailment of the eye, Fortunatus visited Mainz, Cologne, Trier, Metz, and the Moselle, his progress traceable through his poems. Arriving in Metz in 566, he was received at the court of King Sigebert at the time of the royal marriage with Brunhilda (Brunehild). While at court, Fortunatus won praise for his compositions, especially his eulogies. Continuing his pilgrimage, he went to Verdun, Reims, Soissons, Paris, and finally Tours where he prayed at the tomb of St. Martin. From there, he journeyed to Poitiers, meeting the former Queen Radegunda, now a nun and a future saint. Fortunatus served as secretary to Radegunda until her death in August 587. Around 600, he was made bishop of Poitiers, dying a short time later a renowned poet. He produced eleven books of poems; prose, *Lives* of eleven Gallic saints, including the *Vita Radegundis*; a metrical life of St. Martin of Tours; and the elegy *De Excidio Thuringiae*. His six poems on the cross contained the two exceptional works *Vexilla Regis* and *Pange Lingua Gloriosi*. He was also a friend of St. Gregory of Tours.

Forty Martyrs ● Name given to the forty Catholic martyrs who were put to death by the English government between 1533 and 1680 (not to be confused with the Forty Martyrs of the Diocletian persecution). Originally ranked with the English martyrs of the period, these individuals were considered the most likely candidates for sainthood from among the six hundred or so martyrs in England during the period. It was decided in 1960 to pursue the process of canonization for the forty and thereby concentrate the resources needed to conduct a thorough investigation. The forty were chosen from among the one hundred ninety-nine martyrs who were beatified in 1886, 1895, or 1929. The Vatican officials then agreed to accept the requisite two miracles needed by canon law, but for the entire group of martyrs rather than on an individual basis. Among the best known of the martyrs are Margaret Clitherow, Cuthbert Mayne, Edmund Campion, and Robert Southwell. They were canonized by Pope Paul VI on October 25, 1970. Feast day: October 25. (See also **England** and **English Martyrs**.)

Fourteen Holy Helpers ● See **Auxiliary Saints**.

France ● Called the Eldest Daughter of the Church, France has traditionally been a deeply religious nation, despite the often severe troubles and controversies that faced the French Church. It is unclear when Christianity first reached the Roman provinces of Gaul, but a Christian community was present at Lyons from around 177. That year the Romans put to death Ponthinus, the local bishop and a disciple of the famed St. Polycarp. Later that same century, St. Irenaeus of Lyons (d. 200), a gifted theologian, would distinguish himself through his writings.

The Church continued to expand in the third century, establishing some thirty bishoprics by the mid-third century. St. Denis of Paris became the first bishop of that city. In 313, the Edict of Toleration was issued by Constantine and Licinius Licinianus, ending the persecutions in Gaul. The next year, the Council of Arles was convened, but the Church was subsequently troubled by a variety of heresies, including Arianism, Priscillianism, Semi-Pelagianism, and Novatianism. This era also produced some of France's greatest saints, such as Hilary of Poitiers, Paulinus of Nola, Germanus of Auxerre, and Martin of Tours.

By 400, every town or large community had its own bishop, prompting leaders of the Church in Gaul to labor toward the evangelization of the rural areas. Their progress was sharply curtailed by the invasions of the so-called barbarian tribes, most importantly the Visigoths, Vandals, and Franks. Social upheaval and doctrinal irregularities were attendant upon the chronic political problems as the old Roman imperial order was swept away. The conversion of Clovis, king of the Franks, in 496 to the faith marked a major turning point in the history of France. His dynasty, the Merovingians, would rule from 481-751. In 507, Clovis defeated the Arian Visigoths and extended the Frankish realm into southern Gaul. The most important Church figure in this era was St. Gregory of Tours (d. 594), a bishop and gifted historian. Under Clovis's heirs, the Franks continued to expand, reaching out to influence Germanic lands to the east, thereby opening up missionary activity.

The seventh century witnessed the decay of the Merovingians, who degenerated into the so-called "Lazy Kings," generally ineffectual monarchs. Civil wars and unrest were common, and power gradually collected into the hands of the chief ministers, the mayors of the palace. The greatest of these was Pepin of Heristal (d. c. 714).

In 732, Charles Martel defeated a Moorish force at the Battle of Tours, thus saving Christendom from Muslim invasion. The battle was actually more of a skirmish, but it gave the family of Charles enormous prestige and did end any ambitions by the Moors of launching a campaign of conquest north of the Pyrenees.

In 751, the Merovingians finally fell from

the throne as Pope Zacharias gave his approval to Pepin III the Short to become king of the Franks. The next year, papal envoys crowned Pepin king and in 754 he marched into Italy to save Pope Stephen II (III) from the Lombards. Pepin was crowned by the pontiff and in return he gave the pope the Donation of Pepin, which formed the basis of the Papal States. After Pepin's death in 768, he was succeeded by his two sons, Carloman and Charlemagne. Carloman died in 771, making Charlemagne sole ruler of the Franks.

One of the great figures of the Middle Ages, Charlemagne (742-814) would establish the Carolingian Empire, the largest in Europe since the Roman Empire. Under Charlemagne also took place the Carolingian Renaissance, the rebirth of culture and learning. It was guided by such learned figures as Alcuin and fostered learning in the Church and contributed to the cathedral schools and hence to the universities of the West.

On Christmas Day in 800, Pope Leo III crowned Charlemagne emperor. He may not have been pleased with this development, as it gave the pope the claim of granting the title as a kind of *beneficium*; Charlemagne chose to crown his son Louis the Pious himself, an obvious assertion of independence. Charlemagne died in 814 and the empire he had created over many years would not long survive him.

Division and conflict within the Carolingian Empire began soon after Charlemagne's passing and led to the splitting of the vast imperial domain into three parts, a plan largely organized by the renowned Churchman Hincmar of Reims (806-882). The Treaty of Verdun, making the partition official, has come to be considered the start of modern France. Within the country, feudal lords flourished and the Carolingians fell into decline.

The continued deterioration of the Carolingian Dynasty culminated in 987 with its extinction at the hands of Hugh Capet, who founded the Capetian Dynasty (987-1328). The early Capetians were weak, with the main influence wielded by the nobles and Church officials. Meanwhile,

The St. Louis Psalter

monasticism revived in France with the founding in 910 of the Congregation of Cluny.

The Church would continue to reform itself in France during the eleventh century, thanks to the recently established religious orders. French influence in the wider Church would find important expression with the election of Pope Urban II (r. 1088-1099), a Frenchman named Odo of Lagery, a onetime monk of Cluny. His call in 1095 at the Council of Clermont for a crusade would inaugurate centuries of conflict and martial-religious campaigns in the Middle East and elsewhere (see **Crusades**).

In the twelfth century, France produced some of the foremost theologians and writers of the medieval epoch: Peter Abelard (1079-1142), Anselm (d. 1109), and most of all, Bernard of Clairvaux (1090-1153), who would give counsel to and even intimidate popes and kings.

Considered one of the greatest periods in French history, the 1200s were dominated by King St. Louis IX (r. 1226-1270), and the French Church could boast the University of Paris and the birth of Gothic art and architecture that would make possible the spectacular cathedrals of Notre Dame, Chartres, Amiens, and Reims. The University of Paris became the heart of the Scholastic movement; contributors would include Sts. Albertus Magnus (d. 1280) and Thomas Aquinas (d. 1272). Another leading theologian was St. Bonaventure.

The relationship between the Church and State was close during this period owing to the sanctity of King Louis IX. This changed swiftly with the accession of King Philip IV the Fair in 1285. He came into conflict with Pope Boniface VIII (r. 1294-1303) and ultimately humiliated the pontiff in 1303, hastening Boniface's death from maltreatment and consternation. Philip then brought French sway in Europe to its medieval height by persuading Pope Clement V in 1309 to take up residence in Avignon,

thereby launching the Avignon Papacy (1309-1377).

During the Avignon Papacy, called also the Babylonian Captivity, the Capetians died out in 1328 and were replaced by the Valois branch of the royal line. The Hundred Years' War, which began in 1337 and lasted until 1453, was a terrible struggle that would bring France to the verge of absolute ruin and near defeat by the English. It would be saved only by the miraculous appearance of Joan of Arc (1412-1431), who led French troops to victory at Órléans and made possible the final triumph of France in 1453. Centralization would be fostered by Charles VII (r. 1422-1461) and would continue under King Louis XI (r. 1461-1483). The Church was affected in France and beyond by two notable developments: the Pragmatic Sanction of Bourges (issued by Charles VII in 1438) and the conciliar movement, which derived much of its theological basis from the theologians of the University of Paris, such as Jean Gerson, and helped to bring an end to the Great Schism (1378-1417).

The recovery of France as a major European power was fully developed by 1494 with the invasion of Italy by King Charles VIII, precipitating a conflict with the Habsburgs of the Holy Roman Empire that would dominate much of French politics over the next two centuries. The Pragmatic Sanction was effectively replaced in 1516 with the Concordat of Bologna, signed by King Francis I (r. 1515-1547) and Pope Leo X (1513-1521). While granting extensive rights over the Church in France to the crown, the agreement also prevented any inclination of subsequent kings to embrace the Protestant Reformation.

Protestantism nevertheless took root in France, and much of the 1500s was spent in terrible religious and civil strife, collectively known as the Wars of Religion. They ended in 1594 with the conversion to Catholicism of King Henry IV, the first of the Bourbon kings of France. He issued in 1598 the Edict of

Nantes granting toleration to the Huguenots, but the Catholic faith was still the religion of state. Henry then began what has been called the *grand siécle*, or great century, during which France was Europe's major power, both culturally and politically. Absolutism would predominate, thanks to Cardinal Richelieu (1585-1642), who was virtual ruler of the country as chief minister to King Louis XIII (r. 1610-1643). He would involve France in the Thirty Years' War (1618-1648) against the empire; his policies were continued by Cardinal Jules Mazarin (1602-1661). Louis XIV, who came into his majority with the death of Cardinal Mazarin, brought the central control of the French crown to its height, claiming the throne by divine right and pursuing a stern Gallicanist policy toward the Church.

France also profited from the Catholic Reformation and from towering Church figures, among them Sts. Francis de Sales and Vincent de Paul and Cardinal Pierre Bérulle as well as the superb orator Jacques Bossuet and François Fénelon, archbishop of Cambrai. (See also **Descartes, René** and **Pascal, Blaise**.)

The 1700s brought severe hardships to the faith, first from the Enlightenment with intellectuals including Voltaire, Rousseau, and Diderot, and then from the French Revolution, which began in 1789. The *ancien*

King Louis XIV

régime (old regime) was utterly swept away, replaced by the call for *egalité, liberté, fraternité*; with it came sharp restrictions on the Church and debilitating new laws, most notably the Civil Constitution of the Clergy of 1790, which was condemned by Pope Pius VI (r. 1775-1799). In the wars that followed the outset of the revolution the pope was seized and died in exile (see **Pius VI**). The Church, meanwhile, was plunged into a state of schism in France over the new laws, a lamentable condition that would not be rectified until the Concordat of 1801 between Napoleon and Pius VII. (See **Civil Constitution of the Clergy**.)

Napoleon took power in 1799, on November 9 (or 18 *Brumaire* in the French Revolution calendar), becoming first consul and leading the French forces to a smashing victory over the Austrians at Marengo on June 14, 1800, thereby ensuring the survival of his government. Anxious to stabilize the religious situation, he negotiated the concordat with Pius, which he immediately abrogated with the Organic Articles (1802). Napoleon was crowned emperor at Notre Dame in 1804 by Pius, but relations were never cordial, deteriorating further over the succeeding years as Napoleon moved to control the French Church even further. The Papal States were annexed in 1809 to the French Empire and Pius was carried off as a prisoner of the emperor. Pius's freedom was won only as Napoleon fell from power in 1814. The emperor would return briefly in 1815 but would face a final defeat at Waterloo on June 18, 1815.

In the period following Napoleon, the Church enjoyed a revival, partly inspired by the writings of François de Chateaubriand in *Génie du Christianisme* (1802; *The Genius of Christianity*) and as a response to the oppression of the Church by the emperor. Anti-Gallican sympathies would predominate, along with Ultramontanism, which would reach its peak at the First Vatican Council (1869-1870). Within the French Church, a division developed over the value of the ideals and legacy of the French Revolution. In the later years of the 1800s, Modernism became widespread, with such leading advocates as Maurice Blondel, Alfred Loisy, and Lucien Laberthonnière. It would later be condemned by Pope St. Pius X (r. 1903-1914), who called it the "synthesis of all the heresies."

The 1800s also saw in France considerable political changes. The monarchy was restored after the fall of Napoleon under King Louis XVIII (r. 1814-1824). His son Charles X (r. 1824-1830) was replaced by the liberal duke of Orléans, Louis Philippe, who was himself overthrown in 1848 in a revolution. The Second Republic was declared in 1851. The nephew of Napoleon assumed the title Napoleon III in 1852. The Second Republic would survive until 1870 and the crushing defeat of France in the Franco-Prussian War. Napoleon was deposed and the Third Republic declared, but only after bloody fighting in Paris that claimed the life of another archbishop of Paris. The Third Republic would endure until 1940. Its early history was characterized by hostility toward Catholicism. Anticlerical legislation was introduced, the religious orders were harassed and, through the Education Act (1882), teaching was secularized. Catholic education was curtailed and Jesuit houses were closed.

Pope Leo XIII (r. 1879-1903) tried to maintain the agreement signed with France (the Concordat of 1801). His efforts, though, at convincing French Catholics to follow his lead failed in 1892, as the Catholic population was fragmented with many adamantly opposing all Republicanism. The most vocal anti-Republicans were found in *L'Action Française*. Leo's successor, St. Pius X (r. 1903-1914), was confronted by even more anti-Church legislation that reached a climax in 1905 with the Law of Separation. This annulled the Concordat of 1801 and ended the centuries-old association of the Church and State in France. The Church lost its stipends and had its properties seized. Pius protested with an encyclical in 1906 and diplomatic relations were severed until 1921. The Republic was careful not to seem overly vindictive or out to persecute the faithful, but the result of the law was to cause virtual financial ruin for the French Church in the short term. Over time, the French hierarchy and the papacy found that freedom of any state interference in ecclesiastical affairs was a favorable development that had a useful by-product: a greater devotion to the Holy See and the virtual eradication of any lingering Gallican tendencies.

The ensuing years saw the quiet return of the religious orders and the winning of the respect for the clergy because of the courage shown by French priests in the blood-soaked fields of World War I. In the postwar period, Catholic intellectuals flourished, among them Étienne Gilson (1884-1978) and Jacques Maritain (1882-1973), and the Church was in the forefront of providing assistance and relief during World War II and the occupation of France by Nazi Germany. The Church today is considered to be in a state of deep anxiety as it labors to confront and reverse the baleful effects of materialism and the apparently moribund condition of the spiritual life in Western Europe. While the country is nominally a Catholic one, Church attendance is depressingly low and future prospects seem dim. On the positive side is the presence of energetic French Churchmen both in France and in the Curia, such as Cardinal Jean-Marie Lustiger, archbishop of Paris, Cardinal Robert Coffy, archbishop of Marseilles, and Cardinals Roger Etchegaray and Paul Poupard of the Roman Curia.

Frances of Rome, St. (1384-1440) ● Founder of the Oblate Congregation of Tor de'Specchi, also the Oblates of St. Frances of Rome. She is considered the model for the ideal wife and widow. A native of Rome, she wed Lorenzo de'Ponziani in 1347 despite her private desire to join a religious order. A caring and exemplary wife, she also led a firm spiritual life with the help of her husband's brother's wife, Vannozza. The family suffered greatly during the Great Schism, particularly after Ladislas of Naples took Rome in 1408. Frances lived in a habitable part of her ruined palace, husbanding her resources and giving them to the poor. In 1425, with Lorenzo's approval, she founded a society of women to help the poor. The women were not under strict vows, but they were known as the Oblates of Mary. In 1433, the name of the order was changed to the Oblates of Tor de' Specchi after the house in which they resided. Following Lorenzo's death in 1436, Frances entered the congregation and became its superior. She was blessed in her final years by the continuous vision of her guardian angel. Canonized in 1608 by Pope Paul V, she was declared patron of motorists by Pope Pius XI. Feast day: March 9.

Francis I (1494-1547) ● Ruler of France from 1515-1547, a Renaissance figure, patron of the arts, enemy of Emperor Charles

King Francis I of France

V, and a generally ambitious and unscrupulous monarch who was partly responsible for the spread of the Protestant Reformation in Europe. The son-in-law of King Louis XII, he succeeded to the throne with virtually no political experience. Nevertheless, he resumed the Italian Wars and personally led his troops into battle. In 1519, he lost a bid to become Holy Roman Emperor to Charles V, causing a bitter rivalry. Even though he failed at the Field of the Cloth of Gold to secure an alliance with Henry VIII of England in 1520, Francis declared war on Charles in 1521. He was captured at the disastrous Battle of Pavia in 1525, and France was forced to accept the Treaty of Madrid, since he had "lost all save life and honor." After his release, however, the war continued as Francis organized an alliance, the League of Cognac, with Pope Clement VII, Venice, Florence, and Henry VIII against Charles. Years of struggle followed (1527-1529, 1536-1538), but Francis never gained the upper hand. His alliance with Suleiman I, the Ottoman sultan, and his promotion of increasingly Protestant German princes proved not only unsuccessful but also seriously undermined Christian unity at the worst possible time. His failure to rescue Clement from Charles's domination of Rome doomed Henry's hopes of divorce and thus precipitated the loss of England by the Church. While he tolerated humanist and Protestant intellectual circles, he did not permit rampant Protestantism in France, particularly after 1534. Among the notables who received his patronage were Leonardo da Vinci and François Rabelais.

Francis Borgia, St. (1510-1572) ● Spanish Jesuit and the third general of the order, from 1565. A member of the infamous Borgia family, he was the great grandson of Pope Alexander VI and the son of the duke of Gandia. Succeeding to the ducal title in 1543, he was married to Leonora de Castro and became a trusted courtier of Emperor Charles V, being appointed viceroy of Catalonia. He entered the Society of Jesus after the death of his wife in 1546. A friend and adviser of Ignatius Loyola, he was ordained in 1551 at Rome. Francis was responsible for promoting schools and colleges and for providing money for the Collegium Romanum. He subsequently assumed a major role in organizing the foreign missions of the order and was named commissary general of the Jesuits for Spain, Portugal, and the Indies. Succeeding James Laínez as general of the Jesuits, he sent missionaries to Northern and Eastern Europe and worked to bring Catholic Reform. He also edited the rule and the Spiritual Exercises. Clement X canonized him in 1671. Feast day: October 10.

Francis de Sales, St. (1567-1622) ●

Bishop of Geneva, spiritual writer, Doctor of the Church, and patron of the Catholic press. Francis was born in Savoy, in the Château de Sales. He studied at Annecy, in Paris (1581-1588), and the University of Padua (1588-1592), choosing to abandon a potentially brilliant secular career to enter the religious life. Despite his father's opposition, he was ordained in 1593, subsequently being appointed to the post of provost of Geneva. That same year he undertook his first major mission: he went to the Chablais to preach among the Calvinists. His labors and sermonizing lasted for four years and, in the face of great physical danger and challenges, he was largely successful in converting most of the inhabitants. Nominated coadjutor bishop of Geneva in 1599, he was consecrated in 1602 to become bishop of Geneva. He launched a vigorous reform of his diocese, preaching

throughout the parishes, acting as a tireless confessor, and promoting the spread of the catechism. In 1604, he met St. Jane Frances de Chantal. Serving as her spiritual director for several years, in 1610 he founded with her the Order of the Visitation. Francis was the author of numerous and extremely popular devotional writings. Chief among these were the *Introduction to the Devout Life* (1609) and *Treatise on the Love of God* (1616). The *Introduction* began as a small manual for the use by Madame de Charmoisy, his cousin's wife, and was intended to encourage the life of prayer and devotion. It was much respected by a wide cross section of European culture, including King James I of England. One of his most important maxims declared: "It is a mistake, a heresy, to want to exclude devoutness of life from among soldiers, from shops and offices, from royal courts, from the homes of the married." He died at the Visitandine convent of Bellecour, Lyons. Beatified in 1661, he was canonized in 1665 by Pope Alexander VII. In 1887, Pope Leo XIII proclaimed him a Doctor of the Church, and in 1923 Pope Pius XI named him patron of the Catholic press and Catholic writers. Feast day: January 24.

Francis of Assisi, St. (c. 1181-1226) ●

Founder of the Franciscan order and one of the most famous and beloved of all saints. He was born Giovanni di Bernardone, the son of a cloth merchant from Assisi, Pietro Bernardone, and his wife, Pica, who came from a distinguished French family. Until the age of twenty, he worked for his father, receiving the name Francesco from his father's business trips through France. He was very popular in Assisi because of his generosity and his fun-loving, carefree attitude. This changed dramatically in 1202 when Francis joined in a campaign against a rival city, Perugia. Captured in battle, he spent a desolate period in prison. After his release, he found life quite unappealing, his unease only increasing after enduring a lengthy illness. There followed what was called his conversion. He took to prayer and worked among the poor. One day, however, he encountered a leper and turned away, repulsed by the man's grotesque appearance. Stopping himself, Francis gave the man some money and then kissed him. While on a pilgrimage to Rome, he gave his clothes away to some beggars and spent a day begging for alms before St. Peter's.

When Francis returned home to Assisi, he prayed at the Church of San Damiano and heard a command from the crucifix, telling him: "Repair my house, which is virtually ruined." To pay for the repairs in the church, he sold bales of his father's cloth, along with the horse dragging them. Pietro beat Francis and locked him in his room. Francis was released by his mother, and, when his father went to the bishop to demand the money back, Francis stripped off his clothes, saying that they too belonged to his father. Henceforth he dressed in a coarse woolen cloak tied at the waist to commemorate the cloak given to him by the bishop to cover his nakedness.

He spent the next period rebuilding with his own hands the Church of San Damiano. In 1208, while he worshiped at Mass in the nearby town of Portiuncula, he heard the Gospel passage from Matthew (10:7-19, in which Christ sends forth his Apostles to preach) and decided to set out himself. Preaching throughout the area, he soon acquired considerable notoriety and was called *Il Poverello* (The Little Poor Man). Others joined him, some of the earliest and most notable being the merchant Bernard, the canon Pietro, and the famous Brother Giles (St. Giles of Assisi). For them and the others who gathered about him, Francis composed a simple rule of life, called the *regula primitiva*. This rule he took to Rome in 1210 where he won approval for it from Pope Innocent III (r. 1198-1216), whose initial reluctance was melted supposedly by a dream in which he saw Francis holding up the walls of St. John Lateran. So was begun the Franciscan order. Its members practiced rigorous asceticism and extreme poverty, relying upon alms as they wandered across Italy to preach. Under St. Clare of Assisi, a second order of Franciscans was launched in 1212; almost a decade later, around 1221, the third order was established for laypeople, both men and women.

St. Francis of Assisi

Having succeeded in organizing his friars in Italy, Francis decided to travel to other lands around 1214. Choosing to go to the Holy Land, he set out for Palestine but was shipwrecked and then fell ill. In 1219, he reached Egypt, witnessing the siege of Damietta by the crusaders (November 1219) and going to the camp of the sultan of Egypt.

The Muslim ruler was said to have been so impressed with the little friar that he gave him permission to visit the holy places.

Francis returned to Europe to find the order deeply troubled by irregularities and various crises caused by the rapid growth in membership in Italy, Spain, Germany, even Hungary. He reluctantly accepted the fact that a revision in the rule might be needed, undertaking the creation of the revised rule with the help of Peter Cathanii and, after his death in 1221, Elias of Cortona. Pope Honorius III approved the new rule on November 29, 1223. From that time, Francis left the affairs of the order to others, withdrawing from the world. In September 1224, he received the stigmata on Mt. Alvernia in the Apennines. His health and eyesight, already poor, deteriorated rapidly; he died on October 3, 1226, at the Portiuncula, his "little chapel." Pope Gregory IX canonized him a mere two years later, on July 16, 1228. A saint of deceptive simplicity, Francis composed a number of hymns and prayers; the famed "Canticle of the Sun" is attributed to him. He is the patron of Italy, ecologists, and Catholic Action. Feast day: October 4.

Francis of Meyronnes (d. after 1328) ●

Franciscan philosopher and theologian, and an ardent supporter of the ideas of John Duns Scotus. Francis was born in Meyronnes, France, studying under Duns Scotus at the University of Paris. Aside from his many works on Duns Scotus, for which he earned the title "Prince of the Scotists," he founded the so-called Maronitae (Meyronist) school of philosophy, a branch of the Scotist school. His writings include: commentaries on Aristotle's *Physics, Universal and Categories*, and *On Interpretations*; commentaries on the *Sentences* of Peter Lombard; and several treatises, among them *De Formitatibus* (*On Formalities*) and *De univocatione Entis* (*On the Univocity of Being*).

Francis of Paola, St. (1416-1507) ●

Founder of the Minim Friars (from the Latin *Ordo Fratrum Minimorum*) and a noted ascetic. He was born to a poor family in Paola, Italy. Spending a year with the Franciscans at San Marco, he developed a tendency toward austerity and in 1430 became a hermit in a cave near the sea at Paola. There he was joined by two followers around 1435. They established themselves as the Hermits of St. Francis of Assisi, later calling themselves the *Fratres Minimi* (or the "Least Brothers") in 1492. The congregation spread quickly in Western Europe, particularly in Italy, France, Germany, and Spain as well as in Bohemia. Francis, meanwhile, acquired the reputation for deep sanctity and miraculous skills; such were the reports about him that King Louis XI (r. 1461-1483) summoned him to France in the hopes of receiving a cure for his terminal illness. His son, Charles VIII, built monasteries in France and appointed him spiritual adviser. He was canonized in 1519 by Pope Leo X and was named patron of sailors in 1943 by Pope Pius XII. Feast day: April 2.

Francis Regis Clet, Bl. (1748-1820) ●

Missionary to China and a martyr, a member of the Lazarist Missionaries. The son of a merchant of Grenoble, France, he was the tenth of fifteen children. Francis attended the Jesuit College of Grenoble, entering the novitiate of the Congregation of the Mission (or Lazarists) in 1769, and was ordained a priest in 1773. After teaching seminary at Annecy and Paris, he was forced to endure the destruction of the motherhouse of St. Lazaire, where he had taught at the eve of the storming of the Bastille and the onset of the French Revolution in 1789. Forced to flee France, he became a missionary and was sent to China in 1791. There he labored for his remaining years, succeeding in attracting a number of converts but also receiving a number of setbacks: his church and schoolhouse were burned down in 1812, and persecutions were always a threat. In 1819, after evading a number of searches for him and with a large reward on his head, he was finally captured. Enduring terrible sufferings, he was executed by strangulation on February 18, 1820.

Francis, Rule of ● See **Francis of Assisi, St.** and **Franciscans**.

Francis Xavier, St. (1506-1552) ●
Spanish Jesuit and one of the greatest missionaries in the history of the Church whose work in the Far East earned him the title "Apostle of the East Indies" and "Apostle of Japan." Francis was born near Pamplona, in Navarre, to a noble Spanish-Basque family. He went to Paris to study and, while at the university there, he met and came under the influence of St. Ignatius Loyola. On August 15, 1534, at Montmarte, Francis, Ignatius, and five others took vows by which they dedicated their lives to God, promised to embrace chastity and poverty, and pledged to bring the Gospels to the heathen across the world. He was thus one of the very first Jesuits and was ordained with his fellow members in Venice on Midsummer Day, 1537.

In 1541, Francis set sail from Lisbon, Portugal, for India in response to an invitation from King Juan III of Portugal. He and his two companions reached Goa in May 1542, spending the next seven years in missionary labors in the city, among the people of southern India, and throughout Ceylon (modern-day Sri Lanka). His work during this period was more successful among the lower castes of Indian society than the upper (or Brahman) caste. Francis and his fellow Jesuits encountered much difficulty not only among the Hindus (whose religion they did not understand) but also among the Portuguese and Europeans (whose predations against and exploitation of the native populations they found repellent).

In 1549, Francis left Malacca and sailed to Japan. He studied Japanese for a time at Kagoshima and then set out for Kyoto. For two years he taught and attracted converts, departing Japan in 1552 after entrusting the local community to a Portuguese priest. He first went to Goa and then embarked for China where foreigners were forbidden entry. Landing on the island of Shangchwan, he fell ill while waiting for a Chinese junk that was supposed to transport him in secret to the mainland. His hopes of entering China died with him in a small hut on December 2, 1552. His body was taken back to Goa where it was enshrined in the Church of the Good Jesus.

The most traveled missionary since apostolic times, Francis Xavier spent only ten years (1542-1552) in active work. In that time, however, his unflagging zeal and determination took him to a staggering number of lands where he was responsible for the conversion of thousands (Jesuit sources put the number at seven hundred thousand), leaving behind him organized and thriving Christian communities. Pope Gregory XV canonized him in 1622, and Pope St. Pius X named him patron saint of Catholic foreign missions. Feast day: December 3.

Franciscan Controversy ● See under **Franciscans**, following entry.

Franciscans ● Religious order founded by St. Francis of Assisi, known in full as the Order of Friars Minor. The Franciscans were not established as part of a planned program by Francis, since he never intended to found a new religious organization. By the force of his example and the degree of his personal holiness, Francis attracted followers, the first members joining him in 1208. By the next year, their number had grown to twelve, and Francis decided to travel to Rome with them to ask for approval of their rule, the *regula primitiva*, from Pope Innocent III (r.

1198-1216). The pope gave them his approval and each took vows of poverty, obedience, and chastity; the one exception was Brother Sylvester, a priest who received a tonsure. The date of the papal approbation, April 16, 1209, is considered the official start of the Order of Friars Minor.

The early Franciscans resided in Umbria, but the members preached extensively throughout Italy and were characterized especially by their adherence to the rule of poverty. The friars were soon joined by the so-called Second Order of St. Francis, established in 1212 through the desire of St. Clare of Assisi to imitate Francis in his way of life. The women who came to join her were called the Poor Ladies (later the Poor Clares). A third group, comprised of laypeople who wished to share in the goals and life of the Franciscans, received their own rule around 1221; their rule, first written by Francis, then rewritten by Cardinal Ugolino and approved by Pope Honorius III, was the basis of the Third Order of Franciscans.

The order, meanwhile, was growing swiftly, and it was decided to provide further explanations and clarifications of the rule by giving it definite form. The long rule, of twenty-three chapters, was issued in 1221; a shortened version, of twelve chapters, was accepted by Honorius III on November 29, 1223, in the bull *Solet annuere*. The rule stipulated corporate and individual poverty and created the remarkable mendicant structure with its emphasis on both the active and contemplative life. Francis also made certain that the rule took into account the need for foreign missions, the first such declaration for any religious order. On the example of Francis himself, the order would embark on many missionary endeavors around the world so that by the fifteenth century, friars had visited such distant lands as China and Africa. They would be active especially in the New World from the sixteenth century.

As a result of its growth, the Franciscans came to the recognition that it needed better organization. Coupled with this was the increasing belief by many members that the original severity of the rule was impractical. This would become the central crisis facing the order and was present even before Francis' death in 1226. Two main groups among the friars developed: the Spirituals, who desired a precise adherence to the letter of the rule and the spirit of their saintly founder; and the majority of friars, who favored a moderate interpretation. From the start, both sides were intransigent, and the unity of the order was seriously endangered.

A major breach was avoided under the brilliant leadership of St. Bonaventure, superior general of the order from 1257-1274. The matter of the Spirituals was brought before the Holy See, starting in 1310. In 1317-1318, Pope John XXII (r. 1316-1334) decided against the Spirituals; in 1322, he reversed the rule concerning corporate poverty. Many Spirituals, however, refused to accept this command, leaving the order to become the schismatic body known as the Fraticelli. Within the order, the removal of the law against ownership had the effect of fostering wealth, but the 1300s also witnessed a trend toward laxity. Reforms were introduced, leading to the division of the Franciscans into the Observants (who preferred the rules of poverty) and the Conventuals (who wanted the papal decision left as it was). Such was the split that it received formal recognition by the Council of Constance in 1415, an important victory for the Observants.

In 1443, Pope Eugenius IV gave the Observants their own vicar-general, although technically they still belonged to the Franciscan order and thus were joined to the Conventuals. Finally, in 1517, the Observants and Conventuals were separated. Henceforth, the Observants were officially called the Order of Friars Minor of the Regular Observance (shortened to Order of Friars Minor, or O.F.M.); the Conventuals were called the Order of Friars Minor Conventual (O.F.M. Conv.). A third Franciscan order, the Capuchins (Order of Friars Minor Capuchin, or O.F.M. Cap.), was recognized in 1528 (see **Capuchins**).

The Observants fostered a number of additional reforming groups, such as the Capuchins, and also the Discalced, the Reformati, and the Recollects. The latter would play a leading role in the early foundation of the Church in Canada. During the 1500s, the Observants grew enormously, subsequently suffering in the 1700s and 1800s, during the French Revolution, Napoleonic Wars, and in the *Kulturkampf*. Today, the Friars Minor (Observants) are the second largest religious order in the Church, numbering over eighteen thousand members. The Capuchins are the fourth largest, with more than eleven thousand members, while the Conventuals have some four thousand members.

The Franciscans have produced some truly great saints and remarkable theologians. Among the most notable are St. Bonaventure, St. Antony of Padua, St. Bernardino of Siena, St. John Capistran, St. Joseph Cupertino, St. Lawrence of Brindisi, St. Francis Mary of Camporosso, William of Occam, John Duns Scotus, Alexander of Hales, Roger Bacon, the famed travelers Fra Giovanni Pianô Carpini and John of Monte Corvino, and Popes Sixtus IV (r. 1471-1484), Sixtus V (r. 1585-1590), and Clement XIV (r. 1769-1774).

Francisco à Sancta Clara (1598-1680) ● English Catholic theologian. Born Christopher Davenport, he was educated at Dublin and Oxford before his conversion to Catholicism. Leaving England, he journeyed to Douai in 1615 and joined the Franciscans at Ypres in 1617, taking the name Francisco à Sancta Clara. After entering the English Recollects at the newly established convent of St. Bonaventure at Douai in 1618, he was sent to Salamanca University. Returning to Douai, he served as professor of theology at St. Bonaventure. Dispatched to England, he was appointed chaplain to Queens Henrietta Maria and Catherine of Braganza. He was on very good terms with prominent Anglicans and successfully converted many, including Anne, duchess of York. Convinced that a reunion was possible, he authored the *Paraphrastica Expositio Articulorum Confessionis Anglicanae* (published separately in 1634, and as an appendix to his *Deus, natura, gratia*), an attempt to prove that the Thirty-Nine Articles could be interpreted as being in accordance with Catholic teaching. Placed on the Index of Forbidden Books in Spain, the work avoided condemnation by the Holy See only through the intervention of the papal nuncio to England.

Franco, Francisco (1892-1975) ● See **Spain**.

Frankfurt, Councils of ● Site of some sixteen imperial councils, held under the Carolingians, the most famous and important being that of 794. This council was convened by Charlemagne with the approval of Pope Adrian I and was concerned with bringing about improvements in ecclesiastical discipline and condemning the heresy of Adoptionism. In attendance were bishops from the Frankish realm and prelates from Italy, England, and Aquitaine; Adrian was represented by two legates, Theophylact and Stephen. Fifty-six canons in all were passed by the council. The first condemned Adoptionism. The second condemned the decree of the Second Council of Nicaea (787) on the worship of icons, the result of a faulty Latin translation, that seemed to call for the veneration of images to the same degree as the Blessed Trinity. The council had not done this, but the Frankfurt Fathers were certain to make sure no such doctrinal impression could be allowed to remain.

Franks ● See **France**; see also Carolingian Renaissance under **Carolingian Schools; Charlemagne; Clovis; Germany;** and **Holy Roman Empire**.

Franzelin, Johannes Baptist (1811-1886) ● Austrian cardinal and theologian. He was born at Aldein in the Tyrol and, despite his family's poverty, he was sent to the nearby Franciscan College at Bolzano. In 1834, he joined the Society of Jesus at Graz and spent many years studying and then teaching in Austrian Poland. In 1845, he was in Rome where he served as an assistant in Hebrew in the Jesuit College of Rome. Forced to leave Rome because of the Revolution of 1848, Franzelin journeyed to England, Belgium, and France. He was ordained in France in 1849. Returning to the Roman College as a lecturer in 1850, he was appointed in 1853 as prefect of studies in the German College and as a professor of dogmatic theology in the Roman College in 1857. He held this post for nineteen years, acting as a consultant to several Roman congregations and as a papal theologian during Vatican Council I. Despite his protests, Franzelin was raised to the cardinalate in 1876 by Pope Pius IX. A highly respected theologian, he authored numerous treatises, including *De Divina Traditione et Scriptura* (1870; *On Divine Tradition and Scripture*), *De Verbe Incarnato* (1870; *On the Incarnate Word*), and *De Ecclesia Christi* (1887; *On the Church of Christ*).

Fraticelli ● Name used for several heretical sects during the 1300s and 1400s; it was also used in general terms for the mendicant friars, and, more specifically, the Spiritual Franciscans. The word Fraticelli was found principally in Italy and was probably derived from the Italian *frate* (plural: *frati*), the term meaning the members of the mendicants, especially the Franciscans, or the Friars Minor. Its two most frequent applications were for Spiritual

Franciscans, particularly after the condemnation of the followers of Angelo Clareno (d. 1337) in 1317 by Pope John XXII in the bull *Sancta Romana* and for the so-called Michaelites (disciples of Michael of Cesena in the early 1300s). (See also **Spiritual Franciscans**.)

Fredegis of Tours (d. 834) ● Anglo-Saxon monk, writer, and teacher who was also a prominent figure in the famed Palace School of Charlemagne. A native of England, he studied under Alcuin at York and then at the court of Charlemagne. He emerged as one of the most respected scholars at the Palace School of Aachen, where he was known as Nathaniel. While it is highly probable that he remained from 796-804 at the court after Alcuin left to become abbot of Tours, it most likely not true that he was named Alcuin's successor as head of the school. In 804, however, he did follow Alcuin as abbot of Tours. Fredegis authored several poems and a treatise, *De nihilo et tenebris* (*On nothing and darkness*), that was addressed "to all the faithful and to those who dwell in the sacred palace of the most serene prince Charles."

Frederick I Barbarossa (c. 1123-1190) ● King of Germany from 1152-1190 and Holy Roman Emperor from 1155, called Barbarossa (Red Beard) and a formidable enemy of the papacy. The son of Frederick II (duke of Swabia) and Judith (daughter of Henry IX, duke of Bavaria), he was elected German king in 1152 to succeed Emperor Conrad III in the hopes that he might bring an end to the terrible dynastic struggles that had plagued the empire. In 1154, he launched a campaign in Italy, the first of six Italian military adventures. After hanging the disputatious Roman leader Arnold of Brescia and restoring order to Rome, he was crowned emperor on June 18, 1155, by Pope Adrian IV. In Germany, Frederick made as his principal objective the establishing of his political supremacy as a counter to the powerful German princes who posed a chronic threat to imperial authority. Frederick organized imperial territories strategically placed between princely lands, appointing his own agents as governors who were subject only to his will. While he was able to keep in check the dangerous Henry the Lion (duke of Saxony, 1142-1180; duke of Bavaria, 1156-1180), Frederick had less luck with other princes. Turning his attention once more to Italy, Frederick harbored ambitions of promoting imperial rights in the region, using the Diet of Roncaglia (1158) to proclaim his intentions of absorbing Italy into the Holy Roman Empire.

Emperor
Frederick I Barbarossa

Opposition was rallied immediately by Pope Alexander III (r. 1159-1181) and other anti-imperial cities. Alexander excommunicated Frederick in 1160, fleeing to France the next year where he received support from France, England, Spain, and Lombardy. In response, Frederick installed the antipopes Victor IV and Paschal III, invaded Italy in 1166, and marched against the so-called Lombard League, an alliance of Italian cities. His campaign ended in failure, requiring yet another effort in 1174 that compelled the Lombards to sign the Armistice of Montebello. In 1176, however, fighting ensued again and Frederick was severely beaten at the Battle of Legnano. An agreement was reached in 1177 at Anagni with Pope Alexander by which Frederick acknowledged his enemy as the true pontiff. Peace was made in 1183 with the Lombards, although a diplomatic triumph was achieved by the marriage of Frederick's son Henry (VI)

to Constance, heiress of Sicily, in 1186. Three years later, Frederick embarked on the Third Crusade with Richard the Lionhearted of England and Philip II Augustus of France. He drowned while crossing the Salyeh River in Cilicia, his armor preventing him from escaping a watery death. While an avowed enemy of the papacy, Frederick became a near legendary figure in German history, his reign seen as the high point of German unity during the Middle Ages.

Frederick II (1194-1250)
● German king from 1212-1250 and Holy Roman Emperor from 1220 whose long reign marked the zenith of imperial rule in Italy and was distinguished by his often bitter struggle with the papacy. The grandson of Emperor Frederick I Barbarossa and the son of Emperor Henry VI and Constance of Sicily, Frederick was crowned king of Sicily in May 1198 and was placed under the care of Pope Innocent III by his mother, who died a short time later. After marrying Constance of Aragon in 1208, he made a claim to the Germanic crown in 1211, gathering the support of German princes. His rival, Otto of Brunswick, was deposed and in 1212 Frederick was elected king; his position was finally guaranteed in 1214 when Otto was routed at the Battle of Bouvines by Frederick's French allies. Reluctantly crowned emperor in 1220 by Pope Honorius III, Frederick was first required to make a pledge of embarking upon a crusade. Several years were spent consolidating his political position, and Frederick finally set out in 1227 after issuing the Diet of Cremona (1226) by which he

asserted his rights in Italy. An epidemic broke out on his ships and so many soldiers died that Frederick returned to Brindisi. Refusing to believe Frederick's claims of the severity of the plague, Pope Gregory IX excommunicated him in 1228. Brushing aside the pope, Frederick set sail, reaching the Holy Land where he entered into negotiations with the sultan of Egypt. In a major achievement, Frederick won control of Jerusalem, Bethlehem, and Nazareth, entering Jerusalem on March 18, 1229, where he was crowned king of Jerusalem. His supporters proved remarkably few owing to his state of affairs with Gregory, the bulk of his followers being comprised of the Teutonic Knights. In a bizarre turn of events, Frederick was rejected by most of the Christian princes but was recognized by the Muslims.

Returning to Italy, Frederick regained all of the territory that had been seized by his enemies in his absence, signing the Treaty of San Germano in 1230 with the pope, who revoked his ban of excommunication. After issuing a new constitution for Sicily at Amalfi in 1231, Frederick's grand plans for the empire were ruined by the treasonous actions of his son Henry (VII), whom he had installed as king of Germany in 1220. Henry was imprisoned, dying in 1242. Another son, Conrad IV, was made German king in 1237. Frederick routed the Lombards at the Battle of Cortenuova the same year, encouraging him to bring all of Italy under his control. This naturally brought him into conflict with the papacy, a formal break occurring in 1239 when Gregory once more excommunicated the emperor. Frederick marched on the Papal States in 1240, reaching Rome in 1241. He was at the gates of the city when word arrived that Gregory was dead. Negotiations with Pope Innocent IV (r. 1243-1254) collapsed and more fighting followed. Recovering from a series of defeats between 1247 and 1250, Frederick made a remarkable return in both Italy and Germany but died suddenly from dysentery on

December 13, 1250, in Apulia. Within a few short years the Hohenstaufen Dynasty had been extinguished. His rule was very much oriented to the Mediterranean, so much so that he chose as the place of his court Palermo, Sicily, which became a center of Oriental opulence. In Sicily, Frederick instituted broad reforms in law and finance, expanding commerce and industry. Considered by contemporaries as a figure of immense erudition, he was the author of a book on falconry, a poet, and a linguist; he was also a patron of medicine, astronomy, and mathematics.

Free From Rome Movement ● See **Los-von-Rom Movement**.

Free Spirit, Brethren of the ● Term used during the Middle Ages for the members of loosely organized mystical and heretical sects, so-called because they rejected the authority of the Church in favor of religious and doctrinal freedom, rooted in the Spirit. The Brethren probably originated in the thirteenth century and were much reduced by the Inquisition.

Free Thinkers ● Those individuals who reject religious doctrines and truth and will accept no teachings on Christian revelation because they believe in the findings of reason alone. The Free Thinkers as a term first appeared in the early 1700s in connection with the English Deists, particularly in the work "Discourse of Freethinking occasioned by the Rise and Growth of a Sect called the Freethinkers" by Collins. Proponents of free thought, however, argued that freethinking had been around for many centuries, as expressed by the early heretics, who opposed the Church. Among the religious tenets opposed by some Free Thinkers were miracles, external revelation, immortality of the soul, and, in some corners, the very existence of God. Notable members included

Voltaire and Thomas Paine. (See also **Deism** and **Enlightenment**.)

Freemasonry ● Teachings, practices, and principles of the long-secret fraternal organization of the so-called Free and Accepted Masons. The Freemasons were supposedly first established by the builders of Solomon's Temple in Jerusalem, but the historical origins of the organization are found in the Middle Ages when English stonemasons began a religious fraternity under the patronage of St. John the Baptist. They sought to keep and safeguard the secrets of their craft, but toward the end of the medieval epoch its members were devoted mostly to religious instruction. Abolished by King Edward VI in 1547, it reformed, starting in the eighteenth century. The beginnings of modern Freemasonry date to 1717 when the first Grand Lodge was founded in London. The order spread to the Continent and found appeal among the upper classes and intellectual circles. In England, Germany, and elsewhere, Freemasons embraced deistic (see **Deism**) and naturalistic religious views, in keeping with the prevailing currents of thought in the Enlightenment. In other regions — Italy and France especially — they were often distinctly hostile to religion, displaying anticlerical and atheistic tendencies. In the United States, the Freemasons have been devoted in the main to philanthropic activities, claiming as distinguished members George Washington and other Founding Fathers.

Owing to its inveterate hostility in parts of Europe to the Church and its doctrines, authorities long forbade Catholics from joining under pain of excommunication, and numerous popes spoke out against the Masons. The first was Pope Clement XII in 1738. He was followed by Benedict XIV (r. 1740-1758), Pius VII (r. 1800-1823), Pius IX (r. 1846-1878), and Leo XIII (r. 1878-1903). In the revised Code of Canon Law of 1917 under Benedict XV (r. 1914-1922), Canon 2335 prohibits all association with the Masons. A letter in 1974 written by Cardinal Franjo Seper, prefect of the Congregation for the Doctrine of the Faith, seemed to indicate a partial easing of the ban, as the communication was understood in some circles to indicate that Catholics could belong to Masonic lodges so long as the lodges were not anti-Catholic. A clarification was made by the congregation in 1981 and a renewal of the prohibition was issued in November 1983. In the 1983 Code of Canon Law, the penalty of excommunication for those Catholics who join the Masons is not included, although the prohibition remains in force. Bishops are not empowered to grant dispensations from the restrictions. A report by the Committee for Pastoral Research and Practice, National Conference of Catholic Bishops in the United States (June 1985), reiterated the Church's position on Catholics involving themselves in Freemasonry. The 1983 statement sums up Catholic regulations by declaring the principles of Freemasonry to be "irreconcilable with the Church's doctrine."

French Protestants ● See **Huguenots**.

Frequens ● Decree passed by the Council of Constance on October 9, 1417, obliging all future popes to summon councils of the Church at suitable intervals to discuss any problems that might be confronting the faith. Intended to compel the pope and to add teeth to the conciliar acts of the council, the decree was immediately controversial and has been much debated over the centuries as to its legality and effectiveness. (See also **Conciliarism**.)

Friars Preachers ● See under **Dominican Order**.

Fridelli, Xaver (1673-1743) ● Properly Xaver Ehrenbert Fridelli, Jesuit missionary to China. A native of Linz, Austria, he entered the Society of Jesus in 1688 and was sent to China, arriving there in 1705. Aside from his work as rector of one of the four Jesuit churches in Beijing, he is best known for his immense contributions to the cartographical survey that was conducted in China from 1708-1718. With several priests, he created maps for much of the Chinese Empire, and his work was described by the historian Baron Ferdinand von Richthofen in 1877 as "the most comprehensive cartographical feat ever performed in so short a time." Fridelli died at Beijing. (See also **China**.)

Friedrich, Johannes (1836-1917) ●

German Church historian and an outspoken opponent of papal infallibility. He was born in Poxdorf, in Upper Franconia, and was educated at Bamberg and Munich. A noted historian, he taught in Munich from 1862 and was secretary to Archbishop (later Cardinal) Hohenlohe at Vatican Council I (1869-1870). There he came to know Johannes Döllinger, joining him with others in their opposition to Pope Pius IX's definition of papal infallibility. Adhering to the view that infallibility could not be defended historically, Friedrich left the council before its conclusion and was unable to accept its decrees. He gave Döllinger many materials that would be used in writing the "Quirinus" *Letters from Rome*. Excommunicated in April 1871, Friedrich was granted protection by the Bavarian government and was an early leader of the Old Catholics of Germany until the decision to end the requirement of clerical celibacy. He authored numerous works, including *Die Kirchengeschichte Deutschlands* (2 vols., 1867-1869; *History of the Church of Germany*), *Geschichte des Vatikanischen Konzils* (3 vols., 1877-1887; *History of the Vatican Council*), and *Ignaz von Döllinger* (3 vols., 1899-1901).

Friends of God ● See Gottesfreunde.

Froissart, Jean (d. c. 1404) ●

French poet, traveler, and chronicler. Born in Valenciennes, in Hainault, he studied for the priesthood but left that potential career at the age of twenty to organize a chronicle of recent events in France for a patron, Robert of Namur. He was in England by 1361 and won the favor of Queen Philippa. This association helped secure the patronage of both Edward III and Edward the Black Prince. From 1367-1373, he traveled throughout Italy and France, visiting royal courts and the papal residence at Avignon. Returning to Hainault in 1373, he remained there for a number of years until entering into the service of the duke of Brabant (1382). Upon the duke's death a year later, Froissart took up the post of chaplain to Guy de Châtillon, count of Blois. Ordained a canon under Guy, he was a canon at Chimay until his death. His most important work, the *Chroniques*, organized into four books, presents the years 1325-1400 and is a major source of medieval history in general and the Hundred Years' War in particular. A lover of chivalry, Froissart tended to focus on pageant and gallant knighthood instead of the horrors of war when writing his chronicle. The work was much influenced by the writings of Jean le Bel, canon of Liège. Froissart also wrote ballads, rondeaux, and the epic *Meliador* (or *The Knight of the Golden Sun*) in some thirty thousand lines.

Frumentius, St. ●

Fourth-century Apostle of the Abyssinians. He was a Syrian who introduced Christianity to Ethiopia, or Abyssinia. The main source on his life is in the writings of Rufinus of Aquileia (who met Frumentius at Tyre), although he was also mentioned by Socrates, Theodoret, and Sozomen. According to Rufinus, Frumentius was a student of philosophy from Tyre. With a friend, he was captured by the Abyssinians around 340 while returning home from India. Forced to become a government servant in the capital of the Axumite kingdom,

Frumentius ultimately became a royal administrator and tutor of the crown prince. Using his exalted rank, Frumentius worked to convert the Ethiopians. Around 347, he visited Alexandria and made a complete report to St. Athanasius, whereupon he was consecrated a bishop. Athanasius encouraged him to continue his work and to create a translation of liturgical and biblical writings into Ethiopic. A revered figure, he was given the title *Abuna* (Our Father) by his flock, a title used still by the heads of the Ethiopian Church. Frumentius was a definite opponent of Arianism. The historical ties between the Ethiopian and Coptic Churches were largely through his efforts. Feast day: October 27 in the West, November 30 among the Greeks, and December 18 among the Copts.

Fulbert of Chartres, St. (c. 960-1028) ● Bishop of Chartres. An Italian by birth, he possibly came from near Rome and was educated at Reims and Chartres under Gerbert of Aurillac (the future Pope Sylvester II). Appointed in 990 to be the chancellor of the cathedral school of Chartres, he successfully turned the institution into one of the leading educational centers in all of Christendom. He was also respected as a truly learned figure, particularly in the sciences. In 1107, he was named bishop of Chartres, a position that allowed him to serve as a representative of Duke William V of Aquitaine and King Robert II of France on various diplomatic missions. After a fire, Fulbert began repairs on the Chartres Cathedral in 1020 but died before they could be completed. He authored a number of hymns and poems, including *Chorus Novae Jerusalem* (*Choir of the New Jerusalem*).

Fulgentius, St. (d. 533) ● Bishop of Ruspe in North Africa who was an opponent of Arianism and Pelagianism. Fulgentius was born around 462 or 468 at Telepte, Byzacium, in modern Tunisia. Originally a member of the Roman civil service, he became a monk, residing in Africa, Sicily, and Rome. In 507, he agreed to become bishop of Ruspe but was under constant threat of persecution by the Arian masters of Africa, the Vandals, particularly their ruler, King Thrasamund. Around 508, Fulgentius and sixty other bishops were banished to Sardinia, and Fulgentius was elected their leader and chief spokesman. Allowed to return to Africa (c. 515) to engage Arian theologians in a debate, he was banished two years later for his stubbornly Orthodox views. This exile was ended only in 523 by King Hilderic. Fulgentius authored numerous treatises against Arianism and Pelagianism, but of his many sermons only eight are considered authentic. So devoted was he to St. Augustine that he was given the name "abbreviated Augustine." A biography was written by Ferrandus of Carthage. Feast day: January 1.

Gaius ● See **Caius, St**.

Galatians, Epistle to the ● One of the most important of all the letters written by St. Paul, called by some the "magna carta of Christian Liberty." It deals with the controversial issue of whether Christian Gentile converts should be required to become legal Jews first, meaning that they should accept Mosaic law, including circumcision. The Epistle to the Galatians was written around 55 during Paul's third missionary journey, and it is universally accepted that the Apostle is indeed the author. The circumstances surrounding its composition were quite severe for Paul, as the Christian community in Galatia was in a state of crisis. Having established the Church in the region (Acts 16:6), he learned that other preachers had arrived and were instructing the Galatians that to be authentic Christians they must become Jews. This Paul utterly rejects, using his letter to exhort the Galatians not to accept such a false Christianity and to express in clear terms the nature of justification from God, connected to faith in Christ. Paul begins with a serious lamentation (Galatians 1:6-7). He then offers a brief autobiography to demonstrate that the gospel he has preached "came through a revelation of Jesus Christ" (1:12) and that his work among the Gentiles had the acceptance and recognition of the Apostles at Jerusalem: Peter, James, and John. Having defended his authority and the validity of his preaching, the Apostle sets forth the doctrine of justification and its relationship to the law.

He uses as an example Abraham who accepted the promises of God and so established a covenant, one that was not annulled by the law that came centuries later. Paul writes: "Now before faith came, we were confined under the law, kept under restraint until faith should be revealed. So that the law was our custodian until Christ came, that we might be justified by the faith. But now that faith has come, we are no longer under a custodian; for in Christ Jesus you are all sons of God, through faith. For as many of you as were baptized into Christ have put on Christ. There is neither Jew nor Greek, there is neither slave nor free, there is neither male nor female; for you are all one in Christ Jesus. And if you are Christ's, then you are Abraham's offspring, heirs according to promise" (3:23-29). He specifically references circumcision (see **Circumcision Controversy**), declaring: "For in Christ Jesus neither circumcision nor uncircumcision is of any avail, but faith working through love" (5:6). A caution is made, however: "For you were called to freedom, brethren; only do not use your freedom as an opportunity for the flesh, but through love be servants of one another. For the whole law is fulfilled in one word, 'You shall love your neighbor as yourself' " (5:13-14).

Galgani, Gemma, St. (1878-1903) ● Italian stigmatic who was born in Camigliano to poor parents and was forced at the age of nineteen to work as a maid in Lucca because of the death of both her mother and father. Her hopes of becoming a Passionist nun were ended by spinal tuberculosis, but she later claimed to have been cured through the intercession of St. Gabriel Possenti and took several vows in private. Fervently religious, she underwent a number of ecstatic experiences that were investigated by her confessor, Father Germano di San Stanislao Ruoppolo. Between 1899 and 1901 she intermittently received the stigmata and marks of scourging, although she also suffered through bouts of behavior that she attributed to occasional diabolical possession. Much revered after her death, Gemma was soon considered for canonization. While canonization proceedings were opposed by some because of her more erratic episodes, she was nevertheless accepted because of the unquestionable holiness of her life. Beatified in 1933, she was canonized in 1940 by Pope Pius XII. Feast day: April 11.

Galileo (1564-1642) ●

In full, Galileo Galilei, famed Italian astronomer and mathematician who became the center of a major controversy that has long been used by critics of the Church to point to the supposed failures of the

Galileo Galilei

magisterium and the obscurantist tendencies of Church officials. Galileo was born in Pisa, studying at the monastery of Vallombrosa, near Florence. He at first was drawn to the religious life but decided instead to devote himself to science. In 1581, he began medical and mathematical studies at the University of Pisa. Owing to his lack of financial resources, however, he departed school in 1585 without having obtained his degree. In 1589, he was appointed to the chair of mathematics at the University of Pisa where he made enemies because of his sharp wit and his application of empirical observation.

Such was the hostility from adherents of traditional Aristotelians that Galileo withdrew from Pisa and in 1592 settled at Padua. He would remain in this post until 1610, detecting while at Padua the four satellites of Jupiter, a discovery that proved, through observation, the orbit of bodies around something other than the earth. This led to the publication of *Siderius Nuntius* (1610; *Starry Messenger*), advancing his acceptance of the Copernican theory of the solar system. That same year, he was appointed court mathematician and philosopher to the grand duke of Tuscany at Florence. He held this office, albeit nominally, for the rest of his life.

Galileo's work in promoting the Copernican system brought him into conflict with the Holy Office. In 1616, he was warned to cease teaching Copernican theories, and Copernicus's *De revolutionibus orbum coelestium* (1543; *The Revolution of the Heavenly Spheres*) was placed on the Index of Forbidden Books by the Congregation of the Index, *"usque corrigatur"* ("until it was corrected"). The warning was still in force in 1632 when Galileo received permission to publish his *Dialogo dei due massimi sistemi del mondo* (*Dialogue Concerning the Two Chief World Systems*), an attack upon the long-standing Ptolemaic system and a declaration on behalf of the Copernican model. Officials in Rome felt that he had violated the command of the Church, and the book was handed to the Inquisition and placed on the Index of Forbidden Books.

Summoned to Rome, Galileo was placed on trial in 1633. While dealt with respectfully and not mistreated, he was compelled under threat of torture to recant. Pope Urban VIII (r. 1623-1644), at the urging of his nephew

Cardinal Francesco Barberini, made certain that Galileo was not harmed and that his confinement was a comfortable one. After several months, he was released, and he returned to Florence. He published in 1638 a third book, *Discorsi intorno a due nuove scienze* (*Dialogue Concerning Two New Sciences*), a thorough examination of motion and a refutation of Aristotelian physics. He died at Florence on February 15, 1642.

The trial and imprisonment of Galileo were long held up by enemies of the Church to prove that Catholicism was an opponent of scientific progress and that claims to the infallibility of the magisterium are false in the light of subsequent discoveries in science. In the question of infallibility, it is essential to remember that neither Pope Urban VIII nor any Church authorities ever promulgated a decree to the effect that the Ptolemaic system (i.e., a geocentric universe) was official teaching of Catholicism. The Ptolemaic system was merely the accepted explanation of the time by the vast majority of scientists. Church officials were thus mirroring what was believed to be scientific truth.

Galileo was clearly treated improperly by members of the Holy Office, who ought not to have been so averse to potential advances in science, but two mitigating factors can be considered. First, as observed, the current of contemporary thought was in favor of Aristotelian physics and the Ptolemaic system. The modern scientific method, of which Copernicus and Galileo were heralds, was still in its infancy and, as it would later be proved, many of the assumptions made by Galileo were in error. It was thus hardly surprising that members of the Holy Office, advised by learned men who represented the finest of what was then science, should reject much that Galileo proposed. More importantly, the Holy Office recognized the profound theological implications of Galileo's work, perceiving it to be contrary to the theological view of creation; God was seemingly removed from his central place in the universe. Further, Galileo made no effort to harmonize his theories with Scripture and thereby robbed himself of any chance to win over theologians who might otherwise have been disposed to assist him. As the ideas and writings of Galileo were quite innovative and controversial, the Church officials felt obligated to respond in the way they felt best to defend the faith, which was their primary task.

The Church recognized the merits of Galileo's work as early as 1741 when an imprimatur was bestowed. On October 31, 1992, Pope John Paul II publicly declared that the Church had erred in its judgment and a report by a special commission investigating the matter stated: "The philosophical and theological qualifications wrongly granted to the then new theories about the centrality of the sun and the movement of the earth were the result of a transitional situation in the field of astronomical knowledge and of an exegetical confusion regarding cosmology. Certain theologians, Galileo's contemporaries, being heirs of a unitarian concept of the world universally accepted until the dawn of the 1600s, failed to grasp the profound, nonliteral meaning of the Scriptures when they describe the physical structure of the created universe."

Galileo Affair ● See **Galileo**, preceding entry.

Gall, St. (c. 550-c. 645) ● Disciple of St. Columbanus and a Christian missionary. Gall was a native of Ireland, receiving his education at the monastery of Bangor in County Down, becoming one of the twelve companions of Columbanus on the journey to Gaul (France) around 590. While there, he took part in the creation of the monasteries of Luxeuil in the Vosges Mountains. In 610, he went with Columbanus to Switzerland. After they preached to the Alamanni, Gall chose to remain in Switzerland when

Columbanus departed for Italy in 612. Gall became a hermit, refusing the abbacy of Luxeuil and any ecclesiastical rank or honor. The monastery of St. Gall (or St. Gallen) was founded on the site of one of his hermitages. Feast day: October 15.

Gallia Christiana ● Compilation of information on the hierarchy of France, including its bishops and abbots and its sees and abbeys. The work originated in the 1626 publication of the *Gallia Christiana* by Claude Robert. The subsequent 1656 edition was accepted by the Assembly of French Clergy, although approval was not given until a passage suspected of Jansenism was removed. This edition was in four folio volumes: first for the archdioceses, second and third for the dioceses, and fourth for the abbeys. Additional editions, with extensive revisions and improvements, appeared throughout the eighteenth century, including an abridgment in 1774 by Abbé Hugues du Temps, vicar-general of Bordeaux, which appeared under the title *Le clergé de France* (*The Clergy of France*). The *Gallia* has been continually updated, mostly by Benedictine scholars. With its historical records and details of the sees, prelates, abbeys, and major churches dating back to the earliest periods of the French Church, the *Gallia* remains one of the most useful sources on both the ecclesiastical and the secular history of France.

Gallican Articles ● Also Declaration of the French Clergy and Four Articles. Name given to four articles passed on March 19, 1682, by the association of French clergy that established the Gallican position with respect to the authority of the pope in France. Convening to give a response on the part of the French clergy to the dispute between Pope Innocent XI and King Louis XIV of France over the proper control of episcopal appointments and disposition of the revenues of vacant sees, the assembly

(comprising thirty-six bishops and thirty-four deputies) agreed to a document written by Jacques Bossuet (d. 1704) that would have severely curtailed the power of the papacy. Specifically, the Gallican Articles declared:

1. The pope had no jurisdiction in temporal affairs, proclaiming that the king (or rulers in general) were not subject to the Church in matters relating to civil or temporal administration. Nor could the pope demand that citizens abandon their loyalty to the state.

2. The conciliar decrees of the Council of Constance (1414-1418) were reaffirmed.

3. The privileges and rights of the Gallican Church were reiterated.

4. The judgments and declarations of the pope could be resisted until their acceptance by a general council.

Strenuously opposed by the papacy, the Gallican Articles were nevertheless adopted throughout France. Pope Alexander VIII in 1690 condemned them in the apostolic constitution *Inter multiplices*. As the opposition to the articles increased, King Louis revoked them.

Gallican Rite ● Name used for those liturgical rites that were followed in Gaul (France) from the period of the early Church in the region to the adoption of the Roman rite under Charlemagne (r. 768-814). The rites found in Gaul during this period were different from the Roman rite, but they did not have a precise or defined center of origin as compared to the Celtic or Ambrosian rites. The origins of the rite have been the source of debate among scholars, some arguing external influences, others preferring the theory that they developed locally. Sources used for examining the rite include indirect references made by Caesarius of Arles (d. 542), Gregory of Tours (d. 594), and Gennadius of Marseilles (fifth century). Particularly valuable is the *History of the Gallican Liturgy*, traditionally attributed to St. Germanus, bishop of Paris (d. 576). Some critics, however, propose that this work should be dated to the early eighth century and considered the product of a writer in southern France, with a concomitant Spanish influence. Other sources are *Missale Francorum, Missale Gallicanum vetus, Missale Gothicum, Bobbio Missal,* and the *Stowe Missal.* The Maurist scholar Jean Mabillon (1623-1707), also wrote *De Liturgia Gallicana* (1685), which was reproduced in Migne's *Patrologia Latina.*

The liturgy has been characterized as highly expressive, more so than the Roman rite, and the Mass is quite different from other rites, particularly the Celtic and Mozarabic. The prayers indicate a strong tendency against Arianism. In turn, the Gallican rite had an influence upon the Roman rite, specifically in the dedication of churches and altars, the Palm (Passion) Sunday procession, and ordination. The decline in Gallican usage took place gradually as the Roman rite gained ascendancy. While officially abolished by Charlemagne, the Gallican rite lingered in parts of Gaul for some time, its influence stamped subtly upon the Latin Church's liturgical practices.

Gallicanism ● Religio-political theory that asserted the independence of the French Church from the authority of the papacy. Gallicanism had its distant roots in the often intense feelings of nationalism that characterized France during the eighth and ninth centuries, but its intellectual basis was established in the writings during the fourteenth century of French theologians at the University of Paris, most notably Pierre d'Ailly and Jean Gerson. During the troubling era of the Great Schism, Gallicanism found warm support in various religious and political circles, aided by the concept of conciliarism that sought to subordinate the power of the papacy to the general council. A major support came from the French monarchy. In 1398, King Charles VI refused

to give his obedience to the Avignon antipope Benedict XIII (Pedro de Luna), claiming autonomy for the French Church on the basis of certain traditions and rights that he had supposedly rediscovered. These included a special status for the French Church, described as *libertés de l'Église gallicane* — from which Gallicanism derived its name. Further claims were made in 1438 by King Charles VII in the Pragmatic Sanction of Bourges, conditioning papal authority with the royal will and tenets of conciliarism. The sanction was replaced in 1516 by a concordat in which the French crown received the right to nominate Church officials.

Gallicanism continued in varying degrees of popularity until the 1600s when it flourished once more. An important impetus was given through the writings of Pierre Pithou (1539-1596) and Pierre de Marca (1594-1662). In 1682, the Assembly of French Clergy issued the four Gallican Articles, a manifesto of Gallican rights for the French Church that was condemned by Pope Alexander VIII in 1690 and withdrawn in 1693. Nevertheless, Gallicanism continued to find adherents in parts of France, such as among the Jansenists who advanced Gallican ideas in the hope of winning support against the bull *Unigenitus* (1713), issued by Pope Clement XI and condemning one hundred one Jansenist propositions. The last vestiges of meaningful Gallicanism were stamped out in the 1800s through Ultramontanism and especially the declaration of papal infallibility by the First Vatican Council. (See also **Conciliarism, Febronianism, Josephinism,** and **Pistoia, Synod of.**)

Gams, Pius (1816-1892) ● German ecclesiastical historian. Born at Mittelbuch, in Würtemberg, he studied at Biberach and Rottweil (1826-1834), Tübingen (1834-1838), and the seminary at Rottenburg (1838). Ordained in 1839, he was appointed to the chairs of philosophy and general history at

Hildesheim. In 1856, however, he pronounced monastic vows at the Abbey of St. Boniface in Munich, adding the name Pius to the name Bonifacius Gams. He was given a number of posts in the monastery, serving as master of novices, subprior, and prior. Among his many ecclesiastical writings are: *Geschichte der Kirche Jesu Christi im neunzehnten Jahrhunderte mit besonderer Rücksicht auf Deutschland* (3 vols., 1854-1858; *The History of the Church of Jesus Christ with Particular Attention to Germany*); the *Series episcoporum* (1873; with supplement, 1886), a compilation of all bishops in communion with Rome; and the best known of all, *Kirchengeschichte von Spain* (3 vols., 1862-1879; *Church History of Spain*) a methodical account of the Spanish Church, handicapped somewhat by his extensive use of unreliable sources.

Gandolphy, Peter (1779-1821) ● English Jesuit preacher. Also called Peter Gandolphi, he was born in London and educated at the Jesuit College at Liège and at Stonyhurst. Ordained a priest in 1804, he served briefly in Newport, Isle of Wight, and then was transferred to the Spanish chapel in Manchester Square, London. While there, he acquired quite a reputation as a preacher, making many converts but earning censure from his bishop for the irregularity of his methods. His 1812 work, *A Liturgy or Book of Common Prayers and Administration of Sacraments . . . for the use of all Christians in the United Kingdom*, along with his "Sermons in Defense of the Ancient Faith," compelled his ordinary, Bishop Poynter, to suspend him on the grounds of heresy. Gandolphy went to Rome in 1816 and there successfully defended himself. The succeeding episode of the drawn-out apology to Poynter led Gandolphy to resign in 1818 and retire to his family estate in East Sheen.

Garden of the Soul, The ● See under **Challoner, Richard**.

Gardiner, Richard (c. 1482-1555) ● Bishop of Winchester, best known for his role in the persecution of Protestants during the reign of Queen Mary I (r. 1555-1558). Gardiner was born in Bury St. Edmunds, Suffolk, the son of a clothmaker. He studied at Cambridge; from 1525-1549 and 1553-1555, he served as master of Trinity. In 1525, he was appointed secretary to the then powerful figure Cardinal Wolsey, subsequently proving useful to King Henry VIII on several missions to Pope Clement VII in the ultimately fruitless effort to secure an annulment of the king's marriage to Catherine of Aragon.

For his efforts, Gardiner was named principal secretary to the king in 1529 and, two years later, bishop of Winchester. In 1533, he took part in the court that proclaimed the marriage to be annulled, although by this time he had lost Henry's confidence and was increasingly replaced by the ruthless Thomas Cromwell. Nevertheless, Gardiner wrote a defense of royal supremacy over the Church in the treatise *De vera obedientia oratio* (*Bishops' Oration on True Obedience*), in which he also attacked the authority of the papacy. In dealing with the Reformation, however, Gardiner represented a conservative element that was quite alarmed by the movement away from Catholic teachings. He thus had a leading role in the creation of the Six Articles Act of 1539 that sought to impede the spread of Reformist ideas. After the fall of Cromwell in 1540, Gardiner became chancellor of Cambridge and was a prominent Catholic figure on the royal council.

In the atmosphere of the Reform spearheaded by Thomas Cranmer, archbishop of Canterbury, under King Edward VI (r. 1547-1553), Gardiner was distinctly out of favor. He was imprisoned in the Tower of London in 1548 and was deprived of his bishopric in 1551. Edward died in 1553, and Gardiner was released upon the accession of Queen Mary. Restored as bishop, he was also appointed lord chancellor. Despite some misgivings, he presided over the return of England to obedience to the papacy and was a supporter of the persecution of Protestants that began in 1554. To his credit, he opposed and tried to prevent the execution by fire of Thomas Cranmer, despite his personal dislike for the archbishop.

Garibaldi ● See under **Risorgimento**; see also **Italy**.

Garnier, Jean (1612-1681) ● French Church historian, moral theologian, and patristic scholar. A native of Paris, he entered the Jesuits at the age of sixteen in Rouen. He taught theology at the Collège de Clermont at Paris from 1653-1679 and in 1681 was sent to Rome by the order, falling ill on the way and dying at Bologna. Considered one of the most learned men of his time, Garnier authored a number of important works. His *Libellus fidei* (*Petition of the Faith*) was published in 1648 during the Pelagian controversy. In 1673, he edited at Paris the works of Marius Mercator, adding to this edition of the writings seven dissertations on Pelagianism and Nestorianism (including the *Libellus fidei*). Other writings include the *Liber diurnus Romanorum Pontificorum* (a compilation of the pontiffs), a treatise on Pope Honorius defending his orthodoxy, and works on moral theology and Scholastic philosophy.

Gasparri, Pietro (1852-1934) ● Italian cardinal who headed the organization and promulgation of the then new Code of Canon Law (1917). Born at Capovalazza de Ussita, Italy, he was ordained in 1877 and served as a professor of canon law at the Catholic Institute of Paris from 1880-1898. In 1904, he was appointed by Pope St. Pius X (r. 1903-1914) to organize the new Code of Canon Law. His labors took many years, during which he was made a cardinal by Pius

and named secretary of state by Pope Benedict XV (r. 1914-1922). Pope Pius XI (r. 1922-1939) retained him as secretary, and in 1926 Gasparri began the negotiations that led to the Lateran Treaty of 1929 with the Italian government of Benito Mussolini. His successor as secretary of state in January 1930 was Eugenio Pacelli, the future Pope Pius XII (r. 1939-1958).

Gasquet, Francis Neil Aidan (1846-1929) ● Historian and cardinal. Born in London, he was educated at Downside School in Somerset, entering the Benedictine monastery there in 1866. Elected prior of Downside in 1878, he served until 1885 and was notable for his success in improving the priory and the school. Focusing after 1885 on extensive researches, particularly at the British Museum, he authored works on monastic history, including Henry VIII and the English monasteries (1888-1889). In Rome in 1896, he participated in the Commission on Anglican Ordinations. Returning to England, he served as chair of the commission for the reform of the English Benedictines, holding the post of abbot-president until 1914 when Pope St. Pius X made him a cardinal. In 1919, he was appointed prefect of the Vatican Archives. He also was president (appointed in 1907) of the International Commission for the Revision of the Vulgate and was an important figure in securing the appointment of a British minister to the Vatican.

Gassendi, Pierre (1592-1655) ● French priest, philosopher, and scientist. A native of Champtercier, Provence, he studied Latin and rhetoric at Digne and philosophy at Aix. In 1614, he received a doctorate in theology at Avignon and the next year was ordained a priest. On the recommendation of Cardinal Richelieu he was appointed in 1645 by the king to a professorship of mathematics at the Collège Royal of France. Known as the Bacon of France, Gassendi opposed Aristotelianism and promoted a revival of Epicureanism. His major work, *Syntagma Philosophicum* (published posthumously in 1658), presented Epicurean perspectives on philosophy, defending (in Part II) mechanistic explanations of natural phenomena. He also authored works on Epicurus and *Institutio Astronomica* (1647) and is remembered in history for observing the planetary transit of Mercury, an event predicted by Johann Kepler.

Gaudium et Spes ● Last document issued by Vatican Council II (December 7, 1965). The "Pastoral Constitution on the Church in the Modern World" — as it is called in English — is also the longest and has the broadest purpose, namely to provide an extensive final presentation of the aims and hopes of the council while offering guidance to humanity on a variety of pressing subjects. *Gaudium et Spes*, so called from the opening words of the document ("The joy and hope"), was evenly divided into two main parts: the Church's teaching on humanity in the modern era and urgent problems of the times.

The first part starts out: "The joys and the hopes, the griefs and the anxieties of this age" (No. 1) — a clear indication that the Council Fathers were aware both of the positive nature of the modern world and its many dangers and travails. Further, the council places great emphasis throughout on the human existence, a stress that was quite innovative in its presentation: "According to the almost unanimous opinion of believers and unbelievers alike, all things on earth should be related to man as their center and crown" (No. 12). Having developed an analysis of humanity, the document then offered a thorough summary of traditional Church teaching on human life, complete with discussion of sin, the union of body and soul, and the moral conscience.

There is, as well, a genuinely realistic appraisal of contemporary society, noting the pervasiveness of atheism, adding that its spread can be attributed in part to the fault and carelessness of those within the Church whose actions and failures "must be said to conceal rather than reveal the authentic face of God and religion" (No. 19). Toward the fuller understanding of the place of the Church in the modern world, *Gaudium et Spes* emphasizes the harmony that should exist between the Catholic faith and scientific progress because "earthly matters and the concerns of faith derive from the same God" (No. 36). This does not mean, however, that there ought to be no qualifying elements or restraints to science; the Council Fathers add to this positive statement the provision that such research, "within every branch of learning," must be "carried out in a genuinely scientific manner and in accord with moral norms" (No. 36). Finally, the first part makes an ecumenical gesture, noting that the Church "holds in high esteem the things which other Christian Churches or ecclesial communities have done. . ." (No. 40).

Part Two offers the practical application of the Church's teaching and message enunciated in Part One. Most pressing is the council's concern for the family, and its treatment of family life and marriage is the most detailed and extensive in the history of the councils of the Church. This leads to study of the deeply troubling presence of contraception. The council reiterates Church instruction in an affirmation of opposition to contraception that would receive even fuller expression in three years in the encyclical *Humanae vitae*. In the matter of abortion, the document states clearly: ". . .from the moment of its conception life must be guarded with the greatest care, while abortion and infanticide are unspeakable crimes" (No. 51). In its study of culture, in which the council reminds all humanity that culture and civilization are creations of man, it points out his responsibility over it and his duty to seek that which is above, which entails an "obligation to work with all men in constructing a more human world" (No. 57). Here we have a powerful preface or introduction to the next concerns voiced in *Gaudium et Spes*: the questions of economic life, political systems, and war. In building upon earlier social encyclicals, *Gaudium et Spes* discusses economics as vital to human progress and social development, striking the important balance (developed so masterfully in the later writings of Pope John Paul II) between the rights of an individual to possess goods and the obligation to aid the poor (Nos. 63-72). While declaring the autonomous and independent nature of the Church and politics, the Council Fathers do acknowledge: "There are, indeed, close links between earthly affairs and those aspects of man's condition which transcend this world. The Church herself employs the things of time to the degree that her own proper mission demands" (No. 76). The document goes on to state that "the arms race is an utterly treacherous trap for humanity" (No. 81) and "It is our clear duty, then, to strain every muscle as we work for the time when all war can be completely outlawed by international consent" (No. 82).

Gaul ● See **France**.

Gaume, Jean Joseph (1802-1879) ●
French theologian. Born in the Franche-Comté, he was ordained in 1825, serving as a professor of theology, director of the *petit-séminaire*, and a vicar-general for the dioceses of Reims and Montaubon. In 1841, he went to Rome where Pope Gregory XVI conferred on him the rank of knight of the Reformed Order of St. Sylvester. A doctor of theology at the University of Prague, he held a number of additional posts and membership in several scholastic societies and was made a protonotary apostolic in 1854 by Pope Pius IX. Gaume earned considerable notoriety for his opposition to pagan classics in Christian schools, calling

instead for a reading of patristic texts. He was the author of numerous works including *Bibliothèque des classiques chrétiens* (30 vols., 1852-1855; *Library of Christian Classics*), *Pie IX et les études classiques* (1875; *Pius IX and Classical Studies*), *L'Europe en 1848* (1848; *Europe in 1848*), and *Le Manuel des confesseurs* (1837; *Manual for the Confessors*).

Geiler von Kaiserberg, Johann (1445-1510) ● German preacher, known as the "German Savonarola." He was born at Schaffhausen on the Rhine and educated in Ammerswerker in Alsace. From 1465-1471, he lectured on Aristotle in Alsace, and then went to Basel where he lectured on theology in 1476. Journeying to Freiburg, he became rector of the university, but before long his belief that the Church needed to be reformed compelled him to abandon his long association with the academic world. In 1478, Geiler accepted the post of preacher in the Cathedral of Strasbourg. His sermons were remarkably eloquent and enthusiastically delivered. He focused on the errors and abuses found within the Church, but he apparently never considered leaving the faith. One of his most significant complaints was that neither clergy nor laity were willing to work together to bring about a comprehensive reform.

Gelasius I ● Pope from 492-496. He is considered one of the architects of papal ecclesiastical supremacy. Probably from Africa, he was elected the successor to Pope Felix III in March 492. Some question remains, however, as to the his place of origin. Gelasius wrote to Emperor Anastasius that he was *Romanus natus*, but the *Liber Pontificalis* (*Book of the Popes*) noted that he was *natione Afer*. To reconcile these discordant declarations, scholars have proposed that he might have been from Africa but Roman born, or African by birth but a Roman citizen. After his accession, Gelasius steadfastly adhered to the policy of Felix of opposing Constantinople during the Acacian Schism, upholding the supremacy of the Roman See. The Gelasian Doctrine (494), addressed to Anastasius in Epistle XII (*Ad Imp. Anastasium*), presented his views on the relations of Church and State, insisting that both must work together for the good of society, both institutions being divinely created. His writings on the subject shaped much of the subsequent medieval thinking, particularly his belief that there was a natural superiority of the Church in secular matters. Gelasius also authored numerous letters and treatises, including one on the two natures of Christ (*Adversus Eutychen et Nestorium*). The *Decretum Gelasianum* and the Gelasian Sacramentary were both wrongly attributed to him.

Pope St. Gelasius I

Gelasius II ● Pope from 1118-1119. Born John of Gaeta, he was initially an Italian monk at Monte Cassino when, in 1088, Pope Urban II made him a cardinal. The following year, he became the papal chancellor. In 1118, he was elected to succeed Paschal II. The pontificate of Gelasius came during the Investiture Controversy between the Holy Roman Empire and the papacy, the conflict that led Henry V to imprison Paschal. Gelasius was twice forced to flee Rome from the Ghibelline (or pro-imperial) factions of the Eternal City and was actually captured by the pro-imperial Frangipani family. Badly mistreated, he died at Cluny on January 29, 1119, and was succeeded by Callistus II.

General Chapter ● Formal assembly or meeting of the heads, members, or delegates of a religious order or congregation. The purpose of the general chapter is to discuss important issues facing the order, to deal with problems that may have arisen, and to elect new superiors. Its name is derived from the place in a community where the members customarily gathered each day for the reading of a chapter of the rule of the order. According to canon law, the acts of a general chapter are sent to the Holy See for approval or for observation; also, the superior of the order is presented to the pope for confirmation, unless the specific institute has the privilege of not being required to seek such confirmation. The first chapters were introduced by the Cistercian order in 1119 and were declared compulsory upon all orders by the Fourth Lateran Council in 1215.

Genevieve, St. (c. 420-c. 500) ● Also Genovefa, the patroness of Paris. The main source on her is the ancient *Life*, preserved in a number of texts. According to it, the young girl Genevieve dedicated her life to God and received much encouragement from St. Germanus of Auxerre whom she met at Nanterre, near Paris. At the age of fifteen, she was given the veil of a virgin and henceforth adopted a life of prayer and mortification. After the death of her parents, she lived with her godmother in Paris. There she engaged in many charitable works but was criticized viciously by detractors, despite the supportive visit of St. Germanus. In 451, however, Germanus's archdeacon convinced the Parisians that they should listen to the counsel of Genevieve when the Huns under Attila were advancing on the city. By tradition, her prayers saved the city and her intercession continued to work with the Franks, who had blockaded Paris; she managed to bring food to the starving citizens. In 1129, she was invoked by Parisians during an epidemic. The pestilence ended when her relics were carried in a public procession. Feast day: January 3.

Gennadius of Marseilles ● Fifth-century priest and theological historian, best known for his work *De Viris Illustribus*, a continuation of Jerome's book of the same name. Little is known about his life save for the information that he provided about himself in the last of the biographies: "I, Gennadius, presbyter of Marsilia, wrote eight books against all heresies, five books against Nestorius, ten books against Eutyches, three books against Pelagius, a treatise on the thousand years of the apocalypse of John, this work, and a letter about my faith sent to blessed Gelasius, bishop of the city of Rome."

Of these works, the *De Viris Illustribus* is extant. It contains material on one hundred one ecclesiastical writers of both East and West and was completed probably around 480. Ten of the notices were added by later contributors.

Gentiles ● See GLOSSARY; see also **Circumcision Controversy** and **Paul of Tarsus, St**.

Geoffrey of Monmouth (d. 1153) ● Important medieval chronicler and bishop of Asaph. He was probably a Breton, joining a Benedictine monastery, although it is possible that he may have been an Augustinian Canon. A canon and prebendary of the collegiate Church of St. George in the castle at Oxford, he held the position until the church's absorption into the recently

established Oseney Abbey. He witnessed the Oseney Charter of 1129, became archdeacon of St. Teilo's around 1140, and was made bishop of Asaph in 1152, dying before he could assume the office. Geoffrey was the author of a number of works, including: *Prophetiae* (c. 1130-1135), a compilation of the stories about Myrddin (Merlin) the famed wizard; the *Vitae Merlini* (c. 1148-1151), a poem over fifteen hundred hexameters long; and the *Historia Regum Britanniae* (*History of the Kings of Britain*). The *Historia*, Geoffrey's greatest work, was completed sometime after the death of King Henry I (1135). Claimed by Geoffrey to have been a translation into Latin of the older Celtic book given to him by Walter, archdeacon of Oxford, it was largely, according to many scholars, the result of Geoffrey's own imagination. Nevertheless, it emphasized the common origins of the Saxons, Britons, and Normans, introduced the elaborate stories of King Arthur, and directly influenced a host of other writers, such as Geoffrey Gaimar, Robert Wace, Michael Drayton, and William Shakespeare.

George of Cappadocia ● Fourth-century Arian bishop who took possession of the see of Alexandria in Lent 357, a year after the retirement of St. Athanasius. Most of the sources on his life are distinctly hostile to both his Arianism and to what is universally reported as a harsh and ambitious nature. Opposition to his presence as patriarch of Alexandria came not only from Orthodox Christians but from Semi-Arians, who found his extreme Arianism intolerable. He was murdered by an angry mob on December 24, 361. (See also **George, Patron of England**.)

George of Trebizond (1395-1486) ● Greek scholar, humanist, and teacher. While born on Crete, his family came from Trebizond (a town in northeast Turkey on the Black Sea). A professor of Greek in 1420, he spent his remaining years in Italy, traveling and teaching in major cities. At the Council of Ferrara-Florence (1438-1439), he served as an interpreter and adviser to Pope Eugenius IV. Subsequently teaching at Rome, he was granted the patronage of Pope Nicholas V. While there, he translated Aristotle's *Rhetoric*, Ptolemy's *Almagest*, and Plato's *Law*. His quarrelsome and difficult nature, however, ultimately caused a breech with the Roman humanists and he had severe disagreements with Cardinal John Bessarion and Lorenzo Valla. Banished from Rome, he taught at Venice and Naples before returning to the Eternal City where he was imprisoned by Pope Paul II. He died in abject poverty.

George, Patron of England ● Famous saint and martyr whose actual death is undocumented but whose cultus underwent considerable development in the sixth century; today, he is generally accepted as a legitimate historical figure. He may have been martyred in the fourth century near Lydda. While he is not to be confused with the Arian Bishop George of Cappadocia (d. 561), he was possibly mentioned by Eusebius in his *Ecclesiastical History*. The cult of St. George was first seen in the sixth century, spreading throughout England by the eighth. By the twelfth century it had reached such elaborate detail that he was credited with slaying dragons; the thirteenth-century *Golden Legend*, for instance, described St. George's rescue of a maiden from a dragon. During the crusades, he was much revered by the soldiers in the Holy Land and supposedly came to the aid of

St. George, by Donatello

the Christian knights during the Battle of Antioch. He was subsequently named the protector of the Order of the Garter (c. 1347) by King Edward III and patron of England.

Gerald of Wales ● See **Giraldus Cambrensis**.

Gerbert of Aurillac ● See **Sylvester II**.

Gerbillon, Jean François (1654-1707) ● French Jesuit missionary to China. A native of Verdun, he joined the Society of Jesus in October 1670, eventually teaching grammar and the humanities for seven years. In 1685, he was granted permission to join the Jesuits, who had been chosen to establish the French mission in China. They were favorably received by the emperor, and Gerbillon and Bouvet were kept at the imperial court. Gerbillon quickly learned the language and was employed by the ruler on a variety of missions, including the negotiations with the Russians concerning the border of the two large empires. In 1692, Gerbillon was instrumental in securing the promulgation of a decree that granted the right of religious expression. He was also the author of several mathematical treatises and accounts of his travels, most notably *Relations de huit Voyage dans la Grande Tartarie*. Gerbillon died in Beijing.

Gerhard of Zutphen (1367-1398) ● Also Geert Zerbolt van Zutphen, a mystical writer and member of the Brethren of the Common Life. Born at Zutphen, he became a priest and served as a librarian for the Brethren at Deventer in the Netherlands. He was deeply respected for his learning, particularly in moral theology and canon law, authoring several treatises including *De reformatione virum animae* (*Reformation of the Human Soul*) and *De Spiritualibus ascensionibus* (*On the Spiritual Ascents*); two treatises on prayer are attributed to him, as is a treatise on Scripture, all three in the vernacular.

Gerhoh of Reichersberg (1093-1169) ● Notable German theologian and an active supporter of the so-called Gregorian Reform in Germany. Born in Polling in Bavaria, he studied at Freising, Mosburg, and Hildesheim, serving as a *scholasticus* (1119) to the cathedral school of Augsburg and then canon of the cathedral. Appointed by Bishop Hermann of Augsburg, Gerhoh eventually differed with the prelate on ecclesiastical discipline and simony, fleeing to the monastery of Raitenbuch in the diocese of Freising. A reconciliation was effected by the Concordat of Worms (1122) and the acceptance of Bishop Hermann by Pope Callistus II. Thus Gerhoh accompanied Hermann to the Lateran Council of 1123. On his return from Rome, Gerhoh resigned his post, joining the Austin Canons (or Canons Regular of St. Augustine) at Raitenbuch in 1124 with his father and two half-brothers. Ordained a priest in 1126, he was appointed provost of Raitenbuch in 1132 by Archbishop Conrad I of Salzburg. Gerhoh was utilized by Conrad on several missions to Rome, meeting St. Bernard of Clairvaux; he was much respected by Pope Eugenius III, but his relations with subsequent pontiffs were not always so cordial. For his stern support of Pope Alexander III in the disputed election of 1159, he earned the enmity of the imperial party and in 1166 was banished by Emperor Frederick I and forced to flee from the monastery of Reichersberg. He supported enthusiastically the reform of the clergy and defended Orthodox teaching. Among his writings were: the *Liber de aedificio Dei* (1128-1129), on ecclesiastical discipline; *Tractatus adversus Simoniacos*, on simony; a commentary on the Psalms; and letters against the Christological errors of Abelard, Gilbert de la Porrée, and others. (See also **Gregorian Reform**.)

Germain ● See **Germanus**.

German Catholic Center Party ● See **Germany**.

Germanus of Auxerre, St. (d. 448) ● Bishop of Auxerre who made several important journeys to England. Germanus was a native of Auxerre, receiving an education as a Roman advocate (lawyer) and practicing law in Rome before being appointed governor of a part of Gaul (France) by Emperor Flavius Honorius. In 418, he was elected successor to Bishop St. Amator as prelate of Auxerre. A noted ascetic, he was chosen by Pope St. Celestine in 429 to travel to Britain with St. Lupus of Troyes to combat Pelagianism in the isles. At a debate in Verulamium (later St. Alban's), Germanus and Lupus silenced the Pelagians. Returning to Auxerre, Germanus built the Church of St. Alban's and apparently responded to an appeal from St. Patrick (probably one of his former pupils) by sending to Ireland bishops who proved successful in advancing the evangelization of the Irish. Pelagianism rose again in the isles, and Germanus returned in 447, smashing the last of the Pelagians and securing the banishment of the recalcitrant remnant. Around the same time he led the Britons into battle with the Picts and Saxons, teaching them the war cry "Alleluia." At the time of his death, he was in Ravenna pleading the cause of the rebellious Gauls of Armorici, his flock. Feast day: July 31. (See also **Genevieve, St**.)

Germanus of Paris, St. (d. 576) ● Abbot, bishop of Paris, and a political figure in

Merovingian France. A native of Autun (Augustodonum), he became an abbot and was especially known for his charity to the poor. Appointed bishop of Paris in 555 by King Childebert (r. 511-558), Germanus wielded considerable influence at the royal court. Upon Childebert's death, Germanus worked to prevent the bloody power struggle that soon followed; Charibert I was excommunicated for his brutal behavior, and Germanus predicted that Sigebert, king of Austrasia, would die if he continued to use German troops against his brother Chilperic. Sigebert was murdered in 575. Germanus also gave his blessing to the Church of St.-Germain-des-Prés, named in his honor and eventually serving as the site of his tomb. A biography of him was written by Venantius Fortunatus, and two letters by him proved to be of much use to scholars in reconstructing the Gallican rites of the sixth century. Feast day: July 25.

Germany ● One of the major countries of Europe with a long and complex history. The vast regions of Germany stretching beyond the Rhine to the east were a tempting target for expansion by the Roman Empire from the time of Julius Caesar in the first century B.C. Roman efforts to conquer the region, however, proved fruitless as a result of the devastating defeat of Roman forces in the Teutoburg Forest in A.D. 9 and the steadfast obstinacy of what the Romans called *Germania Barbara*. West of the Rhine, Rome was able to create two provinces, called *Germania Inferior* and *Germania Superior*. These provinces would exist in various shapes until the late imperial era and would long be protected from the tribes of the north and the east by a line of strong forts called *limes* (plural: *limites*). Christianity was introduced into the region in the third century, perhaps even earlier than that. Two centers of the early faith were the important cities of Trier (Augusta Trevorarum) and Cologne (Köln; Colonia Agrippina). In the

fourth century, under the favor shown to the Church by Constantine the Great (d. 337), churches were built and, according to legend, St. Helena, Constantine's mother, brought to Trier Christ's robe, which was seized at the Crucifixion.

In the fourth century, pressures mounted on the frontier, and the so-called barbarian tribes burst across the frontiers and pushed into the Western Roman Empire, most notably Gaul. These Germanic tribes, such as the Visigoths, Vandals, and Franks, soon formed kingdoms. The Visigoths and Vandals were converted to Arian Christianity, and from the fifth century launched persecutions of Orthodox Christians. They founded realms in southern France and Spain in the case of the Visigoths, and Africa in the case of the Vandals. The Visigoths were smashed in Gaul by the Franks who under their ruler, Clovis I (d. 511), were converted to Christianity. The Franks proved important patrons of missionaries in Germany, seeing the conversion of the Germanic tribes as both essential and useful for the stability of the region and the promotion of peace. The Frankish leaders cooperated with the papacy and assisted in the sending of missionaries to Germany from Britain, Frankish lands, and elsewhere. Chief among the missionaries was Boniface, the so-called Apostle of Germany who, during the eighth century, brought the faith to numerous tribes and, before his martyrdom in 754, established an ecclesiastical organization. Monasticism was also given impetus along the Rhine. (See **Boniface, St**.)

Under Charlemagne (d. 814), the Franks carved out an extensive empire over the Rhine, making Germany an important part of the Carolingian Empire. The tribes there, such as the Saxons, long remained resistant to subjugation and the faith but were gradually converted. Germany profited from the Carolingian Renaissance, but the unity of the empire was shattered after the death of Charlemagne's son, Louis the Pious in 840.

The empire was divided among his heirs, leading to the Strasbourg Oath of 842, which brought the linguistic division of the Frankish Empire. Feudalism developed and there emerged assorted autonomous duchies such as Swabia, Bavaria, Lorraine, Saxony, and Franconia, which ended the reign of the Carolingian ruler Charles III the Simple, replacing him with Conrad, duke of Franconia in 911. The nobles refused to surrender their authority, and political life was often chaotic, since hereditary succession was not followed. Henry I, duke of Saxony, became German king in 919, launching a dynasty of rulers that would last until 1024. His son, Otto I the Great (r. 936-973), became the first Holy Roman Emperor in 962, inaugurating a system of government that would endure until the 1800s. (See **Holy Roman Empire** for details.)

During this period, the Church continued to flourish and the bishops of Germany came to wield increasing sociopolitical influence and authority. The bishops also emerged as electors of the Holy Roman Emperors. The dominant political question facing the Church in Germany in this era was lay investiture, most characterized by the angry struggle between Emperor Henry IV (r. 1056-1098) and Pope Gregory VII (r. 1073-1085). Further strife ensued in the twelfth and thirteenth centuries between the papacy and the two emperors Frederick I Barbarossa (r. 1152-1190) and Frederick II (1212-1250). The popes ultimately outlasted this dynasty of the Hohenstaufens, bringing about its extinction in 1268 and causing the Great Interregnum in Germany that would not be resolved until 1273 and the election of Rudolf of Habsburg as German king. Dynastic struggles continued until the time of Charles IV (1316-1378), who became emperor with papal support. Crowned emperor in 1355, the following year he promulgated the Golden Bull of 1356, which reformed the election process and instituted seven electors. The Habsburgs took firm

control of the crown, starting in 1438 with the accession of Albert II (r. 1438-1439). This dynasty would remain on the throne until the demise of the Habsburgs in the twentieth century. One of their number, Charles V (1500-1558), would be emperor at the outbreak of the Reformation.

The late medieval Church was characterized by its considerable wealth and the flowering of learning in its universities, such as Cologne (which claimed as early figures Sts. Albertus Magnus and Thomas Aquinas). Involved heavily in the main events of the Church, including the crusades and the Great Schism, Germany was also severely hit by the Black Death in the 1300s. By the 1400s, the German Church was in need of genuine reform owing to a variety of abuses and corruption. These problems, coupled with the desire of many German princes to free themselves from the imperial rule and the rivalries between the princes and the bishops, made Germany fertile ground for the calls by Martin Luther for a general reform of the Church. For political, financial, and social reasons, many German princes and prelates embraced Lutheranism, shattering German unity, both political and religious. The empire, with its concerns in Italy and the Ottoman Turks, and its jockeying for position in the Catholic world with France, remained within the sphere of the Church. This made fighting a war of religion inevitable, as the Lutherans formed the defense pact in Germany called the Schmalkaldic League, which was attacked by Charles V in 1546. Only the Treaty of Augsburg (1555) brought a respite to the fighting with its division of Germany into spheres of Protestant and Catholic influence. The final recognition that unity would not be restored in Germany was made clear by the Council of Trent (1545-1563) with its firm declaration that compromise with Protestantism was not acceptable.

The incomplete political and religious settlements of the sixteenth century only

Abbey of St. Michael, Hildesheim, Germany

made more war a matter of time, and tensions finally erupted into the bloody Thirty Years' War (1618-1648) that brought ruin and devastation to whole parts of Germany. The Treaty of Westphalia (1648) ended the war, affirming the Peace of Augsburg and virtually destroying the Holy Roman Empire, but the hard-won acceptance of Protestantism had come at a disastrous price, with nearly one third of the population having died from fighting, disease, and starvation.

Not all was hopeless for the Church, however, as the Catholic Reformation, under such great leaders as St. Peter Canisius (1521-1597), had done much to revive the faith, most successfully in southern Germany and Austria. The fruits of the reform were visible in the 1600s with the flowering of monasticism and magnificent baroque and rococo art and architecture as expressions of the revitalized faith. The achievement of the Counter-Reformation, though, could not hide the reality that the majority of Germans were Lutherans or

Calvinists, in the main the result of the settlement *cuius regio, eius religio,* by which the faith of a town or region was determined by its ruler, a pragmatic system that would serve as the basis of Josephinism in the 1700s.

The essentially feudal nature of German life remained true throughout the eighteenth century, but, significantly, the seeds of eventual Germanic unity were planted by the rise of the state of Prussia under the Protestant Hohenzollerns, which achieved prominence in the political, military, and cultural affairs on the Continent under its truly remarkable enlightened despot, King Frederick II the Great (1712-1786). While numerous other states continued to exist throughout Germany (for instance, Bavaria and Saxony), Prussia was the preeminent power. It resisted Napoleon in 1806 and had its armies destroyed at the Battle of Jena-Auerstadt. Its shrewd ruler, King Frederick William II, aided by gifted ministers, bided his time, reformed the military, and in 1813 stood as one of the most crucial enemies of France. The Prussians had a major role in the defeat of Napoleon in 1814 and his final fall in 1815 at the Battle of Waterloo.

In the aftermath of the Napoleonic Wars, the Germans increasingly gravitated toward unity, but differences existed as to how it should be fulfilled. Southern (Catholic) Germans desired a Great Germany headed by Austria's Habsburgs while northern (Protestant) Germans saw Prussia as the natural leader. The German Confederation (1815-1866), created by the Congress of Vienna and consisting of the German states and free cities (including Austria), was long dominated by the Habsburgs. In 1848, an effort was made at unifying Germany through the Frankfurt Parliament. Its work came to nothing owing to competing interests and particularly the Revolution of 1848, ruthlessly suppressed by Frederick William IV. His successor, William (Wilhelm) I (r. 1861-1888), took the decisive step of appointing Otto von Bismarck in 1862 as chancellor. Under his leadership, Prussia became the greatest power on the Continent. Austria was defeated in 1866, and in 1870 France was routed in the Franco-Prussian War. On April 14, 1871, in the Hall of Mirrors at Versailles and with the anguished French watching, William was crowned emperor of Germany.

Throughout the 1700s and 1800s, the Church in Germany suffered in various ways from cultural and political developments. The Enlightenment had produced such important philosophers as Hegel and Fichte, and writers such as Johann Wolfgang von Goethe. As in France and elsewhere, the currents of thought, drifting away from Scholasticism and religion, were headed toward skeptical philosophy, positivism, and rationalism with all of their implications for the faith. The Napoleonic Wars and the harsh repression of the French Empire from 1806-1813 imposed severe hardships upon the religious orders. Once German

independence was achieved in 1813, the Church found itself confronted with a hostile Prussian government and other German states that looked upon the Church as a hindrance to cultural unity, since it was under the control of the foreign power of the papacy. This desire for control was exemplified by the imprisonment of Archbishop Droste (d. 1845) in 1837 (see **Droste zu Vischering, Clemens August von**). The Church was further beset by the problems caused by Hermesianism and the *Kulturkampf* implemented by Bismarck in 1870 as a means of furthering state dominance over Prussian and then German life.

German Catholics surprised the government by their support for Droste and their opposition to the *Kulturkampf.* Catholic intellectuals also resisted Marxism and advocated the kinds of social theory and reform that would be so much a part of the encyclical *Rerum novarum* (1891) by Pope Leo XIII (r. 1878-1903). Two notable developments were the creation of the *Gesselenvereine* and the formation of the German Catholic Center Party. The *Gesselenvereine* were Catholic societies devoted to the education, both mental and moral, of young men who were apprentices, journeymen, and other kinds of laborers. The *Gesselenvereine* promoted both educated middle-class workers and good Catholics. The German Catholic Center Party was launched in 1870 as a means of expressing Catholic views and defending Catholic rights in the political sphere. The party would come to the height of its prosperity in the Weimar Republic (1919-1933). Other German Catholics were enemies of Ultramontanism. The most famous of these was Johannes Döllinger (1799-1890), who wrote against the work of the Vatican Council I (1869-1870).

Bismarck was compelled to resign as chancellor at the behest of Kaiser William II (r. 1888-1918). Under William's long rule, Germany enjoyed its prominence in Europe, but the Kaiser's policies brought Germany into war and catastrophic defeat in World War I (1914-1918). The Germans were humiliated in the Treaty of Versailles, and the imperial house fell from power, the Kaiser's government replaced by the Weimar Republic (which was never politically strong). The republic gave the Catholic Center Party its great opportunity to involve itself in the political life of Germany; it would have a major role in the effort to steer the republic away from dictatorship and the unfortunate events that ended with the seizure of power by Adolf Hitler. Most Catholics were unenthusiastic about the party owing to the continued fondness for the now defunct imperial line. Nevertheless, the Catholic Center Party was supported by a number of important Catholic social organizations including the labor unions, Catholic Action, and the Catholic workers' societies. These organizations were devoted to the Catholic cause and to resisting the Communists.

From the start, the republic was beset by difficulties: lingering anger over the acceptance of the demeaning terms of Versailles, mass unemployment, inflation, and the chronic political agitation caused by the extremist parties on the Left and the Right who desired chaos and instability, finding such an environment conducive to the advancement of their radical agendas. A recovery in the economy was achieved after 1925, ending in 1929 with the onset of the Great Depression. In the election that followed, both the Communists and the National Socialists (Nazi Party) under Adolf Hitler made major gains; the National Socialists gathered greater strength in the early 1930s, culminating with Hitler becoming chancellor of Germany in 1933. The Catholic Center Party, pinning its hopes on the Conservatives being able to control Hitler, took the calamitous step of dissolving itself in 1933, leaving the National Socialists in control of the country.

Catholic organizations quickly fell under considerable repression, despite the pledge by Hitler on March 23, 1933 (a few weeks after becoming chancellor), that he considered the Churches, Protestant and Catholic, to be the most crucial elements in the preservation of Germany's national heritage. Having accepted the demise of the Catholic Center Party, Pope Pius XI (r. 1922-1939) recognized the need for some kind of agreement with Hitler to guard the rights of the Church. On July 8, 1933, the pope gave his approval to the now famous concordat with Hitler. This agreement, of course, was soon disregarded by Hitler, who saw the Church as an obstacle to social unity and as an inconvenient opponent to the inhuman policies of his Nazi regime.

In response to Hitler's repressive program, Pius issued in 1937 the encyclical *Mit brennender Sorge*, smuggled into Germany (by a young Francis Spellman, later cardinal and archbishop of New York) and read from Catholic pulpits in March 1937. This condemnation of the Nazis provoked Hitler's anger, but an even more stinging denunciation was in the works when Pius died on February 10, 1939. His successor, Cardinal Eugenio Pacelli (Pius XII, 1939-1958), was a superbly trained and experienced diplomat who had served as nuncio to Germany and was quite fond of the German people. He tried sincerely, desperately, and unsuccessfully to prevent Hitler's drive toward war, and German tanks rolled into Poland in September 1939. World War II brought incalculable suffering to the globe, the ruin and death caused by the conflict surpassed only by the unprecedented terror unleashed by the Nazis throughout all of Europe. With the SS (or *Schutzstaffel*), death squads (such as the *Einsatzgrüppen*), the concentration camps, and the most cruel police system in history under Heinrich Himmler and his dread lieutenant, Reinhard Heydrich, more than six million Jews were exterminated along with millions of Catholics, especially in Poland. Under

Heydrich (assassinated in 1942; see **Czechoslovakia**), the Church was brutally oppressed. Hundreds of priests and nuns were arrested, imprisoned, tortured, and executed. The most famous martyrs of the Holocaust from the Catholic community were Maximilian Kolbe and Edith Stein. Other heroic figures were Cardinal Michael von Faulhaber, archbishop of Munich, Father Rupert Mayer, and Canon Bernhard Lichtenberg. Faulhaber survived several assassination attempts and never ceased to condemn Hitler for his atrocities against Christians and Jews. Pius aided the Church and the Jews as best he could (see **Pius XII** and **Jews and Judaism**), but toward the end of the war he had to move carefully, as Hitler made sounds about seizing the Vatican and evacuating the pope out of Italy.

In the aftermath of the war, the German Church lay, like the rest of the onetime Third Reich, shattered. Cities were rubble and the country cut up into zones of occupation. The Vatican energetically raised aid and encouraged relief programs.

By 1947, it was clear that one Germany would not be possible, a victim of the Cold War between the West and the Soviet Union. West Germany, the Federal Republic of Germany, was created on May 5, 1955. Its principal ruling party, the Christian Democrats, was born out of the vestiges of the German Catholic Center Party. The Church in the postwar period was a model of success as the German dioceses emerged as some of the most prosperous and best run in the entire Church, so much so that they were able to send money to the Third World to assist the faith in those regions. Notable German theologians and prelates played leading roles in the proceeding of Vatican Council II, including the three well-known *periti*, Hans Küng, Karl Rahner, and Joseph (later Cardinal) Ratzinger. In the East, meanwhile, the Church that had survived the Nazis found itself under Soviet domination and then endured oppression under the

Soviet puppets installed as heads of the German Democratic Republic. Priests and nuns were arrested, deported, or executed, seminaries and schools were closed, and total control exercised over the press and communications. The secret police, the SSD (*Staatsicherheitsdienst*), called the "Stassi," were a pervasive and feared part of daily life for all Catholics, both clergy and laypersons. East Germany finally fell in 1990, the Berlin Wall, so long a symbol of division and captivity, torn down by jubilant crowds. The two churches of Germany were united in November 1990 and began participation in the difficult task of uniting the long-separated German people.

Gerson, Jean (1363-1429) ● French theologian, Church reformer, chancellor of the University of Paris, and a spiritual writer who was given the title *Doctor Christianissimus*. Also known in full as Jean le Charlier de Gerson, he was born in Rethel near the Ardennes, studying at the College of Navarre in Paris under Pierre d'Ailly. Earning his doctorate around 1394, he later succeeded D'Ailly as chancellor of Notre-Dame and of the University of Paris. Gerson was concerned by the ongoing Great Schism, which had begun in 1378, but he called for unity and loyalty to Antipope Benedict XIII in two treatises that he wrote while in Bruges (1397-1401) where he had fled to escape the pressures of Paris. Upon his return to Paris, he became a leader of the conciliar movement, attending the Council of Constance as the head of the French delegation. At the council, Gerson contributed to the Four Articles of Constance, the basis of Gallicanism in France, and defeated the proposal of Jean Petite to defend John the Fearless, duke of Burgundy, who had ordered the assassination of the duke of Orléans in 1407. Gerson could thus return to France only in 1419 after the death of John the Fearless. He settled in Lyons where he lived until his death. Aside from his major role in the conciliar movement and formative Gallicanism, he was a mystical poet much respected by Nicholas of Cusa and Ignatius Loyola. The *Imitation of Christ* was, for a time, credited to Gerson. He also authored numerous treatises on conciliarism, moral theology, and the spiritual life. (See also **Conciliarism** and **Gallicanism**.)

Gertrude the Great, St. (d. c. 1302) ● German nun and mystic at the Benedictine convent of Helfta near Eisleben, Saxony, known as "the Great" because of her profound spirituality and her mystical writings. She was taken in by nuns at the age of five, working for a time as a copyist. From the age of twenty-five, however, she received a number of mystical experiences, including visions of the Sacred Heart. Thereafter she adopted a contemplative life, being devoted particularly to the Sacred Heart. She authored the *Exercita Spiritualia*, a collection of prayers, and the highly respected *Legatus Divinae Pietatis*, a magnificent expression of Christian mysticism; Gertrude herself wrote the Second Book of the *Legatus*, the other portions being written from her notes. Feast day: November 16. (See also **Mechtild of Magdeburg, St.**)

Gervase of Canterbury (d. c. 1210) ● Also Gervasus Dorobornensis, a monk of Christ Church at Canterbury and a chronicler. It is possible that he was born at Maidstone, Kent, becoming a monk and, from 1163, serving as a chronicler in the monastery. He was ordained by Thomas Becket, archbishop of Canterbury, as sacristan, holding the post during the 1190s, probably until 1197 when he mentions one Felix as sacristan in the monastery. His writings are of much value in preserving details of the reign of Richard the Lionhearted (r. 1189-1199), and part of the time of King John. His writings were: *The*

Chronicle, covering from 1100-1199; *Gesta Regum*, an abridgment of *The Chronicle*, with the addition of the years from 1199, including the first years of King John; and *Actus Pontificum Cantuariensis Ecclesiae*, a history of the archbishops of Canterbury up to the death of Hubert Walter in 1205. Interestingly, Gervase recorded for the year 1178 the impact on the moon of what is generally believed by astronomers to be a meteor. The resulting crater is called Giordano Bruno.

Gesselenvereine ● See under **Germany**.

Gesta Romanorum ● Latin for *Deeds of the Romans*. An early fourteenth-century collection of short stories or tales, probably assembled in England and written by an unknown author, although it is guessed that he was a priest. The *Gesta* was likely intended to provide preachers with suitable moral anecdotes that could be used to illustrate sermons. Hence there were many themes such as magic and monsters. Very popular throughout the Middle Ages, the tales were used by many writers and poets, most likely Chaucer and Shakespeare.

Gesuati ● Properly the *Clerici apostolici S. Hieronymi*, a congregation of laymen founded by Bl. John Colombini (d. 1367) around 1360. They were mainly devoted to prayer, charity work, and preaching, deriving their name *Gesuati* from the use of "Hail Jesus" or "Praised be Jesus" at the start and end of their sermons. Initially loosely organized, they adhered at first to the Benedictine Rule, later adopting the Augustinian Rule; formal approval of the congregation came in 1367 by Pope Urban V with the provision that they be formed into monasteries. During this period they took to wearing white tunics with a square hood and a grayish-brown cloak. The *Gesuati* spread quickly throughout Italy after Colombini's death, eventually entering France as well. In 1668, however, they were dissolved by Pope Clement IX because they had ceased to be a vital order.

Ghetto ● See under **Jews and Judaism**.

Gibbons, James (1834-1921) ●
Archbishop of Baltimore and the second North American cardinal. Gibbons was born in Baltimore but moved to Ireland with his parents at a very young age, returning to America at the age of nineteen. After working for a time in New Orleans, he entered St. Mary's Seminary and was ordained in 1861. He was appointed secretary to Archbishop Martin Spalding of Baltimore in 1865, assisting Spalding in his preparations for the Second Plenary Council of Baltimore (1866). In 1868, Gibbons was named a bishop with the rank of vicar apostolic for North Carolina. Two years later, he attended the First Vatican Council. Made bishop of Richmond in 1873, he spent four years in the post before succeeding in 1877 James Bayley as archbishop of Baltimore. In 1884, he presided over the Third Plenary Council at Baltimore and in 1886 became a cardinal. At times in sympathy with the ideals of Americanism, Gibbons journeyed to Rome in 1887 and there delivered a sermon in praise of the separation of Church and State. While in Rome, he also succeeded in convincing the Holy See to reverse its condemnation of the Knights of Labor, a large part of whose membership was Catholic. Gibbons was the recipient, as archbishop of Baltimore, of Pope Leo XIII's encyclical *Testem Benevolentiae*, which condemned Americanism. In his later years, he worked to organize several organizational bodies, most notably the National Catholic War Council (1917) and the National Catholic Welfare Conference (1919). His work thus laid the groundwork for the National Conference of Catholic Bishops. A well-known and deeply respected figure on the national scene, Gibbons became arguably the most important religious leader in the country in the early part of the twentieth

century. Theodore Roosevelt in 1917 called him a "venerated and useful citizen." Gibbons was also the author of *Faith of Our Fathers* (1876), an examination of Catholic teachings that became enormously popular and was translated into numerous languages.

Giberti, Gian Matteo (1495-1543) ●
Cardinal and bishop of Verona, one of the foremost proponents of reform at the Council of Trent (1545-1563), which he was unable to attend because of his unexpected death. The son of a Genoese naval captain, he was born in Palermo and in 1513 was admitted to the household of Cardinal Giulio de' Medici (the future Pope Clement VII). Over time he became his secretary, serving also as an adviser to Pope Leo X; in 1521, he was named chief envoy to Emperor Charles V. In 1524, Giberti was named bishop of Verona, but such was his value to Pope Clement that the pontiff compelled him to remain in Rome, so Giberti administered his see through a vicar-general. After the sack of Rome in 1527, he was captured and imprisoned by imperial forces, narrowly avoiding death and finally escaping to Verona the following year. Returning to Rome only periodically during Clement's remaining pontificate, Giberti was recalled by Pope Paul III. In 1536, he was named to the commission charged with launching the reform of the Church, and Giberti's work took him to Trent to prepare for the council. Giberti also authored editions of patristic writings, using his palace at Verona to establish a printing press to produce works of the Greek Fathers.

Gilbert de la Porrée (1076-1154) ●
Scholastic theologian and philosopher and one of the foremost students of the renowned school of Chartres under St. Bernard of Clairvaux. After studying at Poitiers, Gilbert taught at Paris, served as chancellor of the cathedral school at Chartres, and in 1142 was appointed bishop of Poitiers. Gilbert is best known for his controversial teachings

and writings on the Trinity, an extreme form of Universalist thought expressed in his commentary on the *opuscula* (little works) of the sixth-century philosopher Boethius. The opposition aroused by his theories was vociferous, and Gilbert faced charges of heresy by Bernard at the Synod of Reims in 1148. He probably recanted, as no formal condemnation of him was ever pronounced. Among his other works were commentaries on the Psalms and the Epistles of St. Paul; the treatise on Aristotle, the *Liber Sex Principorum*, was attributed to him.

Gilbert Foliot (d. 1188) ● Bishop of London and a noted English ecclesiast. A Norman by descent, Foliot at first entered Cluny, eventually becoming prior. Respected for his austerity and virtue, he was named abbot of Abbeville, abbot of Gloucester, bishop of Hereford, and then bishop of London in 1163. Gilbert opposed the election of Thomas Becket in 1162 as archbishop of Canterbury, declaring that Thomas was unworthy to hold the post, particularly as Thomas had persecuted the Church in the service of King Henry II. Gilbert's disagreement with Becket continued in 1163 and his translation to London; he refused to take a vow of obedience to Canterbury, claiming to have already done so when bishop of Hereford. When Becket broke with Henry, Gilbert sided with the king on the Constitutions of Clarendon, serving also as a royal envoy to Pope Alexander III. Excommunicated by Thomas in 1169, Gilbert appealed to the pope and was supported by the pontiff; the following year, however, he was excommunicated again and was suspected of complicity in Becket's murder, although he was absolved of any involvement in 1172. He died much respected but not well liked.

Gilbertines ● Religious order founded around 1130 by St. Gilbert of Sempringham (c. 1083-1189). The Gilbertines were established while St. Gilbert was working as a parish priest in his native Sempringham. He had hoped initially to establish a monastery, but, as this proved impractical, he provided a conventual life and rule for seven women whom he had once taught. In this he had the support of his bishop, Alexander of Lincoln, and after a year the women were professed. Adopting as closely as possible the Cistercian Rule, Gilbert added lay sisters and brothers to assist in manual labor, recruiting the brothers from among the poor. After a number of years, the fame of the order spread and in 1139 a second house was begun, with more foundations begun soon after. In 1148, Gilbert journeyed to Cîteaux where he asked to have his order incorporated into the Cistercians. This the Cistercians refused to do and Gilbert returned to England and organized the houses under the Augustinian Rule. They were henceforth a double order with each community consisting of nuns and canons as well as regular lay sisters and lay brothers. That same year, papal approval was given. By the time of Gilbert's death, there were nine double monasteries. The only order exclusively of English creation, the Gilbertines were much favored by the crown, although the members maintained a life of simplicity and austerity. Thus, at the Dissolution of the Monasteries under King Henry VIII (r. 1509-1547), only four Gilbertine communities were ranked among the wealthiest monasteries in the realm. The Gilbertines accepted the dissolution of their twenty-five houses without resistance. Members of the order received pensions, and the last master of Sempringham, Robert Holgate, bishop of Llandaff, was made archbishop of York in 1545. Gilbert was canonized in 1202 by Pope Innocent III. Feast day: February 4.

Gildas, St. (d. c. 570) ● British monk and historian, author of the famed work *De Excidio et Conquestu Britanniae*, a history of

Britain from the Roman conquest to his own era. Little is known about Gildas, although according to an eleventh-century source in the Abbey of St.-Gildas-de-Rhuys in Brittany, he was born in Strathclyde. He possibly fled to Wales, journeyed to Ireland and Rome, and established a community in Brittany, the future St.-Gildas-de-Rhuys. His history is notable for being one of the few extant sources on Britain following the departure of the Romans in 410. While hampered by a heavy style and emphasis on the lamentable moral conditions of the time, it remains a valuable historical source.

Giles of Assisi, St. ● See under **Francis of Assisi, St**.

Giles of Rome (d. 1316) ● Also Aegidius Romanus, a philosopher and Scholastic theologian and onetime student of St. Thomas Aquinas. A native of Rome, he entered the Hermits of St. Augustine around 1257, studying in Paris under St. Thomas from 1269-1271. In 1292, he became head of the Augustinian Hermits, administering the order until 1295 when Pope Boniface made him archbishop of Bourges. Despite serving as tutor to King Philip IV the Fair of France (including the authorship for him around 1285 of the popular work *De Regimine Principum*), Giles threw his support behind Boniface in his struggle with the French king. Giles wrote that the pope was deserving not only of supreme ecclesiastical and spiritual power but temporal political authority as well. An ardent Thomist, he authored numerous commentaries on Aristotle and the *Sentences* of Peter Lombard, treatises against

St. Giles of Assisi

Averroism and angels, and *De Summi Pontificis Potestate*, possibly the basis for Boniface's bull *Unam Sanctam*. Giles was given the title of *Doctor Fundatissimus* (the Well-Grounded Teacher, or Doctor) for his genius.

Gilson, Étienne (1884-1978) ● French Thomistic philosopher who was the author of a number of important works on medieval philosophy. Gilson studied at the Sorbonne and in 1913 was appointed professor at Lille, holding chairs at Strasbourg (1917-1920), the Sorbonne (1921-1932), the Collège de France (1932-1951), and, after retirement, professor at the Pontifical Institute of Medieval Studies in Toronto, Ontario. Like Jacques Maritain, he spent his final years in France. Among Gilson's major works were: *Le Thomisme* (1919), an outline on the metaphysics of the Angelic Doctor; *Le Philosophie au moyen âge* (2 vols., 1922), covering the philosophy of the Middle Ages; *La Philosophie de Saint Bonaventure* (1924); and *La Théologie mystique de Saint Bernard* (1934). He also helped to establish the *Archives d'histoire doctrinale et littéraire du moyen âge*, to which he contributed numerous articles.

Giovanni Capistrano ● See **John Capistran, St**.

Giraldus Cambrensis (c. 1146-c. 1223) ● Also known as Gerald de Barri, Gerald the Welshman, and Gerald of Wales, a leading Churchman in Wales and historian. Born to a noble family in Pembrokeshire, Giraldus studied at Paris and was appointed (1175) archdeacon of Brecon, a post he held until 1204. Although he was twice elected bishop of St. David's (in 1176 and 1198), he was never consecrated because of the concerns of the Anglo-Saxon rulers of the isles that he might attempt to free the see from the jurisdiction of Canterbury and to secure supremacy over the Church in southern Wales. Nevertheless, Giraldus agreed to assist King Henry II in preaching the Third Crusade and held several posts under the king. Giraldus was the author of *Topographia Hibernica* and *Expugnatio Hibernice* (works on Ireland); *Itinerarum Cambriae* and *Descriptio*, on Wales; and *De rebus a se gestis*, an autobiography.

Glabrio, Manius Acilius (d. c. 95) ●
Consul in Rome in the year 91. During the reign of Emperor Domitian, he was put to death because of his adherence to Christianity. Glabrio was a member of one of the great noble families of Rome who resided on the Pincian Hills, owning a famous series of gardens. According to the historian Dio Cassius and the writer Juvenal, Glabrio was forced by Emperor Domitian to fight a lion and two bears in an amphitheater in Albano, and then banished for surviving the contest. Finally, around 95, he was executed, an event noted by the historian Suetonius. There seems a very high probability that Glabrio was a Christian, dying, like Flavia Domitilla, for the faith.

Glastonbury ● Famed Benedictine monastery in Somerset, England, traditionally one of the oldest Christian sites in the isles. According to custom, Joseph of Arimathea was the founder of Glastonbury, for it was there that his staff took root and blossomed into the Glastonbury thorn. Historically, Glastonbury was established by the Celts, becoming an Anglo-Saxon monastery in the seventh century under the

patronage of King Ine of Wessex. The monastery was destroyed by the Danes in the ninth century, but it was revived by St. Dunstan, who became abbot in 943 through King Edmund I. Under Dunstan, the Benedictine Rule was adopted and Glastonbury became one of the foremost centers of monastic reform and intellectual development in England. In the mid-1600s, it was demolished on the order of Oliver Cromwell. Glastonbury appeared frequently in legend, particularly in the tales of King Arthur and Queen Gueneviere as well as the Holy Grail and St. Patrick. The Glastonbury thorn, a type of hawthorn, blossoms in May and at Christmas and is found in the Levant. William of Malmesbury wrote a history of Glastonbury in 1135.

Glossator ● Name given to a medieval scholar who wrote commentaries or interpretations, called glosses, on civil or canon law or religious or even rabbinical texts, and the Bible. Legal glosses began probably in the late eleventh century in Bologna where legal experts launched a reconstruction of Justinian's *Digest*. Religious glossators focused on canon law and biblical texts. The standard commentary on the Bible produced during this era was the *Glossa Ordinaria* (or *Glossa Communis*), a work organized into marginal or interlinear glosses, meaning the commentaries appeared in the margins or between the lines. It was generally believed that marginal glosses were written by Walafrid Strabo (d. 849), credited as the first glossator, and the interlinear glosses by Anselm of Laon (d. 1117); actually, both glosses, which appeared together, were the product of a glossator in the school of Anselm of Laon. By the end of the 1100s, the entire Bible was available in the form of glosses. The foremost figure of glosses in canon law was Gratian.

Gnosticism ● Name used for a system of religious thought forming out of various elements that first came into a developed shape in the second century and endured for several centuries. Christian Gnosticism first evolved out of pre-Christian pagan religious currents, influenced by Neoplatonists and pagan philosophers. It was found initially in numerous Christian schools, became increasingly established in various shapes, and by the late second century had splintered from the Christian Church. The sects of Gnosticism varied considerably in their particular doctrines, but they shared certain common characteristics.

Central to Gnostic teachings was the idea of *gnosis*, secret revealed knowledge of salvation. They claimed that the source of the *gnosis* was the secret oral transmission of the knowledge by Christ, either to the Twelve Apostles or to the leader of the sect. In turn, the *gnosis* was transmitted to select members who were determined to be worthy.

To the Gnostics, the universe was sharply divided between spiritual and material worlds, the first representing perfection and goodness, the second imperfection and evil. The world, and hence everything created in it, including humanity, is imperfect. God, to the Gnostics, is a transcendent and spiritual being, meaning that he could not have created the material world. Instead, the material world was created by a lesser god, the Demiurge, derived from the Divine Being through a series of emanations, or aeons. This Demiurge, a creator god, brought the world into being in some manner, a material existence that is imperfect and opposed to the spiritual world. Certain humans, however, contain within them a gift of spirituality, described by some as a spark of the Divine Being. They will be able to achieve salvation and become reunited with the Divine Being through the *gnosis*, secret knowledge of attainment. Christ, to the Christian Gnostics, was a representative of the Divine Being, sent to deliver to the elect the *gnosis*, the path to salvation. Extremely exclusive in nature, Gnosticism thus divided

all of humanity into two main groups, the select (saved) and those of the flesh (damned).

It is a matter of question among scholars as to when the Gnostics first began to trouble the Church. Some feel that reference in several NT books point to efforts to denounce those teachings that came to embody Gnostic ideals. St. Paul, perhaps, confronted them at Corinth and Colossae, and mention might have been made in 1 John. Specific sects can be identified by the second century in the leading centers of the Church — Alexandria and Rome — and to this period belong the most well-known of Gnostic teachers, Basilides, Valentinus, and Marcion. They were challenged within the Church by a number of writers, namely St. Clement of Rome, St. Irenaeus, St. Hippolytus, and Tertullian. These anti-Gnostic spokesmen helped delineate the severe theological differences between the Gnostics and the Church, but they also played a vital role in preserving in their writings information on their opponents, details that were long the main source upon which study of Gnosticism could be based. A major breakthrough in adding to our knowledge thus occurred in 1945-1946 with the discovery of the collection of Coptic texts at Nag Hammadi in Upper Egypt.

Gnosticism, once separated from the Church, survived for several hundred years, finding continued life in the sect of Manichaeism that lasted well into the Middle Ages in the Near East. Gnostic principles were also advanced by the heretical sects of the Bogomils, Cathars, and Albigensians.

Godfrey of Fontaine (d. after 1306) ● French philosopher and theologian who served as a professor and a dean of the University of Paris. His writings include the *Quodlibeta* and the *Scholia*, various annotations on the *Summa Theologiae* of Thomas Aquinas. Godfrey disagreed with Thomas on the idea of identifying essence with existence, disputing with not only

Thomists but with the supporters of John Duns Scotus. Godfrey also opposed the presence of the mendicant friars in the University of Paris.

Golden Bull ● Name given to important decrees or pronouncements, so-called because of the use of gold or some precious metal upon the seal. An example of a golden bull issued by the papacy was the bull granted by Pope Leo X to King Henry VIII giving him the title *Fidei Defensor* (Defender of the Faith). Other bulls involving the Church or its organizations included:

Golden Bull of Rimini (1226) — Issued by Emperor Frederick II, it established rights of jurisdiction over Prussia for the Teutonic Knights.

Golden Bull of 1222 — Issued by King Andrew II, it guaranteed the rights of the clergy and nobility. It also prohibited the imprisonment of any nobles without trial and the collection of taxes from the aristocracy and the Church.

Golden Bull of 1356 — Promulgated by Emperor Charles V, it established the system by which the future kings of Germany should be elected. The bull remained in force until 1806 and the final dissolution of the Holy Roman Empire.

Golden Legend ● Collection of lives of the saints and articles on Christian festivals first compiled by Jacobus de Voragine (d. c. 1298) between 1255 and 1266. Also called the *Lombardica Historia*, it was organized into some one hundred seventy-seven or one hundred eighty-two chapters along the Church calendar. Immensely popular, it was translated into French by Jean Belet de Vigny in the 1300s and underwent numerous other editions. When, however, it was attacked in the 1500s because of historical inaccuracies, particularly by such scholars as Melchior Cano (d. 1560), it fell into disuse. Medieval iconography was much influenced by the work.

Golden Rose ● Ornament made of gold and precious gems in the form of a rose that is traditionally blessed by the pope on the Fourth Sunday of Lent (Laetare Sunday or Rose Sunday) and presented to an individual or community as a token of special papal favor. It is granted in recognition of some special service to the Church or for special devotion. The origins of the Golden Rose are ancient but obscure. Pope Leo IX in 1049 referred to the rose as an old custom. In this century, the rose was presented to the queens of Catholic countries; in those cases where there was not a suitable recipient, it was kept in the Vatican until such time as it could be distributed.

Gordon Riots ● Also called the No Popery Riots. They were a severe series of anti-Catholic riots that gripped London from June 2 to June 9, 1780, so-called because the mob was headed by the fanatical Lord George Gordon and carried flags that declared "No Popery." The violence began when Gordon led a large crowd in a march through London to Parliament to deliver a petition calling for the repeal of the Catholic Relief Act of 1778. Along the route, Catholic homes were sacked and vandalized, the furniture burned in the streets, and the houses put to the torch. Embassy chapels were attacked. As the mobs were largely unopposed by authorities, the violence increased until some unpopular Protestants were being assaulted and fires were set all over the city. As days passed, the rioters attempted to seize the city of London, forcing the hand of the government. Its police and civil branches were inadequate, the government summoned troops into the metropolis. On the express orders of King George III, the crowds were dispersed. Some two hundred ten persons were killed and seventy-five were wounded. Lord Gordon was tried but acquitted of high treason in 1781. He died a lunatic in Newgate prison in 1793. (See **Great Britain**.)

Gorkum, Martyrs of ● Name given to a group of nineteen martyrs who were hanged and mutilated at Brielle in the Netherlands by fanatical Calvinist soldiers called the *Watergeuzen* (Sea-Beggars) in 1572; they are called the Martyrs of Gorkum because most of them were in Gorkum at the time of their capture. Seized in June 1572, nine Franciscans were soon joined by several lay brothers and a group of priests, including a Dominican who had hastened to the city to administer the sacraments to his imprisoned fellow clergy. Cruelly beaten and mistreated by the *Watergeuzen*, the prisoners were transferred to Brielle in groups where they were each ordered to deny papal supremacy and the Blessed Sacrament. They refused, and the local *Watergeuzen* commander had them hanged on July 9, despite a letter from William of Orange that clerics were not to be molested. Beatified in 1673, the martyrs were canonized by Pope Pius IX in 1865.

Görres, Johann Joseph von (1776-1848) ● German Catholic author and an intellectual who became the strongest champion of Catholicism in Germany during the first half of the 1800s. He was born at Coblenz, studying in the city where he was deeply influenced by rationalism. In his younger days he enthusiastically supported the French Revolution, which he thought would free the peoples of Europe; but, after studying in Paris from 1799-1800, he grew disenchanted, calling the city a "flower-bedecked quagmire." From 1800-1806, he taught natural science at Coblenz. He was much shaped by Friedrich Wilhelm Joseph von Schelling (d. 1854), authoring such essays as *"Glaube und Wissen"* (1805; "Belief and Knowledge"). In 1806, he became a lecturer at the University of Heidelberg on history and literature, entering into close association with the leaders and movement of German Romanticism. His support of the Church, however, aroused the anger of the

Protestants in Heidelberg, so Görres returned to Coblenz. Nevertheless, he became immensely popular in Germany for his staunch support of independence during the Napoleonic Wars. In 1814, he launched the first great German newspaper, *Der Rheinische Merkur*, an outspoken paper against Napoleon. In 1816, it was suppressed by the reactionary Prussian government. His unceasing activity in defense of rights, particularly those of the Church in Germany (as in the 1819 pamphlet *Deustchland und die Revolution*), caused a warrant for his arrest to be issued, but Görres escaped to Strasbourg and safety. In 1827, he was offered a professorship at Munich by King Ludwig I of Bavaria, a post that made him one of the foremost Catholic intellectuals in Europe, with the likes of Döllinger and Möhler. From 1828-1832, he helped establish the review *Eos*, originally founded by Herbst (1828), in which contemporary rationalism was opposed by Catholic principles. In 1837, he took up the cause of the archbishop of Cologne, the deposed and imprisoned Clemens August von Droste zu Vischering. Through his treatise *Athanasius* (1834), he helped whip up widespread support not only for the archbishop but for the Church in Germany. *Die Triarier* (1838), another tract, attacked the defenders of the government and was granted special favor by Pope Gregory XVI. Görres's final years were darkened by a scandal surrounding the adventuress Lola Montez, which resulted in the dismissal of several of Görres's friends from the university by King Ludwig in 1847. His vast and important writings were compiled into collected form from 1854-1860.

Gother, John (d. 1704) ● English priest and controversialist. He was born at Southampton and raised a strict Presbyterian. At an early age, however, he was converted to Catholicism, entering the English College in Lisbon in 1668. Ordained a priest in 1682, he returned to England and joined the Catholic Mission in London. There he wrote in defense of the faith during the controversies of King James II (r. 1685-1688). His most famous controversial writing was *A Papist Misrepresented and Represented*, the first section published in 1685, with a second and third part published in 1687. Gother refuted the many erroneous and often vulgar ideas regarding the Church that were being perpetuated. It earned a response from numerous influential Anglican divines, including Edward Stillingfleet (d. 1699). After the so-called Glorious Revolution of 1688, Gother became chaplain at Warkworth Castle; there he received into the Church Richard Challoner and authored several treatises on the transubstantiation and other doctrinal matters. He died while at sea on a voyage to Lisbon.

Gottesfreunde ● German for "Friends of God," a group of fourteenth-century men and women who lived in Switzerland, the Rhineland, and Bavaria and attempted to adopt a Christian existence. The *Gottesfreunde* adhered to strict asceticism and prayer while caring for the poor. While they stressed the need for personal spiritual transformation and union of their souls with God, they largely remained within the Church, drawing much influence from the mystics Johannes Tauler, Henry Suso, and Meister Eckhart.

Gotthard, St. (d. 1038) ● Abbot, bishop of Hildesheim, and a leading figure in monastic reform in Germany. Gotthard was ordained in 990, entering the Benedictines and being appointed abbot in 996 or 997. In his dealings with Henry, duke of Bavaria (the future Emperor Henry II), he so impressed the nobleman that Henry commissioned him to launch monastic reforms throughout the region. In 1022, he became bishop of Hildesheim, continuing his efforts at reforms and working to improve education. The dukes of Bavaria constructed a chapel in his honor at the summit of one of the passes in the Alps; the St. Gotthard pass probably received its name from the chapel. Feast day: May 4.

Gottschalk of Fulda (d. 868) ● Also known as Gottschalk of Orbais, a theologian, monk, poet, known largely because of his controversial ideas concerning predestination. The son of a Saxon count, he was forced by his parents to become an oblate in the Benedictine monastery of Fulda. After spending many years with the monks, including a period of study at Reichenau, Gottschalk was ready to be ordained a deacon. He asked, however, to be freed from his monastic obligations, and his request was granted by a synod at Mainz in 829 over the objections of Rabanus Maurus, who became a devoted enemy. Rabanus succeeded in forcing Gottschalk back into the monastic life, securing his placement at Orbais, in France, and his irregular ordination as a priest at Reims around 838. At Orbais, Gottschalk continued to develop his theological ideas, particularly his views on predestination. He was attacked by Maurus and Hincmar of Reims for heresy and for denying free will and the saving grace of God, being condemned by the Synod of Mainz in 848. Gottschalk was defrocked and imprisoned at the monastery of Hautvilliers. He died there, physically shattered and probably insane, without ever recanting.

Grail Movement ● International movement of laywomen founded in the Netherlands in 1921 by the Jesuit Jacques van Ginneken. Its members are devoted to the spread of Christian values and the development of peoples through religious education, social work, medical service, and apostolic formation. The movement is based upon the principles that the Church is a continuation of Christ's mission entrusted to all of Christ's people, that the laity as the people of God are called to a union with

Christ, and that women are particularly well-suited for a God-centered renewal through their love, the extension of peace, and the establishing of dignity and worth for each human individual. The degree of participation by members varies with their single or married status, although the movement is found throughout the world. The international secretariat is currently located in Mulheim, Germany, while the American headquarters are in Loveland, Ohio.

Grande Chartreuse ● See **Carthusian Order** and **Chartreuse, La Grande**.

Grandmont, Order of ● French religious community first established in 1077 by St. Stephen of Muret (d. 1124). Also known as Grandmontines, the members of this order were devoted to strict poverty and extreme self-discipline, including silence and individual cells. The order eventually spread to England, with three houses, Alberbury, Creswell, and Grosmont. These survived into the second half of the 1400s and the French lasted until the French Revolution.

Gratian (d. c. 1159 or 1179) ● Called the Father of Canon Law, he was a canonist, monk, and author of the important work *Decretum* (also known as the *Concordia Discordantium Canonum*). Gratian was probably an Italian, a Camaldolese monk, and a lecturer at the monastery of Sts. Felix and Nabor in Bologna. His renown is based upon the *Decretum*, a massive collection of thirty-eight hundred texts, conciliar decrees, papal declarations, patristic writings, and apostolic constructions that were supplemented by Gratian's extensive commentary to clarify and to correct various errors and contradictions and to bring the numerous sources into harmony with one another. The *Decretum* was probably completed around 1140, this date accepted by many scholars because of Gratian's

inclusion of material from the Lateran Council of 1139. It soon became the standard work for students of canon law, particularly in the universities of Bologna, Oxford, Paris, and elsewhere. While never given official acceptance by the Church, it was nevertheless an essential source for ecclesiastical law utilized by the curial and canon lawyers; it was also placed in the first section of the *Corpus Iuris Canonici*. While later developments have made the *Decretum* obsolete, it remains a valued work among canonists and historians and was one of the greatest scholarly works in the whole of history of the Middle Ages.

Gravissimum Educationis ● Vatican Council II document promulgated on October 28, 1965, and known in English as the "Declaration on Christian Education." The Council Fathers used the decree to proclaim the inalienable rights of all children to receive education. Among the most important points are: the very grave obligation on parents to ensure a proper education for their family; the need for parents to have freedom of choice in schools, without restrictions, regulations, and coercion; the place of society in imparting a proper education; the obligation of the Church to provide its children with education so that the very lives of the young might be given inspiration by Christ, while offering its assistance in promoting the development of well-balanced individuals; the place of catechetical instruction; the praiseworthy work of teachers, those individuals who labor on behalf of the community through their teaching career; the crucial role of Catholic schools; and the devoting of much attention by the Church to higher education, calling upon all Catholic universities and faculties to be known not for their numbers but their high standards.

Great Britain ● See **England, Scotland,** and **Wales**; see also **Ireland**.

Great Schism ● Also Great Western Schism. See **Schism, Great**.

Greece ● Christianity was brought to Greece in the first century by the earliest leaders of the Church, most notably St. Paul who arrived in the country on his second missionary journey (52-53) with Silas and Timothy. Paul founded the Church at Philippi, the first Christian community on European soil (Acts 16:12), and then went to Thessalonica (17:1), Berea (17:10), and then to Athens (17:15). From there, he traveled to Corinth (18:1) where he was brought before the proconsul of Achaia (Achaea), Gallio. Later, on his third missionary journey (54-58), he spent three months in Corinth. From that beginning, the Greek Church spread swiftly, although the two most prominent communities in the early period were Corinth and Athens. There were a number of bishops in Greece by the second century, as proven by the martyrdoms of several prelates during persecutions. Publius, bishop of Athens, for example, was martyred during the reign of Emperor Hadrian (117-138).

Under the extensive changes in organization that occurred during the reign of Constantine the Great (d. 337), the Greeks were attached to the prefecture of Illyricum, Gaul, and Italy, meaning that its disposition was to be Western. This orientation did not take place, however, and the Greek Church was more Eastern in outlook. Thus, when the empire was divided into East and West in 379, the eastern half of the prefecture (Macedonia, Achaia —including Greece — Thessaly, and other smaller territories) was included in the Eastern Empire. From that time, the Greeks effectively belonged to the Eastern Church, and the patriarch of Constantinople was able to claim jurisdiction over the region, despite the vigorous protests of the popes. Local clergy were most often highly independent in action, frequently siding with their communities against the authorities of Constantinople. This was especially the case in the Iconoclastic Controversy, as the Greeks were highly devoted to their images. The Eastern membership of the Greek Church was certified in 1054 with the schism that erupted between the Eastern and Western Churches. They fully adopted the Byzantine rite and rejected the Roman (or Latin) rite, going so far as to strike the pope's name from their diptychs. When Constantinople fell to the forces of the Fourth Crusade in 1204 and a Latin patriarch was installed over them, the Greeks still retained Eastern custom and suffered persecution from their Frankish overlords until the restoration of the Byzantine Empire in 1261. The Greeks were quite hostile, thereafter, although Greek bishops attended the Councils of Lyons (1274) and Ferrara-Florence (1439) and agreed halfheartedly to the reunion. This, of course, lasted only a short time, and in 1453 the Greek Church fell under the rule of the Ottoman Turks with the capture of Constantinople, cutting off the Orthodox Christians even further from contact with the West. Today, there is a small Catholic population under an archbishop and four dioceses. (See also **Orthodox Eastern Churches**.)

Greek Church ● See **Orthodox Eastern Churches**.

Gregorian Calendar ● Revised (or reformed) calendar that was issued in 1582 by Pope Gregory XIII (r. 1572-1585) and that replaced the long accepted Julian calendar throughout most of Christendom. Owing to substantial improvements in physics and astronomy, by the 1500s it was clear that the Julian calendar, originally designed by Julius Caesar in 46 B.C., was inaccurate; it did not coordinate properly with the rotation of the earth around the sun, and by the 1500s it was ten days out of sync with actual time. Not surprisingly, the ten days were of increasing importance to navigation and agriculture, causing severe problems for sailors, merchants, and farmers whose livelihood depended upon precise measurements of time and the seasons. Pope Sixtus IV (r. 1471-1484) made the first effort to reform the calendar, hiring the astronomer Johann Müller who, unfortunately, was murdered soon after. The work of other astronomers could not gain universal acceptance owing to problems of competing national interests and varying opinions. The Church thus offered the best chance of promulgating a definitive solution to a growing crisis. Pope Gregory XIII commanded that a committee of astronomers look into the matter. Their work formed the basis of the encyclical *Inter gravissimas* (February 24, 1582) by which Gregory commanded that to reform the calendar, the day following October 4, 1582, should not be counted October 5 but October 15, 1582. Leap years were also added to ensure that errors similar to those of the Julian calendar would be prevented. While greeted initially with suspicion by the Protestant countries, the Gregorian calendar was finally recognized as highly accurate and was adopted, although it did not come into use in England until 1752. The Orthodox Church refused to endorse the new calendar, adhering to the Julian, so that feasts fall thirteen days later than those of the Western rite.

Gregorian Chant ● Name given to the form of plain chant that was traditionally believed to have been organized and arranged by Pope St. Gregory I (r. 590-604) from whom its name is derived, although the actual role of Gregory is of considerable question to scholars. The Gregorian chant is the most widely used in the Latin Church and is distinguished from the other chants such as Ambrosian and Mozarabic. It is generally accepted that the chant originated from Jewish sources, subsequently undergoing development as the music of the Roman rite

under the members of the *Schola cantorum*, the school of singers founded by Pope Gregory. It is a vocal form of music, using a conventional scale of eight notes. Very often, the actual tone was dependent upon the Latin text that was being sung. The chant spread quickly from the time of Gregory, being adapted in different regions. Throughout the Middle Ages it became increasingly complex, ornate, and supplemented by musical instruments. Such was its degree of complexity by the eleventh century that only superbly trained choirs could master it. Less and less a means of wide liturgical expression, the chant declined over succeeding years despite an attempt at a revival by the Council of Trent (1545-1563).

The 1800s brought a renewal in appreciation, due largely to the work of the monks of the Benedictine Abbey of Solesmes. Much impetus was given to the study of Gregorian chant by Pope St. Pius X (r. 1903-1914) in the *motu proprio* entitled *Tra le sollicitudini* (1903). The chant was henceforth part of the liturgical movement. Further support for its use was expressed by Pope Pius XI (r. 1922-1939) and Pope Pius XII (r. 1939-1958), and by the Second Vatican Council in the decree *Sacrosanctum Concilium* ("Constitution on the Sacred Liturgy"). Unfortunately, the spread of the vernacular in the liturgy obviated the application of the chant in any wide sense. In recent years, Gregorian chant has enjoyed a renaissance in secular music fields, thanks to the amazing success of the album recorded by the monks of Santo Domingo de Silos in Spain. It was the number one record all over Europe and was a major hit in the United States under the title "Chant" in 1993-1994.

Gregorian Reform ● Name given to an attempted reform of the Church, so-called because of its most important figure, Pope Gregory VII (r. 1075-1085), although the program was launched and fostered by

Gregory's predecessors during the eleventh century. The attempts at real reform probably began as early as Pope St. Leo IX (r. 1049-1054), and were continued by Pope Nicholas II (r. 1059-1061). Among the major issues confronting the Church at the time were simony, the lack of clerical discipline (especially the neglect of clerical celibacy), and the increasingly severe situation of lay investiture. At a synod in 1059, Nicholas II declared Church freedom in papal elections, an important step toward ecclesiastical independence. The foremost reformer, of course, was Hildebrand, Pope Gregory VII. He instituted ecclesiastical changes, adjustments in canon law, and remained steadfast in opposing lay investiture. His reforms were viciously opposed by Emperor Henry IV, sparking one of the most bitter conflicts of the Middle Ages between the papacy and a secular ruler. While he would die in exile, Gregory was instrumental in securing the ultimate independence of the Church from secular interference.

Gregorian Sacramentary ● Important sacramentary (or book of various prayers and texts to be used for the celebration of Mass) traditionally attributed to Pope St. Gregory I the Great (r. 590-604). Also called the *Hadrianum*, the sacramentary was probably composed at Rome (c. 630) and its attribution to Gregory is not correct, as it has within it a Mass for the saint's feast. There are, however, around eighty prayers held to have been composed by the pontiff. The sacramentary is principally known as a result of the copy that was sent (c. 790) to Charlemagne by Pope Adrian I (r. 772-790) at the former's request so as to facilitate further liturgical unity in the lands of the Carolingian Empire. Adrian declares in the letter accompanying the work that it was written by Gregory. The original sacramentary sent by the pope has not survived.

To overcome certain deficiencies in the *Hadrianum*, several supplements were added to it. The chief supplement was the *Hucusque*, so-called from the first word, attributed to both Benedict of Aniane and Alcuin. The *Hucusque* — with other as yet unclear sources — made the *Hadrianum* complete for the entire liturgical year; it was initially separate from the *Hadrianum* but was finally combined with it. Other types of Gregorian Sacramentaries are the *Tridentinum* and the *Paduensis*. With the Gelasian and Leonine Sacramentaries, the Gregorian Sacramentary was an important element in the development of the Roman Missal.

Gregory I the Great, St. ● Pope from 590-604. Last of the Latin Fathers of the Church and founder of the medieval papacy. The son of a senator of Rome and thus a member of a noble (or patrician) family, Gregory embarked upon a very promising secular career and was appointed prefect of the city (*praefectus urbi*) of Rome in 573. He soon renounced this life, however, using his large inheritance to establish seven monasteries, six in Sicily and one in Rome on his own estate. This last community he joined himself around 574, but such was his reputation that in 578 Pope Benedict I appointed him deacon. The next year Pope Pelagius II sent him to Constantinople as *apochrisarius*, or ambassador, with the hope of securing Byzantine help against the Lombards. While at Constantinople, he gained valuable experience in dealing with the Eastern Empire, but he came to the realization that aid would not be forthcoming. Returning to Rome around 585, he served as abbot of S. Andrea, his Roman monastery. Pelagius died in 590, and Gregory was unanimously elected his successor. His efforts at avoiding or preventing elevation proved unsuccessful; he was consecrated, albeit with reluctance, on September 3, 590.

Pope Gregory found the situation facing

Rome and Italy truly severe. Italy was in a state of near ruin, the Lombards were a chronic threat to the Eternal City, and the Byzantines were clearly unreliable allies. While frequently ill from his long-term ascetical practices, Gregory threw himself energetically into solving the problems confronting him. In the face of a virtual vacuum of government authority, Gregory stepped forward and assumed many civil powers, a bold and necessary step that also did much to advance the growing temporal position of the papacy. He undertook a series of charitable services to feed the starving in Rome and reorganized the *Patrimonium Petri* (Patrimony of Peter), the extensive territorial holdings of the Holy See, to improve their financial value and make them more responsive to the needs of the hungry and suffering. Rome was saved from Lombard attack in 592-593 by a peace agreement concluded between Gregory and the Lombard duke of Spoleto. The pope ignored the presence of the Byzantine representative in Italy, the exarch of Ravenna, and wrote a defense of his actions to the emperor. He was careful, though, to recognize the political suzerainty of the Byzantine emperors while disputing zealously the ambitions of the patriarchs of Constantinople to lay claim to the primacy of Christendom, a right held by Rome.

Beyond his reorganization of papal land holdings, Gregory also introduced a number of reforms. He laid down guidelines of religious practice in his *Liber Regulae Pastoralis* (*Book of Pastoral Rules*) and gave a major impetus to missionary activity by sending his reliable agent St. Augustine of Canterbury on a mission to the British Isles in 596. A monk himself, the first to be elected pope, Gregory showed much favor to monasticism, appointing many monks to prominent positions in the papal administration and granting special rights and privileges to the monasteries. He also is credited with the creation of the forms of musical worship that came to be called the Gregorian chant and contributed prayers to the Gregorian Sacramentary, although the collection itself is of a much later date.

A voluminous writer, he authored the *Dialogues* (c. 593), an account of the lives and miracles of the early Latin saints; the *Magna Moralis* (595), an exegetical work on the Book of Job; homilies on the Gospel; and more than eight hundred fifty letters. A sincerely humble individual who called himself *Servus Servorum Dei* (Servant of the Servants of God), Gregory was nevertheless responsible for the wide acceptance by Christians everywhere of the supreme authority of the pope over the Church and the place of the pontiff as a major political figure in Italy and the West. Canonized by popular acclaim after his death (March 12, 604), he was named a Doctor of the Church. With Pope St. Leo I (r. 440-461), he is one of

Pope St. Gregory I the Great

only two successors of St. Peter to be called the Great. Feast day: September 3.

Gregory II, St. ● Pope from 715-731. Originally a priest and treasurer of the Church in Rome, he was elected on May 19, 715, as the successor to Pope Constantine. Gregory's pontificate was marked by the launching of the Iconoclastic Controversy, begun by Emperor Leo III the Isaurian when he issued decrees throughout the Byzantine Empire for the destruction of religious images. The decrees were opposed by Gregory whose relations with the emperor soon deteriorated. Gregory also encouraged the evangelization of Germany, consecrating Boniface (722) and other missionaries. The pope enjoyed generally sound diplomatic dealings with the Lombards and the people of Rome. Feast day: February 11.

Gregory III, St. ● Pope from 731-741. A Syrian by birth, he was the successor to Gregory II and thus the inheritor of the continuing Iconoclastic Controversy with Byzantine Emperor Leo III the Isaurian, who had decreed the destruction of religious images throughout the empire. Gregory continued his predecessor's staunch opposition to the Iconoclasts, condemning them at a council in Rome in 731. The pontiff was then faced with the threat of the Lombards, who exterminated the Byzantine exarchate of Ravenna and thus endangered Rome. Gregory sent a plea for help to Charles Martel and the Franks; while military aid was not immediately forthcoming, the precedent had been established of papal-Frankish political association. Feast day: November 28.

Gregory IV ● Pope from 827-844. A Roman by birth, he was cardinal priest of St. Mark's basilica in Rome at the time of his election as successor to Pope Valentine. He is best known for his mediation between Lothair, king of the Franks, and Louis the Pious, Holy Roman Emperor, supporting

Lothair in his territorial claims. Gregory also instituted the observance of the Feast of All Saints.

Gregory V ● Pope from 996-999. Born Bruno of Carinthia, he was the first German pope. The grandson of Emperor Otto I the Great, he was a cousin of Otto III, serving as chaplain until 996 when he was installed as pontiff, taking the name Gregory and succeeding John XV. On May 21, 996, he crowned Otto emperor, returning the favor of installation. Gregory needed his cousin for political support, however, and, when Otto was recalled to Germany, Gregory was driven from Rome by the powerful nobleman Crescentius II. John XVI was placed on the papal throne in 997 and Gregory was forced to wait until 998 when Otto returned to Italy. John was blinded and imprisoned and Gregory was restored, dying in February of the following year.

Gregory VI ● Pope from 1045-1046. Known originally as Giovanni Graziano (or John Gratian), he came to the papacy by bribing the scandal-ridden Benedict IX to step down because of his highly improper behavior. Gregory, however, was accused of simony by the Council of Sutri, and, under pressure from Emperor Henry III, he abdicated and retired with his private secretary, Hildebrand, the future Pope Gregory VII.

Gregory VII, St. ● Pope from 1073-1085. One of the greatest reformers of the Middle Ages who became embroiled in a conflict with Emperor Henry IV. A native of Tuscany, Hildebrand was born to a poor family and with them moved to Rome when he was still young. After studying at the monastery of Sta. Maria all'Aventino and the Lateran Palace, he was appointed chaplain to Pope Gregory VI (r. 1045-1046), accompanying him into exile at Cologne in 1046. After Gregory's death in 1047, Hildebrand probably entered a monastery, but two years later Pope St. Leo IX (r. 1049-1054) called him to Rome, ordained him a subdeacon, and made him the administrator of the *Patrimonium Petri* (Patrimonium of Peter), signaling the beginning of his rise as a powerful figure in the Church. He wielded enormous influence over succeeding pontiffs — Victor II (1055-1057), Nicholas II (1058-1061), and Alexander II (1061-1073). He was employed as a legate to France and Germany and under Alexander was chancellor of the Holy See. Finally, on April 22, 1073, he was elected to succeed Alexander, postponing his consecration until June 29 and the Feast of Sts. Peter and Paul.

Pope St. Gregory VII

Long committed to the vigorous and comprehensive reform of the Church, Gregory (who took his name from Gregory I the Great) made as his central policy the moral renewal that had been launched by his predecessors and of which he had been an important player. The process of reform took its name from him, being called the Gregorian Reform. Through the Lenten Synods (held every Lent in Rome) and the appointment of stern, loyal papal legates, he attacked simony, Nicolaitism, and many other abuses. Particularly notable was the Lenten Synod of 1074. Rulers of Christendom were enlisted to assist, and Gregory's legates went out to compel reluctant or recalcitrant bishops. This ambitious and far-reaching program caused considerable controversy and opposition among the bishops of France and Germany, but far more violent was the storm created by

Gregory's work at the Synod of Rome in 1075 when he condemned lay investiture.

While some slight gains were made in France and England, Gregory was most concerned with Germany and its young king, Henry IV. The German ruler, facing possible excommunication, convened two synods in 1076, at Worms and Piacenza, to depose the pope. Gregory replied by deposing and excommunicating his obstinate enemy, freeing Henry's subjects from their oath of obedience. Faced by a revolt of the Saxons and unable to muster enough support, Henry submitted and performed a humiliating penance in the snow at Canossa in 1077. The ruler, however, failed to fulfill his pledge and in 1080 Gregory renewed his excommunication. Henry created the antipope Clement III, the former archbishop of Ravenna, and then marched into Italy. Refusing to compromise, Gregory could not prevent the capture of Rome by Henry's forces in March 1084. Normans under the formidable Robert Guiscard rescued Gregory, but their soldiers so outraged the Romans — parts of the city were burned and looted — that the populace drove their pontiff from Rome. He fled to Monte Cassino and then to Salerno where he died on May 25, 1085. His dying words were: "I have loved justice and therefore die in exile." A stern, unbending reformer, Gregory was guided by his absolute, sincere, and pious commitment to the revitalization of the Church. While his work was left unfinished, it would be continued by his successors, in particular Urban II (r. 1088-1099). Considered one of the greatest popes, especially by modern historians, Gregory was beatified in 1584 and canonized by Pope Paul V in 1606. Feast day: May 25.

Gregory VIII <1> ● Pope in 1187. Born Alberto de Morra, he was a native of Benevento from a noble family. A member of the Cistercians, he became a cardinal in 1155 or 1156 and was elected on October 21 to succeed Pope Urban III. His brief pontificate was noted for his attempts at reforming the Roman Curia and preaching the Third Crusade.

Gregory VIII <2> ● An antipope from 1118-1121. Originally Maurice Bourdin, he was a Benedictine monk, bishop of Coimbria, and archbishop of Braga before serving as an envoy of Paschal II to Emperor Henry V around 1117 during the disagreement over lay investiture. Bourdin joined the emperor's camp, however, and was excommunicated by an irate Paschal. When the pontiff died in 1118, Henry secured Bourdin's election as antipope to Pope Gelasius II (1118-1119) and then Callistus II (1119-1121). Gregory was arrested and exiled in 1121, dying around 1137 in prison.

Gregory IX ● Pope from 1227-1241. One of the foremost pontiffs of the Middle Ages, he is best known for his struggle with Emperor Frederick II. A nephew of Pope Innocent III, he was born Ugolino of Segni to a noble family. He studied at the University of Paris and became a noted canon lawyer

and theologian, and was made a cardinal in 1198 by his uncle. Elected successor to Honorius III, he immediately demanded that Frederick fulfill his vow and undertake a promised crusade to the Holy Land. Finally excommunicating the ruler, Gregory's hostilities toward Frederick undermined the emperor's crusade and notable diplomatic achievements. A reconciliation was effected in 1230 with the Treaty of San Germano, but the Roman pontiff excommunicated Frederick again in 1239, launching years of war and conflict. Gregory summoned a general council in 1241, but the fleet carrying the papal entourage was seized by imperial forces and Gregory was besieged in Rome. He died on August 22, 1241, in the midst of the siege. Gregory was responsible for the organization (1234) of papal decretals, known as the Decretals of Pope Gregory IX, including the *Decretum* (*Concordia Discordantium Canonum*) of Gratian. He was also a friend of Francis of Assisi and established the Court of Inquisition in 1232.

Gregory X ● Pope from 1271-1276. A native of Piacenza, he was originally known as Teobaldo Visconti. His election came as a compromise to end the three-year *sedes vacante* following the death of Clement IV in 1268. Not an ordained priest at the time of his election, he was in the Holy Land on a crusade with the future Edward I of England

Pope Gregory X

when word reached him at Acre of his elevation. Returning to Italy, he quickly proved himself a remarkably able pontiff. Repairing the poor relations between the papacy and the Holy Roman Empire, he was instrumental in creating a stable imperial political environment by securing the naming of Rudolf of Habsburg as emperor, inducing other claimants to withdraw to avoid civil war and chaos. He attempted to negotiate a union with the Eastern Church through the Council of Lyons (1274-1275), but his hopes were not fulfilled. Neither were his dreams of another crusade to free Jerusalem. Nevertheless, he succeeded in initiating the important ecclesiastical innovation of electing pontiffs through a system of conclaves. By the terms of his decree *Ubi Periculum* (1274), an assembly of cardinals should be convened to elect a new pontiff, a reform that remedied partially the often chaotic elections that had occurred in the past. (See **Conclave**.)

Gregory XI ● Pope from 1370-1378. He was the last French pontiff and the last of the popes to reside in Avignon as he returned the papacy to Rome in 1377. A nephew of Pope Clement VI, he was born Pierre Roger de Beaufort and, while never ordained a priest, he was appointed a cardinal in 1348 by his uncle. Respected as a canonist, he was elected unanimously in Avignon on December 30, 1370, to succeed Pope Urban V. While he initially considered returning the papacy to Rome, he was forced to delay any plans for a number of years while dealing with other pressing matters. He tried unsuccessfully to negotiate an end to the Hundred Years' War (1337-1453) between England and France and competently waged the War of Eight Saints (1375-1378) with Florence over the Papal States, a conflict ended by the Peace of Tivoli. Finally, in 1377, at the urging of St. Catherine of Siena, Gregory reentered Rome on January 17, 1377, ignoring the displeasure of King Charles V of France, who feared a decline of French influence in papal affairs. Gregory faced much upheaval in the Eternal City during his remaining years of office, but by the time of his death in March 1378 the popes were once more firmly in residence in Rome — there they would remain although the Great Schism would soon follow. Gregory also condemned the teachings of Wycliffe.

Gregory XII ● Pope from 1406-1415. He was responsible for helping to bring an end to the Great Schism that had plagued the Church from 1378. Known originally as Angelo Correr, he served as a bishop and was made a cardinal in 1405 by Pope Innocent VII. Elected to succeed Innocent on November 30, 1406, he was faced with the threat of the antipope Benedict XIII. As part of the effort to solve the ongoing schism, Gregory agreed to accept the Council of Constance, already in session, and abdicate. He stepped down on July 4, 1415, thereby clearing the way for the removal of Benedict and the election of Martin V as pope of a unified Church. The council named Gregory cardinal of Porto, where he died in October 1417.

Gregory XIII ● Pope from 1572-1585. He is best known for his reform of the training of priests in seminaries and for the promulgation of the Gregorian calendar. A native of Bologna, he was born Ugo Boncampagni, studying at the University of Bologna where he taught law from 1531-1534. Ordained around 1539 in Rome, he was so esteemed by Pope Paul III as a lawyer and canonist that he was given numerous posts. Pope Paul IV sent him to France and Brussels, and named him bishop of Vieste. Pius IV used him as an envoy to the Council of Trent from 1561-1563, making him a cardinal in 1565. On May 14, 1572, he was elected pope, as the successor to Pope Pius V. He undertook to promote Church reform, vowing to execute the decrees of Trent and to carry forth the work of the

Catholic Reformation. To advance reform among the clergy, he established numerous seminaries and colleges, especially in Rome, relying upon the Jesuits to supply instructors and spiritual direction. He also promoted missionary activity to the Far East and in lands that had come under Protestant control or influence. In 1582, he issued the Gregorian calendar, correcting the many errors of the Julian calendar that had been in place since 46 B.C. He also organized an improved edition of the *Corpus Iuris Canonici* (1582). Toward the end of his reign, however, papal finances became increasingly strained because of Gregory's extensive building program (including the Quirinal Palace in Rome) and his educational endeavors. The result was enormous suffering in the Papal States and a constant menace from criminal elements that would not be resolved until after Gregory's death.

Gregory XIV ● Pope from 1590-1591. Known originally as Niccolo Sfondrati, he was born at Somma, near Milan, and was educated at Perugia, Padua, and Pavia. A friend of St. Charles Borromeo (d. 1584), he was named bishop of Cremona by Pope Pius IV at the age of twenty-five. He attended the Council of Trent (1562-1563) and was named a cardinal by Pope Gregory XIII in 1583. On December 5, 1590, he succeeded Pope Urban VII after a conclave of some two months. In poor health throughout his pontificate, Gregory generally continued the programs of his predecessors, especially in opposing the Protestant heir to the French throne, Henry

Pope Gregory XVI

III of Navarre, opposition that hastened Henry's conversion to Catholicism. Gregory also tried to bring relief to the long-suffering Catholics of Rome who had endured plague, famine, and constant civil unrest and outlawed betting on papal elections.

Gregory XV ● Pope from 1621-1623. A native of Bologna, he was originally called Alessandro Ludovisi. After studying at Bologna, he entered the Church and participated in a number of important diplomatic missions before becoming archbishop of Bologna in 1612 and a cardinal in 1616 by Pope Paul V. Elected to succeed Paul on February 9, 1621, he came to the papal throne by acclaim (see **Acclamatio**), making him the first Jesuit-trained pontiff. Gregory introduced the secret ballot into papal elections, decreeing in *Aeterni patris filius* (1621) and *Decet Romanum pontificem* (1622) that voting should be in secret, a system that ultimately eliminated political influence and has remained essentially unchanged into modern times. He also established the Sacred Congregation for the Propagation of the Faith through the bull *Inscrutabili* (1622) as a central office for missionary work, particularly in Protestant lands. Under Gregory, Teresa of Ávila, Ignatius Loyola, Philip Neri, and Francis Xavier were all canonized.

Gregory XVI ● Pope from 1831-1846. Known originally as Bartolomeo Alberto Cappellari, he was born in Belluno, Italy, the son of an aristocratic lawyer. Entering the Camaldolese monastery of S. Michele at

Murano, Venice, he was ordained in 1787. At Rome from 1795, he authored in 1799 *Il Trionfo della Santa Sede contro gli assalti dei novatori* (*Triumph of the Holy See Against the Innovators*), upholding the idea of papal infallibility at a time when Pius VI was imprisoned by the French Directory. Made abbot of San Gregorio in 1807, he was forced to flee Rome the following year because of Napoleonic suppression in Italy and the suppression of religious orders. Returning in 1814, he served as vicar-general of the Camaldolese, was made a cardinal in 1825 by Pope Leo XII, and was appointed prefect of Propaganda Fide in 1826. On February 2, 1831, he was elected pope and succeeded Pius VIII. His pontificate was dominated by political upheaval in the Papal States. Austrian troops were needed to help suppress revolutions and papal finances were in a chronic state of disarray because of the need to maintain sizable forces and the remarkably poor administrative skills of the clerics charged with overseeing the Papal States. Gregory's relations with the major powers were thus strained. He was responsible, however, for the promotion of missions, the restoration of the Dominicans and Franciscans in France, and the foundation of the Etruscan and Egyptian museums at the Vatican and Christian museums at the Lateran. His successor was Pius IX.

Gregory of Nazianzus, St. (c. 330-390) ●
Also St. Gregory Nazianzen, called the Theologian and the Christian Demosthenes for his great eloquence, and an important Doctor of the Church who helped defend Orthodox doctrine in the fourth century. Born at Arianzus, near Nazianzus, in Cappadocia (a province in Asia Minor), Gregory was the son of the bishop of Nazianzus. After studying in Athens, he returned to Cappadocia and entered the monastic life, joining the community that had been established by St. Basil in Pontus.

Ordained against his will in 362, he worked for the next years to assist his father, continuing to do so after his own consecration around 370 as bishop of Sasima Cappadocia. He did not take possession of his see but remained an auxiliary bishop to his father. After his father's death in 374, however, Gregory retired to a monastery in Seleucia until 379 when he was summoned to Constantinople where he emerged through his preaching as the main leader of the Orthodox party in its struggle with Arianism. By his oratorical skill, Gregory was able to revive resistance to the Arians, prompting the ultimate summoning of the Council of Constantinople in 381 and the triumph of the Nicene Creed. Named bishop of Constantinople during the council, he was quickly so appalled by the schemes and intrigues of those around him that he resigned his see and retired to Nazianzus. A little later he went to his own land where he spent his last years in prayer and contemplation. Ranked with Sts. Basil the Great and Gregory of Nyssa as one of the Cappadocian Fathers, Gregory played an important role in the final defeat of Arianism. While shy and retiring, he nevertheless accepted responsibility for using his considerable oratorical skill on behalf of Christian orthodoxy. Among his writings were poems, letters, and treatises such as the five *Theological Orations* and the *Philocalia*, which contained excerpts from Origen. Feast day: January 2.

Gregory of Nyssa, St. (c. 335-395) ●
Bishop of Nyssa, brother of St. Basil the Great, and one of the Cappadocian Fathers (with Basil and Gregory of Nazianzus). Born at Caesarea, in Cappadocia, Asia Minor, Gregory was intended for the religious life, but he temporarily abandoned his calling, becoming a rhetorician and marrying a woman named Theosebeia. At the urging of St. Gregory of Nazianzus, however, he was convinced to devote himself to the Church,

being consecrated around 371 as bishop of Nyssa by his brother. After being charged with improper use of church property by the local governor, Gregory was deposed in 376 and exiled for some two years. The real cause of the deposition was the offense taken by the Arians at his strong adherence to the Nicene Creed. Gregory returned to his see after the destruction and death of the pro-Arian emperor Valens in 378. The next year he attended the Council of Antioch where he gained prominence as an outspoken opponent of Arianism. Elected in 380 to be bishop of Sebaste, he protested the appointment. At the Council of Constantinople (381) he was a leader of the Orthodox party, emerging out of the council as a deeply respected Orthodox theologian, one of the most influential in the Eastern Empire. He apparently died a short time after participating in the Council of Constantinople (394) under Nectarius, patriarch of Constantinople and successor to Gregory of Nazianzus. Gregory of Nyssa was a remarkable theologian, philosopher, and writer. Philosophically, he sought a harmony between Christian teaching and the tenets of Platonism and Neoplatonism (see **Neoplatonism** in the GLOSSARY). He was the author of numerous theological treatises, the most famous being the *Catechetical Orations* in which he examined the Trinity and the Incarnation, as well baptism and the Eucharist. He also wrote against Apollinaris and Eunomius. His ascetical works include "On Perfection," "On Virginity," and on the Christian life. Aside from sermons, homilies, and letters, he also composed numerous works on Sacred Scriptures, his exegetical writings covering the life of Moses, a *Treatise on the Work of the Six Days*, and an explanation of the titles of the Psalms. Feast day: March 9.

Gregory of Rimini (d. 1358) ● Philosopher who influenced future thinking, particularly during the Middle Ages and the early Reformation; Martin Luther studied Gregory while at the University of Wittenberg. Born in Rimini, near Venice, he entered the Augustinian Hermits and became general of the order in 1357. He also taught in Bologna, Padua, Paris, and Perugia, emerging as one of the foremost followers of the teachings of St. Augustine. He believed that salvation was entirely dependent upon the grace of God, earning the title *Tortor Infantum* (Infant Torturer), for his stand that all infants who died while unbaptized were doomed to damnation. Gregory also authored a treatise on usury and a commentary on the *Sentences* of Peter Lombard.

Gregory of Tours (c. 539-594) ● Bishop of Tours and the author of the famous *Historia Francorum* (*History of the Franks*). Becoming bishop of Tours in 573, Gregory was remarkably successful in his dealings with the Frankish rulers of the country, particularly King Childebert I of Austrasia from whom he secured spiritual and political protection for the Church. He wielded considerable spiritual and political influence. One of the most respected historians of the Middle Ages, Gregory wrote extensively in vigorous but unpretentious Latin. Aside from the *Historia*, he authored a number of hagiographical works, including *De Vita Patrum* (*Lives of the Fathers*) and *In Gloriam Martyrum*, a study of the miracles of Christ and the Apostles. The *Historia Francorum*, meanwhile, is the primary extant source on sixth-century France. Compiled from eyewitness accounts and firsthand documents, it covers history from the creation to 591, focusing mainly on the year 397 and the rise of the Franks.

Gregory Thaumaturgis, St. (c. 213-268) ● Bishop of Neocaesarea, Greek missionary, and famed "Wonder Worker" (or *Thaumaturgis*). Born at Neocaesarea, in Pontus (modern Turkey), he belonged to a well-to-do family, studying law. He subsequently came under the instruction of Origen at Caesarea, Palestine, who brought Gregory into the Church. Having been educated by one of the leading Christian minds of the era, Gregory was elected bishop of Neocaesarea shortly after his return home. He took up the difficult task of converting the region's pagan population, his work becoming the source for a large body of miracles and legends that provided Gregory with his surname *Thaumaturgis*. During the difficult period of the Decian persecutions (250-251), Gregory was forced to flee to the mountains. A short time after his return, he witnessed (253-254) the terrible invasion of Asia Minor by the Goths, a dark event recorded by Gregory in the Canonical Letter (c. 256), a valuable theological document in which he examined many matters of Church discipline and difficult moral dilemmas caused by the Gothic predations. Around 264, he participated in the first Synod of Antioch at which the heretical teachings of Paul of Samosata were condemned. Aside from the amazing acts with which he has been credited, Gregory is the attributed author of a number of theological treatises. Chief among these was an exposition (in Greek) on Trinitarian doctrine. According to tradition, the work was given to him in a vision of St. John the Evangelist, who appeared with the BVM. Reported by St. Basil in the fourth century, the apparition is considered the first of its kind involving Our Lady. He was also the author of sermons, letters, a panegyric to Origen, and a letter to Theopompus on the impossibility of God, a reply to the philosophical ideas current in Hellenistic thought on the nature of God and his capacity for suffering. The only surviving version of the letter to Theopompus is in a Syriac translation. Feast day: November 17.

Gregory the Illuminator, St. (257-332) ● Apostle and patron saint of Armenia, called the Illuminator because of his bringing the light of the Christian faith to the Armenians.

While Gregory was not the first to preach the Gospel in Armenia (that honor is traditionally held by the Apostles Bartholomew and Jude Thaddeus), he was responsible for convincing the ruler of the Armenians, King Tiridates III to accept Christianity as the national religion. Details about his life are complicated by the general unreliability of accounts written by Armenian chroniclers, such as that of Agathangelos (penned after 456), which embellished their narratives with fantastic tales and legends. It is likely, however, that Gregory was originally a Parthian prince who was raised as a Christian at Caesarea, in Cappadocia. He married and had two sons but then went to Armenia during the persecution of the Church in that country under King Tiridates. Gregory succeeded not only in converting the ruler but inspired him to such devotion that the king sponsored the Church throughout the realm. The Armenian nobles and people quickly followed suit. Gregory then returned to Caesarea where he was ordained and consecrated bishop of the Armenians by Leontius of Caesarea. He continued to preach among the Armenians, establishing bishops and extending Christian influence into surrounding regions, including the Caucasus Mountains. Upon retiring, he was succeeded by his son Aristakes who, in 325, attended the Council of Nicaea. The position of bishop (or *Katholikos*, also *Catholicos*) was for a long period hereditary, remaining in Gregory's family. The many letters and sermons attributed to him are not considered genuine. Feast day: September 30.

Gregory the Wonderworker ● See **Gregory Thaumaturgis, St**.

Grey Friars ● Nickname given to the Friars of the Franciscan order. It is derived from the original color of their habit and was used to distinguish them from the White Friars (Carmelites) and Black Friars (Dominicans).

Grey Nuns ● Nickname given to the Sisters of Charity throughout the world, particularly in North America, France, and Germany. The so-called Grey Nuns of Charity in America were founded in 1737 in Montreal by St. Marie Marguerite d' Youville (1701-1771), the first native Canadian saint (canonized in 1990). The nuns began as a small community devoted to the care of the sick, receiving a rule eight years later, which was first approved by the local bishop in 1754 and by Pope Leo XIII in 1880. The order soon spread throughout North America with several congregations being formed in the 1800s, particularly the Grey Nuns of the Cross (Sisters of Charity of Ottawa) in 1845; the Sisters of Charity of Quebec in 1849; and the Sisters of Charity of Hyacinthe in 1840. Each of these congregations moved into the United States in the late 1800s and remain active in hospital work and health care.

Grignion de Montfort, St. ● See **Montfort, Louis de, St**.

Groote, Gerhard (1340-1384) ● Also known as Geert de (or Gerhart) Groote as well as Gerardus Magnus. The founder of the Brethren of the Common Life, he was a member of a wealthy family of Deventer, in the Netherlands. He was educated in a number of cities including Paris, embarking upon what could have been a remarkably successful academic career. He taught at Cologne and enjoyed a life of great ease and luxury. In 1374, however, he abandoned academic pursuits choosing instead to develop the spiritual life. After spending many years at a Carthusian monastery at Munnikhuizen, near Arnhem, he left around 1377 to become a deacon. Delivering sermons on poverty and the need for reform within the Church, he earned many enemies and in 1383 his license to preach was revoked. The following year, he died of the plague. Prior to his death, however, he attracted followers who were to form the basis of the Brethren of the Common Life; Groote had already formed the nucleus of the Sisters of the Common Life. Highly influential because of his preaching and mysticism, he was a major figure in the spread of the popular ascetic movement, the *Devotio moderna*. A life of Groote was written by Thomas à Kempis.

Gropper, Johann (1503-1559) ● German theologian who became an ardent defender of Catholicism during the Reformation. He studied theology at Cologne University, becoming so distinguished that he earned the nickname *Os Cleri Coloniensis* (Speaker for the Clerics of Cologne). Appointed a canon of Xanten in 1532, he attended the Synod of Cologne (1536), which had been convened by Archbishop Hermann of Wied to oppose the growing influence of the Protestants. There Gropper wrote the *Enchiridion*, a treatise on doctrinal matters such as the sacraments and the Lord's Prayer that was much appreciated by such theologians as Reginald Pole, archbishop of Canterbury, Cardinal Gasparo Contarini, and other theological masters in Cologne. The work was placed on the Index of Forbidden Books in 1596. Nevertheless, Gropper strenuously opposed the movement of Archbishop Hermann toward Protestantism, securing his deposition in 1546. For this, Gropper was made provost of Bonn in 1547 and was offered a cardinalate in 1556 by Pope Paul IV.

Grosseteste, Robert (c. 1175-1253) ● Brilliant intellectual, ecclesiastical reformer, and the bishop of Lincoln. Born in Suffolk, England, he was educated at Oxford and possibly Paris and served as chancellor of Oxford from 1215-1221. The archdeacon of Leicester, he was appointed bishop of Lincoln in 1235. Deeply concerned with reforming the Church, he willingly renounced corrupt or unsuitable abbots, reduced ecclesiastical benefices, and authored a series of *Statutes* to provide specific guidelines for the behavior of the clergy and the administration of dioceses. In 1245, he journeyed to Lyons to attend a council, speaking before Pope Innocent IV on the custom of granting to Italians what were English Church offices. Grosseteste was also one of the most learned men of his age. He studied mathematics, optics, and science, foreshadowing the experimental methods of his pupil Roger Bacon. A Hebraicist and Greek expert, he made translations of Aristotle, St. John of Damascus, and Pseudo-Dionysius. Grosseteste was also a notable patron of the Franciscans, having taught in the Franciscan house in Oxford from 1224-1235.

Guadalupe, Our Lady of ● One of the best-known apparitions of the Blessed Virgin, occurring four times at Guadalupe, Mexico, in 1531. Our Lady appeared for the first time to the Indian Juan Diego (declared Blessed in 1990) on December 12, 1531, at Tepeyac, a hill just outside of Mexico City. The BVM instructed him to go to the local bishop, Juan de Zumárraga, and inform him that she desired a church to be built on the site where she had been seen. The bishop was at first reluctant to believe the earnest visitor, asking for some kind of sign. When Our Lady heard about the bishop's request, she instructed Juan Diego to go and gather roses, even though it was not the season for them. Obediently, he went to the place as told and there found the roses. Gathering them into his cloak (called a *tilma* by the Indians), he returned to the Virgin, who commanded him to go back to the bishop, instructing him not to open the cloak until he reached his destination. Once more before the bishop, Juan Diego unfolded the cloak. The roses fell out, but even more amazing was the life-size depiction of the BVM, exactly as Juan Diego had described her, imprinted upon the *tilma*.

Under Zumárraga's leadership, a church was erected, and the *tilma* soon became an object of great veneration among the Native

Americans in Mexico, helping immeasurably to convert the population to Catholicism. Accepted by the Church, Our Lady of Guadalupe was declared the patroness of New Spain by Pope Benedict XIV who, in a decree in 1754 named December 12 a holiday of obligation and ordered a special Mass and Office. In 1910, Pope St. Pius X designated her the patroness of Latin America. This was extended to patroness of the Americas by Pope Pius XII in 1945. Pope John Paul II in 1988 raised the liturgical celebration on December 12 to a feast for all dioceses in the United States. The *tilma* is today preserved in the Basilica of Our Lady of Guadalupe, which was first dedicated as a shrine church in 1709 and later enlarged and elevated to the rank of basilica. Made of coarsely woven fabric of cactus fiber, the *tilma* is two strips, approximately seventy inches long and eighteen inches wide, sewn together with the stitched seam along the middle of the picture until it nears the face when it turns aside. The Virgin is depicted with the sun, moon, and stars, and an angel beneath the crescent moon. The chief colors are gold, blue-green, and rosy red.

Guarantees, Law of the ● Name given to the law passed on May 13, 1871, that regulated the diplomatic relations between the papacy and the newly established kingdom of Italy. The law remained in effect until the Lateran Treaty of 1929. By its terms, the pope's body was declared sacred and inviolable; the pontiff was to be granted an annual payment of 3,225,000 lire, tax-free, to effect expenses. Further, certain properties of the papacy were retained, specifically the Vatican, the residence of Castel Gandolfo, and the Lateran Palace. Envoys or diplomats to the Vatican were given full diplomatic immunity. Finally, the seminaries of Rome and the six suburbicarian dioceses were to be placed under the authority of the pope, and the pontiff had the freedom of holding all conclaves and ecumenical (or general) councils without Italian interference. Pope Pius IX (r. 1846-1878), of course, refused to acknowledge the law, remaining a "prisoner of the Vatican" to protest the loss of the Papal States.

Guardia Palatina d' Onore ● See **Palatine Guard**.

Guelphs and Ghibellines ● Name given to the two Italian political parties during the 1200s and 1300s. The Ghibellines supported the claims and policies of the Hohenstaufen rulers of the Holy Roman Empire while the Guelphs gave their backing to the papacy. The term Ghibelline came from the Hohenstaufen castle of Waiblingen. The castle was a center of opposition to the German Welf family, a noble Bavarian dynasty that competed for the German throne in the 1100s and 1200s, giving their name to the Guelphs. The terms came into use during the time of conflict between Emperor Frederick II and the papacy (c. 1227-1250), although the actual political factions developed during the reign of Frederick I Barbarossa (1155-1190) when political disputes arose in Italy, particularly in Florence. Florentine Guelphs came to power and waged war upon Pisa and Siena. The losers in such struggles generally faced death or exile while plotting revenge and a return to power. After 1268, and the demise of the Hohenstaufen line, the Ghibellines faced ruthless extirpations and became associated with a desire to resurrect a long-dead imperial position in Italy. The Guelphs, meanwhile, emerged as conservative adherents of the papacy and French-Avignon expansion in parts of southern Italy.

Guéranger, Prosper (1805-1875) ● French Benedictine monk who was influential in reestablishing the Benedictine order in France. Ordained in 1827, he was able to purchase the priory of Solesmes in 1832, working over the next years to be able to reopen it as a formal Benedictine monastery. This he did in 1833 and was named in 1837 by Pope Gregory XVI as the first abbot of Solesmes. As abbot, he became an influential figure in France, working to have the many local variations of the rite replaced by the Roman rite in all of the French dioceses. His writings on liturgical matters included *Institutiones liturgiques* (3 vols., 1840-1851; *Liturgical Institutions*) and *L'Annee liturgique* (9 vols., 1841-1866; *The Liturgical Year*).

Gunpowder Plot ● Infamous plot to blow up the Houses of Parliament and King James I of England in the hopes that Catholics in the kingdom would then rise up and seize the government, thereby restoring the Catholic faith to the isles. The ill-fated conspiracy was organized by Robert Catesby, along with Thomas Percy, Thomas Winter, John Wright, and Guy Fawkes; each was a fanatical Catholic who was disappointed with King James I for not doing enough to promote toleration of religious affairs. To assassinate the government leaders, Catesby rented a cellar that was situated partly beneath the Houses of Parliament, filling it with barrels of gunpowder and assigning Fawkes the task of lighting it. The plot, however, was revealed to authorities by the Catholic nobleman Lord Monteagle who had been warned by his brother-in-law not to attend Parliament on November 5, the day on which James was to be blown up. Fawkes was captured in the cellar and Catesby, Percy, and two other conspirators were killed while fighting with government troops. Survivors were executed on January 31, 1606. Completely unsuccessful, the Gunpowder Plot intensified anti-Catholicism in England, resulting in greater Protestant hatred of popery and the adding of severe punishments in the Penal Code. November 5 was established by Parliament in 1606 as a day of public thanksgiving. It became known as Guy Fawkes Day and was for many years an event of rabid anti-Catholic and antipapal activities.

Guyon, Jeanne Marie Bouvier de la Mothe (1648-1717) ● Known as Madame Guyon, a French quietist author and mystic. Born in Montargis as Jeanne Marie Bouvier de la Mothe, she was ill for much of her childhood, but the devout nature of her parents gave her a considerable religious education. At the age of sixteen, she was married to the wealthy Jacques Guyon, a gentleman twenty-two years her senior and an invalid. He died in 1676, leaving her a widow with three children. She entered into a life of mystical devotion. She had fallen under the influence, meanwhile, of the Barnabite friar Père F. Lacombe (1643-1713), who became her spiritual director and encouraged her to continue her study of quietism, particularly the works of the Spanish quietist Miguel de Molinos (d. 1697). With Lacombe, Guyon traveled throughout France, but her hopes of propagating her mystical ideas were unfulfilled because of opposition from local authorities who suspected her of quietist tendencies. She went to Paris in July 1686 with Lacombe, but by order of King Louis XIV, Lacombe was placed in the Bastille and Guyon was arrested in November 1688. Her release seven months later came after she retracted the doctrines of which she had been writing for a number of years. Through the influence of such friends as Madame de Maintenon and François Fénelon, she became a fixture in the French court and royal circles, and by 1695 she was requesting a formal commission to clear her name. The resulting Conference of Issy (1685) reexamined her writings and condemned her. Imprisoned until 1702, she spent her remaining years in Blois, although Fénelon continued to defend her, especially against Jacques Bossuet. (See **Quietism**.)

Gyrovagi ● Name used by St. Benedict of Nursia for the so-called tramp monks and wandering monks, meaning those monks who were not attached to a monastic community or did not formally reside there. St. Benedict was highly critical of the Gyrovagi because such monks became laws unto themselves, forcing the Church to issue regulations to bring about reform to curtail the practice.

Hadrian I-VI ● For popes of this name, see under **Adrian**.

Hadrian the African, St. (d. 709) ● Monk and abbot and an educational missionary in England. A native of Africa, he was a member of a monastery in Naples and a friend of Pope Valerian who offered him the see of Canterbury. Hadrian declined but was instrumental in having Theodore of Tarsus named instead. In 668, he set out with Theodore for England, eventually becoming the abbot of the monastery of Sts. Peter and Paul. The next decades were spent traveling all over England building schools and promoting the Romanization of the English Church.

Hadrianum ● See **Gregorian Sacramentary**.

Hagenau, Conference of ● Meeting held in Hagenau from June to July 1540 at the behest of Emperor Charles V that brought together the leaders of the Catholic and Protestant causes in Germany. Its purpose was to begin discussions on the points of dispute that existed between the parties with the long-term aim of reconciliation. The conference was a failure, however, because neither side could agree on the definitions or ecclesiastical nature of the Church, preventing any specific examination of doctrinal disagreements. The conference ended without result, although both sides agreed to meet at the planned gathering at Worms, the colloquy called the Disputation of Worms (1540-1541).

Hagia Sophia ● Famous domed basilica of Constantinople (modern Istanbul), also called the Santa Sophia (Holy Wisdom). Considered the supreme example of Byzantine art and architecture, the current Hagia Sophia was actually the third basilica to be constructed on the site. The first was erected in 360 by Emperor Constantius II but was destroyed by a fire and replaced in 415 with a new edifice under Emperor Theodosius II. This too was wrecked, not by fire but during the bloody Nika Revolt in 532 that was so violently extirpated by Emperor Justinian I (r. 527-565). Justinian conceived a much more ambitious church, desiring not only to build a fireproof basilica but a symbol of Byzantine grandeur. Designed by Anthemius of Tralles and Isidorus of Miletus, the Hagia Sophia was constructed from 532-537. At its completion, the nave was one hundred eighty-four feet high and one hundred two feet in diameter. The stunning mosaics and polychrome marbles decorating the interior depicted the Byzantine sociopolitical view of life and their cosmological understanding of Christ as expressed in the theology of the Eastern Church. Especially notable is the skillful use of light. Forty windows at the base of the dome project the illusion that the dome is suspended in midair, the light serving as a bridge from the earth to heaven. Upon the fall of the city in 1453 to the Ottoman Turks, the Hagia Sophia was transformed into a mosque, four slender minarets placed at the corners. In this century, the huge church was first secularized by the Turkish government and then turned into a museum. It remains one

Hagia Sophia

Pius V, proving of great assistance to the English Catholics and helping William Allen to found the English College at Douai.

Hardouin, Jean (1646-1729) ● French Jesuit scholar. Born in Brittany, he

of the greatest buildings in the world and a profound embodiment of faith.

Haito ● See **Hatto**.

Harding, Thomas (1516-1572) ● English controversialist and apostolic legate to England. Born in Combe Martin in Devon, he studied at Oxford, serving there as a fellow in 1536 and Hebrew professor in 1542, an appointment granted by King Henry VIII. Ordained a priest, he became chaplain to Henry Grey, marquess of Dorchester. Initially a supporter of reforms in England, Harding later returned to Catholic teachings upon the accession of Mary in 1553, remaining firm in his beliefs during the reign of Queen Elizabeth I. A doctor of divinity in 1554, he was appointed chaplain and confessor to Bishop Stephen Gardiner. When Elizabeth came to the throne in 1558, Harding was imprisoned, eventually fleeing to Louvain where he served in St. Gertrude's Church and entered into a long controversy with the Protestant bishop of Salisbury, John Jewel. In 1566, Harding was named apostolic delegate to England with Dr. Sander by Pope

entered the Society of Jesus in 1662, devoting most of his life as librarian of the Jesuit Collège de Clermont in Paris. He was the author of several notable works, including *Consiliorum Collectio Regia Maxima*, a collection of the texts of ecclesiastical councils from the earliest days of the Church onward; ready for publication in 1715, its release was delayed by the French government because of Hardouin's ultramontane notes. He also advocated such radical ideas as the one that the NT was written originally in Latin.

Hasslacher, Peter (1810-1876) ● Leading Jesuit preacher in Germany who contributed to the reawakening of the Catholic faith in that country. A native of Coblenz, he attended the University of Bonn as a medical student, taking part in 1831 in the German student movement that led to his seven years' confinement at Berlin, Magdeburg, and Ehrenbreitstein. During this period he underwent a spiritual change by studying the Fathers of the Church. Such was the spiritual transformation that in the spring of 1840 he joined the Society of Jesus.

Ordained in 1844, he preached in the Cathedral of Strasbourg, emerging as one of the foremost preachers in Germany. In 1863, he went to Paris to serve in the St. Joseph's Mission for German Catholics. There he died from overwork and exhaustion.

Hatfield, Council of ● Council of the English Church held in 680 at Hatfield that was concerned with the controversy of Monothelitism. The meeting was convened at the behest of Pope Agatho and was under the presidency of the archbishop of Canterbury, Theodore of Tarsus. It was decided to accept the decrees of the first five general councils of the Church and to condemn Monothelitism.

Hatto (d. 913) ● Archbishop of Mainz and abbot of Reichenau. Hatto wielded considerable power in the territories under control of the Frankish Carolingian Empire. He was an adviser to King Arnulf and served as tutor to the imperial heir, Louis the Child (d. 911). In later years, he secured the election of Conrad, duke of Franconia, as king of the East Franks, working as the primary councillor to Conrad. Hatto was routinely attacked by chroniclers as harsh, cruel, and treacherous. By legend, he was killed by lightning, although the same story was told about him as that of Hatto II, archbishop of Mainz (d. 970). This prelate was supposedly eaten alive by mice as a punishment for massacring starving peasants who had stolen grain. The archbishop's death was connected with the Mauseturm (or Mouse Tower), along the Rhine.

Haydock, George (1556-1583 or -1584) ● English martyr. Born in Cotton Hall, Lancashire, he was educated at the English colleges of Douai and Rome and was ordained in 1581. Sent to England during the English persecutions, he was arrested shortly after arriving in London. Immediately imprisoned in the Tower of London, he was held for a time in "free custody," meaning he was allowed to administer the sacraments to his fellow prisoners. Indicted on February 5, 1583 (or possibly 1584), on charges of conspiracy against the queen, he was condemned on the seventh of the month and executed on the twelfth, at Tyburn, reportedly telling a jeering crowd ". . . I pray God that my blood may increase the Catholic faith in England." Haydock had a particularly passionate devotion to the papacy, drawing in charcoal on his cell walls or door the names and arms of the popes, especially the reigning pontiff, Pope Gregory XIII.

Haymo of Faversham (d. 1244) ● English theologian and friar. A native of Kent, he joined the Franciscans in 1224, teaching for a time at Oxford. A participant in the general chapter of the order in Rome (1239) that deposed Elias of Cortona, he was named in the same year provincial of England and the following year became general of the Franciscans. At his request the so-called Four Masters of Paris wrote the *Expositio Regulae Quattuor Magistrorum* (1241-1242) and, through Pope Innocent IV, he helped revise (1243-1244) the ordinals of the missal, breviary, and a number of prayers, including grace before and after meals. Haymo had also been sent to Constantinople to attempt a negotiated reunion of the Eastern and Western Churches. He died at Anagni and his epitaph read: "Here lies Haymo, highest glory of the English; in his living a brother of the Minors, in ruling them a father."

Heath, Nicholas (d. 1578) ● Archbishop of York who refused to accept the reforms of the Church during the reign of Queen Elizabeth I. Born in London, Heath was educated at St. Anthony's School (London) and at Oxford and Cambridge. After ordination, he served as vicar of Hever, Surrey (1531-1532), and archdeacon of Stafford (1534). Schismatically elected bishop of Rochester in 1539, he was translated to Worcester in 1543 and apparently spent the final years of the reign of King Henry VIII as an accommodationist to the changes in the English Church. By 1550, however, he had become strictly Orthodox, refusing to accept Thomas Cranmer's new form for ordination. As a consequence he was imprisoned, but after the accession of Queen Mary, he was restored to his see. Absolved of wrongdoing in his prior election, Heath became archbishop of York, receiving the pallium in October 1555. Named chancellor in 1556, he proclaimed Elizabeth queen of England two years later but resigned his office the next day. Remaining on the Privy Council for a time, he nevertheless refused to crown her and resisted her claim to be "Governor of the Church" and would not recognize the Acts of Supremacy and Uniformity. Deprived of his see, Heath spent much of his remaining years in the Tower of London, probably dying there in December 1578.

Hebrews, Epistle to the ● Anonymous letter apparently addressed to faltering converts from Judaism that presents a detailed exhortation of the faith and a remarkable examination of the desirability of Christianity over the creed from which the letter's recipients had been converted. The Epistle to the Hebrews was long accepted by many Church scholars as being written by St. Paul.

Despite the popular acceptance, there were a number of important figures who expressed serious doubts about Pauline authorship. Among them were Origen and Tertullian. The date estimated for its composition has varied, with some arguing for a period before the fall and destruction of Jerusalem by the Romans in 70. The latest possible date is 95 or 96 because of the mention made of the letter in the First Epistle of Clement.

The author of the message begins by declaring the greatness and the Incarnation of Christ (1:5—2:18). He then notes that Christ is superior to Moses: "Now Moses was faithful in all God's house as a servant, to testify to the things that were to be spoken later, but Christ was faithful over God's house as a son. And we are his house if we hold fast our confidence and pride in our hope" (3:5-6). Christ is also a high priest, "chosen from among men . . . appointed to act on behalf of men in relation to God, to offer gifts and sacrifices for sins" (5:1). Much of the subsequent text (5:2—10:25) is devoted to Christ as a high priest. The epistle is next concerned with bolstering the faith of its readers, declaring, "But recall the former days when, after you were enlightened, you endured a hard struggle with sufferings, sometimes being publicly exposed to abuse and affliction, and sometimes being partners with those so treated" (10:32-33). He then reminds his audience of Christ's perfection, repairing their "drooping hands" and "weak knees" (12:12). "Let brotherly love continue. Do not neglect to show hospitality to strangers, for thereby some have entertained angels unawares. Remember those who are in prison, as though in prison with them; and those who are ill-treated, since you are also in the body" (13:1-3).

Hecker, Isaac Thomas (1819-1888) ● Founder of the Paulist Fathers (Missionary Society of St. Paul the Apostle) and journalist. Born in New York City, Hecker was the son of a Methodist mother, entering the Catholic Church in 1844. After studying in Europe, he entered the Redemptorists and was ordained in London in 1849. Returning to America, he worked in the missionary field with several other priests, Clarence Walworth, George Deshon, Augustine Hewit, and Francis Baker, their efforts proving extremely successful. Hecker, however, soon encountered difficulties with his own order that disapproved of his request made to Rome for assistance without first securing permission from superiors. Further disagreements resulted in his expulsion from the Redemptorists, but Pope Pius IX (r. 1846-1878) came to his aid, granting dispensations for Hecker and his associates and thereby allowing him to establish in 1858 the Paulist Fathers. Elected superior of the order, Hecker devoted himself to the needs of the new society, but he also lectured, wrote, and promoted Catholic publishing, launching *The Catholic World* magazine, *The Young Catholic* for children, and the Catholic Publication Society, which would become the Paulist Press. He took part in the First Vatican Council and accepted the doctrine of infallibility. He believed there to be a providential alliance between the Catholic Church and the United States of America. In subsequent years, he was involved with the controversy of Americanism. While a devoted American and sympathetic to the views of many liberals in Europe, Hecker was generally sound in matters of doctrine and was a defender of the Holy See. His name, however, became attached to Americanism through a biography that called him the "patron saint" of the cause, prompting Pope Leo XIII (r. 1878-1903) to issue the letter *Testem Benevolentiae*, which condemned certain interpretations of Hecker's work. (See **Americanism**.) His writings included *Questions of the Soul* (1852), *The Aspirations of Nature* (1857), and *The Church and the Age* (1887). The Paulist Fathers grew in the years after Hecker's death in New York and continue their work in missions and pastoral areas.

Hedge Schools ● Nickname given to the method of education adopted by Catholics in the early 1600s in Ireland after the Irish Parliament took steps to suppress primary schooling. In 1695, the Protestant-dominated Irish Parliament passed a decree at the behest of King William III that ended Catholic education; teaching in any organized form was forbidden, and buildings were declared illegal places of assembly for instruction. Even private homes could not be used. To circumvent the laws, educators invented the "hedge schools," a clever means of teaching the faith while expressing a rebellious attitude to the oppressive government. The hedge schools were essentially secluded rural spots where formal teaching was provided for paying students. The name was derived from the customarily chosen spot for classes; the sunny side of a hedge where the natural bank offered not only protection from the wind but also a certain camouflage from authorities. As the fees for the schools were high, many parents could not afford to send their children, and religious education suffered throughout the country. The schools continued until 1760 when the laws were relaxed and the students moved back into buildings.

Hefele, Karl Joseph von (1809-1895) ● German Church historian and bishop of Rottenburg. Born in Würtemberg, he studied at the University of Tübingen (1827-1832) and was ordained in 1833. In 1836, he became *privatdozent* (i.e., a lecturer) in Church history at Tübingen, and full professor in 1840, retaining this post with great distinction until his election in 1869 as bishop of Rottenburg. Given a prominent part in the preparation of (and subsequently the organization of) the First Vatican Council, Hefele was one of the more influential members of the group opposed to papal infallibility, deciding in April 1871, however, to accept and publish the Vatican decrees for the diocese of Rottenburg. A superb scholar and historian, he authored a number of important works, including *Geschichte der Einführung des Christenthums im sudwestlichen Deutschland* (1837; *History of the Introduction of Christianity into Southwestern Germany*), *Der Kardinal Ximénez* (1844; translated into English in 1860) and the monumental *History of the Ecclesiastical Councils* (9 vols., 1855-1890);

the last two volumes were by Joseph Hergenröther.

Hegesippus, St. ● Second-century Church historian. He was probably from Palestine and was a converted Jew, authoring five books of memoirs, in Greek, against the Gnostics, on the true tradition of apostolic preaching. Hegesippus is known only through fragments, mostly preserved in Eusebius's *Ecclesiastical History*, although the work was supposedly found in several libraries in Europe during the 1500s and 1600s, such copies now lost. In the surviving portions, he is concerned with the Church in its early days in Jerusalem and with the first Bishops of Rome, compiling an important succession list of the Roman bishops. He seems to have journeyed to Corinth and Rome, during which he met several bishops as recorded in Eusebius (IV, 22). Feast day: April 7.

Helena, St. (c. 250-330) ● In full, Flavia Julia Helena, mother of Constantine the Great and a renowned patron of Christianity. Helena was born in Bithynia to a poor family of little social status. She was working as a servant, in fact, when she met Constantius I Chlorus (d. 306). As he was not yet prominent politically, their relationship was not discouraged and their subsequent union resulted in the birth of Constantine around 285. In 293, however, Constantius became Caesar (meaning "junior emperor") and found it politically expedient to divorce Helena, marrying Theodora, stepdaughter of Emperor Maximian. Helena withdrew from public life until 306 when her son succeeded Constantius in the imperial system of the tetrarchy (in which there were two senior emperors and two junior emperors). Converted to Christianity, Helena came to enjoy considerable prestige within the empire, especially as her son became sole ruler in 324. The following year, Helena was given the honorific title of *Augusta* and

wielded much influence in the government, with control over part of the imperial treasury. In 326, she went on a pilgrimage to the Holy Land. While there she helped build churches with her money, especially the Holy Sepulchre, the Nativity, and the Ascension. She was also reported to have found the True Cross. After returning to Rome in 330, she died a short time later at the age of eighty, one of the most venerable figures in the Roman Empire. Her tomb was installed in the basilica of Via Labicana. In later traditions, she was given, incorrectly, a background and lineage based in England. Feast day: August 18.

Heliand ● Ninth-century Old Saxon epic poem in alliterative verse, considered the oldest complete work of German literature, whose author is unknown. The work was most likely an effort to make the figure of Christ known to the recently converted Saxons. In it Christ was provided with Germanic origins and the Apostles were described as proud warriors who received rewards from Jesus their King. With the help of his loyal vassals, the Lord establishes his kingdom on earth and throughout the poem appears as the perfect ruler, the ideal sovereign. The poem was some six thousand lines long, covering Christ's birth to the Ascension, with a fragmentary Genesis. According to the Latin *Praefatio*, generally accepted as genuine by scholars, the *Heliand* (*Savior*) was written at the order of King Louis the Pious for his Saxon subjects.

Heloise ● See **Abelard, Peter**.

Hemmerlin, Felix (d. c. 1460) ● Properly Hemerli, and known as Malleolus, a supporter of Church reform. Born at Zurich, he was educated in his native city and then studied canon law at the Universities of Erfurt and Bologna. In early 1412, he became a canon at the collegiate Church of Sts. Felix and Regula at Zurich, taking part in the

Council of Constance in 1415 where he joined the reforming party. Provost at the collegiate Church of St. Ursus at Solothurn in 1421, he undertook a thorough reform of the collegiate clergy, revising their statutes and defending the rights of the Church against municipal authorities. Ordained in 1430, he took part in the deliberations that preceded the general Council of Basel (1431-1449), but his initial enthusiasm was soon dampened. He also met with stiff opposition to reforms in Zurich, suffering an attack by several choir members. He continued to preach reforms, however, calling for an end to simony and concubinage, and attacking Lollardy and the mendicant orders. A supporter of Zurich in its alliance with the Austrians against the Swiss, Hemmerlin was deprived of his ecclesiastical offices and consigned to imprisonment after the reconciliation of the city with the Swiss Confederation. He died, a prisoner, in a Franciscan convent in Lucerne. Hemmerlin authored some thirty polemical treatises.

Henry II, St. (973-1024) ● German king from 1001-1024 and emperor from 1014 who worked to consolidate the political unity of Germany while promoting the German Church. The son of the exiled duke of Bavaria, Henry the Quarrelsome, Henry came to the throne with the full support of the Church, receiving much assistance from Willigis, archbishop of Mainz. Years of conflict followed his accession as he fought to establish himself and the prestige of the empire. He launched several campaigns into Italy, subduing the Italian usurper Arduin of Ivrea and then campaigning against the Lombards and the Byzantines. In 1014, he was crowned Holy Roman Emperor by Pope Benedict VIII. While strengthening the imperial administration, Henry labored to help develop the Church, although his methods at times were autocratic; he interfered with ecclesiastical affairs but kept the support of the papacy through the donation of land and the vigorous enforcement of episcopal celibacy. He also created the see of Bamberg in 1012. Devoted to the faith, he and his queen, Kunigunde, were both canonized, Henry in 1146. During the Middle Ages he was revered as a model of monarchical piety.

Henry IV (1050-1106) ● German king from 1056-1106 whose reign was dominated by his long struggle with the papacy over the controversy of investiture (see **Investiture Controversy**). Henry was only six when he inherited the German throne, the surviving son of Emperor Henry III and Agnes of Poitou. His mother and Archbishops Adalbert of Bremen and Anno of Cologne served as regents during his minority. Upon coming into his majority in 1065, Henry was faced with powerful local dukes whose independence he proved unable to break. He accepted the authority of the pope in 1073 concerning investiture but reversed his policy in 1075 and began appointing bishops. This was opposed by Pope Gregory VII whom Henry deposed at Worms in 1076. Gregory then excommunicated Henry, using considerable political leverage to force Henry to recant. In 1077, Henry accepted a humiliating penance from Gregory in Canossa. His nobles then elected an anti-king, Rudolf of Swabia (1080), sparking a civil war. Excommunicated again in 1084, Henry invaded Italy, removed Gregory, and placed Guibert of Ravenna on the papal throne as Clement II. Gregory would die in exile, but his legitimate successors Urban II (r. 1088-1099) and Paschal II (r. 1099-1118) refused to submit. Faced by the papacy, the German nobles, and his own sons Conrad and Henry, the monarch abdicated in 1105, dying suddenly at Liège in August 1106.

Henry VIII (1491-1547) ● King of England from 1509-1547 under whose rule England broke from the Church. The second son of King Henry VII (r. 1485-1509), he was raised in a bright Renaissance atmosphere, studying French, Latin, and Spanish, and displaying a talent for music and an interest in theology. His brother Arthur died, and the young Henry wed Arthur's widow, Catherine of Aragon, daughter of Ferdinand and Isabella of Spain. Succeeding his father on April 22, 1509, Henry proved an early supporter of the Church against the Reformers, authoring the treatise *Assertio Septem Sacramentorum* (1521; *Defense of the Seven Sacraments*), against Martin Luther that earned for him the title Defender of the Faith from Pope Leo X on October 11, 1521. His position would gradually change, however, as the king grew disenchanted with his wife and increasingly concerned about producing an heir. Only Mary (later Queen Mary, 1553-1558) of the children born to Catherine survived infancy, a disappointment to Henry, who had fallen in love with Anne Boleyn. She would not agree to any relationship save as his queen, an ultimatum that gave impetus to Henry's personal desire for a divorce. There followed the very well-known episode of Henry's attempted divorce that culminated in the fall of the onetime powerful minister Cardinal Thomas Wolsey after he failed to secure an annulment from Pope Clement VII. Frustrated in his hopes, Henry adopted an antipapal position and took England down the road to a separation from the Church.

King Henry VIII of England

Aided by his ruthless minister Thomas Cromwell, Henry embarked upon a hard policy of clerical repression and reduction of papal authority in the kingdom. Various acts were passed to curb papal power and to establish Henry as the head of the Church in England. Progress was made toward this by a variety of laws as well as the subservient agreement of Thomas Cranmer, archbishop of Canterbury. Cranmer declared the marriage to Catherine to be invalid on May 23, 1533, followed a few days later by Henry's marriage to Anne, who was crowned queen on June 1. Clement responded with a bull of excommunication on July 11, declaring the English king's marriage to be null and void.

Along with such laws as the Act of Succession, which brought the executions of Sts. Thomas More and John Fisher in 1535, Henry decreed the Dissolution of the Monasteries in 1536 and 1539, a merciless liquidation of monastic institutions that destroyed bastions of papal loyalty and gave the crown their considerable wealth. Now head of the Church of England, Henry at first seemed to be leaning toward Protestantism, but instead he affirmed that the C of E should retain many central elements of Catholic teachings, a decision made clear by the Six Articles Act of 1539 that repudiated

Protestantism and upheld such doctrines as the transubstantiation, clerical celibacy, and Communion under one species. He did introduce a variety of reforms and founded a number of new bishoprics. The people did not readily accept these changes, and Henry was faced by popular uprisings, the most serious being the Pilgrimage of Grace (1536). In his personal affairs, Henry was unhappy with Anne, who produced only one surviving child, the future Queen Elizabeth I (1558-1603), and in 1536 he had her tried on charges of adultery and treason and beheaded. Ten days later he wed Jane Seymour. She died in 1537 giving birth to Edward (VI). A series of marriages followed: Anne of Cleves (1540), whom he divorced; Catherine Howard, whom he beheaded in 1542; and Catherine Parr (1543), who would survive him. He died on January 28, 1547. England under his successors would move inexorably toward Protestantism.

Henry of Ghent (1217-1293) ●

Theologian and philosopher, noted for his opposition to the systems of Thomas Aquinas and John Duns Scotus. A native of Ghent, he studied at Tournai and later served as a canon, and then as an archdeacon at Bourges (1276) and Tournai (1278). Henry condemned Averroism in 1277 but around 1290 was censured for his protesting the rights and privileges of the mendicant orders by Cardinal Gaetani, the future Pope Boniface VIII. Known as *Doctor Solemnis* (the Solemn Doctor), he authored two main works, *Quodlibita* and an unfinished *Summa Theologica*. Henry is listed as one of the foremost theologians of the so-called Golden Age of Scholasticism, although his place is generally put below Thomas Aquinas, Bonaventure, and John Duns Scotus.

Henry of Langenstein (d. c. 1397) ●

Theologian and philosopher best known for his contributions to the conciliar movement during the Great Schism (1378-1417). While at the University of Paris, Henry authored *Concilium Pacis* (1381), a work presenting the argument that the general council of the Church had greater authority than the pope and was thus empowered to depose the pontiff. The work was important in establishing the legitimacy of conciliarism, particularly as a means of ending the Great Schism. Henry also helped to establish the University of Vienna in 1384 and was an accomplished mathematician. He is also known as Henry the Hesse the Elder.

Herdtrich, Christian Wolfgang (1625-1684) ●

Jesuit missionary to China. Born at Graz, Austria, he entered the Society of Jesus in October 1641. In 1656, he was chosen for the Chinese mission. After working in the Celebes (modern Sulawesi, part of Indonesia) and in several provinces, Herdtrich was called to Beijing in 1671. There he was one of a group of Jesuits in attendance to the Chinese emperor. His writings include a work on Confucius, one of the earliest efforts by a Western scholar to examine Eastern teachings, and perhaps the first ever Chinese-Latin dictionary. He died in China and his epitaph was composed by the Chinese emperor.

Heresy ●

In a broad sense, the holding of beliefs that are contrary to the established and recognized system of theological (or even political) thought. Within the Catholic Church, heresy has a specific meaning and is very clearly delineated by canon law (Canon 751, for example). According to Church law, a heretic is someone who meets the following requirements: valid previous baptism; a profession of being a Christian; the denial or deliberate resistance to the teachings of the Catholic Church on matters it states to have been revealed by God; and the moral culpability that is present as the person in question refuses to acknowledge the so-called doctrinal imperative in the matter in dispute. In essence, heresy is the question or denial of a person concerning the authority of God whose revelation is communicated in the Sacred Scriptures and Sacred Tradition. Canon law stipulates that such a person today may be automatically excommunicated.

Heresy is taken from the Greek *hairesis* (choice) and was initially adopted in Scripture to imply a party or faction (as in Acts 5:17). In 1 Corinthians this was meant in a way that implies division. In this sense it gradually became condemnatory in character in the early Church. Heretical thought has always been present in the faith, ever since its earliest days. St. Paul describes heretics as "false prophets, deceitful workmen, disguising themselves as apostles of Christ" (2 Cor 11:13). There were numerous heresies in the first centuries of the Church, but the major ones were Arianism, Donatism, Manichaeism, Monarchianism, Monophysitism, Montanism, Nestorianism, and Pelagianism. These were strenuously opposed by the Fathers of the Church, such as Ambrose, Augustine, Ignatius, and Cyril of Alexandria. The presence of these heretical sects had in some ways a beneficial effect in that they encouraged, indeed necessitated, the Fathers to undertake careful examination of Orthodox theology and to promote its propagation in order to combat grievous error. Other heresies throughout the history of the Church have included Albigensianism, Lollardy, Lutheranism, Calvinism, Americanism, Modernism (called by Pope St. Pius X the "synthesis of all the heresies"), and according to some, liberation theology.

Hergenröther, Joseph (1824-1890) ●
Church historian and the first cardinal prefect of the Vatican Archives. The second son of a professor of medicine at the University of Würzburg, he attended the university in his hometown and so impressed the local prelate, Bishop Von Stahl, that he was sent to the Collegium Germanicum in Rome. Ordained in 1848, the following year he became a chaplain at Zellingen and then doctor of theology in 1850 at the University of Munich. He taught at Würzburg from 1852 onward, one of a number of eminent scholars, including Franz Hettinger and Heinrich Denzinger. A defender of conservative Catholic ideals, Hergenröther went to Rome in 1868 to assist in the preparation for the First Vatican Council. He defended the resulting definition of papal infallibility, especially against such theologians as Johannes Döllinger, whom he had already attacked in his 1861 *Der Zeitgeist und die Souveränität des Papstes*. As a consequence of this dispute he was never able to hold the post of rector of the university. In 1879, he was named a cardinal and appointed prefect of the Apostolic Archives, the first holder of the office and with the duty of establishing the Vatican Archives and organizing the system of research to be henceforth followed by scholars. His greatest work was the *Handbuch der allgemeiner Kirchengeschichte* (3 vols., 1876-1880), a brilliant treatise on Church history that remained for many years the standard work on the subject. He also continued the writings of Karl von Hefele in his *History of the Ecclesiastical Councils* by compiling the last two volumes in the nine-volume series.

Hermann of Wied (1477-1552) ●
Archbishop of Cologne who became one of the early important converts to Protestantism. Named archbishop and hence elector in 1515, Hermann was a firm supporter of ecclesiastical reform, demonstrating his zeal at the Council of Cologne (1536). An initial opponent of the Reformation, he nevertheless attempted to initiate an aggressive similar movement that was faithful to the Church, proposing many reforms in his work *Einfaltigs Bedencken einer christlichen Reformation* (1545), known also as the *Didgma*, and in an 1548 English edition as *A Simple and Religious*

Consultation of us, Herman, by the grace of God, Archbishop of Cologne. His increasingly Protestant outlook, however, earned the outrage of his archdiocese's population and the grave concern of the Holy Roman Emperor Charles V and Pope Paul III. In 1546, Paul deposed and excommunicated him, and Hermann died in the Lutheran fold.

Hermannus Contractus (1013-1054) ● Also Hermann of Reichenau, Herman the Lame, and Herimannus Contractus, a Christian poet, chronicler, and astronomer. Hermannus was educated at the Benedictine Abbey of Reichenau and was respected as one of the most learned men of his time, despite being so lame (hence the nickname Contractus) that he could barely read or write and was unable to move without assistance. He took monastic vows in 1043 and, using his considerable intellectual gifts, he studied virtually every field of knowledge. Among his many works were: *De Utilitatibus Astrolabii* (*On the Uses of the Astrolabe*) and *De Mense lunari* (*On Lunar Cycles*) in astronomy; *De Divisiones* (*On Division*) and *De Figura Quadrilatera* (*On the Quadrilateral Figure*) in mathematics; poetry; treatises on music; hymns; a martyrology; and a world chronicle from the time of Christ to 1054, the *Chronicon Augiense*.

Hermann von Reichenau ● See **Hermannus Contractus**, preceding entry.

Hermann von Salza ● See under **Teutonic Knights**.

Hermas ● Second-century author, ranked as one of the Apostolic Fathers, whose famed work, *The Shepherd*, was immensely popular in the early Church. Virtually nothing is known about Hermas save what he wrote about himself in his book. According to that he was a Christian slave who had won his freedom from the Roman woman Rhoda who had bought him. Marrying, he became a merchant, acquiring vast wealth, often through unscrupulous means. Penance was done by Hermas and his family when, during a persecution, all of their wealth and property were confiscated. *The Shepherd* is concerned with the Christian virtues and their exercise, stressing the necessity of penance and the forgiveness of sin. An ethical and not a theological work, Hermas did not enter into a deep discussion of doctrine, but he did not distinguish the Son from the Holy Spirit, identified the Holy Spirit with the Son of God before the Incarnation, and claimed that the Trinity only came into being after the humanity of Christ had entered heaven. The book was organized into five visions, twelve mandates, and ten parables. Subject to intense scholarly debate, the date of its authorship is unclear. Hermas says that he is a contemporary of St. Clement of Rome (d. c. 96), but the Muratorian Canon (dated to around 180) lists *The Shepherd* as written by a brother of Pope St. Pius I (r. 140-155); Origen believed Hermas to be the same person mentioned in Romans (16:14). Much beloved in the Eastern regions of the Church, *The Shepherd* was not that well-known in the West, declining in popularity, especially in the East, from the fourth century.

Hermes, Georg ● See **Hermesianism**, following entry.

Hermesianism ● Name given to the philosophical and theological ideas advanced by Georg Hermes (1775-1831), a professor of theology at Münster. Hermesianism had as its objective the accommodation of Catholic teaching to the recent developments of thought in the Enlightenment, specifically the considerable contributions of Immanuel Kant. Hermes believed that through the direct application of reason it is possible to prove the existence of God and thereby also demonstrate supernatural truth. These ideas soon found fertile soil in the academic environment in Germany, and a number of professors became proponents of Hermesianism. A short time after Hermes's death, many of his positions were condemned by Pope Gregory XVI (r. 1831-1846) in *Dum acerbissimas* (1835) and some of his writings were placed on the Index of Forbidden Books. Vatican Council I also condemned Hermesianism, with other similar teachings.

Hermit ● See GLOSSARY.

Hermits of St. Augustine ● See **Augustinian Hermits**.

Hertford, Council of ● Council of the English Church held in 673 with the aim of bringing about ecclesiastical reorganization. Convened at Hertford under Theodore of Tarsus, archbishop of Canterbury, and attended by the English bishops, the council issued ten canons delineating clerical and monastic rights and duties. Among the decrees were: synods were to be held twice a year, or at least once a year, on August 1, at Clovesho; divorce was forbidden except for fornication; monks were not to leave their monastery without the abbot's permission; and bishops were not to intrude upon the dioceses of neighboring prelates.

Hervetus, Gentian (1499-1584) ● French theologian and controversialist. Born near Orléans, he studied in his native city before journeying to Paris where he became tutor to the future French secretary of state, Claude d' Aubespine. Traveling to England, he tutored a brother of Cardinal Reginald Pole, eventually spending time in the Roman house of the cardinal where he concerned himself with Latin translations of the Greek Fathers. After teaching theology at the College of Bordeaux, he returned to Rome and became secretary to Cardinal Cervini, the future Marcellus II. Hervetus accompanied Cervini to the Council of Trent in 1545, delivering an oratory there on

clandestine marriages. Ordained in 1556, he became vicar-general of Noyou and a canon at Reims, preaching against the Calvinists. In 1561, he authored a treatise, *De Reparanda Ecclesiasticorum Disciplina*, calling for the enforcement of episcopal residence as a means of Church reform, and joining a group of theologians combating Protestantism that had been brought together by Cardinal Charles of Lorraine. The following year, he went again to Trent, this time with Cardinal Charles. Aside from his numerous pamphlets and Latin and French translations, Hervetus authored a complete French translation of the decrees of the Council of Trent, *Le saint, universel et general concile de Trente* (1564).

Hesychasm ● Form of mysticism that flourished in the Eastern Church, propagated principally by the monks of Mt. Athos, considered one of the great mystical movements of the Byzantine Church. The aim of the Hesychasts was the attainment of inner quietude (Greek *hesychia*) and a vision of the Divine Light. Popular within the Byzantine Empire from the 1200s to the 1300s, Hesychasm taught that *hesychia* was attainable through the application of rigorous exercises, severe asceticism, prayer, and a perfected will. Especially important was the fixing of the eye on a certain spot or reciting a prayer, the so-called Jesus Prayer, in time with breathing. Most of the Hesychasts were monks, taking their teaching from St. Nicephorus the Hesychast. The movement was defended by Gregory Palamas, but his writings were condemned by two synods in 1342. Nevertheless, Hesychasm was promoted during the reign of Byzantine Emperor John VI Cantacuzenus (r. 1347-1354), who gave high appointments to Hesychasts. Enemies of the movement were excommunicated at the Blackerna Synod (1351) and its doctrine gained ground in the Eastern Church in the latter 1400s until becoming an accepted part of Orthodox tradition. The Hesychasts also traveled to

Russia. The sect never became popular in the West.

Hesychius of Jerusalem, St. ●

Fifth-century Greek presbyter and exegete, the author of numerous biblical commentaries. Little is known of his life with certainty, although he was probably a monk in his early years and, according to Theophanes the Confessor, was a presbyter in Jerusalem in 412. His writings have been lost in part, but many were preserved in edited form and passed on under other names. Thus, the commentary on the Psalms attributed to St. Athanasius was probably the work of Hesychius. He apparently wrote commentaries on the entire Bible and was the author of a lost Church history. (Hesychius should not be confused with Bishop Hesychius of Jerusalem, a contemporary of St. Gregory the Great.) He is a saint in the Greek Church. Feast day: March 28.

Hettinger, Franz (1819-1890) ●

German Catholic theologian, one of the esteemed members of the faculty of the University of Würzburg. Born at Aschaffenburg, he entered the ecclesiastical seminary of Würzburg in 1839, studying there until 1841 when, on the advice of Bishop George Anton Stahl of Würzburg, he went to Rome to study at the German College. Ordained in September 1843, he received a doctorate of theology in 1845. By 1857, he was a professor at Würzburg, becoming professor of dogmatic theology in 1884. His renowned colleagues included Joseph Hergenröther and Heinrich Denzinger. With Hergenröther, Hettinger went to Rome in 1868 to take part in the early work of Vatican Council I. He was named consultor to the theologico-dogmatic commission for the council. In November 1879, he was appointed a domestic prelate by Pope Leo XIII. The author of works on theology, apologetic literature, and Dante, Hettinger was respected throughout all of Europe, receiving honorary degrees from universities in Vienna, Louvain, and Rome. His most famous work was *Apologie des Christenthums* (2 vols., 1863-1867; *Apology for Christianity*), a masterpiece of the apologetic that was enjoyed by theologians and educated readers alike.

Hieronymian Martyrology ●

Famous martyrology, known in the Latin as the *Hieronymianum*, that was probably compiled in the fifth century in Italy. Its name was derived from a statement in the (apocryphal) correspondence that precedes the text that the work was that of St. Jerome. The martyrology gives the date on the calendar year, followed by the name of a saint commemorated on each day, where the saint might be buried, entombed, or venerated, and any appropriate details related to the particular saint.

Higden, Ranulf (d. 1364) ●

Also called Ranulph Higdon, an English Benedictine monk and chronicler. His greatest work, the *Polychronicon*, was a universal history from the creation to around 1342, during the reign of King Edward III of England. Completed around 1350, it was organized into seven books, with additions being made over subsequent years, taking it into the reign of King Richard II (r. 1377-1399). An English translation from the Latin was made by John of Trevisa in 1385 or 1387. Other works by or attributed to Ranulf include *Speculum Curatorum* (1340), *Ars Componendi Sermones*, and *Abbreviationes Chronicorum*.

Hilarion (c. 291-371) ●

Founder of the anchorite life in Palestine. The principal source on his life is a biography about him written by St. Jerome. Hilarion was probably born at Tabatha, in the Gaza, the son of pagan parents. Sent to study at Alexandria, he became a Christian and, at the age of fifteen, was attracted to the life of the hermit by the renown of St. Antony. After spending two months with Antony in the desert, Hilarion returned home, divided his money among the poor, and retired to be an anchorite in the barren desert near Gaza, at Majuma. As his fame for saintliness grew, including reputed miraculous cures and exorcism, Hilarion began attracting followers. To escape the increasingly large crowds, he left the Gaza and returned to Egypt (c. 360), visiting the places where Antony had lived and died. Later, he went to Sicily, Libya, and Cyprus where he died. In his biography, Jerome notes that a chief source on Hilarion was St. Epiphanius, archbishop of Salamis, whom Hilarion had known in the anchorite's later years. Jerome mentions a (now lost) letter from Epiphanius concerning Hilarion.

Hilary, St. ● Also Hilarius. Pope from 461-468. Probably a native of Sardinia, he served for a time as archdeacon to Pope Leo I and was one of his legates with Julius, bishop of Puteoli, at the Latrocinium, the Robber Council of Ephesus in 449. There he protested the condemnation of Flavian, patriarch of Constantinople, and fought for the rights of the Roman see. He was forced to flee the city because of the violence that erupted there, barely escaping unharmed and attributing his safe journey to John the Evangelist, in whose burial site just outside Ephesus Hilary had hidden himself. Elected successor to Leo in November 461, he pursued the policies of his illustrious predecessor, devoting particular attention to Gaul (France) and Spain where he resolved a number of ecclesiastical disputes and

Pope St. Hilary

consolidated the authority of Rome. His synod at Rome in 465 is the oldest Roman synod for which extensive minutes have been preserved. In his dealings with the Eastern Church, Hilary circulated a decretal confirming the Councils of Nicaea (325), Ephesus (431), and Chalcedon (451). Feast day: February 28.

Hilary of Arles, St. (403-449) ●
Archbishop of Arles who became a catalyst in the extending of papal authority over the Church in Gaul. From a family in northern Gaul, he became a monk in Lérins, succeeding St. Honoratus in 428-429 as archbishop of Arles. A supporter of reform, he presided over several councils, including those of Orange (441) and Vaison (442). In 444, he took the important step of deposing Bishop Chelidonius of Besançon and irregularly replacing him with another. This act exceeded his authority as a metropolitan and the entire measure was rescinded by Pope St. Leo I. The pontiff then deprived Hilary of his metropolitan powers and obtained from Emperor Valentinian III recognition that Rome had supreme jurisdiction over the Church in Gaul. Hilary submitted to the papal acts and was not removed from his see. He also authored an extant life of Honoratus and other minor works. Feast day: May 5.

Hilary of Poitiers, St. (c. 315-367) ●
Bishop of Poitiers, a theologian, and a leading opponent of Arianism, called the Athanasius of the West. Hilary was raised as a pagan, receiving an education centered around Neoplatonism. Converted to Christianity, he

was elected bishop of Poitiers around 353 and a short time later he emerged as the main defender of orthodoxy in the West against the Arians. He was condemned for his stand by the Council of Biterrae in 356 and exiled to Phrygia for four years by Emperor Constantius III. In 359, he returned to prominence at the Council of Seleucia where he eloquently spoke out on his own behalf. His oratorical skills were matched by his lasting contributions to the faith through his writings. Aside from his commentaries on the Old and New Testaments, particularly the Psalms, his chief works were *De Trinitate* (*On the Trinity*) and *De Synodis* (*On the Synods*). In 1851, Hilary was named a Doctor of the Church by Pope Pius IX. Feast day: January 13.

Hilda of Whitby, St. ● Abbess of Whitby and an important figure in the Anglo-Saxon Church. A member of a Northumbrian royal family, she was baptized in 627 with her great uncle, King Edwin of Northumberland, by Paulinus, archbishop of York. Made abbess of Harttepool by St. Aidan in 649, she served as tutor to Aelfflaed, daughter of King Oswiu of Northumbria. Oswiu granted to Hilda (c. 657 or 659) land upon which she established the double monastery of Streaneshalch, eventually called Whitby. An ardent supporter of the Celtic Church, she sided with Colman of Lindisfarne in opposition to St. Wilfrid at the Synod of Whitby in 664. While she disagreed with the adoption of the Roman rite, she accepted the decision of the synod and abandoned Celtic customs. Hilda also encouraged the poet Caedmon. Feast day: November 17.

Hildebert of Lavardin (1056-1133) ● Archbishop of Tours, poet, and a literary figure in France. Born in Lavardin and educated at Le Mans, Hildebert was appointed archdeacon in 1091 and bishop of Le Mans in 1096. Disliked by William II Rufus of England, he was captured by the king in 1099 and held prisoner until William's death in 1100. Upon his release, Hildebert returned to Le Mans and built his cathedral. A powerful preacher in his own right, Hildebert defended Church doctrine and ousted Henry of Lausanne, the itinerant preacher, from his diocese because of heresy. Archbishop in 1125, he soon became embroiled in a dispute with King Louis VI and presided over the provincial Synod of Nantes (1137). The author of numerous works, he was especially noted for the high quality of his Latin. His writings included the lives of St. Radegunde and St. Hugh of Cluny, and numerous poems such as *"Vita Mariae Aegyptiacae."*

Hildegard of Bingen, St. (1098-1179) ● German mystic and abbess, called the "Sibyl of the Rhine" because of her many visions. A member of a German noble family, she began experiencing mystical visions at an early age. She was entrusted to the care of a reputed recluse, Bl. Jutta, and, around 1116, was received into the Benedictine community that had grown around Jutta. In 1136, she became abbess of the community, traveling throughout Germany and corresponding with leading figures and personalities of the time, including St. Bernard of Clairvaux and Emperor Frederick I Barbarossa. Through the influence of Bernard, Hildegard secured papal approbation of her visions from Pope Eugenius III. Her community moved to Rupertsberg, near Bingen, between 1147 and 1152, and she established another house in 1165 at Eibingen, near Rüdesheim. She wrote the *Scivias*, a collection of visions, divided into three books, which contained a number of prophecies of disaster. Other works included hymns, scientific treatises, letters, and theological writings. While efforts to secure her canonization were initially unsuccessful, from the 1400s she was listed as a saint in the *Martyrologium Romanum* (or Roman Martyrology). Feast day: September 17.

Hilton, Walter (d. 1396) ● English mystic and devotional writer. He studied at Cambridge before becoming a hermit and eventually joining the Augustinian Canons at Thurgarton Priory. His spiritual writings included the famed *Scala Perfectionis* (1494; *Ladder of Perfection*), a two-volume guide on spiritual attainment. The first book of its kind to appear in England, it remained popular throughout the fifteenth and sixteenth centuries. Other writings include, in English, *Epistle to a Devout Man in Temporal Estate* (1494), *The Song of Angels* (1521), an exposition on the Psalms; and in Latin, four epistles and a *quaestio* on the veneration of images. Hilton may also have been the author of the first three books of the *Imitation of Christ*, attributed to Thomas à Kempis.

Hincmar of Reims (c. 806-882) ● Archbishop of Reims, theologian, and one of the leading prelates of the Frankish Church in the ninth century. Hincmar was the descendant of a noted family of the West Franks and was educated at the famed school of St. Denis in Paris. Through his teacher, Abbot Hildisia, he was introduced into the royal court of King Louis the Pious in 822, serving as well Charles the Bald. When Charles came to the Carolingian throne in 840, Hincmar was retained as counselor, thereby earning the enmity of Charles's rival, Emperor Lothair I. Elected archbishop in 845, Hincmar launched an extensive reform of the diocese, subsequently being acquitted by the Synod of Soissons (853) on the charge of illegally nullifying the acts of his predecessor, an accusation laid by Lothair. Following the death of Lothair II, king of Lorraine, Hincmar personally crowned Charles ruler of Lorraine, an act done over the objection of the pope. Another disagreement with the pontiff came in 876 when Hincmar opposed John VIII's appointment of a papal legate for Germany and Gaul (France). He continued to squabble with other prelates and political leaders until his death while fleeing a Viking attack on Reims. Hincmar participated in the controversy over predestination, attacking Gottschalk of Fulda in his *Ad Reclusos et Simplices*, ultimately eliciting the assistance of John Scotus Erigena. He also authored *Opusculum LV Capitulorum*, defending the rights of a metropolitan over his bishops, and a life of St. Remigius.

Hinsley, Arthur (1865-1943) ● English cardinal and the fifth archbishop of Westminster, noted especially for his work during the years before World War II in opposing Fascism and in the conflict's early period. A native of Yorkshire, he was educated at the English College, Rome, and ordained in 1893. After holding teaching posts at Upshaw College, Durham (1893-1897), and at St. Bede's Grammar School in Bradford (1899-1904), he served as rector at the English College, Rome (1917-1928), and was consecrated titular bishop of Sardinia in 1930. The first apostolic delegate to the African hierarchy (1930-1934), Hinsley fell ill and retired in 1935. That same year, however, he was brought out of retirement and named archbishop of Westminster on the death of Cardinal Francis Bourne. Made a cardinal in 1937, he earned considerable notoriety three years later when he founded the organization Sword and the Spirit, a gathering of Catholics, Anglicans, and Free Churches to opposed totalitarianism. He was especially outspoken against Hitler and provided badly needed spiritual leadership to the English during the dark years of the early phase of World War II.

Hippolytus, St. (c. 170-236) ● Theologian, writer, and antipope in the early Church. A presbyter in Rome, he emerged a controversial and inflammatory figure in the Eternal City, largely because of his opposition to a number of popes, most notably Zepherinus (199-217) and Callistus (217-222) as well as their successors Urban (222-230) and Pontianus (230-235). Hippolytus particularly resisted the teachings of Callistus, possibly establishing himself as an antipope. His struggles with the popes ended only in 235 when, during the persecution of the Church under Emperor Maximinus Thrax, Hippolytus and Pontianus were exiled to Sardinia. Hippolytus died there, possibly in 236 but apparently after reconciling himself with the Roman Christians, for his body was returned to Rome in 236 and given a proper burial. Hippolytus authored a number of works, including commentaries on Daniel and the Song of Songs, a treatise on the Apostolic Tradition, and his greatest writing, *Refutation of All Heresies*, of which Books 4 to 10 are extant. A list of all his works was discovered on a statue of him in Rome in 1551; the statue was probably made during Hippolytus's lifetime. One of the greatest theologians of the West in the third century, he was all but forgotten for many centuries, largely because of his troubles with the popes. Feast day: August 13.

Hippolytus, Canons of St. ● Collection of thirty-eight canons compiled in Greek, perhaps in the middle of the fourth century or around 500. The original Greek text, written in Egypt, is lost, although the canons survive in an Arabic version based on a Coptic translation. Their name was derived from the false attribution of the work to St. Hippolytus. While Hippolytus is not the author, the collection is based on an adaptation of Hippolytus's Apostolic Tradition, and the unknown author follows the general order of his source material. The canons examine disciplinary and liturgical matters such as baptism, prayer, and proper conduct by members of the Christian community. There are no surviving manuscripts of the work earlier than the 1200s. The full title is *Canons of the Church and Precepts Written by Hippolytus, Archbishop of Rome, According to the Ordinances of the Apostles.*

Hitler, Adolf ● See **Germany, Pius XI**, and **Pius XII**; see also **Jews and Judaism**.

Hofbauer, Clement Mary, St. (1751-1820) ● Patron saint of Vienna, the so-called Apostle of Vienna. Born at Tasswitz, Moravia, he was the son of a butcher and grazier, working for a time as a baker's apprentice. Spiritually inclined, he at first hoped to be a hermit but eventually began studying for the priesthood. In 1784, he entered the Congregation of the Redemptorists at Rome and was ordained the following year, at the age of thirty-four. Returning to Vienna, he discovered that the Josephinist laws prevented him from establishing a new house in the city, so he went to Warsaw. There, from 1787-1808, he labored brilliantly among the German-speaking Poles, proving especially successful in his religious and social work. In 1793, he was appointed vicar-general for the Redemptorist house north in the Alps. In 1808, however, Napoleon dispersed the religious communities in Poland, and Hofbauer returned to Vienna where he fought for religious rights, helped establish a new college in the city, and worked to counter the baleful effects of Josephinism. Government approbation of the Redemptorists came shortly after his death. Canonized by Pope Pius X in 1909, he was also declared patron saint of Vienna. Feast day: March 15.

Holiness, His ● Title used today for the pope. During the early Church the term was applied often to bishops, becoming restricted from the seventh century to patriarchs. His Holiness is still applied to patriarchs in the Eastern Church, but in the West, from the 1300s, it has been exclusively borne by the pontiff. From time to time, Byzantine emperors were called His Holiness. (See also **Holy Father**.)

Holland ● See **Netherlands**.

Holy Cross ● See **True Cross**.

Holy Father ● Or more properly, The Most Holy Father, the title used often for the pope. Translated from the Latin *Beatissimus Pater*, it first appeared in English around 1380.

Holy Grail ● Powerful symbol of mystical veneration, perfection, and mystery that came to be identified as the chalice used by Christ at the Last Supper. The Holy Grail was a major element of medieval legend, lore, and literature, appearing variously as a cup, dish, a stone, or even a cauldron into which blood would drip from a bloody lance. It also became closely connected over time with the Arthurian legend. Scholars differ over the possible origins of the Grail legend, some proposing a Celtic or classical mythological origin, others a Christian or Oriental one. Gradually, however, the original elements were united with the tales told of the adventures of Joseph of Arimathea and the arrival of Christianity in the British Isles. The earliest Grail romance was composed around 1180 by Chrétien de Troyes in his *Perceval* or *Conte del Graal*, the start of the great literary tradition that flourished in the late twelfth and early to mid-thirteenth centuries. Other famous Grail stories were written by Wolfram von Eschenbach (*Parzival*), Robert de Boron (*Roman de l'Estoire dou Graal*), and the thirteenth-century prose romance *L'Estoire del Saint Graal* (*History of Grand Saint Grail*).

Pope Leo III

Holy Helpers ● See **Auxiliary Saints**.

Holy Name Society ● Association of Catholic laypeople devoted to the promotion of love and reverence for the name of God and Jesus, and the discouragement of profanity and blasphemies toward the same. The confraternity of men was first founded by the Dominican preacher Bl. John of Vercelli (d. 1283) at the command of Pope Gregory X, who established it at the Council of Lyons (1274), placing its direction in the hands of the Dominicans. The immediate purpose of the confraternity was to counter the rampant blasphemies and vulgarities of the time. In the 1400s, the Spanish friar Didacus (d. 1450) founded an association of the Holy Name of Jesus, a confraternity that merged with the Society of the Holy Name. The society continues to receive rich spiritual endowments from the Church and has worldwide membership reaching into the millions. Members promote the purposes of the association while working to improve their own spiritual state through frequent Communions, devotions, and retreats.

Holy Roman Empire ● Political entity that stretched over much of Central Europe from 800 or 962 until 1806. The Holy Roman Empire was first called that in 1157 and the title Holy Roman Emperor (*Sacrum Romanum Imperium*) was used from 1254. It was called "Roman" because of its claim to the succession of the Roman Empire in the West and "Holy" because of its claims to supremacy over Christendom. The Holy Roman Empire was an evolving institution and was never recognized by the Byzantine Empire; it was also challenged and undermined by such competing states as Spain, France, and England. Further, the understanding of the purpose, powers, and mission of the empire was subject to assorted theories and conflicting ideas by popes, theologians, philosophers, and writers such as Petrarch and Dante.

The origins of the empire are traced to Christmas Day, 800, when Charlemagne was crowned emperor by Pope Leo III as the Frankish king knelt in prayer at St. Peter's. His work restored an order and unity to the West that had not been known since the days of the Roman emperors, but the large Carolingian Empire did not long survive him and the title of emperor lapsed in 924. The empire was restored in 962 under Otto I, who established an extensive realm in Germany and Italy based on feudalism. This feudal tradition required the election of the Holy Roman Emperor by the powerful magnates of Germany, the princes. After 1356, the election was in the hands of electors, comprised of princes and also certain archbishops. By custom the person elected

Charlemagne's chapel at Aachen (Aix-La-Chapelle)

held the title of German king after being crowned at Aachen. This rank was held until the candidate was crowned in Rome by the pope. The heir to the imperial throne was called the "King of the Romans."

The emperors were faced with two main difficulties: the vicissitudes of maintaining political power in Germany against ambitious and combative local nobles and prelates; and the threat posed by the popes, both ecclesiastical throughout Christendom and temporal with the Papal States and in Italy. The struggle with the papacy was characterized by two main crises, the desire of the emperors to exercise influence over the Church in their lands and the ambitions of both parties in Italy. The first was epitomized by the Investiture Controversy and the second by the campaigns of such emperors as Frederick I Barbarossa (r. 1152-1190) and Frederick II (r. 1215-1250). In the political conflicts, the popes were assisted by geopolitical realities confronting the emperors. To focus exclusively on Germany would cause a marked deterioration in Italy, while an interest in Italian affairs could be offset by stirring up trouble in Germany. Frederick II was able to dominate both Italy and Germany while he lived, but after his death in 1250, the papacy proved triumphant, not only breaking imperial rule over Italy but also liquidating the Hohenstaufen Dynasty and causing an interregnum from 1254-1273. In 1273, Rudolf I of Habsburg was elected. His dynasty would compete with the Luxembourg and Wittelsbach Dynasties until 1438 when the Habsburgs took firm control of the crown.

The 1500s saw renewed fighting between the emperors and the papacy, most notably under Emperor Charles V (r. 1519-1556), who sacked Rome in 1527 and imprisoned Pope Clement VII in Castel Sant' Angelo. Under Charles, the empire exercised a policy of aggrandizement that stretched around the world. The century also brought the Reformation, which destroyed the religious unity of the empire, providing as well

Coat of arms of Pope John Paul II

to the German princes the means of rising up against the emperors and furthering their own territorial aspirations. The Thirty Years' War (1618-1648) ruined whole parts of the empire and ended with the Treaty of Westphalia (1648), which dissolved the empire in all but name as the princes enjoyed virtual independence and sovereignty. Wars over succeeding centuries with France and Prussia weakened the empire even further. Finally, in 1806, after smashing the Austrians and their allies the year before, Napoleon terminated the Holy Roman Empire. Henceforth, it was called the Austrian Empire and later the Austro-Hungarian Empire, which collapsed

at the conclusion of World War I. Until 1903, the Austrians continued to attempt to influence the papacy, considering the popes to be mere chaplains to the imperial court. The last case of imperial influence was in 1903 when the cardinals in conclave to elect a successor to Pope Leo XIII were informed that Emperor Franz Joseph would exercise his veto upon Cardinal Mariano Rampolla. Immediately after his election, Pope St. Pius X made illegal any temporal or secular interference.

Holy See ● Term considered synonymous with the Apostolic See that is used to describe the sovereignty, authority, and jurisdiction wielded by the pope and the central administration, spiritual and temporal, of the Church. While the Holy See exercises its jurisdiction in Rome, it should not be confused or considered the same as the Stato della Città del Vaticano (State of Vatican City), which is merely the territorial possession of the papacy as guaranteed by the Lateran Treaty of 1929 and assuring the independence of the Holy See to conduct its universal mission. The Holy See has a dual significance: as a see it denotes the presence of the local bishop's administration or government over a diocese, but the use of "Holy" (or Apostolic) makes clear the unique position of the see. As the successor of St. Peter, the pope is the sovereign pontiff, visible head of the Church, and holder of supreme, absolute jurisdiction over the entire Church, governing with the full authority of St. Peter.

The pope is assisted in the administration of the Church by various aides and organs of government. These are the congregations, the Secretariat of State, tribunals, and commissions, often collectively called the Roman Curia or also known as dicasteries. Through them, authority is transmitted to the entire Church orders or jurisdictions to the bishops, vicars apostolic, prefects apostolic, superiors of the religious institutes, superiors of missions, and others. The function and duties of the Curia are clearly defined in the Code of Canon Law (Canons 330-367) and in the apostolic constitution *Pastor Bonus*, issued by Pope John Paul II on June 28, 1988.

Although it is common parlance to say that diplomats from various countries are posted to the Vatican, it is more correct to state that diplomatic representation is to the Holy See. The Holy See is the world's oldest sovereign state to participate in international relations, remaining so even after the liquidation of the temporal possessions of the papacy in 1870. The popes are represented in many lands by diplomats of various ranks, depending upon the current state of diplomatic relations — representatives may range from apostolic delegates to pro-nuncios to nuncios who enjoy senior status in any diplomatic corps. (For the history of the temporal holdings of the papacy, see **Papal States**; also **Vatican** and **Vatican City, State of**; see also **Cardinals, College of** and **Curia, Roman**.)

The origin of the term and the understanding of its authority is somewhat obscure owing to the use of apostolic see (*sedes apostolicae*) for those churches founded by the Apostles; later the word *sedes* (or "see") was applied to the five great patriarchal sees of Christian antiquity, Rome, Alexandria, Constantinople, Antioch, and Jerusalem. Rome, however, had clear preeminence as seen in the declaration of Pope Gelasius I (492-496): "*Est ergo prima Petri apostoli sedes.*" The *Liber Pontificalis* states under the entry for Pope Leo III (795-816): "*Nos sedem apostolicam, quae est*

caput omnium Dei ecclesiarum, judicare non audemus" ("We dare not to judge the Holy See which is head of all the Churches of God"). Scholars are thus able to trace the application of the term Holy See in denoting the pope and the central administration of the Church. In those times, the 1200s to the 1400s, when, for various reasons, the popes departed Rome, it was accepted that the administration went with him — "*Ubi papa, ibi Curia*" ("Where there is the pope, there is the Curia") — although for a long time there was uncertainty as to where the Holy See was actually fixed. To clarify legal questions arising out of the infrequent but problematic separation of the pope and the Curia, Pope Clement VIII (r. 1592-1605) issued the constitution *Cum ob nonnullas*, establishing the principle that if the pontiff and Curia are separated, the proclamations of both are considered legal, provided that they are in full agreement with each other.

Holy Sepulchre ● Tomb in which Jesus was buried after his crucifixion, and from which he rose. On the site was built the Church of the Holy Sepulchre, which was so constructed as to encompass both the tomb and Golgotha, the exact spot where Christ had died. The Gospel of St. John (19:41) records: "Now in the place where he was crucified there was a garden, and in the garden a new tomb where no one had ever been laid. So because of the Jewish day of Preparation, as the tomb was close at hand, they laid Jesus there." The tomb belonged to Joseph of Arimathea and had a low entry way that led to a vestibule opening onto the actual burial chamber. It was covered by a heavy circular stone.

The site was largely covered over in the early second century (c. 135) as a result of the construction of the Temple of Venus, part of the new pagan Jerusalem that was decreed by Emperor Hadrian (r. 117-135) and that received the Roman name Aelia Capitolina. In 326, Constantine the Great ordered the pagan edifice destroyed and, according to tradition, the tomb of Christ was revealed beneath, along with relics of his death, including the True Cross. With the generous financial support of St. Helena, Constantine's mother, a church was erected under Bishop Macarius of Jerusalem, a magnificent shrine described in considerable detail by Eusebius of Caesarea in his *Vita Constantini* (*Life of Constantine*). This first Church of the Holy Sepulchre was dedicated around 336. In 614, it was burned by the Persians under Chosroes II (r. 590-628) after his capture of Jerusalem. While restored a few years later, it was destroyed by Caliph al-Hakim around 1010. Owing to the Islamic presence in Jerusalem, a general restoration was impossible, so smaller churches were built on the remains of the original shrine. As a result of the seizure of the Holy City by crusader armies in 1099, it became feasible to rebuild the Church. The Latin architects in charge of the project chose a Romanesque design, their work continuing for a good portion of the twelfth century. In 1808, another fire occurred, bringing extensive

Church of the Holy Sepulchre, Jerusalem

damage and necessitating a new round of building in 1810 by local Armenians and Greeks. The present Church dates from this year, although a new rotunda and dome were paid for in 1868 by France, Turkey, and Russia. It is today used by members of the various Christian rites, including the Latin, Coptic, Syrian Jacobite, Greek, and Armenian.

Holy Sepulchre, Knights of the ● See under **Military Orders**.

Holy War ● See **Crusades**.

Homoousios ● Greek for "consubstantial," "of one essence," or "of the same substance."

Defined and accepted by the Council of Nicaea (325), added to the Nicene Creed, and used to describe the relationship of Christ to the Father, *homoousios* was intended to make clear the Church's teaching on the nature of the Second Person of the Trinity, declaring that Christ is of the same substance (or essence) as God the Father. It affirms the full divinity of Christ by stressing his full share in the divine nature of his Father. The word was later in the fourth century understood to apply to the Holy Spirit as the Third Person of the Trinity.

Homoousios was issued by the teaching authority of the Church at Nicaea to give response to the Arians who argued that Christ could be understood to be divine only in the limited sense of being from God, and like God, but not of the same essence as the Father. As the Arians denied that there were three distinct Persons in God, they opposed any term that implied "consubstantial," advancing instead the word *homoiousios*, meaning "like the Father." The only difference in the two words is one letter, the Greek iota, but the theological divergence is absolutely crucial. *Homoiousios* was repudiated by Orthodox theologians and ceased to be supported after the decline of Arianism.

Honorius I ● Pope from 625-638. His pontificate was dominated by the heresy of Monophysitism. A member of a noble family from Campagna, he was elected successor to Boniface IV but took as his model his illustrious predecessor Pope St. Gregory I. Honorius thus gave immediate support to the missionaries in England, pushing for conversion among the Anglo-Saxons and widespread acceptance of the Roman rite. Troubled by the spread of Monophysite tendencies, he responded to a letter from Sergius, patriarch of Constantinople, on whether Christ had one or two natures, by quoting the Chalcedonian model, thereby interpreting Christ's nature as indivisible.

Unfortunately, Honorius used the term "one will" in Christ, causing considerable controversy in the East and West. Honorius was condemned at the Council of Constantinople (680-681) and was attacked for heresy by his successors; the Constantinople condemnation was upheld by Pope Leo II. Opponents of papal infallibility have used Honorius as an example of the unsuitability of the claim. Despite the controversy, Honorius was an energetic pontiff who initiated clerical reform and assumed considerable influence over Italian affairs through his wise management of the Patrimony of Peter.

Honorius II ● Pope from 1124-1130. Originally called Lamberto Scanabecchi, he was made a cardinal by Pope Paschal II in 1117 and was an important representative from Pope Callistus II to Germany, negotiating the Concordat of Worms that brought an end to the Investiture Controversy between the papacy and the Holy Roman Emperors. Elected the successor to Callistus in December 1124, his elevation was opposed by a faction in Rome supporting Cardinal Teobaldo, the antipope Celestine II. Honorius offered to resign, but he was reaffirmed by the cardinals and was duly enthroned. As pontiff, he used the newly established good relations with the empire to promote ecclesiastical reform. He aided the German king Lothair II in 1152, excommunicating Lothair's rival Conrad of Hohenstaufen, the future German king Conrad III. Honorius was less successful with Roger II of Sicily, who defeated an army raised by the pope and compelled him to recognize him as duke of Apulia.

Honorius III ● Pope from 1216-1227. Worthy successor to the brilliant Innocent III. Born Cencio Savelli, to the noble Roman family of the Savelli, he received the post of papal treasurer in 1188 and was made a cardinal priest by Innocent III. Elected on July 18, 1216, he promoted a crusade and labored to reform the Church. To advance the likelihood of a crusade (already endorsed by the Fourth Lateran Council in 1215), Honorius pushed his onetime pupil, Frederick II, to fulfill his vow of going on a crusade, a call that complicated their increasingly strained relationship. Frederick was twice crowned German king by Honorius (1212 and 1215), but his dispute with the pope over Sicily allowed him to evade his vow. Honorius crowned Frederick emperor on November 22, 1220, but still the ruler would not set out, and finally, in 1225, Honorius threatened to excommunicate him. Only the pope's death ended their troubled relationship. Honorius was a patron of the mendicant orders, particularly their tertiary orders and instructed King Louis VIII of France to wage war on the Albigensians of France. He supported the claims of Henry III to the English over those of Prince Louis of France in 1223, and defended the rights of the Church in Bohemia. Honorius authored a collection of decretals, the *Compilatio Quinta* (*Fifth Compilation*), the first compilation of canon law, as well as sermons, letters, a life of Pope Gregory VII, and an extension of the *Liber Pontificalis*. A gifted reformer, he is ranked as one of the foremost of all papal administrators.

Honorius IV ● Pope from 1285-1287. Grandnephew of Pope Honorius III, he was born Giacomo Savelli. Made a cardinal by Urban in 1261, he was unanimously elected the successor to Martin IV on April 2, 1285. Honorius engaged in a conflict with King Peter II of Aragon over control of Sicily, which had been lost to the papacy in 1282. He also gave his enthusiastic support to the mendicant orders, adding to the privileges of the Dominicans and Franciscans and entrusting to them exclusive control of the Inquisition. At the University of Paris, he encouraged the study of Oriental languages to advance the possible reunion of the Western and Eastern Churches.

Honorius of Autun ● Also Honorius Augustodunensis, a twelfth-century theologian and philosopher. Little is known with any certainty about his life, beyond the fact that he probably flourished between 1106 and 1135, that he lived in southern Germany, and that he authored a large body of writings. A long-held theory that he was a native of Autun has fallen out of favor, although Honorius did describe himself (in *De Luminaribus Ecclesiae*) as a "priest and head of the school of Autun." Among his vast corpus of works are writings on philosophy — *De Philosophia mundi*, on God, heaven, and earth, and treatises on the soul; theology — *Eleucidarium* (a summary of Christian theology), *Sigillum Beatae Mariae* (an exposition on the Canticle of Canticles, or Song of Solomon), and *Eucharistion* (on the body and blood of Christ); education — *Summa totius Historiae* (*Summa on the Whole of History*) and *De Luminaribus Ecclesiae* (*On the Windows of the Church*).

Hontheim, Johann Nikolaus von ● See **Febronianism**.

Hormisdas, St. ● Pope from 514-523. An Italian, although he had a Persian name, he was a member of an aristocratic family and had been married prior to ordination, with one son, Silverius (pope himself from 536-537). The successor to Symmachus, he is best remembered for his successful dealings with the Eastern Church, especially bringing an end to the Acacian Schism (484-514). The schism, causing a rupture between the Eastern and Western Churches, had been brought about by the excommunication of Acacius, patriarch of Constantinople, for heresy. Hormisdas was initially unsuccessful in negotiating a settlement with Emperor Anastasius I (r. 491-518), but a breakthrough came with the more flexible Justin I (r. 518-527) and the patriarch of Constantinople, John of Cappadocia. The schism was terminated and the Churches reunited; additionally, Hormisdas secured the acceptance of the *Tome* of Leo I and the decisions of the Council of Chalcedon (451), and recognition of the authority of the Roman see over the Church on the basis of Matthew (16:18).

Hosius of Córdoba (d. 357) ● Bishop of Córdoba (also Cordova) who was an influential Church figure during the reign of Emperor Constantine the Great (sole ruler from 324-337). Also called Ossius, he was elected bishop in 296, suffering in the persecutions of Maximian but surviving to participate in the Council of Elvira (306). From around 313, Hosius was a trusted adviser to Constantine, who had asked him to compile a report on the growing Arian Controversy. After a trip to Alexandria, Hosius returned with such a conclusive and disturbing report that the emperor convened the Council of Nicaea in 325. Hosius may have presided over the council, and it is possible that he introduced the term *homoousios*. Spending the next year fighting Arianism, he attended the Council of Sardica (343), and was exiled by the pro-Arian party for his support of St. Athanasius. At a synod in 357, he agreed to sign a pro-Arian declaration but upon his deathbed recanted and repudiated his signature.

Hosius, Stanislaus (1504-1579) ● Polish cardinal and an important leader in the Catholic Reformation and at the Council of Trent (1545-1563). A native of Cracow, Hosius was of German descent. He studied law at Cracow, Bologna, and Padua, and was ordained in 1543. Consecrated bishop of Chelmo (Kulm) in 1549, he was translated to the diocese of Ermland, in East Prussia, in 1551, embarking on an active campaign to combat the spread of heresy and Protestantism, preaching in Polish, Latin,

and German. At the Synod of Piotrków (1551) he drafted the first version of what was to become the immensely popular *Confessio Catholicae Fidei Christiana* (published in 1552-1553), which was to undergo thirty editions and numerous translations in his lifetime. Called to Rome in 1558 by Pope Paul IV to serve as an adviser on the religious state of Poland and Prussia, Hosius was appointed nuncio to Ferdinand I in 1560 by Pope Pius IV. He then reopened the Council of Trent, rescued Emperor Ferdinand's son Maximilian from the influence of Protestant teachers, and then held a major post at the council in the examination of doctrine as presiding papal legate and cardinal (1561). Returning to Poland, he invited the Jesuits to open a college at Braunsberg, the future Lyceum Hosianum. From 1569, he lived in Rome as the permanent representative of Poland to the Holy See. St. Peter Canisius called Hosius the most gifted writer, most eminent theologian, and the finest bishop of his time.

Hospitals ● Shelters and centers devoted to the care of the sick, orphans, and the aged. Christian hospitals have long been one of the most successful outward expressions of the faith and remain a vital aspect of Catholic service to the world. The first hospitals in a formal sense began in the fourth century in the Eastern Empire, sometime around the reign of Emperor Constantine the Great (d. 337) and certainly before the time of Emperor Julian the Apostate (r. 361-363). Prior to that time, Christians followed the example of Christ and the Apostles and cared for the sick to the best of their individual abilities. An interesting development was the pervasive fulfillment of charitable activity by which the houses of wealthy Christians or local bishops were always open to travelers — Christian or pagan — and to all who were hungry or in need of care. Bishops were often doctors, giving aid to any who might come to the door.

While extensive, this system could not be organized on an ambitious scale so long as the Roman state was devoted to the uprooting of the Church. Thus, when the empire became Christianized, actual hospitals were opened. Examples of early institutions are plague houses opened in 375 at Edessa by St. Ephraem, and the Basilias, the hospital begun by St. Basil in 369 at Caesarea. Over time, the institutions were devoted to specific classes of people, the sick, orphans, the aged, poor, crippled pilgrims, and handicapped or infirm poor who could not work.

In the West, the first hospital was that of Fabiola in Rome around 400. St. Jerome wrote that she would collect the sick from the streets and "nurse the wretched sufferers wasted with poverty and disease" (*Ep.* 77). The hospital was an important institution in the Middle Ages, becoming identified with the monastic orders and congregations and religious orders devoted to ministering to the sick, the so-called hospital orders. During the crusades, the various chivalric orders also aided the sick, especially in the Holy Land, through such groups as the Teutonic Knights and the Order of St. John. Today, the Church is involved in every area of health care, operating hospitals, health-care centers, orphanages, social services, day care, mission hospitals, and special homes. The Catholic Church, for example, is the single largest health-care deliverer in the United States, running more than six hundred hospitals.

Howard, Philip (1629-1694) ●

English-born Dominican and cardinal, commonly called "Cardinal of Norfolk." The third son of Henry Frederick Howard (the future earl of Arundel and Surrey), Howard entered the Dominican order in Italy at the age of sixteen, professing in 1646 and taking the name Thomas. Residing in Naples for a period of his studies, he was chosen to deliver an address in Latin to the general chapter in Rome. His topic was the conversion of England, and his address was so profound the order passed a decree urging its provincials and priors to do all in their power to make converts in England, Scotland, and Ireland. Howard was devoted for the rest of his life to bringing about the return of the homeland to the Church. Ordained in 1652, he was named grand almoner by King Charles II of England to Queen Catherine of Braganza, enjoying a positive influence at the court until the Puritans forced him to leave England. A cardinal in 1675, he became protector of England and Scotland, rebuilt the English College of Rome, and revised the statutes of Douai College. Howard is considered the father and restorer of the English Dominican province.

Hrosvit, St. (d. c. 1000) ●

Also Rosvith, a medieval German poetess and Benedictine nun. Hrosvit was of noble Saxon birth, entering the Benedictine convent of Gandersheim. Her writings, long forgotten from the time of her death, were discovered around 1500 by the German humanist Conradus Celtis (or Celtes) at Ratisbon and were first published a short time later. She was quite familiar with classical literature as well as Scripture, authoring six comedies, eight poems, and two chronicles. The plays were based on the Roman dramatist Terence, were written in Latin, and were intended to repudiate the pagan morality found in classical times. Her poems were concerned with such notable figures as the Virgin Mary, St. Agnes, and St. Basil. The two chronicles covered the achievements of Otto the Great (unfinished) and the history of the Gandersheim Abbey from its foundation to 919. Her plays are notable for their Christian themes wrapped in comedy form.

Huet, Pierre Daniel (1630-1721) ●

French bishop and scholar. A native of Caen, in Normandy, he was the son of a sheriff who had been converted from Calvinism. Orphaned as a baby, Huet studied at Caen, becoming fascinated with René Descartes, although he would later reject Descartes's philosophy, most notably in his 1689 work, *Censura philosophiae Cartesianae*. A friend of Samuel Bockhart (d. 1667), a local Protestant minister in Caen, Huet was inspired and assisted by him in his biblical studies, especially in learning Greek and Hebrew. When Bockhart was invited by Queen Christina of Sweden to the royal court in 1652, Huet was asked to go along. In the Royal Library, he found fragments of the writings of Origen, and thus undertook an edition of Origen, a labor that took years to complete. It was published in 1668. After the brief period in Sweden, Huet spent many years in Caen, although in 1670 he was called to Paris by King Louis XIV to assist in the education of the dauphin and in 1674 he was elected to the French Academy. Ordained in 1676, he became bishop of Avranches in 1689. His large corpus of writings includes philosophy, history, and exegesis.

Hugh of Cluny ● See **Hugh the Great, St**.

Hugh of Flavigny ● Early twelfth-century Benedictine monk and historian. Probably born at Verdun, he was educated at the monastery of St. Vannes at Verdun where he became a Benedictine novice. Hugh later went to the Abbey of St. Benigne at Dijon when the abbot of St. Vannes was forced to leave the monastery and go to St. Benigne as a result of his support of the pope against the antipope Clement III. At Dijon, Hugh made his final vows and in 1096, around the age of thirty-two, he was elected abbot of Flavigny. Differences with the bishop of Autun and his own monks twice caused him to flee Flavigny and finally to abdicate, but the Council of Valence (1100) reinstated him. He seems to have adopted an antipapal position concerning investiture after these

troubles. Hugh was the author of a world chronicle, the *Chronicon Virdunense seu Flaviniacense*, preserved in two books; the first extends to the year 1002, the second covers the years 1002-1112, a very valuable source for the ecclesiastical history of France and the history of Lorraine. Particularly excellent is his account of the election of Victor III in 1086.

Hugh of Lincoln, St. (c. 1140-1200) ● Founder of the first Carthusian monastery in England. The son of the Lord of Burgundy, he was raised with the expectation of serving as a member of the Augustinian Canons near Grenoble; instead he found himself drawn to the more contemplative lifestyle of the recently established Carthusians. In 1160, he took vows at the Grande Chartreuse. Acquiring fame for his learning and character, he was invited by King Henry II of England to establish (1175 or 1176) the first Carthusian community in the isles, at Witham, in Somerset. Hugh served as prior. At the express wish of King Henry, he was made bishop of Lincoln in 1186, although he insisted that before accepting the office he should be freely elected. While opposing many of the policies of Henry and Richard the Lionhearted, Hugh nevertheless maintained their respect and was revered throughout England and elsewhere for his holiness and his charity toward lepers. He died while returning from a trip to Grande Chartreuse. His tomb at Lincoln became a popular pilgrim site. It was ruined by the orders of King Henry VIII. The first Carthusian to become a saint, Hugh was canonized in 1220 by Pope Honorius III.

Hugh of St. Cher (c. 1200-1263) ● Known in the Latin as Hugh de Sancto Caro or de Sancto Theodorico, a Dominican cardinal. Born at St. Cher, he studied at Paris and taught law there before entering the Dominicans in 1225. Provincial and then prior of the Dominican monastery in Paris, he emerged as a trusted adviser to a number of prelates and then the representative of Pope Gregory IX to Constantinople in 1233. Made a cardinal by Pope Innocent IV, he assisted the pontiff at the Council of Lyons (1245). A gifted biblical scholar, he is credited with the first verbal concordance of the Scriptures, a work that served as a model for subsequent concordances.

Hugh of St. Victor (1096-1141) ● French mystic, theologian, and scholar who, with Richard of St. Victor, was a decisive influence upon the Abbey of St. Victor in Paris, helping its development as one of the main centers for mysticism in the West. The nephew of Archdeacon Reinhard of Halberstadt, he entered St. Victor around 1115 and was appointed director of studies in 1133. Known as the *Alter Augustinus* (the Second Augustine), he was a devoted adherent of the great Doctor of the Church, working to combine Augustinian thought with the writings of Dionysius the Areopagite (see **Pseudo-Dionysius the Areopagite**). He created the three stages of the contemplative life, the *cogitatio*, *meditatio*, and *contemplatio*, and authored numerous theological works, including *De Sacramentis Christianae Fidei* (*The Sacraments of the Christian Faith*), the *Didascalion* (a guide to knowledge), and studies in grammar and mathematics. His biblical commentaries addressed the historical nature of the Scriptures and the need to study them in their literal and factual sense.

Hugh the Great, St. (1029-1109) ● Abbot, reformer, and ecclesiast, known also as Hugh of Cluny. He entered Cluny at the age of fourteen and became abbot by 1049, succeeding by unanimous vote the famed St. Odilo. He was soon much respected, emerging as a trusted adviser to some nine popes; he assisted Nicholas II at the Council of Rome (1059) on papal elections, supported Gregory in the Gregorian Reform, and helped organize the First Crusade with Pope Urban II. Under Hugh, Cluny came to its heights of prestige and the cause of monasticism was advanced in the West. He acted as a mediator between Gregory and Emperor Henry IV, especially when Henry humiliated himself before the pontiff at Canossa in 1077. In 1063, Hugh was also instrumental in securing the condemnation of Berengarius of Tours. His writings, mostly lost, included a "Life of the Blessed Virgin." Pope Callistus II canonized him in 1120. Feast day: April 29.

Huguenots ● Name given to French Calvinist Protestants, first used in the 1500s. They were born out of the Reformation, deriving their name from a nickname based on a medieval romance about King Hugo; it was first applied to French Protestants around 1560. The Huguenots took their religious basis from John Calvin (1509-1564), formally organizing themselves on Calvinist lines at the Synod of Paris in 1539. There followed the bloody Wars of Religion (1562-1598) in which the Huguenots fought with the Catholics. The most infamous event of the period was the St. Bartholomew's Day Massacre (1572), a terrible episode that fostered the *Politiques*, the pro-toleration party that worked toward religious peace. This came in 1598 with the Edict of Nantes by King Henry IV, granting religious freedom for all. Under Richelieu, however, there were several Huguenot uprisings (1621-1622, 1625), ending with the crown's capture of La Rochelle in 1628 and the Peace of Alais (1629), stripping Huguenots of virtually all power. Under King Louis XIV, the Edict of Nantes was revoked (1685) and thousands of Huguenots fled to England, Germany, Switzerland, Holland, and America. The Huguenot Church of France was not recognized until 1802.

Humanae Vitae ● Encyclical issued on July 29, 1968, by Pope Paul VI (r. 1963-1978), it concerned itself with the

Church's teachings on marriage and related issues and condemned the use of artificial methods of contraception. Translated to mean "Of Human Life," the encyclical remains one of the most controversial papal pronouncements of the twentieth century and the source of often bitter disagreement among Catholic theologians. It has four main points: new aspects of a perennial problem; the competence of the magisterium to resolve the problem; those doctrinal principles to be maintained; and pastoral directives. Paul, in giving his declaration, restated the traditional teachings of the Catholic Church and was entirely in accord with the teachings and decrees of Vatican Council II promulgated but a few years before. The pope, however, also gave a clear presentation of the unerring magisterium, the basis of Church doctrine concerning the matter to be rooted in natural law, and the essential interconnectedness in the moral sense of abortion, sterilization, and contraception.

The encyclical had its origins in the pressing need by the 1960s to address the number of questions that had arisen concerning birth control owing to various scientific breakthroughs and the rapid proliferation of contraceptive use. Pope John XXIII appointed in 1963 the Commission on Population and Family Life. This was inherited by Pope Paul, who confirmed its work but was soon confronted by a controversy as to its findings, the world press — especially in the United states — playing up the dissent of members who advocated rescinding the Church's teaching, even though the original mandate did not include the provision for advising a reversal of policy. A delay followed the report of the commission, and in the end, Paul remained steadfast to the Church's traditional teaching. The response was vocal and contentious, the result in large measure of the disappointment of proponents of contraception to have their way. Since 1968, *Humanae vitae* has been the subject of

endless debate, but its core instruction has not been altered and has even served as the foundation of stronger denunciations of contraception by Pope John Paul II.

Humani Generis ● Encyclical issued on August 12, 1950, by Pope Pius XII; the Latin title means "The Human Race" and its full English title is "Warning against Attempts to Distort Catholic Truths." The document was an effort to present the need to maintain the integrity of Church teachings and the role of the Church in presenting them, especially in the face of modern types of thought. Pope Pius condemned a number of modern intellectual movements and warned against the degree of accommodation in facing or appropriating modes of new thought. Some elements to be opposed include a willingness to disregard the authority of the Church, a lack of identification of the Mystical Body of Christ with the Catholic Church in communion with the Holy See, contempt for Scholastic philosophy, and unduly liberal interpretations in exegesis. In examining advances in the sciences, the encyclical accepts the feasibility of the theory of biological evolution but rejects a similar theory of relativistic evolution of philosophy. (See also **Modernism**.)

Humbert of Silva-Candida (d. 1061) ● Cardinal and reformer, also known as Humbert of Moyen-Moutier. He became a monk at the monastery of Moyen-Moutier (or Moyenmoutier) in Lotharingia where he acquired a considerable reputation for learning and for promoting reform in the Church. In 1050, he was created cardinal bishop of Silva-Candida by Pope St. Leo IX, subsequently serving as an important adviser to the pontiff on reform. Humbert was especially concerned with the problems of simony, authoring the work *Adversus Simoniacos*. He was also sent by Pope Leo to Constantinople in 1054 as a papal representative to the Eastern Church in a hoped-for reunion of the Churches. Humbert, however, proved undiplomatic in the face of Byzantine intransigence and, on July 16, 1054, excommunicated Michael Cerularius, patriarch of Constantinople, and condemned the entire Greek Church. Under his friend, Pope Stephen IX, he was papal chancellor and librarian for the Roman Church.

Humiliati ● Movement of lay penitents that first developed in Lombardy during the 1100s. The *Humiliati* were men and women who led lives of severe austerity, poverty, and mortification, caring for the sick, including lepers, while calling for extensive reforms in the Church. Often confused with heretical groups such as the Cathars, Patarines, and Waldensians, the *Humiliati* suffered frequent persecution, usually by less discerning secular or ecclesiastical authorities. The Third Lateran Council (1179) forbade them from preaching, a decree upheld and enforced by Pope Lucius III, who excommunicated all violators of the ban. Pope Innocent III, however, gave recognition to the *Humiliati* in 1201, establishing three orders with canons and sisters as well as both celibate and married laity. Over time, the membership suffered from many abuses and St. Charles Borromeo was commissioned by Pope Pius IV to reform it. His efforts were vigorously opposed by a small group of fanatical *Humiliati*; he was attacked and nearly killed in 1569 by one of their ranks, Girolamo Donati Farina. Despite Borromeo's pleas for leniency, Farina and his co-conspirators were executed. By a bull in February 1571, Pope Pius V suppressed the order.

Hungary ● Republic in Central Europe that has long been a Christian land, the Church there surviving the dictatorial Communist regime that oppressed the Catholic faith from 1946 until 1990. It is uncertain when precisely missionaries began to preach among the nomadic tribes of the Danube Valley, but their work probably dated to the fourth century. They were unable to make a lasting impression, however, and there was no organized Church in the wild regions of what became Hungary when the Magyars first poured into the grassy plains of the Carpathians in the ninth century. As the Magyars became settled, Christian missionaries brought the faith from two directions: Germany and the Byzantine Empire. Under King St. Stephen I, a monarchy was established, and the king chose to adopt Western Christianity, forming relations with both the Holy Roman Empire and the Holy See. He founded an ecclesiastical hierarchy, creating a number of dioceses, including the enduring sees of Eger, Kalocsa, and Esztergom. For his labors on behalf of the Church, Pope Sylvester II (r. 999-1003) honored him with the title "Apostolic King." The Hungarian Church was henceforth quite strong and the bishops of the country wielded considerable political influence. The kings thus maintained generally good relations with the papacy, such as the decision of King Ladislas (r. 1077-1095) to support Pope Gregory VII (1073-1085) in his struggle with Emperor Henry IV during the Investiture Controversy.

A golden age in Hungarian history came under the long reign of Matthias Corvinus (1458-1490). After him, however, the kingdom began to deteriorate, culminating in the Battle of Mohács (1526) in which the Ottoman Turks destroyed a Christian army and seized most of Hungary. The Turks remained in control over the country for over a century and a half. Owing to the rule of the Turks and then the invasion of Reformation ideas, the Church underwent a period of severe trial. Its revival was spearheaded by Cardinal Péter Pázmány (1570-1637), who promoted a renewal of the Church and also founded a university at Trnava. Other work was undertaken by the Jesuits. Nevertheless, large parts of the population joined the Protestant cause.

The Turks were expelled in the late 1600s, but their mastery was replaced by the Habsburgs. In the reign of Maria Theresa (1740-1790), an anti-Church policy was adopted in order to effect state control over ecclesiastical affairs (see **Josephinism**). The 1800s saw chronic upheaval against Austrian rule, leading to the Compromise of 1867 by which Hungary gained its own constitution and parliament while part of the wider Austro-Hungarian monarchy. By the end of World War I, Austria-Hungary had been defeated and radicals toppled the government, creating a republic under the presidency of Count Mihály Károlyi. The Church in postwar Hungary began to flourish, an era ended in 1941 with the participation of the country in Hitler's invasion of Russia. The resulting war ended with the ruin of Hungary and the savage occupation by the Soviets who shipped thousands of Hungarians to Siberia for supporting Nazi Germany. Under the Soviet threat, Hungary's government fell to the Communists. In 1946, Catholic organizations were disbanded, followed by the suppression of Catholic schools, colleges, and other institutions. A wave of terror in 1948 saw the arrest of Cardinal József Mindszenty and the murder of Bishop Vilmos Apor of Györ. In 1950, the religious orders were suppressed; thousands of clergy were imprisoned and sent to labor camps, while others were exiled or murdered. The uprising of 1956 freed Cardinal Mindszenty, but the merciless Soviet response reinstalled the Communists. Mindszenty took up residence in the U.S. embassy in Budapest until 1971. An agreement was negotiated with the Holy See in 1964 to "settle" episcopal appointments, but this was soon violated. With the demise of the Communists, a new accord was signed in February 1990 between Hungary and the Holy See, allowing Pope John Paul II to reorganize the nation's hierarchy in May 1993. Currently, well over half the country is Catholic under the care of four archdioceses.

Hus, Jan (c. 1369-1415) ● Bohemian religious reformer who became the center of a major controversy in the fifteenth century foreshadowing the Reformation. Also known as John Huss, he was born in Husinec, studying at the University of Prague. Ordained in 1400, he soon acquired a wide reputation for his preaching. Attracted to the teachings of John Wycliffe, he became associated with Jerome of Prague and a vocal reform movement. His outspoken criticism of abuses in the Church led to his denunciation in Rome in 1407 and a ban on preaching laid upon him by Sbinko von Hasenburg, archbishop of Prague in 1408, upon instructions by Pope Innocent VII. The following year, however, King Wenceslaus IV ousted the Germans from the University of Prague and Hus was appointed rector, instituting Wycliffite doctrines. In 1410, the archbishop of Prague secured a bull ordering the destruction of all Wycliffite materials. Hus was excommunicated in 1410 and again in 1412, and Wenceslaus, needing to repair relations with the Church, removed him from the university. Hus fled to safety among the Czech nobility, writing his main work *De Ecclesiae* (1413; *On the Church*). Finally agreeing to submit himself to a general council, he accepted Sigismund's promise of safe-conduct and journeyed to the Council of Constance. There he was incarcerated by the Dominicans, condemned, and burned at the stake on July 6, 1415. His death enraged radical elements in Bohemia who declared him a martyr and a symbol of Bohemian nationalism. Within a few short years, Bohemia and Moravia were aflame with war. (See **Hussite War, Taborites**, and **Utraquism**.)

Hussite War ● Series of often bitter and bloody conflicts fought from 1419-1436 in Bohemia and Moravia caused by lingering anger in Bohemia over the execution in 1415 of Jan Hus, hostilities between the Hussite nationalist Bohemian party and the Catholic

German inhabitants of the region, and later the divided loyalties of the so-called Hussites (supporters of Hus) who had broken into two camps, the Utraquists (moderates) and the Taborites (radicals). The starting point of the war was in 1419 when the Hussites revolted against the succession of Emperor Sigismund to the throne of Bohemia. They defeated imperial armies in 1420 and 1422, thanks to their brilliant leaders, Jan Zizka and Prokop the Great. The Hussites invaded Silesia (1425-1426) and Franconia (1429-1430). The Council of Basel (1431-1449) offered to the Hussites the Compactata of Prague, giving them a means of returning to the Church. The Utraquists accepted, but the Taborites refused, causing more fighting, this time between the Hussites. The Utraquists were crushed at the Battle of Lipan (1434) and two years later Sigismund became king of Bohemia. The Hussite movement soon died out.

Hyacinth, St. (1185-1257) ● So-called Apostle of the North, a Christian missionary to Poland and Scandinavia. Known to the Poles as St. Iaccho, he was, according to tradition, the son of a nobleman and was born at the castle of Lanka, in Silesia, Poland. After studying at Cracow, Prague, and Bologna, he returned home to Poland for a brief time before setting out to visit Rome with his uncle, Ivo of Konski, bishop of Cracow. In Rome he met St. Dominic (1220) and was one of the first to receive from Dominic's hand at Santa Sabina the habit of the newly established Order of the Friars Preachers, the Dominicans. After making his vows, he was named superior of a band of missionaries to Poland. His labors took him throughout Poland, into Prussia, Pomerania, Lithuania, Denmark, Sweden, and Norway, possibly all the way to the Black Sea, although many details concerning the journey are unclear. Nevertheless, his missionary work was remarkably successful. After his death, the miracles attributed to him were vast in number. He was canonized by Pope Clement VIII in 1594. Feast day: August 17.

Hyginus, St. ● Pope from around 137-140. The eighth successor of Peter and the ninth pope, Hyginus was probably a Greek from Athens, according to the *Liber Pontificalis*. Accounts of the length of his reign and the exact dates vary, often considerably, although both the *Liber* and Eusebius list it as four years long; the Liberian Catalogue puts his pontificate at twelve years, an implausible figure. His reign was noted for the arrival in Rome of the Gnostic heresy that would plague the entire Church. Feast day: January 11.

I

Ibn Baddja (c. 1095-1139) ● Also called Avempace or Ibn Bajjah, a Spanish-Arab philosopher, scientist, and physician, an important predecessor to Averroës. He authored the unfinished treatise *Tadbir al-Mutawakhid* (*Regime of the Solitary*), in which he examined the union of the human soul with the divine. He also wrote a book on botany.

Ibn Gabirol (c. 1021-c. 1058) ● Jewish poet and Neoplatonic philosopher, known in the West as Avicebron and in full as Solomon Ben Judah ibn Gabirol. A revered literary figure during the so-called Jewish Golden Age in Moorish Spain, he attained considerable prominence as a poet, fluent in both Hebraic and Arabic literature. Ibn Gabirol's Neoplatonic writings, particularly his philosophical treatise *Fountains of Life*, influenced the development of philosophy in the West, most notably among Scholastic theologians and later with Baruch Spinoza.

Iceland ● Scandinavian island nation, possessing the oldest democratic state. Owing to their wide ranging martial and mercantile journeys, the Icelanders came into contact with the Christian faith even before missionaries arrived on the isle. The first traditionally accepted native missionary was Stefnir Thorgilsson, who around 996 was commissioned in his work by King Olaf Trygvesson. His work made possible the decision of the Icelandic Parliament, the Althing, to suppress paganism. The actual conversion of the Icelanders, however, took nearly half a century, confirmation of the position of the Church given in 1056 by the appointment of the first bishop, at Skalholt. This see was soon joined by another at Holar. Initially under the jurisdiction of the archbishop of Hamburg, the sees were later placed under the sees of Lund and then Trondheim (1152). Monasteries were also established by the Benedictines and Augustinians, the monks making lasting contributions to the intellectual and artistic life of the island. The Reformation in Iceland was preceded in the fifteenth century by a series of political struggles, plagues, and earthquakes whose demoralizing effects were only aggravated by the unfortunate degree of corruption and neglect on the part of the local bishops. Lutheranism was introduced by several followers of Martin Luther, receiving royal favor from King Christian III of Denmark and Norway, an ardent promoter of reform. Oejmundur Palsson, the last bishop of Skalholt, was imprisoned and his long-time rival Jon Arason, bishop of Holar, was executed on November 7, 1550. The eradication of the Church was achieved gradually, with the retention for many years of the basic elements of ceremony, the Latin usage (until 1686), and the ecclesiastical divisions. Lutheranism, however, was the state religion. Religious freedom was finally granted in 1874. An apostolic vicariate was established in 1929 by Pope Pius XI, replaced in 1968 by a diocese. There is currently a very small Catholic population.

Iconoclastic Controversy ● Also called the Iconoclast Controversy or Iconoclasm, the long dispute within the Byzantine Empire over the veneration of icons that lasted from around 736-842. The Iconoclasts (meaning "breakers of images") used the biblical ban on graven images as their argument against icons, finding considerable support among the Monophysites, Manichaeans, Paulicians, and certain areas of the empire such as Asia Minor where the influence of Islam was being increasingly felt among the populace. While icons remained extremely important to most citizens of the empire, Emperor Leo III the Isaurian in 726 surrendered to Iconoclast pressure and declared all images, icons included, to be idolatrous. His decision was also politically motivated, since the decree permitted greater involvement of the state in ecclesiastical affairs and opened up the Jewish and Muslim population to increased conversions as it removed a long-standing impediment to any embrace of Christianity. Despite widespread discontent, Leo's son, Constantine V (r. 741-775), continued the policy. Leo IV (r. 775-780) and his wife, Irene, who would serve as a regent for Constantine VI, reversed the decree, however, summoning the Seventh General Council at Nicaea in 787 where the icons were restored.

The so-called Second Iconoclastic Controversy began in 814 under Leo V the Armenian (r. 813-820). Icons were to be removed from churches and all buildings, and monks who refused were sent into exile, put in prison, or executed. A respite from oppression came under Michael II (r. 820-829), but his son Theophilus (r. 829-842) launched another round of persecutions. After his death, his widow Theodora, as regent for Michael III, ordered an end to all Iconoclastic practices, a decree widely celebrated by the devout Byzantines that is still celebrated in the Eastern Orthodox Church. The position of the Western Church was firm throughout the controversy that Iconoclasm should be condemned. Pope Gregory III held two synods in Rome against the decrees of Leo III the Isaurian (731), and Pope Adrian I sent legates to the Council of Nicaea (787) to express his support. The entire affair continued to strain relations between the Eastern and Western Churches and was an important event in the schism between them. (See also **Caesaropapism**.)

Ignatius, St. (c. 35-107) ● Bishop of Antioch and an important early martyr. He was probably a Syrian and was possibly a disciple of Sts. Peter and Paul or St. John; it has been proposed that he was the child whom Christ placed among the Apostles in Matthew (18:1-6). Calling himself *Theophoras* (God-bearer), he was either the second bishop of Antioch (according to Origen) or the third (according to Eusebius) after Euodius. Arrested by Roman authorities and sent for execution in Rome, Ignatius was placed in the custody of several soldiers. On the road to the Eternal City, Ignatius began writing epistles (or letters) to the Christian communities of Ephesus, Magnesia, Tralles, Rome, Philadelphia, Smyrna, and a farewell letter to Bishop Polycarp. His letters are of great value on the state of the Church at the time. Ignatius reaffirms the profound honors of martyrdom — "Let me follow the example of the suffering of my God" — and the need to remain firm in the faith. He was granted his wish to die as a devout follower of Christ by being thrown to the wild animals of the Roman circus. The most beautiful of the epistles was that to the Romans. Throughout Church history, the epistles of Ignatius have been held in great esteem. Feast day: October 17.

Ignatius Loyola, St. (1491-1556) ● Founder of the Jesuits, as the Society of Jesus is popularly called. Born Iñigo López de Loyola, he was the youngest son of noble parents; his birthplace was in the family castle of Loyola in Azpeitia, Basque province, Spain. After an education commensurate with his rank, he entered military service. In 1521, at the siege of Pampeluna (Pamplona), he was wounded in the leg by a French cannonball and spent a long time in convalescence; he would remain partially crippled for the rest of his life. During this long and painful period, he underwent a remarkable change, reading the Life of Christ and numerous works on the saints. By March 1522, he was intent on becoming a saint, departing the Loyola castle and embarking on a pilgrimage to the Benedictine monastery of Montserrat. There he confessed his past sins, clothed himself in sackcloth, and placed his sword on the altar of the BVM, dedicating himself to her as a knight. He then went to Manresa where he lived for a time (1522-1523) in a cave. Overcoming scruples, he devoted himself to prayer, mortification, and acquiring deep spiritual insight. As a result of his considerable mystical and spiritual growth, he was able to begin work on his famed *Spiritual Exercises*.

Ignatius left Manresa in February 1523, journeying to Rome and then Jerusalem where he survived entirely through alms and trust in God. Concerned for his welfare, however, the Franciscans suggested that he leave the Holy Land, whereupon he returned to Barcelona. Realizing that he needed to improve his education to make himself better prepared for assisting others, Ignatius spent the next eleven years in studies: at Alcalá de Henares (1526-1527), Salamanca (1527-1528), and Paris (1528-1535). On March 14, 1534, he received a master of arts degree. During this period, Ignatius also gathered around him a group of followers who, like him, were committed to giving their lives to the greater glory of the Church. They came together on August 15, 1534, in the chapel of the Benedictine Monastery of St. Peter, on Montmarte, Paris, where they each took vows of poverty, chastity, and, if possible, a missionary pilgrimage to the Holy Land, with service to the Holy See. At first calling his fledgling association a *compañia*, or company, he changed it to *societas*. So was born the Society of Jesus, the Jesuits.

Ignatius and his six companions went to Italy in 1537 where, on June 24, they were ordained. It soon became clear that a pilgrimage was impossible, so they offered themselves to the Holy Father. Given oral approval by Pope Paul III (r. 1534-1549) in 1539, they drew up a statement for the order, which received papal approbation in 1540 of the *formula instituti* in the bull *Regimini militantis ecclesiae*. Ignatius was elected general the following year and, on April 22, 1541, he received the first solemn profession in the Basilica of St. Paul-Outside-the-Walls in Rome. For the next fifteen years, he continued work on developing and improving the order, drawing up the constitution for the society from 1547-1550. Ignatius founded the Roman College, which later became the Gregorian University; the next year he launched the German College to help prepare priests for endeavors in those lands most under the siege of Protestantism. He died in Rome on July 31, 1556.

One of the boldest innovators in the history of the Church, Ignatius created a religious order distinctly new in its organization, character, and rules. It was well-suited to assist the Church at the time of terrible crisis caused by the Reformation through its loyalty to the Holy See, its stress on education and spiritual development, and its joyous embrace of missionary enterprises. His *Spiritual Exercises*, begun at Manresa but developed over his life, provides a profound set of meditations and rules that will lead to holiness. They have long been recommended as an intensive and successful program of spiritual renewal, taking as their main principles the first declaration: "Man was created to praise, reverence, and serve our Creator and Lord, and by this means to save his soul." Beatified by Pope Paul V on July 27, 1609, he was canonized by Pope Gregory XV on March 12, 1622. Pope Pius XI proclaimed him to be the patron of all spiritual exercises in 1922. Feast day: July 31.

Ildefonsus, St. (d. 667) ● Archbishop of Toledo, author of important writings on the Blessed Virgin. Originally from a noble family, he was possibly a student of St. Isidore of Seville, entering the Benedictine monastery of Agalia, near Toledo. He later became abbot there, attending the Councils of Toledo (653 and 655) before becoming archbishop in 657. Ildefonsus was responsible for a large number of works, of which only four are extant: *Annotationes de Cognitione Baptismi*, a valuable study on the education of catechumens with much material from Augustine, Isidore of Seville, and Gregory the Great; *De Viris Illustribus*, a history of the Spanish Church; *De Itenere Deserti quo Pergitur post Baptismum*, a compilation of the *Annotationes* that unites the progress of the soul after baptism to the wanderings of the Jews in the desert; and *De Virginitate S. Mariae*, a treatise on the Virgin that was an expression of Ildefonsus's deep devotion, the first document on the BVM to come from the Spanish Church. Ildefonsus was also a musician. Feast day: January 23.

Immaculate Conception ● Doctrine affirming the freedom of the Blessed Virgin from sin from the very moment of her conception. As the formal definition of the doctrine proclaimed by Pope Pius IX (December 8, 1854) stated: "We, by the authority of Jesus Christ, Our Lord, of the Blessed Apostles, Peter and Paul and by Our Own, declare, pronounce, and define that the doctrine which holds that the Blessed Virgin Mary, at the first instant of conception, by a singular privilege and grace of the omnipotent God, in consideration of the merits of Jesus Christ, the Savior of mankind was preserved from all stain of original sin, has been revealed by God, and therefore is to be firmly and constantly believed by all the faithful" (*Ineffabilis Deus*).

The doctrine of the Immaculate Conception of Our Lady was not explicitly taught by either the Latin or Greek Fathers, although they made it clear that she was utterly without stain or sin through her purity and holiness. St. Ephraem, for example, declared in the fourth century, "Thou and Thine mother are the only ones who are utterly beautiful in every way. For in Thee, O Lord, there is no stain, and in Your mother no stain." They also compared her to Eve, leaving no question that Mary was free from sin and thereby making implicit her Immaculate Conception.

The Middle Ages brought more specific examination of her sinless state. In the East, the doctrine found wide acceptance and was celebrated as early the seventh century under the title of the Conception of St. Anne. In the West, however, opinion was sharply divided as to whether she had been freed of sin before or after the infusion of her soul into the body. The chief opponent of the concept of an Immaculate Conception was St. Bernard of Clairvaux (d. 1153), who argued that she must have been sanctified after conception, making her holy by birth, not by conception. He was supported by Sts. Thomas Aquinas and Albertus Magnus in the thirteenth century. They were challenged by other theologians, most importantly from among the Franciscans. The foremost of these was the great Franciscan John Duns Scotus (d. 1308), who formulated the concept of preredemption. For his triumphant work, Duns Scotus is called the "Herald of the Immaculate Conception."

The Feast of the Immaculate Conception was approved in 1476 by Sixtus IV and in 1568 it was extended to the entire Church by Pope St. Pius V, who just the year before had excommunicated Michel Baius (1513-1589) for denying that Mary was free from original sin. To give a final definition of the Immaculate Conception, Pope Pius IX launched a commission of twenty theologians in 1848 to study the entire question. The next year, he asked for the opinions of bishops from around the world; they responded almost entirely in favor of the doctrine. Pius then issued the document *Ineffabilis Deus*, which made official Church teaching that the BVM was free from sin at the first moment of her conception by virtue of special grace from God, making her free from the original sin that afflicts all humanity and thus is a recipient in a foreseen manner, of the redemptive merits of Christ. Her preredemption is stated by theologians to have been the infusion of grace at the moment of her soul's entry into her body. This special exemption also made the BVM free of concupiscence and of all sin throughout her entire life.

Index of Forbidden Books ● In Latin, *Index Librorum Prohibitorum.* A list of books and writings that were considered to be contrary to the faith and morals of the Church and that Catholics were forbidden to read. While the Index of Forbidden Books was first officially issued under Pope Paul IV in 1557, the Church had long encouraged the faithful to read good books while discouraging any association with objectionable material. This was done in a formal sense as early as the fifth century when Pope Innocent I in 405 produced a dual list of suggested books for the faithful and condemned works to be avoided. Pope Gelasius I also issued a list in 495. Throughout the Middle Ages, control could be exercised to a high degree owing to the temporal position of the Church and the relatively limited number of books. As printing produced greater numbers of works, Church officials grew increasingly concerned that the proliferation of publishing could lead to works of questionable orthodoxy, outright error, or immoral content.

In 1515, at the Fifth Lateran Council, a law was decreed requiring Catholics to receive approval for any book that was concerned with matters of religion or morality. This was followed in 1557 by the first actual Index of Forbidden Books under Paul IV, published through the Congregation of the Inquisition. In 1571, a central authority was created by St. Pius V to oversee the maintenance of the list. This was the Congregation of the Index. It possessed the right to add new books and to revise the list as circumstances warranted. Officials who examined books were to follow a specific set of guidelines and were to go to considerable lengths to be objective. Nevertheless, by the time of Pope Leo XIII (r. 1878-1903), there were over three thousand books on the Index of Forbidden Books. That pope in 1900 introduced certain changes into the process of review. The congregation survived until 1966 when it was abolished by Pope Paul VI, who also did away with all associated excommunications.

India ● History of Christianity in India is traditionally said to date from the first century A.D. when the Apostle St. Thomas preached in the Kerala region. The converts he supposedly made became the so-called Thomas Christians (see **Malabar Rite**), who were certainly in existence by the fourth century. They were in contact with the Nestorians in the Near East, most notably the patriarch of Baghdad and subsequently joined the Syrian (Jacobite) rite. Thus, when the Portuguese reached India in the early sixteenth century, they found over two hundred thousand Christians in India. From 1510 and the conquest of Goa, efforts were made to bring the Thomas Christians into the Latin rite. While many joined the Roman Church, a large group entered into schism during the seventeenth century. Some were converted in later years through the efforts of the Carmelites. In 1896, the Uniate Thomas Christians received their own bishops.

Meanwhile, a number of religious orders — the Jesuits, Franciscans, Dominicans, and others — carried out missionary programs. The Jesuits from 1542 were most active, thanks to such notables as St. Francis Xavier and Roberto de' Nobili whose innovative methods in adopting Hindu customs and manners were largely criticized (see also **Malabar Rites**). Jesuits were invited to the court of Mogul Emperor Akbar (r. 1556-1605), sending three missions from 1579-1595. They would continue to enjoy the favor of various princes throughout India until the Society of Jesus was expelled in 1759 by the Portuguese.

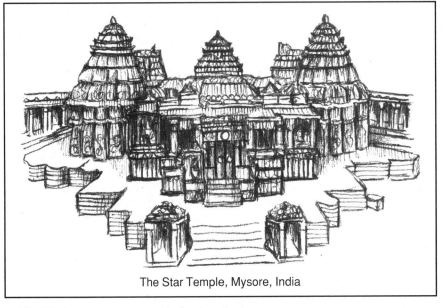

The Star Temple, Mysore, India

The Portuguese were granted extensive rights over the Church in India by the papacy, including the power to nominate bishops for Eastern territories. In 1557-1558, the archdiocese of Goa was established, with two suffragan sees, to advance missionary work. By 1572, there were nearly three hundred thousand Catholic converts. Portuguese inefficiency, however, prompted the Sacred Congregation of Propaganda to appoint vicars apostolic, a move that caused conflict with the Portuguese government which jealously guarded its rights to make appointments. Finally, from 1838-1857, there occurred the Goa Schism. Such was the size of the Catholic population by 1886 (over one million) that Pope Leo XIII (r. 1878-1903) restored the regular hierarchy for India and Ceylon.

While missionary work was impeded in the territories controlled by the English (the British East India Co.) from 1757-1858, other Indian states, under native rulers, prohibited Christian preaching. The dislike of the English rule caused many Indians to regard Christianity in general with suspicion and to mistrust and be hostile to all European missionaries, even non-British Catholics, whom they equated with foreign interests. This antagonism continued in the early twentieth century with the rise of Indian nationalism and hindered the efforts of the Church to increase conversions. The main Catholic populations are in Goa and Kerala; elsewhere, the Church remains largely missionary in disposition, as the vast bulk of the populace is Hindu. Nevertheless, the Church in India has been dedicated to alleviating the staggering poverty of the country; the most famous of all Church figures in the country is Mother Teresa, Nobel Prize winner and founder of the Missionaries of Charity. There are today over fourteen million Catholics. The Church in neighboring Pakistan (independent since 1948) has its own hierarchy (since 1950). The Catholic population in the Muslim country numbers over nine hundred thousand. Joseph Cordeiro (b. 1918) became the first native-born archbishop of Karachi in 1958; he was made a cardinal in 1973 by Pope Paul VI.

Ineffabilis Deus ● Constitution issued on December 8, 1854, by Pope Pius IX that gave definition to the dogma of the Immaculate Conception. (See **Immaculate Conception** for details.)

Infallibilists ● Name used for the majority of bishops and theologians at the First Vatican Council (1869-1870) who supported the principle that the pope, when speaking *ex cathedra* on matters of faith and morality, was infallible due to the special grace of the office of the successors to St. Peter. While opposed by some prelates and liberal elements, the Infallibilists, headed by such respected figures as Cardinal Henry Manning, archbishop of Westminster, ultimately triumphed and secured the promulgation of the decree *Pastor Aeternus* on July 18, 1870. (See also **Infallibility** [following entry] and **Vatican Council I.**)

Infallibility ● The inability to err in teaching on matters of faith and morals. Infallibility should not be confused with inspiration, which implies that God is the chief author of a work that is inspired while infallible denotes providential assistance in which a person is helped but remains the author of an infallible statement. Infallibility may thus be defined as the reception of divine assistance granted to the Church whereby she is preserved from error in teaching on matters of faith and morals. Theology delineates three types of infallibility: the Church, the episcopal college, and the pope. It is taught that God has bestowed upon his people, meaning the Church, a shared infallibility that functions within clear parameters: it is limited to faith and morals; the whole people of God hold a doctrinal point related to these matters; and it is entirely dependent upon the grace of the

Holy Spirit. The Second Vatican Council, in *Lumen Gentium*, declared: ". . . The body of the faithful as a whole, anointed as they are by the Holy One (cf. Jn. 2:20, 27), cannot err in matters of belief. Thanks to a supernatural sense of the faith which characterizes the People as a whole, it manifests this unerring quality when, 'from the bishops down to the last member of the laity,' it shows universal agreement in matters of faith and morals. . . . God's People accepts not the word of men but the very Word of God (cf. 1 Th. 2:13). It clings without fail to the faith once delivered to the saints (cf. Jude 13), penetrates it more deeply by accurate insights, and applies it more thoroughly to life. All this it does under the lead of a sacred teaching authority to which it loyally defers" ("Dogmatic Constitution on the Church," No. 12).

As is clear from the Council Fathers, the infallibility of the Church is a prelude to and is entirely dependent upon the magisterium, the Church's "sacred teaching authority" vested in the bishops, the successors of the Apostles, under the pope, the Successor of Peter and Vicar of Christ, with whom they are in communion. *Lumen Gentium* discussed episcopal infallibility, teaching that the bishops are infallible when they function as a college — provided they are in union with the pope and under his authority or gathered together into a general council in communion with the pontiff and summoned by him.

The most widely known infallibility is that possessed by the pope, borne by him as the successor of Peter. He may speak infallibly on matters of faith and morals through the assistance of the Holy Spirit and under certain conditions, specifically that he make the pronouncement *ex cathedra*: he speaks as pastor and shepherd of all the faithful, with full authority and not in the sense of delivering private opinion as a theologian or expounding some point to a specific segment of the people of God; he speaks on matters of faith and morals; and the doctrine being proclaimed is for the universal Church.

Infallibility has always been present in the Church, as is seen in the sacred writings: John 16:13, Acts 15:28, and Galatians 1:9. A definition was given by Vatican Council I, promulgated on July 18, 1870. The issue and the terms of the definition were hotly debated by many who took part and were attacked by some theologians of the period (e.g., Johannes Döllinger, author of the Quirinus Letters, and Lord Acton), but once proclaimed, the vast majority of prelates accepted the doctrine of infallibility without reservation. Vatican II affirmed the doctrine with a firm declaration in *Lumen Gentium*.

Innocent I, St. ● Pope from 401-417, during whose pontificate Rome was sacked by the Visigoths under Alaric. Innocent was born at Albano, Italy, and was possibly the son of St. Anastasius I. He served Anastasius as his deacon and was elected his successor on December 21, 401. A pontiff of considerable ability, personal strength, and morality, Innocent proved an important figure in establishing the primacy of the Roman see. He demanded, for example, that all disputes within the Church be settled by him, setting important precedents in jurisdiction and authority. In 404, he called for the restoration of St. John Chrysostom as patriarch of Constantinople and later he secured ecclesiastical control over Illyricum, which had passed under Eastern jurisdiction in 388. The heresy of Pelagianism was condemned in 417 and its founder, Pelagius, was excommunicated. Innocent also emerged as a formidable political figure, working to have Emperor Honorius issue decrees against the Donatists. In 410, however, Innocent could not prevent the sack of Rome by the Visigoths, despite his efforts at Ravenna to negotiate a settlement. Returning to Rome in 412 after being spared the horrors of the invasions, his absence was considered providential. Innocent is considered by many

historians to be the first pope, his predecessors ruling with less authority, being counted as Bishops of Rome. Feast day: July 28.

Innocent II ● Pope from 1130-1143. Born Gregorio Papareschi Dei Guidoni, he was a native of Rome. Appointed cardinal by Pope Callistus II in 1122, he served as the pontiff's ambassador to the Concordat of Worms and was elected successor to Honorius II on February 14, 1130. His pontificate was overshadowed by his struggle with the rival claimant Cardinal Pietro Pierleoni, who took the name Anacletus II. Innocent was forced to flee Italy for France and only with the aid of St. Bernard of Clairvaux and German King Lothair II and King Henry I of England was he successful in securing the papal throne. Anacletus continued to trouble Innocent until the antipope's death in 1138. His ally, King Roger II of Sicily, however, sponsored another rival, Victor IV, who ultimately resigned at the behest of Bernard. Roger later captured Innocent (1139) and compelled him to acknowledge the king's rule of Sicily. Innocent also upheld the condemnation of Peter Abelard by the Council of Sens (1140) and configured the rules of the Knights Templars.

Innocent III ● Pope from 1198-1216. One of the foremost pontiffs of the Middle Ages who labored to restore papal supremacy and to bring reform to the Church, he was born Lothair of Segni at Gavignano Castle in Campagna di Roma and was cardinal deacon at Sts. Sergio and Bacco at the time of his unanimous election on January 8, 1198, the very day that his predecessor, Celestine III, died. From the start of his reign, Innocent assumed an exalted position for the papacy, using the title Vicar of Christ to explain his claims of being "set midway between God and man, below God but above man"; however, he stressed his spiritual authority and was reluctant to interfere in temporal matters save where moral issues were concerned. Nevertheless, political involvements and crises filled his reign. He reduced the independence of the Italian aristocracy to restore his control over the Papal States, compelled Philip II Augustus of France to reconcile with his wife, and forced King John of England to accept Stephen Langton as archbishop of Canterbury. The Fourth Crusade, which he supported, turned against his will into a sack of Constantinople, in 1204, but Innocent accepted their overthrow of the Byzantine Empire in the hope that it might lead to a reunification of the Eastern and Western Churches, appointing Thomas Morasini to be the Latin patriarch of Constantinople. An ardent promoter of reform, Innocent introduced changes to the Curia, encouraged reforming councils, and insisted on proper behavior by the clergy. He issued more than six thousand letters and decretals and summoned the Fourth Lateran Council in 1215. His support of the Franciscans and Dominicans made the mendicant orders a viable and recognized source of revitalization within the Church. The Albigensians and other heretics, however, earned his condemnation, but it was only after the murder of his legate in 1208 that Innocent was willing to launch a crusade against them, the so-called Albigensian Crusade. He died suddenly in Perugia on July 16, 1216.

Innocent IV ● Pope from 1243-1254. Known originally as Sinibaldo Fieschi, he was from Genoa, serving as the bishop of Albenga, vice-chancellor of the Roman

Pope Innocent III

Church, cardinal priest of St. Lawrence, and rector of the March of Ancona before his election on June 25, 1243, as successor to Celestine IV after an eighteen-month vacancy. His pontificate was known principally for his often bitter feud with the Hohenstaufen rulers of the Holy Roman Empire, particularly Emperor Frederick II. Forced to flee from Italy after convoking the Council of Lyons (1245), Innocent secured Frederick's excommunication by the council and was instrumental in the rise of Henry Raspe, landgrave of Thuringia, as the German anti-king in 1246. After Frederick's death in 1250, Innocent worked against the other Hohenstaufens, Conrad IV and Manfred, although their ultimate destruction was not brought about until the reign of Clement IV (1265-1268). While criticized for favoritism and heavy taxation to fund his wars, Innocent did launch efforts to evangelize Islam and encouraged King Louis IX (St. Louis) to embark on the ill-fated Seventh Crusade. He also sent missionaries to convert the Mongols.

Innocent V ● Pope from January to June 1276. Known as Peter of Tarentaise, he was the first pontiff to come from the ranks of the Dominicans. Originally from Tarentaise, France, he entered the Dominicans around 1240, studying at Paris from 1255-1259; he later taught there (1259-1264 and 1267-1269). Named French provincial of the order (c. 1264-1267 and 1269-1272), he became archbishop of Lyons in 1271 and a cardinal (c. 1273) by Gregory X whom he succeeded on January 21, 1276. A close friend of St. Bonaventure, Innocent was a pious pontiff who tried to unite the Eastern and Western Churches and launch another crusade to rescue the Holy Land. With Sts. Thomas Aquinas and Albertus Magnus he had a rule of studies for the Dominican order drafted (c. 1259); he also authored a well-known commentary on Lombard's *Sentences*. Pope Leo XIII beatified him in 1898.

Innocent VI ● Pope from 1352-1362. Born Etienne Aubert at Monts, France, he was initially a professor of civil law at Toulouse, before entering the clergy. Subsequently serving as the bishop of Noyon (1338) and Clermont (1340), he became a cardinal in 1342 and cardinal bishop of Ostia in 1352 at the command of Pope Clement VI. He succeeded Clement on December 18, 1352, as one of the Avignon popes. His pontificate at Avignon was preoccupied with two main issues: the deteriorating conditions in the Papal States and the Curia at Avignon. Using Cardinal Gil Albornoz, whom he named vicar-general of the Papal States, Innocent reestablished his authority in the States, a move of future significance, since it prepared the way for the return of the popes to Rome (1378). He introduced numerous reforms to the Curia, but Avignon was increasingly unsuitable as the seat of the papacy. Innocent also negotiated the Treaty of Brétigny (1360) that ended the first phase of the Hundred Years' War between France and England, and attempted to negotiate a union of the Eastern and Western Churches.

Innocent VII ● Pope from 1404-1406. Born Cosimo Gentili de' Migliorati at Sulmona, Italy, he was a teacher at Perugia and Padua prior to his elevation as archbishop of Ravenna (1387), bishop of Bologna (1389), and cardinal (1389), the latter post given to him by Boniface IX whom he succeeded on October 17, 1404. He was troubled from the start by the Great Schism (1378-1417) that had caused the election of the antipope Benedict XIII. Innocent's efforts to end the schism by convoking a council at Rome in 1404 failed, in large measure because of the rebellious attitude of the Romans.

Innocent VIII ● Pope from 1484-1492. Born in Genoa to a Roman senatorial family, Giovanni Battista Cibo was named a cardinal in 1475 by Pope Sixtus IV whom he

Tomb of Pope Innocent VIII

succeeded on August 29, 1484, through the help of Sixtus's nephew Cardinal Giuliano della Rovere (the future Pope Julius II). Innocent was not a particularly good pontiff, acquiring a reputation for immorality and corruption. After depleting the papal treasury to pay for several wars, he sold offices and created new ones to raise money. The papal court was also known as a colorful, profligate center of princes, both secular and ecclesiastical. After his call for a crusade against the Ottoman Turks was unanswered, he negotiated with Sultan Bayezid II, receiving the sultan's brother as a hostage. Innocent also issued the bull *Summis desiderantes* (1484) condemning witchcraft.

His successor was the infamous Borgia, Pope Alexander VI.

Innocent IX ● Pope for two months in 1591. Known originally as Giovanni Antonio Fachinetti, he was born in Bologna, serving as bishop of Nicastro and then papal ambassador to Venice in 1566. After holding several posts under Pope Gregory XIII, he became a cardinal in 1583 and was one of the foremost figures in the pontificate of Gregory XIV (1590-1591). Chosen his successor on October 29, he worked to improve sanitation in the Borgo. He fell ill in the middle of December and died on December 30.

Innocent X ● Pope from 1644-1655. Born Gian Battista Pamphili at Rome, he studied at the Roman College and was a judge at the Rota (1604-1621) before serving as a nuncio to Spain (1626) under Pope Urban VIII, who made him a cardinal *in petto* (i.e., secretly) in 1627; the formal announcement came in 1629. His election as successor to the Barberini pontiff Urban came about through those cardinals anxious to remove the former pope's policies. This Innocent did, condemning, for example, the Peace of Westphalia (1648), which ended the Thirty Years' War, confirming the protest of the papal legate Fabio Chigi in the bull *Zelus domus Dei* (1648). The papal declaration was roundly ignored, however, by a war-weary Europe. He issued the bull *Cum occasione* (1653), which denounced the five propositions from the *Augustinus* of Cornelius Jansen (or Jansenius). His court was dominated by his rapacious sister-in-law Donna Olimpia Maidalchini, a much disliked and feared influence on papal policy. Fabio Chigi, his secretary of state, was named his successor as Alexander VII.

Innocent XI ● Pope from 1676-1689. Known originally as Benedetto Odescalchi, he was born in Como and studied with the Jesuits before mastering law at Rome and Naples, receiving his doctorate in 1639. Made a cardinal in 1645 by Pope Innocent X, legate of Ferrara in 1648, and bishop of Novera in 1650, he acquired a considerable reputation for personal piety, immense charity, and honesty. Retiring in 1654 on the grounds of ill health, his election as successor to Clement X came as a genuine surprise. He would accept only after the cardinals agreed to a fourteen-point program of reform. Much of his pontificate was spent countering the absolutist tendencies of King Louis XIV in dealing with the Church; Innocent opposed Gallicanism, especially the Gallican Articles (1682). Accepting that the Protestants would have to be recognized and dealt with, he disagreed with Louis on the revocation of the Edict of Nantes (1685) and the persecution of the Huguenots. A strong reforming pope, he utilized intelligent taxation, stern cost-cutting, and the aid of Catholic courts to restore papal finances. Doctrinally, he condemned sixty-five laxist propositions of moral theology in the bull *Sanctissimus Dominus* (1679) and sixty-eight quietist propositions in *Coelestis Pastor* (1687), despite his friendship with Miguel de Molinos. A gifted and highly moral pope, Innocent was considered for beatification in the early eighteenth century, but his cause was delayed owing to his somewhat ambiguous stand on Jansenism; he was finally beatified in 1956 by Pope Pius XII.

Innocent XII ● Pope from 1691-1700. Known originally as Antonio Pignatelli, he was born in Spinazzola, Italy, studying at the Jesuit College in Rome. He subsequently served as papal governor of Viterbo, papal ambassador to Tuscany, and papal representative to Poland and Austria. Made a cardinal in 1681 by Innocent XI, he was elected pope on July 12, 1691, after an interregnum of five months. A compromise candidate, he took the name Innocent and vowed to emulate Innocent XI (r. 1676-1689).

Like his predecessor and namesake, Innocent launched a serious effort at reform in the Papal States and Rome, calling for financial moderation and justice for all. Through his pious and diplomatic nature, he succeeded in having King Louis XIV rescind the Gallican Articles (1682) in return for the right to administer vacant French sees. At the behest of Louis, he issued the brief *Cum alias* denouncing quietist propositions in *Maximes des saints* by the French archbishop François Fénélon, a condemnation that extended quickly to all of quietism, including the work of the mystic Madame Guyon. Innocent also passed the decree *Decet Romanum pontificem* (1692), which curbed papal nepotism by proposing that no pope should grant offices or estates to relatives and that only one, presumably deserving, family member should be made a prelate.

Innocent XIII ● Pope from 1721-1724. A noble by birth, Michelangelo dei Conti was the son of the duke of Poli. After schooling at Ancona, he studied with the Jesuits and then entered papal service in the Curia. A papal ambassador to Switzerland and Portugal, he was made a cardinal in 1706 by Pope Clement XI. His election on May 8, 1721, as successor to the long-reigning Clement was unanimous. Eager to improve relations with the major courts of Europe, he granted sovereignty over Naples to Emperor Charles VI and satisfied the French by advancing Guillaume Dubois. He recognized the Old Pretender, James (III), as the true king of England, promising him subsidies upon the return of England to the Church. Innocent also commanded the Jesuits, whom he distrusted, to obey Clement XI's ban on the so-called Chinese rites.

In Petto ● See **Petto, In**.

Inquisition ● Special ecclesiastical tribunal first established in the thirteenth century to help curb the spread of heretical doctrines in Christendom, particularly the Albigensians and Cathars. The Inquisition was initially intended to deal with heresy in a technical, legal method, its penalties remaining entirely spiritual, the most severe being excommunication. The severity of the crisis, however, in the thirteenth century was such that Church officials began to work on close cooperation with secular leaders to inflict increasingly harsh treatment against heretics and those suspected of un-Orthodox tendencies. In 1232, Emperor Frederick II issued an edict against heresy that prompted Pope Gregory IX in 1233 to name special papal inquisitors. This special court was staffed with Franciscans and particularly Dominicans (who had the nickname "Watchdogs of Orthodoxy"), turning heretics over to civil authorities for torture and imprisonment. The contemporary understanding of the need for the Inquisition, coupled with the willingness of Church officials to condone violence and torture, stemmed from the then sincere belief that heresy threatened the good not only of the Church but the state in general. Heresy was thus a crime against the state and the Church. While technically the local board of Inquisition was under the authority of the diocesan bishop, its direction was given by the papacy, and it functioned at the will of the Holy See in France, Italy, and Germany.

The formal permission for the use of torture and various punishments was given by Pope Innocent IV in the bull *Ad extirpanda* with the aim of shattering the stubbornness of defendants and forcing them to admit possible guilt. For those who confessed quickly, penalties ranged from a pilgrimage to the confiscation of goods. Those found guilty of heresy were imprisoned, lost all of their possessions, and could be executed. The normal agent of execution was the local secular authority, and the customary method was burning at the stake. The Inquisition reached its height outside of Spain in the thirteenth century, declining in usage during the next century. In 1542, Pope Paul III created the Congregation of the Inquisition (officially called the *Sacra Congregatio Romanae et Universalis Inquisitionis seu Sancti Officii*) as the final court of appeal. Initially headed by six cardinals, it was reorganized in 1587 under Pope Sixtus V, who increased the number of cardinals to thirteen. Under Pope St. Pius X, in 1908, its name was changed to the *Congregatio Sancti Officii* (Congregation of the Holy Office). Pope Paul VI in 1965 gave it the new name *Congregatio pro Doctrina Fidei* (Congregation for the Doctrine of the Faith), with the task of ensuring, in a positive fashion, the teachings of the Church in such important areas as morality and theology.

Inquisition, Spanish ● Name used for the Inquisition that was established in Spain in the late fifteenth century. It would become a feared element in Spanish life, remaining so until the nineteenth century. The Inquisition was launched in 1478 when Pope Sixtus IV gave his approval to the formation of a tribunal with the aim of rooting out insincere converts among the Jews and Moors who had been recently brought under Christian rule as a result of the *Reconquista*. Technically begun by their Catholic Majesties, Ferdinand and Isabella, the Inquisition's first head was Tomás de Torquemada, a Dominican who would bear the dread title of grand inquisitor. Overall administration was in the hands of the Council of the Inquisition, its members named by the king. The council was assisted by a number of local boards.

After focusing on the Jews and Moors, the so-called Marranos and Moriscos respectively, the Inquisition broadened its powers and jurisdiction, emerging as a strongly centralized means for the crown and Church to regulate Spanish Catholicism and to provide barriers against foreign ideas and the dangerous threat of the Reformation. As a result of the Inquisition, Protestantism

never found a foothold in Spain. The reach of the inquisitors eventually extended to the New World. As a consequence of its violent activities, including torture, imprisonment, and execution, the Inquisition acquired a reputation for cruelty that was subsequently made almost legendary by wild reporting and often exaggerated claims. There can be no question, however, that its use of such brutal methods was more than regrettable. In 1808, Joseph Bonaparte, whom Napoleon had installed on the Spanish throne, abolished the Inquisition, a measure designed to please the populace but which only added to the hate felt by the Spaniards for the French invaders. While reinstated in 1814, the Inquisition was finally suppressed in 1834.

I.N.R.I. ● Letters of the Latin words that were placed on a sign and nailed over the Cross of Christ. They stood for *Iesus Nazarenus, Rex Iudaeorum* (Jesus of Nazareth, King of the Jews). According to the Gospel of John, the sign "was written in Hebrew, in Latin, and in Greek" (19:20).

Instituts Catholiques ● Name given to the five institutes of higher learning in France — at Paris, Lille, Lyons, Toulouse, and Angers — that were established as a result of a French legal declaration of 1875 permitting Christian equivalents to the purely secular state universities of the country. By a law of 1880, however, such schools were not permitted to call themselves universities, although they were ostensibly free. The Paris Institut Catholique emerged as one of the main centers for Modernism in the nineteenth century. (See **Duchesne, Louis** and **Loisy, Alfred**.)

Inter Mirifica ● Vatican Council II document (issued on December 4, 1963, and called the "Decree on the Instruments of Social Communications"), it was concerned with the nature and proper application of the communications media. The document first defines the media as those forms of communication "which by their very nature can reach and influence . . . the whole of society" (No. 1). It then examines how the media should be used in a responsible manner and proclaims the right of the Church to use them as it sees fit — for the care of souls and pastoral formation. The document also declared that "the matter communicated [must] always be true, and as complete as charity and justice allow" (No. 5). To give direction to social communication, the council said that "a pastoral instruction [should] be drawn up. . . . Experts from various countries should assist in this effort. In this way, all the principles and norms enunciated by this council concerning the instruments of social communication may achieve their effect" (No. 23). The result of this call was the publication of *Communio et progressio*, the "Pastoral Instruction on the Means of Social Communication" (January 29, 1971). Currently, the Church is aided by the Pontifical Council for Social Communication, a Vatican council intended to put into practice the furthering of the Church's message of salvation through all the relevant media. First instituted by Pope Pius XII in 1948, it was soon reorganized and then given permanent form in 1959 by Pope John XXIII as a commission. Pope John Paul II made it a council with specified duties in June 1988.

Investiture Controversy ● Name given to the long-running conflict between Church and State over the right, claimed by secular leaders, of investing abbots and bishops with their rings and staffs, receiving from them personal homage before the religious leader was consecrated. The custom was long-standing and was closely associated with lay patronage by the eleventh century when the Church, eager to bring reform, and the papacy, seeking to assert its authority, began to condemn investiture as a violation of the rights of the Church. In 1059, Pope

Nicholas II attacked the practice, followed by Pope Gregory VII, who issued a decree forbidding it. The struggle that ensued with secular rulers was centered mainly around the German kings and the popes, especially Emperors Henry IV and Henry V. The conflict soon involved wider political issues and spread throughout Christendom. St. Anselm, in England, enforced the decree of the Council of Rome (1098), excommunicating anyone who took part in lay investiture and refused in 1100 to give homage to King Henry I of England. Lay investiture was settled through a series of compromises, although the papacy was able to secure a much more favorable position in the negotiations. In England, for example, Henry was given the right to grant investiture and receive homage, but he did not involve himself in ecclesiastical elections. The struggle between the popes and the German kings was resolved by the Concordat of Worms (1122). Secular interference would continue over succeeding centuries, most notably in England and France. (See also **Gallicanism**.)

Iona ● Island in the Inner Hebrides, off the coast of Scotland. A monastery was established there in 563 by St. Columba; it became one of the most renowned centers of learning and an important site for Celtic Christianity. Iona was so named, probably incorrectly, from the Gaelic Iona and was a sacred place before the arrival of Columba. Under him, the island earned a reputation for holiness, and Iona became a popular place of pilgrimage, despite the frequent and savage raids of the Norsemen from 985 until the closing years of the tenth century. During this period the monastery was destroyed by the Norsemen and many inhabitants of the island were killed. Eventually rebuilt, the institution came under the Benedictines in 1203. Such was its status as a holy place that numerous kings of Scotland and Norway were buried there; it was also the temporary resting place of St. Columba.

Ireland ● One of the traditionally great Catholic countries, situated to the west of England. The Irish Church endured often severe persecution under the English, and religion is still the source of violent division in Northern Ireland. The history of the faith in Ireland dates from the early fifth century when Patrick came to the island (c. 400) a captive of Celtic raiders who routinely ravaged the coast of England. Patrick was held as a slave for a number of years, finally escaping and returning to his native England. There he was ordained, going back in 432 to launch the conversion of the Irish.

Ireland in the fifth century was largely pagan, with the bulk of the population devoted to Druidism. It was divided politically into traditional ancient kingdoms known as the Pentarchy (Five Kingdoms), also called the Five Fifths: Leinster, Münster, Connaught, Ulster, and Meath. Each king had control to a varying degree over their local chieftains but gave their obedience to the High King of Ireland. Society was well-ordered, with extensive laws (under the Brehon Laws) and a rich culture that fostered the arts, including music and poetry. Patrick thus found much organized opposition to his preaching the new faith. Despite the danger and enormous hardships that confronted him, he was exceedingly successful. Over some thirty years, he established the Church on a sure footing, built churches, and organized a hierarchy. While he had not been the first missionary to Ireland — that had been Palladius (sent by Pope Celestine I) — he was the most significant.

From around 500, the faith had been so planted that it was feasible to send out from Ireland missionaries to other lands. Among the most notable were St. Columba who journeyed to Scotland, St. Columban in Gaul (France), and St. Gall in Switzerland. Irish missionaries were to have a leading role in

Bronze Celtic crucifix (c. 700s)

the conversion of much of northern Europe. In Ireland, meanwhile, the period from 500-800 was the Golden Age in Irish history. The Church flourished along with peace, the arts, and learning. This era ended from around 795 with the arrival of the Norsemen on the Irish shore. Within half a century the Danish raiders had taken possession of Dublin, Waterford, and Limerick. Along the way, they massacred monks, burned down churches and villages, and carried off the treasures of the kingdoms. Beyond the loss of life, Ireland was deeply wounded by the burning or destruction of a vast body of manuscripts that were the foundation of the progress made in Ireland's education and arts.

The Vikings in Ireland were finally

defeated in 1014 at the Battle of Clontarf when an Irish alliance was finally formed under the famed King Brian Boru. The many years of Norse invasion had left the Irish Church in a state of disarray, as its administrative organization had been severely damaged. Reform was introduced in the twelfth century through the efforts of St. Malachy (d. 1148), archbishop of Armagh. He sought to repair the ecclesiastical leadership in the country, creating several new sees and then traveling to Rome to secure the approval of the Holy See. In 1152, a synod at Kells certified the reforms of St. Malachy. The diocesan structure put in place had four archdioceses (Armagh, Tuam, Dublin, and Cashel) and twenty-eight dioceses.

The twelfth century also witnessed the arrival of the English into the country. The cause of this intervention was the political instability that occurred in the reign of Rory O'Connor, the high king. The king of Leinster, Dermot MacMurrough, refused to submit to King Rory, fleeing to England to seek the assistance of King Henry II. Henry responded in 1169 by sending an English army into Ireland, thereby beginning the English presence in the isle. Henry was proclaimed lord of Ireland and, despite the submission of most of the Irish chieftains, divided up much of Ireland as land grants to his barons. The high king, supported by many chieftains in the north, refused to surrender. The English drove northward and crushed all opposition, finally deposing Rory O'Connor. Religious inspiration was provided during this period by St. Laurence O'Toole, archbishop of Dublin, who called upon the Irish to resist the Anglo-Norman invasion. After his death in 1180, opposition crumbled.

English domination, while bringing certain positive developments for the Irish Church, had a sharply negative effect upon the native inhabitants, since a law was passed prohibiting the advancement of the Irish clergy to high ecclesiastical office. On a brighter note, the English promoted the Cistercian order, which had first come to Ireland in the time of St. Malachy in 1142. Other orders followed in the thirteenth century, namely the Franciscans and Dominicans. They became enormously popular with the people and did much to identify themselves with the simple folk of Ireland. Hatred for the English continued, becoming pronounced in the sixteenth century with the onset of the Reformation.

In 1534, King Henry VIII of England (r. 1509-1547) laid claim to the title of head of the Church in England and Ireland through the Act of Supremacy. This was followed by the Irish Supremacy Act of 1537. The English found support for this action from among the clergy who owed their advancement to the crown. There was no popular sentiment toward reform among the Irish, so that there emerged a clear delineation between the Catholics and Protestants, a sociopolitical reality that would dictate the terms of the Irish-English struggle over the next centuries and would be the cause of enormous bloodshed and suffering. The oppression of Catholics accelerated in the reign of Queen Elizabeth I (1558-1603). Under her, the extensive changes made in England were reproduced in Ireland, the ecclesiastical life of the Church made subject to the state. Catholic landholders were ejected from their land, and there began the process known as the plantation of Ireland. By this, the crown promoted the colonization of Ireland with English and Scottish Protestants. Fighting broke out in the north and, in answer to an appeal from various chieftains, King Philip III in 1601 sent a Spanish force that landed at Kinsale. It was ultimately defeated in 1603 and the English seized such territories as Armagh, Donegal, Derry, and elsewhere, handing the land to Protestants.

In the face of this oppression and the rise of bitter anti-Catholic Puritans, the Irish rose up in rebellion starting in 1641 while England drifted toward its own two Civil Wars (1642-1649). The Confederation of

Kilkenny was formed, restoring the Catholic Church throughout the land and requesting the Holy See to send a papal legate. In 1645, Giovanni Renucci, archbishop of Fermo, reached Ireland, but he returned to Rome after several years as the storm gathered in England and headed toward the island. The second English Civil War ended with the execution of King Charles I and the ascendancy of Oliver Cromwell. Given broad authority by Parliament to crush the Irish rebellion, he landed in Ireland in 1649. His campaign was merciless and pointedly savage: some thirty-five hundred people were massacred at Drogheda alone, followed by thousands more all across the country. The campaign ended in 1652. Thousands of men and women were sent to work in slave conditions in the West Indies, and churches were burned, often with their congregations locked within. More land was given to Protestants and penalties inflicted upon Catholics everywhere.

Some toleration was granted under King Charles II through the Declaration of Indulgence, but this found little support with Parliament. Catholic persecution continued as exemplified by the arrest, trial, and execution of Oliver Plunket, archbishop of Armagh, in 1681. More fighting erupted, starting with the so-called Glorious Revolution of 1688 by which the Catholic king James II of England was deposed in favor of William and Mary. James fled to France and then sailed to Ireland in 1689

where he found a hearty welcome from Catholics. King William III arrived with an army and routed James at the Battle of the Boyne (1690). There followed the Treaty of Limerick (1691), which promised but never bestowed religious toleration. Instead, even more vindictive pogroms were launched against the Catholic faith in the early eighteenth century that had as their objective the virtual obliteration of the Catholic Church. Catholics were excluded from government and most meaningful professions.

Chronic strife pervaded throughout the 1700s, but gradual toleration was felt in the

Rock of Cashel

first years of the 1800s. Irish Catholics were beneficiaries of the various Catholic Relief Acts in England and a major step forward was taken under the guidance provided by Daniel O'Connell and the Catholic Association. O'Connell later became mayor of Dublin and, on April 13, 1829, Catholic Emancipation was proclaimed. The Church hierarchy was reorganized and Paul Cullen (d. 1878) was appointed archbishop of Dublin. Churches were rebuilt and the Irish Catholics jubilantly contributed their limited resources on behalf of the faith.

The Irish Free State was officially declared in 1922. By the Irish Constitution of 1937, the Church was granted many advantages by the government and soon embarked on an age of prosperity compared by Irish historians to the Golden Age of 500-800. The Republic of Ireland was proclaimed in 1949. Today, nearly ninety-five percent of the country is Catholic although Protestant faiths are tolerated. Problems remain in Northern Ireland where violence and religious hatred still seethe between Protestant and Catholic. Ireland is also troubled by chronic economic difficulties, increasing religious indifference, and the slow but relentless promotion of abortion and contraception, an event unthinkable in the devout land only a few years ago.

Irenaeus, St. (c. 130-c. 200) ● Bishop of Lyons, considered the first great Catholic theologian in early Christianity. He was probably born in Smyrna, where he listened as a boy to the magnificent preaching of St. Polycarp. Subsequently studying in Rome, he entered the clergy and became a presbyter in Lyons. When, in 177, he was sent to Rome to take letters to Pope Eleutherius pleading for toleration in dealing with the Montanists of Asia Minor, Irenaeus missed the initial but very severe persecutions of Christians in Lyons. The local bishop, Pothinius, was martyred during the time of oppression. Irenaeus returned the following year and was chosen to head the Church in Lyons, an office he held with great honor until his death. As bishop, he was a vocal defender of Christian orthodoxy, authoring *Adversus omnes Haereses* (*Against All Heresies*), a brilliant attack on Gnosticism. Preserved partly in Greek, the work was translated into Latin, Armenian, and Syriac. He also wrote, in Greek, the *Demonstration of the Apostolic Preaching*, found in an Armenian translation, that was an apologetic work. Feast day: June 28.

Isaac of Nineveh (d. c. 700) ● Also called Isaac the Syrian, a bishop theologian, and a Nestorian. A native of Syria, he was originally a monk in Kurdistan before being

consecrated bishop of Nineveh in modern Iraq by the head of the local East Syrian Nestorian Church. He soon resigned, most likely over doctrinal differences, and retired to a monastery near Rabban Shapur. There he concerned himself with mystical and ascetic writings, originally in Syriac but translated into Arabic, Greek, and Ethiopic. Because of doctrinal divergences from the Orthodox Nestorian view, Isaac's teachings were long unpopular in his later years, although he had considerable influence on Byzantine and Russian theologians over the centuries and helped shape Christian mysticism in the West, through Latin, Italian, and Spanish translations of his works.

Isaac the Great, St. (c. 350-439) ● Famed *katholikos* (also *Catholicos*, or head) of the Armenian Church. He was very important in promoting Armenian cultural independence and a sense of national literature. The son of St. Narses, he was a descendant of St. Gregory the Illuminator. Isaac was educated at Constantinople and, after the death of his wife, he became a monk. In 390, he was appointed *katholicos* of Armenia, the tenth holder of the office. He fostered monasticism among the Armenians, converting his residence into a monastery, and secured the recognition of Constantinople that the Armenian Church had patriarchal rights thereby freeing Armenian Christianity from the control of the Greeks. Isaac was crucial in organizing a group of scholars, with the help of his auxiliary bishop, Mesrop Mastots, that translated Greek and Syriac works, especially the Bible, into Armenian. He also possibly composed Armenian hymns and perhaps the Armenian liturgy. Deposed by the Persians in 425, he was able to regain his see in 432 through popular insistence. He is called St. Sahak in the Armenian Church. Feast day: November 25 and September 9 (Armenian Church).

Ferdinand and Isabella

Isabella of León-Castile (1451-1504) ●
Queen of Castile and Aragon, and consort of
Ferdinand II of Aragon. One of the foremost
monarchs in Spanish history who played a
major role in the unification of Spain and the
spread of the Catholic faith to the New World,
she was the daughter of King Juan II of
Castile. She married Ferdinand in 1469 and
succeeded to the throne of Castile in 1474, in
place of her stepbrother, Henry IV. A civil war
soon erupted over the claim with Juana la
Beltraneja, a conflict not settled until 1479.
That same year, Ferdinand became king of
Aragon and Isabella was declared his
co-ruler, thereby uniting Castile and Aragon.
Over the next years, their "Catholic
Majesties" (from 1481) were engaged in the
final liquidation of the Muslim kingdom of
Granada (1482-1492), which ended with the
Moors' expulsion from Spain. A devout
Christian, Isabella promoted improvements
in the Spanish clergy, especially the rights of
Cardinal Ximénez and the efforts of the
missionary Bartolomé de las Casas in
converting the Indians of the New World. She
also helped establish the Spanish Inquisition
in 1479 and, of course, was a patron of
Christopher Columbus (see **Spain**).

Isidore of Seville, St. (c. 560-636) ●
Theologian, encyclopedist, and archbishop of
Seville. Considered the last of
the Western Latin Fathers, he
was educated at a monastery
headed by his brother St.
Leander after the deaths of
their parents. Leander was a
monk and then Isidore's
predecessor at the see of
Seville, working as an
evangelist to the Visigoths.
Isidore succeeded him as
archbishop around 600,
continuing Leander's work
among the Visigoths and
striving to convert them from
Arianism. He was an adviser
to King Sisibut (r. 612-621) and used
councils to promote theological and
ecclesiastical unity in the Spanish Church.
At the Fourth Council of Toledo (635) he
called for toleration of Jews, uniformity in
the liturgy, and close cooperation between
Church and State. Isidore was especially
opposed to Arianism. A gifted author, he was
deeply respected throughout Europe during
the Middle Ages for his erudition and
sanctity, and his writings were much used by
scholars. Among his works were:
Etymologiae, an encyclopedic compilation of
human and religious knowledge, also known
as the *Origines*; *De natura rerum* (*On the
Nature of Things*); *Sententiarum Libri Tres*, a
manual of Christian doctrine; *Chronica
Majora*, covering history from the creation to
A.D. 615; and possibly the *Hispania collectio*,
a compilation on canon law for the Church in
Spain. Given posthumous honors by the
Eighth Council of Toledo (653), he was
canonized by Pope Clement VIII and declared
a Doctor of the Church in 1722 by Pope
Innocent XIII. Feast day: April 4.

Islam ● Religion established by
Muhammad, the prophet (c. 570-632), one of
the world's great faiths. Considered the latest
of the monotheisms, Islam drew its
influences from both Judaism and

Christianity and is founded upon the sacred book, the *Koran* (*Quran*), claimed by Muslims to have been revealed to Muhammad by Allah, God. Muslims also accept the *Sunna*, the collected *Traditions* (the moral sayings and anecdotes) of Muhammad, which were compiled in the ninth century. A central element of Islamic life are the so-called Five Pillars, five duties that must be fulfilled by every Muslim: one must say at least once, "There is no God but Allah and Muhammad is His Prophet"; one must pray five times each day facing Mecca and attend noonday prayers at the mosque each Friday; alms must be given to the poor; the feast of Ramadan must be kept; and, if possible, one must undertake the pilgrimage to Mecca once in a lifetime, the *Hajj*. The traditional date for the founding of Islam is 622, the flight of Muhammad to Medina from Mecca, called the *Hegira*. From Medina, Muhammad launched his followers, conquering Mecca in 630 without a struggle.

Islamic tower

The Islamic Empire was created from that beginning. It was the spread of Islam that brought it into contact and then conflict with Christianity.

While Islam has definite roots in Christianity (Jesus is included in the list of prophets), the arrival of Islam on the frontiers of the Byzantine Empire was taken as a major threat. The Byzantines resisted the advance in Egypt, but the region fell and most of the subsequent history of Christian-Islamic relations has been characterized by deep-seated hostility, frequent intolerance, and mistrust.

Spain fell to a Muslim host starting in 711 when an Islamic army smashed the Visigoths. The Muslims of Spain, called the Moors, first established an emirate and later a caliphate that represented a rich and highly developed culture, one of the most advanced and enlightened in the West, especially in their capital at Córdoba. The Muslim tide in Western Europe, however, was turned in 732 at the Battle of Tours when a force of Muslims was repulsed in France by Charles Martel. Christian kingdoms in Spain soon began a centuries-long campaign to expel the Moors from the peninsula, called the *Reconquista.* It culminated in the final demise of the last Moorish kingdom in 1492.

Meanwhile, the Byzantines were in regular conflict with the various Islamic dynasties that emerged in the East, and the threat of the Seljuk Turks compelled them to seek the aid of the Western kingdoms and the papacy. Already alarmed by the harassment of the pilgrim trails to the Holy Land by the Turks, Pope Urban II called for a crusade in 1095. The resulting crusading movement would last from 1095 until 1270 and the fall of the last Christian strongholds in Palestine. As a result of the contact between the West and the Islamic East, there occurred the reintroduction of Aristotle to the intellectual life of the Christian Church through the writings of such noted Islamic philosophers as Avicenna and Averroës. These Aristotelian works would have a major impact on Christian theology and serve as the foundation of the vast body of Scholastic thought once they had been synthesized with Orthodox Christian doctrine. Attempts were made to understand Islam from an open-minded perspective by Peter the Venerable and Bl. Raymond Lull, and efforts were undertaken by the mendicant orders. St. Francis of Assisi was the most famous of these, but others would follow, often giving their lives for the conversion of even one soul.

The recognition of a dialogue and open communication between the Church and Islam was expressed by Vatican Council II in the document *Nostra Aetate* ("Declaration on the Relationship of the Church to Non-Christian Religions") when it declared that the Church looks upon the Muslims with esteem.

Pope John Paul II has continued the important dialogue, and the Vatican efforts in recent years have included meetings between Islamic officials and the Pontifical Council for Interreligious Dialogue and a message of greeting in 1993 at the close of Ramadan from Cardinal Francis Arinze, president of the Council for Interreligious Dialogue.

Italy ● One of the foremost traditionally Catholic countries, Italy contains within it the Vatican City State (which is located in Rome, the capital of Italy). The Church was born at a time when Italy was the homeland of the Roman people, masters of the known world. The Italian peninsula itself had been acquired by Rome gradually and was comprised of a number of native peoples, including the Etruscans, Latins, Sabines, Apulians, and others, held together by Roman law and the advantages of the Roman franchise, which brought the full protection of law (the rights used by St. Paul in Acts 22-28). At the time that St. Peter first came to Italy, around A.D. 42, Italy was divided into eleven districts; Rome was excluded from this system by virtue of its special position as capital of the empire. Peter made his see in Rome and was martyred there around 64 by Emperor Nero (for other details, see **Peter, St.**). By this time, however, that faith had already begun to spread throughout Italy, finding converts among all the classes (see **Domitilla, Flavia**). While it may stretch believability to give credence to the claims of most of the Italian churches concerning their apostolic origins, it is possible to accept the assertion of Eusebius of Caesarea that the Church was found throughout Italy prior to the time of Constantine the Great. Persecutions had been severe at times, as seen in the martyrdom of popes and others, and the sending of many Christians to the dread mines of Sardinia.

Toleration was formally granted in 313 by Constantine the Great. Italy had already lost its legal and cultural preeminence in the empire. Nevertheless, a well-developed

Church organization was in place, dominated and led by the see of Rome with its bishop, the pope. This leadership would permit the faith to survive the next dark centuries when Italy was overrun by Germanic tribes, including the Visigoths, Vandals, and Ostrogoths. Rome was sacked in 410 and 455 and much of the rest of the peninsula was repeatedly looted, burned, and laid waste. The Roman Empire in the West finally fell in 476. Into the political void stepped the papacy, which used the resources of the Church to ease suffering, provide food, and rebuild shattered towns and churches. From the political developments of the fifth through the eighth centuries were born the Papal States (States of the Church), which controlled much of central Italy. (See **Papal States**.)

The chronic threat posed by the Lombards convinced the popes to seek the aid of the Franks. Pepin the Short intervened in 751 (see **Donation of Pepin**) and in 800, on Christmas Day, Pope Leo III crowned Charlemagne emperor. Italy soon came under the hegemony of the Carolingian Empire, but after the empire's disintegration in the ninth century, the peninsula slipped into chaos. The empire's recovery, starting with Otto I, inaugurated the Holy Roman Empire and would precipitate centuries of conflict between the papacy and the German emperors over interests in Italy. (See **Holy Roman Empire** and **Investiture Controversy**.) This is not to say, however, that Italy was culturally or politically united, for sharp divisions existed between the north (where city-states were formed, the central duchies, the Papal States) and the south (where the Normans came to rule in the eleventh century, finally replaced by the Hohenstaufen Dynasty, the Angevines of Naples, and then the Aragonese kings of Sicily). The northern city-states (Venice, Milan, Siena, and Florence) were assiduous in resisting imperial expansion in Italy but also struggled with one another, were

plagued with internal conflict, and were frequently at odds with the papacy. (See also **Guelphs and Ghibellines** and **Venice**.) The Church, including the papacy and the hierarchy, was deeply involved in the political and cultural life of the Italians.

The Church fostered the arts and education, the mendicant orders of the Dominicans and Franciscans found deep support among the people, and Rome stood as the very heart of the Christian civilization of Europe. The universities, such as those of Padua and Bologna, gave much support to the papacy while assisting in the development of law. Meanwhile, Venice and Genoa emerged as formidable maritime powers, and the cities of Florence, Siena, and Lucca became commercial centers.

From the height of the medieval papacy under Innocent III (r. 1198-1216), the authority of the papacy slowly submitted to the French crown in the fourteenth century during the Avignon period (1309-1377). During this time, the Papal States and Rome sank into disorder, with papal control restored between 1350 and 1370 by Cardinal Gil Albornoz. Shortly after the return of the pontiffs in 1377 to Rome, the Church was racked by the Great Schism, severely damaging its prestige. The schism was finally resolved in 1417 with the election of Martin V (r. 1417-1431).

The fifteenth century would witness the Italian Renaissance, which flourished especially in Florence and Rome. While the arts, literature, and scholarship underwent a wondrous flowering, the Italian Church suffered from a high degree of apathy and corruption owing to the lamentable lifestyles of the popes (Sixtus IV, Innocent VIII, Alexander VI, and Leo X), the lavishness of the papal court, the spread of humanism, and the dissolute moral order of the times. (In sharp contrast were such saints as Frances of Rome, Bernardine of Siena, and John Capistran.)

The Church proved itself remarkably

capable of self-reform and revitalization, so that the Protestant Reformation, in particular Calvinism, never gained a lasting foothold in Italy. The causes of reform were: the gifted reforming popes of the sixteenth century (Paul III, Pius IV, St. Pius V, and Sixtus V); the Council of Trent (1545-1563); the Society of Jesus (or Jesuits); the Inquisition, especially under Pope Paul IV; the new emphasis on the religious life; and the work of the reformers and saints such as St. Charles Borromeo, St. Robert Bellarmine, and Cardinals Giovanni Caraffa (later Paul IV), Marcello Cervini (later Marcellus II), Reginald Pole, and Gasparo Contarini. (See also **Reformation, Catholic [and Protestant]**.)

While the Church was reformed and strengthened, Italy itself was to suffer from political disintegration, the habitual battleground between France and the Habsburgs. By the eighteenth century, foreign powers dominated the peninsula save for the Papal States, which were criticized for the incompetence of their administration. Spanish Bourbons came to rule in Naples, Sicily, Piacenza, and Parma; the Austrians would control Modena, Tuscany, Milan, and Mantua; and the venerable states of Venice and Genoa were markedly deteriorated. To these were added the states of the Church, the territories of the House of Savoy, and the kingdom of Sardinia. Despite this fractured political situation, the Italian Church in the seventeenth and eighteenth centuries was vibrant, producing St. Alphonsus Liguori, St. Paul of the Cross, and such scholars as Pietro Ballerini, Cardinal Henry Noris, Ludovico Muratori, and Giovanni Mansi.

The French Revolution and the Napoleonic Wars (1796-1815) swept away the old order, although the Congress of Vienna (1814-1815) restored much of the pre-Revolution establishment, including the Papal States. Austria enjoyed a preeminent position in northern Italy, but it was soon confronted by the nationalist movement that would come to be called the Risorgimento. (See **Risorgimento**.)

The architect of Italian national unity was Camillo Cavour (1810-1861), Italian statesman and premier of the kingdom of Sardinia. Through his grand scheme, the unification of the entire peninsula was achieved (except for Rome itself) by 1860 under the rule of King Victor Emmanuel II. The capital was Florence from 1860-1870. On September 20, 1870, Rome itself fell, ending the temporal holdings of the papacy. With the words *"Finalment i sum"* ("At last, here I am"), Victor Emmanuel took up residence in the Quirinal Palace, the possession of Pope Pius IX (r. 1846-1878) just days before he declared himself a "prisoner of the Vatican." The difficult relations between the Holy See and the Italian government were not formalized until 1929 and the signing of the Lateran Treaty. (See also **Lateran Treaty, Pius IX,** and **Pius XI**.)

The Lateran Treaty proved possible because of the rise in Italy of the Fascists under Benito Mussolini, who was anxious to win the good will of the Church. By the terms of the adjoining concordat, the often anticlerical measures of the Italian government were reversed and Catholicism was declared the religion of state. Relations cooled considerably between the Fascists and Pope Pius XI (r. 1922-1939) toward the end of the 1930s, and throughout the war, Pius XII (r. 1939-1958) conducted a cautious campaign of resisting Fascist oppression and aiding the Jews without causing a disastrous reprisal from the Italians and the Nazis. Mussolini fell in 1943 and Rome was liberated the next year.

In the postwar years, Pius was active in leading the Church's opposition to Communism, working to secure Communist defeat in Italian elections. This policy was largely abandoned in succeeding years, and it was a sign of the times when Pope John Paul I (1978) met with the Communist mayor of Rome. A new concordat with Italy was reached in 1984 by Pope John Paul II. Today, the Italian Church is confronted with the dilemma of falling church attendance and rising divorce rates, despite the fact that nearly ninety-seven percent of the country is Catholic. Also ominous is the rapid increase in the median age of the country owing to declining birth rates. (See also **Bruno, Giordano; Charlemagne; Dante; Frederick II; Gregory VII, St.; Gregory IX; Henry IV; Holy See; Honorius III; Innocent III; Matilda of Tuscany; Medici, House of; Monarchia Sicula; Petrarch; Pistoia, Synod of; Renaissance; Rienzi, Cola di; Roman Empire; Rome; Sarpi, Paolo; Savonarola, Girolamo; Sicilian Vespers; Vatican;** and **Vatican City, State of.**)

Ivo of Chartres, St. (c. 1040-1116) ● Bishop of Chartres, ranked as one of the most learned canonists of his era. He studied at Paris and at Bec (under the famed Lanfranc), and was prior of the Canons Regular of St. Quentin before being elected bishop of Chartres in 1090, an appointment approved by Pope Urban II. Two years later, he was imprisoned by King Philip I of France for opposing the king's plans to divorce his wife to marry Countess Bertrade of Anjou. His release was secured largely through public outrage, and the pope excommunicated Philip. In 1104, however, while attending the Council of Beaugency, Ivo proposed that the ban upon Philip be lifted. Ivo was a very important figure in the development of canon law, particularly through his three treatises, the *Collectio Tripartita*, the *Decretum* (seventeen books), and the *Panormia* (eight books). A collection of extant letters has survived, among them notable ecclesiastical and religious issues as well as two dozen or so sermons. Feast day: May 23.

J

Jacobite Church ● Name given to the Syrian Monophysite Church, which was derived from its founder, Jacob Baradaeus (c. 500-578), bishop of Edessa. Jacob Baradaeus (so-called from his nickname Baradai, or "ragged") traveled throughout the Middle and Near East as a missionary, preaching, ordaining priests, and organizing what was to become the national Church of Syria. The Jacobite Church had its origins in the Monophysite movement that refused to accept the pronouncements of the Council of Chalcedon (451) on the two natures united into one Divine Person of Christ. The name Jacobite was not adopted until the Second Council of Nicaea (787). Repressed by the laws of the Byzantine Empire, the Jacobites welcomed the invasion of the Arabs in the mid-seventh century, although they suffered severely under the Islamic rule in the succeeding centuries. The Jacobite Church survived, however, and its patriarch since 1959 has resided in Damascus, Syria, ruling over three dioceses. There are four in Syria, two in Iraq, two in Turkey, one in Jerusalem, and one in the United States (New Jersey).

Jacobus de Voragine (c. 1230-1298) ● Archbishop of Genoa, hagiographer, and historian, best known as the author of the *Golden Legend*. A native of the village of Varozze, near Genoa, he entered the Dominicans in 1244. Provincial of Lombardy from 1267-1285, he was instructed by Pope Nicholas IV to free Genoa from the ban that had been placed upon it for giving help to the Sicilians in the struggle with King Charles of Naples. Among his writings were: the *Chronicon Genuense*, a chronicle on Genoa; numerous sermons; *Defensorium contra Impugnantes Fratres Praedicatores*, a defense of the Dominican order; and *Legenda Aurea* (the *Golden Legend*), also called the *Lombardica Historia*, a collection of saints' lives and articles on Christian festivals, written between 1255 and 1266 and organized according to the Church calendar. Intended to foster piety, the *Golden Legend* was very popular in style and was translated into French by Jean Belet de Vigny in the fourteenth century and into other languages after the invention of the printing press. Its historicity was condemned by Melchior Cano (1509-1560). His cultus was ratified by Pope Pius VII in 1816.

Jacopone da Todi (c. 1230-1306) ● Franciscan poet and mystic, known originally as Jacopo Benedetti. A wealthy lawyer (he studied at Bologna), he was converted to severe asceticism in 1268 when, upon the death of his wife, he discovered that she wore a hair shirt under her beautiful and expensive clothing. Drawn to the Franciscans, he became a tertiary and then, around 1278, a lay brother. Later, as a member of the Spiritual Franciscans, he wrote satirical poems against Pope Boniface VIII and was excommunicated and then imprisoned in 1298. Released by Pope Benedict XI, he retired to the monastery of Collazone. Jacopone composed mystical works, a reflection of his own deep spirituality. His compositions included the *Laudi spirituali* and were both in Latin and Umbrian; he was once credited with the

445

Stabat Mater. The depth of his mystical works might have led to his consideration for canonization but for his satirical writings against Boniface VIII.

James, St. (d. c. 62) ● Called the Lord's brother, leader of the Christians of Jerusalem, and an important figure in the early Church. James is quite often confused with St. James the Less (Son of Alphaeus) and shares with that James the feast day May 3, with St. Philip. According to St. Paul, James received a singular appearance of Christ (1 Cor 15:7) after the Resurrection, subsequently becoming a prominent leader among the Christian community of Jerusalem with St. Peter. His prominence is attested by the mention made of him by Paul in Galatians (1:19) and the fact that he presided over the crucial Council of Jerusalem concerning Paul's preaching to the Gentiles (Acts 15). His authority was only heightened after the departure of Peter from the city (Acts 12) to escape Herod Agrippa I and the beheading of St. James the Greater by that same king. He was also visited by Paul (Acts 21:18) on his last visit to Jerusalem. While not described as such in the NT, James is traditionally considered the first bishop of Jerusalem on the basis of a report by Clement of Alexandria as recorded by Eusebius of Caesarea in the *Ecclesiastical History*. Clement calls him the Just, perhaps because of his desire to adhere to some element of Jewish law. He was apparently put to death by the Sanhedrin in 62. The second-century historian Hegesippus described his death, preserved in the *Ecclesiastical History* of Eusebius. According to him, James was thrown off a tower in the Great Temple of Jerusalem and then beaten to death. The Jewish historian Josephus in the first century wrote that James was stoned. His symbol in art is a club or heavy staff.

His name was attached to a number of apocryphal writings. Among these are: the Apocalypses of James, two works found in the codices of the Nag Hammadi; an Epistle of James, also found at Nag Hammadi; the Liturgy of St. James, traditionally ascribed to him; and the so-called Infancy Gospel or the Book of James, also known as the Protoevangelium from the sixteenth century, that was based on the Gospels of Mark and Luke. James was also proposed as the author of the NT Epistle of James.

James, Epistle of St. ● First of the Catholic Epistles with those of Peter, John (1-3), and Jude, meaning that they were accepted by all churches (by the understanding of the West) or addressed to all churches (by the thinking of the East). The letter of James is considered essentially a sermon that relies upon familiarity with the Gospels and biblical teachings, and most importantly the words of Christ, to give exhortation to his readers to maintain their faith and to endure temptations and persecutions with steadfastness. James describes himself as "a servant of God and of the Lord Jesus Christ," addressing the epistle "To the twelve tribes in the Dispersion." It is clear from his elegant Greek style of writing that James was either a Hellenic Christian or a convert from Hellenistic Judaism. The exact authorship, however, remains a mystery, although there is a long tradition — unsupported from the first century — that James "the brother of the Lord" and the first bishop of Jerusalem was responsible for it. The writer was educated and apparently a figure who wielded authority with the Church. It dates from sometime probably in the first century, scholars disagreeing on the specific time, some prefer earlier, circa 40, because of the relatively unsophisticated theological framework, others arguing for a later date but not, most agree, after the turn of the century. First mentioned by Origen, it grew in popularity and usage until finally receiving the status of being canonical by the Council of Hippo in 393.

James begins by making an appeal for perfect steadfastness, writing, "Blessed is the man who endures trial, for when he has stood the test he will receive the crown of life which God has promised to those who love him" (1:12). Much of the remaining text is devoted to giving readers presumably familiar with Christ's teachings a guide to moral and proper Christian behavior. He discusses "doers of the word, and not hearers only" (1:22), proclaiming, "Religion that is pure and undefiled before God and the Father is this: to visit orphans and widows in their affliction, and to keep oneself unstained from the world" (1:27). Next he charges that one should hold no favoritism in faith, preferring the rich over the poor: "Is it not the rich who oppress you, is it not they who drag you into court?" (2:6). Faith, James states, is connected to works (2:14-26). The tongue, meanwhile, "is a fire" (3:6), while one who has wisdom from God controls the tongue — "But the wisdom from above is first pure, then peaceable, gentle, open to reason, full of mercy and good fruits, without uncertainty or insincerity" (3:17). (See also **Anointing of the Sick**.)

James the Greater, St. (d. 44) ● Also James the Great, the son of Zebedee, brother of St. John, and one of the Twelve Apostles. James is called the Greater to distinguish him from James the Less, the name not denoting any ecclesiastical or honorific superiority but simply implying that he was older than James the Less or of greater height. A native of Galilee, he became a follower of Christ and, with his brother, displayed tremendous zeal (Lk 9:49, 54; Mk 10:37). Christ gave the two brothers the name "Boanerges, that is, sons of thunder" (Mk 3:17). James was a member of the small group of disciples, with John and Peter, witnessing the raising of Jairus's daughter (Mk 5:37; Lk 8:51), the Transfiguration (Mk

9:2), and the Agony in the Garden of Gethsemane (Mk 14:32-33; Mt 26:37). James and John's memorable exchange with the Lord concerning drinking from Christ's cup is recorded in Mark (10:35-40).

He was the first Apostle to suffer martyrdom, being beheaded at the command of King Agrippa I of Judaea in 44. His death, recorded in Acts (12:2), is the only one pertaining to the Twelve Apostles to be reported in the NT. According to long Spanish tradition, James was able to preach before his death in Spain, and thus became one of the most popular Spanish saints. It was generally accepted in Spain that his body was translated to Santiago de Compostela, one of the foremost of all pilgrim sites. Feast day: July 25.

James the Less, St. (d. 66) ● Son of Alphaeus, called the Less or the Lesser to distinguish him from James the Greater, who was older or taller. James is often confused with James, the "Lord's brother," although there is a certain tradition that they might be one and the same person. (For the activities of this James, see under **James, St.**) He is mentioned several times in the Gospels. Mark (15:40) describes "James the younger" as the son of Mary, a woman, who, with Mary Magdalene, stood and witnessed the Crucifixion, and calls this Mary "the mother of James" a little later (16:1). In Matthew (27:56) he is again called by implication the son of the woman Mary. Little else is known of him, unless the possibility of his being the aforementioned James is accepted. He shares the same feast day as St. Philip: May 3.

Jane Frances de Chantal, St. (1572-1641) ● Foundress of the Order of the Visitation. Born to a noble family in Dijon, she wed at twenty the Baron Christoph de Rabutin-Chantal. While their marriage was a happy one, he died in 1601, leaving her a widow with four children. In 1604, she met St. Francis de Sales, who agreed to serve as her spiritual director, beginning one of the most remarkable of saintly associations. She agreed in 1607 to assist Francis in the founding of a new religious order of women, and in 1610 she assumed the post of spiritual director in the establishment in Annecy of the Congregation of the Visitation for young women and widows. The order was designed to offer the spiritual life to those women who, because of various reasons, were unsuited for more severe and rigorous ascetic orders, and St. Jane proved superbly skilled in defending and promoting the new communities of the Visitation Sisters. She devoted herself to the care of the sick and poor while establishing new communities. By the time of her death there were eighty-six houses. St. Vincent de Paul said that she was "one of the holiest people I have ever met on this earth." Beatified in 1751, she was canonized in 1767 by Pope Clement XIII. Feast day: August 21.

Jansenism ● Heretical system of theology that was first established by Cornelius Jansen (1585-1638), bishop of Ypres, and subsequently developed and propagated throughout the seventeenth century by its adherents, the Jansenists, until suppressed

Pope Innocent X

by ecclesiastical and secular authorities. The roots of Jansenism are found in the theories of Michel Baius (or Michel de Bay; 1513-1589), who advanced a heretical interpretation of St. Augustine, most notably on original sin. His ideas were condemned by Pope St. Pius V in 1567 and Pope Gregory XIII in 1579. Nevertheless, he influenced Cornelius Jansen in the writing of his most famous work, the *Augustinus*, a commentary on St. Augustine's teaching on grace, published two years after Jansen's death. The publication aroused considerable controversy and opposition. It found support, however, among many theologians in France and the Low Countries. Chief among them was Jean Duvergier de Hauranne (the Abbé de St.-Cyran, more commonly known as simply St.-Cyran), Jansen's friend, who won to his side the nuns at Port-Royal, under Mère Angelique, near Paris. Port-Royal was henceforth the heart of the Jansenist cause. St.-Cyran was succeeded in 1643 after his death by Antoine Arnauld, who authored several works in defense of Jansen's theories while contributing to the development of the system of Jansenism.

Jansenism was essentially a pessimistic view concerning the state of humanity, denying that humans have freedom of the will to accept or reject the grace of God. Further, it claims that Christ did not die for all people, that humans cannot keep all of the commandments, and that only the most worthy should even receive the Eucharist. The crux of Jansenism was laid out in 1649 by Nicholas Cornet, a theologian of the Sorbonne, in Paris, in a set of five propositions. These were extracted from the *Augustinus*: (1) As the grace of God is lacking, some commandments are impossible even for the just; (2) interior grace can never be resisted because of our fallen state; (3) a person does not need freedom from necessity to merit or demerit in the state of a fallen nature; (4) Semi-Pelagians heretically taught that grace could be accepted or rejected by the human will; and (5) Christ did not die for all humanity. Jansenists thus pessimistically believed that persons had no freedom and that free will is drawn to do evil; a special grace, one that cannot be resisted, is required for salvation, but salvation is of a rigidly determined kind in which God chooses selectively to save some people while denying his mercy to a majority of mankind. Not surprisingly, the Jansenists were proponents and practitioners of a harsh and rigorous moral lifestyle. Despite preaching doctrines contrary to the Church, they did not deny the authority of the Church and went to some lengths to remain within the faith.

The Sorbonne attacked them in 1649, followed by Pope Innocent X with the bull *Cum occasione* in which he condemned the five propositions. A defense of Jansenism ensued, highlighted by the writings of Blaise Pascal. In his *Lettres provinciales*, he expounded Jansenist views while launching a clever, satirical criticism of the Jesuits. When adherents claimed that the five propositions did not represent Jansen's own views, Pope Alexander VII in 1656 renewed the papal condemnation and added the point that they were held by Jansen. He also imposed a formulary of submission, which many of the nuns of Port-Royal would not sign.

To ease the crisis in France, Pope Clement IX (r. 1667-1669) permitted Jansenists to sign the formulary but maintain a respectful silence on the propositions. This so-called Clementine Peace or Peace of the Church did not long endure, for more Jansenist controversy erupted in the next years. Pasquier Quesnel's book *Réflexions morales* (1693) reaffirmed Jansen's teachings and caused Pope Clement XI (r. 1700-1721) to issue the bull *Unigenitus* condemning one hundred one propositions from the *Réflexions*. The vast majority of French clergy accepted the bull, but the Jansenists stubbornly refused to adhere to Church commands. King Louis XIV, who at first found Jansenism a useful tool in advancing Gallicanism, eventually tired of the incessant squabbling. He suppressed Port-Royal in 1709, and royal policy for the rest of the century was one of persecution.

The dispersed Jansenists fled to other countries where their tenets found fertile ground, such as in the Netherlands where a schism took place when Pope Clement XI removed a pro-Jansenist vicar apostolic. The Jansenists responded in 1723 by electing their own bishop (see **Old Catholics**). The heresy was also seen in the Synod of Pistoia (1786) and in so-called Moral Jansenism, a type of rigorism that was opposed by Pope St. Pius X (r. 1903-1914).

Januarius, St. (d. early fourth century) ● Bishop of Benevento and patron saint of Naples, Januarius is generally believed to have been martyred during the persecution of Roman Emperor Diocletian in 305. Beyond the fact that he died in Naples, possibly at Pozzuoli, the later stories about him are unreliable. He is best known for his remarkable relic, a glass vial, that contains his blood. Eighteen times a year, the powdery, solid blood liquefies, a unique phenomenon that defies science and is the source of much attraction to the faithful. Crowds routinely gather to witness the ceremony, usually headed by a group of old women, called the *zie di San Gennaro* (the aunts of St. Januarius). The earliest recording of the liquefaction of the Blood of St. Januarius is 1389. Feast day: September 19 (old); January 1 (with several other saints).

Japan ● Asian country into which Christianity was introduced in 1549 by the great Jesuit missionary St. Francis Xavier. He landed on Kyushu with two fellow Jesuits and soon learned of the present political situation in which the local lords (*daimyo*) exercised extensive powers and that little authority was in the hands of the emperor, despite his traditionally accepted divine origins. Francis thus concentrated on winning the confidence of the *daimyo* in the area. Successful, he mastered Japanese and took his preaching into the neighboring island of Honshu, the main island in the chain of Japan. He encountered opposition from the Buddhists but was soon making converts. His work was carried on and furthered by the Jesuit Alexander Valignano, who arrived in 1579. This remarkable missionary opened a school to teach newly arrived mission workers, established seminaries, and promoted vocations for the Jesuits among the inhabitants. Around 1580, there were over one hundred fifty thousand converts cared for by eighty missionaries. To guarantee that Japan remained in the sphere of Jesuit activity, Pope Gregory XIII (r. 1572-1585) decreed in 1585 in *Ex pastorale officio* that the Japanese missions were the exclusive territory of the Society of Jesus. Two years later, the first diocese was created at Funai (modern Oita).

Japanese fears that the Christians were merely a prelude to European invasion — military and cultural — caused an ultimately severe response from authorities. Christianity was discouraged starting in 1587, although conversions continued until 1596-1597; the Franciscans arrived in 1593, followed by the Augustinians and Dominicans. Their more aggressive style in winning converts, as compared to the subtle and more methodical processes of the Jesuits, deeply concerned Toyotomi Hideyoshi (1536-1598), then master of the country. In 1597, the same year as the arrival of the first bishop, Pierre Martinez, S.J., the government launched a persecution. The most famous martyrs were Paul Miki and his companions. Miki, a Jesuit, along with twenty-five other priests and laymen, were crucified at Nagasaki. They were canonized in 1862 by Pope Pius IX, making them the first canonized martyrs of the Far East (Feast day: February 6).

Sporadic persecutions were conducted over the next years, erupting in 1613 with the sharp campaign under the shogun Tokugawa Ieyasu (1542-1616), who considered Christianity to be detrimental to the good of Japan and the social order he was instituting. The next year, all missionaries were expelled and Japanese converts were commanded to abjure the faith. Long-simmering Christian resentment culminated in the 1637 uprising by Christians. This was mercilessly put down and the once flourishing Church in Japan seemed dead, as foreigners were forbidden from entering the country on pain of death.

This long-standing policy was ended in 1853 with the arrival of American Commodore Matthew Perry. Japan grudgingly negotiated treaties with other countries and in 1859 an agreement was reached removing many restrictions on worship by foreigners. Total religious toleration was not permitted until 1890. In 1859, priests from the Paris Foreign Missions Society landed and were stunned to discover thousands of Christians, descendants of the original converts who had secretly kept the faith alive. Surviving more persecutions from 1867-1873, the Church gradually emerged once more. A vicariate apostolic was installed in 1866, replaced in 1891 by an archbishopric and three suffragan sees. By 1910, there were thirty Japanese prelates. World War II caused all non-Japanese clergy to depart the country; those that remained were imprisoned. The Church grew rapidly in the postwar period. A second province was begun in 1959 for Nagasaki, and the following year, Pope John XXIII named Peter Doi, archbishop of Tokyo, a cardinal. There are currently half a million Catholics in Japan in three archdioceses. Pope John Paul II visited the country in 1981.

Jerome, St. (c. 342-420) ● Doctor of the Church and biblical scholar. Known in full as Eusebius Hieronymus, he was born at Stridon, near Aquileia, Italy. He studied in

Rome where he was baptized around the age of eighteen, although he had been raised as a Christian. After baptism he traveled to Gaul and then returned to Aquileia where he devoted himself to an ascetical life. Around 374, he set out on a trip to the East. At Antioch, he dreamed that Christ spoke to him, saying, "*Ciceronianus es, non Christianus*" ("You are a Ciceronian, not a Christian"), a condemnation of his preference for Roman literature to Christian. Choosing to live in the deserts of Syria to do penance, he became a hermit for four or five years, mastering Hebrew. On a trip to Antioch, he was ordained, proceeding from there to Constantinople.

In 382, Jerome was back in Rome, coming to the attention of Pope Damasus. He served as the pontiff's secretary and was a popular figure among the Roman nobility, claiming the friendship of such noblewomen as Marcella, Paula, and the latter's daughters, Eustochium and Blaesilla. Marcella, Paula, and Eustochium were later canonized. At the death of Damasus in 384, Jerome went back to the East. He visited Antioch, Palestine, and Egypt with Paula and Eustochium, settling in Bethlehem in 386. He spent the rest of his life in study and scholarly pursuits, also heading a community of men that had been established.

One of the greatest scholars of the early

St. Jerome,
from Chartres Cathedral

Church, Jerome utilized his long and comprehensive education to make extremely important literary contributions to the faith. His chief work was the translation of the Bible from Hebrew into Latin, which began at the suggestion of Pope Damasus. Aside from his translation of the OT, he revised the existing Latin translations of the NT. This endeavor took some fifteen years (c. 390-405), and was recognized by the Church as essential to the producing of the Vulgate. He also wrote: commentaries on the Old and New Testaments, demonstrating his vast erudition and familiarity with Hebrew; a continuation of the *Historia Ecclesiastica* (*Ecclesiastical History*) of Eusebius of Caesarea, carried down to 378; *De viris illustribus* (392), presenting the leading ecclesiastical writers of the previous years; numerous letters, sent to the most notable leaders of the time; translations of Origen; and various controversial treatises. A spirited and at times intemperate figure, Jerome entered eagerly into the controversies then facing the Church — Arianism, Origenism, and Pelagianism. His harsh and unbending writings against Origen caused a quarrel with his old friend Rufinus of Aquileia. He was much disturbed by the sack of Rome in 410 by the Visigoths, seeing it as the demise of the Roman world. Ranked since the eighth century among the Fathers and Doctors of the Church, he is called the Father of Biblical Science. His symbol is the red hat, from the tradition that Damasus created him a cardinal; another symbol is a lion resting at his feet. Feast day: September 30.

Jerome Emiliani, St. (1481-1537) ●

Founder of the Somaschi (or Clerks Regular of Somascha), Jerome was born in Venice and was ordained in 1518 after a time in the army. A devoted worker among the poor and sick, he established hospitals and orphanages, founding in 1532 the Somaschi, at Somasca, in northern Italy, an order of clerks regular who follow the Rule of St. Augustine and care for the poor and suffering. The order was formally constituted by Pope Pius IV in 1568. Jerome was canonized in 1767 by Pope Clement XIII, and in 1928, Pope Pius XI named him patron saint of orphans and abandoned children. Feast day: July 20.

Jerome of Prague (c. 1365-1416) ●

Bohemian philosopher, reformer, and theologian who was much influenced by Jan Hus and John Wycliffe. A native of Prague, Jerome studied at the University of Prague where he worked with Jan Hus, and at the University of Oxford, where he studied the teachings of John Wycliffe. Returning to Prague in 1401, he emerged as the leading advocate of the Wycliffite doctrines, subsequently teaching at Paris (1405), Heidelberg (1406), and Cologne (1406), but in each case was driven from the post by appalled local Church officials. In 1412, he led a march in Prague during which the decree of the antipope John XXIII, allowing the sale of indulgences, was burned. Going with Hus to the Council of Constance in 1415, he was arrested, imprisoned, and burned at the stake. He supposedly died singing hymns to the Blessed Virgin.

Jerusalem ●

Holy city situated in Palestine, held sacred by three different faiths: Christian, Jewish, and Muslim. It was first inhabited sometime in the fourth millennium B.C. and was called Salem when it served (c. 2100 B.C.) as the capital of King Melchizedek (Gn 14). According to the Book of Joshua (15:63), the inhabitants were known as Jebusites; they were conquered around 1000 B.C. by David, who established his capital, Jerusalem. His son, Solomon, built the Great Temple of Jerusalem. Captured and destroyed by King Nebuchadnezzar (597 and 586 B.C.), the city, along with the Second Temple, was not rebuilt for many years.

The Roman conquest of the region came in 64 B.C. under Pompey the Great. Thereafter, for many centuries Palestine and hence Jerusalem would be under the control of Rome, ruled for a time by its local vassals. Chief among these was Herod the Great (r. 37-4 B.C.), who built the Third (and final) Temple. The Christian history of Jerusalem commences with the brief ministry of Christ. In Jerusalem occurred the crucifixion, death, and resurrection of Our Lord. The Apostles remained in the city, preaching after the Pentecost. After they departed for other lands, they came together once more around A.D. 49 at the Council of Jerusalem. The head of the Church there, ranked as the first bishop of Jerusalem, was St. James. He was condemned by the Sanhedrin and martyred around 62.

The bloody Jewish Revolt that began in 66 ended in 70 with the siege of Jerusalem by the Romans under the future emperor Titus. In the bitter fighting, the Temple was destroyed and the city utterly ruined. Most of the population was forced to move, so no effort was undertaken to rebuild on any appreciable scale. Even more suffering was caused by the Jewish rebellion from 132-135 during the reign of Hadrian. After its suppression, the remains of Jerusalem were renamed Aelia Capitolina and a temple to Jupiter Capitolinus was erected on the site of the Great Temple. Jews were forbidden to enter the city, so the Christian community was comprised almost exclusively by Gentiles. The see of Jerusalem was far from important in the ensuing centuries, compared with Antioch or Alexandria. Its status in the Eastern Church changed, however, after the visit of St. Helena around 326. She paid to build churches, and the number of pilgrims visiting the holy places increased significantly (see **Holy Sepulchre** and **Pilgrimage**). Finally, at the Council of Chalcedon (451), the see of Jerusalem was removed from the jurisdiction of Caesarea and declared a patriarchate.

Pilgrims continued to visit during the Middle Ages. It was the loss of safe and easy access to the city in the late eleventh century that helped encourage the launching of the First Crusade. The Seljuk Turks menaced the pilgrim trails, and the Muslims, since the seventh century, had been masters of the entire region. A crusader army captured Jerusalem in 1099, leading to the founding of the Latin kingdom of Jerusalem (see also **Crusades**). In 1187, Muslim forces took back the city, thanks to the brilliant leadership of Saladin. It would remain a possession of Islamic rulers (including the Mamelukes and Ottoman Turks) until World War I (1914-1918) when it was taken by the British. Today, Jerusalem is part of Israel, although its political disposition is a matter of ongoing negotiation between the major parties with historical and religious interests. The main Christian site is the Church of the Holy Sepulchre. (See **Jerusalem, Council of;** also **Jerusalem, Patriarchate of** [following entries]; see also **Patriarch**.)

Jerusalem, Council of ● Earliest council of the Church, dated to around 49, that was convened to discuss some of the issues then facing the faith, under the direction of the Apostles. The immediate question facing the early Christian Church concerned the regulations of the OT and the degree to which Jewish tradition needed to be adopted by the many Greek converts to Christianity,

particularly as the early Christian liturgy was derived from Jewish ritual. It was decided by Paul, Barnabas, and Titus to present the situation to the Apostles in Jerusalem, most notably Peter and James, the bishop of the city. There followed the Council of Jerusalem, a private session in which it was decided that Jewish traditions (circumcision, dietary restrictions, and Jewish rituals) should not be forced upon Gentile converts. Additionally, it was determined that there was no difference between Jew and Gentile in the eyes of the Church, although this view was opposed by some of the Jewish converts, called Judaizers. The decisions of the council, after an invocation of the Holy Spirit, helped open the Church to a rapid expansion beyond the Jewish people. The decrees were sent to Church communities in Syria and Cilicia and led to a hierarchical organization of the Church leadership, with three descending grades: bishop, priests, and deacons. Chapter 15 of the Acts of the Apostles recorded a clear account of the council.

Jerusalem, Patriarchate of ● See of Jerusalem. Currently the seat of several patriarchs, Jerusalem was elevated to the rank of a patriarchate by the Council of Chalcedon in 451 because of the enormous spiritual importance of the city. During the crusades, a Latin patriarch of Jerusalem was established (along with Antioch, Alexandria, and Constantinople), but with the demise of the Christian status in the Holy Land by the middle of the thirteenth century, the patriarchate was in name only. On July 23, 1847, however, Pope Pius IX, by virtue of the bull *Nulla Celebrion*, reconstituted the patriarchate of Jerusalem. The patriarchate of Jerusalem was led into schism in 1453, following the fall of Constantinople to the Ottoman Turks, in part because of the traditional ill will of Jerusalem's see for that of Constantinople after the latter see was given status and preeminence in the East in the fifth and sixth centuries. Today, the city of Jerusalem is the seat of several patriarchs: the Eastern Catholic, the Latin Patriarch, the Eastern Orthodox, and the Ancient Oriental.

Jesuit Reductions ● Term derived from the Spanish word for settlements (*reducciónes*) that came to be applied to mission settlements established by the Society of Jesus in South America, particularly in Uruguay and Paraguay, between 1607 and 1768. The Jesuit reductions eventually numbered in the hundreds and generally consisted of several thousand natives formed into self-sufficient communities that was remarkably free of the exploitative tendencies of many Spanish officials in the New World. While the reductions were not unique to the Jesuits nor established by them originally, those run by the members of the Society of Jesus were by far the most prosperous and resulted in the conversion of some seven hundred fifty thousand converts to the Church. As part of the desires of many governments to extirpate the Jesuits, false accusations of political plotting and ambition by the order were used to suppress the reductions in the eighteenth century.

Jesuits ● Properly the Society of Jesus, the order of clerks regular founded at Paris in 1534 by St. Ignatius Loyola with six companions. Throughout the succeeding centuries, the order would endure great hardships, including suppression, but would long be respected as a bastion of orthodoxy, loyalty to the papacy, and excellence in scholarship, education, and missionary labors. The Jesuits had their origins in the group of followers who gathered around Ignatius while he studied at the University of Paris. The original six were St. Francis Xavier, Bl. Peter Faber, Alphonse Salmeron, Simon Rodríguez, Nicholas Bobadilla, and Diego Laynez. Loyola and the six cemented their union in 1534 by gathering in a Benedictine chapel on Montmarte and taking vows of chastity and poverty, and a promise to embark, if possible, on a pilgrimage to the Holy Land. As the latter was to be impractical, the group journeyed to Rome to offer itself to the service of the papacy. Formal approbation for the new religious order was given by Pope Paul III on September 27, 1540, in the bull *Regimini militantis ecclesiae*. They were given the name Society of Jesus, and Ignatius was elected the first general. In 1550, Ignatius submitted the constitution for the Society.

As reflected in the motto of the Jesuits, *Ad majorem Dei gloriam* (abbreviated AMDG; "To the Greater Glory of God") the order, as envisioned by Ignatius, had the duty of working for the honor of God and to save men. Toward this end, the members would aid the reform of the Church and offer

Pope Clement XIV: suppressed the Jesuits

themselves to missionary efforts around the globe. Beyond the vows of chastity, obedience, and poverty, the Jesuits took a special oath of obedience to the Holy See, placing themselves entirely at the disposal of the popes, going forth immediately and without question wherever he might command. For the fulfillment of these tasks, Ignatius desired priests who were superbly educated and trained, highly disciplined but exceedingly rational and cultivated in the faith. Jesuits were not to accept any preferments or offices unless specifically pressed upon them by the pope, and their habit was to be simple and without any distinction. For the education of the priests, the order, in 1599, launched a system of studies called the *Ratio Studiorum* (in full, *Ratio atque Institutio Studiorum Societatis Iesu*; see **Ratio Studiorum**).

The formation and rapid spread and development of the Jesuits provided the Holy See with a useful instrument in the launching and propagation of the Catholic Reformation. Jesuits, such as St. Peter Canisius, Laynez, and others were to be instrumental in bringing reform to the Church in Central and Western Europe and in halting the spread of Protestantism. They revived the faith in Austria, Poland, Lithuania, parts of Germany, and Hungary. In France, they emerged as gifted defenders of papal authority, also advancing the Church's as well as the pope's interests in the British Isles (England, Scotland, and Wales). The activities of the Society in England and Scotland form a heroic chapter in the history of the order, as dozens of members were to be put to death during the Elizabethan era, including St. Edmund Campion, John Ogilvie, and Robert Southwell. The sixteenth century also produced brilliant Jesuit theologians, such as Canisius, St. Robert Bellarmine, Francisco Suárez, and Luis de Molina, and Jesuits had a part in the deliberations of the Council of Trent. Other notable Jesuits of the time were St. Francis Borgia, Claudius Acquaviva, and St. Aloysius Gonzaga.

On the basis of their excellent educational skills, the Society of Jesus became one of the foremost teaching orders. The first college was begun in 1548 by Ignatius at Messina. By the end of the century, they had founded over a hundred colleges. The Jesuits taught not merely in universities and colleges but all over Europe. They preached, gave catechetical instruction, and were committed to the education of the poor and the bolstering of the faith wherever it might be in danger of being replaced by Protestantism. Invited into countries to form schools and open educational centers in missionary territories all over the world, the Jesuits prior to their suppression in 1773 were operating fourteen universities, some six hundred colleges, and nearly two hundred seminaries.

The society was also deeply and eminently involved in the missionary campaigns of the Church from the mid-sixteenth century. In the fulfillment of their duties in the missions, the Jesuits encountered often bitter opposition not only from native peoples or governments but also from colonial regimes, other orders, secular clergy, and business (or mercantile) elements who resented the Jesuit efforts to keep indigenous populations free from exploitation. Areas of enormous Jesuit success were Japan, China, and North America. The greatest of their missionaries was St. Francis Xavier (1506-1552), but a few of the many other truly remarkable mission figures were St. Peter Claver, Matteo Ricci, Robert de Nobili, Antonio Vieira, Luis de Valdivia, Eusebio Kino, St. Isaac Jogues, and Bl. Charles Spinola. (See also **Chinese Rites, Malabar Rites,** and **Jesuit Reductions**.)

By the mid-eighteenth century, the Society of Jesus was known across the globe as a corps of devoted supporters of the papacy and a leading voice in the Church for missionary zeal and adherence to the teachings of the faith. Their loyalty to the Holy See, determination to remain independent of national or secular interference, and the power they wielded in the missions had created many enemies in Europe and its colonial lands. Protestants, in Germany and England most of all, hated the order for its intellectual assaults on Protestant thinking. Gallicanists and Jansenists, joined by the leading lights of the Enlightenment, attacked the Jesuits from a variety of positions (see, for example, **Jansenism** and **Pascal, Blaise**). And the Spanish and Portuguese crowns disliked Jesuit independence and habitual interference in the running of the colonies in Central and South America. One by one, various states launched persecutions and then expelled the order: Portugal (1759), France (1764), Spain (1767), and Naples (1768). The expulsions demonstrated the worst excesses of the Enlightenment and the absolutist tendencies of governments at the time, since the priests were cruelly ejected. Not content with the ruthless humiliation of the society, France, Spain, Portugal, and Naples pressed the Holy See to suppress the entire order.

The crisis for the popes had long been building. For years, the worst calumny had been reported about the Jesuits, and Pope Benedict XIV (r. 1740-1758) had ordered an investigation into its activities in Portugal. This was followed by expulsions. In answer to a possible compromise in France, Clement XIII (r. 1758-1769) had declared, *"Sint ut sunt aut non sint"* ("Let them be as they are or not at all"). The countries put further pressure on Clement XIV (r. 1769-1774). Under threat of a total break in relations with these Catholic monarchies, the pontiff issued the brief *Dominus ac redemptor* (1773), which suppressed the Society of Jesus and dealt a calamitous blow to education and the missions. The only places where the Jesuits found safety were Prussia and Russia where the brief was not allowed to be published. They also benefited from the state of affairs in England where the English had no interest in enforcing the brief and in which the local officials were prevented from acting by laws concerning Praemunire.

The Jesuits were thus not entirely destroyed, and in 1780, under the protection of Catherine the Great, the members in White Russia opened a novitiate. In 1801, Pope Pius VII (r. 1800-1823) granted permission for onetime Jesuits to be affiliated with their associates in Russia. Other members followed suit in parts of Europe and the United States, a preparatory event to the decision of Pope Pius to issue the bull *Sollicitudo omnium ecclesiarum* (August 7, 1814) by which the Jesuits were fully restored.

The return of the Jesuits as a recognized order did not immediately mark their full restoration to prosperity. Indeed, even with the sanctuary and protection they had enjoyed for the previous years, they were less than one hundred strong. Nevertheless, the appeal of the Jesuits caught on throughout the first half of the nineteenth century and their numbers steadily increased. As with the size of the order, the scope of its work long remained limited, the consequence of scant resources and the frequently omnipresent anti-Jesuit hostility and presence of laws restricting the work of the order. As membership grew, the Society of Jesus returned to its missionary endeavors. They were routinely singled out for persecution, arrest, or even death in areas undergoing political upheaval in the twentieth century, including Russia, China, Spain (during the Civil War), and Mexico.

In the years prior to the Second Vatican Council, the Jesuits numbered over thirty-five thousand. Today, there are more than twenty-three thousand members, making them still the largest religious institute in the Church. Aside from missionary and education work, they are involved in academic writings, including periodicals and journals. They also operate Vatican Radio. The order has been embroiled in some controversy over the last decades over its direction and purpose. Owing to the questions concerning its activities, Pope John Paul II took the unusual step of postponing the election of a successor to Pedro Arrupe, the controversial general. In 1981, the pope made Paolo Dezza, S.J. (cardinal in 1991), the head of the society until an election would be permitted. On September 13, 1983, Father Peter-Hans Kolvenbach was elected. Traditionally, the superior general was a powerful figure in Rome, earning him the nickname the Black Pope.

Jews and Judaism ● Members of the oldest of the great monotheistic religions of the West. The Jews are members of the faith and considered the historical parent of both Christianity and Islam. Judaism in its widest sense can refer to both the religion of the Jews and their culture — political, social, and historical. In the religious sense, Judaism is a complex of teachings based on the Talmud and the Old Testament, with a fundamental belief in the omnipotence of God and his law, the Torah (which was granted to his Chosen People, Israel). The father of Israel was Abraham, and its leader, the recipient of the Torah, was Moses. In the ancient period of Judaism, the Jews were divided into sects: the Pharisees, Sadducees, and Essenes. Contemporary or modern Judaism is divided into three groups: Orthodox, Reform, and Conservative. The Orthodox Jews are considered the most theologically conservative; they are also the oldest of the current sects. The Conservative Jews seek a moderate course in religion. The Reform Jews, generally viewed as the most liberal of all Jews, first formed in the eighteenth century in Germany; they advocate the use of the vernacular and changes in ritual. All members of Judaism, however, are generally united in their loyalty to the Jewish homeland, the State of Israel.

The relationship between Christianity and Judaism, and, specifically the Church and the Jews, is a long one, complicated over the centuries by the close interconnectedness of the Church and society and the often pervasive anti-Semitism that was found in most elements of life. While many unfortunate episodes did take place from time to time — most true in the Middle Ages — the Church has always tried to teach restraint and understanding toward the Jews. These teachings were not always followed by Christians, and the history of the Jewish people in Europe has thus been a tragic one.

The Christian faith was born in the Jewish community, and its first converts were found among them. The Apostles were Jews and the first Christians adhered to the Jewish faith. The spread of the Church, however, was soon a source of some consternation to Jewish religious authorities prior to the destruction of the Great Temple of Jerusalem in A.D. 70. They looked upon Christianity as a heretical sect within Judaism. Local officials were thus not ill-disposed to Roman measures against the Christians and there was some tension between the groups. Gradually the Church reached out to the Gentiles, after the momentous Council of Jerusalem (c. 49) and through the preaching of St. Paul.

In the succeeding centuries, both Judaism and Christianity would suffer. The Jews would have their temple destroyed, suffer forced migration by Roman authorities, and in whole parts of the empire be forbidden from even entering a province or city on pain of death, the result of several unsuccessful rebellions, such as the bloody and ill-fated uprising of Simon Bar Cochba in the early second century. Christianity, meanwhile, spread across the Roman Empire and flourished despite often ruthless persecutions. Toleration of the faith was finally decreed in 313 with the Edict of Milan, by which Christianity was granted a favored position and emerged as the creed of the Roman civilization.

As Christianity was the religion of state

from the fourth century, there was mounting social pressure to join the Church and to look upon membership as helpful for social advancement. Conversions to other belief systems, such as Judaism and paganism, were discouraged. Unfortunately, this discouragement caused some Christians to consider abuse and injury tolerable activities. Thus, Jews were beaten, humiliated, and accused by the uneducated of the responsibility for Christ's death. The Church taught that this was not so, preaching Christ's words on the Cross: "Father, forgive them; for they know not what they do" (Lk 23:34).

As a result of often rampant anti-Semitism, the Church found it difficult to disabuse many people of the notion that brutal treatment of the Jews was morally wrong. The declaration of the papacy could not be clearer than the words of Pope St. Gregory the Great when he decreed that Jews were not to be molested and were to be allowed to dispose of their property. Still, the culture of the times was generally anti-Semitic. The Jews suffered from legal disabilities, were forced out of the feudal system that prevailed, and were the targets of wild and even ridiculous accusations: the murder of Christ, poisoning wells and water to spread the plague, and the performing of ritual murders — they supposedly murdered young Christian boys and made unleavened bread with their blood (see **William of Norwich, St.**). Hatred was exacerbated by the presence of Jews in banking, with charges of usury. Jews were thus regularly subject to pogroms and were compelled to live in ghettoes, walled parts of a city where they were to remain. Ghettoes became a fixture of European culture, with one even in Rome. This was established in 1556 by the severe Pope Paul IV (r. 1555-1559). It would be the last ghetto to be closed in Europe, in 1870, although the Warsaw ghetto created by the Nazis in World War II would become infamous. Coupled with their physical

separation from the community, Jews were ordered to wear distinctive marks on their clothing.

The brutalities against the Jews in the Middle Ages paled in comparison to the Holocaust, in which six million persons died under the Nazis. The Church throughout the Nazi period spoke in defense of the Jews, with several prelates, such as Cardinal Michael Faulhaber of Munich, risking their lives. Pope Pius XI issued the encyclical *Mit brennender Sorge* (1937) attacking Nazism, and Pope Pius XII went to great lengths to save and protect Jews in Italy and elsewhere. (See **Pius XII**.)

Serious efforts to be reconciled with the Jews were propelled by the birth of Israel (1948) and the conscious efforts of the modern popes. Pope Pius XI condemned anti-Semitism in 1938 and Pope John XXIII in 1960 met a Jewish delegation with the words, "I am Joseph your brother." Vatican Council II in *Lumen Gentium* made note of the special relationship between Catholics and Jews, calling them "a people most dear." Much progress was made under Pope John Paul II. *Notes on the Correct Way to Present the Jews and Judaism in Preaching and Catechesis in the Roman Catholic Church* was issued in 1985. Further, after many years of negotiation, diplomatic relations have been launched between Israel and the Holy See, an event marked by the arrival of Israeli representatives at the Vatican in 1994.

Joachim of Fiore (c. 1132-1202) ● Also Joachim of Flora, a mystic and apocalyptic writer. Born at Celico, Italy, he went on a pilgrimage as a young man to the Holy Land and was there converted to a deeply religious life. Upon his return to Italy, he entered the Cistercian order and was elected abbot of Corazzo in 1177 against his will. Around 1191, he resigned his abbacy, withdrew to a strictly contemplative life, and devoted himself to writing. Residing at first at the Abbey Casamari, he moved to Fiore, in

Calabria, where he established a monastery for himself and the group of disciples who had gathered around him. This community received papal sanction in 1196 from Celestine III. It developed into a prominent religious institute, the Order of San Giovanni in Fiore. The author of several important works, Joachim died before securing papal approval for his writings; he left explicit instructions, however, for his successors to seek the Holy See's decision and then abide by it. Some of his views were subsequently condemned by the Lateran Council (1215) and the Council of Arles (1263). His three main works were *Liber Concordiae Novi ac Veteris Testaménti*, the *Expositio in Apocalipsim*, and the *Psalterium Decem Cordarum*. In these, he developed a Trinitarian philosophy of history in which it is viewed in three great periods of riding spirituality. The ages (*status*) were the Father, the Son, and the Spirit. The last period would see the creation of new religious orders to convert the entire world and thus usher in the *Ecclesiae Spiritualis*. His teachings were extremely influential, especially among the more radical or extreme religious groups, such as the Spiritual Franciscans and the Fraticelli, who declared themselves Joachim's prophesied religious orders and then called for revolutionary reform.

Joan, Pope ● Legendary female pontiff who supposedly reigned for two years as Pope John VIII, between the pontificates of Leo IV and Benedict III, roughly between 855 and 858; some versions have Pope Joan elected in the year 1100. Dismissed as total fabrication by scholars and called a Roman fairy tale by the German historian Johannes Döllinger, the story was nevertheless quite popular in the Middle Ages. According to the legend, she was a talented scribe who, disguised as a man, advanced through the ranks of the Curia and secured election as pope. After a brief rule, however, she gave birth to a child

while in procession to the Lateran and was stoned to death. First recorded by the Dominican chroniclers Jean de Mailly and Stephen of Bourbon, the story soon spread through the writings of the thirteenth-century Polish Dominican Martin of Troppau. Probably originating from lingering accounts of women who dominated the papacy, such as the tenth-century Theodora and her daughter Marozia, Pope Joan can be dismissed, aside from all the other reasons, by the fact that the interregnum between Leo IV and Benedict III was much less than two years. Pope Joan was used in the sixteenth century to promote antipapal sentiment and anti-Catholicism by Protestant polemicists and even as late as the nineteenth century was being used by enemies of the papacy and Catholicism.

Joan of Arc, St. (c. 1412-1431) ● Maid of Orléans, or *La Pucelle*. A patron saint of France, she emerged from absolute obscurity to lead the armies of France to victory against the English at Orléans. The daughter of a peasant in Domremy, Champagne, Joan began hearing the voices of St. Michael, St. Margaret, and St. Catherine. They told her to save France. Initially unsuccessful in convincing the commanding officer of Vaucouleurs that she was sincere and genuine (1428), she was able to use fulfilled prophecies to gain an audience at the royal court of the uncrowned King Charles VII of France. In the famous episode, she stupefied the disguised dauphin and soon after won the approval of theologians at Poitier. Named commander of the forces gathered to relieve the besieged city of Orléans, she put on white armor and led the French to a stunning victory. The breaking of the siege led to Charles's coronation at Reims on July 17, 1429, and to the ultimate defeat of England in the Hundred Years' War (1337-1453). More campaigns followed, but Joan was finally captured by the Burgundians near Compiègne and sold to the English. Tried before a tribunal at Rouen headed by Pierre Cauchon, bishop of Beauvais, she was condemned for heresy and witchcraft on May 30, 1431, and burned at the stake. Pope Callistus ordered a careful examination of her trial and she was declared innocent of all charges in 1456. Canonized on May 9, 1920, by Pope Benedict XV, she is the second patron of France. Feast day: May 30.

Jocists ● Common name for the Catholic movement of factory and industrial workers, known officially as the Jeunesse Ouvrière Chrétienne (J.O.C.). It was established after World War I in Brussels by Abbé Joseph Cardijn (1882-1967; made cardinal in 1965). Taking inspiration from the Church's social teachings, especially Pope Leo XIII's encyclical *Rerum novarum*, the Jocists endeavored to bring Christian morality into modern industry and to educate young workers about the life and doctrines of the Church. Known as the J.O.C. from 1924, the movement spread to France in 1926 and corresponding or similar organizations also developed: Jeunesse Agricole Chrétienne (J.A.C., for agricultural worker), Jeunesse Maritime Chrétienne (J.M.C., for sailors), Young Christian Workers, and Young Christian Students. The Jocists are organized usually into sections, centered on parishes, with groups of thirty to forty sections constituting a regional federation.

St. Joan of Arc

General organization is patterned after the structure of reflections and suggested activities contained in the writings of Cardinal Cardijn.

Jogues, Isaac ● See **North American Martyrs**.

John, St. ● Apostle. Called "The Beloved Disciple," he was the author of the Fourth Gospel, three Epistles, and the Book of Revelation. John was a Galilean, the son of Zebedee, brother of James the Greater, with whom he was called Boanerges (meaning "sons of thunder") in Mark (3:17). John was originally a fisherman and was probably a follower of John the Baptist before becoming a disciple of Jesus. Among the disciples he, James, and Peter, formed the inner circle around Jesus; they thus were present at the raising of Jairus's daughter (Mk 5:37), the Transfiguration (Mt 17:1), and the agony in the Garden (Mt. 26:37). Despite his reputation for excitability, John, with his brother (Mk 10:35-41; Lk 9:54), was also very generous, offering in Matthew (20:22) to drink from Christ's cup. Further, it is accepted that John was referring to himself in the Fourth Gospel when he wrote of the disciple "whom Jesus loved," reclining on Our Lord's bosom at the Last Supper (13:23); to whom he entrusted Mary at the Crucifixion (19:26); who ran with Peter to the tomb after the Resurrection (20:2-8); and who proclaimed to Peter, "It is the Lord!"

when Christ revealed himself at Tiberias (21:7). John is mentioned in the Acts of the Apostles, with Peter at the Temple (3:1, 11), before the Sanhedrin (4:1-21), and later in Samaria (8:14). St. Paul (Gal 2:9) calls John, with Peter and James, a "pillar" of the Church in Jerusalem.

According to tradition, John traveled and took up residence in Ephesus. He was eventually exiled to Patmos "on account of the word of God and the testimony of Jesus" (Rv 1:9); this exile took place during the reign of Emperor Domitian (81-96). It was here that he wrote Revelation, subsequently returning to Ephesus under Nerva (96-98) where he wrote the Gospel and Epistles. The Church has long upheld the authorship of John concerning the Gospel, although debate has taken place in modern times among scholars who question the identity of John as author. Its apostolic nature, however, is not suspected. He apparently died at Ephesus of old age, the only disciple known with some reliability not to have been martyred, although some experts point to inconclusive evidence that he may have been put to death with St. James. A later story, deemed apocryphal, told that he went Rome and was hurled into a cauldron of boiling oil, emerging unscathed. Until 1960, the event was commemorated as part of the Feast of St. John at the Lateran Gate (*ante portam Latinam*) on May 6. His symbol is the eagle. Feast day: December 27.

John, Epistles of ● Three relatively short letters traditionally attributed to St. John, author of the Fourth Gospel. The basis of the assessment is the similarity in style, vocabulary, and theme. The possible dates of the epistles are placed between 92 and 100, although they may have been written later.

First Epistle: The longest of the three letters, this epistle is viewed by many scholars as a kind of guide to the Fourth Gospel. It is addressed to the "little children," members of the Church that John had founded and is concerned with the problems that have arisen in the community. These seem centered on the denial of Christ's humanity; John proclaims: "Beloved, do not believe every spirit, but test the spirits to see whether they are of God; for many false prophets have gone out into the world. By this you know the Spirit of God: every spirit which confesses that Jesus Christ has come in the flesh is of God, and every spirit which does not confess Jesus is not of God" (4:1-3).

Second Epistle: A letter most closely related to the Third Epistle but one also, as noted, almost certainly by the author of the Fourth Gospel. Both this epistle and the third are begun with the citation of "the Elder." In this epistle John gives encouragement to his readers to "love one another" (5). That the problems discussed in the First Letter remains is clear from his warning, "For many deceivers have gone out into the world, men who will not acknowledge the coming of Jesus Christ in the flesh; such a one is the deceiver and the antichrist" (7).

Third Epistle: Like the Second Epistle, this is written under the name of "the Elder," but it is the only one of the three to be addressed to an individual, Gaius. The letter is concerned with one Diotrephes, a member of the community of the local Church to whom this communication is directed who "likes to put himself first" and "does not acknowledge my authority" (9). John, writing to Gaius, most likely a prominent leader in the local Church, promises to deal with Diotrephes when he next visits.

John I, St. ● Pope from 523-526. The first pontiff to visit Constantinople, he had been born in Tuscany and was a senior deacon at the time of his election as successor to Pope Hormisdas. A close friend of the philosopher Boethius, he had been instrumental in ending the Acacian Schism (484-519), an event that reunited the Eastern and Western Churches. The reunion was not pleasing to King Theodoric of the Ostrogoths, who had been acting as a protector and patron of the papacy. Thus, when Byzantine Emperor Justin issued his edict against Arianism, the ruler instructed John to negotiate a settlement, as Theodoric was himself of an Arian persuasion. When John failed, he was imprisoned and died, probably of starvation at Ravenna. His epitaph noted that he was a "victim for Christ." Feast day: May 27.

John II ● Pope from 533-535. John is remembered most for his condemnation of Nestorianism and for being the first pontiff to change his name after election. A native of Rome, he was already quite old when, as a priest of S. Clemente, he was elected as successor to Boniface II. As his name, Mercurius (or Mercury), was that of a pagan god, he changed his name to John, the first pope to do so, although the practice did not become common until much later (see **Sergius IV**). At the request of Emperor Justinian I, he excommunicated Nestorian monks at Constantinople (March 534).

John III ● Pope from 561-574. Possibly known originally as Catelinus, he was the son of a Roman senator. Elected to succeed Pelagius I, his pontificate was dominated by the Lombard invasions of Italy, during which time the records of his reign were destroyed. Pressed for help, John called upon the Byzantine general Narses for aid, but the Romans, believing that Narses had connived with the Lombards, responded by forcing John to hide in the catacombs until the

Pope John VII, from a Roman mosaic

general died in 573. He conducted all official business in the church of SS. Tiburtius and Valerian.

John IV ● Pope from 640-642. A Dalmatian, he was archdeacon of Rome at his election to succeed Severinus. His main action was to continue the papal condemnation of Monothelitism. He also defended his predecessor Honorius I on the matter of the unity of Christ's will, and opposed the Celtic dating of Easter, sending a warning to the Irish bishops against Pelagianism.

John V ● Pope from 685-686. A Syrian from Antioch, he had distinguished himself as one of the three representatives of Pope Agatho to the Third Council of Constantinople (680-681). He was elected unanimously, but virtually nothing is known about his reign save that he strove to maintain papal supremacy over Sardinia and was revered for his care of the poor.

John VI ● Pope from 701-705. Originally a Greek, he gave protection to the Byzantine exarch Theophylact when the latter caused an uprising of Italian militia. Around 702, Duke Gisulf of Benevento invaded Campania, forcing John to expend large amounts of money to ransom the hostages and to bribe the duke into withdrawing. John also ordered that the deposed Wilfrid of York be restored to his see (704).

John VII ● Pope from 705-707. A Greek, he was the first pontiff to be the son of an official of the Byzantine Empire — his father,

Plato, was responsible for maintaining the imperial palace on the Palatine Hill in Rome. Elected to succeed John VI, he enjoyed excellent relations with the Lombards, allowing him to restore Roman churches and to act as a patron of the arts. Noted for his devotion to the Virgin Mary, he was buried in the chapel of the BVM. His reign, artistically, was much influenced by the Byzantines, as seen in his choice of church decorations.

John VIII ● Pope from 872-882. Elected after the death of Adrian II, he had been a Roman by birth and an important archdeacon in the service of Adrian and his predecessor St. Nicholas I whom John sought to emulate. By recognizing the condemned Photius, patriarch of Constantinople, John secured a resolution to the disputes between the Eastern and Western Churches. Much troubled by the raids of the Saracens from southern Italy, he created a papal fleet and took command of the forces intended to stop the Muslim raids. Eventually, however, he had to buy them off but not before a defensive wall was built around St. Paul's Basilica. He crowned Charles the Bald emperor on Christmas Day, 875, and was forced in 876 to excommunicate conspiring Roman nobles, including the future Pope Formosus. The missionary efforts of St. Methodius among the Slavs was promoted, and he sanctioned the use of Slavonic in the liturgy. He was also the first pope to be assassinated, when he was poisoned and then beaten to death by the members of his intrigue-filled court.

John IX ● Pope from 898-900. Born at Tivoli, he was a Benedictine monk or abbot who had been ordained by Pope Formosus and thus was counted as a member of the Formosan party in Rome. After the death of Theodore II in November 897, John IX was elected by the Formosan party and, with the help of Lambert of Spoleto, king of Italy, the newly elected Sergius (backed by the

anti-Formosans) was expelled and ultimately excommunicated; he would return in 904 as Sergius III. Summoning synods at Rome and Ravenna, he exonerated Formosus and condemned the so-called Cadaver Synod of Pope Stephen VI (VII) in 897, which had tried Formosus' corpse on various charges; the acts were destroyed and all deposed clergy were restored. John also confirmed the *Constitutio Romana*, whereby emperors maintained their rights on papal elections.

John X ● Pope from 914-928. The archbishop of Ravenna, John was chosen the successor to Lando as a result of the direct influence of the Theophylact family of Rome, most notably the imperious Theodora (d. c. 916). Most of his pontificate was spent challenging the Saracens of southern Italy who were a chronic threat to Rome. He joined an alliance with the Byzantine emperor Constantine IV and Berengar I of Italy, and, with the additional support of the Theophylacts and the duke of Spoleto, the Saracens were crushed in 915 at the Battle of Garigliano River. John blessed the rule of the Order of Cluny and had improved relations with the Eastern Church. He also rebuilt the Lateran and was profuse in his decoration of it. Inevitably, however, his independent-minded rule, free of the Roman nobles, ended his reign. Marozia, daughter of Theophylact, had him overthrown, placed in Castel Sant' Angelo, and finally suffocated with a pillow.

John XI ● Pope from 931-935. A pontiff during one of the darkest periods in papal history, he was the son of Marozia, the daughter of Theophylact and a member of the ruthless Crescentii family, and her supposed lover, Pope Sergius III. Elected through the dominating influence of the Crescentii and Marozia, John was a mere tool of his mother. Alberic II, John's half-brother by Marozia, overthrew her around 933 and imprisoned John. He died in custody either in December

935 or January 936. His successor was Leo VII.

John XII ● Pope from 955-964. The son of Alberic II of Spoleto who dominated Roman life and had imprisoned John XI, John XII was elected at the age of eighteen. He attempted to find a counterbalance to the dangerous northern Italian rulers King Berengar II and his son Adalbert by allying himself with Otto I the Great. He crowned Otto at Rome in 962 and agreed to the *Privilegium Ottonianum*, which confirmed the rights of the emperors in papal elections. Regretting his alliance, John unwisely connived with Berengar and was deposed by Otto in 963, replaced by Pope Leo VIII. John returned in 964, punished the Roman supporters of Otto, and removed Leo. Otto soon marched back into Italy and John died, mysteriously, as the emperor was on his way. John's reign had done much to weaken the papacy.

John XIII ● Pope from 965-972. Called the Good for his piety and learning, he was elected pope through the patronage of Emperor Otto I the Great. This naturally displeased the Roman nobles, who kidnapped John and held him until his rescue by imperial troops. John had a subsequently peaceful pontificate. He crowned Otto II in 967 and his wife in 972. John also supported the Cluniac reform.

John XIV ● Pope from 983-984. Known originally as Pietro Canepanova, he was bishop of Pavia at the time of his election through Emperor Otto II. His elevation as pontiff was opposed by the powerful Crescentii family of Rome, who supported the antipope Boniface VII. When Otto II died in December 983, the exiled Boniface returned to Rome and, with the aid of the Crescentii, imprisoned John at Castel Sant' Angelo before finally murdering him on August 20, 984.

John XV ● Pope from 985-996. He owed his elevation to the harsh influence of the powerful Roman nobleman Crescentius, thus marking a revival of the Crescentii family, especially after the sudden death of the scandalous Boniface VII in 985. After enduring years of Crescentii domination, John appealed to Emperor Otto II for help but died before imperial aid could arrive. John's pontificate was notable for the establishment of the practice of solemn canonization. In 993, John solemnly canonized Bishop St. Ulrich of Augsburg, the first canonization by papal decree.

John XVI ● Antipope from 997-998. An ally of the Roman nobleman Crescentius II, Giovanni Filagato became antipope to Gregory V. Once enjoying the favor of Emperor Otto II and his widow, Empress Theophano, he accepted Crescentius' offer of the papacy against the candidate, Gregory, chosen by Emperor Otto III. Otto marched on Italy and captured both John and Crescentius. Crescentius' bloody career of dominating the papacy finally ended with his decapitation. John was blinded, mutilated, and placed in a monastery. He died around 1013.

John XVII ● Pope from June 16 to December 6, 1003. He was elected by the Crescentii family, particularly the head, Crescentius III. His virtually anonymous pontificate was spent under their total domination. John was originally known as Giovanni Siccone.

John XVIII ● Pope from 1004-1009. A Roman, Giovanni Fasano was the cardinal priest of St. Peter's at the time of his election to succeed John XVII. His rise was through the powerful Crescentii family; he may have been connected to the Crescentii through blood relatives. Unlike his predecessor, John enjoyed a certain independence from the Roman tyrants, although his departure from the throne in 1009 remains a mystery. He may have retired or was compelled to step down, one of the few pontiffs to die out of office. John died a monk in June or July 1009 at St. Paul-Outside-the-Walls.

John XIX ● Pope from 1024-1032. The brother and successor to Pope Benedict VIII, Count Romanus was a member of the Tusculani family that was then dominating Roman political life. A layman at the time of his election, he was infamous and offensive to the Romans because of his rapacious habits. His main act was to crown Conrad II Holy Roman Emperor on Easter, 1027.

John XX ● There is no Pope John XX in historical records.

John XXI ● Pope from 1276-1277. A native of Lisbon, Peter Juliani was a scholar and highly respected teacher of medicine before his election. He authored medical treatises on the eye, and various works on logic, theology, and philosophy; he was also the physician to Pope Gregory X. That pontiff made him bishop of Braga and cardinal bishop of Tusculum in 1273. On September 8, 1276, he was elected to succeed the briefly reigning Adrian V. He was killed when the ceiling of the papal palace at Viterbo collapsed on him on May 20, 1277. His successor was his principal adviser, Cardinal Orsini, Nicholas III.

John XXII ● Pope from 1316-1334. The second pope to reside in Avignon, he was originally called Jacques Duèse and was born at Cahors, France. A scholar in canon law, he taught at the University of Paris and served as bishop of Avignon before his election in Carpentras after a nearly two-year interregnum following the death of Clement V. Elderly, ill, and seemingly doomed to a brief reign, he appeared to be a suitable compromise candidate but soon surprised his electors with drive and energy. He

reorganized the Curia, founded new dioceses, promoted learning, codified Church law, sponsored missionary work in Asia, and improved papal finances. A major episode of his reign came with the growing conflict of the Spiritual Franciscans and the Conventuals of the order over the question of holding property. John sided with the Conventuals, and the Spiritual Franciscans fled to Louis IV, king of Bavaria, a ruler who had opposed John's election. Louis captured Rome and in 1328 placed a Franciscan on the papal throne, Nicholas V. John imprisoned and excommunicated Nicholas, leading to a reconciliation with Louis. John issued the bull *Docta Sanctorum* (1322), the first major papal declaration on Church music. He also canonized Thomas Aquinas, established the Feast of the Trinity (1334), and added a third row of jewels to the papal tiara, following the addition of the second row by Nicholas II. His only failing was his often shocking nepotism, although he himself practiced a frugal and simple lifestyle.

John XXIII <1> ● Antipope from 1410-1415. Born at Naples, Baldassare Cossa was a recipient of a doctorate from the University of Bologna before entering into the service of the Curia. Made a cardinal in 1402 by Pope Boniface IX, he served as papal representative to Bologna from 1403-1408. As the Church continued to suffer from the Great Schism (1378-1417), the Council of Pisa (1409) tried unsuccessfully to resolve the crisis, declaring Pope Gregory XII and antipope Benedict XIII deposed, and electing a third claimant, antipope Alexander V. Upon Alexander's demise in May 1410, John was elected his successor. Convinced by Emperor Sigismund to convene the Council of Constance in 1414, John refused to accept its declaration that all the rival popes should resign. Fleeing Constance dressed as a layman, he was captured and imprisoned, remaining incarcerated even after acknowledging the election of Pope Martin V, until 1419, when Martin made him cardinal of Tusculum. He died at Florence on November 22, 1419.

John XXIII <2> ● Pope from 1958-1963. One of the most popular of all pontiffs, he was best known for launching Vatican Council II (1962-1965). Angelo Giuseppe Roncalli was born in 1881 at Sotto il Monte, near Bergamo, Italy, to a family of peasant farmers. He studied at the seminary of Bergamo and then at the S. Apollinaire Institute in Rome (from 1901), being ordained in 1904. Appointed secretary the next year to Bishop Radini-Tedeschi of Bergamo, he also taught Church history at the seminary. At the start of World War I in 1914, he was conscripted, eventually serving as a chaplain. After the war, he was named by Pope Benedict XV national director of the Congregation for the Propagation of the Faith. Devoting much of his spare time to historical research, most notably on his own diocese and St. Charles Borromeo (1538-1584), he had researched in the Ambrosian Library, coming into contact with its greatest director, Achille Ratti, the future Pope Pius XI (r. 1922-1939). In 1925, Pius made him titular archbishop of

Areopolis and apostolic delegate to Bulgaria, holding the same post from 1934 in Turkey and Greece.

Having acquired an excellent reputation for his dealings with the Orthodox Church, he was transferred in 1944 to the very difficult post of nuncio to France. He was quickly confronted with the demands of the recently reconstituted French government that thirty-three bishops be removed for collaboration during the German occupation. Roncalli investigated and suggested to the accused bishops that they resign. He negotiated concessions from the French over the financing of schools and called for the humane treatment of German prisoners in the tense period of repatriation. In 1952, he became a permanent observer for the Holy See at UNESCO (United Nations Educational, Scientific, and Cultural Organization). The next year, Pope Pius XII made him a cardinal and patriarch of Venice. While there, he was a very popular figure, known for his wit, cordiality, and approachable pastoral style. After the death of Pius on October 9, 1958, Roncalli was not considered a strong contender to succeed to the throne of Peter, but, on October 28, 1958, he was elected on the twelfth ballot.

Pope John XXIII

Largely thought by observers to have been a compromise candidate (he was seventy-seven at the time), John XXIII proved full of surprises.

One of his first acts was to rescind the regulation since the time of Sixtus V (r. 1585-1590) that fixed the number of cardinals at seventy. His subsequent appointments internationalized the College of Cardinals and brought the number to eighty-seven. On January 25, 1959, he declared his desire for three main goals to be achieved: a diocesan synod, a revision of canon law, and an ecumenical council. The synod was held in January 1960 and was a foreshadowing of the greater council to come in its effort to revitalize the life of the Roman diocese. Canon law revisions were to be the task of a pontifical commission (begun in March 1962). The ecumenical council, which he called the Second Vatican Council (answering suggestions that he simply reconvene the First Vatican Council, which had never adjourned), was to prove the most important event in the history of the Church since the time of the Council of Trent. (For full coverage of the council, see **Vatican Council II**). Said by John to be an inspiration of the Holy Spirit, the council was the fullest expression of the pope's vision of *aggiornamento* (renewal), a new vibrant presentation of the faith.

Beyond the council, John made numerous other efforts to bring reform and revitalization. He issued several notable encyclicals: *Ad Cathedram Petri* (1959), *Mater et Magistra* (1961), and *Pacem in Terris* (1963), which preached "universal peace in truth, justice, charity, and liberty." He thereby took the first steps toward a dialogue with the Soviet bloc that would become the *Ostpolitik*. In ecumenical affairs, he established the Secretariat for Christian Unity (1960) under Cardinal Augustin Bea with the aim of reaching out to the other Christian denominations. He also sent observers to the World Council of Churches and was highly sensitive to Jewish concerns. In liturgical matters, John approved new rubrics for the breviary and missal (1960), inserted the name of St. Joseph in the Canon of the Mass (1962), and permitted the use of the vernacular in the liturgy of the Melkites.

Known throughout the world as a simple, kind, and genuinely earnest pastor, John XXIII became almost legendary for his humor and peasant's common sense. He cultivated the good will of all nations through his honest acts of goodness, be it meeting with pilgrims to St. Peter's or visiting prisoners in the Regina Coeli Prison. Long in poor health, John fell ill after the closing of the first session of the Council (December 1962) and died on June 3, 1963. He had made Giovanni Battista Montini, archbishop of Milan, a cardinal and had given him a prominent role in organizing the council; Montini would succeed him as Pope Paul VI.

John Baptist de la Salle, St. (1651-1719)
● Educator and founder of the Institute of the Brothers of Christian Schools. He was born at Reims, the son of a noble family, entering the service of the Church in 1662. Named a canon of Reims in 1667, he studied for the priesthood, including two years (1670-1672) at St.-Sulpice in Paris, and was ordained in 1678. The following year, he took part in the creation of two schools in Reims, becoming increasingly concerned with the education of the children of poor families. He realized, however, that a religious disposition should be cultivated first among the teachers. Gathering instructors to his own house, he attempted in 1681 to introduce community life but was resisted, and the project failed. He tried again the following year, this time making greater progress. In 1683, he resigned his canonry and gave away his fortune to the poor, devoting himself exclusively to the training of his young men. These would be the foundation of the Brothers of the Christian Schools.

John Baptist took over a free school in the

Parisian parish of St.-Sulpice in 1688, the site of the remarkable work of Jean Jacques Olier, founder of the Society of St.-Sulpice. There, in 1699, John Baptist opened Sunday schools. Such was the renown of his work that he was asked by King James II of England to educate the young boys at his court. A school was opened in Rome in 1700. His work did cause difficulties with the established education authorities who opposed his innovations. In 1702, the archbishop of Paris refused to recognize him as the head of the institute, although he remained in control of its activities until 1717. By 1690, it had been decided that the institute should not have priests and should be constituted entirely by lay brothers. This decision was confirmed in 1693 with the first rule. Today, the Brothers of the Christian Schools (F.S.C.) continue their educational and charitable work; they are the largest religious institute of lay brothers, numbering some eight thousand worldwide. (They should not be confused with the Congregation of Christian Brothers, C.F.C., founded in Ireland in 1802 by Edmund Ignatius Rice.) His most famous pupil was St. Dominic Savio (1842-1857), a young man who died before his fifteenth year and whose biography was written by John Bosco. He was canonized in 1954 by Pope Pius XII and is the patron of choirboys. (Feast day: March 9.)

Beyond his spiritual contributions, John Baptist de la Salle was a gifted pioneer in the field of education. He was the first to create colleges devoted to teacher training as opposed to traditional seminary instruction. Students were taught using the so-called simultaneous method and learned not in Latin but in the vernacular. Especially influential was his school at St.-Yon, begun in 1705, which came to serve as the model for much in modern secondary education. His chief writing on the subject of education was *Conduite des écoles chrétiennes* (1720; *The Conduct of Christian Schools*.) Pope Leo

XIII canonized him in 1900. Feast day: April 7.

John Bosco, St. (1815-1888) ● Also known as Don Bosco. Founder of the Salesian order, he was born in Piedmont, the son of a peasant couple. His father had died when he was only two, so his mother had raised him. From around the age of nine, he aspired to the priesthood with the ambitions of devoting his life to children. The first part of his dream was fulfilled in 1841 when he was ordained. He was sent to the Valdocco suburb of Turin where he soon attracted hundreds of youths to his chapel and evening classes. He then opened a boarding house with his mother for apprentices, followed by workshops where various trades were taught, such as shoemaking and tailoring. From that beginning grew a congregation to advance Bosco's work, founded in 1859 and named by Bosco the Salesians after his deep admiration for St. Francis de Sales. In 1872, Bosco established a similar congregation for women near Genoa with St. Mary Mazzarello (d. 1881) called the Daughters of Mary, Help of Christians. By the time of his death, the congregation had nearly a thousand priests and some nine hundred sisters. His work among the poor children was characterized by infinite patience and a minimum of restrictions or penalties; Bosco once claimed that he could not remember ever actually punishing one of his youths. His labors were accomplished in the face of often considerable hostility from authorities and indifference from local Church officials. Pope Pius XI canonized him in 1934, declaring, "In his life the supernatural almost became natural and the extraordinary, ordinary." Feast day: January 31.

John Capistran, St. (1386-1456) ● Properly Giovanni Capistrano, a Franciscan friar and famed preacher. A native of Capistrano, he studied at Perugia where, in

1412, he was made governor by King Ladislas of Naples. Captured and imprisoned in a war with the family of the Malatestas, he was given a vision of St. Francis that caused him, upon his release, to enter the Franciscan order. Ordained in 1420 or 1426, he soon began preaching, earning considerable fame in Italy. In 1429, however, he was charged and acquitted with fellow Observant Friars on charges of heresy concerning the poverty of Christ. In 1451, Pope Nicholas sent him to Austria to attempt the conversion of the Hussites. He later journeyed to Hungary where he offered his help to oppose the seemingly unstoppable advance of the Ottoman Turks. With the renowned general Hunyadi, John raised an army that defeated the Turks and raised the siege of the city of Belgrade in July 1456. John died of the plague on October 23, 1456. Beatified in 1694, he was canonized in 1724. Feast day: October 23.

John Chrysostom, St. (c. 347-407) ●
Bishop of Constantinople and a Doctor of the Church. John was born in Antioch, studying law under the great pagan orator Libanius in his native city. He also studied theology under Diodore of Tarsus, the head of the Alexandrian School. Drawn at a young age to a life of monasticism, he was unable to become a monk because of the poor health of his widowed mother Anthusa, and then by his own deteriorating physical condition, brought on by his rigorous adoption of a

St. John Chrysostom

strict ascetic lifestyle as a hermit (from around 373 to 381). Made a deacon in 381, he was ordained a priest in Antioch in 386 by Bishop Flavian. Given the task of preaching to the Christian community, he proved so magnificent that his sermons earned him the title *Chrysostom*, or "Golden-mouthed." His homiletic topics varied from the Bible to the moral reformation of society, establishing him as the foremost orator of the age. During the period 386-398, his preaching was devoted to the Antiochenes and included no less than eighty-eight sermons on the Gospel of St. John. Offered the see of Constantinople, he at first refused, but in 398 he was consecrated bishop. His brief episcopate was marked by incessant difficulties with the intrigue-filled imperial court. While the Byzantine masses adored his moral exhortations, the aristocracy greeted him with suspicion, most notably Empress Eudoxia, who viewed his sermons as personal attacks. Theophilus, bishop of Alexandria, soon connived against John, and the empress supported the bishop. In 403, she convened a council that condemned and removed John from office. Reconciled a year later, he was soon banished again in June 404, exiled to Isauria, in the Taurus Mountains. (See also **Oak, Synod of the**.) His letters for help went largely unanswered by fellow Churchmen, save for Pope Innocent I, who tried courageously to save him but to no avail. Surviving longer than expected, John was moved to Pontus, and was forced to travel in bad weather. Falling ill, he died on September 14, 407. He is honored with the title Doctor of the Church and Doctor of the Eucharist for his beautiful witness to the Real Presence. His writings include the treatise *On the Priesthood*. Feast day: September 13 in the West; November 13 in the East.

John Climachus, St. (c. 579-649) ● Also called John of the Ladder. A Byzantine ascetic and writer, he was a member of the monastery of St. Catherine in the Sinai. After spending time as a monk in the Sinai, he retired from monastic life to become a hermit. He was later chosen abbot of the Sinai around 639. A spiritual writer, he authored the *Ladder of Paradise* (or *Ladder of Divine Ascent*), a guide to the acquisition of Christian ideals of spiritual perfection. The book was divided into thirty chapters, each a step along the ladder, culminating with the divine union. His writings were particularly influential among the Hesychasts.

John Duns Scotus, Bl. (c. 1266-1308) ● Franciscan theologian and philosopher, called *Doctor Subtilis* (the Subtle Doctor). He was born in Scotland, probably at Maxton, near Roxburgh, although few details are known of his early life. Around 1280, he entered the Franciscans and studied theology at Oxford under William de Ware. Ordained in 1291, he continued his studies at Paris. He subsequently taught at Oxford, Paris, and Cologne; he and fellow supporters of the papacy were temporarily exiled by King Philip IV the Fair of France during his dispute with Pope Boniface VIII. In 1307, he went to Cologne, perhaps to escape persecution, dying there the next year.

Duns Scotus was a highly influential theologian, establishing a school of thought called Scotism, that would be largely adopted by the Franciscans and would have a wide following during the Middle Ages. His writings are complicated by the fact that he made revisions of them, and he had attributed to him a number of works. Chief among his writings were his commentaries on the *Sentences* of Peter Lombard, extant in three editions: the first was organized by Duns Scotus himself from the notes of his lectures; the second was called the *Opus Oxoniense* (*Oxford Work*), based on his lectures at Oxford; and the third, the *Reportatio Parisiensia* (*Parisian Papers*), was from his Paris lectures. He also wrote commentaries on Aristotle and *Quaestiones Quodlibetales* (*Selected Questions*).

Known as the Subtle Doctor, Duns Scotus created a system of considerable complexity. He affirmed the traditionally held tenets of Augustinianism as per the long-standing custom of his order, but he was quite modern in his outlook. He thus adopted many points of Aristotelianism that were very much in vogue during the period — the way having been shown by St. Thomas Aquinas — and took other farsighted positions such as the use of deduction (foreshadowing Descartes) and mathematics as a basis of the sciences. While he agreed with Thomas Aquinas that reason was not contradicted by revelation, he departed from Thomism by de-emphasizing the essential roles of reason and the intellect in favor of God's love and will. He also promoted the doctrine of the Immaculate Conception, the first theologian of note to proclaim this teaching. Duns Scotus ultimately replaced St. Bonaventure as the greatest of the Franciscan theologians; he was beatified by Pope John Paul II in 1993.

John Eudes, St. (1601-1680) ● French Jesuit and founder of the Sisters of Our Lady of Charity of Refuge and the Congregation of Jesus-Mary, called the Eudists. Born in Ri in Normandy, he was educated at the Jesuit College of Caen and, having been accepted by the superior general of the Oratory (1623), he was ordained in 1625. During the terrible outbreak of plague, John was noted for his courageous care of victims, thereafter working as a missionary in the country. In 1641, he established the Sisters of Our Lady of Charity to care for fallen women; it was entrusted in 1644 to the Visitandines of Caen. In 1643, he founded at Caen the Congregation of Jesus-Mary, an association of priests devoted to the guiding of seminaries. Devoted to the Sacred Hearts of Jesus and Mary, John authored *Le Coeur admirable de la Mère* (1670) and introduced to the congregation a feast in honor of the Sacred Heart of Mary in 1648; with St. Margaret Mary Alacoque, he was responsible for initiating devotion to the Sacred Heart of Jesus. He also authored *La Vie et royaume de Jésus* (1637; *The Life and Realm of Jesus*). The Eudists were nearly wiped out in the years of the French Revolution, but they were reconstituted in 1826 and continue to function as educators in South America, Europe, and the United States and Canada. Beatified in 1909, John was canonized in 1925 by Pope Pius XI. Feast day: August 19.

John of Ávila, St. (1500-1569) ● Apostle of Andalusia, a Spanish mystic reformer, and brilliant preacher. Jewish-born near Toledo, he studied law at Salamanca (1514-1515) but soon found himself drawn to a religious life. For three years he adhered to a life of prayer and austerity before studying theology at Alcalá under the great Spanish Dominican Dominic Soto (1494-1560). Ordained in 1525, he initially prepared for missionary work in Mexico, but in 1528 Archbishop Hernando de Contreras of Seville asked him to remain in Spain to revive the faith in Andalusia. Preaching from 1529, he soon attracted huge crowds with his sermons and was investigated by the Inquisition on charges of heretical teaching of excessive rigorism, denunciations of wealth, and exaggerations. Acquitted and acclaimed in 1535, he continued his Andalusian ministry. After nine years, he returned to Seville and then preached in Córdoba, Granada, and

numerous towns throughout the kingdom. Renowned for his sermons, he was an ardent proponent of clerical reform, especially celibacy, and directly influenced such future saints as Francis Borgia, Luís of Granada, John of God, and Teresa of Ávila. He was also a trusted adviser to Teresa and helped organize (1537) the University of Granada. An associate of the Jesuits, he did much to foster the growth of the order in Spain, dying before he could fulfill his hope of becoming a member. Among his writings are *Audi Filia* (c. 1530), a treatise on Christian perfection addressed to a young nun, Doña Sancha Carillo, and spiritual letters. Beatified by Pope Leo XIII in 1894, he was canonized in 1970 by Pope Paul VI. Feast day: May 10.

John of Damascus, St. (c. 675-749) ● Syrian theologian and writer, a Doctor of the Church. Also called Johannes Damascenus or John Damascene, he was born in Damascus, the son of an official of the local Islamic government, the caliphate. A Christian, he succeeded his father as chief representative of the Christian community (the *Logothete*) to the Caliph. In 719, however, he was compelled to step down from his government post because of his faith, entering a monastery near Jerusalem where he devoted himself to prayer and writing. He was a prolific author, writing some one hundred fifty works on theology, religious education, philosophy, and hagiographies. Between 726 and 730 he composed a spirited defense of the veneration of icons against Emperor Leo III and the Iconoclasts. His two foremost works were *Sacred Parallels* and *Fount of Wisdom*. The latter work, divided into three parts, was known to such later theologians as Peter Lombard and St. Thomas Aquinas, especially the section on the Orthodox faith, *De Fide Orthodoxa*. John thus earned a place in the development of Christian theology. He was declared a Doctor of the Church by Pope Leo XIII in 1890. Feast day: December 4.

John of God, St. (1495-1550) ● Founder of the Order of Charity for the Service of the Sick, also called the Brothers Hospitallers. A native of Portugal, John spent much of his early life as a soldier, suddenly repenting for his violent ways around the age of forty. Hoping to die a martyr in North Africa, he was disappointed and so wandered through Spain selling holy pictures. Finally, after hearing one of the profound lectures of St. John of Ávila, who became his spiritual adviser, John gave himself to the care of the sick and the poor. He rented a house in Granada (1537) and his work for the disadvantaged soon attracted others. Called John of God by Bishop Sebastián Ramírez de Fuenleal of Tuy, Spain, he won approval for his order. His successor, Antonio Martino, drafted a rule for the members. Papal approval came from Pope St. Pius V in 1572 and the order had the financial support of King Philip II of Spain. It soon spread throughout parts of Europe and then the world. The Brothers of the Hospitallers of St. John of God (O.H.) continue to work in hospital-related areas. John was canonized in 1690 by Pope Alexander VIII and declared by Pope Leo XIII in 1886 to be patron of hospitals and the sick; he is also considered a patron of booksellers and printers. Feast day: March 8.

John of Jandun (d. 1328) ● Philosopher and one of the foremost interpreters of Averroism at the University of Paris. Born in the Champagne region of France, he worked as a lecturer on Aristotle and was the author of an important commentary on several works by Aristotle. He also wrote a treatise on Averroism, displaying his Averroist tendencies, including a defense of the theory of the twofold truth — what may be true in theology may be false in philosophy and vice versa. An associate of Marsilius of Padua, he defended imperial policy against the Avignon Papacy and was, with Marsilius, excommunicated in 1327.

John of Matha, St. ● See under **Trinitarians**.

John of Monte Corvino (1246-1328) ● Franciscan friar and the founder of Catholic missions in China. Born at Monte Corvino, he entered the Franciscans and devoted himself for a number of years to the conversion of some of the tribes from the East, concentrating his efforts partly on the Asiatic hordes of Persia. In 1289, he was entrusted by Pope Nicholas IV with a mission to China to deliver letters to Kublai Khan. He set out with the Dominican Nicholas Pistoia and the merchant Peter of Lucalongo. Arriving in India in 1291, the trio was soon reduced by one with the death of Nicholas. John, however, reached China in 1294, just in time to learn of Kublai's death. Nevertheless, he managed to secure excellent relations with the new khan. In 1299, John built a church in Beijing and was later joined by other Franciscans. He was consecrated archbishop of Beijing in 1308 and was revered, even by the Mongols, for his saintliness.

John of Parma (1209-1289) ● Minister-general of the Franciscan order who attempted to restore the order to its original discipline and founding principles. A native of Parma, he entered the Franciscans possibly around 1233. Ordained a priest, he taught theology at Bologna and Naples, and attended the First Council of Lyons (1245). Elected minister-general in July 1247, he held the post until February 1257. During his period of government, he traveled extensively, visiting the Franciscan provinces and promoting discipline. He was forced to deal with the often bitter disputes between the mendicant orders and the University of Paris over the place of the mendicants in the school, writing a letter, with Dominican Master General Humbert of Rome, that called for harmony between the two orders in the face of the common threat. Charged with association with the teachings of Joachim of Fiore, John was eventually acquitted of heresy but resigned in 1257. He retired to a hermitage where he devoted himself in seclusion to penance and prayer, with the exception of a mission to the Byzantine Empire in 1289.

John of Ragusa (1380-1443) ●

Dominican theologian. Born John Stojkovic in Ragusa, he entered the Dominicans at a young age and in 1420 became a master of theology at the University of Paris. In 1426, he was named procurator-general of the order, residing in Rome. Trusted by Martin V, he was appointed papal theologian for the General Council of Basel (1431), chosen to open the council in place of Cardinal Giuliano Cesarini and delivering the inaugural sermon and several morning exhortations against the Hussites. John then served as a legate, in 1435 and 1437, to the Council of Constantinople with the aim of uniting the Eastern and Western Churches. It was John who was probably most responsible for the decision of Emperor John VIII Palaeologus to send an embassy to work toward the brief and ill-fated reunion with the West. While he remained faithful to Pope Eugenius IV, it is possible that he was made a cardinal by the antipope Felix V. He received from Eugenius the bishopric of Argos. His extensive writings include: a treatise against the Hussites; a history of the Council of Basel; an account of his travels in the East, preserved by Leo Allatius; and a record of his embassy to Constantinople, included in the account of the Council of Basel. He should not be confused with John of Ragusa (Cardinal Giovanni Domenici; d. 1419), who took part in the Council of Constance.

John of St. Thomas (1589-1644) ●

Spanish Dominican theologian, so-called because of his remarkable and profound devotion to the teachings of Thomas Aquinas. Born in Lisbon, he was originally named John Poinsot, studying at the Universities of Coimbra and Louvain before entering the Dominicans of Madrid in 1612 or 1613 and taking the name John of St. Thomas. He served as professor of philosophy and theology at the University of Alcalá, and he was named in 1630 and 1640 to the two principal chairs of theology and philosophy respectively. A renowned teacher, he was the foremost interpreter of the system of the Angelic Doctor, declaring on his deathbed that in the thirty years of labors he had never taught or written anything contrary to St. Thomas. He refused all honors offered to him and accepted the post of confessor to King Philip IV in 1643 only through religious obedience. His main writings were: *Cursus Theologica* (9 vols., 1637-1667), a brilliant commentary on the *Summa Theologiae*; a compendium of Christian doctrine, in Spanish; and a treatise on a happy death, also in Spanish.

John of Salisbury (c. 1115-1180) ●

Bishop of Chartres, humanist, and philosopher. A native of Salisbury, he studied at Paris under some giants of the era, including Peter Abelard. After further study at Chartres, he served in the Papal Curia before returning to England where he worked as a secretary to Theobald, archbishop of Canterbury, holding the same position under Thomas Becket. As secretary to Becket, he aided the prelate in his struggle against King Henry II and was thus exiled to Reims with Becket from 1163-1170. When Becket was murdered in 1170, John was present in the Cathedral of Canterbury, although he did not witness the terrible event. In 1176, with the aid of King Louis VII of France, he became bishop of Chartres. A highly enlightened prelate, he was one of the first medieval authors to write with familiarity of Aristotle's work on logic, the *Organon*. He also wrote the *Pelicraticus*, a treatise on the state; the *Metalogicon*; promoting the study of logic and metaphysics; a collection of Becket's correspondence; a collection of his own letters; and the *Historia Pontifica*, a record of his years in Rome.

John of the Cross, St. (1542-1591) ●

One of the greatest mystical theologians in the history of the Church and founder of the Discalced Carmelites. A Doctor of the Church, he is known as the "Doctor of Mystical Theology." He was born Juan de Yepes y Álvarez in the city of Fontiveros, Castile. His father died shortly after his birth, so John was raised by his mother, Catalina Álvarez, but he was able to study at the Jesuit school in Medina, becoming an apprentice at the age of fifteen in the hospital of Our Lady of the Conception. In 1563, he entered the Carmelite order in their monastery in Medina del Campo, taking the name John of St. Matthias. After profession, he was sent to the Carmelite monastery near the University of Salamanca where he studied theology from 1564-1568. He was ordained in 1567.

John was much troubled by the laxity he saw in the Carmelite order, receiving permission from his superiors to adhere privately to the rigorous life established by the original rule. He was drawn to the Carthusians but was dissuaded from this by St. Teresa of Ávila. She was then establishing her reformed convents of the Carmelites and, having received permission to found two monasteries or reformed friars, she encouraged John to join her. He eagerly entered into the movement and soon after created the first Discalced monastery in Duruelo, at which time he adopted the name John of the Cross.

His remaining life was devoted to promoting the reform and writing, although his years were to be sorely troubled. From 1571-1572, he was rector of the monastery at Alcalá and from 1572-1577 confessor of the convent of the Incarnation at Ávila where Teresa was prioress. He faced opposition to his work from within the Carmelites, as many disagreed sharply with the Discalced, refusing to acknowledge the validity of their institutions. After the general chapter of the so-called Calced Carmelites in 1575 at Piacenza, John was seized and in December 1577 was imprisoned by the Calced Carmelites in a tiny cell in a monastery in Toledo. He escaped nine months later by a makeshift rope on the Feast of the Assumption and made his way to the monastery of El Calvario, in Andalusia. The separation of Carmelites into Discalced and Calced was achieved a short time later (1579-1580). Rector (1579-1582) of the college he had begun at Baeza, he next was rector in Granada and prior at Segovia. In 1585, however, Nicola Doria was elected superior of the Discalced Carmelites, and his policies proved so harsh that John felt compelled to oppose him at the chapter held in June 1591. Doria stripped him of all offices and banished him to the monastery of La Penuela in Andalusia. He died on December 14, 1591, in the monastery of Ubeda.

St. John of the Cross was a theologian, a mystic, and a poet, each of these finding profound expression in his writings. The foundations of his mystical treatises were his poems, to which he added extensive and theologically rich commentaries. His chief works are the *Spiritual Canticle*, the *Ascent of Mount Carmel*, the *Living Flame of Love*, and the *Dark Night of the Soul*. These are now spiritual classics by which John presented the stages of development of the human soul through purgation ("the night of the senses"), illumination ("the night of the spirit") and the transforming union, the latter described in the *Living Flame* with its accompanying commentary. Beatified in 1675, he was canonized in 1726 by Pope Benedict XIII; Pope Pius XI declared him a Doctor of the Church in 1926. Feast day: December 14.

John Paul I ● Pope from August 26 to September 28, 1978. A much beloved but very briefly reigning pontiff, his death after thirty-three days came as a shock to the Church, especially given the euphoria that had surrounded the weeks following his election. Albino Luciano was born on October 17, 1912, in Forno di Canale (modern Canale d' Agordo), the son of a poor worker. Educated at the minor seminary in Feltre and the seminary of the diocese of Belluno, he was ordained on July 7, 1935. Serving as a curate at Belluno, he taught at the seminary and, after World War II, studied at the Pontifical Gregorian Seminary (the Gregorian) in Rome, receiving a doctorate in theology. His doctoral thesis was on the Italian philosopher Antonio Rosmini-Serbati. Appointed vicar-general of the diocese of Belluno in 1947, he was appointed bishop of Vittorio Veneto in December 1958. A participant in the Second Vatican Council, he also took part in the Synod of Bishops (1971, 1974, and 1977) and was vice-president of the Italian Bishops' Conference from 1972-1975. Named by Pope Paul VI the patriarch of Venice on December 15, 1969, he became a cardinal on March 5, 1973. Elected by the largest conclave in history, he chose the name John Paul as a reflection of his immediate predecessors and the promise to carry on their work. Warm and engaging, John Paul ended the traditional papal coronation and was

Pope John Paul I

installed by receiving his pallium. During his pontificate he delivered a mere nineteen addresses. He died of a heart attack and was succeeded by Karol Wojtyla, Pope John Paul II.

John Paul II ● Pope from 1978; the first Polish pope and the first non-Italian pontiff since the reign of Adrian VI (1522-1523). Karol Wojtyla was born on May 18, 1920, in the town of Wadowice, Poland, the son of a retired army lieutenant. His mother died while he was still young, and the family was a poor one. He attended the local primary school and then the high school, entering the Jagiellonian University in Cracow in 1938. His field of study was literature and Polish language, but he also distinguished himself as a gifted sportsman, a poet, and a fine performer in amateur theater. Owing to the seizure of Poland in 1939 by the Nazis, the university was closed, and Karol ended up working in a limestone quarry and a chemical factory. Throughout, he continued his studies through an underground association and took part in a secret theater club.

After his father's death in 1942, and having survived two near fatal accidents, Karol chose to enter the priesthood. He studied theology in the clandestine program adopted by the church in Poland in order to circumvent the Nazis. In August, 1946, he graduated and was ordained a priest on November 1, by Cardinal Adam Sapieha, archbishop of Cracow. He was then sent to the University of St. Thomas Aquinas (Angelicum) in Rome, earning a doctorate in theology in 1948. His dissertation was on St. John of the Cross.

Returning to Poland, he worked as a parish priest from 1948-1951 and then studied philosophy at the Jagiellonian University. A lecturer at the Cracow seminary, he was also appointed in 1956 a professor of ethics at Lublin. Two years later, Pope Pius XII appointed him auxiliary bishop to the see of Cracow (titular bishop of Ombi). On December 30, 1963, Paul VI named him archbishop of Cracow. Four years later, on June 26, 1967, he was created a cardinal. As a bishop, he had authored a treatise on sexuality, *Love and Responsibility*, and had been an active member of the preparatory commission for Vatican Council II. He attended all four sessions of the council and took part in the postconciliar commissions. A firm adherent of the decrees of the council, he implemented the reforms and in 1971 was elected a permanent member of the council of the Roman Synod of Bishops. A well-known figure in Europe, he traveled extensively to North America (including the Eucharistic Congress in Philadelphia in 1976), the Middle East, Asia, and Africa. Meanwhile, back in Poland, he worked with the Polish primate, Stefan Wyszyski, to promote political liberty and to give inspiration to Catholics against the Communist regime.

On October 16, 1978, Wojtyla was elected pope by the conclave, choosing a successor to the briefly reigning John Paul I. He was elected most likely on the eighth ballot and took the name John Paul II in deference to his predecessor. Like John Paul I, he was not crowned pope but was installed in a simple ceremony on October 21, proclaiming his devotion to the continued promotion and authentic interpretation of Vatican II.

From the very start of his pontificate, he demonstrated his desire to be "a witness for universal love," spending much of the next few years in extensive travels: Mexico, Poland, Ireland, the United States, Turkey, Zaire, Congo, Ghana, the Ivory Coast, Kenya, Upper Volta, France, Brazil, Germany, the Philippines, and Japan. Tensions were quite high in Poland, however, owing to the Solidarity movement under Lech Walesa, the declaration of martial law by the Polish government, and the chronic threat posed by the Soviet Union. In the midst of these crises, an assassination attempt was made upon John Paul on May 13, 1981, by Mehmet Ali

Pope John Paul II

Agca, while the pope was being driven through St. Peter's Square. A long recovery period followed, but in 1982, he resumed his globe-trotting, traveling to Britain, the first pontiff ever to visit the isle. That same year, he went to Fátima to give thanks to the Blessed Mother for his survival. His unceasing trips since the time of his recovery have made him the most traveled pope in history and the most recognized leader in the entire world. Some of the most significant have been to South Korea (1984), Oceania (1986), the United States (1987, 1993), Scandinavia (1989), Mexico and Czechoslovakia (1990), Poland, Hungary, and Brazil (1991), Latvia, Lithuania, and Estonia (1993).

Deeply concerned with doctrinal orthodoxy and the genuine interpretation of Vatican II in the postconciliar Church, John Paul has been extremely active in voicing his concerns over troubling issues. In 1979, he spoke at the Puebla Conference in Mexico about liberation theology and approved instructions on that movement that were prepared by the Congregation for the Doctrine of the Faith in 1984 and 1986 (see **Liberation Theology**). He has moved against such radical priests as Leonardo Boff, Hans Küng, Charles Curran, and Edward Schillebeeckx, O.P. At the same time, in the face of the intransigence of Archbishop Marcel Lefebvre (d. 1991), he decreed the prelate's excommunication in 1988. On a more positive note, the pope has presided over *The Catechism of the Catholic Church* (1994), the first since the Roman Catechism of the sixteenth century, and issued the encyclical *Veritatis Splendor* (1993), which concerns itself with pressing concerns in moral theology and is a superb expression of the pontiff's complex mind. These measures, coupled with John Paul's forceful personality and his determination to provide a steady course for the direction of the faith, have restored much of the Church's vitality and organization that had been lost in

the turbulent years following the close of Vatican Council II.

Highly experienced in the areas of marriage, sexual ethics, issues of human rights, and economic justice, John Paul has been unequivocal in reaffirming the Church's teaching on matters of reproduction while providing new insights into the nature of the family, the relationship between husband and wife, and the vital sacredness of all life. This position was most seen in his opposition to the Cairo Conference (1994) on Population Growth sponsored by the U.N.

Concerning the internal administration of the Church, he codified the new Code of Canon Law for the Western Church in 1983 and the new Code for the Eastern Churches in 1990. In 1988, he issued the apostolic constitution *Pastor Bonus* (effective March 1, 1989) by which the Curia was reorganized. He has continued to increase the international nature of the College of Cardinals and the Curia, and had made a point to foster collegiality and to convoke synods for the good of the Church.

In the field of ecumenism, John Paul has carried on the work of Paul VI in reaching out to all the faiths and promoting Christian unity, declaring in 1984 that the commitment to religious unity was irreversible. Under his leadership, ecumenism has taken many strides in the last decade, and the pontiff has pointed to the commonality of baptism, prayer, and the Scripture, while remaining firm in refusing to permit the sharing of the Eucharist. One of the happiest and most fruitful achievements of his ecumenism is his relationship with Judaism. In 1986, he visited a synagogue in Rome and in 1994 normalized relations with Israel.

John Paul's pontificate has witnessed one of the most tumultuous periods in history. The pope has had the once unthinkable opportunity to reestablish the Church in the onetime lands of Communist Eastern Europe, including Hungary, Poland, the

Baltic States, and even Russia. Deeply committed to religious freedom, human rights, economic and social justice, and to alleviating the suffering of the poor and afflicted, the pope has regularly used his travels as a platform to address these issues. His social concerns have been the subject of several encyclicals: *Laborem exercens* (1981), *Sollicitudo Rei Socialis* (1987), and *Centesimus annus* (1991). In other affairs, he negotiated a new concordat with Italy (1984), formalized relations with the United States (1984), embarked upon a new diplomatic era with Mexico (1992), and has promoted peace in war-torn Yugoslavia.

Karol Wojtyla was one of the most accomplished and superbly educated cardinals ever to be elected to the throne of St. Peter and was the youngest pontiff, fifty-eight at his election, since Pius IX in 1846. The holder of multiple degrees and a brilliant philosopher and theologian, he is also a poet, playwright, and avid skier, whose enjoyment of the slopes was curtailed only in 1994 after a hip injury from a fall in the apostolic apartments. He is fundamentally aware of the place of the Church in the modern world and has concentrated much effort to preparing the faithful for the challenges and opportunities of the next millennium. (See also **Communism, Ecumenism, Ostpolitik, Poland**, and TABLE 8.)

John Scotus Erigena (d. c. 877) ● Irish philosopher and scholar. Winning the favor of Charles the Bald, king of the West Franks, John was appointed head of the palace of Laon, subsequently taking part in two controversies involving Gottschalk of Fulda and the Eucharist involving Paschasius Radbertus. The author of the *De Divisione Naturae*, he proposed that nature was divided into four general categories, beginning and ending in God. The treatise was condemned in 1210 at Paris and 1225 at Sens (by Pope Honorius III) for its tendencies

toward pantheism. John may have gone to England in his later years at the invitation of King Alfred the Great and was associated, probably erroneously, with the revival of learning that occurred at Alfred's court. He also translated the writings of Dionysius the Areopagite (see **Pseudo-Dionysius**) into Latin along with those of the Greek Church officials, and wrote a number of exegetical works.

John Vianney, St. ● See **Vianney, John, St.**

Joinville, Jean (c. 1224-1317) Properly Jean de Joinville, a French historian, author of the famed *Histoire de Saint-Louis*. Joinville accompanied Louis IX on the Seventh Crusade (1248-1254) to Egypt and with him was captured by the Muslims. Captive and in confinement with the king, Joinville became a good friend of Louis, remaining so upon their return to France. He refused, however, to embark on Louis's ultimately fatal expedition in 1270 but served as an important witness to Louis's canonization in 1282. At the request of Queen Jeanne of Champagne and Navarre, wife of King Philip IV the Fair, he began a biography of Louis, presenting the finished work to Louis X. The biography is a charming and generally objective source on both Louis and the Seventh Crusade. He also wrote a *Credo* (1252), a compilation on his personal beliefs.

Joseph Calasanz, St. (1556-1648) ● Also Joseph Calasanctius, a Spanish priest and the founder of the Piarists (Order of the Pious Schools). The son of Don Pedro Calasanza and Dona Maria Gastonia, he was born in Aragon and studied at the Universities of Valencia and Alcalá. Ordained in 1583 by the bishop of Urgel and known in religion as "*a Matre Dei*," he spent several years working in Spain and then, in 1592, he went to Rome where he won the patronage of Cardinal Marcantonio Colonna, who employed him as a theological adviser and tutor to his nephew. While in Rome, he undertook numerous charitable works, especially caring for poor and homeless children. In November 1597, he opened the first public free school in Europe and in 1602 established the Order of Piarists in the rented house at S. Andrea della Valle. The school was transferred in 1612 to the Torres palace adjoining S. Pantaleone and there Joseph spent his remaining years. He was canonized by Pope Clement XIII on July 16, 1767. Feast day: August 25.

Joseph of Arimathea, St. ● The "good and righteous man" (Lk 23:50) and the man "who was also himself looking for the kingdom of God" (Mk 15:43) who, after the Crucifixion, requested the body of Christ from Pontius Pilate and provided a proper burial for Our Lord. Called also "Councillor" (cf. Lk 23:50) he was described as a disciple by John, who "secretly, for fear of the Jews, asked Pilate that he might take away the body of Jesus, and Pilate gave him leave" (19:38). Joseph had a role in the foundation of the Christian community of Lydda, according to the apocryphal Gospel of Nicodemus and was later given a preeminent place in medieval literature pertaining to the Holy Grail. He appeared in Robert de Barron's early thirteenth-century romance *Joseph d' Arimathie* and in William of Malmesbury's *De Antiquitate Glastoniensis Ecclesiae* (twelfth century; relating the story of Joseph's arrival in England with the Grail and the building of the first church on the isle at Glastonbury, although the passage on Joseph was added in the thirteenth century), and Thomas Mallory's *Morte Darthur* (fifteenth century). Feast day: March 17.

Joseph of Cupertino, St. (1603-1663) ● Italian Franciscan. The son of a carpenter in Cupertino, he was born Joseph Desa. Because of his severe ignorance he was refused entry into the Conventual Friars Minor and was dismissed by the Capuchins on account of his clumsiness and awkwardness. Finally, the Franciscans at La Grotell, near Cupertino, took him in as a stable boy. He was ordained in 1628 and thereafter was blessed with miracles and ecstasies, including the well-accounted phenomenon of levitation. He was also able to read the consciences of those whom he met. So profound was his effect upon the Lutheran duke John Frederick of Brunswick that the nobleman was converted to Catholicism. Within his communities, however, his levitation and ecstasies were found to be disruptive and Joseph lived for most of his remaining years in private seclusion, being removed to quiet convents, including the Conventual house at Orsimo in the March of Amona. There he ended his days as one "whose conversation was in heaven." He was canonized in 1767 by Pope Clement XIII. Feast day: September 18.

Joseph the Hymnographer, St. (c. 810-886) ● Prolific Greek hymn-writer. He is considered the composer of one thousand canons, some two hundred being compiled in the *Menaion*, the twelve liturgical books in the Eastern Church containing the variable parts of the Divine Office for immovable feasts. Revered in the Eastern Church as a saint, his feast day is April 3.

Josephinism ● Also Josephism, the theories forming the basis of the religious policy and reforms launched by Joseph II, Holy Roman Emperor from 1765-1790 and from whom its name is derived. Joseph was influenced in formulating his policies by his mother, Maria Theresa, and took elements of Gallicanism and Erastianism as his guiding principles. In essence, Josephinism advocated the supremacy of the state in matters of religion, with control over the Catholic Church in all its affairs, including appointments. In practical application, Joseph adopted ideas from Febronianism which argued that the pontiff should have limited ecclesiastical authority.

Through Josephinism, the emperor sought to place state regulations upon the Church within the Holy Roman Empire. In cooperation with the bishops, he reorganized dioceses, stipulated the number of Masses that could be celebrated, and seized many schools that were replaced by state-controlled institutions. The seminaries were also brought under the state, substituted with government-controlled centers with the aim of producing clerics fully indoctrinated in Josephist policies. Hardest hit were the religious orders. Severe limits were placed on the number of religious who could reside within the lands of the empire. Monasteries were taken away from the authority of the pope and then dissolved on the grounds that monks and nuns spending their days in prayer were useless to society. In 1781, the Act of Toleration was passed formalizing the suppression of the religious orders and monasteries, granting supposed full freedom to religious organizations, and stipulating that all papal pronouncements, decrees, or statements should be subject to government approval prior to publication in imperial territories.

Pope Pius VI (r. 1775-1799) protested the policies, actually traveling to Vienna in 1782 to make his point. Despite the wild reception given to the pontiff on his route to Vienna, Joseph remained firm and Pius returned home without a lessening of the state of affairs. Josephinism continued until the emperor's death, although resentment and resistance were found in the Netherlands and Hungary. After Joseph's passing, Josephinism entered into a long period of decline, as Europe was faced with the French Revolution and then the Napoleonic Wars. It was reintroduced under Emperor Francis II and would not be repudiated until the mid-nineteenth century.

Josephus, Flavius (c. 37-c. 100) ● Jewish historian. Probably born in Jerusalem, he was the descendant of Jewish priests, studying Jewish law, living for three years in the desert as a disciple of the hermit Bannos, and becoming a Pharisee in 64. A patriot, he joined the cause of the Jews in the first period of the Jewish Revolt (66-70) against the Romans. Placed in command of Galilee, his authority was constantly undermined by rivals leading to the fall of the city of Jotapata in Galilee and Josephus' capture by the Romans under Vespasian in 67. Known to Vespasian and his son Titus, Josephus was spared, especially after predicting Vespasian's rise as emperor. For the rest of the Roman campaign, Josephus worked as a translator, witnessing the fall of Jerusalem in 70. Much favored by the Flavians (hence the name "Flavius"), Josephus moved to Rome, was granted a pension by the imperial family, and devoted himself to literary efforts. His two major works were the *Jewish Antiquities* (finished in 93 or 94) and the *Jewish War* (compiled in 73 and rewritten in Greek in 75-76). Josephus was much read by the Fathers of the Church, especially St. Jerome, as they utilized his biblical narratives. Josephus mentioned Christ in a passage on St. James. The famous reference in *Antiquities* (XVII, 3.3, "a wise man if indeed one should call him a man") was probably not authentic, being an addition or interpretation by a Christian after the time of Eusebius of Caesarea (d. c. 340).

Judaizers ● Name given to the first-century Christian converts who believed that it was necessary for all Gentile Christians to become full and legal Jews, observing the Mosaic law, in order to experience full Christianity. They called, for example, for the enforcement on all Christians of such practices as circumcision, and the distinction between clean and unclean meats. Their name meant "to live in the Jewish manner," and they are considered the first heretical sect or the earliest internal crisis that had to be faced by the Church. The Judaizers caused the convening of the first Church council (c. 49), the Council of Jerusalem, at which the Apostles and other Christians called together by them reached the decision that Gentiles should be received into the family of the Church. (cf. Acts 15:10-11). The Judaizers quickly declined in influence and eventually disappeared in the period following the destruction of the Great Temple of Jerusalem (70). The principal opponent of the Judaizers in the Church was St. Paul.

Jude, St. ● Apostle and popular saint. Venerated as the patron of hopeless situations, he is mentioned as a disciple in several lists in the NT. In Luke (6:16) and Acts (1:13) he is called Judas of James; in John (14:22) he is known as "Judas (not Iscariot)." Also named Thaddeus (or Thaddaeus), he was mentioned as such in Matthew (10:3) and Mark (3:18). He is considered in tradition to be the brother of St. James the Less and was long reputed to be the author of the Epistle of St. Jude, although scholars today doubt that St. Jude was actually the writer. In John (14:22-23), Jude had a memorable exchange with Christ. According to early traditions about him, including the apocryphal "Passion of Simon and Jude," he and Simon preached in Persia where they were martyred. Feast day: October 28, with St. Simon.

Jude, Epistle of ● One of the "catholic" letters of the NT, so-called because it is addressed not to any one local Church or individual but to the universal Church. The relatively short epistle is concerned with warning the faithful about false teachers who had gained admission into the Church and "who pervert the grace of our God into licentiousness and deny our only Master and Lord, Jesus Christ" (v. 4). The author is very clear in his rejection of such persons: "These are grumblers, malcontents, following their own passions, loud-mouthed boasters, flattering people to gain advantage" (16); they "defile the flesh, reject authority, and revile the glorious ones" (8). He reminds his readers to remember the promises of judgment, exhorting the faithful to keep themselves "in the love of God; wait for the mercy of our Lord Jesus Christ unto eternal life" (21).

The epistle is written by one who identifies himself as "Jude, a servant of Jesus Christ and brother of James." According to tradition, he is identified with the Judas described in Matthew (13:55) and Mark (6:3) as one of the brethren of Jesus. Some scholars hold the view that Jude was a pseudonym. Origen and St. Jerome both held that he was the Apostle of Luke (6:16) while Acts (1:13) claims it was "Judas the son of James." Its date has been the subject of considerable question owing to the lack of any internal evidence. As the Second Epistle of Peter mentions the Epistle of Jude, it can be naturally deduced to have been written before 2 Peter, meaning it can be dated to sometime before 100. Possible suggested dates are around 80 or 90, although prior to 70 has been proposed owing to the absence of any reference to the destruction of the Great Temple of Jerusalem in that year.

Julian of Norwich (c. 1342-after 1413) ● English mystic. Also called Juliana of Norwich, author of the famous work *Revelation of Divine Love*. Few details of Julian's life are known except for the fact that she was an anchoress who spent her days in prayer. Starting in May 1373, she was the recipient of a series of visions concerning the Holy Trinity and the Passion. The *Revelation* was composed to detail what she had seen but was written some twenty years later. One of the most remarkable and profound works on mysticism, it was written with the aim of stressing Divine Love as the source of ending all problems of existence.

Julian the Apostate (c. 332-363) ●
Emperor of Rome from 361-363. Known in
full as Flavius Claudius Julianus, he was the
last pagan ruler of the Roman Empire and an
opponent of Christianity. Born at
Constantinople, he was the son of Julius
Constantius, half-brother of Constantine the
Great, and Basilina, a daughter of the
governor of Egypt. His father was murdered
in 337 in the palace massacre that followed
the death of Constantine. Julian was spared
only because of his age. Despite an education
along Christian lines, he remained a devoted
pagan in his private life. Chosen in 355 to be
given the rank of caesar (or junior emperor)
by Emperor Constantius, he proved a gifted
general, inflicting severe defeats upon several
Germanic tribes such as the Franks and the
Alamanni. In 360, Julian was declared
emperor by his troops, becoming ruler of the
empire in 361 because of the death of
Constantius from fever in Cilicia. Julian
immediately embarked upon a deliberate
policy of renouncing Christianity, earning the
historical title of "the Apostate." He
dismissed Christian teachers, ended state
subsidies for the Church, promoted pagan
worship, and was willing to do everything
possible to curb the growth of the faith short
of outright oppression. Julian was not
supported by the majority of the citizens in
the empire. He died on June 20, 363, during
a campaign against the Persians, from a
wound he suffered in battle.

Juliana Falconieri, St. (1270-1341) ●
Foundress of the Third Order of the Servites.
Born to a noble Florentine family, she was
much influenced in her early life by her uncle
St. Alexis Falconieri, one of the seven
founders of the Servite order. After the death
of her father, Juliana received, around 1385,
the habit of the Third Order of the Servites
from St. Philip Benizi, general of the Servites,
thus making her the foundress of that order.
At first permitted to remain in her mother's
house, Juliana and several companions

moved in 1305 into their own house, which
became the first convent of the Sisters of the
Third Order of the Servites. Juliana remained
superior until her death. Revered as a saint
almost immediately after her death, she was
canonized in 1737 by Pope Clement XII.
Feast day: June 19.

Julius I, St. ● Pope from 337-352. A
strong opponent of Arianism, Julius spent
much of his reign upholding Christian
orthodoxy against the Arians. Julius was
elected on February 6, 337, as successor to
St. Mark after an interregnum of four
months. He gave refuge in Rome to St.
Athanasius of Alexandria in 339 after the
bishop had been deposed and expelled from
his see by the Arians. Julius reaffirmed
Athanasius' right to the see at the Council of
Rome in 340, and then convoked the Council
of Sardica (342-343) to combat Arianism and
to bolster the West against its spread. The
council gave Julius acknowledgment of his
supreme ecclesiastical authority, particularly
the right to judge cases involving episcopal
sees. Emperor Constantius II, an Arian,
confirmed Julius's restoration of Athanasius,
a statement of Julius's abilities as pontiff.
Letters from Julius were preserved in
Athanasius' *Apology Against the Arians.*
Feast day: April 12.

Julius II ● Pope from 1503-1513. A
remarkable pontiff, general, and patron of
the arts, Julius was one of the most powerful
figures of his era. A nephew of Pope Sixtus IV
(Francesco della Rovere), Giuliano della
Rovere was born in Albissola, near Savona,
in 1443. Living for a time at a house for
Conventual Franciscans under the care of
his uncle, Giuliano was made a cardinal
upon Francesco's election in 1471. A highly
influential figure in the pontificate of Sixtus,
he was utilized on numerous missions by his
generous relative, receiving extensive
holdings and offices. Recognizing, however,
that the circumstances were not ideal to

secure his own election as successor to his uncle, Giuliano used bribes and influence to ensure the election of Innocent VIII in 1484. Throughout Innocent's reign, he continued to exert enormous power in papal affairs, his place in Rome suffering a major setback in 1492 with the election of his bitter enemy, Rodrigo Borgia, as Alexander VI. Fearing his murder, Julius fled to France and King Charles VIII of France. Although a formal reconciliation was made between them in 1498, Giuliano chose to reside in hiding in northern Italy, safe from the pope and his dangerous relatives. Upon Alexander's death in 1503, Julius returned to Rome and remained there throughout Pius III's brief reign. On November 1, he was finally elected pope by unanimous vote.

From the start of his pontificate, Julius devoted himself wholeheartedly to reestablishing a strong, independent, vibrant papacy, free from foreign domination. While the methods he used were often violent, he succeeded in his ambitions. Such was his ardor in pursuing military solutions that

Pope Julius II

Guicciardini, the Florentine historian, noted that there was nothing of the priest about him except for the dress and the name. As a preliminary means of improving his position, Julius succeeded in driving Cesare Borgia, son of Alexander VI, out of Italy in 1504, launching his campaigns against Perugia and Bologna. This was followed by his joining the League of Cambrai against Venice (1509), in which the Venetians were defeated with the help of France. In 1511, Julius turned on the French, forming the Holy League with Spain, England, Switzerland, and Venice. King Louis XII responded by convening a council of rebellious cardinals to depose Julius at Pisa in 1510. Julius was declared suspended by the cardinals who had moved to Milan in 1512. Such setbacks were offset by the Fifth Lateran Council (1512-1517) at which the Pisan Council and the Pragmatic Sanction of Bourges were condemned, and the support of Emperor Maximilian secured the papal cause. His death from fever on February 21, 1513, left many crises unresolved but the Papal States considerably stronger and financially more sound than when he found them.

A sensual and difficult man, known as *"Il terrible"* (he had fostered three daughters as a cardinal), Julius did institute reforms in the Church. His constitution *De fratrum nostrorum* (1505) declared void all pontifical elections secured by simony. His greatest contributions were as a patron of Renaissance masters. He promoted the works of Michelangelo (especially in the Sistine Chapel) and Raphael as well as Bramante, one of the most important of all papal-sponsored artisans. In 1506, Julius laid the cornerstone for the new St. Peter Basilica, although the indulgence for the project was the occasion some years later for the ninety-five theses of Martin Luther. Desiderius Erasmus attacked Julius as being too warlike in his *Moriae Encomium* (*Praise of Folly*) and Michelangelo composed a scathing poem about him. He was succeeded in the papacy by Giovanni de' Medici, Leo X.

Julius III ● Pope from 1550-1555. Called a Renaissance pontiff, Julius was a patron and protector of Michelangelo, but he also promoted Church reform. Born Giovanni Maria Ciocchi del Monte, he was a native of Rome, studying at Perugia and Siena. Made archbishop of Siponto in 1511, he was a trusted figure in the reigns of Clement VII and Paul III. In 1527, with the sack of Rome, he was briefly held as a hostage by imperial forces. Later, in 1545, as a cardinal, he opened the Council of Trent as its co-president and a papal legate. On February 7, 1550, he was elected pontiff after a stormy conclave. Anxious to bring reform, he reopened the Council of Trent on May 1, 1551, but, after its sixteenth session, the proceedings were suspended owing to severe political difficulties. The pope encouraged the recently established Society of Jesus, confirming its constitution (1550), and establishing the Collegium Germanicum (1552) under Jesuit instructors, to train German secular priests to return and engage in the evangelization of their homeland. A lover of the arts, Julius named Michelangelo chief architect of St. Peter's and the gifted composer Palastrina the choirmaster. Disappointed in his final years by failing to bring reform, Julius spent much of his time enjoying banquets, art, and hunting.

Julius Africanus, Sextus (d. c. 240) ● Christian writer, the author of a *History of the World*, he was considered a father of Christian historiography. Probably a native of Jerusalem, Julius enjoyed the favor of the Severan Dynasty of the Roman emperors, most notably Elegabalus (r. 218-222) and Alexander Severus (r. 222-235). Under the latter, he played a major role in the creation of a public library in the Pantheon of Rome. He was the author of two letters: the first was to Origen, disputing the authenticity of the

story of Susanna, which was answered by Origen and preserved in Origen's works making it the only completely extant writing by Julius; the second was addressed to a certain Aristides on the two genealogies of Christ as given by Matthew (1:2-19) and Luke (3:23-38). His main work was the aforementioned world history, dated to perhaps between 212 and 221. It attempts to unite the account of the Bible with Roman and Greek history, carrying events from the creation (5499 B.C. by Julius's calculations) to A.D. 221. The first effort at Christian historiography, the work is quite important, particularly as it is the basis of Eusebius's *Ecclesiastical History* and was a vital source for later Byzantine historical writings. It is now known only in fragmentary form. Julius also wrote the *Embroidered Girdles*, an encyclopedic guide to miscellaneous sciences, natural history, and medicine, dedicated to Severus Alexander, in twenty-four books.

Justin Martyr, St. (c. 100-165) ● Early Christian theologian and one of the foremost of all apologists. Justin was born in Flavia Neapolis in Samaria to a pagan family. After spending many years of his life studying paganism, he grew dissatisfied and, at the age of thirty, found Christianity. He taught at a school in Ephesus and, around 135, engaged in a famous disputation or debate with Trypho the Jew, the basis for Justin's later work, *Dialogue with Trypho the Jew.* Moving to Rome, he opened a place of learning for Christians, claiming as one of his pupils the theologian Tatian. By now a learned Christian, Justin began to defend his faith in clear and brilliant fashion, utilizing his extensive familiarity with pagan teachings to provide an educated Roman audience with reasoned arguments for the moral and intellectual superiority of Christianity. His *First Apology* (c. 155) was written for Antoninus Pius, Marcus Aurelius, and Lucius Verus, defending the faith against various charges and accusations. The *Second Apology* was written for the senate and again refuted assorted charges. Around 165, the imperial government finally took action against him. He and several followers were arrested, ordered to make sacrifices, and, upon their refusal, were scourged and beheaded. The greatest of the early apologists, Justin was remarkable for his effort to unite Christian faith with reason. An extant account of his death was the *Martyrium S. Iustini et Sociorum.* Feast day: June 1.

Justinian I (483-565) ● Byzantine Emperor from 527-565 who has been called the "Last Roman" and the "First Byzantine Emperor" and was responsible for the return of the empire to greatness. The nephew of Emperor Justin I (r. 518-527), he was named caesar (or junior emperor) in 525 and co-emperor in 527. Upon the death of Justin on August 1, 527, he became sole emperor. The primary focus of much of his reign was the reinstitution of the Roman Empire in the West, using such talented generals as Narses and Belisarius to recover large portions of the Western provinces that had been lost to the Germanic kingdoms. Italy, parts of Spain, Dalmatia, and areas of North Africa were reclaimed. His policy, however, particularly using diplomacy and tribute to keep the dangerous Persians at bay, emptied the imperial treasury, requiring such heavy taxes that there occurred the Nike Revolt of 532, an uprising that he and his wife Theodora suppressed ruthlessly. His main achievements were in acting as a patron of the Church. In Constantinople, he built the Santa (or Hagia) Sophia, one of the greatest churches in Christendom, and other basilicas were erected elsewhere, particularly at Ravenna. An advocate of Caesaropapism, Justinian was an advocate of Christian orthodoxy, persecuting the Montanists, and encouraging the conversion of pagans. In 552, he summoned the Second Council of Constantinople in an effort to reconcile the Monophysites. Of particular note was his codification of Roman law, called the Code of Justinian, which became the source for much of modern civil law and influenced the development of canon law. Within a decade of his death, most of the lands reclaimed during his reign were lost once more.

Emperor Justinian I

Kalands Brethren ● In German and Latin, respectively, *Kalandsbruder* and *Fratres Calendarii.* Religious organizations or associations found in considerable number in northern and central Germany that met routinely to promote prayer (especially for the dead) and works of charity. Their name was derived from the custom of the clergy of separate deaneries to hold their meetings on the first day of each month, *Kalendae.* The gatherings became much more organized from the thirteenth century, and the associations came to include priests and laypersons, both men and women. The head of each organization was customarily the dean. Flourishing in the fourteenth and fifteenth centuries, the Brethren spread from Germany to Denmark, Hungary, Norway, and France. Decline set in during the sixteenth century with numerous abuses becoming commonplace. Most of the associations were eradicated as a result of the Reformation and the rest died out over succeeding years.

Kant, Immanuel (1724-1804) ● German philosopher, ranked among the greatest and most influential philosophers in history. He was born at Königsberg, lived a quiet life in that city, taught logic and metaphysics in the local university, and devoted himself to the development of his vast system of thought. His chief works were *Critique of Pure Reason* (1781), *Foundations of the Metaphysics of Ethics* (1785), *Critique of Practical Reason* (1788), *Critique of Judgment* (1790), and *Religion within the Boundaries of Pure Reason* (1793-1794). These were the foundation of a program so extensive and

complicated that it defies summary and is considered by some philosophers to have been the result of nearly deliberate obscuration. Kant did not attempt to organize his ideas into a specific system. This was done by others, such as Georg Wilhelm Friedrich Hegel (1770-1831) and Johann Gottlieb Fichte (1762-1814), creating what is called Kantianism (or Kantism). In broad terms, he sought to find alternatives to the Continental rationalism of Descartes, Leibniz, and Spinoza, and the empiricist philosophy of David Hume, John Locke, and George Berkeley. He distinguished between those things of our experience (*phenomena*) that can be placed into the realm of our understanding (such as causality) and things in themselves (called *noumena*) that are beyond the grasp of the intellect. To explain this inability of the intellect, Kant established the antinomies. These are contradictions of various principles that are beyond resolution (e.g., that God exists and does not exist). He argues that while we cannot know *noumenal* things ("things in themselves"), we can know that they exist. In matters of morality, Kant advanced the notion of the categorical imperative, stating that one should act so "as to treat humanity, whether in your own person or that of another, in every case as an end in itself, never as a means." The freedom of the will guided by absolute duty he believed should be the basis of moral order, although it is pointed out by critics that the application of the principle of absolute duty is difficult in terms of specific norms.

Many elements of Kantianism are considered quite at odds with Christian philosophy and points of Catholic theology. In his moral structure, his adherence to freedom of the will and absolute duty run counter to the ethical norms expounded by the magisterium, boundaries of conduct that would be viewed as severe infringements of the personal freedom Kant espoused. Further, Kant's notion that certain kinds of knowledge such as the existence of God are unattainable by human reason is in conflict with traditional Church teaching, especially as expressed by St. Thomas Aquinas.

Kells, Book of ● Magnificent illuminated manuscript of the Gospels in Latin. So named after the monastery of Kells in County Meath, Ireland, and also called the Book of Columba, probably because it was written in the monastery of Iona in honor of that great saint. The book was most likely produced in the eighth century. The tradition, however, that claimed the book to have been a possession of St. Columba is now known to be erroneous because of the confirmation of the date of the manuscript. Arguably the greatest of all illuminated manuscripts, it contains the Four Gospels, a fragment of Hebrew names, and the Eusebian Canons. Written in black, red, purple, or yellow ink, it was the work of two scribes, otherwise unknown, and was apparently left unfinished. So renowned was its beauty that there was a long-standing tradition that the Book of Kells could only have been written by the angels. It is preserved in the Library of Trinity College, Dublin. (See also **Manuscript Illumination**.)

Kempe, Margery (c. 1373-after 1433 or 1439) ● English mystic and author of the *Book of Margery Kempe*. The daughter of John Burham, mayor of Lynn, she was born in Norfolk. Marrying John Kempe, burgess of Lynn, she bore him fourteen children, but in 1413 they both took a vow of chastity before Philip Repingdon, bishop of Lincoln. Shortly after an episode of mental instability, she

began receiving visions and so took a pilgrimage with her husband to Canterbury. Around 1413, they journeyed to the Holy Land, Rome, Germany, and Spain. An ardent opponent of pleasure, she was accused of Lollard heresy but was ultimately acquitted. She received encouragement from Julian of Norwich. Her autobiography, the *Book of Margery Kempe*, describes her mystical experiences and her travels. From about 1432-1436, it was dictated to clerks owing to Kempe's illiteracy. Only one manuscript of the book is now known to exist.

Kempis, Thomas à ● See **Thomas à Kempis**.

Kentigern, St. (d. 603) ● "Apostle of Scotland." Also called St. Mungo. According to some sources, he was of British royal descent, raised in Scotland, in a monastic school on the Firth of Forth. He established a Christian community in Scotland around 550, receiving much help in his missionary work through the patronage of the king of Strathclyde. Kentigern was forced to flee to Cumberland and Wales in the face of the inevitable pagan counterreaction, founding in Wales the monastery of St. Asaph. Finally allowed to return to Scotland, he restored Christian practices around Glasgow.

Ketteler, Wilhelm Emmanuel, Baron Von (1811-1877) ● Bishop of Mainz. He was an outspoken defender of Church freedom from the German government and an ardent promoter of the rights of workers. A native of Münster, he was preparing to enter the service of the Prussian bureaucracy when, in 1837, he was so appalled by the persecution of Archbishop Droste of Cologne, that he resigned. Ordained in 1844, he was elected to the Frankfurt Parliament in 1848, distinguishing himself for his knowledge of contemporary social conditions. At the Catholic Conference of Mainz (October 1848), he made the famous declaration that religion needs freedom and freedom needs religion. Named by Pope Pius IX to the see of Mainz, Ketteler quickly inflicted ecclesiastical defeats upon the highly Josephist government of Hesse, securing the independence of his seminary. His remarkable work in social areas was reflected in his *Die Arbeiterfrage und das Christenthum* (1864; *The Labor Question and Christianity*). A participant in the First Vatican Council (1869-1870), he opposed the dogmatic definition of papal infallibility and departed the council before any votes on the matter were taken. Ketteler accepted the decrees of the council in August 1870. He also opposed the *Kulturkampf.*

King's Confession ● Also Scot's Confession. Protestant declaration written by John Craig (d. 1600) in 1581 reaffirming that Protestantism was the creed of Scotland. Drafted out of fear that "Popery" might return to Scotland, the Confession, known in full as "A Short and General Confession of the True Christian Faith and Religion according to God's Will and Acts of our Parliament," was signed by King James VI and his entire household and all the clergy in the kingdom. Reaffirmed over the next years, it was the foundation for the National Covenant (the Covenant of Scottish Presbyterians) of 1638. This should not be confused with the Scottish Confession, the first Confession of Faith for the Reformed Scottish Church that was adopted by the Scottish Parliament in 1560.

Klesl, Melchior (1552-1630) ● Austrian cardinal and statesman. Became for a time the most powerful figure in the Holy Roman Empire. Born in Vienna, Klesl was the son of Protestants. After studying at the University of Vienna, however, he and his parents were converted, through the influence of the Jesuits (particularly the Jesuit court chaplain, Father George Scherer). Receiving minor orders in 1577, he became a doctor of

philosophy in 1579 and provost of St. Stephen's in Vienna. Ordained to the priesthood a short time later, he served as chancellor to the bishop of Passau, so impressing Emperor Rudolf II that he was appointed court chaplain and imperial councillor; the ruler also gave Klesl instructions to promote the Catholic Reformation. In 1598, he was named bishop of Vienna (consecrated in 1614), and made a cardinal, first *in petto* (1615) and then publicly in 1616 by Pope Paul V. A trusted adviser to Matthias, king of Hungary and Bohemia, he helped secure his election as Holy Roman Emperor (1612) and was named head of the privy council. In this capacity Klesl ran most of the affairs of the empire, promoting the Catholic Reformation. He also worked to bring religious peace, a conciliatory policy much opposed by the German Catholic princes, especially Archduke Ferdinand. When the cardinal suggested making concessions to the Bohemian Protestants, he was removed by the princes in 1618 and imprisoned. Restored as bishop in January 1628, he decreed that the Feast of the Immaculate Conception should be observed in his diocese. He died in Vienna and was buried in St. Stephen's.

Knights of Columbus ● World's largest fraternal organization of laymen. It was founded in 1882 in New Haven, Connecticut, by Father Michael J. McGivney with the aim of uniting Catholic men to foster and promote genuine Catholicity and civic activities. The knights are devoted to numerous programs of public service including charities, social welfare, educational scholarships, and the providing of aid in times of war, tragedy, or disaster. While existing in complete harmony with the Church, the society is organized under a supreme knight, with an executive board, a supreme council, and a number of subordinate or state councils. The knights have traditionally been especially generous in donations to the Holy See. The society's chief publication is the magazine *Columbia.*

Knoblecher, Ignatius (1819-1858) ● Priest and missionary in Africa. A native of the German region of Carniola he was ordained a priest in 1845 and was selected the following year by the Congregation of Propaganda to serve in the recently established vicariate apostolic for Central Africa. After spending a number of months studying Oriental rites in Lebanon and Syria, Knoblecher departed Cairo in September 1847, in the company of Maximilian Ryllo, S.J., the pro-vicar apostolic of Central Africa and four other missionaries. They arrived in Khartoum in February 1848, and there erected a school for young people whom they had freed from slavery by literally buying them at the local slave market. Ryllo died a short time later and Knoblecher succeeded him as pro-vicar. He spent the next years making expeditions into Central Africa, encountering fierce opposition from European merchants and slave traders. Increasingly ill from the climate and the diseases of the regions, Knoblecher was forced to leave Africa, dying on the way home. His accounts of his travels provided valuable insights into missionary work on the continent.

Know-Nothing Movement ● Also Know-Nothingism, a political movement in the 1850s in the United States that was a largely secret manifestation of Nativist sentiment against immigrants, especially Catholics. The Know-Nothings had their origins in the eastern cities of the country where predominantly Protestant areas witnessed with alarm the arrival of large groups of immigrants who were, by and large, from Catholic countries. Seen as a genuine threat to their way of life and fearing a loss of political power, the Protestants formed themselves into a revived version of the

Nativist Party, stemming from the American Republican Party (formed in New York in 1843). Gradually, a variety of secret parties sprouted up in the early 1850s, formed together under the collective nickname of Know-Nothings because all inquiries of supposed members were met with the declaration that they "knew nothing." They sought the election of only Nativist candidates, worked to form a twenty-five-year residence qualification for citizenship, and wanted a ban on all foreign-born persons holding elected office. Particular scorn and vitriol were reserved for Catholics. The Know-Nothings did very well in the 1854 election, especially in Massachusetts and Delaware, and in 1855 they adopted the name American Party, abandoning much of their secrecy. That same year, Abraham Lincoln wrote to Joshua Speed that if the Know-Nothings succeeded in gaining control of the country, the Declaration of Independence would read: "All men are created equal except negroes, foreigners, and Catholics." The party was torn apart by the slavery issue and the movement declined in popularity, remaining active until 1860 in the border states. The anti-Catholic and antiforeign laws were repealed over the next years. Many ideas of the Know-Nothings were borrowed by the American Protective Association in the 1890s and the Ku Klux Klan in the 1920s.

Knox, John (c. 1513-1572) ● Scottish reformer and founder of Scottish Presbyterianism. Originally a Catholic priest, he came under the influence of the Scottish reforming figure George Wishart and eventually became a Protestant. From 1549-1554, he preached in England and was a participant in the revision of the Book of Common Prayer. He went into exile with the succession of Mary I, residing in Geneva where he consulted with John Calvin. Emerging as a leader of the reforming party in Scotland, he preached bitterly against the pope's authority and the creeds of the Church, especially attacking Mary, Queen of Scots. After her abdication in 1567, Knox preached the sermon at the coronation of King James and was a prominent friend of the regent, the earl of Moray. His position declined after Moray's assassination in 1570, but he had succeeded in making Scotland a Protestant land. Outspoken, narrow-minded, and full of vicious anti-Catholic fanaticism, Knox was nevertheless a gifted and fearless promoter of the Scottish Reformation.

St. Maximilian Kolbe

Knox, Ronald Arbuthnott (1888-1957) ●
Catholic apologist and convert. The son of Edmund Knox, bishop of Manchester, he was educated at Eton and Balliol College, Oxford, and became a member of the Anglo-Catholic movement. In 1913, he authored the satirical poem *Absolute and Abitofhel* in the style of John Dryden, which was a clever attack on the symposium "of Christian belief in terms of modern thought." Drawn to the Church, he was formally received into the faith at Farnborough Abbey in 1917. The following year, he published *A Spiritual Aeneid*, an autobiographical work. In 1919, he was ordained. After teaching at St. Edmund's College, Ware, and serving as a chaplain to Catholic undergraduates at Oxford (1926-1939), Knox resigned to devote himself to a translation of the Bible. The NT was finished in 1945 and the OT in 1949; the entire volume was issued in 1955. Called the Knox Version of the Bible, this edition relied upon a heightened literary quality and a greater use of prose. Monsignor Knox also wrote *Some Loose Stones* (1913), *On Englishing the Bible* (1949), and detective stories.

Kolbe, Maximilian, St. (1894-1941) ●
Franciscan priest, theologian, and martyr. Maximilian Maria Kolbe was born near Lodz, Poland. originally called Rajmund Kolbe, he entered the Franciscan Conventuals in 1907 and was sent to Rome in 1912 where he studied at the Gregorian (Pontifical Gregorian University). Ordained in 1918, Kolbe was distinguished by his devotion to Mary, founding in 1917 the sodality of the Militia of Mary Immaculate and later establishing the monthly publication *The Knights of Mary Immaculate*. In 1927, he also began the so-called City of Mary Immaculate, a center devoted to Marian devotion that spread to Japan and India. While he was a gifted mathematician and scientist, Kolbe was best known for his work in journalism, earning the enmity of the Nazis for his anti-Nazi writings. When Poland fell in September of 1939, Kolbe was arrested for what the Nazis considered illegal activities. Released, he was picked up again in February 1941 for giving aid to Jews and assisting members of the Polish underground. Sent to Auschwitz, Kolbe, as prisoner 16670, was subjected to especially brutal treatment because he was a Catholic priest. An SS guard, for example, attempted to beat him to death, leaving his broken body in a wood. Surviving, Kolbe gave comfort to his fellow prisoners, reminding them that there was glory in the Cross. One

day, ten men were picked by the SS to be starved to death in reprisal for a prison escape. Kolbe stepped forward and asked to be chosen in the place of Franciszek Gajowniczek, a onetime sergeant in the Polish army who was married. Surprisingly, the SS officers agreed, and Kolbe joined the others. As his fellow prisoners died, Kolbe prayed for each, aiding them in their final hours. Greatly disturbed by Kolbe's patience and calm forbearance, the guards hastened his demise by injecting him with phenol. He died on August 14, 1941, and was cremated. Pope Paul VI beatified him on October 17, 1971, and Pope John Paul II canonized him on October 10, 1982, declaring him a martyr. Feast day: August 14.

Kraur, Franz Xaver (1840-1901) ●
Ecclesiastical historian. Born in Trier, he studied in his hometown and elsewhere, and was ordained in March 1864. In 1872, he became professor extraordinary of the history of Christian art at the University of Strasbourg and in 1878 succeeded Johann Alzog as professor ordinary of Church history at Freiburg. He was supported by the government in a candidacy for an episcopal see, but the opposition of ecclesiastical leaders prevented its fulfillment, largely because of his statements affirming that the state should be free from interference from Church officials. Among his many works were: *Geschichte der christlichen Kunst* (2 vols., 1896-1900; *History of Christian Art*), although the last section was completed by Joseph Sauer (1908); *Roma sotteranea* (1873; *Subterranean Rome*); and *Realencyklopaedie der christlichen Altertumer* (2 vols., 1882-1886; *Encyclopedia of Christian Antiquities*). His religio-political ideas led to the formation of a society in 1909 to further them.

Ku Klux Klan ● Called also by its initials KKK. A secret society formed in 1866 in Pulaskie, Tennessee, that became the "Invisible Empire of the South," a racist and virulently anti-Catholic terrorist organization. Initially begun as a club for veterans of the Confederate army after the Civil War, the Klan was initially concerned with protecting white interests in parts of the South from carpetbaggers and scalawags (Northerners seeking to profit from the ruin of the Confederacy) and recently emancipated and enfranchised blacks. Through threats and then violence, the Klansmen terrorized their opponents into leaving. By wearing white hoods to shield their identities, Klansmen became a dreadful and pervasive presence in many communities, solidifying their brotherhood with strange rituals and appointing as their chief a Grand Wizard, seconded by a hierarchy that included Grand Dragons and Grand Titans. While technically disbanded in 1869 because of its gratuitous violence, the continued activities of members prompted the passage of the Force Act (1870) and the Ku Klux Klan Act (1871). The Klan declined in membership from then on, after peaking at half a million in the late 1860s. A revival of the society occurred in 1915 with the organization started up in Atlanta, Georgia. To its antiblack message was added hatred for the Jews and Catholics. By 1924, there were around five million members, with popularity only being fueled in the South with the unsuccessful presidential bid of the Catholic Democrat Alfred E. Smith. Owing to scandals, internal squabbles, and the Great Depression, the Klan declined once more and was dissolved in 1944. Two years later, it started up yet again, surging in the 1960s in the era of civil rights legislation and protests. They violently opposed the Civil Rights Act of 1964 and were responsible for much of the bloodshed that accompanied its enforcement by the federal government.

Kulturkampf ● German for "culture war." It was used for the harsh harassment of the Catholic Church by the Prussian state starting in 1871. The *Kulturkampf* had its origins in the unification of the German Empire that had been achieved by the ruthless Prussian minister Otto von Bismarck. Anxious to root out and destroy any element in German life that might pose a threat to the unity of the empire, he looked upon the Church as a foreign intruder that demanded loyalty to the distant authority of the Holy See, only recently bolstered by Vatican Council I. In 1871, Bismarck launched his sweeping program by closing down the Catholic department of the Prussian Ministry of Public Worship. The next year he appointed the pugnacious Paul Ludwig Falk (1827-1900) as minister of public worship. Falk ousted the Jesuits, Redemptorists, and other religious orders, seized control of Catholic schools, and in 1873 issued the infamous May Laws that sharply curtailed the powers of the Church in German lands and took over the seminaries. When confronted with opposition to this repression from the clergy and German people, he imprisoned several prelates, most notably Cardinal von Ledochowski of Posen.

Pope Pius IX resisted the *Kulturkampf* by annulling the May Laws and promulgating the denunciatory encyclical *Quod nunquam* (February 5, 1875), to which Bismarck responded by advancing his measures against the religious orders and cutting off all money from the state to the Church in Germany. The minister soon came to realize, however, that the *Kulturkampf* had a directly opposite effect from the one he wanted. Catholics throughout the land were energized in their opposition and in proclaiming a revival of the religious life in German lands. While the idea of the *Kulturkampf* spread to some other German states, others chose to support the Church. In Bavaria, along the Rhine, and in staunchly Catholic areas of Prussian Poland, Catholics formed into a political party, called the *Centrum*, or Center Party. Its rapid rise convinced Bismarck of the need to find a face-saving way to rescind his policies. The means presented themselves with the accession of Pope Leo XIII (r. 1878-1903), who began his pontificate by making conciliatory gestures to the Prussians. A new concordat was negotiated, and by 1887 the majority of the anti-Catholic laws had been repealed.

Küng, Hans (b. 1928) ● Swiss priest and controversial theologian. Küng was born in Sursee, Switzerland, studying at the Gregorian University and the Catholic Institute of Paris. He was ordained in 1954. First coming to prominence as a result of his theological dissertation *Justification: The Doctrine of Karl Barth and a Catholic Reflection* (1957), he was appointed a professor of theology at Tübingen University in 1960. During Vatican Council II (1962-1965) he served as one of the *periti*, the theologians who provided technical assistance to the Council Fathers. His book *The Church* (1967) was concerned with Church reform, a recurring theme in his early writings. In 1970, he was appointed head of an ecumenical institute at Tübingen, the same year that he published his highly controversial *Infallible? An Inquiry*, a study of the dogma of papal infallibility on the hundredth anniversary of the declaration by Vatican Council I of its definition. Increasingly outspoken in questioning Church teaching, Küng came into disagreement with authorities in Rome and Germany, especially in his public disagreement with papal declarations on contraception, in particular Pope Paul VI's *Humanae vitae*. His writings during the 1970s continued to distinguish him as a leading voice of theological dissent. Criticized for his views and for being deliberately unwilling to compromise with authority, he remained intransigent during the first year of the pontificate of John Paul II and in 1979 was deprived of his position as a recognized theologian.

Labarum ● Military standard used by the Christian emperors of Rome. First adopted by Constantine the Great as the result of a vision in 312, it was described by Eusebius of Caesarea as "a long spear, overlaid with gold, with a crossbar giving it a cruciform shape." It was most likely adopted from a typical cavalry standard. The traditional pagan emblems were replaced, however, by a Christian monogram: a gold wreath around the symbol of Christ's name, two letters, X and P (standing for the first two letters of the Greek XPIETOE, or Christ), and called the *Chi-Rho*. On Constantine's banner used victoriously at the Battle of the Milvian Bridge, the Latin phrase *"In hoc signo vinces"* ("By this sign you will conquer") was hung upon a purple banner. Subsequently, the *labarum* became the standard of the Western Empire, serving as the banner of the Eastern Empire as well after the defeat of Licinius at the Battle of Adrianople in 324 by Constantine.

Labbe, Philippe (1607-1667) ● Jesuit Church historian. A native of Bourges, he joined the Society of Jesus in September 1623, later holding a chair of theology. Labbe authored some eighty works, including: *Sacrosancti Oecumenici Tridentini Concili . . . canones et decreta* (1667), a valuable compilation on the Council of Trent; and, most importantly, *Sacrosancta Concilia ad Regiam Editionem exacta*, a collection of Church councils, published in 1671-1673, although the outstanding volumes were finished by the Jesuit Gabriel Cossart.

Laberthonnière, Lucien (1860-1932) ● Notable Modernist theologian. A member of the Oratorians (ordained in 1886), he taught at the college at Juilly and the École Massillon in Paris; in 1900, he became the rector of the Juilly College. Among his writings were *Essais de philosophie religieuse* (1903; *Essays on Religious Philosophy*) and *Le Réalisme chrétien et l'idéalisme grec* (1904; *Christian Realism and the Idealism of the Greek*). Both were put on the Index of Forbidden Books. He also edited the *Annales de philosophie chrétienne* and participated, with Maurice Blondel, in an attack upon *Action Française*. Laberthonnière was a staunch opponent of Thomas Aquinas and the Aristotelian-Thomistic tradition in the Church, preferring instead the ultimately incompatible fusion of Greek idealism and Christian thought. In 1913, he was forbidden from any further publication.

Laborem Exercens ● Encyclical published in 1981 by Pope John Paul II and given the English title "On Human Work." An important contribution to the Church's social doctrine, *Laborem exercens* provides a powerful synthesis of Church teaching concerning economic ethics and the rights of all persons to do meaningful work. The third encyclical of Pope John Paul, it strives to make clear the dual but equal nature of labor, namely that there exist two meanings or proper understandings of work: the objective sense and the subjective. In the objective meaning can be found the broad understanding of labor contributing to society in the production of goods and services, an activity that is most often divorced or quite separate from the personal life of the worker. Subjectively, work is the personal realization of individual worth and a crucial expression of the image that a person has of God in the world.

John Paul then examines the lamentable reality that in both the broad economic systems of capitalism and Marxism the objective aspect of labor has far outweighed the subjective, causing a tendency to treat work merely as a means of advancing economic growth without concern for the inherent worth and dignity of the worker. This unfortunate circumstance is reflected in laws, customs, and labor organizations that do nothing to advance the personal value of the worker or foster a societal recognition of the value of the individual laborer. The solution, the pope writes, lies in the development of an abiding respect for the worker and the personal nature of the labor, a process known as socialization (which is not to be confused with socialism). In the capitalist state, this means that the forces driving economic life should be respectful of the social significance and personal meaning of work, as they give a sense of identity and dignity to the laborer. In Marxist states, socialization implies the need for the government to reduce its omnipresent role in the lives of workers. This latter point, with its obvious implications in application, was taken by many in Eastern Europe to mean the formation of unions and the establishment of fair and equitable standards of labor.

La Chaise, François D' Aix de (1624-1709) ● French Jesuit priest and confessor to King Louis XIV. From Aix, he entered the Society of Jesus in 1649, and taught at the College de la Ste. Trinité at Lyons before serving as rector at the school and then provincial. In 1675, he succeeded to the post of confessor to the French king. In his position, he advocated the king's

termination of an illicit relationship with Madame de Montaspan and had a hand in ending Louis's affair with Madame de Maintenon. While he supported the revocation in 1685 of the Edict of Nantes, La Chaise did not connive to bring this about, nor did he in any way condone the use of violence against the Huguenots as had been widely reported. Even Voltaire admitted to his mildness and abiding humility. King Louis granted him a tract of land in Paris that was converted in 1804 into a cemetery, the Père Lachaise.

Lacordaire, Jean Baptiste Henri (1802-1861) ● French Dominican who was ranked as the foremost preacher in the nineteenth century. Born near Dijon, he lost his faith early while in school, and studied law at Dijon and Paris, attracting considerable attention as an orator. By 1824, however, he had regained his faith and was determined to devote his life to the Church. In May 1824, he entered the seminary of Issy and was ordained in 1827. The following year, he was appointed chaplain to the Convent of the Visitation in Paris and in 1830 he began contributing to the periodical L'Avenir, headed by Félicité Lamennais. His association with it ended in 1832 when it was condemned by Pope Gregory XVI and, while disappointed, he submitted completely to the decision. Lacordaire then began to give public lectures on religion, first at the Collège Stanislas (1834) although these were denounced for their liberalism. In 1835-1836, he gave two series of conferences at Notre-Dame, announcing a short time later, however, his intention to retire. At Rome, in 1839, he entered the Dominican order, deciding then to return to France and reestablish the Dominicans. At Nancy, in 1843, he established the first Dominican house since the order's suppression in 1790. Named provincial in 1850, he was elected to the French Academy in 1860. His most

important work was *Conferences de Notre-Dame de Paris* (4 vols., 1844-1851).

Lactantius (c. 245-323) ● In full, Lucius Caecilius Firmianus Lactantius, one of the greatest of all Christian apologists. From Africa, he entered the service of Emperor Diocletian, receiving an appointment from him as a teacher of rhetoric in Nicomedia. In 300, however, he was converted to Christianity and, under the laws of persecution of the time, he was removed from office. Later, Constantine named him tutor to his son Crispus. Lactantius authored a number of books to propagate the faith: from 304-311 he wrote the *Divinae Institutiones* (*Divine Institutions*), presenting many facets of Christian doctrine with particular emphasis in attracting Latin leaders; *De Mortibus Persecutorum*, a very detailed and often lurid or grotesque account of the death of the persecutors, sent to them by God in punishment for their attacks on Christ's followers. The description of the death of Emperor Galerius was notably vivid. Two other books were *De Opificio Deo*, on the existence of God, and *Ira Dei* (*The Wrath of God*).

Laetentur Coeli ● Latin for "Let the heavens rejoice." Used as a title for two documents, otherwise unrelated. The first was a Greek Formulary of Union that was approved by the Council of Chalcedon (451) and that presented the orthodox doctrine on the Person of Christ, including the unity of the Person, the distinction of the natures, and the *Theotokos* (or "Mother of God" but literally "bearer of God"). It was sent originally in 453 by Cyril of Alexandria to John, bishop of Antioch, to establish the basis of reunion after John had sided with the teachings of Nestorius. The second *Laetentur* was a bull issued by Pope Eugenius IV on July 6, 1439, that decreed the formal union of the Eastern and Western (or Greek and Latin) Churches, as negotiated at the Council of Florence. While signed by the Greek and Latin representatives, the reunion would be a brief one.

Laicism ● Idea prominent during the nineteenth century that the administration of the Church, including its ecclesiastical, civil, and even spiritual affairs should be conducted by the laity. In this system, the role and importance of the clergy, especially the magisterium, is reduced or removed entirely. An expression of a severe form of secularism — with its promotion that human society should be conducted without concern for religion — laicism was foreshadowed by Gallicanism and Febronianism. Many of the more radical supporters of laicism bordered on anticlericalism, with its virulent and erroneous opposition to any Church influence on social or political spheres. Laicism was condemned by Pope Pius IX on December 8, 1864, in the *Syllabus of Errors*.

Laic Laws ● Broad series of laws enacted in France between 1875 and 1907, culminating with the Law of Separation of 1905. Aimed at effecting a complete separation of Church and State, and stemming from the Gallican traditions and radical anticlericalism, they were called laic because they were intended to transfer or "restore" power to the laypeople at the expense of the clergy. The reasons given by the government for its promulgation included charges that the French clergy were avowed enemies of the Republic, were ignorant, and were backward in outlook, especially in the face of new scientific developments. Additionally, the Republicans pointed to the antidemocratic sentiments of many conservative Catholics and Catholic organizations. The result of the laws was the severe secularization of education in which all religious were removed from the process of learning; moreover, prohibitions were placed on religious education, private schools received no financial support from the state, the Church had restricted rights of property holdings, and services could not be conducted without the permission of secular officials.

In the policy of *ralliement*, Pope Leo XIII (r. 1878-1903) issued the encyclical *Nobilissima Gallorum gens* (1884) in which the French hierarchy was encouraged to cooperate as best as possible. There followed a brief mitigation of the laws, but new difficulties resulted from such social crises as the struggle between the radicals and conservatives in the Dreyfus Affair. Under the leadership of Justin Combes, a law was written that "all religious associations must obtain special authorization to operate in France." With no choice in the matter, Pope St. Pius X (r. 1903-1914) severed relations between France and the Holy See. The law proposed by Combes became the Law of Separation, passed in 1905. The decree ended all appropriations for public worship, the extreme laicization of French life, and the termination of the idea of national faith. This state of affairs with the Holy See remained in effect until 1920 when relations were stabilized. While the Catholic faith remains the predominant religion of France, the Laic Laws had a very deleterious effect on the Church of France ("the eldest daughter of the Church") throughout the twentieth century. (See **France**.)

Laínez, James (1512-1565) ● Also called Laynez. Second general of the Society of Jesus, he was the successor to St. Ignatius Loyola, and a Castilian by birth. Laínez studied at the University of Alcalá, receiving a licentiate in theology in 1532. The following year, at Paris, he met Ignatius Loyola and became one of the earliest founders of the Jesuit order. In August 1534, he took his vows, as one of seven, in the chapel of St. Denis, on Montmarte. Pope Paul III subsequently gave his blessing for their ordinations, acting as an admirer and patron of the fledgling order, choosing three Jesuits,

including Laínez, to serve as theologians at the Council of Trent. Laínez took a prominent part in the discussions of grace and justification, refuting many of the propositions of Martin Luther and the Protestants; such was the brilliance of his ideas on justification that the council adopted some by unanimous decree in January 1547. Upon Loyola's death in 1556, Laínez succeeded him as vicar-general of the society and then in 1558 as general. Much of his time in office was spent expanding the order and its works, while continuing to speak at the Council of Trent (1562-1563) on doctrinal matters and papal justification. He died in Rome.

Lambert of Hersfeld (c. 1024-after 1077) ● Medieval historian. Few details of his life are known with certainty. He was from Franconia or Thuringia and in March 1058 entered the Benedictine monastery of Hersfeld, in Hesse, and was ordained a priest the following year. Twice he departed the monastery, once without permission when he left for a pilgrimage to the Holy Land, and then, in 1071, at the orders of the abbot, he spent some weeks looking at the reformed monasteries of Sieburg and Saalfeld; he was impressed with the reform that had been introduced. His most important work was the *Annales Lamberti*, a chronicle of world events from the creation to 1077. The first portion, to 1040, is essentially a recreation of earlier annals; from 1040-1068 the coverage is more extensive, including eyewitness accounts; and from 1068-1077 Lambert emerges as a brilliant historian, using eloquent classical style and what was, for many centuries (especially between 1525 — the release of the first edition — and the nineteenth century), considered an entirely objective source on the struggle between Emperor Henry IV and Pope Gregory VII. The work was criticized by Leopold von Ranke (d. 1886) as being biased and full of falsifications. Lambert also authored *Vita Lulli*, a biography on

Archbishop Lullus of Mainz, and other historical works.

Lambruschini, Luigi (1776-1854) ●

Italian cardinal and statesman who served as secretary of state and was one of the greatest diplomats of the nineteenth century. Born near Genoa, he entered the Order of the Barnabites and, because of his intelligence and learning, was appointed as a consultor to several Roman congregations. In 1815, he served as secretary to the famed Cardinal Ercole Consalvi to the Congress of Vienna. Rising rapidly, he was named archbishop of Genoa (1819) and papal nuncio (1827) to France. Owing to the Revolution of 1830, he journeyed to Rome and was made a cardinal in 1831 by Pope Gregory XVI. Appointed secretary of state, he proved remarkably skilled in diplomacy, especially in advancing a firm papal policy toward the Prussian government concerning the imprisonment of Archbishop Clemens August von Droste zu Vischering of Cologne; his eloquent vehemence caused the recall of the Prussian minister to Rome, Christian Bunsen. A leading candidate to succeed Gregory, Lambruschini received a majority of votes but not enough to secure election in the conclave. Giovanni Maria Mastai-Ferretti was then chosen instead, taking the name Pius IX. As Lambruschini disagreed with him on constitutionalism in the Papal States, he resigned his post. The cardinal barely escaped Rome in the Revolution of 1848, as he was the object of much hatred by Roman radicals for his controversial views.

Lamennais, Félicité (1782-1854) ●

In full, Félicité-Robert de Lamennais. French religious and political writer and priest. Born at St.-Malô, he belonged to a prosperous family and was well-read as a youth, although his study of such writers and philosophers as Rousseau caused him to reject any thoughts of personal faith. Gradually, however, he was brought into the Church, mainly through the efforts of his brother Jean Marie (d. 1860), a priest. In 1804, he was given the post of mathematics professor at the local episcopal college. Having seen the effects of the French Revolution on society, both Félicité and his brother recognized the need for a Catholic revival in the country to rebuild the social system. Thus, in 1808, he published *Réflexions sur l'état de l'eglise en France pendant le 18e siecle et sur sa situation actuelle* (*Reflections on the State of the Church in France During the 18th century and Her Present Situation*), an ambitious call for reform that attacked the rationalism of the previous years and the social anarchy that had been caused by atheism and anticlericalism. His views, especially his Ultramontanism, forced his flight from Napoleonic France in 1815. The following year, he was ordained a priest and in 1818 published the first volume of what is considered his most important work, *Essai sur l'indifference en matière de religion* (*Essay on Indifference toward Religious Matters*). In this famous writing, he attacked indifference and argued in favor of the Church authority that was widely supported by Ultramontanists. The *Essai* gave much needed encouragement to Catholic apologists and was the cause of numerous conversions. While many of his views were greeted with suspicion in some theological circles, Lamennais was ranked as the foremost figure among the French clergy. He followed the successful first volume with two more (1820, 1823) in which he elaborated a philosophical system of certitude. He proposed that there is no certitude to be derived from individual reason, rather it comes from the general reason, described by Lamennais as the *sens commun*, or common sense. It is the testament of the entire human race. He went on to state that the doctrines of the Church have been found, under various forms or disguises, throughout the world. Criticized from several sides, he wrote *Defense de l'Essai* (1821), which won an imprimatur from authorities in Rome. In a visit to the Eternal City, he was warmly received by Pope Leo XII (r. 1823-1829), who considered for a time making him a cardinal. While a dedicated enemy of Gallicanism, Lamennais was willing to unite many elements of contemporary liberalism with Catholicism, demonstrating this tendency in his 1829 work, *Des progrès de la Révolution*, in which he pointed to the inevitable revolution in the country and called for a complete separation of Church and State and full equal rights for the Church. He perceived considerable threats to the faith and, to promote its defense in the face of Gallicanism and the hostility of the government, he established the *Congregation de St. Pierre* in 1828, although this proved a brief venture cut short by the revolution of 1830. Lamennais also founded the newspaper *L'Avenir* (1830-1831) with Jean Baptiste Henri Lacordaire and Charles de Montalembert. His increasingly liberal ideas soon proved unpopular in both French social and ecclesiastical circles, and the disfavor of Pope Gregory XVI caused him to suspend the paper's operations. His ideas were then condemned by Gregory's encyclical *Mirari vos* (1832). Lamennais responded with his *Paroles d'un croyan* (1934), which questioned papal authority in secular affairs and was the talk of Europe. When the pope issued the condemnatory encyclical *Singulari nos* (1834), Lamennais left the Church and was to be disappointed even further in his liberal hopes with the rise of Louis-Napoleon in France. He died away from the Church, despite the efforts of Pope Pius IX to reconcile him.

Lamentabili ● Decree issued by the Holy Office on July 3, 1907, condemning a list of sixty-five propositions that were considered errors derived from the teachings of the Modernists. Approximately half were drawn from the writings of Alfred Loisy (1857-1940), a French Modernist biblical scholar. Among the errors were: that the Jesus of history was inferior to the Jesus of faith; that he did not possess always a consciousness of his Messianic dignity; that there were limits to his knowledge; that he might have been in error; that the supremacy of Rome was divinely established; and that modern Catholicism could not be reconciled with science unless it is changed or transformed into a type of nondogmatic Christianity. The decree was followed on September 8, 1907, by the encyclical *Pascendi dominici gregis*, from Pope St. Pius X.

Lance, Holy ● Renowned relic. The subject of numerous legends, it was the lance supposedly used to pierce the side of Christ: "But one of the soldiers pierced his side with a spear, and at once came out blood and water" (Jn 19:34). Throughout history there have been a number of holy lances, the most famous in legend being that of Longinus, the centurion who wielded the spear (see under **Longinus**). The earliest reference to the spear was made sometime in the sixth century when it was seen by St. Antoninus in Jerusalem. It was subsequently mentioned by St. Gregory of Tours and Cassiodorus. While it fell into the hands of the Persians in 615, the tip was saved and taken to Constantinople and was preserved in an icon in the Hagia Sophia; it was subsequently given to King St. Louis IX of France in 1241. A relic of the St.-Chapelle in Paris, it was kept with the crown of thorns, disappearing during the French Revolution. The surviving part of the lance taken by the Persians was seen in Jerusalem and surfaced in Constantinople in the tenth century. Captured by the Turks in 1492, it was sent to the pope as a gift from the sultan and has been held in St. Peter's ever since. Other lances have been found, the most notable being those of Longinus and the one found at Antioch in 1098 by members of the First Crusade who supposedly used it to defeat a

Muslim army at the so-called Battle of the Lance. (See also **Relics**.)

Landus ● Pope from 913-914. Also called Lando, he was the son of a wealthy Lombard count and was elected to succeed Anastasius III probably through the influence of the House of Theophylact that was then dominating Roman political life.

Lanfranc (c. 1005-1089) ● Scholar, theologian, profound intellectual, and archbishop of Canterbury. A native of Pavia, Italy, he studied as a lawyer and traveled to France (c. 1030 or 1035), teaching there and then entering in 1042 the Benedictine monastery of Bec, in Normandy. He was the prior in 1045, and then named abbot of St. Stephen's in Caen in 1063. In 1070, he was appointed to the see of Canterbury, working with the regime of William I the Conqueror to reform the English Church. Lanfranc, however, was careful to maintain his own ecclesiastical independence. Among his writings were commentaries on the *Trivium* (grammar, logic, and rhetoric; now lost), St. Paul, and Psalms; and the much read *De Corpore et Sanguine Domini* (c. 1070, *On the Body and Blood of God*), which was a sharp criticism of the teaching on the Eucharist by Berengarius of Tours. Lanfranc also transformed Bec into a renowned monastery and was vital in securing the succession of William II Rufus in 1087 to the English throne.

Langton, Stephen (d. 1228) ● Theologian and archbishop of Canterbury who played a major role in the events leading up to the signing of the Magna Carta. Born in England, he was educated at Paris and there became a friend of the future Pope Innocent III (r. 1198-1216). Named a cardinal by him in 1206, Langton was chosen to succeed Hubert Walter for the see of Canterbury, an appointment opposed by King John. There followed a bitter dispute that was ended only in 1213 with Langton's arrival in England and the lifting of the papal interdict and the excommunication of John. Langton supported the barons against John, serving as a royal counselor at Runnymeade in June 1215. His name appeared on the Magna Carta. In 1218-1219, he gave his support to King Henry III and the regency against the barons. Langton authored a famed commentary on the *Sentences* by Peter Lombard as well as commentaries on the *Historia Scholastica* of Peter Comestor, and the Old and New Testaments. He also secured the withdrawal of the papal legate to England so that Canterbury stood as the *legatus natus* of the pope in the isle.

Laodicea, Canons of ● Group or set of sixty canons dating to the fourth century. May have been the subject-headings of the canons that were issued by councils earlier in the century, particularly the Council of Nicaea (325) and the otherwise unknown Council of Laodicea. The canons are concerned with such subjects as heresies (Novatianism, Montanism, etc.) and the list of the scriptural books considered canonical. The Epistle of St. Paul to the Laodiceans is an apocryphal Latin epistle, included in many Latin manuscripts of the NT from the sixth through fifteenth centuries. Scholars generally agree that it dates to the fourth or fifth century and was probably written in Greek.

Lapsi ● Latin for "fallen." It denoted those individuals who had denied their Christian faith during times of persecution by the Roman government. Early Church teaching held that apostasy was an unforgivable sin, but, by the third century, the problem of the *lapsi* had grown so acute that a means of finding readmission for the repentant had to be found. St. Cyprian of Carthage (d. 258), confronted by the Decian persecutions (launched by Emperor Trajanus Decius), made the decision to readmit the *lapsi* but only after a suitable period of penance. Cyprian recognized three classes of the *lapsi*: *thurificati* — those who gave incense at pagan ceremonies; *sacrificati* — those who took part in pagan sacrifices; and *libellatici* — those who went so far as to secure certificates that they had conformed to legally required pagan practices. Cyprian's decision was vigorously opposed by the Novatianists, who were unbending in resisting the readmission, opposition that led them to open schism. Several councils took up the issue of the *lapsi*, including Elvira (306), Arles (314), Ancyra (314), and Nicaea (325).

La Salette, Our Lady of ● Title given to the Blessed Virgin commemorating her appearance on September 19, 1846, to two children, Melanie Calvat and Maximin Giraud, in La Salette, near Grenoble, France. The BVM gave the children a message that was only partially revealed by them to the public. The known portion was a call for people to repent, with the promise of dire punishment should lives of humility, penance, and prayer not be adopted. Melanie revealed in 1849 the entire message to the Holy See, a declaration that has never been disclosed. The bishop of Grenoble first approved devotion to Our Lady of La Salette in 1851; popes since St. Pius X have also given their approval.

Lateran Basilica ● Basilica of St. John Lateran (San Giovanni in Laterano). The Cathedral Church of Rome and one of the four major patriarchal basilicas of Rome, its full name is the Patriarchal Basilica of the Most Holy Savior and St. John the Baptist at the Lateran. The basilica is situated upon the Caelian Hill on land that was once owned by the Lateranii family who owned a palace that came into the possession of Emperor Constantine the Great in the early fourth century. Around 313, he gave the palace to Pope St. Melchiades along with an adjacent basilica. The site became the residence of the popes from that time until 1309 and the departure of the papacy to Avignon. The basilica was converted into a five-aisle church from 1314-1318, being dedicated to the Redeemer. As the Cathedral of the Pope, Supreme Pontiff and Pastor of the Universal Church and Bishop of Rome, the Church's position was one of enormous prominence, bearing the title that is found upon its walls: *Omnium urbis et orbis ecclesiarum mater et caput.*

Virtually destroyed by an earthquake in 896, it was rebuilt by Pope Sergius III (r. 904-911), lasting until 1308 and surviving a terrible fire. Repaired by Popes Clement V (r. 1305-1314) and John XXII (r. 1316-1334), it burned down again in 1360. This time Pope Urban V (r. 1363-1370) oversaw the reconstruction. Extensive restoration work was needed after the return of the popes from Avignon in 1378. A major rebuilding of the interior was paid for by Pope Innocent X and implemented by Francesco Borromini (1599-1667) in 1646. The north façade was constructed by Domenico Fontana (1543-1604) for Pope Sixtus V and the east façade for Pope Clement XII around 1734 by Alessandro Galilei (d. 1737). Until 1870 most of the popes were crowned in the Lateran Basilica, the coronation being moved to St. Peter's as a result of the tensions between the popes and the Italian government over the seizure of the Papal States. Aside from the remains of the original Lateran Palace, the basilica also is distinguished by adjoining cloisters, built by the family of the Vassallette in the thirteenth century, a magnificent baptistery dating to 432 and the reign of Pope Sixtus III (432-440), and a striking baldacchino dating to the thirteenth century. The basilica remains the church of the pope in his capacity as Bishop of Rome. The most well-known of the ceremonies held there is the Maundy Thursday washing of the feet.

Lateran Concordat ● See **Lateran Treaty**.

Lateran Councils ● Five Church councils held in the twelfth through sixteenth centuries, so-called because they were convened in the Lateran Palace in Rome.

First Lateran Council (1123): The ninth ecumenical council, summoned by Pope Callistus II to confirm the Concordat of Worms and thereby end the Investiture Controversy. The council also promulgated twenty-two disciplinary canons.

Second Lateran Council (1139): The tenth ecumenical council, convened by Pope Innocent II to condemn the antipope Anacletus II and the followers of Arnold of Brescia after the schism that occurred with Innocent's election.

Third Lateran Council (1179): The eleventh ecumenical council, convoked by Pope Alexander III in 1179 to extirpate all trace of the schism of the antipope Callistus III. Most importantly, the council promulgated a decree concerning papal elections that provided for the election of the pope by the College of Cardinals, with a two-thirds majority required. A treaty with Frederick I Barbarossa was ratified and each bishopric was required to conduct a school for clerics.

Fourth Lateran Council (1215): The twelfth ecumenical council, convened by Pope Innocent III, considered one of the most important Church assemblies before the Council of Trent. Among its declarations were annual confession, a definition of the doctrine of transubstantiation, Communion during the Easter season, condemnation of the Cathars and Waldenses, and the requiring of Muslims and Jews to wear specific attire. (See also **Ecumenical Councils**.)

Fifth Lateran Council (1512-1517): Summoned by Pope Julius II in response to the antipapal council summoned in Pisa by a number of cardinals opposed to Julius and through the influence of King Louis XII of France. The decrees of the Pisan Council

were invalidated and a number of reforms were launched.

Other councils were held in the Lateran, most notably those in 649 (against Monothelitism), 823, 864, 900, 1102, 1105, 1110, 1111, 1112, 1116, and 1725 when Pope Leo XIII summoned the bishops directly dependent on Rome as their metropolitan with the object of suppressing Jansenism and confirming the bull *Unigenitus*.

Lateran Treaty ● Treaty and concordat between the Holy See and the Italian government of Benito Mussolini signed on February 11, 1929. The agreement established the State of the Vatican City as a sovereign state, the sovereign independence of the Holy See in international affairs, and the Holy See's jurisdiction in Vatican City. Recognition extended as well to extraterritorial holdings such as Castel Gandolfo and the Lateran Church. The Italian government also confirmed the Catholic religion as the only faith of Italy, called for Catholic education in schools, gave freedom for Catholic Action, and compensated the Holy See for the loss of the Papal States by paying seven hundred fifty million lire in cash and one billion lire in five-percent negotiable government bonds. In return, the Holy See recognized the loss of the Papal States, the Italian state, and Rome as the capital of Italy. Also, before taking possession of their dioceses, all bishops were to take an oath to the king. The main representative of the Holy See in the negotiation was Cardinal Pietro Gasparri. Confirmed by the Italian Constitution of 1948, the treaty was renegotiated in the 1980s; by the new terms the clergy ceased to receive a government salary and mandatory Catholic instruction was ended. (See also **Holy See** and **Vatican City, State of**.)

Latrocinium ● "Robber Council." Name used for the Council of Ephesus convened in August 449 by Emperor Theodosius II to discuss pressing matters of ecclesiastical discipline. While the synod had the approval of Pope Leo I, the time between the summoning and the opening of the council was so short that few Western bishops were in attendance and Leo could not appoint a representative. The heretical bishop, Dioscorus of Alexandria, a supporter of Monophysitism, came to dominate the proceedings with the result that the Marian title *Theotokos* (Mother of God) was repudiated, Nestorian doctrines were advanced, the *Tome* of Leo was insulted, and the rights of the pope were ignored. The acts of the council were subsequently reversed by the Council of Chalcedon (451). The name Latrocinium (Latin for "band of robbers") was derived from Leo's letter to the Empress Pulcheria in which he described the council as *non iudicium sed latrocinium*.

Lawrence, St. (d. 258) ● Roman martyr and one of the most famous martyrs of the early Church. Lawrence (also spelled Laurence) was one of the seven deacons of Rome during the reign of Pope St. Sixtus II, dying a mere four days after the pontiff. According to tradition as preserved by St. Ambrose, Prudentius, and others, Lawrence was ordered by the prefect to hand over the treasures of the Church, whereupon he gathered the poor and sick, presented them to the Roman official, and said, "Here is the treasure of the Church." He was then supposedly executed by being roasted on a grid. Scholars prefer to maintain that he was beheaded like Sixtus II. Lawrence was buried on the road to Tivoli, on the Via Tiburtina, and a chapel was built on the site in the early fourth century, where the church of St. Lawrence-Outside-the-Walls currently stands. He is mentioned in the Canon of the Mass. Feast day: August 10.

Lawrence of Brindisi, St. (1559-1619) ● Franciscan Capuchin preacher who had great influence in the years just after the Reformation. Born Cesare de' Rossi in Brindisi, Italy, he studied at Venice with the clerics of St. Mark's after the death of his father around 1571. In 1575, he entered the Capuchins under the name Lorenzo and studied at the University of Padua. He was subsequently active on behalf of the order, holding a number of posts and preaching extensively in Europe, especially among the Protestants (Lutherans) and Jews. Appointed chaplain to the imperial army in 1601 that was then fighting in Hungary against the advancing Ottoman Turks, Lawrence served as a leading adviser (see also **John Capistran, St.**) and a source of tremendous inspiration to the soldiers, once leading an army into battle armed only with a crucifix. Among his writings were sermons, commentaries on Genesis and Ezekiel, and three volumes of religious polemics. Canonized in 1881 by Pope Leo XIII, he was proclaimed a Doctor of the Church in 1959. Feast day: July 21.

Leander, St. (d. c. 600) ● Bishop of Seville and the elder brother of St. Isidore whom he preceded as bishop. Leander was probably born in Carthage around 534, emigrating to Seville with his family that same year. He entered a Benedictine monastery and possibly became a bishop in 579. Exiled by the Arian Visigoth king Leovigild, he journeyed to Constantinople and there authored several works against Arianism, making the acquaintance of the future Pope St. Gregory I the Great in 582 when the latter was serving as legate to Constantinople from Pope Pelagius II. The two became good friends and maintained a cordial correspondence. His principal achievements as bishop were the conversion of King Reccared and many Visigoths from Arianism and presiding over the Synod of Toledo. Little of his writings survive, among them a monastic rule for women (*De institutione virginum*) for his sister and a homily for the synod. Feast day: February 27.

Lebwin, St. (d. c. 770) ● Also Liafwin. Apostle of the Frisians, missionary, and patron of Deventer, Holland. An Anglo-Saxon by birth, he was educated in a monastery and, after ordination, embarked upon missionary work among the Germans. Welcomed by Gregory, bishop of Utrecht, Lebwin was sent to preach to the tribes in modern Westphalia. He soon attracted many converts, building a chapel on the west bank of Yssel, followed by a church in Deventer. The pagan Saxon reaction was severe: the church was burned and Lebwin barely escaped with his life. Returning to the area, Lebwin managed to secure from the Saxons respect for the rights of the faith. The church at Deventer was then rebuilt, only to be burned again before 776.

Leclerq, Henri (1869-1945) ● Noted Benedictine scholar. A native of Tournai, Belgium, he became a naturalized French citizen. Entering the Benedictines, he professed at Solesme and was ordained in 1898. Among his vast writings are *L'Afrique chrétienne* (2 vols., 1904), *L'Epoque chrétienne* (1906), *Monumenta Ecclesiae Liturgica* (4 vols., 1900-1913), an early liturgical history, and *Histoire des Conciles* (10 vols., 1907-1939).

Lefebvre, Marcel (1905-1991) ● Controversial French archbishop and founder of the Priestly Society of St. Pius X. A native of Tourcoing, France, he studied at Sacred Heart College in his home city and the French Seminary in Rome and was ordained in 1929. He served for a short time at Lille but in 1932 was sent to Gabon where he held a missionary post until 1946. In 1948, he was appointed archbishop of Dakar, Senegal. Departing Senegal in 1962, he was an eminently successful superior general of the Holy Ghost Fathers. Taking part on the preparation for Vatican Council II, he was an outspoken supporter of traditional Catholicism. As recommendations for retaining less innovative reforms were rejected by the bishops, Lefebvre became increasingly disenchanted with the council, ultimately condemning the reforms of Vatican II as heretical. In 1969, he established the so-called Priestly Confraternity of St. Pius X in Fribourg, Switzerland. This was followed in 1970 with the creation of a seminary at Ecône, in Switzerland, to train priests in preconciliar Catholicism. In the face of Lefebvre's intransigence, Roman authorities withdrew approval of the order and Pope Paul VI suspended him. Lefebvre disregarded this command, continuing to ordain new priests; he also began making his society international by organizing throughout Europe.

As a resolution could not be reached between the Lefebvrists and Rome, Pope John Paul II excommunicated him in 1988 after Lefebvre ordained four bishops. Lefebvre died on March 25, 1991, without reconciling with the Church. The Society of St. Pius X continued after his death. Its leadership claims millions of members. Vatican authorities estimate half a million, with two hundred fifty priests and almost as many seminarians. It is especially active in France but is found in Germany, England, and the United States. The members are considered to be in a state of schism.

Le Nourry, Denis-Nicholas (1647-1724) ● Maurist ecclesiastical historian. A native of Dieppe, Normandy, he was educated by the priests of the Oratory (Oratorians) and entered the Benedictine order in Jumieges in 1665. After ordination he was sent to Rouen and the Abbey of Bonnenouvelle. There, with John Garet, he produced an edition of Cassiodorus (1679), and with Jean du Chesne and Julien Bellaise, and later Jacques du Frische, an edition of St. Ambrose. His principal work was *Apparatus ad Bibliothecam Maximam Veterum Patrum et Antiquorum Scriptorum* (2 vols., 1703 and 1715), an exhaustive series of dissertation on the Fathers and their writings and eras; it was intended as an aid to the Lyons *Bibliotheca* (collection) of the Fathers.

Leo I, St. ● Pope from 440-461. One of the two popes, with St. Gregory I (r. 590-604), to be given the title "the Great." Little is known with certainty about his early years. He was born in Rome, served as a deacon, and was a pronounced opponent of Pelagianism. While serving as a deacon, he wielded considerable influence during the reigns of St. Celestine I (422-432) and Sixtus III (432-440) and was elected the successor to Sixtus while away in Gaul. He was consecrated on September 29, 440, and took as the primary policy of his long pontificate the aggrandizement of the papacy throughout Christendom, the full recognition of the primacy of the Bishop of Rome as the successor of St. Peter. He maintained the obedience of those dioceses around him and then worked to secure his jurisdiction over the sees in Gaul (France) and Spain; he was also successful in winning the trust of the African bishops by providing them with advice and regulations aimed at curbing various irregularities then afflicting the Church there. An important development came with Leo's obtaining from Emperor Valentinian III (r. 425-455) a rescript granting him full jurisdiction over the West. He thus received vast powers in the Western Empire, and, although his authority was not recognized in the East, such was the force of his personality and the heightened *gravitas* of the papacy that Leo was inexorably drawn into the major theological crisis that had erupted in the Eastern Empire over the nature of Christ. He sent his famous *Tome* to Flavian of Constantinople on June 13, 449, condemning Eutyches and elucidating clearly the important teaching that Christ had two natures in his one Person. Three legates were sent to the Council of Ephesus (449) where the pope fully expected the *Tome* to be read. Instead, it was rejected, Eutyches was fully

restored to favor, and Flavian deposed as patriarch. Leo called the Council of Ephesus the Latrocinium, or Robber Synod, and used his full weight to reverse its acts. At the Council of Chalcedon (451), his *Tome* was read and given full approval, the decrees of Ephesus were rescinded, and the doctrine concerning the Person of Christ formally proclaimed. Chalcedon marked a major triumph for Leo, particularly the declaration by the council members that "Peter has spoken through Leo. . . ." In keeping with his principle concerning the Roman see, however, he rejected Canon 28 of the Chalcedonian decrees granting broad patriarchal rights to Constantinople.

Leo was also of enormous help to the increasingly weak imperial government. When, in 452, Attila the Hun was poised to sack all of Italy, the pope bravely met him at Mantua and convinced him to withdraw. Three years later, the Vandals under King Geiseric arrived, and Leo greeted him at the gates of Rome. While unable to prevent the sack of the city, he did win from Geiseric the promise not to burn or massacre. He died on November 10, 461, and was buried in St. Peter's. Of his writings, there are extant one hundred forty-three letters and ninety-six sermons; he may have contributed prayers to both the Leonine and Gelasian Sacramentaries. In theological matters, he is considered a strong advocate of orthodoxy, even if he was not particularly original. Pope Benedict XIV (r. 1740-1758) declared him a Doctor of the Church. Feast day: November 10.

Leo II, St. ● Pope from 682-683. Although he was elected in December 681 or January 682 to succeed St. Agatho, he did not receive confirmation from Byzantine Emperor Constantine IV, and was thus consecrated only in August 682. Leo was Sicilian by birth and was much respected for his fluency in Greek and Latin. His main act as pope was to ratify the decision of the Council of

Constantinople (680) that condemned the heresy of Monothelitism. Feast day: July 3.

Leo III, St. ● Pope from 795-816. A Roman by birth, Leo was unanimously elected to succeed Adrian I, although he soon encountered severe opposition from many Romans, especially partisan supporters of the recently deceased pontiff. Matters finally turned violent on April 25, 799, when a mob attacked him, nearly cut out his tongue and put out his eyes, and shut him up in a monastery. The pope escaped to Charlemagne (742-814), who refused to accept any deposition of Leo by the Romans. Returning to Rome from Paderborn, Leo was restored by the Franks and cleared by Charlemagne of all charges made by the rebels. On Christmas Day, 800, Leo crowned Charlemagne, establishing the precedent that all Holy Roman Emperors should receive their crown from the pope, thereby allying the papacy with the Western Empire. While forced to reign in the shadow of Charlemagne, Leo proved an admirable administrator. He also confirmed the correct nature of *filioque* but asked that it not be read in public so as not to offend the Greeks. Leo died on June 12, 816. Feast day: June 12.

Leo IV, St. ● Pope from 847-855. A native of Rome, Leo was a Benedictine monk before being appointed subdeacon and then cardinal priest. Upon the death of Pope Sergius II, Leo was elected unanimously and consecrated soon after. His main concern as pope was the constant peril facing Rome from the Saracens, who were raiding the Eternal City, including a damaging attack in 846. The allies routed a Saracen force in a naval battle near Ostia. To prevent additional threats, Leo fortified Civitavecchia, which was renamed Leopoli in his honor (854). His other main involvement was in punishing Archbishop Hincmar of Reims because the prelate had excommunicated an imperial vassal without papal approval. Leo also permitted Hincmar's suffragan bishops to appeal against the archbishop directly to Rome. Feast day: July 17.

Leo V ● Pope from August to September 903. His career and the nature of his election are obscure, questions arising from the fact that he was not apparently a member of the Roman clergy. While much respected for his goodness, his reign was cut short by his deposition by Christopher, a member of the palace clergy who threw him into prison. It is possible that Christopher had Leo strangled, although it is more likely that both Christopher and Leo were executed by Pope Sergius III, who had removed Christopher from the throne.

Leo VI ● Pope from May to December 928. Elected the successor of the deposed and imprisoned John X, Leo owed his election to the powerful Marozia and the Crescentii family who were dominating Roman political life. He died before John and was succeeded by the equally brief reigning Stephen VII (VIII).

Leo VII ● Pope from 936-939. Chosen by Duke Alberic II of Spoleto to succeed the deposed and imprisoned John XI, Leo was probably a Benedictine and a native of Rome. An ardent supporter of reform, Leo gave encouragement to Odo of Cluny and pushed for reform among the clergy in Germany. Leo did not favor the forced conversion of the Jews of Mainz by Archbishop Frederick, but he did not prohibit the expulsion of any Jews who refused to become Christian.

Leo VIII ● Pope from 963-965. His much troubled pontificate began on December 5, 963, when the Roman synod that had just deposed John XII was instructed by Emperor Otto I to elect by acclamation the much respected layman Leo. Hastily ordained, Leo was immediately beset by the supporters of John who rose up after Otto's departure from

Rome. A synod organized by the restored John officially deposed and excommunicated Leo. When John died, the Romans refused to acknowledge Leo as a candidate, preferring the popular Benedict (V). Otto could not accept this development, marching into Rome, suppressing all opposition, and restoring Leo in June 964. Leo died the next year.

Leo IX, St. ● Pope from 1049-1054. Born Bruno of Egisheim, he was a native of Alsace and a son of Count Hugh of Egisheim. Educated at Toul, he served as a canon of the cathedral and, from 1026-1027, bishop of Toul. He was elected to succeed Damasus II largely through the influence of Emperor Henry III. A gifted pontiff, Leo pursued both a genuine reform of the Church and an improvement of the Church's temporal position. One of the founders of what came to be called the Gregorian Reform, he was aided in his efforts by Hildebrand (the future Gregory VII) and Peter Damian. The Roman Curia was expanded, papal legates were sent out to the courts of Europe, and reforming councils were convened in France, Germany, and elsewhere. In 1053, Leo launched an ill-fated campaign against the Normans in Sicily and was defeated and captured. Held for nine months, Leo negotiated his release with what were probably extensive concessions. His campaign, however, strained relations with the Byzantine Empire, culminating in the

Pope St. Leo IX

final breach in 1054, the historical and ongoing schism between the Eastern and Western Churches beginning with this date. Feast day: April 19.

Leo X ● Pope from 1513-1521. One of the most famous of the so-called Renaissance popes, Leo was born Giovanni de' Medici, the second son of Lorenzo de' Medici. Born in Florence he was educated in his father's court and at the University of Pisa (1489-1491). While appointed a cardinal in 1489 by Alexander VI, he was not officially invested until 1492 and completion of his studies at Pisa. After the exile of the de' Medicis from Florence in 1494, Giovanni wandered from 1494-1500, journeying to France, Holland, and Germany. From 1500, he was back in Rome and emerged as a powerful figure in the pontificate of Julius II. In 1511, he was named a legate to Bologna; in 1512, he helped reclaim de' Medici control over Florence; on March 11, 1513, he was elected Julius's successor. Only thirty-eight years old when chosen as Leo X, he soon distinguished himself as the most lavish of the Renaissance popes. Work proceeded on St. Peter's basilica, the arts were encouraged, and large additions were made to the Vatican Library. While moral and religious in his personal life, Leo was extremely free with papal funds, squandering Julius's vast fortune and ignoring needed reform in the Church to prevent the growing dissent that came to be embodied in Martin Luther, whom Leo excommunicated in 1520. In 1516, he signed the Concordat of Bologna with Francis I of France, establishing Church-State affairs in France to replace the Pragmatic Sanction of Bourges. He was famous for the declaration made at the start of his pontificate, "Let us enjoy the papacy which God has chosen to give us."

Leo XI ● Pope in April 1605. Alessandro Ottaviano de' Medici was born in Florence to a branch of the famed de' Medici family. A nephew of Pope Leo X, he was a disciple of St. Philip Neri and so impressed Gregory XIII that he was created bishop of Pistoia in 1573, archbishop of Florence in 1574, and cardinal in 1583. Elected on April 1, 1605, to succeed Clement VIII, the seventy-year-old pontiff was ill when chosen, dying on April 27.

Leo XII ● Pope from 1823-1829. Successor to the remarkable Pius VII, Annibale Sermattei della Genga was born near Spoleto to a noble family. Ordained in 1783, he was appointed private secretary to Pius VI, subsequently serving as the papal representative to Lucerne, Cologne, and a number of royal courts in Germany. Made a cardinal in 1816 and vicar-general of Rome in 1820, he was elected pope on September 28, 1823, in opposition to the Austrians by the so-called Zelanti, conservatives who were against the moderate reforms of Cardinal Ercole Consalvi, the secretary of state. Leo proved a generally stern pontiff, resisting the spread of liberal ideas, especially in matters of doctrine. He condemned Freemasonry and strengthened the papacy's political control over the Papal States. His measures reduced taxation within the States, but the precarious financial situation remained. While the European powers feared a sharp reversal of Pius VII's conciliatory foreign policy, Leo actually came to an understanding of the value of sound relations, going so far as to seek the advice of Consalvi. Concordats were

Pope Leo XIII

negotiated with Hanover (1824) and the Netherlands (1827); he also promoted the emancipation of Catholics in England.

Leo XIII ● Pope from 1878-1903. Successor to Pope Pius IX (r. 1846-1878) and predecessor of Pope St. Pius X (r. 1903-1914), Gioacchino Vincenzo Pecci was born in Carpineto, near Rome, a son of a family of Italian minor nobility. Before his ordination in 1837, he studied at Viterbo (1818-1824), the Roman College (1824-1832), and the Academy of Noble Ecclesiastics (1832-1837). The next year, he was named governor of Benevento (1838-1841) and then governor of Perugia (1841-1843). In 1843, he was sent by Pope Gregory XVI (r. 1831-1846) as nuncio to Belgium. At this time, he was made a titular archbishop. Appointed bishop of Perugia in 1846, he was elevated to the cardinalate in 1853 by Pope Pius IX. In Perugia, he was outspoken in his promotion of Thomism, founding (1859) the Academy of St. Thomas Aquinas, and in his resistance of the anticlerical tendencies of the Sardinian government after its seizure of Perugia in 1860. Pius named him camerlengo in 1877, and the next year, on February 20, 1878, he was elected pope on the third ballot. He was probably chosen as a compromise temporary candidate, especially given his age (he was sixty-eight) and his supposed poor health. He thus surprised many observers by his energetic pontificate, his cautious, careful, and conciliatory policies, and his excellent health — his reign would last twenty-five years and would have two main concerns: turning the Church toward recognition of the social problems created by the industrial revolution and attempting to resolve the lingering crises in relations between the Church and various secular powers.

Clearly desirous of reestablishing the temporal power of the papacy that had been irrevocably lost in 1870, Leo commanded that no Catholics should participate in Italian elections. In Germany, he was able to reverse Pius's intransigence toward Bismarck, thereby allowing the minister to ease the *Kulturkampf* without political loss of face. His hope of winning German support against Italy was a failure, however, and papal foreign policy received setbacks in England (where diplomatic efforts were rebuffed) and in France (where anticlerical legislation and anti-Catholic measures deeply troubled the French Church).

Leo had long been concerned with social issues, coming into contact with the implications of the industrial age while visiting London, Paris, and elsewhere when serving as a Vatican diplomat; he was also much impressed with the labors of St. John Bosco. He rejected utterly socialism, Communism, and anarchy as leading inevitably to oppression and being inconsistent with Christian charity. Socialism was denounced in *Quod Apostolici muneris* (December 28, 1878), but the pope recognized that more than denunciatory proclamations were needed. A clear social policy for the Church was thus enunciated in the encyclical *Rerum novarum* (May 15, 1891), which has been called the Charter of Catholic Social Doctrine (by Pope John XXIII) and earned Leo the title of the "workers' pope." This dialogue, while crucial, was carefully tempered by the pontiff with sound doctrine. He thus maintained the heart of the policies of Pius IX, condemning Freemasonry in *Humanum genus* (1884) and keeping tight control over the central administration of the Church.

With his doctrinal efforts, Leo promoted Thomism and learning and missionary activities throughout the world. In the encyclical *Aeterni Patris* (1879), Leo gave a profound affirmation of the greatness and value of St. Thomas Aquinas. Advancing Catholic scholarship, he gave impetus to scientific and astronomic studies, and, in a significant gesture, opened the Vatican Archives in 1883 to all scholars, not just Catholic ones. He also established a guide for biblical research in the encyclical *Providentissimus Deus* (1893). Hierarchies were created in various countries, including North Africa, India, and Japan; his pontificate brought some two hundred forty-eight new sees, twenty-eight of them in the United States (see also **Americanism**). He died on July 20, 1903.

Leopoldine Association ● Missionary aid society. Established in Vienna, Austria, in 1829, largely through the efforts of Frederic Résé (the future first bishop of Detroit) with the aim of assisting in the development of the Church in the United States. Deriving its name from Leopoldine (d. 1826), daughter of Francis I of Austria and empress of Brazil, the society provided funds for the creation of new dioceses and parishes, helped to defray other costs, and assisted German-speaking immigrants and clergy in the United States. The work of the association was most helpful in the mid-nineteenth century, declining thereafter as the American Church became better organized and on firmer financial ground. The activities of the Leopoldine Association were suspended in 1921.

Lepanto, Battle of ●
Important naval engagement. Fought on October 7, 1571, between the Ottoman Turks and a fleet of the allied Christian forces, the battle ended the threat of Turkish naval supremacy in the Mediterranean. The Turks had been increasingly a danger to Christendom in the Mediterranean in the years just prior, especially launching campaigns against Venice with the aim of driving the Venetians from the area of the eastern Mediterranean.

Marques de Santa Cruz, commander at the Battle of Lepanto

The Venetians responded by forming an alliance with Pope St. Pius V and King Philip II of Spain, with Pius providing the principal moral leadership. Philip's brother, Don Juan (or John) of Austria, commanded the allied fleet, taking it into combat against the Turks under Ali Pasha (also spelled Pasa) in the Gulf of Patras, near Lepanto (Naupaktos). After hours of bitter fighting, some fifteen thousand Turks were dead, one hundred seventeen galleys captured, and ten thousand Christian galley slaves freed. In celebration and thanksgiving, Pope Pius instituted a special feast of the Virgin Mary; from 1573, October 7 has been kept as the Feast of the Rosary. G. K. Chesterton (1874-1936) authored a well-known poem on Lepanto.

Le Quien, Michel (1661-1733) ● French historian and theologian. A native of Boulogne, he studied at Paris and entered the Dominican convent of St. Germain in 1681. With the exception of several short trips, Le Quien never left Paris. Among his important works are: *La Nullité des ordinations anglicanes* (2 vols., 1725) and *La Nullité des ordinations anglicanes démontrée de nouveau* (2 vols., 1730), both on Anglican Orders in response to Pierre Courayer's apologetic work on the subject; *Oriens Christianus* (3 vols., 1740, posthumously), an ambitious work on the Eastern Churches; and *Johannis Damasceni opera omnia* (2 vols., 1712), an edition on the works of St. John Damascene.

Lessius, Leonard (1554-1623) ● Flemish Jesuit theologian. Born in Brecht, near Antwerp, he studied at the University of the Louvain, apparently becoming a doctor of philosophy at the age of seventeen. In 1572, he joined the Society of Jesus, teaching philosophy at Douai from 1574-1581 and at Louvain from 1585-1600. He was a student in Rome of the famed Jesuit theologian Francisco Suárez. After retiring from teaching he was asked by his superiors to publish his lectures on theology. His vast literary output included works on theology, morals, and ascetics. Chief among his writings were: *De justitia et jure* (1605), examining the moral considerations of economics; *De gratia efficaci* (1610), on grace; and numerous works on moral theology. He also participated in the major controversies of the day, most notably on grace; in 1587 the Louvain Theological Faculty censured thirty-four of Lessius' theses. Lessius was much respected, however, by Pope Urban VIII and St. Francis de Sales for his sanctity.

Libellatici ● Name used for those Christians who, during the Decian persecutions (of Emperor Trajanus Decius) of 249-251, purchased from officials of the

Roman state the required certificates, called *libelli pacis*, that declared that the holder had made the required sacrifices to pagan idols. The Christians who acquired the certificates had not in fact made any sacrifices but had used money to buy their safety. Condemned by the Church, the *libellatici* were ranked among the *lapsi*, those who had turned from the faith during the persecutions. Their punishment and required penance, however, were lighter than those of the Church who had made sacrifices. (See also **Lapsi**.)

Liber Censuum ● Name given to the register of the Roman Church that made an extensive accounting of the titles owed to the papacy by various dioceses, cities, monasteries, and kingdoms. It was first compiled by Cencio Savelli (the future Pope Honorius III), who was then serving as secretary, or *camerarius*, to Popes Clement III (r. 1187-1191) and Celestine III (r. 1191-1198). The *Liber* also contains a list of dependent bishoprics and monasteries.

Liber Diurnus Romanorum Pontificum ● Collection of important ecclesiastical documents customarily prepared and used by the papal chancery until the eleventh century. Scholars have disagreed as to when the *Liber diurnus* began, although it was probably sometime in the seventh century, possibly in the reign of Honorius I (r. 625-638). Early collections relied on the formularies of earlier papal documents such as those of Gelasius I (r. 492-496) and St. Gregory I (r. 590-604). Among the models contained within the *Liber* were letters relating to the death, election, and consecration of popes; the election of bishops; and the conferring of the pallium on archbishops. Used until the eleventh century, the collection was gradually replaced by new compilations that were better suited for the contemporary needs of the papal administration. While used as a source by canonists of the twelfth century

such as Gratian, it eventually fell into total disuse and was all but forgotten.

Liber Pontificalis ● Latin for *Book of the Popes*, it is a compilation of papal biographies from St. Peter to the second half of the fifteenth century (c. 1464). The earliest series of biographies on the popes — from St. Peter to Felix III (IV) (d. 530) — was written almost certainly by a Roman presbyter during the reign of Boniface II (r. 530-532). The main sources used for these early entries were the Liberian Catalogue (Latin: *Catalog Liberianus*) and a list most likely dependent upon the Liberian Catalogue; other historical writings were no doubt consulted, including the Roman Acts of the Martyrs. The early biographies were generally short, increasing in length with each of the subsequent editions. The first collection in the complete form of the *Liber Pontificalis* dates to Stephen V (r. 885-891). Additions were then frequently made, in a different style, down to the times of Eugenius IV (r. 1431-1447) and Pius II (r. 1458-1464). The collection, particularly the later biographies, is a valuable source of information on the development of the papacy. The individual entries contain details about the origin and birthplace of the pope, the length and decrees of his pontificate, notable ecclesiastical and civil events, important ordinations, renovations of churches, the death and burial of the pontiff, and the time of *sede vacante*.

Liber Septimus ● Name given to three different canonical collections.

1. Known to historians and canonists as the *Liber Septimus*, the officially titled *Constitutiones Clementis V* (or *Clementinae*) was promulgated by Clement V in March 1314. As Clement died soon after, some question existed as to its validity, although John XXII promulgated it again in 1317 in the bull *Quoniam nulla* (October 23, 1317).

2. The *Septimus Liber Decretalium* was a

collection of canons organized by the sixteenth-century canonist Pierre Mathieu and published in 1690. He arranged the canons according to the order presented in the Decretals of Gregory IX but containing some decretals of later pontiffs, including Sixtus IV (r. 1471-1484) and Sixtus V (r. 1585-1590).

3. The *Liber Septimus* drawn up by Cardinal Pinelli, prefect of the special congregation appointed by Sixtus V, was officially known as the *Decretales Clementis Papae VIII* but called the *Liber Septimus* by Pinelli, a name subsequently used by Benedict XIV. Instructed to make up the defect of official codification of canon laws that was lacking from the time of the *Constitutiones Clementis V* as promulgated by John XXII in 1317, the new collection was submitted in 1598 to Clement VIII, who refused to give his approval. Paul V also refused to approve it. The reasons for papal hesitation stemmed from political considerations, as a number of states refused to accept some of the constitutions that were included. (See also **Canon Law**.)

Liber Sextus Decretalium ● Canonical collection organized by Guillaume de Mandagot (bishop of Embrun), Ricardo Petroni (vice-chancellor to the pope), and Berenger Fredoli (bishop of Beziers) at the command of Pope Boniface VIII and approved by him in the bull *Sacrosanctae* on March 3, 1298. It replaced or abrogated all previous general laws from the time of Gregory IX to the accession of Boniface (September 5, 1234 to December 24, 1294), save for those maintained as being in force through their being added or included in the collection. The name *Liber Sextus* was given by Boniface to indicate that it was a continuation of the five books of the Decretals of Gregory IX and because six is a perfect number.

Liber Usualis ● Book of Gregorian chants for the Ordinary and Propers of Masses,

chants for rites and special Masses, and chants of the Divine Office. Edited by Benedictine monks of Solesme, the chants of the *Liber* are of great historical value and, while the book is currently out of print, it can be used in Masses today.

Liberals, Catholic ● Term used to describe the intellectuals of the nineteenth century who attempted to reconcile the doctrines and teachings of the Church with the liberal ideas that emerged out of the French Revolution, in particular political and social reform and regulating relations between Church and State. Liberalism, also called ecclesiastical liberalism, had its origins in the ideas of Josephism, Febronianism, and Gallicanism, although many of the liberals preferred to argue that they took their inspiration from the positive aspects of the French Revolution — such as freedom of speech and democracy — rather than the anti-Catholic and persecutory tendencies of the various movements. Catholic liberalism had its foundation in 1828 in Félicité Lamennais (d. 1854). With Jean Baptiste Henri Lacordaire (d. 1861) and Count Charles de Montalembert (d. 1870), Lamennais founded the newspaper *L'Avenir* (*The Future*), with the banner "God and Freedom." Their views were attacked as proclaiming the absolute autonomy of humankind in the moral and social order. Condemnation by French bishops caused the liberal Catholics to appeal to Pope Gregory XVI (r. 1831-1846). He also rejected their liberal ideas in the encyclical *Mirari vos* (1832), and future briefs by Pope Pius IX as well as encyclicals by Pius IX, Leo XIII, and St. Pius X continued to point out the errors of liberalism. The most severe condemnation, of course, came in the constitution *De Fide* of Vatican Council I (1869-1870) and the encyclical *Quanta cura* (1864) with the attached *Syllabus of Errors* by Pope Pius IX. Lacordaire declared, however, "I die a penitent Catholic, but an impenitent liberal."

Liberation Theology ● Movement within the Church attempting to unite theology with a program of social liberation that includes opposition to the economic and political oppression of the poor, promotion of minority rights, women's liberation, and in some cases the violent overthrow of repressive regimes. Liberation theology was launched in 1973 with the publication of *A Theology of Liberation: History, Politics, and Salvation* by Gustavo Gutiérrez, a Jesuit priest from Peru. The work brought together a number of ideas that had been finding currency in various circles within the Church and in universities, and that had been very aggressively advanced by participants in the 1968 meeting in Medellín, Colombia, of the Latin American Episcopal Conferences. Gutiérrez proved to be only the first of many writers and theologians to contribute ideas to the movement christened "Liberation Theology." One of the most outspoken modern authors has been the former Franciscan Leonardo Boff.

In a broad sense, the adherents of the movement advocate a vigorous new approach to theology in which the primary focus of the Church is on social deliverance, the freeing of poor people across the world through the application of the resources of the Catholic Church. The consequence of this orientation has been noted by many observers as leading inevitably to a reduction of theology as the expression of the message of salvation to an intellectual foundation for the introduction of socialist or even Marxist programs of sociopolitical restructuring. In the revision of Catholic doctrine, Christ ceases to fulfill his glorious mission as the Son of God and is instead a human revolutionary deliverer whose time on earth was to serve as the expression of the liberation of the weak and the oppressed. The Church ceases to be the Mystical Body of Christ, becoming a vehicle for social revolution, its concerns exclusively on the crises and problems of this world, with little or no consideration of the ultimate and vital salvation of all humanity. Central to this entire project is the reinterpretation of sin away from a personal offense against God toward a grave crime against society.

Pope Paul VI noted the danger posed by such a theological outlook when he proclaimed, "The Church connects but never equates human liberation with salvation in Jesus Christ." Pope John Paul II, who had long experience with Marxist theory as a prelate in Communist Poland, has been even more specific throughout his pontificate. In his address to the Third General Conference of the Latin American Episcopate (January 28, 1979), the pope emphasized the truth that the Church is bound "to proclaim liberation in its integral and profound meaning, as Jesus proclaimed and realized it." The pope, who has been totally committed to the cause of the poor and suffering, subsequently ordered a thorough investigation of liberation theology by the Congregation for the Doctrine of the Faith. Its findings were released in two documents: "Instruction on Certain Aspects of the Theology on Christian Freedom" (1984) and "Instruction on Christian Freedom and Liberation" (1986). The first reiterated the grave reservations of the Holy See, pointing out: "The theses of the 'theologies of liberation' are widely popularized under a simplified form, in formation sessions or in what are called 'base groups' which lack the necessary catechetical and theological preparation as well as the capacity for discernment." The second reminded the faithful that liberation in its fundamental nature has always been taught by the Church and is not the exclusive possession of a single group or set of theologians. Liberation theology continues to find wide support among many religious in Central and South America, Africa, and Asia, although it has lost much of its urgency due to the collapse and discrediting of Communism. (See also **Social Encyclicals**.)

Liberatus of Carthage ● Sixth-century archdeacon and historian. Much trusted by the bishops of Africa, he was frequently a representative in their dispute over the edict of Justinian I against the Three Chapters (544). His main work, however, was to author an important history of the Nestorian and Monophysite Controversies of the period. The history is called *Breviarium causae Nestorianorum et Eutychianorum* (*A Short Account of the Affair of the Nestorians and Eutychians*) and is a useful source on the two heresies.

Liberius ● Pope from 352-366. The first pontiff not honored in the calendar, whose pontificate was troubled by the Arian Controversy. A Roman deacon, he was elected on May 17, 352, to succeed Pope St. Julius I, coming under immediate pressure from the ardently pro-Arian emperor Constantius II. The emperor demanded that Liberius sign the condemnation of St. Athanasius of Alexandria and, when he refused, Constantius had him banished (355) to Beroea and the Arian archdeacon Felix (II) named as antipope in his place. In 357, Liberius submitted to the will of the emperor. Having made concessions to Constantius, Liberius was allowed to return to Rome. The nature of the concessions is unclear, but Liberius probably subscribed to some kind of heretical formula, although St. Jerome and St. Athanasius both agreed that any assent was given under duress and therefore was not valid. There remained, however, the uncomfortable presence of Felix (who died only in 365) and Liberius's own severely impaired credibility. He was not involved at the Council of Rimini (359), which resulted in a compromise with the Arians, but, after Constantius' death in 361, Liberius voided the Rimini decrees and received in 362 the recognition of his authority by several Eastern bishops. Liberius built the famous Basilica Liberiana on the Esquiline Hill, the foundation for the present-day Santa Maria Maggiore.

Lindisfarne ● Famed island located off the coast of Northumbria, the site of Lindisfarne Abbey. Known as the Holy Island from the eleventh century, the monastic community was founded there in 635 by St. Aidan, who had come from Iona, and was soon established as a base for missionary activity. In the aftermath of the Synod of Whitby (664), many of the English and Scoto-Irish monks left the abbey to protect the end of the Celtic traditions on the Church of the country. The island was twice attacked and pillaged by Viking raiders (793, 875), forcing the monks to flee temporarily and then to repair extensive damage to the community. In 995, the island's bishopric was transferred to the see of Durham, but the monks continued to reside at Lindisfarne until the reign of King Henry VIII and the Dissolution of the Monasteries.

Linus, St. ● Pope from 67-76. Accepted as the immediate successor of Peter as Bishop of Rome. Aside from leading the Christians of the Eternal City, little is known with certainty about him. Both Irenaeus and Hegesippus listed Linus as the successor to Peter, having been entrusted with the office by Peter and Paul. Eusebius supported the earlier writings of the historians. Eusebius and Irenaeus further identify Linus with the so-called companion of St. Paul who sends greetings from Rome to Timothy in Ephesus (cf. 2 Tm 4:21). He is listed among the martyrs named in the canon of the Mass. Feast day: September 23.

Lithuania ● Baltic republic that once dominated much of the region of the Baltic Sea. The area that became Lithuania was long a pagan stronghold, steadfastly resisting in the twelfth century the advance of the Teutonic Knights and their allies, the Livonian Knights (see under **Military**

Orders), who had seized Estonia and Latvia and were driving ever eastward. The unification of the Liths occurred during this era in order to facilitate their stand against the violent conversions brought by the Teutonic Knights. Despite this hostility, Christianity penetrated into Lithuania during the thirteenth century, and in 1251 Grand Duke Mindaugas was baptized. He was given recognition in 1253 by Pope Innocent IV and the Church was given its first foundation. The pagan counterreaction from 1263 and the duke's murder proved so extreme that the faith was not able to secure a firm hold over the country until the late fourteenth century. This came about largely by the marriage of the Lithuanian grand duke Jagiello with Jadwiga, heiress of the Polish crown. Under the Jagiello Dynasty, Lithuania reached its greatest extent of power, smashing the Teutonic Knights in 1410 at the Battle of Tannenberg (or Grünwald). By the terms of the Treaty of Torun (Thorn), the knights surrendered Pomerania. Polish culture gained ascendancy in Lithuania in the fifteenth century, meaning that the Christian faith was of Western orientation. Both the Polish influence and Roman Church contributed to the Lithuanian determination to resist any interference from the east, the rising grand duchy of Moscow under its ambitious ruler Ivan III (r. 1462-1505).

The spread of Reformation ideas was not a widespread problem for Lithuania, as the faith was quite strong. In the face of continued Russian expansion, the grand duchy was absorbed into Poland in 1569, marking definitively its decline as a northern European player. Poland also deteriorated so that in the partition of the kingdom in the years 1772-1795, Lithuania was seized by Russia. The Church there from that time came under much pressure from the Russian Orthodox Church, but Lithuanians resisted fiercely, seeing the Orthodox clergy as invaders. In 1918, Lithuania won its independence from Russia and then repulsed an attack by the Bolsheviks. In the grim years before World War II, the Lithuanians were forced to permit Russian military bases (1939) and then endured forced admission into the Soviet Union (1940) by Joseph Stalin.

The Communist era (1940-1991) brought harsh repression, with deportations to Siberia, arrest, torture, imprisonments, and murders of clergy and laypersons. The Church, however, proved astonishingly resilient and was nurtured in underground ways by the people who found in it both a sense of hope and a powerful means of resisting a foreign oppressor. From 1982, there was a gradual easing of tensions and persecutions so that Bishop Vincentas Sladkevicius, under Communist watch since 1957 and restricted in his movements, was allowed to return to his see. Other ecclesiastical reorganization was permitted in 1989. Independence for Lithuanians was achieved finally in 1991.

Little Flower ● See **Thérèse of Lisieux, St**.

Little Flowers of St. Francis ● In Italian, the *Fioretti di San Francisco*. It is a collection of tales and legends about St. Francis of Assisi and his companions, dating to around 1375. The *Little Flowers* was an anonymous translation made in Tuscany of some fifty-five chapters of the Latin work *Actus Beati Francisci et Sociorum Eius* by Fra Ugolini Boniscambi, along with other useful sources, most notably the "Five Considerations of the Holy Stigmata." The work is an invaluable source on the early stages of the Franciscans.

Liturgical Movement ● Movement in the Church that seeks to revitalize the liturgy in modern life and to promote a renewal of active participation by Catholics everywhere in the Mass, the sacraments, the Divine Office, and other forms of worship, although such liturgical renewal has been a constant throughout the history of the Church. The origins of the modern liturgical movement can be credited to the French Benedictine monk Prosper Louis Guéranger (1805-1875), who authored numerous liturgical works, including *Institutions liturgique* (3 vols., 1840-1851) and *L'année liturgique* (9 vols., 1841-1866), a comprehensive and devotional study of the Church calendar. The movement's main drive was initiated by Pope St. Pius X (r. 1903-1914), who encouraged the revival of the Gregorian chant and was especially an advocate of frequent and early Communion. In the spirit of his call, the movement found support in much of Europe and the United States. Pope Pius XII (r. 1939-1958) in the encyclical *Mediator Dei* (November 20, 1947) stressed both the place of the liturgy and the vital need for participation by the faithful. His initial reforms of the liturgy laid the groundwork for the changes implemented by Vatican Council II in the "Constitution on the Sacred Liturgy" (*Sacrosanctum Concilium*) promulgated on December 4, 1963.

Liutprand (c. 922-c. 972) ● Also Liudprand or Liutprand of Cremona, Italian chronicler and bishop of Cremona. Made a bishop by the ruler Otto I in 961, Liutprand took part in the synod that deposed John XII. Sent by Otto to Constantinople in 968, Liutprand was unsuccessful in negotiating a marriage between Otto II and a Byzantine princess. Among his notable works were: *Antapodosis* (*Revenge*), a history from 888-958; *Historia Ottonis* (*History of Otto*); and *Relatio de legatione Constantinopolitana* (*Account of the Mission to Constantinople*). He is the main source of information on Italian history during the era.

Loisy, Alfred (1857-1940) ● French biblical scholar and linguist, considered the founder of Modernism. Born in Ambrières, France, Loisy studied at the diocesan seminary of Châlons-sur-Marne and at the Institut Catholique in Paris. Ordained in 1879, he centered his studies on the Bible and a revitalization of biblical interpretation. His writings as professor of Sacred Scriptures at the Institut Catholique soon aroused much opposition and in 1893 his severe criticism of traditional Catholic theology led to his removal from the professorship and confinement to teaching Oriental languages. From 1900, he taught at the École Pratiques des Hautes Études, authoring in 1902 *L'Évangile et L'Église* (*The Gospel and the Church*). His work, which stressed the guiding hand of the Spirit with a resulting spiritual charisma, was both a sharp reply to the German historian Adolph von Harnack and a highly controversial argument for the intuitive powers in religious experience. Condemned by the archbishop of Paris, *L'Évangile* and Loisy's other writings were placed by Pope St. Pius X on the Index of Forbidden Books. While he submitted in 1904, he broke from the Church in 1907 and was excommunicated in 1908. Loisy served as professor of the history of religion from 1909-1930 at the Collège de France.

Lollardy ● Name given to the movement of followers of John Wycliffe (or Wyclif; d. 1384). Also used for the adherents of radical preachers, usually among the lower classes, or, less properly, for any critics of the Church. The name Lollard was probably derived from the Latin *lollium* (tares) but may have come from the Old Dutch word *lollen* (to sing), emerging as a phrase meaning mumbler of prayers; first used in 1382, it became an official term in 1387. The first Lollards were the intellectual supporters of Wycliffe at Oxford, including such men as Nicholas of Hereford and Philip Repington. As developed, Lollardy taught that the principal authority for the faith was the Bible, with every person possessing the right of interpretation. Pilgrimages, celibacy, and many traditions of the Church were attacked.

The morality of the priest determined the validity of his acts.

The so-called Wycliffites were suppressed by Archbishop William Courtenay of Canterbury in 1382, launching a series of aggressive steps, including the promulgation of the statute *De Haeretico Comburendo* (1401). These measures effectively eradicated the academic support for Lollardy, but the movement soon spread among the poor, who were inspired by the militant preachers. After the crushing of the revolt of Sir John Oldcastle in 1413, however, popular Lollardy declined. Nevertheless, it influenced the development of the Hussites and Lutheranism.

Lonergan, Bernard (1904-1984) ● Canadian priest and Thomist. Born in Canada, he entered the Jesuits after graduating from high school, studying at Heythorp College in London and the Gregorian University of Rome. Ordained in 1936, he earned a doctorate in theology at Rome and then returned to Canada where he taught theology from 1940-1953. From 1953-1965, he taught at the Gregorian. Owing to poor health, including a lung operation in 1964, he became less active but continued to write and to lecture, at Regis College, Toronto, from 1965-1975, and Boston College from 1975-1983. Ranked with Joseph Maréchal (1878-1944), Karl Rahner (1904-1984), and Emeric Coreth (b. 1919) as one of the most important figures in so-called Transcendental Thomism, Lonergan promoted a different method for theology, working to harmonize Thomistic thought with the demands of the modern age. While acknowledging and embracing the theological foundation of Thomas Aquinas on which all theologians must rely, Lonergan, like his fellow Transcendental Thomists, accepted as well the contributions of other sources — from Kant to phenomenology to Maurice Blondel. His two chief works were *Insight: An Enquiry into Human Understanding* (1957) and *Method in Theology* (1972).

Longinus ● The centurion, according to tradition, who was in charge of the crucifixion of Christ and pierced Our Lord's side. He was supposedly converted that instant, becoming the first Roman Christian, and his spear emerged as one of the most revered of all Christian relics, known generally as the Holy Lance or the Lance of Longinus. Longinus was said to have left the legions, wandering across the empire with his lance. The spear itself faded into obscurity, reappearing from time to time in legend and in fact. Often confused with other lances of Christian lore, the spear of Longinus may be the so-called Maurice (or Mauritius) Lance that was part of the Habsburg regalia and is currently in the Hofburg, Vienna. Other legends associate it with Joseph of Arimathea's journey to England and with the Holy Grail. (See also **Holy Grail; Lance, Holy**; and **Relics**.)

Loreto, Holy House of ● One of the most important of all the Marian shrines. Located in Loreto, Italy, near the Adriatic port city of Ancona, it is traditionally accepted as the home of the Holy Family, the house in which Mary resided at the time of the Annunciation. The Holy House, actually more of a room, was attested to by a number of writers, including St. Epiphanius in the fourth century, the Venerable Bede, and St. Willibald in the eighth century. Preserved in Jerusalem in an extensive basilica built by St. Helena, the Holy House was visited by King Louis IX of France in 1251, only a few years before the fall of the city to the Mamelukes who, in 1263, destroyed the church. Somehow miraculously spared, its existence in 1289 was attested to by Ricoldo di Montecroce, a pilgrim and author of an account of his pilgrimage to the Holy Land. In 1291, the house suddenly appeared in the town of Tesatz, in Dalmatia, the story swiftly circulating that it had been transported by angels from Palestine. Three years later, it was discovered to have moved to its present site at Loreto, its transportation again attributed to angels. The small shrine soon began to attract pilgrims, its fame spreading quickly throughout Christendom. In 1310, Pope Clement V issued a bull granting a special indulgence to German pilgrims. A basilica was built around it in the mid-fifteenth century, replaced during the pontificate of Pope Sixtus V (1585-1590). This magnificent shrine still stands and has been visited by numerous saints and popes, such as Pius IX, St. Pius X, John XXIII, and John Paul II. In a letter published on September 7, 1993, Pope John Paul II celebrated the seven hundredth anniversary of the house at Loreto. Our Lady of Loreto is the patroness of homes and was named by Pope Benedict XV to be patroness of air travelers and aviators.

L'Osservatore Romano ● See **Osservatore Romano, L'**.

Los-von-Rom Movement ● German title meaning "free from Rome." Used for an anti-Roman political and religious movement first established in Austria in 1897 that then spread throughout the Pan-Germanic territories. Fostered by German nationalists, the Los-von-Rom movement derived its name

from the student cry heard at the Deutscher Volkstag (1897) in Vienna. Its primary purpose was to draw Roman Catholics away from the Austrian Church and lure them into the Protestant Churches of Germany. This was accomplished by such organizations as the Ulrich-Hutta Bund, which spread vicious propaganda against the Church, especially of being anti-German and pro-Slavic in its sympathies. As many as seventy-five thousand Catholics left the faith, even though the movement soon revealed itself to be not only anti-Catholic but anti-Christian in ideology. The kind of pseudo-Germanic national Church favored by the leaders of Los-von-Rom foreshadowed many of the ideas promoted by the National Socialist, or Nazi, Party. While fading before World War I, the movement resurfaced in postwar Germany and also arose in other non-Germanic countries such as Mexico and Belgium.

St. Louis IX of France

Louis IX, St. (1214-1270) ● King of France from 1226-1270. Honored as one of the greatest monarchs in French history and revered as the embodiment of Christian ideals of chivalry and piety, he was the fourth son of Louis VIII and Blanche of Castile. He was crowned at Reims and spent his minority (1226-1234) under the regency of his able mother. Assuming control of the state in 1234, Louis wed Margaret of Provence, a union that produced eleven children. In 1244, Louis took up the cross and embarked on the Seventh Crusade (1248-1254). Campaigning in Egypt, he was defeated and captured at El Mansura (1250), winning his freedom from his Muslim captors only with the payment of a ransom. Louis remained in the Holy Land until 1254, returning to France after the death of his mother. Reforming the government, Louis prohibited private warfare, distributed taxes more evenly, and extended the right of appeal to the crown. Convinced of the need to return to a crusade, in 1270 he launched the disastrous Eighth Crusade. After capturing Carthage, he fell ill during an outbreak of the plague, dying on August 25, 1270. Renowned for his honor and chivalry, Louis was also a great patron of churches, constructing St.-Chapelle in Paris and aiding Christian cities in Syria. He also supported various religious houses and the mendicant orders. Pope Boniface VIII canonized him in 1297. Feast day: August 25.

Lourdes, Apparitions of ● Series of eighteen apparitions of the Blessed Virgin from February 11 to July 16, 1858, in the rock cave of Massabielle, along the Gave River, near Lourdes in the French *département* of Hautes-Pyrénées. Our Lady appeared to fourteen-year-old Bernadette Soubirous (canonized on December 5, 1933, by Pope Pius XI), instructing her to drink from a spring beneath the rocks of Massabielle. While only mud was at first apparent, water began to flow from the spot to the Gave. The water, possessing no discernible or unusual properties, soon acquired a reputation for having miraculous powers, and pilgrims began flocking to the site. In her final appearance to Bernadette, the BVM declared, "I am the Immaculate Conception."

To fulfill the wishes of Our Lady, a chapel was built at the site that became a great basilica in 1901 and was joined by an underground church in 1958. Found today at Lourdes are medical bureaus and a hospital staffed by volunteers from around the world who assist the sick and the lame in reaching the healing waters. It is estimated that some six million pilgrims visit Lourdes each year. The Church officially approved Lourdes as a pilgrim site in 1862, and the feast of the apparitions on February 11 was extended by Pope St. Pius X to the entire Church. It is now an optional memorial in the revised calendar.

Lucian of Antioch, St. (d. 312) ● Theologian, scholar, and martyr. A presbyter in Antioch, Lucian authored numerous works on the doctrines of the Church and the Bible, his writings in Greek so respected that they were accepted texts by most of the sees of the East. Unfortunately, little of his output is extant, although it is believed that the second of the four creeds issued by the Council of Antioch (341) may have been composed by Lucian. He also founded the important theological school that claimed as students Arius and Eusebius of Nicomedia. Feast day: October 13 (East), January 7 (West).

Lucifer of Cagliari (d. 370 or 371) ● Also Lucifer of Sardinia. Bishop of Cagliari and one of the Church's greatest and most outspoken opponents of Arianism. At the Council of Milan (354) he refused to condemn St. Athanasius and was imprisoned by Emperor Constantius II for several days in the imperial palace before being banished to Egypt. Throughout, he continued his attacks on Arianism in general and the emperor in particular. Released by the general amnesty of Emperor Julian in 362, Lucifer had spent much of his period of exile writing defenses of Orthodox Christianity against the Arians. His works included: *De non conveniendo cum haereticis* (*On his refusal to meet with the heretics*); *Pro S. Athanasio*, a defense of Athanasius; and *De regibus apostacisis*, an attack on Constantius. After his release, Lucifer traveled to Antioch and then returned to his see in Cagliari.

Lucius I, St. ● Pope from 253-254. The successor to St. Cornelius, he was a native of Rome and shortly after his election as pontiff was banished to Civitavecchia, Italy, by Emperor Trebonianus Gallus. Shortly after Valerian (r. 253-260) became emperor, however, Lucius was allowed to return to Rome. Based on one of the letters of St. Cyprian, Lucius continued the policy Cornelius promulgated of allowing those Christians who had apostatized during the persecutions to be readmitted to the Church after a suitable penance. He thus opposed the antipope Novatian and the rigorists. According to the *Liber Pontificalis*, he was martyred by decapitation, although the tradition of the Liberian Catalogue states that he died of natural causes. An epitaph on his tomb in Greek has survived. Feast day: March 4.

Lucius II ● Pope from 1144-1145. Known originally as Gherardo Caccianemici, he was a native of Bologna. Named a cardinal by Pope Callistus II in 1124, and chamberlain to Innocent II, he was elected on March 12, 1144, to succeed Celestine II. He made peace with Roger II of Sicily, who had invaded papal territory, but the revolt of the population of Rome, who resented ecclesiastical domination of the city, became so troublesome that Lucius took up arms to suppress it. The rebels, led by Giordano Pierleoni, brother of antipope Anacletus, put up stiff resistance; as a result, the pontiff died of injuries received in combat.

Lucius III ● Pope from 1181-1185. Known originally as Ubaldo Allucingoli, he was a native of Lucca, Italy, and a Cistercian monk. Named a cardinal by Pope Innocent II and the cardinal bishop of Ostia and Velletri by Adrian IV, he was a trusted adviser to

Alexander III whom he succeeded on September 1, 1181. Owing to difficulties with the Romans, Lucius had himself crowned at Velletri and spent most of his pontificate outside the Eternal City. While relations with Emperor Frederick I Barbarossa were strained, he did secure his promise to participate in the Third Crusade and his support at the Synod of Verona (1184). The synod decreed the extermination of heretics. Lucius died at Verona on November 25, 1185.

Lucy, St. ● Fourth-century virgin martyr. It is known with certainty that Lucy was martyred in Sicily, Italy, most likely during the persecutions launched by Emperor Diocletian. The accompanying traditions cannot be verified, although the story is both detailed and well-known. She was supposedly a native of Syracuse who was denounced as a Christian by her rejected suitor. Subsequently, she was saved miraculously from a brothel and execution by fire, dying finally by a sword thrust to the neck. The date of her martyrdom has been fixed at 304. Her veneration dates from the fourth century, and she is included in the Canon of the Mass. The patroness of eyes, she is invoked against eye diseases and is depicted holding two eyes in a dish. Feast day: December 13.

Ludolph of Saxony (d. 1378) ● Also Ludolph the Carthusian, a spiritual writer. There is very little information on his early life, and even his place of origin is unclear, despite the surname "of Saxony." According to a story probably originating in the sixteenth century, he first entered the Dominicans and then, in 1340, joined the Carthusians in Strasbourg. Named prior in 1343 of the Charterhouse in Coblenz, Ludolph resigned his post in 1348, spending the rest of his life as a simple monk in Mainz and Strasbourg. At times erroneously credited with the authorship of the *Imitation of Christ*, Ludolph authored two important works, a "Commentary on the Psalms" and the much read "*Vita Christi*," not a biography of Christ but a series of spiritual dissertations or meditations on the life of Christ, from the eternal birth in the Father to the Ascension.

Ludwig Mission Association ● In German, *Ludwig-missionsverein.* Organization established in Bavaria in 1838 to give aid to missionary activities in North America. The founder was the German-born priest Frederic Résé, who would become first bishop of Detroit. He had begun the Leopoldine Association and was an active servant of the North American missions. Through financial grants, help was provided to the religious orders working in the growing American Church; money was also sent to the Franciscans caring for shrines in the Holy Land. By 1921, over a million dollars had been given to the Church in the United States.

Luis of Granada (1504-1588) ● Spanish Dominican spiritual writer. Born in Granada and originally known as Louis Sarriá, he entered the Dominicans in 1524. After studying at the College of San Gregorio in Valladolid, he worked for eleven years in Córdoba (1534-1545) to restore the Dominican convent there. Invited to Portugal in 1555, he served as provincial of the Portuguese Dominicans from 1556-1560 and as confessor to the Portuguese nobility. A renowned preacher, he declined the

St. Luke

archiepiscopal see of Braga. Luis authored a number of books on the spiritual life, most notably the *Libro de la oración y meditación* (1554; *Book on Prayer and Meditation*) and the *Guía de pecadores* (*Guide for Sinners*). Much influenced by Erasmus and Savonarola, his writings were placed on the Index of Forbidden Books in Spain in 1559. A revised edition of his work was published in 1567, and it was translated into French, English, and Italian. Luis also authored biographies of John of Ávila and Bartholomew of the Martyrs, two personal acquaintances whom he greatly admired.

Luke, St. ● Author of the Third Gospel and the Acts of the Apostles. Luke was a Greek Gentile, born perhaps in Antioch and was a physician by profession, a detail confirmed by the passage in Colossians (4:14) in which Paul speaks of him as "Luke the beloved physician." A convert to Christianity, possibly one of the first in Antioch, he apparently accompanied Paul on the Second Missionary Journey from Troas to Philippi (Acts 16:10-17), on the Third Missionary Journey from Philippi to Jerusalem (Acts 20:5—21:18), and on the Italian Journey, including the famous episode of the shipwreck off Malta. While in Rome he remained with Paul during his captivity. Paul notes Luke's presence on three different occasions, in Colossians (4:14), 2 Timothy (4:11), and Philemon (24). In Timothy, Paul writes that "Luke alone is with me." That Luke was with Paul on the journey can be deduced from passages in

Acts (16:10-17; 20:5—21:18; 27:1—28:16) in which he, as the author, writes in the first person plural ("we"). The second-century Anti-Marcionite Prologues (attached to the Gospels of Mark, Luke, and John — possibly Matthew, although it was lost) declared that Luke wrote his Gospel in Greece. His authorship is affirmed by tradition as well as such major sources as the Muratorian Canon, Tertullian, Origen, Irenaeus, Jerome, and Eusebius. The Gospel was probably composed around 70-85. The Acts, also attributed to Luke, was penned, according to the Anti-Marcionite prologues, in the region of Achaea, a Roman province in the area of Greece. The date has been long debated by scholars. He was said to have died in Greece, unmarried, at the age of eighty-four, "full of the Holy Spirit." This tradition differs from various *Acta* that report his martyrdom; experts consider these to be unreliable and legendary. His relics were supposedly translated from Thebes in Boeotia (in the Balkans) to Constantinople by Emperor Constantius II in 356-357. Luke is the patron saint of doctors and also of painters, this from the belief in medieval times that he painted a picture of the Virgin Mary that was preserved in the Santa Maria Maggiore, Rome. The work actually dates to a later period. Luke, however, was a genuine painter of words, his writings standing forth as the most vivid and literary of the works of the NT. His narratives, especially of the birth of Christ and in detailing the universal nature of Christ's redemptive labors, are excellent literary creations beyond their spiritual and exegetical importance. His symbol is a winged ox. Feast day: October 18.

Lull, Raymond (d. c. 1316) ● Also Ramon Llull or Lullus. Catalan philosopher and mystic, known as *Doctor Illuminatus* (the Enlightened Doctor), he was a native of Majorca. He entered the service of King James I of Aragon, married, and had two children. At the age of thirty, however, he experienced mystical visions and joined the Third Order of St. Francis. He traveled to North Africa and Asia Minor to convert the Muslims and, while living in Majorca, he studied Arabic and Muslim philosophy. A prolific writer, Lull composed poetry and works on philosophy and mysticism. His most famous book, collectively called *Ars Magna* (or *The Great Art*), was comprised of the treatises *Liber de ascensu et descensu intellectus* (*The Book of the Ascent and Descent of the Intellect*) and *Arbor scientiae* (*The Tree of Knowledge*). A mystic of great depth, he is considered a predecessor of St. Teresa of Ávila and St. John of the Cross. According to tradition, he was stoned to death by Muslims in Bougie, North Africa.

Lumen Gentium ● Document issued by Vatican Council II on November 21, 1964, and given the English title "Dogmatic Constitution on the Church." One of the two dogmatic constitutions published by the council (with *Dei Verbum*), it is to be distinguished from the "Pastoral Constitution on the Church in the Modern World" (*Gaudium et Spes*), released on December 7, 1965, whose purpose it is to make clear the nature of the Church as "a sacramental sign and an instrument of intimate union with God, and of the unity of all mankind" (No. 42). *Lumen Gentium* (Latin for "Light of the Nations") is organized into a number of chapters, from "The Mystery of the Church" to "The Role of the Blessed Virgin Mary, Mother of God, in the Mystery of Christ and the Church." To the conciliar document was added a "Prefatory Note of Explanation" at the order of Pope Paul VI. Its aim is to give additional clarification on collegiality by reemphasizing the essential requirement of communion with and dependence on the Bishop of Rome for the full exercise of authority by the bishops. Additional interpretation was given by a number of postconciliar documents, including *Ministeria Quaedam* (1973), the declaration of the

Congregation for the Faith *Mysterium Ecclesiae* (1973), and *Ad Pascendum* (1973).

Luther, Martin (1483-1546) ● German priest who launched the Protestant Reformation. Luther was born in Eisleben, in the county of Mansfield, the son of a miner. Educated initially at the cathedral school of Magdeburg, he subsequently studied at Eisenach and then Erfurt. He completed the master's examination in 1505 and began a study of law. That same year, however, he entered the Augustinian friars in their monastery at Erfurt, said to have been in fulfillment of a vow he had made during a violent storm. Ordained in 1507, he was sent to lecture at the University of Wittenberg. In 1510, he was sent to Rome and was appalled by the spiritual laxity and what he felt was the severe state of moral decline. Returning to Wittenberg in 1511, he continued studies and received a doctorate in theology as well as the post of professor of Scripture. In 1515, he became a vicar of the Augustinians.

Martin Luther

On the basis of his studies and extensive thinking, Luther reached the conclusion that the Church was in great need of a genuine and complete reform. He also was convinced that the hope of sinners was in the grace of God and redemption by Christ, through faith. This idea of justification on faith alone came about after the famous "Tower Experience" (*Turmerlebnis*), a kind of revelation, placed to between 1512 and 1515. Over the next years, he would formulate doctrines increasingly at variance with traditional Church teachings, actually breaking with the faith in 1517 when he protested the preaching of Johann Tetzel of the indulgence granted by the papacy to help pay for the building of the new St. Peter's Basilica. To proclaim his disagreement he posted his ninety-five theses on the door of the Schlosskirche at Wittenberg. The theses spread swiftly through Germany and found wide support in humanist circles while causing a storm of controversy with Church authorities. Additionally advocating many elements of German nationalism and state control of the German Church, he found backing from secular leaders. Elector Frederick III of Saxony provided protection.

Church officials attempted to enforce monastic discipline, but Luther used a chapter at Heidelberg (1518) to continue his attacks. He was thus tried at Rome and ordered to appear before Cardinal Cajetan at Augsburg. After refusing to recant, he fled to Frederick III, and negotiations that followed with Carl von Miltitz, a representative of the pope, proved fruitless.

Relations deteriorated steadily. In 1519, he rejected the primacy of the pope and the next year published three major reform works, denouncing clerical celibacy and formulating many Lutheran doctrines. On June 15, 1520, forty-one of his theses were declared heretical by the bull *Exsurge Domine*. Luther responded by burning the bull, whereupon he was excommunicated by Pope Leo X (r. 1513-1521) on January 3, 1521, in the bull *Decet Romanum pontificem.*

That same year, he was summoned to the Diet of Worms where a ban was placed upon him. The elector of Saxony then had him taken to safety at Wartburg. There he wrote pamphlets and began to translate the Bible into German, an important influence in forming German religious unity and a major contribution to German language. While at Wartburg, his ideas continued to be accepted throughout Germany, doing considerable harm to Catholic cohesion and practice, especially among many of the clergy.

The Peasants' War (1524-1525) cost him some degree of his popularity as he urged the German princes to suppress the violent activities of the peasants who had erupted into open revolt. In 1525, he married a former nun, Katharina von Bora, fathering six children. In his later years, he was involved in numerous controversies with other Reformers who had begun to express divergent opinions on theological points, such as the Eucharist. His disagreements with Zwingli and Calvin would ultimately divide the Protestants into the Lutheran and Reformed Churches. Luther gave his blessing to Philipp Melanchthon's authorship of the Augsburg Confession, presented at the Diet of Augsburg in 1530, but was not in favor of a reunion with the Catholic Church. Throughout the 1530s he took a largely secondary place in the broad process of the Reformation that had engulfed Central Europe. The religious crisis that was caused by Lutheranism created several political opportunities as German princes adopted Lutheran teachings in part because of the power that could be secured through conversion. Tension finally erupted into a civil war between Emperor Charles V and the Protestants of the Schmalkaldic League. Luther died just before the fighting began, on February 18, 1546, while visiting Eisleben. (For the subsequent history of Lutheran ideas, see under **Reformation, Catholic [and Protestant]**; see also **Lutheranism** in the GLOSSARY.)

Lyons, Councils of ● Two general councils convened at Lyons.

1. The Council of Lyons (1245) is counted as the thirteenth ecumenical council, summoned by Pope Innocent IV to address a number of problems facing the Church. This included the continued schism with the Byzantines, the invasion of Hungary by the Mongols (Tatars), the decline of morality among the clergy, and the troubled relations between the popes and Emperor Frederick II. The emperor was deposed by the council, an act that was based on four charges: sacrilege, disturbing the peace, suspicion of heresy, and perjury.

2. The Council of Lyons (1274) is counted as the fourteenth ecumenical council, convoked by Pope Gregory X to bring moral reform and a desired union of the Eastern and Western Churches. The main achievement of the council was the acceptance by the Byzantine delegates of Emperor Michael VIII Palaeologus of the supremacy of the pope and the articles of faith of the Western Churches. The union proved short-lived, however, as another rupture took place in 1289. Among those in attendance were five hundred bishops and such notables as St. Bonaventure, St. Albertus Magnus, and Peter of Tarentaise (the future Innocent VI). St. Thomas Aquinas died en route to the council.

Lyons Rite ● Also Lyonnais rite. Modified form of the Roman rite that developed throughout the Middle Ages and was preserved locally in the archdiocese of Lyons, France. The rite probably began in the ninth century, was purged during the 1700s, and partially restored in 1864 by Pope Pius IX. Major differences included the offering of the bread and wine as one at the offertory, the use of ashen, or gray, as the Lenten liturgical color, and different preparatory prayers from those used in the Tridentine Mass. The High Mass of the Lyons rite had numerous ministers: the bishop was joined by six priests, seven deacons, seven subdeacons, and seven acolytes, all in full vestments.

Mabillon, Jean (1632-1707) ● Scholar and member of the Benedictine Congregation of St. Maur (the Maurists). Born at St.-Pierremont, in Champagne, France, he studied at the Collèges des Bons Enfants in Reims, subsequently entering a seminary in 1650. Three years later, however, he withdrew, entering instead the Maurist Congregation at the Abbey of St. Remy in Reims; he professed in September 1654. In 1664, he joined the Abbey of St.-Germain-des-Prés where he would spend the rest of his life. A brilliant scholar, he was the author of numerous works including: the *Acta* of the Benedictine saints (9 vols., 1668-1701, with the patristic scholar Jean Luc d'Achéry); the first four volumes of the Benedictine *Annales* (1703-1707), covering the years to 1066; and an edition of St. Bernard of Clairvaux (2 vols., 1667). He also defended the members of the religious in *Traité des etudes monastiques* (1691).

Macarius, St. <1> (d. c. 334) ● Bishop of Jerusalem and an ardent opponent of Arianism. Named bishop in 312, he took part in the Council of Nicaea (325) and possibly had a part in drafting the Nicene Creed; he also may have had a "passage of arms" with his metropolitan, Eusebius of Caesarea, concerning the rights of their sees. That he opposed Arianism was confirmed in the harsh letter from Arius to Eusebius of Nicomedia preserved by Theodoret in his *Ecclesiastical History*. Macarius was instructed by Emperor Constantine the Great to build the Church of the Holy Sepulchre in Jerusalem. He also erected with the bishop of Palestine a church in Mamre. Feast day: March 10.

Macarius, St. <2> (d. c. 390) ● Also Macarius the Egyptian and Macarius the Great. One of the Desert Fathers who helped foster monasticism in Christianity. He was born in Upper Egypt and, at the age of thirty, he retired to the desert of Scete, or Scetis (the Wadi-el-Natrun), where he soon attracted followers. The colony of hermits became a renowned place of monasticism, and Macarius's reputation for sanctity, intelligence, and healing powers quickly spread. Ordained a priest around 340, he was noted by writers of the era as particularly gifted in preaching and spiritual guidance. He supported St. Athanasius against the Arians and then, in 374, he was banished to an island in the Nile by Athanasius' replacement as bishop of Alexandria, Lucius. Macarius later returned and spent his remaining years in the desert.

While the sources on Macarius mention nothing of his literary output, a body of works, called at times Macarian literature and subscribed to him, was preserved in later manuscripts. The most notable of these is a collection of fifty spiritual homilies. Also attributed to him is the letter "To the Friends of God," addressed to younger monks. Jacques Paul Migne in Volume 34 of the *Patrologia Graeca* preserved the Macarian literature, and many scholars have examined the possible influence upon Macarius and the sources of the so-called Macarian writings. Feast day: January 15.

Macarius Magnes ● Late fourth-century Christian apologist, author of the *Apocritica*. Nothing is known concerning his life, although he has been considered possibly to be identified with Macarius, bishop of Magnesia, who accused Heraclides, bishop of Ephesus, of Origenism at the so-called Synod of the Oak (Chalcedon, 403). The *Apocritica* was a defense of the faith against a pagan philosopher, written in the form of a dispute, in five books. The work was used in the ninth century by the Iconoclasts to defend their doctrines.

Macedonianism ● Heresy begun in 360 by several Arian bishops who taught that there existed within the Trinity a hierarchy of Persons. The heresy derived its name from the bishop of Macedonius (d. c. 362), an Arian who became bishop of Constantinople around 342. His reign was marked by harsh repression of Orthodox Christians and the promotion of the Trinitarian heresy. According to the heretical doctrine, instead of an equality among the Persons of the Trinity, the Second Person was declared inferior to the First, and the Holy Spirit inferior to both the First and the Second. In 360, Macedonius was deposed and banished; the heresy, with others, was condemned at the First Council of Constantinople (381). (See also **Pneumatomachians**.)

Macrina, St. (c. 330-379) ● Also Macrina the Younger. Granddaughter of St. Macrina the Elder and sister of Sts. Basil the Great, Gregory of Nyssa, and Peter of Sebastea. Betrothed at an early age to a lawyer, she was soon deprived of marriage by his death, henceforth devoting herself to her family. She had a profound influence upon her brothers, especially Peter, who became bishop of Sebaste and Basil whom she convinced to give up a potentially great secular career for the priesthood. Macrina also succeeded her mother St. Emmelia, as the head of the Christian community on the river Iris in Pontus, situated on a family estate. The main account of her life was written by her brother Gregory in his *Vita Macrina Junioris*, including a touching picture of his time with her at her death. Feast day: July 19.

Magic ● See **Occultism** in the GLOSSARY; see also **Astrology**.

Maimonides, Moses (1135-1204) ● Jewish philosopher and medical writer. One of the foremost Jewish intellectuals of the Middle Ages who had a profound effect upon the writings of St. Albertus Magnus and Thomas Aquinas. Born and educated in Córdoba, he was forced to flee in 1149 when the city was captured by the Muslim troops of the Almohades. With his family, he settled in Fez, Morocco, leaving in 1165 to travel to Palestine and then to al-Fustat (Cairo), in Egypt. While in al-Fustat, Maimonides served as court physician to Saladin and his son, Al-Afdal', enjoying the position of leader of the Jewish community. He composed his first work at sixteen, a treatise on the terms used in logic and metaphysics. Other writings include: *More nevukhim* (1190; *Guide for the Perplexed*); *Mishe Torah* (c. 1180; *Torah Reviewed*), a work on the Talmudic code; and the *Kitab al-Siraj* (1169), a commentary on the Mishnah, the first section of the Talmud. He was known to Jewish writers as Rambam, from the consonants of Rabbi Moses ben Maimon.

Malabar Rite ● Properly Syro-Malabar rite. One of the rites considered distinct by the Congregation for the Oriental Churches and listed under the broader Chaldean rite. The Malabar Christians of the rite are also St. Thomas Christians and reside in India. They claim their Church was first founded by St. Thomas the Apostle. He was believed to have been martyred near modern-day Madras, but there is little evidence to indicate that a Christian community had been established before the sixth century.

Cosmas Indicopleustes (a sixth-century geographer) mentions in his writings that there were Christians in the country prior to 550. The Portuguese discoverers and merchants who first encountered the so-called Syrian Christians found them using Syriac in their liturgy. The Christians in India gave their allegiance to the papacy at the Synod of Diamper (1599), although a separation occurred in 1653, largely resolved in 1662.

The Malabar rite uses the Syriac and Malayalam languages in its liturgy, although a number of Roman customs have been adopted, most notably Communion under one species. It was derived from the Antiochene rite. The calendar is the same one used by the Roman Church. Currently, there are nineteen dioceses and two archdioceses under the jurisdiction of the Malabar Christians. There are also mission churches in the United States, especially Chicago.

Malabar Rites ● Not to be confused with the Malabar rite. Controversy that erupted in the 1500s in the Jesuit province of Malabar, in India. The problem was similar to that of the Chinese rites in that Hindus who had been converted to Christianity were permitted to retain a number of customs and Brahmin observances in their Christian practice in order to alleviate disorientation in the increasing familiarity with the faith and to prevent cultural isolation. The Jesuits, particularly the great missionary Roberto de Nobili, were generally careful to weed out any objectionable practices, but, as with the Chinese rites, a controversy ensued, led mostly by the Dominicans and Franciscans. The Holy See was at first willing to uphold the Malabar rites in 1623, but it insisted that certain changes be made to ensure the liturgy did not disagree in any way with the accepted liturgy of the Church. In 1712, however, the rites were forbidden. The Jesuits appealed the decision numerous times, resulting in confirmation of the 1712 decision in 1727 and 1734. After further examination, Pope Benedict XIV issued a bull, *Omnium Sollicitudinum* (September 12, 1744), obliging the missionaries to swear an oath relating to the rites. Pope Pius XII dispensed of this oath in 1940 with the stipulation that the missionaries observe in other matters the directives of Benedict XIV.

Malachy, St. ● Archbishop of Armagh, papal legate, and famous figure in Irish history. Known as Máel Máedoc Úa Morgair in the Gaelic, Malachy was largely responsible for bringing the Roman liturgy to Ireland by laboring to introduce the reforms of Gregory VII. Often bitterly opposed by antipapal elements in the country, he was nominated archbishop in 1129 but could not secure his see. He thus journeyed to Rome seeking his pallium, meeting there with St. Bernard of Clairvaux, and being appointed papal legate in 1139. Pope Innocent II, however, would not grant the pallium until Ireland was more secure. After a second trip to Rome, Malachy received the pallium at last, dying on his way home at Clairvaux. St. Bernard, who held him at his death, authored a biography of Malachy. The so-called Prophecies of Malachy are supposed glimpses into the future of the papacy; they have been attributed to Malachy but they probably date to the late sixteenth century. A motto is given for every pope, from Celestine II (r. 1143-1144) to the last pontiff, Petrus Romanus (Peter the Roman), of whom Malachy reportedly wrote: "In the last persecution of the Holy Roman Church will reign Peter the Roman who will feed his flock among many tribulations; then the seven-hilled city will be destroyed and the terrible Judge will judge all humanity." Feast day: November 3.

Malalas, John (d. c. 578) ● Byzantine chronicler. Also called John Rhetor and John Scholasticus, patriarch of Constantinople. He was the author of the eighteen-volume *Chronographia*, a useful history of the ecclesiastical and secular history of the period, extant to 563. It was much used by succeeding writers.

Maldonado, Juan (1533-1583) ● Also Maldonatus. A Spanish theologian and exegete, he was born outside Madrid at Casas de Reina and studied at the University of Salamanca, entering the Society of Jesus in 1562. He was ordained the following year. In 1562, he began teaching at the recently opened University of Clermont in Paris where his lectures acquired for him a reputation for brilliance. His lectures from 1570-1576 were especially notable, particularly in 1574, as he was attacked by members of the Sorbonne for impugning the Immaculate Conception. This was disproved and in January 1575 the bishop of Paris completely vindicated him. Nevertheless, he departed the city and subsequently held a number of posts within the Jesuits. He died in Rome. Chief among his works were brilliant commentaries on the Gospels (2 vols., 1596-1597). Of great importance was Maldonado's work in reviving and repairing theology in Paris and in refining Latin, rescuing it from a severely deteriorated condition of usage. All of his works were published posthumously.

Malebranche, Nicholas (1638-1715) ● French Oratorian philosopher and theologian. Born at Paris, he was a son of a secretary to King Louis XIII, first studying at home owing to a slight deformity and being prone to illness. He eventually entered the Collège de la Marche and then studied theology at the Sorbonne. After declining a canonry at Notre Dame, he chose to enter the Oratorians at Paris, eventually focusing on philosophy and theology. He was drawn to these fields by his reading of René Descartes, expressing himself as a Cartesian and relying upon Descartes in the formulation of his own system. Like Descartes, Malebranche held

that matter cannot act upon the mind. The mind, however, is unable to produce its own ideas, necessitating a creative process from some power. God, he argues, is the cause of human knowledge. God, he goes on to say, is so intimately connected to the soul by his presence that he is the place of ideas, which are themselves spiritual beings. The mind is the recipient of knowledge from God to the degree that God is willing to reveal it. God so wills this because he displays his greatness in the most direct and simple manner possible, a principle described by Malebranche as *simplicité des moyens*. He is one of the foremost spokesmen, with the Belgian Arnold Geulincx (d. 1669), of occasionalism, an effort to reconcile the dualism of the system established by Descartes. In his occasionalism, Malebranche has our certainty concerning the world entirely dependent upon God's revelation, but in keeping with his principle of *simplicité*, God is the cause of our sensations and "the place of our ideas." Further, the principle requires that our first, and simplest, idea is that of the infinite. Malebranche is thus also an adherent of ontologism, which claims that God is the source of all validation of all human ideas. His chief writings are: *Recherche de la Vérité* (1674; *On the Search for Truth*), *Traité de la nature et de la grâce* (1680; *Treatise on the Nature of Grace*), and *Méditations chrétiennes et métaphysiques* (1683; *Christian Meditations and Metaphysics*). He was much criticized by Antoine Arnauld (1612-1694), Jacques Bossuet (1627-1704), and Archbishop François Fénelon (1651-1715). Bossuet described Malebranche's system as *pulchra, nova, falsa* — "beautiful, new, false."

Malines Conversations ● Series of meetings occurring between Catholic and Anglican theologians from 1921-1926. The talks were organized at the encouragement of the English High Churchman Lord Halifax (1839-1934), who had previously worked to promote possible union between the Catholic Church and the Church of England. The Malines Conversations were presided over by Cardinal Désiré Mercier of Belgium (the meetings were held in his see of Malines, Belgium) and were conducted with the acceptance of the Holy See and the archbishop of Canterbury. A number of points were agreed upon, including the often contentious point that the pope should be given a place of honor. The encyclical *Mortalium Animos* (January 1928) by Pope Pius XI, which forbade Catholics from participating in such efforts at reunion as the Faith and Order (a part of the ecumenical movement), ended any additional progress in the meetings. However, the dialogue would ultimately continue. (See also **Anglican-Roman Catholic International Commission**.)

Malta, Knights of ● See under **Military Orders.**

Mandaeans ● Gnostic sect. Also called the Nasoreans, they developed in the first and second centuries in modern Jordan. Based on surviving writings, particularly the *Ginza* (*Treasure*) dating to the seventh or eighth century, they were similar in their teachings to those of the Manichaeans, with elements of Christian thought interwoven. Also known as the Christians of St. John, the Mandaeans much revered John the Baptist.

Manharter ● Religio-political sect that arose in the Tyrol, Austria, in the early nineteenth century. It was founded by the priest Kaspar Hagleitner of Aschau, who refused to take the oath of allegiance to the edicts of Napoleon who had conquered part of Austria in 1809 and demanded the obedience of all authorities, secular and religious. Hagleitner declared that any priest who took the oath was excommunicated by the act. He was soon supported by many Austrian patriots, and the Manharter was

thus established. Its name was derived from the surname Manhart used for the parish magistrate, Sebastian Manzl, one of the heads of the movement.

The members of Manharter at first refused to associate with any cleric who had taken the oath, but they later condemned French and German bishops, proclaiming themselves to be the only true Catholics and loyal adherents of Pope Pius VII. They eventually refused to rejoin the Church after the fall of Napoleon and only Pope Leo XII was able to win them back in 1826. Some members even then would not return, but the sect died out in succeeding decades.

Manichaeans ● Religious sect founded by a Persian named Mani (or Manes) in the third century. It spread throughout the East and was even found in the Roman Empire. Little is known about Mani (c. 215-276) save that he was born in Ctesiphon, beheld visions, and began preaching a new religion in the lands of the Persian Empire where the creed of Zoroastrianism predominated. Most likely because of local opposition, Mani left Persia for India around 242. Having enjoyed some success in preaching during his journey, he returned to Persia and secured the toleration and even friendship of the Persian monarch Shapur I. His successor, Varahran I, however, persecuted Mani and his followers; Mani was imprisoned and then put to death, his disciples banished from the realm.

The so-called Manichaeans soon spread the faith throughout the eastern regions of the Roman Empire, succeeding so swiftly in winning adherents that Diocletian condemned the creed in 297. Christians and Neoplatonists also attacked it, but the Manichaeans found fertile ground across the empire, with believers even in Rome. St. Augustine was a member for nine years, attaining the rank of Hearer. In the West, Manichaeism died out gradually, although scholars have long debated its degree of influence on later heresies such as the

Cardinal Henry Manning

Albigensians and Bogomils. In the East, the Manichaeans survived until the fourteenth century.

The followers of Mani believed that there was an eternal struggle between good and evil, between the darkness and the light. When darkness intruded upon the realm of the light, there occurred an intermingling of the mortal with the divine, a mixture trapped in matter. The light was found in the brain. Humanity was to practice strict asceticism in order to begin the process of releasing the trapped light. Those who became Hearers hoped to achieve rebirth as the Elect, those blessed few who had overcome the need for the transmigration of the soul. Jesus, they felt, was the Son of God, but he had come to earth to save his own soul because of Adam. Jesus, Buddha, and other holy figures were sent to help humanity in attaining spiritual freedom. Sources on the Manichaeans include the writings of the Church Fathers and Manichaean fragments preserved in various documents, especially the texts discovered in Turfan, Turkestan, early in the

twentieth century and papyri of Coptic origin found in Egypt in 1935.

Manning, Henry Edward (1808-1892)
● English cardinal and the second archbishop of Westminster. Born at the estate of his uncle in Copped Hall, Totheridge, Hertfordshire, he was the son of William Manning, M.P. Educated at Harrow and Oxford, he initially hoped for a career in banking and the Parliament but the bankruptcy of his father convinced him to pursue a different course. After working as a clerk in the colonial office, he was elected to a fellowship at Merton College in 1832, becoming a deacon. In 1833, he married Caroline Sargent, although she died in 1837. An archdeacon in 1841, he was gradually drawn to the Tractarian movement and subsequently became a leader of the Oxford movement, especially after the conversion of John Henry Newman in 1845. Following the support given to the Rev. George C. Gorham by the Judicial Committee of the Privy Council, Manning despaired of salvaging Anglicanism and was received into the Catholic Church in 1851. Ordained the same year by Cardinal Nicholas Wiseman, the first archbishop of Westminster, he studied for two years at Rome. In 1865, Manning was named Wiseman's successor, proving subsequently to be an ardent supporter of papal infallibility at the First Vatican Council (1869-1870). Named a cardinal in 1875, he took part in the conclave that elected Pope Leo XIII (1878). His interest in social work made him a prominent figure in England, especially in 1889 when he mediated the London Dock Strike, and his funeral was one of the largest London had ever witnessed.

Mansi, Giovanni Domenico (1692-1769)
● Italian archbishop of Lucca and scholar. A native of Lucca, he was a member of an Italian noble family who entered the Clerks

Regular of the Mother of God in 1710. He spent the next years actively engaged in study until 1765 when he was named archbishop of Lucca. Mansi's principal literary work was centered in the reediting of ecclesiastical writings; his name appears on the title page of ninety folio volumes, although he was generally unoriginal in his annotations, usually because of the hurried pace of his labors. His only notable original work was the *Tractatus de casibus et censuris reservatis* (1724), which had troubles with the Index of Forbidden Books.

Manuscript Illumination ● Illustration (or illumination) of parchments or vellum, with drawings or miniature paintings. Manuscript illumination represents some of the greatest art forms produced in medieval Europe from the so-called Dark Ages to the fifteenth century. The early types of such manuscripts first appeared in the eastern provinces of the Roman Empire and were of a Christian nature. The practice spread throughout the declining Western Empire and took root in the recently Christianized areas of Northumbria, in Britain, and Ireland. The monasteries of these regions produced magnificent examples of illuminated manuscripts, chief among which were the Books of Kells, Durrow, and Lindisfarne. Continued development took place during the Carolingian Renaissance with the creation of manuscripts of high

Manuscript illumination

quality and sophistication by the monks of Regensburg, Reims, Winchester, and Paris. A peak was reached during the Romanesque at the monastery of Reichenau in Switzerland. From around 1200, the art became centered increasingly in the decoration of miniatures for books, especially the Book of Hours and the Bible. An individualized and sumptuous art form, illumination was often a rich demonstration of faith, adding visual appeal to religious texts; in that capacity, it enhanced the deep devotion that went into the work of the monks of Europe in producing copies of Scripture and other important religious writings. Illumination ended abruptly with the rise of printing.

Marburg, Colloquy of ● Meeting convened at Marburg by Philip, landgrave of Hesse. Held from October 1-3, 1529, its aim was to create a united confederation of Reformers out of the various Protestant groups of the time. Held in the castle at Marburg-on-the-Lahn, the colloquy was attended by such figures of the reform movement as Martin Luther, Huldrych Zwingli, and Philipp Melanchthon. Agreement was reached by the delegates on fourteen of fifteen Marburg Articles that had been drawn up by Luther, but Luther and Zwingli could not agree on the point concerning the Eucharist — Zwingli remained adamant in opposing the Lutheran doctrine of the Real Presence of Christ in the Eucharist. As both sides were intractable, the colloquy was a failure, although the articles led to the Augsburg Confession (1530).

Pope St. Marcellus I

Marcellina, St. (d. 398) ● Only sister of St. Ambrose. Probably born in Trier, she assisted in the education of her brothers and in 353 received from Pope Liberius the veil of consecrated virginity. Later, after Ambrose had become bishop of Milan (374), he summoned her to Milan and was given much help in fostering the spiritual life among the maidens of the city. Ambrose dedicated to her the *De Virginibus* (377), his work on virginity in three parts. She survived her brother for a short time and was buried in the crypt under the altar of the Ambrosian Basilica. Feast day: July 17.

Marcellinus, St. ● Pope from 296-304. His reign was marked by the renewal of the persecution of Christians by the government of Emperor Diocletian. A Roman by birth, Marcellinus was elected to succeed St. Caius and enjoyed several years of peace before the return of violent imperial oppression. While denied by St. Augustine, it is possible that Marcellinus was guilty of apostasy. Hence his name was omitted from official lists of popes, and he perhaps was removed or deposed. His death on October 25, 304, left the Church in some disorder and a successor, St. Marcellus I, was not elected until May 308. He was buried in the cemetery of St. Priscilla, Rome. Feast day: April 26.

Marcellus I, St. ● Pope from 308-309. From Rome, Marcellus was elected to succeed St. Marcellinus after an interregnum of some four years. His main act was to impose penances on those Christians who had become apostates during the severe persecutions under Emperor Diocletian. His decision caused rioting in the streets of Rome, only adding to the difficulties of the Church at the time, coming on the heels of the possible apostasy of Marcellinus. In 309, Marcellus was banished by the ultra-pagan Emperor Maxentius, dying a short time later.

Marcellus II ● Pope from April to May 1555. Originally known as Marcello Cervini, he was born in Montepulciano, Italy. A gifted scholar, he was made a cardinal in 1539 by Pope Paul II whose nephew, Cardinal

Alessandro, Cervini had tutored. In 1545, he was named one of the co-presidents of the Council of Trent (with the future Pope Julius III and Cardinal Reginald Pole). Elected to succeed Julius III, he chose to retain his baptismal name and was welcomed eagerly as a possibly great leader in reforming the Church. While he immediately took steps to curb nepotism and to begin reforms, Marcellus suffered a stroke and died.

Marcionism ● Heresy that became quite popular throughout the Roman Empire during the second century. It was developed by the heretic Marcion (d. c. 160), who was originally from Sinope in Pontus, Asia Minor. The son of a bishop (according to St. Hippolytus), Marcion was excommunicated for immorality. Around 140, however, he left Sinope and journeyed to Rome where he initially joined the Christian community. By 144, however, he had left the Church and was gathering his followers into a separate body. Excommunicated, he renounced the Church and devoted himself to founding a new one based on his own radical interpretation of Scripture. Aside from this edition, he wrote the book *Antitheses*, providing his disciples with a comprehensive guide to faith. A genuinely gifted preacher and a superb organizer, he traveled throughout the Roman Empire, attracting numerous converts from all social classes. His church was characterized by fanatical devotion to its founder, the practice of stern asceticism, and the maintaining of rigid discipline, including the forbidding of marriage. His success can be seen in the number and geographical locations of his opponents in the Church — Tertullian (in Carthage), Bardesanes (at Edessa), and Dionysius (at Corinth), to name a few. While a threat to the orthodox teachings of the Church, by the late third century Marcionism had been absorbed by Manichaeism.

The central theme of Marcionism was that as Christianity is a Gospel of Love, the Law is entirely excluded. Thus, the God of the Old Testament (which Marcion rejected), being the God of the Law, had no place in the Christian faith, which was established by the God of Love, the God of Jesus Christ. He contrasted the cruel and despotic God of the Law with the loving, caring, merciful God of Love. Christ, to him, is the Son of God, but only in name is he distinct from the Father. As matter is itself evil, Christ was not born into the world, rather he descended to earth from heaven in an unreal form and preached a new doctrine of Love to replace the doctrine of the Law. His death was not to redeem all humanity but only a few. Marcion did not accept the Old Testament, but he also rejected whole parts of the NT because of their Jewish content or influence. He accepted only ten epistles of St. Paul (whom he honored) and portions of the Gospel of Luke. The Apostles were deceived and led away from the truth by the Jews. While his writings are not extant, scholars are able to know much about them through the early Christian historians and authors, in particular Tertullian in his *Adversus Marcionem* and *De praescriptione haereticorum*; other sources include Irenaeus, Origen, and Clement of Alexandria.

Marcus Aurelius (120-180) ● Roman emperor from 161-180. One of the foremost intellectual figures of the Roman Empire. The adopted son of Emperor Antoninus Pius, he was much favored by Pius's predecessor, Hadrian. On March 7, 161, he succeeded Antoninus Pius, taking as his colleague Lucius Verus. Having received a brilliant education, Marcus claimed as teachers such notables as Alexander of Cotiaeon and Cornelius Fronto. Apollonius of Chalcedon also introduced him to Stoicism, a belief that was strengthened in Marcus by the Stoic Junius Rusticus Claudius Maximus. His Stoic philosophy was clearly displayed in his *Meditations*, the emperor's maxims, meditations, and confessions. Aside from his major military campaigns, especially the bloody Marcomannic Wars (c. 166-175, 177-180), Marcus was much concerned about the spiritual well-being of the empire. His Stoicism caused him to disagree ethically and philosophically with Christianity. His opposition to the faith, however, was the occasion of a number of important apologetic writings, most notably those of Athenagoras and Theophilus of Antioch; other lost apologies were written by Melito of Sardis, Claudius Apollinaris, and Pope St. Melchiades. He died while on campaign and was succeeded by his demented son Commodus.

Margaret Beaufort (1443-1509) ● Lady Margaret, countess of Richmond and Derby, and the mother of King Henry VII of England. Margaret was the daughter of John Beaufort, first duke of Somerset. In 1455, she married Edmund Tudor (half-brother of King Henry VI), and their son, Henry, was born in 1457. He would bring an end to the bloody dynastic struggle in England, the Wars of the Roses, establishing the long-standing Tudor Dynasty that would include Henry VIII and Elizabeth I. Margaret also helped arrange Henry's union with Elizabeth of York, thus connecting the two warring sides. A patron of religious houses, she supported as a "Sister" such institutions as Westminster and Durham. Under the influence of her spiritual adviser, John Fisher, she also established the Lady Margaret Professorship at Oxford and Cambridge, founded Christ's College, Cambridge, and provided an endorsement for St. John's College, Cambridge, in her will. Fisher also guided her deep spiritual life; she took religious vows and devoted herself to a life of prayer and devotion.

Margaret Mary Alacoque, St. (1647-1690) ● Member of the Visitandine order and an Apostle of the Devotion to the Sacred Heart of Jesus. Born in Lhautecour, France, she suffered during her childhood

from paralysis, and was forced to remain in bed for years, frequently enduring cruel treatment from her unsympathetic family. In 1671, she entered the convent of the Visitation in Paray-le-Monial, taking her final vows in November 1672. Later, she became novice mistress and assistant superior, but in December 1673 she received a number of visions of Our Lord, in which he appeared with his Sacred Heart visible, surrounded by a crown of thorns and flames. He frequently appeared before her and gave her the mission of establishing the devotion to the Sacred Heart of Jesus. Faced at first with criticism from her community, Margaret persevered and eventually won recognition from even her most severe detractors. She was canonized by Pope Benedict XV in 1920. Feast day: October 16.

Margaret of Scotland, St. (c. 1045-1093) ● Scottish saint and queen consort of King Malcolm III Canmore (r. 1058-1093). Raised at the Hungarian royal court where her father, King Aetheling, lived in exile, she returned to England in 1057. In 1066, she fled to Scotland after the defeat of the Saxons at the Battle of Hastings, marrying Malcolm III around 1070. Deeply religious, she was an influential figure in instituting religious reforms, including conformity with the Gregorian Reform. She was canonized in 1250 by Pope Innocent IV. Feast day: June 10.

Mariana, Juan de (1536-1624) ● Controversial Spanish Jesuit historian who was best known as the author of *De rege et regis institutione* (1599), which discussed the killing of despots. A native of Toledo, he joined the Society of Jesus in 1554 and was ordained in 1561. He subsequently taught at Rome and then Paris, returning to Spain (c. 1574) because of illness. His greatest literary work was the *Historiae de rebus Hispaniae* (1592) a comprehensive history of Spain. A later edition, the *Historia general de España* appeared in 1601; it was the translation of the work into Spanish. His *De rege*, a political treatise, caused a major controversy by its advocating assassination in certain circumstances. The storm of indignation was particularly pronounced in France, and the book was publicly burned. The general of the Jesuits also ordered that no Jesuit teach that it is by any means lawful to kill rulers. Mariana's later writings on political subjects earned his arrest in 1610 and his brief imprisonment. While much defamed by detractors of his *De rege*, Mariana was justifiably honored for his excellent history of Spain.

Marianus Scotus (d. c. 1082) ● Irish monk and chronicler, known originally as Moel-Brigte (Gaelic for "Servant of Brigit"). Originally a member of the Benedictines, he was banished from Ireland for breaking several monastic rules. As a result, he entered an Irish monastery in Cologne in 1058 and was ordained the following year. Marianus was the author of the *Chronicon*, a Latin chronicle covering world history from the creation to 1082. Very popular during the era, it is of value to scholars in preserving details of Irish monasticism in the eleventh century.

Marinus I ● Pope from 882-884. A native of Tuscany, in Italy, he was twice sent as a papal emissary to Constantinople representing Pope Adrian II (r. 867-872) and John VIII (r. 872-882). John made him bishop of Caere (modern Cervateri, Italy). Upon John's assassination, he was elected pope. Little about his pontificate is known with certainty, although he did engage in a number of discussions with Photius, the condemned patriarch of Constantinople. Marinus is often listed incorrectly as Martin II.

Marinus II ● Pope from 942-946. A Roman by birth, he was elected to succeed

Stephen VIII (IX) through the influence of Alberic of Spoleto, the powerful nobleman who ruled Rome. Marinus's pontificate was completely dominated by Alberic, although the pontiff did pursue a policy of Church reform. He is often incorrectly listed as Martin III.

Maritain, Jacques (1882-1973) ● French Thomist philosopher who had a major role in reviving the study of St. Thomas Aquinas. Born in Paris to a wealthy Protestant family, he studied at the Sorbonne where he was influenced by the French philosopher Henri Bergson (1859-1941). In 1906, he was converted to Catholicism with his wife, Raïssa, who was herself an accomplished author and philosopher. He studied at Heidelberg from 1907-1908, focusing on biology, but he was soon drawn to the vast body of works by Thomas Aquinas; a major impetus was his reading of Pope Leo XIII's encyclical *Aeterni Patris* (1879), which fostered Maritain's devotion to the great saint. He lectured on Thomist philosophy at universities all over Europe, including Louvain, Geneva, Milan, Oxford, and the Angelicum in Rome, and held chairs at the Institut Catholique, Paris (1914-1933), the Institute for Medieval Studies, Toronto (1933-1945), and Princeton (1948-1952). From 1945-1948, he held the post of ambassador from France to the Holy See. In 1958, the Jacques Maritain Center was opened at the University of Notre Dame in Indiana. Three years later, he took up residence with the Little Brothers of Jesus in Toulouse, becoming a Little Brother himself in 1970.

Considered by many to be one of the foremost exponents and interpreters of Aquinas, Maritain was especially concerned with applying in a practical manner Thomism to modern concerns or trends of thought. He thus applied Thomistic philosophy to contemporary developments in art, politics, sociology, education, and philosophy. His

Thomism, however, was shaped by a number of other philosophers, and he took into consideration the important strides made in scientific fields. He stressed the transcendent nature of the human person within the political community, declaring that democracy must support human freedom. His most important writings include: *La Philosophie bergsonienne* (1914), a critique of Henri Bergson; *Art et scolastique* (1920; *Art and Scholasticism*); *Distinguer pour unir, ou les derés du savoir* (1932; *Degrees of Knowledge*); *Frontieres de la poésie et autre essais* (1935; *Art and Poetry*); *Man and the State* (1949); and *La Philosophie morale* (1960; *Moral Philosophy*).

Mark, St. <1> ●
Evangelist and traditionally accepted author of the Second Gospel. Also known at times as John Mark, he was a cousin of Barnabas and thus was a Jew. An early convert and member of the Christian community of Jerusalem, he joined his cousin and St. Paul on the First Missionary Journey, but, for some reason that did not at all satisfy Paul, he left them in Pamphylia (Acts 15:37-38). This caused a breakup between Barnabas and Paul, and the former took Mark with him on a journey

St. Mark, by Donatello

to Cyprus (15:39). Mark was subsequently with Paul in Rome, his presence attested to in Colossians (4:10), 2 Timothy (4:11), and Philemon (24). He was also with Peter in Rome (1 Pt 5:13). According to Papias, who wrote in the second century, he was the interpreter of St. Peter. Scholars are in agreement that the Gospel attributed to Mark was probably written in the Italian peninsula during this period, if not in Rome itself. Eusebius, in the *Ecclesiastical History*, wrote that Mark later went to Alexandria. He preached there and was the first bishop of the local Church. The story that he was martyred in Alexandria during the reign of Emperor Trajan is considered unreliable. Mark is also connected with Venice, the association the result of his relics being brought to Venice in 829 and placed in the original church of St. Mark's (San Marco). His symbol, the winged lion, subsequently became that of the city and the onetime Venetian Republic. It has graced the coats of arms of three popes in this century: St. Pius X (1903-1914), John XXIII (1958-1963), and John Paul I (1978); each had served as patriarch of Venice before their election. Feast day: April 25.

Mark, St. <2> ● Pope from January to October 336. According to the *Liber Pontificalis*, Mark (or Marcus) was a Roman by birth who was responsible for decreeing that the bishop of Ostia should have the right to consecrate the new pope (or Bishop of Rome). He may also have established two new churches, that of San Marco in Rome and the one built over the catacomb of S. Balbina on the Via Ardeatina (no longer in existence). Constantine the Great may have mentioned Mark (who was then a member of the Roman clergy) in a letter to Pope St. Melchiades (r. 311-314). He succeeded St. Sylvester and was followed by St. Julius I. Feast day: October 7.

Marks of the Church ● Four distinctive characteristics of the Church: one, holy, catholic, and apostolic. They declare the Church to be the true faith, the instrument of salvation in the world, founded by and belonging utterly to Christ, the one Church, as opposed to other rival claimants of Christianity. These marks were first enumerated by the First Council of Constantinople (381) in the formalization of the Nicene Creed and were reaffirmed by the Council of Trent (1545 1563), a desirable and necessary step in the wake of the Protestant Reformation. The Church is: *one* because its members are united in faith and doctrine, under the pope; *holy* because it offers the means of receiving sanctifying grace and because it was founded by Christ and is animated by the Holy Spirit; *catholic* because it is universal, meaning that it is intended for all peoples in all places of the world; and *apostolic* because of the unbroken line from the apostles to the bishops whose teaching authority, the magisterium, can be traced to the eternal and unquestionable teachings of Christ. A number of Catholic writers, most notably St. Robert Bellarmine, added other marks of the Church. St. Robert declared that there are fifteen; the four marks, however, could stand uniquely on their own.

Maronites ● Members of the Maronite Church. One of the Eastern Catholic Churches, meaning that it is in communion with Rome, the Maronite rite is found in Lebanon, Syria, Egypt, Cyprus, and elsewhere (the United States, Brazil, and parts of the British Commonwealth). According to Maronite historians, the Maronites date to the time of St. Maron, from whom the Church derives its name. Maron's followers founded a monastery on the Orontes River in Syria. Other historians, however, argue that the Maronites date to the seventh century when the monks of St. Maron's monastery adopted a fiercely independent stand in the face of the Monophysite heresy then afflicting much of the Eastern Church. The Monophysite response was reportedly severe, as over three hundred monks were massacred for remaining loyal to the decrees of the Council of Chalcedon (451). During this period they were in contact with the Holy See.

The date customarily given for the birth of the Maronite Church is 681, for it was that year during which the Council of Constantinople was held. As loyal supporters of the Byzantine emperors, the Maronites possibly adopted the heretical tenets of Monothelitism under the influence of Emperor Heraclius. In 681, however, the council condemned the heresy. The Maronites contend that they renounced Monothelitism and remained orthodox; other scholars differ on this, citing, among various sources, St. John Damascene (d. 749), who called them heretics. Regardless of the specific circumstances that led up to it, by 685 the monks and bishops of the area elected their own patriarch, although the first known patriarch is said to date to 1121. Around this time, they moved from Syria to the mountainous territories of Lebanon where they existed as an independent church under their patriarch.

The twelfth century brought to the Levant the crusader armies and with them came representatives of the Western Church from which the Maronites had been essentially cut off for centuries. After the crusaders established good relations with them, they made the decision in 1182 to enter virtually en masse (some forty thousand) into communion with Rome. They have remained so ever since, especially from the time of the Lateran Council in 1215 during which the patriarch Jeremias al Amshiti visited Pope Innocent III and received from him the pallium. Pope Gregory XIII (r. 1572-1585) bestowed the pallium upon Patriarch Michael and in 1584 founded the Maronite College in Rome, where many distinguished scholars studied, including the Assemani, a family of noted Maronite Orientalists (Joseph Simonius, Stephen Evodius, Joseph Aloysius, and Simon) of the eighteenth and nineteenth centuries. The Maronites follow the Antiochene rite and their liturgical languages are Syriac and Arabic, and have suffered considerably in Lebanon during recent political turmoil there.

Marriage ● Institution by which a man and a woman enter into lasting union with the aim of procreating and fostering the love that they have for each other. Marriage was not instituted by Christ, but he elevated it to the dignity of a sacrament in recognition of its fundamentally good nature and as a means of helping spouses to attain Christian perfection, raise their children in the faith, and encounter Christ in a unique way while assisting the Church through their married lives. For these reasons, then, the Church is quite clear that marriage should be a sacrament when the contract is between two consenting, baptized persons; formal recognition of its status came in 1215 at the Fourth Lateran Council, although Christian writers, such as St. Augustine, had called it a sacrament prior to that time.

In the very early Church, the Christian members generally adhered to traditional wedding customs. Among the Roman upper classes this was a solemn and pagan ceremony called *confarreatio;* among the lower classes (the plebeians) a more basic, common-law marriage was known as the *usus.* Christians would have dispensed with the pagan elements and probably managed to include references to the faith. Most importantly, they would have received the recognition, approval, and blessing of their union by the local Church elders. This was noted by St. Ignatius in a letter to Polycarp.

From the fourth century, it became customary for marriages to be blessed by a priest, and it was decreed that those members of the lower orders should have their marriages certified. From these rituals evolved the actual liturgical celebration itself, the earliest evidence of which dates probably from the reign of Pope Damasus (366-384). The bride was led to the altar by her father and was then covered, with the groom, by a veil while the priest gave them his blessing. There was no set liturgy or formula to be followed at the time. In the East, and later in the West, it was common practice to place wreaths upon the couple's heads, a beautiful ceremony that was described by St. John Chrysostom in his homily on 1 Timothy 9.

By the Middle Ages, the ceremony had become quite formalized, including the willing exchange of vows before the priest and in front of witnesses. The vows had to be given by consent or the marriage was considered invalid. There was, however, no universal law within the Church that could be used to determine the validity of the marriage contract. Nevertheless, there were numerous canons enacted over the centuries, and the nature of the seriousness of regulations can be seen in the now well-known, albeit unsuccessful, attempt by King Henry VIII of England (r. 1509-1547) to divorce Catherine of Aragon. An important legal enactment on the validity of marriage was that of *Tametsi*, issued in 1563. Questions continued until the time of Pope St. Pius X (r. 1903-1914), who issued a decree concerning the requirements for validity in marriages, namely the presence of the pastor or bishop of the location where the marriage took place, if said place was outside the parish of the couple. Vatican Council II introduced numerous reforms, including granting permission to use rituals in keeping with local custom and the establishing of rituals to be used for marriage between a Catholic and non-Catholic. It is the clear and consistent teaching of the Church that a valid, sacramental, consummated marriage is indissoluble by any power save death.

Marsilius of Padua (d. 1342-1343) ● Author of the controversial political treatise *Defensor Pacis* (*Defender of Peace*). Born in Padua, Marsilius was educated at the University of Paris, spending time in northern Italy and at Avignon. He probably practiced medicine in Paris from 1320, authoring *Defensor Pacis* between 1320 and 1324; he was assisted in his work by John of Jandun. As the work caused a major controversy, Marsilius fled to the safety of the court of the recently excommunicated Louis IV of Bavaria, joining Louis in the state of excommunication the following year by decree of Pope John XXII. He accompanied Louis on his Italian expedition (1327-1329) and helped remove John XXII in favor of the antipope Nicholas V. Marsilius held the post of imperial vicar during the period. His remaining years were spent in Munich as part of Louis's court. His work was a remarkably original and influential treatise on political theory. Based on Aristotle, it foreshadowed not only the Reformation but formative democratic theory. According to Marsilius, the state, not the Church, was the unifying fabric of society. As such, the state must be derived from the people and should be superior to the Church. Meanwhile, the authority of the Church came from the general council that, ideally, should be comprised of clergy and laymen. These were,

of course, radical ideas in medieval times. (See **Conciliarism**.)

Martianus Capella ● Also Matthew Capella. Fifth-century Latin writer from Africa. A pagan, he authored the influential work *De nuptiis philologiae et Mercurii* (*The Marriage of Philology and Mercury*), a long allegory with an extensive treatment of the liberal arts. During the Middle Ages it was used as a kind of introduction to the liberal arts in schools and was mentioned by Gregory of Tours in the sixth century as a manual of education.

Martin I, St. ● Pope from 649-655. Born in Todi and an individual of strong will and determination, he was elected to succeed Pope Theodore I in July 649 without the approval of Byzantine Emperor Constans II Pogonatos. He also did not wait for Constans's approval to be consecrated, an act that incensed Constans, who thereafter refused to accept Martin as the legitimate pontiff. In an effort to end the ongoing controversy of Monothelitism, Martin convened a Lateran council (649). The heresy was condemned, as were Constans's decrees, the *Typos*, which had forbidden any discussion on the matter. Constans had Martin arrested and deposed on June 15, 653. The pope was taken to Constantinople and, despite poor health, was brutally humiliated and exiled to Crimea. He died at Chersonesus, Crimea, on September 16, 655. Soon venerated by the Roman Church, he was ranked as the last papal martyr. Feast day: April 13.

Martin II ● See **Marinus I**.

Martin III ● See **Marinus II**.

Martin IV ● Pope from 1281-1285. Born Simon de Brie, he served as chancellor and keeper of the great seal and was a trusted adviser to King St. Louis IX of France. A cardinal under Pope Urban V, he owed his election on February 22, 1281, as successor to Nicholas III, largely to the considerable influence of Charles of Anjou. He chose the name Martin IV, although he was only the second pontiff to bear that name, as the result of a mistake in the thirteenth-century lists of popes in which Marinus I and Marinus II were counted as Martin II and Martin III respectively. Owing his advancement to Charles, Martin was a dutiful adherent of his policies. He restored Charles to the kingdom of Naples and agreed with him that a reunion of the Eastern and Western Churches should be undertaken by military means. As relations with the Byzantines were understandably poor, Martin excommunicated Emperor Michael VIII Palaeologus in 1282, thereby ending any chance of negotiated reunion that had occurred at the Council of Lyons. Never liked by the Romans — he had been forced to hold his coronation in Orvieto — Martin died outside of Rome, at Perugia.

Martin V ● Pope from 1417-1431. His election brought an end to the Great Schism that had troubled the Church since 1378. Born Oddone Colonna, he studied at Perugia and was named a cardinal by Pope Innocent VII. He helped organize the Council of Pisa (1409) and was unanimously elected by the Council of Constance on November 11, 1417. Considered a mild individual, he soon proved himself remarkably determined in restoring unity to the Western Church and reviving the fortunes of the papacy. The Curia was reformed and papal authority in the Papal States strengthened, particularly after the defeat in 1424 of the dangerous soldier Braccio de Montone. While he summoned the Council of Pavia in 1423, he moved quickly to curb its possible effectiveness, finally securing its dissolution; by these moves he rejected conciliarism and reestablished the papacy as the supreme authority in the Church. Martin was opposed during his reign

by the antipopes Benedict XIII and Clement VIII. He also organized a crusade against the Hussites and attempted to mediate an end to the Hundred Years' War between France and England.

Martin, Gregory (d. 1582) ● Translator of the Douai-Reims Bible from Latin into English. Born in Sussex, England, he was noted for being one of the original scholars of St. John's College, Oxford, in 1557 (with, among others, Edmund Campion). After serving as a tutor in the family of the duke of Norfolk, Martin departed England and, having decisively turned to Catholicism, entered Douai as a possible candidate for the priesthood in 1570. Ordained in 1573, he went to Rome in 1576 to assist William Allen in the founding of the English College there. He remained in Rome for two years before journeying to Reims where Allen had moved the college owing to political difficulties. Martin then devoted himself to translating the Vulgate into English; the first work, the Reims NT, appeared in 1582. Because of a shortage of funds, the OT did not appear until 1609. In his labors Martin was assisted by several individuals. Martin also authored a number of other works and died of consumption on October 28, 1582. (See also **Douai-Reims Bible**.)

Martin of Tours, St. (c. 316-397) ● Patron saint of France. One of the major figures in the development of Western monasticism. The son of a pagan soldier, he was born in Pannonia. Forced to enter the Roman imperial army, he was compelled toward charitable acts. Once, when sharing his cloak with a beggar, he was struck with a vision of Christ who told him to depart the military and pursue a spiritual life. Abandoning the army, he journeyed through northern Italy and the Balkans. By 360, he had become an associate of Hilary of Poitiers, founding the first Gallic monastery near Hilary's city. As a result of his labor, he was consecrated bishop of Tours in 371-372. He did not cease to work to promote monasticism, however, and he was responsible for the conversion of numerous inhabitants of Gaul. An influential figure, he was nevertheless unable to prevent the execution of Priscillian in 386 by Emperor Magnus Maximus. Already revered as a miracle worker in his lifetime, he was one of the earliest nonmartyrs to be venerated by the Church. Feast day: November 11.

Martyr ● Person who is willing to suffer persecution, torture, and even death rather than renounce the faith. Derived from the Greek word for witness, the martyr has been deeply honored by the Church because of his or her willingness to suffer great hardship, humiliation, and the ultimate sacrifice, one's life, in the name of Christ. It is the greatest testament possible of an individual's faith. The first Christian martyr was the deacon St. Stephen who was stoned to death by a mob for confessing his devotion to Christ. Presiding over the crowd was Saul. In the early Church the term martyr was generally used for those individuals who had given their lives. The Apostles were thus martyrs, serving as great example for future generations who were likewise persecuted and killed.

Particularly notable in developing the special place of martyrdom in the early Church were the letters of St. Ignatius of Antioch to the Ephesians, Romans, and the Smyrnaeans. Written while Ignatius was on his way to Rome to be put to death, the letters stressed Ignatius' desire to achieve martyrdom because through it he would be able most perfectly to imitate Christ. Another remarkable account was that of Perpetua, who suffered martyrdom with her slave Felicity in 202. In the work the *Passio SS. Perpetuae et Felicitatis* (*Passion of Sts. Perpetua and Felicity*) martyrdom is called a second baptism.

While the era before the promulgation of the Edict of Milan (312) is commonly considered the time of greatest persecution and martyrdom (particularly the oppressions of Emperor Trajanus Decius and Diocletian), the Church has been blessed with believers giving their lives as witnesses to the faith throughout its entire history. Martyrs have been found in all corners of the world — from Japan and China to Russia and Germany and to the Americas. Especially notable periods of persecution have occurred just in this century: the staggering cruelty of Nazi Germany, producing such magnificent figures as Maximilian Kolbe and Edith Stein, who died in German concentration camps; the dehumanizing and barbaric acts of Communism around the world, such as in the so-called Soviet Empire, creating such heroic opponents to tyranny as Cardinal Mindszenty and Cardinal Trotka, who were voices for a repressed Church, speaking for millions who suffered for the faith — from simple workers in Poland who desired basic rights to priests and nuns in the prisons of Siberia, former Czechoslovakia, Bulgaria, and elsewhere.

Martyrology ● Name given to a list or catalog of martyred saints, customarily arranged in the order of their feast days as organized in the liturgical calendar. Martyrologies were originally mere calendars on which were inscribed the names of the martyrs, with a few details, such as where the martyrdom took place. There were local martyrologies with listings for the churches of a particular place such as those of Rome (fourth century) and Carthage (early sixth century). It is generally accepted that the first martyrology was the Hieronymian Martyrology, dated to the mid-fifth century and purportedly compiled by St. Jerome.

Increased development in the style and structure of the martyrologies took place during the Middle Ages and are thus valuable sources of history. Among the most notable medieval martyrologies are those of the

Venerable Bede (eighth century), Ado (ninth century), and Usuard (ninth century). These works, particularly from the ninth century, provided descriptions of each martyr's life, writings from the Church Fathers, and other interesting facts or material so as to make the calendar complete.

Mary Magdalene, St. ● First-century follower of Christ. She was called Magdalene from perhaps Magdala, near Tiberias, on the west shore of Galilee. There is some question as to her identity, with debate centering on the presence of three possibly distinct women: Mary Magdalene, the unnamed "sinner" of Luke (7:36-50), and the sister of Martha and Lazarus in Luke (10:38-42) and John (11). In the Eastern Church, these three persons were considered unique, different women, but in the Western Church, they were accepted as one and the same woman — Mary Magdalene. St. Ambrose observed that it was better to leave this matter unresolved and today it is a matter of general acceptance that her identity is uncertain in this area.

In the NT, Mary Magdalene is clearly identified as being among the women who accompanied Christ and ministered to Him (Lk 8:2-3). There it was also stated that she had been healed of seven devils cast out (also in Mk 16:9). She is reported to have been at the foot of Christ's Cross (Mt 27:56; Jn 19:25; Mk 15:40; and Lk 23:49). Next, she witnessed the placing of Christ in the tomb and was the first recorded eyewitness of his resurrection. John (20:1-18) described in some detail her remarkable experience at Christ's tomb, where she met the risen Lord and carried from him a message to the disciples: "I am ascending to my Father and your Father, to my God and your God" (20:17).

The subject of many legends in the early Church, she was much venerated during the Middle Ages as a figure of penance and atonement. Medieval stories about her were numerous, including a popular one that had her journeying to France with Martha and Lazarus, originating in the ninth century. Feast day: July 22.

Mary Magdelen de' Pazzi, St. (1566-1607) ● Italian Carmelite mystic. A native of Florence, Mary displayed early on deep spirituality, vowing perpetual virginity at the age of ten. In 1582, she entered the Carmelite Convent of Santa Maria degli Angeli in Florence. In the midst of a very severe illness she was professed on May 28, 1584, subsequently receiving forty days of ecstasy at the end of which it was doubtful she would survive. Recovering miraculously, she held a number of posts in the convent but continued to be subject to intense mystical episodes, including five years (1595-1590) of total desolation. She died on May 25, 1607, after three years of intense suffering. Pope Clement IX canonized her in 1669. Feast day: May 27.

Mary, Queen of Scots (1542-1587) ● Also Mary Stuart, the only legitimate child of King James V of Scotland and Mary of Guise, being crowned queen of Scotland six days after birth upon the death of her father. Owing to efforts by Tudor England to compel a union through a marriage between Mary and young Edward VI, she was sent to France in 1548, receiving a superb education. One of the most beautiful women in Europe, she married the dauphin Francis in 1558 and the next year became queen consort of France when her husband succeeded Henry II as King Francis II of France. Francis died prematurely in 1560 and, after negotiations, Mary sailed home to Scotland in 1561, her ships avoiding capture by the vessels sent out by Queen Elizabeth I, who was staunchly opposed to the presence of a Catholic ruler in Scotland who also had a legitimate claim to the English throne.

While hated by many Protestants, especially John Knox, Mary was able to win over much of the population and nobility with her policy of moderation, although she was a devoted Catholic and a loyal supporter of the pope. Hoping to strengthen her claim to the crown of England, in 1565 she wed her cousin Henry Stuart, Lord Darnley, a match acceptable to both Philip II of Spain and the Holy See. She gave birth to the future king James VI of Scotland (James I of England), but her marriage to Darnley was a disaster, as she found him to be a reprehensible consort. He entered into a conspiracy with Scottish nobles that led to the murder of one of Mary's favorites, David Rizzio, a clandestine representative of the papacy. She fled to loyal nobles, and the next year Darnley was assassinated, most likely by James Hepburn, earl of Bothwell. He, however, was acquitted and, having entered into an affair with the queen, divorced his wife and wed Mary. This marriage was rejected by the pope and most European courts and caused the Protestant Scottish lords to rise in open revolt.

Queen Mary I of England

Her army was defeated at Carberry Hill; the queen was imprisoned, Bothwell fled to Denmark (where he died in an insane asylum), and young James VI was crowned king under the regency of the earl of Murray. Protestantism was declared the country's religion and Catholicism was suppressed. Escaping from prison in 1568, Mary raised an army but was again crushed in the field, seeking sanctuary with Elizabeth in England. Seized and incarcerated by the English, she was tried by a commission on a set of severe accusations that relied upon the highly questionable Casket Letters (supposedly written by Mary to Bothwell) for their foundation. Acquitted, she received a supportive letter from Pope St. Pius V. Her confinement continued, as Elizabeth lived in dread of her relative. Spies watched her every move and read every letter, their vigilance rewarded in 1586 when they discovered a communication from her implicating her in a plot against the English queen. Condemned, she was beheaded at Fotheringhay on February 8, 1587, displaying remarkable courage and dying with the knowledge that her son would almost certainly follow Elizabeth on the throne. When the pope made indications that he might beatify Mary, Elizabeth ordered all the possessions of the Scottish ruler to be destroyed to prevent their use as relics.

Mary Tudor (1516-1558) ● Also Mary I. Queen of England from 1553, she restored, albeit briefly, England to the Catholic faith. The daughter of King Henry VIII (r. 1509-1547) and Catherine of Aragon, she was exceedingly well-educated and was long the recognized heir of the throne. Henry attempted to marry her to the dauphin (or royal heir) of France and then betrothed her in 1522 to Emperor Charles V as part of the Treaty of Windsor that had been negotiated through Cardinal Wolsey, Mary's godfather. Mary soon fell out of favor with the king who was determined to be rid of Catherine. She was harshly treated during the divorce proceedings and, in the period of Queen Anne Boleyn's ascendancy, she was forcibly separated from her mother. Catherine died in 1536 and Anne Boleyn was executed a short time later. Having survived this dark period, Mary — called "the King's natural daughter" — was terribly scarred emotionally. Under Henry's third wife, Jane Seymour, she was brought back into favor, signing in 1536 under pressure from the ruthless minister Thomas Cromwell a document that renounced her Catholicism and acknowledged that the marriage of Henry and Catherine had been against God's law. She did not read the document, and the imperial ambassador privately protested that it had been gained by compulsion. By the time of Henry's death in 1547, she had, through her friendship with the king's last wife, Catherine Parr, been named second heir in the royal will, after young King Edward VI and ahead of Elizabeth.

King Edward died in 1553 and Mary succeeded to the throne after extirpating a Protestant uprising that tried to install Lady Jane Grey. Enthusiastically supported by the followers of the Catholic Church, she proscribed the Protestant faith but was careful to treat her non-Catholic subjects with leniency. Crowned by Stephen Gardiner, bishop of Winchester, she was soon a disappointment to many by her marriage to King Philip II of Spain, a union that proved childless and was quite unpopular among the English. Dissatisfaction produced a plot against her, headed by Thomas Wyatt. Henceforth, her rule proved increasingly severe, distinguished by a persecution of Protestants. Papal authority was reestablished in early 1555 with the arrival of Cardinal Reginald Pole, but the persecutions, especially the restoration of heresy laws and the burning of Thomas Cranmer, archbishop of Canterbury, and Hugh Latimer, bishop of Worcester, lost her the support of the people and greatly bolstered the Protestant cause. Philip left England in frustration at the failure of their royal marriage, returning in 1557 to bring England into an alliance and war against France. This conflict resulted in the humiliating loss of Calais (1558), a blow from which Mary never recovered. She died on November 17, 1558, at St. James Palace, a much hated figure and was succeeded by Elizabeth under whom England would be irretrievably lost to the faith. Known in memory as "Bloody Mary," she was responsible for the deaths of some two hundred seventy-seven persons at the stake, the result of what Catholic and other historians recognize to be an unfortunate and misguided zeal.

Massillon, Jean-Baptiste (1663-1742) ● French bishop and noted preacher. Born in Hyères, in Provence, he studied in his native town and in Marseilles before entering the Oratorians (Congregation of the Oratory) at eighteen. After teaching in Pèzenas, Marseilles, and Montbrison, Massillon taught philosophy and theology at Vienne (1689-1695), during which time (1691) he was ordained. Acquiring a reputation as a gifted preacher in Vienne and elsewhere, he was appointed in 1695 to be director of the seminary of St.-Magloire, being removed a year later for devoting too much time to preaching. His eloquence in 1699 at the Oratory of Paris was such that he was honored with the widely held opinion that his skill was equal to that of the brilliant preachers Bossuet and Bourdaloue. His preaching at the court of King Louis XIV in 1699 caused the French monarch to declare that he had previously been very pleased with the preacher, but now he was displeased with himself. King Louis was henceforth a devoted listener until the king suspected him of Jansenism or some other fault. He was restored to the court in 1717 after Louis's death and named bishop of Clermont. Among his greatest orations were the funeral orations for Louis XIV (1715), the archbishop of Lyons (1693), and "On the Fewness of the Elect" (1704).

Master of the Sacred Palace ● In Latin, *magister sacri palatii*. Title given to the priest who serves as the theological adviser to the pope. The master was first appointed in 1218 by Pope Honorius III. He chose St. Dominic and it was thus established that Dominicans (the "watchdogs of orthodoxy") should always hold the post, although care has always been taken that the person chosen is the most eminent of all available candidates in theology and canon law. Among his duties are advising the pontiff on theological or canonical matters and organizing any preaching for him; he also advises the Curia. By custom, he lives in the Vatican.

Mater et Magistra ● Latin for "Mother and Teacher." Encyclical issued by Pope John XXIII and given the English title "On Christianity and Social Progress." Dated May 15, 1961, to commemorate the seventieth anniversary of *Rerum novarum*, it was concerned with the important issues of social justice, human rights, political and economic inequalities, and the concerns of underdeveloped nations. One of a number of social encyclicals, it helped present Catholic social doctrine in terms of systematically applying the writings of the Fathers of the Church, Scripture, and revelation to the pressing concerns of the modern era. *Mater et Magistra* stressed that an individual is the "foundation, cause, and end of all social institutions," and therefore such institutions

Countess Matilda of Tuscany

must serve the needs of the individual. (See also **John XXIII** and **Social Encyclicals**.)

Matilda of Tuscany (1046-1115) ● Countess of Tuscany, she was an important ally of Pope Gregory VII and his often bitter disputes with Emperor Henry IV during the Investiture Controversy. In 1077, Matilda's castle was the scene of Henry's humiliation in requesting and receiving in the snow the pope's absolution. When the emperor was excommunicated in 1080, she sent funds to Rome to assist Gregory in the conflict. Continuing to support the papacy after Gregory's death in 1085, she married Welf V, duke of Bavaria in 1089, thereby cementing her position as a leader of the Guelph (or pro-papal) party. At first leaving her lands to the papacy, she made peace with Henry V in 1110 and changed her will to leave him the strategically placed territories. After her death, ownership of her land became yet another source of contention between the popes and the emperor.

Matthew, St. ● Apostle and Evangelist. Traditionally ascribed author of the First Gospel, Matthew was a tax-collector (or publican) in Capernaum who received the call of Christ, "And he rose and followed him" (Mt 9:9; cf. 10:3). In the Gospels of Mark (2:14) and Luke (5:27), he is called Levi, the former saying that he was the son of Alphaeus. Matthew (or Levi) gave Christ a feast in his house where the exchange between Our Lord and the Pharisees concerning his eating with tax collectors and sinners occurred (Lk 5:29-32). Matthew appears in the four lists of the Apostles that are given in three of the Gospels (Mt 10:3, Mk 3:18, and Lk 6:15) and the Acts of the Apostles (1:13). Aside from the attributed authorship of the Gospel and the gathering of a collection of Christ's sayings in Hebrew credited to him by the first-century bishop of Hierapolis, Papias, little is known with certainty about his later career. Eusebius of Caesarea in the *Ecclesiastical History* states that he preached to his fellow Jews. Numerous other traditions, generally unreliable, have him suffering martyrdom in Ethiopia, Persia, or Pontus. Feast day: September 21.

Matthew of Aquasparta (d. 1302) ● Franciscan theologian and cardinal. Also called Matteo Aquasparta, he was born in Aquasparta, in Umbria, Italy. Entering the Franciscans, he studied at Todi and at Paris under St. Bonaventure. Named in 1280 as successor to John Peckham as *Lector sacri Palatii apostolici* (i.e., official teacher of the Papal Curia), he was elected minister-general of the Franciscans in 1287. After the accession of Pope Nicholas IV in 1288, the onetime Franciscan superior general elevated Matthew to the cardinalate. He held several posts under Boniface VIII and supported him in his struggle with the Colonna. A gifted philosopher and theologian, he was a marked supporter of Augustinianism. He authored *Quaestiones disputatae*, sermons, and biblical commentaries.

Maurice, St. ● *Primicerius* (commander) of the Theban Legion, which — according to tradition — was massacred at Agaunum by Emperor Maximian for refusing to make sacrifices to the gods. The legion was made up almost entirely of Christians, including its commander, Maurice. It had been summoned from its posting in Africa to help suppress an uprising of local tribes called Bagaudae, in Gaul (modern France). When, after proving victorious, the soldiers were ordered to make sacrifices, they refused. In punishment, every tenth soldier was put to death, but the legionnaires still refused and Maximian ordered a general massacre, Maurice among them. While largely legendary, the story was most likely based on the true events that occurred around 287. Maurice is invoked against gout and is the patron saint of soldiers, cloth makers, and dyers. Feast day for the Theban Legion martyrs: September 22.

Maurists ● Congregation of the Benedictine order. First established in 1618 (or 1621) at St. Maur, the Maurists were begun as a result of the efforts to institute reforms and were based on the reformed Congregation of St. Vannes. At a general chapter of the congregation, in 1618, it was decided that some kind of separate congregation should be developed. The new body was named the Congregation of St. Maur, receiving formal approval on May 17, 1621, from Pope Gregory XV. It was supported by both King Louis XIII and Cardinal Richelieu. The Maurists soon developed a reputation for attracting brilliant scholars, and the congregation became known for its work in historical research and especially hagiography. The Maurists produced such eminent scholars as Jean Mabillon and Bernard de Montfaucon (the founders of Greek and Latin paleography) as well as Jean Luc d'Achéry. The congregation suffered from a relaxation of discipline and a taint of Jansenism toward the end of the eighteenth century, with the result being a loss of public trust, despite the continuing of the work of its scholars. In 1790, however, came the suppression of the religious orders in France as a result of the Revolution. After the years of the Revolution and Napoleon came to an end, the survivors of the Maurists attempted to restore the congregation (1817). Their efforts were not approved by the Holy See and Pope Pius VII put an end to the Maurists' revival.

Maxentius (279-312) ● In full, Marcus Aurelius Valerius Maxentius. A Roman emperor in Italy and Africa from 306-312, he was one of the last ardent pagans to come to the imperial throne. The son of Emperor Maximian and his wife Eutropia, Maxentius was bypassed in the imperial succession in 305 when the co-rulers Diocletian and Maximian retired in favor of Galerius and Constantius I Chlorus (the father of Constantine the Great). Maxentius was not named caesar, or junior emperor, a slight that caused him to instigate a revolt in Rome, aided by the Roman and the Praetorian (or imperial) Guard. Proclaimed emperor in 306 by the Romans, he thwarted several attempts to oust him, clinging to power until 312. He was finally defeated and killed at the Battle of the Milvian Bridge (312) by Constantine, one of the most famous engagements in the history of Christianity. While a devoted pagan, Maxentius was generally tolerant of Christians in an effort to maintain his popularity among all classes, although many chroniclers subsequently called him a pagan tyrant.

Maximus the Confessor, St. (c. 580-662) ● Byzantine theologian who was also known as Maximus the Theologian and Maximus of Constantinople. A native of Constantinople and a member of a noble Byzantine family, he served as a respected secretary of Emperor Heraclius before becoming a monk around 614 at the monastery of Chrysopolis. In 626 and the Persian invasion of the region, Maximus fled to Africa. There he became an outspoken opponent of Monothelitism at African synods and at the Lateran Council of 649. In 653, however, Maximus and Pope St. Martin I were arrested

Cardinal Jules Mazarin

by Emperor Constans II and, as they refused to accept his decrees, the *Typos*, were exiled. Martin was sent to Crimea and Maximus was sent to Thrace. Brought back to Constantinople in 661, he once again refused to yield and so his tongue and right hand were chopped off and numerous humiliations were heaped upon him. Banished to the area around the Black Sea, he died on August 13, 662. One of the great theologians of the Church, Maximus is honored with the title of "The Theologian" and is ranked as a Doctor for his contributions to the theology of the Incarnation. The author of some ninety works on theology, mysticism, and dogma, his theological brilliance was displayed in such writings as his *Opuscula theologica et polemica* (*Short Theological and Polemical Treatises*); the *Ambigua* on Gregory of Nazianzus; and the *Mystagogia*, a study on symbolism that was an important entry in liturgical literary history.

Mazarin, Jules (1602-1661) ● French cardinal and statesman. The virtual ruler of France from around 1641, Mazarin was born at Piscina, in Abruzzi, Italy. Educated by the Jesuits, he studied at the University of Alcalá, receiving a doctorate of law around 1622 at Rome. Known at the time as Giulio Mazarini, he entered into the service of the papal army and soon secured promotion. Pope Urban VIII (r. 1623-1644) admired his diplomatic abilities, appointing him representative in negotiating an end to the war of the Mantuan Succession (1628-1630). His work there gained the notice of Cardinal Richelieu in France. Mazarin was named vice-legate at Avignon (1632-1634), proving so pro-French in his sympathies that Urban removed him, whereupon he went to Richelieu to whom he offered his services. Naturalized as a French citizen in 1639, he was officially commissioned in 1640. The next year, on December 16, 1641, he was created a cardinal, largely through the influence of his patron whom he replaced as prime minister in 1642. Through the cooperation of Queen Mother Anne of Austria, Mazarin, like Richelieu before him, was able to acquire near total control of the state until his own death, his time of power extending from the final years of the reign of King Louis XIII well into the long era of Louis XIV (r. 1643-1715). Crucial to his political endurance were his humility, gentle manner, genuine ability, and his intimate relationship with Queen Anne. The nature of this intimacy was the subject of much speculation, including the possibility that the two had entered into a morganatic marriage. Though never ordained a priest, he did hold the see of Metz (1653-1658) and headed several abbeys.

As prime minister, Mazarin adhered to the framework built by Richelieu, working to advance the political and military fortunes of France while seeking the defeat of the House of Habsburg. He helped negotiate the Treaty of Westphalia (1648) ending the bloody Thirty Years' War and the Peace of the Pyrenees (1659), which closed the protracted struggle between France and Spain. At home, however, he faced constant struggle owing to the Fronde (1648-1653), a series of conflicts with the Parlement arising out of his hard financial and centralizing policies. The Fronde of the Parlement (1648-1649) ended with a compromise while the Fronde of the Nobles, or Princes (1650-1653), was much more serious. Attacked in a series of pamphlets called Mazarinades, the cardinal went into banishment from 1651-1652, but the ultimate triumph of the crown allowed Mazarin to prepare much of the ground that would facilitate Louis's rise as an absolute monarch.

In religious affairs, Mazarin put the interests of France before those of the Church. He labored to reconcile the Huguenots for the good of the country and guaranteed the position of Protestantism in Europe with the Treaty of Westphalia. Relations with the papacy became strained from 1644 with the election of the pro-Spanish Innocent X (r. 1644-1655) when the cardinal gave refuge to several discredited cardinals of the Barberini family. An enemy of the Jansenists, however, he promulgated Innocent's decrees against them, most notably the constitution *Cum Occasione* (1653).

Mazarin Bible ● Also called the Gutenburg or Forty-two-line Bible. Probably the first published by Johannes Gutenburg, taking its name from its place of discovery in the library of Cardinal Jules Mazarin (d. 1661). The Bible was printed from movable type in Mainz around 1456. Called the Forty-two-line Bible because it had folio pages in two columns of forty-two lines each, it was also distinguished for its gothic type and hand-illumination.

Mechitarists ● Or the Benedictine Armenian Antonines, a congregation of

Armenian Benedictines in communion with Rome and using the Armenian liturgy that was first established in 1701 at Constantinople by the priest Mechitar Petrosian (1676-1749) of Sebaste (modern Sivas). The community, which had its rule based on the Rule of St. Benedict, was forced out of Constantinople in 1703, and they went first to Morea and then the island of San Lozzaro, Venice, in 1717. This property was granted to them by the Venetian Republic, and the community became known as the *Ordo Mechitaristarum Venetiarum*. In 1772, a number of monks moved to Trieste, finally settling in Vienna around 1810. The Mechitarists are noted for their work in scholarly areas, making important contributions to the study of Armenian literature and philology. They were responsible for producing invaluable histories, dictionaries, and periodicals, fostering a rebirth of Armenian culture in the nineteenth century. They have publishing houses (in Vienna and Venice) and maintain a number of houses; the Viennese Mechitarists were active in missionary work.

Mechtild of Magdeburg, St. (1210-c. 1285) ● Famous German mystic. Born to a noble Saxon family, she experienced at the age of twelve her first mystical visitation from the Holy Spirit. Inspired by her desire for humility, she joined (c. 1230) the Beguine community in Magdeburg where she was placed under the spiritual direction of the Dominicans. There her life of intense prayer and asceticism led to her receiving visions and, by the order of her confessor, she undertook to write them down. In 1270, she joined the Cistercian convent in Helfta where she remained for her last years. Her visions were recorded in the book generally known as *Das fleissende Licht der Gottheit*, derived from the title God purportedly had declared for it, *Vliessende licht miner gotheit in allu die herzen die da lebent ane valscheit* (*Light of my divinity, flowing into all hearts that live*

without guile). Begun in 1250, it was translated into Latin in 1290 (6 vols.). *Das fleissende* had a lasting impression on German mysticism. Mechtild of Magdeburg should not be confused with St. Mechtild of Hackeborn-Wippra (c. 1240-1298), who was responsible for the education of St. Gertrude the Great and was also at Helfta. Feast day: November 19.

Medici, House of ● Italian noble family that controlled the city of Florence from the fifteenth century until 1737, produced four popes, became connected by marriage to several royal houses, and was the foremost patron of the arts in European history. The Medicis first became prominent in the early 1200s as bankers and merchants. Through alliances and ruthless political ambition, they came to dominate the Florentine state, maintaining the fiction of the city's democratic constitution while standing as patrons of Florence's preeminent position as the leading center of the Renaissance. Cosimo de' Medici (1389-1464) was the first de' Medici to rule the city, while his grandson, Lorenzo de' Medici (1449-1492), called *Il Magnifico*, became the foremost personality of Renaissance Italy. Two queens of France, Catherine (1519-1589) and Marie (1573-1642), both came from the house, as did Pope Leo X (Giovanni de' Medici, r. 1513-1521), Clement VII (Giulio de' Medici, r. 1523-1534), Pius IV (Giovan Angelo de' Medici, r. 1559-1565), and Leo XI (Alessandro de' Medici, r. April 1-27, 1605).

Medina, Bartholomew (1527-1581) ● Also Bartolomé de Medina, a Spanish Dominican theologian, called the Father of Probabilism. A native of Medina, he entered the Dominicans and studied at the University of Salamanca with Dominic Báñez, Melchior Cano, and Dominic Soto. After teaching at Alcalá, Medina took up a chair of theology at Salamanca, spending from 1576 until the death of his brilliant instructor in the field.

The main focus of his writings was St. Thomas Aquinas, especially commentaries on the *Summa Theologica*. While known as the Father of Probabilism, it is uncertain whether Medina was indeed the founder of this important doctrine in moral theology. Scholars have differed over the years as to his place in the establishing of the doctrine, but Medina himself examined the question in his commentary on the *Prima Secundae* of the *Summa*. (See **Probabiliorism** and **Probabilism**; see also **Salmanticenses**.)

Medjugorje ● Town in Bosnia-Herzegovina where apparitions of the Virgin Mary have been reported since 1981. The first appearance was supposedly in June 1981 to six young people on a hillside next to the town. She was subsequently said to have appeared in the Church of St. James in Medjugorje and in other spots some distance from the community. According to the individuals who claim to have witnessed the events, Our Lady delivered a series of secret messages, calling upon all persons to pray, do penance, and practice personal conversion for world peace. The apparitions soon came under official scrutiny, and a commission appointed by the local bishop published its findings in 1984; no verification could be made as to the authenticity of the events. The bishop, however, expressed his grave doubts, a view not personally shared by the archbishop of Split-Makarska, who stated his private (or unofficial) opinion that the apparitions were of a supernatural inspiration. A more formal investigation was undertaken by the Church of Yugoslavia in 1987. By a vote of 19 to 1, the Yugoslav bishops declared in a statement issued on January 2, 1991, that no confirmation could be made of the supernatural apparitions. The fame of Medjugorje has continued to spread, however, attracting many pilgrims from across the world who continue to visit, despite the dangers of the civil war raging across much of the Balkans. The town has

survived the fighting and many believers point to the "miraculous" day when a bomb landed next to the church but did not explode, mystifying local U.N. soldiers.

Melanchthon, Philipp (1497-1560) ● German scholar, humanist, and a leading figure of the Protestant Reformation. Born Philipp Schwarzerd at Bretten, Germany, he studied at Heidelberg and Tübingen. In 1518, he was named the first professor of Greek at the University of Wittenberg. Developing a friendship with Martin Luther, he became an ardent defender of Luther's ideas, participating in the Leipzig Dissertation. In 1521, he authored the *Loci communes*, which presented the first organized treatment of the principles of the Reformation. He also took part in the Diet of Speyer (1529), the Colloquy of Marburg (1529), and especially the Diet of Augsburg (1530). Moreover, he authored the Augsburg Confession (1530), but it was rejected, ending Melanchthon's hope for a reconciliation with the Church. A gifted scholar, he was familiar with many humanists, acting as their liaison with Martin Luther.

Melania the Elder, St. (d. 410) ● Grandmother of Melania the Younger. A member of a wealthy Roman class of patricians, she was widowed at the age of twenty-two, thereafter devoting herself to a life of prayer and penance. In 372, she departed Rome and journeyed to the Holy Land where she became close to St. Jerome and where she established a double monastery on the Mount of Olives just outside of Jerusalem. After her return to Rome (397), she was forced to flee Italy in the face of the invasion of the Visigoths. She died in Jerusalem. Feast day: June 8.

Melania the Younger, St. (d. 439) ● Granddaughter of Melania the Elder who was much influenced by her in forsaking her patrician (noble) class and embarking upon an ascetic life. She renounced her wealth and, with her husband Pinianus, devoted herself to prayer. When Italy was invaded by the Visigoths in the early fifth century, she fled to Africa and then, joined by her husband, she entered Bethlehem before going to Jerusalem. There, just like her grandmother, she founded a monastery on Mt. Olive. Pinianus died seven years before his wife. Feast day: December 31.

Melchers, Paul (1813-1895) ●

Archbishop of Cologne and a cardinal. Born in Münster, in Westphalia, he studied law at Bonn and Munich and was ordained in 1841. Named bishop of Osnabrück in 1857, he was promoted to archbishop of Cologne in 1866 by Pope Pius IX. While personally opposed to the idea of papal infallibility and leaving the First Vatican Council in 1870 before the fourth solemn session (owing to the start of the Franco-Prussian War), he nevertheless accepted the dogma and proclaimed it in an address on July 24, 1870. He subsequently took steps to remove opposition to the doctrine among the professors of Bonn. An opponent of *Kulturkampf*, he was imprisoned for six months because of his excommunication of two priests who had joined the Old Catholics. Upon learning that authorities planned to depose him (1875) he took refuge with the Franciscans and ran his diocese for ten years from the monastery. To bring peace, he voluntarily resigned, retired to Rome, and was made a cardinal by Pope Leo XIII in 1885. Before his death, he entered the Jesuits.

Melchiades, St. ● Pope from 311-314.

Also known as Miltiades, he was probably a native of Africa and was elected successor to St. Eusebius on July 2, 311. His election came after the issue of the Edict of Toleration by Emperor Galerius (311), meaning that for the first time the Church was to be officially tolerated by Roman officials. The position only improved in the period immediately

following, for Emperor Maxentius, eager to cultivate popular favor, restored Church property that had been seized in the Diocletian persecutions. There followed in 313 the Edict of Milan. Melchiades certainly knew Constantine the Great, no doubt greeting him after the Battle of the Milvian Bridge (October 312). From Constantine, he received the palace of Empress Fausta, what was to become the papal palace of the Lateran. While the Church was no longer persecuted, Melchiades was confronted with the Donatists whom he had condemned at a Lateran synod in 313. He was ranked as a martyr because of the earlier sufferings in persecutions. He died on January 10, 314. Feast day: December 10.

Melchite Rite ● Also spelled Melkite, the

name given to those Christians who adhere to the Byzantine rite but are in communion with Rome. The Melchites originated in the fifth century among the Christians of Syria and Egypt who refused to accept Monophysitism, embracing instead the decrees of the Council of Chalcedon (451), which condemned the heresy. They were subsequently called Melchites by the Monophysites, a term from the Syriac meaning "emperor's men"; used at first for Orthodox Egyptian Christians, it spread in application to all adherents of Chalcedon before becoming synonymous with the members of a particular sect. As they were united with the patriarch of Constantinople, the Melchites joined in the schism between the Eastern and Western Churches that began in 1054. Many Melchites came to promote reunion with Rome, however, and over time a separate hierarchy was developed. Finally, in 1724, a formal union was made with Rome under Cyril VI, patriarch of Antioch. Another patriarch was elected for the Orthodox Melchites. The Melchites are headed by the patriarch of Antioch, with patriarchal vicariates in Egypt, Jerusalem, Sudan, Iraq, and Kuwait. They are also in Europe, Asia, America, and Australia. The liturgy is in Arabic with readings in Greek.

Melitian Schism ● Also, less properly, the Meletian Schism, a fourth-century schism that occurred in the Church of Alexandria. The name was taken from the early fourth-century bishop of Lycopolis who was declared in schism with the Christian Church. It began as a result of the pointedly severe persecutions of Emperor Diocletian (r. 284-305). Melitius found that existing regulations were too lenient for those Christians who had renounced the faith to be accepted once more into the community. After expressing his concerns to Peter, bishop of Alexandria, Melitius decided that the response from authority was not acceptable. He thus began ordaining his own priests and was excommunicated. To the surprise of Peter, however, Melitius had many adherents, his reputation only enhanced by the harsh period of labor in the mines; Peter, meanwhile, was put to death. The Council of Nicaea (325) did not condemn the Melitians, and they were integrated back into the Church. Fanatical adherents lasted until the eighth century until their eradication by the Muslims.

Melitius of Antioch (d. 381) ● Bishop of Antioch, he was a source of considerable controversy in the mid-fourth century over the see of Antioch. Melitius, the bishop of Sebaste (modern Sivas), was translated from his see to that of Antioch around 360, at the time when the diocese was still in the throes of considerable theological upheaval from the major heresy of Arianism. As Melitius had made promises to both parties in the city, he was soon embroiled in trouble after his election, since the two sides both looked to him to be a partisan. Of a mild, peaceful, and religious disposition, he was forced to decide his theological loyalties before Emperor Constantius II who, upon hearing Melitius's

orthodoxy, exiled him. There followed a bitter division within the city and, upon Melitius's return under Emperor Julian (362), his claim to the see was disputed, particularly as an opposing claimant, Paulinus, had entered the picture. Banished several more times and censured over possibly questionable theological views, Melitius was finally restored in 378. He died fully reconciled with the Church in 381 while presiding over the Council of Constantinople. The followers of Melitius came to be called Melitians and these efforts were denoted the Melitian Schism, not to be confused with the Melitian Schism in Egypt in the early fourth century. The pro-Melitian bishop Flavian was recognized as bishop of Antioch in 398 by Pope St. Siricius.

Melkite Rite ● See **Melchite Rite**.

Mendicant Orders ● Name given to those religious orders requiring of their members a vow of poverty, a renunciation of worldly possessions, and a willingness to beg or work for food. The mendicant orders were born in the twelfth century out of the sincere movement within the Church to counter the rampant corruption and materialism of the times and to adopt lifestyles that were truly faithful to the Church's call for poverty, charity, and a total dependence upon the providence of God. Two monumental figures gave solid foundation to the mendicant movement: St. Francis of Assisi (1181-1226) and St. Dominic (1170-1221); they established respectively the Franciscans and the Dominicans. They were later joined by the Carmelites and the Augustinians. While opposed by many priests and prelates, the mendicants soon grew immensely popular, especially among the poor, and the orders gradually received the enthusiastic support of the papacy, which granted the right to hear confession and to preach, with other exceptions from local episcopal authority. Through their efforts, the Church in the thirteenth century underwent considerable reform, and the orders produced some of the greatest figures in the history of the Church, among them St. Thomas Aquinas, St. Bonaventure, St. Teresa of Ávila, St. John of the Cross, and John Duns Scotus. The name mendicant came from the Latin *mendicare* (to beg), and friar, which was used to distinguish the mendicants from monks, was derived from *frater* (brother), a reference to their closeness to the average people and their humility.

Mercedarians ● Order of Our Lady of Mercy. This congregation was first established by St. Peter Nolasco in 1218. The order was devoted to the care of the sick, but its main purpose was to rescue Christian captives from the Muslims, even going so far as to offer themselves as replacements for the hostages. St. Peter founded the Mercedarians as the result of a vision of the BVM, who asked him to work for the ransom of captured Christians. Encouraged by his confessor, St. Raymond of Peñafort, he found support from a number of noblemen who joined the congregation and followed a rule drawn up for them by St. Raymond. Pope Honorius III gave his approval, which was reconfirmed in 1230 by Pope Gregory IX, who gave the Mercedarians the Rule of St. Augustine. St. Peter was the first superior, holding the title of commanding general until his death in 1258. The order spread through France, England, Germany, Spain, and Portugal, and several members sailed with Columbus in 1492. They subsequently established numerous houses in the New World. An order of nuns for the congregation was begun in 1568. The Mercedarians continue to work around the world.

Mercier, Désiré Joseph (1851-1926) ● Belgian cardinal, philosopher, and a leading figure in Neo-Scholasticism. Born in Braine-l'Alleud, Belgium, he studied at Malines and Louvain and was ordained in 1874. From

1877-1882, he taught at the seminary of Malines. In 1882, he was named first professor at the University of Louvain in the program of Thomist philosophy that was being promoted by Pope Leo XIII and that had been launched by the pontiff's encyclical *Aeterni Patris* (1879). Such was the popular reception to Thomistic revival that Mercier, with Leo's support, established the Institut Supérieur de Philosophie at Louvain. The institute quickly became an important center for Neo-Scholasticism, particularly through its publication *Revue Néoscolastique*. Named by Pope St. Pius X archbishop of Malines in 1906, Mercier was elevated to cardinal the next year. He earned international notoriety for speaking out during World War I on behalf of Belgium, especially protesting the German burning of Louvain. His tour of the United States in 1919 to raise money for the city was a considerable success. In his later years, Mercier was an advocate of Christian unity, helping to organize the Malines Conversations (1921, 1923, 1925), which propelled a Catholic-Anglican dialogue. He was the author of numerous works on philosophy, including a manual on modern Scholastic philosophy.

Merry del Val, Rafael (1865-1930) ● Spanish cardinal who held the posts of secretary of state and secretary of the Holy Office. The son of a Spanish diplomat, he studied under the Jesuits in Namur and Brussels before attending Ushaw College at Durham and the Accademia dei Nobili in Rome. Ordained in 1888, he became a trusted representative of Pope Leo XIII, serving on the pontifical commission that was examining the question of Anglican Orders (1896) and negotiating with the Canadian government a settlement on the Catholic schools that became necessary as a result of the Manitoba Laws (1890). Appointed a bishop in 1900, three years later the newly elected Pope St. Pius X elevated him to cardinal and named him secretary of state. In this position, he was quite able and distinguished himself in supporting Pius's strong stand against Modernism. He assisted Monsignor Umberto Benigni in his work to establish the *Sodalitum Pianum*, the effort to reduce Modernist influences in the Church. Later, Pope Benedict XV named him secretary of the Holy Office. He was buried in St. Peter's, close to Pius X.

Mersenne, Merin (1588-1648) ●

Scientist, philosopher, mathematician, and a member of the Order of Minims. A native of Oize, Maine, France, Mersenne entered the mendicant orders in 1611 at Paris, subsequently teaching at Nevers and then Paris. A brilliant mathematician, he endeavored to find a formula that would encompass all prime numbers, his efforts resulting in the so-called Mersenne numbers. Accomplished in his field, he was nevertheless best known for his enormous contribution as a link between the leading scientists and philosophers of his time including Descartes (a former schoolmate), Pascal, Galileo, and Pierre de Fermat. Mersenne vigorously opposed astrology and alchemy and was a defender of Galileo and Descartes.

Merton, Thomas (1915-1968) ●

Immensely popular American writer and poet, he was a longtime member of the Trappists. Born in France to parents who were artists, Merton was orphaned at the age of sixteen. After wandering for a time in France and England, he won a scholarship to Cambridge (1933-1934) but was dismissed after only one year because of his improper lifestyle and lack of discipline. Moving to America, he attended Columbia University, receiving a bachelor's in literature and poetry in 1937, and then a master's in 1939. Baptized into the Church in 1938, he underwent a profound conversion and in 1941 entered the Trappist Abbey of Our Lady of Gethsemane, near Bardstown, Kentucky.

Ordained in 1949, he served also as a master of novices. In 1965, however, he was allowed by the community to adopt a solitary lifestyle away from the abbey itself. He lived in a small house in the adjoining hills where he focused on the mystical life and studied the mysticism of Eastern philosophers. His increased interest in the East led to a tour of Asia where he met with numerous Eastern religious leaders, including the Dalai Lama. While in Bangkok, Thailand, he died by accidental electrocution while bathing.

Merton was one of the most widely read Catholic authors of the twentieth century. He first achieved fame for an autobiographical account of his spiritual journey to the Trappists, *The Seven Storey Mountain* (1948), a book so successful that he later renounced much of it because he found it unequal to his developed skills as a writer and his heightened mysticism. Permitted to fulfill his vocation through writing, he authored numerous books, including poetry, and hundreds of articles. Among his most important works were *Ascent to Truth* (1951), *Mystics and Zen Masters*, *No Man Is an Island* (1955), and *Faith and Contemplation* (1962). The issues he covered — including race relations, militarism, nuclear weapons, Eastern mysticism, and ecumenism — made him at times a controversial figure, but he remains an influential and significant contributor to contemporary discussions of mysticism and spirituality.

Methodius ● See under Cyril and Methodius, Sts.

Methodius of Olympus, St. (d. 311?) ●

Probably bishop of Olympus (in Lycia, Asia Minor), possibly bishop of Tyre, and generally held to be the first major opponent of Origenism. Very little is known about Methodius; Eusebius, for example, does not mention him in his *Ecclesiastical History*, most likely because of Methodius's opposition to Origen. Jerome describes him as bishop of

Olympus and Tyre, although the second posting was not supported by Eusebius, who mentions Tyrannio as the bishop (*Historia Ecclesiastica*). In all likelihood, however, Methodius was martyred in Tyre, in 311. His major writings included: "Symposium or, On Virginity" (in Greek), with a concluding hymn on Christ as the Bridegroom of the Church; "On Free Will" (in Greek) attacking certain Gnostic doctrines; and "On the Resurrection" (in Greek), in which he upheld that the body used by the living will be reawakened and incorrigible at the time of the resurrection, a view in opposition to Origen. These works have been preserved either entirely ("Symposium") or, in the case of the other two, in large fragments, in their original Greek. Other works are known only in Slavonic translations. Among these are treatises on the OT references to lepers, and OT customs concerning food.

Metochites, George (d. c. 1328) ●

Byzantine historian and theologian. The representative of Byzantine Emperor Michael VIII Palaeologus to Pope Gregory X, Metochites took part in the efforts to bring about a reunion of the Eastern and Western Churches. At the Council of Lyons (1274) he helped draft the decree of union, but his hopes of meaningful restitution of Christian unity were dashed when Emperor Andronicus II reversed Byzantine policy. Metochites was arrested and exiled to Nicomedia. His *Historia dogmatica* is an invaluable source on the schism between the Churches.

Mexico ●

Central America republic in which the Church long suffered from disabilities and regulation but in which the faith has flourished. Mexico was the site of two of the most important pre-Columbian cultures of Mesoamerica: the Aztec Empire and the Maya. The Maya were already in a relative state of decline at the start of the sixteenth century, and the Aztec realm had been beset by political difficulties in the years prior to the Spanish arrival in the region. One of the last rulers of the Aztecs, Montezuma, was anticipating some kind of disaster to befall his empire (he had been warned of this by his priests) when the Spanish arrived in 1519. The Spaniards, under Hernando Cortés, destroyed the Aztec Empire, besieging the Aztec capital of Tenochtitlan, slaughtering thousands of natives, and finally strangling the Aztec ruler.

Within a few years of the Spanish conquest, Catholic missionaries had begun entering into Mexico, most notably the Franciscans. They were joined by the Dominicans and, later, by the Jesuits. While working closely with Spanish colonial authorities, the missionary orders did distinguish themselves by their resistance to the brutal enslavement and exploitations of the Indians, their learning the native languages, and their willingness to endure enormous hardships in bringing the faith to the distant corners of Mexico. As the Church became more established, the missionary priests and friars came increasingly into conflict with the secular clergy, who desired full control over the ecclesiastical affairs and resented the extensive powers of the religious orders who had been granted a bull in 1521 giving them authority to preach. The conflict between the secular clergy and the religious orders would rage for some years until it was finally settled in Mexico in 1583 with the triumph of the secular clergy. Henceforth the secular clergy would be closely allied with Spanish authorities and identify closely with its interests. This was due in large measure to the right enjoyed by the crown in making ecclesiastical appointments and the high degree of patronage that was attendant on Spanish colonial society.

Among the native population, meanwhile, missionary activity continued throughout the sixteenth century. A diocese was created in 1530 in Mexico City, which became the heart of missionary endeavors. Through the often violent policies of the colonial officials, many conversions were made by force so that while most of the population was quickly baptized, their faith was far from sincere; as a result, throughout Catholic history in Mexico many elements of Aztec or pre-Columbian ritual have endured in some parts of the country, mixed with the faith. Aside from disease, slavery, exploitation, and war, the native population suffered in the early period of the Inquisition, which was approved by King Philip II in 1569 for Mexico. Eventually, authorities ceased dragging the Indians before tribunals because they decided that the Indians were of limited intelligence.

On the positive side, the Church did much through its missionaries to save many Indians from death and enslavement and to preserve vital portions of Mesoamerican culture, art, and history. Equally, friars traveled to northern Mexico and beyond, bringing the faith with them into California, Texas, and New Mexico. A lasting boost to conversions and the fostering of sincere devotion among the simple people was the appearance in 1531 of Our Lady of Guadalupe. The shrine built in her honor remains the most important religious site in Mexico. The Church also had near total control over education, and Mexico City became one of the foremost centers of learning in the New World.

The Spanish domination of Mexico would last for nearly three centuries, deteriorating gradually throughout the 1700s as the gulf widened between the Spanish ruling class and the native classes that were joined by the mestizos and Creoles (descendants of Native Americans and Europeans). Unrest broke out into a full-scale rebellion in 1810 with the uprising of many priests led by Father Miguel Hidalgo y Costilla and, after his execution, by Father José Maria Morelos y Pavón. While suppressed in 1816, it proved only the first of several revolts, culminating in the 1821 declaration of Mexican independence. By the terms of the independence, the Church received a special status and had enormous sway in political life. This changed in subsequent years, as a republic was proclaimed in 1836 and various liberal regimes came to power. Anticlericalism became commonplace, made even more strident by the lingering hostility over the Church's activities with Spanish colonial government. After the Mexican-American War (1846-1848), the political instability led to the dictatorship of Antonio López de Santa Anna (of the Alamo fame). He was toppled by a liberal regime whose anti-Church legislation sparked an armed struggle called the War of the Reform (1858-1861). The laws issued by the government included the forced selling of Church land. Mexico's educational system was deeply affected. While the liberal forces won the War of the Reform, the conflict had so debilitated Mexico that the French were able to intervene in 1861 and install their puppet, the Austrian duke Maximilian, on the Mexican throne.

The French finally pulled out of Mexico in 1867 and Benito Juárez became president. His successor, Sebastián Lerdo de Tijada, was toppled in 1876 by Porfirio Diáz who would remain dictator for thirty-four years. A civil war ended his regime, but more bloodshed ensued. Finally, a constitution was issued in 1917 that placed severe restrictions on the Church: there could be no criticism of the government, only Mexicans could be clergy, the Church was not permitted to own property, and any privileges were stripped away.

The situation became worse from 1923 when the papal legate was expelled. The administration of Pluarco Calles (1924-1928) launched a wave of persecution that sparked a popular uprising called the Cristeros Rebellion. Coupled with the repressive measures of local governments, the Calles regime and its successors had forced the Church into very difficult times, with only a few priests remaining in the country. The persecution prompted Pope Pius XI to stand firm against them and to issue several encyclicals, *Iniquis afflictisque* (1926) and *Acerba animi* (1932). An easing of the situation began in 1940 as the rigid anticlerical laws ceased to be enforced with enthusiasm. Gradual improvement in relations between Mexico and the Holy See led to the formation of full diplomatic ties in 1992. This was followed by the final easing of many of the handicaps under which the Church had long suffered. The faith of the country is profoundly deep, as was seen in the nearly frenzied greeting given to Pope John Paul II in 1979 and 1993. However, social unrest, poverty, economic challenges, and corruption still plague the country. A symbol of the difficulties was the murder of Cardinal Juan Jesús Posadas Ocampo, archbishop of Guadalajara, on May 24, 1993. (See also **Central America** and **Liberation Theology**.)

Michael Cerularius (d. 1059) ● Patriarch of Constantinople. His reign (1043-1058) is generally marked as the final breach between the Eastern and Western Churches. A favorite member of the court of Emperor Constantine IX Monomakhos, Michael had first come to prominence by assisting Constantine in his effort to depose Michael IV (r. 1034-1041). When the plot failed, both Michael and Constantine were banished. Although a mere monk, Michael was given a place of high honor by Emperor Constantine upon his accession in 1042. The following year, Constantine named him patriarch, to succeed Patriarch Alexios. An ardent defender of the Greek Church, Michael adopted an often bitter anti-Latin

stance, so much so that in 1054 the equally intractable Cardinal Humbert of Silva-Candida excommunicated him while on a visit to Constantinople. Michael responded with his manifesto declaring the independence of the Byzantine Church. The formal, irreconcilable schism between the Churches dated from this year. Emperor Isaac I Comnenus found him overly ambitious, however, and he was removed and exiled in 1058.

Michelangelo (1475-1564) ● In full, Michelangelo Buonarroti. One of the foremost of all Renaissance artists, he was born in

Michelangelo

Caprese, Tuscany, the son of Ludovici and Francesca Buonarroti Simoni. At the age of thirteen, he was apprenticed to Domenico Ghirlandaio of Florence, studying art under him for a time and then in the school sponsored by the de' Medici in the Medici Gardens. While living in the house of Lorenzo de' Medici (Lorenzo the Magnificent), he encountered poets, scholars, artists, philosophers, and others. Reading Dante and Petrarch, meeting Pico della Mirandola, and others, he acquired a high degree of erudition.

From 1496-1501, Michelangelo worked in Rome, sculpting the "Pietà." He returned to Florence in 1501 where he received a commission from the city to create the huge "David," which became one of the wonders of the city. In 1505, he was summoned to Rome by Pope Julius II. The pope commissioned him to execute his tomb, a project that would take some thirty years to complete, in large measure because of the numerous undertakings of the intervening period.

Julius gave him the task of painting the Sistine Chapel, which was finished in 1541. Michelangelo took to this commission only with great personal reluctance, as his first love was not painting but sculpture. Julius was also a hard master, their relationship a fascinating mixture of contentiousness and abiding mutual respect.

Back in Florence from 1520-1534, he worked for the Medicis on their tombs, in the sacristy of S. Lorenzo and the Medicea-Laurenziana Library, enjoying the patronage of the Medici popes Leo X (r. 1513-1521) and Clement VII (r. 1523-1534). In 1529, he gave his considerable skills as an engineer to the city of Florence in its defense during the siege. After the fall of the Florentine republic, Michelangelo returned to Rome, itself recovering from the devastating sack by imperial troops in 1527. While in Rome, he painted the "Last Judgment" in the Sistine Chapel (1534-1541), executed frescoes in the Pauline Chapel (1542-1550, commissioned by Pope Paul III), and in 1546 was appointed the chief architect of St. Peter's Basilica, succeeding Sangallo (see **St. Peter's Basilica**). He died in Rome on February 18, 1564.

The genius of Michelangelo extended from painting and sculpture to architecture and literature (including poetry and prose). He was the author of highly expressive and original sonnets. Among his other famous works were: sculpture — the "Drunken Bacchus," "Moses" (originally intended for the tomb of Julius II), and the "Pietà di Palestrina" in the cathedral of Florence; painting — "The Holy Family"; architecture — the cornice of the Farnese Palace, in Rome, work on the Capitoline Hill, Rome, the design for the Church of S. Giovanni de'Fiorentini, and the Dome of St. Peter's.

Migne, Jacques Paul (1800-1875) ●

French priest and publisher best known for his work in preserving the writings of Latin and Greek ecclesiastical authors. Born at St.-Flour, he studied theology at Orléans and was ordained in 1824. The next year, he became pastor of the parish of Puiseaux, serving until 1833, resigning his post after a disagreement with the local bishop over Migne's publication of the pamphlet *De la liberté*. Migne went to Paris and there established the journal *L'Univers Religieux* (later *L'Univers*), editing it until 1836. He also founded an ambitious printing house, the Imprimerie Catholique, that he hoped to devote to the publishing of theological works that might be affordable in price and thus accessible to a broad ecclesiastical market. From 1836, he released a number of theological volumes, of moderate price, including *Scripturae Sacrae Cursus Completus* (28 vols., 1840-1845), on Sacred Scripture; *Demonstrationes Evangeliques* (20 vols., 1842-1853), a collection of apologetic writings; and *Theologiae Cursus Completus* (28 vols., 1840-1845), a massive compilation on theology. His chief work was the *Patrologia*, in two collections: *Patrologia Latinae Cursus Completus* (217 vols., 1844-1855) and *Patrologia Graecae Cursus Completus* (81 vols., 1856-1861). The first was a collection of Latin Church writers from the earliest period until the pontificate of Pope Innocent III (r. 1198-1216). The second gathered the works of Greek ecclesiastical writers until the Council of Florence (1438-1439). While the huge collection contained a large number of printing errors and lacked at times an ideal judgment in the choice of editions used for the text, the *Patrologia* nevertheless offered what quickly became the standard work in the field and remains an invaluable reference source. A terrible fire in 1868 destroyed the printing house and the plates for the *Patrologia*. Migne attempted to rebuild, but his program was impeded by the Franco-Prussian War in 1870 and he ultimately found it impossible to regain his former publishing position.

Milan, Edict of ● Decree issued around 313 by Emperor Constantine the Great and Licinius Licinianus, effectively ending the persecution of Christianity within the Roman Empire. The edict marked a new era for the Church and would lead to the eventual supremacy of Christian belief in the affairs of the empire. Constantine the Great, the leading force behind the decree, laid the groundwork for an empire-wide granting of freedom to Christians by first passing legislation in the provinces under his control. His declaration went beyond the Declaration of Toleration that had been issued by Emperor Galerius in 311, in which Christians received full rights of worship and other privileges. Using his considerable political influence, he pushed his colleague emperors to adopt similar measures, winning the agreement of Licinius who was seeking an ally against Maximinus Daia. The two met at Milan (Mediolanum) early in 313, formulating their famous decree, although it was not declared publicly nor was it really an edict. In June 313, Licinius published formally at Nicomedia the letter that had been agreed upon earlier in the year. The edict was hailed by Christian chroniclers, particularly Eusebius and Lactantius.

Milic, Jan (d. 1374) ● Also John Milic or Milic of Kromerz, a Czech pre-Hussite reformer. Originally the head of the chancery of Emperor Charles IV, Milic was ordained around 1350. Seized with an overpowering spirit of reform, he resigned his post, gave up all earthly powers and possessions, and began to preach in Prague. He called for Church reform and a return to spirituality. Arrested and imprisoned by the Inquisition in 1367, he received absolution from Pope Gregory XI in 1373, subsequently preaching before the College of Cardinals. During his time in prison, he authored a call for reform entitled *Libellus de Antichristo* (*Booklet on the Antichrist*).

Military Orders ● Collective name given to the chivalric, monastic, and political military organizations that were first organized during the Middle Ages, most often to take part in the crusades to the Holy Land, to carry out the martial evangelization of Eastern Europe, or to assist in the *Reconquista* in Spain. Most of the orders died out centuries ago, but some have survived and are today important Catholic organizations. The major military orders were:

Brothers of the Sword: See **Livonian Knights** [this entry].

Calatrava, Knights of: The greatest of the chivalric Spanish orders. Launched in the twelfth century at the fortress of Calatrava (which had been abandoned by the Knights Templar) by Abbot Ramón Sierra, with a band of monks and soldiers. After the abbot died in 1164, the monks departed, but the soldiers chose to remain, creating a military force to defend Calatrava. The knights were granted papal approval as an actual order, adopting the Benedictine Rule and taking vows of poverty, chastity, and obedience.

The Calatravan Knights expanded their field of operation over the next years, coming to wield much prestige and wealth in Spain, their authority centered in Castile. After participating in the terminal phases of the *Reconquista*, they came under the control of their Catholic Majesties, Ferdinand and Isabella, in 1489. In 1523, Pope Adrian VI gave the office of grand master to Emperor Charles V. It then emerged as an honorary order reserved for noblemen. The honorary order of nuns was founded in 1219.

Holy Sepulchre, Knights of the: An order launched during the First Crusade (1095-1099), receiving approval in 1122 from Pope Callistus II. The purpose of the knights was originally to defend the Basilica of the Holy Sepulchre in Jerusalem, but they also helped fight against the Muslims in the Holy Land and to provide protection to the pilgrims journeying to the sacred places. The knights were forced to leave Jerusalem in

1244. In 1847, Pope Pius IX (r. 1846-1878) reconstituted the order. It is today one of the most prominent of all chivalric organizations, with five grades. It grants all five grades to women. Its grand master is a cardinal, appointed by the pope. The full title of the order is the Equestrian Order of the Most Holy Sepulchre of Jerusalem.

Hospitallers, Knights: See **Malta, Knights of** [this entry].

Livonian Knights: Also known as the Brothers of the Sword or the Knights of the Sword, an order begun in Germany (c. 1202) by Albrecht von Buxhovden, bishop of Riga. They were charged with defending the Christian colony of Livonia and Christianizing the rest of the country and areas along the Baltic. Considerable progress was made until 1236 when they were surprised by a host of Lithuanians and nearly destroyed. The survivors formed an alliance with the Teutonic Knights (1237-1239), ensuring their survival until the sixteenth century.

Malta, Knights of: The name used from 1530 for the military order that was established in the late eleventh century to care for pilgrims to the Holy Land; still in existence, it is one of the most respected honorary bodies in the Church. Originally known as the Knights Hospitallers, the Order of the Hospital of St. John, or the Knights of Jerusalem, the first organization was born around 1070 out of the hospital that was begun to care for travelers to the Holy Land. With the onset of the First Crusade (1095-1099), it adopted a military function in the struggle against the Muslims, receiving papal approval in 1113 from Pope Paschal II. Along with the Templars, the Knights Hospitallers were participants in all of the major military campaigns of the crusades,

Marienburg, headquarters of the Teutonic Knights

helping to defend Acre until its fall in 1291 to the Mamelukes. They then retreated to Cyprus. In 1310, they conquered Rhodes, making it their headquarters.

Over the next years, the Knights of Rhodes (as they were now known) benefited handsomely from the uprooting of the Templars (1312) and became politically, financially, and militarily powerful throughout the Mediterranean. Their ships were one of the main defenses against the Ottoman Turks. In 1480, Rhodes itself was besieged by a huge armada under Sultan

Muhammad II, or Mehmet II the Conqueror (r. 1451-1481), who captured Constantinople. The knights, led by Pierre d'Aubusson, though outnumbered, repulsed the Turks. This proved only a respite, for Sultan Suleiman the Magnificent took the island in 1522. Ejected from Rhodes, the knights were granted Malta by Emperor Charles V in 1530. They would remain in control of the island until 1798 when Malta was seized by Napoleon as part of his Egyptian campaign.

The order managed to survive in relative obscurity throughout the first part of the nineteenth century. Its headquarters were opened in Rome in 1834, and in 1879 Pope Leo XIII restored the office of grand master. The Knights of Malta henceforth were a religious body fully approved by the Holy See. Today, the knights continue to work to provide assistance to the poor and promote hospital and charitable endeavors. There are four main classes: Knights of Justice; Knights of Obedience; Knights of Honor and Devotion, and of Grace and Devotion; and Knights of Magistral Grace. Members are found in more than a hundred countries. It is recognized in international law as a sovereign entity and thus maintains diplomatic relations with over fifty countries including the Holy See, on which it is dependent as a religious order (and independent as a sovereign entity). The current grand master — with the title Most Eminent Highness and with the rank of cardinal — is Fra' Andrew Willoughby Ninian Bertie.

Our Lady of Montjoie, Knights of: A Spanish order launched in 1176 in the Holy Land. Its founder was named Count Rodrigo, a onetime member of the Knights of Santiago. Approved in 1180 by Pope Alexander III (r. 1159-1181), they eventually possessed extensive holdings in Castile and Ascalon. Its headquarters were at Montjoie, outside of Jerusalem, until the loss of the Holy Land to the Muslims.

St. John of Jerusalem, Hospitallers of: See **Malta, Knights of** [this entry].

Santiago, Knights of: An order begun in 1158 in Castile, Spain, with the purpose of fighting against the Moors. Papal approval was granted in 1175 and the next years were spent in active campaigning against the Moors. After acquiring considerable wealth, the knights came to own holdings in England, Palestine, France, and Hungary. Its most notable grand master was Alvaro de Luna (master from 1445-1453), who won the Battle of Higuera (1431). The order was singular in allowing its members to marry.

Sword, Knights of: See **Livonian Knights** [this entry].

Templars: Also called the Knights Templar or the Poor Knights of the Temple of Solomon, one of the best known of all military orders during the Middle Ages. The Templars were begun around 1119 in the Holy Land when a group of knights gathered together under the French knight Hugh de Payens; they took their name from the section of Jerusalem that was given to them by King Baldwin II of Jerusalem, traditionally said to be near the former Temple of Solomon.

Following the Augustinian Rule, the knights proved a courageous and adroit organization. They took possession of the fortress of Acre and held it until 1291, proving the last crusader stronghold in Palestine until ejected by the Mamelukes. They then retreated to Cyprus and concentrated on amassing vast powers, riches, and holdings. To protect themselves from interference and overly prying eyes of local rulers, the Templars instituted secret codes and other measures of private activity. Owing to their wealth, influence, and secrecy, they created formidable enemies, the foremost of whom was King Philip IV the Fair of France. Using his domination of the papacy, Philip pushed Pope Clement V to permit accusations against the Templars (such as devil worship of the idol Baphomet, sodomy, and murder). The pope suppressed the order in 1312 and its leadership was arrested. The last grand master, Jacques de Molay, was burned at the stake. The possessions of the knights were liquidated and seized by the crowns of various realms.

Teutonic Knights: In German, *Deutschen Ordens* (German Order); in Latin, *Ordo Domus Sanctae Mariae Teutonicorum* (German Order of the Hospital of Holy Mary). One of history's greatest and long its most feared military order, the Teutonic Knights were begun in 1190 at Acre as a group of charitable knights, lay brothers, and priests funded by the merchants of Bremen and Lübeck. After taking part in military operations in Syria and elsewhere in the Holy Land, it was granted formal approval in 1199 by Pope Innocent III. Its first great grand master, Hermann von Salza (master from 1209-1239), took the knights out of the Holy Land to Europe and set the order on the course of advancing Christianity in Eastern Europe. (The first grand master was Heinrich Walpoto.) In 1225, they were invited by the Polish duke Conrad of Mazovia to conduct campaigns in Prussia against pagan tribes. The knights demonstrated merciless determination against the Prussians, massacring most of the population and Christianizing what was left by the sword. The order then encouraged German immigration and became virtual master of the region, only adding to their prosperity and power through grants of land and the promotion of trade (by permission of the Holy See in 1263). By 1309, the knights owned an extensive feudal realm stretching along the Baltic.

From their headquarters at Marienburg, Prussia, and in close alliance with the Livonian Knights, the Teutonic Order drove eastward, against Lithuania and Russia. Dreaded by the Lithuanians and disliked by the Poles who had misgivings about their ambitions, the knights earned lasting enmity on the part of the Lithuanians by continuing their war with them even after the Christianization of the country. The Poles and Lithuanians united in 1386 and in 1410 defeated the Teutonic Knights at the Battle of Tannenberg (Grünwald), effectively breaking the power of the German Order.

Decline set in soon after and, following another war with the Poles (1454-1466), the knights accepted the Treaty of Thorn (Torun), leaving them only East Prussia and vassal status to the Poles. In 1525, Grand Master Albert of Brandenburg accepted Protestantism and transformed the lands of the order into a hereditary duchy, thereby forming the foundation of the state of Prussia. Many knights remained Catholic, reconstituting themselves in Catholic Germany. They fought valiantly against the Turks in Austria in the seventeenth century but were disbanded in the early 1800s by Napoleon. A new order was later begun with honorary duties. Their chief church is the Kirche des Deutschen Ordens in Vienna. (See also **Crusades**.)

Millenarianism ● Called also at times Chiliasm, it is a belief that Christ will return and reign for a thousand years. Meaning "one thousand" as derived from the Latin, it has its basis in an overly literal interpretation of the passage in the Book of Revelation (20:6) in which John writes: "Blessed and holy is he who shares in the first resurrection! Over such the second death has no power, but they shall be priests of God and of Christ, and they shall reign with him a thousand years." Instead of accepting a spiritual meaning for the passage in Revelation, some Christians adopted a faulty, literal interpretation, making assumptions that the millennium actually refers to a thousand-year reign. Such a view is still accepted by some denominations such as the Jehovah Witnesses. The Church teaches that the sense of the thousand years must be understood from the perspective of St. Paul (Eph 5:4-5; Col 3:1); and only through participation in faith and grace can one share in the resurrection of Christ.

Milner, John (1752-1826) ● English Catholic apologist. A native of London, Milner was sent at the age of twelve by Bishop Challoner to the English College at Douai. There he studied for the priesthood and was ordained in 1777. Sent back to England, he became pastor of Winchester, holding this position for over twenty years, during which he established a school and rebuilt the chapel. He was particularly known for his work in caring for the large numbers of French clergy who had fled France at the outset of the French Revolution. In 1803, he was consecrated titular bishop of Castabala and named vicar apostolic of the Midland District. His main claim to notoriety, however, was in his extensive writings, as an apologist. While causing tension in some circles, his works were staunch defenses and ardent promotions of the Catholic faith. Among his writings were "Letters to a Prebendary" (1800), *The End of Religious Controversy* (1801-1802, published in 1818), "Appeal to the Catholics of Ireland" (1809), and "Elucidation of the Conduct of Pius VII" (1802).

Miltiades, St. ● See **Melchiades, St**.

Miltitz, Carl von (c. 1480-1529) ● German papal nuncio and chamberlain. A native of Meissen, he was the son of the nobleman Sigismud von Miltitz, studying at Mainz, Trier, and Meissen before journeying to Rome in 1514 or 1515. Appointed a papal chamberlain and notary, he also acted as an agent of Frederick, elector of Saxony. When it became clear that the efforts of Cardinal Cajetan were unsuccessful in silencing the work of Martin Luther, von Miltitz was chosen to enter into negotiations with the vocal reformer. He traveled to Germany on the pretense of taking the Golden Rose to Frederick, an award the elector had long coveted (see **Golden Rose**). His first meeting with Luther was held in Achtenburg from January 4-6, 1519. Luther was cooperative but refused to recant. He did accept an examination by Archbishop Richard of Trier. Miltitz then went to Leipzig where he reproached Johann Tetzel, the infamous preacher of indulgences. The crisis caused by Luther had progressed too far, however, and the two subsequent meetings, at Liebenwerda (October 1519) and Lichtenburg (October 1520), came to nothing. Miltitz died by accidental drowning on November 20, 1529, and was buried in the cathedral of Mainz.

Milvian Bridge, Battle of the ● Famous military engagement fought in late October 312 between the forces of Constantine the Great and Maxentius. The battle established Constantine as master of the western regions of the Roman Empire, but it also guaranteed the eventual supremacy of Christianity as the foremost creed of thc cmpire.

Mindszenty, József (1892-1975) ● Hungarian cardinal who stood as one of the foremost resisters of Communism in Eastern Europe. Mindszenty was named cardinal in 1946, but he soon confronted the Communist regime of Hungary, which was demanding the nationalization of the Hungarian Church. As he remained steadfast in his opposition, despite the cruel repression of the clergy and his own abuse by the Hungarian police, he was imprisoned in 1949. Freed in 1956 during the unrest of the country, he was granted asylum with the U.S. legation in Budapest, remaining a virtual prisoner on American soil as the persecution of the Hungarian Catholics continued. His departure from Hungary was finally arranged in September 1971 as part of the Holy See's policy of *Ostpolitik*. He journeyed to Rome and was the honored guest of Pope Paul VI, before taking up residence in Vienna. In his final years, the cardinal traveled extensively to publicize the plight of Hungarian Catholics. He died in Vienna.

Minims ● From the *Ordo Fratrum Minimorum*, an order established in 1435 by St. Francis of Paola. The Minims were much inspired by St. Francis of Assisi, practicing a severe form of personal humility and declaring themselves to be the most humble of all religious communities. The Minims wore black and took a perpetual vow of abstinence from all fish, meat, and dairy products, especially cheese. Their first rule, derived from that of St. Francis, was approved by Pope Alexander VI in 1493; a revised version appeared in 1501. The Minims spread rapidly throughout Europe, reaching their peak in the sixteenth century.

Minucius Felix ● Second-century Christian apologist. Probably from Africa, he is the author of *Octavius*, an eloquent defense of Christianity, in Latin, presented in the form of a conversational debate between the Christian Octavius and the pagan Caecilius. The work brilliantly refutes the charges against the Church.

Miracle Plays ● See under **Plays**.

Mit Brennender Sorge ● German for "With Burning Anxiety," an encyclical issued on March 14, 1937, by Pope Pius XI, "To the Bishops of Germany: On the Church and the German Reich." Largely overlooked because of the concordat that Pius had negotiated with Hitler in 1933, the encyclical was a strong denunciation of Nazism, noting that the Nazis had broken several points of the concordat and were actively involved in anti-Catholic and anti-Christian programs such as the removal of the OT from schools and the promotion of the so-called German National Church. The encyclical was read from the pulpit of every German Church on March 21, 1937.

Modernism ● Movement that developed within the Church in the late nineteenth century. It attempted to reconcile the teachings of the Church with modern advances in science, historical and biblical research, and philosophical trends by altering Catholic doctrine through innovation and reinterpretation; because of the errors that were advanced by many of its differing proponents, the movement was called by Pope St. Pius X (r. 1903-1914), "the synthesis of all the heresies." Modernism originated in the atmosphere of revived learning that was fostered by Pope Leo XIII (r. 1878-1903), in which he gave encouragement to the study of science, current sociopolitical processes, and philosophy. Some intellectuals, however, attempted to adopt many of the trends in the thinking of the period to meet the criticisms of theology and the Scriptures. The most influential non-Catholic system then being advanced was Kantianism, from the works of Immanuel Kant (1724-1804), which advanced the ideas of the subjective nature of natural knowledge and the unknowableness of God by natural means. On the basis of much in Kantianism, the Modernists came to consider religion a matter of personal and collective experience, claiming that faith comes naturally from within and is part of human nature that occurs naturally. It is a "religious feeling" or "a kind of motion of the heart," instinctual and inexpressible in any naturalistic definition of religion. The Modernists denied revelation, Scripture, and Church authority, rejecting also the credibility of the Christian faith as supported by historical documentation and miracles. In its most extreme form, it questioned the very divinity of Christ, describing the Church as a sociological institution and Scripture a kind of literature.

While Modernism appeared in a spontaneous fashion in various places, some scholars consider its foundation to rest with the professors at the Institut Catholique, the most famous being Louis Duchesne

(1843-1922). It is a matter of debate as to whether the movement was ever organized, but it did have a large set of important contributors. Among them were Alfred Loisy (1857-1940), Maurice Blondel (1861-1949), Lucien Laberthonnière (1860-1932), Édouard le Roy (1870-1954), Romolo Murri (1870-1944), Antonio Fogazzaro (1842-1911), George Tyrrell (1861-1909), and Friderich von Hügel (1852-1925).

Pope St. Pius X opposed Modernism very strenuously, condemning it in the 1907 decree *Lamentabili* (July 3) and the encyclical *Pascendi dominici gregis* (September 8). These were followed by the *motu proprio Sacrorum antistitum* (1910), requiring an anti-Modernist oath from the clergy. The steps against the Modernists were carried out so vigorously in the next years that a call for moderation was made by Pope Benedict XV (r. 1914-1922).

Möhler, Johann Adam (1796-1838) ● German theologian. Born in Igersheim, he studied at Ellwangen and then Tübingen before entering the seminary of Rottenburg. Ordained in 1819, he held various posts until 1828 when he was appointed professor of theology at Tübingen. He remained at the university until 1835 when he was named to the theological faculty at the University of Munich, lecturing on the exegesis of the NT. In 1838, the king of Bavaria granted him the Order of St. Michael and made him dean of Würzburg Cathedral. He died before he could assume his duties. A remarkable scholar and theologian, Möhler authored a number of important works that stimulated an ecclesiastical and theological revival in the German Church. Chief among his writings was *Symbolik* (1832; English translation, 1843), a profound study on the necessity of finding God only through the Church established by Christ. He also wrote *Die Einheit in der Kirche* (1825; *Unity in the Church*), a life of Athanasius (2 vols., 1827); a Church history (3 vols., 1867-1870); and

Neue en Untersuchung der Lehrgegensätze zwischen Katholiken und Protestanten (1834; *New Examination of the Doctrinal Differences Between Catholics and Protestants*). Möhler was also an advocate for the ultimate reunion of the Protestant and Catholic Churches.

Molina, Luis de (1535-1600) ● Spanish Jesuit theologian and founder of the theological system on grace called Molinism. Born to a noble family at Cuenca, New Castile, Spain, he entered the Society of Jesus at the age of eighteen, studying at Alcalá and then Coimbra, Portugal. After completing his theological and philosophical courses, he was appointed professor of philosophy at Coimbra, serving from 1563-1567, and then chair of theology at Evora, from 1568-1583. He retired in 1590 to his native city of Cuenca to concentrate on continued study and writing. Shortly before his death he took up the post of professor of moral theology in a school recently opened by the Jesuits in Madrid. Aside from his commentary on the *Summa Theologiae* of St. Thomas Aquinas, the first such work written by a Jesuit, Molina's chief and most controversial contribution to theology was the *Concordia* (1588), known in full as the *Concordia liberi arbitrii cum gratiae donis, divina praescientia providentia, praedestinatione et reprobatione*, a complex examination of the difficult issue of reconciling grace and free will. The *Concordia*, in its long and complicated text, formed the basis of the system of Molinism.

Molina was concerned with answering the questions of how efficacious grace (*gratius efficax*), which includes the consent of free will, derives its accepted infallible effect, and how in spite of the efficacy of grace the freedom of the will is not at all impaired. Molinism offered an explanation that, while safeguarding the dogmas of the supremacy and causality of grace and the freedom of the will, was nevertheless at variance with the position of Thomism, which also ensured the safety of those essential points of dogma. The system, as elaborated in the *Concordia*, emphasizes the unrestrained freedom of the will without in any way subtracting from the dignity and efficacy of grace. This was the exact opposite of the Thomistic view, which argued the infallible efficacy of grace without impairing in any way the freedom of the will. In reply to the charge made by Thomists that Molinism gave undue power to human freedom and placed limits upon the supremacy of God, the Molinists presented the doctrine of *scientia media*. In this was stated that God possesses a special knowledge by virtue of his infallibility through which is foreseen from all eternity what response of the human will might be under every circumstance when grace is offered to it. This foreknowledge guides God in the determining of what kind of grace will be given to each person. The Molinists thus argued that it is entirely on God's pleasure alone that the final determination of granting grace rests; he decides who will receive it and who will not. In the dispute that emerged between the Jesuits (who largely adopted Molinism) and the Dominicans (who rejected it), the *scientia media* was one of the key battlegrounds, for through it the Molinist position was given its foundation in terms of direct theological application of its principles.

Molinism was opposed from the start by the Dominicans and other conservative theologians who felt, as noted, that it impaired God's supremacy over his creatures and reduced the efficacy of grace, and that the *scientia media* was a pure invention of Molina and hence a dangerous innovation. A prominent leader of the Dominicans during this period was Dominic Báñez (1528-1604). The dispute eventually reached Roman authorities and in 1594 Pope Clement VIII imposed silence upon both parties. In 1598, he established the *Congregatio de Auxiliis* (1598-1607), which never reached a formal decision and allowed Molinism to be taught in theological programs of study.

Molinos, Miguel de (1640-1696) ● Founder of quietism, the condemned theory of total abandonment to God to the degree that heaven and hell become inconsequential because the perfect soul is incapable of sin and is completely absorbed in God. Molinos was born in Muniesa, Spain, near Saragossa. He studied and was ordained at Valencia, journeying to Rome in 1662 as the procurator for the cause of beatification of the Ven. Jeronimo Simón. Once there, he established himself at the church of Sant' Alfonso, ingratiating himself with many of the most powerful and influential figures in Rome. His teachings soon drew accusations of heresy led by the Jesuits and Dominicans. His very capable defense, however, led to censure for his accusers, but in May 1685 the Holy Office secured his arrest and subsequent imprisonment. On September 3, 1687, he was declared a heretic, sentenced to life imprisonment, compelled to wear penitential garb, and instructed to make confession four times a year. In the bull *Coelestis Pastor* (November 2, 1687), Pope Innocent XI condemned sixty-eight propositions by Molinos. A number of prelates and clergy were caught in the affair, as they had come to practice his quietist doctrines or were in sympathy with him. Chief among his writings was *Guida spirituale* (1675; *Spiritual Guide*). (See also **Fénelon, François.**)

Monarchia Sicula ● Right exercised by the rulers of Sicily, particularly from the sixteenth century. It granted to them the final jurisdiction in matters of religion, since they were free from any influence of the papacy. The custom of Sicilian independence had its origins in the late eleventh century with the issuing of a bull in 1098 by Pope Urban II addressed to King Roger I of Sicily. By its terms, the pontiff agreed to appoint no papal legates without the council of the court and to execute through the court any ecclesiastical decrees or acts. These were subsequently confirmed and clarified by Pope Paschal II. The nature of feudalism in Sicily thus reduced to subservience the Church in the island, but the de facto supremacy of the secular ruler was never formally invoked until the time of Ferdinand II of Aragon, who became king of Sicily in 1468. He had issued the *Liber Monarchiae*, proclaiming his power over the Sicilian Church. King Philip II tried unsuccessfully in 1578 to win complete recognition of the *Monarchia Sicula* from Pope Pius V, but in 1597 the *Index monarchiae Siculae* was appointed, a permanent judge in ecclesiastical matters, from which there was no appeal to the pope. Various pontiffs attempted to negotiate an end to the right, with little success, until finally, in 1867, Pope Pius IX revoked it. The formal revocation from the Italian government came in 1871.

Monarchianism ● Name used by Tertullian to describe heretical theological theories of the second and third centuries. He called them "monarchian" because they placed great stress on the unity, or monarchy, of the Godhead. Monarchianism originated out of a severely orthodox concern for affirming in doctrine a strict monotheism; however, the movement's adherents were drawn into heresy because of the failure to give recognition to the independence of the Son and the Spirit. As developed, there were two major forms of Monarchianism — Adoptionism and modalism. The Adoptionists argued that Jesus was human, receiving divine power from God at some point while on the earth; the modalists, or Sabellians, proposed that the Godhead was undifferentiated, assuming the apparently independent roles of Father, Son, and Spirit in offering salvation. The Council of Nicaea (325) would retain the orthodox tenets of Monarchianism —that there was a unity of the Godhead — while insisting upon the Trinity of individual Persons in the one nature.

Monasticism ● Religious life by which an individual leaves the world and enters into a community whose members, monks, devote themselves to the service of God through prayer, contemplation, solitude, and self-denial. Monasticism has been one of the oldest and most enduring traditions of the Church, both East and West, and the faith has profited enormously from the work of monks throughout its long history. It was not a Christian invention, however, as monastic customs existed in the pre-Christian world, including the Essenes and in the East. In Asia, it was highly developed, most remarkably so in China and Japan. The origins of Christian monasticism date to the second half of the third century (c. 270) in Egypt. There members of the Christian communities, under the influence of Clement of Alexandria and Origen, strove to achieve states of perfection by withdrawing from the world and severing all associations with people and material attachments. They prayed, fasted, labored, studied the Scriptures, and performed penitential exercises to cleanse their souls and bodies. Of these first anchorites (the name used for those who resided in the desert, in cells, or in caves), the greatest was St. Antony (d. c. 356). He attracted other persons and hermits to his way of life and so earned the title Father of Monasticism.

The anchorite life would flower in the Egyptian desert, but it was soon joined by another form of monasticism, the one that would create the basis of the formal monastic orders in later years. This was cenobitism, the life by which a group of like-minded men or women came together to reside in a community under the authority of an abbot or abbess. To St. Pachomius (d. 348) is given credit for the formulation of both the initial concept of the cenobitic life and the first monastery in Upper Egypt.

The appeal of the monastic system swiftly spread across Christian lands and was given extensive theological foundation by St. Basil the Great, who provided two monastic rules. He also insisted that such communities should not only be concerned with labor but with learning. This innovation served to heighten even further the appeal of monasticism so that the official presence of monasteries as contributors to the intellectual life of the Church became highly desirable. Other significant contributions were made by St. Jerome (d. 420), St. Ambrose of Milan (d. 397), St. Martin of Tours (d. c. 399), and especially St. Augustine (d. 430). Under their influence, monasticism in the East became quite important, with respect shown to abbots and notable monks.

In the West, meanwhile, monastic life took longer to take shape, in part because of the loose organizational structure that was in place, creating a situation in which monasteries followed the specific rules laid down by their individual abbots. The more successful and practically applicable rules acquired influence or were adopted *in toto* by other houses. Still, the West lacked a sense of unification. This was provided in large measure by St. Benedict of Nursia (d. c. 550), the so-called founder of Western monasticism. He provided his monks with a useful and eminently flexible rule (see **Benedict, Rule of**) that encapsulated the guiding principles of earlier customs while striving to take consideration of the realistic needs of his monks. Such was the excellence of his rule that it swept across the West and facilitated the rise of the Benedictine order as a major contributor in the civilization of Europe.

St. Gregory the Great

Meanwhile, monasticism reached Ireland from Gaul and flourished to a special degree. Ireland soon emerged as one of the truly great centers of monastic life, Irish monks proving so numerous and zealous that they set out to convert other lands, including Scotland and parts of Germany, Switzerland, and northern Gaul, founding significant houses such as Luxeuil in Gaul and St. Gall in Switzerland. These missionaries were joined by monks from England and the lands of the Franks, so that the faith was brought to Poland, Hungary, Scandinavia, and elsewhere by such missionaries as St. Willibrord (d. 739), St. Boniface (the Apostle of Germany, d. 754), and St. Anskar (the Apostle of the North, d. 865).

During the Carolingian era, bringing with it the so-called Carolingian Renaissance, the development of monastic culture, proceeded steadily. Despite the opposition of St. Benedict of Aniane (d. 821), the Benedictine houses continued to place heavy emphasis on learning and culture, including the arts (such as manuscript illumination). Throughout the Carolingian Renaissance, monasteries became important centers of education, and such sites as Canterbury, Reichenau, St. Gall, Fulda, Malmesbury, and elsewhere were active cultural hubs, providing the surrounding areas with art, learning, and economic involvement, in the absence of any meaningful or substantial civil centers. As a consequence of this, monasteries gradually acquired wealth, influence, and prestige, their abbots receiving royal favors and political rights.

A general reform of the monastic life was begun in 910 with the founding of Cluny, marking what is considered the zenith of monasticism in the West from the tenth through the thirteenth centuries. The Cluniac Reform, with its call to greater prayer (choir office) and unity among the houses, found wide appeal and by 1100 there were several thousand Cluniac houses. Cluny would have a profound effect on the Church, serving as an example of the extent of restored spiritual vigor that was attainable. The Gregorian Reform of the eleventh century, especially under Pope St. Gregory VII (r. 1073-1085), drew much inspiration from Cluny.

At the same time, monasteries remained rich cultural places. Monks were chroniclers and historians (such as Matthew Paris and Gervase of Canterbury), theologians (St. Bernard of Clairvaux and William of St. Thierry), artisans, and even architects. Abbot Suger of St. Denis (d. 1151) would serve as regent to King Louis VII of France, and his church at St. Denis would be a vital element in the flourishing of Gothic architecture. As a result of the work of the Cistercians, advances were made in agriculture and animal husbandry. While most agreed that the secular involvements of the monks had a generally positive influence — St. Bernard of Clairvaux, for example — many members of the monastic orders desired a return to the religious and spiritual simplicity of earlier times. Thus were founded the stricter orders of the Carthusians, Camaldolese, and Vallambrosians, and the heightened pursuit of seclusion by the Cistercians.

From the thirteenth century, decline set in throughout Western monasticism. The causes were found in the widespread relaxation of rules, a frequent mediocrity on the part of the abbots, and, most of all, the flowering of the mendicant orders (particularly the Dominicans, Franciscans, and Carmelites), who drew away many potential members to their new call of service to the Church. A revival of the Benedictine order took place in the late fourteenth century, but such reforms did little to prepare monasticism for the onslaught of the Protestant Reformation.

Martin Luther was vicious in his attacks upon monasteries, and in those lands where the reformation took hold, monasteries were suppressed, monks expelled or executed, and the treasures — both cultural and intellectual — were routinely carried off, burned, or destroyed. The worst damage was done in the Scandinavian countries and in England where King Henry VIII (r. 1509-1547) pillaged and dissolved the communities (see **Dissolution of the Monasteries**).

The Council of Trent (1545-1563) and the

Catholic Reformation brought strong decrees of reform, centralization, and revitalization that not only saved monasticism in the West from possible extinction but gave it new life and direction. Two of the foremost congregations born out of the Catholic Reformation were the Maurists (the Benedictine Congregation of St. Maur, founded in 1621), which focused on scholarship (see **Mabillon, Jean**), and the Trappists (Cistercians of the Strict Observance, O.C.S.O.) begun at La Trappe in 1662 by Abbot Armand de Rancé (1626-1700).

Having endured the cataclysm of the Reformation and then the challenges of the Enlightenment, the monasteries were faced next by the French Revolution and the devastating Napoleonic Wars (1796-1815). Monastic houses were wiped out in France, Switzerland, Germany, and elsewhere. In the years that followed, a rebirth of monasticism took place, extending throughout the nineteenth century. Distinguished leaders, including Dom Prosper Guéranger, oversaw the creation of new houses in France, Belgium, England, America, and Australia. Today, the monastic orders continue to make large contributions to the Church. The Benedictines are one of the largest religious orders with some nine thousand members worldwide; thousands more belong to the Trappists, Cistercians, Carthusians, and Camaldolese.

Monica, St. (331-387) ● Mother of St. Augustine of Hippo. Born probably in Thagaste, she was raised a Christian, marrying a local official named Patricius. She bore three children before his death, the eldest being Augustine. Anxious for her son to succeed, she was surprised and disappointed by the contempt he felt for Christianity and she was upset by his affair with an unknown woman. She prayed earnestly for his conversion, remembering the declaration of a clergyman to whom she

had told her troubles, "It is impossible that the son of so many tears will be lost." When Augustine journeyed to Rome in 383, Monica followed, first to the Eternal City and then Milan. There she came under the influence of St. Ambrose. Her son's conversion was the source of great joy to Monica, after which she retired to Cassiciacum. Deciding to return to Africa, she made it only to Ostia, where she died. Augustine recorded a long series of dialogues with her in *De Ordine* and *De Beata Vita*. Her relics were transferred in 1430 by Pope Martin V from Ostia to Rome. Feast day: August 27.

Monita Secreta ● Alleged secret instructions that were supposedly sent by Claudius Aquaviva, the fifth general of the Society of Jesus, to the superiors of the order, providing them with the blueprint to be followed in increasing the influence of the society. According to the ultimately discredited orders, the programs included using every possible means — legal and moral or otherwise — to add wealth, prestige, and territories to the holdings of the order; included were the conniving to take lands from widows and luring into the order of rich young men who would then hand over their estates. First appearing in Cracow in 1612 and purporting to be a translation from the Spanish, the *Monita Secreta* were quickly denounced as an absolute fabrication both by the Jesuits and the important prelate, Bishop Lipski of Cracow, in 1616. Acknowledged today as false and scurrilous, they were actually the work of Jerome Zahorowski, a Pole who had been discharged from the Jesuits in 1613.

Monophysitism ● Also Monophysism. A heresy of the fifth and sixth centuries teaching that there was but one nature in the Person of Christ, a divine one. It was opposed to the orthodox doctrine established at the Council of Chalcedon (451) in which the doctrine of the two natures of Christ was upheld. Stemming in part from a reaction to Nestorianism, it found development in the writings of the monk Eutyches (d. 454), who was condemned by the synod at Constantinople. Subsequent views among theologians ranged from highly radical (Julian, bishop of Halicarnassus, d. c. 518) to moderate (Severus, patriarch of Constantinople, 553). Condemned at the second Council of Constantinople (553), the Monophysites continued to find support in Syria, Armenia, and especially among Coptic Christians in Egypt. Several attempts were made to effect a reconciliation, such as the efforts of Emperors Zeno (r. 474-491) and Justinian I (r. 527-565), but the Monophysites remained firm. Any hopes of a reunion were ended with the Islamic conquest of Syria and Egypt. (See also **Monothelitism**, following entry.)

Monothelitism ● Also Monothelism. A heresy of the seventh century claiming that Christ possessed two natures but one will. The doctrine originated in the theological effort to secure a reconciliation of the Monophysites with Orthodox Christianity in the hope of organizing a unified religious force against the inroads of the Persian Empire and later the Islamic armies. Emperor Heraclius (r. 610-641), in meeting with the Monophysites, stated the idea that Christ was endowed with two natures but only one will. He received support from Sergius, patriarch of Constantinople, and, in part, from Pope Honorius I, who wrote the famous opinion about Christ's one will. This view was then condemned by his successors, causing a breach with the Eastern Church. An important theological correction of Monothelitism was written by St. Maximus the Confessor (d. 662), in which he argued that the number of Christ's wills is a function of the nature of Christ and not his unity of person. Monothelitism was condemned by several councils, most importantly the Council of Constantinople (680), which affirmed that Christ had two wills, divine and human.

Montalembert, Count Charles (1810-1870) ● In full, Charles-Forbes-René, count of Montalembert, a French historian and liberal. Born in England, he was the son of a French soldier who had served in an English cavalry regiment and had announced to King Louis XVIII that the French monarchy had been restored with the fall of Napoleon. Montalembert grew up in England but studied in Paris and developed a liberal philosophical tendency that soon brought him into contact with Félicité Lamennais and other prominent Catholic liberals. While on a visit to Ireland in 1830, Montalembert received the early ideas for the newspaper *L'Avenir* (*The Future*), which was established by Lamennais in October 1830. He met Lamennais in November 1830 and thereafter energetically helped the paper. The controversial publication soon compelled him to go on a trip to Rome to attempt to secure papal approval. Pope Gregory XVI, however, issued the encyclical *Mirari vos* (1832). Montalembert submitted immediately and ultimately ceased his association with de Lamennais. Remaining a liberal, Montalembert authored a number of historical works and other writings, including *Les Moines d' Occident* (5 vols., 1860-1867) on the origins of monasticism that had begun as an effort to write a biography of St. Bernard of Clairvaux.

Montanism ● Heresy that originated in the latter half of the second century in the region of Phrygia (in Asia Minor). An apocalyptic and semimystical movement, it was started by a prophet from Phrygia named Montanus. He believed that a holy Jerusalem was soon going to descend upon the Phrygian village of Pepuza and, with the help of two disciples, Prisca and Maximilla, he preached intense asceticism, personal purity, fasting, and a burning desire to suffer martyrdom. Montanists, as the members of the movement were called, accepted the idea that such a lifestyle was essential to prepare for the impending return of Christ and because sins after birth could not be forgiven. While opposed by many bishops in Asia Minor, Montanism spread throughout the region and by the third century the movement had become organized into a virtual Church. It achieved its greatest success in 207 with the conversion of Tertullian to their cause. The leadership was ultimately excommunicated and the movement died out in most of the Roman Empire. It lingered in Phrygia for several centuries before finally disappearing.

Monte Cassino ●

Famed monastery situated on a hill between Rome and Naples. It is the principal house of the Benedictine order and one of the cradles of Western monasticism. Monte Cassino was founded around 529 by St. Benedict of Nursia after his flight from Subiaco to escape the cruel treatment given him by the priest Florentius. Assisted by Sts. Maurus and Placid, he found the hill to be perfectly suited to his needs; it had been one of the pieces of land given to him by Placid's father, Tertullus. Benedict took up residence in one of the towers of a wall that had surrounded a onetime temple to Apollo, using this as the basis of the community that was subsequently established.

The history of the monastery since the death of Benedict is one of prayer and work, interrupted by periods of war and other catastrophes, natural and man-made. Monte Cassino was sacked a number of times during the Middle Ages: by the Lombards (580), the Saracens (884), the Normans (1046), and the troops of Emperor Frederick II (1239). The attack in 1239 compelled the family of young Thomas Aquinas to withdraw him from the monastery and send him to the

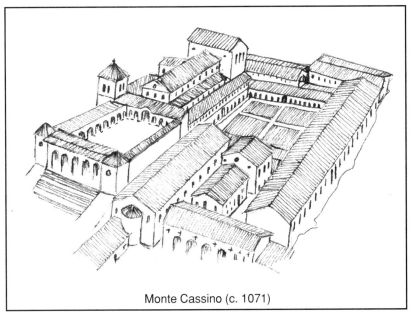

Monte Cassino (c. 1071)

University of Naples. An earthquake struck in 1349, but the damage caused by this natural disaster was nothing compared to the wholesale destruction of Monte Cassino in 1944 during World War II. Its vast and important holdings of art and books were spared annihilation in the conflict, and Pope Paul VI consecrated the new buildings on October 24, 1964. Among the most notable abbots were Petronax (seventh-eighth century), Desiderius (eleventh century), and Oderisius (also eleventh century). (See also **Benedictines**.)

Montfaucon, Bernard de (1653-1741) ●

French Maurist scholar who is generally credited as the founder of Greek paleography. Born in the Château de Soulage, Languedoc, France, he entered the Académie des Cadets at Perpignan at the age of thirteen, in anticipation of a military career. He subsequently fought in the Battle of Marienthal in 1673 and fell ill in Saverne. As the result of a vow made to the Blessed Mother, he gave up the military life and in 1676 entered the Benedictine Congregation of St. Maur. Sent to Toulouse, he studied Greek at the Abbey of Soreze and was then moved to various houses before being sent to Paris in 1687. There, at the Abbey of St.-Germain-des-Prés, Montfaucon participated in the great work of the Maurists, initially assisting in the preparation of an edition of the Greek Fathers. He also studied Coptic, Syriac, Hebrew, and Chaldean and was appointed in 1694 as curator of the numismatic collection of the abbey. In 1698, he embarked on a tour of Italy to study important manuscripts, receiving a warm reception in Rome, most notably by Pope Innocent XII. A brief period as procurator-general in Rome ended in 1701 with his return to France. His remaining years were devoted to study. An important scholar, he was largely responsible for the study of Greek texts and helped lay the foundation for modern archaeology. His chief writings included the monumental *Palaeographia Graeca* (1708), *L'Antiquité expliquée et representée en figures* (10 vols., 1719; *Antiquity Explained and Represented in Figures*), and *Monuments de la Monarchie française* (5 vols., 1729-1733; *Monuments of the French Monarchy*), with a dedication to King Louis XV.

Montfort, Louis de, St. (1673-1716) ● Also known as Grignion de Montfort. A noted missionary and founder of the Sisters of Wisdom, he was born at Montfort in Brittany. He studied at the Jesuit College of Rennes and was ordained in 1700. From an early time, he devoted himself to the care of the sick and the poor, serving from 1701-1703 as chaplain of the hospital in Poitiers. There, in 1703, he established the Sisters of

Wisdom to nurse the sick among the poor and to teach in schools that were free for the poverty-stricken. A talented preacher, he soon began working as a missioner to French towns and cities, encountering opposition from both secular and religious leaders who disliked his methods and Jansenists who feared his sermons. Nevertheless, he was a very popular figure among the people, so much so that around 1715 he was able to found the Company of Mary, a congregation of priests to continue his important work. He is the author of *Traité de la vraie devotion á la Saint Vierge* (*Treatise on True Devotion to the Blessed Virgin*), which was lost for several hundred years but was rediscovered in 1842. Since that time, it has been printed in many languages. Montfort was canonized by Pope Pius XII in 1947. Feast day: April 28.

Mont-St.-Michel ● Benedictine monastery. Situated just off the Normandy coast in France near the town of St. Malo, it is distinguished for being connected to the mainland by a causeway accessible only at low tide. Mont-St.-Michel was first established as an oratory by St. Aubert, bishop of Avranches. According to tradition, St. Aubert founded the oratory at the command of St. Michael the Archangel. A monastery was built in 966, but the original buildings were reinforced by a fortress and walls. The structures facing the sea, called *La Merveille* (1203-1208), remain truly magnificent Gothic creations. Besieged during the Hundred Years' War, the monastery-fortress was never captured. The monks were thrown out during the French Revolution and the monastery was converted into a political prison. Leased to the bishop of Avranches (1183), the French government took over the site in 1872 as a national monument. In 1922, it once again became a place of worship.

Morality Plays ● See **Plays**.

Mont-St.-Michel

More, Dame Gertrude (1606-1633) ● English Benedictine nun. More was the daughter of Cresacre More (grandson of St. Thomas More) and daughter of Elizabeth Gage (sister of the chamberlain of Queen Mary, Sir George Gage). Born in Essex, England, she was largely raised by her father after the death of her mother. In 1623, she entered at Cambrai the English Benedictine congregation as one of the first postulants. Her novitiate was much troubled by personal doubts, and with reluctance she made her final vows on January 1, 1625. Continued hesitations and temptations plagued her until she came under the influence of Dom Augustine Baker, who taught her in the formulation of the interior life. In 1629, despite her young age, she was nearly made abbess, but she was nevertheless honored as the foundress. She died on August 17, 1633. Her writings were published after her death and include *The Holy Practice of a Divine Lover, or the Saintly Ideot's Devotions* (1657) and *Ideot's Devotions* (1658), to which was added her *Apology*, explaining her method of prayer and defending her spiritual guide.

More, Thomas, St. (1478-1535) ● Lord chancellor of England, humanist, scholar, and one of the most famous martyrs. He was born in London, the son of Sir John More, a lawyer and later a judge, and Agnes Granger. After attending St. Anthony's School in London, he became a page (c. 1490) in the household of John Morton, cardinal and archbishop of Canterbury. Around 1492 he was sent to Oxford where he began to study Greek, beginning a lifelong interest in the classics. After two years, however, he left Oxford at his father's request and transferred to the study of law in 1496. In 1501, he was called to the bar, lectured at Furnivall's Inn for several years, and in 1504 was elected to Parliament. While still very interested in Greek and classicism — he attended lectures on Aristotle by Linacre — he was also drawn to a life of great spirituality. He lectured on Augustine's *City of God*. Thomas, however, decided against a clerical life or celibacy, marrying Jane Colt in 1505, perhaps on the advice of his spiritual adviser, John Colet. He had three daughters and one son. Jane died in 1511, and that same year Thomas married the widow Alice Middleton. Throughout this period he was a close associate of such notables as William Grocyn and Desiderius Erasmus.

More's rise as a statesman began in 1510, one year after the accession of King Henry VIII (d. 1547). He held numerous posts in swift succession: undersheriff of London (1510); part of a mission to Flanders (1515), described in *Utopia*; a member of a mission to Calais (1517); master of requests and a royal councillor (1518); a companion to King Henry on his famous trip to the Continent during which the monarch met King Francis I of France and Emperor Charles V on the Field of the Cloth of Gold (1520); knighted (1521); speaker of the House of Commons (1523); high steward for the University of Cambridge and chancellor of the duchy of Lancaster (1525); and in 1529, chancellor of England to succeed Cardinal Wolsey who had fallen from royal favor for failing to secure a divorce between Henry and Catherine of Aragon.

More resigned as chancellor on May 16, 1532, because of his irreconcilable opposition to the king's divorce. He chose to live in retirement but was deprived of virtually his entire income. When he refused to take the Oath of Succession he was arrested and sent to the Tower of London on April 17, 1534. While in prison for over a year he devoted himself to prayer, authoring *Dialogue of Comfort against Tribulation* (published in 1553) but leaving unfinished the *Treatise upon the Passion* (published in 1557). Doomed even before the start of the trial, he was convicted and condemned on July 1, 1535, largely through the perjury of

Richard Rich (later chancellor himself). More was beheaded on July 6, 1535.

One of the foremost intellectuals of his time, More was a prolific writer. His works in Latin, aside from *Utopia*, were epigrams, translations of Lucian's dialogues (1506), and a defense of King Henry's treatise *Assertio Septem Sacramentorum* (on behalf of the sacraments), which had been attacked by Martin Luther. More's treatise *Responsio ad convitia Martin Lutheri* (1523) was released under the pseudonym Gulielmus Rosseus. His works in English included a translation from the Latin of the life of Pico della Mirandola; *The Four Last Things* (1522); *Dialogue Concerning Heresies and Confutation of Tyndale's Answer*, his entry into the debate over the English Reformation and a refutation of the work of the Protestant William Tyndale; and a *History* of Richard III, which did much to establish that ruler as a villain of history. His chief writing was, of course, *Utopia*, composed in Latin in 1516 while More was in Europe. First published in Holland, it was translated thirty-five years later into English. A brilliant criticism of contemporary English society, it offers a fictional island nation called Utopia where an ideal republic exists that is governed by the natural law. Throughout, he satirizes the customs and systems found in Europe. *Utopia* has two parts; the first part, written after the second (describing Utopia), is an introduction in which More meets the traveler Raphael Hythloday, who tells him of Utopia. Beatified in 1886, he was canonized in 1935 by Pope Pius XI, although he was long revered as a great martyr. Feast day: June 22, with St. John Fisher.

Morin, Jean (1591-1659) ● French Oratorian priest and learned scholar. Born at Blois, in central France, on the Loire, Morin was raised a Calvinist but was converted by Cardinal Duperron in 1617. He entered the Oratorians in Paris the following year. After holding several posts, including attendance upon Queen Henrietta of France in England (the wife of King Charles I) in 1625, Morin returned to Paris. There he devoted himself to scholarly research, assuming such a reputation for learning that Pope Urban VIII summoned him to Rome; he spent nine months serving as an important adviser (1639-1640) on the possible reunion of the Eastern and Western Churches. Recalled to Paris at the behest of Cardinal Richelieu, Morin was frequently consulted by the Assembly of French Clergy. Among his writings were: *Commentarius historicus de disciplina in administratione sacramenti Poenitentiae* (1651), on the sacrament of penance; *Commentarius de sacris Ecclesiae ordinationibus* (1655), on holy orders; and *Excercitationes biblicae de Hebraei Graecique textus sinceritate . . .* (1663), on the Bible.

Morone, Giovanni (1509-1580) ● Italian cardinal and bishop of Modena. A member of an important noble family of Milan, he was named at the age of twenty to the see of Modena by Pope Clement VII, an appointment that caused some difficulties with Cardinal Ippolito d'Este, who had been promised the see himself. Morone was thus unable to occupy his episcopal office until 1532, and then only by paying off the cardinal. He soon distinguished himself as a skilled diplomat, holding a number of prominent positions as a representative: to France for Clement VII in 1529; to Milan for Paul III in 1535; and to Germany in 1536 for Paul, at the court of the future Emperor Ferdinand I. As a nuncio, he took part in the Diets of Hagenau (1540), Ratisbon, or Regensburg (1541), and Speyer (1542), distinguishing himself as a member of the moderates in the matter of dealing with Luther and the Reformists. On June 2, 1542, Morone was made cardinal by Pope Paul III, and later in the year was honored with Cardinals Parisie and Pole in being appointed president of the forthcoming Council of Trent. He did not, however, participate in the early

sessions, since he was sent as a legate to Bologna. Under the stern Pope Paul IV, however, Morone's moderate views and reputation for liberality caused his imprisonment in 1557 in Castel Sant' Angelo. He remained confined until 1560 when a complete reexamination of the case against him for heresy was ordered by Pope Pius IV; Morone was cleared of all charges. Pius subsequently used him to promulgate the decrees of Trent. He was later sent on a diplomatic mission to Genoa (1576), served as a papal legate at the Diet of Ratisbon (1576), and was cardinal protector of England (1578-1579).

Motet ● Type of musical composition in polyphonic style. Customarily a three-voice composition arranged in a rhythmic pattern, the motet was established on the basis of melodies found in the Gregorian chant. The origin of the name, however, is obscure, the most commonly accepted derivation being from the French *mot* (word) or the Latin *motus* (movement). It is believed that the motet was early on restricted to France; the oldest specimens of motets in sacred music are preserved in a manuscript of the work *Ars compositiones de motetis*, by Philip de Vitry, bishop of Meaux, written around 1320. A number of years passed, however, before other composers undertook to produce motets; these fifteenth-century figures of note included Dunstable, Dufay, and Brasart. Development of the polyphonic motet was heightened from the late fifteenth to the early sixteenth centuries (c. 1480-1520), with notable composers being Josquin Despréz and Eleazar Genet. The height of motet composition came from around 1560-1620 with the magnificent works of Palestrina, Byrd, and especially Orlandus Lassus. Lassus alone composed some eight hundred motets. Instrumental accompaniment became commonplace in the late seventeenth century, enduring in the form until the reign of Pope St. Pius X; through his *motu proprio* in 1910, he revived the polyphonic motets of the early eras, marking a return to unaccompanied music.

Mother Teresa ● See **Teresa, Mother**.

Mozarabic Rite ● Non-Roman liturgical rite that was in use in Spain from the earliest period of Christianity in the Iberian Peninsula until the eleventh century. The term Mozarabic is not itself entirely appropriate, as it normally refers only to those parts of the peninsula that fell under the control of the Moors from 711; nevertheless, Mozarabic came to be used for the rite that was present in the region and has never been replaced by a more suitable name. The rite developed very early in the Church in the peninsula, with references made to it by various national councils and in the writings of St. Leander, bishop of Seville (d. c. 600 or 601), St. Ildefonsus, archbishop of Toledo (d. 667), and especially St. Isidore of Seville in his *De ecclesiasticis officiis*, one of the most valuable sources for details on the rite; there is also a letter written by Pope Vigilius (c. 554). The councils were concerned most with establishing a uniformity to the rite, an effort clear from the decrees of the Fourth Council of Toledo in 633. Further development took place under the guidance of several archbishops of Toledo who, along with others, composed Masses and added innovations and contemporary flavor to the services. Only one service book is extant from the years prior to the invasion of Spain by the Muslims in the eighth century, the *Verona liber orationalis*. The influence of the rite was found in the Gallican liturgy.

Efforts were made starting in the eleventh century to end the use of the rite and to replace it with the Roman rite. Popes Alexander II (r. 1061-1073) and Gregory VII (r. 1073-1085) attempted to abolish it, and at the Council of Burgos (1080) the Roman rite was ordered adopted by the churches in the kingdoms of León and Castile. Pockets of adherents remained, however, such as the six parishes in Toledo that demanded its retention after the conquest of the city from the Moors in 1085. Cardinal Francisco Ximénez de Cisneros, archbishop of Toledo (1495-1517), secured papal approval for the Mozarabic rite to be used in the cathedral and the six parishes; he also had a missal (1500) and a breviary (1502) to be printed. The rite has survived into modern times, with interest in recent years reviving the hopes of some who wish to see many of its elements used in a Spanish liturgy. A Mozarabic Mass was celebrated during the proceedings of Vatican Council II. Today, it is customarily reserved to semiprivate celebration in a chapel of the Toledo Cathedral.

Munificentissimus Deus ● Apostolic constitution issued on November 1, 1950, by Pope Pius XII, giving formal definition to the doctrine of the Assumption of the Virgin Mary. According to the constitution, Pius wrote: "By the authority of Our Lord Jesus Christ, of the Blessed Apostles Peter and Paul, and by Our Own authority, We pronounce, declare, and define as divinely revealed dogma: The Immaculate Mother of God, Mary ever Virgin, after her life on earth, was assumed, body and soul to the glory of heaven" (III, 44). While causing some controversy with the Orthodox Church and some Protestant denominations, especially the Anglican Church, the constitution was widely proclaimed in the Church as proclaiming the place of the BVM in the life of the Church. Further, it demonstrated profoundly the important role of tradition in the functioning of the Church's magisterium.

Muratori, Ludovico Antonio (1672-1750) ● Italian theologian and scholar as well as discoverer of the so-called Muratorian Fragment. After an early education by the Jesuits, Muratori studied at the University of Modena. Ordained in 1694 or 1695, he was summoned by Count Charles Borromeo to the famed Ambrosiana (the Ambrosian Library) in Milan. There he distinguished himself for his work in collecting previously unedited ancient writings. In 1700, Rinaldo I, duke of Modena, named him as librarian and archivist in the Library of Modena. This position he held until his death, although on 1716 he was also named provost of Sta. Maria della Pomposa, serving until 1733. A historian and theological writer, Muratori authored a vast body of works. Among his chief works were: *Rerum Italicarum Scriptores* (25 vols., 1723-1751; *Writings on Italian Affairs*); *Antiquitates Italicae Medii Aevi* (6 vols., 1738-1748), on Italian medieval history; *Annali d' Italia* (12 vols., 1744-1749), on general Italian history; and *Liturgica Romanum Vetus* (2 vols., 1748). Attacked by some circles for his theological writings, he was investigated by the Spanish Inquisition, but protection was given him by Pope Benedict XIV. He was also much esteemed by Cardinal Giovanni Ganganelli, the future Pope Clement XIV. (See also **Muratorian Fragment**, following entry.)

Muratorian Fragment ● Also called the Muratorian Canon, it is the oldest surviving list of canonical NT writings, written in Latin and dated to the second century. The list was found by Ludovico Muratori in the Ambrosian Library of Milan and was published in 1740. It is generally assumed that it was composed by St. Hippolytus and has been dated to the late second century because of references to Pope St. Pius I (r. 140-155), Basilides, and Marcion, all belonging to that era. Some eighty-five lines long, the fragment includes the four Gospels, the Acts, thirteen letters of Paul, the pastoral letters of 1 and 2 Timothy and Titus, Philemon, the letters of Jude, two letters of John, the Wisdom of Solomon, the Apocalypse of John, the Apocalypse of Peter, and the *Shepherd* of Hermas (listed as a book of private devotions). Written in poor Latin, the manuscript is indeed fragmentary, since the beginning is missing, as is probably the ending.

Music ● Music used by the Church in liturgical services or to give glory and praise to God as well as to foster the edification of the worshipers. Church music has always played a part in the liturgical services of the Church, a fact noted by Pope St. Pius X in 1903: "The Church has always recognized and honored progress in the arts, admitting to the service of religion everything good and beautiful discovered by genius in the course of ages — always, however, with due regard to the Liturgical laws."

Experts in Church music note that the use of music is traced to Christ himself. At the Last Supper he sang hymns with his disciples (Mk 14:26). In Jewish custom, music had a major role in the religious activities in the Temple and the daily lives of the Jews. It was not surprising, then, that music should find its way into the nascent Christian communities. Singing, however, was probably influenced by various external factors, such as new conversions from among Gentiles who did not know the Jewish songs, and the need for restraint in the face of persecutions. That singing did occur in the early Church is regularly attested by writers during the period: Tertullian, Eusebius of Caesarea in the *Ecclesiastical History*, St. Jerome, and St. Augustine. It was customary to sing (or at least recite) psalms; St. Athanasius insisted on their being recited while Ambrose promoted the antiphonal singing of psalms.

From the foundation established with Jewish hymns, psalms, canticles, and other compositions, there was developed a broader system of musical expression, in large part through the formation of the *schola cantorum*, the singing school of Rome under Pope St. Gregory I the Great (r. 590-604). The chief musical form of the Middle Ages for the Church was monody, which is defined as a single, unaccompanied melodic line. Monody is better known under the name plainsong (plainchant) or, more popularly, Gregorian chant. Plainsong (*cantus planus*) would undergo continued usage until the advent of polyphony, but by that time it had grown decidedly due to abuses of composers and a willingness to experiment beyond its original simple form. Polyphony replaced plainsong in the fifteenth century and was increasingly adopted for liturgical celebrations. This process could not be reversed, despite the efforts of the Council of Trent (1545-1563) to encourage Gregorian chant. The first Catholic hymnbook was published in 1537, marking the increase of congregation singing. The rise of singing in the vernacular opened a new era that continued into modern times and was characterized by a loss of the vital interconnectedness of music with the liturgy itself. The ornamental nature in much of contemporary Church music was noted by Pope St. Pius X in his *motu proprio* of November 22, 1903.

Vatican Council II, in the "Constitution on the Sacred Liturgy" (*Sacrosanctum Concilium*), stressed the need for Church music: "Liturgical action is given a more noble form when sacred rites are solemnized in song, with the assistance of sacred ministers and the active participation of the people" (No. 113). Moreover, "Composers, filled with the Christian spirit, should feel that their vocation is to cultivate sacred music and increase its store of treasures" (No. 121). The instruction on music to be used in the liturgy is the *Musicam Sacram*, issued by the Sacred Congregation of Rites; it provides the essential norms to be followed in preparing for the use of liturgical music. (See also **Ambrosian Chant**, **Gregorian Chant**, and **Motet**.)

Mystery Plays ● See under **Plays**.

Mystici Corporis Christi ● Encyclical issued on June 29, 1943, by Pope Pius XII. It examines in deep theological terms the description of the Church as the Mystical Body of Christ. As Pope Pius wrote: "If we would define and describe this true Church of Jesus Christ — which is the holy, catholic, apostolic, Roman Church — we shall find no expression more noble, more sublime or divine than the phrase which calls it 'the mystical body of Jesus Christ.' This title is derived from and is, as it were, the fair flower of the repeated teachings of Sacred Scriptures and the holy Fathers." Christ is the head of the Church and "It was on the tree of the cross, finally, that he entered into possession of his Church. . . . Christ must also be acknowledged head of the Church for this reason that, since supernatural gifts have found their supreme fullness and perfection in him, it is from the fullness that his mystical body receives."

The Church is mystical because of that crucial union between Christ and the Church: "It is far superior to any other human societies, it surpasses them as grace surpasses nature, as things immortal are above all those that perish." The Church is a "Body" because it was Christ who "began the building of the mystical temple of the Church when by his preaching he announced his precepts; he completed it when he hung glorified on the cross; and he manifested it and proclaimed it when he sent the Holy Spirit, the Paraclete, in visible form on his disciples." Pope Pius also used the encyclical to warn all Catholics about falling into errors that could endanger the faith. He concludes by commending the Church to the protection of the Blessed Virgin.

Mystics ● See TABLE 9.

Nag Hammadi ● Site in Upper Egypt, approximately sixty miles south of Luxor. There, in 1945, in a onetime pagan cemetery, a clay jar containing thirteen papyrus codices was discovered. Eleven of the codices were completely intact, including their original leather bindings. The codices preserved a virtual Gnostic library of treatises; thus the Nag Hammadi find was the most important of all discoveries related to Gnosticism, as it provided scholars with firsthand writings by the Gnostics on their own doctrines. Previously they had been known only through the often severely critical works of Church Fathers. Interestingly, the various treatises were written in Coptic and were almost certainly translated from the Greek. Among the more notable works contained within the codices were the Apocalypses of James (preserved on the fifth codex) and the apocryphal Epistle of James (on the first codex); all three of these were influenced by Gnostic teachings.

Scholars have noted that the portrait given of the Gnostics and their doctrines by patristic writings was based upon the Nag Hammadi papyri and was a remarkably accurate one. The papyri are preserved in the Coptic Museum of Cairo.

Nails, Holy ● Relics purported to be the nails used to crucify Christ. Generally held to be quite difficult to authenticate, there have been around thirty different nails that some have claimed to belong to the original set used on Calvary. Among the most famous of the nails were the ones supposedly used in the bridle of Constantine the Great's horse, the one added to his imperial diadem, and the one dipped into the Adriatic to calm a raging storm (as recorded by Gregory of Tours). The questions surrounding the nails have been compounded by the issue of how many nails were actually used, with some scholars traditionally accepting three, others preferring four. Medieval treatments of the Crucifixion often depicted four nails, a number supported by historical writers. Later medieval art only depicted three nails, supported by such works as the poem *Christus patiens* (attributed to St. Gregory of Nazianzus).

Nantes, Edict of ● Edict issued by King Henry IV of France on April 13, 1598. It stipulated the rights of the French Protestants, the Huguenots. By its terms, the Huguenots possessed complete freedom of private worship and freedom of public worship in certain towns. Further, around two hundred cities were granted to the Protestants to fortify and defend, and royal subsidies were granted to Protestant schools. Justice was to be applied with strict fairness by the courts and government. Breaches of the edict occurred throughout the seventeenth century, particularly during the time of Richelieu (1585-1642). King Louis XIV ultimately revoked the edict on October 18, 1685.

Napoleon Bonaparte (1769-1821) ● Emperor of France from 1804-1814 (and again briefly in 1815). Brilliant military figure and the preeminent political leader in Europe in the early nineteenth century, Napoleon

Bonaparte was born in Ajaccio, Corsica, one year after Corsica became a French possession. Thereby born a Frenchman, he studied at the École Militaire in Paris and subsequently received a commission as an artillery officer. A true military genius, he applied his vast talents, with a ruthless ambition and self-will, to advancing his career. His progress was astonishingly swift: in 1794, he helped break the English siege of Toulon; that same year he suppressed a royalist uprising thus saving the Republic; and in 1795, he was given command of the bedraggled army of Italy. In a series of swift campaigns (1796-1797) he destroyed the Austrians in Italy and forced upon them the Treaty of Campo Formio (1797). His campaigns also made possible the removal of Pope Pius VI from Rome and the looting of the Vatican, the first of several outrages committed against the Church under Napoleon and his minions. In 1798, he invaded Egypt, won the Battle of the Pyramids, and then withdrew to France where he took the leading part in the coup d'etat of 18 *Brumaire* (November 9) by which he became virtual ruler of France through the foundation of the Consulate (1799-1804).

Napoleon Bonaparte

control over it. He found the authority of the pope over the French Church quite irksome and made as a chief target of his religious policy the rendering of the French clergy compliant. He thus entered into negotiations with Pope Pius VII (r. 1800-1823), ultimately reaching the Concordat of 1801, to which he cunningly added the Organic Articles enabling the state to exercise extensive controls over the Church. The basic tenets of the concordat, however, would remain in place for a century.

In 1804, Napoleon proclaimed himself emperor, convincing Pius to come to Paris and crown him. The assumption of the imperial dignity sparked another round of European wars. The Austrians and Russians were routed at Austerlitz in 1805, the Prussians at Jena-Auerstadt in 1806, the Russians again in 1807, and the Austrians once more in 1809. This last campaign was exceedingly difficult for Napoleon, made even more so by fact that by now he was engaged in a full war in Spain, which he had invaded in 1808. Spanish opposition, already bitter over nationalistic feeling, was fueled to greater depths of hostility over Napoleon's treatment of the Church in the years since the concordat. These sentiments were echoed in staunchly Catholic areas such as Belgium.

As consul, Bonaparte recognized the necessity and desirability of improving relations with the Church, especially after the difficult years of the French Revolution. As a dictator, he preferred to have one state religion to unify the people and then to enjoy

Napoleon suppressed many monasteries in Spain and elsewhere, and closed Church schools and universities, which he looked upon as beds of resistance to his government. Far more severe was his policy against the papacy. Owing to papal intransigence, Napoleon sent an army into Rome in 1808, and the next year the Papal States were added to the French Empire. Pius was soon arrested and deported to Grenoble and then Savona. In 1812, the pope was moved to Fontainebleau where he remained in uncomfortable incarceration until 1814 and the fall of Napoleon from power. The emperor's political and military demise began with the cataclysmically disastrous invasion of Russia that witnessed the destruction of the *Grande Armée*, a host that had numbered at one point half a million men. In 1813, the Allies (Russia, Austria, Prussia, Saxony, Sweden, and others) defeated the emperor at Leipzig and then, in early 1814, captured Paris after finally overcoming Napoleon's smaller army in a campaign in France that displayed his still formidable military prowess. He would return from exile at Elba in 1815 to fight the famed Waterloo Campaign, losing the battle and his crown on June 18, 1815, to the English under the duke of Wellington and the Prussians under Field Marshal Gebhard von Blücher.

He died on May 5, 1821, on St. Helena, the island off the African coast where he had endured years of often melancholy banishment. Remembered today as one of history's greatest generals, Napoleon in his own time was hated by Catholics all over Europe. Ruthlessly determined to subject the Church to his will, he perceived its value to his regime as a formidable element in society and a source of influence and prestige as a willing ally. His view of the Church was summed up by the statement "I don't see in religion the mystery of the incarnation, but the mystery of the social order." As for himself, he had a sincere faith in his own abilities and was utterly pragmatic in matters of creed: "In Egypt I was a Mohammedan,

here I shall be a Catholic, for the good of the people. I do not believe in religions."

Natalis, Alexander (1639-1724) ●
Controversial Dominican theologian. Known also as Alexander Noël, he was born in Rouen, entering the Dominicans there in 1654. After completing his studies at the Sorbonne in Paris in 1675, Natalis was to remain in the city for most of his remaining life. A theologian with sympathies for Jansenism, he took part in the appeal against the bull of Pope Clement XI, *Unigenitus* (1713), which had condemned the Jansenist propositions. He submitted to the papacy. Far more controversial was his chief work, *Selecta historiae ecclesiasticae capita* (24 vols., 1676-1686; *Selected Chapters of Ecclesiastical History*). Condemned by Pope Innocent for its Gallicanism, and placed on the Index of Forbidden Books, the work was revised and reissued under the title *Historia ecclesiastica veteris et novi testamenti* (*Ecclesiastical History of the Old and New Testaments*) in eight volumes. The work was not actually removed from the Index, however, until 1734.

Nazism ● See under **Germany;** see also **Fascism** in the GLOSSARY.

Necedah, False Apparitions of ●
Apparitions of the Virgin Mary that supposedly occurred in the small town of Necedah, Wisconsin, in 1950. They were claimed to have occurred to a Mrs. Fred Van Hoof, who told Church authorities that she had been visited routinely by the BVM. The Church investigation resulted, however, in the declaration that the apparitions were entirely unfounded, based on falsified testimony, potential personal profit, and a refusal to accept the authority of the Church.

Nemours, Treaty of ● Treaty promulgated by King Henry III of France (r. 1574-1589). It outlawed Calvinism in France. Issued at the behest of the Catholic League in the country, it made clear the often bitter conflict between the Protestants and Catholics and was aimed specifically at the Calvinists because of their hopes to impose their Protestant reforms on all of France. (See also **France**.)

Neo-Caesarea, Council of ● Council held in the Cappadocian town of Neocaesarea in Asia Minor early in the fourth century (c. 315). The proceeding passed fifteen canons on marriage and Church discipline.

Neo-Scholasticism ● Name given to the revival of Scholastic thought in the nineteenth and twentieth centuries. Neo-Scholasticism has as its objective the restoration of medieval Scholasticism in the intellectual life of the Church. The Catholic thinkers who have advocated it have been careful to make the distinction, however, that Neo-Scholasticism does not imply the wholesale adoption of medieval or antiquated systems which, in that unaltered form, would be highly inappropriate and ill-suited to the changes and challenges confronting the world since the Golden Age of Scholasticism in the thirteenth century. Rather, they hope to put traditional Scholasticism to use by harmonizing it with modern science and developments. Central to this endeavor is the recognition of the so-called eternal philosophies (*philosophia perennis*), certain universal truths that were taught and elucidated by the Schoolmen such as Sts. Bonaventure, Albertus Magnus, and, of course, Thomas Aquinas. These truths are always applicable, and all that must change is the method used in presenting them; thus Neo-Scholastic (or Neo-Thomist) instructors took traditional Scholastic teachings and reconciled them with modern curricula and academic styles such as the use of the vernacular instead of obtuse and difficult Medieval Latin.

The movement had its origins in the dark years of oppression that accompanied the French Revolution and Napoleonic Wars (1796-1815). As the Church had suffered terribly in the wars, the repressive tendencies of Napoleon, and the ongoing application of the tenets of the Enlightenment, scholars and Church leaders searched for the means to revitalize Catholic thought in a spiritually shattered Europe. They turned to the Schoolmen, finding much support from across the world in the Philippines where Thomism had been taught in a largely undiluted form at the University of Manila. Early proponents included Coroldi (d. 1892) of Italy, Stöckl (d. 1895) of Germany, and Dormet de Vorges (d. 1910) of France. Its greatest encouragement came from the papacy, most notably Pope Leo XIII (r. 1878-1903), who issued the encyclical *Aeterni Patris* exhorting the study of Thomas Aquinas upon all students of theology. He made Thomas the patron of Catholic universities, a preeminence reemphasized by Pope Pius XI in the encyclical *Studiorum Ducem* (1923) and Pope John Paul II in the apostolic constitution *Sapienta Christiana* (1979). In the twentieth century, Neo-Scholasticism received further development in the works of Desiré Mercier (1851-1926), Etienne Gilson (1884-1978), and especially Jacques Maritain (1882-1973). There were also the Transcendental Thomists Joseph Maréchal (1878-1944), Karl Rahner (1904-1984), Bernard Lonergan (1904-1984), and Emeric Coreth (b. 1919), and the non-Aristotelian and highly Augustinian Alphonse Gratry (1805-1872). In the years after Vatican Council II, Neo-Scholasticism and Neo-Thomism have largely declined within many Catholic intellectual circles. (See also **Scholasticism** and **Thomism**.)

Nero (37-68) ● Roman emperor from 54-68. The son of Agrippina the Younger and the Roman nobleman Domitius Ahenobarbus, Nero became the adopted heir of Emperor Claudius through the ruler's marriage to Agrippina. Nero is infamous in

Christian history for launching what is generally considered the first of the persecutions of the faith. His program of persecution probably stemmed from a need to find a scapegoat to throw before the Roman mobs following the burning of large parts of Rome in 64. The Christians were charged with setting fire to the city. Their property was confiscated to pay for the rebuilding and many, apparently, were put to death. According to accepted tradition, both Sts. Peter and Paul were executed during Nero's reign, although Paul had probably earlier made an appeal to the emperor from the trial before Festus at Caesarea as recorded in Acts (25:11). (See also **Roman Empire**.)

Nestorianism ● Widespread Christian heresy. Found in the East, it proposed the idea that there were two separate persons in Christ, one divine, one human, united in a voluntary manner. Nestorianism took its name from the fifth-century patriarch of Constantinople, Nestorius, who first propagated the doctrine. Nestorians differed from orthodox teaching by denying that Christ was a single person, both God and man, objecting as well to the title of the Virgin Mother as Mother of God (*Theotokos*). They further held that only Christ the man had died on the Cross.

Nestorianism was opposed by a number of important prelates, headed by St. Cyril of Alexandria. It was condemned at the Council of Ephesus (431) and Chalcedon (451), but Nestorius enjoyed support among the many Eastern bishops. They refused to accept the condemnations, breaking with the Church and forming an independent sect. Nevertheless, Nestorius was exiled in 436 to Upper Egypt; he died there several years later.

The Nestorian (or Persian) Church formed over time, particularly in Persia (modern-day Iran), with its intellectual base in Nisibis. Missionary activities were conducted in Iraq, Egypt, India, and even China. The Nestorians fared well under the Muslims after the conquest of Persia in the eighth century, receiving recognition as a definite religion. With the Mongols, however, came severe oppression, culminating in the bloody massacre under Tamerlane in the fourteenth century. In 1445, the Nestorians of Cyprus were reunited with the Church and in 1559 the Nestorian Church of Malabar recognized the supremacy of Rome. (See also **Malabar Rite** and **Three Chapters**.)

Netherlands ● European constitutional monarchy, known in unofficial usage as Holland. During the time of the Roman Empire, the region that became the Netherlands was occupied by the tribes of the Batavi and the Frisians. It came under the control of the Franks from around the fifth century. Missionaries from Irish, Anglo-Saxon, and Frankish lands arrived in the area around the early seventh century. Evangelization was spearheaded by St. Willibrord (658-739), the so-called Apostle of Frisia, who was consecrated archbishop of the Frisians in 695. The Christian community came under the influence and jurisdiction of the see of Utrecht, held by Willibrord from 695-739. The bishop of Utrecht would be a leading political and social potentate in Holland throughout the Middle Ages. During much of the medieval epoch, the chief secular leaders were the counts of Holland. They were replaced in the fifteenth century by the dukes of Burgundy, who themselves became part of the House of Habsburg in 1492. At the start of the sixteenth century, the bishops of Utrecht were challenged as temporal rulers, finally surrendering their nonecclesiastical claims in 1526 to Emperor Charles V.

Charles, in 1555, gave the Low Countries, including the Netherlands, to his son, King Philip II of Spain. His rule, including the implementation of the Inquisition, was manifestly unpopular, made even more so by the spread of Reformation ideas.

Lutheranism was not especially prevalent, but French Calvinism was very active, becoming most pronounced from 1572. Philip's efforts to cultivate good will among the Catholics through the creation of several new sees and the elevation of the see of Utrecht to an archbishopric could not prevent the formation of the Union of Utrecht (1579) by various states in the area (Belgium, the Netherlands, and some northern provinces), culminating in the declaration in 1581 of independence. Years of struggle followed, dragging on into the Thirty Years' War (1618-1648), and ended only in 1648 when the United Provinces was recognized. Catholics were much oppressed in the seventeenth century, with numerous legal handicaps, so that the Catholic population was soon much reduced. Further difficulties were soon encountered with the spread of Jansenism, leading in 1702 to the schism of Petrus Codde (1648-1710), vicar-general and titular archbishop of Philippi, and his followers, prompting the rise of the Old Catholics. There was thus a mere marginal Church organization in the Netherlands from 1702, this unfortunate state of affairs ending only in 1853 with the full restoration of the archiepiscopal see of Utrecht. The Church in the Netherlands remained largely isolated until the early twentieth century. A marked revival followed and the Catholics of the country became well-known for their highly progressive outlook. In the years before and after the First Vatican Council, the Catholics of Holland were among the most liberal in all of Europe, and some elements at times were distinctly hostile to the Holy See and its efforts to restore obedience and adherence to orthodoxy.

Netter, Thomas (d. 1430) ● English Carmelite theologian. A native of Saffron Walden, Essex, he joined the Carmelites in London, studying at London and Oxford. He served as confessor to King Henry V of England; Henry is traditionally said to have died in his arms in 1422. Netter then acted as tutor and spiritual adviser to King Henry VI, journeying with him to France in 1430 where Netter died, at Rouen, on November 2, 1430. A much respected theologian, Netter served as a representative to the Council of Pisa (1409), the Council of Constance (1414-1418), and to Poland (1419). His writings were centered on refuting the doctrines of the Wycliffites and Hussites, particularly his large treatise *Doctrinale antiquitatum fidei ecclesiae catholicae*, a brilliant defense of Catholic doctrine.

Neumann, John Nepomucene, St. (1811-1860) ● Fourth bishop of Philadelphia and the first canonized American bishop. Born in Bohemia, he studied at the University of Prague and was a distinguished scholar, completing his education there in 1835. While preparing for ordination, he was inspired to journey to America by the remarkable letters sent by Father Frederic Baraga (later bishop of Marquette) to the Leopold Missionary Society. Arriving in America in 1836, he was ordained in New York on June 25 of that year and would spend the next four years in active missionary work among the Germans around Niagara Falls. In 1840, he joined the Redemptorists, becoming the first of their number to be professed in America (1842). Ten years later, at the suggestion of Archbishop Francis Kenrick of Baltimore, Neumann was consecrated bishop of Philadelphia (March 28, 1852). As bishop, he worked strenuously to improve education; at the time of his consecration there were two parochial schools in the diocese, but by the time of his death they numbered nearly a hundred, making him an important figure in the organization of the American Catholic school system. He erected some fifty churches and advanced the work on the cathedral for the city and was the first American bishop to introduce the Forty Hours Devotion in 1853. Having had a major role in the First Plenary Council of Baltimore in 1852, he was invited to Rome by Pope Pius IX in 1854 to take part in the formal definition of the dogma on the Immaculate Conception. Beatified by Pope Paul VI in 1963, he was canonized in 1977. Feast day: January 5.

Neumann, Therese (1898-1962) ●
Germanic mystic and stigmatic. Born in Konnersreuth, Bavaria, she had a normal childhood until the age of twenty; after assisting in putting out a fire, she fell ill and the next year went blind. Her sight was restored in 1923 on the beatification day of Thérèse of Lisieux. When, in 1925, Thérèse was canonized, Neumann regained the ability to walk. The following year, she began receiving visions and the first apparent marks of the stigmata appeared during Lent. The wounds commonly bled on Fridays and were particularly active during the last two weeks of Lent. The remarkable occurrences, coupled with her severe absorption and trances, soon attracted visits and the first of the Church's investigations in 1927. Other efforts to look into her case were rebuffed by her, citing the opposition of her father. Nevertheless, thousands of pilgrims visited her in Konnersreuth, most notably after World War II. Of note was Neumann's claim that after 1922 she ate no solid food and after 1927 no food at all so long as she received daily Communion. The Church never made any pronouncements concerning her, although she has been the subject of much discussion and controversy.

Newman, John Henry (1801-1890) ●
Leader of the Oxford movement, prominent convert to Catholicism, and a cardinal. He was born in London, the son of a London banker. At the age of seven, he entered the Ealing School and while there became initially attracted to the antireligious writings of Voltaire (1694-1778) and the Scottish philosopher David Hume (1711-1776), one

day announcing his disbelief in God and divine revelation. His master at the school persuaded him to read the writings of John Calvin (1509-1564), and Newman underwent a kind of conversion, reading the Bible with enthusiasm. In 1817, he enrolled at Trinity College, Oxford, and was converted to Anglicanism. In 1822, he became a fellow of Oriel and two years later was ordained a deacon. He was then appointed vice-principal of Alban Hall (1825) and vicar of St. Mary's, Oxford (1828). As a preacher, he attracted a wide following with his superb oratory; the crowds only increased after his resignation in 1832 from his tutorship at Oxford owing to a dispute over religious duties.

From that time, as Newman's belief in Anglicanism declined, he became a leading figure in the Oxford movement and acquired national notoriety for his writings entitled *Parochial and Plain Sermons* (1834-1842) and his contributions to the *Tracts for the Times* (1833-1841). He advocated a position for the Anglican Church that he characterized as the *via media*; this meant that Anglicanism held a middle ground between Romanism (with its papal infallibility) and Protestantism (with its lack of restraint for private judgment). This perspective was more fully developed in the *Lectures on the Prophetical Office of the Church* (1837) and *Lectures on Justification* (1838). Finally, he caused a firestorm of controversy in the Anglican Church with "Tract 90" in which he argued that the Thirty-Nine Articles should be interpreted in a manner in keeping with the Council of Trent. To him, the Thirty-Nine Articles were not directed against the leadership of the Catholic Church but the political supremacy of the papacy. Condemned by Anglican authorities, Newman resigned from St. Mary's, ended his association with Oxford, and retired to the village of Littlemore with several friends. His four friends entered the Church over the next several years, largely under Newman's influence, but he did not join himself until 1845. On October 9 of that year he wrote to his sister: "I must tell you what will pain you greatly. This night Father Dominic, the Italian Passionist, sleeps here. . . . I shall ask him to receive me into what I believe to be the One Fold of the Redeemer." He then issued a defense of his decision, *Essay on the Development of Christian Doctrine* (1845).

Newman traveled to Rome after his baptism and was ordained in 1847. He entered the Congregation of the Oratory of St. Philip Neri and received permission from Pope Pius IX to open an oratory in Birmingham in 1849. From 1851-1858, he served as the first rector of the Catholic University of Dublin, finally resigning in 1858. In 1864, he became embroiled in a controversy with the Protestant clergyman Charlie Kingsley (d. 1875), who had slandered both Newman and the priesthood in an article. After several unsatisfactory exchanges, Newman released his *Apologia pro vita sua* (1864), a magnificent religious autobiography examining his religious thoughts to the time of his reception into the Church. It is also one of the greatest autobiographical works in the English language, and the primary source for the history of the Oxford movement. In 1870, he wrote *A Grammar of Assent*, a profound survey on the psychology of faith. Other writings included: *Loss and Gain* (1848, a novel); *Callista* (1856, a novel); *The Dream of Gerontius* (1866, in book form), a poem expressing the departure of a soul to God that was set to music by Edward Elgar (1857-1934); and *Idea of a University* (1852), containing Newman's vision of a liberal education.

Cardinal John Henry Newman

In 1877, Newman was elected an honorary fellow of Trinity College. Two years later, in recognition of his service to the Church, Pope Leo XIII made him a cardinal deacon. He chose as his motto, *"Ex umbris et imaginibus in veritatem"* ("Out of the shadows and images into the truth"). His elevation was greeted with genuine enthusiasm in England and elsewhere, and was considered a significant gesture by the Holy See to the English Catholics. Newman died at Edgebaston, Birmingham, where he had spent his final years, on August 11, 1890.

Nicaea, Council of ● Two ecumenical councils convened in 325 and 787 respectively. The First Council of Nicaea is ranked as the first of twenty-one general councils of the Church.

Nicaea, First Council of: A council convened by Emperor Constantine the Great (d. 337) with the principal aim of resolving the Arian Controversy. Recognizing that Arianism had created a major storm in he eastern half of the Roman Empire, Constantine decided not to leave the matter in the hands of local Church councils but to summon bishops from all over. While advice was probably given by Hosius, bishop of Córdoba (Cordova), Constantine was most responsible for organizing the council, including the generous gesture of granting free transportation for the bishops who were attending. The site chosen was the imperial summer palace at Nicaea, on the Bosporus, in Bithynia. It was attended by over three hundred bishops, although the names of only two hundred twenty are known. The main

Western representatives, besides Hosius, were the bishops of Milan, Dijon, and Carthage and the two papal delegates on behalf of Pope Sylvester I (r. 314-335). The traditionally accepted date for the start was May 20, 325. It went on until the end of August. The president was probably Bishop Hosius, although some historians argue that it may have been Eustathius, bishop of Antioch.

After a brief opening statement by Constantine, the Council Fathers set to work. It would appear that a creed of Arian disposition was proposed by Eusebius of Nicomedia and rejected; Eusebius of Caesarea then offered his own. With the insertion of the term *homoousios* (see **Homoousios**), this was adopted, although this was not the creed finally promulgated (see **Nicene Creed** for other details). Only two bishops, Theonas of Marmarica and Secundus of Ptolemais, refused to subscribe to the Nicene Creed and its anti-Arian anathemas and both were deposed. The council then dealt with other pressing topics, including a resolution of the Melitian Schism and the fixing of the date of Easter for the Churches in the East and West (thus ending the Paschal Controversy), and the readmission of the Novatianists and Paulinians (followers of Paul of Samosata) to the Church. Privileges were also accorded to the sees of Alexandria, Antioch, and Jerusalem. While the council was supposed to bring a close to the Arian Controversy, this hope proved fleeting; the crisis would continue throughout the fourth century. Unfortunately, the *acta* of the council are lost. The only extant documents are the twenty canons it issued, the creed, and the synodal letter.

Nicaea, Second Council of: The seventh ecumenical (general) council, convened by Empress Irene in order to resolve the Iconoclastic Controversy. The proceedings were launched by the Byzantine empress at the behest of Tarasius, patriarch of Constantinople, who, at his election in December 784, had declared his request for a council. Both Empress Irene and Tarasius wrote to Pope Adrian I (r. 772-795) asking his support in the summoning of a council. He responded affirmatively and promised to send two legates, with the proviso that the false council of 753 be condemned — the Iconoclast Synod of Hieria.

On August 17, 786, the bishops gathered at the Church of the Apostles in Constantinople. They were soon dispersed, however, by an uprising of the Iconoclasts, assisted by some members of the army. Empress Irene suppressed the revolt, and the next year, on September 27, 787, with Tarasius presiding, the council finally met, in the church of St. Sophia in Nicaea. The patriarchs of Alexandria and Jerusalem could not attend, but their representatives proclaimed their full support of the condemnation of the Iconoclasts. Adrian's letter to Irene and Tarasius was read, and the council promulgated a decree stating that various kinds of images could be set up, but they were to be given veneration or honor and not worshiped, since the act of worship belongs only to God. The Iconoclasts were then condemned. There were also twenty-two disciplinary canons concerned with the clerical life of simplicity and diocesan administration. (See **Iconoclastic Controversy**.)

Nicene Creed ● Name given to two creeds, the first issued by the Council of Nicaea (325) and the second by the First Council of Constantinople (381). The original Nicene Creed was composed by the Nicaean Council Fathers in an effort to respond to the need for a clear statement of faith in their struggle with the Arians. It is relatively simple and is distinguished by its use of the term *homoousios* (consubstantial) in describing the nature of Christ, a word much opposed by the Arians. The second creed, also called the Nicene-Constantinople Creed, is the one used today as the profession of faith in the liturgy. It was more precise and sophisticated in its theological expression than the first creed, with added declarations on the Church, the resurrection, baptism, and eternal life. Unlike the first creed, the second Nicene Creed contains no anathemas; the first creed, fighting as the Fathers were against Arianism, included four anathemas.

Nicephorus, St. (d. 829) ● Byzantine theologian and patriarch of Constantinople. A respected official at Constantinople, he retired from public life to a monastery, although he did not become a monk. Recalled by Emperor Constantine VI, he was appointed patriarch. An ardent opponent of the Iconoclasts, he was deposed by the Iconoclast emperor Leo V the Armenian and exiled to a monastery near Chalcedon for his firm stand at the Iconoclast Synod in Constantinople. His chief writing was the *Apologeticus major* (817), a study on Iconoclasm; his other works included *Chronological Tables* on religious and civil offices until 829 and *Breviarium Nicephori* (*Nicephorus's Short History*), on Byzantine history from 601-796. Feast day: March 13 (West), June 2 (East).

Nicephorus Callistus (c. 1256-c. 1335) ● Byzantine historian, theologian, and priest of the Hagia Sophia (Santa Sophia). Probably born in Constantinople, he was a priest and teacher of rhetoric and theology. He also became a monk in later life, but he is best remembered for his writings. Chief among his works was the *Ecclesiasticus historiae* (*Church History*), detailing in eighteen volumes the history of Christianity from the birth of Christ to the death of Emperor Phocas in 610; an appendix of five volumes summarizes additional events to the demise in 912 of Emperor Leo VI the Wise. He also wrote on Byzantine liturgy.

Nicholas I, St. ● Pope from 858-867. A Roman by birth, he was the son of a nobleman. The most respected and trusted figure in the pontificate of Benedict III, he was elected to succeed him on April 24, 858, proving himself a formidable spokesman for papal power and a dominating figure in his time. In 863, he involved himself in the controversy involving the Eastern Church. Ignatius, patriarch of Constantinople, had made an appeal to Nicholas after having been deposed by Emperor Michael III and replaced by Photius. Nicholas sided with Ignatius, excommunicating Photius and thereby beginning the so-called Photian Schism. In the West, Nicholas supported the right of suffragan bishops to appeal to the pope against their metropolitans, restoring a bishop of Soissons against the wishes of Hincmar, the formidable archbishop of Reims. He also refused to grant a divorce to King Lothair II of Lorraine, who was anxious to separate from his wife. Not only did Nicholas stand firm, he deposed the archbishops of Cologne and Trier after they had given their permission to the king. His successor, Adrian II, ordered that Nicholas's name be among the prayers said at Mass. Feast day: November 13.

Nicholas II ● Pope from 1059-1061. Known originally as Gerard, he served as bishop of Florence (from around 1045) until his election as successor to Pope Stephen IX (X). As pontiff, Nicholas had a major role in establishing the groundwork for the important Gregorian Reform of the Church that would find fullest expression under Pope St. Gregory VII (r. 1073-1085). Elected through reforming cardinals under the influence of Hildebrand (the future Gregory VII), he was chosen in opposition to the antipope Benedict X. He summoned the Lateran Council of 1059 and there promulgated his new decree on papal elections that the cardinals should elect the pope. The council also condemned concubinage, clerical marriage, and lay investiture. These moves to reduce imperial influence were the cause of much controversy in Germany, further fueled by Nicholas's alliance with the Norman rulers of Italy. He died on July 26, 1061.

Nicholas III ● Pope from 1277-1280. A native of Rome, Giovanni Gaetano was a member of the Orsini family and, prior to his election on November 25, 1277, as successor to Pope John XXI, had served as cardinal deacon of S. Niccoló in Carcere. His election came after an interregnum of some six months, although he was much opposed by the supporters of King Charles of Sicily whose policies Pope John had sought to limit, with the help of Gaetano. Nicholas continued to work for the strengthening of the papacy, especially in the Papal States. As he had served in 1261 as protector of the Franciscans, under Pope Urban IV, Nicholas was in an excellent position to help resolve the internal problems that were besetting the Franciscan order on the question of poverty.

Nicholas IV ● Pope from 1288-1292. Born Girolamo Masci, he was the first member of the Franciscans to be elected pope. He had joined the Franciscans at an early age and in 1274 succeeded the great St. Bonaventure as general. Named a cardinal by Pope Nicholas III, he was chosen unanimously by the College of Cardinals to bring an end to the interregnum that had endured for nearly a year following the death of Pope Honorius III. He at first refused, but on February 22,

1288, the cardinals elected him again and this time he accepted. In an effort to bring peace to Sicily, Nicholas negotiated peace between France and Aragon. While hopes of organizing a crusade never came to fruition, he did mount an effort to secure an alliance with the Mongols, sending missionaries to the court of Kublai Khan. These friars would be the first missionaries to China; Nicholas also sent missionaries to the Near East and Africa.

Pope Nicholas V

Nicholas V ● Pope from 1447-1455. A remarkable pontiff, his pontificate was noted for its intellectual achievements, but its final period was overshadowed by the fall of Constantinople in 1453. Born Tomaso Parentucelli, he was named papal legate to the Diet of Frankfurt and a cardinal in 1446; the following year he was named bishop of Bologna. On March 6, 1447, he was elected to succeed Eugenius IV as a compromise candidate, ending the schism then plaguing the Church by receiving the submission of the antipope Felix V and the Council of Basel. One of the first so-called Renaissance popes, Nicholas founded the Vatican Library, was an enthusiastic patron of scholars, humanists, and artists, and restored many churches, most notably St. Peter's. He crowned Frederick III as emperor, the last coronation to be held in Rome. In 1453, however, Nicholas was forced to put to death several conspirators who had planned to assassinate him. This bad news was followed in June 1453 by the arrival of word that Constantinople had fallen to the Ottoman

Turks. Both probably hastened his death on March 24, 1455; he died extremely disappointed that the Christian West was so apathetic in its response to the fall of Constantinople.

Nicholas, St. ● One of the most popular of all saints, he is best known as the patron of children, who call him Santa Claus. Virtually nothing is known about him with any certainty. He was certainly the bishop of Myra in the fourth century in Lycia, Asia Minor, but for the most part, he is known in legend. For example, he supposedly saved several young girls from prostitution by throwing bags of gold at their windows during the night. Stories about him spread across the East, so that churches dedicated to him multiplied. There was one at Constantinople in the sixth century and, thanks to trade and pilgrims, Nicholas came to be honored in the West in the eleventh century. His good deeds toward children helped lay the foundation for the Father Christmas stories and the later development of Santa Claus. His feast day on December 6 is still celebrated in some areas with gift giving. He is also called Nicholas of Bari after the removal of his relics from Myra to Bari, in Apulia, Italy, by Italian merchants.

Nicholas of Cusa (1401-1464) ● German theologian, humanist, mystic, and cardinal. A brilliant expert in canon law, he was ordained in 1430 and took part in the Council of Basel (1431-1449) where he was conspicuous in his efforts to bring about a reconciliation between the Church and the supporters of Jan Hus. In 1437, he served as a representative of Pope Eugenius IV to the imperial court at Constantinople to negotiate a hoped-for reunion between the Eastern and Western Churches. A strong advocate of the papacy, he was rewarded for his labors in 1448 by Nicholas V with his elevation to the rank of cardinal. Two years later, he was named papal legate to the German lands.

Under Pope Pius II he became vicar-general, promoting reform in Rome. A model for the so-called Renaissance man, he was a mathematician, scientist, artist, and philosopher; among his writings were: *De Concordatia Catholica* (1453; *On Catholic Concordance*), a detailed work on Church reform; four dialogues on wisdom and the soul (1450); and *De Docta Ignorantia* (1440; *On Learned Ignorance*).

Nicholas of Hereford (d. c. 1417) ● Supporter of reform in the English Church and a follower of John Wycliffe. A fellow at Queen's College, Oxford (c. 1374), his support of Wycliffite doctrine and his attacks on papal authority culminated with his condemnation and excommunication on July 1, 1282. He fled London with the help of the duke of Lancaster, appealed to Pope Urban VI, but was once again condemned and sentenced to prison. Unlike other Wycliffites, he was spared execution, possibly because of the long-standing favor shown English academics by the pope. Escaping briefly in 1385, he was imprisoned once more, recanting in 1391. Henceforth an opponent of heresies, he was appointed inquisitor against Lollardy, resigning his post in 1417 to enter the Carthusians. His most notable achievement was the role he had in the translating of the Bible into English. He translated the OT, which was later revised by Wycliffe and John Purvey.

Nicholas of Lyra (c. 1270-1349) ● Franciscan scholar and highly respected biblical expert. A native of Vieille-Lyre, France, he entered the Franciscans around 1300 and became regent of the University of Paris around 1309. A decade later he was elected general of the Franciscan order. His chief writing was the *Postillae perpetuae in universam S. Scriptorum* (*Commentary to the Universal Holy Scripture*), a fifty-volume work on the Bible that was both popular and highly influential, the first printed commentary of its kind. It may have had an influence in the formulation of Luther's ideas concerning the Bible. Nicholas also founded the College of Burgundy in Paris around 1325.

Nicholas von Flüe, St. (1417-1487) ● Swiss mystic and ascetic who was also known as Brother Klaus. Born near Lake Lucerne, he served for a number of years as a judge and scholar, fighting in two wars on behalf of his native land. Married to a woman named Dorothy, he fathered ten children. In 1465, however, he retired from public life and then, in 1467, he gave up his family to become a hermit in the Ranft Valley. He attracted many people who sought to take inspiration from his remarkable goodness. Around 1481, he was consulted by leading political figures in Switzerland who hoped he might prevent a Swiss civil war. His suggestions were soon adopted in the Compromise of Stans. He was canonized in 1947 by Pope Pius XII. Feast day: March 21.

Nicole, Pierre (1625-1695) ● French theologian and controversialist and a supporter of Jansenism. A native of Chartres, he studied at Paris, receiving a bachelor of theology degree in 1649. A short time later, he joined Port-Royal, then an intellectual center of Jansenist teachings. An associate and ally of Antoine Arnauld, Nicole assisted in numerous Jansenist writings. When, however, Arnauld was exiled in 1679, Nicole accompanied him to Belgium. He returned to Paris only in 1683, after submitting to the archbishop of Paris. In later years, he defended Catholic teachings against Protestant attacks and authored a refutation of quietism. Among his writings were a Latin translation of Blaise Pascal's *Lettres Provinciales* (1659; *Provincial Letters*), *Le Perpétuité de la foi catholique touchant l'Eucharistie* (1664; a defense of the Real Presence and transubstantiation against

Calvinist teachings), and *La Traité de la grâce générale* (1715; a treatise on grace).

Nicolo de' Tudeschi (1386-1445) ● Also called Abbas Siculus, Panormitanus, and *abbas modernus*. A Benedictine expert in canon law, he was a Sicilian by birth. He entered the Benedictine order in 1400, studying at the University of Bologna; among his teachers was Francisco Zabarella, the great Italian canonist. Nicolo subsequently taught at Parma, Siena, and Bologna; he also served as abbot of the monastery of Maniacio, near Messina. After several years (1433-1435) of service in Rome, he became bishop of Palermo and was soon an ally of the antipope Felix V, who made him a cardinal in 1440. The writings of Nicolo included the *Tractatus de concile Basiliensi*, on the Council of Basel, which he had attended on behalf of King Alfonso of Aragon. In the work, he defended the superiority of the council to the pope. His most important works were on canon law, most notably on the Decretals of Pope Gregory IX (*Lectura in Decretales*). He was known as the *Lucerna Juris* (Lamp of the Law). The name *abbas Siculus* was used for him to note his Sicilian birthplace and *abbas modernus* to distinguish him from *abbas antiquus*, an earlier canonist of the thirteenth century.

Nider, John (1380-1438) ● Dominican theologian. Born in Swabia, he joined the Dominicans in Colmar, subsequently studying at Paris and Cologne. He taught at Vienna (1425-1427) and was elected prior of the Dominican convent in Nurenburg in 1427 and Basel in 1431. As a legate to the Council of Basel (1431-1449) he served on several missions at the behest of the council to the Hussites, in hopes of reconciling them to the Church. Later, he supported the continuation of the council's proceedings but changed his position when Pope Eugenius remained firm in his decree that the council be dissolved. In 1436, he returned to the University of Vienna and resumed his lectures. A gifted and famous preacher, Nider was also an advocate of genuine Church reform. His chief writings included *Formicarius* (5 vols., 1602; a treatise on important philosophical and theological issues) and numerous theological works.

Nilus, St. (d. c. 430) ● Also Nilus of Ancyra. Founder of a monastery in Ancyra and a writer. A native of Ancyra, Nilus studied at Constantinople under St. John Chrysostom. He then established a monastery in Ancyra (modern Ankara) and wrote a number of important works on ascetic and moral subjects. Nilus also maintained a very extensive correspondence with many notable contemporaries; most of his letters are extant. Nilus was long confused with the same named Nilus of Sinai, who became a hermit on Mt. Sinai. Feast day: November 12.

Ninety-Five Theses ● Name given to the ninety-five statements on the abuses of the Church. They were nailed to the main door of All Saints Church in Wittenberg, Germany, on October 31, 1517, by Martin Luther. The complaints by Luther included such topics as papal authority, indulgences, and the place of faith and good works. This event is considered the launching point of the Protestant Reformation. The theses, which were written in Latin, were soon translated into German and published extensively in German-speaking territories. The publication of Luther's declarations was assisted by the rise of the printing press, thus facilitating the spread of reforming opinions. (See also **Luther, Martin**.)

Ninian, St. (d. c. 432) ● Also Ninias, the first Apostle of Scotland. The earliest source on Ninian is the Venerable Bede's *Ecclesiastical History*. According to tradition, he was the son of a British chieftain, educated at Rome, and consecrated a bishop by Siricius (c. 394). On his way to

Christianize the Picts, he met St. Martin of Tours. So influenced was he by Martin that later, while building a church at Whithorn and learning that Martin had died, he dedicated the church to him; the structure was the White House, most likely because it was built of white stone. Ninian also established a monastery in Whithorn for himself and his monks. This served as a useful center for spreading Christianity among the Picts and within a century of Ninian's death it was a leading site for learning and monasticism. Ninian was buried at the church in Whithorn and his tomb was a popular pilgrim site; no relics have survived. Feast day: September 16.

Nomocanons ● Collection of ecclesiastical law compiled from both secular and canon law. It is used in the Eastern Church. Nomocanons had their origin in the custom of the fourth- through sixth-century Roman emperors passing decrees and legislation that influenced or had jurisdiction upon both civil and ecclesiastical spheres. Emphasis, for example, was placed upon clerical discipline in both the Code of Theodosius and the Code of Justinian. As these civil laws could be compared with similar enactments in canon law, it became useful to bring both together into collections so that by the seventh century the laws had combined to form the Nomocanons. The earliest form of a compilation was ascribed to John Scholasticus (d. 577), although the first actual collection dates to the reign of Byzantine Emperor Heraclius (610-640). This, called the collection in "Fourteen Titles," was eventually supplanted by the revised edition by Photius in the ninth century. A commentary was written on the Nomocanons by Theodore Balsamon (d. late 1100s), Greek patriarch of Antioch, who lived in Constantinople; this work was subsequently attached to the accepted Nomocanon of Photius. Such collections were also introduced into the Russian Orthodox Church.

Nonnus of Panopolis ● Early fifth-century reputed author of two poems in Greek hexameter. The first was concerned with the mysteries of Bacchus, the second a "Paraphrase of the Fourth Gospel." Virtually nothing is known about Nonnus beyond these poems, although it is believed that he was a pagan at the time of his writing the first poem and was converted during the intervening period of the second. Only 3,750 lines of the "Paraphrase" are extant. Its value stems from the analysis made of the original text of the Bible used by Nonnus in writing the poem; otherwise both works are of limited interest and merit.

Norbert, St. (c. 1080-1134) ● Archbishop of Magdeburg and the founder of the Premonstratensian Canons, or the Norbertines (also called the White Canons). Born in Xanten, Germany, he was the son of Heribert, count of Gennep, making him related to the German imperial family. Holding several ecclesiastical posts at the court of Frederick, bishop of Cologne, and Emperor Henry V, he distinguished himself for his enjoyment of worldly affairs and steadfastly refused ordination. In 1115, however, he underwent a complete conversion. He placed himself under Cuno, abbot of Siegburg, who directed his spiritual development; he was ordained by the bishop of Cologne. Attempting to promote reform among the clergy of Xanten, he encountered severe opposition and insults and was accused at the Council of Fritzlar of improper innovations in 1118. Resigning his offices and selling his estates, he walked barefoot to meet with Pope Gelasius. The pontiff granted him permission to preach through northern France and, with the help of Bartholomew, bishop of Laon, he established the Order of Premonstratensians in 1120. The order received recognition in 1126 by Pope Honorius. Named archbishop of Magdeburg that same year, he later (1132-1133) supported Pope Innocent II against the antipope Anacletus. Pope Gregory XIII canonized him in 1582. Feast day: June 6.

Noris, Henry (1631-1704) ● Cardinal and head of the Vatican Library. Noris was of English blood, but he was born in Verona. He studied under the Jesuits at Rimini, entering there the Order of Augustinian Hermits. After studies at Rome, he taught at Pesaro, Perugia, and Padua, authoring two controversial books, *Historia Pelagiana* (*History of Pelagianism*) and *Dissertate de Synodo V Oecumenica* (*Dissertations on the Fifth Ecumenical Council*) in 1673. The first was a history of the Pelagian Controversy and the second was, with the *Vindiciae Augustinianae*, a defense of Augustinian doctrines on grace. While initially approved by the Holy See, the writings were attacked in 1676 for supporting the errors of Michel Baius and Cornelius Jansen. Acquitted of the charges by the Holy See, Noris was appointed assistant librarian in the Vatican (1692) and cardinal in 1695 by Pope Innocent XII. In 1700, he became head of the Vatican Library. His works continued to cause controversy, however, and were placed on the Index of Forbidden Books by the Holy Office. Pope Benedict XIV officially removed his name from the Index in June 1748.

North American Martyrs ● Eight Jesuits martyred between the years 1642-1649 during their efforts at bringing the Gospel to the Native Americans in modern upstate New York and southeastern Canada. These remarkable and inspirational men are venerated at two shrines, one in Auriesville (New York) and one in Canada. The North American martyrs are: René Goupil, a lay medic (d. 1642); Isaac Jogues (d. 1647); Jean Lalande (d. 1647); Jean de Brébeuf (d. 1649); Antoine Daniel (d. 1649); Gabriel Lalemant (d. 1649); Charles Garnier (d. 1649); and Noël

Chabanel (d. 1649). They were canonized in 1930 by Pope Pius XI. Bl. Kateri Tekakwitha, the Lily of the Mohawks, was brought into the faith by the Jesuits and is also honored at the shrine in Auriesville.

Norway ● Country in northwestern Europe where Christianity was introduced during the ninth and tenth centuries and was given much encouragement and patronage by several kings, most notably Hakkon I, who reigned from 934-961, and his immediate successors. Final conversion came under Olaf II Haroldsson (r. c. 1015-1030), who built churches, founded schools, and attempted to make the Christian faith accepted throughout the kingdom. After his murder in 1030 by rebels, he was considered a saint. His rule made possible further missionary work and the establishing of a number of dioceses. Local bishops were under the metropolitan jurisdiction of the archbishop of Lund until 1152 when the papal legate, Nicholas of Albano, transferred authority to the see of Trondheim. The groundwork for the eventual loss of Norway to the Church was laid around 1519 by King Christian II, who suppressed a large number of the monasteries in the country. His successor, Christian III, was an energetic supporter of Lutheranism, but the Reformation was introduced fully only after 1537 and the domination of Norway by the Danes. Harsh measures were taken against the Church, and some prelates escaped to safety; others were imprisoned or executed. The faith endured until the early seventeenth century, but it was finally virtually extirpated by the ruthless anti-Catholic laws of the Danish

St. Isaac Jogues

overlords. Only in 1845 was Catholicism tolerated. A prefecture was created in 1869 by Pope Pius IX. Greater freedom was possible after 1897 when various legal handicaps were lifted. The Catholics in Norway were cared for by an apostolic vicariate (1892-1932), after which there were three territories administered by the Congregation for the Propagation of the Faith. Today, there is a small Catholic population in a country still overwhelmingly Lutheran.

Nostra Aetate ● Document of Vatican Council II that was promulgated on October 28, 1965, and called in English the "Declaration on the Relationship of the Church to Non-Christian Religions." While positively affirming the common solidarity of humanity and rejecting all forms of intolerance and prejudice, the Council Fathers specifically discussed and praised the other world's major faiths, including Buddhism, Islam, and Hinduism. Special attention, however, was paid to Judaism, in recognition of the people of the OT, the historical roots of Christianity in the Jewish faith, and the age-old and often pervasive anti-Semitism found within the culture of the West. The decree refuted in certain terms such claims as a collective guilt for the crucifixion and death of Christ. Anti-Semitism in all of its forms was utterly rejected. The document was especially embraced by the German bishops. (See also **Jews and Judaism**.)

Notre Dame de Paris ● Famous cathedral situated on the Île de la Cité, Paris, considered one of the foremost Gothic cathedrals ever constructed. It was conceived by Maurice de Sully, bishop of Paris, and had its foundation laid by Pope Alexander III in 1163, on the site of an earlier Roman temple and two later Christian churches. As was the custom of the Middle Ages, construction took hundreds of years to complete, with work progressing in stages: the altar was finished in 1189; the choir and

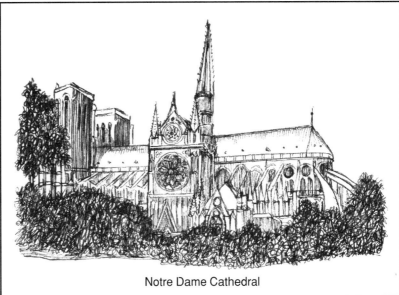

Notre Dame Cathedral

west front in 1240; and the remaining chapels and work in the fourteenth century. Originally it was planned that the twin towers should have spires placed upon them, but these were never added. Extensive restorations were made in 1845. Of particular note are the rose windows, dating from the thirteenth century.

Novatian (d. c. 257-258) ● Theologian and presbyter who established the popular schismatic sect of Novatianism. Probably a convert to Christianity, Novatian served as a presbyter in Rome and was the author of an orthodox treatise on the nature of the Trinity. A rigorist in matters of readmission for lapsed Christians, he came to oppose vigorously the policy of the Church in allowing those Christians who had denied their faith to repent and return to the fold, particularly after the harsh persecutions of Emperor Decius (r. 249-251). When, in 251, St. Cornelius was elected as successor to Pope St. Fabian, Novatian allowed himself to be elected Bishop of Rome as a rival, making him the first of the antipopes. Condemned by Cornelius and a synod of Rome, Novatian died during the persecution of Emperor

Valerian (r. 253-260). Novatian's followers persisted, however, in their belief that those who had fallen from the faith should never be allowed to repent because their sin was unpardonable in the eyes of God. Formally condemned by the Council of Nicaea in 325, the Novatianists survived into the fifth century.

Nuncio ● Also apostolic nuncio. Name used for the permanent diplomatic representative of the Holy See to a country. By custom, the nuncio was once sent only to those countries that had a large and important Catholic population. As a senior diplomat, the nuncio is automatically given the rank and precedence of the dean of the diplomatic corps in the capital in which he is serving. As with other diplomatic representatives — pro-nuncios and internuncios — the nuncio also fulfills important duties as an apostolic delegate, meaning he is the representative to the local churches of a country. He thus assists in the nomination of bishops, gives advice and aid to local bishops, assists those religious communities of pontifical rank, and confers with (but does not belong to) the episcopal conference of a country. The nuncio resides in what is called the nunciature, the formal diplomatic residence that enjoys diplomatic right and immunity. Among the apostolic nuncios currently in service around the world are those in Austria, Belgium, and Italy. Superbly trained and highly experienced diplomats, nuncios are usually archbishops. The papal representative to the United States is a pro-nuncio, as he is not the dean of the diplomatic corps.

Nuremburg, Declaration of ● Protest made by a group of Catholic German intellectuals against the decrees of Vatican Council I (1869-1870). The declaration was the result of a meeting held in Nuremburg in August 1870 and attended by such notables as Johannes Döllinger (1799-1890), Franz Reusch (1825-1900), and Johannes Friedrich (1836-1917). They protested that the Vatican Council was not a true ecumenical council and, more importantly, that the pope (Pius IX) had no right to issue decrees on papal infallibility and that infallibility would eventually lead to severe curtailing of civil rights within the Church. As no satisfactory response to them was forthcoming from the Church officials, most of the supporters of the declaration entered the so-called Old Catholic Church.

Oak, Synod of the ● Synod held in 403 in a suburb of Chalcedon known as the Oak where St. John Chrysostom was removed from his post as patriarch of Constantinople. The result of efforts by members of the imperial court to depose the stubborn bishop, the council was convened with the full approval and connivance of Emperor Arcadius (r. 395-408). Presided over by Paul, exarch of Heracles, the council found John guilty of twenty-nine totally fabricated charges, whereupon the emperor exiled him to Bithynia. While John would be recalled soon thereafter, a more permanent banishment was organized in 404. Interestingly, his recall by the empress was brought about by severe public outrage, including riots in Constantinople and an earthquake.

Observantines ● Also Observants. More properly, the *Fratres de Observantia*, the name given to those Franciscans who proclaim their obedience to the original Rule of St. Francis as approved in November 1223 by Pope Honorius III. Largely inspired by the so-called Spiritual Franciscans, they became a separate order from the Franciscans in 1517 but were later themselves divided. In 1897, the various branches were combined into the Order of Friars Minor. (See **Franciscans** for other details.)

Odilo of Cluny, St. (c. 962-1048) ● Fifth abbot of Cluny who had a major influence upon the Cluniac order. A descendant of the nobility of Auvergne, he first entered the seminary of St. Julien in Brionde, but in 991

he joined Cluny. In 994, he was ordained and succeeded Mayeul as abbot. He soon proved himself a highly capable head of the monastery, advancing the reforms of the Benedictine institutions, increasing the number of Cluniac houses, and spreading their influence across Europe. Under him the number of Cluniac houses rose from thirty-seven to sixty-five; of these, twenty-three were newly reformed houses. A remarkable traveler, Odilo took part in several synods and was highly respected by popes (John XIX and Benedict IX each offered him the see of Lyons) and emperors. He was also instrumental in concluding the Truce of God and established All Souls' Day (November 2), which was later to be adopted by the entire Church. Canonized in 1063, he was much revered in the Middle Ages; his relics were burned, however, in 1793 during the French Revolution. Feast day: January 1.

Odo of Cluny, St. (d. 942) ● Second abbot of Cluny, he was an important figure in the promotion of the Cluniac reform. Born in Tours to a Frankish knight, Odo was raised in the family of William, duke of Aquitaine, entering the monastery of Baume (909) under the influence of St. Berno. In 927, he was named the successor of Berno as abbot of Cluny, subsequently proving instrumental in the rise of Cluny in reforming the monasteries of Christendom. Such was his esteemed position that Pope John XI authorized him to promote reform among the monasteries of France and Italy. He penned a number of notable works: three books of *Collationes* (moral essays), an epic poem on the Redemption, twelve choral antiphons in honor of St. Martin of Tours, and a biography of St. Gerald of Aurillac.

Oecumenical Councils ● See **Ecumenical Councils**.

Olaf II Haraldsson, St. (c. 995-1030) ● Known as St. Olaf, he was the king of Norway from 1015-1030. He completed the Christianization of the country and became its patron saint. A descendant of King Haraldsson II Fairhair and the son of a nobleman (or *jarl*), he was raised a pagan, taking part in a number of raids against England from 1008-1011. After traveling for a time in Spain and France, he served King Ethelred II of England, fighting the Danes. Converted to Christianity, he was baptized in 1013. Returning to Norway in 1015, he claimed the throne by defeating his rival, working to reduce the influence of the Danes and Swedes. His most important policy, however, was to promote the spread of Christianity. In this he was quite successful, but his efforts to unite the kingdom brought severe opposition from the nobles who disliked his often harsh methods. Overthrown in 1028 in favor of Cnut the Great, he fled to Russia. In 1030, he attempted to regain the throne but was killed at the Battle of Stiklestad. Canonized a short time later, he became an immensely popular saint, the patron of Norway. Churches were dedicated to him throughout England where he was known as St. Olave. Feast day: July 29.

Old Catholics ● Name given to the members of numerous local churches composed of onetime Catholics who refuse to acknowledge the infallibility of the pope as defined by the First Vatican Council in 1870. The Old Catholics maintain that only they are keeping the true Catholic faith alive. The movement began among many German Catholic intellectuals in response to the decree on infallibility. A series of conferences, including the one held in Nuremburg in August 1870, resulted in a denunciation of Pope Pius IX and the infallibility doctrine, but as it was clear the Holy See was quite unprepared to initiate changes, such noted reformers as Johannes Döllinger (1799-1890), Franz Reusch (1825-1900), and Johannes Friedrich (1836-1917) took the decisive step of breaking with Rome. They were joined by like-minded individuals from German-speaking countries and by elements of the Anglican and Lutheran Churches; support also came from parts of Germany where the Church had faced chronic difficulties due to implementation of anti-Roman policies such as the *Kulturkampf* in Prussia. The organization of the Old Catholics was established from 1874-1875 at Bonn, largely under the guidance of Döllinger. They took their apostolic succession from the so-called Church of Utrecht, which had been formed in 1724 by the separation from Rome of three bishops. Doctrinally, the Old Catholics reject papal supremacy, accept only the first seven ecumenical councils, oppose the veneration of saints and relics, and accept both clerical marriage and mixed marriages. They are found mostly in Europe, and their work in the United States is centered mainly in minority communities of European descent.

Olier, Jean Jacques (1608-1657) ● Founder of the seminary and Society of St.-Sulpice. Born in Paris, he studied under the Jesuits at Lyons (1617-1625) and was encouraged to enter the priesthood by St. Francis de Sales. Subsequently studying in Paris (1625-1627) and at the Sorbonne in Paris (1627-1630), he was plagued by failing eyesight. He made a pilgrimage to Loreto, however, and was completely cured. Converted to a spiritual life at the same moment, he at first looked into entering the Carthusians but was instead drawn to the priesthood. Instructed by St. Vincent de Paul he was ordained in May 1633. Olier now devoted himself to the arduous task of reviving religion in France. With the spiritual guidance of Vincent and Père de Condress, superior of the Oratory, Olier embarked on a mission across the country. An effort to establish a seminary at Chartres (1641) failed, but in December 1641, Olier and several associates began a seminary in Vaugirard, in Paris. The next year, Olier was placed in charge of the parish of St.-Sulpice, with the objective of founding a seminary and Christianizing the Sorbonne. As the parish was a large one and had been overrun with the worst and most pitiful elements in society, Olier worked unceasingly to care for the sick and the poor, to revive the faith, and to promote a free Catholic education. In the midst of these programs, Olier also enjoyed success in converting many French nobles and members of the upper classes. Such was his influence that the English king Charles II was brought into the faith. Olier's other great achievement was in establishing the seminary of St.-Sulpice. This community became the model for many other diocesan seminaries, and members of the Society of St.-Sulpice were sent to other dioceses to help install similar programs. In 1657, Olier even sent several priests to Montreal in Quebec, Canada. He authored numerous spiritual writings and was considered a saint by Vincent de Paul, who was with him at his death at St.-Sulpice on April 2, 1657. (See also **Sulpicians**.)

Olivetans ● Branch of the Benedictine order founded in 1319 by Giovanni Tolomei (St. Bernard Ptolomei). The Olivetans were first established on a mountain near Siena by Tolomei, assisted by two former Sienese political leaders, Patricio Patrici and Ambrogio Piccolomini. They at first adopted a very austere lifestyle, so much so that after several years they were charged with heresy. Summoned before Pope John XXII at Avignon, Tolomei not only secured papal

approval but was sent to receive a rule from Guido di Pietromala, bishop of Arezzo. This prelate had once had a dream or vision in which Our Lady had told him to give white habits to the monks who were kneeling before her. The bishop thus gave the three monks white habits and the Benedictine Rule. Tolomei was henceforth called Bernard and the mountain renamed Monte Oliveto. The new congregation spread to other sites, and the Olivetans were known for their austere lifestyles, including, for a long time, abstaining completely from wine. St. Bernard Ptolomei died in 1348. The Olivetans were brought into the Order of St. Benedict in 1960.

Olivi, Pierre (d. 1298) ● Also Petrus Johannis, a Spiritual Franciscan, theologian, and writer. Born at Serignan, in Languedoc, France, he entered the Friars Minor in Béziers at the age of twelve. After studying at Paris, he returned to Languedoc. There he earned a reputation for strict observance of the Franciscan Rule and was thus asked in 1279 by Pope Nicholas III to give his opinion on Franciscan poverty. A supporter and leading spokesman for the Franciscan rigorists, Olivi was accused of heresy at the general chapter in 1285 at Strasbourg. The following year, seven learned friars censured thirty-four of his propositions and seized his writings. After ably defending himself, however, he was rehabilitated by the general chapter at Montpelier in 1287, served as a lector on theology by the order, and died on March 14, 1298, after making a profession of faith. Unfortunately, soon after his death, his followers displayed such exaggerated veneration of him and so revered his tomb that steps had to be taken by the order; in 1318, his tomb was destroyed. This came after the Chapter at Lyons (1299) burned his writings and the Chapter of Vienne (1311) issued the decretal *Fidei catholicae fundamento* against three points of Olivi's teachings (although he was not mentioned by name: the moment Christ's body was transfixed by the lance; the union of the soul within the body; and the baptism of infants). Pope John XXII also condemned his *Postilla super Apocalypsim* in 1326, after it had been used by Louis the Bavarian in his well-known Appeal of Sachsenhausen (1324). His writings, which were forbidden by the Franciscans, included biblical commentaries, studies of the Franciscan Rule, and theological works.

Optatam Totius ● One of the decrees of Vatican Council II, promulgated on October 28, 1965. Known in English as the "Decree on Priestly Formation," it is concerned with the training of priests and the fostering of priestly vocations. Stressing the need for a priesthood that is "vitalized by the spirit of Christ" (Preface), the decree calls for care in preparation of potential members of the priestly ministry. Among suggested steps to achieve this are recognizing the importance of stable seminaries, revising and updating the program of studies, and the continuation of studies by priests after ordination. Above all, the decree hopes to facilitate the preparation of priests full of "that truly Catholic spirit by which they can transcend the borders of their own diocese, nation, or rite, be accustomed to consulting the needs of the whole Church, and be ready in spirit to preach the gospel everywhere" (No. 20). It has been the subject of ongoing debates as to the effectiveness of the actual implementation of the decree. Pope John Paul II examined the continuing process of priestly formation in his *Pastores Dabo Vobis* (1992), a postsynodal apostolic exhortation, "To the Bishops, Clergy, and Faithful on the Formation of Priests in the Circumstances of the Present Day."

Optatus, St. ● Late fourth-century bishop of Mikvis and Numidia, North Africa. Little is known about him beyond his authorship of the treatise against Parmenian, a Donatist

and successor to Donatus as bishop of Carthage. Optatus had probably been a pagan convert to Christianity and was mentioned by St. Augustine in *De Doctrina Christiana* (40). According to St. Jerome (in *De viris illustribus*, CX), the treatise was in six books (seven are extant, including a later Book VII) and was written during the reigns of Emperors Valens and Valentinian (363-375). Book I was concerned with the founding of Donatism; Books II-VI were centered in examining the Donatist controversy. Optatus argues that while there is agreement between the Donatists and Catholics on the necessity of a united Church, the Donatists cannot claim to be a "catholic" Church because they lack acceptance by the universal faith; the Church, he notes, cannot be limited to North Africa but must be everywhere (*catholica*) in the world. Book V also argues against Donatist teachings on baptism; proposing the faith of the baptizer is unimportant because it is God who confers the grace; the idea of baptism by one outside the Church had been rejected by the Donatists, and Optatus actually anticipated St. Augustine in his analysis. Book VII, of which Jerome was apparently unaware, was added to a later edition. Optatus called for unity and extols the willingness of Catholics to accept the Donatists back into the faith. There was also an appendix containing a dossier of heretical documents related to the origin of Donatism that was compiled by a scholar sometime in the middle of the fourth century.

Opus Dei ● Latin for "Work of God." Worldwide association of Catholics that was first founded in Madrid, Spain, in 1928 by Monsignor Josemaría Escrivá de Balaguer y Allia (beatified in 1992). Opus Dei has as its aims the attainment of Christian perfection that is the universal call for all people, the giving of theological and ascetical formation for its members so as to lead to personal sanctity in their daily lives, and the enabling of them to carry on a personal apostolate in their conduct of work. Opus Dei is made up of two main sections, one for men and another for women. Both contain single and married members, under the direction of a president general. Priests for the association are chosen from among the laymen, although diocesan priests are permitted to be members through the Priestly Society of the Holy Cross while remaining under the authority of their bishops and continuing their regular diocesan assignments.

Opus Dei was given first formal approval in 1947 by Pope Pius XII, who declared it universal, thereby permitting it to function internationally. By 1964, members were found in over fifty countries. On November 28, 1982, Pope John Paul II declared it to be a personal prelature, with the full title Prelature of the Holy Cross and Opus Dei, a clear statement of papal favor. It is customarily inserted into dioceses with the local ordinary having jurisdiction over the chapter within his diocese. Members are thus directed in their religious activities while retaining full freedom in their other, secular affairs. Currently, there are nearly eighty-two thousand members worldwide, with almost fifteen hundred priests and three hundred fifty seminarians.

Orange, Councils of ● Also called the Councils of Arausio (the Roman name for Orange). Two nonecumenical councils held at Orange in southern France; they occurred in 441 and 529.

First Council of Orange: Convened on November 8, 441, it was presided over by St. Hilary of Arles, and attended by sixteen other bishops. It issued thirty canons on the administration of the sacraments, the right of sanctuary, relations between bishops, clerical marriage, widows and virgins, and the holding of subsequent councils.

Second Council of Orange: More important than the synod held in 441, this was convened on July 3, 529, presided over by St. Caesarius of Arles, and attended by thirteen other bishops. The council is notable for being the first in Gaul (France) to deliberate upon matters of doctrine on grace and free will as they pertained to the controversy of Semi-Pelagianism. The resulting *capitula* (propositions drawn from St. Augustine and St. Prosper of Aquitaine) issued by the council (twenty-five in number) were based on a series of *capitula* sent by Pope Felix IV (III). The acts of the council defined doctrine against the Semi-Pelagianism in the causes and necessity of grace, the functioning or operation of grace prior to justification, the operation of grace in baptism or justification, the functioning of grace after justification, and the universal necessity of grace. Pope Boniface II approved the acts on January 25, 531. They were also used by the Council of Trent (1545-1563) to condemn Martin Luther.

Oratorians ● More properly, Congregation of the Oratory (C.O.). Founded formally by St. Philip Neri at Rome in 1575, the name was derived from the oratory of San Girolamo, Rome, where an original community of priests had gathered around St. Philip. He devoted his efforts to giving shape to the congregation that would attract more priests who customarily said Mass and, with devotions and hymns, preached four sermons daily. Having begun his work in 1564, St. Philip found by 1575 that his community was in need of a rule and a church that it might call its own. So, from Pope Gregory XIII, Philip obtained permission to take over the church of S. Maria in Vallicella. The priests of the Oratory were to live under obedience but were to be bound by no vows. Further, the founder was adamant that even should the majority of members wish to take vows, the minority should possess the property; nor, he felt, should the houses that might be founded ever cease to be utterly independent, declaring, "Let each house live by its own vitality, or perish of its own decrepitude." The rule was given approval in 1612 by Pope Paul V, with a provost elected for three years by those members who had been in the congregation for ten or more years. The object of the congregation was proclaimed to be prayer, preaching, and the sacraments. It spread throughout Italy and then into Spain, Portugal, and Poland before reaching South America and Asia. Surviving the terrible period of the French Revolution and Napoleonic Wars, the Oratorians rebuilt and once more flourished. John Henry Newman brought them into England in 1848 when he established the Oratory at Old Oscott, followed by one the next year in London. They maintained the strictly autonomous nature of their houses until 1942 when the still independent communities were formed into a confederation. Their aim remains pastoral work, preaching, and the fostering of development among the young and students. There are currently nearly five hundred members worldwide.

A French Congregation of the Oratory was founded in 1611 by Cardinal Pierre de Bérulle, based on the Oratory begun by St. Philip Neri and adopting many elements of the rule and constitution of the original congregation. Bérulle's main alteration was to create a central organization for the houses under a superior general. It was intended to promote the fulfillment of the priestly life by its members; although not a teaching order, it did engage the direction of colleges and organized seminaries in accordance with the commands promulgated by the Council of Trent. Nevertheless, its chief aim was, as described by the French cardinal Adolphe Perraud, "the pursuit of sacerdotal perfection." Surviving the Jansenist tendencies of some of its members, including two superior generals, the Oratorians were effectively suppressed by the French Revolution. In 1852, they were reestablished through the work of Father Auguste Gratry (1805-1872) and Father L. Pétot (d. 1887). Among its most notable

members were St. John Eudes, Jean-Baptiste Massillon, and Nicholas Malebranche.

Ordericus Vitalis (d. c. 1142) ● Benedictine historian. Born in Shrewsbury, he was the son of a French priest and an English woman. While still a boy, he was sent to St. Evroult, the Benedictine monastery in Normandy. Here he would remain for the rest of his life. He is best known for his *Historia ecclesiastica*. This began originally as a history of St. Evroult, but it developed into a full account of the Church from the birth of Christ to 1141. The history is noted for its extensive use of sources, including William of Poitiers and Fulcher of Chartres; it is a valuable source for details on contemporary society (c. 1082-1141).

Orders, Holy ● Sacrament conferring spiritual grace and power upon a man through the imposition of a bishop's hands, permitting the man to carry out the ordained ministry. Also known as the major orders (as compared to the minor orders), there are three forms of the sacrament, the diaconate, priesthood, and episcopate; it should be remembered, however, that while there are three forms of the sacrament there is only one sacrament that is administered, with higher sacramental effects. The sacrament may be conferred upon any baptized male, although ordination would be illicit were it bestowed upon a person before the age of reason. A baptized male may be ordained a priest without ordination to the diaconate, but a baptized male may not be validly consecrated a bishop unless he has already been ordained a priest. Further, as the sacrament leaves an indelible mark upon the soul of the recipient, it is received only once.

The sacrament of holy orders was first instituted by Christ at the Last Supper when he offered his body and blood under the appearance of bread and wine, commanding the disciples, "Do this in remembrance of me" (Lk 22:19) Having established the sacrament, however, the specific grades of ministers developed only slowly in the early Church. In the Acts of the Apostles and the Epistles of St. Paul, there is little clear information on a delineated hierarchy of bishops, presbyters, and deacons. The various ministerial terms such as *episcopoi* (bishop) and *presbyteroi* (presbyter) were applied in Scripture interchangeably. Nevertheless, within the NT the appellations applied are of a more semantic nature than any reference to authority, and within Scripture there is a distinct presence of the three ministerial grades, becoming clearer toward the end of the apostolic age.

In 1 Timothy 3:1-7, Paul gives a description of the characteristics of the ideal bishop, and in the same epistle (3:8-13), he writes of the needed qualities in deacons.

Essential to the hierarchical system of the Church leadership was the presence of the bishop (*episcopoi*) for each community. He presided over a college of priests (*presbyteroi*). That this system was in place by the second century is attested by St. Ignatius of Antioch (d. 107) in a letter to the Smyrnaeans.

The sacraments, save for baptism and marriage, were customarily administered by the bishop, or by a priest so delegated by the bishop. Over the succeeding centuries, as the Church grew in size and the power and duties of the bishops increased, the priests were permitted to administer more of the sacraments. This was most true once the parish system within the diocese was fully in place. The priests thus came to administer all of the sacraments except for confirmation and holy orders, which were always to remain the domain of the bishops.

Theologians eventually asked the question whether Christ himself had instituted the grades (or ranks) of priests — priests and bishops — or if this had been laid down by the Apostles. The Council of Trent took up the question, decreeing in Canon 6 of the *Canons on the Sacrament of Orders*: "If anyone says that in the Catholic Church there is not a hierarchy, divinely instituted and consisting of bishops, priests, and ministers, let him be anathema."

Extensive changes were introduced by Vatican Council II. The reforms extended to the ceremonies and texts of ordination, the diaconate, the subdiaconate, and the minor orders. The decree of the Vatican Council was implemented by an apostolic constitution as well as several apostolic letters by Pope Paul VI. He established a new rite for ordinations of bishops, priests, and deacons, and reformed the minor orders with the *motu proprio Ministeria quaedam* (1972). The subdiaconate was suppressed and its duties assumed by the acolyte and the reader. The diaconate was also clarified and given a place of heightened importance. It was henceforth to have two forms, permanent and transitional. The permanent diaconate was for those who would have perpetual celibacy and for those who were married (see **Deacon** in the GLOSSARY). The second diaconate was transitional in that it was a preparatory stage for the priesthood.

Ordines Romani ● Books used during the Middle Ages giving instruction to the clergy on the performance of rituals according to the Roman rite. The *ordines* were often compiled with one ceremony in mind (and here would be called *Ordo*), such as the rites of baptism, marriage, and the consecration of a church. The earliest of the surviving *ordines* are preserved in manuscripts dating from the eighth to twelfth centuries. The first printed collection was the *Ordo Romanus Vulgatus*, edited by George Cassander and published at Cologne in 1561. This was reprinted in 1568 and was reedited by Melchior Hittorp and was thus called the *Ordo Romanus of Hittorp*. The most valuable of the *ordines* were collected by Jean

Mabillon (1632-1707) into his *Museum Italicum* (1689). These fifteen *ordines* were of varying form and organization.

Oresme, Nicole (c. 1320-1382) ● French philosopher, bishop of Lisieux, and mathematician. A native of Normandy, he studied at Paris and served as grand master of the College of Navarre (1356) and dean of Rouen (1367); in 1377, he became bishop of Lisieux. Much respected by King Charles V of France, he served as adviser to the monarch and was encouraged by the king to promote learning in France. Oresme wrote in both Latin and French, examining such subjects as economics, mathematics, natural sciences, theology, and politics. Of particular importance were his commentary on the economics and politics of Aristotle; *De Moneta* (*On Coinage*), an early (1360) scientific study on numismatics; and his writings on mathematics. Oresme's studies with Jean Buridan of moving bodies foreshadowed the work of Leonardo da Vinci and Copernicus.

Organic Articles ● Law issued by Napoleon Bonaparte in April 1802. The law's aim was to regulate public worship in France and secure control of relations between Church and State. The law was comprised of seventy-seven articles relating to Catholicism and forty-four to Protestantism. It was presented by Napoleon, then first consul, to the Tribunate and the legislative body of the government at the same time that he requested them to vote on the Concordat of 1801 that he had negotiated with Pope Pius VII. Naturally accepted, the two were published as law and were henceforth considered to be inseparable by the French government until 1905. A sharp and entirely nonnegotiated change in the agreement between Napoleon and the pope, the Organic Articles were declared by Pius on May 24, 1802, to have been promulgated without his prior knowledge and to be unacceptable

without considerable alterations. Among the terms of the Organic Articles were: the right of authorization by the government over the publication and execution of papal documents in France; rights over clerical dress, which was to be "in the French fashion and in black"; state regulation over public processions; partial control by the state over seminaries, including the teaching of the Gallican Articles; rights of interference by the state in some appointments; and the institution of regulations on parish boundaries and stipends for the clergy. While many of the articles became virtually dead and ceased to be enforced, they were not fully abrogated until 1905 when the concordat was terminated by a new law separating Church and State in France.

Orientalium Ecclesiarum ● Known in English as the "Decree on the Eastern Catholic Churches," it was issued by the Second Vatican Council on November 21, 1964, and became law on January 22, 1965. The decree has, among its goals, the declaration of the full rights and equality of the Eastern communities of the Catholic Church, while at the same time making positive statements toward the separated Eastern Churches (the Orthodox Christian Churches). Members of the Eastern Catholic communities are given encouragement to remain steadfast in their faith and to preserve always their customs and proper liturgical rites. The council sought to give reassurance of the full intention of the Church in the West to have the utmost respect for their brethren in the Eastern Church and that Catholics in the West would be urged to study and become acquainted with the other rites of the Catholic Church. Beyond these broad assurances, the decree covers such legal matters as: the declaration as valid of all marriages between Eastern Catholic and non-Catholic Christians, when performed by a validly ordained priest; the reception of non-Catholic Christians into the

Catholic Church with the simple profession of faith; the points of shared worship between the Catholic and non-Catholic Eastern Churches. The simplifying of the process of reception would have important ramifications for the rebirth of the Catholic Church in Ukraine in the early 1990s following the collapse of the Soviet Union. *Orientalium Ecclesiarum* also makes clear the hope of the council that a reunion between the Catholic and Orthodox Churches will one day take place.

Origen (c. 185-254) ● In full, Origenes Adamantius. An influential early teacher, theologian, exegete, and writer, he was born probably in Egypt, perhaps Alexandria, to Christian parents. His father, St. Leonidas, taught him extensive elements of the faith and made him memorize passages from the Scriptures. (Leonidas was martyred around 202.) Further education came under the famed teacher Clement of Alexandria, head of the Catechetical School of Alexandria. Around the same time as his father's death, Origen succeeded Clement as director of the school, since Clement had been forced into exile by the Romans. He remained in the post for some twenty years, even after the end of the persecution; he taught philosophy, Scripture, and theology but at the same time improved his own knowledge of pagan philosophy by attending lectures by the noted philosopher Ammonius Saccas, founder of the school of Neoplatonism. Origen also adopted a strict asceticism, castrating himself in a very extreme interpretation of the passage in Matthew (19:12).

In 212, he traveled to Rome and then to various places in Greece, Palestine, and Arabia. While in Palestine, Origen was invited by several local bishops to preach in their churches. Origen accepted their request, despite being a layman, an action that angered Bishop St. Demetrius of Alexandria, who ordered him to return to Alexandria. On another visit to Palestine around 230, he was ordained a priest by the bishops of Jerusalem and Caesarea. Demetrius, even more angry and feeling that his rights had been violated, held two synods. Origen was exiled from Alexandria and commanded not to exercise his priestly duties. Given sanctuary at Caesarea, he opened another school in 231 and added to his already considerable reputation through his writing and instruction. Sometime in 250, however, he was arrested during the Decian persecution. Imprisoned and tortured, he was shattered physically and never recovered his health after his release in 251. He died a few years later at Tyre.

Origen was the author of a vast corpus of writings. Unfortunately, few of his works have survived, extant mostly in fragments or generally unreliable Latin translations from the original Greek. His scriptural writings include: numerous Commentaries of the Old and New Testaments and the *Hexapla* (or sixfold Bible), that was used by St. Jerome in his creation of the Vulgate. Other works are: *Contra Celsum* (*Against Celsus*), an apology against the pagan cynic Celsus; *Exhortation to Martyrdom*, a plea to his friends to remain firm in the faith during the persecutions; and perhaps his most important book, *First principles* (c. 225), an effort to compile a comprehensive manual on dogmatic theology, one of the first in the history of the Church. It is known today only in two Greek fragments and an unreliable Latin version translated by Tyrannius Rufinus (d. 410). This manual became the focus of the Originist controversy.

Origen was accused by St. Jerome and others of certain heretical tendencies. Others defended him, however, and the majority of the Eastern bishops considered him a defender of the faith. His name nevertheless became attached to a doctrinal system, Origenism, incorporating various unorthodox elements of his teaching. Widely read in the years after his death, Origen attracted many adherents who propagated some of his more extreme theories, ultimately causing the Origenist controversy of the fourth century. The chief enemy of Origenism was St. Jerome, who helped secure the condemnation of Origen's radical teachings by Pope Anastasius I in 400. Elements of Origenism would endure into the sixth century.

Orléans, Councils of ● Six national, rather than general, councils held in Orléans between 511 and 639. Council I was convened by King Clovis in July 511. It established the right of sanctuary and forbade divination (see **Sanctuary, Right of**). Council II, under King Childebert, met in June 533, and decreed new, tougher regulations on marriage and declared marriages between Jews and Christians illegal. Council III was held in May 538; it excommunicated any cleric who might fail in leading a celibate life and determined certain impediments to marriage. Council IV, in 541, considered the emancipation of slaves. Council V, in October 549, condemned Nestorianism and Eutychianism and prohibited simony. Council VI, held under King Clovis II in 639, condemned and exiled a supporter of Monothelitism. Two other councils, in 1022 and 1478, were convened in Orléans.

Orosius, Paulus ● Fifth-century Christian apologist. Also known simply as Orosius, he was probably born in Bracara, modern Braga, Portugal. Entering the Church at an early age, he was ordained and set off for Africa in 413 or 414. There he became a friend of St. Augustine, who sent him to Palestine in the hopes of gaining the support of St. Jerome against the Pelagians. In 415, however, Bishop John of Jerusalem held a council in Jerusalem, upholding the teaching of Pelagius. Orosius spoke out against Pelagius but was then accused of possible heresy. In response, he wrote the *Liber apologeticus*, providing a detailed account of

the Jerusalem council and an examination of the main points against Pelagius. Returning to Africa in 416 with a letter from St. Jerome, Orosius authored, at Augustine's behest, the *Historiarum adversus paganos* (417), the first universal Christian history, in which Orosius argued that the Roman Empire had suffered as many calamities before Christianity as after; this refuted claims that the empire had been punished with disasters as a result of abandoning pagan beliefs. The work is particularly useful in the information it provides for the years after A.D. 378 and was used frequently during the Middle Ages as a guide to history. King Alfred the Great even translated it into Anglo-Saxon.

Orsi, Giuseppe (1692-1761) ● Italian cardinal and theologian. Born in Florence, he was a member of a noble Florentine family, studying under the Jesuits and entering the Dominicans in February 1708. After holding various posts, he was sent to Rome in 1732 as professor of theology at the College of St. Thomas. Two years later, he became an adviser to Cardinal Neri Corsini, nephew of Clement XII. Named master of the sacred palace in 1749 by Pope Benedict XIV, he held the post for ten years when, on September 24, 1759, he was appointed cardinal by Pope Clement XIII. Among his numerous writings were apologetics, history, and dogmatics. His chief work was the *Storia ecclesiastica*, a history of the Church (20 vols., 1747-1761) that Orsi was able to bring down to the sixth century; a twenty-first volume was finished by a onetime pupil, and the Dominican scholar F. Becchetti continued the work to 1587.

Orthodox Eastern Churches ● Broad name given to the churches of the Eastern rite, which withdrew from communion with the Holy See throughout the history of the Church. (Also referred to simply as Orthodox Church and similar variants.) While they do not accept the primacy of the pope, differ from the Latin (or Catholic) Church on various points of theology, and recognize only the first seven ecumenical (or general) councils, they retain nevertheless, the character of valid Christian (or Mother) Churches, possessing complete liturgies, hierarchy, and doctrines. They may be considered as well descendants of the foundational sees of the East: Constantinople, Antioch, Alexandria, and Jerusalem.

The wide communion of Orthodox Churches is principally comprised of self-governing, or autocephalous, Churches under the authority of patriarchs. Chief among them is the oecumenical (or ecumenical) patriarch, the patriarch of Constantinople. While he is given the position of honorary primacy, he does not rule over the other Churches; his jurisdiction extends only to his own patriarchate, although he is able to summon assemblies of the Orthodox leaders and controls the so-called Holy Canons of the Autocephalous Churches. In this is kept a listing of those recognized churches of the Orthodox communion. The entire Orthodox Church may be divided along the following lines:

Greek Orthodox: The Churches under this jurisdiction are based in the patriarchates of Constantinople, Alexandria, Antioch, and Jerusalem, each with its own specific territorial authority. To these are added the Churches of Sinai, Greece, and Cyprus, which are also autocephalic.

Russian Orthodox: This largest of the Orthodox communities is under the patriarchate of Moscow and claims members throughout the former Soviet Union. It has traditionally wielded enormous influence in the lives of the Russian people and, since the fall of Constantinople in 1453, has been the most powerful participant in the communion. (See also **Russia**.)

Slavic Churches: The patriarchates of Serbia, Bulgaria, Romania, and Georgia. These were born out of the missionary labors of Sts. Cyril and Methodius, the Apostles of the Slavs, in the ninth century. They developed into national churches, and, under the influence of Constantinople became part of the Orthodox Church with the breach in 1054.

Other Churches: These include the Churches of Poland, Albania, Cyprus, Czechoslovakia, Latvia, Lithuania, Hungary, Finland, Estonia, China, and Japan.

In liturgical practice, these churches are almost exact in all essentials to the Eastern Catholic Church. They follow generally the Byzantine rite. This was the rite of St. James of Jerusalem and the churches of Antioch and was revised under Sts. Basil and John Chrysostom. It has been characterized historically by its expression in liturgical terms of Eastern theology, a practice that contributed to the early gulf that developed with the Western Church, where theology was more concerned with the construction of rational thought within the deposit of revealed truth. The Catholic Church recognizes as valid all of the Orthodox sacraments as well as the ordination and consecration of Orthodox priests and bishops respectively. The Catholic also gives respect to the Orthodox Church for its immense contributions to monasticism, spiritual theology, and, like its Western counterpart, its abiding love for the Mother of God (*Theotokos*). This does not lessen, however, the serious differences between the Churches, most pointedly in the areas of papal authority, the *Filioque*, and the Immaculate Conception. (For details, see **Schism, Eastern**.)

The last decades have seen an improvement in the relations between the Orthodox and Catholic communities, with both sides entering into good faith discussions. Of special note was the meeting between Pope Paul VI with Ecumenical Patriarch Athenagoras I before the patriarch's death in 1972. Pope John Paul II has striven for better relations, the desirability of friendly dialogue and cooperation becoming even more urgent with the fall of Communism and the opening up of the lands of the onetime Soviet bloc to proselytizing. Tensions have increased, however, as Orthodox and Eastern Catholics have disagreed over property ownership and rights of preaching.

Osservatore Romano, L' ● In Italian, *The Roman Observer*. Daily newspaper of the Holy See and the most important publication of the Vatican, it is called "the official newspaper of the pope." It was founded in July 1861 as an independent newspaper by four Catholic laymen. One of its founders was Marcantonio Pacelli, the grandfather of Pope Pius XII. Purchased by Pope Leo XIII in 1890, it is owned by the Holy See and is answerable to the Office of Information and Documentation — part of the Secretariat of State — in all matters of policy and editorial control. Administered by the members of the Salesian Congregation of St. John Bosco, *L'Osservatore Romano* has a director and editor-in-chief, a small editorial board, and a staff of local reporters that covers Rome and various foreign stories. There are no overseas correspondents, but the paper avails itself when needed of episcopal conferences around the globe or other sources.

Every day, except Sunday, at 3:00 P.M., the paper is published, although much of the audience reads one of the weekly editions, published in English, French, Portuguese, Spanish, German, Italian, and Polish. These editions are available worldwide by subscription and each "foreign" language edition has its own editor.

L'Osservatore Romano has one of the most familiar mastheads of any newspaper, including the mottoes *"Unicuique suum"* ("To each his own") and *"Non praevelalunt"* ("They shall not prevail"), reminders of the terrible events in 1870 when the Papal States were lost and when the paper last ceased, albeit temporarily, to be published. Extremely devoted and utterly loyal to the Holy See, it

provides approved translations of encyclicals, speeches, and other papal documents; also, there are listings of appointments, daily calendars, planned trips, consistories, and assorted announcements. The only part of the paper considered "official," however, is the front-page column *Nostre Informazioni*, with formal announcements and any news that the Holy Father wishes released. With a circulation of around fifty thousand, the paper nevertheless enjoys considerable influence and is read with great interest by Church leaders, governments, scholars, and so-called Vaticanologists.

Ostpolitik ● Policy first adopted by Pope Paul VI in his relations with the countries of the Soviet Bloc that attempted to improve the plight of Catholics in Eastern Europe through negotiations and a rapprochement. The roots of *Ostpolitik* were planted in the reign of Pope John XXIII (r. 1958-1963), who made a conscious decision to end the distinctly hostile attitude of the papacy toward Communism under Pope Pius XII. John used his natural charm and the services of some truly remarkable Vatican diplomats to begin thawing relations between the Holy See and the Soviet Union. Reversing Pius's declaration that Communism was an evil that could not be negotiated with, John encouraged discreet communications between the Vatican representatives and diplomats of the Soviet bloc and provided further inspiration and justification by his encyclical *Pacem in Terris* (1963).

It was Paul VI who formalized the policy, finding two crucial architects in Agostino Casaroli (later cardinal) and Cardinal Franz Koenig, archbishop of Vienna (1956-1985). Koenig provided important links to the Communist regimes of Eastern Europe, and Casaroli, under Paul, became the first Vatican official to travel extensively in the Soviet bloc. As a leading figure in the Council of Public Affairs of the Church, Casaroli distinguished himself as a talented diplomat.

Made titular archbishop in July 1967, he was the chief negotiator for the Holy See, visiting Hungary, Czechoslovakia, Poland, and Bulgaria. The short-term goal of easing the harsh treatment was achieved in some areas, as witnessed by the 1972 release of Cardinal Mindszenty of Hungary.

The election of a Polish cardinal as pope in 1978 signaled a new era in *Ostpolitik*, for the figure succeeding to the papal throne had long experience in dealing with the oppressive regimes of the Soviet Empire. Karol Wojtyla, as Pope John Paul II, not only retained Casaroli's services but promoted him to succeed Cardinal Jean Villot as secretary of state in 1979. Cardinal Casaroli continued to negotiate with the Eastern bloc, but the policy of constructive engagement used by the pontiff in such cases as dealing with the Soviets over their 1979 invasion of Afghanistan and threats of intercession in Poland over Lech Walesa and the Solidarity movement led to what may have been a KGB-inspired assassination attempt in 1981 by Bulgarian operatives using Mehmet Ali Agca.

The pope remained firm in his stand that the Church be granted freedom in Poland and Eastern Europe, a position only strengthened by his personal popularity in the East and the determination of the West to face down Soviet aggression. That this policy was vindicated was seen in 1989 with the visit of Mikhail Gorbachev to the Vatican and the appointment of bishops by the Holy See to long empty sees in Eastern Europe. The final fruition of *Ostpolitik* would be achieved in the next years as the Soviet Empire crumbled and Communist regimes fell from power, an event unthinkable but a few years before. With the apparent demise of the Soviet bloc came new dangers and opportunities for the Church in Eastern Europe, with new policies of *Ostpolitik* formulated by Cardinal Casaroli and, after his retirement in 1990, by Cardinal Angelo Sodano, the current secretary of state.

Oswald, St. (d. 642) ● King of Northumbria (633-642) and martyr. The son of King Ethelfrith (d. 616), Oswald was the rightful heir to the throne but, upon his father's death, was prevented from taking the throne by Edwin, king of the East Angles. Fleeing to Scotland, Oswald was converted to Christianity by the monks of Iona, thereafter working to promote the faith. Returning home in 633 after Edwin's passing, he defeated King Caedwalla to secure his claim, traditionally proving victorious because of the help given his troops by the wooden cross he erected on the battlefield. His reign was spent increasing the size of his kingdom and spreading Christianity among his subjects. On December 5, 642, however, he was routed and slain by King Penda of Mercia at the Battle of Maserfeld, near modern Shrewsbury. His head was supposedly deposited in the tomb of St. Cuthbert in 875; it was there when the tomb was opened in 1828. Oswald was revered as a martyr, particularly during the Middle Ages. Feast day: August 9.

Ottaviani, Alfredo (1890-1979) ● Powerful and influential Italian cardinal. Long the head of the Sacred Congregation of the Holy Office, and one of the most prominent conservative voices at Vatican Council II, he was born in Rome and studied at the Christian Brothers School in Rome and then the Pontifical Roman Seminary and Pontifical Institute of Canon and Civil Law. Ordained in 1916, he taught at the Lateran University and the Urban College. In 1928, Ottaviani was appointed undersecretary of the Sacred Congregation for Extraordinary Ecclesiastical Affairs; the next year he became *sostituto*, or substitute secretary, of the Secretariat of State. Pope Pius XII named him a cardinal deacon in 1953 and Pope John XXIII placed him in charge of the Sacred Congregation of the Holy Office in 1959. Under John, he held the post of head of the theological commission that was preparing the way for the Second Vatican Council. He worked to preserve as much as possible traditional Catholicism within the wider context of conciliar reform, warning of the potentially disastrous consequences that might arise from some of the liturgical innovations that were introduced. Ottaviani was also an outspoken opponent of Communism. His motto was *Semper idem.*

Otto I (912-973) ● German king from 936 and emperor from 962. Generally held responsible for the founding of the Holy Roman Empire, he was the son of King Henry I; he succeeded his father in 936 but faced years of struggle with the nobles of Germany and his younger brother, Henry. After solidifying his hold on power, he invaded Italy in 951, defeated Berengar II, claimed the iron crown of the Lombards, and wed Adelaide, widow of King Hugh of Italy, thereby attaching Italy to his large territorial possessions. In 955, he routed the invading Magyars at the Battle of Lechfeld, thereafter extending Germanic influence beyond the Oder River. Under his rule, the German towns increased in prosperity. Otto believed in a close political and social relationship between his dynasty and the Church, with the state dominating the ecclesiastical sphere and making it subject to the will of the emperor. Toward this end he created new dioceses (Magdeburg and Brandenburg and in parts of Denmark), made the imperial court the ecclesiastical heart of Germany, and interfered directly with the papacy. He instructed Pope John XII to crown him emperor in 962 and, when John proved to be too independent of mind, he deposed the pontiff in favor of Leo VIII in December 963.

Otto III (980-1002) ● German king from 983 and emperor from 996. The son of Emperor Otto II and the Byzantine princess Theophano, he was elected king at the age of three and spent a miserable time in the guardianship of Henry I the Quarrelsome,

former duke of Bavaria. In 984, however, when Theophano became regent, she promoted a close relationship between Church and State, but by the terms of the imperial understanding of the alliance, the Church, particularly the papacy, were to be subordinated to the will of the emperor. In 996, Otto invaded Italy, placing the German Bruno of Carinthia on the papal throne as Pope Gregory V. While Bruno promoted reform, he could not long survive without direct imperial protection. So, in 997, Gregory was deposed by the Roman nobleman Crescentius in favor of John XVI. Otto returned to Italy, reinstated Gregory, and put Crescentius to death. Otto then remained in Rome, appointing his tutor Gerbert of Aurillac to be Gregory's successor as Pope Sylvester II (r. 999-1003). Otto died at a young age, his dreams of a grand, spiritually guided empire shattered by uprisings in Rome and severe political foment among the German nobles.

Otto of Freising (d. 1158) ● Bishop of Freising and one of the greatest of all medieval historians. The son of St. Leopold III (margrave of Austria) and Agnes (daughter of Emperor Henry IV), Otto was also the uncle of Emperor Frederick I Barbarossa. After attending the University of Paris, he and fifteen other noblemen entered the Cistercian order in Morimond around 1132. After several years, he was elected abbot but was appointed bishop of Freising in 1137 or 1138; in any case, he retained the Cistercian habit. As bishop, he promoted monastic reform, improved education, and was active (as an imperial prince) in negotiating a peace between his nephew Frederick and the papacy. Otto took part in the Second Crusade with his half-brother Emperor Conrad III in 1147-1148. A gifted historian, he authored a number of important works, including the *Gesta Friderici I imperatoris* (1156-1158; a history of the early part of Frederick's reign) and a *Chronicon*

(1143-1146; a universal history in eight books, based on notable medieval chronicles and histories, and dedicated to Isingrim, believed to be abbot of Ottobeuren). In the *Chronicon*, Otto presented modified views of the conception of St. Augustine that the City of God was in a struggle with the world.

Oxford Movement ● Movement of leading intellectuals of the Church of England. Originating and focused in Oxford University that lasted from 1833 until around 1845, it had as its aim the restoration of certain principles of religious heritage that members of the movement felt had been lost. The Oxford movement hoped to bring back to the Church of England those elements of worship of a Catholic nature without, of course, the concomitant defect (from the Anglican perspective) of allegiance to Rome. Its origins can be traced to the growing tension within the C of E between the High Church, which tended toward more Catholic liturgical viewpoints, and the Low Church, which was more Protestant in outlook, preferring less formal sacramental life and a presbyterial versus episcopal form of government. Many High Churchmen were alarmed by the spread of liberal ideas in theology and feared government involvement in church affairs such as the plan to suppress a number of bishoprics in Ireland.

The movement was launched in July 1833 by Dr. John Keble, who spoke out in favor of High Church (or "Catholic") ideals such as the Book of Common Prayer and apostolic succession. He was soon joined by John Henry Newman and Edward Bouverie Pusey. Newman began the *Tracts for the Time*, a series of leaflets to elucidate the tenets of the members. The first was published on September 9, 1833, and was entitled "Thoughts on the Ministerial Commission respectfully addressed to the Clergy." Others followed soon after, earning the movement the early name of Tractarianism, as its growing list of leaders and new supporters contributed tracts of their own. Among the most important Tractarians, besides Keble, Newman, and Pusey, were William Ward, J. D. (Bernard) Dalgairns, Isaac Williams, Richard Froude, Frederick Faber, Charles Marriott, Robert Wilberforce, and Richard Church.

While many Anglicans were sympathetic with the principles advocated by the movement, others in the liberal wing of the Church attacked it as an effort to advance Romanism. Opposition became especially acute after the 1841 publication of Newman's "Tract 90," which sought to give an interpretation of the Thirty-Nine Articles in a Catholic light. Newman retired to Littlemore, as it was increasingly clear to various members that a reform of the C of E would not be possible and that only by returning to the Roman Church could they find a true expression of the Catholic faith. William Ward, Frederick Faber, and several others were received into the Catholic Church on February 13, 1845, followed by Newman that same year, on October 9. Further conversions took place in the years to follow, especially after the Gorham Case, in which much offense was given to High Churchmen owing to the doctrinal views of the Rev. George C. Gorham, who had been chosen in 1847 as bishop of Exeter. The movement, meanwhile, continued to spread, despite much antipathy for it from the established C of E. While it faded as a force within English life, it did accomplish a reemphasis upon the importance of liturgical ceremony and worship as a vital part of Anglicanism.

Ozanam, Antoine Frédéric ● See **Vincent de Paul, St.**

Pacca, Bartolomeo (1756-1844) ● Italian cardinal and statesman. He distinguished himself in the service of Pope Pius VI (r. 1775-1799) and Pius VII (r. 1800-1823). Pacca was born in Benevento, the son of the Marchese di Matrice. After an early education by the Jesuits at Naples, he studied at the Clementine College in Rome and the Academy of Noble Ecclesiastics. Pius VI appointed him nuncio to Cologne in 1785, soon consecrating him titular archbishop. As nuncio he came into conflict with the archbishop of Cologne who, with the archbishops of Mainz, Trier, and Salzburg, issued the so-called *Emser Punktation* (1786), which sought to curtail papal authority in German lands. Pacca resisted all such measures, promoting the work of all defenders of the Holy See. When the Rhine provinces were invaded by the French, Pacca fled to Trier where he was received and recognized by the archbishop. Named in 1794 nuncio to Portugal, his time of service there was generally uneventful, although in 1801 he was promoted to cardinal. In 1808, after Pius bowed to pressure from Napoleon and removed Cardinal Ercole Consalvi and several other pro-secretaries of state, Pacca was chosen pro-secretary, working to maintain stable relations with the French emperor. When the pontiff was seized, however, and removed from Rome, Pacca accompanied him to Florence but was there separated and spent time in harsh confinement. Released in 1813, he rejoined Pius and, after the fall of Napoleon in 1814 was appointed camerlengo. While Consalvi was at the Congress of Vienna, Pacca had the task of restoring the government of the Papal States. His remaining years were spent in various posts in the Curia. Pacca is also remembered for urging Pope Pius to reestablish the Society of Jesus in 1814.

Pacem in Terris ● Encyclical issued on April 11, 1963, by Pope John XXIII, "On establishing universal peace in truth, justice, charity, and liberty." Meaning "Peace on Earth," *Pacem in Terris* was a notable encyclical because it was addressed for the first time not only to all Catholics but to all people of goodwill. It set forth the necessary conditions for the establishment of peace on earth, stressing an existing order between persons and the state, as well as the respectful relationship between nations.

Pachomius, St. (d. 346) ● Egyptian saint and founder of Christian cenobitic (or communal) monasticism. Born near Thebes, Egypt, he was raised a pagan and served in the Roman legions in North Africa. After leaving the legions in 313, he was converted to Christianity, withdrawing into the desert near Thebes. There he lived for a time as a disciple of the noted hermit Palemon (or Palaemon). He then established a community of monks by gathering together the various hermits of the area. This monastery, situated on the Nile at Tabenissi, in the Thebaid, soon attracted many followers. Pachomius drew up a rule for the monks that called for a life of work and prayer. It was the first such rule in the history of monasticism and was to prove so remarkable and flexible that by the time of his death Pachomius had founded over ten monasteries for both men and women. His rule, further, was to have a major influence on such innovators as St. Basil, St. Benedict, and John Cassian. Pachomius is revered by the Eastern and Western Churches as well as by the Coptic Church. Feast day: May 14.

Pagi, Antoine (1624-1699) ● French Church historian and uncle of François Pagi. Born in Rognes, he studied with the Jesuits at Aix before entering the Franciscan monastery at Arles, making his profession in 1641. Elected provincial in 1653, he served in the post three other times but was especially devoted to the study of history. His main work was to bring about a correction of the numerous errors in the *Annales ecclesiastici* of Cesare Baronius (1538-1607). The resulting work was the *Critica historico-chronoligica in universos annales ecclesiasticum em. et rev. Caesarius Card. Borinii*, called the *Critica historico-chronologica*, for short. The first volume appeared in published form in 1689, although the complete work, edited by François Pagi and in four volumes, was published posthumously in 1705. Other writings included the *Dissertatio hypatica* (1682; a study of the electoral process of Roman consuls) and an edition on the sermons of St. Antony of Padua. François Pagi (1654-1721), the nephew of Antoine, was born in Lambere, in Provence, France. Aside from editing the *Critica historico-chronoligica*, he authored the *Breviarium historico-chronoligica illustriora Pontificum romanum gesta*, a history of the popes to 1447 (4 vols., 1717-1727).

St. Gregory Palamas

Pagninus, Santes (1470-1541) ● Dominican biblical scholar. From Lucca, in Tuscany, he entered the Dominicans around 1486 at Fiesole, where he studied under Savonarola. Summoned to Rome in 1516 by Pope Leo X, he taught at the free school of Oriental languages until 1521 and the death of his papal patron. He then spent time in Avignon before settling in Lyons. His principal achievement was the first ever translation of the entire Bible into Latin from the original Hebrew and Greek texts. Published in 1528, the new Bible was also noteworthy for its division of the chapters into verses and its literal adherence to Hebrew. Despite its often crude style, the Bible was often reprinted in numerous editions by both Catholics and Protestants. Pagninus also wrote the *Thesaurus linguae sanctae* (1529; *Thesaurus of Sacred Language*).

Palamas, Gregory, St. (d. 1359) ● Byzantine monk and leading spokesman for the mystical sect of Hesychasm. Born in Constantinople, he entered the monastic community of Mt. Athos around 1316. There he became adept at Hesychast techniques of prayer and meditation. The advance of the Ottoman Turks forced Palamas to flee Mt. Athos; he went to Thessalonika where, in 1326, he was ordained. Eventually returning to Mt. Athos, he became involved in a controversy with theologians of the Greek and Latin Churches over Hesychasm. Excommunicated in 1344, he was restored by Emperor John VI Cantacuzenus, who made him bishop of Thessalonika. In 1351, the Blackerna Synod in Constantinople declared his teachings to be entirely orthodox. Canonized in 1368 and declared a Doctor of the Orthodox Church, his work was instrumental in propagating Hesychast precepts. Feast day: November 14 (in the East).

Palatine Guard ● In full, the Palatine Guard of Honor (*Guardia Palatine Honoria*). An honorary military body founded in 1850 by Pope Pius IX who merged two preexisting papal units, the *Milizia Urbana* and the *Civica Scelta*, the Palatine Guard was ranked below the Swiss Guard. Initially a military unit, in 1870 it was given a more ceremonial function, in keeping with the reduction of the temporal power of the papacy. It was seen at all major ceremonies and a squad of the Palatine Guard maintained a careful watch during all ceremonies (or the election of new popes). During World War II in the final days of Benito Mussolini's control over Italy, Pope Pius XII permitted the ranks of the unit to keep hundreds of young Roman men from being pressed into the armed forces of Fascist Italy. As with the Noble Guard, the Palatine Guard was disbanded in September 1970 by Pope Paul VI. By custom, the force was recruited from among only Romans; it was an unpaid, all-volunteer unit, but, unlike the Noble Guard, it was open to members of all social classes.

Palestrina, Giovanni Pierluigi da (d. 1594) ● Major Italian composer, called the first composer of the Catholic Church. Born in Palestrina, he supposedly spent his youth selling his family's vegetables in Rome by singing. Such was the beauty of his voice that the choirmaster of the Santa Maria Maggiore undertook to train him in music. His formal career began in 1544 when he became choirmaster and organist in Palestrina. By 1551, such was his reputation that Pope Julius III (r. 1550-1555) summoned him to Rome and eventually named him choirmaster of the *Capella Giulia*

(Julian Chapel) of St. Peter's. In 1554, Palestrina dedicated to the pope his first compositions, a volume of Masses for four voices. Pope Julius, in 1555, rewarded him with an appointment to the papal choir, despite the regulation that all members must be in the holy orders (Palestrina was married at the time). Palestrina, however, was forced to resign later in 1555 upon the accession of Pope Paul IV, as the new pontiff ordered all regulation be adhered to vigorously. Despite a small pension, the enforced departure created a major heartache for the composer, but, recovering his health, he became director in October 1555 of the choir of St. John Lateran. There he remained until 1561 when, after a dispute over his salary, he accepted a post with the choir of Santa Maria Maggiore where he worked until around 1571. Having secured the patronage of St. Charles Borromeo, Palestrina in 1570 was named composer to the papal chapel by Charles's uncle, Pope Pius IV. The following year, he was also appointed choirmaster of St. Peter's. Over the next years, he composed music for the Oratory of St. Philip Neri (a longtime spiritual adviser and friend), and composed magnificent funereal music following the 1580 death of his wife. In his final period, from 1581, he wrote extensively for his patron, Prince Buocampagni, nephew of Pope Gregory XIII.

Among the large number of compositions by Palestrina are: *Improperia (Reproaches)*, first performed in 1561; the *Missa Papae Marcelli*; motets and *laudi spirituali* for St. Philip Neri; twenty-nine motets on words from the "Canticles of Canticles," which earned him the title Prince of Music; the superb *"Lamentations"*; and the *"Stabat Mater"* for double chorus. A deeply spiritual person whose development was fostered by St. Philip, Palestrina found rich expression for his devotion, spirituality, and immense musical gifts in the compositions that are virtually unmatched in Church music and that embodied the new vigor within the

Church in the years of the Catholic Reformation. Palestrina secured for himself a permanent place in the history of sacred music.

Palladius (c. 365-425) ● Bishop of Helenopolis and important historian. Probably from Galatia, Palladius became a monk in Egypt and then in Palestine; he was, for a time a pupil in Egypt of Evagrius Ponticus. In 400, he journeyed to Constantinople where St. John Chrysostom, patriarch of the city, made him bishop of Helenopolis in Bithynia. He proved a vocal supporter of Chrysostom, being exiled in 406 to Egypt because of it when the patriarch himself was deposed and banished. During the next six years of exile, Palladius wrote a defense of his friend, the *Diologus de Vita S. Joannis Chrysostomi* (*Dialogue on the Life of St. John Chrysostom*). Finally around 412 he was allowed to return to Asia Minor and, in 420, he completed the famous Lausiac History. Dedicated to Lausus, the chamberlain in the court of Emperor Theodosius II, the Lausiac History was a detailed and valuable account of the history of monasticism to the fifth century. While sometimes dubious at times in its accuracy, the work was a sincere effort, relying upon Palladius's own experiences and preserving vital information on early monastic life in Egypt and Palestine.

Palladius, St. ● Fifth-century missionary in Ireland. First bishop sent among the Irish by Pope Celestine I (r. 422-432). The main source on Palladius and his activities is the chronicles of St. Prosper of Aquitaine. According to him, Palladius was able to convince Celestine in 429 to send Germanus, bishop of Auxerre, to Britain to stamp out the Pelagians. In 431, according to Prosper, Palladius was consecrated a bishop by Celestine and sent to Ireland to be their first prelate (*primus episcopus*). It is probable that he held the post of deacon of Rome before his consecration, but it is uncertain as to whether he was of Roman or British descent. The Bollandists held that he was a Briton, in keeping with the traditions found in the British isles. The mission of Palladius in Ireland included work to convert the inhabitants and to establish churches, but he apparently met with only limited success, departing Ireland for Scotland where he subsequently died. At least three churches have been assigned to his work, but the seventh-century life of Patrick in the *Book of Armagh* clearly mentions the difficulties he encountered.

Pallavicino, Pietro (1607-1667) ● Italian cardinal and historian. A member of a noble Italian house, he surrendered any claim to aristocratic title and began studying for the priesthood at a young age. Obtaining doctorates in philosophy and theology, he was appointed to several posts by Pope Urban VIII (r. 1623-1644) and was much respected in Rome. The fall of his friend Giovanni Ciampoli, a papal secretary, from favor, however, caused Pallavicino to be exiled to various postings until in 1637 he entered the Jesuits. From 1639-1651, he taught at the Collegium Romanum, becoming a highly respected expert in theology, consulted often by Pope Innocent X (r. 1644-1655). During this period he wrote a defense of the Jesuits against the accusations raised concerning the activities of the society and a disputation of the *Pars Secunda* of the *Summa Theologica* by St. Thomas Aquinas. His chief work came after 1651, when he was assigned by Innocent the task of continuing the work of previous historians in organizing a massive history of the Council of Trent (1545-1563). The result was a most important and authoritative history of the council, *Istoria del Concilio di Trento* (2 vols., 1656-1657 and published in later editions), written in reply to Paolo Sarpi's (1552-1623) vituperative history on the council, *Historia del Concilio Tridentino*

(1619). Named cardinal *in petto* by Pope Alexander VIII (r. 1655-1667) in 1657, his appointment was made public in 1659.

Pammachius, St. (d. c. 409) ● Roman senator and friend of St. Jerome. Following the death of his wife, Paulina, in 397, Pammachius, a devoted Christian, began to wear religious garb and embarked on works of charity. Among his noteworthy acts were the construction of a hospice in Porto, at the mouth of the Tiber, in conjunction with St. Fabiola; and the founding of the church of Sts. John and Paul (although this may have been started by his father). Such was the esteem in which Pammachius was held by St. Jerome that the great writer dedicated to Pammachius a number of works. Pammachius, however, complained at times about Jerome's vituperative style, especially Jerome's book against Jovinian. St. Augustine also thanked Pammachius for a letter to the Africans — where Pammachius owned property — calling upon them to oppose Donatism. Feast day: August 30.

Pamphylius of Caesarea, St. (d. 309) ● Martyr and author who much admired Origen and was highly respected by Eusebius of Caesarea. Probably born in Berytus, Pamphylius studied at Alexandria and finally settled in Caesarea. There he was ordained a priest and established a noted school for the study of theology. Aside from his work copying the Scriptures, Pamphylius was devoted to transcribing and defending the works of Origen. Eusebius, for example, possessed numerous commentaries on Origen that had been compiled by Pamphylius; Pamphylius also composed an *Apology* for Origen in five books (Eusebius would add a sixth volume). The *Apology* has only one book that is extant, in a Latin version made by Rufinus of Aquileia. The magnificent library collected by Pamphylius at Caesarea survived at least until the seventh century but was probably destroyed by the Muslims when they captured Caesarea in 638. Pamphylius himself, however, was arrested in 307 as part of the severe persecution of the faith in the Roman Empire; he was martyred by beheading in February 309. Feast day: June 1.

Papabile ● Italian term used for a cardinal or prelate who is considered a possible or even likely candidate to become pope in an upcoming conclave or at the eventual passing of a reigning pontiff. It is noted by longtime watchers of papal elections, however, that "he who goes into a conclave a pope, comes out a cardinal," a maxim proven by the last two elections, in which Albino Luciani and Karol Wojtyla were elevated to the papacy in 1978 as John Paul I and John Paul II respectively. Neither cardinal was considered *papabile*.

Papacy ● Term having several ecclesiastical meanings. It can denote the office of pope, the successor of St. Peter and Vicar of Christ, the supreme head of the Catholic Church. It also signifies the temporal power of the pope in matters of historical and political importance; today it is more limited in this sense to the place of the pope as temporal ruler of the State of Vatican City. Papacy also refers to the length of a pope's reign (also called a pontificate) or to the list of succeeding pontiffs since Peter.

Papal Bull ● See **Bull**.

Papal Coronation ● Formal coronation of the newly elected pope, one of the two most important ceremonies of any pontificate — the other being the solemn obsequies surrounding a pontiff's death. The ceremony surrounding the installation of a new pope in the early Church was probably a simple affair, growing more elaborate over the centuries in keeping with the increased position of the papacy in the temporal affairs of the West. The two main symbols of the coronation were the tiara and the pallium.

The papal tiara symbolized the supremacy of the papacy over the entire Church and the pallium was worn to denote his position as Bishop of Rome. The placing of the tiara on the head of the new pope was accompanied by tremendous pomp and circumstance right up to the latter twentieth century. The earliest version of the tiara was most likely used for the coronation of Nicholas II in 1059. A second level, or layer, was added to the tiara by Pope Benedict VIII (r. 1294-1303), and a third was attached over the next years.

By the 1500s, the coronation was standardized, so much so that it remained virtually unchanged until the reign of Pope John Paul I (1978). The new pontiff was carried into St. Peter's on the *sedia gestatoria*, surrounded by the extensive and ornately colorful papal court and nobility, The crown was then placed upon his head, with the following being pronounced: "Receive this tiara adorned with three crowns; know that thou are the father of princes and kings, victor of the whole world under the earth, the vicar of Our Lord, Jesus Christ, to whom be the glory and honor without end."

The last time that entire ceremony was held in traditional manner was the coronation of Pope Paul VI in 1963. In the succeeding years of his reign (1963-1978), major changes occurred in the papal household. The Palatine and Noble Guards were disbanded (1970), the *ciborra*, or papal fan, and the *sedia gestatoria* were used only rarely, and the elaborate, regal court was trimmed considerably. With the election of Albino Luciani as John Paul I, he took the step of ending formal coronations with the tiara. Instead, greater emphasis was placed upon the pallium, to stress the pastoral image he chose to project. Entering into his decision were the monarchical rather than religious connotations of the tiara. Pope John Paul II accepted his predecessor's decision and was installed with the pallium, formalizing a new era in the installations, versus the coronation of a new pontiff.

Papal Decorations ● Properly pontifical decorations. Those honors granted to laypersons by the Holy See in recognition of special or exemplary service to the Church or society in general. There are various types of papal decorations, ranging from classes of knights, medals of honor, and the military religious orders. The pope has always enjoyed the privilege of conferring upon individuals symbols of his pleasure or recognition of honor. Among these were titles of nobility — count, marquis, and prince — along with making the choice of making the title personal or hereditary. While frequently bestowed in previous times, the ranks of nobility effectively died out during the pontificate of Pope Paul VI (1963-1978) as part of his streamlining of the papal administration and court. Other types of medals include:

Knighthood: There are five orders of knighthood bestowed by the Holy See — The Supreme Order of Christ, Order of the Golden Spur, Order of Pius IX, the Order of St. Gregory the Great, and the Order of St. Sylvester. The Order of Christ is reserved for Catholic rulers or heads of state. The Order of the Golden Spur was supposedly founded by Pope St. Sylvester I (r. 314-335); eventually falling into disrepute, it was revived in 1905 by St. Pius X. It is not restricted to Catholics, but the membership may not exceed one hundred. The Order of Pius IX was begun in 1847 by Pope Pius IX and may be granted to non-Catholics. The Order of St. Gregory the Great was formed by Pope Gregory XVI (r. 1831-1846) originally to honor those persons who were of great help in the defense of the temporal authority of the Holy See. It was later extended to those persons not immediately subjects of the Papal States who distinguished themselves by their loyalty to the Holy See and for other virtues (such as piety and generosity). It has two divisions, civil and military, each division possessing three degrees: knights, knights commanders, and knights of the Grand Cross. The Order of St. Sylvester was also begun by Pope Gregory XVI, in 1841. Pope St. Pius X in 1905 divided it into two orders, the Golden Militia and St. Sylvester. The former is the Order of the Golden Spur mentioned previously.

Medals of Honor: This group of papal decorations does not confer any kind of knighthood upon the recipient; they are given to men and women who have merited recognition through their services to the Church. Customarily, the decoration is awarded by the secretary of state by diploma. The two best known are the *Pro Ecclesiae et Pontifice* (For the Church and the Pontiff) and the *Benemerenti* (For Him Who Deserves It). The *Pro Ecclesiae* was started in 1888 by Pope Leo XIII to commemorate the fiftieth anniversary of his ordination to the priesthood. The *Benemerenti* is awarded for service of a special nature to the Church. There are also two decorations not bestowed by the Holy See but given its approval: the Lateran Cross, given by the chapter of the Basilica of St. John Lateran, Rome, and the medal of the Holy Land. (See also **Golden Rose**.)

Military Religious Orders: See **Malta, Knights of** and **Holy Sepulchre, Knights of the** under **Military Orders**.

Papal Elections ● See **Conclave**.

Papal Flag ● Official flag of the Vatican. The papal flag consists of two equal fields, divided vertically, of white and yellow. The yellow field is blank and is closest to the flagpole. The white field is decorated with the insignia of the papacy, a triple tiara, and the crossed keys. The tiara symbolizes the spiritual authority of the supreme pontiff and the keys, one silver and one gold, denote the power of the keys given to St. Peter. There is also an inscription in Italian, "State of the City of the Vatican."

Papal Guard ● See **Palatine Guard** and **Swiss Guard**.

Papal Knights ● More properly, Pontifical Order of Knighthood. Honorary titles granted to laypeople by the pope for notable or important service to the Church, the ranks of the order, by precedence, are: The Supreme Order of Christ, The Order of the Golden Spur, The Order of Pius IX, The Order of St. Gregory Great, and The Order of St. Sylvester. The titles may be granted by the pontiff, but it is customary that only the first two are bestowed by him; the other three are granted by the Secretariat of State to worthy persons based on the recommendation of the diocesan bishop of the candidate. These titles are further delineated by rank: baron, knight, prince. There are also two surviving ecclesiastical, but not papal, orders of knighthood that are recognized by the Holy See: Sovereign Military Order of St. John of Jerusalem, of Rhodes, and of Malta (generally called the Knights of Malta) and the Equestrian Order of the Holy Sepulchre of Jerusalem (known as the Knights of the Holy Sepulchre). (See also **Papal Decorations**.)

Papal Legate ● Officially appointed representative of the pope. According to the document *Sollicitudo Omnium Ecclesiarum* (June 24, 1969) issued by Pope Paul VI, papal representatives receive the duty of

Papal flag

representing the pontiff "in a fixed way in the various nations or regions of the world." Traditionally, the highest form of legation is the *legate a latere*, who is sent as a personal representative of the pope for a specific event or in some very important matter. This legate is always a cardinal and is granted often special powers. A historical example of the *legate a latere* was the dispatching of Cardinal Giovanni Battista Caprara by Pope Pius VII to France in 1801 to execute the concordat with Napoleon Bonaparte. The other types of papal representatives are: nuncio, sent to countries with full diplomatic relations with the Holy See; internuncio, a representative in special circumstances or an ambassador ranked below the nuncio; pro-nuncio, a representative to a country having full diplomatic relations with the Holy See but where the diplomat does not carry the position of being dean of the diplomatic corps; apostolic delegate, the personal representative of the pope to the Church in a country with which the Holy See does not have diplomatic relations; charge d'affaires, a papal agent, customarily not possessing the episcopal dignity, who heads a diplomatic delegation to a country that has neither a nunciature nor an apostolic delegation. (For other details, see under **Nuncio** and **Pro-Nuncio**.)

Generally, papal legates — be they nuncios, internuncios, pro-nuncios, or other ranks — are expertly trained diplomats with long service and experience in the diplomatic corps of the Holy See. They are normally prepared in the Pontificia Academia Ecclesiastica (Pontifical Ecclesiastical Academy), the diplomatic school in Rome. After graduation, they are appointed as secretaries to diplomatic missions around the world.

Popes have made use of the legate since the early periods of Church history, although probably the first known sending of such representatives was in 325 when legates appeared at the Council of Nicaea on behalf of Pope Sylvester I. During the fourth century, the official representative of a pope was called the *apocrisiarius* (or *responsalis*). His main functions were to defend the rights of the pope, prevent the spread of heresy, and enforce clerical discipline. Such a legate was commonly present at the Byzantine court in Constantinople, eventually disappearing in the eighth century during the Iconoclastic Controversy, temporarily revived by Pope Leo III (r. 795-816) to represent him at the court of Charlemagne (d. 814). At the same time as the *apocrisiarius* were the *legati nati* (perpetual legates), who originated in the post of apostolic vicar under Popes Damasus I (r. 366-384) and Siricius (r. 384-399). The *legatus natus* was a prelate who occupied a see in a given country but who also fulfilled certain duties as a papal legate, most notably the promotion of ecclesiastical affairs, enforcement of decrees, and the maintaining of relations with the Holy See. The powers of the *legati nati* were initially considerable, declining throughout the Middle Ages until virtually disappearing in the twelfth century.

As the *legati nati* proved increasingly unable to effect reform or curb local abuses and infringements of Church rights by secular rulers, the Holy See found it expedient to appoint certain special envoys. These legates were more reliable than *legati nati* and came to be called *legati missi*. They were sent to represent the pope at special occasions, to negotiate or meet with kings and emperors, and, eventually, to head the provinces of the Papal States, such as Bologna. In the thirteenth century, the *legati missi* became known as nuncios, the title that has endured into modern times.

Papal Letters ● Pronouncements, letters, or decrees issued by pontifical authority. Papal letters can be written for public or private reading and vary considerably in order of importance. Because of the primary position of the Bishop of Rome in the early

Church, it was only natural that they should communicate their views and decisions on matters confronting the faith. Customarily, the early popes sent letters either of their own initiative or when their judgment was required by synods or individual prelates. Aside from the epistles written by St. Peter, the first letter by a pope known with certainty was that of St. Clement I (r. 88-97) to the much troubled Corinthians. Other references to papal writings of this kind over the next centuries have been preserved in the works of various Christian chroniclers, but few are extant in partial or complete form.

From the fourth century, however, and the rise of the Church to religious prominence in the Roman Empire, the number and nature of papal letters changed. The popes were involved in all aspects of life, but the differing nature of the issues brought about new categories of letters: legal matters were discussed in *decretas* or *sententiae* (for opinions) or *praecepta*; dogmatic topics were presented in *epistolae tractoriae* or *tomi* (a tome). There was also the *epistola synodica*, which could denote a letter published by a pope in connection with the advice of a Roman synod or Roman presbyter or a letter sent by a newly elected pope (or a newly elected bishop) by which he notified the other bishops of his elevation. Unfortunately, the majority of papal letters from the first millennium are lost, with only a few surviving in a state of complete preservation, namely letters by Popes St. Leo I, St. Gregory I, and St. Gregory VII. The first comprehensive attempt to collect the letters was compiled by Dionysius Exiguus early in the sixth century.

Papal letters grew considerably in number during the Middle Ages and, according to Gratian, it was accepted that each letter of a general nature had authority over the entire Church. The names used for the different types of letters included: *edictum, statutum, decretalis,* and *constitutio*; in specific cases they were called *mandata, responsa,* and *rescripta*. Changes in the style of the documents and also the method by which they were sealed brought about the difference between such documents as bulls and briefs; less important seals were used for briefs while bulls, of weighty matters, had seals stamped in wax or lead (or even gold), placed in a case, and attached to the document by a cord. Almost all the papal letters since the thirteenth century are preserved — specifically from the pontificate of Innocent III (1198-1216), owing to the excellence of papal archives or through their inclusion in the *Corpus Juris Canonici*. Papal letters are still issued in considerable number, varying in nature and importance. They can be encyclicals, apostolic constitutions, *motu proprio*, epistles, exhortations, and decrees.

Papal States ● Also called the Pontifical States and the States of the Church. Temporal possessions ruled over by the pope in Italy and, for a time, in France, until 1870. According to tradition, the temporal holdings of the Holy See originated in the *Patrimonium Petri* (Patrimony of Peter), extensive grants of land in Italy, Corsica, Sardinia, Sicily, and Africa that were granted to the Church by the imperial government under Constantine or were donated by wealthy Christians. The property was administered by the popes and marked a significant addition to papal authority and revenue, money that was then used to aid the poor of Rome and to help repair the city after disasters or invasions. Over ensuing centuries, new possessions would be added as the popes took upon themselves the government of whole parts of Italy as the Roman Empire collapsed. The term *Patrimonium Petri* would be applied in the Middle Ages not only to the possessions around Rome but to all of the Papal States. (See also **Donation of Constantine**.)

The Papal States themselves were born in the eighth century when Pope Stephen II (III) (r. 752-757) asked for the aid of the Franks against the Lombards. This request led to the Donation of Pepin in 756, giving to the

Church even more land, roughly equal to the old Byzantine exarchate of Ravenna and the so-called Pentapolis (a stretch of territory along the Adriatic coast comprised of Ancona, Senigallia, Pesaro, Rimini, and Faso). As formidable feudal lords, the popes ultimately came to rule parts of Emilia-Romagna, the Marches, Umbria, Latium, and the French sites of Avignon and Venaissin. The Papal States added to the prestige of the papacy and allowed the popes to speak on equal temporal terms with the other monarchs of Christendom. The Papal States, however, also involved the papacy in often bloody conflicts in Italy for new possessions, to defend the old ones, or to put down independent-minded vassals or brigands who commonly infested the cities and regions under papal authority (see **Sixtus V**). One of the principal enemies of the popes was the Holy Roman Emperor, who made the Papal States a battleground in the twelfth to thirteenth centuries over such issues as the inheritance of Countess Matilda of Tuscany and the Investiture Controversy.

Toward the end of the Middle Ages, papal powers declined and some parts of the Papal States, notably Romagna, resisted papal agents. This crisis only deepened in the fourteenth century while the popes resided at Avignon and later during the Great Schism (1378-1417). The popes were able to restore their control in the mid-fourteenth century under the remarkable generalship of Cardinal Gil Albornoz. Full reclamation of prestige would not be achieved until the time of Pope Julius II (r. 1503-1513).

The French Revolution and the Napoleonic Wars would witness the cruel seizure of Rome in 1808 and the annexation of the Papal States to the French Empire in 1809. Cardinal Ercole Consalvi negotiated the restoration of the Papal States on behalf of Pope Pius VII (r. 1800-1823), thus beginning the final phase of their history. Over the ensuing decades, the Papal States came under increasing pressures from the drive for Italian unification (see **Risorgimento**), culminating with the seizure by Sardinia of Bologna, Romagna, and the Marches, in 1860. Only Rome was left to Pope Pius IX (r. 1846-1878) and this remained safe only by the presence of French troops. When, in 1870, the French withdrew to fight the Prussians, Rome fell, ending the Papal States. By the terms of the Lateran Treaty of 1929, the Holy See had restored to it temporal possessions consisting of the State of the Vatican City and other extraterritorial holdings such as Castel Gandolfo. (See **Lateran Treaty** and **Vatican City, State of**.)

Paris, Matthew (1200?-1259) ● English Benedictine monk and chronicler. He entered the Benedictine monastery of St. Alban's in January 1217, remaining attached to the community until his death, although he frequently traveled to London and the Continent. He once journeyed to Norway with letters from King St. Louis, king of France, for King Haakon IV. In the course of his trip, Paris became a good friend of the Norwegian monarch. The monk was also a favorite of King Henry III of England and was treated with considerable respect by the monastic or ecclesiastical communities he visited. One of the greatest of the English chroniclers, his principal work was the *Chronica majora*, a history of the world from the creation until 1259. While the portion to 1235 was largely derived from the *Flores Historiarum* of Roger of Wendover, the coverage for the years 1235-1259 is definitely an original work by Paris and remains a valuable source on events in the period. Paris additionally wrote the *Historia minor*, a compendium of the *Chronica* from 1067-1253, with major revision; a life of Stephen Langton is also attributed to him.

Pascal, Blaise (1623-1662) ● French mathematician, physicist, and apologist. Born in Clermont-Ferrand, he was the son of a local official. His mother died when he was four, and his father moved the family to Paris in 1631 and then to Normandy in 1639. He was educated by his father and sisters, displaying early on a remarkable intelligence and interest in scientific experiment. In 1646, he first came into contact with the Jansenists, developing a relationship with the Jansenist community of Port-Royal; his sister would enter the convent of Port-Royal in 1651 and in his later years, from 1655, Pascal regularly visited it. His scientific work included investigations into the air and liquids, and his contributions to mathematics varied from advances in geometry to the foundation of calculus. A deeply religious individual, however, he is best known for two works: *Pensées* and *Lettres provinciales*. *Pensées* (1670; *Thoughts*) was a published collection of his thoughts in the form of notes. He had perhaps hoped to write a book defending Christianity as early as 1654 and his so-called second conversion. This one was released posthumously and was subsequently reedited. It represents a brilliant analysis of the faith, providing a new, innovative technique in apologetics. *Lettres provinciales* was a series of letters published between 1656-1657 attacking the Jesuits. They were written in response to the condemnation by the Sorbonne of Antoine Arnauld and vigorously defended the Jansenists. Known in full as *Lettres écrites à un provincial*, they numbered eighteen in all, assailing the Jesuits, questioning the theories on grace that were then being advanced such as Molinism by the Society of Jesus, and promoting the rigorous moral system of Jansenism. Much influenced by Jansenist thinking, Pascal adhered to the idea that faith was absolutely essential and morality stems from the redemptive power of Christ. He accepted that human nature was incapable of correct behavior because of original sin. The *Lettres provinciales* was condemned in 1657 by the Congregation of the Index. Despite his doctrinal errors and his harsh criticism of the Jesuits, Pascal

made legitimate contributions of the examination of the soul in the *Pensées*.

Pascendi Dominici Gregis ● Encyclical issued on September 8, 1907, by Pope St. Pius X, "On the doctrines of the Modernists." Translated as "Feeding the flock of the Lord," the encyclical was concerned with the dangers posed to the Church by Modernism, called by Pope Pius X, "the synthesis of all heresies," and followed closely the promulgation of the decree against the Modernists, *Lamentabili* (July 3, 1907). *Pascendi* opposed specifically several threads of Modernist thinking, including the idea that revelation and doctrine evolved in conjunction with the development of humankind, that no absolute knowledge of God is attainable by the human mind, and that belief in God only arises out of the necessity for humans to believe in some kind of Supreme Being. Against these, Pius positively stated a reaffirmation of the eternal and immutable nature of revelation, the unassailable truth of the Scriptures, the value and importance of the magisterium, and the divine origin of the Church as established by Christ. With *Lamentabili* and the Oath against Modernism (issued on September 1, 1910) that was taken by all clergy and instructors in seminaries, the pontiff took deliberate steps to eradicate Modernism from the Church, particularly in the important spheres of education and priestly formation.

Paschal I, St. ● Pope from 817-824. A native of Rome, he was ordained by Leo III and was serving as abbot of St. Stephen's monastery at the time of his election on January 24, 817, to succeed Stephen IV (V). His reign was dominated by two issues: the relationship between the papacy and the Holy Roman Empire, and the controversy over the Iconoclasts in the Byzantine Empire. Paschal, negotiating with Emperor Louis I, was granted considerable independence for the

Holy See from imperial interference by the emperor, receiving from him recognition that the popes owned the Papal States and were free in elections. In return, however, Louis spearheaded reform in monastic and diocesan life and required notification of the election of a new pope to be made to the emperor. Of particular note was the crowning in 823 of Louis's son Lothar in Rome; by it the tradition of imperial coronation was formalized, including the handing of a sword to the new emperor by the pope, signifying the temporal authority to overcome evil. Lothair's presence in Rome stirred anti-Frankish sentiment, and Paschal was forced to take an oath of purgation to clear himself of possible complicity in the murder of two Frankish officials by members of the Curia. His efforts to oppose the Iconoclastic policies of Emperor Leo V were unsuccessful, and Iconoclasm became a problem between the Eastern and Western Churches. Paschal also constructed several churches in Rome. Feast day: May 14.

Paschal II ● Pope from 1099-1118. Born Rainerius in Bieda di Galeata, near Ravenna, he entered a monastery while still a boy, eventually becoming abbot. Pope St. Gregory VII appointed him cardinal around 1078 and he served as legate to Spain for Urban II. On August 13, 1099, he was elected to succeed Urban, taking the name Paschal. While eager to continue the reform of Gregory and to promote the crusader spirit like Urban, Paschal found his reign dominated by the Investiture Controversy. Negotiations led to a resolution of the crisis in England and France, but Holy Roman Emperor Henry IV and then his son Henry V remained intractable. Henry IV was excommunicated at the Council of Rome (1102), and Paschal found it convenient to support Henry V in his ultimately successful revolt against his father. The new emperor proved just as determined on the question, however, and deliberations at the Synods of Guastalla

(1106) and Troyes (1107) could effect no resolution. Paschal finally condemned Henry, but the invasion of Italy by an imperial army brought about an agreement at Sutri in early 1111. It was totally unacceptable to the German bishops, and their vigorous complaints to the emperor led to the seizure and imprisonment of the pope. Brutalized, Paschal acceded to Henry's demands, crowning him on April 13, 1111, and agreeing to lay investiture. The next year, this treaty was voided by the Lateran Council of 1112, and Paschal excommunicated Henry in 1116. Forced into exile by the ever-troublesome Romans, Paschal went to Benevento; he died in Castel Sant' Angelo on January 1, 1118, after finally returning to the Eternal City. His death came with the Investiture Controversy unresolved.

Paschal Baylon, St. (1540-1592) ● Franciscan lay brother who was noted especially for his devotion to the Blessed Sacrament. Born at Torre-Hermose in Aragon, to peasant parents, Paschal spent his early life as a shepherd. In 1564, however, he entered the Franciscan order, spending his remaining years as a lay brother. While never educated in any formal sense, he acquired a reputation for wisdom and was frequently consulted by the lowly and the great. Once, while journeying through France, he engaged and defeated a Calvinist preacher in a debate on the Eucharist, so thoroughly destroying Calvinist doctrine that he was forced to flee for his life from an angry Huguenot mob. Paschal was canonized in 1690 and was declared the heavenly protector of all Eucharistic congresses and associations by Pope Leo XIII (r. 1878-1903) in the apostolic letter *Providentissimus Deus*. Feast day: May 17.

Paschasius Radbertus, St. (c. 785-c. 860) ● Benedictine abbot and theologian. A native of Soissons, he entered the Benedictine monastery of Corbie, studying under the remarkable Abbot Adalhard and his brother Wala. In 822, he journeyed with Adalhard to Saxony, establishing in Westphalia the monastery of New Corbie. Elected abbot of Corbie around 843, Paschasius attended the Council of Paris (847) but retired in 849 to devote himself to writing and studying. Among his works were a life of Adalhard, poems, letters, and the important treatise *De Corpore et Sanguine Domini* (831; *On the Body and Blood of Christ*), on the doctrine concerning the Eucharist. While revised in 834, the work was the occasion of a major controversy over the Eucharist involving Ratramnus and extending into the tenth century.

Passionists ● In full, the Congregation of the Discalced Clerks of the Most Holy Cross and Passion of Our Lord Jesus Christ. Religious order founded by St. Paul of the Cross (1694-1775). Originally called Paul Francis Danei, he was the son of a poverty-stricken noble family, leading a deeply religious life of prayer until 1720 when he received a vision and was inspired to establish a religious body to give honor to the passion of Our Lord. At Castelazzo where he was granted his inspiration, he undertook a forty-day fast, was given the habit of the Passion by his bishop, and wrote up the rule that would later be adopted by the new institute. Permission was granted by Pope Benedict XIII to initiate a congregation in 1725, and two years later the pontiff ordained both St. Paul and his brother John Baptist. The two then worked in the hospital of St. Gallicano before leaving Rome and retiring to Mt. Argentaro where they opened the order's first house. Others soon joined and the foundation on the mountain became the cradle for the Passionist Congregation. Approval of the rule was given on May 15, 1741, by Pope Benedict XIV, and in 1744 St. Paul opened a second house near Vetralla. Further confirmation and approval was given by Pope Clement XIV in November 1769 (later

signs of papal favor were granted by Pope Pius VI in 1775). St. Paul remained in Rome from 1769, dying there on October 18, 1775. He had served as superior general of the Passionists since 1747 and was considered one of the greatest preachers in the Church. The Passionists grew rapidly, working for the sanctification of members and others through the practice of devotion to the passion of Our Lord. The Passionists thus have not only vows of poverty, chastity, and obedience but also a vow to promote devotion to the Passion. Today, the Congregation of the Passion (C.P.) continues to conduct missions and retreats. They currently number some twenty-five hundred worldwide. St. Paul also founded the Sisters of the Cross and Passion (C.P.), known as the Passionist Nuns in 1771. In the brief of Pope Pius IX for Paul's beatification in 1852 the pope wrote: "Although continually occupied with the cares of governing his religious society, and of founding everywhere new houses for it, yet he never left off preaching the Word of God, beginning as he did with a wondrous desire for the salvation of souls." Pius IX canonized him in 1867. Feast day: October 19.

Passion Plays ● Type of religious drama that originated during the Middle Ages and that depicts the passion of Christ. The most famous and enduring of the Passion plays is that of Oberammergau, Bavaria, Germany. The Passion play had its origin in liturgical activities during the Easter season in which readings were made from the Gospels in Latin on Christ's suffering, crucifixion, death, and resurrection. These were gradually adapted by communities to make them of a more popular nature and hence more accessible to the common people, who most often did not speak or understand Latin. Adaptations fostered the use of German and led to the staging of various plays that might present scenes from the OT, the last judgment, and such New Testament topics as the life of Mary Magdalene and the Last Supper. The more specialized Passion play made its appearance in the fourteenth century. Notable early examples include the Vienna Passion, the Frankfurt Passion, the St. Gall Passion, and the Celtic Passion. The period of highest development was from 1400-1515 during which the play spread to neighboring countries, most notably Spain and France. The most influential plays and the most consistently elaborate were those held in the region of the Tyrol.

From around 1515, however, the plays declined in both quality and content, suffering suppression during the Reformation. As they were expressions of a sense of community and urban opulence, the Passion plays at their height were an excellent demonstration of sociopolitical life in the cities, especially in the fifteenth century when nobility and patricians were actively involved and paid for the plays. When, during the sixteenth century, the upper classes increasingly withdrew from participation, the staging of the plays fell to lower classes, with the inevitable result that the artistic and spiritual quality of the plays declined in direct proportion to the levels of sophistication and education of the producers and audience. The chief surviving play, of course, is that of Oberammergau. Its earliest mention occurs in 1633 when the inhabitants of Ammergau pledged to stage a play once every ten years should the community be spared the ravages of the plague. When the town was bypassed by the epidemic, the people held the first Play in 1634. Since that time, it has continued and attracts people from all over the world. An entirely local production, the Passion play is presented without any amplification equipment, the performers relying entirely on the superior natural acoustics.

Patriarch ● Title borne by high-ranking ecclesiastical officials, it is used today most often for the recognized heads of the various Eastern (or Oriental) Churches. A patriarch is the title of a bishop with the highest possible rank in the hierarchy of his jurisdiction. This means that he is superior to all primates, metropolitans, and bishops within his patriarchate. He is answerable and subject to, however, the pope. By custom, the patriarch is the successor to one of the first great sees that were established in the time of the Roman Empire, namely Rome, Constantinople, Alexandria, Antioch, and Jerusalem.

The name patriarch (Latin *patriarcha*) was derived from the Greek meaning "father" or chief of a race or tribe. In the early Church, it was sometimes used as an honorific appellation for certain bishops, becoming an accepted or official title only gradually. The Council of Nicaea (325) gave official recognition to three patriarchs: the bishops of Alexandria, Antioch, and Rome. The successor to St. Peter had, naturally, the first place among the patriarchs while those of Antioch and Alexandria emerged because of the evolution of the metropolitan system of provinces in which it was logical for the bishops of the largest and most important cities of the East to have prominence. The Council of Nicaea gave the bishop of Alexandria an honorary primacy in recognition of the large numbers of visitors to the Holy City; total promotion would come later. The rise of Constantinople as the chief city of the empire in the fourth century prompted its bishop and his supporters to agitate for patriarchal status second only to Rome, if not its approximate equal. The Council of Constantinople (381) thus declared: "The Bishop of Constantinople shall have the primacy of honor after the Bishop of Rome, because it is the New Rome." Despite opposition from the Holy See, the canon was granted de facto acceptance because of the favor shown the see by the Eastern emperors. The Council of Chalcedon (451) created two patriarchs, the long-desired one for Constantinople and one for Jerusalem, formed by slicing away parts of the patriarch of Antioch. Pope St. Leo I refused to accept the canon of Chalcedon (28) that gave Constantinople a second place to Rome, and the popes would resist this until 1215 and the Fourth Lateran Council. By that time, of course, Constantinople had fallen to the crusaders, and the patriarch was a Latin. From the time of the Eastern Schism in 1054, the status of the patriarchs declined sharply in power and influence, with the exception of the pope, who remained one of the most central figures in the West. The deterioration of the Eastern patriarchies was only exacerbated by the multiplication of patriarchies arising out of the crusades — with such new offices as the Latin patriarch of Jerusalem — and the break with central authorities by heretical groups such as the Copts, Nestorians, and Jacobites, which in turn sprouted their own patriarchates.

Today, the pope remains the first of patriarchs over the Catholic hierarchy of the Church, with the titles Bishop of Rome and Patriarch of the West. The Latin rite has several titular patriarchates. These are the patriarchs of Lisbon, the East Indies, the West Indies, and Venice. The patriarchate of the West Indies has been empty since 1963 while that of Venice has produced three pontiffs in the twentieth century, Popes St. Pius X (r. 1903-1914), John XXIII (r. 1958-1963), and John Paul I (1978). During the crusades, as noted, Latin patriarchates were established for the Latin-rite Christians in the Holy Land. These were Antioch, Jerusalem, Alexandria, and Constantinople. A constant source of irritation to the Eastern Christians, the Latin patriarchs eventually became titular officeholders after the loss of the Crusader States to the Muslims. Pope Pius IX reconstituted the patriarchate of Jerusalem for the Latin rite in July 1847 with the bull *Nullo Celebrior*. The patriarchates of Constantinople, Antioch, and Alexandria were finally abolished in 1964 by Pope Paul VI, a significant gesture to the Eastern Churches.

There are currently multiple Eastern patriarchates, with a patriarch often present for each of the various Eastern, or Oriental, rite Churches. They are: Alexandria (Coptic); Antioch (Syrian, Maronite, and Greek Melkite, the latter bearing the title "Greek Melkite Patriarch of Alexandria and Jerusalem"); Babylonia (Chaldaeans) and Cilicia, or Sis (Armenian), properly called the *Katholikos*. Each is elected by the bishops of the rite but is approved by and receives the pallium from the pope. The Orthodox Churches are also headed by patriarchs, who exercise authority in their respective jurisdictions for the Greek, Russian, Serbian, Romanian, Bulgarian, and other communities. These patriarchs are the heads of some fifteen communities or autonomous Churches. Chief among them, enjoying a primacy of honor (but not jurisdiction), is the oecumenical (or ecumenical) patriarch of Constantinople.

Patrick, St. (c. 389-461) ● Patron saint of Ireland and one of the most famous missionaries. Patrick (or Patricius) was a native of Roman Britain, the son of a Roman citizen by the name of Calpurius who was also a deacon. He was born at a site called Bannavem Taburniae (it is otherwise unknown) and was named in full Magnus Sucatus Patricius. While raised a Christian, he was not significantly devout. At the age of sixteen, he was captured by Irish raiders and taken to Ireland where he was made a slave. For six years Patrick labored as a sheep herder among the people, "living beside the Wood of Voclut, which is near the Western Sea" (modern Killala, in County Mayo). During this time, he underwent an intense spiritual conversion and in the summer of 407 was told to make his escape.

Patrick set out on a journey of some two hundred miles, finally reaching the southeastern coast. There he managed to convince a group of sailors to transport him away from the country. According to tradition he sailed to the Continent where he spent some time wandering, ultimately reaching home a very different person from the one carried away years before. Absolutely convinced of his call to become an ordained minister, he embarked upon a rudimentary course of study. He regretted that he did not have the opportunity for a formal education, making his feelings clear in his *Confession.* Nevertheless, he mastered the principles of faith and became very familiar with Sacred Scriptures. It is possible that he spent some time in Gaul (France) under St. Germanus of Auxerre, but many scholars believe that his training was exclusively (or almost so) in Britain. Regardless of his actual course of studies, he would prove a brilliant missionary.

Patrick was not the first bishop appointed to bring the faith to the Irish. That honor goes to Palladius who, in 431, was sent to Ireland by Pope Celestine I (r. 422-432). Palladius either died or proved unsuccessful and some time after 431, Patrick was appointed to take his place. He spent the rest of his life among the Irish preaching, establishing the faith, organizing clergy, monks, and nuns, and winning the abiding confidence of the Irish chieftains. His two lasting contributions were his skillful union of the Christian faith with the Irish-Celtic cultural orientation, and his promotion of

St. Patrick

native clergy that would continue after his death. In essence, he became Irish and, through his heartfelt, simple, and very conservative style of preaching, he won the hearts and minds of the people. Sometime before his death, he made Armagh his primatial see, thereby establishing it as the religious heart of the island. There are many questions concerning the life of St. Patrick, a difficulty exacerbated by the general unreliability of the main sources on his life including the Irish *Annals,* the *Breviarium Tirecham,* and the *Life of St. Patrick* by Muirchu. Patrick himself wrote a *Confession* (a moving personal testimony of faith) and the *Letter to Coroticus,* a troublesome chieftain who is the subject of much historical debate. The accounts of his life are at times heavily embellished with fantastic stories and legend. Nevertheless, Patrick is one of the most beloved saints in the world, the recipient of national holidays in many countries, including Ireland and the United States. Feast day: March 17. (See also **Breastplate of St. Patrick**.)

Patrimonium Petri ● See under **Papal States**.

Patriotic Association of Chinese Catholics ● Organization founded in July 1957 by Communist China. Its aim is to maintain a façade of Catholic activity in the country while effectively cutting off all

Chinese Catholics from contact with Rome and legitimate Church authority. Pope Pius XII condemned the false Church in 1958, and few Chinese laypeople or priests actually joined. The government pressed on, however, by creating a skeletal hierarchy that same year through the consecration of several priests by four legitimate bishops. From this foundation, the Patriotic Association expanded the hierarchy by having over twenty bishops "elect" themselves between April 1958 and November 1959. Such consecrations, performed without the permission of the Holy See, are considered valid but illicit. There were more than sixty such bishops by 1983, creating a serious obstacle to productive discussions between the Chinese government and the Vatican representatives of the Holy See, although efforts were made in 1993 to establish what the Vatican called "indirect contacts" to improve relations. The Patriotic Association claims to have a membership of 3.5 million, a number that cannot be confirmed.

Patron Saints of Countries ● See TABLE 10.

Paul I, St. ● Pope from 757-767. A native of Rome, he was the brother of Pope Stephen II (III). Ordained a deacon by Pope Zacharias, Paul was appointed to the papal government by his brother, whom he was elected to succeed on May 29, 757. Paul's reign was dominated by his struggles with King Desiderius of the Lombards and Byzantine Emperor Constantine V. Facing the potential eradication of the Papal States by the Lombards, Paul allied himself with the Frankish king Pepin the Short, thereby securing a powerful ally in the Frankish dynasty that would soon be ruled by Charlemagne. With relations between the papacy and the Byzantine Empire already deteriorating because of Byzantine dealings with the Lombards, Paul was forced to exacerbate the situation even further by

protesting the Iconoclast policies of Emperor Constantine V. Feast day: June 28.

Paul II ● Pope from 1464-1471. Born Pietro Barbo in Venice, he was the nephew of Pope Eugene IV (r. 1431-1447), advancing quickly through the ecclesiastical ranks through Eugene's patronage. In 1440, at the age of twenty-three, he was made cardinal and in 1456 governor of Campania. Elected successor to Pope Pius II on August 30, 1464, he proved an active pontiff, particularly in European affairs. Opposed to the Pragmatic Sanctions of Bourges, he made repeated condemnation of the decree by King Charles VII of France. In dealing with the Utraquist national Church of Bohemia, Paul pressed George of Podiebrad, king of Bohemia, to curb their activities. When the ruler refused, Paul excommunicated him and supported King Matthias Corvinus of Hungary in his campaign against Bohemia, crowning him king of Bohemia in 1469. He earned the enmity of the humanists in Italy by purging the Roman Academy in 1468, outraging the members by putting to torture one of their members, Bartolomeo Platina, on charges of criminal conspiracy. Despite this episode, Paul was a decided patron of humanists and learning, helping to open the first of the printing presses of Rome. Concerned with the advance of the Ottoman Turks into Europe, he attempted to launch a crusade against them but was very disappointed in the lack of any enthusiastic response from the Holy Roman Emperor Frederick III.

Paul III ● Pope from 1534-1549. Considered the first pontiff of the Catholic Reformation, Paul was responsible for convoking the Council of Trent in 1545. Born Alessandro Farnese in Canino, Italy, he studied at Rome and in Florence, spending time in the circle of Lorenzo de' Medici the Magnificent. Advancement in the Church came through the patronage of Cardinal

Rodrigo Borgia, particularly after Borgia's election as Pope Alexander VI in 1492; part of Borgia's patronage was due to the fact that Farnese's sister, Giulia, was his mistress. Appointed cardinal in 1493, he held subsequently a number of important posts, including dean of the Sacred College under Pope Leo X (r. 1513-1521). He was finally ordained a priest in 1519 and was unanimously elected successor to Pope Clement VII on October 13, 1534.

Long known for his worldly habits and tastes — he fathered three sons and a daughter — before ordination, Farnese reformed himself and was forever after devoted to genuine reform in the Church. As pope, he became identified with bringing genuine reformation, embarking on a vigorous campaign that was in sharp contrast to his predecessor's inactivity in the face of rampant Protestantism. Paul elevated a number of genuinely gifted Church leaders to the cardinalate: Reginald Pole, Gian Pietro Caraffa (the future Paul IV), and Marcello Cervini (the future Marcellus II), among others, directing them to prepare the way for the Council of Trent, which opened on December 13, 1545. At the same time, Paul supported the activities of new religious orders, most notably the Jesuits, giving his approval to them in the bull *Regimini militantis ecclesiae* (1540). The Inquisition was restored in 1542 under the name Congregation of the Roman Inquisition, or Holy Office. Less successful was his relationship with King Henry VIII of England. Paul excommunicated the monarch on December 17, 1538, but the act only isolated England further from the Church because

the pontiff failed to secure support for sanctions from other nations.

A Renaissance pope in favor of the arts, Paul was a great patron of artists and scholars. He commissioned Michelangelo to complete the "Last Judgment" in the Sistine Chapel and to continue the construction of St. Peter's. At times an inveterate nepotist, he suffered in his later years from the death of his son and the defection of his grandson Ottavio to the service of the Holy Roman Emperor Charles V, taking with him two duchies heretofore the possession of the papacy.

Pope Paul III

Paul IV ● Pope from 1555-1559. Born Giovanni Pietro Caraffa, he belonged to a prominent family of Naples and received an excellent education through the patronage of his uncle, the formidable Cardinal Oliviero Caraffa. His uncle secured for him admission into the papal court, and he rose swiftly: bishop of Chiete (Theate) from 1506-1513, legate (for Pope Leo X) to England from 1513-1514, and nuncio to Spain from 1517-1520. Desiring, however, to pursue a life of asceticism, he resigned his numerous benefices in 1524 and helped establish the Congregation of Clerks Regular with St. Cajetan (d. 1547) that came to be called the Theatines after Caraffa, who served as first general of the congregation. Caraffa was henceforth one of the Church's most prominent promoters of reform. Named by Pope Paul III to a committee to reform the papal court, he was soon elevated to cardinal (1536) and appointed archbishop of Naples (1549). While gifted intellectually and a master of Hebrew and Greek, Caraffa was also hard and unbending, with little interest in the work of other cardinals such as Pole, Contarini, or Morone. Caraffa headed the reinvigorated Inquisition for Paul III and quickly made it a feared organization in Italy. Named dean of the Sacred College of Cardinals in 1553 by Pope Julius III, he went into the conclave to elect a successor to Marcellus II (r. April 9-May 1, 1555), with little prospect of becoming pope. Emperor Charles V, however, stated in clear terms that he would not tolerate Caraffa, a bitter enemy of Spain, to be pontiff. Nevertheless, Caraffa was elected in the face of the emperor's demands and, as Paul IV, was hailed as a potentially great reforming pope.

Pope Paul would prove to be a disappointment. In matters of foreign policy, he was thoroughly disliked by the Spanish and Austrian Habsburgs, who did not even bother to consult him in the abdication of Emperor Charles V and the election of Ferdinand I (r. 1558-1564). The pontiff pursued a disastrous policy in England, first antagonizing Queen Mary and the English Catholics by refusing to sanction the arrangement formulated by Cardinal Pole for the restitution of confiscated Church property. Pole was relieved as papal legate. When Queen Elizabeth came to the throne, Paul indelicately refused her claim to the throne on the grounds of her illegitimacy, wrecking any hopes of a good diplomatic start of what proved a very long reign for the English queen.

As a reformer, the pope was virulently anti-Protestant, preferring to rely on a medieval style of Church government. He would not consider reconvening the Council of Trent (suspended in 1552), believing it faster and simpler to promulgate reform by his own decrees, although he did formulate plans to organize a commission to replace the council and assist in reform matters. His chief instrument was the Inquisition, which, under Cardinal Ghislieri (later Pope St. Pius V), wielded vast powers. No prelate or individual was beyond his reach, and even Cardinal Giovanni Morone was dragged before it and then imprisoned in Castel Sant'

Angelo. In 1559, Paul also launched the *Index Prohibitorum Librorum* (see **Index of Forbidden Books**), confined the Jews of Rome to their ghetto and made them wear distinctive marks and clothing, and promoted his relatives, especially his nephew Carlo, to prominent positions. While eventually ousting them from their offices, he had damaged severely his reputation for scrupulousness. On the positive side, Paul did lay the groundwork for the very substantial reforms of Pius IV and Pius V, and his careful choices of cardinals would benefit the Church for years to come. By the time of his death, he was hated by the Romans who greeted his death on August 18, 1559, with riots; a mob stormed the office of the Inquisition to free its prisoners and a statue of him erected at the start of his pontificate was torn down.

Paul V ● Pope from 1605-1621. A Roman by birth, Camillo Borghese was a descendant of a prominent Sienese family; his father was a law professor. After studying law at Perugia and Padua, he entered into the service of the Curia, distinguishing himself as a respected canonist. His rise in the papal government was steady, culminating with his appointment in 1596 to cardinal by Pope Clement VIII. He was also named cardinal vicar of Rome. Known as a legalist without any particular allegiance to any party, Borghese was considered a suitable compromise choice to succeed Pope Leo XI whose reign had lasted but a few weeks in April 1605. Thus, while only fifty-two years old, he was elected on May 16, 1605, taking the name Paul (V). His legal training and habits would serve him throughout his pontificate.

A believer in the rights of ecclesiastical jurisdiction of the Church and the authority of the Holy See, Paul quickly came into conflict with the Italian states, especially Naples, Genoa, Savoy, and Venice. Only the latter chose to stand firm and on April 17,

1606, the pope pronounced a state of excommunication for the doge and the Venetian state. Most of the Venetian clergy sided with the republic save for the Jesuits, Theatines, and Capuchins who were expelled, and the position of Venice was defended by the Servite priest Paolo Sarpi, a bitter enemy of the papacy. Cardinals Bellarmine (St. Robert Bellarmine) and Baronius stood on behalf of the Church's claims. The crisis continued for nearly a year and might have erupted into war but for the mediation of France and Spain. Paul withdrew the censure and was forced to admit that traditional methods of papal rule were ineffective. Further, the Jesuits were not permitted back to Venice. In 1606, Paul wrote to King James I of England in a friendly letter, imploring him not to persecute Catholics for the rash actions of a few in the Gunpowder Plot (November 1605). His hopes of improved relations, however, were dashed by the Oath of Allegiance, which contained certain declarations absolutely unacceptable to the pope, who denounced it in 1606 and 1607. Matters were complicated even further by the archpriest Robert Blackwell, who advised his followers to take the oath and was replaced in 1608. The Thirty Years' War (1618-1648) began toward the end of Paul's reign, placing him in a difficult position because of his determination to adhere to the Peace of Augsburg of 1555. Nevertheless, he gave subsidies to Emperor Ferdinand II and the Catholic League to wage war upon the Protestant princes of Germany.

Devoted to reform, Paul energetically enforced the decrees of the Council of Trent, ordering home those prelates, even cardinals, who should not have been absent from their sees. He gave approval to the Congregation of the Oratory in 1612 that had been founded by St. Philip Neri (whom Paul would beatify) and the French Oratory established by Pierre de Bérulle. Paul concerned himself with doctrinal matters in two major incidents: he ruled in 1607 that the continuing debate over grace that had been caused by Molinism (see Molina, Luis de) should be suspended, thereby permitting Molinism to be taught; he also censured Galileo Galilei for teaching the theories of Nicolaus Copernicus concerning the solar system.

While somewhat of a nepotist, Paul appointed relatives who were very capable. They nevertheless amassed very considerable fortunes, one nephew, Cardinal Scipione Borghese, spending lavishly to build the sumptuous Villa Borghese. Among Paul's other notable achievements were his adding immeasurably to the Vatican Library by making possible the first collections that became the Vatican's secret archives and the completion at long last of St. Peter's Basilica, an edifice nearly a century in the making, with the end of the work on the nave, portico, and façade. The façade bears the name PAVLVS V BORGHESE. Paul beatified Francis Xavier, Ignatius Loyola, Teresa of Àvila, and others, and canonized Charles Borromeo and Francis of Rome.

Paul VI ● Pope from 1963-1978. Giovanni Battista Montini was born at Concesio, near Brescia, the son of a lawyer and political editor of the Catholic paper *Il cittadina di Brescia*. He was a sickly child but demonstrated an aptitude for reading. Entering the seminary, he studied mostly from home and was ordained on May 29, 1920. From there, he went to the Gregorian University in Rome and in 1922 worked in the Secretariat of State before serving briefly in 1923 in the Warsaw nunciature. Back in the secretariat, where he would remain, he devoted himself to the students of Rome and in 1931 taught diplomatic history in the Pontifical Ecclesiastical Academy. That same year, he was made a domestic prelate to the Holy See. In 1937, he became an assistant to Cardinal Eugenio Pacelli (the future Pope Pius XII), accompanying him to the Eucharistic Congress at Budapest in 1938. Pacelli was elected pope the next year, and in

Pope Paul VI

1944, following the death of Cardinal and Secretary of State Luigi Maglione, Pius did not appoint a new one. Montini was named pro-secretary for the internal affairs of the Church, distinguishing himself for leading relief efforts in the closing phases of World War II. In 1952, he was named pro-secretary of state but declined elevation to cardinal in December 1952. Almost two years later, in November 1954, Pius sent him to Milan as its archbishop; unfortunately, Pius died in 1958 without giving Montini the red hat.

As archbishop of Milan, Montini proved both energetic and deeply concerned with the pressing social problems of that enormous see and the need to repair the terrible damage caused in the war. After Pius's death, he was considered a possible candidate to succeed him, despite being only an archbishop. Angelo Roncalli was elected instead as John XXIII. The new pontiff named Montini one of the first new cardinals of the pontificate and gave him a prominent place in the preparations for Vatican Council II. During the first session of the council in

1962, he spoke only twice. Nevertheless, having made many positive statements about the process of reform, he was a leading candidate to succeed John, who died on June 3, 1963. In the conclave, he was elected (on the fifth ballot) on June 21, 1963, taking the name Paul (VI). The day after his elevation, he promised to continue the council as John had intended it, and to seek peace and unity among Christians.

Paul's immediate order of business was to reconvene the council that had been suspended at the death of his popular predecessor. The second session was begun on September 29, 1963, demonstrating certain Pauline innovations such as the admission of laymen. Other changes would include the admission of women religious, the creation of a press committee, and the naming of moderators. After more than two years of extensive and often contentious deliberations, he closed the council on December 8, 1965. Three of his most notable actions during the council were the announcing of the establishment of a permanent Synod of Bishops, the declaration of the BVM as the Mother of the Church, and the adding to the "Dogmatic Constitution on the Church" (*Lumen Gentium*) a note clarifying the statements concerning the collegiality of bishops.

After the council was brought to a close, Paul declared an extraordinary jubilee (or Holy Year) to last from January 1-May 29, 1966. It was his hope that during this celebration the faithful might be given extensive instruction in the reforms introduced by the council and that the Church might be thereby renewed and the changes begun in a positive fashion and atmosphere. He was to be confronted from the very start with the colossal changes wrought by the documents of Vatican II and the challenge of steering the Church toward a universally authentic interpretation of the decrees. Toward this end, he set up a large number of commissions and promulgated many statements. Paul struggled to hold to the frequently difficult road of reform; he faced opposition from prelates who resisted the changes and others who accelerated the process to such a degree that serious disorientation was occurring in Europe and the United States. To assist the process of revitalization, Paul introduced extensive changes in the Curia and the papal government. Finances were reorganized, and he fixed the retirement age at seventy-five for priests and bishops. Cardinals over eighty years of age should also retire, give up all curial offices, and be prohibited from participating in papal elections. The pope gave confirmation to the secretariats for the Promotion of Christian Unity, Non-Believers, and Non-Christian Religions. In keeping with his promise of adopting collegiality, he convened the Synods of Bishops in 1971, 1974, and 1977. Finally, to make manifest his determination to curb the perquisites of the papal court and its ancient pomp, he reduced the size of the court, abolished many centuries-old traditions (such as the Noble Guard), and sold a magnificent tiara that had been presented to him by his former flock in Milan, using the money for the poor.

Paul was sincerely devoted to the cause of Christian unity and ecumenism. In 1964, he would stun the world by his journey to Jerusalem (January 4-6) where he met with Oecumenical Patriarch Athenagoras I. The next year, on December 7, 1965, he had read a joint statement with the patriarch expressing regret over the mutual excommunications that had been pronounced in 1054 and that had caused the schism that still divided the Eastern and Western Churches. In a moment fraught with symbolism, he exchanged an embrace with the envoy of the patriarch. He met with Michael Ramsey, archbishop of Canterbury, in March 1966 and with the patriarch again in July 1967 in Istanbul. Later, in April 1977, he and Donald Coggan, archbishop of Canterbury, released the joint pledge of continued effort toward reunion. This progress was somewhat offset by Paul's canonization over Anglican objection of the Forty English Martyrs in October 1970 and the failure of the archbishop to secure a statement on intercommunion.

Until the globe-trotting pontificate of Pope John Paul II, Paul was the foremost traveler in the history of the Church. As a cardinal, he had visited the United States, Ireland, and parts of Africa. After his election, he made his trip to Jerusalem (1964), spoke at the UN to plead for peace (1965), attended the Eucharistic Congresses in Bombay (1964) and Bogota (1968), undertook a pilgrimage to Fátima (1967), and went to Uganda (1969), Australia (1970), the Philippines (1970), and elsewhere. In the Philippines, he was nearly assassinated by a knife-wielding assailant.

Inclined toward mysticism and superbly well-read (his massive collection of books was legendary in the Vatican service), Paul was especially fond of contemporary French theological thought. While desirous of bringing a reforming progressiveness to the Church, he was ever careful to avoid dangerous innovation and revitalization that was not in keeping with the council. His encyclicals epitomized this position: *Ecclesiam Suam* (1964), *Mysterium Fidei* (1965), *Populorum progressio* (1967), *Sacerdotalis caelibatus* (1967), and *Humanae vitae* (1968). This last, famed encyclical provoked so bitter and heated a debate that Paul was forever after saddened and wary. His decree on marriage, *Matrimonia mixta* (March 31, 1970), was greeted with the same cynicism and hostility that had surrounded *Humanae vitae*.

The encyclical on birth control was to prove what some saw as a turning point in his pontificate. His remaining years were to be filled with journeys and pronouncements of hope — such as the naming of Sts. Teresa of Ávila and Catherine of Siena to be Doctors of the Church (1970) — but he was deeply troubled by crises in the Church (such as the stand of Marcel Lefebvre and the dissent over contraception) and international or political upheaval, most tragic of all being the kidnapping and death of the Italian Christian Democrat leader Aldo Moro in May 1978. Paul's last public appearance was, in fact, the funeral of his good friend. The pope's health soon failed. He died at Castel Gandolfo on August 6, 1978.

Paul of Samosata ● Third-century bishop of Antioch and a noted heretic. From Samosata, he entered the service of Queen Zenobia of Palmyra, probably working in some government position, adding to what was already a substantial personal fortune. Named to the see of Antioch around 260, he soon acquired a reputation for heretical views, most notably on the Person of Christ. Paul supported a version of Monarchianism, arguing that Christ, the Savior, is essentially a man, one of the Two Persons, with the Son of God. Condemned by several synods in Antioch, he was able to retain his post until 268 or 270 when he was finally deposed. His followers took the name Paulianists and were required by the Council of Nicaea (325) to be rebaptized into the faith before being accepted once more as members of the Church.

Paul of Tarsus, St. (d. c. 67) ● Apostle of the Gentiles. One of the greatest mystics, writers, and missionaries in the history of the

St. Paul

Church, he was born in the town of Tarsus, in the Roman province of Cilicia. Known originally as Saul, he was a Jew of the tribe of Benjamin but also possessed Roman citizenship. While in Tarsus, he studied Greek and Latin and was raised as a Pharisee (Acts 26:5). He was sent at some time to Jerusalem where he studied "at the feet of Gamaliel" the famed rabbi (Acts 22:3), coming to appreciate the Torah and forging what were strong ties to Jerusalem. Paul was thus the recipient of an excellent education and a solid scriptural foundation so that he would be without question the most erudite and learned figure in the early Church.

After returning to Tarsus almost certainly before Christ's public ministry, he first encountered the faith several years after the Crucifixion, by which time the Church had been established in the Holy City. Saul was an inveterate enemy of the creed and was present in the year 36 at the martyrdom of St. Stephen; he guarded the clothes of those who stoned Stephen and "was consenting to his death" (Acts 7:58—8:1). He was "still breathing threats and murder against the disciples" (Acts 9:1) when he set out for Damascus to arrest Christians. On his way he received his famed conversion, an event described in three places in the Acts of the Apostles (9:1-19, 22:5-16, and 26:12-18). For Paul — as he would soon be called (Acts 13:9) — the theological encounter with the light could not have been greater. With overwhelming clarity he understood that the Jesus whom those he persecuted worshiped was God. This identification would change his life and would influence every element of Pauline theology.

Left blind by the light, Paul was taken to Damascus where he sat in darkness for three days. Baptized by the imposition of hands by Ananias (9:17), Paul accepted the spiritual and the intellectual challenge offered to him by God and had restored his sight. Departing Damascus (an event described in Galatians 1:17 but mentioned in Acts), Paul spent several years in Arabia in prayer and meditation. He then returned to Damascus and began preaching the faith. Owing to the danger of being seized by the governor of King Aretas of Nabataea and the murderous intentions of the local Jews (Acts 9:23-25; 2 Cor 11:32), Paul made a secret escape from the city, lowered down a wall in a basket.

Meeting with St. Peter in Jerusalem, where Barnabas testified on his behalf to the suspicious disciples, he spoke "boldly in the name of the Lord," and then went to Caesarea and Cilicia (Acts 9:30; Gal 1:21-24). After several more years, perhaps around 45, Paul was at Antioch where the Holy Spirit declared: "Set apart for me Barnabas and Saul for the work to which I have called them" (Acts 13:2). A short time later, Paul and Barnabas, along with Mark, set out on what is called the First Missionary Journey. They sailed to Cyprus and then to Asia Minor where, to Paul's disappointment, Mark left their company. It was on the early part of this journey that Paul assumed the leadership in the missionary activity, his name changing from Saul to Paul in this part of the narrative. He preached and founded Christian communities in Antioch, Pisidia, Iconium, and elsewhere. By custom, he began with the Jewish inhabitants, speaking at the local synagogue, but he devoted great effort to the Gentiles who were routinely receptive to his words: "They were glad and

glorified the word of God" (Acts 13:48). At Lystra, where he cured a cripple, Paul and Barnabas were revered by the crowd as gods (Acts 14:8-18). His labors also caused local disturbances, and at one point he was stoned by a mob and left for dead (Acts 14:27). Nevertheless, the return of Paul and Barnabas to Antioch (c. 49) brought with it Paul's joyous declaration that the Gentiles were eager for conversion and that "he had opened a door of faith" to them (Acts 14:27).

St. Paul, however, did not find the entire Christian community overjoyed at his news and there followed the often bitter episode over the adherence of Gentile converts to Jewish precepts such as those governing eating and especially circumcision. Paul disagreed with those who believed that all members of the community should adhere to Jewish custom, since he saw such practices as not essential to salvation (he declared, for example, that circumcision had been replaced by Christ with baptism), and a hindrance to new Gentile conversions. The controversy was resolved in his favor by the Council of Jerusalem around 49 and, henceforth, Paul would be the foremost missionary to the pagan world. (See **Circumcision Controversy; Jerusalem, Council of**; and **Judaizers**.)

Around 50, Paul set out on the Second Missionary Journey, an undertaking begun with Silas that would last some five years. He traveled to Tarsus and then revisited the churches of Asia Minor. Timothy joined him at Lystra (Acts 16:1-3). It is possible that at this time he converted the Galatians (see **Galatians, Epistle to the**). His hopes of preaching in Bithynia were somehow circumvented and, instead, Paul was told in a vision to go to Macedonia. He crossed the Hellespont and thus brought the faith into Europe. Reaching Philippi, he made his first convert, a Macedonian named Lydia, who came from Thyatira (Acts 16:14-15), in whose house he stayed. Imprisoned briefly for exorcising a slave girl of a "spirit of divination" (Acts 16:16-18), Paul journeyed to Thessalonika, Beroea, and then Athens. In Athens he encountered Greek philosophers, including Stoics and Epicureans. They listened to his words but were largely unmoved (Acts 17:16-34), and Paul moved on to Corinth. He stayed there for some time, well over a year, firmly establishing the Christian community there. Leaving Greece, he sailed to Palestine and met with the Apostles in Jerusalem.

The Third Missionary Journey began soon after (around 55). He paid another visit to Asia Minor and then went to Ephesus, staying for two years and teaching in the "hall of Tyrannus" (Acts 19:4-10). Numerous converts were made, and Paul most likely spent part of the time in neighboring areas, such as Philadelphia, Colossa, and Laodicea. While at Ephesus, he also wrote his first letter to the Corinthians. His departure proved necessary owing to the riot of silversmiths upset at the shrinking business in the shrine of the goddess Diana.

Going in 57 to Philippi, in Macedonia, he authored his letter to the Galatians and his second letter to the Corinthians. Proceeding to Corinth, he wrote his magnificent letter to the Romans, but he kept his sojourn a short one, his intention being to gather money to relieve the hunger now afflicting the mother Church of Jerusalem (Rom 15:25-26; 1 Cor 16:3). Traveling home, he met the elders of the Church at Ephesus in Miletus, bidding them a tearful farewell tinged with the premonition of imprisonment and martyrdom (Acts 20:17-37).

Back in Jerusalem, he was attacked by his Jewish enemies, beaten by a mob, and rescued from death only by a squad of Roman soldiers. Subsequently brought before the Sanhedrin (Acts 22:30—23:10) on charges of bringing Gentiles into the Temple, he skillfully divided the council by noting his own origins as a Pharisee. Enjoying the rights of a Roman citizen, he was sent to Caesarea for trial before the governor. The procurator

Felix put him in prison for two years (58-60), and the trial was held only under Felix's successor Porcius Festus. Paul, as was his right, appealed to Caesar; so off to Rome he went, after meeting and much impressing King Herod Agrippa. Under Roman guard, he sailed for Rome and was shipwrecked on the island of Malta (Acts 27-28), eventually reaching the Eternal City. Here he was warmly received by the city's Christians and permitted to reside, at his own expense, for two years in a house. He wrote his letters to the Colossians, the Philippians, Philemon, and perhaps the Ephesians (the so-called Captivity Epistles) while in Rome. When finally tried, he was acquitted.

His remaining life is quite obscure, the chronology reconstructed from tradition and his later letters. He probably visited Spain and then perhaps revisited Syria, Palestine, Asia Minor, Greece, and Crete. Arrested again, he was taken back to Rome, kept in close confinement, and apparently knew his death was imminent, as is clear from his second letter to Timothy (in particular 4:6-8). He was martyred around 67 by Emperor Nero, most likely beheaded as reported by Tertullian. According to the apocryphal Acts of St. Paul, his place of martyrdom was on the left bank of the Tiber; he was said to have been buried in a cemetery on the Via Ostia owned by a Christian named Lucina, the site where the Basilica of S. Paolo Fuori le Mure (St. Paul-Outside-the-Walls) would be built.

St. Paul had a genuinely colossal role in the formation of Christian theology through his Epistles, written in the very drama of the moment during his eventful and so fruitful missionary endeavors. His letters comprise approximately one-third of the NT and provide vibrant testimony to his extensive conception of the great divine plan of the Father, carried through by his Son in his incarnation, life, death, and resurrection. Paul's theology extends into the whole of the Mystical Body of Christ and encompasses such decisive issues as faith, baptism, the

Holy Spirit, grace, predestination, free will, the Eucharist, and the full attainment of perfection through the mature Christian life. Paul's works specifically were Romans, 1 and 2 Corinthians, Galatians, Ephesians, Philippians, Colossians, 1 and 2 Thessalonians, 1 and 2 Timothy, Titus, and Philemon. (See also under individual letters as well as **Acts of the Apostles; Jerusalem;** and **Peter, St.**)

Paul of the Cross ● See **Passionists**.

Paul the Hermit, St. (d. c. 347) ● Also Paul of Thebes. First traditionally accepted Christian hermit. According to the *Vita Pauli* by St. Jerome, Paul was from the Thebaid in Egypt, going into the desert during the Decian persecutions of 249-251. There he lived for the remainder of his remarkably long life, in a cave, his days of prayers of penance interrupted only once, by a visit from St. Antony, who had been sent to find Paul to learn humility from his predecessor in the arid land. Later, after Paul's death, Antony would bury Paul in the cloak that had been given to Antony by St. Athanasius. Two lions were said to have helped dig his grave. Scholars note that the *Vita Pauli*, in both Latin and Greek versions, is the only source on Paul's life; it is thus open to question as to the accuracy of the account, although there is little doubt that St. Paul actually lived. Feast day: January 15.

Paula, St. (347-404) ● Roman widow and close associate of St. Jerome. A member of a noble Roman family, Paula was married to a Roman senator who died when she was around thirty-two, leaving her with five children. A devout Christian, she spent the next years in prayer and personal devotion, largely through the influence of Sts. Marcella and Jerome. Around 382, however, she became determined to travel to the Holy Land and to settle into a monastic life near Bethlehem. She departed Rome in September

385, journeying to all the pilgrim sites in the East before residing in Bethlehem. With her traveled St. Eustochium, her daughter, who would remain forever at her mother's side. Paula and Eustochium had prominent roles in Jerome's exegetical labors and in the establishing of the dual communities for men and women. The chief source for information on her is the correspondence of St. Jerome. Feast day: January 26. St. Eustochium continued her work, dying in Bethlehem around 419. Feast day: September 28.

Paulicians ● Name of a dualistic heretical sect found in the Byzantine Empire. The name was probably derived from the extreme devotion to St. Paul, or it was used by their opponents to associate them with the teachings of Paul of Samosata. The origins of the sect are somewhat obscure, although it was probably begun around 657 in the Manichaean village of Kibossa by Constantine of Mananalis in Armenia. The small group soon spread to parts of Armenia, earning imperial displeasure; persecution came under Emperor Constantine II Pogonatos (r. 668-685). The sect's founder, Constantine, was arrested and stoned to death while preaching in Asia Minor. The Paulicians continued to grow, reaching their height of influence in the ninth century, but they faced persecutions from the Byzantine Empire and were shattered militarily in 872 by the troops of Emperor Basil I. The Paulicians who survived the persecutions went to Bulgaria and elsewhere, having an influence on the development of the Bogomils. They believed that there were two fundamental principles: a good God and an evil God; the first is the ruler of the world to come and the second the master of the present world. By their reasoning, then, Christ could not have been the Son of God because the good God could not take human form. The Paulicians did revere the Gospels because of the value they placed on Christ's teachings.

Paulinus of Aquileia, St. (c. 726-802) ● Bishop of Aquileia. Born to a Roman family in Cividale (Friuli), he was educated in the local Church school, eventually becoming its master following his ordination. Known for his learning, he secured the favor of Charlemagne and was invited to the Frankish court in 776. There he became an acquaintance of such famous figures as Alcuin and Petrus of Pisa. As a master of grammar, he contributed to the revival of learning in the West. In 787, Charlemagne named him bishop of Aquileia. Paulinus was subsequently involved in the condemnation of Adoptionism, particularly at the Councils of Ratisbon (792), Frankfurt (794), and Friuli (796). He also promoted missionary work among the surrounding pagan tribes. Among his writings were books against Adoptionism, an account of an expedition he accompanied against the Avars, and poetry. Feast day: January 11.

Paulinus of Nola, St. (c. 353-431) ● Bishop of Nola and a famous Christian poet. Meropius Pontius Paulinus was born in Bordeaux, a member of a wealthy senatorial family. He studied under the noted poet Ausonius, embarked on a political career, and served as a consul (378) and governor of Gallia Cisalpina (381). With a bright future in government ahead of him, Paulinus surprised his friends and associates by announcing in 390 that he had been baptized by St. Delphinus, that he was giving away his fortune, and that he and his wife, Therasia, were entering into a life of severe asceticism. Ordained in 395, he became bishop of Nola in 409. A poet of great talent, he used poetry as an expression of his Christian faith; most of the poems were devoted to the martyr St. Felix while others were on psalms and John the Baptist. He wrote a whole panegyric to celebrate the victory of Emperor Theodosius I over the usurper Eugenius in 394. Paulinus enjoyed a varied correspondence with some of the most prominent Christians of his era,

including Augustine, Ambrose, and Martin of Tours. Feast day: June 22.

Paulinus of York, St. (d. 644) ● Important missionary in England and the first bishop of York. Paulinus was sent by Pope Gregory I in 601 to assist in the work of St. Augustine of Canterbury. After laboring for years in Kent, he was consecrated bishop of Kent in 625 and served as escort to the Kentish princess Ethelburga when she was wed to Edwin, king of Northumbria. Two years later, Edwin was converted to the Christian faith, thereby ensuring the conversion of Northumbria. Paulinus was soon installed as bishop of York, working closely with Edwin to foster the spread of Christianity in the region. Edwin, however, was slain in battle in 633 with the pagan ruler Caedwalla. Paulinus was forced to return to Kent, serving as bishop of Rochester. Feast day: October 10.

Paulus Diaconos (d. c. 794) ● Lombard historian. Called Paul the Deacon and a native of Friuli, he was a member of a noble Lombard family and served as a tutor to Adalberga, daughter of the Lombard king Desiderius. After the destruction of the Lombard kingdom in 774 by Charlemagne, Paulus entered the Benedictine monastery of Monte Cassino. His brother, however, was implicated in an anti-Frankish plot and was sent as a prisoner to France. In 782, Paulus visited Charlemagne to ask for his brother's release. The ruler was favorably disposed toward this but only on condition that Paulus enter the imperial court of Aachen. He spent the next several years with Charlemagne's brilliant court, finally returning to Monte Cassino around 787; he remained there for the rest of his life, authoring his most important work, the *Historia Langobardorum* (*History of the Lombards*), covering the Lombards from 568-744; it is a major source on the events of the period because of the excellent use of sources. Paul also wrote a

Historia Romana, which was a continuation of the *Breviarum* of Eutropius. Also known as Paulus Levita, he is considered the Father of Italian History.

Pázmány, Péter (1570-1637) ●

Hungarian cardinal, theologian, scholar, and preacher. Born to a noble Hungarian family, he was raised a Calvinist, but his stepmother, a devout Catholic, was able to bring him into the Church. He became a Catholic in 1583 and in 1587 entered the Jesuit novitiate, studying at Rome under St. Robert Bellarmine. After teaching theology at Graz, Pázmány returned to Hungary in 1607. Thereafter his rise in the Hungarian Church was swift, culminating in his appointment as archbishop of Esztergom (1616) and then cardinal primate of Hungary. Pázmány long labored to improve the Church in his native land: he established schools and seminaries, promulgated the decrees of the Council of Trent, and introduced the *Missale Romanum*. A preacher of brilliant skill, Pázmány was largely responsible for rescuing Hungary from the domination of Protestantism.

Peace of Augsburg ● See **Augsburg, Peace of**.

Peace of God ●

Movement established in medieval Europe, beginning in the late tenth century. It attempted to curb the violence of the era and to make roads and cities safer for pilgrims and traveling merchants. The Peace of God was first decreed in 989 in Charroux, stipulating that there were peasant rights and insisting upon codes of behavior for all knights and soldiers, guaranteeing the safety of traders and the sanctuary of churches. Additional steps were taken in the eleventh century with the so-called Truce of God. This new step in reducing bloodshed produced armistices in blood feuds, prohibiting fighting from Wednesday night until Monday morning, and was enforced by bands of militia and threats of ecclesiastical punishment. First pronounced at the Council of Elne in 1027, the Truce of God was reinforced in 1095 by the Council of Clermont, which extended the prohibitions from the start of Advent until eight days after the Feast of the Epiphany. Rarely effective, both the Peace and Truce of God did have an important role convincing knights under threat of Church punishment to expiate their sins of violating the Peace of God by embarking on a crusade. The movement also demonstrated the pervasive cultural influence of the Church in the daily life of Christians, particularly as a means of taming the savage and brutal instincts of the feudal establishment.

Peasants' War ●

Bloody uprising of the peasants in southern and central Germany from 1524-1525. The causes of the revolt are much disputed, the result over the centuries of biased analysis by reporting steeped in religious prejudice. It is generally agreed, however, that the terrible war began as the result of economic hardships suffered by the peasant classes in the early sixteenth century. The difficulties were most acutely felt in the German states, and the unease of the peasant populace was only heightened by the call for total reform made by Martin Luther and his adherents. The hopes of the average people were dashed by the failure of the meeting of officials at Speyer (September 1524), which was unable to bring about the popularly desired reform of the German Church and political life.

Led by such anarchists as the Anabaptist Thomas Münzer (d. 1525) and Hans Müller, the uprising began in the Black Forest region of Germany and soon spread through Franconia, Swabia, and Alsace. The rebels issued the so-called Twelve Tables at Memmingen in March 1525, demanding the abolition of serfdoms, equality in taxes, and extensive religious reforms. Such was the unstable nature of the peasant mobs, however, that savage violence soon erupted, with rebel gangs burning down churches and castles, massacring nobles and clerics, and sacking monasteries. The initial demands were forgotten as the new radical leadership of the mobs called for the total liquidation of the Church and State.

Among those who insisted that harsh measures be taken against the revolt was Martin Luther. He had originally advocated the very social reforms that had been the expressed desire of the rebel leaders, and, until April 1525, he had served as a mediator between the various German princes and the peasant leaders; but soon after, he was so sickened by the brutality and potential collapse of all order that he encouraged the princes to take all necessary steps to end the fighting and chaos. He authored a pamphlet against the rebels, and his support of the princes outraged many in the revolt who had earnestly felt that their actions had been endorsed by Luther.

By May 15, 1525, Münzer and his host were routed by the combined forces of the princes, and Münzer was put to death. Over succeeding months, the peasants were mercilessly crushed, and the situation was used by the nobles to increase their power and delay any meaningful reforms in social and political life.

Pecock, Reginald (c. 1395-1460) ● Also spelled Peacock, bishop of Chichester and a theologian. Born in Wales, Pecock was educated at Oxford University and was ordained in 1421. A much respected scholar, he was appointed master of Whittington College, London (1431), rector of St. Michael's-in-Riola, bishop of St. Asaph (1444), and bishop of Chichester (1450). An opponent of Lollardy, he authored a number of works against them, including *The Book of Rule of Christian Religion* and, most importantly, *The Repressor Over Much Blaming of the Clergy*, an apology for the Church and an attempt to convert the Lollards. His theological tendency toward the idea that the natural law was superior to the Scriptures provided considerable ammunition against him for his enemies, most notably the Yorkists, who disliked Pecock's involvement with the Lancastrians. In 1457, he was accused of heresy by his enemies and Archbishop Bourchier allowed proceedings against him. Condemned on November 28, Pecock successfully appealed to Pope Callistus III, but the pontiff's untimely demise (along with the refusal of Bourchier to promulgate the pope's bull exonerating Pecock) caused Pecock to be confined at the Abbey of Thorney where he died, despite recanting and resigning his see. Although Pecock was generally considered an orthodox theologian, his writings and thinking were much distorted by his enemies.

Péguy, Charles Pierre (1873-1914) ● French poet and philosopher who had considerable influence on French Catholic writers of the twentieth century. Born in Orléans to a poor family, he was educated in his native city and at Paris, at the *École Normale Superieure*. Marrying in 1897, he used some of his wife's money to start a bookstore, which became a center in Paris for writings in support of Captain Alfred Dreyfus. A devoted Dreyfusard, Péguy was also an ardent social reformer, attempting to defend both his Catholicism and socialism in his journal *Cahiers de la Quinzaine* (*Notebooks of the Fortnight*), which he began publishing in 1900. His most important writings included the drama *Jeanne d'Arc* (1897) and the poem *Le Mystére de la charité de Jeanne d'Arc* (1910). A patriot, he joined the French army at the start of World War I and was killed at the Battle of the Marne on September 5, 1914.

Pelagia, St. (d. c. 311) ● Virgin and martyr, known as Pelagia of Antioch. Often confused with the unhistorical Pelagia the Penitent, St. Pelagia was a fifteen-year-old girl in Antioch who was caught up in the persecutions of the Christians during the time of the Diocletianic oppression of the early fourth century. When soldiers came to arrest her, she threw herself from a rooftop to preserve her virginity. Plunging into the sea, she was killed instantly. Her existence is confirmed by the writings of both St. Ambrose and St. John Chrysostom, and she is listed among the virgin martyrs of the Canon of the Mass found in the Ambrosian rite of Milan. Feast day: June 9.

Another Pelagia, called the Penitent, is known in Christian legend. She was supposedly a dancer in Antioch who was converted by Bishop Nonnus of Edessa after hearing one of his sermons. Dressing as a man, she went to Jerusalem and lived as a hermit on the Mount of Olives until her death. Feast day: October 8.

A third Pelagia, of Tarsus, is also found in legend. She was supposedly a virgin who was forcibly betrothed to a son of Emperor Diocletian. When she refused both the son and the emperor, she was supposedly roasted to death in a red-hot bull made of brass. Feast day: May 4.

Pelagianism ● Heresy originating in the fifth century. It derived its name from the British monk Pelagius (c. 355-425), who gave the movement much of its theological basis. Pelagianism can be defined as a series of heretical propositions concerning grace, ultimately denying both the supernatural order and the necessity of grace for salvation. Among its other tenets were: Adam still would have died even if he had not sinned; the fall of Adam injured only Adam and not the entire human race; a newborn child is in the same state as Adam prior to the Fall; the human race will not die as a result of Adam's sin, but it will not rise on the Last Day because of Christ's redemption; the law of the Jews (or Israel) will permit individuals to reach heaven in the same way as the Gospel.

The monk arrived in Rome around 380. He found the Romans shockingly lax in their moral attitudes and blamed the cause on the Church's teachings on grace. He believed that the Augustinian position of grace being dependent upon the divine will was incorrect and gave humanity no personal reason to avoid sin. Instead, he argued that humans were responsible for their own actions. In this he was supported by the lawyer Celestius and a number of Romans. Around 410 and the sack of Rome by the Visigoths, Pelagius and Celestius journeyed to Africa. There they were vigorously opposed by St. Augustine, who especially disagreed with Pelagius's concept of an individual's essentially good moral nature and his understanding of the person as a free and autonomous individual who can achieve sanctity through unaided human effort. In 411, Pelagius was condemned by the Council of Carthage. While vindicating himself at a synod in Jerusalem, he was condemned again, with Celestius, at two councils, in Carthage and Milevis, in 416. At the behest of the African bishops, Pope Innocent I excommunicated them. Celestius then chose to go to Rome where he was able to convince Pope Zosimus to reopen the affair. At the Council of Carthage (May 418) they renewed their condemnatory position, issuing nine canons concerning Augustine's doctrine on original sin and denouncing Pelagius. Zosimus, who had at first found Pelagius to be innocent and had released the *Libellus fidei* (*Brief Statement of Faith*), reversed himself. In the *Epistola Tractoria*, he reiterated Pope Innocent's position. Pelagius subsequently disappeared from history, although Pelagianism continued to be advocated by Celestius who, with his followers, was condemned by the Council of Ephesus (431). Pelagianism endured in parts of the West, most notably Britain and Gaul. (See also **Semi-Pelagianism**.)

Pelagius I ● Pope from 556-561. The pontificate of Pelagius was overshadowed by his own remarkable work as a deacon to

Popes St. Agapetus I, St. Silverius, and Vigilius. Born in Rome, he accompanied Agapetus I to Constantinople in 536 and was appointed by him legate to the Byzantine capital. Agapetus died soon after, and Pelagius returned to Rome the following year, upon the banishment of Pope Silverius by Empress Theodora, but was soon back in Constantinople with the accession of Vigilius. While there, he served as a close adviser to Emperor Justinian I and was soon embroiled in the so-called Three Chapters Controversy that would dominate the next years. In 546, however, Pelagius acted as vicar of Rome while Pope Vigilius was in Constantinople; he presided over the defense of the city during the siege of King Totila and the Ostrogoths. When the Eternal City fell, he was crucial in preventing a merciless massacre. On the matter of the Three Chapters, meanwhile, he remained firm in his refusal to endorse Justinian's condemnation of them, enduring excommunication and imprisonment. A reconciliation was effected in 555, and soon after with Justinian's full support he was elected pope to succeed Vigilius. He could not be consecrated until April 16, 556, owing to opposition in the West, and his reign was troubled by a schism that would continue until 610. Of great significance was his recognition by Justinian as the de facto ruler of Rome, a step that was crucial in establishing the temporal power of the papacy, particularly in Italy. Pelagius also rebuilt Rome, repairing the damage done by the Goths.

Pelagius II ● Pope from 579-590. Born in Rome, Pelagius was a Goth by descent. Elected to succeed Benedict I in August 579, he came to the papacy during the Lombard siege of Rome. Eager to find support against the Lombards, Pelagius first sent a plea to the Byzantine emperor Tiberius, but when the Byzantines were not in a position to send aid because of a conflict with the Persians, the pope took the momentous step of asking

for assistance from the Franks. Peace was subsequently negotiated in 585 through the Byzantine exarch of Ravenna. Pelagius also promoted a building program in Rome.

Penance ● Also confession or reconciliation. The sacrament by which a penitent makes contrition, confesses one's sins, and demonstrates a desire to perform those deeds that will make satisfaction or atonement for his or her transgressions. Absolution for the sins is given by a priest. It is accepted by the Church that Christ instituted the sacrament of penance when he proclaimed to the Apostles on Easter Sunday night: "If you forgive the sins of any, they are forgiven; if you retain the sins of any, they are retained" (Jn 20:23). Christ thus conferred upon the Apostles the power to forgive sins and the authority to withhold absolution in those cases where it is warranted.

In the early Church, there was no specific form for the sacrament, but most of the first churches followed the teachings of St. Paul (e.g., 1 Cor 5:3-5; 2 Cor 2:7-11) in which is stressed the power of the keys, namely the authority to bind and loose — placing the sinner under ban of excommunication and then reconciling the sinner. Initial custom, as evidenced by the *Didache* and James (5:16), may have been in some areas to make confession of sins in public. While public admission of sins was used at times, this probably ceased early on and by the fifth century was discouraged by authorities, as evidenced by Pope St. Leo I the Great who, in 459, condemned the public reading of a chart containing the sins of the penitents. Confession was made by a sinner in the early Church to a bishop of the local community. When the size of the Christian population grew — as in Rome, Antioch, and, from the fourth-century Constantinople — the penitents made confession to a priest penitentiary.

In some regions, it was common for a

severe sinner (those guilty of apostasy, adultery, and murder) to be enrolled as a so-called public penitent. They would be dressed in sackcloth, a garment made of goat hair, and be covered with ashes to give visible symbol of separation from the faithful. During Mass, such persons were kept away from the Offertory, Prayers of the Faithful, and the Eucharist (with the catechumens); penitents also had to fast and contribute alms to the poor. They were reconciled according to Pope Innocent I (r. 401-417) on the Thursday before Easter. In the cases of those guilty of lesser transgressions, they performed penances that included fasting, prayers, and almsgiving.

A practice of penance in Celtic lands developed in a manner different from that found on the Continent. The minister of reconciliation was customarily the priest abbot of the monastery dominating the area or a priest monk in one of the surrounding churches. Penances were also much more severe in the Celtic Church. A person guilty of serious sins might be exiled, forced to wander with a pilgrim's staff. For those who have made minor transgressions, punishments might include extreme prayer, fasts, or living on bread and water for a prescribed time. The Irish monks also fostered two other innovations: the permitting of repeated penance and the

Angel locking the Gate of Hell (c. 1100s)

granting of immediate absolution with penance to be performed later. The first rule was born out of the idea that a person should have only one public penance and that further public penance should not be allowed so as not to give confusion to the catechumens. The second rule reversed the standing practice of doing penance and then receiving absolution. The Celtic practice of immediate absolution subsequently became very popular, fostered throughout Europe by the missionary endeavors of the Irish monks.

During the Middle Ages, theologians in the Western Church gave recognition of penance as a sacrament of the Church. They often disagreed and speculated, however, as to the element of the sacrament granting the actual grace of forgiveness. Peter Lombard in the twelfth century, for example, proposed that absolution by the priest was to make clear to the sinner that sins have been forgiven by the grace of the person's sorrow. This was contrary to the thinking of Hugh of St. Victor (d. 1141), who stated that it was by the priest's absolution that sins were forgiven. Further analysis was made by both St. Bonaventure and St. Thomas Aquinas. They stipulated that, in keeping with the terminology of Aristotelianism, the matter of the sacrament was in the act of the penitent and the form of the sacrament was the absolution of the minister. Penance was subsequently defined as a sacrament at the Council of Lyons in 1274.

Further and extensive clarification of the sacrament was made by the Council of Trent (1545-1563), issuing some nine chapters and fifteen canons on penance. These were considered quite important in the face of the Reformers, who were de-emphasizing the place of the priest, going so far as to declare the minister as unnecessary. The council stated that all Christians should confess their mortal sins, both by number and species, to a priest who was empowered to grant absolution. Vatican Council II reaffirmed the teachings of Trent but also placed emphasis on the healing nature of the sacrament of penance and introduced changes in the rite. The Church today, as stipulated in the Code of Canon Law, requires that all Catholics should confess their mortal sins at least once a year; venial sins should also be confessed. (See also **Donatism, Novatian,** and **Jansenism**.)

Pentecost ● Feast celebrating the descent of the Holy Spirit on the Apostles. The name is derived from the Greek (*he pentekoste*), meaning the fiftieth day, an allusion to the fact that it occurs fifty days after Easter. Pentecost was the name used in Tobit (2:1) and 2 Maccabees (12:32) for the Hebrew Shabuoth, or Feast of Weeks, a festival that was on the fiftieth day after Passover when the fruits of the first harvest were offered to the Lord in thanksgiving (Dt 1:16). It was mentioned in Exodus (23:16) as one of the three pilgrimage fasts, with Passover and Tabernacle. The Shabuoth also commemorates the giving of the law by God to Moses on Mt. Sinai. In the Christian Church, Pentecost assumes its importance from the descending of the Holy Spirit, an event recorded in Acts (2:1-4). In the early Church, the common understanding of Pentecost was the entire time from Easter

until Pentecost Sunday. During the period no fasting was permitted, the Alleluia was sung with greater frequency, and all prayers were made standing.

Perfectae Caritatis ● Vatican Council II document promulgated on October 28, 1965, the "Decree on the Appropriate Renewal of Religious Life" (as it is called in English) is concerned with adapting the religious life to the demands and conditions of modern times; it also calls for the renewal of the religious orders but without the loss of the essential elements of the consecrated life and role of the religious. A number of important points were to be followed in bringing this about: the Gospels are to serve as the central guide in renewal; the spirit and intention of the founders of each of the religious orders should be reemphasized; the members of the religious orders should each be fully aware of the problems and challenges facing the contemporary Church; each religious institute should participate in the active life of the Church to the degree established by its charter; and all members of the institutes must remember that their lives as religious are to be guided by the principle of charity, obedience, and poverty, and to be a religious is not a career or activity but a complete way of life. *Perfectae Caritatis* has been the source of considerable debate within the Church over its implementation. Questions about it led to the formation of the *Consortium Perfectae Caritatis* in 1971 to assist women religious in the formation of the religious life in keeping with the intention of *Perfectae Caritatis* and while obedient to the teachings of the Church.

Periti ● Latin plural of the term *peritus* (expert) and used for experts within the Church in various ecclesiastical matters. They are consulted by those offices of the Church to whom their service is of value. The *periti*, for example, played a major consultative role in the proceedings of the

Second Vatican Council and continue today to be used by some Congregations of the Roman Curia. The term *peritus* is also used in canon law for any expert who acts as a witness in an ecclesiastical trial; such a *peritus* would be the ecclesiastical equivalent of an expert called in a secular trial to provide some kind of expert testimony, as noted in the Code of Canon Law (Canons 1574-1581).

Persecutions, Catholic ● For details on the individual persecutions launched against the Catholic Church, the reader is encouraged to consult the numerous geographical entries (i.e., **Japan, Russia, France,** etc.) and such entries as **Communism, Kulturkampf, Josephinism,** and **Reformation, Protestant**.

Persecution, Christian ● See under **Roman Empire**.

Persons, Robert (1546-1610) ● Also Robert Parsons, the English Jesuit who helped organize Catholic activities in Elizabethan England. Born in Nether Stowey, Somerset, Persons was raised an Anglican, becoming a fellow at Balliol College, Oxford. Because of his Catholic sympathies, however, he was forced to resign his position. He departed England and was received into the Church at Louvain in 1575. That same year, in Rome, he joined the Society of Jesus and in 1580 was chosen, with Edmund Campion, to return to England to lead the Jesuit mission. Over the next year, he worked to promote the Catholic cause, preaching and establishing a printing press. The 1581 arrest of Campion compelled him to flee to the Continent; he would not return to England. Persons subsequently worked with Cardinal William Allen to improve conditions for the much persecuted Catholics of England. In 1588, he was sent to Spain, where he was deeply respected by Philip II and succeeded in establishing a number of seminaries and schools for English Catholics, including Valladolid (1589), Seville (1592), and Madrid (1598). The author of a number of controversial writings, his best known work was the *Christian Directory*. Originally called the *Book of Christian Exercise*, the *Directory* was first published in 1582 and was a spiritual treatise that became popular with both Catholics and Protestants. He died in the English College, Rome, on April 15, 1610.

Pétau, Denis (1583-1652) ● Also Dionysius Petavius, a prominent French Jesuit theologian and scholar. Born in Orléans, he studied in his native city and then at Paris where he became a friend of the great scholar Isaac Casaubon. In 1605, he entered the Society of Jesus, subsequently teaching at Reims and La Flèche (1611-1621), and the Collège de Clermont in Paris (1621-1644). His remaining years were spent teaching in Paris, acquiring a wide reputation for his learning and scholarship. His vast writings covered a wide variety of subjects: history, philosophy, theology, and chronology, and included: *De doctrina temporum* (1627), a thorough study of chronology that was a major revision of Joseph Scaliger's *De emendatione temporum* (1583); and his *magnum opus*, the *Dogmata theologica* (the first three volumes published in 1644, the last two in 1650), a large treatise on theology. His work in the field of dogmatic theology earned him the title Father of the History of Dogma.

Peter, St. ● Simon Peter, Prince of the Apostles, Vicar of Christ, founder of the see of Rome, and the first pope. Peter was the brother of Andrew, and like him, was a fisherman. As reported in John (1:44), he was born in Bethsaida, a small community in Galilee near Lake Tiberias. Called to become a disciple by Jesus, his call is described variously in the Gospels (Mt 4:18-20; Mk 1:16-18; Lk 5:1-11; Jn 1:40-42), but in

Matthew and Mark, he and Andrew are described as fisherman whom Christ called from their livelihood. The story of Peter catching so large an amount of fish that he fell down at Jesus's knees is told in Luke's account; Jesus responded to his humility by saying, "Do not be afraid; henceforth you shall be catching men" (5:10). After being called by Jesus, Peter would forever after be first in all lists of the Apostles. In the Johannine account, Jesus gives to him a new name: "So you are Simon the son of John? You shall be called Cephas" meaning the rock (1:42). Translated into Greek, this becomes *Petros* and hence Peter. Later, in Matthew (16:13-20), when Peter proclaims at Caesarea Philippi that "You are Christ, the Son of the living God," Jesus gives to him the most important promise of the keys of the kingdom of heaven.

St. Peter

Peter was a member of the inner circle of the disciples, with James and John. He was thus present at the raising of Jairus's daughter (Mk 5:37), the Transfiguration (Mt 17:1-8), and the Agony in the Garden of Gethsemane (Mk 14:33; Mt 26:37). He was clearly one of the leaders, if not the foremost, of the disciples, speaking for them in saying to Christ (Jn 6:68-69) that "Lord, to whom shall we go? You have the words of eternal life; and we have believed, and have come to know that you are the Holy One of God." He also helped to organize the Last Supper. During it (Lk 22:31-32), Christ gives him encouragement to "strengthen your brethren."

Throughout the Passion accounts, Peter figures quite prominently. He refuses to allow Jesus to wash his feet (Jn 13:6-9). When the Master is arrested, he cuts the right ear off a slave of the high priest Malchus (Jn 18:10-11). Later that night, as Jesus had predicted (Mt 26:34), Peter denied Christ three times. Remembering Jesus' words, Peter "went out and wept bitterly" (Mt 26:75). After the Resurrection, Peter, with the "other disciple" (most likely John), went immediately to the tomb after being told by the women. The "other disciple" reached the tomb first but did not enter, waiting for Peter (Jn 20:3-10). As reported in Luke (24:34) and 1 Corinthians (15:5), the first appearance of the risen Christ was to Peter, before all of the other Apostles. Further, when Christ appeared before the disciples at Tiberias, he gave Peter the famous commands to "Feed my lambs. . . . Tend my sheep. . . . Feed my sheep" (Jn 21:15-17). In the time that was to follow after the Ascension, Peter was to be the unquestionable head of the Apostles and the Church that Christ had founded. The position of Peter is made abundantly clear in Acts. He was the guiding hand in choosing a replacement for Judas Iscariot (1:15-22). He spoke first to the crowds that had gathered after the descent of the Holy Spirit at Pentecost (2:14-41). Peter was the first Apostle to perform miracles in the name of Our Lord (3:1-10). And he passed judgment upon the deceitful Ananias and Sapphira (5:1-11). Of the disciples, he was the greatest miracle worker, his very shadow healing the sick (5:15).

Peter was also an important impetus in bringing the Gospel to the Gentiles. He baptized the pagan Cornelius (10:1—11:18) and was one of the leaders, with James, at the Council of Jerusalem, which made possible the preaching to Gentiles, permitting the Church to become universal. St. Paul mentions his visit to Antioch (Gal 2:11-21), including the rebuke by Paul for bowing to the circumcision party and curtailing his association with Gentiles. He may have visited Corinth, on the basis of a reference by Paul of a party of Cephas in that city's Christian community (1 Cor 1:12).

Peter's years prior to his martyrdom are obscure. Nevertheless, there is long and accepted tradition connecting him with Rome. The saint himself makes apparent reference to being in the Eternal City in his first Epistle (5:13) by noting that he writes from Babylon, a common metaphor for Rome. St. Paul makes note of an Apostle in Rome before himself in Romans (15:20). It is known with certainty that Peter died in Rome and that his martyrdom came during the reign of Emperor Nero, probably around 64. The testimony of the writers of the early Church is quite extensive, including Origen (who, as told in Eusebius's *Ecclesiastical History*, reported that Peter was crucified upside down at his own request), Eusebius of Caesarea (who writes of Peter's pontificate as lasting some twenty-five years), St. Clement I of Rome, St. Ignatius, and St. Irenaeus. The latter, in his *Adversus haereses* (*Against Heresies*), is clear in stating that Peter founded the Church in Rome and what is Christian belief is that which is accepted by the Church in Rome, begun by Peter and Paul. Thus, from the earliest days of the Church, Peter has been recognized as the Prince of the Apostles and as such, the see that he founded, namely Rome, has enjoyed the position of primacy in the Catholic Church, the test of communion with the Roman Church being recognition of the ecclesiastical supremacy of the Petrine see and the legitimate authority of the Bishop of Rome over the universal Church as the successor to Peter. The traditional symbols of Peter are the keys of the kingdom, depicting his primacy over the Church; he is also represented by an inverted cross, a boat (for the barque of Christ, which he guides), and the cock (for the triple denial of Christ). Feast day: June 29, with St. Paul. (See also **Apostolic See; Apostolic Succession; Bishop of Rome; Holy See; Peter, First [and Second] Epistle of; Peter, Tomb of; Primacy of the Pope; Quo Vadis?; Rome;** and **St. Peter's Basilica**.)

Peter, First Epistle of ● One of two letters in the NT traditionally attributed to the Prince of the Apostles, St. Peter. It was written in a particularly flowing Greek style and was intended for the Christian communities of Asia Minor (Pontus, Galatia, Cappadocia, Asia, Bithynia), who were enduring persecution. Aside from offering general encouragement to the converts, Peter provides exhortations to his readers to endeavor to live in holiness. Peter writes: "You know that you were ransomed from the futile ways inherited from your fathers, not with perishable things such as silver and gold, but with the precious blood of Christ, like that of a lamb without blemish or spot. He was destined before the foundation of the world but was made manifest at the end of times for your sake" (1:18-20). His commands include the abstaining "from the passions of the flesh that wage war against your soul" (2:11), maintaining "good conduct among the Gentiles" (2:12), being "subject for the Lord's sake to every human institution" (2:13), and working for good relations between wives and husbands (3:1-7). He continues: "Since therefore Christ suffered in the flesh, arm yourselves with the same thought, for whoever has suffered in the flesh has ceased from sin, so as to live for the rest of the time in the flesh no longer by human passions but by the will of God." (4:1-2). The letter was carried to the churches by Sylvanus (Silas). It was written from Rome, called by Peter "Babylon" (5:12), and has been dated to around 66, after the persecution of Christians by Emperor Nero in the wake of the fire that destroyed much of the Eternal City. Some scholars have questioned Peter's authorship of the epistle and the second one under Peter's name, but most accept the first while acknowledging that questions persist concerning the second.

Peter, Second Epistle of ● Second letter in the NT traditionally attributed to St. Peter, although scholars have long questioned whether Peter was the actual author, preferring a hypothesis that can account for the composition without demeaning the validity of its teaching or impugning the honesty of the members of the early Church. These doubts are found in the considerable differences of style between the two epistles ascribed to Peter and the knowledge and familiarity of the author with all of the writings of St. Paul, a comprehensiveness that would most likely have been virtually impossible while Peter still lived. Scholars therefore argued that the Prince of the Apostles had given his message to a trusted friend or disciple who then composed the letter and placed Peter's name upon it so as to make clear the authority from which the teachings of the epistle flowed. Such a use of the name of Peter was in no way dishonest and, in fact, was a common literary practice during the era. Further, the meaning of the letter, accepted as significant and genuine by the Church as written under the guidance of the Holy Spirit, made the letters worthy of inclusion in the NT. A short letter, the work is concerned with warning Christians to be aware of false teachers and not to have unrealistic expectations about the coming of Christ.

Peter, Tomb of ● Resting place of St. Peter, traditionally accepted as being on the Vatican Hill and long held to be beneath St. Peter's Basilica, specifically below the main altar of the great church. The search for the actual tomb of Peter has been one of the more remarkable efforts in the history of the Vatican in the twentieth century. When constructing his first basilica in honor of Peter, Constantine the Great (d. 337) chose to build over the spot where the first pope was actually interred. This area was a cemetery, and the emperor commanded that the foundation be laid over the tombs, rather than going to the expense of moving the bodies. The tombs were thus filled in and the edifice was erected above them, effectively preserving them virtually intact. Workers laboring in the sixteenth century on the new St. Peter's unearthed some of the burial chambers, but they did not pursue any investigations owing to time, respect for the dead, and popular stories about curses — and so, the new St. Peter's Basilica was built and the tombs forgotten.

In 1939, shortly after the death of Pope Pius XI, arrangements were made to place the pope's remains in the crypt beneath the basilica. Diggers broke through the floor and found extensive remains, including early structures and the long-lost Roman cemetery. At the command of Pope Pius XII, a thorough investigation was undertaken. The studies continued through the 1940s, reaching an electric climax when archaeologists found, on the lowest level, beneath the altar of the basilica, a simple grave covered with a slab. Inside were the bones of an older man with bits of fabric that were colored gold and purple. The conclusion was both obvious and inescapable — this was the shrine built by Constantine, and these were the bones of Simon Peter.

Pius XII was skeptical, especially given the placement of the bones in a position right at the edge of the grave. Among the notable experts deserving mention for the efforts in deciphering the mystery of the bones and tombs was Margherita Guarducci, an expert of inscriptions at the University of Rome. She was an important figure in the researches over the next decades, culminating in the final determination by Church authorities that these were the bones of Peter. In his Christmas message for 1950, Pius XII proclaimed that the evidence indicated that the tomb had been found. From this vague starting point, a testament to the necessary restraint and caution that is exercised in a case such as this, came the final declaration on June 26, 1968, by Pope Paul VI that these were, indeed, the final remains of Peter. Experts continue to question whether the bones are authentic beyond doubt, but the tour of the tomb is one of the highlights to any visit to St. Peter's Basilica, even if the public is not allowed to see what is believed to be the tomb of the first Vicar of Christ.

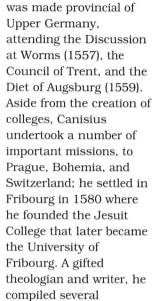

St. Peter Canisius

Peter Canisius, St. (1521-1597) ● Also Petris Kanis, Jesuit theologian and Doctor of the Church, the so-called Second Apostle of Germany. Canisius was born in Nijmegen, in the Netherlands, studying theology at Cologne and Mainz. He joined the Society of Jesus in 1543 and was much influenced by the Jesuit Pierre Lefevre. At Cologne he founded the Jesuit colony and was active in opposing the Protestantism of Archbishop Hermann of Wied. He subsequently taught at Cologne, Ingolstadt, and Vienna, and later established colleges in Munich, Innsbruck, Dillingen, Würzburg, Augsburg, and Vienna. As his fame grew for learning and skill in reversing the spread of Protestantism, he secured the patronage of Archduke and later Emperor Ferdinand. Canisius received from him in 1552 the see of Vienna, but he was instructed by his superiors to decline, as his efforts were needed elsewhere. In 1556, he was made provincial of Upper Germany, attending the Discussion at Worms (1557), the Council of Trent, and the Diet of Augsburg (1559). Aside from the creation of colleges, Canisius undertook a number of important missions, to Prague, Bohemia, and Switzerland; he settled in Fribourg in 1580 where he founded the Jesuit College that later became the University of Fribourg. A gifted theologian and writer, he compiled several catechisms, most notably the *Summa Doctrinae Christianae* (or the *Catechismus Major*), published in 1555. A brilliant presentation of Catholic dogma, it was the chief work of the Catholic Reformation and was printed in some four hundred editions over the next two centuries. Canisius was a major figure in halting the tide of Protestant fervor, particularly in German lands and throughout parts of Austria. The title of Second Apostle of Germany is well deserved, for he not only defended the Church but promoted a reformed and revitalized Catholic faith in lands that otherwise would have been lost. He was canonized by Pope Pius XI in 1925 and given the unprecedented honor of being named a Doctor of the Church at the same time. Feast day: December 21. (See also **Germany** and **Reformation, Catholic**.)

Peter Cantos (d. 1197) ● French theologian. Also called Peter the Chanter, he was probably born near Beauvais, although his birthplace may have been Reims. He studied at Reims and Paris, subsequently teaching in the cathedral school in Paris. Named cantor around 1184, he held a number of trusted positions as a judge and was elected bishop of Tournai by the clergy in 1191. This was annulled by the bishop of Reims, however, and in 1196 Peter refused the post of bishop of Paris. That same year he was elected dean of the cathedral chapter of Reims, dying at the Cistercian Abbey of Long Pont while on his way to assume his duties. Peter authored commentaries, or glosses, on virtually all of the books of the OT and the entire NT; particularly notable is his work on the Gospels. He also wrote the *Summa de sacramentis*, a valuable source for information on the religious customs of the era, and the *Verbum Abbreviatum*, a study on virtue that was addressed to clergy and monks.

Peter Chrysologus, St. (406-450) ●
Bishop of Ravenna. Born in Imola, he studied in his native city and was named bishop of Ravenna in 433. Known for his personal sanctity and his remarkable oratorical skills, he was much esteemed by Emperor Leo I the Great and Empress Galla Placidia. He was called Chrysologus (golden-worded), a title given to him to make him the equivalent of John Chrysostom (golden-mouthed) in the West. The heresiarch Eutyches wrote Peter in 448 following Eutyches's condemnation by the Synod of Constantinople, but Peter wrote back calling for obedience to the Roman see. Peter's homilies were collected by Felix, bishop of Ravenna, in the eighth century; they numbered one hundred seventy-six and covered biblical texts, the Apostles' Creed, and the Blessed Virgin. The main source for his life is the *Liber Pontificalis Ecclesiae Ravennatis* (ninth century) by Agnellus. In 1729, Pope Benedict XIII named him a Doctor of the Church. Feast day: July 30.

Peter Claver, St. (1580-1654) ● So-called Apostle of the Negroes, he labored to convert and care for the slaves of the New World. The son of a Catalonian farmer, he studied at the University of Barcelona and in 1602 entered the Society of Jesus in Tarragona. While studying at Majorca in 1605, Peter came under the influence of St. Alphonsus Rodríguez, who convinced him to undertake missionary work in the New World. Peter arrived in Cartagena in 1610 and at once found his calling. He pledged himself to be "the slave of the negroes forever," working ceaselessly to ease the brutal and terrible conditions faced by the West African slaves brought to the Spanish colonies. He routinely rowed out to the crowded, filthy slave ships, bringing food and comfort to the slaves. Despite humiliations from local officials and colonial society, he valiantly defended slave rights and reportedly baptized some three hundred thousand Africans. Beatified in 1850 by Pope Pius IX, he was canonized on January 15, 1888, by Pope Leo XIII; in 1896, he was also proclaimed patron of Catholic missions among the blacks. Feast day: September 9.

Peter Comestor (d. c. 1178) ● Influential theological and biblical scholar. Probably born in Troyes, he served as the dean of the cathedral chapter of the Church of Notre-Dame at Troyes from around 1148-1164. Named (c. 1164) to be chancellor of the University of Paris, he was reportedly pointed out to Pope Alexander III by a cardinal as being one of the most learned men in France. In 1169, he retired to the Abbey of St. Victor where he died. Aside from his commentaries on the Gospels, a commentary on St. Paul, and allegories on the Scriptures, Peter's chief work was his highly influential *Historia Scholastica*, dedicated to Guillaume aux Blanches Mains, bishop of Sens. The *Historia* is a sacred history from the creation to the end of the events described in the Acts of the Apostles.

He used most of the books of the OT, but he also consulted pagan authors and such writers as Flavius Josephus. The work became the standard text for biblical history during the Middle Ages, with numerous editions, commentaries, and translations used by students. It was still popular in the fifteenth century and earned Peter the title *magister historiarum* (master of history). Peter also enjoyed a high reputation for his sermons.

Peter Damian, St. (1007-1072) ●
Cardinal and Doctor of the Church. A native of Ravenna, he endured a hard childhood and worked for a time as a swineherd to a cruel brother. Another brother, archpriest of Ravenna, recognized his intelligence and piety and provided him with an education at Ravenna, Faienza, and finally Parma. It is generally accepted that his kind brother's name was Damian and that Peter added it to his own in memory of his sibling's great charity. In 1035, Peter entered the Benedictines in Fonte-Avellana, authoring in 1051 the *Liber Gomorrhianus*, dedicated to Pope St. Leo IX and attacking the many vices of the contemporary clergy, particularly clerical marriage. Around 1053, he wrote the *Liber Gratissimus*, a defense of the legitimacy of simoniacal ordinations. An ardent supporter of Church reform, he fought against simony, concubinage, and other abuses, and was named in 1057 cardinal bishop of Ostia. He also wrote letters and sermons. While never formally canonized, his cultus began shortly after his death, and his feast day was extended to the entire Church in 1828 by Pope Leo XII. At the same time he was named a Doctor of the Church. Feast day: February 21.

Peter de Bruis (d. c. 1126 or 1132) ●
Also Peter de Bruys, a heretical priest. Somewhat obscure, Peter was apparently removed from his office for his views on the Mass, infant baptism, and the veneration of the cross; he particularly inflamed his opponents by burning crosses. Preaching in parts of France, most notably Provence, he acquired a wide following among the people who took to calling themselves Petrobrusians. The movement was short-lived, however, for Peter was condemned and hurled into flames at St.-Gilles, near Nîmes by a mob. The main source on Peter are Peter Abelard's *Introductio ad Theologiam* and Peter the Venerable's *Tractatus adversos Petrobrusianos Haereticos*.

Peter Gonzalez, St. (d. 1246) ●
Popularly known as St. Elmo, the patron saint of mariners. Born in Astorga, Spain, he was a nephew of the bishop of Astorga, who saw to his education. Entering the Dominicans, Peter soon achieved great renown as a brilliant preacher, speaking before large crowds and attracting the attention of King Ferdinand III of León. With the king, Peter took part in an expedition against the Moors. His lifework, however, was to preach among the poor, particularly bringing the faith to the seafaring people of the Spanish coasts. A patron saint of seamen, he was considered their protector; the electrical discharge occurring during storms called St. Elmo's fire was named after him, although the balls or streaks of fire were also thought to be the souls of the dead and in ancient times were identified by Roman sailors as the gods Castor and Pollux. St. Peter Gonzalez was buried in the cathedral of Tuy. He should not be confused with the fourth-century St. Erasmus, also called St. Elmo (feast day: June 2), who is ranked among the Auxiliary Saints. Feast day: April 14.

Peter Lombard (c. 1100-1160) ●
Bishop of Paris and one of the most influential authors of the Middle Ages through his work the *Book of Sentences* (or simply *Sentences*). Petrus Lombardus was born in Italy, studying at Bologna, Reims, and Paris; he

subsequently taught at Paris. Described by Otto of Freising with Robert of Melun as *magistri scholares*, Peter took part in the Council of Reims (1148) where he spoke against Gilbert de la Porrée. Around this time he authored the *Sentences*. Around 1159 he was named bishop of Paris, holding this office only briefly; his successor was Maurice de Sully, founder of the present Cathedral of Notre-Dame. He also wrote commentaries on the Psalms and the Pauline epistles as well as sermons and letters.

The *Sentences* earned Peter the title "master of the sentences" (*magister sententiarum*) and secured for him lasting fame during the medieval epoch. Becoming the standard text for theological study, it was a collection of the Church Fathers, opinions of respected theologians, and important scriptural traditions. It was divided into four books: on God and the Trinity; on the creation and sin, with angels, demons, and the fall of man; on the Incarnation; and on the sacraments and the Four Last Things — death, judgment, heaven, and hell. Numerous commentaries were made on the work, including one by Thomas Aquinas, and it remained the essential textbook in the universities until finally superseded by the *Summa Theologica*. Attacked at various times by such theologians as Walter of St. Victor, the *Sentences* were upheld as orthodox by the Fourth Lateran Council (1215).

Peter Martyr, St. (1205-1252) ● Also Peter of Verona, inquisitor and patron saint of inquisitors. A native of Verona, he was the son of Cathari parents, but he adhered to the faith, entering the Dominicans in 1221 under the influence of St. Dominic. In 1251, he was named inquisitor of northern Italy by Pope Gregory IX. His work among the Cathari proved surprisingly successful; many were converted while others were driven away from the country. While journeying to Milan he was assassinated, reportedly writing on the ground as he died, "*Credo in Deum*" ("I believe

in God"). Feast day: April 29. He should not be confused with Peter Martyr (d. 1562), the Reformer who was imprisoned during the reign of Queen Mary of England.

Peter Mongus (d. 490) ● Also Peter Mongo (or the Stammerer), patriarch of Alexandria and an ardent Monophysite. A deacon of the Monophysite patriarch Timothy Aelurus of Alexandria, Peter succeeded him in 477 but was soon driven from the see by orders of Emperor Zeno (r. 474-491). After agreeing to Zeno's theological formula of 482, the *Henotikon*, Peter was restored. He thereafter worked for the cause of the Monophysites, securing the condemnation of the Council of Chalcedon (451) and continuing the persecution of the Melchites. Excommunicated by the pope, he threw his support behind Acacius, patriarch of Constantinople, and encouraged his successors in the so-called Acacian Schism with Rome. His death in 490 prevented his inevitable deposition. The name Peter became a symbol of Monophysite sympathies and its renunciation, with others of the heresy, was necessary for complete reunion with the Church.

Peter Nolasco, St. ● See **Mercedarians**.

Peter of Alcántara, St. (1499-1562) ● Spanish mystic and the founder of the Discalced Franciscans of Spain. Born in Alcántara, Spain, Peter Garavito was the son of a lawyer; his mother was of a noble family. After studying at Salamanca, he entered the Franciscans of the Strict Observance in 1515 and was ordained in 1524. Over the next years he preached extensively to the poor of the Estremadura province. In 1538, he was elected provincial of St. Gabriel (Estremadura), introducing reforms to the life of Strict Observance. When these proposals were vigorously opposed by members of the order, Peter stepped down and retired to an ascetic lifestyle near Lisbon, Portugal. He was soon joined there by other Franciscan friars, and a community was established that would, in 1560, be connected to the province of Arabida. Peter, meanwhile, returned to Spain in 1553, founding around 1556 the convent of Pedrosa that was to be the basis for the so-called Alcantarine Franciscan congregation. Such was Peter's reputation for spirituality that he was often consulted for advice. Peter was especially important in encouraging St. Teresa of Ávila in her attempted reforms of the Carmelite order and in her establishing the monastery of Ávila in 1562. St. Teresa's autobiography is the main source on Peter's life and gifts. He was canonized in 1669 by Pope Clement IX and was the reputed author of a much translated treatise on prayer. Feast day: October 19.

Peter of Alexandria, St. (d. 311) ● Bishop of Alexandria and a martyr. A much respected prelate, especially by Eusebius, Peter was elected bishop of Alexandria in 300. In the severe persecution launched by Emperor Diocletian over the next years, Peter was forced to go into hiding, returning after several years and subsequently compiling a series of canons concerned principally with the *lapsi* and the regulations to be followed for readmission into the Church. These canons were later ratified by the Council of Trullo (692) and were adopted into the canon law of the Eastern Church. Another persecution, however, began in 306 and during Peter's enforced absence from Alexandria the see was taken over by Bishop Melitius, thereby causing the so-called Melitian Schism. After returning to Alexandria in 311, he was arrested by the Romans in the persecution of Emperor Maximian and beheaded. Aside from his canons, a number of fragmentary writings have been preserved that were purportedly by his pen. Feast day: November 24 (in the East) and November 26 (in the West).

Peter of Blois (d. c. 1212) ● French poet, humanist, and theologian. A native of Blois, he probably studied at Tours, Bologna, and Paris; it is possible that while in Paris he was a student of William of Salisbury. After serving as tutor to the future King William II of Sicily, he left Sicily (1167) and traveled to France and then England, securing a post as a trusted agent in the diplomatic service of King Henry II of England. Appointed chancellor to the archbishop of Canterbury in 1176, he participated on several missions to the popes in the disagreement between the archbishop and his monks. Removed after the death of Henry in 1189, Peter served for a time as secretary to Eleanor of Aquitaine (1190-1195) and was later archdeacon of London, although his letters, particularly one to Pope Innocent III in 1198, noted his lack of personal funds, despite the high positions of honor he had held. Widely known for his letters, he also authored treatises on history, politics, and theology.

Peter of Poitiers (c. 1130-1205) ● French theologian. Born in Poitiers, he studied at Paris where he became an important scholastic theologian, professor, and lecturer, succeeding Peter Comestor as chair of scholastic theology. Also chancellor of the Church of Paris, he showed much concern for the poor students of the city and was known for his extensive correspondence with Popes Celestine III (r. 1191-1198) and Innocent III (r. 1198-1216). Among his writings were commentaries on several OT books (Exodus, Leviticus, Numbers, and Psalms), abridgments of the chronologies and genealogies of the Bible (attributed), and several books of sentences that were synopses of his lectures.

Peter the Hermit (d. 1115) ● French preacher, best known as a leader and promoter of the People's Crusade of 1096. Born in Amiens, he was a gifted speaker, his eloquence attested by a number of chroniclers of the era, particularly Albert of Aachen and William of Tyre. He preached the First Crusade but probably only after the official call by Pope Urban II at the Council of Clermont (1095) and was instrumental in organizing the ill-fated People's Crusade. After reaching Nicaea in October 1096, with the main body of the crusade, Peter left to go to Constantinople in the hopes of winning aid from the Byzantine Empire. While he was away, the Seljuk Turks massacred the defenseless pilgrims. The pitiful survivors were gathered together by Peter, who brought them into the main host of crusaders under Godfrey de Bouillon. During the siege of Antioch (1098) Peter attempted to flee the army, but he was caught, brought back, and thereafter remained with the Christian forces. He entered Jerusalem in 1099 after its capture. Returning to Europe, he helped establish the Augustinian monastery of Neufmoûtier in modern Belgium. (See also **Walter the Penniless**.)

Peter the Hermit

Peter the Venerable (d. 1156) ● Abbot of Cluny, he was called the Venerable for his gentle nature, saintliness, and wisdom. Also known as Peter of Montboissier, he was a member of a French noble family, entering the Congregation of Cluny at the age of seventeen. After serving as prior in several houses, he was elected the eighth abbot of Cluny in 1122, introducing many reforms. He made extensive changes in the finances of the order and the system of education; he traveled extensively in England, Spain, and Italy. To aid in conversion among the Muslims, Peter made the unprecedented suggestion that the *Koran* (*Qu'uran*) be translated into Latin. He also provided refuge for Peter Abelard after his condemnations at the Council of Sens (1140). Among his writings were treatises against the Jews and Peter de Bruys as well as poems and sermons. St. Bernard of Clairvaux was a friend.

Peter Urseolus, St. (928-c. 987) ● Also Peter Orseolo. Doge (or chief magistrate) of Venice, he helped rebuild churches and was renowned for his charitable work. A member of the powerful Venetian family of the Orseoli, Peter earned much notoriety in his service for the Venetian state, particularly his military activity against the pirates. When, in August 976, the doge Pietro Candiano was assassinated and his palace burned, Peter was elected to replace him. Convinced to accept despite personal misgivings about Candiano's demise, Peter set to work repairing the damage caused by the fire — it had not only wrecked the palace but had burned several churches. Money was paid to all of the victims and the Candiano family was convinced to refrain from seeking the political revenge so common in Venetian life. In September 978, he stepped down as doge and secretly departed Venice, entering a Benedictine monastery at the base of the Pyrenees. There he remained for his final days. St. Peter Damian wrote that Peter had been guilty of complicity in the assassination of Candiano, but this assertion is generally held to be without foundation. The cult of Peter that had long venerated him as a saint was ratified by Pope Clement XII in 1731. Feast day: January 10.

Peter's Pence ● Annual collection taken among Catholics throughout the world that is intended to assist in the maintenance of the Holy See and papal charities. The collection began in the eighth century and was traditionally a tax of a penny on each household. Arising in England, it was largely found in the English isles during the Middle Ages, and was known in the Anglo-Saxon as the *Romfeoh*. According to one tradition, Peter's Pence was first collected by King Offa of Mercia, who confirmed the gift to papal legates at the Synod of Chelsea (787). Another story claims that Peter's Pence originated with King Alfred the Great of Wessex, when he imposed the tax throughout the English kingdom in 889. While found in some northern kingdoms in Christendom, it continued, with some periods of inactivity, in England throughout the medieval epoch, until finally abolished by King Henry VIII in 1534. The collection did not survive the Reformation in Europe, but a revival occurred in the nineteenth century. The cause was the flight from Rome of Pope Pius IX to Gaeta in 1848. Money was donated in France, Ireland, Germany, and elsewhere to aid the pope in exile. After the liquidation of the Papal States in 1870, Peter's Pence became one of the most important sources of revenue for the Holy See. Today, the collection is part of the annual plea by bishops; each diocese sends the funds to Rome. It is noted by observers that, as the donation is voluntary, the amount sent in is an excellent barometer of the popularity of the reigning pontiff.

Petit-Didier, Matthieu (1659-1728) ● Benedictine historian and theologian. A native of Lorraine, he studied at the Jesuit College of Nancy before entering the Benedictines in 1675. Elected abbot of Bouzanville in 1699, he was unable to take possession because the duke of Lorraine gave the abbey to his own brother; in 1715, he was again elected abbot, this time of Senones. In 1725, he was named a bishop by Pope Benedict XII, largely as a reward for his work, *Traité sur l'autorité et l'infallibilité du pape* (1724; *Treatise on the Authority and Infallibility of the Pope*), a work banned in France that was particularly pleasing to Benedict because of Petit-Didier's previous opposition to the bull *Unigenitus*. He also wrote on the Council of Constance, on the OT, and on morality. His brother, Jean Joseph Petit-Didier (1664-1756), was a Jesuit theologian.

Petite Église ● French for "Little Church," it was used by the Catholics in France who refused to accept the Concordat of 1801 between Napoleon Bonaparte and Pope Pius VII. The members recognized only those bishops who refused to resign their sees as per the terms of the agreement. The *Petite Église* was rendered meaningless after the restoration of 1815 when all the schismatic bishops were restored to the Church. The only exception was the bishop of Blois, who functioned as spiritual adviser to the Little Church until his death in 1829. The movement declined rapidly thereafter.

Petrarch (1304-1374) ● Italian poet and humanist. An important transitional figure between the Middle Ages and the Renaissance, he was born Francesco Petrarca at Arezzo, the son of a Florentine notary. His family had been exiled from Florence by the Black Party of the Guelphs of the city and in 1311 moved to Avignon, in Provence. Petrarch thus studied at Montpellier before going on to Bologna. He returned to Avignon in 1326. In 1330, he took minor orders but fathered two illegitimate children, Giovanni (b. 1337) and Francesca (b. 1343). With several members of the Colonna family, he journeyed to Italy in 1336, reaching Rome the next year. He found

Rome preferable to Paris because it encouraged the revival of classical traditions in poetry. In 1341, he was awarded in the Eternal City the crown of the poet laureate. Traveling for a time, he enjoyed the patronage of the rulers of Milan, Venice, and Padua. He was in Venice from 1362-1367. His friend Boccaccio presented him in 1366 with a translation of Homer's poems into Latin. From 1367, he divided his time between Padua and Argua, dying in Argua on July 18 or 19, 1374, supposedly found with his head resting on a manuscript of the Roman poet Virgil.

Petrarch was considered by his contemporaries to be the greatest scholar of the age, the first of the humanists, and a poet surpassed in Italian literature only by Dante. A brilliant classicist, he finished a text of Livy by his twenties that earned him the name Father of Humanism. His earliest poems date to 1318 or 1319, although he was most proud of his Latin verse, letters, and biographies. His Latin works included: *Africa* (begun in 1338 or 1339), on Scipio Africanus and the Second Punic War; *De viris illustribus* (begun in 1338-1339 and revised in 1341-1343); *De vita solitaria* (1346; with additions in 1347); *De otio religioso* (1347; revised in 1357), a defense of monasticism; and *Secretum meum* (1342-1343), a series of dialogues between himself and St. Augustine in the presence of Truth. Among his Italian works were: *Canzoniere* (first edition 1340, second edition 1373), one of his master works consisting of sonnets, ballads, and madrigals; *Trionfi* (begun in 1351 and later revised), telling the poetic story of the development of the soul toward fulfillment in God; and *Rime in vita di Laura* as well as *Rime in morte di Laura*, describing his abiding love for his beloved Laura, a chaste (or platonic) love for a woman whom he first saw on Good Friday in 1327 in Avignon. She would be a deep inspiration for his poetry.

Petto, In ● Special means used by the pope to elevate an individual to the rank of cardinal. *In petto* means "in secret"; the practice is also called *in pectore*, "in the breast." By this custom, a pontiff names a new member of the College of Cardinals in secret, usually owing to sensitive political considerations in which publicly declaring an individual to be a cardinal could be potentially inflammatory. The use of designating a cardinal *in petto* was probably begun by Pope Martin V (r. 1417-1431). The cardinal in question normally does not know about his new status, but he is considered a cardinal from the time the pope so designates him using papal authority. The seniority of the cardinals dates not from when his elevation is made public but from the moment of the pope's decision in secret; yet, he has no duties, authority, or status until such time as formal open recognition is given. However, if the pontiff dies before publicly declaring the elevations of *in petto* cardinals, all such promotions are considered utterly void, especially as it may be assumed no one knew about them anyway. Further, no papal statement or will is legally permissible for advancement to the Sacred College after a pope's death. After falling into disuse under Popes Pius XII (r. 1939-1958) and John XXIII (1958-1963), the creation of *in petto* cardinals was revised under Pope Paul VI, who sought to give his discreet support to a number of prelates enduring totalitarian oppression in Eastern Europe. Chief among the *in petto* cardinals was Frantisek Tomasek of the former Czechoslovakia (currently Czech Republic and Slovakia).

Pflug, Julius von (1499-1564) ● Bishop of Naumburg at the onset of the Protestant Reformation. Born near Leipzig, he studied at Leipzig, Padua, and Bologna, and then held posts in Mainz and Messeburg, was deacon of the Cathedral of Meissen, and provost of the College Church of Zeitz. Because of his diplomatic skills and training in humanism,

Pflug was often consulted in confronting the Protestants, although he hoped for a peaceful resolution to the religious crisis caused by the Reformers. He took part in a number of conferences, including Leipzig (1534) and Ratisbon (1541). Elected bishop of Naumburg-Zeitz in 1541, Pflug was unable to take control of his see because of the Protestant sympathies of the elector of Saxony. Only after the elector's defeat at the Battle of Mühldorf (1547) did Pflug actually enter his diocese. He found the diocese in lamentable condition because of the Protestants — including a shortage of unmarried priests. His hopes to have a successor named to the see in 1561 went unfulfilled and, despite his efforts at strengthening the faith, he proved to be the last bishop of Naumburg.

Philemon, Epistle to ● Letter written by St. Paul to Philemon, a Christian slave owner of Colossae, in Phrygia. It sought to reconcile him with a runaway slave named Onesimus who had become a Christian himself. Paul composed his epistle while in prison, although where the place of incarceration might have been cannot be determined. He may have been in Rome, Caesarea, or Ephesus. While there, however, he became a father of sorts to the slave Onesimus. This individual had run away and had apparently stolen from his master or done him some harm. The Apostle writes in the hopes of bringing them back together, but he does not exercise any apostolic rights; rather, he asks him as "Paul, an ambassador and a fellow prisoner also for Jesus Christ," Paul tells Philemon, "I am sending him back to you, sending my very heart. I would have been glad to keep him with me, in order that he might serve me on your behalf during my imprisonment for the gospel; but I preferred to do nothing without your consent in order that your goodness might not be by compulsion but of your own free will" (12-14). He asks Philemon to receive back

Onesimus "no longer as a slave but more than a slave, as a beloved brother, especially to me but how much more to you, both in the flesh and in the Lord. So if you consider me your partner, receive him as you would receive me" (16-17). In the message, Paul elucidates the principles that permitted the Church to transform Roman society and virtually eradicate slavery as an institution.

Philip, St. ● Apostle. Mentioned in the Acts of the Apostles (1:13) and in some detail in John (1:43-51), describing him as coming from Bethsaida, the city of Andrew and Peter. He was among those surrounding John the Baptist at the moment the Baptist pointed to Christ and called him the Lamb of God. Jesus subsequently called for Philip to join him with the words, "Follow me." Philip then convinced Nathaniel to become a disciple. In John, he is present in several episodes, including the feeding of the multitude (6:5-7); the desire of several Greeks to meet Jesus (12:21-23); and when he said to Jesus, "Lord show us the Father, and we shall be satisfied," to which Jesus replied, "Have I been with you so long, and yet you do not know me, Philip? He who has seen me has seen the Father. . ." (14:9). Elsewhere in the Gospels, Philip is included among the twelve Apostles sent out by Christ, and is ranked fifth in three different lists, after the brothers Peter and Andrew and James and John (Mt 10:2-4; Mk 3:14-19; Lk 6:13-16). His activities in later years are uncertain, doubts being compounded by the confusion in tradition of Philip with Philip the Evangelist, one of the seven deacons appointed in Acts (6). Bishop Polycrates of Ephesus (second century) wrote of Philip as being buried in Hieropolis with his two daughters. He died apparently of natural causes, although there is a tradition that he suffered crucifixion. Feast day: May 3, with St. James the Less.

Philip II Augustus (1165-1223) ● King of France from 1180-1223, he was one of the foremost monarchs of the Middle Ages who was responsible for increasing the size of his realm, destroying the English Angevin Empire on the Continent, and strengthening the ties between the Church and the crown. The son of King Louis VII and Adela of Champagne, he was crowned on September 18, 1180. After suppressing a rebellion by the count of Flanders and the House of Champagne, Philip turned his attention to his main enemy, the English. Defeated by King Richard the Lionhearted of England in a series of engagements between 1194-1198, Philip was saved from potential disaster by Richard's death in April 1199. Henceforth faced with King John, Philip captured vast English possessions in France, including Anjou, Maine, Normandy, and Brittany. He then routed King John's allies under Otto IV of Germany at the Battle of Bouvines in July 1214, an engagement that marked the supremacy of France in Western Europe. Meanwhile, domestically, Philip consolidated royal power at the expense of the feudal nobility. He gave extensive rights to towns and merchants, to the effect that by the end of his reign, France was prosperous and moving decidedly away from feudalism, to the aggrandizement of the monarchy.

In dealing with the Church, Philip shrewdly recognized its value as an ally in uniting the country and reducing the power of the nobility. He thus carefully cultivated excellent relations with the clergy. Cathedrals were constructed, considerations made of Church reaction to royal policy, and campaigns were launched against nobles who were persecuting local clergy. Philip also took part in the Third Crusade with Richard the Lionhearted and Emperor Frederick I Barbarossa and helped support the Albigensian Crusade in southern Toulouse, which made possible the eventual seizure of Toulouse. Thus, while not saintly like his grandson St. Louis IX (r. 1226-1270), Philip nevertheless gave the Church a legitimate place in the political and cultural life of the kingdom of France.

Philip IV the Fair (1268-1314) ●
Formidable king of France (r. 1285-1314). Known for his cruel treatment of Pope Boniface VIII, he was the successor to King Philip III. Philip was devoted to the centralization of the French kingdom and was much concerned with the raising of revenue to fund his campaigns against England to strengthen the monarchy. Toward this end, he summoned the first meeting of the Estates General and ordered an emergency tax on the clergy (see **Estates General**). He soon came into conflict with Pope Boniface in 1296 over the tax, but Boniface capitulated the following year when Philip deprived the papacy of a valuable source of revenue at the time he forbade the export of precious metals from France. More difficulties with Boniface began again in 1301, however, when Philip arrested Bishop Saisset for inciting rebellion against the king. When Philip remained firm, Boniface issued the famous bull *Unam Sanctam* (1302), which led to the seizure of the pope at Anagni in 1303. The humiliation of the pope hastened Boniface's death that same year and permitted the eventual election of Pope Clement V (r. 1305-1314), a Frenchman who would transfer the papacy to Avignon, thereby launching the so-called Babylonian Captivity and marking the ascendancy of the French in papal affairs. Philip also dominated the French Church and mercilessly suppressed the Knights Templar in order to seize their vast holdings and financial assets.

Philip Neri, St. (1515-1595) ● Apostle of Rome. A missionary and founder of the Congregation of the Oratory, Philip was born in Florence and educated by the Dominicans at San Marco. He was apprenticed into the family business, but at the age of eighteen he left for Rome to give himself entirely into the service of God. In Rome, he worked as a tutor and adopted a rigorously austere life. In 1535, he began studying philosophy and theology. Giving these up after three years to focus on charitable endeavors, he organized a lay brotherhood that prayed together and cared for the sick and pilgrims to the city. At night, Philip lived in prayer, often residing in the catacomb of San Sebastiano on the Appian Way. It was here in 1544 that he experienced an ecstasy, which is said to have enlarged his heart. His lay group, the Confraternity of the Most Holy Trinity, became a major presence in the city over the next years. Ordained a priest in 1551, he joined a community of San Girolamo where he earned considerable fame as a confessor, possessing the skill of actually reading the hearts of visitors. He also conducted religious discussions and addresses for young men, laying the groundwork for what became the Congregation of the Oratory, as the community was joined by other priests and laypersons desirous of joining. Approval of the Oratory was given in 1575 by Pope Gregory XIII. Philip was already one of the most respected and revered figures in Rome, his counsel bearing enormous weight with popes, kings, and cardinals as well as the people of the city and simple peasants. He emphasized love and spiritual perfection for all members of the Church, his message reaching out to laypeople to the same degree as clergy; he was distinguished by the abiding gentleness of his nature and his imperturbable happiness. Pope Gregory XV canonized him in 1622. Feast day: May 26.

Philippians, Epistle to the ● Letter written by St. Paul demonstrating not only his abiding love for the Christian community of Philippi ("whom I love and long for, my joy and crown," 4:1) but his joyousness in Christ even while in prison. Philippi, in Macedonia, was Paul's first missionary success in Europe, his work there chronicled in Acts (16:11-40). From that time on, he was especially close to his flock there, receiving from them through one named Epaphroditus a gift delivered while he was in prison. He thus writes to thank them for the gift (4:18) and to address certain difficulties that had been encountered by the Philippians. After mentioning his imprisonment, in which he describes advancing the Gospel (1:12), he gives encouragement to his readers to endure and "be worthy of the gospel of Christ" (1:27-28). Paul warns against false teachers, telling the Philippians, "Look out for the dogs, look out for the evil-workers, look out for those who mutilate the flesh," (3:2) and reiterates, "Rejoice in the Lord always; again I will say, Rejoice" (4:4). While Paul wrote his epistle from prison, it is unclear exactly where. References to the praetorium and to "Caesar's household" (4:22) would indicate Rome, placing the date to the early 60s. Most scholars accept this location, but some prefer Ephesus or Caesarea.

Philippines ● Group of some seven thousand islands in southeast Asia that is currently a republic with a very large Catholic population and a highly active Catholic hierarchy. The Philippines were first visited by Europeans in 1521 under Ferdinand Magellan. The conquest of the islands commenced in 1564 by the Spanish with the arrival of Miguel Lopez de Legaspi. The Church, which found the native population quite receptive to the faith, advanced right along with the military and secular Spanish authorities. Under Spanish rule, the Church enjoyed a close relationship with the government, although the authorities long worked to control ecclesiastical appointments and thus influence policy.

As the power of the empire waned in the nineteenth century, the influence of the local hierarchy increased. An independence movement led by José Rizal flourished in the late 1800s, but freedom for the Philippines would not be acquired for many years. As a result of the Spanish-American War, the

United States in 1898 secured control of the islands. In 1902, the Church, already troubled by anticlerical sentiment because of a popular charge that the religious orders had been too closely allied with the Spanish, was faced with the Aglipay Schism that attracted a million Filipino Catholics and resulted in the loss of Church property until 1906 when a U.S. court returned it to proper authorities. The founder of the schism, Father Gregorio Aglipay (d. 1941), was ultimately reconciled with the faith, and his movement dwindled over the decades.

Philippine independence was finally achieved in 1935 with the inauguration of Manuel Quezon y Molina (1878-1944). The islands suffered severely under Japanese occupation from 1941 until their famous liberation by General Douglas MacArthur from 1944-1945. As per the agreement with the United States, full independence was granted in 1946 and the completion of a transition period that began with the creation of the Commonwealth in 1935. In later years, the Church was confronted by the undemocratic regime of Ferdinand Marcos, who was replaced in 1986 by open elections.

Philo (c. 30 B.C.-A.D. 50) ● Known as Judaeus (the Jew), Philo was a writer and philosopher who became one of the most respected figures in Hellenistic Judaism during the first century A.D. Born in Alexandria to a wealthy Jewish family, Philo was well-read in Greek and was sent to Rome in 39-40 as an envoy to Emperor Gaius Caligula. There he attacked the Roman prefect of Egypt, Flaccus, and defended the rights of the Jews; the events of the delegation were recorded in *Legatio ad Gaium* (*Embassy to Gaius*) and *Contra Flaccum* (*Against Flaccus*). Little else of his life is known with certainty. A gifted philosopher and exegete, Philo influenced subsequent theological thought in Alexandria's Christian community, particularly Clement of Alexandria and Origen, through his allegorical interpretation of the OT and his presentation of Jewish thought in terms of Platonic philosophy. His writings included expositions on Jewish law, philosophical treatises, and apologies.

Philomena, St. ● Assumed name of a martyr whose bones were apparently discovered in 1802. What was believed to be the tomb of St. Philomena was found on May 25, 1802, in the catacomb of St. Priscilla; the bones of an adolescent girl were unearthed, and the name Filumena (Philomena) was found on an earthenware slab found at the entrance. Although there was no mention made of Philomena in the early accounts of the martyrs, the relics of the assumed virgin martyr were transferred to the church of Mugnano, near Naples, on June 8, 1805, and there soon began a widespread cultus, including reports of miracles. To give body to the veneration, a nun in Naples wrote an entirely fictitious story of Philomena's martyrdom. Pilgrims soon appeared at the church, although her name was never added to the Roman Martyrology. Inevitably, archaeological study soon began raising questions about the entire tomb and scholarly opinion reached the nearly unanimous conclusion that the bones were not of Philomena and that whoever had been buried in that spot had probably not died a martyr. Her feast was suppressed in 1860 and the shrine was dismantled, an excellent demonstration of the use of solid archaeological scholarship in verifying the authenticity of a site, particularly when supporting evidence is wanting.

Philostorgius (d. c. 433) ● Ecclesiastical historian and an ardent Arian. A native of Cappadocia, Philostorgius resided in Constantinople. As a writer, he was much influenced by Eunomius, the Arian bishop of Cyzicus. His principal writing was a continuation of the work of Eusebius of Caesarea with a *History of the Church*, in

Greek, covering the years from around 150-425. Examining Christianity from an Arian perspective, the *History* survived only in fragmentary form and in an epitome by Photius; the epitome is decidedly hostile.

Photius (c. 820-891) ● Patriarch of Constantinople from 858-867 and from 877-886. He was the cause of a major controversy between the Eastern and Western Churches, the so-called Photian Schism. Born in Constantinople, he was the son of noble parents who had apparently suffered during the Iconoclast period in the city; the tales of Photius's birth recounted by Symeon Magister cannot be taken seriously, particularly the supposed prophecy of a bishop that Photius would become patriarch but cause much evil. According to his own letters, Photius had an early inclination toward the monastic life, but instead, he began a secular career. He served as an imperial secretary and, around 838, served as an ambassador to the caliph at Baghdad. Much respected at the imperial court, he was thus chosen by Emperor Michael III in 858 to succeed Ignatius, patriarch of Constantinople, who had been deposed by imperial order. Only a layperson, Photius was hastily ordained and consecrated. There followed the Photian Schism.

Ignatius refused to abdicate or to recognize his removal, and the emperor was forced to convene a synod in Constantinople to resolve the crisis. Pope Nicholas I sent several legates to the proceedings, but, under the pressure exerted by the Eastern bishops, they accepted Ignatius' deposition and recognized Photius. Nicholas refused to accept Photius, however, and in 863 deposed Photius and his supporters. The Byzantines thereupon ignored the papal letter of deposition until 867 when Photius attacked the *filioque* of the creed and the presence of Latin missionaries in Bulgaria; he also convened a Council of Constantinople (867) to declare the pope excommunicated.

That same year Emperor Michael was assassinated. His replacement, the stern Emperor Basil I, deposed Photius and reinstated Ignatius, who would remain patriarch until his death in 877. Photius, already rehabilitated and serving as tutor to Basil's children, was once more made patriarch, holding the post until 886 and the accession of Leo VI as emperor. Photius then probably retired voluntarily and died in a convent in Armenia. Ranked as one of the foremost scholars of his time, he authored numerous works, including treatises on theology and philosophy as well as letters and sermons. His most important writing was a treatise on the Holy Spirit that provided Byzantine theologians much of their dogma and oppositional material to the doctrines of the Western Church. One of the most important figures in the long and bitter schism between the Latin and Greek Churches, Photius became a symbol for the Byzantines, who steadfastly refused to be reconciled with the Western Church. (See also **Orthodox Eastern Churches**.)

Pianô Carpini, Giovanni (c. 1182-1252) ● Franciscan friar and one of the greatest travelers of the Middle Ages. Born in Pian di Carpine near Perugia, Italy, he entered the Franciscans and took part in the order's second mission to Germany in 1221 with Caesar of Spires. In 1245, he was chosen by Pope Innocent IV to undertake an embassy to the Mongols. Pianô Carpini set out in early 1246 with several companions, including Benedict of Poland and Stephen of Bohemia. Journeying through Russia, they reached the camp of Batu Orkhan in the spring of 1246. This powerful leader of the Horde in the West gave the friars permission to continue through the vast Mongol Empire, providing them a squad of soldiers to ensure their safety. In August 1246, they reached the camp of the Great Khan and were in time to witness the coronation of Khan Güyük. They left in November, bearing a letter from Güyük to the pope, reaching Kiev on June 9, 1247. Pianô Carpini then went on to Lyons where he delivered his letter; he was later made archbishop of Antivari. Writing down the account of his travels, he produced the impressive *Historia Mongalarum* (*History of the Mongols*) and *Liber Tartarum* (*Book of the Tartars*), detailed records of Mongol life, customs, and history that, aside from geographical errors, were of considerable scholarly value. Curiously, they were largely ignored by contemporaries and were known mainly in abstract form in the writings of Vincent of Beauvais.

Pico della Mirandola, Giovanni (1463-1494) ●

Italian humanist, philosopher, and theologian, he was considered the first Christian intellectual to utilize the mysteries of the *Cabala* (an esoteric work of Jewish mystical thought) to defend Christian doctrine. A native of Mirandola, Italy, near Ferrara, he was the son of Italian nobility. He studied at Bologna and Padua, also mastering Hebrew, Arabic, and Aramaic during his travels in France and Italy. A student of the *Cabala*, he hoped to use such esoteric teachings to prove Christian teachings, compiling some nine hundred theses from various sources to support his often highly unorthodox understandings of theology. He intended to defend his propositions in 1486 before a gathering of scholars in Rome, but a papal commission looking into them determined that some of the theses were heretical; Pope Innocent VIII denounced thirteen of them, and the planned gathering was forbidden. While authoring an *Apology* for the theses, Pico fled to France and then settled in France where he remained for the rest of his life under the patronage and protection of the Medicis. He was officially absolved of heresy by Pope Alexander VI in 1492 and died under the influence of Girolamo Savonarola, who dressed him in the robes of a Dominican on Pico's deathbed.

Pierre d'Ailly (1350-1420) ●

Also Petrus de Allaco, French cardinal, theologian, and philosopher. Born in Compiègne, he studied at Navarre and Paris, becoming a doctor of theology in 1380. Noted for his commentaries on the *Sentences* (1373), he soon acquired considerable notoriety for his writings and ideas while authoring a number of treatises on philosophy and theology. Named in 1384 director of the College of Navarre, he represented the school in a delegation to antipope Clement VII in 1389. That same year, he became chancellor of the University of Paris; King Charles VI soon made him confessor as well as treasurer of St.-Chapelle. Appointed bishop of Le Puy in 1395 and bishop of Cambrai in 1397, he devoted himself to finding a solution to the Great Schism that had troubled the Church since 1378. In 1409, he attended the Council of Aix and called for the convening of a general council. In attendance at the Council of Pisa (1409), he supported the election of the third pope, Alexander V, and was made cardinal by Alexander's successor, antipope John XXIII. After assisting in the Council of Rome (1412), he took part in the Council of Constance that finally brought an end to the schism with the election of Pope Martin V in 1418. D'Ailly had wielded much influence over the council, securing the application of many of his ideas concerning the powers of the general council over the papacy. For his work, Martin named him legate to Avignon where he eventually died.

Highly respected in his time, D'Ailly was the author of some one hundred fifty works on the reform of the Church, theology, philosophy, Scriptures, and mysticism; he also studied astrology. Two notable works were the *Tractatus super Reformatione Ecclesiae* (1416; on Church reform) and *Imago Mundi* (*The Appearance of the World*). The *Tractatus* had considerable influence upon the Reformers in England and Germany, and the *Imago Mundi* presented D'Ailly's firm conviction that the West Indies could be reached from the West. Christopher Columbus read *Imago Mundi* and was much encouraged by it in his own planned explorations. (See also **Conciliarism** and **Gallicanism**.)

Pilate, Pontius (d. after 37) ● Procurator of Judaea from 26-36. He gained eternal notoriety for his condemnation and crucifixion of Jesus. Pilate was appointed procurator to succeed Valerius Gratus, inaugurating his time as governor by infuriating the Jews of Jerusalem when he marched through the city carrying images of Emperor Tiberius, in direct contradiction to Jewish law. Later, he used money from the sacred treasury of the Jews to finance improvements of the city's water supply, suppressing the resulting riots with much bloodshed. Even more disastrous was the crushing of an uprising of the Samaritans in 36. Such was the loss of life that the Jews appealed to Pilate's superior, Lucius Vitellius, governor of Syria, who wrote to Tiberius. The emperor recalled Pilate to Rome; he reached the Eternal City after Tiberius's death in 37 and the accession of Gaius Caligula. According to Eusebius, in the *Ecclesiastical History*, Pilate committed suicide. Other sources, most notably Josephus and Philo, were extremely hostile to him, a reflection of his steps against the Jews. The later Christian accounts of his activities, in keeping with the tone of the Gospels, were more sympathetic, stressing Pilate's efforts to acquit Jesus. The Abyssinian Church considered him a saint, while the Coptics ranked him a martyr. Pilate's wife, Claudia Procula, was thought to have become a Christian, as mentioned by Origen; the Greek Church placed her feast on October 27.

The Christian tradition of Pilate begins, of course, with the Gospels. All four Gospels provide details of Pilate's trial of Christ (Mt 27:11-26; Mk 15:1-15; Lk 23:1-25; Jn 18:29-40). Aside from Christian accounts by Eusebius, Origen, and others, Pilate was the central figure in a considerable body of apocryphal literature and Christian lore. Chief among these were the so-called *Mors Pilati* and the *Acts of Pilate*. The *Mors Pilati* supposedly recounts his death, noting that when he was thrown into the Tiber, the water would not accept the body, hurling him back onto the land; the rejection by waters would continue in other places until his final internment in a mountain near modern Lucerne, Switzerland. The *Acts of Pilate*, an apocryphal work on the trial and death of Christ, probably dates to the fourth century, although some scholars prefer to date it to the second century. Around the fifth century, the *Acts* were combined with the "Descent of Christ into Hades," a supposed description of Christ's time among the souls of hades. The two manuscripts were known at times as the Gospel of Nicodemus and helped influence the medieval play "Harrowing of Hell." Legends concerning Pilate were also found in Germany.

Pilgrimage ● Journey to a place considered holy. Normally undertaken as an act of personal devotion, the reasons for a pilgrimage may vary from an act of penance or thanksgiving for the fulfilling of a promise, to the hope of physical or spiritual cure, to the begging of some important favor or request. The custom of the pilgrimage is an old one and is found in both the Christian and Islamic faiths. The first of the Christian pilgrimages probably began in the second century as members of the Church traveled to Jerusalem and Rome to commemorate the sacred events in the Holy City or to remember the martyrdoms in the Eternal City, particularly those of Sts. Peter and Paul. The two most famous of the early pilgrimages were made by St. Helena, mother of Emperor Constantine the Great, to Jerusalem in 325 and St. Jerome to the Holy Land. Of particular value in presenting details of such journeys in the early Church is the *Peregrinatio Etheriae* (the *Pilgrimage of Etheria*) written by a Spanish nun in the late fourth century. It describes her journey to Egypt, the Holy Land, through Asia Minor, and Constantinople.

As the Church grew more established and prosperous, major sites in Rome, Jerusalem, Bethlehem, and elsewhere became important shrines and powerful places for worship. Deeply meaningful acts of faith were performed by humble and simple Christians who would set out from their native lands, cross often dangerous territories, and then pray before the tombs of the Apostles Peter and Paul in Rome or at the Church of the Holy Sepulchre. The average medieval pilgrim would set out with a priest's blessing and would wear clearly distinguishing clothing, often adorned with the shell of a scallop, the symbol of the pilgrim. From around the eighth century, it became a custom to impose a pilgrimage upon a person as penance for some crime or transgression. As various sites in the Holy Land fell under the control of the Muslims, the pilgrimage became increasingly perilous, especially after 1000 when the Seljuk Turks threatened the main pilgrimage routes. The disruption of the pilgrimages, in fact, became a factor in the calls for a crusade to be launched to liberate Jerusalem from Islamic occupation. In Europe, meanwhile, there developed a host of pilgrim sites, a reflection of the very real faith of the people of Christendom and the economic advantages to a community of having a popular shrine in the city or environs. Aside from Rome, the chief pilgrim centers were

A pilgrim

Santiago de Compostela, Assisi, Tours, Fulda, and Canterbury (which was immortalized by Geoffrey Chaucer in his *Canterbury Tales*). The pilgrimage declined in the sixteenth century because of the Reformation, and the frequent wars of the 1500s and 1600s prevented the large migrations of believers that characterized an earlier age. The Catholic Reformation, however, reinvigorated the appeal of the pilgrimage. Today, millions of faithful from all over the world continue to make meaningful trips to Rome, Assisi, Compostela, and to the Marian shrines (Lourdes, Fátima, Guadalupe, etc.) found on several continents. Catholics receive encouragement in this from the modern popes who have made their own pilgrimages.

Pio, Padre ● See under **Stigmata**.

Pisa, Council of ● Council convened in 1409. It hoped to bring about a resolution of the Great Schism that had plagued the Church since 1378; it would fail completely and actually exacerbate the crisis. As the papacy was divided into two rival camps in Rome and Avignon, it was the hope of cardinals from both sides to organize a council that would resolve the presence of two popes, Benedict XIII and Gregory XII. Delegates came from most of the courts of Europe and was well attended by cardinals from both factions; in all, there were some two hundred bishops and seven hundred theologians. Declaring itself to be properly canonical, the council invited both popes to present their cases before the delegates, but they refused to appear. The council then took the step of declaring both Benedict and Gregory deposed, proceeding, however, to elect a new pontiff, Cardinal Pietro Philarghi, who took the name Alexander V. When both Benedict and Gregory refused to abdicate, and the Church found itself not with one pope but three, the council was dissolved by Alexander, having failed to resolve the schism. While defended by such conciliarists as Pierre d'Ailly and Jean Gerson, the council of Pisa is not counted as an official ecumenical council because of the severe irregularities of the proceedings and because it was not summoned by the pope. The council did lay the groundwork for the future Council of Constance (1414-1418), which did bring an end to the Great Schism.

Pistoia, Synod of ● Synod convoked in 1786 under the presidency of the Jansenist bishop Scipione de'Ricci (1741-1809) of Pistoia. Held under the influence of Grand Duke Leopold of Tuscany (r. 1765-1790), who supported both Gallicanism and Josephism, the synod passed some sixty-five decrees that would later be decreed as heretical. The grand duke sent encouraging but nevertheless very clear messages to the several hundred priests who were gathered at the synod, stressing his desire that they enact reforms that comported with his own views. As his soldiers had taken up residence across the street from the building where the synod was holding its deliberations, the results were far from surprising. De'Ricci secured the priests' agreement and support for the Gallican Articles of 1682; they proposed that Church authority was derived only from the entire body of the faithful, declared bishops to be independent of the papacy, and condemned the use of Latin Church services. Reaction to the irregular synod was severe. Ricci was deposed and later submitted to the Holy See, largely because of the promulgation of the famous bull *Auctorem fidei* on August 28, 1794, by

Pope Pius VI; the bull condemned eighty-five of the articles passed by the Synod of Pistoia and in general the tenets of Jansenism.

Pithou, Pierre (1539-1596) ● Influential French writer and theologian who helped codify Gallicanism. Born in Troyes, he was the son of a Calvinist lawyer, studying at Paris, Bourges, and Valence, and entering the bar in Paris in 1560. At the eruption of the Second War of Religion in France, he fled France and went to Troyes. As a Calvinist, however, he was forbidden from practicing law and so went to Sedan, a Protestant district, where he undertook legal work for the duke of Bouillon. After traveling to Switzerland, he returned to France in 1570 and became a Catholic following the St. Bartholomew's Day Massacre of August 1572. A supporter of the future King Henry IV (r. 1589-1610) in his struggles with the Catholic League, Pithou dedicated to the monarch the first edition of his important work, *Les Libertés de l'église gallicane* (1594; *The Freedom of the Gallican Church*), which helped organize the tenets of Gallicanism in eighty-three articles and was the basis for the Gallican Articles of 1682. Pithou also composed the *Satire Ménippée* (1593) and prepared an edition of the *Corpus Juris Canonici*.

Pitra, Jean Baptiste François (1812-1889) ● French scholar, theologian, archaeologist, cardinal, and Vatican librarian. Educated at Autun, Pitra was ordained in December 1836, subsequently teaching at the *petite seminaire* of Autun from 1836-1841. During this period, he earned considerable scholarly notoriety for his decipherment in 1839 of the so-called "Inscription of Autun," probably a third-century gravestone inscription that preserved early belief in baptism, the communion of saints, and eternal life. As early as 1840, Pitra hoped to join the Benedictines, but it was not until 1841 that he was allowed to enter the novitiate in Solesme. Making his profession in February 1843, he was soon appointed prior of St. Germain in Paris where he collaborated with Jacques Paul Migne in the *Patrologia Latina*, a vast work on Latin ecclesiastical writers to the time of Pope Innocent III (r. 1198-1216), which was published in two hundred twenty-one volumes from 1844-1864. Traveling extensively in search of unpublished manuscripts on early Church history, he became a renowned expert on the Byzantine Church and attracted the attention of Pope Pius IX who, in 1858, sent him on a mission to Russia to study the libraries. Returning to France in 1860, he was summoned to Rome the following year to be consulted by the pope. In 1861, he was named a cardinal and in 1869 was appointed Vatican librarian. A brilliant scholar and one of the most respected members of the College of Cardinals, Pitra authored numerous works including: *Spicilegium Solesmense* (4 vols., 1852-1858), a collection of unpublished writings by the Fathers of the Church; *Juris ecclesiastici Graecorum historia et monumenta* (2 vols., 1864-1868), a collection of the canonical writings of the Greeks; and *Hymnographie de l'église grecque* (1867), a treatise on the hymnography of the Greek Church. He also authored two supplementary works to the *Spicilegium Solesmense*.

Pius I, St. ● Pope from around 140-155. He was ranked by St. Irenaeus as the ninth successor to St. Peter and hence the tenth pope. According to the Liberian Catalogue and the Muratorian Canon, Pius had a brother named Hermas, the reputed author of the book *The Shepherd*, while the *Liber Pontificalis* states, probably with less authority, that Pius was born in Aquileia. His pontificate was troubled by the presence of various heretics in Rome, most notably the Gnostics Valentinus and Cerdon. He was also visited by St. Justin. The tradition that he was martyred is generally held to be without foundation. Feast day: July 11.

Pius II ● Pope from 1458-1464. Born Enea Silvio Piccolomini near Siena, he studied there and was inspired to enter the monastic life by the sermons of St. Bernardino of Siena. Persuaded against this by friends, he instead studied under the great humanist Francesco Filelfo (1398-1481) at Florence, acquiring knowledge of the classics and poetry. In 1431, he attended the Council of Basel as secretary to the bishop of Fermo, subsequently serving other prelates, most notably Cardinal Albergati whom he accompanied to the Congress of Arras in 1435. Summoned to Vienna in 1442 by Emperor Frederick III, who was impressed with his political skills, Enea was crowned poet laureate and employed in various capacities. Meanwhile, he belonged to the opposition party of Pope Eugenius IV, supporting for a number of years Amadeus of Savoy, who had been elected as the antipope Felix V. Gradually moving away from Felix, Enea was formally reconciled with Eugenius in 1445 in conjunction with a personal moral transformation. Promoted to several ecclesiastical posts, he was created a cardinal by Pope Callistus III in 1456. Two years later, on August 19, 1458, he succeeded Callistus as pope. His reign was centered on the promotion of a crusade against the Ottoman Turks who had captured Constantinople in 1453, a hope that was never fulfilled. Pius also gave his patronage to humanists and issued the bull *Execrabilis* (January 18, 1460), which condemned all appeals from the pope to an ecumenical council. He authored an autobiography, the only public memoirs ever written by a pontiff.

Pius III ● Pope from September 22 to October 18, 1503. A nephew of Pope Pius II, Francesco Todeschini Piccolomini was born in Siena. He was made archbishop of Siena in 1460, although he was only twenty years old and a deacon; then in March of that year he was named cardinal deacon of S. Eustachio. He subsequently served as legate to the March of Ancona, cardinal protector of England and Germany, and legate to Germany. Avoiding Rome during the worldly pontificates of Sixtus IV and especially Alexander VI, he was elected successor to Alexander by a conclave that could not agree on one of the more prominent candidates. The cardinals clearly did not expect him to live long, suffering as he did from gout and premature aging. He took the name Pius in honor of his uncle. His pontificate was briefer than even the cardinals expected: he died a mere ten days after his coronation and was succeeded by Giuliano della Rovere, Julius II.

Pius IV ● Pope from 1559-1565. Best known for reconvening and completing the work of the Council of Trent (1545-1563). Born in Milan, Giovanni Angelo Medici (no connection to the Florentine House of de' Medici) was the son of a Milanese notary. He studied medicine and law at Pavia and completed his education in Bologna in 1525. Traveling to Rome in 1526, he entered papal service, holding several curial positions. In 1545, he was named archbishop of Ragusa and then cardinal in 1549 by Pope Paul III. Known as a reliable Churchman, he was appointed papal legate to Romagna and a member of the tribunal of Pope Julius III. He departed Rome, however, in 1558 after coming to differ with Paul IV's hostility toward Spain. The next year, at the four-month-long conclave to choose Paul's successor, Medici was picked on December 25, 1559, taking the name Pius (IV).

Not generally considered an avid reformer, he began his pontificate by reversing Paul's often harsh rule; Cardinal Giovanni Morone was released from incarceration, a revision of the Index of Forbidden Books was ordered, and new, more cordial relations were fostered with Spain and the Holy Roman Empire. Many Romans were pleased by his decision to bring to trial two of Paul's unscrupulous nephews, Cardinal Carlo Caraffa and Giovanni Caraffa, duke of Palino; both were executed on March 5, 1561. Pius was himself guilty of nepotism, but his elevation in 1560 of his nephew St. Charles Borromeo (1538-1584) proved most fortuitous.

On November 29, 1560, Pius issued the bull *Ad ecclesiae regimen* reconvening the Council of Trent, which had been suspended without conclusion in 1552. The members assembled at Trent on January 18, 1562. Under the pope's strong will and determination and the leadership of Cardinal Morone (named president in early 1563), the council returned to the broad agenda of reform. After its twenty-fifth session, on December 4, 1563, the council came to a close; Pius gave confirmation formally of its decrees on January 26, 1564, and then issued the bull *Benedictus Deus* (June 30, 1564) granting formal confirmation. Most of his remaining years were devoted to implementing the work of the council and making sure that Church reforms took hold. To check the spread of Protestantism, he allowed the chalice (meaning Communion in both hands) for Catholics in Germany, Hungary, Austria, and elsewhere in 1564; this measure, rescinded by his successors, could not stop the Protestants from increasing in Germany, England, and France. In 1564, he released the revised Index of Forbidden Books. He also reformed the Rota, the Sacred Penitentiary, and the Camera and required the *Professio fidei Tridentinae* (Profession of the Tridentine Faith) to be taken by all ecclesiastical officials. Owing to the necessity to raise taxes on the Papal States, his popularity sank in later years. He died on December 9, 1565, and was succeeded by Pope St. Pius V.

Pius IV, Creed of ● Properly the *Professio fidei Tridentinae*, it was a profession of faith that was imposed upon all ecclesiastical officeholders by Pope Pius IV through the bull *Injunctum nobis* (November 13, 1564). Based on the decrees issued by the Council of Trent, it contained a lengthy list of doctrines, including such important teachings as: the seven sacraments, the Mass, purgatory, obedience to "the Roman Pontiff, Vicar of Christ, and successor to Blessed Peter, Prince of the Apostles"; the apostolic and ecclesiastical traditions of the Church; and the Sacred Scriptures. A slight revision was made in 1887 by Pope Pius IX to include the primacy of the Roman pontiff and his infallible teaching authority. The creed was used until 1967 when, under Pope Paul VI, a simpler version was adopted.

Pius V, St. ● Pope from 1566-1572. Born Antonio Ghislieri to a poor family of Bosco, Italy, he labored as a shepherd until the age of fourteen when he joined the Dominicans and took the name Michele. He studied at Bologna and was ordained in 1528, thereafter serving as a lecturer for sixteen years. Appointed inquisitor for Como and Bergamo, he so distinguished himself that by 1551, at the urging of Cardinal Giampietro Caraffa (later Pope Paul IV), Pope Julius III named him commissary general of the Inquisition. Caraffa was elected pope in 1555 and was a patron of Ghislieri's rapid rise: Ghislieri was made bishop of Nepi and Sutri (1556), cardinal (1557), and then grand inquisitor (1558). His zeal as an inquisitor and his long association with the Caraffa caused a certain amount of disfavor with Paul's successor, Pius IV. Upon his death, however, Ghislieri was supported by most of the Sacred College of Cardinals and was unanimously elected on January 7, 1566.

Pius declared immediately that the main object of his reign was to continue Church reform, particularly through the aggressive implementation of the decrees of the Council of Trent. He led by example, continuing in his sternly austere life, including the wearing of

his coarse robes under his papal raiment. With the very able help of St. Charles Borromeo (1538-1584) he brought extensive changes to the papal court, steadfastly refusing to engage in any kinds of nepotism. In keeping with the commands of Trent, he published the Roman Catechism (1566, which was translated into various languages), the revised Roman Breviary (1568), and the Roman Missal (1570); he also established a commission in 1568 to revise the Vulgate and commanded a new edition of the works of St. Thomas Aquinas (1570), whom he declared a Doctor of the Church (1567). Very active in fostering the faith, he promoted personally the Tridentine reforms in Italy and ordered them published throughout the Catholic world, even to distant points of India, Africa, and the New World. His willingness to use the Inquisition kept Italy entirely free of the threat of Protestantism, and in 1571 he created the Congregation of the Index to add weight to the Church's position against dangerous works. In the matter of foreign policy, he was able to achieve the formation of a league between Spain and Venice that resulted in the decisive triumph of the Christian navies against the Ottoman Turks at the Battle of Lepanto on October 7, 1571. Pius declared that day to be the feast day of Our Lady of Victory (later changed to the Feast of the Rosary) in thanks for the intercession of Our Lady in the engagement that effectively broke Turkish supremacy in the Mediterranean. Less successful was his decision to excommunicate (and claim to have deposed) Queen Elizabeth I of England in February 1570, an act that only proved the inability of such proclamations to be effective in Reformation Europe and that made worse the plight of English Catholics. Pius died on May 1, 1572. Throughout his reign he remained devoutly religious and wholeheartedly devoted to the reform of the Church. Both aspects of his character shaped his every step as pope. While the Inquisition was quite harsh, and the Jews of the Papal States found no relief from exclusionary laws and a hard atmosphere (they were largely expelled from the Papal States), Pius's work left the Church much stronger than when he found it, and his continuation of the Catholic Reformation would be felt for centuries to come. Beatified by Clement X on May 1, 1672, he was canonized by Clement XI on May 22, 1712. Feast day: April 30.

Pius VI ● Pope from 1775-1799. His reign witnessed the French Revolution. Born Giovanni Angelo Braschi at Cesena, in Emilia, Italy, he belonged to a noble but poor family. He was educated by the Jesuits and studied at Cesena and Ferrara, receiving a doctorate of law. Braschi then became secretary in 1740 to Cardinal Antonio Ruffo, who was then legate of Ferrara. Named a papal secretary in 1755, he was ordained in 1758 and appointed by Pope Clement XIII treasurer of the Apostolic Chamber, or Camera, in 1766; Clement XIV named him to the cardinalate in 1771. Four years later, after a conclave lasting one hundred thirty-four days, he was elected Clement's successor on February 15, 1775. His early period as pope was distinguished by his patronage of the arts, spending lavishly on the Museum of Pio-Clementine in the Vatican and on the sacristy of St. Peter's. He also made an expensive attempt to drain the Pontine marshes of Rome.

Pius was confronted by the spread of atheism and secularism, and was especially troubled by the introduction of dangerous ideas influenced by Febronianism into the lands of the empire by Emperor Joseph II. Josephism, as it was called, challenged the authority of the pope and secularized numerous monarchies, with the local Church under state control. Gravely concerned, Pius traveled to Vienna in 1782. Along the way, huge and enthusiastic crowds greeted him, but he could gain no concessions from the determined ruler. Febronianist thinking soon appeared in parts of Germany and in Tuscany where Joseph's brother, Grand Duke Leopold II (later emperor from 1790-1792), held power and was desirous of freeing himself from papal influence. In September 1786, even more bad news struck when the Synod of Pistoia under Bishop Scipione de'Ricci gave its support to Leopold and adopted the Four Articles of 1682 (see **Gallicanism**). Pius finally took steps: Ricci was compelled to resign and Febronianism was condemned in the bull *Auctorem fidei* (1794). On the continuing question of the Jesuits who had been suppressed under Clement XIV, Pius at first tried to pressure Frederick II of Prussia (r. 1740-1786) and Catherine II the Great of Russia (r. 1762-1796) into adopting Clement's decree of suppression. Catherine remained firm in her granting refuge to the Jesuits, ultimately receiving Pius's secret approval.

By far, the most explosive crisis of the pontificate was the Revolution in France. At first careful to avoid a major eruption of hostility with the Revolutionary government, Pius declined action on the Civil Constitution of the Clergy (1790), but when an oath was demanded, the pope condemned the constitution in 1791 as heretical. Relations soon deteriorated. France seized the papal holdings of Avignon and Venaissin (1790), and in 1797 the young general Napoleon Bonaparte annexed the Papal States. In the

Pope Pius VI

arbitrary peace that followed (the Peace of Tolentino, 1797), Pius had to accept the loss of large slices of papal land (Romagna, Bologna, and Ferrara) as well as treasures and manuscripts. The situation did not improve, however, and that same year the French general Mathieu Léonard Duphot was killed while stirring up a riot in Rome, a disaster that allowed the French to enter the Eternal City under General Louis Berthier (later Napoleon's chief of staff) on February 10, 1798. Pius was deposed as head of state and a Roman Republic was established. The pope was forced to leave Rome and was incarcerated in Florence from where, on March 28, 1799, he was moved by troops of the French Directory over the Alps to Briançon and then to Valence in July. He died there on August 29, 1799. At the close of his pontificate, one of the longest in the history of the papacy, the future of the papacy seemed bleak. Having left provisions for the election of a successor under such dire circumstances, the handsome and highly cultured Pius helped ensure the survival of the popes in an age soon dominated by Napoleon and bloody national wars. His successor was Pius VII (r. 1800-1823).

Pius VII ● Pope from 1800-1823. His pontificate was dominated by the Napoleonic Era. Luigi Barnaba Chiaramonte was born to noble parents in Cesena, in Emilia, Italy. He entered the Benedictine order at the age of fourteen, taking the name Gregorio. After studying at Padua and Rome, he became a professor of theology at Parma. From 1766-1775, he was a professor at the Abbey of St. John in Parma; the following six years, from 1775-1781, found him teaching at St.

Pope Pius VII

Anselm's in Rome. In 1782, he was named bishop of Tivoli, from where he was transferred three years later to Imola. That same year (1785) he was made a cardinal. Highly respected and known for his receptivity to current trends of thought, he became a compromise candidate for the papacy after the death of Pius VI and was elected on March 14, 1800, by the conclave convened in Venice. Pius was very much aware that the central crisis facing him was France, under the control of Napoleon Bonaparte. To assist him, the pope appointed the genuinely brilliant statesman Ercole Consalvi (1757-1824) as his cardinal secretary of state.

Consalvi negotiated with Napoleon the Concordat of 1801, which the French leader promptly violated by adding to it the Organic Articles (1802), tightening his hold over the French Church. Another concordat was negotiated in 1803 with the Italian Republic, but a similar agreement for the Church in Germany proved elusive, and the secularization of Church property in 1803 was a cause of much concern to the pope. Hoping to win concessions from Napoleon, Pius accepted his invitation in 1804 to travel to Paris to crown him emperor, putting aside the advice of the Curia, which was against it. Pius said the Mass at the coronation of Napoleon on December 1, but no modifications in policy were forthcoming. War broke out again the next year, and the emperor was disappointed that Pius could not be cajoled into giving his support.

As Pius was determined to effect a neutral stance in the struggle that pitted Catholic powers, relations with the French Empire deteriorated steadily. Napoleon forced Pius to remove Consalvi in June 1806. The pope's refusal to be bullied, however, prompted Napoleon to occupy Rome in February 1808 and annex the remains of the Papal States in 1809. On June 10, 1809, Pius in the bull *Quum memoranda* excommunicated all persons involved in the annexation, whereupon Napoleon had him arrested (July 5) and moved from Rome to Grenoble and then Savona. Isolated from his advisers, Pius was compelled to agree in 1811 to the irregular process of instituting bishops by their metropolitans without the recognition of the pope, a measure intended by Napoleon to give him even greater control over the French Church. In 1812, Pius was transferred to Fontainebleau. There he was subjected to even further ill treatment and, both exhausted and ill, he accepted the so-called Concordat of Fontainebleau, making numerous concessions to the emperor, on January 25, 1813. Two months later, he retracted his signature.

Finally released on March 10, 1814, with the fall of Napoleon, Pius returned to Rome on March 24. After a brief flight to Genoa in 1815 with the escape of Napoleon from Elba, he came back on June 7. Renowned in Europe for his brave resistance to the emperor, Pius enjoyed heightened prestige and international favor. He reappointed Consalvi on May 7, 1814, sending him to the Congress of Vienna (1814-1815) where he won the nearly complete restoration of the Papal States. Concordats were arranged with a number of states, including Prussia (1821), Bavaria (1817), and Russia (1818). In rebuilding the Papal States, he and Consalvi introduced various governmental, judicial, and financial reforms.

His main concern, of course, was rebuilding the shattered Church in Europe. On July 31, 1814, he reinstituted the Society of Jesus. His later years saw his continued opposition to intellectual currents that fostered atheism and indifferentism. Pius was also a patron of the arts and learning. A kind, gentle, and genuinely courageous pontiff, he guided the Church through a tumultuous period, using piety and forbearance to outlast the threats of the French Revolution and Napoleon. He died on August 20, 1823, and would be succeeded by Pope Leo XII (r. 1823-1829).

Pius VIII ● Pope from 1829-1830. Francesco Saverio Castiglione was born to a noble family in Cingoli, near Ancona. He studied at Orsimo, Bologna, and Rome, becoming a respected expert on canon law. Appointed by Pope Pius VII in 1800 to be bishop of Montalto, he was to enjoy the complete confidence of the pontiff. From 1808-1814, he was imprisoned for refusing to swear allegiance to the French government in Italy and was named a cardinal in 1816. Pius VII made it clear that he hoped that Castiglione would succeed him, once, according to Cardinal Wiseman, telling Castiglione during some business, "Your Holiness Pius VIII may one day settle this affair." While a leading candidate in 1823, Pius VII was succeeded by Pope Leo XII. On March 31, 1829, however, he succeeded Leo, and to no one's surprise, he took the name Pius VIII. His pontificate, while brief, was not without activity. He reversed Leo's stern policies toward the Papal States, recognized the new regime in France under King Louis Philippe after the Revolution of 1830 and the deposition of King Charles X (r. 1824-1830), and was able to accept the Roman Catholic Relief Acts in England, which passed in April 1829. He also approved the decrees of the first Council of Baltimore (October 1829).

Pius IX ● Pope from 1846-1878. His pontificate, the longest in history, witnessed the demise of the Papal States and the end of the temporal power of the papacy, and Vatican Council I. Giovanni Maria Mastai-Ferretti was born in Senigallia, in the March of Ancona, the fourth son of a count. After overcoming epilepsy as a child, he studied at Viterbo and Rome, being ordained in 1819. From 1823-1825, he took part in a papal mission to Chile; in 1827, he was appointed archbishop of Spoleto and in 1832 bishop of Imola. Known for his open mind and considered by many to be liberal with strong Italian nationalist tendencies, he was made a cardinal in 1840 by Pope Gregory XVI and was a leading candidate to succeed him at the conclave of 1846. After two days, he was elected pope. Pope Pius IX inaugurated his reign with measures that seemed to confirm his liberal reputation: an amnesty was declared for political prisoners, reforms were ordered for the Papal States, and he expressed his support for the movement of Italian unity. Wildly popular for these steps, he embraced other concessions toward democratic measures in his government of the Papal States, but he made it clear that he had no intention of surrendering his authority to a constitutional regime and then angered reactionaries by adopting a neutral stand in the war that erupted to oust the Austrians from Italy. Denounced as a traitor, Pius was faced with a crisis that grew violent with the murder of his prime minister, Count Rossi, on November 15, 1848. Besieged on the Quirinal by rebels, he adopted a disguise and fled to Gaeta on November 24. A Roman republic was established in February 1849, and Pius appealed for aid from the Catholic powers. He returned to the Eternal City on April 12, 1850, with the help of French troops. Having endured a humiliating setback from liberals, he now adopted politically conservative policies for the Papal States with the capable help of Secretary of State Cardinal Giacomo Antonelli.

Despite his valiant efforts to resist the grinding process of the Risorgimento, Pius was forced to watch the rise of Piedmont and the gradual unification of Italy. The Papal States were lost in 1860 after the defeat of the papal forces at the Battle of Castelfidardo, so that all he ruled was Rome. The last temporal possessions fell to Italian soldiers on September 20, 1870. The pope was given assurances of the inviolable nature of the Vatican and his person by the Law of Guarantees (May 13, 1871), but Pius protested vehemently and declared himself a prisoner of the Vatican from which he would never leave. He issued the decree *Non expedit* (1868) forbidding Catholics from participating in Italian political affairs, thus beginning the conflict that would not be resolved until 1929 and the Lateran Treaty.

While overshadowed by the demise of the temporal holdings of the Church and apparently a political disaster, Pius's long reign was also filled with remarkable vitality and energy, and was noted for its many successes in ecclesiastical areas. He restored the hierarchy in England (1850) and the Netherlands (1853), negotiated a number of concordats with various states in Europe and beyond, and worked with bishops to respond to the loss in political power by devoting even greater emphasis to spiritual concerns. Gallicanism and Josephism were thus ended and a centralization of papal authority was increasingly felt, facilitated by improved transportation and communication.

Pius gave the papacy an important restoration of purpose and strength through several notable measures. In 1864, he denounced several errors that had sprung up in Church teaching with the encyclical *Quanta cura* to which he attached the *Syllabus Errorum*. He gave a definition of the Immaculate Conception (1854), providing a flowering of Marian devotion. Most importantly, he convened the First Vatican Council (1869-1870), which, while cut short in 1870, pronounced against atheism, materialism, liberalism, and pantheism, and declared the definition of papal infallibility. (See **Vatican Council I**.) His tumultuous reign saw the transformation of the Holy See into a spiritual domain, but his efforts to improve that status for the papacy allowed it to recover brilliantly from the catastrophes of 1860 and 1870. His reign ended one long era in the history of the popes and began another. Known for his charm, wit, kindness, and forbearance, he was genuinely respected throughout the world for standing firm in his principles. Such was the anticlerical sentiment in Rome, however, that a mob tried unsuccessfully to hurl his body into the Tiber after his death on February 7, 1878. In 1985, his cause for possible canonization was opened.

Pius X, St. ● Pope from 1903-1914. The last pontiff to be canonized and the first since Pius V in 1712, Giuseppe Melchiore Sarto was born in Riese, Upper Venetia, the son of a postman and a seamstress. His early education was at Riese and Castelfranco; in 1850, he entered the seminary in Padua and was ordained in 1858. He then spent the next years as curate of the parish of Tombolo. In 1867, he was named pastor of Salzano where his remarkable zeal and pastoral skills earned his appointment as canon in the Cathedral of Treviso in 1875. His subsequent rise was swift: spiritual director and rector of the Treviso seminary; chancellor of the Treviso diocese (1878); provost of the Cathedral of Treviso (1879); and bishop of Mantua (1884). He found Mantua's diocese in a state of crisis. The seminary had been closed, there were no vocations, and the populace was indifferent owing to rampant anticlericalism and liberalism. Over the next years, Sarto restored the seminary and completely revitalized the Church in the area. In recognition of his magnificent work in Mantua, Sarto was elevated to the cardinalate in June 1893 by Pope Leo XIII. He was then chosen to serve as patriarch of Venice, a post he held for ten years with genuine distinction, winning the respect and love of the populace through hard work and cooperation with both local and central government. Leo died on July 20, 1903, and in the ensuing conclave, a veto was used by Emperor Franz Joseph I (1848-1916) to prevent the possible election of Cardinal

Pope St. Pius X

Mariano Rampolla. The cardinals declared that such secular interference was intolerable and proceeded with the balloting. Cardinal Sarto at first resisted the votes that were given on his behalf, but he finally accepted the wishes of his fellow cardinals and was elected on August 4, 1903, taking the name Pius (X) in honor of other popes who had fought against oppression.

Pius chose the motto *"Instaurare omnia in Christo"* ("To restore all things in Christ"), announcing his obvious intention to be a pastoral pontiff in contrast to his gifted but political predecessor, Leo XIII. In dealing with the difficult states of Europe, however, he was often compelled to issue hard pronouncements in defense of the Church. With his secretary of state, Cardinal Rafael Merry del Val (1865-1930), he staunchly protested the anti-Catholic measures by the French government causing a break in relations in 1904. He denounced the Law of Separation (1906) and thereby caused severe hardship in the French Church, but his position made it possible for the Church to be free of secular interference in France and

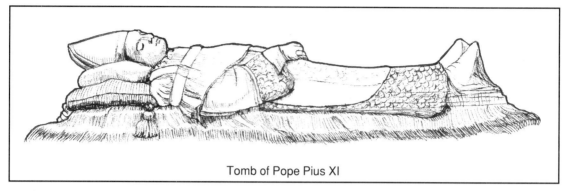

Tomb of Pope Pius XI

much stronger in the long term. Similar protests were made to the Portuguese government in 1911 when it too separated Church and State.

In matters of doctrine, Pius was a conservative condemning Modernism in the decree *Lamentabili* (July 3, 1907), the encyclical *Pascendi dominici gregis* (September 8, 1907), and the *motu proprio Sacrorum antistitum* (September 1, 1910), by which all clergy were required to take an oath against Modernism, called by Pius the "synthesis of all the heresies." A stern program was thus launched to expunge the contemporary Church of all Modernist tendencies. He also condemned the Le Sillon movement in France in 1910, the group begun by Marc Sangier, which worked for a synthesis or adaptation of Catholic teaching with the ideals of the French Revolution. Pius's main achievements were constructive, for he brought extensive reforms to the life of the Church. The Curia was reorganized through the decree *Sapienti consilio* (1908), the Code of Canon Law was codified (promulgated in 1917 under Benedict XV), and Church music was reformed, including the restoration of the Gregorian chant to the liturgy in 1903, a major impetus to the liturgical movement. The breviary was revised (by *Divino afflatu* in 1911), and Catholic Action was established on a sure footing through the encyclical *Il fermo proposito* (1905). Of all his reforms, he is best known for his wholehearted encouragement of daily Communion, earning him the title Pope of Frequent Communion. Having predicted the outbreak of World War I, he was powerless to stop it and died of a broken heart on August 20, 1914, only a few weeks after its commencement. Revered in his lifetime, he was beatified on June 3, 1951, and canonized on May 29, 1954, by Pope Pius XII. Feast day: August 21.

Pius XI ● Pope from 1922-1939. A native of Desio, near Milan, Ambrogio Damiano Achille Ratti was the son of a manager of a silk factory. Ordained at the Lateran on December 27, 1879, he received three doctorates from the Gregorian University and from 1883-1888 he taught dogmatic theology at the seminary of Milan. In 1888, owing to his remarkable scholarship and his paleographic ability, he was elected to the staff of the Ambrosian Library of Milan where he became prefect in 1907. From 1911-1918, he worked at the Vatican Library, first as pro-prefect, then prefect. As prefect, Ratti was responsible for the systematic cataloging of its many collections. At the command of Pope Benedict XV, he was sent in 1918 as an apostolic visitor to Warsaw, Poland, receiving the post of nuncio at the request of the Polish government. He was bestowed the Order of the White Eagle by the Poles for remaining in Warsaw in 1920 during the invasion in August of that year by the Bolsheviks. Recalled in 1921, he was made archbishop of Milan and on June 13, 1921, was elevated to the cardinalate. Although a cardinal for only some seven months, he was elected Pope on

February 6, 1922, to succeed Benedict, taking the name Pius (XI).

Pius took as his motto "To seek the peace of Christ through the reign of Christ," and throughout his pontificate he was an advocate of peace in a world heading toward global cataclysm. He worked to bolster the Catholic faith everywhere, issuing the encyclicals *Ubi arcano* (1922) to launch Catholic Action, *Divini illius Magistri* (1929; on education), and *Quadragesimo anno* (1931; on a variety of social issues). Particularly significant to him was the institution of the Feast of Christ the King. He also encouraged the missions and promoted the work of the Pontifical Academy of Sciences and the Vatican Observatory. His notable canonizations included Thérèse of Lisieux, John Fisher, Thomas More, Bernadette Soubirous, and John Bosco; Robert Bellarmine, John of the Cross, Albertus Magnus, and Peter Canisius were made Doctors of the Church.

Much of his pontificate was occupied with foreign matters. Chief among his many achievements was the Lateran Treaty of 1929, ending the Roman Question and creating the Vatican City as an independent state. His early secretary of state, Cardinal Pietro Gasparri, was succeeded in 1930 by Cardinal Eugenio Pacelli, who would travel extensively on his behalf dealing with international issues and crises. Pius condemned Communism sharply in the encyclical *Divini Redemptoris* (1937), and his opposition to Communism prompted him to negotiate with Adolf Hitler a concordat in 1933. The agreement, entered into with ultimately meaningless promises from Hitler, earned criticism for Pius and gave Nazi Germany considerable prestige in some circles. Nazi persecution, however, only intensified, and Pius released the condemnatory encyclical *Mit brennender Sorge* (1937), denouncing Nazi Germany for its treatment of the Church, its anti-Christian policies, and its repeated violations of the concordat. His relations with the Fascist regime in Italy likewise suffered toward the end of the late 1930s as Mussolini drew closer to Hitler's program and introduced Nazi racist policies in 1938. In 1929, Pius also reached an agreement with Mexico, ending the disagreement between Church and State that had existed since 1926 and reopening at last the churches, although Church-State tensions continued.

A truly learned pontiff, Pius was a formidable personality who willingly applied an imperious nature in the fulfillment of his papal duties and for the good of the Church. He was the first pope to use the radio to speak to the faithful. His reign would be overshadowed by the terrible events that would occur under his successor, Eugenio Pacelli (Pius XII), but he left the Church in a very strong position to face and weather the storm that would finally break seven months after his death. He died on February 10, 1939.

Pius XII ● Pope from 1939-1958. His long reign covered the difficult years of World War II and its aftermath. Eugenio Maria Giuseppe Giovanni Pacelli was a Roman by birth, a member of the highly respected Pacelli family, which had long been in the service of the papacy. He studied at the Gregorian University, the Capranica College, and the S. Apollinaire Institute in Rome, receiving holy orders in April 1899. He entered papal service in 1901, soon proving of enormous assistance to Cardinal Gasparri in the codification of canon law. Named secretary of extraordinary ecclesiastical affairs in 1914, he was made titular archbishop of Sardes in 1917 by Pope Benedict XV and sent as apostolic nuncio to Bavaria. As nuncio, he represented Benedict in working for peace and was appointed in 1920 as nuncio to the German republic. In this capacity he concluded a concordat with Bavaria (1924) and Prussia (1929). On December 16, 1929, he was elevated to the cardinalate by Pope

Pius XI (r. 1922-1939), who then named him to succeed Cardinal Gasparri as secretary of state (February 7, 1930). He soon proved an energetic and highly capable servant to Pius XI, traveling extensively, with visits to the United States (1936; he conferred with President Roosevelt), France (1935 and 1937), Argentina (1934), and elsewhere. His most famous diplomatic mission was to negotiate the concordat in July 1933 with Nazi Germany. As Europe was plunging into chaos, the cardinals who assembled at the conclave in early 1939 to elect a successor to Pius XI immediately turned to the foremost diplomat of the Church. Pacelli was elected on the third ballot (the first secretary of state to be chosen since Clement IX, 1667-1669) on March 2, 1939.

Pope Pius XII

As Pope Pius XII, he struggled to prevent the start of the war, speaking out on radio in August to plead for peace. On September 1, 1939, Germany invaded Poland. Pius's first encyclical, *Summi Pontificatus* (October 20, 1939), called upon humanity to restore God to his rightful place. In his Christmas allocution for 1939, he declared five principles of peace, the Five Peace Points: a true Christian Spirit among nations; recognition of the rights of every nation; true disarmament; recognition of the rights of minorities; and the creation of an international court to guarantee peace.

Pius maintained a position of neutrality in the long war but spoke out in favor of peace and, more importantly, devoted all available resources to ease the suffering of refugees through the Pontifical Aid Commission. When, in 1943, the regime of Mussolini fell and Rome was occupied by Nazi troops, Vatican City was opened to a flood of refugees, including Jews. Pius has been criticized for failing to speak out against the indescribable treatment of the Jews by Nazi Germany, an attack on the pope that was epitomized by the vicious play "The Representative" by Rolf Hochhuth. This is a charge unsupported by Pius's record. In 1943, he ordered sacred vessels to be melted to help pay a ransom to the Germans to keep the Jews of Rome safe; they had been ordered to pay one million lire and one hundred pounds of gold. The Vatican churches, basilica, and Church properties were opened to give shelter; there were fifteen thousand Jews at Castel Gandolfo alone, and thousands more at nearly two hundred different sites. Pius also denounced Nazi policies and atrocities. Pius believed that more explicit and provocative moves would be dangerous, especially as Hitler had made certain threats about removing the pontiff from the Vatican. The Church in Nazi lands was also being severely persecuted (millions of Catholics, including nuns and priests, would die in the Holocaust), and Pius was gravely concerned about the loss of even more innocent life. After Rome's liberation, the chief rabbi of the city, Dr. Israel Zolli, expressed his immense gratitude to Pius for his bravery and for having saved so many

Jews in very difficult circumstances. Dr. Zolli entered the Church soon after, dying a Catholic in 1956.

In perhaps the most memorable moment of Pius's pontificate, he greeted the Allied army that liberated Rome in the summer of 1944, transfixing the soldiers and jubilant people who flooded St. Peter's Square to celebrate the city's freedom. Having weathered the terrible storm of the war, Pius turned his attention to the postwar world. When Cardinal Luigi Maglione, his secretary of state, died, Pius assumed the post himself, receiving principal assistance from two talented monsignori, Domenico Tardini and Giovanni Montini, the future Pope Paul VI. Pius recognized both the heightened prestige of the papacy coming out of the struggle and the incalculable degree of devastation and ruin throughout Europe. He continued to use the Church's resources to aid those in need and also spoke out against Communism, which was making much unfortunate progress in European states, most notably in Eastern and Central Europe.

In matters of the Church, Pius was able to preside over the continued expansion of the faith all over the world. He was responsible for thirty-three canonizations, excavations beneath St. Peter's Basilica, and the issuing of a number of notable encyclicals: *Mystici Corporis Christi* (1943), *Divino afflante Spiritu* (1943), *Mediator Dei* (1947), *Humani generis* (1950), and *Ad Caeli Reginam* (1954). In all, he issued forty-one encyclicals. He also decreed the apostolic constitution *Christus Dominus* (1953), relaxing the Eucharistic fast, and used the *motu proprio Sacram Communionem* (1957) to promote attendance at evening Masses; these reforms anticipated many of the changes brought by Vatican Council II. One of the foremost pontiffs of modern times, Pius was a deeply revered figure in and out of the Church. His death at Castel Gandolfo on October 9, 1958, would signal the end of an era in the Church. His successor, John XXIII (r. 1958-1963), would launch the *aggiornamento*.

Plainsong ● See **Gregorian Chant**; see also **Music**.

Platina, Bartolomeo (1421-1481) ● Italian humanist and Vatican librarian. Originally named Sacchi, he was renamed Platina after the place of his birth near Cremona. After studying at Florence, he journeyed to Rome in 1462, most likely a member of the body of scholars accompanying Cardinal Francesco Gonzaga. There he joined other humanists at the Roman Academy, particularly Pomponius Leto. When, however, Pope Paul II suppressed the academy in 1468, Platina wrote an insolent letter to the pontiff and was arrested on charges of conspiracy and tortured. Released in 1469, he came back into papal favor under Sixtus IV (r. 1471-1484). The pope appointed him papal librarian in 1475, and for Sixtus, Platina compiled the famous *Lives of the Popes*, the *Vitae Pontificum Platinae historici liber de vita Christi ac omnium pontificum*, published in Venice in 1479. The first comprehensive guide to papal history, the work was an impressive effort, although lacking in critical scholarly examination. A misunderstanding of references made in the book to Halley's Comet and certain exhortations made against the Ottoman Turks by Pope Callistus III in 1456 led to a widespread myth that the pontiff had excommunicated the comet, an error repeated frequently by writers and astronomers of the 1800s.

Plays ● Various types of dramas popular throughout the Middle Ages and after. Presenting elements of Christian morality or lessons of truth, there were two main types of plays, Miracle and Morality.

Miracle Plays: Also called Mystery Plays, these were religious dramas that flourished especially during the Middle Ages, ultimately finding their fullest expression in the Passion Plays (see **Passion Plays** for other details). They probably emerged as depictions, written by individuals, of certain parts of the liturgy or the Bible, and came to present the life of a saint, stories from the Bible (especially the Gospel), and important teachings of the faith. The plays were kept deliberately simple and were staged with the intention of appealing to the generally uneducated, who could learn basic tenets of doctrine and important truths about morality where otherwise no such knowledge or education could be offered them. Customarily, the plays were performed outdoors by a troupe of actors. The main difference between the Miracle and the Mystery Play was that the latter was more concerned with notable events from the Old and New Testaments. The plays declined in the sixteenth century and developed into the Morality Plays. One of the most interesting Mystery Plays was the Play of the Crucifix, written by the otherwise unknown York Realist.

Morality Plays: Popular dramas that developed out of the Miracle (or Mystery) Plays in the fifteenth and sixteenth centuries. They were intended to present important moral truths to the audience most often comprised of simple, uneducated people. In presenting these moral tenets, the plays utilized characters personifying moral characteristics (i.e., Beauty, Perseverance, Knowledge, etc.). Each has an impact on the soul of an individual, either for good or ill. The plays culminated in the salvation of the central character. The foremost Morality Play was the anonymous drama *Everyman*, written around 1485 and first printed early in the 1500s. Everyman, the main character, represents the Christian. He meets Death but asks for time to prepare himself. He seeks the aid of Goods, Fellowship, and others, but they all fail him, so he turns to Knowledge and Good Deeds. Knowledge gives him some help and Everyman finally achieves salvation with the assistance of Good Deeds. The Morality Play is considered a significant precursor to English drama of the sixteenth century, most demonstrably Shakespeare.

Plethon, Georgius Gemistus (c. 1355-1450) ● Greek philosopher and humanist. Called Plethon because he was considered a reincarnation of Plato, he studied at Constantinople and at the Ottoman court of Adrianople, later establishing a school of esoteric religious study in Misra. A supporter of Neoplatonism, he convinced Cosimo de' Medici to open the Platonic Academy of Florence, an institution that was to have a major role in creating the atmosphere that would foster the Renaissance. Plethon served as a councillor to Byzantine Emperor John VIII Palaeologus (r. 1425-1448) and was a member of the Byzantine delegation to the Council of Ferrara-Florence (1438-1445), the last, abortive effort to unite the Eastern and Western Churches.

Pliny the Younger ● In full, Gaius Plinius Caecilius Secundus. Son of the writer and encyclopedist Pliny the Elder, he earned lasting historical fame for his correspondence with his friend Emperor Trajan. Pliny served in a number of government posts, enjoying the confidence of Trajan, who sent him to Bithynia as a special legate from 111-113. Pliny sent to Trajan nearly two hundred fifty letters, including one hundred twenty-one before and after his posting to the province of Bithynia. The letters reveal the cordial friendship between them, but they have also preserved vital glimpses of the era, including government administration and, most importantly, imperial views of Christianity. One of these *epistolae* reflected Pliny's concern for the legality of persecuting Christians. Sent around 112, the letter asks whether the Christian should be executed for being Christian or for committing specific crimes. His ambivalence stems from the fact that investigations into their activities revealed that Christians were actually decent people. Trajan decided against any toleration, but the ruler did agree that any prosecutions should not be made arbitrarily nor initiated because of wild, unreliable, or anonymous accusations.

Plotinus (205-270) ● One of the leading Neoplatonic philosophers of the Roman Empire. Plotinus, who influenced the development of Christian thought and mysticism, was probably born in Egypt, studying at Alexandria under the philosopher Ammonius Saccas. Around 244-245, he moved to Rome where he worked as a teacher. Plotinus authored essays, fifty-four of which were gathered by his student Porphyry and later published in the fourth century under the title *Enneads*. He believed in the source of all creation called by him the One. Union with the One was the essential goal of all persons, a unification that was attainable through meditation and contemplation. While similar to Christian mysticism in the attainment of spiritual union, Plotinus was unaware of the necessity of divine grace, relying instead upon the unaided labors of the human soul. He was nevertheless much read by Christian writers and had an influence upon such figures as St. Augustine and Dionysius the Pseudo-Areopagite.

Plunket, Oliver, St. (1629-1681) ● Archbishop of Armagh and the last Catholic martyr of England. Born to noble parents in Loughcrew, County Meath, Ireland, Plunket studied at Rome where he was ordained, serving there as a professor of theology at the College of the Propaganda Fide. He also served as the representative of the Irish bishops to the Holy See. In 1669, Clement IX appointed him archbishop of Armagh and primate of Ireland. Arriving in Ireland the following year, he found the Irish Church in terrible disarray owing to the harsh persecution of the English. He labored incessantly to revive the faith, to reorganize the Church, and to improve the level of education in his diocese and elsewhere. He placed much emphasis upon clerical discipline and adherence to the decrees of the Council of Trent. His relations with the Protestants were generally excellent until 1673 when persecutions were renewed. The next years were increasingly hard, culminating in anti-Catholic fervor caused by the so-called Popish Plot (1678; also known as the Titus Oates Plot). Arrested in 1679, he was imprisoned in Dublin Castle. The subsequent trial in London proved an absolute legal farce and, to no one's surprise, he was found guilty of treason; on July 1, 1681 he was hanged, drawn (or disemboweled), and quartered before a crowd at Tyburn, London. His head was taken to Rome in 1684 but was returned to Ireland in 1722; it has since been preserved at St. Peter's Church, Drogheda. Plunket was beatified in 1920 and canonized in 1975 by Pope Paul VI. Feast day: July 11.

Pneumatomachians ● Greek for "enemies of the Spirit." Members of a fourth-century heretical sect that denied the divinity of the Holy Spirit, they were largely organized by the middle of the fourth century and were officially condemned by Pope Damasus in 379 and subsequently anathematized in 381 by the Council of Constantinople. Through the writings of ecclesiastical historians like Socrates and Sozomen, the Pneumatomachians were considered virtually identical to the heretics who followed Macedonius and were even described as disciples. While their views were doctrinally similar and the sect almost certainly contained onetime members of the Macedonians, the Pneumatomachians were dated after the deposition of Macedonius in 360 and should be identified entirely with the Macedonian sect. The Pneumatomachians were extirpated by the end of the fourth century.

Poissy, Colloquy of ● Conference held in Poissy, France, in 1561, it was summoned by Catherine de' Medici in the hopes of initiating a dialogue between the Catholics and Protestants of the country. The Catholic delegation was headed by Cardinal de Tournon and the Protestants by the Calvinist theologian Theodore Beza. Among the issues discussed were the state of religious affairs and doctrinal matters such as the Eucharist. While no agreement was reached on any significant point, the colloquy did lead to the edict of 1562 granting recognition of French Protestantism.

Poland ● Eastern European country with a traditionally strong devotion to the Church. Christianity first arrived in Poland probably in the late ninth century and soon spread among the Slavic peoples in the region. It was furthered by the political unification of Poland under the Piast dynasty starting with Mieszko I (r. 960-992). He was baptized in 966, marrying a Catholic princess from Bohemia. Under his son Boleslav I (r. 992-1025), campaigns were waged against the pagan peoples from Prussia and Lithuania who had invaded Poland, and the Church received vigorous development. The first see was established in 968. This was followed in 1000 with the erection of Gniezno as the metropolitan see. The succeeding centuries brought severe sociopolitical upheaval as the kingdom sank into civil war. Anti-Christian oppression broke out in the eleventh century, but the Church endured and flourished, with a rise in churches and monasteries, and increases in the native clergy. Such was the routine degree of mayhem and destruction caused by the civil strife that in 1180 the Synod of Leczyca passed decrees against those who were plundering churches. The thirteenth century brought the recognition of the need to curb the dangers of the Prussian pagans and so, in 1237, the Teutonic Knights (founded in 1228) were invited into Poland. They would remain a factor in Polish life (and along the Baltic) for some time. During this same period, Poland was beset by further dynastic struggles and the Mongol invasions, during which the Church stood as a powerful force for order and stability, winning the love of the people of the villages.

The Reformation in the 1500s thus found appeal mostly among the urban population and the nobility; the latter saw the adoption of Protestantism as an excellent way to curb the traditional powers of the Church and Royal House. The nobles joined such new organizations as Lutheranism and the Bohemian Brethren, but Protestantism made little progress among the peasants. For a time, the reform of the Polish Church was resisted by some officials, such as the papal legate, but the Catholic Reformation was finally embraced, its momentum spearheaded by the Jesuits who were established in Poland in 1565. (See also **Hosius, Stanislaus**.) The Ruthenian Church, long of the Orthodox communion, was united formally with Rome in 1596. The Catholic Reformation in the country went far to restore Catholic unity, a common bond that would prove of great value to the Poles in the coming centuries, as the once mighty kingdom would face invasions by the Swedes, Russians, and Turks and then partition by its neighbors. The Catholic uniformity, however, also promoted a high degree of intolerance toward the Protestants and the recently converted Ruthenians and Armenians. Although formal religious toleration was not decreed until 1767 and the Confederation of Radom, such toleration was not put into practice until the formation of the constitution of May 3, 1791.

The partition of Poland in 1772-1773 among Austria, Prussia, and Russia brought considerable hardship to the Church. In the Russian region, the Latin-rite Christians faced restrictions at the hands of the Orthodox minority, and the Uniate Catholics were compelled (eventually accepting in

1831) to return to the Orthodox Church. In the other regions, Catholics were restricted by the Prussians and endured state control by the Austrians. These difficulties would continue until 1919 when an independent Polish state was established allowing the Church to revive. Then, in 1939, Poland was invaded by both the Soviet Union and Nazi Germany. The event marked the start both of World War II and the descent of a grim period of occupation during which millions of Jews and Catholics died from war, starvation, oppression, and genocide.

The Black Madonna of Czestochowa, Jasna Gora

Repression of the Church was unabated with the Soviet occupation, which proved a mere prelude to the Communist seizure of Poland.

The Communist regime, guided by their Soviet masters, introduced sharply atheistic policies and a campaign of suppression and liquidation of the Church. Hundreds of priests, nuns, and bishops were arrested and imprisoned, including Cardinal Stefan Wyszynski. He was released in 1956 by the new regime of Wladyslaw Gomulka, which made numerous concessions to the Church and signed an agreement in late 1956 between Church and State. The Church, in return, cooperated, recognizing that the alternative was a brutal Soviet crackdown. Religious freedom or toleration was not remotely in place, of course, as atheism was still enforced and harsh laws and regulations would remain in force for decades.

What many consider a turning point not

only for Poland but for all of Eastern Europe came in 1978 with the election of Karol Wojtyla as Pope John Paul II. Wojtyla, cardinal and archbishop of Cracow, had proven a formidable figure in dealing with the Communists, and his elevation was a major encouragement to all who resisted the Polish government. The Church gave much support to the Solidarity movement, which won recognition in 1980 but was then outlawed in 1981 with the imposition of martial law under the threat of Soviet invasion. Martial law was lifted in 1983 and the Communist regime deteriorated steadily. Full freedom was granted to the Church in 1989 and a democratic constitution was adopted for the country the following year. A new concordat was signed in 1993 between the Holy See and the Polish government.

Pole, Reginald (1500-1558) ● English cardinal, archbishop of Canterbury, and an important figure in sixteenth-century English ecclesiastical history. The son of Sir Richard Pole and Margaret, Countess of Salisbury, he was born in Stourton Castle, Staffordshire, and was a cousin of King Henry VII of England; his mother was also a niece of King Edward IV. Educated at Oxford University and Padua, he enjoyed the patronage of King Henry VIII, who not only paid for his schooling but gave him a number of preferments in the Church. A friend of Thomas More and Erasmus, Pole seemed destined for greatness in the service of King Henry. The monarch, however, was soon embroiled in his efforts to secure a divorce from Catherine of Aragon, offering Pole the see of York (or Winchester) in the hopes of

Cardinal Reginald Pole

placing an ally in a prominent Church position. Loyal to Pope Clement VII, who was opposed to the divorce, Pole declined Henry's offer, departing the country for Padua in 1532. In 1536, Pole wrote the treatise *Pro ecclesiasticae unitatis defensione* (*In Defense of Ecclesiastical Unity*), a comprehensive attack on Henry's policies toward the English Church and a defense of papal authority.

The treatise made it impossible for Pole to return home, but in 1536 he was summoned to Rome by Pope Paul III. The reforming pontiff, searching for talented men, placed Pole on a commission that was charged with bringing reform to Church discipline; the commission produced the important *Consilium de emendanda ecclesia* (1557), the blueprint for Church reform. From 1537-1539, he served Pope Paul on missions to France and Spain. While failing to create a unified front against Henry, his activities caused the king to issue an Act of Attainder against the Pole family; Pole's brother was executed in 1538, followed by his mother in 1541. The following year, he was named one of the three prelates to preside over the forthcoming Council of Trent; the council opened in 1545 and would ultimately reject Pole's efforts to negotiate a compromise with the Lutherans on the doctrine of justification. Much esteemed by his fellow cardinals, he was nearly elected pope in 1549 following the death of Paul; Julius III was ultimately chosen. The pope sent Pole back to England as papal legate upon the demise of Edward VI and the accession of Queen Mary in 1553. Landing in Dover in November 1554 after the lifting of the long-standing Act of Attainder, Pole officially brought the country back into the Church. Thereafter, he wielded enormous power in the regime of Mary; on March 22, 1556, he was made archbishop of Canterbury. He was not involved in any of the excesses of Mary toward the English Protestants, but his failure to oppose the executions has been criticized. Despite personal devotion to the pope, Pole was stripped of his office as legate in 1557 by Paul IV at the outbreak of the war between King Philip II of Spain and the papacy, a conflict that made Mary an enemy of the pope. He died on November 17, 1558, a mere twelve hours after the passing of the queen. A pious and passionately Catholic prelate, Pole was also a devoted reformer and humanist.

Polycarp, St. (c. 69-c. 155) ● Bishop of Smyrna and martyr. One of the most important figures in Christian Asia during the second century, Polycarp is considered an intermediary link between the apostolic age and that of the patristic; St. Irenaeus, for example, wrote that Polycarp had known St. John and others who had actually seen the Lord. A defender of Christian orthodoxy, he was an opponent of such heretical groups as the Marcionites and the pseudo-Gnostic sects such as the Valentinians. Aside from his famed martyrdom, recounted in the *Martyrium Polycarpi*, few details of his life are extant. St. Ignatius of Antioch wrote him a letter of encouragement while Ignatius was being led to Rome to be martyred. Polycarp himself wrote a surviving epistle to the Philippians, calling upon them to keep their faith intact. The letter is of great importance because it verifies the existence of NT texts during the period. Polycarp quotes passages from Matthew and Luke, the Acts of the Apostles, and the first letters of Peter and John. Arrested in Smyrna shortly after returning from a trip to Rome to discuss the date of Easter, Polycarp refused to recant the faith, declaring that he had served Christ for

eighty-six years. He was burned alive. According to Eusebius, the date of his martyrdom was 167 or 168, but other sources put the date at 155 or 156; traditionally, the day was February 23. The *Martyrium Polycarpi* (*The Martyrdom of Polycarpus*), dated to the mid-second century, was a letter sent to the Christian community of Philomelium from the Christians of Smyrna describing Polycarp's death. It is considered the oldest reliable account of a martyrdom. Feast day: February 23.

Polycarpus ● Name given to a canonical collection dated to the first half of the twelfth century. It was composed by Cardinal Gregorius; there are conflicting dates as to when he did the work, ranging from 1104-1106 to around 1120 or 1124.

Pomponazzi, Pietro (1462-1525) ● Italian Renaissance philosopher. Born in Mantua, he became a teacher of philosophy at Padua, Ferrara, and Bologna, distinguishing himself for his opposition to the philosophical system of Averroism. He relied upon the second century A.D. Aristotelian commentator Alexander Aphrodisias for many of his ideas, presenting doctrines of Aristotelian thought that were often contrary to contemporary Scholasticism. For example, he argued that according to Aristotle miracles were impossible and the soul was mortal, perishing after the death of the body. His chief writings are: *De immortalitate animae* (1516; *On the Immortality of the Soul*); *De Fato* (published posthumously in Basel; *On Fate*), and *De Incantationibus* (published posthumously; *On Enchantments*). He also authored an *Apologia* (1518) and a *Defensorium* (1519), the latter against the attacks made upon him by the future Cardinal Gasparo Contarini.

Ponce, John ● See **Punch, John**.

Pontian, St. ● Pope from 230-235. First pontiff to abdicate. According to the *Liber Pontificalis,* he was a native of Rome and the son of Calpurnius. He became pope on July 21, 230, succeeding Pope St. Urban I. While few details of his pontificate have been preserved, it is known that a synod held in Rome confirmed the condemnation of Origen by the Church of Alexandria (231-232). This was almost certainly convened by Pontian. In 235, however, a new persecution was launched by Emperor Maximinus I Thrax. Directed not against all Christians but only the leaders of the Church, the persecution singled out Pontian as one of its first victims. Banished with Hippolytus to Sardinia, Pontian took the unprecedented step of abdicating on September 28, 235. He died on Sardinia at some unknown later date. Pope Fabian (r. 236-250) brought the remains of Pontian and Hippolytus back to Rome. Feast day: November 19.

Pontifex Maximus ● Latin for "supreme pontiff," it is today reserved for the pope. In the religion of ancient Rome, the *pontifex maximus* was the chief priest of the Roman religion who headed the college of priests and wielded enormous religious authority and influence, including fixing the dates of festivals and the organization of the calendar. When Rome was under the control of Julius Caesar, the office of *pontifex* was combined by him with that of dictator. The Roman emperors subsequently assumed the role of *pontifex maximus*; the last ruler to do so was Emperor Gratian (r. 367-383), who terminated the office as part of his antipagan measures. He presented the title to the pope in 375 in recognition of the pontiff's supreme authority over the Christian Church. Henceforth, the title pontiff or supreme pontiff has been born by the Bishops of Rome (i.e., the Vicars of Christ). Its common usage, however, dates from the late Middle Ages.

Today, it remains one of the many titles of the pope (with Vicar of Christ, Patriarch of the West, Servant of the Servants of God, etc.), although it is used less frequently than other titles in keeping with the de-emphasizing of the monarchical characteristics of the papacy that began in the reign of Pope Paul VI (1963-1978) and continued in the brief pontificate of Pope John Paul I (1978).

Pontiff ● See **Pontifex Maximus**, preceding entry.

Pontifical Academy of Sciences ● Academy composed of internationally respected scientists, including Nobel laureates. It advises the pope on scientific matters, provides him with research and materials for his addresses on relevant scientific issues, promotes research, and fosters the place of science in the Church. The academy was first established in Rome on August 17, 1603, by Pope Clement VIII under the title Linceorum Academia (The Academy of the Lynxes), so-called from the traditional depiction of lynxes as symbols of intellectual achievement. Among the early members was Galileo Galilei. In 1847, it was reorganized by Pope Pius IX and given the name Pontificia Academia dei Nuovi Lincei; this was subsequently seized by the Italian government in 1870 and renamed the Academia Nationale dei Lincei. Recognizing the need to have a scientific academy, Pope Leo XIII reconstituted the body in 1887. In 1922, Pope Pius XI ordered that the academy meet in the Vatican Gardens, specifically in the magnificent garden retreat of the Casino of Pius IV. Pius also gave the academy its present shape with the issue of the charter *In Multis Solaciis* (October 28, 1936). It was called the Pontifical Academy of Sciences and had a membership of seventy. Scientists were chosen for life, were named by the pope, and were picked exclusively for merit on the basis of scientific or mathematical achievement;

they do not have to be Catholics. Pope Pius XII granted the members the title Excellency, and Pope John XXIII appointed honorary members. Pope John Paul II increased the membership in 1985-1986 by appointing fifteen additional scientists. There are currently scientists from nearly thirty countries in the academy. They are joined by a number of Vatican officials, including the director of the Vatican Observatory, the prefect of the Vatican Library, and the prefect of the Vatican Archives.

Pontifical Biblical Commission ●
Commission instituted by Pope Leo XIII on October 30, 1902, by the apostolic letter *Vigilantiae*. Its task is the study and examination of Scripture so that it "should everywhere among us receive that more elaborate treatment which the times require and be preserved intact not only from any breath of error but also from all rash opinions." Known in its official Latin title as *Pontificia Commissio de Re Biblica*, in its initial years, the commission responded to many questions concerning biblical studies that were presented to it, the *responsa* (or replies) answering such important queries as possible authorship of the Pentateuch by Moses. A major change in the nature of the commission came in 1943 with the promulgation of the encyclical *Divino afflante Spiritu* by Pope Pius XII, which encouraged the work of biblical scholars and promoted heightened scholarship and communication in the field of biblical studies. The commission responded to the encyclical by working to be more open, setting the stage for the post-Vatican II restructuring of the commission by Pope Paul VI with his *motu proprio Sedula Cura* (June 27, 1971). The commission was henceforth composed of theologians who promoted biblical study and conducted research. It is today under the authority of the Congregation for the Doctrine of the Faith and has as its president the prefect of the congregation.

Pontifical Institutes of Higher Learning
● See TABLE 11.

Pope ● Title derived from the Greek *pappas* (Father). It is used in the Western Church for the Bishop of Rome as the head of the universal Church, the Vicar of Christ, the Roman pontiff, and the successor to Peter. The term is also used in the Eastern Church (Orthodox Church) for priests and bishops, and is also applied to the Coptic patriarch of Alexandria, but it is best known when designating the supreme head of the Roman Catholic Church. It is customary to refer to the supreme pontiff as "His Holiness the Pope." The office is covered in detail in Canons 331-333 of the Code of Canon Law. (For details on this office, consult the following entries: **Acclamatio; Acta Apostolicae Sedis; Annuario Pontificio; Apostolic See; Apostolic Succession; Bishop of Rome; Bull; Bullarium; Collegiality; Conciliarism; Conclave; Curia, Roman; Decretals; Encyclical; Holy See; Liber Pontificalis; Papacy; Papal Coronation; Pontifex Maximus; Rome; Social Encyclicals; Vatican; Vatican City, State of; Vicar of Christ;** and **Vicar of Peter;** see also under individual popes).

Popery ● Harsh and often virulent name used in England by anti-Catholic elements to describe the teachings and practices of the Church. The term was probably coined in the early days of the Reformation in England and became common by the middle of the sixteenth century and the break with Rome under King Henry VIII (r. 1509-1547). In 1673, the so-called Declaration Against Popery was made mandatory on all members of Parliament. The M.P.'s had to take an oath against such Catholic doctrines as the transubstantiation and the invocation of saints. It was replaced in 1778 by a less antagonistic oath, but the spirit of antipopery was still rampant, as was evidenced by the Gordon Riots of June 1780, during which

Catholic homes were looted and burned by mobs carrying signs reading "No Popery."

Popes ● See APPENDIX 1.

Popes, False ● See **Antipope**.

Popes, Titles of ● The popes bear a number of titles by virtue of the extensive jurisdiction and multiple offices they possess. The titles are: His Holiness the Pope, Bishop of Rome, Primate of Italy, Archbishop and Metropolitan of the Roman Province, Patriarch of the West, Vicar of Jesus Christ (or Vicar of Christ), Successor of St. Peter, Vicar of St. Peter (superseded in the 1200s by Vicar of Christ), Prince of the Apostles, Supreme Pontiff (*Pontifex Maximus*), Servant of the Servants of God, and Sovereign of the State of the Vatican City.

Popish Plot ● Also commonly known as the Oates Plot. An entirely fabricated conspiracy concocted in 1678 by two Englishmen, Titus Oates and Israel Tonge, alleging that the Jesuits were planning to assassinate King Charles II (r. 1660-1685) in order to secure the accession of Charles's Catholic brother, the duke of York (the future King James II, r. 1685-1688). A onetime Anglican cleric who had been converted to Catholicism but expelled from several Jesuit seminaries on the Continent, Oates was pushed to even greater discontent by an acquaintance, Tonge, a rabid anti-Catholic. It has been suggested by some scholars that Tonge was the inventor of the subsequent fabrication, but, in any case, he certainly assisted Oates in its development. Finding allies in the anti-Catholic Parliament, Oates was able to present to the government entirely false charges against the pope, the Jesuits, and their Catholic allies. Brought before the king, Oates was questioned by the skeptical Charles and found wanting in both character and any reliable particulars concerning the plot. Despite the absence of any credible evidence, the charges were accepted by members of Parliament who made Oates a national hero and spread antipapist fervor throughout the land. Catholics were arrested all over England, including several Jesuits and St. Oliver Plunket, archbishop of Armagh and the primate of Ireland. Oates was soon unable to maintain his believability and the entire plot was revealed as a fraud. No respectable English historian has ever accepted any truth to the charges, but the plot remains a clear example of anti-Catholicism in the isles and the dangers faced by English Catholics. Oates died in 1705.

Populorum Progressio ● Encyclical issued on March 26, 1967, "On the Development of Peoples," by Pope Paul VI. It addressed the Church's teaching on economic justice while placing it in the very real context of contemporary economic systems. Serving as an extension or elucidation of the social doctrine expressed in the "Pastoral Constitution on the Church in the Modern World" (*Gaudium et Spes*) of Vatican Council II, Paul stressed the need for social and economic justice in the distribution of goods and particularly the development of the third world countries. He argued that the first world, the wealthy and developed countries, were obligated to help the poor and the needy not merely out of charity but out of the recognition of the justice of the act. Such assistance must lead to economic improvement and complete development of poor nations, although he placed much emphasis on what he termed authentic development. In this the pope meant that a fullness of growth should be promoted that includes more than the fostering of financial and material wealth. There should be religious, cultural, intellectual, and family development that enriches all people, makes the citizens of the countries active participants in the world community, and makes possible the realization of the moral, intellectual, and spiritual potential of each individual. Pope Paul offered concrete suggestions such as the redistribution of trade between the wealthy and poor countries and the imposition of limits on free trade to prevent exploitation. This was one of Paul's most important and widely read encyclicals.

Porphyry (c. 233-c. 305) ● Neoplatonic philosopher and a vocal opponent of Christianity. Born probably in Tyre or, less likely, in Batanea, Palestine, he was originally called Malchus (from the Syrian-Phoenician name for king, *melech*). While studying in Athens under the Greek philosopher Cassius Longinus, he took the name Porphyry, a derivation of the Latin for giant. From 262-263, he studied at Rome under Plotinus, becoming his greatest pupil. Porphyry remained in Rome as a teacher and the foremost Neoplatonist of his era. He edited the *Enneads* of Plotinus and authored a biography of his former teacher, also writing works on philosophy including treatises on Plato, Aristotle, and Theophrastus, and technical studies such as music, logic, the philology of Homer, and astrology. Of particular controversy was his *Isagoge*, an introduction to the logic of Aristotle. It was translated into Latin by Boethius in the sixth century; the translation and Boethius's commentaries were the source of considerable uproar over the definition of universals, but the work became an accepted source of study in the schools of the Middle Ages. An adherent of Plotinus's ideas concerning the nature of the soul, stressing the virtues that he felt necessary for the purification of the soul and its union with what Plotinus termed the One. A student of contemporary religions, he was an enemy of Christianity because of the Christian Church, which he considered to be unpatriotic. While he respected Christ as a teacher, he wrote the fifteen-book treatise *Against the Christians*; Eusebius of Caesarea responded with a refutation and in 448 the writings of Porphyry were banned, surviving largely in fragmentary form.

Portiuncula ● Italian for "small portion." Name given today to a tiny chapel within the Basilica of Our Lady of the Angels, in Assisi. The Portiuncula is of enormous importance in the early history of the Franciscan order and in the life of St. Francis of Assisi. The area where the Portiuncula was initially situated was called Santa Maria degli Angeli at the start of the 1200s. It was there, within a few miles from Assisi, that Francis received his vocation on February 24, 1208, where he largely resided, and where he died on October 3, 1226. What was to become the Portiuncula was originally a small, ruined chapel on a piece of land that was given to Francis and his first followers by the monks of the nearby Benedictine monastery of St. Benedict. Francis, however, would accept this "*portiuncula*," or "small portion" of property, only on condition that some kind of rent be paid for its use; to this day the monastery is given rent.

This spot became the cradle of the Franciscans, for Francis and his brethren repaired the church, and the saint made it the center of his activities. For example, St. Clare received her habit in the Portiuncula in 1212. At the time of his death, Francis commended the chapel to the care of the order. It soon attracted a great many pilgrims and became surrounded by a number of buildings. These were torn down in the reign of Pope St. Pius V (r. 1566-1572) and replaced by the magnificent basilica that built over the Portiuncula, the Basilica of Our Lady of Angels. A papal basilica, it was damaged by an earthquake in 1832. The entire complex remains an important pilgrim site.

The Portiuncula Indulgence derives its name from the Portiuncula where, at first, it was limited. According to custom, it was established by Francis in 1216 after he received a vision of Our Lady, surrounded by angels, in which it was decreed that a plenary indulgence could be obtained for the deceased as often as a person might visit the chapel on August 2. While direct evidence is lacking that Francis established the indulgence himself in 1216, the custom was certainly accepted in the thirteenth century. The oldest surviving document on the matter dates to 1277 and is a testament made by Bl. Benedict of Arezzo that he had been told by one of the first companions of Francis, Brother Masseo, of Francis' announcement of the indulgence's declaration by Pope Honorius III at Perugia. Other testimony, however, does not explain that absence of corroborative evidence from the period 1216-1277. Nevertheless, in 1480, Pope Sixtus IV extended it to all churches of the first and second order; Pope Gregory XV in 1622 extended it even farther, to any faithful who visited all Franciscan churches, be they associated with the first, second, or third order of St. Francis. On May 1, 1939, it was decreed that any pastor could request the Portiuncula Indulgence for his parish from the Sacred Penitentiary, so long as he had the permission of the local bishop.

Port-Royal ● Famed Cistercian abbey. It became prominent in the 1600s as a center for French Jansenism. The convent of Port-Royal-des-Champs was first founded in 1204 some sixteen to seventeen miles southwest of Paris, in the valley of the Chevreuse. By the start of the seventeenth century, the convent had declined severely in discipline, undergoing a very thorough reform

Mère Angelique Arnauld

under the abbess Mère Angelique Arnauld (starting in 1608), who was much influenced by St. Francis de Sales. Port-Royal soon began to attract novices from all over, and Mère Arnauld sent sisters all across the country to bring reform. In 1626, the sisters moved out of Port-Royal owing to unhealthy conditions, migrating to a new house in Paris in the Faubourg St.-Jacques that came to be called Port-Royal-de-Paris. The abbey soon renounced the jurisdiction of Cîteaux and placed itself under the archbishop of Paris, and the sisters took the name Daughters of the Blessed Sacrament. They came under the spiritual direction in 1636 of Abbé de St.-Cyran, and Port-Royal-de-Paris was turned into a major site of Jansenist teachings. Port-Royal soon attracted various Jansenists who sought the solitary life of prayer and study. They opened a small school for boys in 1646 and then restored in 1648 the original Port-Royal that had been abandoned years before. There followed the persecution of the Jansenists, during which the small schools were closed, novices expelled from Port-Royal, and, as the residents of the abbey steadfastly refused to sign the condemnation of Jansenist teachings — except for a few — the more vocal sisters were sent to various communities. The Peace of the Church was signed in 1669, Port-Royal-de-Paris was set aside for the nuns who had returned to the Church, and Port-Royal-des-Champs was used for the recalcitrant Jansenist sisters. This situation remained relatively tranquil until the late seventeenth century when the Jansenist controversy erupted once more. By a bull of Pope Clement IX (1705), Port-Royal-des-Champs was officially suppressed; in 1709, the last nuns were expelled, and the following year, the buildings of Port-Royal were burned to the ground.

Portugal ● Republic in the Iberian Peninsula, neighboring Spain. Long before the birth of an independent Portugal, Christianity arrived in the area, being introduced sometime before the fourth century. It took root and the Church there grew strongly, although, like the rest of the peninsula, it was troubled by the fifth-century barbarian invasions, including those of the Visigoths and the Germanic Suebi. They were followed by the Moorish invasions in 711. During this early period, the Church was also troubled by several heresies, including the Arianism of the Visigoths, Priscillianism, and Pelagianism.

The foundations for the Portuguese state were established in the eleventh century with the Christian reconquest of the region under King Ferdinand I of Castile, who captured the city of Coimbra in 1064. His son Alfonso VI made Henry of Burgundy count of Coimbra around 1095. Portuguese independence was won by Henry's son Alfonso I, who declared himself king of Portugal in 1139; Lisbon was won in 1147 with the aid of crusaders and mercenaries. Papal recognition was not secured until 1179, however, owing to a disagreement with the Holy See, which was only the start of long-term tensions between Portugal and the papacy. Antipapal sentiment was especially pronounced under King Sancho I (r. 1185-1211), causing a conflict only briefly resolved in 1210. Monastic influence was meanwhile strong, thanks to the Cistercians — and the rise of the mendicant orders in the 1200s helped improve the position of the papacy. Portugal was conspicuous in its support of Pope Urban VI (r. 1378-1389) during the early phase of the Great Schism, but this was due

in the main to its hostility toward Spain, which backed Urban's rival.

Thanks to the work of Henry the Navigator and such explorers as Vasco de Gama, Cabral, and Francisco de Aleida, by the end of the fifteenth century Portugal was a major commercial power and would soon forge a large overseas empire. Missionaries set out for distant lands on Portuguese ships and then labored to spread the faith in India, Africa, and South America. As was seen in such places as Brazil, the success in conversions by the missionaries was offset by the rapacious, exploitative, and cruel secular administration of the colonies. Back home, owing to extensive reforms of the local Church in the 1400s, the Reformation had no influence at all. The Inquisition became quite influential, to put it mildly, in the sixteenth century.

As its empire declined, Portugal fell under the control of Spain in 1580, remaining beneath the Spaniards until 1640 when a struggle for independence was launched. This ended in 1668 with a triumph for Portugal, marking a defeat for the papacy, which had supported Spain. In the middle of the next century, the Jesuits were expelled from the country and colonies and, under, the formidable anticlerical minister Sebastiano Pombal (1699-1782), the government claimed extensive control over the Church until Pombal fell from power in 1777 and was exiled. The 1800s brought a conflict between the Church and the liberals of the country. A concordat in 1886 signaled a victory for the Catholic cause, but the revolution of 1910 resulted in the expulsion of the religious orders, the seizure of Church property, and other harsh measures. The Catholic Church was disestablished first in Portugal (1911) and then the colonies (1913). The situation eased slightly around 1918, with relations between the government and the Holy See finally formalized in 1940. Under General Salazar, another concordat was negotiated by which property was restored and the Church granted some rights in education; the Church remained largely subservient. Today, the country is over ninety percent Catholic. Its one cardinal is the patriarch of Lisbon.

Praemunire ● Series of statutes issued in the fourteenth century delineating the rights and privileges of the English crown against all forms of possible interference by the Holy See. First promulgated in 1353, Praemunire declared that it was illegal to take any case out of the kingdom to the papal courts that should be tried before an English court. Additional penalties and details of the law were added in 1365 and 1393. King Henry VIII used Praemunire in 1529 to reject the work of Cardinal Thomas Wolsey as the papal legate, claiming that Wolsey represented papal interference in English affairs. Praemunire thus became an important element in the issue of the Act of Supremacy. Praemunire was used repeatedly by Queen Elizabeth I (r. 1558-1603) to persecute Catholics. The statutes were repealed finally in 1967 by the Criminal Law Act.

Pragmatic Sanction ● In Latin, *pragmatica sanctio*. Edict originating in the Late Roman Empire that was issued by the emperor. Among the subsequent pragmatic sanctions issued by rulers were several related to the Church.

Pragmatic Sanction of Bourges: A pronouncement issued on July 7, 1438, by King Charles VII of France and the French clergy, although the clergy was under the direct influence of the monarch. The pragmatic sanction formalized the rights of the clergy against the papacy; the French Church claimed control over ecclesiastical appointments, appeals to the Holy See, and the right of determining the validity of papal bulls. While technically revoked by King Louis XI in 1461, the sanction remained in effect until finally annulled by the Concordat

of Bologna (1516) signed between King Francis I of France and Pope Leo X.

Pragmatic Sanction of Germany: A decree promulgated in March 1438 by the German princes at the Diet of Frankfurt that declared their official state of neutrality in the controversy between Pope Eugenius IV (r. 1431-1447) and the Council of Basel over conciliarism. The diet, however, reconvened in Mainz in March 1439, adopting some of the conciliar decrees of Basel, reserving the privilege to adopt further changes. The designation "pragmatic sanction" is not considered correct, since the decree was not accepted or confirmed by the Holy Roman Emperor.

Premonstratensian Canons ● In Latin, *Canonici Regulares Praemonstratenses.* Abbreviated O. Praem., the order is also called the Norbertines or, in England, the White Canons (from the color of their habits). Founded by St. Norbert in 1120 at Premontre, near Laon, France, the Premonstratensians attempted to combine the active life of the religious with the strict, prayerful life of a contemplative. Their success in this effort contributed enormously to the creation of the environment in the 1100s that made possible the rise of the mendicant orders with their austere but active friars. The order at first adopted the Rule of St. Augustine, but because of Norbert's close friendship with St. Bernard of Clairvaux and the natural ties that developed with the Cistercians, the Premonstratensians practiced rigorous asceticism. Papal approval was granted in 1125 by Pope Honorius II, and the canons soon spread over Western Europe. Members became especially important in missionary work in parts of Eastern Europe, eventually wielding considerable influence in Hungary. In later years, the rules of the order were relaxed so that a number of reforms had to be made and several essentially independent congregations were established. The French Revolution was particularly hard on the White Canons, and the order had virtually ceased to exist in the years following the Napoleonic Wars (1796-1815). A revival came in the twentieth century, most notably in Belgium. The Canons came to the United States in 1893 and currently operate several houses.

Presbyterorum Ordinis ● This document, whose English title is the "Decree on the Ministry and Life of Priests," was issued on December 7, 1965, by the Second Vatican Council. *Presbyterorum Ordinis* stresses the important share of priests in Christ's ministry and calls upon all priests to remain devoted to the ministry. Accordingly, they should remain in obedience and a state of charity with their bishop; strive to make the word of God central to their very being; administer the sacraments and prayer with diligence; celebrate the Eucharist every day; promote the role of laypeople in the Church; and, in keeping with the example of Christ, remain devoted to their vows of priestly celibacy. The decree was careful to confirm the vows of celibacy in the Latin Church, although it added provision for those priests lawfully married and noted that the nature of the priesthood does not demand celibacy. The spirit and intention of the decree was elaborated upon by the 1990 Synod of Bishops, which gave the "The Formation of Priests in the Circumstances of the Present Day." On April 7, 1992, Pope John Paul II issued his apostolic exhortation *Pastores Dabo Vobis* (I Will Give You Shepherds) on the subjects covered by the synod. (See also **Orders, Holy**.)

Prester John ● Legendary Christian king of the East who was the subject of many stories by medieval chroniclers. The tale of Prester John first entered into medieval awareness during the crusades, probably in the late eleventh and twelfth centuries. According to early accounts, he was supposedly a Nestorian king-priest who had marched with an army to assist the First Crusade in the liberation of the city of Jerusalem from Islamic domination. The story was first recorded by Otto of Freising in his *Chronicon* (1145) and was based on a report provided about Prester John to the papal court by Bishop Hugh of Gebal concerning the king's triumph over the Persians. He was almost certainly referring to a crushing defeat inflicted upon the Seljuk Turks by a Mongol army. Subsequent stories told of a King David of India who routed various Islamic hosts. It is believed that the person to whom the tales actually referred was Genghis Khan.

The historian Alberic de Trois-Fontaines recorded in the thirteenth century that in 1165 a letter reached a number of European courts from Prester John. Among the supposed recipients were Emperors Frederick I Barbarossa and Manuel I Comnenus. The letter was totally fictitious, but Pope Alexander III accepted the reality of Prester John and sent a message to him; the end result of the communication is unknown. The search for Prester John, however, became the aim of many travelers in the 1200s and 1300s. These efforts had the unforeseen consequence of establishing contacts with the Mongol Empire. Later medieval stories changed Prester John's realm from the east to Abyssinia (Ethiopia), a region confused at times with India.

Primacy of the Pope ● Supreme, universal authority of the pope as successor to St. Peter. The primacy of the pope extends to him supreme jurisdictional authority by virtue of his office, including his powers as teacher, legislator, and head of the Church. As recorded in Matthew (16:18), St. Peter received his primacy from Christ when the Savior told him that he was to be the rock on which Christ would build his Church. Peter received the primacy from the risen Lord when Christ told him "Feed my lambs. . . . Tend my sheep. . . . Feed my sheep" (Jn

21:15-17). Based on these passages and the acceptance of the see of Rome as the primatial see of the Church, the pope was given primacy over Christendom because Peter was the supreme head of the Church to whom all the Apostles, Paul included, were subordinate. A formal definition of this primacy was made by Vatican Council I by building on the previous work of the Second Council of Lyons (1274) and the Council of Florence (1439); the council defined Peter's successor in the primacy to the Bishops of Rome, declaring that the Bishop of Rome is thus possessor of the primacy. Such authority is based on the historical fact that Peter worked and died as bishop of the Eternal City and, more importantly, that Christ or the Holy Spirit decreed that Peter and his successors are vested with universal jurisdiction.

Priscillianism ● Heretical sect originating in Spain during the fourth century, subsequently growing in popularity in the Western Roman Empire. Its name was derived from its principal spokesman, Priscillian. Apparently based on Gnostic-Manichaean teachings, the doctrine was first introduced into Spain by an Egyptian named Marcus. One of the early disciples was the Spanish layman Priscillian. Described by Sulpicius Severus as a man of noble birth and eloquence, he began to teach a severely ascetic and pseudo-Christian creed. While few details of his teaching have been preserved, the developed theology of the Priscillianists was much influenced by Gnostic-Manichaean dualism; they attempted to reconcile much of the OT but rejected the narrative about creation. A number of apocryphal books of the Scriptures were accepted as absolutely genuine.

Priscillian was able to use his oratorical skills to rally support from among many Spanish bishops. Orthodox Church leaders, however, attempted to secure his condemnation, but at the Council of

Saragossa (380), only the followers were censured. Priscillian was soon ordained bishop of Ávila and was then bolstered by the backing he received from Emperor Gratian. Gratian was assassinated in 383, and his successor, Magnus Maximus, reversed imperial policy to placate Orthodox Christians whose support he needed politically. In 384, Magnus allowed Priscillian to be condemned at the Council of Bordeaux. A tribunal of lay officials presided over the trial, proceedings much opposed by St. Martin of Tours, who protested the interference of a secular court in ecclesiastical affairs. Priscillian and several followers were executed in 385, an event that made them revered as martyrs and that promoted the spread of the sect even further in Spain. The Council of Toledo (400) launched a campaign to reconcile the Priscillians to the Church, a program interrupted and partly thwarted by the sociopolitical upheaval caused by the invasion of Spain by the Vandals in the early fifth century. Such was the resulting revival of Priscillianism that a letter was sent by Orosius to St. Augustine to enlist his aid in suppressing it. Pope Leo I the Great (r. 440-461) promoted anti-Priscillian activities, particularly councils convened in 446 and 447. Decline began in the sixth century, dying out after the Council of Braga in 561.

Probabiliorism ● System in moral theology proposing that in cases where there is doubt concerning the lawfulness or unlawfulness of an action, it is lawful to accept the opinion favoring liberty only when that opinion is more probable than the opinion favoring the law. A more rigorist system than that of probabilism, it was long held by theologians in centuries before the time of Bartholomew Medina (1527-1580), the Spanish Dominican theologian who gave definition to probabilism. It was revived in the 1600s to counter the popular acceptance of probabilism and what many theologians felt was a tendency toward laxity (or laxism) in moral theology. Receiving much impetus from Popes Alexander VII (r. 1655-1667) and Innocent XI (r. 1676-1689), the probabiliorists secured the support of many theologians, especially among the Dominicans. In 1656, the general chapter of the Dominicans urged all members to adopt probabiliorism; they were joined by a number of Jesuits, Franciscans, Augustinians, Carmelites, and many Benedictines. The Jesuit theologian Thyrsus Gonzalez of the University of Salamanca wrote *Fundamentum Theologiae Moralis* (1670-1672), a work supporting probabiliorism. Withheld by the Jesuit general from publication, it would eventually be released, in 1694. In the meantime, Pope Innocent XI decreed in 1680 that the order permit probabiliorists to write in opposition to probabilism. Gonzalez himself became general in 1687. The system was thus generally accepted until the second half of the eighteenth century. At that time, the renowned moral theologian St. Alphonsus Liguori abandoned it for probabilism. Probabiliorism soon declined in use and was virtually abandoned in the 1800s.

Probabilism ● System found in moral theology holding that in those cases where question exists concerning the lawfulness or unlawfulness (or licitness or illicitness) of an action, it is permitted to follow an opinion that is solidly probable in favor of liberty, even when the opposing view against liberty is even more probable. Probabilism is based on the principle that in any situation where there are grave doubts concerning a law, that doubtful law does not bind a person to its adherence. Probabilists argued that solid probability could be determined where the application of reason is such that a group of theologians could give an accurate and acceptable judgment so long as their opinion does not run counter to authoritative teaching or decisions and does not neglect to

consider or resolve important arguments in the discussion. While intended to assist persons in resolving matters of conscience, probabilism was attacked for lacking objective norms or criteria in the determination of the probability of a law or moral obligation. It was opposed by such groups of moral theologians as the so-called rigorists, probabiliorists, and equiprobabilists.

Probabilism did not exist as a specific system before the sixteenth century, although probabilist proponents have pointed out that the Church Fathers and eminent theologians applied probabilism to resolve contemporary questions on morality, citing as examples St. Augustine and especially St. Thomas Aquinas who stated that a precept does not bind a person save through the application or medium of knowledge. The formal development of probabilism came through the work of the Dominican Bartholomew Medina (1527-1580) a Spanish professor of theology at the University of Salamanca. In his commentary on the *Summa* of St. Thomas Aquinas (1577), he presented this most important concept: "*Si est opinio probabilis, licitum est eam sequi, licet opposita probabilior sit*" ("If an opinion is probable, it is licit to follow it, even if the opposing opinion is more probable"). The system remained generally accepted teaching until the middle of the 1600s; it was utilized by both Dominicans and Jesuits and further developed by such theologians as Gabriel Vázquez and Francisco Suárez. While there were critics who opposed it on the basis of potential laxism, it was not until the 1650s and the Church response to Jansenism that the system was the cause of controversy.

In 1653, theologians at Louvain condemned probabilism, and the counter system of rigorism came into fashion. Blaise Pascal attacked the system in his *Lettres Provinciales*. While these were condemned by Pope Alexander VII in 1657, rigorism was not given papal disapproval until 1690, by Alexander VIII. Probabiliorism (arguing that it is not lawful to act on the less safe opinion unless it can be considered more probable than the safe opinion) came also into use during the mid-seventeenth century, largely due to the promotion of it by Alexander VII and Innocent XI. The Dominicans in 1656 urged it upon all members. By the middle of the 1500s it was accepted by most major orders, including the Franciscans. Thyrsus Gonzalez, a Jesuit theologian and professor at Salamanca, wrote *Fundamentum Theologiae Moralis* (1670-1672), supporting probabiliorism. He was opposed by his own order and the book was published only in 1694, after Gonzalez's election as general of the order and the issuance of a decree by Pope Innocent XI in 1680 to allow the Jesuit probabiliorists to write in favor of the system.

The controversy continued until the time of St. Alphonsus Liguori (1696-1787). After abandoning probabiliorism, he became an adherent of probabilism, defending it in his treatise on the subject in 1749. In 1762, he altered his opinion, preferring to embrace equiprobabilism, relying nevertheless on probabilist teaching as the basis of his system. Because of St. Alphonsus' position as a Doctor of the Church and his place in moral theology, probabilism and equiprobabilism remained the prevailing systems studied by moral theologians into the late twentieth century and its reappraisal of all processes of moral analysis.

Procopius of Caesarea (d. c. 562) ● Byzantine historian, ranked as one of the greatest of Greek historians. Born in Caesarea, he accompanied the Byzantine general Belisarius on his campaigns against the Vandals and Ostrogoths as well as the Persians, serving as secretary. His chief writings were: *History of the Wars*, a thorough account of the military ventures he personally witnessed and an excellent source on the reign of Justinian I (527-565);

Justinian's Buildings (completed c. 558), a survey of the emperor's programs of construction, including the Santa Sophia (or Hagia Sophia); and the *Anecdota*, also called the *Arcana historia* (*Secret History*), a critical and often ugly history of the emperor and court that was not intended for publication. Often bitter and decidedly harsh, the *Anecdota* was merciless in its criticism of Justinian, Empress Theodora, the imperial government, and the Byzantine Church. It was first published in 1623.

Pro-Nuncio ● Representative or papal legate to a country having diplomatic relations with the Holy See. The pro-nuncio has the dual task of representing the Holy See to the secular government of the country and to serve as a valuable liaison to the Church in the same nation. Pro-nuncios are customarily titular archbishops and diplomats of long service, extensive experience, and superb training. They differ from nuncios in a technical diplomatic sense; nuncios are recognized as the dean of the diplomatic corps in the country in which they are serving; pro-nuncios are assigned to posts where this status and prerogative is not recognized, a custom that has been in practice since 1965. The majority of papal ambassadors are pro-nuncios, a demonstration of the active role the Holy See plays in establishing relations with new nations or with countries previously unwilling to normalize diplomatic ties.

Prosper of Aquitaine (d. c. 463) ● Also known as Prosper Tiro. A theologian and a defender of St. Augustine's doctrines on grace and predestination, Prosper was born somewhere in Gaul (Roman France), moving to Marseille (Massilia) sometime before 428. Living there as a monk, he became deeply concerned about the rise of Semi-Pelagianism, deciding to write to Augustine concerning the controversy. The letter, sent in 428, prompted Augustine to compose two treatises, *De praedestinatione* (*On Predestination*) and *De dono perseverantiae* (*On the Gift of Perseverance*), escalating the Semi-Pelagian Controversy. Around this time, Prosper authored a letter to a certain Rufinus, actually a short treatise on grace and free will, and a poem, the *Carmen de ingratis*, on grace, that was over one thousand hexameters in length. In the period following the death of Augustine (430), Prosper also wrote several works in defense of Augustine; these included an attack on Vincent of Lérins and defenses of Augustinian doctrine, especially those in *De praedestinatione* and *De dono perseverantiae*. In 431, he went to Rome to enlist the help of Pope Celestine I, and the pope wrote the letter *Apostolici Verba*, addressed to the bishops of Gaul, exhorting them to support Augustine. Returning to Gaul, Prosper wrote against John Cassian. He later served as secretary to Pope St. Leo I and authored important works: *Epigrammata ex sententiis sancti Augustini* (excerpts from the writings of St. Augustine) and a *Chronicle* (or abridgment of St. Jerome's *Chronicle*, covering history from the creation to A.D. 378).

Providentissimus Deus ● Encyclical issued on November 18, 1893, by Pope Leo XIII. Intended to provide impetus to the study of the Bible, it has been called the "Magna Carta of Biblical Studies." *Providentissimus Deus* was written to encourage scholars to continue the work that had recently been done in biblical studies, particularly the application of new methods in critical analysis, archaeology, and the study of the language used originally in the writing of the Scriptures. The encyclical stressed, however, the divine inspiration of the Bible, reaffirming declarations of both the Council of Trent and Vatican Council I. It made clear that the Scriptures were written under the influence of God upon the intellect and was thus composed through the

authorship of God, at the dictation of the Holy Spirit. Pope Leo also promoted the reading of the Bible by laypeople, but he reminded them to approach the Scriptures with piety and reverence. The encyclical was ratified and developed further by two subsequent encyclicals, *Spiritus Paraclitus* (September 15, 1920) by Pope Benedict XV, and especially *Divino afflante Spiritu* (September 30, 1943) by Pope Pius XII. (See also **Pontifical Biblical Commission**.)

Provisors, Statute of ● Law passed in England in 1351 under King Edward III. It attempted to limit the power and influence of the papacy in the kingdom by curtailing the practice of so-called papal provision, meaning the nomination by the pope of persons to fill vacant ecclesiastical offices without first securing the consent of the king. A law that was in keeping with the long tradition in England resisting papal appointments to episcopal benefices, the Statute of Provisors was prompted by English concern over the domination of the papacy by the French, a situation epitomized by the fact that the reigning pontiff, Clement VI, was French, and that the popes continued to reside in Avignon. The laws stated that the king and lords should declare benefices and not the "Bishop of Rome." It was followed in succeeding years by a series of new statutes. The statute of 1353 established Praemunire; a third in 1365 confirmed the statute of 1353; and a fourth in 1389 declared benefices accepted in a manner different from those of the earlier statutes should be forfeited. The Statute of Provisors was essentially ignored and generally forgotten until the 1500s. King Henry VIII (r. 1509-1547) used the statute to assume control over the English Church. The practice of provision was renewed briefly under Queen Mary but was ended by Queen Elizabeth I (r. 1558-1603).

Prudentius (c. 348-c. 410) ● In full, Aurelius Clemens Prudentius. Important Christian poet known for his hymns and apologies. Born in Spain, he studied law and then held several prominent positions in the government of Emperor Theodosius. He went into seclusion around 392 and henceforth devoted himself to poetry. Among his compositions were: *Peristephanon*, giving praise to martyrs; *Contra Symmachum*, a polemic intended to refute the brilliant speech delivered by the pagan orator Symmachus in favor of the return to the senate of the pagan altar of victory; and the *Psychomachia*, a study of Christian asceticism presented in an allegorical struggle between good and evil. The *Psychomachia* was very influential in the development of medieval literature.

Pseudo-Dionysius the Areopagite (fl. c. 500) ● Also Dionysius the Pseudo-Areopagite, a Syrian monk and mystical theologian who attempted a synthesis of Christian and Neoplatonist thought. A number of writings attributed to him became highly popular during the Middle Ages owing to the acceptance of them as possessing apostolic authority. He was identified as Dionysius the Areopagite, a person converted by St. Paul on his second missionary journey as described in Acts (17:34). A number of other references were made, such as by Eusebius, who declared him the first bishop of Corinth. Nothing else is known about him, but from an early time the treatises attributed to him gained a wide following and came to exercise a lasting and pervasive influence in medieval theological thought. They possessed virtually unquestioned authority from the time of Pope St. Gregory I (r. 590-604). Initially translated by John Scotus Erigena, they were eventually

mentioned by such notables as St. Thomas Aquinas, St. Bonaventure, St. Albertus Magnus, Meister Eckhart, and Hugh of St. Victor. The high position of Pseudo-Dionysius was finally questioned in the sixteenth century by several scholars. In the 1800s, it was generally accepted that the writings were not of apostolic origin. Rather, they dated to the late fifth century and were apparently composed under the influence of Emperor Zeno (r. 474-491) during the Monophysite Controversy. The four treatises were originally written in Gaul and were later translated into Latin under the following titles: *Caelestis hierarchia* (*On the Celestial Hierarchy*), *Theologica mystica* (*On Mystical Theology*), *De divinis nominibus* (*On the Divine Names*), and *Ecclesiastica hierarchia* (*On the Ecclesiastical Hierarchy*). While deeply imbued with Neoplatonism, the treatises were quite obscure in style, perhaps purposely so, and the precise theological positions of the author cannot easily be determined. (See **Neoplatonism** in the GLOSSARY.)

Punch, John (1603-1670) ● Also erroneously referred to as John Ponce. An Irish philosopher and theologian, he was born in Cork, Ireland. He left his native land while a youth and journeyed to Belgium where he entered the Irish Franciscans in Louvain. After studying at Cologne, Louvain, and Rome, he taught at Lyons and Paris, acquiring a reputation for being an expert on the philosophical system of John Duns Scotus (d. 1308). His works included: *Cursus philosophiae* (1643) and *Integer cursus theologia* (1652), both on the Scottish school of philosophy; and *Commentarii theoligici in quatuor libros sententiarum*, a commentary on the *Sentences* that was much respected by contemporaries.

Q Document ● Term referring to a possible or hypothetical written source that was said to have been used by both Matthew and Luke in the composition of their Gospels. The Q is derived apparently from the German *quelle* (source). The theory is the result of efforts to resolve questions concerning the similarities between the Gospels according to St. Matthew and St. Luke but that are not present in the other Synoptic Gospel, that of St. Mark. The commonality of passages is especially pronounced in the recording of Christ's sayings, the Temptation of Christ, and in the account of John the Baptist. For example, in Matthew (3:12) John proclaims, "His winnowing fork is in his hand, and he will clear his threshing floor and gather his wheat into the granary, but the chaff he will burn with unquenchable fire." In Luke (3:17), meanwhile, it is written, "His winnowing fork is in his hand, to clear his threshing floor, and to gather the wheat into his granary, but the chaff he will burn with unquenchable fire."

The theory of a possible Q Document was first suggested by the scholar C. H. Weisse in 1838, receiving development in the work of other eminent historians and biblical scholars such as Adolf Harnack and Burnett Streeter. The Q Document was postulated to be an actual work, written in Greek, containing the sayings of Christ and related materials; it was, according to theory, the primary source used by both Matthew and Luke in the writing down of their Gospels, in conjunction with oral traditions. The possible existence of the Q Document was widely accepted in many scholarly circles, finding

widest enthusiasm among Protestants. Many Catholics in the middle of the twentieth century subscribed to the idea, and the point was made that even should such a collection have existed, it would in no way reduce or impugn the historical validity of the Gospels, their freedom from error, or their divine inspiration. In modern times a number of questions have been raised about the possible existence of the Q Document. Chief among these is the insurmountable fact that no such work has ever been found or mentioned in any other source.

Quadragesimo Anno ● Encyclical issued on May 15, 1931, by Pope Pius XI. It reaffirmed the teachings of Pope Leo XIII on social justice and noted the fortieth anniversary of Leo's encyclical *Rerum novarum*, "On Capital and Labor." The encyclical of Pius echoed and stressed many of the important points of his predecessor, but it placed within the context of the teachings a heightened sense of urgency because of the ongoing global depression with its terrible effects upon large segments of the world's population. It condemned the evils of unconstrained and unprincipled capitalism; noted the unacceptability of the Socialist state with its collectivism, statism, and anti-Catholicism; and called for fundamental reorganization of society, one based on respect for both the worker and the employer. Pius proposed as an example of this cohesive, organic society the trade or guild system that flourished in the Middle Ages.

Quadratus, St. (fl. second century) ● Earliest known Christian apologist. Nothing is known about him with any certainty save for a fragment of an apology he wrote around 124 that is preserved in a passage of Eusebius's *Ecclesiastical History*. According to Eusebius, Quadratus was a disciple of the Apostles, called by him *auditor apostalorum*. Other references, such as that of St. Jerome, who identified him with Quadratus, bishop of Athens of the second half of the second century, are considered erroneous. Quadratus addressed his apology to Emperor Hadrian from Asia Minor. It was written during a persecution and sought to defend the faith by arguing the truth of Christ's teaching through the miracles performed by the Savior. Some scholars have proposed that it is possible to equate Quadratus's apology with the second-century Epistle to Diognetus that opposed paganism and Judaism. Feast day: May 26.

Quadrivium ● See GLOSSARY.

Quam Singulari ● Decree issued on August 8, 1910, and promulgated officially on August 15, 1910, by the Sacred Congregation of the Sacraments. It provided the regulations on the appropriate age at which children should be admitted to First Communion. By the conditions established in the decree, Holy Communion, following First Confession, should be received at the appropriate age of discretion, a time judged to have been reached by the indication that a child has begun to utilize reasoning powers and by the ability to determine right from wrong. The decree stressed that children should not be forced to memorize theological terms that are meaningless to them, but they should know the importance of Communion, recognize it as the Body of Christ, and treat it devoutly. (See **Eucharist** and **Penance**; see also **Pius X, St.**)

Quanta Cura ● Encyclical issued on December 8, 1864, by Pope Pius IX, meaning "What Great Care." The encyclical promulgated the famous *Syllabus of Errors*, condemning the doctrines of liberalism, which was attached to it. *Quanta cura* also examined contemporary errors concerning the relationship of Church and State, reiterating the divine foundation of the Catholic Church and its full independence from secular authority. (For further details, see **Syllabus of Errors**.)

Quentin, Henri (1872-1935) ● French Benedictine biblical scholar. Ordained in 1902, he was appointed in 1907 by Pope Pius X to the pontifical commission charged with revision of the Vulgate. He was largely responsible for the subsequent text of the Pentateuch. Among his scholarly writings were: *J. D. Mansi et les grandes collections consiliares* (1900), on the work of the canonist Giovanni Domenico Mansi (1692-1769) in collecting material on Church councils; and *Les Martyrologes historiques du moyen âge* (1908; *The Historical Martyrologies of the Middle Ages*).

Quesnel, Pasquier (1634-1719) ● French theologian and a leading defender of Jansenism. A native of Paris, he studied theology and philosophy at the Sorbonne, entering the Congregation of the Oratory in 1657. Ordained in 1659, he was soon appointed director of students, authoring a guidebook (published in 1671), *Abrégé de la morale de l'Évangile* (*Epitome of the Morals of the Evangelists*); subsequent editions and revisions were published under the title *Le Nouveau Testament en français, avec des réflexions morales sur chaque verset* (1687-1692; *The New Testament in French, With Moral Reflections on Each Verse*), commonly called *Réflexions morales*. In 1675, he published a complete edition of the writings of Pope St. Leo I, a highly scholarly work that was nevertheless placed on the

Index of Forbidden Books because the notes included questions on papal infallibility and the primacy of the Roman See. An adherent of Jansenist teachings, Quesnel was removed from Paris in 1681 and sent to Orléans. Three years later, he was expelled from the Oratorians and, refusing to sign the anti-Jansenist decrees of the order, he fled to Belgium and lived in exile in Brussels with Antoine Arnaud. Imprisoned in 1703 by the archbishop of Malines, he escaped after a brief time and fled to Holland. Settling in Amsterdam, he devoted his remaining years to a defense of Jansenism and his *Réflexions morales*. The work was a major source of controversy, promoting considerable conflict between Jansenists and the Holy See. Condemned in a brief by Pope Clement XII in 1708, it was formally condemned by the constitution *Unigenitus* (September 8, 1713) by Pope Clement at the urging of King Louis XIV. This was followed in 1718 by the bull *Pastoralis officii* (August 28, 1718), issued against those, Quesnel included, who had refused to accept *Unigenitus*. *Unigenitus* condemned one hundred one sentences from *Réflexions morales*, including the idea that without grace the sinner is capable only of evil; without grace a person is incapable of loving anything save one's ultimate condemnation; and that prayers by a sinner are new sins. Quesnel steadfastly refused to accept the papal condemnations, denying that his writings were heretical, and calling upon a general council to prove him innocent.

Quiercy, Synods of ● Also Councils of Quiercy, they were several synods held at Quiercy, near Laon, in the ninth century. At the time, Quiercy was a residence of the Carolingian kings and was known as *palatium Carissiacum*. The first synod was convened in 838 and condemned some of the opinions of Amalarius of Metz and compelled the bishop of Le Mans to allow monks to return to a monastery from which he had expelled them. More important was the synod of 849. Convened under the formidable Hincmar of Reims, it deposed Gottschalk of Fulda and ordered his imprisonment in Hautvilliers. At the next synod, in 853, Hincmar secured a renewal of Gottschalk's condemnation and the issue of the four chapters, or *capitula*, on the question of predestination. These were: the predestination of some to eternal life; the liberation through grace of evil tendencies by the free will, which had been lost by Adam and restored by Christ; the intention by God that all people should be saved; and that Christ suffered and died for universal redemption. The *capitula* were renounced two years later by the Council of Valence. Two other minor synods were held in 857 and 858.

Quietism ● Doctrine exhorting, in its broadest sense, the need for that attainment of perfection through a process of spiritual annihilation and the absorption of the will by God. In its most specific or restricted sense, it was a doctrine developed by Miguel de Molinos (d. 1696) and advocated by the noted quietists Madame Jeanne Marie Guyon (1648-1717) and François Fénelon, archbishop of Cambrai (1651-1715). The distant origins of quietism can be traced to certain practices in the East, especially India where Pantheistic Brahmanism flourished. It was found in tendencies among the Greeks, and was later adopted in various forms by the Bogomils, Hesychasts, and the Beguines and Beghards. Molinos expounded his quietist teachings in his *Dux spiritualis* (1675). Sixty-eight propositions were subsequently taken from this work and others and condemned by Pope Innocent XI in his bull *Coelestis Pastor* (November 19, 1687). Among the propositions that were condemned were: man must annihilate his power and abandon himself entirely to God; by ceasing its activity the soul is able to annihilate itself and return to God, who resides in it after it is transformed; through such abandonment, the utter passivity of the soul brings about a lack of concern for salvation, and heaven and hell; external works of charity are to be eschewed as being wasteful occupations of the senses. Such activities to be resisted include the recitation of prayers and honors given to the Virgin Mary and the saints. Only nondiscursive prayer or meditation should be adopted. Once a state of annihilation has been attained, sin becomes impossible for the individual because such a person is completely in God. Curiously, while such a perfected human might be tempted and even commit externally sinful deeds, he or she is free from any guilt, as the person's will has ceased to exist. Additionally, such a person must ever be on one's guard to avoid being distressed by these distractions lest a disruption occur in the state of so-called mystical death.

Although condemned, quietism soon found adherents, even in the Church. Among them were Pietro Petrucci (1636-1701), a cardinal whose works on the spiritual life were examined by the Inquisition and in 1688 fifty-four propositions were proscribed; François Malaval (1627-1719), a blind layman; and the Barnabite François Lecombe, the spiritual director of Madame Guyon.

Quiñones, Francisco de (c. 1480-1540) ● Spanish cardinal. Born to a noble family of León, he received an education as a page in the service of Cardinal Ximénez, entering the Franciscans around the age of sixteen. He planned to embark on a journey with a fellow Franciscan to the missions of America in 1521, but this venture was cut short by the companion's death and the election of Quiñones as commissary general of part of the order. In 1523, he was elected general of the Franciscans, proving an active head, promoting heightened discipline, increased education, and missionary activities in Mexico. Quiñones proved an important figure in the protracted negotiations that resulted from the sack of Rome and the imprisonment of Pope Clement VII by the troops of Emperor Charles V in 1527. As a relative of the emperor, Quiñones helped negotiate the release of the pontiff and the subsequent Treaties of Barcelona (1527) and Cambrai (1529). He stepped down as general in December 1527 to be of greater assistance to the pope and to prevent his papal duties from interfering with a smooth running of the order. He was then appointed cardinal, earning the nickname Cardinal of the Holy Cross from the titular see of S. Croce in Gerusalemme. He is particularly remembered for his reform of the Roman Breviary.

Quinque Viae ● Latin for Five Ways. Used for the five arguments used by St. Thomas Aquinas to prove the existence of God, they were first presented in the *Summa Theologica* (Part I, Question 2, Article 3). Each of the ways seeks to demonstrate that God's exists by showing the effects of his being upon the nature of the cosmos; from these effects it is possible to conclude his existence. The First Way is concerned with motion and change in the universe, arguing that whatever is in motion must have been moved by something else. The Second Way postulates cause and effect; because in nature there is no way something can cause itself, the inevitable first cause, or efficient cause, is God. The Third Way argues that God is the necessity in all things, as everything derives its existence from God. The Fourth Way offers the idea of various degrees of perfection or goodness; Thomas here states that all things are good or perfect by varying degrees and that only one thing is truly, absolutely perfect: God. The Fifth Way is concerned with the finality, or ultimate goal, of things; God can be detected through the recognition that in the order of the universe there is to be seen some goal or direction, and this source or direction is God. From these ways, Thomas presents the case that there must be a Prime Mover, a perfect being, an unmoved mover, that is the cause of all creation and the reason for which we owe our own existence.

Quirinus ● Name used by Johannes Joseph Ignaz von Döllinger (1799-1890) for a series of sixty-nine letters. They were published from 1869-1870 in the *Augsburger Allgemeine Zeitung* concerning Vatican Council I. The letters from Quirinus were written in opposition to the proceedings of the Vatican Council that were leading to the definition of papal infallibility that was desired by Pope Pius IX and the majority of cardinals in attendance. Döllinger, as Quirinus, made clear his extreme disagreement with the proposed definition, but the letters remain, nevertheless, a valuable source on the council and a remarkable embodiment of the intellectual reasoning used by those such as Döllinger, Lord Acton, and others who were against papal infallibility. (See **Döllinger, Johannes**, for further details.)

Quo Vadis? ● Legend based on a passage found in the apocryphal Acts of Peter, written around 190. It presented the supposed flight of Peter from Rome during the terrible Neronian persecutions. According to the tale, Peter was walking away from the Eternal City when he suddenly met Christ on the Appian Way. The Apostle asked him: *"Quo Vadis, Domine?"* ("Where are you going, Lord?"). Christ relied, "I am going to Rome to be crucified once more," whereupon Peter turned around and returned to Rome to suffer martyrdom with the Christians of the city. He was subsequently crucified, upside down because of his declaration that he was unfit to die in the same manner as his Lord. A small church on the Appian Way, Santa Maria delle Piante, was built to commemorate this event. It is commonly called *Domine Quo Vadis. Quo Vadis?* was also used as the title of the 1899 novel by Henryk Sienkiewicz.

Rabanus Maurus (d. 856) ● Abbot of Fulda, archbishop of Mainz, writer, and noted theologian. A native of Mainz, he entered the Benedictine monastery of Fulda at an early age and was ordained a deacon in 801. After studying at Tours under Alcuin (where he earned the name Maurus in memory of St. Benedict's favorite pupil), Rabanus returned to Fulda where he taught and later was made master of the monastic school there. Through his skills the school emerged as one of the foremost centers of learning in the Frankish Empire, and Rabanus was renowned as a teacher. Ordained a priest in 814, he was elected abbot of Fulda in 822, working to increase the material and spiritual wealth of the monastery. Rabanus retired in 842, probably under pressure from King Louis the German with whom he had not been on the best of terms. After spending several years in prayer at Petersburg, he was reconciled with King Louis and in 847, named archbishop of Mainz. Aside from several provincial synods concerning clerical discipline, the doctrine of predestination, and the rights of the Church, Rabanus distinguished himself as archbishop by his great charity; the *Annales Fuldensis*, for example, recorded his work to care for the poor and hungry during a famine in 830. One of the most learned figures of his age, Rabanus wrote commentaries on the Scriptures; poetry; *De clericorum institutione*, a manual for clerics on the sacraments; *De universo*, a twenty-two-book encyclopedic work based on the *Etymologiae* by St. Isidore of Seville; and an attack on Paschasius Radbertus.

Rahner, Karl (1904-1984) ● German theologian and priest who exercised considerable influence on students of twentieth-century theology. Born in Freiburg in Breigau, Baden, Germany, Rahner joined the Society of Jesus in 1922, following his brother into the religious life. Ordained in 1932, he studied at Freiburg and Innsbruck and was appointed in 1936 to the faculty of the University of Innsbruck. After the interruptions caused by World War II, he returned to Innsbruck in 1948 and was promoted the next year to professor of dogmatic theology. In 1952, he served as editor of the *Enchiridion Symbolorum* of Denziger and from 1957-1965 helped edit the *Lexicon für Theologie und Kirche* (10 vols.). Highly respected in the Church, he served as a *peritus* (theological expert) at Vatican Council II. Rahner was also a professor at the Universities of Munich and Münster. His major writings included: *Sacramentum Mundi* (1968-1970), *Geist in Welt* (1939; revised in 1957; *Spirit in the World*), and *Hörer des Wortes* (1941; *Hearers of the Word*). Rahner was very much shaped in his philosophical outlook by Joseph Maréchal (1878-1944), the Belgian Jesuit philosopher and theologian, and Martin Heidegger (1889-1976), the German existentialist. Rahner studied under Heidegger in Freiburg. An exponent of what has been termed supernatural existentialism, Rahner interpreted Thomistic teaching in terms of existentialism, arguing that knowledge proceeds from sensible impressions.

Rainald of Dassel (d. 1167) ● German chancellor of the Holy Roman Empire and archbishop of Cologne. He wielded considerable influence during the reign of Emperor Frederick I Barbarossa (German king from 1152 and emperor from 1155-1190). Rainald was the son of a Saxon count, studying at Hildesheim and Paris. Serving as provost in the churches of Petersburg, Hildesheim (twice), and Münster, he declined the offer to become bishop of Hildesheim, most likely because he had aspirations of entering the imperial court. In 1153, he took part in the delegation sent by Frederick I to Pope Eugenius III during which he demonstrated marked abilities. Three years later, he was appointed imperial chancellor, thereafter enjoying a powerful say in the policies of the Holy Roman Empire. He promoted the cause of the German king, especially in its involvement in Italy, and was eager to reduce the power of the papacy in secular and ecclesiastical matters. Thus, at the Diet of Besançon (October 1157), Rainald rejected the term *beneficium*, which had been used by Pope Adrian to imply that the crown had been conferred upon Frederick by the papacy. Rainald instead advanced the idea that the emperor ruled independently and owed his rule only to God and the princes who had elected him. Appointed archbishop of Cologne in 1159, Rainald continued to support the imperial cause in Italy and, after the death of Adrian (1159), gave his support to the antipope Victor IV against Pope Alexander III. Over the next several years, he embarked on several missions to France and England in an effort to secure support for Victor. These were largely unsuccessful, however, and in 1163 Alexander III excommunicated him. Nevertheless, after Victor's death in 1164, Rainald, on his own initiative, moved swiftly to have a new antipope elected, Paschal III; by this move he ensured a continuation of the struggle between Frederick and the papacy, a conflict that might otherwise have been resolved. In

1166-1167, he took to the field and campaigned in Italy, defeating a much larger force than his own in Tuscany. He then marched on Rome but died of malaria near the Eternal City after an epidemic broke out among his troops. He is also remembered for advocacy of the canonization of Charlemagne and for bringing to the cathedral of Cologne the bones of the Three Wise Men, relics that drew pilgrims to Cologne. Rainald was buried in the cathedral of Cologne.

Rambler, The ● Monthly Catholic journal in England from 1848-1862, which served as a major source of discussion and controversy among English Catholics concerning many of the social and ecclesiastical issues of the day. According to the last issue published under the name *The Rambler* (May 1862), the periodical was begun "on 1st of January 1848 as a weekly magazine of home and foreign literature, politics, science and art. Its aim was to unite an intelligent and hearty acceptance of Catholic dogma with free inquiry and discussion on questions which the Church left open to debate and while avoiding, as far as possible, the domain of technical theology, to provide a medium for the expression of independent opinions on subjects of the day. . . ." It was published on a monthly basis from September 1, 1848, to February 1, 1859; starting in May 1859, it was published every two months until May 1862 when it ceased printing, although the quarterly journal *The Home and Foreign Review*, with the same editorial staff, was begun in July of that year.

The Rambler was organized under the influence and leadership of some of England's foremost Catholic converts and liberal Catholics, including John Acton and the future cardinal John Henry Newman. The actual founder was J. M. Capes, and editorial work was done by Lord Acton and especially Richard Simpson. As *The Rambler* itself noted: "We at first endeavoured to restrict it to topics of social and literary interest, without entering directly into the graver problems of moral or political philosophy, but the events of the time and the circumstances of English Catholicism compelled us more and more to open our pages to investigations of a deeper and more complex nature." These writings soon brought the journal into disagreement with the hierarchy of the English Church. Writers were particularly critical of the Ultramontanism of William George Ward (1812-1882) and Henry Manning (1808-1892, later archbishop of Westminster); the journal criticized Cardinal Nicholas Wiseman, leading ultimately to *The Rambler*'s suppression in 1862. The subsequent *Home and Foreign Review* was also antagonistic to the English hierarchy and survived only until April 1864.

Rancé, Jean-Arnaud de Bouthillier de (1626-1700) ● Abbot and reformer of the Abbey of Notre Dame de la Trappe. Born in Paris, he was the son of a councillor of state, was a godson of Cardinal Richelieu, and was originally to enter the Knights of Malta. Owing to the poor health of his brother, however, he was entered into the religious life in order to ensure the family's saving of a number of benefices that were possessed by his older brother. When his brother died in 1637, Rancé received in succession the position of canon of Notre Dame de Paris, abbot of La Trappe, and other offices. Ordained in 1651, he succeeded the following year to the extensive estates of his family owing to the death of his father. Known for his fondness of hunting and feasts, he was nevertheless appointed archdeacon by his uncle, the archbishop of Tours, was elected to the Assembly of French Clergy, and was chaplain to Gaston, duke of Orléans. Over the next years, however, he underwent a conversion and in 1662 disposed of his possessions, visiting the Abbey of La Trappe. With the king's permission, he made his profession and became abbot regular of La Trappe. Thereafter, he was devoted to

reforming the monastery. He also took part in physical labor and authored several important spiritual works including *La traité de la sainteté et des devoirs de la vie monastique*. His severe asceticism led some to accuse him of Jansenist leanings, a charge refuted by Rancé's signing of the anti-Jansenist formula and the various letters and pamphlets of his that were published by Jacques Bossuet. He retired in 1693 and died on October 27, 1700.

Raphael (1483-1520) ● Italian name: Raffaello Santi or Raffaello Sanzio. One of the most famous of all the painters of the Italian Renaissance, Raphael was born in Urbino. He was the son of Giovanni Santi, the court painter and poet to the duke of Urbino. From around 1499-1504, Raphael worked under Perugino of Perugia; his influence upon Raphael was clear in such early works as the "Crucifixion," "The Three Graces," and "The Espousals of the Virgins." From 1504-1508, he was in Florence, becoming an associate of such notables as Massaccio, Leonardo da Vinci, Michelangelo, and Fra Bartolomeo. Summoned to Rome in 1508, he entered into the service of Pope Julius II, working in the Eternal City until his death. For the popes, he erected a series of panels in the Sistine Chapel, with themes from the Acts of the Apostles; the Sistine Madonna; and, for Pope Leo X, the portraits of Baldassare Castiglione. In 1514, Pope Leo appointed him successor to Bramante as chief architect of St. Peter's. Raphael died with his last work, "The Transfiguration," left unfinished; his death has traditionally been attributed to a wild debauch.

Ratio Studiorum ● Term for the comprehensive educational system used by the Jesuits, or Society of Jesus. It is an abbreviation of the official title for the system: *Ratio atque Institutio Studiorum Societatis Iesu* (Method and System of the Studies of the Society of Jesus). The extensive program of studies evolved over a period of time in the late 1500s and was devised in order to fulfill the crying need for an organized system of education that was acutely felt in the recently established Jesuit colleges throughout Europe. Under the Jesuit general Claudius Aquaviva, who served from 1582-1615, the *Ratio Studiorum* took definitive shape; early drafts were made in 1586 and 1591, culminating in the approved draft of 1599. The final version was the result of a long consultation throughout the order and the entire Church and was a remarkable work. It provided the regulations for the teachers and officials of the order and divided education into the broad categories of theology (including dogmatic and moral theology, canon law, ecclesiastical history, and the Scriptures), philosophy, and the so-called *studia inferiora* (the lower departments, such as grammar and rhetoric); much stress was also placed on Latin and Greek in order to facilitate a proficiency in the languages of the Church but also to improve both the mind and faculties of reasoning that resulted from such linguistic mastery. Thomas Aquinas was the chief source for theological training. Despite criticisms of the *Ratio* by some in the nineteenth and twentieth centuries, the system utilized by the Jesuits during the centuries after its introduction made the order one of the most successful in the Church and one of the most theologically orthodox and steadfastly loyal to the Holy See. The *Ratio* ratified in 1599 remained essentially unchanged until 1773 and the suppression of the society.

When the order was reestablished in 1814, it was decided that a reappraisal should be made of the *Ratio* to ensure that it was in keeping with current intellectual life. The resulting *Ratio Studiorum* of 1832, while never fully approved, was published and adopted. The original system was left essentially unchanged, although the *Ratio* did permit greater emphasis on various colleges devoting study to the history, language, etc., of native countries. The order since that time has promoted the adoption of the *Ratio* to modern needs, and a formal system of training is largely limited today to the study of theology and philosophy.

Ratisbon, Conference of ● Meeting held in Ratisbon (modern Regensburg) from April 27 to May 22, 1541. Convened at the behest of Emperor Charles V, it brought together three Catholic and three Protestant theologians. Its aim was to find common ground in the theological controversies of the time and thereby create an environment for possible reunion. The Catholic representatives were Johann Eck, Johann Gropper, and Julius von Pflug; the Protestants in attendance were Martin Bucer, Philipp Melanchthon, and Pistorius. While agreement was reached on a number of subjects, the conference ultimately failed because of the opposition of Martin Luther and the deterioration of the political system in Germany.

Ratramnus (d. 868) ● Benedictine monk and theologian of the monastery of Corbie, France. Little at all is known about Ratramnus except for his writings, particularly his treatise on the Eucharist, *De corpore et sanguine Domine* (*On the Body and Blood of Christ*). Written at the suggestion of Emperor Charles the Bald, the treatise opposed the thinking of Paschasius Radbertus on the Real Presence in the Eucharist. Ratramnus distinguishes between the invisible substance of the true body and blood of Christ and the visible appearance of the Eucharist that seems to remain unchanged from the time before the consecration. Owing possibly to confusion concerning Ratramnus's interpretation of the Eucharist, the work was condemned by the Synod of Vercelli in 1050 and virtually forgotten by the end of the Middle Ages. It was rediscovered in the sixteenth century, however, by Protestant Reformers who argued that Ratramnus called for a symbolic presence in the Eucharist. Despite its use by St. John Fisher in the preface of his work *De veritate corporis et sanguinis Christi in Eucharistia adversus Joh. Oecolampadium* (1527; a treatise against the German reformer Johannes Oecolampadius), intended to defend Catholic orthodoxy, the work was placed on the Index of Forbidden Books in 1559 (removed in 1900). Ratramnus also wrote a defense of St. Augustine's doctrine on predestination and *Contra Graecorum Opposita* (*Against Greek Opposition*), an attack on the Eastern Church.

Raymond Nonnatus, St. (c. 1204-1240) ●

Spanish missionary of the Mercedarians. Born in Catalonia, he supposedly received the name Nonnatus because he was taken from the womb after his mother's death (*non natus*, or not born). Marked at an early age for his piety, he was given permission by his father to enter the Mercedarians in Barcelona, being enrolled personally by St. Peter Nolasco. Named a ransomer by the order, he journeyed to Algiers and secured the release of many slaves. When his money ran out, he surrendered himself as ransom, living for a number of years as a slave and enduring many hardships and cruelties. Causing much consternation to his captors because of his preaching, he was thrown into prison for eight months. To prevent further teaching of the faith, his captors had a red-hot spike driven through his lips and a padlock inserted to close his mouth at the discretion of his masters. Finally ransomed by his order, he returned to Spain in 1239 and was appointed a cardinal by Pope Gregory IX. Summoned to Rome, he died in Cardona, near Barcelona. His name was placed on the Roman Martyrology in 1657 by Pope Alexander VII, and he is considered the patron saint of midwives. Feast day: August 31.

St. Raymond Nonnatus

Raymond of Peñafort, St. (1185-1275) ●

Dominican friar and canonist. Born near Barcelona, he studied and then taught there for around fifteen years. In 1210, he departed the city for Bologna where he finished his studies in canon law; he held a chair at Bologna from 1218-1221, returning to Barcelona at the urging of the bishop there. After serving as a canon, he entered (1222) the Dominican order in

Barcelona. He wrote for the order the *Summa de casibus poentitentiae*, a manual on canon law for confessors that was to have a major influence on the system of penance. After serving as a theologian to Cardinal Abbeville in 1229, Raymond was summoned to Rome by Pope Gregory IX, who named him chaplain and grand penitentiary. The pope also instructed him to collect and reorganize the papal decretals that had been multiplying over the previous years. His brilliant work was promulgated in the bull *Rex Pacificus* (September 5, 1234), and the pontiff declared that only Raymond's collection should be considered official and authoritative. Declining the offer of the archiepiscopal see of Tarragona, Raymond returned to Spain in 1236. Two years later, he was elected general of the Dominicans, reforming the constitution before retiring in 1240. He then worked to convert Muslims and Jews, organizing a school of Arabic and Hebrew studies to assist in this effort. He also suggested to St. Thomas Aquinas that he write the *Summa Contra Gentiles*, to assist theologians and missionaries in the efforts of winning converts from among the non-Christians. Pope Clement VIII canonized him in 1601. Feast day: January 7.

Raymond of Sabunde (d. 1432) ● Also spelled Sebonde, Sabonde, and Sebon. A Spanish philosopher, he was born in Barcelona. He taught philosophy and theology at the University of Toulouse and was the apparent author of several books on theology and philosophy. Only one has survived, the *Liber Naturae sive Creaturarum*, more commonly known as *Theologia Naturalis*. Originally written in Spanish and published in 1484, it was soon translated into French and Latin and enjoyed enormous popularity in the 1500s. A vigorous defense of it was made in 1569 by Michel de Montaigne, but it was placed on the Index of Forbidden Books in 1595. Raymond attempted to synthesize both theology and philosophy, arguing that because humanity is the link between the natural and the supernatural world, it should be possible for human reason to arrive at even the greatest mysteries of revelation.

Recusancy ● Practice found among the English Catholics during and after the reign of Queen Elizabeth I (1558-1603), in which they refused to participate in the services of the Church of England. From the Latin *recusare* (to refuse), the recusants were rarely punished prior to 1570, largely because of uncertainties among the English Catholics as to what they should do with regard to the ceremonies of the C of E. The major event that ended this period was the promulgation of the bull *Regnans in excelsis* (1570) by Pope Pius V, in which Elizabeth was formally anathematized. Henceforth, large numbers of Catholics were recusants, receiving encouragement and support from among the Jesuits who arrived in English towns to bolster the faith in the Protestant lands. Laws were already in place to combat recusancy, having been passed under the Acts of Uniformity of 1549, 1552, and 1559, but these were soon revised to include increasingly harsh penalties against those "Popish Recusants" who were "not repairing to some Church, Chapel or usual places of Common Prayer to hear Divine Service." Some adherents of recusancy were put to death, others were imprisoned, banished, had their lands and properties seized, or were severely fined. Recusants continued to be punished until the end of the eighteenth century, although courts in the 1700s rarely inflicted the most cruel sentences possible. In 1791, during the reign of King George II, the crime of recusancy was officially abolished by the Catholic Relief Acts, although certain disabilities remained that would not be lifted until the twentieth century.

Redemptorists ● Common name for the members of the Congregation of the Most Holy Redeemer. A society of priests founded in Italy on November 9, 1732, by St. Alphonsus Liguori, the Redemptorists were intended by their founder to be a missionary society, devoted to preaching and evangelizing among the poor. After its establishment in Scala, near Amalfi, the order soon spread out and in 1749 received approval from Pope Benedict XIV under the title Congregation of the Most Holy Redeemer, and the next year approval was given for a community of nuns.

Reformation, Catholic ● Also Counter-Reformation. The broad movement of reform within the Catholic Church lasting from the early 1500s until around 1648.

While the term Counter-Reformation is regularly used, it is rejected by many because it implies that Catholic reform was merely a response to the Protestant Reformation. The spirit of genuine Catholic reform existed before the dawn of the Protestant movement. The Church, however, was certainly in need of reform at the start of the early 1500s. It suffered from moral decadence, corruption (including simony, laxity, the peddling of indulgences, obsession with money, and the seeking of temporal gain), the poor example set by the so-called Renaissance popes (Sixtus IV, Alexander VI, Julius II, and Leo X), and the vice displayed by princely bishops. Among priests, celibacy was ignored and severe doctrinal irregularities were commonplace. Exacerbating the situation was the institutionalized nature of the corruption and the close identification of the

Pope St. Pius V

Church in many countries with the crown, thus giving the hierarchy little incentive to promote reform or constructive change.

Calls for reform were made from a number of quarters within the Church, but these proved limited in their effectiveness and reach. Among those who called for steps to be taken were St. Catherine of Siena, Nicholas of Cusa, and Christian humanists such as Erasmus. The papacy made several attempts, although the dissolute nature of the pontificates of the Renaissance popes undermined their viability. Cardinal George d'Amboise, for example, was named by Alexander VI (1492-1503) papal legate to France and charged with improving the religious orders. He was only partially successful. The Fifth Lateran Council, held from 1512-1517, was intended by Julius II and Leo X to bring real change. Unfortunately, disputes among members, the scandalous state of affairs in the Holy See, and the obstinate opposition of many Church leaders rendered it ineffective. Other fleeting reform programs were introduced by Pope Adrian VI (r. 1522-1523) and the disastrous Clement VII (r. 1523-1534).

By the end of Clement's pontificate, the Protestant Reformation was widespread in Europe, but the enormous challenge of Catholic reinvigoration was already being faced by groups of earnest reformers. These included new or reformed orders and formidable, committed Churchmen. The orders were the recently founded Theatines (1524), Barnabites (1530), Somaschi (1533), and Capuchins (1528). By far the greatest of the era's orders would be the Society of Jesus (the Jesuits), launched by St. Ignatius Loyola in 1534. (See **Jesuits**; see also **Ignatius Loyola, St.; Laínez, James**; and **Peter Canisius, St**.) Further progress would be made through the Oratorians, established in 1564 by St. Philip Neri.

The Church itself was finally able to embark on a universal, aggressive reform with the election of Pope Paul III (r. 1534-1549) as successor to Clement. He found in Rome and elsewhere humanists, prelates, and theologians eager to assist him and was thus able to appoint to the College of Cardinals such princes of the Church as Gasparo Contarini, Reginald Pole, Giovanni Caraffa (the future Paul IV), and Jacopo Sadoleto. Paul appointed them to a commission with the task of preparing an agenda of what Paul hoped to be an expansive general council and presenting the report on current abuses in the Church. Their study, called *Consilium delectorum cardinalium et aliorum prelatorum de emendada ecclesia* (Advice of the Appointed Cardinals and other prelates concerning the Reform of the Church), was a blunt and severe indictment of the Curia, the contemporary hierarchy, the clergy, and even the papacy. Paul anticipated many of their suggestions and brought changes in the papal court and Curia, and then used the cardinals to set the tone and direction of his momentous council. This was to be the Council of Trent (1545-1563). (For details, see under **Trent, Council of**.)

Paul III was followed by more aggressive reforming pontiffs, most notably Paul IV (r. 1555-1559), Pius IV (r. 1559-1565), St. Pius V (r. 1566-1572), Gregory XIII (r. 1572-1585), and Sixtus V (r. 1585-1590). The Council of Trent drew to a close under Pius IV, but its work and its profound spirit were carried on in the next decades as the pontiffs implemented its decrees with vigor and with the help of such great saints as Peter Canisius and Charles Borromeo. St. Pius V, for example, revised the Roman Breviary

(1568) and the Roman Missal (1570), published the Roman Catechism (1566), and personally visited the basilicas of Rome to exhort the clergy to adopt the reform. Gregory XIII fostered education and missions, and Sixtus V brought extensive administrative changes in the Curia and the papacy.

The success and sweeping nature of the Catholic Reformation can be seen in a number of ways. There was a flowering of theological writing and thought as seen in the work of Italian and Spanish theologians (Melchior Cano, Dominic Báñez, Dominic Soto, Francisco de Vitoria, and Francisco Suárez). Foreign missions were vastly expanded, thanks in large measure to the Jesuits (see **Francis Xavier, St.**). Spiritual fervor and the vital Christian life flourished through St. Teresa of Ávila, St. Vincent de Paul, St. John of the Cross, St. Catherine of Ricci, St. Ignatius Loyola, and St. Francis de Sales. The religious orders continued to grow and prosper, most notably the Jesuits, Ursulines, and the innovative Discalced Carmelites. Protestantism was effectively halted in parts of Germany, Austria, Poland, Italy, and elsewhere. The lives of the average Catholics were improved in matters of faith, thanks to the broad eradications of abuses, the reenergized clergy, and the reaffirmation of the doctrines of faith. The depth of reform and the passionate responses it inculcated in the hearts and minds of Catholics all over found expression in the triumphant, elaborate, and even ostentatious ornamentation of churches, in paintings, sculpture, and architecture. A few of the gifted artists of the Counter-Reformation were Peter Paul Rubens (1577-1640) in Flanders, El Greco (1541-1614) in Spain, and Giovanni Lorenzo Bernini (1598-1680) as well as Michelangelo Caravaggio (1573-1610) in Italy.

The end of the Catholic Reformation came toward the termination of the Thirty Years' War and the signing of the Treaty of

Westphalia (1648). While Protestantism was now fully recognized and the zeal of the reforming movement faded somewhat from the middle of the seventeenth century, the work of the Council of Trent was complete and the Church blessed with renewed vigor. (See also **Bellarmine, Robert, St.; Cajetan, St.; Campion, Edmund, St.; Charles V; Cochlaeus, Johannes; Eck, Johann; Fisher, John, St.; France; Francis I; Francis Borgia, St.; Germany; Holy Roman Empire; Hosius, Stanislaus; Italy; Jerome Emiliani, St.; Luther, Martin; More, Thomas, St.; Poland; Ratio Studiorum; Reformation, Protestant; Religion, Wars of; Renaissance; Spain;** and **Ximénez de Cisneros, Francisco.**)

Reformation, Protestant ● Religious revolution that took place in the 1500s and 1600s. It shattered the unity of Christianity and had the most far-reaching implications for the political, religious, social, and intellectual life of Europe. The Reformation effectively divided Christians into two large groups, the Catholics (remaining in communion with the Holy See and the Roman Church) and Protestants (members of various Christian bodies that had formed after separation from the universal Church). While the traditional starting date of the Protestant Reformation is placed at October 31, 1517, the day that Martin Luther nailed his ninety-five theses to the door of All Saints Church (the *Schlosskirche*) in Wittenberg, it had its origin in events dating back to the fourteenth century. Among the causes of the reform movement were: the severe decline of authority and prestige of the papacy as a result of the Avignon Papacy (the

Babylonian Captivity), the Great Schism (1378-1417), the flourishing of conciliarism, and the often scandalous pontificates of Sixtus IV, Alexander VI, and Leo X; the spread of heretical movements like the Hussites and Wycliffites; the decay and corruption in some quarters of the Church; the mediocrity and deteriorated condition of Christian theology; and the pervasiveness of humanism and secularism that was fostered by the philosophers and scholars of the Renaissance.

Many in the Church were aware of the crying need for a broad program of reform, but the implementation of genuine revitalization had not been manifestly successful and little had been accomplished. Among the efforts to reform the Church were the convening of the Lateran Council in 1512, the propagation of the movement for spiritual renewal called the *devotio moderna* (modern devotion), that was so exemplified by the Brethren of the Common Life; and the examples of the zealous saints and reformers of the 1300s through 1500s, such as St. Catherine of Siena and Cardinal Ximénez, archbishop of Toledo. There were also the Christian humanists, such as Erasmus and St. Thomas More, who sharply criticized the Church but found a break with Rome

Pope Leo X

unthinkable. All of these attempts, however, proved ineffective, in large measure because of the lack of enthusiasm and interest on the part of the papacy.

Outside of the Church, events were also leading to an anti-Church environment. In the wake of the reduced power of the papacy, many secular states were anxious to increase their independence from the Church. In

France, the Pragmatic Sanction of Bourges (1438) curtailed papal influence, as did the Statute of Provisors and the Statute of Praemunire in England. In Germany, the princes continued to search for a means of breaking the ascendancy of the Holy Roman Emperors and forge for themselves territories free from the influence of both the empire and the hierarchy of the Church. Religious sentiment among all the classes was marked by cynicism and disillusionment through humanism, the depopulation and social chaos caused by the Black Death, and the failings perceived by the faithful on behalf of the local clergy and the Church leadership. Resentments of various kinds and in varying degrees of fervor were thus simmering in whole parts of Christendom, needing only a spark to ignite a wide conflagration. The flame was provided by Luther.

Martin Luther's posting of the ninety-five theses was occasioned by his protest of the crude and corrupt selling of indulgences by the hyperbolic Dominican preacher Johann Tetzel, but his theses also represented his deep-seated convictions that faith was sufficient for justification, that good works for justification were unnecessary, and that the claims of supremacy by the popes was questionable. He would also attack transubstantiation, clerical celibacy, and the religious orders. The theses were soon spread across Germany, their proliferation assisted by the printing press, and a controversy soon erupted. Catholic theologians sharply criticized Luther, who responded by securing the protection and patronage of the elector Frederick the Wise of Saxony and hardening his position. At the public debate held in Leipzig with Johann Eck in 1519, Luther denied the authority of the pope, declaring that Scripture alone was his guide. The next year, he authored important treatises elucidating his theological position, and his defiance brought his excommunication by Pope Leo X (r. 1513-1521) in the bull *Exsurge Domine* (June 1520).

The breach with Rome now having taken place, efforts to heal it, such as the Diet of Worms (1521), failed. Luther sought safety from arrest by going to Wartburg Castle (under Frederick the Wise) where he translated the NT into German. Lutheranism found wide acceptance throughout Germany: monasteries and convents were closed, the Mass was abolished, and anti-Roman Churches were launched. Even more significantly, German princes and cities in Hesse, Saxony, Mansfeld, Pomerania, Brandenburg, and elsewhere rose up, declared for Luther, and severed their ties with Rome. Luther's backing of the princes in the Peasants' War (1524-1525) would be decisive in cementing the commitment of the princes to the Protestant cause and their willingness to utilize a rejection of the Church to further secular control of political and social affairs and to break free of the Holy Roman Empire.

Tensions mounted within the empire, and the Holy Roman Emperor Charles V undertook a genuine effort to secure a peaceful resolution. These included the Diets of Speyer (1526 and 1529, the latter assembly helping to coin the name Protestants), the Diet of Augsburg (1530), and the Diet of Ratisbon (1541). The failure of these led to the outbreak of fighting between the empire and the German princes who had organized themselves into the Schmalkaldic League. A provisional religious settlement was reached in 1548 with the Interim of Augsburg, accepted by the Diet of Augsburg (1548). This was replaced in 1555 by the Peace of Augsburg with its establishment of the governing principle *"Cuius regio eius religio"* (literally, "In a prince's country, a prince's religion"; in other words, "The religion of the prince determines the religion of the region"). The peace made formal the religious division of Germany and the recognition of Lutheranism, an event abhorrent to many in the Church.

Lutheranism was also adopted in other

parts of Europe, most notably in Scandinavia. It was advanced by King Christian III of Denmark and Norway in 1536, bringing with it the relentless extirpation of the Church. Similar events occurred in Sweden where Lutheranism became synonymous with the independence movement. The Swedish Lutheran Church thus developed as the state religion and was different in its orientation from the rest of Scandinavia.

Protestantism, meanwhile, was to undergo its own divisions, as embodied in the doctrines of Huldrych Zwingli (1484-1531) and John Calvin (1509-1564) as well as the Anabaptists. Zwingli based his ideas on Lutheranism, but he differed with Luther on a number of doctrinal points. The differences in the movement compelled Protestant leaders to debate their theology at the Colloquy of Marburg (1529), but Luther and Philipp Melanchthon could not reach agreement with Zwingli and Johannes Oecolampadius. Henceforth, Protestant unity itself would be impossible. Zwingli differed with Luther most significantly on the doctrine of the Eucharist, arguing only a symbolic presence by Christ. His teaching was embraced in Zurich, Switzerland, spreading over much of Swiss territory and southwestern Germany. Zwingli was killed in 1531 in a battle with Catholic Swiss cantons, and the intellectual heart of Protestantism moved from Zurich to Geneva where the foremost theologian of the Reformation, John Calvin, had emerged.

The influence of Calvin, especially through his famous treatise *The Institutes of Christian Religion* was enormous. His systematic theology was more developed than that of either Zwingli or Luther and was centered on the idea of predestination for the elect; he accepted only baptism and the Eucharist, postulating a spiritual presence of Christ in the sacrament. His moral ascendancy was total in Geneva, forming a rigid theocracy in the city that would endure even after his

death. Elsewhere, Calvinist doctrine inflamed Protestants in France, the Netherlands, and England. In France the rapid proliferation of reforming ideas precipitated the bloody Wars of Religion (1562-1598) that would rip the country apart and lead to the Edict of Nantes (1598). Calvinism also shaped the direction of Protestantism in Scotland (with John Knox). (See also **England** and **Scotland**.)

The resolution of the religious question through the Peace of Augsburg did not bring lasting peace to Europe. Religious and political struggles would continue into the seventeenth century and would cause the enormously destructive Thirty Years' War (1618-1648). This conflict was ended by the Treaty of Westphalia (1648), which signaled the end of the Protestant Reformation. The effects of this vast movement, however, were felt in every facet of European life. Christian unity was irretrievably shattered, the state amassed greater power and authority, the religious outlook in whole parts of the West was forever changed, long periods of harsh intolerance and bigotry were initiated, and the political structure in Germany and the Holy Roman Empire was altered. For the Catholic Church, while the Reformation brought incalculable sorrow, it also spurred the faith to continue the Catholic (or Counter) Reformation and to embark on an aggressive defensive posture that would endure into the modern era. (See also **Albert of Brandenburg**; Augsburg Confession under **Augsburg, Diet of; Cajetan, St.; Charles V; Clement VII; Cochlaeus, Johannes; Contarini, Gasparo; Eck, Johann; Hus, Jan; Leo X; Miltitz, Carl von; Paul III; St. Bartholomew's Day Massacre; Sadoleto, Jacopo; Worms, Diet of;** and **Wycliffe, John**.)

Regimini Ecclesiae Universae ●
Constitution published on August 18, 1967, by Pope Paul VI and taking formal effect in March 1968. Its aim was to reorganize the Roman Curia. Meaning in English "Guides of

the Universal Church," the constitution was the result of a four-year study begun in 1963 to examine potential reorganization of the Curia. It served also as the basis of the modification in curial organization undertaken by Pope John Paul II that was ordered in the apostolic constitution *Pastor Bonus*, published on June 28, 1988, and taking effect on March 1, 1989.

Regimini Militantis Ecclesiae ● Bull issued on September 27, 1540, by Pope Paul III. It gave formal approval to the Jesuit order. Meaning "Guides of the Militant Church," the bull recognized the organization and rule of what it called the Society of Jesus, stating its concerns to be preaching and strengthening the faith by educational and confessional work. The society was to enjoy special protection from the popes but was to be obedient to the papacy as well as to the rule and the superior. (See **Jesuits** for other details.)

Regina Coeli ● Latin for "Queen of Heaven." Given to the BVM, *Regina Coeli* is also the opening to an antiphon to the Virgin Mary that is sung or chanted during the Easter season. It is recited in the Divine Office (or Liturgy of the Hours), after Compline, from Holy Thursday to the Saturday that follows Pentecost Sunday. It is also used instead of the Angelus during Eastertide, and is to be recited standing, at the three prescribed times, 6:00 A.M., noon, and 6:00 P.M. The author of the *Regina Coeli* is unknown, although legend attributes it to Pope St. Gregory the Great (r. 590-604). The pontiff was said to have heard the angels singing it; he supposedly added the versicle, or lost line. Scholars generally agree that the hymn probably dates from the twelfth century. It was first used by the Franciscans in their Office, after Compline. The popularity of the *Regina Coeli* increased as a result of the decision of Pope Nicholas III (r. 1277-1280) to replace the Office books used in the churches of Rome with ones based on the Office of the Franciscan Order.

Reginald of Piperno (d. c. 1290) ● Dominican theologian, best known as the devoted companion and assistant of St. Thomas Aquinas. A native of Piperno, Italy, he entered the Dominicans in Naples. Around 1259, he was chosen by Thomas to serve as his assistant and confessor in Rome, remaining the Angelic Doctor's faithful companion and friend until Thomas's death in 1274. Thomas dedicated several works to him and cured him of a fever through prayer. In 1272, Reginald taught with Thomas at Naples and, two years later, was at the saint's deathbed, hearing his friend's final confession. Two years later, he delivered the final oration for Thomas. Returning to Naples, he served as successor to Thomas in the Dominican school and was subsequently an important source of testimony in the process of Thomas's canonization. He collected all of the saint's writings and recorded four *opuscula*, or lectures by Thomas, including the lectures on St. John and the Epistles of St. Paul. Reginald is also considered by some scholars to have been responsible for compiling the supplement to the *Tertia Pars* (or *Third Part* of the *Summa Theologica*), although other scholars prefer to attribute the work to Peter of Auvergne or Henry of Gorkum.

Regnans in Excelsis ● Bull issued on February 25, 1570, by Pope St. Pius V declaring Queen Elizabeth to be formally excommunicated. The bull pronounced the English ruler to be a heretic and a usurper, thereby absolving her subjects of any obligation to obey her or the laws she might promulgate. It was issued after a trial was held at Rome in which it was determined that she was a heretic, based upon the testimony of a number of English Catholic exiles. *Regnans in Excelsis* was a recognition that

England was irretrievably lost to the Catholic faith.

Regulae Juris ● Latin for "rules of law." The name was given to a set of general principles or maxims, ninety-nine in number, that were collected into the *Corpus Juris Canonici* over a period of time in the 1200s. The axioms were of considerable importance in formulating subsequent canon law, although there has been serious question as to whether the *Regulae Juris* was ever officially accepted as law. Eleven rules were inserted by Pope Gregory IX (r. 1227-1241) at the end of the fifth book of *Decretals* (the *Decretals of Pope Gregory IX* that had been compiled by Reginald of Peñafort and published in 1234). Eighty-eight were added by Pope Boniface VIII (r. 1294-1303) at the end of the *Liber Sextus Decretalium*. Generally, the maxims are applicable to all legal matters or are concerned with specific legal points such as trials or benefices. Whether accepted as law or not, the *Regulae Juris* are of such a remarkable nature and display such wisdom that their study and application were inevitable and desirable. The German canonist Johann Reiffenstuel (1642-1703) held them in high regard, even commending canonists to memorize them. Among the *regulae* are: "What concerns all must be approved by all" (Rule 29); "One in silence seems to give assent" (Rule 43); "The crimes of the individual must not be held against the Church" (Rule 76); "No one can be held to the impossible" (Rule 6); "What is not allowed the defendant, is to be denied to the plaintiff" (Rule 32); and "The truth must not be hidden simply to avoid a scandal" (Rule 3). (See also **Canon Law**.)

Reiffenstuel, Johann Georg (1642-1703) ● German canonist and theologian. Considered one of the foremost experts on canon law in Church history, he was born in Kaltenbrunn and entered the Reformed Franciscans of Bavaria in November 1658,

taking the name Anacletus. He taught theology at Freising (1665), Landshut (1667-1668), and Munich (1671-1680). From 1683, he taught at Freising, also organizing the episcopal library at the request of the bishop of Freising, who had appointed him (1692) director of diocesan education. Aside from his canonical work, Reiffenstuel authored the *Theologia Moralis* (1692) on moral theology. He is best known, however, for his writings on canon law, most notably the *Jus Canonicum universum* (1700; *Universal Canonical Law*), a superb study that went through numerous editions and is still considered one of the best works on the subject; some editions also contained the *Tractatus de regulis juris* (first published in 1733). (See also **Regulae Juris**.)

Reims, Synods of ● A large number of synods convened in the city of Reims. The first was held sometime between 624 and 630 and is considered the same as that referred to having been held at Clichy around 626. Notable synods included: 873, presided over by Archbishop Wilfer, which introduced reforms; 1049, presided over by Pope St. Leo IX, another reforming council; 1119, which accepted peace between Pope Callistus II and Emperor Henry IV; 1164, convened by Pope Alexander III to promote a crusade against Emperor Frederick I Barbarossa; 1528, to condemn Luther; and 1564, to implement the decrees of the Council of Trent. Other synods were held in 991, 1115, 1148, 1407, 1583, 1849, 1853, and 1857.

Relics ● Remains of saints or sacred objects — cloth or other items — that were once in contact with the saints' bodies. The Church recognizes three classes of relics. The first is an actual part of the saint's body. The most revered type of relic, it is to be given particular veneration. Relics of martyrs are often placed in the altar stone at the consecration of an altar in a church. The second class of relic is an item actually worn or used by a saint during his or her lifetime. The third class is an item that has merely been touched to a first-class item. Most often, third-class relics are cloth.

Relics became important at an early date in the history of the Church, stemming from the veneration of martyrs. The earliest evidence of a relic is provided in the *Martyrium Polycarpi*, which, in the second century, described the bones of St. Polycarp as being like precious stones. The cult of relics then spread in the Eastern and Western Churches. In the East, however, the veneration of relics was overshadowed to some degree by the veneration of icons. Formal approval was given by the Second Council of Nicaea in 787, which condemned all people who hated relics, and by the Council of Constantinople in 1084.

Owing to the crusades with their concomitant religious fervor, the number of relics increased enormously from the eleventh through twelfth centuries, as supposedly sacred relics were brought to Europe from the Holy Land. Many of these were quite remarkable, being placed in magnificent reliquaries. Others, however, were of dubious authenticity, sold by unscrupulous individuals to prey upon the sincere devotion of gullible Christians. Such an activity as selling a relic is of course forbidden by Church law, punishable by excommunication. Abuses in the selling and distribution of relics was an unfortunate propaganda device used by the Reformers to point to supposedly superstitious practices by the Church, proving a useful device for King Henry VIII of England (r. 1509-1547) in his suppression of the monasteries. Current canon law (c. 1190) deals with the veneration and proper care of relics. Powerful relics include the True Cross, the Holy Grail, the so-called Holy Lance, and the relics of Santiago de Compostela.

From the time of the first visits to the catacombs by members of the early Church, relics have been venerated by large groups of the faithful who most routinely undertake pilgrimages to where the relics are to be found, such as Santiago de Compostela.

Relief Acts, Catholic ● Also Catholic Emancipation Acts. A series of laws that gave religious freedoms of varying degrees to the Catholics of England and Ireland, they were first passed in 1778. The acts reversed over two centuries of often severe anti-Catholic laws that limited or forbade completely Catholic worship and the holding by Catholics of any position of authority in the government, the military, or law. By the first act of 1778, Catholics were allowed to own property after taking an oath of loyalty and operators of schools could live without fear of imprisonment if caught. The reaction in many circles of English life was harsh, erupting violently in the Gordon Riots, in which Catholic homes were burned and looted. Further relief came in 1791 when it was declared that Catholics were no longer to be persecuted under the Act of Supremacy and the Statutes of Recusancy. Catholic worship was officially tolerated and some Catholics were, albeit grudgingly, permitted to receive posts in the armed forces. Two years later (1793), freedoms were given to Irish Catholics; they were granted admission, for example, to the universities.

The most important of the Relief Acts came in 1829 with the Roman Catholic Relief Acts, passed under the forceful leadership of Arthur Wellesley, duke of Wellington (of Waterloo fame), who served as prime minister from 1828-1830 and had previously been an opponent of Catholic Emancipation. By this bill, the broad prohibitions in English society were removed. Henceforth, they were no longer legally barred from holding positions in the government, law, or other professions where crippling disabilities had been present. Certain stipulations did remain, however, such as the refusal of the state to accept the validity of marriages performed by the

Catholic Church. In 1926, these last disabilities were lifted by the government, although Catholics still suffered from anti-Catholicism and bigotry. Unchanged, of course, was the law demanding that the king or queen of England be of the Church of England, in keeping with the monarch's position as head of the C of E. Other important officeholders forbidden from being Catholic are the lord chancellor, keeper of the great seal, and any regent.

Religion, Wars of ● Series of often bloody civil wars fought in France from 1562-1598. The struggle was characterized by fighting between Catholics and Protestants (Huguenots) but were complicated by political machinations and intrigue between the crown and the powerful nobles of the country that were routinely motivated by concerns only superficially connected with the faith. Throughout, both sides engaged in cruel treatment of the enemy and routine massacres of helpless civilians.

The first war began in 1562 and was the result mainly of the spread of Protestantism in France and the alarm of Catholic leaders, particularly the House of Guise, which was to assume a major leadership position in the Catholic cause. It ended the next year with the Protestants in a position of advantage. Two more wars soon followed, from 1567-1568 and 1568-1570. A fourth war, from 1572-1573, was launched by the infamous St. Bartholomew's Day Massacre. It was followed by another conflict, from 1574-1576, ending in the Edict of Beaulieu, proclaiming freedom of worship in France.

Attempting to unite against the Protestants, the Catholics formed the so-called League, precipitating another struggle in 1577. More fighting occurred in 1580 and 1585 — the War of the Three Henrys — a political and religious dispute over the succession involving King Henry III, Henry of Navarre (later King Henry IV), and Henry of Guise. Henry of Navarre's accession

in 1589 prompted the League to ally itself with Spain. Henry defeated the alliance and entered Paris in 1594. He then negotiated peace with Spain in the Treaty of Vervins and issued the Edict of Nantes (1598), thereby finally bringing peace to France. Much of Europe, however, would soon be engulfed in a similarly bitter conflict, the Thirty Years' War (1618-1648). (See also **France**.)

Reliquaries ● Containers or repositories for keeping and displaying relics. From the earliest times of the Church when relics were first venerated, reliquaries to keep the remains of saints or other sacred objects safe from harm were probably created. Unfortunately, little information has survived on how such containers were built, and even their names are general or broad (*capsa, capsella, arca*, etc.), with perhaps little differentiation from the *arcae* used for holy oil and the Eucharist. Reliquaries developed rapidly in the Western Church, both in keeping with the proliferation of relics and as an ornate cultural expression of devotion. This was particularly true during the Middle Ages, from which period a very large number of reliquaries have been dated. Many reliquaries were made of solid gold or silver, were decorated with precious gems, and often took a form to symbolize the relic for which the reliquaries were created, such as a hand, an arm, or a head. Among the most remarkable are the shrine of the Three Kings in the treasury of Cologne Cathedral; the Ursula Shrine at Bruges, with superb decorations by the painter Hans Memling (c. 1430-1494); the reliquaries of Sts. Peter and Paul in the Lateran; and the one containing a piece of the True Cross found in the cathedral in Limburg, Germany. (See also **Relics**.)

Remigius, St. (c. 438-533) ● Also Remi. The Apostle of the Franks, noted for his baptism of King Clovis I of the Franks and for converting the Frankish people, he was the son of Emile, count of Laon. He studied at Reims and was so renowned for his intelligence and holiness that he was appointed archbishop of Reims at the age of twenty-two. He thereafter devoted himself to the spread of Christianity in Gaul (Roman France), establishing sees at Tournai, Laon, Arras, Therouanne, and Cambrai. On excellent terms with Clovis, he brought the ruler into the faith, traditionally baptizing him in Reims on December 24, 498, in the presence of most of the Frankish army. Feast day: October 1.

Remigius of Auxerre (d. c. 908) ●

Benedictine monk, theologian, and commentator. A student of Heiric at the monastic school of St. Germain, Auxerre, Remigius subsequently taught at St. Germain, Paris, and Reims. He authored commentaries on the Bible, on *De Consolatione Philosophiae* by Boethius, and on Martianus Capella. He also wrote on theology. His commentaries and glosses were much read during the Middle Ages and were influential in the development of the seven liberal arts in the Christian setting of the medieval university.

Cosimo de' Medici, one of the great patrons of the Renaissance

Renaissance ● Period of

history in Europe stretching from approximately the 1300s until the 1500s. One of the most significant eras in the history of the West, the Renaissance is considered a major transition from the medieval epoch to the modern world. The Renaissance can be characterized by a flowering or rebirth in cultural and intellectual pursuits, but it also brought extensive development in economic, political, and scientific life. It had, as well, a profound impact upon religious life, the ultimate effects of which are still felt in the Church. In the short term, the Renaissance produced humanist tendencies, a de-emphasizing of religion in the activities of the Renaissance man, and the creation of the atmosphere in northern Europe that would foster the Protestant Reformation.

Rerum Novarum ● Encyclical "On Capital and Labor" issued by Pope Leo XIII on May 15, 1891, which presented the Church's teachings on social justice and morality as pertaining to capitalism and labor. Written in the face of severe poverty and economic injustice, *Rerum novarum* called for all people to return to the Church and its message, declaring the Church to be important in reminding the social classes of their duties to one another and to the precepts of justice. Pope Leo defended the rights of private property, but he noted that such ownership could be rescinded when necessitated by the common good. The right to own land should be possible for workers, but it could be feasible only when workers enjoy certain rights — such as the formation of labor unions — and receive decent wages. The encyclical further declared that the foremost duties of the heads of state "should be to make sure that the laws and institutions, the general character and administration of the commonwealth, shall be such as to produce of themselves public well-being and private prosperity." *Rerum novarum* is considered the foundation of the so-called social justice movement in the Church, marking the Church's involvement in relevant and pressing social issues. On the fortieth anniversary of *Rerum novarum* Pope Pius XI published the encyclical *Quadragesimo anno* (May 15, 1931), another important social encyclical. (See also **Centesimus Annus**.)

Restitution, Edict of ● Declaration made by the Holy Roman Emperor Ferdinand II on March 6, 1629. It attempted to restore to the Church the property that had been seized from it in Germany by the Protestants during the Reformation. The edict had been issued as the result of recent military victories during the Thirty Years' War (1618-1648), including the compelling of the Protestant leader Christian IV of Denmark to agree to the Treaty of Lübeck (1629). The Protestant princes, however, refused to restore any Church lands and bloody fighting commenced once more. (See **Thirty Years' War** for other details.)

Retz, Jean François Paul de Gondi de (1613-1679) ● Cardinal and archbishop of Paris. A leader of the French noble rebellion called the Fronde from 1648-1653, he was born in Montmirail to a noble family. He was chosen early for a career in the Church, studying under the Jesuits and then at the Sorbonne. Named in 1643 to be coadjutor to the archbishop of Paris (who happened to be his uncle), Jean François de Gondi, he was ordained a priest and thereafter embarked on a virtually political career. He joined the Fronde, a rebellion of French aristocrats against Cardinal Mazarin and Anne of Austria, regent for King Louis XIV, shifting his allegiance through intrigue. For example, he accepted the arrest of the prince of Condé in 1650 but then changed his position and worked to secure the prince's release and the exile in 1651 of Mazarin. Reconciled with the royal court, he was nominated for the cardinalate, a nomination approved by Pope Innocent X in 1652. Mazarin, meanwhile, had returned and Retz was imprisoned. When his uncle died in 1654, Retz used a

proxy to secure the archiepiscopal see of Paris, escaping from prison in August 1654 and working to gain the see from exile. He traveled to Spain and then Rome, participating in the conclave that elected Alexander VII. Finally returning home in 1662 after Mazarin's death, he was again reconciled with the king, resigning his see in return for the Abbey of St. Denis. Over his remaining years, he took part in the conclaves that elected Clement IX (1667), Clement X (1670), and Innocent XI (1676). His *Memoirs*, written in retirement, are considered a classic of French literature.

Reuchlin, Johannes (1455-1522) ● German humanist and classical scholar. A native of Pforzheim, he studied Greek and Latin at Freiburg, Paris, and Basel, studying law at Orléans and receiving his licentiate of law from Poitiers in 1481. The next year he accompanied Duke Eberhard of Württemberg on a visit to Italy, serving as his translator. While in Florence, he entered into an association with the Platonic Academy. He returned to Italy in 1490 and in the meanwhile had begun (1485) mastering Hebrew. In 1496, Reuchlin fled from the service of the counts of Württemberg to Heidelberg owing to the hostility of Eberhard's successor, Eberhard VI. He served for a time as an adviser to the elector, and in 1498 returned to Italy. There, with the help of a group of Jewish intellectuals, he perfected his Hebrew, subsequently contributing a number of important books on the language. After Eberhard VI's deposition, he returned to Stuttgart and subsequently served as an imperial judge of the Swabian Confederacy (1502-1512) and a professor at Ingolstadt (1520-1521) and Tübingen (1521-1522).

His extensive writings marked him as one of the leading scholars of his era. Among his chief works on Hebrew was the important grammar and lexicon manual *De Rudimentis Hebraicis* (1506; *On the Fundamentals of*

Hebrew). He promoted the study of the OT, undertook an examination of Cabalistic teachings (which he attempted to reconcile with Platonism) in several works, including *De Verbo Mirifico* (1494) and *De Arte Cabalistica* (1517), and saved Hebrew literary works from being burned. This latter effort brought Reuchlin into sharp conflict with the Jewish convert Johann Pfefferkorn and the Dominicans of Cologne. Reuchlin believed that Jewish writings should not be burned because of their value to scholars. He authored a satire *Epistolae Obscurorum Virorum* (1515-1517; "Letters of the Obscure Men"), a demonstration of the opposition of humanists to the Scholastics. Initially acquitted of heresy in 1516, he was condemned in 1520 by Pope Leo X. His ideas and writings were much used by the early Reformers, but Reuchlin remained steadfast in his devotion to the Church, repudiating both Martin Luther and his grandnephew Philipp Melanchthon; he attempted to alienate Melanchthon from Luther's influence.

Revelation, Book of ● Final book of the NT, which is also known as the Apocalypse. One of the most vivid and eloquently poetic books of the NT, the Book of Revelation was probably written during the reign of Emperor Domitian (r. 81-96), who was responsible for the persecution of the Church and was considered a second Nero, the infamous emperor (r. 54-68) who had launched the first real oppression of Christians. It was composed on the Island of Patmos by an author named John whose identity has been the source of considerable study and speculation by scholars. Custom has it that John was St. John the Evangelist, this claim apparently supported by similarities in the use of such phrases as "the Lamb" in Revelation (5:6) and "the Lamb of God" in the Gospel of St. John (1:29). Experts, however, have noted the differences in style and Greek spellings as well as other internal indications, and have concluded that authorship by St. John is unlikely. If John, then, was not the Evangelist, he was most likely an educated Christian from Asia Minor who had, apparently, been exiled to Patmos by Roman officials under Domitian.

Revelation is divided into two parts, a preface of pastoral letters to seven cities in Asia Minor comprising the first three chapters and then the very demanding visions taking up the remaining nineteen chapters. The letters are sent to the Seven Churches in Asia Minor — Ephesus, Smyrna, Pergamum, Thyatira, Sardis, Philadelphia, and Laodicea — and are intended to be read to the entire congregation of each place. They are both positive and admonishing, as with the letter to the Church of Pergamum (2:12-17) in which the Christians are praised for keeping the faith but warned that some have drifted.

Chapters 4-22 present an unrelenting set of prophetic visions, describing the travails and suffering to be visited upon the faithful, culminating with the descent of a "new heaven and new earth; . . . And I saw the holy city, new Jerusalem, coming down out of the heaven from God, prepared as a bride adorned for her husband. . ." (21:1-2). Recurring throughout is potent symbolism, such as the breaking of the seven seals, the sounding of the seven trumpets announcing seven disasters, the seven plagues, and the seven bowls. Rich apocalyptic events ensue, including the woman who is crowned with twelve stars and brings forth a child, "one who is to rule all the nations with a rod of iron" (12:5); the beasts from the sea and the earth; and the city of Babylon, understood by the description of seven hills to mean Rome. The number of the Beast whom all are forced to worship, 666, is generally understood to refer to Emperor Nero whose name, when given Hebrew numerical equivalents for each letter, adds to 666. Babylon, of course, is destroyed and evil is vanquished.

Ricci, Matteo (1552-1610) ● Italian Jesuit and founder of the Catholic missions in China. He was born at Macerata, Italy, in the Papal States, studying in his native town and Rome before entering the Society of Jesus on August 15, 1571, at the Roman College. Aside from his studies in theology and philosophy, Ricci also undertook an extensive program in astronomy, science, and mathematics, fields of interest that would be of the utmost importance in his later work in China. Requesting to be sent to the Asia missions, Ricci received permission from his superiors, setting sail from Lisbon on March 24, 1578. He arrived in Goa (a former Portuguese colony) in September where he spent several years teaching. In 1582, he was summoned to Macao and there told to begin preparations for missionary labors in China. He mastered Chinese, specifically Mandarin, and in September 1583 set out for Chao-K'ing, the local capital of the province of Canton, with Father Michel de Ruggieri.

The priests wisely adopted a subtle program of introducing themselves to the Chinese, refraining from any actions that might give insult to their hosts and remaining ever mindful of the rich and proud culture they were attempting to evangelize. Ricci found that an excellent way to ingratiate himself and, at the same time, secure the trust and interest of the Chinese was to engage them in scientific discourse. He would provide them with maps of the world and soon introduced the first elements of the faith. Much progress had been made by 1589, but that year a local official evicted Ricci and his assistant, a young priest. Father Ruggieri had returned to Europe; he would die there in 1607. Ricci traveled to other cities in Canton, reaching Nanking in 1595 where he was initially unsuccessful in establishing himself. Returning in 1599, he finally won acceptance from the local mandarins (public officials) and the following year set out for Beijing. There he was received by the emperor in 1601. Ricci remained in the capital until his death, repeating his successful program for winning the respect of the Chinese by impressing them with his scientific knowledge before promoting Christian doctrine, especially as he found that his hosts normally advanced to that important matter on their own.

The methods used by Ricci to attract converts involved, however, many innovations that would subsequently be the cause of considerable controversy, namely his free adoption of the Chinese lifestyle and the adaptation of certain practices, such as the use of Chinese terms for heaven (*T'ien*) and Heavenly Lord (*Shang-ti*) to describe the True God, and ancestor worship or veneration. Ricci himself used the phrase *T'ien-chu* (Lord of Heaven) finding it, as well as *Shang-ti* and *T'ien*, to be an acceptable title that approximated the cultural understanding of the Supreme God. After Ricci's death, the controversy surrounding such Chinese rites would prompt Pope Clement XI (r. 1700-1721) to issue judgments against them in 1704 and 1715. Ricci's contribution was nevertheless immense. He sensitized missionaries to China to their customs and culture, advanced a Western understanding of Chinese life, and authored several important works. Chief among these was *The True Doctrine of God* (1595) in Chinese, describing his missionary activities; he also composed a Chinese Catechism, which became the standard for missionaries and a Chinese translation of the Ten Commandments.

Richard of Middleton (fl. late 1200s) ● Also Ricardus of Media Villa or Richard of Middletown, a Franciscan theologian. Little is known about his life, and scholars are uncertain as to his place of birth. Some argue in favor of Middleton in Oxfordshire or Middleton in Northamptonshire; others prefer France or even Scotland. After possibly studying at Oxford, he most likely attended the University of Paris, receiving in 1283 a bachelor's degree in theology. Having entered the Franciscans, he was appointed by the general to the committee that was charged with examining the writings of Pierre Olivi. The date and circumstances of his death are unknown. His writings include a commentary on the *Sentences* of Peter Lombard (c. 1281 and 1285), *Quaestiones Quodlibetales*, and *Quaestiones Disputates*. He was remarkable for his willingness to support the theological system of St. Thomas Aquinas against Augustinianism, an acceptance quite contrary to traditional Franciscan teachings. He also studied hypnotism, mentioning it in his *Quodlibeta*. A number of other works have been attributed to him.

Richard of St. Victor (d. 1173) ●
Scottish-born mystical theologian. He entered the monastery of St. Victor and was professed under the first abbot, Gilduin. There he studied under the great scholastic theologian Hugh of St. Victor, subsequently becoming prior in 1162. His tenure as prior was noteworthy for the upheaval at St. Victor caused by the improper conduct of the abbot Ervisius, who earned a censure from Pope Alexander III; Richard received a letter from the pontiff to the community and its prior. Chief among his writings was the treatise *De Trinitate*, in six books, although much attention is paid to his contributions to mystical theology. His two most important works on mystical contemplation were the *Benjamin maior* and the *Benjamin minor*, in which he detailed the stages of divine contemplation. The stages were divided among the powers of the soul: imagination, reason, and intuition or intelligence. As it ascends toward God, the soul undergoes the final stages before coming into the Divine Presence, the names given to them being *dilatio* (delay), *sublevatio* (lightening), and *alienatio* (separation). Richard also stressed the utilization of speculative reasoning and

Cardinal Richelieu

secular knowledge in the process of spiritual development. His writings also extended into exegesis. Richard had considerable influence upon medieval mysticism, particularly St. Bonaventure and Jean Gerson. He is ranked by Dante as one of the greatest teachers in the history of the Church.

Richelieu, Armand Jean du Plessis de (1585-1642) ● French cardinal and chief minister to King Louis XIII. One of the most able and ruthless political figures of the seventeenth century, he was born in Paris to a noble family. He was originally intended to pursue a military career, but in 1605 his brother Alfred stepped down as bishop of Luçon to enter the Grande Chartreuse, and young Armand Jean was named in his place by King Henry IV. After studying under Bishop Cospéan of Aire, he was ordained and consecrated bishop in Rome on April 17, 1607. As bishop of Luçon, he distinguished himself by his efforts to convert Protestants and his zeal in promoting reform through the appointment of the Capuchins and

Oratorians as preachers. In 1614, he was named to the Estates General to represent the clergy of Poitou. While there, he called for the Church to be exempt from taxation, the punishment of Protestants who usurped church, the promulgation of the decrees of the Council of Trent in France, and the summoning of prelates to the royal council. Having won the confidence of both Marie de' Medici, the queen mother, and Louis XIII, he was appointed secretary of state on November 30, 1616. The assassination of his patron, the courtier Concini, led to Richelieu's dismissal. He retired to the priory of Coussay in June 1617 and was then exiled to Avignon in 1618. While in this state of casual disgrace, he wrote a defense of the Catholic faith against the Huguenots (1617) and the *Instruction du chrétien* (1619), a catechism that was to enjoy enormous popularity.

Finally recalled in 1619, he was successful in negotiating a reconciliation between the king and his mother (1620). On November 3, 1622, by a brief issued by Pope Gregory XV, he became cardinal. On April 16, 1624, he once more became a member of the council of ministers; on August 12, 1624, he was made its president. Assuming increasing political power, by 1628 he was master of France with the title chief minister, running the entire government. He pursued two broad policies: the unification of France and opposition wherever possible to the power of the Spanish Habsburg Empire in Europe. These positions required considerable pragmatism and diplomatic skills, for in France he opposed the Huguenots whom he considered a dangerous political threat, but, elsewhere, he allied himself with the German Protestant princes then fighting the Thirty Years' War (1618-1648) against the empire. He curbed conspiracies in the court by putting to death several prominent enemies, and through the capitulation of the Huguenot stronghold La Rochelle and the harsh Peace of Alais (June 1629) he smashed the Huguenots and

efficiently extirpated Protestant political ambitions. His foreign policy — giving aid to the Protestants, most notably Gustavus Adolphus, king of Sweden — not only hurt the imperial cause but severely impeded papal hopes of restoring the Church in German lands and elevated France as a European power.

While an enemy toward Jansenism (he expelled the solitaires from Port-Royal-des-Champs), he acted with cool independence from the Holy See, humiliating Pope Urban VIII in 1636 by neglecting to participate in a Catholic conference in Cologne sponsored by the pope. Earlier in 1624, he had seized the strategically important Alpine Valley of Valtelina from a papal peace-keeping force. Worse yet, the cardinal upheld Gallican principles concerning the taxation of the French Church. Interestingly, Richelieu was ever advising the king only to appoint qualified and suitable bishops and, from 1629, as abbot of Cluny, he launched a reform of the Benedictine order. A patron of the arts and sciences, he founded in 1635 the Academie Française. A complex ecclesiast and statesman, he used both his spiritual and political authority to aid the state, leaving France a legacy of monarchical absolutism and a leading place in the affairs of Europe.

Rienzi, Cola di (1313-1354) ● Also called Rienzo, he was a tribune of the Romans who became master of the Eternal City through his promise to restore Rome to its lost greatness. The son of a Roman shopkeeper, he was born in Rome, leaving the city around 1323 to live in Anagni with his uncle. In 1333, he returned to the city where he became a notary. Sent to Avignon in 1343 as a representative to Pope Clement VI of the party of Rome that had managed to acquire political power, he was appointed by Pope Clement to the office of papal notary. Returning to Rome in 1344, he began plotting a major conspiracy to seize control.

Backed by the Romans, he assumed the title of tribune and broad dictatorial powers in 1347. While unhappy about not being consulted, Clement accepted the development. Having driven many of the nobles out of the city, Rienzi instituted reforms in taxes and justice. He soon conceived a far-reaching plan to unite all of Italy and thereby alienated many who had tolerated his increasingly grandiose lifestyle. The papal legate convinced the nobles of Rome to reclaim their lost supremacy. They marched on the city in November 1347 and were repulsed with considerable losses. The populace, however, had lost its faith in him and, coupled with a papal bull denouncing him, the nobles attacked once more, this time toppling him. After spending two years in the safety of the Spiritual Franciscans in Abruzzi, he journeyed to Prague in 1350 to meet with Emperor Charles IV. After several wild prophecies, he was thrown into prison for two years, being released in 1352 by Pope Clement after an appeal was made by Petrarch for mercy. When, in 1353, the new pope, Innocent VI, decided to send Cardinal Gil Albornoz to Italy, he permitted Rienzi to accompany him. The Romans, again tired of political anarchy, welcomed him back with triumph on August 1, 1354. His new reign was to prove brief. Harsh taxes, ill-advised executions, and the inveterate hatred of the Roman aristocracy, most notably the House of Colonna, caused a riot on October 8, 1354. After failing to quiet the mob, he tried to flee, was discovered, and murdered. His body was dragged through the streets and left for two days on the Piazza San Marcello before being burned.

Ripalda, Juan Martínez de (1594-1648)
● Spanish Jesuit theologian. Born in Pamplona, he joined the Society of Jesus in 1609 and then taught philosophy at Salamanca and moral theology at the Imperial College of Madrid. Ranked as one of the foremost theologians of his era, he was the author of a number of notable works. Chief among them is *De Ente Supernaturali*, a treatise of supernatural topics that is a classic in the field; published in three volumes, it included an attack on Michel Baius in the third volume. The dates of the volumes are 1634, 1645, and 1648.

Risorgimento ● Italian for "resurgence" or "revival." Movement (c. 1815-1870) that brought about Italian unification and resulted in the loss of the Papal States. The Risorgimento began developing after the fall of Napoleon and the spread of disappointment among Italians that they were to remain a divided people. The Congress of Vienna (1814-1815), for example, ended the states created by the Napoleonic Wars (1796-1815) and restored the former rulers, thereby carving Italy into separate states, largely under the control of Austria. Conservative, and much opposed to nationalistic Italian tendencies, these states were soon confronted by a number of secret societies, such as the Carbonari. The Italian societies calling for unification were broadly divided into three groups: a republican national party that exhibited anticlerical tendencies, founded in 1831 by Giuseppe Mazzini; a pro-papal party that desired an Italian confederation under the popes; and a moderate party favoring rule of the House of Savoy, the heads of the Italian state of Piedmont-Sardinia. The last group was led by the statesman Camillo Cavour (1810-1861). Revolutions in 1848-1849 were suppressed by the Austrians, but they caused Pope Pius IX to flee Rome for Gaeta. He would be returned to the Vatican with the help of the Austrians. The leadership in the drive for Italian unity now passed to the Sardinians. With their ally, France, they defeated the Austrians in 1859 and by the Treaty of Villafranca di Verona secured control of Lombardy. This was followed in 1860 with the annexation of Parma, Tuscany, Modena, and Romagna. In conjunction with the Garibaldi, whose troops were conquering the Two Sicilies, the Sardinians seized the Marches and Umbria. Victor Emmanuel II was crowned king of Italy in 1861, an event that made virtually inevitable the demise of the Papal States. Venetia was added to Italy in 1866, leaving only the Papal States of Rome and Latium, which remained under French control until 1870. That year, Italy took control of the Papal States, ending the temporal holdings of the papacy save for the Vatican City and

St. Rita

other minor possessions. The loss of the Papal States was never recognized by Pope Pius IX and the so-called Roman Question remained unresolved until 1929 and the Lateran Treaty.

Rita of Cascia, St. (1386-1456) ●

Augustinian nun. Rita was born in Roccaporena, Italy, demonstrating from an early time a desire to become a nun. At her parents' wish, however, she accepted marriage to a man described in the biographies as cruel and harsh. For eighteen years she was a caring and devoted mother and wife, but, with his murder, she was widowed suddenly. Desirous still of entering the religious life, she asked permission to join the Augustinian nuns at the convent in Cascia. At first refused because she was a widow, Rita was finally admitted, traditionally as a result of divine intervention. Her years as a nun were known for their austerity, prayerfulness, and

self-mortification. Canonized by Pope Leo XIII on May 24, 1900, she was known in Spain as *La Santa de los impossibles*. Her symbol is roses, and she is depicted with roses and figs. Feast day: May 22.

Rite ● For coverage of rites (Alexandrian, Antiochene, Coptic, Roman, etc.) see under individual rites.

Rituale Romanum ● Latin for Roman Ritual, the official authorized book for the celebration of the Roman rite. The *Rituale Romanum* contains all the prayers and ceremonies that are to be used in the administration of the sacraments as well as other liturgical functions. The parts of the *Rituale* include Rite of Marriage, Rite of Baptism for Children, Rite of Funerals, Rite of Religious Profession, Rite of Christian Initiation of Adults, Rite of Anointing and Pastoral Care of the Sick, Holy Communion and Worship of the Eucharist Outside Mass, and Rite of Penance. It thus contains all services to be performed by priests that are not in the missal or breviary.

Early versions of the work were the sacramentary (in the West) and the euchologion (in the East); they included all activities of the priest, involving the liturgy, sacraments, blessings, and the appropriate rites; the sacramentary contained the contents of both the Roman Ritual and the pontifical. There evolved in the West a clarification of books, categorized by the services to be held. The sacramentary was replaced by the missal and further books appeared: the pontifical, with bishop's functions (confirmation, ordination, etc.) and the ritual, or *Rituale Romanum*, with priest's functions (penance, matrimony, baptism, etc.). There was no official book as is known today throughout the Middle Ages, so that instead a priest relied upon a wide variety of sources and handbooks. These varied by diocese and were called the *Rituale, Manuale*, or the *Sacramentale*. An effort was made by the papacy in the 1500s to bring some kind of uniformity to the manuals, but no standard work was ever authorized. An important event came in 1614 when Pope Paul V published the first edition of the official ritual, based on a handbook organized by Cardinal Giulio Antonio Santorio in 1586. This new *Rituale*, however, was not imposed on the Church, since the only accepted version and numerous other manuals continued to exist. A revision of the *Rituale Romanum* was undertaken in 1752 by Pope Benedict XIV. Further revised editions were published over succeeding centuries. The current authorized edition of the *Rituale Romanum* is updated periodically by the Holy See through the Congregation for the Sacred Rite. (See also **Rubrics**.)

Robert of Kilwardby (d. 1279) ●

Archbishop of Canterbury and cardinal. His early life is obscure, but it is certain that he did study at Paris and most likely Oxford. He taught at Paris and authored a number of notable works on philosophy and science, including *De divisione scientiarum* (*On the Division of the Sciences*), as well as commentaries on the *Institutiones grammaticae* by Priscian. After returning to England, Kilwardby entered the Dominicans, studying at Oxford. From 1261-1272, he was provincial of the order in England. A short time after leaving that office, he was chosen by Pope Gregory X to be archbishop of Canterbury. Consecrated on February 26, 1273, he received the pallium on May 8. As

archbishop he proved to be exceedingly active in charitable works and in visiting all of the regions under his jurisdiction. Of particular note was his visit to Oxford University in 1277, which resulted in the condemnation, with the university masters, of thirty propositions that were held to be contrary to the faith; the chief object of the condemnation were a number of views held by St. Thomas Aquinas, and Kilwardby's measure, issued as it was by a Dominican, was a severe blow to the supporters of Thomas and Thomism. In 1278, Kilwardby was named a cardinal and transferred to the see of Porto and Santa Rufina. He died the following year, on September 11, in Viterbo.

Robert of Melun (c. 1100-1167) ●

English scholar and theologian. He studied at Paris under Hugh of St. Victor and probably Peter Abelard, subsequently teaching at Melun, near Paris, from where his name was taken. Among his pupils were John of Salisbury and Thomas Becket, and his position of respect among contemporary theologians can be discerned from the adulatory statements made by John of Salisbury in the *Metalogicus*. In 1148, he took part in the Synod of Reims that condemned Gilbert de la Porrée. Through the influence of Thomas, his former pupil, he was appointed bishop of Hereford in 1163. Among his writings were a *Summa Sententiarum* on the *Sentences*, *Quaestiones de Divina Pagina*, and *Quaestiones de Epistolis Pauli*. The *Summa*, left unfinished, is a remarkable work in formative Scholasticism.

Robert of Molesme, St. (c. 1029-1111) ●

Benedictine abbot and reformer who was the founder of the Abbey of Cîteaux. Born in Troyes, to noble parents, Robert entered at the age of fifteen the Benedictine Abbey of Moutier-la-Celle, near Troyes. He became prior and in 1068 succeeded as abbot of St. Michael-de-Tonnerre. After failing to institute extensive reforms in the community, he retired in 1071 and returned to Moutier-la-Celle. Meanwhile, a group of hermits living in the forest of Collan desired Robert to become their leader. He had at first refused their request, but, after securing the pope's blessing, the hermits won Robert's agreement and in 1074 Robert introduced them to the monastic life. The following year, Robert moved his monks to the monastery that he had established in Molesme. At first quite austere, Molesme soon grew in wealth and prosperity. Discipline became lax and Robert tried unsuccessfully to reinstitute the vigor that had characterized previous years. He resigned as abbot but returned, remaining until 1098 when, giving up in the face of the recalcitrant monks, he received permission to establish a new order. With twenty-one monks he founded a new community: Cîteaux, which was formally begun on March 21, 1098. The monks of Molesme appealed to the pope to have Robert brought back. He once more entered Molesme and the monastery emerged as a leading center for reform. The abbey survived until the French Revolution. Robert died on April 17, 1111. Pope Honorius III in 1222 permitted his veneration in the church of Molesme; this was extended to the whole Church a short time later. Feast day: April 29.

Roch, St. (c. 1295-c. 1378) ● Also Rock, or Rocco. Known as the healer of plague victims, he was supposedly born in Montpellier, France, amazing his family because of the red cross found on his chest at birth. According to the stories told of his life, he was journeying through Italy when, in the town of Aquapendente, he encountered many victims of the plague. He healed the suffering and repeated the miracle at Modena, Parma, and Mantua. Stricken himself at Piacenza, he recovered but was then not recognized by his relatives in Montpellier. Thrown into prison for being an alleged spy, he died there, his identity not revealed until after his death, when his captors discovered his identification on a piece of paper and the distinctive red cross. Roch, according to one story, was invoked against the plague in 1414 during the Council of Constance. His relics were moved to Venice in 1485. Revered still in France and parts of Italy for protection from disease, he is portrayed in art in the company of a dog. Feast day: August 16.

Rock, Daniel (1799-1871) ● English ecclesiologist and antiquarian. Born in Liverpool, he studied at St. Edmund's College before receiving the distinct honor of being one of the first students sent to Rome to reopen the English College. He was ordained in 1824 and graduated the next year. Returning home, he held a number of posts, including chaplain to Sir Robert Throckmorton of Buckland. He was also a member of the so-called Adelphi, a group of priests in London who successfully worked for the restoration of the Church hierarchy in England. As a result of this, he was elected in 1852 one of the first canons of Southwark. Among his writings were *Hierurgia or the Holy Sacrifice of the Mass* (1833) and *The Church of Our Fathers* (3 vols., 1849-1854), a remarkable and monumental study on medieval liturgical practices, especially the Sarum rite.

Rolle de Hampole, Richard (d. 1349) ● English hermit and mystic. Born at Thornton, in Yorkshire, he studied at Oxford and Paris before entering into the life of a hermit on the estate of a friend, John Dolton of Pickering, in 1326. Over the next years he devoted himself to strict contemplation, attaining a high degree of spiritual perfection. He then wandered through England, finally settling in Hampole. He served as a spiritual guide to the nuns of the nearby Cistercian convent. His tomb was the site of reported miracles, but his cause was never pursued. His prolific writings were much read in the fourteenth and fifteenth centuries. These include: *De emendatione vitae* (on the perfection of life) and *De incendio amoris* (on the flame or heat of love), treatises that were translated in the 1400s into Middle English; commentaries on the Scriptures; letters; and lyric poems. He was long the attributed author of the poem "the Pricke of Conscience."

Roman Catholic ● See GLOSSARY.

Roman Curia ● See **Curia, Roman**; see also APPENDIX 2.

Roman Empire ● One of the largest and most enduring empires in history. It survived in the West from 27 B.C. until A.D. 476 and the fall of the Western Empire; in the East, the imperial realm would last through the Byzantine Empire until 1453 and the fall of Constantinople to the Ottoman Turks. Christianity was born in the Roman Empire and would be preached, developed, and then flourish in its provinces and cities. The faith would enter into a titanic struggle with pagan Rome and, after centuries of persecutions and martyrdoms, it would prove triumphant. The victory of the Christian Church would facilitate its emergence as the creed of the Roman world.

The imperial government first looked upon Christianity as a minor sect of Judaism. While it was tolerant of the creed, Rome was suspicious of the Christians, counting them — with the Jews — among the purveyors of strange Eastern practices and rites; since the time of the peculiar cult of Cybele (whose members routinely castrated themselves in bloody ceremonies), the Eternal City had been hostile to such cults. The legal position of Christianity changed as it became clear that Christianity was distinct from Judaism, a recognition that Jewish leaders had been striving to achieve. Christians were already under criticism for their practices: they refused to associate or take part in pagan cults and would not make sacrifices to the emperors. This was repellent to Romans, who practiced a cult of state by which religious ceremonies were patriotic exercises intended to further and aid the imperial state. Rumors and accusations were also spread about the Christians, sometimes deliberate untruths about them, other times genuine misunderstanding of Christian tenets (e.g., cannibalism, human sacrifice, or incest). (See **Tacitus**.)

The date generally chosen to mark the persecution of the faith is A.D. 64, the year in which Emperor Nero (d. 68) blamed the Christians as easy scapegoats for the fire in Rome. His pogrom proved short-lived, and in the following years, Christians suffered in persecutions only irregularly. The degree and size of the oppression varied according to the local governors, popular sentiment, and the wills of the individual emperors. The emperors most responsible for persecutions were Domitian (81-95), Trajan (98-117), Antoninus Pius (138-161), Marcus Aurelius (161-180), Septimius Severus (193-211), Trajanus Decius (249-251), Valerian (253-260), Diocletian (284-305), and Galerius (305-311). The martyrdoms during these centuries were numerous, including popes and simple, sincere Christians who were willing to die rather than make sacrifices to the emperor and thus abjure their faith.

The persecutions prompted Christian writers to pen apologies on behalf of the creed (see **Apologists**). They also provided some truly touching accounts on the martyrs, such as those of St. Irenaeus and the letters in the second century from the Church of Lyons to those of Asia, Rome, and Phrygia. The extent of conversions all along the Roman social strata was seen in the conversions of Flavia Domitilla and the Theban Legion and the soldiers of Sebaste.

Roman officials looked with some frustration at the rapid growth of Church membership. Local Church leaders (such as Sts. Polycarp and Melito) were well-respected, and popular civic figures as well as many governors and regional or city officials were reluctant to execute them. The last, desperate effort at extirpating Christianity came in the late third and early fourth centuries, under Emperors Diocletian and Galerius. Both came to realize the futility of mass executions. Galerius, the prime mover in Diocletian's campaign, trumpeted his surrender in 311 with his own Edict of Toleration. Two years later, Constantine the Great and Licinius Licinianus published the Edict of Milan. (See also **Alexandria; Byzantine Empire; Catacombs; Colosseum; Constantine the Great; Constantinople; Italy; Paul of Tarsus, St.; Rome;** and **Vatican**.)

Roman Martyrology ● In Latin, the *Martyrologium Romanum*. Official martyrology of the Church containing the complete and authorized list of saints venerated by the faithful. The Roman Martyrology had its basis in the Martyrology of Usuard, the most commonly used source for lists of martyrs throughout the Middle Ages. Compiled by the Benedictine monk Usuard of St.-Germain-des-Prés, in Paris, in the ninth century, the Martyrology of Usuard was widely read, but there developed numerous versions and adaptations during the medieval epoch. In an effort to standardize the martyrology for the Church, a committee of scholars was convened in the late 1500s to compile a new work. This ten-person board included the historian Cesare Baronius (1538-1607). The result of their efforts was the Roman Martyrology, issued in 1584 by Pope Gregory XIII. It officially replaced all other martyrologies but was itself revised to keep it current with canonizations and advances in historical research. Revisions were undertaken by Popes Urban VIII (1630), Benedict XIV (1748), Pius IX (1870), Pius X (1913), and Benedict XV (1920), and after Vatican Council II (1962-1965). The martyrology contains some six thousand

saints and blesseds honored by the Church; additions are made through the decrees of beatification and canonization issued by the Congregation of the Causes of Saints.

Romanos Pontifices ● Apostolic constitution issued by Pope Leo XIII on May 8, 1881. It defined the relationship in England between the hierarchy and the religious orders. The constitution was the result of a controversy between the recently established hierarchy (as a result of the restoration of the hierarchy under Pope Pius IX in 1850) and the various religious orders over matters of jurisdiction and discipline. The dispute could not be resolved locally, so Cardinal Manning proposed in 1877 to submit the question to Rome. Manning later suggested that a commission be appointed by Pope Leo. This was done in 1880 and the final report was issued in January 1881. The resulting constitution, *Romanos Pontifices*, gave clear definition to the relations between bishops in England and Scotland with the religious orders. It covered such topics as the use of religious in parochial duties, the control over temporal goods, and the status of exemption of religious from episcopal jurisdictions. Such was the success of the constitution that it was extended for the United States (1885), Canada (1911), South America (1900), and other mission territories.

Romans, Epistle to the ● Letter written by St. Paul to the Christian community of Rome with the hope of preparing his readers for his eventual arrival in the Eternal City with the intention of proceeding on to Spain (1:13; 15:22, 24, 28). His epistle, first in the canonical order of the writings in the NT, reveals Paul as one who clearly identifies himself as "an apostle to the Gentiles" (11:13). The circumstances surrounding its composition indicate that Paul had been working for several years to continue his missionary work but also to raise contributions from the churches of Asia

Minor and Greece for those in need in Jerusalem. He was apparently finished with this task and was also reaching the point of concluding his missionary labors in the eastern Mediterranean. Thus, Paul was at last in a position to undertake a Western journey, one that would take him to Rome (1:13) and then to Spain. His letter, to lay the groundwork for his arrival, was probably written in Corinth (or Cenchreae) in the winter, between 54 and 58 (most likely 57-58); he notes that "Macedonia and Achaia have been pleased to make some contribution for the poor among the saints at Jerusalem" (15:26) and he is planning to go to the Holy City with the funds. The longest of his epistles, it is also notable for being the only one addressed to a Church that he did not establish, his awareness of this being stated in kind words (15:14). He also observes that he is reluctant to "build on another man's foundation" (15:20).

One of his greatest works theologically, the letter makes clear the intent of its author immediately after the introduction: "For I am not ashamed of the gospel: it is the power of God for salvation to every one who has faith, to the Jew first and also to the Greek. For in it the righteousness of God is revealed through faith for faith; as it is written, 'He who through faith is righteous shall live' " (1:16-17). He stresses the vital need for justification by the faith (1:18—4:25) and the receiving of grace and freedom from sin

St. Paul

(5:1—8:39). Paul then discusses the place and the duties faced by Christians.

Romanus ● Pope from August to November 897. Born to Gallese parents near Civita Castellana, Italy, he was a cardinal priest when elected to succeed Stephen VI (VII). Chosen at a time of considerable chaos because of the murder of his predecessor by the supporters of the dead Pope Formosus (whose body Stephen had exhumed, tried, and humiliated), Romanus proved to be favorably disposed to the pro-Formosan party. He ordered Formosus' body reclaimed from the Tiber, where it had been floating, and given proper burial. He also most likely took steps toward nullifying Stephen's irregular acts; these would not be formally nullified until the reign of John IX (r. 898-900). Based on a recension on the *Liber Pontificalis*, it is believed that Romanus was deposed and probably confined to a monastery where he died at some unknown date. He was succeeded by the equally brief reigning Theodore II.

Rome ● Currently the capital of Italy, the onetime chief city of the Roman Empire, and one of the most important cities in the history of the West. Rome is also the center of Christendom, the diocese of the Bishop of Rome and hence the primatial see of the Roman Catholic Church. Called the Eternal

City, the area of the seven hills that were to become Rome was a gathering place in ancient Italy for the Etruscans, Latins, and Sabines. According to tradition, the city itself was founded in 753 B.C. by Romulus. It would be ruled until around 500 B.C. by Etruscan kings, the last of whom, Tarquinius Superbus, was replaced by the Roman Republic. The republic endured until the first century B.C., carving for Rome a vast Mediterranean empire. Increasingly corrupt, the republic was brought to an end by the civil war (49-45 B.C.) that was won by Julius Caesar, who became dictator. His assassination precipitated another series of wars (44-31 B.C.), ended by the triumph of Octavian (later Emperor Augustus) at the Battle of Actium (31 B.C.) over Mark Antony and Cleopatra. Octavian ruled from 27 B.C. to A.D. 14, formally establishing the Roman Empire. This empire would survive in the West until 476 and in the East (in the form of the Byzantine Empire) until 1453 (see **Byzantine Empire**). It was also within this empire that Christ was born and that Christianity was founded and first spread.

The city of Rome symbolized for the Roman people and indeed for the inhabitants of the empire the greatness of Roman civilization and achievement. It was literally true that all roads led to Rome, and the metropolis came to epitomize the political, artistic, architectural, and cultural accomplishments of the Roman people. It was also the gathering place for all the social and religious innovations that arose within the empire and, inevitably, Christianity found its way there. The faith was at first viewed by the cosmopolitan Romans as just another cult from the East that routinely became popular in the city.

It is unclear at what time Christianity first entered the city, but the most significant date in the early history of the Roman Church was 42. In that year, Peter arrived and established the Christian presence that could never be eradicated by Roman authorities.

While probably away from his flock for periods of time, Peter nevertheless endured persecution as leader of the Christians of Rome and was finally put to death around 64 by Emperor Nero — traditionally being crucified upside down on the Vatican Hill. (See also **Peter, Tomb of**.)

From the time of the early Church, Peter enjoyed the position of primacy over the faithful and, as the recognized Vicar of Christ and the first Bishop of Rome, his successors would be inheritors of his ecclesiastical supremacy. The see of Rome was Petrine and the Bishops of Rome derive their supremacy from the undisputed fact that Peter founded the diocese of Rome. This position would be further enhanced by the prestige of being bishop of the capital of the empire and through the temporal and spiritual place of the bishops in governing the entire, universal Church. The term Roman Catholic Church is thus based upon the central place of the Bishop of Rome as head of the Church and the unquestionable fact that the faithful look to Rome for spiritual leadership and guidance. (See also **Holy See** and **Primacy of the Pope**.)

Over the centuries following Peter's martyrdom, the Bishops of Rome acquired increasing influence within the city, attendant upon the growth of the Christian population. They were regularly singled out in persecutions and were genuinely feared by Roman authorities; Emperor Trajanus Decius, for example, once remarked that he would rather learn that he faced a usurper with many legions than hear of another bishop in Rome. The position of the bishops was only strengthened by the final victory of Christianity in 313 with the granting of toleration. In the next years, Emperor Constantine the Great lavished gifts and property upon the Roman Church, assisting in making the bishops prosperous and growing participants in the affairs of the city's administration.

The temporal authority of the bishops

St. Peter's Basilica

realistically dates to the fifth century when, in the face of the collapse of imperial rule, the bishops assumed responsibility for the welfare of the people and the city. Thus, Pope St. Leo I the Great (r. 440-461) saved Rome from destruction by Attila the Hun and negotiated a relatively bloodless sack of the city in 455 by the Vandals. The popes could not prevent the final demise of the Western Empire in 476, but they did struggle to feed the starving Romans and to negotiate with the barbarian rulers of Italy for the good of the Church.

Rome declined in importance during the next centuries as political power resided in Ravenna under the Byzantines. This changed significantly in the next centuries with the rise of the papacy. Under such pontiffs as St. Gregory I the Great (r. 590-604), Rome was made the capital of the Papal States, and universal recognition was given to the Holy See and the whole fabric of Western civilization would be unthinkable without the spiritual and the temporal presence of the supreme pontiff. Rome itself would still endure great hardships, however, including pillage by the Muslims in 846 and chronic political chaos in the tenth century when local noble houses (such as the Crescentii, Orsini, Colonna, and Theophylact) vied for supremacy, appointing, deposing, and murdering popes to gain advantage or fleeting supremacy.

The reforms of Pope Gregory VII (r. 1073-1085) did little to improve the climate, and the popes regularly found the Romans irascible and even violent. In the 1200s, the popes decided it was convenient — and physically advisable — to reside outside the city, which was beset by feuds and civil disorder. This situation was followed by the Avignon Papacy (the Babylonian Captivity, 1309-1377) during which the popes, under French domination, resided in Avignon. The absence of the papal court was a disaster for Rome economically and socially. The city sank into ruin, the population shrinking drastically through plague, brigandage, and despair. The return of the popes in 1377 brought little improvement owing to the Great Schism (1378-1417).

In 1417, Pope Martin V was elected, ending the Great Schism. He reinvigorated the city from 1420, marking the advent of the Renaissance in the Eternal City. His successors, most notably Nicholas V (r. 1447-1455), Pius II (r. 1458-1464), and Sixtus IV (r. 1471-1484) brought stability and attracted to the city artisans and scholars. Renaissance grandeur would reach its zenith under the popes of the sixteenth century, epitomized by Pope Julius II (r. 1503-1513), who would grant commissions to Michelangelo, Bramante, and Raphael.

The Renaissance popes beautified the city, but their enthusiasm for humanism, art, and frequent bouts of decadence contributed to the spread of the Reformation and the need for serious Church reform. Further, the political interests of the papacy brought disaster in 1527 when Rome was sacked by the troops of Emperor Charles V and Pope Clement VII was imprisoned for a time in Castel Sant' Angelo. A brilliant revival was achieved under Paul III (r. 1534-1549), Pius IV (r. 1559-1565), St. Pius V (r. 1566-1572), Gregory XIII (r. 1572-1585), and especially Sixtus V (r. 1585-1590). The Catholic Reformation cleansed much of the papal court, ended the infamous corruption, and transformed Rome into one of the artistic jewels of Europe. Under Sixtus, a massive program of building and beautification brought a flowering of baroque architecture that is still visible today. Rome was henceforth a place of artists, scholars, intellectuals, and saints, profiting economically and politically from the government of the popes as heads of the Papal States.

The political process that would ultimately bring the demise of the Papal States began in 1798 when French troops occupied the city and removed Pope Pius VI (r. 1775-1799). His successor, Pius VII (r. 1800-1823), would endure imprisonment by Napoleon and the seizure of Rome by the French Empire until 1814. While the Papal States were restored in 1814, there followed the Risorgimento, which climaxed in Italian unification in 1870. The Papal States were lost in 1860 and Rome in 1870. Pope Pius IX declared himself a "prisoner of the Vatican," and the conflict between the Holy See and the Italian government — called the Roman Question — would be settled only in 1929 with the Lateran Treaty. Today, the pope remains the Bishop of Rome, his cathedral the Basilica of St. John's Lateran. Within the city are more than four hundred churches. (See TABLE 12; see also **Dissidio, Italy, Risorgimento, Vatican,** and **Vatican City, State of**.)

Romuald, St. (c. 950-1027) ● Founder of the Camaldolese order. Born in Ravenna, to a noble family, at the age of twenty he witnessed his father kill a man in a duel, an act that so appalled Romuald that he fled to the Abbey of S. Apollinaire. Such was his determination to lead a rigorously ascetic life that he found the abbey insufficient in its observances. He requested, and received, permission to retire to Venice. There, under the hermit Marinus, he lived as a strict ascetic, eventually wandering through Italy, establishing hermitages and monasteries. In 1005, he went to Val-di-Castro, residing there for two years and prophesying at his departure that he would one day return there — to die. His most famous foundation was that of the community of Campus Maldoli, or Camaldoli, which would become the center for the Camaldolese order. Romuald finally returned to Val-di-Castro in 1026, dying there traditionally on June 19, 1027, alone in his cell. His body was found incorrupt in 1466. His feast was fixed by Pope Clement VIII to February 7, in 1596; it would be changed later. St. Peter Damian, a disciple, authored a biography. In it, probably due to an error, it was claimed that Romuald lived to be one hundred twenty years old. Feast day: June 19.

Rosary ● Devotional prayer honoring the Blessed Virgin Mary, it is usually recited on a string of beads, which is divided into five sets, known as decades, with ten smaller beads and one large bead. On each smaller bead is recited a Hail Mary and on the larger bead is said the Our Father (*Pater Noster*). Customarily, the Rosary is a devotion to the fifteen mysteries, with the recitation of the fifteen decades. On most occasions, one-third (or five decades) is said at one time. Thus, the mysteries are divided into three groups, the Joyful, Sorrowful, and Glorious Mysteries. Each decade is preceded by an Our Father and a Glory Be.

According to tradition, the Rosary was first made popular by St. Dominic (1170-1221), who sought the aid of Our Lady during the travails and bloodshed of the Albigensian Crusade in southern France. As reported in the stories told in honor of the Feast of the Holy Rosary (October 7), Dominic was commanded to preach the Rosary among the heretics. The saint was thereafter its most ardent promoter, his special status noted by several popes, including Leo XIII who, in an encyclical, *Laetitae sanctae* ("Commending Devotion to the Rosary"), on September 8, 1893, recognized as historical fact Dominic's role in establishing the Rosary.

Roscellinus (c. 1050-c. 1125) ● Also Roscelin and Roscellinus Compendiensis. Monk, theologian, and philosopher, he is best known as the founder of nominalism. A native probably of Compiègne, he studied at Soissons and Reims, later teaching at Besançon. Among his pupils was Peter Abelard. The writings of Roscellinus are almost exclusively known through the hostile works of his critics, St. Anselm, John of Salisbury, and Abelard. He also communicated with Lanfranc and St. Ivo of Chartres. In 1092, he was accused of tritheism at the Council of Soissons, a charge based on his proposition that the Trinity was composed of three separate deities. While he denied that such was his doctrine, he retracted the idea to avoid excommunication. While not necessarily the originator of nominalism, he was given much credit by the chronicler Otto of Freising, who wrote that Roscellinus was *"primus nostris temboribus sententiam vocum institut," sententia vocum* being the contemporary name for nominalist ideas — namely that universals were only words (*flatus vocis*), that only individual things existed. If he did not, in fact, originate nominalism, then he was at least one of its strongest defenders.

Rose of Lima, St. (1586-1617) ● First saint of the Americas. Born Isabel de Flores y del Oliva in Lima, Peru, she was the daughter of Spanish parents. In 1597, she took the name Rose at her confirmation because as an infant her face had supposedly been transformed by a mystical rose. Owing to the poverty of her family, she helped by growing flowers and making beautiful lace and embroidery. The focus of her life, however, was absolute devotion and severe self-mortification. Her reverence for Jesus, the Virgin Mary, and the Blessed Sacrament included fasting, strict penances, daily Communion, and countless hours of prayer. Her interior desolation and severe temptations were accompanied by the persecution of her by her family and friends. She refused, however, to cease her mortification or to be married, taking a vow of perpetual virginity. Finally overcoming her parents' objections, she joined the Third Order of St. Dominic around 1606. She died on August 30, 1617, from the severity of her penances, offering all to Our Lord for the souls in purgatory and the forgiveness of sins against Him. Beatified in 1668 by Pope Clement IX, she was canonized by Clement X in 1671, the first American to be so honored. Her concerns for the plight of the Native Americans of Peru and slaves made her the foundress of care for Indians and the poor in her country. Feast day: August 23.

Rosmini-Serbati, Antonio (1797-1855)

● Italian philosopher, theologian, and founder of the Institute of Charity. Born in Rovereto, Italy, he was initially educated at home, subsequently studying at the University of Padua. Ordained in 1821, the following year he received a doctorate in theology at Padua. In 1823, he journeyed to Rome where he received encouragement from Pope Pius VII to begin a reform and a revitalization of philosophy. This would become one of Rosmini-Serbati's principal undertakings, and he also would be encouraged by Popes Leo XII, Pius VIII, Gregory XVI, and Pius IX. From 1823-1826, he focused on the study of St. Thomas Aquinas and in 1828, at the suggestion of Maddalena di Canossa (foundress of the Daughters of Charity), he established the Congregation of the Fathers of Charity, called later the Rosminians, devoted to improving the spiritual and educational lives of the faithful through teaching and preaching. The Rosminians

St. Rose of Lima

were approved by Pope Gregory XVI in 1839 and soon spread to England, the United States, and elsewhere.

Rosmini-Serbati was a supporter of the Risorgimento, the movement to unite all of Italy, but he opposed those elements in the cause that exhibited anticlerical and antipapal tendencies. Sent to Pius IX in 1848-1849 as an envoy of the House of Savoy, he attempted to negotiate a concordat with the pontiff on the part of the Piedmont. Pius named him as one of his advisers examining the definability of the Immaculate Conception. In 1848, he accompanied Pius into exile at Gaeta following the revolution in Rome in November of that year. Rosmini-Serbati eventually left Gaeta in the face of Austrian victories against the revolutionaries. Two of his works, meanwhile, *Delle cinque piaghe della sancta Chiesa* (1848; *Of the Five Wounds of the Holy Church*) and *La Constituzione secendo la giustizia sociale* (1848; *A Constitution Based on Social Justice*), were placed on the Index of Forbidden Books in 1849. He submitted at once and retired to Stresa, learning just before his death that the works had been cleared by a papal commission.

As a philosopher and theologian, he penned several notable works. *Nuevo saggio sull'origine delle idee* (3 vols., 1830; *The Origin of Ideas*) was supplemented in 1836 by *Il rinnovamento della filosofia in Italia* (*The Revitalization of Philosophy in Italy*). He also wrote *Massime di perfezione Cristiana* (1830; *Maxims of Christian Perfection*). He considered philosophy to be a science of ultimate reasons or the grounds of human knowledge. He developed a complex system, Rosminianism, that argued for the idea of ideal being, distinguishing degrees of being by their completeness. Deriving from elements of St. Augustine, St. Thomas Aquinas, Plato, Descartes, Kant, and Hegel, Rosiminianism was attacked by critics for its ontologism and apparent pantheism. While his works were cleared by a papal commission in 1854, Pope Leo XIII issued a partial condemnation of his forty propositions in 1887-1888. The future Pope John Paul I (r. 1978), Albino Luciani, wrote his doctoral thesis on Rosmini-Serbati. Today, Rosmini-Serbati is largely unknown outside of Italy.

Rota ● Properly *Rota Sacra Romana* (Sacred Roman Rota). The court of the highest appeal in the Church, used for presiding and judging those cases brought before the Holy See, the Rota was established in the second half of the 1200s, subsequently deriving its name from the round tables used by the judges while they resided in Avignon in the 1300s. The officials also customarily sat in individual desks arranged in a circle. Its authority extended to both civil and ecclesiastical cases, reaching its height of influence and power in the fifteenth and sixteenth centuries. Gradually, however, its jurisdiction became limited to civil matters, especially by the 1700s. This development presented serious problems for the Rota's continuing functioning after 1870 and the final demise of the Papal States and the unification of Italy. Its activities ceased entirely under Pope Pius IX (r. 1846-1878) and did not begin again until 1908 when it was reconstituted by Pope St. Pius X in the bull *Sapienti Consilio*. Today, the Rota is best known for its handling of appeals concerning marriages. The number of these cases is enormous, especially as there are appeals made from all over the world. It also handles cases of ecclesiastical law, and those cases made on specific appeal from other ecclesiastical courts. In this capacity, it is a court of first instance in disputes involving abbots, heads of religious orders, and bishops. It is also a court of appeal for cases tried in episcopal tribunals. There are certain cases that, because of their special nature or gravity, are not handled by the Rota and are passed on directly to the pope. The court is normally composed of judges who are priests possessing at least a doctorate in civil and canon law. The judges, known as auditors (*auditores*) come from all over the globe. Their head, known as a dean, is considered, as with other courts, *primus inter pares*. Lawyers appearing before the Rota are required to have a doctorate in canon law and be graduates of a school of special training operated by the Rota. Contrary to popular thought, most of the advocates who appear before the Rota are laypersons.

Rubrics ● Directives, precepts, or liturgical provisions found in the missal, including the sacramentary and lectionary, and in the Roman Ritual (*Rituale Romanum*) to assist bishops, priests, and deacons in the administration of sacraments and sacramentals. The preaching of the Word of God, and in the Eucharistic liturgy, the rubrics are, based on the clearly noted context, either mandatory or directive. The name is derived from the fact that the rubrics are always printed in red (Latin *rubrica*, red earth). The rubric had its etymological origins in the Roman term *rubrica*, denoting the red earth that was used by carpenters to mark wood with lines to aid in cutting. The name was also used by the great Roman jurists for the red letters under which various legal collections and pronouncements were gathered. Over time, the red letter came to denote not the text but remarks and guides in studying the text; it was in this sense that the rubric was adopted into liturgical collections. Their application by the Church has been difficult to trace owing to the oral traditions by which they were transmitted and the local character of the observances. Organization of the rubrics in a meaningful sense began in the fifteenth century. Under Pope Leo X, the rubrics of the Roman Missal were edited, and so-called rubricists researched early collections and versions. The official *Rituale Romanum*, published in 1614 under Pope Paul IV, used its rubrics from those of the handbook of Cardinal Giulio Antonio Santorio, which was itself the basis of the *Rituale*. The *Rituale* also marked the formal utilization of rubrics in liturgical books to which they correspond instead of being gathered into separate compilations or guidebooks. This innovation, dating from the time of Pope Pius V (r. 1566-1572), made rubrics an important source of directives in the performance of ceremonies and the administering of sacraments. Interpretations, alterations, the removal of abuses, and the issuing of authentic liturgical books — with rubrics — falls under the purview of the Congregation for Divine Worship and the Discipline of the Sacraments, known originally as the Congregation of Rites as established by Pope Sixtus V in 1588.

Rufinus of Aquileia (c. 345-410) ● Also Tyrannius Rufinus. Christian scholar and monk. Born to Christian parents, he was educated at Rome but was not baptized until around the age of twenty-five while living for a brief time in Aquileia as a monk. He became a close friend of St. Jerome during this period. Around 371, he journeyed to the East, visiting Egypt and studying at Alexandria. From the Egyptian ascetics, he came to appreciate Origen. Going on to Jerusalem, he used his own money to establish a monastery on the Mount of Olives. After a return visit to Egypt, he went back to Italy in 397, settling in Aquileia. His friendship with Jerome was wrecked because of Rufinus's adherence to Origenism, even

after the condemnation of Origen as a heretic. As Jerome was an absolute opponent of what he deemed the unacceptably unorthodox doctrines of Origen, the breach between them could never be settled. Rufinus was the translator, into Latin from Greek, of numerous writings, including those of Origen, St. Basil, St. Gregory of Nazianzus, and Eusebius of Caesarea. He also authored an *Apology*, in two books, to an attack made upon him by Jerome. Rufinus died in Sicily after fleeing the invasion of Italy by the Visigoths.

Ruinart, Thierry (1657-1709) ● French theologian and historian. Born in Reims, he entered the Maurist Congregation at the Abbey of St.-Remy at Reims on October 2, 1674. Such was the reputation he soon acquired as a scholar that the great Jean Mabillon (1632-1707) asked for him as an assistant. Thus, in 1682, Ruinart went to the Abbey of St. Germain-dcs-Prés, near Paris, where he worked with Mabillon, becoming one of the foremost Church historians of his time. His greatest work was *Acta primorum Martyrum sincera et selecta* (1689), a vast collection of the martyrs that Ruinart accepted as genuine. While modern scholarship has found some individual documents to be lacking in authenticity or genuineness, the collection remains nevertheless an impressive labor. He also published an edition of the works of St. Gregory of Tours, collected (with Mabillon) the eighth and ninth volumes of the *Acta Sanctorum Ordinis Sancti Benedicti* (1700-1701), and wrote a comprehensive study of the persecution of Orthodox Christians under the Vandals in Africa, as part of the publication in 1694 of Victor of Vita's *Historia persecutionis Vandalicae*.

Russia ● Land with a long history of Christianity largely dominated in its religious life since 1054 by the Orthodox Church. While Christianity has suffered terribly in

Russian lands, most severely in the twentieth century under Communism, it has had a special place among the Russian people, becoming over the centuries an important element in the vast country's sociopolitical development. Christian missionaries first preached in Russian territories during the ninth and tenth centuries. In 988, Emperor Vladimir was converted and baptized, declaring Christianity to be the state religion. To further the Christian faith, he invited priests from the Byzantine Empire into his realm; they established an initially Greek hierarchy but were eventually replaced by a native clergy. In 1054, the Russian Church sided with the Byzantines in its conflict with the Western Church, remaining an ally of the Eastern Church after the formal launching of the Great Schism.

The Mongols began their invasion of Russia in 1237, bringing massive destruction. In attempting to extirpate the faith, the Mongols put to death several Russian princes who refused to give up their faith. The Mongols would remain a chronic threat over the next years. In 1329, meanwhile, the important monastery of Valamo was founded on an island in Lake Ladoga. This would prove a major development in Russian monasticism (originally started in the eleventh century), which came to occupy a leading part in society after the creation of the monastery of the Most Holy Trinity at Sergavo.

In the 1300s, a new Russian state began to emerge out of the chaos and carnage of Old Russia, which had virtually been destroyed by the Mongols. This new state was centered in the grand duchy of Moscow. The grand duchy under Ivan III finally freed itself of Mongol domination in 1480. The Russian Church soon became divided between two main metropolitans: Kiev and Moscow. Steadfastly resistant to the Western Church, the Russians refused to accept the union of the Churches that was negotiated at the Council of Florence in 1439. In 1448, still declining to acknowledge the union, the Russians elected their own metropolitan of Moscow, without the approval of the Byzantines. From that date, the Russian Church became autocephalous.

During the sixteenth century, Russia's grand duchy of Moscow continued its expansion. In 1547, Ivan IV, called the Terrible (1530-1584), crowned himself tsar (czar), launching Russia's eastward expansion. He also kicked one of his sons to death and executed St. Philip II of Moscow. In 1503, the Russian monasteries split into two parties: those who favored ownership of property and those who desired to follow a vow of poverty. A reform of religious life was undertaken in 1551 through the Council of the Hundred Chapters.

In 1589, Moscow received its first patriarch, under Job (1589-1605). This major step for the Russian Church was offset in 1586 by the Synod of Brest-Litovsk through which a large part of the Orthodox population around Kiev entered into communion with Rome. Many were subsequently convinced, often through force and intimidation, to return to the Orthodox faith. Under the Patriarch Nikon (d. 1681), liturgical reforms were attempted, including the revision of service books that caused a breach in the Orthodox Church, as resistance to the changes brought the start of the so-called Old Believers.

In the 1700s, Czar Peter the Great (r. 1682-1725) ended the office of patriarch, replacing him with the Holy Synod through the Spiritual Regulation of 1721. As the czar had control over nominations and the power of dismissing its members, the imperial court came to dominate the Church. Throughout the century, anti-Catholic persecutions became increasingly oppressive, most notably in Poland, which had been gradually absorbed into the Russian Empire. Meanwhile, the Jesuits were given sanctuary by Catherine the Great (d. 1796) after the suppression of the order in 1773 by Pope

Clement XIV. The Catholics, identified by the Russian government with unwanted nationalist tendencies in Poland and elsewhere, and perceived as troublesome because of their loyalty to the papacy, continued to be repressed throughout the 1800s.

In 1917, the czarist government was overthrown by the Russian Revolution. Before long, the Bolsheviks under Lenin came to power, formed the Communist Party, and established the Union of Soviet Socialist Republics. Under the Communists, there was introduced one of the most despotic, atheistic, and merciless anti-Christian programs in history. Communist hatred for religion of all kinds compelled them to launch attacks against all the faiths, including the Russian Orthodox, Catholics, Jews, and Muslims.

The war against religion was conducted with a dual strategy: through outright oppression and the insidious use of bureaucracy and law. Technically, worship was still permitted, but the government seized all Church buildings, declared it illegal to teach religion to anyone under the age of eighteen, closed seminaries, and used every opportunity to denigrate, slander, and abuse religion through propaganda. In matters of state police oppression, the faith endured a virtually unprecedented degree of suffering. Such was the scale that by the outbreak of World War II in 1939, the clergy of the Catholic and Orthodox Churches had been horribly reduced with few churches left open. The Orthodox Church was in a slightly better position owing to an understanding reached with the Soviets in 1927 by Sergius, metropolitan of Moscow, and its patriotic stand in the invasion of Russia by Hitler in 1941. In a move to bolster morale, Stalin took the surprise step of giving a variety of concessions to the Orthodox, actually opening the churches — which were filled during the bleak winter of 1941-1942 when the Nazis were at the very door of Moscow.

Sergius was elected patriarch in 1943, coinciding with the creation of two state councils: one for the Orthodox Church and another for other creeds, including the Catholic Church. The tolerant policy, however, that Stalin found expedient in the war was ended after the Soviet victory in 1945. Soon after, there descended the Iron Curtain and began the Cold War with the West. This would remain in place for many years, with special animosity evidenced toward Catholics because of the absolutely uncompromising attitudes of Popes Pius XI (r. 1922-1939) and Pius XII (r. 1939-1958). During this time, from 1917-1959, according to reliable estimates, two and a half million Catholics were put to death or died in prison camps in Siberia or elsewhere; fifty-five bishops and thirteen thousand priests were killed. Another ten million Catholics, including some two hundred bishops and thirty-two thousand priests, were placed in prison or various types of cruel incarceration. Throughout, the faith endured, particularly in Ukraine and Lithuania.

With the accession of Pope John XXIII in 1958, a reversal of papal policy took place. A dialogue was cautiously pursued, leading to the program called *Ostpolitik* that was to be developed and encouraged throughout the pontificate of Paul VI (r. 1963-1978). (See **Ostpolitik**.) A more aggressive style was to characterize the early period of the reign of Pope John Paul II (r. 1978-), who had an almost immediate disagreement with the Soviets over the question of Poland and the Solidarity movement. According to most experts, the Soviets responded by masterminding the assassination attempt on the pontiff in 1981 that was probably carried out by the Bulgarians. Although considered unthinkable at the time of his election, John Paul II has presided over the Church while witnessing the fall of Communism and the dissolution of the Soviet Empire. To promote the faith, he reestablished the hierarchy for the Byzantine Catholic rite in Ukraine in

1991 and appointed several apostolic administrators for the Russian Federation and several of the recently formed independent republics. Tension has been present between the Catholic and Orthodox Churches in Russia over a number of issues, such as the right of proselytizing, legal status, and ownership of property. (See also **Eastern Catholic Churches** and **Orthodox Eastern Churches**.)

Ruysbroeck, Jan van (1293-1381) ●
Flemish mystic. One of the foremost mystical authors of the Middle Ages, he was called the Admirable Doctor or the Divine Doctor. Born in Ruysbroeck, near Brussels, he left his family around 1304 to study at Brussels, living with his uncle, John Hinckaert, the devout canon of Ste.-Gudule. Ordained perhaps in 1317, he served in Ste.-Gudule until 1343. An important event during this period of service was his controversy with a woman named Bloemardinne who was active in Brussels. Ruysbroeck wrote several treatises (not extant) to refute her teaching and pamphlets, and he makes frequent reference in later writings to such heretical movements as the Brethren and to false mystics. In 1343, he retired from Ste.-Gudule and founded the Augustinian Abbey of Groenendaal. He became prior there in 1349 and wrote all of his works save for the first, *The Kingdom of the Lovers of God*. His writings include *The Book of Supreme Truth, The Seven Steps of the Ladder of Spiritual Love, The Mirror of Eternal Salvation, The Sparkling Stone, The Book of the Spiritual Tabernacle*, and *The Spiritual Espousals*. Many of these were translated from the Flemish into Latin and had a major influence on subsequent mysticism, most notably the spiritual movement of the *devotio moderna*. Among those shaped by his works or at least familiar with them were Gerhard Groote, Johannes Tauler, Henry Suso, and Thomas à Kempis. He was beatified in 1908.

Sa, Manoel da (1530-1596) ● Portuguese Jesuit theologian. After studying for a time at the University of Coimbra, Sa entered the Society of Jesus at the age of fifteen. He then taught theology at Coimbra and at Gandia where he acted as a tutor to St. Francis Borgia, who was, at the time, duke of Gandia. In 1557, he began serving as professor at the Roman College. He was appointed by Pope St. Pius V a member of the commission charged with preparing the approved edition of the Septuagint. At the same time, Sa continued various apostolic efforts, including the founding of several houses for the Jesuits in northern Italy and working at Loreto and Genoa. Among his writings were commentaries on the Scriptures and the treatise *Aphorismi Confessariorum* (1595), a kind of manual for casuistry. It was censured in 1603, for a number of maxims were held to be irregular and placed on the Index of Forbidden Books. After corrections were made, it served as a popular source for information on moral theology.

Sabellianism ● Also called modalism, it is one of the two forms, with Adoptionism, of the theological movement of Monarchianism in the second and third centuries. The Sabellians took their name from the theologian Sabellius, who expounded modalist ideas. The Sabellians argued that the Godhead was essentially undifferentiated in its internal nature. Sabellius was probably excommunicated in 217 and died most likely unreconciled to the Church. Little else is known about him. (See **Monarchianism** for other details.)

Sabinianus ● Pope from 604-606. Also called Sabinian, he was born near Viterbo. Sent in 593 to Constantinople as the nuncio of Pope St. Gregory the Great, Sabinianus disappointed the pontiff because he proved incapable of standing firm against the clever Byzantines, particularly Emperor Maurice (r. 582-602) and the patriarch John IV. Recalled to Rome, he was elected to succeed the mighty Gregory most likely in March 604. Imperial approval did not arrive from Constantinople, however, for several months, and he was not consecrated until September 13. The two main crises of his pontificate were the threat of the Lombards and a famine. Unlike his predecessor, Sabinianus refused to give away grain from the papal granaries. Instead, he sold it, an act that made him quite unpopular with the Romans. Thus, there were demonstrations at his funeral so that the procession had to go outside the city walls to reach St. Peter's where he was entombed. Sabinianus also reversed Gregory's preference for monks in filling various posts.

Sacraments ● For information on the sacraments, see under the following: **Anointing of the Sick; Baptism; Confirmation; Eucharist; Marriage; Orders, Holy**; and **Penance**.

Sacred Heart of Jesus ● Physical heart of Christ to which great devotion has been given by the faithful over the centuries. The Sacred Heart is a powerful sign and symbol of the inexhaustible love of and mercy that were poured out for humanity by God through the pierced heart of his Son. It is a symbolizing of Christ's love for the Father and all humankind in three ways: the divine love shared by Christ with the Father and the Holy Spirit, manifested through his perishable body; the profound, burning love that was infused into his soul, which strengthened and enriched the human will of Christ and enlightened and magnified its acts through the knowledge taken from that which was infused and the beatific vision; and the sensible love of Christ who, in his humanity, was the possessor of the greatest possible powers of feeling and sensory perception.

Devotion to the Sacred Heart developed out of reverence for the humanity of Christ and the recognition of the human nature of God's love for all people. While not defined theologically until the 1700s, devotion to the Sacred Heart began in the Middle Ages, probably originating out of veneration for the wound in Christ's side. A number of mystics helped develop the devotion, including St. Bernard of Clairvaux (1090-1153), St. Bonaventure (1221-1274; especially in his treatises *Vitis mystica* and *De ligno vitae*), St. Mechtilde (1212-1280), St. Gertrude (1256-1302), St. Catherine of Siena (1347-1380), Julian of Norwich (c. 1342-after 1413) and St. Francis of Rome (1384-1440). Important promotion of the devotion was made by St. Francis de Sales (1567-1622), who stressed it to the Visitandines and St. John Eudes (1601-1680). By far the most important figure in fostering wide acceptance of the Sacred Heart was St. Margaret Mary Alacoque (1647-1690), a Visitandine nun who received visions of the Sacred Heart at Paray-le-Monial from 1673-1675 and a set of twelve promises. Through her, the devotion became widely popular among Catholics; through her Jesuit spiritual director Claude de la Colombière, the Society of Jesus began advocating the Sacred Heart through France and made it part of their institute, especially in the Apostleship of Prayer. The liturgical observance of the feast was authorized by Pope Clement XIII in 1765. Pope Pius IX extended the feast in 1856 to the universal Church; Pope Leo XIII elevated it to a "double feast of the first class" and in 1899 consecrated humanity to the Sacred Heart; Pope Pius XI revised the feast in 1928; and further revisions of the feast were made in the Roman calendar in 1969. The feast is celebrated as a solemnity on Friday of the second week after Pentecost.

Sacrosanctum Concilium ● The first official document to be promulgated by Vatican Council II, on December 4, 1963, it is known by its English title as the "Constitution on the Sacred Liturgy." Its aim was to introduce a process of liturgical renewal. The desire for a careful examination of the liturgy did not simply commence with the deliberations of the council but had as its basis the ongoing study and research of the question for many years by the Holy See. For example, Pope St. Pius X (r. 1903-1914) instituted a number of directives aimed at liturgical renewal, such as the restoration of Sunday as the center of the liturgical observance each week, and, most importantly, urging the reception of Communion early and often in the lives of all Catholics. Pope Pius XII (r. 1939-1958) issued the important encyclical *Mediator Dei*, calling the liturgy the foundation of the Church's spiritual life, and stressing the Mass as the Church's primary or principal prayer. He also gave encouragement to heightened participation by the congregation through vocal prayer and frequent Communion and the reading of the Divine Office, which he considered a complementary activity to the Mass. It was thus both inevitable and desirable that the Second Vatican Council should take up the vitally important work of liturgical renewal as part of its wider considerations and endeavors.

The final decree, issued under Pope Paul VI, began with "General Principles for the

Restoration and Promotion of the Sacred Liturgy" (ch. 1), including "I. The Nature of the Sacred Liturgy and Its Importance in the Church's Life"; "II. The Promotion of Liturgical Instruction and Active Participation"; "III. The Reform of the Sacred Liturgy" (with its general principles, principles drawn from the hierarchical and communal nature of the liturgy, and principles for adapting the liturgy to the culture and traditions of nations); "IV. The Promotion of Liturgical Life in Diocese and Parish"; and "V. The Promotion of Pastoral-Liturgical Action." The constitution then concerned itself with "The Most Sacred Mystery of the Eucharist" (ch. 2); "The Other Sacraments and the Sacramentals" (ch. 3); "The Divine Office" (ch. 4); "The Liturgical Year" (ch. 5); "Sacred Music" (ch. 6); and "Sacred Art and Sacred Furnishings" (ch. 7).

As with many other enactments of Vatican Council II, *Sacrosanctum Concilium* has been the subject of considerable debate concerning its implementation and the direction that such a process has taken. In his apostolic letter on the constitution, dated December 4, 1988, Pope John Paul II celebrated the twenty-fifth anniversary of its promulgation by noting the continuing importance of liturgical renewal that has begun "in accordance with the conciliar principles of fidelity to tradition and openness to legitimate development." The pope, however, made note at that time of the very real problem of abuses and liberties taken with the liturgy on the one hand, and the stubborn refusal of some to accept liturgical reforms as they were formally intended by the Church authority on the other. His Holiness observed that the liturgical renewal, authentically interpreting the constitution through a harmonious dialogue between competent authorities in Rome and the local conferences of bishops, is not the source of the problem in the liturgical controversy, but it is the result of indifference on the part of many members of the faith, a rejection of the meaning and correct interpretation of the constitution, and unacceptable and outlandish innovations in the liturgy. The Holy Father has stressed the need for the liturgy to provide a ritual experience.

Sadoleto, Jacopo (1477-1547) ●

Cardinal, humanist, and reformer. Born in Modena, he was originally intended by his father to follow in the legal profession. But he instead chose to devote himself to classical studies and philosophy. Going to Rome, he secured the favor of Cardinal Caraffa and was appointed a secretary to Pope Leo X in 1513. Four years later, he was appointed bishop of Carpentras, near Avignon. Noted for his remarkable learning and outstanding personal nature, he was much respected by his contemporaries. A special focus of his concerns was reconciliation with the Protestants. Summoned to Rome in 1535 by Pope Paul III, he was appointed to a special commission charged with the reform of the Church that included Reginald Pole and the future Paul IV (Giampietro Caraffa); that December, Sadoleto was made cardinal at the same time as Pole and Caraffa. They subsequently drew up, with Cardinal Contarini, the *Consilium de emendanda Ecclesia*, the blueprint for the reform of the Church that laid the groundwork for the Council of Trent. Around this time, he tried without success to bring back to the Church the reformer Philipp Melanchthon (1497-1560) and the city of Geneva. Sent as a legate in 1542 to King Francis I of France, he failed to effect a reconciliation between the king and Emperor Charles V. From 1543, he was one of the closest advisers to Pope Paul III. Among his writings was a commentary on the Epistle to the Romans, which was banned from publication in Rome because of its questionable opinions on the doctrine of grace. It was subsequently corrected.

Sahagún, Bernardino (c. 1499-1590) ●

Spanish missionary, historian, and

archaeologist. A native of Sahagún, León, Spain, he studied at Salamanca where he took his final vows. Sent in 1529 to Mexico, he became one of the earliest missionaries to the recently conquered region, remaining there until his death. In an effort to be able to communicate with the native peoples and to advance his work of conversion, Sahagún learned the Aztec language. His mastery of the tongue prompted his superiors to encourage him in compiling a comprehensive study of the Aztec people, including their language, history, and culture. The result was the invaluable *Historia de las cosas de Nueva España* (*History of the Things of New Spain*). It was not actually published until 1829 (in three volumes) in Mexico owing to concerns among Spanish authorities that it preserved too much of the Aztec culture and would thus encourage the recently and forcibly converted indigenous populations to return to traditional Aztec religious practices. Political considerations were also taken into account as Sahagún was quite critical of the activities of the rapacious and cruel conquistadors. His *Historia* remains a vital source on life in Mesoamerica during the 1500s, preserving vital glimpses of Aztec life before the cultural obliteration brought about by Spanish colonial policies. Sahagún also wrote a grammar of the Aztec language and a dictionary, in Aztec, Spanish, and Latin.

St. Bartholomew's Day Massacre ●
Massacre occurring throughout Paris and other French cities on the night of August 23-24, 1572, and lasting several days during which thousands of Huguenots (French Protestants) were killed. One of the most infamous events in French history and a bloody episode in the Wars of Religion that plagued France in the sixteenth century, the Massacre of St. Bartholomew's Day had its origin in the growing concerns of Catherine de' Medici, mother of King Charles IX, and the Catholic House of Guise with the political power of the Protestant nobleman Gaspard

de Coligny. On August 22, 1572, they attempted to assassinate Coligny. The assassination misfired, however, and Coligny was only wounded. The inevitable investigation would have revealed Catherine's role and so, to prevent a severe political defeat, she convinced Charles to order the deaths of the Huguenot leaders in France, a task made simpler by the fact that many of them were in Paris for the wedding of Henry of Navarre, the future Henry IV. Catherine and Charles were assisted by Henry, third duke of Guise and the duke of Anjou (later King Henry III). The massacre began in Paris with the murder of the Protestant nobles; only Henry of Navarre and the prince of Condé were left alive. The fury of the Catholics erupted as mobs roamed the city, brutally killing Huguenots. The deaths continued even after a royal order of August 23 called for an end to the bloodshed, and it spread to the provinces. Huguenots were murdered in Orléans, Bordeaux, Lyons, Bourges, and elsewhere. It is unclear as to how many Protestants were killed; conservative estimates put it at two thousand while the Huguenot writer of the era, the duke of Sully, claimed seventy thousand. While greeted as a triumph over Protestantism by King Philip II of Spain and Pope Gregory XIII, the massacre polarized the Protestant countries of Europe and provoked a new wave of fighting in France.

St.-Cyran, Abbé de (1581-1643) ● Or simply St.-Cyran. Originally Jean Duvergier de Hauranne, St.-Cyran was a French religious leader and one of the founders of Jansenism. Born in Bayonne, France, he studied at the Sorbonne and the Jesuit College of Louvain from which he graduated in 1604. It was probably while at the Louvain that he became a friend of Cornelius Jansen. Over the next years he devoted himself to the study of early Christian writers, especially St. Augustine. In 1617, St.-Cyran went to Poitier where Bishop de la Rochepasay made him part of the canonry and priory of Bonneville. Three years later, he was appointed commendatory abbot of St.-Cyran, although he spent little time at the abbey. Residing in Paris, he became a familiar figure to many of the most prominent figures of the time, including Richelieu, St. Vincent de Paul, and Jean Jacques Olier. Associated with the Jansenists of Port-Royal and the Arnauld family, St.-Cyran served from 1633 as the spiritual adviser to the convent of Port-Royal and emerged as a major leader of the Jansenist cause. Such was the opinion of French officials concerning his power that Richelieu declared him to be more dangerous than six armies. The cardinal placed him in the *donjon* (prison) in Vincennes. St.-Cyran remained there from 1638-1643, after Richelieu's death. His release allowed a triumphant return to Port-Royal where he learned of the condemnation by Rome of the *Augustinus* of Jansen. He promised a harsh response but died before carrying it out. Among his writings were *Théologie familière*, a treatise on Jansenist teachings that was condemned by the Holy Office in 1654, and *Lettres chrétiennes et spirituelles*, written while in prison and published posthumously in 1645 in Paris.

St. John of Jerusalem, Hospitallers of ● See under **Military Orders**.

St.-Omer ● The Jesuit College founded around 1593 by Robert Persons (1546-1610) at St.-Omer in Artois, near Calais. Founded by Parsons to educate Catholic laity from England, St.-Omer had its roots in a small school run by him at Eu, Normandy. The few boys from that school were soon joined by other English youths so that within ten years the enrollment had reached over a hundred students; within thirty years the number had more than doubled. Fires in 1684 and 1725 led to extensive improvements and increases in the size of the entire compound. St.-Omer received encouragement from the French

government in 1678 (when Artois passed into French control) until 1762 when the Jesuits were expelled from France. Rather than be taught by secular priests, the students agreed to move to Bourges where studies were resumed until the suppression of the Society of Jesus in 1773. Refusing to give up, the boys went to Liège where the local bishop permitted ex-Jesuits to continue teaching. Fleeing from France in 1793 because of the French Revolution, they were eventually allowed to return to England owing to the modification of penal laws. St.-Omer, meanwhile, was used by the English clergy of Douai as a preparatory school until they also returned to England in 1795. St.-Omer was later sold to the French government. St.-Omer, like Douai, was an important site of Catholic education for adherents of the faith in exile from England.

St. Peter's Basilica ● Largest church in the world and arguably the greatest example of Christian architecture. St. Peter's Basilica is situated in northwestern Rome, on Vatican Hill, over an ancient burial ground traditionally accepted as the site where the body of St. Peter was placed after his crucifixion. There have been two basilicas, the first built by Emperor Constantine the Great (d. 337); the second, dating from the 1500s, is the one still standing. The first basilica was erected probably between 320 and 350 and was an expression both of Constantine's wholehearted patronage of the Church and his desire to honor St. Peter. It was soon joined by other smaller churches, hospitals, cemeteries, and places to stay, emerging as one of the preeminent pilgrim centers in all of Christendom. There was no initial altar and the main architectural focus was the tomb-shrine located beneath the *baldacchino* in the apse. It was not until the pontificate of St. Gregory I the Great (590-604) that various additions and repairs were needed, especially to fix the damage done by earthquakes and pillaging by raiders, such as the Saracens. By the late Middle Ages, however, the basilica was in a serious state of decay. Pope Nicholas V (r. 1447-1455), the great humanist pontiff, therefore decided to construct a new one. He chose a cross design for the basilica and Bernardo Rossellino (d. 1464) was picked as its architect. All plans ceased upon Nicholas's death and nothing further was done until the memorable pontificate of Julius II (1503-1513).

Pope Julius launched a building project that would take over a century to complete, with thirteen architects and twenty popes needed to bring it to fruition. The pope accepted the initial design of Donato Bramante (d. 1514), laying the cornerstone on April 18, 1506, on which was inscribed: "Pope Julius II of Liguria in the year 1506 restored this basilica, which had fallen into decay." Money to pay for the work was to be provided by the sale of indulgences, an action that would have major implications in Luther's call for reform. At Julius's passing in 1513, the project was halted, and Bramante's own death the next year marked some twenty years of inactivity as popes were more concerned with other matters. Pope Clement VII, for example, had to endure the sack of Rome in 1527 by imperial troops. In 1534, Pope Paul III appointed at last a new architect, Antonio da Sangallo (d. 1546). Sangallo's modified plan to give the original Greek cross design more of a Latin cross shape was rejected by his successor Michelangelo, who restored the simpler Greek cross. By Michelangelo's death in 1564, the drum of the dome was

completed. Other architects would follow: Piro Ligorio, Giorgio Vasari, Giacomo Barozzi, and Giacomo della Porta. The latter finished the dome during the reign of the famed Sixtus V (1585-1590), who was responsible for many architectural achievements in the

Baldacchino of St. Peter's Basilica

Eternal City. Pope Paul V (1605-1621) employed Domenico Fontana and Carlo Maderno to conclude the work on the actual building, ordering the last remains of the old Constantinian basilica to be torn down. Maderno constructed the current façade, built with two extra bays on each side to support bell towers. These were to be added by Bernini (d. 1680), who lost much face

745

when the towers began to sink; the towers were torn down and only the façade remains, notable for its pillars and the inscription IN HONOREM PRINCIPIS APOST. PAVLVS BORGHESIVS ROMANVS PONT. MAX. AN. MDCXII PONT. VII (In Honor of the Prince of the Apostles, Paul V Borghese, Roman, Supreme Pontiff, in the Year 1612, the Seventh of His Pontificate). Pope Urban VIII consecrated the church on November 18, 1626. He would be responsible for much of the interior decoration that is today still a wonder to the visitor, including the sumptuous *baldacchino* by Bernini over the high altar.

St. Peter's is still the most recognized church in the world. While not the cathedral of the Bishop of Rome (that being St. John Lateran), it is nevertheless used as the site of the important liturgical functions of the papacy, including funerals, installations (or coronations), canonizations, and other important Masses or feasts.

Salesians ● In full, Salesians of St. John Bosco (or the Salesians of St. Francis de Sales, S.D.B.). A religious congregation founded at Turin in 1859 by St. John Bosco (or Don Bosco), the Salesians are dedicated to the education of boys and young men, especially among the poor, with the additional aim of educating them toward entering the priesthood. The society derived its name from St. Francis de Sales (1567-1622), who provided Don Bosco the inspiration to work among the orphaned and poor children of Turin. He began his work soon after ordination in 1841, settling in the Turin suburb of Valdocco and establishing what he called "festive oratories" (where he taught the catechism and said Mass for them) and night classes. The program faced much opposition initially from the local Church and city officials but soon proved so popular and successful that it spread to neighboring cities. In 1857, Don Bosco drew up rules to form the growing society into a religious congregation. Two years later, he

summoned the members of the society to a general chapter and placed the society under the patronage of St. Francis de Sales, giving the congregation its name. Formal approval was given in 1874 by Pope Pius IX, long a benefactor of the Salesians. The order quickly grew into an international one, sending members all over the world including South America. Two missions were begun in New York, in 1898 and 1902; the first United States mission, however, was in 1898, in San Francisco. The Salesians, with over seventeen thousand members in the world, remain the third largest order in the Church. The Salesian Sisters, known in full as the Daughters of Mary Help of Christians (F.M.A.), was founded in 1872 at Mornese, Italy, by Don Bosco and St. Mary Mazzarello. It performed the same mission for girls that was carried out by the Salesian Fathers. They arrived in the United States in 1908.

Salisbury, Use of ● See **Sarum, Use of**.

Salmanticenses ● Group of Discalced Carmelites who authored the *Cursus theologicus Summam d. Thomae complectens*, a vast commentary on the *Summa Theologiae* of St. Thomas Aquinas. Intended to serve as a comprehensive course of study on Scholastic philosophy and theology, the work took some eighty years to complete and was compiled from around 1631-1712. The authors were long thought to have been anonymous Carmelites, but their identity is now known: Antonio de la Madre de Dios (c. 1583-c. 1637), Juan de la Anunciación (1633-1701), Domingo de Santa Teresa (1604-1660), Diego de Jesús (1570-1621), Antonio de San Juan-Bautista (1641-1699), Ildefonso de los Angeles (1663-1737), and Francisco de Santa Ana (d. 1707). The work done by these scholars has long been considered one of the highest levels of Thomistic Scholasticism and was used as the standard source for the training of theologians in Thomism. The Salmanticenses also wrote the *Cursus Salmanticensis Theologiae Moralis* (1665-1724), a comprehensive treatise on moral theology that was highly esteemed by St. Alphonsus Liguori.

Salutati, Coluccio (1331-1406) ● In full, Coluccio di Piero di Salutati. Italian humanist and long-serving chancellor of Florence, he was a native of Tuscany. He studied at Bologna and then served as the chancellor of the Commune of Todi, chancellor of Lucca, and then secretary to Pope Urban IV. In 1375, he was elected chancellor of Florence, an office he would hold for thirty years, until his death. Aside from his varied and often complex political involvements, Salutati was involved energetically in the intellectual life of the city and hence played a role in the early Renaissance. The great humanist scholar Manuel Chrysoloras came to Florence during this period, and Salutati secured for him a pension of a hundred *florins* a year. He also worked to collect Latin manuscripts and advanced scholarship in the field of classical studies. Salutati composed Latin verse and epigrams and several treatises. Anneas Sylvius (the future Pius II, r. 1458-1464) observed that by his own time, Salutati had been much obscured by other (Renaissance) writers.

Salvian (fl. mid-fifth century) ● Christian writer, also known as Salvianus Massiliensis. Born perhaps in Germany (near Cologne) to Christian parents, he married a pagan woman named Palladia, who was converted to Christianity; the couple then agreed to live apart in continence to devote their lives to prayer. Around 420 or 430 he went to Lérins where he became an ascetic under the direction of Honoratus. He later went to Massilia (modern Marseilles) and was reported by Gennadius of Marseilles to be a priest in the Church. Of the works by Salvian mentioned by Gennadius, only two treatises

and nine letters are extant. *De gubernatione Dei* (also *De presenti judico*) was written after 439 and was a treatise in eight books devoted to providing an explanation for the invasions of the Roman Empire by the Germanic hosts. He contrasted the depraved but Orthodox Roman Christians with the vital, virtuous but Arian barbarian hordes. A moralist in keeping with the Roman tradition dating to the historian Tacitus (d. c. 117), he called upon contemporary society to reform itself and become pure in the faith. The other treatise, *Ad ecclesiam*, exhorted Christians toward charity and to make the Church their heir.

Sanchez, Thomas (1550-1610) ● Spanish Jesuit theologian. Born in Córdoba, he joined the Society of Jesus in 1567, having overcome their initial refusal owing to a speech impediment. He served as master of novices in Granada and taught theology, but most of his life was devoted to his writings. His chief work was *Disputationes de sancti matrimonii sacramento* (1602), a comprehensive examination of the sacrament of marriage, or matrimony. Ranked as one of the foremost treatises on the subject, it suffered nevertheless the curious fate of being placed on the Index of Forbidden Books. This was caused by the publication in 1614 of a Venetian edition that omitted a small section concerning the power of the pope to grant legitimacy to the children of a marriage declared invalid because of a stipulation in canon law. This passage was opposed by the Venetian Republic. Sanchez also wrote the *Opus morale in praecipta Decalogi* (published posthumously in 1613), a manual on casuistry based on the Decalogue. It was left unfinished, the author reaching only the Second Commandment. While attacked for supposed laxity (by Blaise Pascal in his *Lettres provinciales*, for example), the work merely considered the concept of mental reservations (*restrictio* *mentalis*) and did not consider them applicable in every case.

Sanctuary, Right of ● Also called right of asylum. A custom found in Christian lands, especially during the Middle Ages, it allowed a criminal or some fugitive to seek refuge in a church. The practice evolved out of Roman law in which a bishop was able to intercede on a criminal's behalf, thereby ensuring the individual's safety. Sanctuary took various forms in medieval Europe — in Germany, for example, the Church would surrender a fugitive after being guaranteed that no harm would come to their ward — receiving its most extensive development in England where two forms existed: that of every church and sanctuary by royal charter. A church was able to provide protection for a criminal, meaning that the royal officials could not enter into the actual church or possibly even come into a certain set territory surrounding it. Individual customs were used so that a person might have to be seated upon a throne, or *frithstool*, before being recognized, or had to grab the large ring or knocker on the church door. In cases where there was a territorial sanctuary, the precise limits were marked out (usually a mile in diameter) by numerous sanctuary crosses that state officials could not cross while in pursuit of a wanted person. While the individual could not be forcibly extracted from a church, secular officials could starve him into submission after forty days if the so-called oath of abjuration was not taken. This oath, made before a coroner, permitted the fugitive to travel unmolested to a seaport and to embark on a trip into exile. Certain crimes naturally did not apply, such as high treason or sacrilege; for violent crimes like murder, a limited sanctuary was available to give adequate time for arranging suitable compensation to the victim or surviving family members.

Royal or secular sanctuary was established out of a royal charter that recognized certain places to which a person could flee. There were many such sites in the kingdom regulated by local magnates who would grant a place of safety in return for an oath of fealty and compensation, if applicable. The royal charter, bestowing a far more desirable form of sanctuary, was possessed by at least twenty-two churches, including Westminster, York, Norwich, Durham, and Winchester. This sanctuary should not be confused with that possessed by all churches. Gradually curtailed with the centralizing tendencies of the absolutist Tudors, sanctuary virtually ceased with the Reformation in England under King Henry VIII (r. 1509-1547). Besides ambassadorial houses, which gave some aid to the hunted, the last surviving sanctuary was the Whitefriars, London, abolished in 1697; sanctuary for crimes had been ended in England by an act of King James I in 1623. Throughout Europe, sanctuary was terminated by the late 1700s.

Sander, Nicholas (1530-1581) ● Also Sanders. An English Catholic historian, he was born at Charlwood, in Surrey, studying at Winchester and Oxford. Graduating in 1551, he participated in the reform of the university but was forced to flee from England in 1559 after the accession of Queen Elizabeth I. Ordained in Rome around 1560, he authored for Cardinal Moroni the "Report on the State of England." Sander then attended the Council of Trent in the position of theologian to Cardinal Hosius. After the council, he accompanied the cardinal to Poland, Prussia, and Lithuania. In 1565, he went to Louvain where he joined the numerous Catholic exiles who had gone there, including his mother and sister. He served as professor of theology and became involved in the controversy surrounding Bishop John Jewel's *Apologia Ecclesiae Anglicanae* (1562), a defense of the Church of England. Sander published in response *The Supper of the Lord* (1565), *A Treatise of*

Images (1566), *The Rock of the Church* (1567), and his chief work, *De visibili monarchia ecclesiae* (1571). His writings in support of English Catholics did much to establish the exiles as a real and devoted community while making Sander one of the chief leaders of the Catholic refugees. In 1567, he was granted, with Thomas Harding and Thomas Peacock, the power to return heretics to the Church. Summoned to Rome in 1572, Sander was thought to be on his way to the cardinalate, but Pope St. Pius V died before he arrived; Gregory XIII instead named him an adviser on English affairs. The next year, he went to Spain to enlist the aid of King Philip II in the struggle with Elizabeth. In 1579, he sailed to Ireland and, as a papal representative, caused an uprising against England. The result was a bloody, fruitless insurrection during which Sander died from exhaustion. He left unfinished the short book *De schismate Anglicano* (*De Origine ac Progressio Schismatis Anglicani*), first published in Cologne by E. Rishton in 1585. It provides many useful details on the events of the period from the Catholic view.

Santa Maria Maggiore ● One of the great basilicas of Rome, situated on the Esquiline Hill. According to tradition, the church was founded in 352 by Pope Liberius as the result of a dream in which the Virgin Mary commanded him to build a church where he found snow. To his surprise, snow fell on the Esquiline on August 5, in the middle of a severely hot summer. In the snow could be seen the footprints of Our Lady. The event was long celebrated as the Feast of Our Lady of the Snows (August 5), now called the Dedication of the Basilica of St. Mary. The day is celebrated by having thousands of white petals float down from the ceiling during a service. Originally rose petals, the petals used today are usually from dahlias. The present-day church was begun under Pope Sixtus III around 432 on the site of a former Roman basilica. Enlarged during the

fifth century, the church was the site of several notable events during the Middle Ages, such as the kidnapping of Pope Gregory VII by enemies in 1075 while the pontiff was saying Christmas Mass and the crowning of Cola di Rienzo as tribune in 1347 was taking place. Extensive modifications and additions were made during the Renaissance and Baroque eras. An obelisk was added by Pope Sixtus V in 1587; a gilded ceiling, supposedly using gold brought from America by Christopher Columbus, was installed as a gift by Pope Alexander VI (r. 1492-1503), and the beautiful façade was erected in 1743 by Ferdinando Fuga by command of Pope Benedict XIV. Also found are magnificent mosaics, dating from the fifth century (in the nave) and the late 1200s and early 1300s (in the apse). Santa Maria Maggiore is the largest of the eighty churches in Rome dedicated to the BVM.

Santiago de Compostela ● City in Galicia, Spain, renowned for its shrine to St. James. During the Middle Ages, Santiago de Compostela was one of the most important pilgrimage centers in all of Christendom, behind only Rome and Jerusalem. According to tradition, the tomb of St. James was discovered around 813 through supernatural inspiration. St. James had supposedly been martyred in Jerusalem (c. 44) and his bones taken to Spain where they were interred in the part of the country he had evangelized. An earthen church was constructed over the tomb by the ruler of Asturias, Alfonso II. This was replaced with a stone edifice in the reign of Alfonso III, and the entire site became a source of tremendous inspiration to the Christians of Spain in their efforts to defeat the Moors and reclaim all of the peninsula to the faith. Pilgrims soon began visiting the shrine; however, in 997, the entire town, but not the tomb, was destroyed by the Moors under Al-Mansur. Recaptured, the town was rebuilt and in 1075 King Alfonso IV of

León-Castile began the magnificent cathedral. Consecrated in 1211, the cathedral had later additions made to it that included a Baroque west façade and a Romanesque portico. Santiago de Compostela remains one of the great pilgrim sites.

Santiago, Knights of ● See under **Military Orders**.

Sardica, Council of ● Council summoned around 343 by Emperor Constans and Constantius II in an effort to resolve the doctrinal crisis that had been caused by the Arian controversy and the deposition of St. Athanasius as patriarch of Alexandria. Convened at Sardica (modern Sofia), in Dacia, the council was intended to be an ecumenical one, but the few Eastern bishops who actually arrived refused to take part because they were unwilling to recognize Athanasius and other excommunicated prelates who were in attendance and were recognized by the Western bishops. The president of the council, Hosius of Córdoba, failed to negotiate a compromise, and only the Western bishops came together; the Eastern prelates met in Philippopolis. The Council of Sardica restored Athanasius and lifted all censure or deposition from Asclepas, bishop of Gaza, and Marcellus of Ancyra. Further, several Eastern bishops were

Santiago de Compostela

deposed and excommunicated for grave irregularities in leaving the conciliar proceedings. While the council passed a series of well-known canons on discipline that were sent to Pope Julius I, it failed entirely in its purpose. No resolution was achieved in the crisis, and the Eastern bishops were further alienated from the colleagues in the West. (See **Arianism**.)

Sarpi, Paolo (1552-1623) ● Servite antipapal historian, author of the *Historia del concilio Tridentino*. A Venetian by birth, he entered the Servite order at the age of thirteen, taking the name Fra Paolo in place of his birth name, Pietro. After spending a number of years teaching theology, philosophy, and canon law, he was ordained in 1574. In 1579, he was elected provincial of the Servites in Venice, subsequently serving as procurator-general, residing in Rome from 1585-1588. Sarpi returned to Venice and soon began acquiring his reputation for an anti-Roman bias. He was accused of being overly sympathetic with various Protestant elements and thus earned the suspicion of the Curia, which refused him on three different occasions elevation to the episcopate after nominations were made by the Republic of Venice in 1593, 1600, and 1601. These setbacks seemed only to have hardened Sarpi's feelings toward Rome and the papacy, an opinion encouraged by the Venetians and their doge Leonardo Donato. He was granted special protection by the Venetian state and was appointed theological consultor to the republic. During the conflict between Venice and Pope Paul V (r. 1605-1621) Sarpi was an ardent partisan of the republic, using his influence to render meaningless the interdict that had been placed upon Venice by the pope. It would be revoked in April 1607. That same year, Sarpi was excommunicated and in October was nearly assassinated. The plot has been frequently attributed to his enemies in the Church, but evidence remains inconclusive. He continued to serve as adviser and to function as a priest until his death, despite the state of being excommunicated. His antipapal views found bitter expression in the *Historia del Concilio Tridentino* (published in London in 1619 under the pseudonym Pietro Soave Polano). A history of the Council of Trent, the work is a savage attack on the papacy, claiming that the council was nothing more than a conspiracy to prevent reform of the Church. While using much authoritative material, the *Historia* is rendered virtually useless by its vindictiveness and mean-spirited perspective. A refutation was authored by Pietro Pallavicino.

Sarum, Use of ● Also Use of Salisbury. A set of modifications or adaptations of the Roman liturgy that was used at the cathedral of Salisbury during the Middle Ages. They were supposedly inaugurated by St. Osmund (d. 1099), although their actual usage did not begin until a much later date. Richard Poor (d. 1237), bishop of Salisbury, first compiled

a collection of services relating to the Use of Sarum, providing a comprehensive directory. A revision in the fourteenth century, called the New Sarum Use (or New Use of Sarum), included a number of changes that had been made in the calendar. From around the 1200s, the Use of Sarum became increasingly popular in the dioceses of

Salisbury Cathedral (c. 1220)

England, spreading by the middle of the fifteenth century to the dioceses of nearly all of England and Wales, and parts of Ireland. The so-called Sarum Breviary was imposed in 1543 by the Canterbury Convocation (the provincial assembly of the clergy of the Church of England) on the province of Canterbury. The books containing the Use of Sarum were important sources of material for the first Book of Common Prayer, the Prayer Book of Edward VI (1549).

Satis Cognitum ● Encyclical issued on June 29, 1896, "On the unity of the Church," by Pope Leo XIII. The encyclical stressed the genuine desirability of Christian unity and the sincere hope of the Church for an eventual reunion of all of Christendom. Nevertheless, Pope Leo made it clear that such a reunion must be rooted in the recognition of the pope as the sole source of spiritual and ecclesiastical jurisdiction and the acceptance of the Holy See's primacy over the Church. The pontiff wrote: "It is the duty of the Church to carry to all men of all ages the salvation won by Jesus Christ and all the blessings that flow from it. It is therefore necessary, in accordance with the will of its founder, that it should be the only Church in the whole world for all time. . . . The episcopal order is considered to be in proper union with Peter, as Christ commanded, if it subordinate to Peter and obeys him . . . it is false, and in obvious contradiction to the divine constitution, to say that the individual bishops, but not the bishops as a whole, should be subject to the jurisdiction of the Roman Pontiff. . . . This power over the college of bishops, of which we have been treating, is clearly mentioned in the Scripture, and the Church has never failed to recognize it and to bear witness to it." *Satis Cognitum* was followed on September 13, 1896, by the bull *Apostolicae Curae* declaring the Anglican Orders to be invalid.

Saul ● See **Paul of Tarsus, St**.

Sava, St. (c. 1176-1235) ● Also Sabas. Patron saint of Serbia, he was born Rastko, the third son of the Serbian ruler Stephen Nemanja. In 1191, he journeyed to Mt. Athos and there entered a monastery, taking the name Sava. He was joined there in 1196 by his father, who had abdicated in favor of his eldest brother Stephen. With his father, Sava established the monastery of Khilandar (Hilandar) on Mt. Athos. This monastery emerged as the heart of Serbian cultural life.

Returning to Serbia in 1208, Sava opposed his brother's policy of promoting the Western Church in Serbia and his close political alliance with the papacy. Through the help of the patriarch of Nicaea, Sava was consecrated the first archbishop of the Serbian Church in 1219, marking the birth of an independent Church for the Serbs. Under Sava's leadership the Serbian Church turned to the East for inspiration, rejecting the Western (or Latin) Church. Sava also promoted learning and built churches. Feast day: January 14 in the Serbian Church.

Savonarola, Girolamo (1452-1498) ● Italian religious reformer, preacher, and, from 1494-1498, master of the city of Florence. Born and educated in Ferrara, he joined the Dominicans in 1474, supposedly after hearing a moving sermon on repentance by an Augustinian. Devoted to a rigorous ascetic life, he was conscious of the moral decay of the times, composing in his first year in the order the poem "On the Decline of the Church." After serving in Bologna as instructor of novices, he was sent around 1482 to Florence and the priory of San Marco. Appalled by the immorality and what he considered the pagan atmosphere of Renaissance Florence, he began preaching, denouncing the sins of the times. In August 1490, he launched an apocalyptic style of preaching that soon brought a large following. His prophecies of doom captured the imagination. The following year, he was made prior of San Marco, soon denouncing Lorenzo de' Medici, even though the Medici family had been great patrons of the monastery, and predicting Lorenzo the Magnificent's fall. This came in 1494 with the ouster of the Medicis from power in the face of the advance of King Charles VIII of France into Italy. Savonarola greeted the French ruler as the means of restoring reform to the Church. Charles was welcomed into the city and, after his departure, the Florentines established a quasi-republic. Based on

Savonarola's social and political doctrines, the new constitution of Florence laid down a theocratic democracy with a great council and laws adhering to those of Christ. Savonarola did not interfere directly with the affairs of political life, but his influence was supreme — and his severe views were ever present in the daily goings-on of the city.

Savonarola preached incessantly on the abuses and failings of the Church. He reformed the monastery of San Marco, founded a brotherhood of young people that policed the morals of the city, and held public burnings in the monastery of immoral items such as playing cards, portraits of nude or beautiful women, and pagan writings or poetry. His sermons grew increasingly extreme, however, as his hopes increased of leading a movement in Italy and then all of Christendom to revitalize the Church. Attacks on the Curia and Pope Alexander VI led the pontiff to summon Savonarola to Rome in 1495 to face questions on his prophecies. Claiming ill health, the monk refused to leave the city, prompting a papal brief that forbade him from preaching. This Savonarola refused to follow, delivering an especially vicious sermon against the Church of Rome. On May 13, 1497, Pope Alexander VI excommunicated him. Disregarding the condemnation, he continued to preach against the Church, but his enemies inside the city were now considerable owing to the severity of his measures and his radicalism.

Savonarola

A Franciscan challenged one of Savonarola's followers to an ordeal of fire to disprove the prophecies, a challenge that was never met. With two of his disciples, Savonarola was arrested and imprisoned. After being tortured and confessing to lies and personal ambition, he was condemned to death. Although he retracted his confession, he and his two followers were hanged in the market of Florence and on May 25 their bodies were burned. His large following melted away immediately after his arrest. While he challenged the papacy and was both fanatical and disobedient, he was not considered a heretic. Among his writings were theological treatises, a *Compendium revelationum*, and the *Triumphus Crucis de fidei veritate* (*The Triumph of the Cross*), a well-written apology for Christianity. The *Dialogo della verita* and several sermons were later placed on the Index of Forbidden Books. Savonarola was considered erroneously by some of the Reformers to be a precursor of the Reformation. A statue was thus erected of him in Worms at the foot of the monument to Luther. He was much revered by St. Catherine of Ricci.

Scala Sancta ● Also the *Scala Pilati*. Latin for Sacred Stairs, the *Scala Sancta* is a staircase of twenty-eight steps made of Tyrian marble that is located near the Church of St. John Lateran (Italian: San Giovanni in Laterano) in Rome. The stairs are covered with wood and are housed in a building across from the basilica on the east side of the Piazza di San Giovanni that contains parts of the old Lateran Palace of the popes. The *Scala Sancta* (or *Scala Santa* in Italian) are reputed to be the steps of Pilate's *praetorium* in Jerusalem that were traversed by Christ on the way to his interrogation by the Roman procurator. They were said to have been brought to Rome from Jerusalem by St. Helena around 326, although the earliest mention of them is in the seventh century. Known during the Middle Ages as the *Scala Pilati*, they were part of the Lateran Palace until its destruction by Pope Sixtus V (r. 1585-1590). He ordered them moved to the present site where they lead to the *Sancta Sanctorum*, the old private chapel of the popes in the Lateran Palace. The *Scala* were covered with wood so that no foot may step upon them. To ascend to the *Sancta Sanctorum*, they may be climbed only by persons on their knees. Pilgrims continue to visit the site, especially on Good Friday. The chapel was built in 1278 by Pope Nicholas III.

Scaramelli, Giovanni (1687-1752) ●

Italian Jesuit writer. Born in Rome, he entered the Society of Jesus in September 1706 and was ordained in 1717. Aside from the missions and preaching in which he was engaged for many years, Scaramelli devoted himself to spiritual writings. Among his works were: *Direttorio ascetico* (1754; *Ascetic Directory*), a series of treatises on Christian perfection, obstacles to its attainment, the cardinal virtues, and the theological virtues; *Discernimento de'spirit* (1753; *Discernment of the Spirit*); and *Direttorio mistico* (1754; *Mystic Directory*), a guide to mysticism and spiritual direction that was intended to complete the work begun in the *Direttorio ascetico*. The *Direttorio ascetico* is still considered a classic work in the study of Christian perfection.

Scarampi, Pier Francesco (1596-1656) ●

Oratorian and papal representative. Born in Piedmont to a noble family, he was intended by his parents to join the military but instead entered the religious life after a visit to Rome. He was admitted to the Oratory of St. Philip Neri in November 1636. In 1643, Pope Urban VIII sent him to Ireland at the request of Father Luke Wadding, the envoy of the Irish Confederation to Rome. Scarampi was to represent the pope to the Supreme Council of the Irish Confederation. Scarampi was greeted with great enthusiasm by the Irish, who soon implored the pontiff to make Scarampi an archbishop and apostolic nuncio to Ireland. Scarampi declined these honors. Recalled to Rome in 1647 by Pope Innocent X, Scarampi was replaced as nuncio, taking his leave from what contemporary writers described as a tear-filled crowd. He sailed from Ireland with five Irish youths who planned to enter the priesthood; one of them was Oliver Plunket, the future martyr and archbishop of Armagh. Scarampi died while caring for plague victims in Rome.

Schall von Bell, Johann Adam

(1591-1666) ● Jesuit missionary to China and astronomer. A native of Cologne, he was born to a prominent family of the city. He studied at Rome and there joined the Society of Jesus on October 20, 1611. The next years were devoted to the study of philosophy and theology; however, desiring to embark on missionary labors, he requested permission to go to China. In April 1618, he set sail from Lisbon, reaching China in 1619. Having also studied the latest developments in astronomy, Schall was soon able to impress the Chinese with his astronomical knowledge and was granted an important post in the Chinese government to assist in reforming the Roman calendar. Schall benefited from the 1611 decree that enlisted the aid of the foreign missionaries in calendar revision and requested the translation of Western books on astronomy. Around 1630, he was summoned to Beijing to assume the duties of the recently deceased Father Terrentius, who had spearheaded missionary reforms of the calendar. Schall's work was much assisted by the fall of the Ming Dynasty (1368-1644) and the rise of the Manchus, who established the Ch'ing Dynasty. Winning the confidence of the new rulers, Schall was named director of the Imperial Board of Astronomy. He also subsequently served as a powerful adviser to the Manchu emperor Shun-chih (r. 1644-1661), who called Schall *ma fa*, or grandfather. Schall was thus able to propagate the faith and to build a church in Beijing in 1650. The emperor gave the Jesuits the additional privilege of being allowed to preach everywhere. The emperor's son would later prove favorable to the Western faith, but there occurred in the short term a counterreaction to the Christian missionaries that began with the death of Shun-chih and the assumption of power by a board of regents. In 1664, Schall was arrested and charged with the murder of the emperor. Condemned to death with several fellow Christians, he was spared because of an earthquake that struck the day after the sentence was passed; five Chinese Catholics were put to death, however. Schall, who had already suffered a stroke, died in Beijing on August 15, 1666. A few years after his death, he was formally exonerated of all charges, one of the first important acts of Shun-chih's son when he reached his majority. While

A Byzantine mosaic

overshadowed by Matteo Ricci, Schall made important contributions to advancing the Christian cause in China.

Scheeben, Matthias Joseph (1835-1888) ●
German theological writer. Born in Mechenheim, near Bonn, he studied at the Gregorian University in Rome and was ordained in December 1858. From 1860, he taught theology at the seminary of Cologne. In his numerous writings he devoted himself exclusively to mysticism, with speculations on grace, hypostatic union, and the beatific vision. His works on divine grace included *Natur und Gnade* (1861; *Nature and Grace*), *Die Herrlichkeiten der göttlichen Gnade* (1863; *The Glory of Divine Grace*), and *Quid est Homo*, a new edition of the original work by Casini. He also authored *Die Mysterien des Christenthums* (1865-1897; *The Mysteries of Christianity*), pamphlets in defense of Vatican Council I, and the important *Handbuch der katholischen Dogmatik* (1873-1882; *Handbook of Catholic Dogma*), a major contribution to theology based on Thomistic teaching but utilizing all possible sources. Scheeben opposed the anti-Infallibilists, particularly Döllinger, and was an ardent supporter of the doctrine of papal infallibility of Pope Pius IX that had been promulgated by the First Vatican Council.

Schism ● Greek for "tear" or "division." The term is used to denote the conscious and willful separation of a group from the unity of the Church and thus also from communion.

Schism differs from heresy in that it is not based on doctrinal differences to begin with and there is no loss of orders for clerics within the schism; bishops can ordain priests, and priests can still celebrate the sacraments. While heresy is contrary to the faith and is a sin against the faith, schismatics commit a sin against charity. The canonical penalty of obstinate schismatics is excommunication. Schisms have occurred throughout much of the history of the Church. It was probably first used in a formal way by St. Irenaeus (second century) in his work *Adversus omnes Haereses*. Among the early schisms were those of the Novatianists and the Donatists. The two most famous were the Great Schism (which plagued the Western Church) and the Eastern Schism (which divided the Eastern and Western Churches). The Eastern Schism caused the virtually irreparable breech between the Churches, especially after 1054 when Cardinal Humbert of Silva-Candida, legate of Pope Leo IX, traded condemnations with the patriarch of Constantinople, Michael Cerularius. The Church recently has faced schism caused by the actions of Archbishop Marcel Lefebvre (d. 1991) and the schismatic Priestly Society of St. Pius X, headed since 1983 by Father Franz Schmidberger. In *Lumen Gentium*, the Second Vatican Council declared: "The Church recognizes that in many ways she is linked with those who, being baptized, are honored with the name of Christian, though they do not profess the faith in its entirety or do not preserve unity of communion with the successors of Peter" (No. 15).

Pope Urban VI

Schism, Eastern ● Long-running schism dividing the Eastern (or Orthodox) and Western (or Roman Catholic) Churches. The so-called Eastern Schism — from a Western perspective — formally erupted in 1054, although events had been leading to it for many centuries, the causes being traced to the wide differences that had developed between the East and West in matters of culture, politics, jurisdiction, language, and even some elements of doctrine. Among the early signals of an ever-widening gulf were: the disputes over Arianism in the fourth century; the attempts by the patriarchs of Constantinople to increase their authority over the East and rival the see of Rome in the Church; the Acacian Schism of the fifth century; the controversy over the Three Chapters in the sixth century; the use of the *Filioque* (And the Son) in the West on a regular basis throughout the lands of the Franks in the ninth century; the claims of Charlemagne (d. 814) as emperor in the face of Byzantine opposition; the crisis caused by Photius, patriarch of Constantinople; and the decline of the Byzantine Empire as a major power both in Europe and the Middle East. As the atmosphere of mistrust and mutual suspicion had been created, it was perhaps inevitable that one further dispute would bring about a full rupture. This took place in 1054.

Patriarch Michael Cerularius of Constantinople (d. 1058), a virulent opponent of the Latins, attempted to curb the inroads made by the Latin rite in Italian territory held by the Byzantines and hence under his jurisdiction. He ordered all churches in the region to adopt the Byzantine rite. This sparked a controversy.

Pope St. Leo IX (r. 1049-1054) attempted to resolve the situation through negotiation, sending to Constantinople the legate Humbert of Silva-Candida. He matched Michael's hostility with his own and the ill will on both sides was brought to a head in 1054: Humbert excommunicated Michael, placing the bull on the altar of the Hagia Sophia in Constantinople and the patriarch responded with his own anathema.

Pope Gregory XII

The efforts to bring the Byzantines back into communion were hindered by the long-standing animosity of the two sides, exacerbated by the overthrow of the empire in 1204 by the Fourth Crusade and the installation of the Latin Empire of Constantinople. Some success was achieved at the Council of Lyons (1274) and especially Florence (1438-1439), but the unwillingness of the Byzantine people and clergy to accept reunion doomed any long-term progress toward reunion. The capture of Constantinople in 1453 by the Ottoman Turks rendered reunion virtually impossible. Relations improved between the Catholic and Orthodox Churches in the middle of the twentieth century, under the inspiration of Popes John XXIII and Paul VI and Ecumenical Patriarchs Athenagoras I and Dimitrios I. (See **Orthodox Eastern Churches**.)

Schism, Great ● Also known as the Great Western Schism or the Western Schism. The conflict that divided the Church in the West from 1378-1417, it began shortly after the death of Pope Gregory XI in 1378 (the pontiff known for ending the Avignon period, the so-called Babylonian Captivity) and the election of Urban VI (r. 1378-1389). The conclave that resulted in the election of Bartolomeo Prignano as Urban had been conducted under intense pressure from the Roman mobs to choose an Italian and thereby break the French lock on the papacy. Urban, an Italian, only added to the unease of the French cardinals by deliberately alienating them. He then raised questions among the other members of the College of Cardinals by behaving with arrogance and displaying at times what appeared to be mental instability. A group of cardinals thus took the decisive step of declaring the election to be invalid on the grounds of irregularities and coercion. In his stead, they supported Robert of Geneva, antipope Clement VII, who took up residence at Avignon.

The Church quickly split into two camps. Urban was supported by the Holy Roman Empire, Scandinavia, England, Hungary, and most of Italy. Clement was backed by France, Spain, Scotland, Sicily, and Savoy. The crisis did not end with Urban's death in 1389 but would continue under his successors Boniface IX (1389-1404), Innocent VII (1404-1406), and Gregory XII (1406-1415). Clement, meanwhile, died in 1394 and was followed by Pedro de Luna, antipope Benedict XIII (1394-1423). Neither side was willing to summon a general council to resolve the crisis, but adherents of conciliarism proposed that a council was the only effective solution. Conciliarists were able to promote and finally secure the convening of a council, at Pisa in 1409, but its deliberations only complicated matters by electing a third pope, Antipope Alexander V (1409-1410). He would be succeeded by Antipope John XXIII (1410-1415) who, to his credit, was receptive to the urging of Emperor Sigismund that another council be summoned. The result was the Council of Constance (1414-1418), which brought an end to the schism by accepting the resignation of Gregory XII, deposing Benedict and John, and electing Cardinal Oddo Colonna as Martin V, the first sole pontiff in some thirty-nine years.

Schlegel, Karl Wilhelm Friedrich von (1772-1829) ● German writer and Catholic apologist who helped inspire the early German Romantic movement. A native of Hanover, he studied at the University of Göttingen and then at Leipzig. After settling in Jena with his brother August Wilhelm von Schlegel (1767-1845), who would also be a champion of the Romantic movement, Friedrich moved to Berlin in 1797 where he developed a friendship with his future wife, Dorothea, daughter of Moses Mendelsohn, and became a leader of the Romantic movement. He married Dorothea in 1804 and in 1809 they became Catholics. That same year he was made a secretary in the court and state chancellory in Vienna. While in Vienna, Schlegel delivered a series of lectures on modern history (1810-1812) in which he defended the concept of medieval imperialism against the government of Napoleon. Schlegel also spoke out bitterly against the French emperor and lectured on ancient and modern literature. He was in Frankfurt from 1815-1818, as part of the Austrian legation, returning to Vienna and editing the journal *Concordia* (1820-1823). He was an advocate of a restored Christian culture, working with St. Clement Maria Hofbauer and others to promote a Christian state and Christian ideals. Among his writings were *Philosophie der Geschichte* (2 vols., 1828; *Philosophy of History*) and *Die Geschichte der alten und neuen Literatur* (1815; *The History of Ancient and Modern Literature*).

Schoenstatt Movement ● Apostolic movement founded in Schoenstatt, Germany, in 1914 by Father Joseph Kentenich, S.A.C. The movement led to the establishing of five secular institutes: one for laymen, two for women, and two for priests. Its purpose is to promote spiritual development in the Christian life and combat the dangers of materialism and secularism by cultivation of and adherence to the developed Christian ideals. Members also stress devotion to the Virgin Mary. Central to the movement are the lay institutes. Members promote religious education while maintaining the Christian life in the day-to-day activities of marriage, parenting, and work. Father Kentenich's Schoenstatt Sisters of Mary, begun in 1926, is now the largest of the secular institutes. It received pontifical rights in 1948 and arrived in the United States in 1949. The Secular Institute of Schoenstatt Fathers, for priests serving the Schoenstatt movement, was begun in 1965. It received approval as a secular institute in June 1988.

Schola Cantorum ● Latin for "choir school" or "school for singers," the *schola cantorum* trained singers and taught mastery of liturgical musical tradition. In the early Church, it was customary that the music used in worship would be provided by the clerics themselves, with the support and assistance of the congregation. This practice came to be replaced by a more organized and systematic use of singers actually trained in music. The need for training led to the creation of actual schools where students could be instructed in voice, composition, and instrument. It is suggested that Pope Hilarius (r. 461-468) founded the first *schola cantorum*, but scholars generally agree that, based on the writings of John the Deacon, it can be argued that Pope Gregory I the Great (r. 590-604) established the school in Rome on a solid basis. The course of study was reportedly quite extensive for the time, and a complete period of preparation took nine years. Students mastered singing and plainsong. The house that Gregory donated to the *schola* was rebuilt by Pope Sergius II in 844. He had been trained in the school, as were a number of successors. The idea of the *schola cantorum* soon spread from Rome, becoming institutionalized in the great cathedrals (York, Worcester, and others), and monasteries (Malmesbury, Molesme, and elsewhere), thereby permitting the standardizing of Church music in the West. Many *scholae* died out after the Middle Ages when churches began using paid singers. Some *scholae* continued to function, part of the important work of maintaining study and appreciation of the magnificent musical history of the Church. The name *schola cantorum* is also used for a select group of singers who chant the more complicated or elaborate portions of liturgical music. The place and continued appreciation of the *schola cantorum* was made clear by Vatican Council II when it declared in the "Constitution on the Sacred Liturgy" (*Sacrosanctam Concilium*): "The treasure of sacred music is to be preserved and fostered with very great care. Choirs must be diligently promoted, especially in cathedral churches." (See **Music**.)

Scholastica, St. (d. 543) ● Sister of St. Benedict of Nursia. Almost nothing is known about her save a mention made of her in one of St. Gregory the Great's *Dialogues*. She dedicated herself at an early age to God and came to live in some kind of convent near Monte Cassino and her brother. According to Gregory, she and Benedict would meet once a year at a house close to Monte Cassino where they would discuss matters of spiritual importance. She died three days after her yearly reunion with Benedict. When Benedict died some four years later, around 547, he was buried in the same grave as his sister. Feast day: February 10.

Scholasticism ● Broad term describing an extensive system of theology and philosophy that developed in medieval Europe in the schools and universities. It had as its goal a greater understanding and exploration of revealed truth and Church doctrine through the application of reason, analogy, and careful analysis of faith. First applied pejoratively in the 1500s by Renaissance intellectuals, Scholasticism was attacked by some philosophers as monolithic and uniform; in reality, Scholastic thought was remarkably varied in its expression, and was a rich and profound testament of the reason and faith of the great minds who devoted their lives to its propagation.

Scholasticism was born and flourished in a long period of deep faith. It was advanced and developed by Churchmen and its greatest achievements were on behalf of the Church, reaching its zenith under the Angelic Doctor, St. Thomas Aquinas (d. 1274). The history of Scholasticism can be divided into specific eras: medieval Scholasticism (eighth through fifteenth centuries), the Catholic Reformation (1520-1640), and Neo-Scholasticism (nineteenth and twentieth centuries). Within these long eras there were numerous periods of development so that Scholastic thought was an ongoing process characterized by the efforts of specific members of the movement, known generally as the Schoolmen.

The origins of Scholasticism are traced to the writings of St. Augustine of Hippo and other early Church Fathers as well as Cassiodorus and Boethius. St. Augustine was especially influential with his emphasis on dialectics and such works as *De Praedestinatione Sanctorum* and *De Doctrina Christiana*. His maxim *"Ergo intellige ut credos, crede ut intelligas"* ("Understand in order to believe, believe in order to understand") was used by John Scotus Erigena, one of the leaders of the revival of learning in the ninth century. He was one of the first philosophers to make a distinction between Holy Scripture and reason (*ratio*), considering reason to be essential for human understanding of doctrine.

The next centuries saw the rapid development of the monastic schools, leading in the eleventh century to the rise of the cathedral schools, important centers of learning that made possible the universities of Christendom that would become bastions of Scholastic enterprise. Key members of this period were Anselm of Canterbury, Anselm of Laon, Hugh of St. Victor, William of Champeaux, Gilbert de la Porrée, Peter Lombard (author of the *Sentences*), and Peter Abelard. Notable schools were found in Chartres and St. Victor.

Thanks to the traditions of Arab philosophers, a new era was launched in the thirteenth century with the spread of Aristotle's writings throughout Europe. Initially translated from the Greek and Arabic, Aristotelian treatises were highly prized jewels for many years, gradually becoming more available throughout the 1100s and receiving full appreciation in the 1200s. The writings of Aristotle (called "the Philosopher" by the Schoolmen) gave foundation and impetus to the so-called Golden Age of Scholasticism in the 1200s that would witness the synthesis of Christianity with a meaningful and feasible undertaking through the reaching of harmony between the Augustinians (loyal adherents of Augustinianism who rejected all Aristotelian ideas not in agreement with those of St. Augustine) and the Latin Averroists (followers of the Arab philosopher Averroës and other Arab commentators who embraced pure, undiluted Aristotelianism). The chief architects of the synthesis were the Dominicans. It was foreshadowed in the work of St. Albertus Magnus and accomplished by Thomas Aquinas. Aquinas then brought Scholasticism to its crowning moment with the *Summa Theologiae*.

During his life, St. Thomas was opposed by other theologians, most notably from among the Franciscans who stressed Augustinianism. The leading Franciscans were St. Bonaventure (a friend of Thomas Aquinas), John Duns Scotus, and William of Occam. Occam was especially important in centering his arguments against Aquinas in nominalism (the concept that forms were mere abstractions from specific example) versus realism (that forms had reality in and of themselves); he was largely a factor in the decline of Scholasticism in the fifteenth century that would be hastened by the rise of humanism and natural science as embodied in the Renaissance.

Scholasticism was far from dead, however, as it endured in the Dominican houses and was adopted by the Jesuits in the sixteenth century. This so-called Renaissance Scholasticism, while overshadowed by the Renaissance and the Protestant Reformation, produced some truly great theologians and philosophers. Among them were: Dominic Báñez, John of St. Thomas, Cajetan, Francisco de Vitoria, and Francisco Sylvester de Sylvestris, called Ferrariensis — all Dominicans; and Francisco de Toledo, Gabriel Vázquez, Luis de Molina, Juan de Mariana, and Francisco Suárez — all Jesuits. The Jesuits and Dominicans were involved during this period in several controversies such as grace and predestination. While upheld and honored by the Council of Trent, Scholasticism had ceased to be a guiding force in the Church. Its revival would not come until the 1800s when it burst forth once more in the movement known as Neo-Scholasticism. (See also **Neo-Scholasticism** and **Thomism**.)

Schottenkloster ● German name meaning Scottish (or Scotch) monastery. The name used for the monastic institutions established on the Continent by Irish and Scottish monks. The monasteries were an important element in advancing the evangelization of Germany, and the presence of Irish-Scottish monks in German lands would continue until the middle of the nineteenth century. The earliest Schottenkloster was founded probably toward the end of the fifth century at Sackingen in Baden by the Irish monastery St. Fridolin. He also began the monastery in Constance. St. Columbanus (c. 543-615) was responsible for numerous monasteries with the help of his twelve companions. The successor to Columbanus and his disciples spread the Schottenklosters across Western Europe, including France, Switzerland, Belgium, and Germany. Among the most notable monasteries created by the Irish and Scottish monks were St. Gall in Switzerland, Ebersmünster in Upper Alsace, St. Martin in Cologne, and Altomünster in Upper Bavaria. Around 1072 several Scottish monks began to live in the church of Weih-St. Peter in Ratisbon. This became the monastery of St. Jacob in Ratisbon, which was named by Pope Innocent III in 1215 the motherhouse of the newly constituted congregation of the Schottenkloster comprised of a group of abbeys in Würzburg, Nuremburg, Vienna, and elsewhere that had sprung from St. Jacob in Ratisbon. Decline set in during the 1300s and 1400s so that several houses were withdrawn from the congregation and repopulated with German monks. The dwindling number of Irish and Scottish monks was bolstered in the 1500s by exiles from the British Isles as a result of the Reformation. By 1803, the only surviving Schottenkloster was St. Jacob in Ratisbon. Although permitted in 1827 to accept novices, its irreversible state of decline prompted Pope Pius IX to issue a brief suppressing the last of the Schottenklosters, bringing an end to over fifteen hundred years of contributions to the Continental monastic life by Irish and Scottish missionaries.

Scotland ● Part of the United Kingdom with a long history of fierce independence from English rule. Christianity came to the rugged regions of Scotland in the late fourth century under St. Ninian (d. c. 432), who erected the first stone church in the country at Whithorn. He also conducted missionary work among the Picts and prepared the way for the influential evangelizing effort of St. Columba (d. 597). Under his leadership, Iona became from 563 the chief center of missionary work until replaced around 635 by Lindisfarne under St. Aidan. The Church as established in Scotland belonged to the influence of the Celtic Church, remaining so until 664 when the Synod of Whitby found in favor of the Roman usage after which Celtic customs declined and finally died out.

The Scottish Church soon after passed into obscurity and darkness owing to the invasion of the British Isles by Norse raiders. During the period, however, unity in the Church was achieved on a relatively national scale with recognition of the primacy of the bishop at Dunkeld; the national seat was later transferred to St. Andrews. Under King David I (r. 1124-1153), the Church in Scotland was increasingly brought into contact and conformity with the faith on the Continent. This was promoted by the arrival of various religious or monastic orders and the founding of new dioceses. Ever present was the intense determination of the Scots, and their clergy, to remain free of English domination. The Church thus represented patriotic tendencies and resisted all attempts to place Scottish dioceses under the ecclesiastical jurisdiction of Canterbury and York. At the same time, the powerful Scottish prelates were often at variance with the nobility and the ruling families of the kingdom.

The late Middle Ages were a difficult era, for the Church, like Scotland itself, endured the invasion by King Edward I of England (r. 1272-1307), the Black Death in 1349, which wiped out over thirty percent of the population, and then the civil war that followed the assassination in 1437 of King James I. During the fifteenth century, Lollardy became popular in some circles and laid the groundwork for the Reformation in the sixteenth century. The atmosphere was further poisoned by the decay that had set in throughout much of the Church and the active involvement of many prelates in the political struggles.

The Reformation was resisted in its early stages, but the execution at the stake of Patrick Hamilton (1528) and George Wishart (1546), two Scottish reformers, widened the appeal of the movement. In retribution for his role in the death of George Wishart, Cardinal David Beaton was murdered in 1546, thus depriving the Church of an influential voice. John Knox (d. 1572) soon emerged as the prominent leader in the Scottish Reformation, and it was a measure of his success that by the time of the arrival of Mary, Queen of Scots, in 1561, Catholicism had been virtually exterminated in the Lowlands. Knox launched vituperative attacks on Mary, and her defeat in the struggle with the Protestant Lords of the Congregation brought the near extinction of the faith throughout all of Scotland. In 1560, the Reformed Church of Scotland was established, severing papal supremacy in the country. Protestantism was then made the religion of state (see **King's Confession**) and the Catholic Church suffered from harsh intolerance and legal disabilities.

As in Protestant England, the Catholic faith was kept alive through the courage of those priests who were willing to risk torture and death. In 1653, a Scottish Mission was launched, under a prefect apostolic; the Church was later aided (in the 1800s) by the "heather" priests — clergy trained in secret in the heather country. Finally, starting in 1793, various disabilities were gradually lifted. Over succeeding years, further laws were rescinded. By 1800, there were thirty thousand Catholics and in 1827 Pope Leo XII added a new vicariate to the Scottish Mission, which now had several divisions. The Catholic population soon rose to seventy thousand. On March 4, 1878, Pope Leo XIII,

fulfilling the desire of his predecessor Pius IX, issued the bull *Ex Supremo Apostolatus apice*, reestablishing the hierarchy with two archbishoprics, St. Andrews and Edinburgh. Currently, there are some seven hundred fifty thousand Catholics in Scotland. (See also **Aidan, St.; Beaton, David; Celtic Church; Easter Controversy; Lindisfarne; Margaret of Scotland, St.; Mary, Queen of Scots; Ninian, St.;** and **Whitby, Synod of**.)

Scot's Confession ● See **King's Confession**.

Sebaste, Forty Martyrs of ● Famous Roman martyrs put to death around 323 in Sebaste (modern Sivas), Lesser Armenia, as part of the persecution of Christians under Emperor Licinius Licinianus. The martyrs were part of the XII Legion, the "Thundering Legion," stationed in Sebaste when orders arrived that all Christians in the East were to renounce their faith, on pain of death. Forty soldiers refused to do so and were subjected to various threats and persuasions. When they remained firm, the order was given for them to be stripped and placed out on the ice of a frozen pond. To add to their torment, hot baths and fires were prepared in the pond bank where they could see them. The pagan commander then yelled that should they renounce their faith the fire and the baths could be enjoyed by the increasingly frozen soldiers. Only one Christian broke from his companions, but he was replaced by another soldier who, inspired by the legionnaires' bravery and a dream about angels, walked out onto the ice and sat down. By the next morning, most of the Christians were dead. Those still alive were executed. The tale of the martyrs was recounted by St. Basil of Caesarea and St. Gregory of Nyssa. Feast day: March 10.

Sebastian, St. ● Famed Roman martyr of whom nothing is known beyond the fact of his death. The sources for his martyrdom include the *Depositio Martyrum* of the Chronographer of 354 and St. Ambrose. From them, it is clear that Sebastian probably came from Milan, was put to death, was buried on the Via Appia, and was already revered in Milan in the fourth century. According to legend, Sebastian was an officer in the Imperial Guard under Emperor Diocletian. Discovered to be a Christian, he was sentenced to death, the sentence to be carried out by archers from Mauretania. The arrows, however, failed to kill him because he was healed by Irene, widow of the martyr St. Castulus. When Diocletian heard of this apparent miracle, he ordered Sebastian to be clubbed to death. Sebastian became one of the most famous of all early martyrs through the magnificent depictions of him by Renaissance painters. His symbol is the arrow. Feast day: January 20.

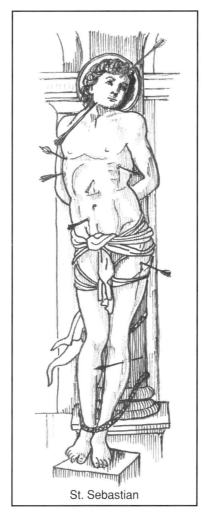

St. Sebastian

Sede Vacante ● Latin for "the see is vacant." Used for a period during which a see is unoccupied. In its broad sense, *sede vacante* refers to a period when a diocese is without a bishop due to death, resignation, or retirement. Customarily, the see is governed by an apostolic administrator, a caretaker who oversees the day-to-day running of the diocese. Such an administrator usually cannot make important personnel changes or decisions. In its specific meaning, *sede vacante* is used for the interregnum caused by the death of a pope. During this time, the daily affairs of the Church are run by the camerlengo, the Vatican chamberlain, with the assistance of the College of Cardinals. The interregnum ends with the election of a new pontiff in a conclave.

Sedulius Scotus ● Ninth-century Irish grammarian and scriptural commentator, he was also called Sedulius the Younger to distinguish him from the poet Coelius Sedulius, who composed the *Carmen Paschale*. Born in Ireland, Sedulius journeyed to Liège and, under Emperor Lothair I (r. 840-855), he entered the Irish colony of teachers and most likely held the post of tutor to Lothair's two sons Charles and Lothair. He authored commentaries on the *Isagoge* of Porphyry, the Epistles of St. Paul, and the Gospel of St. Matthew; around ninety poems; and the treatise *De Rectoribus Christianis*, a guide to the instruction of Christian rulers, one of many such works that would appear in the Middle Ages. It is possible that in his later years he journeyed to Milan.

Segneri, Paolo (1624-1694) ● Italian Jesuit preacher. Born in Nettuno, Italy, he entered the Society of Jesus in 1637 after studying at the Roman College. Ordained in 1653, he soon became one of the foremost preachers in Italy, traveling through the main cities of the peninsula, especially in Tuscany and the Papal States. His sermons from the pulpits of the great cathedral drew great crowds, appealing to the masses through the beauty of his phraseology, his devotion to God, and his personal sanctity. While criticized at times for poor taste, his sermons remain some of the finest orations to be found in the history of the Italian Church. Chief among his works was *Quaresimale* (1679), a collection of sermons delivered in Lent. They were much admired by Antonio Pignatelli; when he became Pope Innocent XII he summoned Segneri to Rome and asked him to preach before the pontiff. Segneri opposed both probabilism and quietism.

Semi-Arianism ● Also Semiarianism. Fourth-century heresy arising out of Arianism. Holding a modified position to that of the Arians, it attempted to bring theological agreement between the Arians and Orthodox Christians. In a broad sense, the Semi-Arians were in the majority among conservative Christians during the fourth century, and in a stricter sense were the adherents of the doctrinal party headed by Basil of Ancyra around 358. They believed a doctrinal view contrary to that of the Arians concerning the nature of Christ, but the Semi-Arian position was far from orthodox. Specifically, while the Arians proposed that the Son and Spirit derived their divinity from the Father and the Trinity was composed of three separate essences, the Semi-Arians argued that the Son was like the Father, using the term *homoiusios* (like). This was still at variance with the Orthodox Christians, who preferred the term *homoousios* (of the same substance). While condemned in 381 at the Council of Constantinople, the Semi-Arians gave inspiration to the Pneumatomachians and the Monarchianists. (See **Heresy**.)

Semi-Pelagianism ● Heresy emerging in the fifth century out of Pelagianism. It argued that while grace is necessary for salvation it is merited and made efficacious by the human will. The founders of the movement were monks in the south of France, who came to represent the countermovement to the doctrines of St. Augustine. They attempted to strike a middle ground between the teachings of Augustine and Pelagius on the question of grace. Their ideas were developed in the early fifth century through the writings of John Cassian, receiving support from St. Vincent of Lérins. Semi-Pelagianism spread throughout the monasteries of southern Gaul (France) and was taught by the monks of the region in the fifth and sixth centuries. After subsiding briefly in the late fifth century, Semi-Pelagianism erupted anew in controversy through the writings of St. Faustus of Riez, who authored *De Gratia* (c. 470; *On Grace*) at the request of Leontius, bishop of Arles, to refute the idea of predestination. His Semi-Pelagian views, while initially approved by the Council of Arles in 472 or 473, were now attacked by theologians in the East and the West.

Semi-Pelagianism was initially opposed by one of St. Augustine's disciples, Prosper of Aquitaine. He authored two works in defense of Augustinian doctrine, *Contra Collatorem* and *Responsiones ad Capitula Objectionum Gallorum*, written in reply to St. Vincent of Lérins and the Semi-Pelagians. By the sixth century and the controversial *De Gratia*, the opponents of the heresy secured the support of the papacy. Pope Felix IV (r. 526-530) instructed the influential St. Caesarius of Arles to condemn Semi-Pelagianism at the Second Council of Orange in 529, a condemnation reaffirmed by Boniface II, successor to Felix. From that time, the Semi-Pelagians argued that mankind must be inherently, or natively, empowered to take the vital step toward salvation, but as a consequence they denied the absolute necessity of God's gracious empowerment of the will to accept salvation. This placed them in opposition to St. Augustine, the accepted authority by the Church on these theological questions. During the controversy between Dominicans and Jesuits over the doctrine of grace in the 1500s, the term Semi-Pelagianism was used by supporters of the Dominican theologian Dominic Báñez (1528-1604) for the teachings of the Jesuit Luis de Molina (1535-1600). (See also **Heresy** and **Molina, Luis de**.)

Sens, Councils of ● Councils held at Sens in northern France. The first was convened around 601 or 602 as part of the campaign against simony that was launched by Pope St. Gregory I the Great. It was notable because of the boycott of St. Columbanus, who opposed the planned discussion of the date of Easter that was then dividing the Church in England. There were numerous other councils. Of these the most important was in 1140 when Archbishop Henri Sanglier presided over the condemnation of Peter Abelard for heresy. Peter appealed to Pope Innocent II, but the sentence was confirmed through the influence of St. Bernard of Clairvaux.

Septuagint ● Known to scholars as LXX, it is a translation of the Hebrew OT into Greek that was inherited and adopted by the early Church. The Septuagint is traditionally attributed to the desire of King Ptolemy II Philadelphius of Egypt (r. 285-249 B.C.) to have a copy of the sacred book of the Jews for his recently established library at Alexandria. The translation from the Hebrew into Greek was accomplished by seventy-two scholars (hence the name *Septuagint*). They labored supposedly for seventy-two days and at the end of that time, the translation was widely praised for its accuracy and was placed in the famed library, the repository for the virtual sum total of all learning in the ancient world. The story is considered by scholars to be legendary, based on an almost certainly apocryphal letter from Aristeas to his brother Philocrates. It is now generally agreed that the LXX took a considerable

period to be given shape and that the stories relating to the work done by the translators was embellished over succeeding years. For example, the tale spread that not only was Ptolemy responsible for having the Pentateuch translated but the entire OT as well. Further, experts have determined that not all of the translation was done in Alexandria and that different sets of translators were at work.

Regardless of its origins, the Septuagint was welcomed enthusiastically by the Jews of Alexandria and soon spread throughout the entire Greek-speaking world. In the case of several Jewish historians, it became a valuable resource. Both Philo and Josephus used it, as did many rabbis in Palestine. Thus by the time of Christ, the work was recognized as a legitimate text, permitting its use by the Gospel writers. The Septuagint also had the positive influence of securing a wide readership among the Gentiles of the Hellenic lands, promoting the spread of such ideas as the expectation of the Messiah. When Christianity began to propagate in Greek-speaking countries, many Gentiles were already familiar with important concepts of the OT and were thus receptive to the teachings of the Gospels of Christ.

The LXX was an important book for the early Christian authors. As noted, the writers of the NT used it, quoting it on a number of occasions. It became the accepted OT of the Church and was declared by some Christian authorities to have been inspired. The Church Fathers took it as their standard text, preferring it to the Hebrew versions of the OT. It was also the basis for the Old Latin version of the OT, although recensions and corrections were made by Origen, St. Lucian of Antioch, and the Egyptian bishop Hesychius in order to purify the text as much as possible of the many errors or changes that had crept in owing to the wide diffusion of copies throughout the Church. The first published edition of the LXX appeared in the Complutensian Polyglot Bible of Cardinal

Ximénez, printed from 1514-1518 but not published until 1521. The Septuagint there appeared with both the Hebrew and the Latin Vulgate. Another important edition was that published by Cardinal Caraffa under Pope Sixtus V in 1587 to assist in the preparation of the Latin Vulgate edition, which had been ordered by the Council of Trent. It should be noted that the Jews regarded the Christian use of the LXX to prove the fulfillment of the OT prophecies by Christ to be wholly improper. They thus ceased any utilization of the text. The Septuagint also remains the accepted version of the OT in the Greek Church.

Seraphic Order ● Name sometimes used for the Franciscan order (O.F.M.). It is derived from a vision by St. Francis of Assisi of a seraph on Mt. Alverna during which he received the stigmata.

Sergius I, St. ● Pope from 687 701. Born in Palermo to a Syrian family, he was ordained in Rome and was a respected priest under Popes St. Leo II and Conon. At the death of the latter in September 687, the election was split into factions, one favoring the archdeacon Paschal, the other wanting the archpriest Theodore. When no solution could be achieved, the electors (government officials, army officers, and the clergy) chose Sergius. The new pope was accepted by the exarch of Ravenna, John Platyn, but only by paying the bribe that had been promised by Paschal. As pope, Sergius proved capable and energetic. He promoted the Church in England, baptizing Caedwalla, king of the West Saxons, in 689 and granting the pallium to Brithwald of Canterbury in 693. St. Willibrord was consecrated bishop of the Frisians in 695, thereby advancing the missionary work done by him in Frisia. In his dealings with the Byzantines, Sergius rejected several of the decrees passed by the Council of Trullo (692) that tolerated clerical marriage and elevated Constantinople to the ecclesiastical equal of Rome. Sergius also introduced the chant *Agnus Dei* to the Mass. Feast day: September 8.

Sergius II ● Pope from 844-847. A member of the Roman nobility, he held various posts under his predecessors, culminating with his appointment as archpriest by Pope Gregory IV. When Gregory died on January 25, 844, the Roman mob chose the popular deacon John to be the next pontiff, but the aristocracy decided upon the elderly and sick Sergius. The troops of the nobles then stormed the Lateran, dispersed the populace, and spared John only because Sergius asked for mercy. His hastily organized consecration was performed without the approval of Emperor Lothair I, a slight that brought down the wrath of the Franks. Sergius managed to settle the issue but only after reaffirming the supremacy of the emperor and his rights of ratification. Suffering from gout, the pontiff left most of the papal administration to his brother, Bishop Benedict of Albano, launching an unfortunate episode of unscrupulous dealings and simony. The Romans were convinced that what happened in August 846 was punishment for their vices: Saracens landed at the mouth of the Tiber and stormed the city; St. Peter's and St. Paul's were looted, a catastrophe, as the treasures of both basilicas were carried off. Sergius was also responsible for enlarging St. John Lateran. His successor was Pope St. Leo IV.

Sergius III ● Pope from 904-911. A Roman by birth, he was made a deacon by Pope Stephen V (VI) and a bishop by Pope Formosus, despite his personal dislike of Formosus. Thus, after the death of Formosus in April 896, he took part in the infamous Cadaver Synod that was presided over by Pope Stephen VI (VII), exhuming and trying the rotting corpse of Formosus. As these proceedings annulled all previous ordinations by the deceased pope, Sergius was ordained a priest by Stephen. Elected to succeed Theodore II in early 898, Sergius was soon deposed by the partisans of Pope Formosus. He returned some years later with the help of Duke Alberic of Spoleto, overthrowing the antipope Christopher, who had himself deposed Pope Leo V. Consecrated on January 29, 904, Pope Sergius soon embarked on a remarkably violent and unfortunate pontificate. Both Christopher and Leo were strangled and his own reign he declared to have begun in 897, thereby proclaiming John IX, Benedict IV, and Leo V to have been usurpers. All of the condemnations of Formosus were reaffirmed, causing much havoc among the clergy, as Sergius demanded that all ordinations be redone. He then resorted to violence to enforce his demands. In this he was aided by the rapacious and ambitious Roman nobleman Theophylact. This Roman consul and his cruel wife Theodora would come to dominate the papacy over the next years, bringing the Holy See into one of its darkest periods. For Sergius's part, he relied upon Theophylact for political support, supposedly fathering a son, the future John XI, by Theodora's fifteen-year-old daughter Marozia. He was succeeded by Pope Anastasius III. Sergius was also responsible for completely restoring the Basilica of St. John Lateran.

Sergius IV ● Pope from 1009-1012. The son of a shoemaker, he was born Peter in Rome. Bearing the nickname Buccaporci (Bucca Porci — "Pig's Snout"), he served as bishop of Albano from 1004-1009 and was then elected to succeed John XVIII, being consecrated on July 31, 1009. As it was not appropriate for him to take the name Peter, he chose instead to be called Sergius (IV). He probably owed his election to the considerable influence of the Crescentii family, but throughout his pontificate he promoted relations with the ruler Henry II of Germany as a means of reducing the political power of the Crescentii. He was also known for his care of the poor during a famine in Italy. His passing on May 12, 1012, was soon followed by the demise of John II Crescentius, dictator in Rome from 1003, prompting historians to speculate on the timing of these deaths, particularly as Sergius's successor, Benedict VIII, was a member of the Tusculani, a rival family of the Crescentii. The custom of the newly elected pontiff's changing his name is generally considered to have begun with Sergius IV, although several popes had done so previously (e.g., John XII, from Octavius, and John XIV, from Peter Campenora). From that time, however, the choosing of a name became common practice. Two notable exceptions were Adrian VI (Adrian Florensz, r. 1522-1523) and Marcellus II (Marcello Cervini, r. 1555).

Sergius I, Patriarch of Constantinople (d. 638) ● Patriarch from 610-638. One of the leading spokesmen for Monothelitism, he devoted much of his time attempting a reconciliation with the Monophysites. Toward this end, he crafted a doctrine which stated that Christ had two natures but one will. Soon opposed by a number of prelates in the East, Sergius appealed to Rome. Pope Honorius I used the occasion to issue his controversial opinion on the one will of Christ (see **Honorius I**). After modifying his doctrine, Sergius secured approval from two synods at Constantinople in 638 and 639. The Council of Constantinople (681) ultimately rejected and condemned Sergius's teachings. Sergius was also known for his support of Emperor Heraclius in his wars. During the conflicts between the Byzantines and the Avars and the Persians, Sergius served as regent (622-628) and donated the Church treasury to fund Heraclius's campaigns.

Servites, Order of ● Also the Servants of Mary (from its Latin name, *Ordo Servorum BVM*), it is a mendicant religious order established in 1240 by seven Florentine men who had devoted themselves to the Virgin Mary. The seven formed themselves into a confraternity called the *Laudesi* (Praisers of Mary) and in 1233, while praying on the Feast of the Assumption, they received an apparition of the BVM. She instructed them to withdraw from the world and to give themselves entirely to prayer. The seven first established themselves near the convent of Friars Minor in a Florentine suburb, but they soon moved to Monte Senario to the north. There they were visited again by Mary, who told them to adopt the black habit and to follow the Rule of St. Augustine. They added vows of obedience, chastity, and poverty. Early approval was secured for the order in March 1249 by Cardinal Raniero Capocci, papal legate to Tuscany, followed by the appointment of a cardinal protector, Guglielmo Fieschi, by Pope Innocent IV. The Servites spread quickly throughout Italy but encountered much opposition from within the Church. The Council of Lyons (1274) enforced the decree of the Fourth Lateran Council (1215) forbidding new religious orders; Pope Innocent V informed the Servite general St. Philip Benizi (1267-1285) in 1276 that the order was suppressed. Innocent died a short time later and one of his successors, John XXI (r. 1276-1277), decided to allow the Servites to continue. Formal papal approval came under Benedict XI, who issued the bull *Dum levamus* (February 11, 1304). The early rapid growth of the Servites was largely due to the work and leadership of St. Philip. Under him houses were established throughout Europe. By the early fourteenth century, the Servites had been established in Hungary, Bohemia, and Poland, with missionaries going to such distant lands as India. The Servites were also joined by a Second Order (the Servite nuns) and a Third Order, founded in 1306 by St. Juliana Falconieri. Members of the Servites are devoted to the propagation of devotion to the Mother of God, with particular attention to the Sorrows of the Virgin. They recite the Rosary of the Seven Sorrows and are devoted to apostolic ministry.

Servus Servorum Dei ● Latin for "Servant of the Servants of God." A title of the popes used by them for official documents. It was first applied by Pope St. Gregory I the Great (r. 590-604) and was adopted by his successors. It did not come into general use, however, until the ninth century and has been an exclusive title of popes since the twelfth century.

Seton, Elizabeth, St. (1774-1821) ● First American-born saint. Founder and first superior of the Sisters of Charity, she was born in New York and was the daughter of non-Catholics. Her father was professor of anatomy at Columbia College and a well-known official of the health authorities of the Port of New York and her mother was the daughter of an Anglican minister. Her mother died in 1777 and Elizabeth, with her sisters, was educated by her father. When he remarried, Elizabeth came to be very fond of her stepmother. On January 25, 1794, she wed William Magee Seton, working with her sister-in-law to perform various missions of mercy. The death of her father in 1801 was the source of great grief, adding to the considerable financial strain that had begun in 1798 with the passing of her father-in-law after his business failed. Her husband's health soon deteriorated, necessitating a journey in 1803 to recover his strength. He died in Pisa on December 27, 1803, and Elizabeth lived with business friends of her husband, the Filicchi brothers, and their families. During this time she became attracted to the Catholic faith, returning home in May 1803. The prospect of her conversion was most distressing to her Anglican friends, but, aided by her friend Antonio Filicchi and advised by Jean Louis Lefebvre de Cheverus (first bishop of

Boston), she entered the Church on March 14, 1805.

To be able to care for her children, Elizabeth opened a boarding house for some boys at a nearby Protestant school, the necessity for money being especially acute because of the hostility of her relatives and the dwindling funds left by her husband. Early in 1806, meanwhile, her sister-in-law, Cecilia Seton, expressed a desire to become a Catholic. Her powerful family and friends were so outraged that moves were made to have Elizabeth expelled from New York. Perceiving the volatile conditions in the city, Elizabeth proposed to travel to Canada and there enter a convent, a plan rejected by Bishop John Carroll of Baltimore. Instead, she went to Baltimore in 1808, opening a school

St. Elizabeth Seton

next to the chapel of St. Mary's Seminary. She was soon joined by other women, and in June 1809 the little community was transferred to Emmitsburg to take over a house that had been established to care for poor children. Having become the head of a nascent religious community, Mother Seton asked the local bishop to request from the Sisters of Charity of St. Vincent de Paul rules by which the members could live. This rule was approved by Archbishop Carroll in January 1812. Against her will, Elizabeth was elected superior. All of the sisters took their vows on July 19, 1813. They soon spread to other cities. Mother Seton continued to work up until the time of her death in Emmitsburg on January 4, 1821. She was beatified in 1963 and was canonized

by Pope Paul VI on September 14, 1975. Feast day: January 4.

Seven Sleepers of Ephesus ● Seven legendary Christian men who were said to have been walled up in a cave near Ephesus after taking refuge during the Decian persecution (c. 230). They then supposedly awoke during the reign of Emperor Theodosius II (408-450) two hundred years later and were revered as giving proof of the resurrection of the dead. After being received by the emperor and explaining the significance of their sleep, they died. Theodosius gave them a magnificent burial and declared free all bishops who might have been imprisoned for adhering to the doctrine of the Resurrection. The legend of the Seven Sleepers was known in the sixth century, becoming enormously popular during the Middle Ages. Surviving versions were recorded in numerous forms, including Greek, Coptic, and Syriac. The site declared at Ephesus to be the tomb was a favorite pilgrim site until the conquest of Asia Minor by the Turks. Feast day: July 27.

Severinus ● Pope from May to August 640. A Roman by birth, he was the son of Avienus, perhaps a member of the nobility. Elected in October to succeed Honorius I, he sent envoys to Constantinople to secure confirmation of his election by Byzantine Emperor Heraclius (r. 610-641). The Byzantines responded that Severinus's confirmation was contingent on his acceptance of the *Ecthesis*, the decree declaring the Monothelite doctrine that Christ had only one will. This the pontiff would not do, remaining firm even after the Greeks besieged the Lateran and the exarch Isaac plundered the papal vaults. Only in May 640 were Severinus's envoys able to secure the pope's confirmation. It is unclear whether Severinus ever made a declaration of his position concerning the *Ecthesis*, as the reports of his stern position on the two wills of Christ are not entirely reliable. Already ill when finally accepted as pope, he died barely two months after his consecration. He was buried in St. Peter's.

Sheen, Fulton J. (1895-1979) ●
Archbishop and beloved preacher who had a huge following on radio and television. Born in El Paso, Illinois, he was baptized Peter but chose to use his mother's maiden name. After studying at St. Victor's College and Seminary in Bourbonnais, Illinois, he entered St. Paul's Seminary, Minnesota, where he was ordained on September 20, 1919. He then attended The Catholic University of America and won his Ph.D. from the University of Louvain in 1923. Still more studies followed at the Sorbonne and the Angelicum, after which he taught at St. Edmund's College, Ware, England. In 1925, his doctoral thesis, *God and Intelligence in Modern Philosophy*, was published, winning him the Cardinal Mercier Prize for International Philosophy. Returning to the United States, he served as a curate at St. Patrick's in Peoria before being appointed to teach at The Catholic University of America. He held this post from 1926-1950 during which he rose to national notoriety as one of the most eloquent Catholic preachers. A regular on ABC's "Catholic News Broadcast," he attracted millions with his theological depth, spoken with consummate skill and in terms that were comprehensible to the average person, Catholic and non-Catholic. Named in 1950 director for the Society for the Propagation of the Faith, he

spent the next years raising millions of dollars for Catholic missions. In 1951, he was made an auxiliary bishop of New York, under Cardinal Spellman. That same year, he launched the amazingly successful television program "Life Is Worth Living" for the ABC network; the show, running in the early 1950s, became the number one program in the ratings. Sheen appeared on the cover of *Time* magazine and won an Emmy. In 1966, Pope Paul VI appointed him bishop of Rochester, but he remained there only three years, resigning in 1969. He then traveled constantly throughout the world. Before his death, he was made a titular archbishop. The author of over sixty books, he was especially known for his best-selling *Life of Christ* (1958).

Shroud, Holy ● See **Turin, Shroud of**.

Sicard (1160-1215) ● Bishop of Cremona, papal legate, and historian. A native of Cremona, he was made a subdeacon by Pope Lucius III in 1182. Ordained in Cremona, he succeeded to the see of his city in 1185. He served as papal representative on several occasions and was a confidant of Emperor Frederick I. The author of a *Chronicon*, a history of the world to 1202 (later revised to cover the additional years to 1213), Sicard was an important source on the crusade of Frederick I. He also compiled a collection of canons and wrote a treatise on the liturgy.

Sicilian Vespers ● Name given to a rebellion in 1282, and the resulting war, by the Sicilians against the rule of King Charles I (Charles of Anjou), the French king of Naples and Sicily. Caused by the bitter hatred among Sicily's population for the French officials in charge of the island, especially after Charles decided to move his seat of rule from Palermo to Naples, the rebellion took its name from the bloody events that were launched in a church just outside Palermo during Vespers on March

30, 1282. Although an uprising had been planned and organized by John of Procida, an agent of King Pedro (Peter) of Aragon (a rival of Charles for the Neapolitan kingdom), the actual rebellion began prematurely and apparently spontaneously with the murder of several French soldiers in the church. Word soon spread and riots broke out, followed by a general massacre of the French in Palermo. Soon, more than two thousand men, women, and children had died and all of Sicily was in revolt. Aragonese troops landed in August to occupy the island, thereby launching the War of the Sicilian Vespers. Charles was backed by Pope Martin IV, the Guelph party of Italy, and France; the Aragonese had the support of the Ghibellines. Years of desultory fighting followed, ended in 1295 by the Treaty of Anagni, which allowed King James II of Aragon, son of King Pedro, to make peace; he renounced his claim to Sicily. His brother Frederick (III), however, became king of Sicily at the insistence of the Sicilians, finally securing his crown by the Peace of Catabellotta (1302).

Sidonius Apollinaris (c. 430-479) ● In full, Gaius Apollinaris Sidonius. One of the last of the great Roman poets and bishop of Auvergne (modern Clermont). Born to a noble senatorial family in Lugdunum (Lyons), he was raised a Christian and became connected to the imperial family by his marriage to Papianilla, daughter of Avitus, who was crowned emperor in July 455. In his father-in-law's honor, Sidonius delivered a panegyric on New Year's Day, receiving as a reward the honor of having a statue erected in the Forum of Trajan in Rome. Avitus soon fell from power, and Sidonius was reluctant to accept his successor, Majorian. Finally relenting, he composed a second panegyric, delivered to the emperor in Lugdunum in 458. Holding some office until 461 in Rome, he went into retirement until 467 when he was appointed by the city to lead a delegation to the new emperor, Anthemius. He gave a third panegyric, this time to Anthemius, in early 468 and was appointed prefect of the city. Returning to Auvergne in 469, he was asked to become bishop of Auvergne. He accepted with reluctance but worked energetically to counter the dominating influence of the Goths, especially under King Euric, successor to King Theodoric II of the Visigoths. Briefly imprisoned by the king in 475, he was released and died in Auvergne, having been restored to his episcopal duties. Aside from his remarkable panegyrics, Sidonius composed a large number of poems, his works being preserved in the *Carmina* (Songs). He also enjoyed a wide correspondence with friends, his letters collected in the *Epistulae*. While criticized for his lack of originality in his composition, Sidonius was nevertheless one of the final flickering literary lights in the moribund Western Roman Empire.

Sigebert of Gembloux (d. 1112) ● Benedictine historian and chronicler. Born near Gembloux in Belgium, he was educated at the Abbey of Gembloux, entering the Benedictines there before teaching at the Abbey of St. Vincent in Metz. He returned to Gembloux in 1070 and resided there until his death. Among his extensive writings were: a poem on the martyrdom of St. Lucia; a poem on the martyrdom of the Theban Legion; a history of the abbots of Gembloux; *De scriptoribus ecclesiasticis*, a compilation of one hundred seventy-one ecclesiastical writers and their works; and a chronicle of the world, the *Chronicon sive Chronographia*, covering from 381-1111, a useful source on medieval history, particularly the years in which Sigebert lived. He also became involved in the Investiture Controversy, authoring three treatises on the subject: one is lost, the second is a polemic in favor of King Henry IV against Pope St. Gregory VII, and the third is in support of imperial investiture against Pope Paschal II.

Siger of Brabant (c. 1235-c. 1282) ● Theologian, philosopher, and the leading spokesman for Latin Averroism in the 1200s. A native of Brabant, he probably served as a canon at the cathedral of Liège before teaching at Paris from around 1266. As a prominent lecturer at the University of Paris, Siger gathered support for the propagation of an interpretation of Aristotelianism that integrated the ideas of Avicenna and Averroës into a philosophy they called Latin Averroism. They soon encountered opposition from within the university, particularly from the mendicant orders who disagreed with many of their ideas, such as the theory of the two truths which stated that what is true in theology could be false in philosophy and vice versa. Siger disputed his teachings with such notable contemporaries as St. Bonaventure and St. Thomas Aquinas. Condemned for heresy in 1270 by Stephen (Étienne) Tempier, bishop of Paris, he resisted all proceedings against him for several years until finally summoned before the Grand Inquisition of France in 1276. Fleeing to Italy with several followers, he made an appeal to the Papal Curia. At Orvieto, he was stabbed to death by his mentally disturbed secretary, as noted in a 1284 letter by John Peckham, archbishop of Canterbury. Aside from his numerous commentaries and *quaestiones* on the writings of Aristotle, Siger authored two notable treatises, *De anima intellectiva* (*On the Intellectual Soul*) and *De aeternitate mundi* (*On the Eternity of the World*). In the first, Siger postulated that there was only one intellectual soul for all of humanity, a concept vigorously refuted by St. Thomas in his *De unitate intellectus contra Averroistas*. In *The Divine Comedy*, Dante placed Siger among the twelve sages in the Heaven of Light, a curious honor given Dante's admiration for Thomas Aquinas, who had devoted such effort to refuting Siger and defeating Averroism.

Sigismund, Emperor (1368-1437) ● Holy Roman Emperor from 1433. An important figure in organizing the ecclesiastical means by which the Great Schism (1378-1417) was finally brought to an end. A son of Emperor Charles IV, Sigismund first secured the throne of Hungary (from 1387) by his marriage to Mary of Hungary. As king, he was forced to devote a number of years to defeat the ambitions in Hungary of the ruling House of Naples. In 1396, he embarked upon a crusade against the Ottoman Turks in the Balkans, leading an army to a crushing, humiliating defeat at Nicopolis; his troops were virtually entirely wiped out and Sigismund barely avoided capture. Returning home, he attempted to seize Bohemia from his half-brother, Wenceslaus IV. Sigismund imprisoned his half-brother in 1401 but was forced to release him because of domestic trouble in Hungary. He was finally able to secure sole rulership of Bohemia in 1419. Meanwhile, he was crowned German king in 1411, distinguishing himself with his war with Venice (1412-1413). Of greater importance was Sigismund's desire to restore unity to the Church. Through his influence, the Council of Constance (1414-1418) was convened, culminating with the conclusion of the Great Schism in 1417 by the election of Pope Martin V. During the council, Sigismund probably had a role in seizing Jan Hus in 1415 and having him burned at the stake for heresy. Crowned emperor in 1433, he inspired a reputation for being chivalrous and genuinely concerned for the welfare of the Church. He was for many years troubled by the Hussites in Bohemia, receiving formal acceptance by the Bohemians only in 1436.

Silverius, St. ● Pope from 536-537. The son of Pope Hormisdas (before the future pontiff entered the priesthood), Silverius served as a subdeacon in Rome before his election to succeed Agapetus I. Consecrated in June of 536, he owed the papacy to the influence of King Theodahad, the last

Ostrogothic ruler of Italy (r. 534-536), who was anxious to secure a pope whom he might be able to intimidate and use during what he expected to be the forthcoming invasion of Italy by the forces of Emperor Justinian I (r. 527-565) and the Byzantine Empire. At first opposed by the Roman clergy, as related in the *Liber Pontificalis*, Silverius was finally accepted for the sake of unity and under the threat of Theodahad. The pope, however, soon became a victim of the complex political situation of the times. Empress Theodora, wife of Justinian, attempted to win Silverius to the cause of Monophysitism and, failing that, worked for his deposition to secure the papacy for Vigilius, the Roman deacon in Constantinople who had already made certain promises concerning Monophysitism. General Belisarius, the Byzantine commander, tried without success to convince Silverius to abdicate and so used forged letters to accuse the pontiff of conspiring with the Goths — who were by now besieging the city — to hand over the city. On March 11, 537, Silverius was deposed, degraded to the rank of monk, and deported to Patara, in Lycia, on the coast of Anatolia. The bishop of Patara, however, protested to Justinian the pope's innocence. The emperor sent Silverius back to Rome, but the unscrupulous Vigilius, who now reigned as pope, connived with Theodora to seize Silverius shortly after his return to Rome. The deposed pope was taken to the

St. Simeon Stylites

island of Palmaria, near Naples, where he finally abdicated on November 11, 537. Silverius died on December 2, 537, and was buried on the island. His passing had been hastened by the terrible conditions in which he was forced to live and the brutal treatment, including starvation, given him by his captors. His grave became renowned for miracles and cures. Feast day: June 20.

Simeon of Durham (d. c. 1130) ● Also Symeon. An English Benedictine chronicler, Simeon entered the Benedictines in Jarrow (later moved to Durham in 1083) and was professed around 1085 or 1086. He was subsequently given the office of precentor. His chief work was the *Historia ecclesiae Dunelmensis*, written between 1104 and 1108, on the history of the bishops of Durham down to 1096. He was also probably the author of the *Historia regum Anglorum et Dacorum*, a history of England from 732-1129, relying on earlier chroniclers except for the years 1119-1129.

Simeon Stylites, St. (d. 459) ● First of the *stylitae* (or hermits of the pillar), the remarkable ascetics in the Eastern Church who chose to reside on the tops of pillars. Born on the northern frontier of Syria, Simeon entered a monastery in Eusebona, near Antioch, but his extreme asceticism convinced his fellow monks that he was ill-suited to a community life. Simeon departed the monastery and then for three years lived in a hut, initiating the practice of fasting during Lent while standing continually upright to the limit of his strength. Finding this lifestyle insufficient, Simeon had a pillar set up with a platform at the top. The first version was only nine feet high, but, as he found that this left him too close to the pressing crowds who came to see him, he increased the height to about fifty feet. He remained there until his death. Simeon, however, was not entirely withdrawn from the world as he allowed some visitors — via a ladder — and wrote letters to a wide variety of people. He also preached to crowds who would assemble below him. While unusual in the expression of his deep faith, Simeon had a wide and enduring influence, capturing the imagination of his contemporaries. His remains were a source of disagreement between Antioch and Constantinople, and a church and monastery were built in his honor. The buildings surrounded a court containing St. Simeon's pillar. Feast day: January 5, in the West; September 1, in the East. A second Simeon Stylites, called St. Simeon the Younger, also lived on a pillar near Antioch for some sixty-eight years, dying in 597. Feast day: May 24. (See also **Daniel, St.**)

Simon, St. ● Called "the Less," he was one of the twelve Apostles whose name appears in the lists of the Apostles contained in the Gospels and the Acts of the Apostles. He is described by Matthew (10:4) and Mark (3:18) as Simon the Canaanite or the Cananaean; and by Luke (6:15) and in the Acts (1:13) as "Simon who was called the Zealot" and "Simon the Zealot." These names distinguished him from Simon Peter but had the same general meaning in Hebrew or Aramaic, both being derived from the Hebrew term *qana* (zealous). While some scholars propose that Luke's references to him imply a onetime membership in the Zealots, others argue that he was simply devoted to the law. Nothing is known with certainly about his early life, his years as a preacher, or how he died. According to the apocryphal *Passio Simonis et Judae* (*Passion of Simon and Jude*), Simon was martyred in Persia after preaching in the region. Traditionally, he is venerated with St. Jude (Thaddeus) and in the West, his feast day, October 28, is shared with Jude; in the East, his feast day is separate, on May 10. His symbol is the saw, as he was said in legend to have been sawed to pieces.

Simon, Richard (1638-1712) ● French biblical scholar, he was considered the founder of the modern method of biblical criticism. A member of the Oratorians from 1662-1678, he authored the well-known work *Histoire critique du Vieux Testament* (1678; *Critical History of the Old Testament*), a scholarly examination of the OT that soon caused considerable controversy because of Simon's denial that Moses was the author of the Pentateuch. Removed from the order because of his views, Simon also had his work placed on the Index of Forbidden Books. Nevertheless, he professed strict orthodoxy and was a vigorous opponent of both Jansenism and the biblical theories of Baruch Spinoza.

Simon, Yves René (1903-1961) ● French Thomistic philosopher. Born in Cherbourg, France, he studied at Paris and secured a doctorate in philosophy in 1934. In 1938, he became a visiting professor at the University of Notre Dame in Indiana, remaining in the United States during World War II. Becoming an American citizen in 1946, he joined the faculty of the University of Chicago in 1948, teaching there for the next eleven years until a forced retirement from illness in 1959. A friend of Jacques Maritain, Simon wrote extensively on political philosophy, earning the title Philosopher of the Fighting French for his study of intellectual freedom and democracy and the crises besetting Europe during the 1930s.

Simon Magus ● First-century sorcerer. According to the Acts of the Apostles (8:9-24), Simon practiced magic in the city of Samaria and so amazed the people that they declared, "This man is that power of God which is called Great."

Simon, however, was drawn to Christianity and was baptized by Philip. Later, when Sts. Peter and John arrived in Samaria, Simon offered them money in return for the power of transmitting the Holy Spirit, receiving a stern rebuke from Peter. Simon thus became the basis for the sacrilege of simony, the buying and selling of ecclesiastical offices or sacred things. There is no mention of Simon Magus again anywhere in the NT, but he quickly became a figure of false repentance in the second century and was almost universally described by early Church writers as having continued in his false and evil ways, the first heretic, or the Father of Heresies. Such declarations outside the NT are considered entirely legendary, without any historical substantiation. St. Justin Martyr (second century) wrote of Simon as a man who claimed divine power, adding that he journeyed to Rome during the reign of Claudius (41-54), attracting many followers. These adherents supposedly erected a statue to him on an island in the Tiber with the inscription *"Simoni Deo Sancto"* ("Simon the Holy God") at its base. When recovered in the 1500s, the base was actually determined to read *"Semoni Sancto Deo Fideo,"* a dedication to a Sabine god of early Rome. St. Hippolytus in his *Philosophumena* recounted Simon's struggle with Peter and Paul and how, in a desperate effort to recapture his dwindling following, he had himself buried, promising to arise from the earth in three days. He naturally died beneath the ground. Similar tales were recounted in the apocryphal Acts of Peter and the writings of the apologist Arnobius (fourth century). Here Simon plunges to the earth after attempting to fly.

He was also the source for a Gnostic sect in the second and third centuries.

Simon of Sudbury (d. 1381) ● Archbishop of Canterbury and chancellor of England. Born in Sudbury, in Suffolk, England, he studied law at Paris. After serving as a chaplain to Pope Innocent VI (r. 1352-1362), Simon returned to England in 1356 as a papal nuncio. In 1361, he was appointed bishop of London, becoming a close associate of the powerful English nobleman John of Gaunt, duke of Lancaster. His translation in 1375 to the see of Canterbury brought him into conflict with Courtenay, bishop of London, who opposed his ties with the Lancastrian party. In 1377, he crowned Richard II king of England and was soon involved in the controversy surrounding John Wycliffe. Owing to Wycliffe's support among the Lancastrian party, especially John of Gaunt, Simon was hesitant in launching proceedings against him, and did so only at the command of the pope. Made chancellor in 1380, his imposition of the poll tax helped cause the Peasants' Revolt in England in 1381. Forced to seek refuge in the Tower of London with the king, Simon stepped down as chancellor. A mob stormed the Tower anyway on June 14, carried him away from Tower Hill, and beheaded him. His head was stuck on a spike on London Bridge as was the custom of the era for those deemed traitors. After the suppression of the revolt, his head was removed and, with his body, was buried in Canterbury. He was revered by many as a martyr, and chroniclers noted his goodness and the courage he displayed in facing death.

Simon Stock, St. (c. 1165-1265) ● Also Simeon Stock. One of the first persons from England to join the Carmelites, he was later its general. Born in Kent, he supposedly entered into the life of a hermit at the age of twelve, residing in the hollow of a tree before becoming an itinerant preacher. After several years he entered the Carmelites, who had recently arrived in England. According to custom, he journeyed to Jerusalem and spent some time on Mt. Carmel. While these details are of dubious historicity, it is known with certainty that in 1247, despite his age, he was elected the sixth Carmelite general, displaying much vigor and earning the reputation for being the greatest of the generals in the history of the Carmelites. Under his leadership, the order spread throughout Europe, especially in England. Houses were founded in the university cities of Paris, Oxford, Cambridge, and Bologna, and Simon won papal approbation for his alteration to the rule that had been made to adapt the order to European life. As the Carmelites were still much opposed by the secular clergy, the members prayed to the Virgin Mary. She appeared to Simon in 1251, instructing him to seek the aid of Pope Innocent IV. On January 13, 1252, Pope Innocent issued a letter of protection for the order. Later Carmelite writers also recorded that Mary gave the scapular to Simon, declaring to him, *"Hoc erit tibi et cunctis Carmelitis privilegium, in hoc habitu moriens salvabitur"* ("This shall be the privilege of you and for all Carmelites, that whosoever dies in the habit shall be saved"). He is also the attributed author of two hymns, *Ave Stella Matutina* and *Flos Carmeli*. The surname Stock was added considerably after his death, most likely in honor of the tradition concerning the tree trunk in which he lived for a time. Feast day: May 16.

Simony ● The buying or selling of spiritual things. A sin in which temporal goods are considered of equal value to spiritual goods and are thus offered in the hopes of acquiring through money or treasures those things of the spirit that belong to God. The name simony is derived from Simon Magus, the magician in Acts (8:18-24) who attempted to buy from the

Apostles the power of conferring the gifts of the Holy Spirit.

The two types of recognized simony are those that violate Church or ecclesiastical law and those that are contrary to divine law. The receiving of money in return for a benefice or office in the Church violates canon law. The granting of prayers only in return for money is against divine law and is considered a serious offense. The sin of simony was largely unknown in the early Church, becoming a problem only after the end of the Roman persecutions and the acquisition by the faith of wealth, property, and social influence. The earliest legislation on it was issued by the Council of Chalcedon (451) in which the second canon forbade ordination for money. Specific regulation came to include all transactions involving benefices and payments for prayers, oils, sacred objects, and Masses (save for accepted or authorized Mass offerings). These strictures not withstanding, simony became widespread in the Middle Ages and was denounced vigorously by Pope St. Gregory VII (r. 1073-1085). Very severe penalties were inflicted upon abusers, and many medieval Church writers called simony the most terrible of crimes. The Third Lateran Council (1179) condemned it, as did St. Thomas Aquinas. Pope Julius II (r. 1503-1513) proclaimed that any pope elected through simony should be declared invalid, a decree rescinded in 1904 by Pope St. Pius X in the constitution *Vacante Sede*. Simony declined as a scandalous problem after the Middle Ages and the Renaissance through the diligence of the Catholic Reformation, the work of the Council of Trent, and the changing nature of the position of the Church with regard to the sociopolitical organization in the secular environment. Pope Pius IX, in the constitution *Apostolicae Sedis* (October 12, 1869), stipulated the cases in which excommunication would apply to simoniacs. Canon law continues to attach penalties to any cleric guilty of simony.

Simplicius, St. ● Pope from 468-483. His pontificate coincided with the fall of the Roman Empire in the West in 476. Born in Tivoli, he succeeded St. Hilarius (Hilary) on March 5, 468. The early part of his reign was spent combating the spread of Monophysitism in the Eastern Empire, which had gained the upper hand in Constantinople through the usurpation of Byzantine Emperor Basiliscus in early 475. Several prominent sees were filled with Monophysites and both the *Tome* of Leo and the Chalcedonian Christology were condemned. The deposition of Emperor Basiliscus by Zeno in August 476 did not guarantee a return to orthodoxy for Zeno and the patriarch Acacius promulgated in 482 the *Henotikon*, the conciliatory document that was approved by the Monophysites but could not satisfy Simplicius because of its harsh comments on Chalcedon and the omission of the positive declaration on the two natures of Christ. There thus erupted the Acacian Schism that would last until 519. In the West, meanwhile, the last Roman Emperor, Romulus Augustus, was deposed in September 476 by the German chieftain Odoacer. In the short term, the final, inevitable demise of the Roman Empire precipitated the rise of the Germanic kingdoms in Italy, but over the next years the papacy would grow increasingly influential in the West now that the central western authority of the emperors was eradicated. Simplicius thus worked to advance papal authority. He also built several churches in Rome and reorganized the clergy of Rome. Feast day: March 10.

Siricius, St. ● Pope from 384-399. A native of Rome, he was made a deacon by Pope Liberius (r. 352-366) and served under Pope St. Damasus I (r. 366-384) whom he succeeded in December 384. Although disliked by St. Jerome and overshadowed in history by the dominating personality of St. Ambrose, bishop of Milan, Siricius was a remarkable pontiff, responsible for several innovations that strengthened the papacy. Chief among these was the issue of letters that made clear the claim of popes as having primacy over the Church. These letters, the earliest decretals (*decretalia*) ever promulgated by a pontiff, were concerned with ecclesiastical discipline and such matters as ordinations, penance, and baptism. The first decretal, dated to February 385, was sent to Bishop Himerius of Tarragona in response to his question on discipline.

Siricius' reply included the important command of clerical celibacy, marking the first decree on this issue. Other decrees were sent to the African Church, accompanied by severe penalties for all who would not recognize his authority. In his dealings with the East, he demonstrated a willingness to intervene in matters he considered of vital interest. Thus, he worked to resolve the Melitian Schism in Antioch and preserved the influence of Rome in the region of Illyricum when the see of Constantinople began looking ambitiously at it as a place to expand its influence. While he opposed Priscillianism, the pontiff chastised the imperial usurper Maximus for putting Priscillian to death; in dealing with heretics he shared St. Ambrose's desire that the penitent be given mild punishments. He dedicated the Basilica of St. Paul's in 390, an event commemorated on a plaque still surviving in the Roman church. Feast day: November 26.

Sirmond, Jacques (1559-1651) ● French Jesuit scholar. A native of Riom, France, he joined the Society of Jesus in 1576. From 1581-1590, he served as a professor in Paris; one of his students was St. Francis de Sales. In 1590, he was called to Rome to hold the post of private secretary to the Jesuit general Claudius Aquaviva. At the same time, he cultivated an association with some of the most remarkable figures of his era, including

Cesare Baronius and St. Robert Bellarmine. He assisted Baronius in some of his researches. Returning to France in 1608, he was rector of the Paris College (1617) and then confessor to King Louis XIII (1637). His extensive scholarly writings included editions of the Greek and Latin Fathers, such as Paschasius Radbertus, Hincmar of Reims, Theodoret, and Ennodius. He also wrote *Concilia antiqua Galliae* (1629), on the ancient councils.

Sisinnius ● Pope in early 708. A Syrian by birth, he was elected successor to Pope John VII and was consecrated probably on January 15, 708, although his election most likely occurred in October 707. The delay was caused by the failure of the Byzantine representative (exarch) to grant approval. Said to have been a person of strong character, he was severely ill by the time of his consecration, surviving only a few weeks. His only recorded act was to consecrate a bishop for Crete. He died on February 4, 708.

Sistine Chapel ● Principal chapel of the Vatican Palace, called also the Pope's Chapel. It was built by Pope Sixtus IV (r. 1471-1484) from which its name is derived and is one of the most visited sites in the Vatican because of the incomparable decorations found on its walls and ceilings, the most famous, of course, being the frescoes by Michelangelo. The chapel was erected from 1473-1481 and the sidewall frescoes from 1481-1483. The early artists who contributed to the decorations were Perugino, Botticelli, Domenico Ghirlandaio, Cosimo Roselli, Pinturicchio, Benedetto Ghirlandaio, Luca Signorelli, and Bartolomeo della Gatta. These masters did not decorate the ceiling, which was left painted blue with stars. Determined to improve upon this state of affairs, Pope Julius II (r. 1503-1513; nephew of Sixtus IV) commissioned Michelangelo to paint the ceiling and west wall behind the altar. The ceiling fresco took from 1508-1512 and the

"Last Judgment" behind the altar from 1536-1541.

In one of the most significant artistic events of the twentieth century, the frescoes of Michelangelo underwent a complete restoration that removed the centuries of candle smoke and dirt that had dulled the original colors. The project, lasting fourteen years, was funded by Japanese Nippon Television and was headed by Fabrizio Mancinelli of the Vatican Museum and Gianluigi Colalucci, chief Vatican art restorer. Although a small group of art historians complained that the restoration had betrayed what they believed to be the purposefully grim spirit of the work, the consensus of expert opinion was that the frescoes had been restored to the original vibrancy and magnificent color that had been beheld for the first time by Pope Paul III in 1541 when the "Last Judgment" was completed. In celebrating the project's conclusion in April 1994, Pope John Paul II observed that in gazing upon the "Last Judgment," "We are dazzled by splendor and the fear." The chapel is also used for the very special occasion of the conclave, when members of the Sacred College of Cardinals gather beneath Michelangelo's frescoes to elect a new pope. At this time, the chapel is fitted with a special stove to allow the ballots to be burned, the smoke, either white or black, informing the expectant crowds in St. Peter's Square and around the world whether a new pontiff has been chosen.

Sistine Choir ● Known officially as *Il Collegio dei Capellani Cantori della Capella Pontificia*, it is the choir that performs at those functions presided over by the pope. The Sistine Choir had its origins probably in the *schola cantorum* established in the fourth century to provide training to singers of the papal choir. Under Pope St. Gregory I the Great (r. 590-604) a permanent choir was established at St. John Lateran. This was soon joined by a similar group of singers at

St. Peter's, although it is believed that this second choir was to serve as a preparatory body for singers who might receive appointment at the Lateran, which was more important. The choir of the Basilica of St. Peter's had thus been in existence by the start of the 1200s. It subsequently suffered from separation from its master. Pope Innocent IV (r. 1243-1254) chose not to take the *schola cantorum* when he departed Italy in 1244 during his struggle with Emperor Frederick II. As Innocent's flight to Genoa in June 1244 had been secret, it was hardly surprising that the choir did not go with him. A more permanent kind of separation took place during the Avignon period of the papacy. Pope Clement V (r. 1305-1314) not only neglected to summon the papal choir but, being French, formed a new one in Avignon. This body, which favored new trends in Church music, was ultimately amalgamated by Pope Gregory XI (r. 1370-1378) with the surviving *schola* when the pope returned to Rome in 1377. The head of the choir was henceforth the *magister capellae*.

The Sistine Choir began its formal existence in the pontificate of Pope Sixtus IV (r. 1478-1484), founder of the Sistine Chapel. The *schola cantorum*, or the *capella pontifica*, became the *capella sistina*. By a bull, dated November 1483, he established their number

Pope St. Sixtus I

at twenty-four. His nephew, Pope Julius II (r. 1503-1513), would not only create the magnificent surroundings of the Sistine Chapel by commissioning Michelangelo, he would also revive the concept of the preparatory choir for the Sistine Choir. This was the *capella Julia*, the Julian Choir, which performs at all important functions in St. Peter's Basilica. The Julian Choir was formally established by a bull issued in February 1512. An important development came under Pope Leo X (r. 1513-1521) when he named a *magister capella* who was a fully trained musician rather than a cleric who was familiar with music. Pope Paul II (r. 1534-1549) introduced a constitution by which candidates were examined by the whole choir. This basic constitution, promulgated by a bull in November 1545, has remained until today. Some reforms, especially in finances, were undertaken by Pope Pius XI (r. 1922-1939) and John XXIII (r. 1958-1963). Two other papal choirs are those of St. John Lateran and Santa Maria Maggiore.

Sixtus I, St. ● Pope from c. 115-125. Known in early sources as Xystus, he reigned for around ten years, although the specific dates vary; Eusebius, for example, gives two different figures in the *Ecclesiastical History* and the *Chronicle*: 119-128 and 114-124 respectively. According to the *Liber Pontificalis*, he was Roman by birth, being elected as the successor to Pope St. Alexander I. He is commemorated as a martyr and was supposedly buried on Vatican Hill, near St. Peter's Tomb, a claim that cannot be substantiated.

Sixtus II, St. ● Pope from 257-258. Known also as Xystus II, he was perhaps a Greek by origin, as recorded in the *Liber Pontificalis* and was said to be peaceful and conciliatory. He thus brought peace between Rome and the churches of Roman Africa and Asia that had been temporarily broken over the controversy concerning the rebaptism of heretics. Elected to succeed Pope St. Stephen I, Sixtus was confronted immediately with the severe persecution of Christians that had been launched by Emperor Valerian. He managed to avoid arrest and execution, but his task as pastor to the Church was complicated by the new decrees issued in 258 that singled out all bishops and deacons for the most harsh treatment. Sixtus was finally arrested on August 6, 258, while seated on the episcopal chair delivering an address to the faithful in the cemetery of Praetextatus, on the Appian Way. Sixtus was then beheaded with the four deacons who had been in attendance; two more died on the same day, followed by one more, Lawrence by name. Sixtus was buried in the crypt for popes in the cemetery of Callistus, receiving an epitaph in hexameter

Pope Sixtus IV

a hundred years later from Pope St. Damasus I. Behind his tomb was placed the bloodstained chair on which Sixtus had been executed. Much revered as a martyr, his tomb was visited by pilgrims as late as the eighth century. Feast day: August 6.

Sixtus III, St. ● Pope from 432-440. Also known as Xystus III, he was a Roman by birth. Prior to his election, Sixtus had served under Popes Zosimus, Boniface I, and Celestine I. Questions arose concerning his possible leanings toward Pelagianism, but he accepted the condemnation of Pelagius and communicated his opposition to St. Augustine. Elected to succeed St. Celestine, he approved the acts of the Council of Ephesus (431) and worked with much vigor to restore unity in the Eastern Church that had been threatened with dispute between St. Cyril of Alexandria and John of Antioch begun during the Council of Ephesus over the Nestorian Controversy. Sixtus was much pleased with the reconciliation that was reached in 433. He also defended the rights of the papacy in Illyricum in the face of the local ambition of the bishops and the interference of Proclius, patriarch of Constantinople, and restored the Basilica of Santa Maria Maggiore (originally called the Basilica of Liberius) while enlarging the Lateran Basilica with a new baptistery. Feast day: March 28.

Sixtus IV ● Pope from 1471-1484. Born Francesco della Rovere near Savona, Italy, to poor parents, he was educated by the Franciscans and entered the order, subsequently studying at the University of Padua and the University of Bologna. He served as lecturer in Padua, Bologna, Pavia, Siena, and Florence, was a highly respected theologian, and was elected general of the Franciscan order on May 19, 1464. Promoted to cardinal in September 1467 by Pope Paul II, he devoted himself over the next years to theological pursuits, authoring treatises on the Precious Blood and the Immaculate Conception. Attending the conclave following the death of Paul in July 1471, he emerged as a surprise favorite and was elected in August 1471 in part through the influence of the duke of Milan, taking the name Sixtus.

As pontiff, Sixtus was vigorous in temporal affairs, proving a marked contrast to the theologian and devout Franciscan who had been elected. Spending vast sums on grand entertainments in Rome, he became caught up in the political machinations in Italy and was an unfortunate and severe nepotist. Two nephews were immediately made cardinals, one of whom, Giuliano della Rovere, would become Pope Julius II (r. 1503-1513). Many other members of the family were given lavish favors and offices. At the same time, he promoted the arts, bringing to Rome some of the finest artists and architects of the time. He rebuilt whole stretches of the city, widened and paved many streets, and erected the Sistine Bridge (across the Tiber). Chief among his artistic achievements was the Sistine Chapel that would become so famous as a result of his nephew's pontificate. Sixtus is also

Pope Sixtus V

considered the second founder of the Vatican Library and the organizer of the Vatican Archives, both institutions of long historical value and importance.

Soon after his election, Sixtus hoped to launch a new crusade against the Ottoman Turks. He sent legates to the major courts of Europe, but the response was lukewarm and the campaign resulted in little gain for Christendom. He failed also in negotiating a reunion with the Russian Church. In 1478, meanwhile, he was drawn into a two-year war with Florence as a result of the conspiracy of the Pazzi. This plot, organized by Sixtus's nephew Cardinal Rafael Riario with the cognizance of the pope, caused the murder of Giuliano de' Medici. The two years of fighting with Florence were compounded by Sixtus's efforts to obtain Ferrara for another nephew by having the Venetians attack Ferrara. More fighting compelled the Italian cities to force Sixtus into making peace in 1484, a bitter disappointment to the pope and his nephews. His tomb in the Vatican Grottoes was decorated by Antonio del Pollaiuolo.

Sixtus V ● Pope from 1585-1590. A remarkable reforming pontiff who is best known for his creation of the Roman congregations to assist in the governing of the Church. Born in Grottammare, in the March of Ancona, Felice Peretti was the son of a gardener. According to custom, young Felice worked as a swineherd. He was sent to the Franciscan convent of Montalto at the age of nine, entering the order three years later. After studying at Montalto, Ferrara, and Bologna, he was ordained in 1547 at

Siena, becoming a successful preacher and winning the friendship and patronage of several cardinals, including two future popes, and Sts. Philip Neri and Ignatius. Swiftly promoted, he was appointed in 1557 counselor to the Inquisition in Venice by Pope Paul IV. His enthusiasm in the execution of his office was displeasing to the Venetians who demanded his recall in 1560 but was reappointed by Pius IV at this time. He was then made counselor to the Holy Office in Rome, a professor at Sapienza, and grand procurator and vicar apostolic for the Franciscan order. In 1565, he traveled to Spain with Cardinal Buoncampagni (later Pope Gregory XIII) to investigate Archbishop Carranza of Toledo; during the trip the two came to dislike each other, a hostility that would become quite pointed in Gregory's pontificate (1572-1585). Back in Rome in 1566, Peretti was made a bishop by Pope St. Pius V; in 1570, the pope made him a cardinal. Throughout the reign of Gregory, he remained away from the government of the Church, devoting himself to study. At the conclave of 1585, however, he was elected pontiff after only four days, taking the name Sixtus (V) in honor of Sixtus IV, a fellow Franciscan. The story, generally disproved, was told that he entered the conclave on crutches and supposedly was elected by cardinals who thought he would not live long. After being elevated, he then dropped the crutches and displayed his true vigor. While almost certainly an untrue tale, Sixtus nevertheless amazed his contemporaries with his energy.

His first major effort as pope was to launch an often brutal and wholly merciless campaign against the roving bands of brigands who had infested Italy, especially the Papal States. He put to death thousands of bandits, some sources putting the number at twenty-seven thousand, and within two years the entire Papal States were entirely free of outlaws and were the safest territory in Europe. He then focused on papal finances, using a firm policy of spending and taxation to save money wherever possible; to make additional money, he sold various offices and used all available means to amass funds.

At the same time, he spent lavishly on public works. A few of his notable achievements in Rome included the completion of the cupola of St. Peter's, the building of the Lateran Palace, raising various obelisks, establishing a hospice for the poor, erecting the Vatican Library, and reviving the great aqueduct system of Rome, thereby supplying water for the city by the Aqua Felice. By widening many of the streets Sixtus was able to connect directly the seven major pilgrimage churches, altering the very organization of the city.

Particularly important were the reforms of the Curia and the College of Cardinals. On December 3, 1586, he issued the bull *Postquam Verus* limiting the number of cardinals to seventy. This was followed on February 11, 1588, by the bull *Immensa aeterni Dei*, establishing fifteen congregations, administered by cardinals who worked under the authority of the pope while easing many of the burdens the pontiff carried in the increasingly varied and difficult papal government and administration of the Church. These arrangements remained essentially unchanged until the reforms of Vatican Council II. He also reintroduced the requirement that bishops make a regular visit to the Holy See, submitting a report on the state of their diocese. These *ad limina* visits continue today. Called the Iron Pope for his determination and indomitable will, Sixtus left a lasting legacy for the Church through his innovations and reforms. For Rome, he was able to transform the city into a magnificent baroque metropolis.

Slavery ● Social and economic institution by which segments of a population or an entire race is held in various types of servitude. It is an inherently inhuman system that has been actively opposed by the Church. Christianity first developed in an empire that not only promoted and accepted slavery as a legitimate part of the fabric of Roman life but had a complex set of laws and customs governing the practice. As slavery was an ingrained or natural part of the social system of the time and Christian converts were raised in this system, the issue of slavery was not an important one to the nascent Church, which was struggling for its very existence. Christian teachings, however, laid the groundwork for the transformation rather than the obliteration of the practice: first by emphasizing the fair recognition of mutual rights and obligations between master and slave and then by the spread of the doctrine of equal worth and commonality of all people who have accepted Christ. An example of the former concept was given by St. Paul in his Letter to Philemon in which he seeks to reconcile Onesimus — a runaway slave and now a Christian — and his master Philemon, a Christian in Phrygia. The latter teaching is given magnificent expression by Paul in his Letter to the Galatians (3:27-28). By example and by gently preaching, the Church was able to create an atmosphere within the empire that made the institution of slavery morally unacceptable, in a manner similar to the program against the savage sport of gladiatorial combat.

Slavery underwent a rebirth after the demise of the Roman Empire in the fifth century and the conquest of Europe by the so-called barbarian peoples, many of whom kept slaves or engaged in slave trade. Once again, the Church worked indirectly to end the institution through the efforts to evangelize these cultures. Christian doctrine had a civilizing influence that combined with the manorial system to eradicate slavery almost completely by the 1200s. In the place of slaves developed the social class of the semi-free serf with its own characteristics and limitations.

After centuries of European decline, slavery erupted once more as the result of the extensive discoveries made by Spain and Portugal in the New World. When it became a matter of terrible commerce to seize native peoples and carry them off to work on plantations, in mines, or elsewhere, the slave trade became a worldwide industry, with sources for the brutal business found in Africa and the Americas. Contrary to long-held misconceptions, the Church was an outspoken enemy of slavery over the centuries, from popes and cardinals to missionaries and theologians. In 1537, Pope Paul III — in response to the common enslavement of the Indians and the ruthless seizing of their territory —excommunicated those persons who took part in the slave trade among the Native Americans. The Jesuits in the Americas were much feared and hated by Spanish government officials because of their efforts to protect the rights of the native peoples.

The nineteenth century was a particularly active period for the Church against the slave trade. Pope Gregory XVI in 1838 wrote to the bishops of Brazil to commend Brazil on having at long last outlawed slavery. Of lasting importance was the founding of the Anti-Slavery League in France by Cardinal Lavigerie in 1890 whose Congregation of the White Fathers (Missionaries of Africa) has long labored to end slavery in Africa, often at great personal risk. The Church continues to fight slavery of all kinds, be it through the chains of iron or the chains of spiritual, intellectual, or economic repression and oppression.

Social Encyclicals ● See TABLE 12.

Society of Jesus ● See **Jesuits**.

Socrates (c. 380 B.C.-c. 450 B.C.) ● In full, Socrates Scholasticus, an important Greek Church historian, author of the immensely valuable *Historia Ecclesiastica*. A native of Constantinople, he studied by his own account under the grammarians Hellodius and Ammonius and received the title *scholasticus*, taken by scholars to mean he was a lawyer. While he almost certainly visited other cities and regions of the Eastern Empire, he spent most of his life in Constantinople, confessing in his writings that the great city's affairs took much space in his work. The first layperson to author a history of the Church, Socrates hoped to create a continuation of the *Ecclesiastical History* by Eusebius of Caesarea down to his own era. Relying on Tyrannius Rufinus (d. c. 410), Gelasius of Caesarea (d. 395), and St. Athanasius (d. 375), as well as extensive collections and sources, Socrates organized his work into seven books, each corresponding to the reign of an Eastern Emperor. The books thus covered the periods of: Constantine (r. 306-337), Constantius II (r. 337-361), Julian the Apostate and Jovian (r. c. 360-363), Valens (r. 364-378), Theodosius the Great (r. 379-395), Arcadius (r. 393-408), and the years 408-439 in the reign of Theodosius II. Extensive revisions were made as a result of Socrates's discovery of the writings of St. Athanasius, proving the numerous errors in the work of Rufinus. While not particularly interested in theological questions and sympathetic to both Novatianists and Byzantine culture, Socrates's history was generally objective and impartial in its assessments. The straightforward and at times rather bland narrative was in contrast to and deliberately a reversal of the elaborate style of Byzantine historical composition in his time. Two serious failings in the *Ecclesiastical History* are its neglect of the Western Church (and errors in the coverage that is given) and the credulous nature of some of his accounts, particularly related to miracles and omens. Socrates was nevertheless one of the most valuable source for the medieval Church on its history in the fourth and fifth centuries, and he remains a reliable chronicler for modern historians.

Soissons, Council of ● Council held in Soissons in 1121 under the presidency of Conon, the papal legate and bishop of Palestrina. It is known mainly through Peter Abelard's understandably bitter account of the proceedings in his *Historia Calamitatum* and was convened to condemn Abelard's book *Theologia Summi Boni*, which contained the error of Sabellianism. Abelard was not allowed to defend the work, which was burned by order of the council. Another Council of Soissons had been convened in 1092 to condemn the tritheistic teachings of Roscellinus.

Sollicitudo Omnium Ecclesiarum ● Papal document issued by Pope Paul VI on June 24, 1969. It details the nature and functions of papal representatives throughout the world. The pope declared that papal representatives "receive from the Roman pontiff the charge of representing him in a fixed way in the various nations or regions of the world." The purposes and activities of the various ambassadors are given, including apostolic delegates, nuncios, pro-nuncios, internuncios, and those clergy or laypeople who are part of the pontifical mission that is attached to some international organization or who participate in various congresses or conferences. The representatives are to act "under the guidance and according to instructions of the cardinal secretary of state to whom he is directly responsible for the execution of the mandate instructed to him by the Supreme Pontiff."

Sollicitudo Rei Socialis ● Encyclical issued on December 30, 1987, by Pope John Paul II, "On Social Concerns." Published on the twentieth anniversary of Pope Paul VI's encyclical *Populorum Progressio*, *Sollicitudo Rei Socialis* continues to examine the moral obligation of all nations to promote the complete and multifaceted development of each person in the world. Pope John Paul noted the need for the more wealthy and developed countries to recognize the increasing gap between the rich and poor on the earth and to take heed of the dangers that are concomitant in such inherently destabilizing sociopolitical situations. He calls upon the wealthy nations to have respect for the needs and rights of developing regions and to take decisive steps toward fulfilling their obligations as leaders on the planet to facilitate their common goal in a manner that is complete and in keeping with the respect accorded to others of the human family who, as images of God, are entitled to a full share in the riches and beauty of life. Such actions, however, must be more than economic advancement. John Paul strikes a middle ground that is separate from the polar economic systems of capitalism and socialism, or Communism. He decries the myth that social order can be built upon a headlong pursuit of profit or in the creation of collectivist central authority; both, he points out, are dehumanizing. He adds that there is an essential interdependency in the world and that international development must be undertaken with an aim of freedom in solidarity with other peoples and nations, and, equally, in a religious communion with God.

Somaschi ● Name given to an order of clerks regular founded in 1528 by St. Jerome Emiliani. It is devoted to charitable work and adheres to the Rule of St. Augustine. The name was derived from the motherhouse in Somasca near Venice, Italy. Formal approval was given in 1568 by Pope St. Pius V. The Somascan Fathers (C.R.S.) continue to work among the poor and ill, with over five hundred members worldwide.

Soter, St. ● Pope from around 164-174. According to the *Liber Pontificalis*, he came from Campania, Italy, and was elected to succeed St. Anicetus. Eusebius of Caesarea preserved in the *Ecclesiastical History* part of a letter from St. Dionysius, bishop of Corinth, to Soter acknowledging the pope's letter and gifts to the faithful in Corinth. Dionysius also promised to read Soter's letter during services, recognizing the pontiff's advice on matters of theology. During his pontificate, Easter was introduced to Rome as an annual festival. Soter is traditionally revered as a martyr, although no account of his death is extant. Feast day: April 22.

Pope St. Soter

Soto, Dominic (1494-1560) ● Also Domingo de Soto. A highly respected Spanish Dominican theologian, Dominic was born in Segovia. He studied in his native city, at Alcalá, and at Paris before becoming a professor of philosophy and teaching at the College of San Ildefonso from around 1520. By 1524, he was widely acclaimed for his learning and remarkable gifts, but he suddenly resigned his chair and entered the Dominicans in Burgos. After his novitiate, he was appointed professor at the convent of St. Paul, Burgos. In 1532, he was summoned to Salamanca University where he held the chair of theology until 1545 when Emperor Charles V chose him to be one of the imperial theologians at the Council of Trent. At the council he represented as well the Dominican order, first in place of the recently deceased general Albertus Casaus and then on behalf of the newly elected general Franciscus Romaeus. At Trent, Soto distinguished himself by upholding Thomistic doctrine on the question of grace and original sin. Confessor to Emperor Charles around 1547, he declined the offer of the see of Segovia and instead returned in 1550 to Salamanca. Two years later, he succeeded at the university to the principal chair of theology that had been held by Melchior Cano. He resigned in 1556. Among his many works were: the *Summulae* (1529), a manual on logic; *De natura et gratia* (completed while at Trent), dedicated to the Council Fathers, on grace and original sin; and commentaries on Aristotle (1544), the Epistle to the Romans, and the *Sentences* (1557-1560); there were also treatises on theology and philosophy.

South America ● See **Argentina, Brazil, Central America, Chile, Inquisition, Liberation Theology, Spain,** and **Umbanda**.

Southwell, Robert (1561-1595) ● Jesuit missionary, poet, and martyr. Born in Horsham, St. Faith's, Norfolk, he was the grandson of a prominent figure in the court of King Henry VIII. Raised a Catholic, he was sent to Douai and attempted to enter the Society of Jesus, at first being rejected. In October 1578, he was given admission, taking his vows in 1580. After ordination in 1584, Southwell became prefect of studies at the English College in Rome. In 1586, he returned to England where he was appointed chaplain to Anne Howard and her husband, the earl of Arundel. The latter had been imprisoned in the Tower of London for recusancy. Residing in secret in the Arundel estate and visiting other houses of Catholics, Southwell adopted various disguises to travel around the country. He was finally arrested in 1592 at Uxenden Hall, Harrow, reportedly betrayed by a Catholic girl named Anne Bellamy, daughter of the owner of the house

in which Southwell was arrested while celebrating Mass. Tortured and abused in the Tower, he refused to confess the whereabouts of other Jesuits and was thus tried in 1595 for treason and executed by being hanged and quartered. Southwell was a popular poet, using his piety as inspiration for his compositions. Among his most notable works were "Triumphs over Death," "The Burning Babe," "Short Rule of Good Life," "Hundred Meditations," and his longest poem, "St. Peter's Complaint." He was much respected by later religious poets and earned the admiration of Ben Johnson.

Soviet Union ● See **Russia**; see also **Communism** and **Ostpolitik**.

Sozomen (c. 400-c. 447 or 448) ● Important historian of the early Church. Salamanes Hermeios Sozomenos (his Greek name) was a native of Bethelia, near Gaza, in Palestine. He was raised by a Christian, claiming that his grandfather had become a Christian by witnessing a miracle performed by St. Hilarion. Educated by the monks of the region, he traveled to Constantinople to work as a lawyer, deciding to author a history of the Church. The result was the *Historia Ecclesiastica*, intended by Sozomen to be a continuation of the history written by Eusebius down to his own day and thus covering the period 323-425. Sozomen dedicated the work to Emperor Theodosius II, dividing it into nine books, organized according to the reigns of the emperors. He almost certainly used as a source the writings of the older Socrates. When compared with Socrates, Sozomen is considered superior in style but inferior in the nature of his literary construction and his understanding of the details and significance of many of the events and theological controversies that he was reporting. He focused, however, considerable attention on missionary activities, particularly the introduction of Christianity among the Armenians, Goths, and Saracens. He also examined the early monasteries and preserved important documentary material that is to be found nowhere else.

Spain ● Catholic country in the Iberian Peninsula. Christianity was born in Spain in the first century through the works of some of the earliest missionaries. According to tradition, the first Christian preachers were St. Paul and St. James. They and their successors found the presence of Roman culture (Spain, or Hispania, being part of the Roman Empire) helpful in assisting in the spread of the faith. Henceforth, Christianity would be an indelible element in the life of the Spanish people. The Church was organized sufficiently by the fourth century to have several important councils, including Elvira (c. 306) and Toledo (400). The Spanish Church also produced the influential figure of Hosius of Córdoba (d. 357), who was an adviser to Constantine the Great and presided over the Council of Nicaea (325).

The fifth century brought the invasion of the peninsula by the so-called barbarians, most likely the Visigoths who crossed south over the Pyrenees from Gaul and settled in the Roman territory of Spain. Devoted Arians, they brought some suffering to the Orthodox Christians but were gradually converted to Catholicism by the late sixth century. An important step was taken in 589 when King Reccared of the Visigoths at the Third Council of Toledo abjured Arianism. The Visigoths would endure until the lightning invasion of Muslims in the eighth century.

The Muslims poured into Spain from North Africa and destroyed the Visigoth kingdom. They then made an attack into Gaul (or France) in 732 but were repulsed at the Battle of Tours by Charles Martel. The Muslim armies then decided to consolidate their position in the peninsula and thus formed the so-called Moorish states. These kingdoms, such as the emirate (later caliphate) of Córdoba and the Nasrid kingdom of Granada, would become highly developed and culturally rich centers of art and learning. Scholars from all over Europe, including Jews and Christians, studied under the Moors (as the Spanish Muslims were called), and the Moorish kingdoms would make lasting scientific contributions (such as algebra) and artistic masterpieces (such as the Alhambra). The intermingling of the Moorish and Christian cultures would also create the so-called Mozarabic, a rich amalgamation of the two that would foster art, architecture, music, and even religious practice. (See **Mozarabic Rite**.)

The Moorish conquest of Spain was not unopposed by Christians, nor was it free of oppression and persecution. Gradually, the Christians who had fled to the north of the peninsula united together and formed the kingdom of Asturia in the eighth century. This led to the moving of the capital to León in the tenth century, which was to be the launching site of the centuries-old effort of expelling the Moors called the *Reconquista*. The *Reconquista* traditionally began with the Christian triumph at the Battle of Calatanaor in 1002. It would culminate in 1492 with the final demise of the kingdom of Granada, which had been destroyed by troops of Ferdinand and Isabella, their Catholic Majesties, who had united the crowns of Castile and Aragon. That same year, Columbus discovered the New World and made possible the conquest of the Americas and the rise of Spain as the foremost empire in Europe.

The Church during this period was closely allied with the Spanish crown, a cooperation that would be most manifest in the instituting of the Inquisition in the late 1400s. The Church worked in concert with civil authorities to enforce strict Christian orthodoxy and to reduce the traditional influence of the Jews who were expelled in 1492. The presence of the Inquisition, however, also insulated Spain from the reforming ideas and the dangers characterized by the Protestant Reformation in the 1500s.

In 1516, the Spanish crown passed to the grandson of Ferdinand and Isabella, Charles V, the Habsburg prince who became the Holy Roman Emperor. Spain thus became part of the Habsburg Empire, stretching from the New World to Italy, Austria, the Spanish Netherlands, and Germany. Charles abdicated in 1556 and was succeeded by his son Philip. As Philip II (r. 1556-1598), he made Spain a formidable Catholic bastion against Protestantism, although for political reasons he was, like his father, frequently at odds with the papacy. Nevertheless, he waged a war against heresy through the Inquisition and fostered the Catholic faith. This would be highly successful in Spain but would be a failure in the Low Countries.

The Spanish Church was to have a major place in the Council of Trent, contributing many influential Council Fathers and theologians. They subsequently helped promote the Catholic Reformation. In Spain itself, the faith was quite active and vibrant, despite the image of stultification and oppression owing to the seeming ubiquitousness of the Spanish Inquisition. The sixteenth century, for example, would produce the genuinely brilliant theologians Dominic Báñez (d. 1604), Dominic Soto (d. 1560), Melchior Cano (d. 1560), and Francisco de Vitoria (d. 1546). It would also witness the profound work of the mystics St. Teresa of Ávila and St. John of the Cross.

The once mighty Spanish Empire declined in the seventeenth century, a state of deterioration demonstrated in 1643 by the crushing defeat of a Spanish army at the Battle of Rocroi against the French. In 1700, the Spanish Habsburg kings died out and the Bourbon Dynasty came to the throne under King Philip V. The Bourbons would be adherents of the worst trends of the Enlightenment, including anticlericalism and rationalism. Despite the indomitable spirit

and abiding faith of the Spanish people, the Bourbons oppressed the Church and, under King Charles III (r. 1759-1788), the Jesuits were expelled. Spain also pushed for the suppression of the Jesuits entirely. (See **Jesuits** for other details.)

The early nineteenth century brought the invasion of Spain by Napoleon, starting in 1808. The country would be a battleground from 1808-1814 — the Peninsula War — during which the local members of the Spanish Church, especially the monks, priests, and nuns, led popular uprisings that were marked by their brutality against French troops. The French response was often bloody, but the guerrilla struggle needed resources and aided the campaigns of the English forces under the duke of Wellington. The Bourbons, who had been replaced by Napoleon with his brother Joseph, were restored in 1814.

According to the 1812 Constitution, steeped in French ideas of liberalism, the Church was severely suppressed and much suffering was caused to the leaders and devoted of the faith. Much hated by the Spaniards, the 1812 Constitution was abandoned by King Ferdinand VII. His death in 1833 would bring a long series of civil wars as liberal and conservative factions vied for political power. Political struggles were to characterize much of the remaining century, as the once vast Spanish Empire collapsed in the wake of numerous wars of independence. Instability would carry over into the twentieth century, culminating in the dictatorship of Primo de Rivera in 1923. He was followed in 1931 by the Spanish Republic, which promulgated stringent anticlerical decrees, nationalized Church property, secularized the schools, and dissolved the Jesuits. Pope Pius XI protested with the encyclical *Dilectissima nobis* (1933).

The Spanish Civil War began in 1936, raging for three bloody years and bringing ruin to much of the country. In the fighting between Loyalists (leftist pro-Republican) and the Nationalists (rightists of the Falange party), over seven hundred fifty thousand men, women, and children perished, along with some six thousand priests and other religious. In the end the Republicans were defeated and Francisco Franco was able to assume dictatorial powers. His regime would last until his death in 1975. (See **Franco, Francisco**.) The Church was largely on the Nationalist side during the civil war, and Franco attempted to cultivate the goodwill of the Church, even while maintaining stern control over social and political life. A concordat was signed in 1953 between Franco and the Holy See that declared Catholicism to be the state religion. This was changed in 1976 with the new constitution that revised the previous concordat and disestablished Catholicism while granting full religious toleration. In the years since the Second Vatican Council, the Spanish Church has promoted religious liberty, economic justice, and democratization. It has also developed and nurtured its traditional ties to the Church of Central and South America. (See also **Opus Dei**.)

Specola Vaticana ● See **Vatican Observatory**.

Spellman, Francis Joseph (1889-1967) ● Cardinal and influential archbishop of New York. Born in Whitman, Massachusetts, Spellman studied at Fordham University and the North American College, Rome, where he was ordained on May 14, 1916. After several years of service in the archdiocese of Boston, he returned to Rome in 1925 and was appointed to the Vatican Secretariat of State. In 1932, he was named auxiliary bishop of Boston, a post he held until 1939 when Pope Pius XII made him archbishop of New York. A close friend of Pope Pius, Spellman proved an invaluable representative of the Holy See to the United States administration of President Franklin Delano Roosevelt during World War II, especially when the pope was compelled to maintain neutrality during that war. Further, as military vicar (bishop ordinary of the army and navy), he was able to be of use to Roosevelt in various missions where his diplomatic skill and remarkable fluency in languages could be of great value to American interests. A candidate to serve as papal secretary of state after the war, he was made cardinal in 1946, emerging as the most powerful Church figure in the country. A devoted anti-Communist, he supported American involvement in Vietnam and promoted U.S. policy in Asia and Latin America. At Vatican Council II, he took part in the debates and gave his backing to the "Declaration on Religious Freedom" (*Dignitatis Humanae*). As archbishop, Spellman was active in defending Catholic rights advocating censorship in films, speaking out against contraception, and working for the place of the Church in American life. A poet and novelist, he also made translations of a number of works on theology from the original Italian.

Speyer, Diet of ● Assembly convened on February 21, 1529, by Emperor Charles V at the behest of Pope Clement VII. It marked a sharp Catholic counterreaction in the Holy Roman Empire to the rise of the Reformers. The diet was dominated by the Catholic majority of princes and electors who issued legislation that terminated the toleration of Lutheranism in lands with a Catholic majority while insisting on toleration of Catholicism in lands with a Lutheran majority. Anabaptists and adherents of Huldrych Zwingli were not to be tolerated anywhere. This resulted on April 19, 1529, in the Protest of Speyer signed by a number of prominent delegates to the diet, including the elector John of Saxony, landgrave Philip of Hesse, and the representatives of fourteen cities. They defended religious toleration and inaugurated the use of the term "Protestants."

Spinoza, Baruch (1632-1677) ● Also Benedict de Spinoza. A Dutch philosopher, he was born in Amsterdam and was a member of a family of Jewish merchants, originally known as Baruch, later changing it to Benedict, the Latin equivalent. Raised in the Jewish faith, he was intended to become a rabbi, advancing swiftly in the study of the Talmud and Hebrew. His questions and sharp independence of thought led to the study of such controversial figures as Thomas Hobbes, René Descartes, and Giordano Bruno and his increasing isolation from the Jewish community. In 1656, he was excommunicated from the Jews of Amsterdam and forced to leave the city. He traveled to various places, surviving by working as a lens grinder and finally settling in the Hague in 1670. His life as a philosopher was remarkable as to the degree to which he worked alone, his solitary labors producing a complex and profound philosophical system. Fundamental to this system is the belief that God or Nature is the eternal or infinite substance from which all things come. God or Nature (*Deus sive Natura*) is the cause, the *natura naturans* (nature that natures or naturing nature) that leads by causes to *natura naturata* (nature that has been natured). While the infinite substance possesses an infinite number of attributes, humanity is able to comprehend two, thought (*cogito*) and extension (*extensio*); one is the essence of mind and the essence of body. In matters of religion, Spinoza denied a personal God who influences events and lives, arguing instead a broad pantheism in which God or Nature is intimately connected with all things, existing in all things as all things exist in God and flow directly from God. In ethics, Spinoza was a determinist, denying that freedom could exist and proposing a relativist position, looking at every event as part of a wider system described by Spinoza as "under the species of eternity." During his life, Spinoza only published two works, *Principles of Cartesian Philosophy* (1663) and *Tractatus Theologico politicus* (1670). The posthumous treatise *Ethica ordine geometrico demonstrata*, an examination of ethics using geometrical logic, appeared in 1677. One of the most difficult works in all of philosophy, it is divided into five parts: *"De Deo"* ("Concerning God"); *"De Natura et Origine Mentis"* ("Concerning the Nature and Origin of the Mind"); *"De Origine et Natura de Affectum"* ("Concerning the Origin and Nature of the Emotions"); *"De Servitute Humana seu de Affectum Viribus"* ("Concerning Human Bondage and the Strength of the Emotions"); and *"De Potentia Intellectus seu de Libertate Humana"* ("Concerning the Power of the Intellect or on Human Freedom"). A number of letters are also extant. Spinoza exercised considerable influence on later philosophers, especially during the 1800s, including Kant, Hegel, Nietzsche, Schelling, and Leibniz.

Spiritual Franciscans ● See under **Franciscans;** see also **Beghards; Bonaventure, St.; Elias of Cortona; Joachim of Fiore; John of Parma; Olivi, Pierre;** and **Ubertino of Casale**.

Stained Glass ● Windows of colored glass. They had an important role in the decorative arts during the Middle Ages, particularly in the 1100s and 1200s. Stained glass evolved slowly over time in Western Europe, finding early application during the architectural periods described as the Carolingian (ninth and tenth centuries). Stained-glass windows made during these eras were generally small, increasing in size throughout the Romanesque, finding full and often magnificent expression in Gothic architecture (1200s through 1400s). The improvements made in architecture during the Gothic — for example, the introduction of support ribs and flying buttresses — gave much greater strength to massive constructions, but they also permitted innovation in the use of enlarged windows. Widened windows brought greater light into the churches, allowing artisans to undertake the use of stained glass to decorate sumptuously the open areas. Much as the Gothic cathedral came to epitomize in physical form the power and stature of the grand medieval Church, so did the stained-glass windows represent the deep spirituality and devotion of the times, particularly as the windows were often decorated with depictions of saints, ecclesiastical symbols, or colorful, intense religious themes intended to foster prayerfulness and inspire reverence. Stained glass was also used for the preservation of important coats of arms belonging to prelates and high Churchmen.

Stanislaus, St. (1030-1079) ● Patron saint of Poland and bishop of Cracow. Also known as St. Stanislaw, he was a member of a noble Polish family, born in Szczepanow and studying at Gniezno and probably Paris. After being nominated by Pope Alexander II, he was elected bishop of Cracow in 1072. Subsequent events remain a source of debate among Polish historians. Stanislaus soon came into conflict with King Boleslaus II the Bold of Poland, reproaching the king for cruel behavior and immorality and joining the opposition party of the king's policies. It is uncertain whether Stanislaus joined the plot spearheaded by German-Bohemian nobles to depose Boleslaus, but in 1079 the bishop was seized on the charge of treason and condemned to death. When Boleslaus's knights refused to murder the prelate, the king was forced to do the deed himself. Stanislaus was stabbed to death in the chapel of St. Michael in Cracow. Some scholars have argued that Stanislaus had been a plotter against the king, while others state that he was a victim of a rapacious ruler. Stanislaus was canonized in 1253 by Pope Innocent IV. Feast day: April 11.

Stapleton, Thomas (1535-1598) ● English controversialist. Born in Henfield,

Sussex, Stapleton was educated at the Free School, Canterbury, at Winchester, and at Oxford; he became a fellow in January 1553. Under Mary he received the prebendary of Chichester Cathedral in 1558, fleeing England upon the succession of Queen Elizabeth rather than conform to the reinstituted new religion. Stapleton went to Louvain and then Paris where he studied theology. Back in England by 1563, he was called upon by Anglican authorities to issue a renunciation of papal authority. Refusing to do this, he was stripped of his prebendary, returning to Louvain. In 1568-1569, Stapleton moved to Douai where he taught theology and assisted William Allen in his work of making Douai a safe haven for English Catholics; from 1585, he lectured in theology at the Jesuit College, although he did not finish his novitiate for the Society of Jesus and ultimately returned to Douai. King Philip II gave Stapleton the professorship of Scriptures at Louvain in 1590, and soon after he was appointed dean of Hilverenbeeck. Having impressed Pope Clement VIII with his theological writings, Stapleton was invited to Rome, finally accepting in 1597 when the pope offered to make him a protonotary apostolic. While it was anticipated that he would be made a cardinal, the opposition of the Jesuits at the English College ended any chance of his promotion. An energetic and skillful controversialist, he composed numerous works, including *Principiorum fidei doctrinalium demonstratio* (1578), a defense of the faith; *Apologia pro rege Philippo II* (1592); *Antidota Evangelicae* (1595); *Antidota Apostolica contra nostri Temporis Haereses* (1595); and *Tres Thomae*, on the three Thomases — the Apostle, Thomas Becket, and Thomas More.

States General ● See **Estates General**.

States of the Church ● See **Papal States**.

Stein, Edith, Bl. (1891-1942) ● Carmelite nun, convert, philosopher, and spiritual writer. Stein was born into a Jewish family in Breslau. At an early age she abandoned Judaism (1904), becoming a self-proclaimed atheist. Studying philosophy at the University of Göttingen, she became a student of the philosopher Edmund Husserl and his school of philosophical thought called phenomenology, in which phenomena are investigated and described as they are experienced, without any external theorizing about causes and unexamined preconceptions. A brilliant student, she served as Husserl's assistant at the University of Freiburg in Breisgau. There she secured her doctorate in 1916 and acquired a reputation as one of Europe's leading philosophers and a major figure in phenomenology. As a philosopher, Stein attempted to examine phenomenology from the perspective of Thomistic thought. Her conversion to Catholicism was propelled by her reading of the autobiography of St. Teresa of Ávila. Baptized on January 1, 1922, she gave up her post in Freiburg to teach in a Dominican school in Speyer, remaining there from 1922-1932. In 1932, she was named lecturer at the Educational Institute of Munich, but owing to the rise of the Nazis in Germany she was forced to resign her position.

She entered the Carmelite order at Cologne in 1934, taking the name Sister Teresa Benedicta a Cruce. As the Nazi persecution intensified, she was smuggled out of Germany into the Netherlands in 1938 where it was hoped she would be safe. In 1942, however, with Germany occupying Western Europe, she was arrested with her sister Rosa (also a convert) as a part of Hitler's order against all non-Aryan Catholics. Taken to Auschwitz, she displayed compassion for her fellow prisoners and was put to death in a gas chamber on August 9 or 10, 1942. Among her major writings were: *Endliches und ewiges Sein* (*Finite and Eternal Being*), a metaphysical synthesis of Thomism and phenomenology; *Studie uber Joannes a Cruce: Kreuzeswissenschaft* (1950; published in English in 1960 as *The Science of the Cross*). Other writings were collected and published, and the study of her work is promoted by the Archivum Carmelitanum Edith Stein at Louvain, Belgium. Her cause was opened in 1962; in 1987, Pope John Paul II beatified her during a visit to West Germany. Feast day: August 10.

Stephen, St. ● Traditionally the first martyr for the Christian faith and one of the most revered of all martyrs. His death is recounted in the Acts of the Apostles (6-7). Stephen is first mentioned (6:5) as being one of the seven deacons chosen by the Apostles and ordained by them with the duty of taking care of charitable works among the poor. Stephen was the first deacon to be listed and became the most famous of the group picked because they were "of good repute, full of the Spirit and of wisdom" (6:3). Prior to his appointment as a deacon, Stephen's life is obscure. As his name is Greek, it has been theorized that he was a Hellenist, meaning one of the Jews born in a distant land whose native language was Greek. This is disputed by the tradition started in the fifth century that Stephen was merely a Greek equivalent of the Aramaic Kelil, possibly Stephen's original name, as inscribed upon a stone slab found in his tomb. Further support is given to Stephen's Jewish origin by the list of the deacons in which Nicolaus is described as a "proselyte of Antioch" (Acts 6:5), making the obvious assumption that the other deacons are Jews. Nothing is known of his conversion. His ministry as a deacon appears to have been centered among Hellenist converts. A remarkable preacher, he performed miracles and was described as being full of grace and power. Opposed by a group of Jews in Jerusalem, he was brought before the Sanhedrin where he delivered the profound testament in Acts (7:2-53). Enraging his

Jewish enemies, Stephen was seized, dragged out of the city, and stoned to death according to the precepts of Mosaic law. The witnesses laid their garments at the feet of the young man named Saul, the future St. Paul. As he was being stoned, Stephen prayed, "Lord, Jesus, receive my spirit" (7:59), asking Christ's forgiveness for his attackers. While it was written that Saul "was consenting to his death" (8:1), the martyrdom had a lasting influence upon him. Stephen was buried by "devout men" who "made great lamentation over him" (8:2). His tomb was long forgotten until its discovery by Lucian in 415 and a church was built in his honor just beyond the Damascus Gate by Empress Eudoxia (r. 455-460). Feast day: December 26.

Stephen I, St. <1> (977-1038) ● First king

of Hungary. Ruled from 997-1038 and introduced an ambitious program of Christianization. The son of the Magyar chieftain Geza, Stephen succeeded him in 997. Having been raised a Christian and marrying in 996 the daughter of Duke Henry II of Bavaria, Stephen actively promoted the faith, routing the pagans (called Black Hungarians) when they rebelled against missionaries and forcibly converted them. The Church emerged as a powerful social force in Hungary and an important means of establishing political unity. In 1000, he was anointed king, traditionally receiving the cross and crown from Pope Sylvester II; the crown would become famous and a symbol of the Hungarian state. Stephen promoted learning, built churches, was a patron of missionary activity, and created a fit standing army. Much revered for his devotion, Stephen was canonized in 1083. Feast day: August 16 (August 20 in Hungary).

St. Stephen I, king of Hungary

Stephen I, St. <2> ● Pope from 254-257.

A native probably of Rome, the son of Jovius, Stephen was an archdeacon serving in the Eternal City when in 254 Pope St. Lucius I, at the moment of his martyrdom, entrusted the care of the Church to him. Stephen was then consecrated, traditionally on May 12, 254. His pontificate is best known through the controversies that were so troublesome during the period, the details of which were preserved in the letters of St. Cyprian of Carthage. Shortly after becoming pope, Stephen was urged by Faustinus, bishop of Lyons, to move against Marcian, bishop of Arles, for adopting certain Novatianist practices, most notably refusing to give Communion to penitent *lapsi*, those Christians who had returned to the Church after making sacrifices to the gods during persecutions. When Stephen took no immediate action, Faustinus appealed to the influential Cyprian. The Carthaginian wrote to the pontiff (in a preserved letter) asking him to support the Gallic prelates. A second controversy with Cyprian involved Stephen's restoration of two Spanish bishops, Martial of Merida and Basilides, who had been accused of denying the faith. The Spanish bishops protested this decision, appealing to the African Church and Cyprian. A synod of bishops there confirmed the deposition, arguing that

Stephen had been deceived by Basilides owing to the fact that he was "situated at a distance, and ignorant of the true facts of the case." A third dispute was over the question of whether baptism by heretics was valid. Stephen upheld the tradition that such a baptism was valid, requiring schismatics only to receive absolution; Cyprian and the bishops of Africa and elsewhere argued that baptism was only valid within the Church and that schismatics needed to receive another, proper, Catholic baptism. In this matter Stephen remained adamant, threatening to excommunicate the bishops of Africa and Asia Minor if they persisted in performing second baptisms. Cyprian responded by organizing a council at Carthage in 255 and writing a treatise in defense of rebaptism. Stephen refused to receive envoys from the African bishops, and it seemed that a schism would soon erupt. The crisis may have become even more severe had Stephen not died on August 2, 257. His passing came during the persecutions of Emperor Valerian, although Stephen is not generally considered a martyr, the evidence for this claim being doubtful. Stephen is notable for being the earliest pope to make formal claim to the primacy of Rome on the basis of the declaration of Christ to Peter. He was buried in the cemetery of Callistus on the Appian Way, and his remains were later moved by Pope St. Pius I to a monastery founded in Stephen's honor. Feast day: August 2.

Stephen (II) ● Roman priest elected pope to succeed Pope St. Zachary (r. 741-752) in late March 752. Properly elected, he was installed in the Lateran Palace but died four days after his elevation, before his consecration as Bishop of Rome. As the canon law of the time considered a pontificate to have begun at the moment of consecration, Stephen was not included in most lists of popes. He was not recognized as pontiff by medieval historians or the *Liber Pontificalis*. In the sixteenth century, however, when the custom was established that a person was pope from the moment of election, Stephen was counted as a legitimate successor to Peter and listed until 1961 when the Holy See removed his name and instead changed the numbering system used for his namesakes. Thus his successor Stephen, who ruled from 752-757, is numbered Stephen II (III).

Stephen II (III) ● Pope from 752-757. A Roman by birth, Stephen was appointed a deacon by Pope St. Zacharias (r. 741-752). When, after a few days, Zacharias's successor Stephen (II) died without being consecrated, Stephen was unanimously elected pope. He is numbered Stephen II (III) to reflect the confusion in some lists over the question of the validity of Stephen (II) owing to the lack of consecration. The pontificate of Stephen II (III) is significant, for during it the papacy was able to free itself from the dominating influence of the Byzantine Empire and to lay the groundwork for the Papal States. Facing the threat of the Lombards under their ruler Aistulf (r. 749-757), Stephen made the important decision of appealing to the Franks. In 754, he crossed the Alps and conferred with the Frankish king Pepin III the Short. Having despaired of help from the Byzantines, Stephen pleaded with the Franks for aid, securing the promise from Pepin to protect the Church in Rome. Stephen anointed Pepin in late July 754 at St. Denis. The Franks then marched into Italy, defeated the Lombards, and forced Aistulf to cede to Stephen extensive lands that had been seized from the Byzantines in Italy. Once the Franks departed, however, the Lombards renewed their attacks on the areas around Rome, laying siege to the Eternal City on January 1, 756. Pepin returned to Italy, once again crushed the Lombards, and gave Stephen the former Byzantine possession of Ravenna, the onetime exarchate of Pentapolis (Rimini,

Fano, Ancona, Senigallia, and Pesaro), and other lands. Thus was born the temporal power of the papacy through the so-called Donation of Pepin. The Papal States would henceforth be of considerable importance to the papacy, surviving until 1870. Stephen also built hospitals for the poor.

Stephen III (IV) ● Pope from 768-772. A Sicilian, he was raised in Rome and served as a Byzantine priest in the city at the time of his election and consecration (August 7, 768) to replace the deposed antipopes Constantine and Philip. He was unable to prevent the harsh treatment given to the deposed papal claimants and their adherents, but the synod he convened in the Lateran in April 769 burned Constantine's acts, declared his ordinations to be invalid, and sentenced the now blinded usurper to perpetual penitence in a monastery. Stephen and the bishops at the synod also took the important step of forbidding the participation of laypeople in papal elections or the elevation of a layperson to the papacy. His remaining pontificate was troubled by the cunning Lombard king Desiderius who worked to alienate the pope from his ally Charlemagne and the Franks; Desiderius secured the marriage of his daughter to Charlemagne and managed the removal of two powerful papal officials, Christopher and Sergius, and the subsequent massacre of the Frankish party in Rome by the pro-Lombard chamberlain Paul Afiarta. Stephen's ill-advised alliance with Desiderius was proven a strategic error in 771 when Charlemagne repudiated his marriage to Desiderius's daughter. He is considered a saint in some martyrologies.

Stephen IV (V) ● Pope from 816-817. A member of a noble Roman family, he was raised in the Lateran and had known in his youth both Popes Adrian I and Leo III; the latter had ordained him a deacon. Elected to succeed Leo in June 816 (consecrated on June 22, 816), he immediately instructed the Romans to take an oath to Emperor Louis the Pious (r. 814-840), sending several envoys to the emperor to announce his election. Stephen then met with Louis in October 816, being received with great pomp. The pope crowned Louis (October 18) thereby inaugurating the tradition of papal consecration, an act that concretized the formal relationship between the popes and the Frankish emperors. For the emperors, they were able to point to their special position with the popes, claiming succession to the Roman emperors; for the popes, they took as their prerogative the privilege of crowning and anointing the emperors and being able to call upon them for aid. Returning to Rome, Stephen brought with him the nobles who had been banished to Gaul by Charlemagne in 800 for conspiring against Leo III.

Stephen V (VI) ● Pope from 885-891. His pontificate took place during a time of famine, threats from Saracen raiders, and the political disintegration of the Carolingian Empire. A nobleman of Rome, he had been educated by Zachary, a relative who was also a bishop and chief librarian for the Holy See. Made a cardinal by Pope Marinus I (r. 882-884), he had a reputation for personal holiness and was thus unanimously elected to succeed Pope St. Adrian III. His consecration in September 885 was without imperial confirmation, but Emperor Charles III the Fat did not press the matter. The emperor was deposed in 887 by Arnulf, king of the East Franks, depriving Stephen of much needed help to curb Saracen attacks in Italy and to reduce the violent political struggle between the noble families. A short time later, the extensive Carolingian Empire broke apart, forcing Stephen to find a new protector. He chose Guido (Guy) III of Spoleto, an ambitious nobleman who would prove very troublesome to the Church over the next years. To combat famine, he used his own family's funds, since the papal treasury was empty. He also secured the exile of Photius, the patriarch of Constantinople, and made what was later proven to be a mistake by opposing the Slavic liturgy in Moravia, a move that drove the Slavs into the fold of the Eastern Church and would precipitate the evangelization of Russia by the Orthodox Church. His successor was the ill-fated Formosus.

Stephen VI (VII) ● Pope from 896-897. Stephen gained historical infamy for convening the so-called Cadaver Synod in 897, one of the bleakest and most lurid episodes in the history of the papacy. A Roman by birth, he was made bishop of Anagni, perhaps against his will, by Pope Formosus and was then elected successor to Boniface VI in May 896. Rome at the time was filled with considerable strife as various factions vied for supremacy, a struggle that inevitably impacted upon the papacy. Stephen belonged to the House of Spoleto, which was headed by Guido (Guy) of Spoleto who had been crowned Holy Roman Emperor in 891 by Pope Stephen V (VI); his son Lambert had been crowned co-emperor by Pope Formosus. When, however, Formosus crowned Arnulf as Holy Roman Emperor, the Spoleto party felt betrayed. Thus, when Boniface died, the Spoletans secured Stephen's elevation, launching a pogrom against the partisans of Pope Formosus. Their campaign did not cease with the living, as Stephen was compelled or convinced to stage the gruesome trial of his deceased predecessor. Convening the Cadaver Synod, Stephen had Formosus exhumed and his body propped up in a chair to answer various charges; a deacon was appointed to speak for the rotting corpse. Found guilty, Formosus's body was stripped of its vestments, mutilated (two fingers were cut from the right hand), and thrown into the Tiber. The decrees of Formosus were annulled and his ordinations declared invalid, an act that rendered Stephen's own consecration void. A short

time later, an earthquake struck and the Roman mob, made uneasy by the horrific proceedings of the synod, revolted against the pope. Deciding that Stephen had served his purposes, the Spoletans had him imprisoned and strangled. A series of dominated pontiffs followed in succession.

Stephen VII (VIII) ● Pope from 928-931. A Roman, he was a priest of St. Anastasia at the time of his election to succeed Leo VI. He owed his election to Marozia, the formidable matron of the House of Theophylact in Rome, and his pontificate (December 928-February 931) was dominated by her. He wielded no authority and was widely acknowledged to be a mere interim pontiff until Marozia's son John (XI) was old enough to install on the papal throne. The only noteworthy act of his reign was to issue certain privileges to monasteries in France and Italy.

Stephen VIII (IX) ● Pope from 939-942. A Roman by birth, he was serving as cardinal priest of Sts. Silvestro and Martino at the time of his election as successor to Pope Leo VII. His pontificate was completely dominated by Alberic II, prince of the Romans and virtual ruler of the city from 932-954. While severely limited in his authority in Rome, Stephen did manage to support King Louis IV of France (r. 936-954) in his struggle with the Frankish nobles, threatening the nobles with excommunication should they recognize Louis as their monarch. He died probably as a result of angering Alberic over some matter; the prince most likely had him imprisoned, mutilated, and left to die. A false story was later told that he was of German descent.

Stephen IX (X) ● Pope from 1057-1058. Known originally as Frederick of Lorraine, he was the son of the duke of Lorraine and cousin to Pope St. Leo IX (r. 1049-1054). Appointed chancellor and librarian of the Roman Church around 1051, he was utilized by the pontiff on several missions, including the ill-fated effort at reconciliation with the Eastern Church in 1054. Owing to poor relations with Emperor Henry III, he entered the monastery of Monte Cassino in 1055 and was elected abbot two years later. Made a cardinal by Pope Victor II, he supported several candidates to succeed Victor (d. 1057), including Hildebrand (the future Pope St. Gregory VII) and the harsh cleric Humbert of Silva-Candida. To his surprise, he was elected, taking the name Stephen (after St. Stephen I whose feast day coincided with his own election, August 2). While he reigned only briefly, Stephen was an important promoter of what came later to be called the Gregorian Reform. He summoned a synod in Rome to condemn simony, made St. Peter Damian a cardinal, and enthusiastically utilized the talents of the brilliant reforming leader Hildebrand. It had been his hope to renew negotiations with the Greeks, but his death cut short any plans. He also proposed a campaign against the troublesome Normans in southern Italy. On his deathbed, Stephen requested that the cardinals wait for the return of Hildebrand (who was on a mission to Germany) before electing his successor so as to ensure the elevation of another reforming pontiff.

Stephen Harding, St. (d. 1134) ● Abbot of Cîteaux and an English monastic reformer. Born in Dorsetshire, England, he studied at the monastery of Sherborne, at Paris, and at Rome. Returning from Rome, he spent time at the monastery of Molesme where, impressed with the abbot of St. Robert, he joined the monks. In 1098, he was chosen to be one of the monks who were to go to Cîteaux. Subsequently serving as prior, he was elected abbot in 1109. Despite shrinking numbers, Stephen insisted that the community continue its strict observance. Just as it seemed that the monastery should die out, St. Bernard of Clairvaux with thirty companions arrived in 1112. This new development led to the prosperity of Cîteaux

and necessitated the founding of other communities. By the time of Stephen's death, thirteen houses had been established. To assist in the organization of the houses, Stephen instituted the Charter of Love (*Carta Caritatis*), the regulations covering the government of the monasteries tied to Cîteaux, which was approved by Pope Callistus II in 1119. Feast day: April 17. (See also **Carta Caritatis** and **Cîteaux**.)

Stigmata ● The rare phenomenon in which some or all of the wounds of Christ appear on the body of an individual, that is, the person receives wounds on the hands, feet, side, and forehead; these wounds will bleed spontaneously from no apparent source and at times profusely. There is also the invisible stigmata, without any visible wounds, such as that received by St. Catherine of Siena (d. 1380). The Church takes the stand that authentic stigmatization is a sign of the special favor of God, and, over the centuries, it has established certain objective criteria for the determination of the validity of a stigmata. These include: the bleeding of the wounds and pain occurring on certain days or during those days connected with the Passion, such as Fridays and feast days; the location of the wounds corresponding to the five wounds and not the result of hysterical bleeding or hypnotically induced blood sweat; there is actual bleeding that continues and does not begin and end abruptly; the wounds are removed or away from the blood vessels but do truly bleed, thus eliminating the possibility of a person simply injuring himself or herself to induce hemorrhaging or blood loss; the wounds do not become infected and will not respond to any medical treatment; and, of great importance, the person must be determined to possess both heroic virtue and special devotion to the Cross. Based on the evidence of those who have been blessed with the stigmata, the phenomenon occurs in individuals who have advanced greatly in the spiritual life and enter into states of ecstasy. They endure enormous suffering, physical and spiritual, in preparation for the arrival of the stigmatization. The suffering continues during the time of stigmata.

Throughout history, there have been three hundred thirty known cases of the stigmata appearing in some way on persons. Of these, sixty have been canonized or declared blessed, an indication both of the care the Church takes in examining the event thoroughly and that the presence of the stigmata is not sufficient of itself for canonization. The first recognized and most famous stigmatist was St. Francis of Assisi (d. 1226), who received the wounds while in ecstasy on Mt. Alverina on September 17, 1224. Among the other better known recipients of the stigmata are Padre Pio, St. Gemma Galgani, Anne Catherine Emmerich, and Theresa Neumann. The term stigmata comes from the Greek *stigma* (tattoo mark).

Stylites ● Term from the Greek for "pillar," used for the solitary ascetics who chose to live on the tops of pillars. Such rigorous individuals probably originated in the early Church, as St. Gregory of Nazianzus (329-389) told of a hermit who remained standing for many years at a time and Theodoret (d. c. 466) told of a solitary who lived for ten years in a tub that was suspended in the air by two large pillars. The stylites themselves took as their founder St. Simeon Stylites (d. 459), who chose to reside at the top of a pillar at first nine feet and then fifty feet high. He was the inspiration to such subsequent stylites as St. Simeon the Younger (d. 597) and Daniel (d. 493). By custom, the stylite would spend his time on a platform at the top of a pillar, often with a small hut. Ideally, they would sleep standing up, but many chose a small corner or support on which they could lean. Food was brought to them by students or friends. Most of their time was occupied with prayer, although they also frequently gave sermons,

counseled many on spiritual matters, and arbitrated in conflicts or controversies, usually of a theological nature. Found throughout Syria, the lands of the Eastern Empire, and Egypt, stylites flourished until the twelfth century. One of the most extreme forms of spiritual devotion, the pillar life was the subject of numerous accounts by writers.

Suárez, Francisco (1548-1617) ●
Prominent Jesuit theologian, called *Doctor Eximius* (the Special [or Remarkable] Doctor). A native of Granada, he joined the Society of Jesus in June 1564 and received holy orders in 1572 after studying at Salamanca. Subsequently teaching philosophy and later theology at Ávila, Segovia, Valladolid, Rome, Alcalá, Salamanca, and Coimbra, he became one of the era's foremost theologians. Pope Gregory XIII (r. 1572-1585) attended his first lecture in Rome in 1580, and Pope Paul V (1605-1621) employed him both as an adviser and to refute the errors in the writings of King James I of England. A gifted master of Scholastic thought, Suárez gave his name to his own school, Suarism, differing in a number of points from Thomism. Among the principles of Suarism are: the pure potentiality of matter; the difference between the essence and the existence of created beings; the Incarnation of the Word as inevitable, even if Adam had not committed sin; and the heightened or superior grace of the Blessed Virgin when compared with that of the saints or angels. His vast corpus of writings includes: *De Verbo Incarnato* (1590; *On the Incarnate Word*), a commentary on the first twenty-six questions of the *Tertia Pars* of the *Summa Theologiae* of St. Thomas Aquinas; *De Mysteriis Vitae Christi* (1592; *On the Mysteries of the Life of Christ*); *Disputationes Metaphysicae* (1597; *Metaphysical Disputations*), on the metaphysics of Aristotle and St. Thomas that enjoyed wide readership, even among Protestants; *Varia Opuscula Theologica* (1599), which attempted to find a means of

resolving the controversy on grace then occurring between the Dominicans and the Jesuits; *De Virtute et Statu Religionis* (1608-1609), a study of the religious life, with particular attention paid to Jesuits; *De Legibus* (1612), a brilliant study on natural and civil law examining questions found in the *Summa*, which was to have an influence on subsequent developments, in law, earning Suárez the title of one of the founders of international law.

Suetonius (c. 69-c. 140) ● In full, Gaius Suetonius Tranquillus. One of the most famous Roman historians. Born in Hippo, Africa, he served in various posts in the empire, including director of the Imperial Library under Emperor Trajan (r. 98-117) and secretary to Emperor Hadrian (r. 117-138). Among his writings were the important biographical collections, *De Viris Illustribus* (*Lives of the Great Men*), on major Roman literary figures and *De Vita Caesarum* (*Lives of the Caesars*). In the biography of Emperor Claudius (r. 41-54), Suetonius became the first pagan writer to mention Christianity with the passage *"Iudaeos impulsore Christo assidue tumultuantes Roma expulit"* ("As the Jews, at the instigation of Christus, constantly rebelled, he [Claudius] drove them from Rome").

Succession, Act of ● Decree passed in 1534 under King Henry VIII of England (r. 1509-1547). It required all subjects to take an oath acknowledging the king's marriage to Anne Boleyn as "true, sincere, and perfect." St. Thomas More and St. John Fisher refused to take the oath and were arrested. Both were beheaded in 1535 as traitors.

Suger (c. 1080-1151) ● Abbot of St.-Denis in Paris and an influential figure in promoting the Gothic style of architecture in Western Europe. Born probably near St.-Denis, he entered the monastery there around 1091, studying with the future King Louis VI. After completing studies at several other monastic institutions, Suger was named in 1106 secretary to the abbot of St.-Denis. In the service of Louis VI by 1118, he was sent to the court of Pope Gelasius II in southern France and then to that of Pope Callistus II in Rome. While in Rome (1121-1122), Suger was elected abbot of St.-Denis, subsequently attending the First Lateran Council (1123) and so impressing Pope Callistus that the pontiff invited him to Rome, in all likelihood with the intention of elevating the abbot to the cardinalate. Suger's trip to Rome was ended abruptly, however, while at Lucca where word arrived of the pope's death. From 1127-1137, he was devoted to a successful reform and reorganization of the monastery. At the same time, Suger remained a loyal and trusted figure in the royal court under both Louis VI and Louis VII. Regent to Louis VII during the king's absence while on crusade, Suger proved remarkably capable, improving taxation and curbing the rebellious attitudes of the nobles. Upon Louis's return in 1149, the abbot was named Father of the Country. Suger wrote a number of historical works, including *Vita Ludovici Grossi regis* (a history of King Louis the Fat); *Historia Ludovici VII* (on Louis VII); and *Liber de rebus in administratione sua gestis*, a memoir of his monastic government. In rebuilding the church of St.-Denis, Suger helped to introduce many crucial elements to Gothic architecture, a style of building that would soon dominate in Europe.

Sulpicians ● Properly the Society of Priests of St. Sulpice (S.S.), the Sulpicians are a congregation of priests founded in 1641 by Rev. Jean Jacques Olier (1608-1657) that is devoted to the education of priests and seminarians. The Sulpicians were founded in the Parisian parish of St.-Sulpice by Olier, who hoped to create a community of diocesan priests following a common life that would assist in the formation of active, educated, and spiritually trained priests. The congregation evolved out of the seminary, which Olier had moved into the St.-Sulpice area to assist in the reform of the once morally deprived neighborhoods of the parish. The seminary became so successful that Olier allowed several priests to assist other dioceses in the creation of similar houses of priestly formation or to aid in the reform of the seminaries along the line found at St.-Sulpice. The Sulpicians thus spread out across France, and in 1657 Olier sent several members to Canada. Papal approval came in 1664 from Alexander VII. In France, the congregation long enjoyed much influence in the Church, although the French Revolution brought much suffering, a difficult era ended only in 1801 with the restoration of the order by the concordat signed by Pope Pius VII and Napoleon Bonaparte. During the period of the Revolution, the general of the Sulpicians, Jacques André Émery, looked for a place to find refuge for many of the priests. After consulting with Cardinal Dugnani, papal nuncio to Paris, Émery interviewed with Bishop John Carroll in London, in 1790, receiving enthusiastic acceptance of his offer to launch a theological seminary in Baltimore. Four Sulpicians arrived in Baltimore in 1791, purchasing on the city's outskirts a small tavern that became St. Mary's, the first seminary in the U.S.

Sulpicius Severus (c. 360-c. 420) ● Historian and ecclesiastical writer. Born in Aquitaine, he received an excellent education and became a lawyer. Marrying the daughter of a wealthy consular family, he had a bright future ahead of him. His wife, however, died prematurely, and, encouraged by his friend Paulinus of Nola and inspired by St. Martin of Tours, Sulpicius renounced his life. Becoming a disciple of St. Martin in southern Gaul (France), he authored the immensely popular life of St. Martin, written during the saint's lifetime but not published until after Martin's death in 397. Especially read during the Middle Ages, the hagiography influenced much of subsequent hagiographies. According to the fifth-century historian Gennadius, Sulpicius was ordained a priest and in later years took upon himself the punishment of silence for having been tempted temporarily toward Pelagianism. His other works were a *Chronicle*, or *Historia sacra* (published after 403, a sacred history covering from the creation to A.D. 400 but omitting the historical events recounted in the NT), two dialogues, and three letters.

Supremacy, Act of ● Act decreed in 1534 that declared Henry VIII of England and his successors the head of the English Church with the title of being "the only supreme head in the earth of the Church of England, called *Anglicana Ecclesia.*" The act was intended to place the Church in England under direct control of the crown with the particular aim of abolishing papal authority and influence in the kingdom. Upon the succession of Queen Mary in 1553, the Act of Supremacy was rescinded. The repeal of the act was upheld by Queen Elizabeth I (r. 1558-1603), but the first legislative act of her reign was the new Act of Supremacy of 1559. While the enactments under Henry were essentially reinstituted under a revised form, the new act changed the formal title of the monarch to "the only supreme governor of the realm, and all of her highness's other dominions and countries, as well as in all spiritual or ecclesiastical things or causes temporal."

An oath was required of all clergy and public officials that they accept the act and would be obedient to the crown. Those who refused could be charged with treason; because of their refusal, St. Thomas More (1478-1535) and St. John Fisher (1469-1535) were both arrested, imprisoned in the Tower, and beheaded. (See also **Congé d'Élire**.)

Suso, Henry (c. 1295-1366) ● Also Heinrich Suso, a famed German mystic and an important figure among the *Gottesfreunde* (Friends of God). Born Heinrich von Berg probably in Constance, Swabia, to a noble family, he entered as a young man the Dominican order in Constance. After a number of years he underwent a remarkable conversion and henceforth developed a deep and abiding spirituality. From around 1322-1325, he studied under Meister Eckhart in Cologne, returning (c. 1326) to Constance to teach. The first of his works, *Das Buchlein der Wahrheit* (*The Little Book of Truth*), was published around 1327, a defense of Eckhart, whom he much admired, and an attack upon the Brethren of the Free Spirit. The following year, he wrote *Das Buchlein der ewigen Weisheit* (*The Little Book of Eternal Wisdom*), a book of practical meditations that became the most popular work on mysticism in the 1300s and 1400s until the *Imitation of Christ* by Thomas à Kempis (d. 1471). Owing to his continued support of Eckhart (who had been condemned by Pope John XXII in 1329), Suso was censured by his superiors and then stripped of his teaching position. He later became a preacher, especially in Switzerland, and the Upper Rhine, and was a much respected spiritual adviser, most notably among the Dominicans and the *Gottesfreunde* in Constance who had been exiled to Diessenhofen, Switzerland, by the German king Louis IV of Bavaria. Subjected to considerable persecution, he was transferred around 1347 to Ulm where he died. Suso also wrote *Horologium sapientiae* (*Clock of Wisdom*), a Latin translation of the *Little Book of Eternal Wisdom*; several sermons; a life of the Dominican nun Elsbeth Stägel (d. 1360); and a letter. He was beatified by Pope Gregory XVI in 1831. Feast day: March 15.

Sweden ● A Scandinavian country where the Christian faith first made contact with the Swedes through the voyages and raids of the Vikings. While the Norsemen pillaged churches and were long devoted pagans, Christianity proved an attractive creed because of its cultural associations with the prosperous nations of the south. The earliest concerted program of evangelization was undertaken by St. Anskar (d. 865) who, among his varied missionary pursuits, was permitted by the Swedes to preach in their land in 830. He returned around 853 as archbishop of Hamburg-Bremen to continue the Christianization of the kingdom, his work furthered by his successor, Archbishop Rimbert. The civil wars that soon plagued the country effectively wrecked their work so that the Church could not be reestablished until early in the eleventh century. German and English missionaries preached across Sweden, laying the basis for the subsequent creation of bishoprics. The see of Lund was given metropolitan rank in 1104, and in 1152 the first national synod was held under the direction of Bishop Nicholas of Albano, papal legate. Shortly after, Uppsala was made a diocese; its first bishop was Henry, an Englishman who died in Finland in 1158 on a missionary crusade. In 1164, Uppsala became an archdiocese.

The church in Sweden throughout the Middle Ages wielded extensive powers in social and political affairs. Its influence was furthered by several enactments freeing clerics from the oath of loyalty to secular authority and the payment of taxes. Notable during this period was St. Brigit (or Brigitta), mystical writer and founder of the Brigittine order.

The wealth and strength of the Church made it a target for criticism, and its involvement in the bloody civil war made many prelates unpopular. Swedes were thus disposed toward the anti-Catholic policies of King Gustavus Vasa, who waged a war of independence from Denmark and was crowned king in 1523. Gustavus permitted the launching of a reform movement. Luther's pupil Olavus Petri preached against the Church, and in 1524 the king broke off relations with the Roman Curia. Sweden did not, however, embrace the entire Lutheran program. Rather, a Swedish Church was created, retaining much of the Catholic structure while adopting Lutheran doctrines. An effort was made in the reign of King John III (1569-1592) to forge a reunion with Rome, but it proved fruitless. In 1593, the government accepted the Augsburg Confession; in 1617, Catholics were forbidden from entering the country. This situation remained essentially unchanged until 1781 when King Gustavus III granted the free exercise of religion. A vicar apostolic was appointed in 1783 by Pope Pius VI, although his work was much impeded by laws forbidding native Swedes to enter the Church. While these were technically ended in 1860 and 1873, there remained many obstacles to conversions. The 1873 law, for example, allowed persons to leave the Lutheran Church, but membership is presumed by the state unless an individual provides specific notice of intent to enter another denomination. Virtual religious freedom has existed since 1952. A diocesan structure was introduced to local Church organization the following year. Despite pervasive anti-Catholic sentiment, relations between the Church and the Swedish Church have improved in the reign of Pope John Paul II.

Swiss Guard ● The *Guardia Svizzera Pontificia*, the famed bodyguard of the popes, recruited from the Catholic Swiss cantons and first established by Pope Julius II (r.

Swiss Guard

1503-1513) around 1505. Also called the *Cohors Helvetica*, the Swiss Guard was created as the result of an agreement reached by Julius with the cantons of Zurich and Lucerne in which he contracted several hundred well-trained soldiers to serve as a guard. The first troops arrived in Rome on January 21, 1506, marching to St. Peter's Square through the Porta del Popolo under their first commanding officers, Peter Hertenstein and Gaspar de Silinon. There they received the pope's blessing. The anniversary of the occasion is celebrated every year. The uniform given to the Swiss Guard was possibly designed by Michelangelo, although some scholars have argued that the Swiss entered into papal service wearing their distinctive uniform. Today, the blue-and-gold-striped uniform, with fluffy beret and high ruffled collar, is known the world over.

Recruitment of the guard is generally limited to Catholics from Switzerland. If found acceptable for service, the potential guardsman signs up for two years, although he is able to leave at any time after giving notice of three months. After eighteen years a person is eligible for a pension equal to half pay, this increases to full pay after thirty years. The guard has a barracks just inside St. Anne's Gate and its own chapel. The whole corps is commanded by a colonel with three other officers. There are also a chaplain, over twenty other noncommissioned officers, two drummers, and some seventy guardsmen who carry halberds, the tall axe-tipped poles used especially for crowd control on hot Roman summer days. The guardsmen are also trained to use more modern weapons that are kept at easy-to-reach spots, although in the event of a major breach of the peace, the Vatican will rely on the gendarmerie, or more properly, the *Vigilanza*, assisted by Italian police. The Swiss Guard's presence around the pontiff is ubiquitous, however, and a squad travels with him wherever he goes. That the guardsmen have historically been willing to die in the service of the pope was proven in 1527 when the troops of Emperor Charles V sacked Rome and St. Peter's. The guard put up a valiant defense of the Vatican to protect Pope Clement VII, and nearly one hundred fifty were killed in a brutal fight in St. Peter's Square, buying time for Clement to escape over the *loggia* to the safety of Castel Sant' Angelo. The dead included the guard commander and his wife who were tortured and put to death in their quarters. Among the imperial troops were good Catholic mercenaries. Every year, May 6 is still commemorated in honor of the fallen guardsmen. On that day also new members are given their oath and entered into the corps.

Switzerland ● Central European republic comprised of twenty-two cantons united into a confederation. Known as Helvetica and Rhaetia to the Romans, the territory that would later become Switzerland was first conquered by imperial legions under Julius Caesar in 58 B.C. Christianity was introduced probably in the fourth century, and early bishoprics included those of Geneva, Chur, and Sion. The devastating barbarian invasions began in the fifth century. The Germanic tribes were soon converted, and the Burgundians in 515 established the monastery of St. Maurice, beginning the tradition that Switzerland's monasteries were truly remarkable centers of learning and culture. Two of the most famous are St. Gall and Einsiedeln. Meanwhile, the diocese of Constance, begun in the seventh century, stood as a bastion against the pagan tribes of the Alamanni, who would not be converted until the ninth century.

From the eleventh century, the area was held by various feudal lords, most notably the Habsburgs and the House of Savoy from the 1200s. The hard rule of the Habsburgs led to the union in 1291 of the cantons of Uri, Schwyz, and Unterwalden. They were joined by other cantons, and the Swiss Confederation fought a long conflict with the Habsburgs for independence. The Swiss won battles at Morgarten (1315), Sempach (1386), and Näfels (1388), securing virtual independence in 1499. Very active during the period were the various orders such as the Benedictines, Carthusians, Franciscans, and Dominicans. The most notable Swiss religious figure was Nicholas von Flüe (1417-1487), the hermit and statesman now honored as the patron saint of Switzerland.

From the 1500s, the Swiss were deeply involved in the religious strife that plagued Europe. In 1519, the Reformation came to the country with Huldrych Zwingli who, with John Calvin, made the country one of the hearts of Protestantism and Geneva the intellectual capital of the Reformation. Switzerland was also made a battleground between the Catholic and Reforming parties, dividing the beautiful alpine land: Zurich and Geneva joined the Protestant cause while the mountain cantons, along with Fribourg and Lucerne, remained loyal to the Catholic faith. Zwingli was killed in 1531 in a battle with Catholics, and Calvin, the absolute moral and political dictator of Geneva, died in 1564. The Catholic Reformation, launched in 1570, brought civil war that would continue until the eighteenth century. During the nineteenth century, the radicals secured a governmental program that introduced anti-Catholic measures that were opposed by the Catholic cantons and sparked the Sonderbund War (1847). Their defeat by federal forces brought a constitution in 1848 that transformed Switzerland into a federal state, bringing with it the seizure of many monasteries and the expulsion of the Jesuits. In 1973, the laws against the Jesuits and the monasteries were repealed. Today, the six dioceses are directly subordinate to the Holy See, with almost half the country belonging to the Catholic faith. The Catholic cantons are also the source of recruitment for the Swiss Guard.

Syllabus Errorum ● See **Syllabus of Errors**, following entry.

Syllabus of Errors ● In Latin, *Syllabus Errorum*. A list of eighty propositions published on December 8, 1864, by Pope Pius IX (r. 1846-1878) that had been previously condemned in earlier declarations. The *Syllabus of Errors* was attached to the encyclical *Quanta cura* covering a host of modern errors already specifically censured and the *Syllabus* itself gave no direct condemnation, relying instead upon the document where the error itself was first censured. One of the most famous pronouncements of Pius IX, the *Syllabus* was organized into ten main categories: (1) Pantheism, Naturalism, and Absolute Rationalism; (2) Moderate Rationalism; (3) Indifferentism and Latitudinarianism; (4) Socialism, Communism, Secret Societies, Bible Societies, and Liberal-Clerical Societies; (5) The Church and Its Rights; (6) Civil Society and Its Relation to the Church; (7) Natural and Christian Ethics; (8) Christian Marriage; (9) The Temporal Powers of the Pope; (10) Modern Liberalism. Typical propositions that were condemned included such statements as: "Men can find the way to salvation, and they can attain salvation in the practice of any religion; Protestantism is merely another form of the same true Christian religion, and it is possible to please

God just as much in it as in a Catholic Church; the Christian faith is opposed to reason; divine revelation is not only useless but is even harmful for human perfection; and human reason, in total independence from God, is the sole judge of truth and error, good and evil. It is autonomous, and by its own natural power is adequate to care for the good of all men and nations."

The *Syllabus* was the cause of considerable controversy, especially in Europe. Its publication was forbidden in France on January 1, 1865, although this decree was reversed a short time later; liberals, both secular and ecclesiastical, were outraged. In the dogmatic constitution *De Fide Catholica* (1870) of Vatican Council I, many points of the *Syllabus* found incorporation and henceforth became part of Church teaching, an important step in resisting the spread of Modernism and indifferentism.

Sylvester I, St. ● Pope from 314-335. His pontificate coincided with the final victory of the Christian faith over the Roman Empire. According to the *Liber Pontificalis*, he was a Roman. It is likely that he endured persecution under Emperor Diocletian (r. 284-305) and was a presbyter in Rome when elected to succeed Pope St. Melchiades, being consecrated on January 31, 314. While he reigned during some of the most important years in the history of the Roman Empire, he did not play a major role in the transformation of imperial lands into a Christian domain. This was in large part because of the dominating personality of Emperor Constantine the Great, who launched the vast program of Christian favor and frequently involved himself in ecclesiastical affairs. While Constantine was consistently courteous to the Bishop of Rome, he did not acknowledge any special primacy for the see. Thus, at the Council of Arles (314), to examine the claim of Caecilian to be bishop of Carthage, Sylvester was not asked to preside. He did not attend owing to the demands of his new office, but in an important recognition of his special position, the council sent him a letter detailing its proceedings and given expression of Sylvester's primacy. He was also not asked to preside over the Council of Nicaea (325) but did receive an invitation to attend. Sylvester once again did not attend, but his two legates were given genuine respect, being allowed to sign the acts of the council ahead of everyone else save for the president, Hosius of Córdoba. Significantly, he was able to preside over the creation of the first great churches of Rome — the Basilica Constantiniana (later St. John Lateran), St. Peter's, and St. Paul's — the

Pope St. Sylvester I

result of the generous patronage of Constantine. Sylvester also figured in legends concerning his conversion of Constantine and his curing the emperor of leprosy. In return, the ruler supposedly gave him the Donation of Constantine (*Donatio Constantini*), granting him supremacy over the West and spiritual authority over the East. The donation is now known to be a forgery dated to the eighth century, but during the Middle Ages it was acknowledged as entirely authoritative, even by enemies of the papacy, until the 1500s. Feast day: December 31, in the West; January 2, in the East.

Sylvester II ● Pope from 999-1003. The first Frenchman to succeed to the papacy, he was a great scholar and statesman. Born Gerbert of Aurillac, near Aurillac, Auvergne,

he studied in France and Spain before journeying to Rome. There he gave a favorable impression to Pope John XIII, who recommended him to Emperor Otto I. The emperor sent him to Reims where the archbishop, Adalbero, named him to head the cathedral school. His reputation for learning quickly grew, so that in 980, while visiting Emperor Otto II in Ravenna, he debated Otric, the master of the cathedral school of Magdeburg. In 983, Otto appointed Gerbert abbot of the Monastery of Bobbio near Genoa. He soon returned to Reims (984), assisting Hugh Capet in becoming king of France (r. 987-996). Upon the death of Adalbero, Gerbert hoped to succeed him as archbishop of Reims, but Hugh nominated instead Arnulph, illegitimate son of King Lothair (r. 954-986). Arnulph soon proved unreliable and Hugh secured his deposition in 991. Gerbert was elected in his place at the Synod of St.-Basle. Pope John XV refused to acknowledge Arnulph's removal, sending a legate to suspend Gerbert in 995. At a synod in July of that year, Gerbert's elevation was declared illegal, whereupon Gerbert went to the court of Emperor Otto III. He became a teacher to the ruler and accompanied him to Italy for his coronation. In 998, the lingering questions over the see of Reims were decided when Pope Gregory V named him archbishop of Ravenna. The following year, Gregory died and Gerbert was elected his successor, partly through the influence of his friend Emperor Otto III.

Taking the name of Sylvester in honor of

Pope St. Sylvester (r. 314-335) because of that earlier pontiff's excellent relations with Constantine the Great, he proved a capable defender of papal rights while maintaining sound relations with Otto. He worked to cure simony and clerical marriages, and strengthened the Church in Hungary and Poland; he traditionally sent the famed Crown of St. Stephen to the Hungarian monarch in 1000. Sylvester also promoted education and was himself renowned for hi74 knowledge of astronomy, mathematics, science, and Latin.

Sylvester III ● Pope from January 20-March 10, 1045. Known originally as John, he was serving as bishop of Sabina when Pope Benedict IX was forcibly deposed in September 1044. After long negotiations and machinations, particularly on the part of the family of the Crescentii, John was elected pope in January 1045. His brief pontificate was immediately troubled by the deposed Benedict, who excommunicated his successor. On March 10, Sylvester was compelled to step down; deciding to ignore the excommunication by Benedict, he returned to his see in Sabina. Benedict, meanwhile, sold the papacy to Giovanni Graziano, Pope Gregory VI. At the subsequent Synod of Sutri (1046), Sylvester, Benedict, and Gregory were all declared deposed and replaced by Suidger, bishop of Bamberg, Pope Clement II. Sylvester continued to serve as bishop of Sabina until just before his death. He is considered in some lists to have been an antipope, particularly if the deposition of Benedict was not legal.

Sylvester IV ● Antipope from 1105-1111. Originally known as Maginulfo, he was established as a rival to Pope Paschal II by supporters of King (later Emperor) Henry V during his bitter fight with the pope over investiture. Immediately ousted from Rome, he never wielded much influence and was removed in 1111 after an agreement was reached between the king and the pope.

Sylvestrines ● Minor religious order that was founded in 1231 by St. Sylvester Gozzolini, on Monte Feno, near Fabriano, Italy. The Sylvestrines adopted a version of the Rule of St. Benedict, but St. Sylvester placed much emphasis on the strict observance of poverty by all members. Given formal approval in 1247 by Pope Innocent IV, the Sylvestrines possessed eleven houses by the time of Sylvester's death in 1267. The houses of the order are today independent of the Benedictine Congregation, with communities in Italy, the United States, and elsewhere; a mission was established in Ceylon (modern Sri Lanka) in 1855.

Symmachus, St. ● Pope from 498-514. According to the *Liber Pontificalis*, he was a native of Sardinia. Baptized in Rome, he was ordained a deacon and elected on November 22, 498, to succeed Pope Anastasius II. Immediately consecrated Bishop of Rome, he was considered a candidate elected in opposition to the Byzantines. While chosen by a majority of the Roman clergy, Symmachus was opposed by some clerics who convened in the Basilica of Santa Maria Maggiore and elevated the archpresbyter Laurentius to the papacy. The two popes agreed to submit their claims to King Theodoric of the Ostrogoths. He confirmed Symmachus and Laurentius submitted, receiving from the pontiff the diocese of Nocera, Campania. At a synod in Rome (499), it was declared that any cleric who might campaign to acquire votes for election to the papacy during a pope's lifetime should be deposed; clerics should also refrain from holding any meetings that might lead to securing votes before the death of a pontiff. In 501, King Theodoric visited Rome, receiving the thanks of the Romans, but he was soon confronted by the pro-Byzantine Laurentian party, which accused

Symmachus of simony, fornication, and irregularities in the calendar. As the opponent faction seized the Lateran, Symmachus was forced to reside for several years near the Church of St. Paul-Outside-the-Walls. A synod was to be held between May and June 502, but Theodoric insisted that a proper investigation be held. A second session was finally convened on September 1, 502, but Symmachus and his aides were attacked by a mob of Laurentian sympathizers. Several priests were killed, and Symmachus fled to St. Peter's from which he refused to budge. Several more sessions resulted in the declaration by the majority of bishops that Symmachus was free of blame and that the property of the Church was to be given to him. Laurentians, however, continued to remain obstinate, recalling Laurentius to Rome where he took up a seat at the Lateran. Theodoric finally took steps against the Laurentians in 506-507, and Laurentius retired from Rome. In other matters, Symmachus took part in the Acacian Schism (484-519) between Rome and Constantinople, expelled the Manichaeans from Rome and burned their books, and confirmed the primatial rites of the see of Arles over the Gallican and Spanish Churches. To make clear the position of the archbishop of Arles as metropolitan, Symmachus bestowed upon Archbishop Caesarius of Arles the pallium, the first known instance of the granting of the pallium by the Holy See upon a prelate outside of Italy.

Synesius (c. 370-c. 413) ● Bishop of Ptolemais and a Neoplatonic philosopher. A native of Cyrene, he was a member of an ancient family of the city, studying at Alexandria under the famed Neoplatonic philosopher Hypatia (d. 415). After a brief time in the army, he returned to Cyrene where he studied philosophy and mathematics and was sent on a mission to Constantinople to make an appeal to Emperor Arcadius to relieve taxes. In 403, at Alexandria, he married a Christian woman and had several children. Much respected, Synesius was elected bishop of Ptolemais in 410, but he was reluctant to give up his wife and to abandon a number of philosophical views such as the preexistence of the soul. Despite these misgivings, Synesius was consecrated bishop by Theophylus, bishop of Alexandria. His time as bishop was troubled by invasions and personal tragedies, including the deaths of his three sons. His death preceded the tragic murder of Hypatia. The writings of Synesius included: *De Providentia* (*On Providence*), a political pamphlet written while in Constantinople; *De regno* (*On Kingship*), an oration delivered before Emperor Arcadius around 399; *Cynogetics* (not extant), a manual on dog breeding; *De insomnius*, a treatise on dreams; some one hundred fifty letters; and ten hymns. The letters are of lasting importance because of the details they preserve of Synesius' own life and era.

Synod ● Gathering or assembly of clergy and possibly laity that is today recognized to be of two types, as per the revised Code of Canon Law: the Synod of Bishops and the diocesan synod. The *synodus* (synod) first received mention in the Apostolic Canons (late fourth century), joining the term *concilium*, which was used by Tertullian in the third century. From that time, the synod and the council were synonymous and are today still essentially interchangeable. When, however, all the bishops are gathered together under the authority of the pope, the synod or council is declared a *sancta synodus*, a general (or ecumenical) council.

Synod of Bishops: An assembly of bishops representing the world's episcopal conference that is customarily held every three years and is presided over by the pope. While the broad purpose is to promote a close unity and association between the pontiff and his bishops, specific topics can be discussed at the will of the pope. Usually one subject is considered in great detail, but discussions of other matters also take place. From these synods, a number of apostolic exhortations have been issued, such as the postsynodal apostolic exhortation *Pastores Dabo Vobis* (I Will Give You Shepherds) issued by Pope John Paul II in 1992.

The Synod of Bishops was chartered by Pope Paul VI on September 15, 1965, in the document *Apostolica sollicitudo.* According to the Vatican Council II decree *Christus Dominus* (October 28, 1965), "Bishops from various parts of the world, chosen through ways and procedures established or to be established by the Roman Pontiff, will render especially helpful assistance to the supreme pastor of the Church in a council to be known by the proper name of Synod of Bishops" (No. 5). Membership is based on the election of representatives, but certain bishops are appointed by the pope and others are given the right of participation by Church law. A permanent body, even though it is assembled only occasionally, the Synod of Bishops is supported by a secretariat provided by an advisory council of fifteen members, twelve of whom are elected and three appointed by the pope. The secretariat conducts all communications with the Church's episcopal conferences and solicits suggestions from bishops concerning future topics the pope as president of the synod might consider worthy of examination. The synod is covered in the 1983 Code of Canon Law in Canons 342-348. Since its inception in 1967 the topics covered by synodal assemblies have been:

∗1967 (September 29-October 29): "The preservation and strengthening of the Catholic faith, its integrity, its force, its development, its doctrinal and historical coherence."

∗1969 (October 11-28): Relations between the pope and the bishops, centered on the nature of collegiality, the relationship of the bishops and their conferences to the pope, and the relationship of the bishops and conferences to one another.

∗1971 (September 30-November 6): The ministerial priesthood and justice in the world.

∗1974 (September 27-October 26): The evangelization of the modern world.

∗1977 (September 30-October 29): Important issues in catechetics; the synod issued the first synodal statement, a "Message to the People of God."

∗1980 (September 26-October 25): Matters related to the Christian family, including reaffirmation of *Humanae vitae* and the indissolubility of marriage; on the basis of its recommendation, Pope John Paul II issued a charter of family rights (1983).

∗1983 (September 29-October 29): Penance and reconciliation in the mission of the Church; the synod issued a statement on October 27, declaring that "the Church, as sacrament of reconciliation to the world, has to be an effective sign of God's mercy."

∗1985 (November 24-December 8): A review of Vatican Council II, examining the work of the council, the degree of implementation of its decrees, and the continued means of bringing reform and revival in the Church within the spirit of Vatican Council II; the final report of the synod noted that there have been unfortunate developments as a result of improper or superficial interpretation of the council's decrees.

∗1987 (October 1-30): The vocation and mission of the laity; Pope John Paul II responded to the assembly with the apostolic exhortation *Christifideles laici* (January 30, 1989; The Christian Faithful Laity).

∗1990 (September 30-October 28): The Formation of Priests in Circumstances of the Present Day; Pope John Paul II responded to the proceedings with the apostolic exhortation *Pastores Dabo Vobis* (April 7, 1992; I Will Give You Shepherds).

∗1994 (October 2-October 29): The

Consecrated Life in the Church and in the World. Its dominant themes stressed the consolidation of the consecrated life with the decrees of Vatican Council II, the recognition of the charism of the consecrated life, the search for the balancing of new forms with the traditional ways of consecrated life, and the promotion of the activities of the religious among the poor and needy, without impinging on the work of laypeople.

Diocesan Synod: An assembly of representatives of the body of the faithful within a diocese, the bishop, priests, religious, and laity, with the purpose of examining and taking action on certain relevant matters and issues confronting the diocese. Diocesan synods have been of considerable importance in the history of the Church, as many of the canons issued by them to deal with assorted crises faced by the Church became accepted law. This type of synod dates from the fourth century, serving as a means for prelates and clergy to come together to resolve problems. Over succeeding centuries, the synod became more specific in its choosing of participants: membership became restricted to the priests and related religious of a diocese who were summoned by their bishop for a reason, usually to offer council on the needs of the faithful within the diocese. The Council of Trent required that a diocesan synod be convened once a year. The Code of Canon Law of 1917 required a diocesan synod at least once every ten years.

By the terms established in the revised Code of Canon Law (1983), the synod is convened by a bishop when he deems it necessary. At least one priest is selected from each vicariate and representatives from the religious communities of the diocese are chosen, as are suitable members of the laity. Such persons are normally elected, but the bishop has the right to appoint any other participants he deems desirable. Of importance is the nature of the synodal delegates. They possess only consultative status, as the bishop alone is the legislator and any synodal decrees must be ratified and promulgated by him. The Code of Canon Law covers diocesan synods (460-468). (See also **Councils, Ecumenical Councils**, and **Collegiality**.)

Synoptic Question ● Problem examined by biblical scholars concerning the relationship between the first three Gospels — Matthew, Mark, and Luke. These three works are called synoptic because of the similarities in the texts. When these Gospels are placed into columns and carefully ordered, a process known as a synopsis, there are many clear agreements in the verbal structure and general organization. The term synopsis was first used for the three Gospels from the time of Johann Griesbach (1745-1812), an NT scholar who was the first expert to make critical literary analysis of the Gospels. The question relates to uncovering the cause of the apparent concordance. It is generally accepted today that there was some kind of literary association among the three Gospels, but the specific details of such a dependence are elusive and scholars have been forced to make a series of hypotheses to explain them. Among these are: the possible presence of an older, lost source, called the Q Document; that Mark's Gospel was earlier than those of Luke and Matthew and was used by them; and that Matthew's was the earliest of the three Gospels. The latter position was taken by the biblical commission established in 1902 by Pope Leo XIII (r. 1878-1903). As none of the hypotheses have been accepted universally, no solution to the Synoptic Question has yet been reached. (See also **Q Document**.)

Syrian-Malabar Rite ● See **Malabar Rite**.

Taborites ● Name given to radical members of the Hussite movement in Bavaria during the 1400s. They took their name from the biblical Mt. Tabor, using it to christen their fortress south of Prague. The Taborites took the most extreme view of Hussitism, arguing that the Bible was the principal source of faith, denying the Real Presence, and taking the Eucharist under both species. While opposed by the moderate Utraquist Calixtines among the Hussites (who also favored Communion in both kinds), the Taborites fought along their side during the Hussite Wars. They were well-trained and feared in battle, especially under General Jan Zizka. In 1434, however, they refused to accept the Compactata of Prague and were attacked by the now allied Catholics and Calixtines. At the Battle of Lipan (1434), they were destroyed and their leader Procopius killed. The fortress of Tabor was not captured until 1452.

Tacitus (c. 55-c. 117) ● In full, Cornelius Tacitus. A Roman historian, his *Annals* contains one of the first non-Christian accounts of the persecutions of the Christians. Considered the last of the great classical Roman historians, he probably came from Gaul (France) or was of Gallic descent, reaching the high social position of senator during the reign of Vespasian (69-79). He later served as consul in 97 and in 112-113 was appointed proconsul of Asia. The extant writings of Tacitus are: *Dialogus de Oratoribus* (*Dialogue on the Orators*); *Germania* (*De origin et situ Germanorum, On the Origins and Country of the Germans*);

Historia, an account of the events on the empire from 69-96 under Emperors Galba, Otho, Vitellius, Vespasian, Titus, and Domitian; and *Annals*, a history of Rome following the death of Emperor Augustus in A.D. 14 to the reign and possibly the death of Emperor Nero in 68. Of the sixteen original books, eleven are extant, although there may have been more. In the *Annals*, Tacitus wrote of the persecution of Christians by Nero. According to him, the emperor used them as a scapegoat for the fire in Rome of 64, even though the historian believed the Christians to be innocent of the matter. He considered Christians, however, to be followers of a "detestable superstition" (*exitiabilis superstitio*). (See also **Suetonius**.)

Talleyrand (1754-1838) ● In full, Charles Maurice de Talleyrand-Périgord. Prince of Benevento and bishop of Autun, he was a formidable French minister and ambassador who wielded considerable influence in the regimes of Napoleon Bonaparte and the restored royal House of the Bourbons. Born in Paris to a prominent family, he entered holy orders owing in part to lameness caused by an accident in his youth. After studying at the Collège d'Harcourt, he was ordained a priest (1775) despite being quite unfit morally. Appointed a court priest, he became agent-general of the French clergy in 1780. Two years later, the Assembly of French Clergy chose him promoter and then in 1785 secretary. Notorious for his dissolute lifestyle, he was able to secure an episcopal see only by the scheming of his father, Count Daniel de Talleyrand. He was consecrated on

January 16, 1789, as bishop of Autun. A leading adviser to King Louis XVI, he supported the dissolution of the assembly but then skillfully joined the movement that launched the French Revolution in 1789. His participation in the harsh treatment of the Church and his acceptance of the reforms forced upon it led to his excommunication in 1789 by Pope Pius VI. Banished by the Revolution, he fled to England and then journeyed to the United States. Returning to Paris in 1796, he became foreign minister under the French Directory (1797-1799) and then Napoleon (1799-1807). As a self-serving but ruthlessly capable minister to Napoleon, Talleyrand enjoyed immense power in imperial Paris until 1807, when he resigned over serious policy differences with the emperor. Thereafter he was a diplomat and adviser, secretly working to assist the Austrians against the interests of his master. Because of the severe opposition of Talleyrand to Napoleon's war in Spain, the minister was removed in 1809 and retired in disgrace to his residence in the Rue St. Florentin. His patience was rewarded in 1814 with the fall of Napoleon. Talleyrand was a prominent leader in bringing about the restoration of the Bourbons under Louis Philippe, who appointed him minister of foreign affairs. At the time of his death in May 1838, he gave a solemn declaration of penance for the errors that "troubled and afflicted the Catholic Apostolic and Roman Church."

Tallis, Thomas (1514-1585) ● English musician who was considered the foremost composer of sacred music before Richard Byrd (1543-1623) and like him a Catholic organist in the service of Queen Elizabeth I (r. 1558-1603). It is not certain where he was raised and educated, but in 1532 he was serving in Dover Priory. At one time a chorister at St. Paul's Cathedral in London, he became organist of Waltham Abbey in 1536. In 1540, this office was lost through the dissolution of the abbey under King Henry VIII (r. 1514-1547). Two years later, he was named a gentleman of the Chapel Royal, remaining in this post through the reigns of Henry, Edward VI, Mary Tudor, and Elizabeth. Owing to his talent and the personal favor shown his music by Queen Elizabeth, Tallis was able to remain a Catholic and avoid severe penalties for adhering to the faith. By 1575, he was joint organist in the Chapel Royal with William Byrd, receiving with him a monopoly for printing music and music paper in England. Called the Father of English Cathedral Music, Tallis was a prolific composer, creating music in both Latin and English, and adapting brilliantly to the introduction of the English liturgy. His Latin compositions included the magnificent forty-part motet *Spem aliam non habis*, the seven-part *Misere nostri*, and the five-part Mass *Salve intemerata*; his English compositions were often originally Latin works altered to fit the needs of the Anglican liturgy. His *Lamentations*, especially the first setting, is one of his greatest pieces. Tallis's keyboard compositions were largely preserved (eighteen of twenty-three extant pieces) in the Mulliner Book of the mid-sixteenth century. Tallis died in Greenwich on November 23, 1585.

Tardini, Domenico (1888-1961) ● Cardinal and secretary of state under Pope John XXIII. A native of Rome, he was ordained on September 20, 1912, subsequently serving as professor of sacramental theology and liturgy at the Roman Seminary and at the Propaganda College. His promotions were rapid: a member of the Congregation for Extraordinary Ecclesiastical Affairs (1921), assistant in the Italian Catholic Youth Organization (1925), undersecretary in the Congregation for Extraordinary Affairs (1929), and an official of the Congregation for Russia (1933). A consultor for the Congregation for the Oriental Church (1937), he then became secretary for the aforementioned Congregation for Extraordinary Ecclesiastical Affairs (1937). Pope Pius XII named him pro-secretary of state in 1952. Tardini administered the external affairs of the Church, working closely with Monsignor Giovanni Battista Montini (the future Pope Paul VI), who was in charge of the internal affairs of the Church as another pro-secretary. As Pius held the office of secretary of state for himself, both Tardini and Montini were directly under the pope. After the election of Pope John XXIII in 1958, Tardini was one of the twenty-three new cardinals appointed by the new pontiff, holding the post of secretary of state. While more conservative in his outlook than Pope John, Tardini proved a loyal supporter of his policies, assisting in the crafting of the encyclical *Mater et Magistra* (1961) and in organizing the upcoming Second Vatican Council. Tardini was also the founder of the Casa Nazareth, a home for orphaned children. He died on July 30, 1961.

Tarasius, St. (d. 806) ● Patriarch of Constantinople. The son of the prefect of Constantinople, he was a trusted secretary in the service of Empress Irene, regent for Emperor Constantine IV (r. 780-797) at the time of the death of Patriarch Paul IV in 784. While still a layperson, Tarasius was acclaimed by a crowd of people outside the imperial palace to succeed Paul, a move no doubt organized by Irene. In speaking to the people, Tarasius declared that he felt unworthy of the office and that, should he accept the post, a new effort would have to made to restore the unity of the Christian Church, as a separation had developed between the Eastern and Western Churches. Securing the agreement of the imperial government, Tarasius was consecrated patriarch on December 25, 784. Although Pope Adrian had serious misgivings about the elevation of a layperson to the patriarchate, he gave his recognition to Tarasius because of the new patriarch's orthodox views. A short time later, the Second Council of Nicaea (the seventh ecumenical council) was convoked in 787 under the presidency of Tarasius, a council that marked the restoration of reunion with the West. Tarasius' remaining years were much troubled. He was attacked by a group of rigorist monks, supported by Theodore of Studios, for being tolerant of and even encouraging simony. He also refused to acknowledge or accept Constantine VI's divorce of his wife, but Tarasius was once again criticized by Theodore, this time for not pursuing the matter with vigor. In 802, the patriarch crowned Emperor Nicephorus, who had removed Irene. An ascetic who was devoted to the care of the poor, Tarasius was venerated as a saint after his death. Feast day: February 25.

Tatian (fl. second century) ● Christian apologist and writer. Of Assyrian descent, Tatian studied Greek rhetoric and philosophy and was converted to Christianity sometime between 150 and 165. Joining the community of Christians in Rome, he became a pupil of Justin Martyr. Tatian remained at least outwardly orthodox during this period, but after Justin's death (c. 165) he displayed tendencies toward Gnosticism, journeying to the East (c. 172) where he probably founded the sect of Encratites, comprised of Gnostic ascetics. His writings were listed by Eusebius of Caesarea in the fourth century and are now lost except for the *Oratorio ad Graecos* (*Discourse to the Greeks*) and the Diatesseron. The *Oratorio* was an apology for Christianity that condemned Hellenic civilization and argued that the Christian faith was superior to Greek philosophy. The Diatesseron, a history of the life of Christ, was presented in a continuous narrative and harmonized the four Gospels. It was an important source of doctrine for the Syrian Church into the fifth century.

Tauler, Johannes (c. 1300-1361) ● German Dominican and mystic. A native of Strasbourg, he entered the Dominicans there in 1315 and was one of the Rhineland mystics. While studying at the University of Cologne, he came under the influence of Meister Eckhart (whom he had heard preaching in Strasbourg) and Henry Suso. It is possible that he studied at Paris and then returned to Cologne; it is more likely that he went back to Strasbourg from Cologne and then journeyed to Basel where he remained from 1339-1347. During his time in Basel, Tauler entered into a close association with the *Gottesfreunde* (Friends of God). He returned to Strasbourg (c. 1347-1348) and there became a well-known preacher, also acquiring fame for his care of the unfortunate victims of the Black Death in 1348. Although a large number of works have been ascribed to him, Tauler's genuine surviving body of writings is limited to several sermons and two letters. His mystical teaching was based mainly on the doctrine of Thomas Aquinas. Central to his mysticism was the *visio essentiae Dei*, the blessed contemplation on the nature of God. Unlike Aquinas, Tauler believed that divine knowledge was attainable in this life and thus should be the sole object of all people; he also believed that help is given in this effort by grace, and love is the way to God. Martin Luther valued highly Tauler's sermons, and Tauler was considered a forerunner of the Protestant Reformers; Catholic scholars note, however, that he always remained devoted to the faith and was conspicuous in avoiding heresy. (See also TABLE 9.)

Taxa Innocentia ● Decree issued by Pope Innocent XI on October 1, 1678. It placed regulations on taxes and fees that might be demanded or also accepted by an episcopal chancery office for assorted writings or acts. Bishops were not to receive, charge, or accept any fee or gift in return for ordinations, benefices, or matrimonial dispensations. A fee, if approved by the Holy See, could be placed upon the work in expediting certain documents save for permissions to say Mass, to preach, or to administer the sacraments, among other activities. A modification of the decree was issued in June 1896 by the Sacred Congregation of the Council. By its terms, a tax or fee could be imposed in cases involving benefices or sacraments, but no fee could be asked in the actual conferring of the sacraments themselves.

Te Deum ● Or *Te Deum Laudamus* (Thee God, We Praise). An ancient Latin hymn, it is traditionally sung on an occasion of great joy or thanksgiving. According to legend, the *Te Deum* was first composed spontaneously by Sts. Ambrose and Augustine at the latter's baptism. This story is today generally rejected by scholars, and the hymn is now attributed to the missionary bishop of Remesiana, St. Nicetas (d. 414). Some prefer to argue that it originated liturgically and was perhaps taken from the service of the Paschal Vigil. Its use in Matins (now the Office of Readings) is attested by the Rule of St. Benedict (sixth century), although the earliest known use of the title *Te Deum Laudamus* was in the Rule of St. Caesarius of Arles (early sixth century). Today, the hymn is sung at the conclusion of the Office of Readings on Sundays, feasts, and solemnities, but it is best known for being sung on special occasions. Typical episodes include a great triumph of peace, a canonization, or the election of a pope. Two famous celebrations were the liberation of Paris in 1944 (in which a *Te Deum* was sung in Notre Dame Cathedral with Charles de Gaulle in attendance, despite the considerable danger from German snipers) and the controversial ordering of a *Te Deum* by Pope Gregory XIII after the St. Bartholomew's Day Massacre in France in 1572.

Teilhard de Chardin, Pierre (1881-1955)

● French Jesuit theologian and scientist. He was born in Sarcenat, France, near Clermont, and entered the Society of Jesus at Aix-en-Provence in 1899, embarking on a long period of theological training and receiving holy orders in 1912. During World War I, he served as a medical corpsman in the French army. Afterward, he focused his educational attentions on science, earning a doctorate in paleontology in 1922. In 1923, he began his work in China, where he soon acquired a wide reputation for his contributions to paleontology. He later worked in India but after 1939 concentrated on writing, including both theological and spiritual efforts. At his death, however, only his scientific papers had been published. His body of theological and spiritual books remained unpublished until after his death owing to the refusal of his superiors and Church authorities to have them released. After their publication, the Congregation of the Holy Office in July 1962 issued a warning about them because of the questions that surrounded many of Teilhard's ideas and the confusion that they might cause among uneducated Catholics.

His first major book was *Le Milieu divin* (written in 1927, published in 1957; *The Divine Milieu*), an effort to express his own religious experience. His chief work, the one considered most expressive of his complex theology, was *Le Phénomène humain* (1955; *The Phenomenon of Man*), written during the 1930s and 1940s. He began the work with a warning that it was not a theological treatise, but rather a scientific memoir. The book, however, presented the heart of his vision of creation and was quite innovative. Teilhard accepted a positive view of the universe, which he saw as an ongoing evolutionary process of movement toward systems of increasing complexity. In humanity, the complex evolution of life led to the development of consciousness and then self-consciousness. Evolution, however, does not cease with self-consciousness, for the evolutionary process moves toward higher levels of consciousness. This process of human consciousness implies that humanity is no longer merely a part of evolution, functioning within the laws of nature, but has a part, with natural processes, in directing evolutionary progress. All evolution is pointed toward a final, eschatological point, called the *divinus terminus* or Omega Point in which the universe is gathered into God. Since the Incarnation, this movement has been part of the "Christification" of the universe. Teilhardism, as his system is called, has been the source of considerable debate in the years since the publication of his books. He himself understood that there were ambiguities in them and that the writings should be carefully examined and even more thoughtfully and cautiously disseminated. His optimistic exploration of an evolutionary process finding consummation in God has certainly found appeal and is of interest to those seeking a synthesis or affinity between Church teaching and the wide cosmological questions facing modern scientists. Teilhard spent his last years in the United States, dying in New York on April 10, 1955.

Tekakwitha, Kateri, Bl. (1656-1680) ●

Daughter of a Mohawk chieftain. A convert to Catholicism, she was called "The Lily of the Mohawks." Kateri was born in a Mohawk village in Ossernenon (modern Auriesville, New York). Her father was the chief of the Tortoise clan and her mother, a Christian, was a member of the Algonquins who had been taken captive by the Mohawks in a raid. Both parents, with an infant brother, died in 1660 during a smallpox epidemic. She was left by this outbreak orphaned, scarred severely, and suffering from poor eyesight. Raised by an uncle, she was considered a highly desirable woman to marry because of her father, but she soon dismayed her Mohawk companions by refusing to wed.

In 1677, she first came into contact with French Catholic missionaries who had been allowed to preach among the Iroquois according to the peace terms established between the French and the Indians after many years of fighting in the Mohawk Valley. While not yet ready to be baptized, Kateri had been deeply impressed by the Jesuit missionaries and had begun to adopt the tenets that they preached. In 1669, she was adamant in rejecting a marriage that had been arranged for her and further alienated the Mohawks of the village by refusing to consider any other possible matches and by moving toward conversion starting in 1675.

Her desire to become a Christian came to the attention of Father Jacques de Lamberville, who gave her formal instruction. She was baptized on Easter 1676. The next year, owing to hostility from members of the tribe, she fled her village with the help of Christian warriors and sought refuge in the Sault Mission on the Richelieu River. Her final three years were spent in prayer and self-mortification. The Jesuits at the mission considered Kateri the recipient of an advanced mystical union with God, noting her asceticism and her gifts of contemplation. She fell ill and died on April 17, 1680. According to reports from those who attended her funeral, the scars that had long been present on her face disappeared, replaced by a beautiful countenance. Miracles were soon reported through her intercession. In April 1943, she was declared Venerable by Pope Pius XII; Pope John Paul II beatified her in June 1980. Feast day: June 14 (in the United States).

Telesphorus, St. ● Pope from around 125-136. A martyr and the seventh successor to St. Peter, he was a Greek according to the *Liber Pontificalis*. That source also claims that Telesphorus introduced the use of the *Gloria in excelsis* to the Christmas midnight Mass. Scholars considered this dubious, relying instead

upon the testimony of St. Irenaeus who declared that he suffered martyrdom gloriously. Eusebius of Caesarea, in his *Ecclesiastical History*, placed the start of the pontificate of Telesphorus at the twelfth year of the reign of Hadrian (128-129) and his death in the first year of the reign of Emperor Antoninus Pius (138-139). This is considered inaccurate by several years. Feast day: January 5.

Templars ● See under **Military Orders**.

Tencin, Pierre (1680-1758) ● In full, Pierre-Guérin de Tencin, a French cardinal and statesman. Born in Grenoble, he studied under the Oratorians of Grenoble and then at the Sorbonne in Paris. Appointed vicar-general of Sens, he became a trusted protégé of Cardinal de Rohan when he accompanied him to the conclave of 1721 that elected Cardinal Conti (Pope Innocent XIII). Remaining in Rome, Tencin became an influential figure in the pontificate of Benedict XIII (r. 1724-1730), who consecrated him archbishop of Embrun in June 1724. He launched an extremely active persecution of the Jansenists at the provincial synod held at Embrun in 1727, including the suspension of Bishop Jean Soanen, the eighty-year-old prelate of Senez (Sens), who had appealed against the bull *Unigenitus*. In part because of his pogrom against the Jansenists, he was made cardinal in 1739, serving in Rome as French ambassador until 1742, when he finally took possession of the see of Lyons to which he had succeeded two years earlier. In September 1742, King Louis XV made him minister of state. He retired in 1782. His sister was Claudine-Alexandrine Guérin de Tencin, the profligate writer, patroness, and social figure during the reign of King Louis XV; she was also a mistress for a time of the minister and dissolute Cardinal Guillaume Dubois (d. 1723).

Ten Thousand Martyrs ● Two large groups of martyrs listed in the Roman Martyrology. The first martyrs, listed for June 22, were supposedly soldiers in the Roman legions who, with their commander, Acacius, were crucified on Mt. Ararat: *In monte Ararath passio sanctorum martyrum decem milia crucifixorum.* While they were entirely legendary, their relics were said to have been found and brought to Europe during the crusades. A second group of martyrs, for March 18, refers to those Christians put to death at some point during the persecutions of Emperor Diocletian (303). Eusebius of Caesarea, in the *Ecclesiastical History,* and Lactantius, in *De Mortibus Persecutorum,* both mention the martyrs, although the number is considered an exaggeration.

Teresa, Mother (b. 1910) ● Sister, foundress, and Nobel Prize winner. Called Mother Teresa of Calcutta, she has devoted most of her life to the care of the "poorest of the poor." She was born Agnes Gonxha Bojaxhiu at Skopje, Macedonia, the daughter of an Albanian grocer. At the age of seventeen, she entered a congregation of Irish Loretto sisters, arriving in Ireland in 1928 to begin training. A mere six weeks later she set sail for Calcutta, India, where she taught at St. Mary's School, an institution for the daughters of prosperous families. After a number of years, however, she asked permission to give up her teaching and devote herself to caring for the poor of the city. Granted approval by authorities, she adopted the sari as her dress and, barefooted, began tending to the sick, teaching the children of the slums, and caring for the dying so as to allow them to pass into the next life with dignity. Having impressed the local authorities, she was granted her request of a small hostel that became the cradle of her new religious order begun in 1948. She had already been receiving help from various sources, but the desire of young women to join her made the foundation of an order of nuns inevitable. Formal approval was granted by Pope Pius XII in 1950 for the Order of the Missionaries of Charity. Mother Teresa, who had adopted Indian citizenship in the same year, provided the sari as the habit of the sisters. In 1965, special status as a pontifical congregation was granted by Pope Paul VI, meaning that the nuns were answerable only to the pope.

From the one hostel located near the temple of Kali, in Calcutta, the order established a wide variety of hospitals, schools, and shelters as well as places for lepers, especially the leper colony Shanti Nagar, near Asansol, India. For her efforts on behalf of the most unfortunate, the Indian government awarded Mother Teresa with the order of *Padmashri,* or Lord of the Lotus, its honor for those who have aided the people of India. Pope Paul VI, an enthusiastic supporter of her endeavors, asked Mother Teresa to open a hostelry in the Vatican in 1968 and in 1971 gave her the first ever Pope John XXIII Peace Prize. In 1979, she won the Nobel Peace Prize. Today, despite frequent bouts of poor health, she continues to travel the world, speaking on the rights of the poor and on the dangers of abortion and contraception. Her order is now in nearly thirty countries, including Tanzania, Great Britain, Australia, the United States, and even Jordan.

Teresa of Ávila, St. (1515-1582) ● Also St. Teresa of Jesus. A Spanish Carmelite nun and mystic, she was the first woman to be declared a Doctor of the Church. Born Teresa de Cepeda y Ahumada in Ávila, Spain, she came from a well-respected family. Educated by Augustinian nuns, she entered the Carmelite convent of the Incarnation at Ávila in 1535. Falling ill, she returned to her family for a time but, upon recovery, once more entered the convent. There, despite her love of prayer, she was a carefree nun in keeping with the generally lax conditions that prevailed within the community. Members were allowed to own property and enjoyed contact with others outside the convent. In 1555, however, she underwent a conversion while praying before a statue of the scourged Christ. Thereafter she progressed as a mystic, being visited by "intellectual visions [of Christ] and locutions," meaning images that were impressed or communicated upon her mind rather than her senses. At first she received very poor counsel from her spiritual advisers, but gradually sound advice and guidance were given to her by St. Peter of Alcántara, St. Francis Borgia, and especially the remarkable Dominican Dominic Báñez.

St. Teresa of Ávila

In 1558, Teresa was convinced of the need to bring reform to the Carmelite order and return it to its original austerity. She proposed to adopt a religious life of prayer, penance, and work, securing permission from Pope Pius IV to open a convent for Carmelite reform. The foundation of St. Joseph's convent in 1563 caused a near riot because of the severity of opposition from local secular and religious leaders who disapproved of her innovations and the fact that the house was not to be endowed but would exist entirely through charitable donations. In 1567, Teresa was given backing by John Baptist Rossi, the Carmelite prior general, who instructed her to found more convents. That same year, she met the profound mystic Juan de Yepes y Alvarez (St. John of the Cross). He would launch the Carmelite reform for men, opening in 1568 the first of the Discalced Carmelite monasteries in Ávila.

Teresa continued to establish new houses over the next years, but like St. John of the Cross, she eventually encountered severe difficulties within her own order. In 1575, owing to the disagreement between the Discalced and the so-called "Calced" (or "Shod") Carmelites — those members who did not adopt the revived Primitive Rule — Teresa was ordered to cease the creation of new monasteries and to retire to a convent in Castile. The case and accounts of her work had been presented to her superiors in Rome improperly and with considerable exaggeration. Her friend John of the Cross was actually imprisoned in 1577. Facing possible imprisonment and with the threat of the Inquisition bearing down upon her, Teresa was suddenly rescued by the intervention of King Philip II of Spain, a great admirer, who gave the Discalced Carmelites his protection. This independence was confirmed by Pope Gregory XIII in 1580. Teresa, despite her shattered health, once more set to work. She fell ill at Alba de Tormes and died there on October 4, 1582.

From the time of her conversion in 1555, she had continued to make progress in the mystical life, preserving her profound experiences in her autobiography *Vida* (1565, *Life*). With the magnificent works *Relations* and *El Castillo Interior* (*The Interior Castle*), she was responsible for preserving one of the greatest bodies of mystical writings in the history of the Church. In 1572, her spiritual development led to her "spiritual marriage," considered the highest level of mystical attainment. She was also the recipient of the extraordinary piercing of her heart; the fact of this occurrence was proven after her death, when her heart was found to have been pierced. Her writings on her experiences are full of deep insights and Thomistic influence, but they remain intensely personal; she did not adhere to any school of mysticism, and she never intended to be the founder of a new one. Amazingly practical and focused, she also wrote *The Way of Perfection*, for the Carmelite nuns, to serve as a guide to prayer and the attainment of virtue, and the *Book of Foundations*, recounting her labors. Beatified in 1619, she was canonized in 1622 by Gregory XV. Pope Paul VI named her a Doctor of the Church in 1970. Feast day: October 5.

Teresian Martyrs of Compiègne ●

Sixteen beatified martyrs executed on July 17, 1794, during the Reign of Terror (1793-1794). The martyrs were Carmelite nuns, lay sisters, and two servants, under the prioress Madeleine-Claudine Ledoine (b. 1752) and the subprioress Marie-Anne Brideau (d. 1752). Arrested by the government, they were sentenced to death by the guillotine. Just before their deaths, the sisters renewed their baptismal and religious vows and sang the *Veni Creator*. Unlike the usual merriment that accompanied the terrible executions by guillotine, the deaths of the sisters were greeted by the crowd with absolute silence. The first to die was the novice Marie-Geneviève Meunier (b. 1765), followed by the other nuns; the prioress was the last to be executed. The others were Marie-Anne Piedcourt (b. 1715), Anne-Marie Madeleine Thouret (b. 1715), Marie-Antoinette (or Anne) Hanisset (b.

1740), Marie-Françoise Gabrielle de Croissy (b. 1745), Marie-Gabrielle Trézel (b. 1743), Rose-Chrétien de la Neuville (b. 1741), Anne Petras (b. 1760), Marie Claude Cyprienne Brard (Catherine Charlotte Brard, b. 1736), Angélique Roussel (b. 1742, a lay sister), Marie Dufour (b. 1742, a lay sister), Juliette Vérolot (b. 1764, a lay sister), Catherine Soiron (b. 1742, a lay servant), and Teresa Soiron (b. 1748, a lay servant). After their executions, the sisters were placed in a sandpit in a cemetery in Picpus. On the basis of several miracles, they were beatified on May 27, 1906, by Pope St. Pius X. From a play by French novelist Georges Bernanos (1888-1948), composer Francis Poulenc (1899-1963) wrote an opera on the Teresian Martyrs, *Dialogue des Carmélites* (1957), considered one of the finest operas of the twentieth century.

Tertullian (c. 160-c. 222) ● In full, Quintus Septimius Florens Tertullian. Apologist, theologian, and controversialist. Born in Carthage, North Africa, he was the son of a Roman soldier, probably a centurion. Raised as a pagan, he studied law and was also learned in Latin and Greek literature. He became a lawyer and adherent to Stoicism before settling in Rome where he acquired an excellent reputation as a jurist. Appalled by the state of social decay, he was drawn to Christianity, perhaps attracted by the steadfastness of the Christian martyrs. Converted around 195-196, he returned to Carthage and became a defender of the new faith, also devoting his time to teaching. According to St. Jerome, Tertullian was ordained as a presbyter around 200. By 207, however, he had become disillusioned with the African Church, turning to the Montanist movement, which offered a strict morality and a rigorous lifestyle. He formally joined the Montanists in 211, but even they were not sufficiently rigorist for Tertullian; he left the heretical sect and established his own group, called the Tertullianists. While he wrote against Catholic teaching during his Montanist period, he did retain many orthodox beliefs. These, however, are not considered acceptable for usage in the defense of Catholic teaching, only his orthodox writings being applicable. Thus, in examining the many works of Tertullian, a division must be maintained between his Catholic and Montanist periods.

His orthodox writings include: the famous *Apologeticus* (c. 197), a popular treatise refuting the charges then being hurled against Christianity; *Ad nationes* (*To the Nations*), an apology on which was based the *Apologeticus*; *Ad martyres* (*To the Martyrs*), in praise of martyrs; *De praescriptione hereticorum* (c. 200; *Prescription Against the Heretics*), attacking heresies then facing the faith; *De spectaculis* (*On Shows*), about pagan spectacles; *De oratione* (*On Prayer*); *De baptismo* (*On Baptism*); *De paenitentia* (*On Penance*); *De Testimonio animae* (*On the Testimony of the Soul*), a declaration of the natural recognition of the existence of God; *De cultu feminarum* (*On the Apparel of Women*); and *Adversus Marcionem* (207; *Against Marcion*), a relentless criticism of the heretic Marcion, in five books and his doctrine concerning the nature of Christ.

His works as a Montanist include: *De idolatria* (*On Idolatry*), a strict interpretation of Christian morality; *De carne Christi* (*On the Flesh of Christ*); *De resurrectione carnis* (*On the Resurrection of the Flesh*); *De fuga in persecutione* (*On Flight in Persecution*); *De exhortatione castitatis* (*On the Exhortation to Chastity*); *De jejunio* (*On Fasting*); *De monogamia* (*On Monogamy*); *Ad Scapulam* (*To Scapula*), an open letter dated to 212 and sent to the proconsul of Africa, Scapula, condemning his persecution of Christianity. His last known treatise was *De pudicitia* (*On Modesty*), questioning the measure of Pope Callistus I in making more lenient the penance required of Christians.

Considered the first true theologian of the West, he is distinguished as the first Christian author to compose chiefly in Latin. He utilized in his theology a clear, superbly organized, and legally exact mind, creating a comprehensive body of Latin terms that was ideally suited to the spread of the Christian faith throughout the West and the rapid development of theology. His contributions would earn him the eventual title of Father of Latin Theology and would influence the theological life of the Western Church for the next millennium. He mistrusted philosophy, holding it to be the source of all heresy, using it only as a tool rather than as a source of truth. Disliked by many early writers because of his apostasy, Tertullian is today recognized as a figure of true genius and lasting import.

Testem Benevolentiae ● Apostolic letter dated January 22, 1899. It was addressed to Cardinal James Gibbons (1834-1921), archbishop of Baltimore, by Pope Leo XIII (r. 1879-1903), condemning the movement of Americanism. While Pope Leo had initially been receptive to Americanism, the controversy stirred by some of its propositions and the publication of the biography of Isaac Hecker, founder of the Paulists, prompted him to take a decisive step toward protecting the Church from the movement's errors. His letter was courteous, praising the devotion and spirit of the American Church, but it was also firm in its declaration that the faith must not be compromised to promote conversions and that it would be a serious error to relax or minimize essential points of doctrine or even the deposit of faith in order to adapt to contemporary circumstances. Pope Leo made reference to the First Vatican Council, which made clear that the faith is not a doctrine open to speculation, like philosophy, dependent upon the will and imagination of private individuals and consciences. Modifications in response to the needs of prevailing conditions and the demands of time and place must be undertaken not by individuals but on the judgments of the Church's teaching authority. The letter went on to point out the errors in Americanism, concluding with the exhortation toward unity with the Church and urging resistance to any tendency that might lead to the unfortunate development of a national Church in the United States. (See **Americanism** for further details.)

Tetzel, Johann (1465-1519) ● Also called Tezel, a German Dominican preacher. His efforts to promote indulgences contributed to the outbreak of the Protestant Reformation. Tetzel was born in Perna, Germany, entering the Dominicans at Leipzig in 1490. A few years later, he was appointed inquisitor, first for Poland and then Saxony. In 1503, he began working as a preacher of indulgences, traveling throughout Germany until at least 1510 by which time he was commissary in Strasbourg, going to Nuremburg and Würzburg; he was a well-known figure in parts of Germany and was thus the natural candidate in 1516 to preach indulgences to assist in the construction of St. Peter's, Rome. He was named commissary by Archbishop Albert of Mainz for the territories of Magdeburg, Halberstadt, and Meissen. While forbidden to preach in Wittenburg by command of the elector Frederick III the Wise of Saxony, Tetzel appeared in Jüterborg, near Wittenburg, in the spring of 1517. There followed a now famous episode on October 31, 1517, in which Martin Luther protested the unscrupulous practice of selling indulgences by nailing the ninety-five theses to the church door of Wittenburg. Although Luther admitted in a letter to Archbishop Albert that he had pondered protesting the abuses in indulgences, the episode of the ninety-five theses has long been held to have been instigated specifically in response to the activities of Tetzel. In reply to Luther, Tetzel issued in April 1518 the *Vorlegung*, an attack on Luther's position and a defense of the Church. This was joined the next month by a

set of fifty theses published (May 1518) under Tetzel's name (possibly written by the theologian Konrad Wimpina). The theses were principally concerned with the authority of the Church. Unable to rally any popular support for his position, Tetzel withdrew toward the end of the year to Leipzig. In January 1519, he was bitterly castigated by the papal nuncio Carl von Miltitz (d. 1529), dying in Leipzig on August 11, 1519. (See also **Reformation, Protestant.**)

Teutonic Knights ● See under **Military Orders**.

Theatines ● Properly the Congregation of Clerics Regular (C.R.), the Theatines are a religious order of men founded in 1524 in Rome by St. Cajetan (1480-1547) and Gian Pietro Caraffa (the future Pope Paul IV), then bishop of Theate from which the name was taken. Approved by Pope Clement VII on June 14, 1524, the Theatines were intended to work toward the reform of the Church by countering the damage done by Martin Luther and the Reformers, invigorating the virtuous life among the laity, and reviving and reforming the clergy. Members adhered to a strict vow of poverty and lived under a severe rule, but the order grew swiftly. New houses were established in Italy, spreading to Spain, France, Portugal, and elsewhere. Their labors on behalf of reform in Europe were of considerable help in promoting the Catholic Reformation and resisting the inroads of Protestantism in Catholic lands. The Theatines also distinguished themselves in conducting the earliest papal missions in distant regions, including Peru, Borneo, and Sumatra. The symbol of the order is a cross, chosen by St. Cajetan because he consecrated the new order to the Cross of Christ. There are currently over one hundred fifty Theatines in the world. The Theatine nuns were established in 1583 by Ursula Benincasa under the name of Sisters of the

Immaculate Conception of the Virgin Mary; they remain limited to Naples and Sicily.

Theban Legion ● See **Maurice, St**.

Theobald (d. 1161) ● Also called Tedbald. Archbishop of Canterbury, he was a Norman by descent. He entered the Benedictine monastery of Bec, becoming prior in 1127 and abbot in 1137. Elected archbishop on December 28, 1138, he was consecrated on January 8, 1139, journeying to Rome where he was granted the pallium and participated in the Second Lateran Council (1139). During the civil war in England between Matilda and Stephen de Blois over succession to the throne, he initially hesitated in supporting either party but finally gave his backing to King Stephen, whom he crowned in 1141. As archbishop, Theobald helped to introduce civil law into England, establishing a law school at Canterbury that was to influence the subsequent development of English law. Among the brilliant scholars attracted to his household was Thomas Becket. Some difficulties were encountered by the appointment by Pope Innocent II of Henry Blois, bishop of Winchester, as papal legate, since Henry opposed Theobald over the question of appointments, most notably that of St. William of York as archbishop of York, which Theobald did not desire. In 1143, with the election of Pope Celestine II (r. 1143-1144), Henry was not reconfirmed as legate, and in 1150 Theobald was named to that post by Pope Bl. Eugene III (r. 1144-1153), perhaps on the recommendation of St. Bernard of Clairvaux. Two years earlier, Theobald had defied King Stephen and attended a council in Reims. His property was then confiscated and he was exiled, causing the pope to place England under an interdict. Although ignored save in Canterbury, the interdict prompted a reconciliation between the king and the archbishop. In 1151, he convened a council in London. The next year, he refused to crown Stephen's son Eustace and was again forced to flee. Succeeding in reconciling Stephen with Henry (II) of Anjou, he brought an end to the civil strife in the country, crowning Henry king in 1154. His remaining years were spent in good relations with the court, largely because of Thomas Becket, now chancellor of England. Confiding to his secretary, John of Salisbury, that he hoped Thomas would succeed him as archbishop, Theobald died on April 18, 1161. Buried in Canterbury Cathedral, he was found sixteen years later to be incorrupt, a discovery that added to his reputation for personal holiness.

Theodicy ● Term meaning "the justification of God." It was first used by Gottfried Wilhelm Leibniz in his *Essais de Théodicée sur la bonté de Dieu* (1710). Leibniz tried to prove that the evil in the world is not incompatible with the goodness and omnipotence of God, further declaring that despite its evils, the world remains the best of all other possible worlds. His concept of theodicy was in part a response to the wider philosophical discussion of the era relating the origins and existence of evil and a specific answer to the writings of the skeptic Pierre Bayle (1647-1706) and his *Dictionnaire historique et critique* (1695-1697), in which Bayle postulated that evil was not compatible with the goodness and omnipotence of God.

Supporting Leibniz in his so-called optimism theory, other philosophers of the 1700s began describing as theodicies their own examinations of the question of evil. As their studies expanded into other areas (e.g., proof of the existence of God), the entire field of the philosophical treatment of God came under this increasingly broad category. By the nineteenth century, theodicy was virtually synonymous with the school of natural theology (*theologia naturalis*) and has thus been defined as the science that treats of God through the application of reason alone, using nature as the lone source of proof, in marked contrast to theology, which utilizes supernatural revelation.

Theodore I ● Pope from 642-649. The son of a bishop, he was a Greek born in Jerusalem. More than likely going to Rome from the Holy Land to flee the invasion of the area by the Arabs, Theodore was elected to succeed Pope John IV, probably because the electors wished to ensure that the next pontiff would be eager to continue opposition to Monothelitism and had some ties to the Eastern Church. Theodore was consecrated on November 24, receiving swift confirmation from the exarch of Ravenna. As anticipated, the pope was devoted throughout his pontificate to resisting Monothelitism. A forceful individual, he wrote to Emperor Constans (r. 641-668) inquiring why the controversial decree *Ecthesis* had not been rescinded despite the opposition to it by Pope John IV and the repudiation of the decree that Christ had only one will by its own promulgator, Constans's predecessor, Emperor Heraclius. Theodore also refused to recognize Paul II, patriarch of Constantinople (641-653), until he had rejected the *Ecthesis* and canonically deposed his predecessor Pyrrhus I (638-641). Though resisted at Constantinople, Theodore's efforts were widely received in Africa and Palestine. The deposed patriarch Pyrrhus recanted in 645 but once again lapsed into Monothelitism in 648. The

Pope Theodore I

following year, he was joined in excommunication by Patriarch Paul. Constans, meanwhile, had issued a decree that abrogated the *Ecthesis*, the infamous edict known as the *Typos* that forbade all discussion of the issues concerning the number of wills in Christ. Condemned vigorously in the West, the *Typos* may have been anathematized by Theodore (it is uncertain) before his death but was certainly condemned by his successor, Pope St. Martin I. Theodore was known as an energetic builder of churches and a generous patron of the poor.

Theodore II ● Pope in December 897. Elected to succeed the short-reigning Romanus (August-November 897), he was even more so, his pontificate lasting a mere twenty days. A pontiff convinced of the need to restore some semblance of order to the politically charged and chaotic situation involving the papacy of the time, he annulled the acts of the so-called Cadaver Synod (January 897), officially restoring Pope Formosus and giving his body, which had been abused in the proceedings, a decent burial in its original tomb at St. Peter's Basilica. He also reinstated those clerics who had been degraded by Pope Stephen VI (VII). The cause of his death and date are unknown.

Theodore of Amasea, St. (d. 306?) ● Roman martyr. He was called Tyro (or Tiro) because he was a soldier in the *Cohors Tyronum*, a military unit stationed in Amasea where he was martyred. According to tradition, he was serving in the legions when a decree of Galerius and Maximian was issued demanding sacrifices by all to the gods. When he refused, he was granted a short period of reflection by his judges; supposedly he used the time to burn down a temple of Cybele. Once again arrested, he was tortured and either burned at the stake or roasted in a furnace. While the story is suspect, a St. Theodore was revered from the fourth century, and his body, buried in Euchais, was transferred to Brindisi in the twelfth century. He is honored there as a patron saint, and his head is enshrined in Gaeta. Feast day: November 9.

Theodore of Mopsuestia (c. 350-428) ●
Ecclesiastical writer, Bible exegete, theologian, and bishop of Mopsuestia. Born in Antioch, he studied at the renowned school of rhetoric in the city under the pagan orator Libanius. While there, he met and became a friend of St. John Chrysostom and Maximus, the future bishop of Seleucia. Around 369, influenced by the example of Chrysostom, Theodore entered the school run by Diodore (Diodorus), later bishop of Tarsus. There Theodore entered into an ascetic life, departing briefly and returning at the passionate urging of Chrysostom who had sent him two letters begging his reconsideration. Ordained sometime between 383 and 386, he left Antioch around 392 to join Diodore in Tarsus and was named bishop of Mopsuestia that same year, probably through Diodore's influence. He remained bishop until his death. During the controversy involving Chrysostom at Constantinople, he stood by his friend.

While friendly to the Pelagians and perhaps influenced by them, he accepted the condemnation of Pelagianism and was largely considered by his contemporaries to be an adherent of orthodoxy. Theodore was the author of a vast body of works, including exegetical commentaries (on the Old and New Testaments) and theological treatises such as *De Incarnatione* (fifteen books, written in Antioch around 382-392), on the Incarnation; *De Sacramentis* (one book now lost), on the sacraments; and *De Spiritu Sancto* (two books, now lost), on the Holy Spirit, against the Macedonians. His biblical commentaries are known for their high critical standard; he applied scientific, historical, and philological methods in marked contrast to the allegorical interpretations of Scripture used by members of the Catechetical School of Alexandria. Theologically, he proposed that Christ had two natures, divine and human, but his use of terms in making his position clear was at times ambiguous, as was to be anticipated in the era before the Council of Chalcedon (451). His views on the Incarnation were subsequently condemned at the Councils of Ephesus (431) and Constantinople (553). Theodore, however, had a major influence upon the Nestorians, earning the title, with Diodore, *patres Nestorii blasphemiae* (Fathers of the Nestorian Blasphemy). He was revered, however, by the Nestorians who called him the Interpreter and looked upon him as one of their most important sources for doctrine. The rediscovery of many of Theodore's works in modern times has forced a careful reappraisal of the often harsh criticism of his views by historians and contemporary theologians.

Theodore of Studios, St. (759-826) ●
Also Theodore of Studium and Theodore Studites, he was an abbot, monastic reformer, and an outspoken critic of Iconoclasm. Theodore studied to be a monk under his uncle, St. Plato, abbot of Saccudium, a monastery in Bithynia (Asia Minor) near Mt. Olympus. Entering the monastery around 780, he succeeded his uncle as abbot in 794 when Plato abdicated in his favor. Banished to Thessalonika

because of his vocal opposition to the adulterous marriage of Emperor Constantine VI, Theodore was recalled in 797 after Constantine's deposition by his mother, Irene. Two years later, owing to the constant threat posed to Saccadium by the Arabs, he moved his monastery to Studios, in Constantinople. Through his forceful, imaginative, and spiritual leadership, Studios emerged as the religious and monastic heart of the Byzantine Empire. He was exiled again from 809-811, this time by Emperor Nicephorus I, being recalled in 811 after the emperor's death in 811. Emperor Leo V the Armenian succeeded to the throne in 813, reviving Iconoclast policies and compelling Theodore to oppose the destruction of the icons. Seized and abused, he was banished to various distant spots, and Studios was filled with Iconoclast monks. Returned to Constantinople in 820 by the command of Emperor Michael II, Theodore learned that no change in Iconoclast policies was to be forthcoming and so remained in opposition to the government. He passed away without ever returning to Studios as its abbot, dying just outside of Constantinople. One of the great figures in the history of Eastern monasticism, Theodore was revered for his sanctity, indomitable will, and preaching leadership. Special praise is given him for championing at deep personal sacrifice the rights of the Church. He authored a *Catechesis magna* and *Catechesis parva*, hymns, polemics against Iconoclasm, spiritual orations, and over five hundred letters. Theodore was also a talented calligrapher. Feast day: November 11.

Theodore of Tarsus, St. (c. 602-690) ●
Archbishop of Canterbury. Born in Tarsus in Cilicia (modern Turkey), he was a Greek by descent, receiving his education at Tarsus and Athens before journeying to the Eternal City. At Rome, he was chosen by Pope Vitalian in 667 to succeed to the see of Canterbury, and was consecrated by the pontiff on March 26, 668. Setting out for England, he was accompanied by St. Benedict Biscop and St. Hadrian the African, in part to assist him in the fulfillment of his duties but also to make certain that Theodore adhered to strict orthodoxy. Arriving at Canterbury in May 669, Theodore set out to promote unity in the English Church, convening two notable synods, at Hereford (673) and Hatfield (680). By making episcopal appointments, reforming the Church in England, and working to improve learning, Theodore established himself as primate of England and solidified the metropolitan status of the see of Canterbury. According to the Venerable Bede, Theodore was distinguished for having "visited all the island, wherever the tribes of the Angles inhabited," and for being "the first archbishop obeyed by all the English Church." Feast day: September 19.

Theodoret of Cyrrhus (c. 395-c. 458) ●
Bishop of Cyrrhus (Cyprus), theologian, and controversialist. A native of Antioch, he was supposedly dedicated from birth to the religious life and was educated by the monks Macedonius and Peter. At the age of twenty-three, he gave his fortune to the poor and became a monk in the monastery near Apamea. Despite his personal objections, he was made bishop of Cyrrhus in 432. As bishop, he was active among the non-Christian population of his diocese and opposed heresy, once burning two hundred copies of the Diatesseron of Tatian. He also built churches and public works.

Around 430, Theodoret involved himself in the Nestorian controversy, emerging as a steadfast supporter of Nestorius against St. Cyril of Alexandria. He published a disputatious work against Cyril in 430, receiving an apology from the Alexandrian bishop in reply. The following year, at the Council of Ephesus (431), Theodoret continued to back Nestorius (and John of Antioch), taking part in the deposition and anathematization of Cyril. The creed, which brought about the reconciliation between John and Cyril (c. 432), was probably drawn up by Theodoret, but the bishop of Cyrrhus refused to accept the agreement because it would have required the condemnation of Nestorius. Reconciled with John in 435, Theodoret once more entered into conflict with Cyril two years later, when Cyril declared Theodore of Mopsuestia and Diodore of Tarsus the *patres Nestorii blasphemiae* (Fathers of the Nestorian Blasphemy). When Dioscorus succeeded Cyril as patriarch of Alexandria (following Cyril's death in 444), he secured an edict against Theodoret and accused him of Nestorianism. While Theodoret wrote the polemic *Eranistes* in response, Dioscorus managed to have his enemy forbidden to attend the Latrocinium, the so-called Robber Council of Ephesus (449). At the council, Theodoret was deposed and sent into exile. He appealed to Pope St. Leo I, who declared his deposition to be invalid and, after the accession of Emperor Marcian in 450, Theodoret was allowed to return to his diocese and then was invited to the important Council of Chalcedon (451). There he agreed to the anathematization of Nestorius, although he acquiesced only in the condemnation of the errors that Nestorius might have taught. His remaining years were generally peaceful. Theodoret authored exegetical works, including commentaries on the Psalms and the Epistles of St. Paul; apologetics; polemical treatises; letters; the *Historia Ecclesiastica*, a Church history continuing the work of Eusebius of Caesarea to 429 — it would be used by Theodorus Lector in his *Historia tripartita*, in the sixth century; *Historia religiosa*, biographies of thirty monks and hermits; and a collection of heretical fables dealing with Nestorianism, Eutychianism, and Arianism.

Theodoric the Great (d. 526) ● King of the Ostrogoths from 471-526, he emerged as one of the foremost rulers of the early medieval era. The son of an Ostrogoth chieftain, he was raised in Constantinople as a hostage, since his people were federated allies to the Byzantine Empire. Succeeding as chief in 471, he alternated between being an ally and an enemy of the emperors. In 481, however, Emperor Zeno appointed him a patrician, in part to begin attempting a restoration of political order in Italy in the wake of the final demise of the Roman Empire in the West in 476. In 489, Zeno commissioned Theodoric to destroy the German chieftain Odoacer, the general who had overthrown the last Western Emperor, Romulus Augustulus. Odoacer was defeated and slain at Ravenna in 493, and Theodoric laid claim to supremacy in Italy. As master of Italy, Theodoric ruled his Roman subjects with moderation, using Roman officials (including the scholars Boethius and Cassiodorus) in his government, maintaining useful Roman institutions, promoting the arts and learning, and working for good relations with the Orthodox Christians of Byzantium and Italy. Theodoric was an Arian, but not until his final years did he persecute Orthodox Christians, responding in a harsh manner to the anti-Arian program of Emperor Justinian I (r. 527-565), most notably with the execution of Boethius (c. 524). He was buried in a magnificent tomb at Ravenna.

Theodorus Lector (fl. sixth century) ● Byzantine Church historian, he was the author of two important works, the *Historia tripartita* and a *Church History*. A reader at the Hagia Sophia in Constantinople, Theodorus wrote the *Historia tripartita* from around 520-530. An epitome of the writings of the fifth-century chronicles of Sozomen, Socrates, and Theodoret of Cyrrhus, Theodorus's history presented the principal events of the Church from 313-439 (the reign of Constantine I to Theodosius II). Known in the original Greek (translated) as *Selections from the History of the Church*, it brought together accounts from each of the writers chosen by Theodorus for their excellence and superiority to parallel passages found in the other two. The unusual passages, however, were noted and discussed in the margins, thereby heightening the value of the entire work for future scholars. The *Church History*, or *Ekloge*, was a continuation of the *Historia tripartita*, continuing the account by his own pen from the death of Theodosius II (450) to the accession of Emperor Justin I (518). Unfortunately, only fragments of this work have survived, preserved in part in the *Patrologia Graeca* of Jacques Paul Migne.

Theodosianus, Codex ● Latin for Theodosian Code, it is a massive compilation of laws. Promulgated on February 15, 438, by Emperor Theodosius II, it collected and codified in sixteen books the numerous decrees and enactments of previous years. The codex was accepted as law in the Western Empire and was one of the foundations for the subsequent Code of Justinian of the sixth century. Book XVI of the codex was concerned with the affairs of religion, stipulating penalties for heresy and forbidding the practice of paganism. It also delineated the position of Church and State. (See also **Canon Law**.)

Theodosius I the Great (d. 395) ● Roman Emperor from 379-395. Called the Great because of his devotion to and promotion of Christianity, he was born in Cauca, the son of the formidable imperial nobleman Count Theodosius. His rapid military and political career seemed cut short in 375 when his father was executed, probably for treason; however, Theodosius was summoned by Emperor Gratian in 378 to serve as a general on the frontier following the annihilation of a Roman army under Emperor Valens by the Goths at the Battle of Adrianople. His

campaign against the Goths was so effective that Gratian named him emperor of the Eastern Empire on January 19, 379. He concluded peace with the Goths in 382 and in 387 crushed and beheaded the usurper Magnus Maximus who had overthrown Theodosius' co-emperor Gratian (383). While in the Western Empire, Theodosius became a close supporter of St. Ambrose, archbishop of Milan, receiving from him enormous support and influential encouragement in the liquidation of lingering elements of paganism and the creation of an Orthodox Christian state. In 391, pagan temples were closed and pagan practices were outlawed. A brief revival of paganism occurred under the usurper General Arbogast, who had elevated Eugenius, a onetime teacher, to the throne in 392. In 394, at the bloody Battle of Frigidus, Theodosius routed Arbogast and Eugenius, uniting both imperial domains. In dealing with the faith, Theodosius worked to reduce the presence and influence of the Arians, expelling them from the government and closing their churches. A broad decree was passed for the empire forbidding all heresies, including Manichaeism. Theodosius, however, refused to carry out severe punishments because, as the historian Sozomen wrote, "he did not desire to punish, but only to frighten his people, that they might ponder, as he did, Divine matters." One unfortunate episode resulted in his brief excommunication by St. Ambrose; he put seven thousand people to death in Thessalonika for civil disorder and had to make atonement before absolution could be granted. Convened under his auspices, the First Council of Constantinople in 381 attempted to negotiate a settlement, without result, between Arians and Orthodox Christians. His funeral oration (*De obitu Theodosii*) was preached by St. Ambrose.

Theodosius II (401-450) ● Roman emperor of the East from 408-450. Longest reigning ruler in the history of the Roman

Empire, he was born in Constantinople, the son of Emperor Arcadius and grandson of Emperor Theodosius I the Great. Succeeding to the throne in 408, he was under the regency of the powerful Praetorian prefect Anthemius from 404-414 and then his own sister Aelia Pulcheria from 414-416. Aelia, however, remained the most formidable figure in the imperial court until the mid-440s when she was eclipsed for a time by the eunuch Chrysaphius Zstommas. Theodosius was much concerned with matters of law, religion, and education. He founded the University of Constantinople (425), with departments in Greek, Latin, law, and philosophy. In 438, he promulgated the *Codex Theodosianus*, the Code of Theodosius, a monumental compilation in sixteen books that would be an important foundation for law in the West and the Code of Justinian in the East. In dealing with the Church, Theodosius was proof of the degree to which Christianity had become a central part of the imperial administration and society. He convened the Council of Ephesus (431) and, despite his personal piety, he was convinced by Chrysaphius to grant toleration of the Monophysites. He died on July 28, 450, after falling from his horse just outside of Constantinople.

Theodulf (c. 750-821) ● Bishop of Orléans. He was a theologian and a member of the famous court of Charlemagne at Aachen that promoted the Carolingian Renaissance. A Goth by descent, Theodulf was born in France and was received into the court at Aachen sometime before 794, ranked only behind Alcuin in respect. Charlemagne granted Theodulf the see of Orléans (c. 798) and the abbacy of Fleury. As bishop he promoted reform among the clergy and the building of schools. In 818, however, he was deposed and banished to Anger after being accused of conspiring against King Louis the Pious. An important theologian in the Frankish Empire, Theodulf wrote a

number of theological works, including *De Spiritu Sancto*, on the Holy Spirit, a treatise on baptism, and probably an exposition on the Mass and the creed. In *De Spiritu Sancto*, Theodulf took part in the dispute over the *Filioque*, defending the doctrine of the procession of the Holy Spirit from the Son as well as the Father at the behest of Charlemagne. As a poet, he composed *Versus contra judices* (against the harshness of Frankish law) and *Carmina* (providing a vivid description of the court). His hymn *Gloria, laus, et honor* ("Glory, Praise, and Honor") became the processional for Palm Sunday in the Western Church.

Theognostus (fl. late third century) ● Greek theologian, ecclesiastical writer, and head of the Catechetical School of Alexandria. Theognostus became head of the Alexandrian school around 265, probably succeeding Dionysius the Great. His chief work was the *Hypotyposeis* (*Outlines*), a theological compendium in several books. Intended to be used by students, the work was heavily influenced by Origen and was supported by St. Gregory of Nyssa. St. Athanasius of Alexandria used it in his conflict with the Arians during the fourth century. Owing to severe opposition to it by Photius, patriarch of Constantinople, in his *Myriobiblion*, an extensive account of the *Hypotyposeis* was preserved.

Theophanes, St. (758-817) ● Byzantine chronicler and martyr in defense of the veneration of icons. A native of Constantinople, he was the son of a Byzantine imperial official, raised at the imperial court after the early deaths of his parents. Married in 770, he convinced his wife to remain a virgin, and in 799 they separated by mutual consent so that they could each enter into the religious life. Theophanes joined a monastery near Cyzicus, later building a monastery on his own lands and founding an abbey at

Sigriano, near the monastic institution of Cyzicus where he had previously resided. Becoming abbot, he participated in the Second Council of Nicaea (787) and gave his signature to the decree in defense of sacred images. Summoned to Constantinople by Emperor Leo V the Armenian (r. 813-821), he was pressured to renounce the acts of the council. Refusing, Theophanes was imprisoned for two years and then banished to Samothrace where he survived a mere seventeen days, dying in March 817. He was the author of a *Chronicle*, covering the years 284-813, written at the request of his friend George Syncellus (d. 810). The *Chronicle* used the previous works of Socrates, Sozomen, and Theodoret, as compiled by the *Historia tripartita* of Theodorus Lector, and the writings of George Syncellus.

Theophilus of Alexandria (d. 412) ●

Patriarch of Alexandria from 385-412. Few details are extant concerning his early life, and St. Jerome wrote that he was not known as a public teacher before 385. Elected patriarch in 385, he proved a bishop of considerable talent, but he was described as unscrupulous in his efforts at aggrandizing the see of Alexandria and violent in his opposition to paganism. In 390, he seized from the pagans a small temple and destroyed several others, inciting riots in the streets. After a number of Christians were killed, he retaliated by leading a mob that destroyed the temple of Serapia (Serapeum), building a church upon the site of the ruins. Originally an adherent of Origenism, he completely revised his position between 398 and 400, probably as a result of a sharp quarrel with the archpresbyter Isidore, a well-known ally of the Origenists in Alexandria. Condemning the Origenists at a synod in Alexandria in 401, he ordered and participated in the burning of the monastery housing monks who adhered to Origenist teachings, abusing the survivors. The three hundred monks fled to Palestine and then to Constantinople where they were given protection by St. John Chrysostom. There soon began a bitter struggle between Theophilus and Chrysostom, culminating with Theophilus's manipulation of the Synod of the Oak (403) to secure the condemnation and banishment of Chrysostom on wholly specious charges. In the period that followed, the prelate was able to elevate the prominence of the Alexandrian see at the expense of the patriarchate of Constantinople in the affairs of the Eastern Church. While criticized for ruthless ambition and severity, he is honored as a saint by the Coptic Church. He was succeeded as patriarch by his nephew St. Cyril.

Theophilus of Antioch (fl. second century) ●

Bishop of Antioch and a leading Christian apologist. Of the writings of Theophilus, the only extant work is the *Ad Autolycum*, an apology for Christianity. According to this he was a convert from paganism. The *Ad Autolycum* was organized into three books, most likely written at different periods, examining the Christian concept of God, Scripture accounts of the origin of man, and the superiority of the Christian creation to the myths of pagans. Theophilus was also responsible for the introduction into literature of the word "triad" in describing the Godhead: God (the Father), the Word, or *Logos* (Jesus), and Wisdom (the Holy Spirit). Among his lost writings were treatises refuting Marcion and Hermogenes, several catechetical books, and a number of commentaries on the Gospels and Proverbs. He was elected bishop of Antioch around 170.

Theophylact of Ochrida (d. c. 1109) ●

Byzantine exegete and archbishop of Ochrida in Bulgaria. Born in Euboea, he was a pupil of Michael Psellus and served as tutor to the future Emperor Constantine VII Porphyrogenitos, son of Emperor Michael III. Appointed bishop of Ochrida in 1078, he promoted Christianity among the Bulgars and defended his flock against the harsh imperial program of taxation. He authored numerous letters on the state of affairs among the Bulgars, making frequent referrals to the highly uncivilized nature of the inhabitants and lamenting that he had been sent to such a depressing land. In the ongoing schism between the Eastern and Western Churches, Theophylact maintained a conciliatory position. Writing *Allocutio de eis quorum Latini incusantur* (Address on the Matters for Which Latins are Attacked), a severe criticism of his fellow Greeks for their harsh treatment of Western Christianity, he argued that such Latin practices as clerical celibacy and the use of unleavened bread for the Eucharist were of no major consequence doctrinally and should not be allowed to stand in the way of union between the Churches. He was also the author of a series of commentaries on parts of the OT and all of the NT except for the Book of Revelation.

Theotokos ● Greek for "bearer of God," it is one of the titles given to the Blessed Virgin, the principal title of her in the Greek Church. It dates back to the third century, was probably first used by Origen, and was subsequently accepted by the Greek Fathers of the Church. While opposed by Nestorius and his followers on the basis that it was incompatible with the full humanity of Christ, it received the enthusiastic endorsement of St. Cyril of Alexandria and was officially sanctioned by the Councils of Ephesus in 431 and Chalcedon in 451. The Latin word *Deipara* most approximates *Theotokos* etymologically, but scholars note that the term *Dei Genetrix* more fully represents the meaning — "Mother of God."

Thérèse of Lisieux, St. (1873-1897) ●
Called the Little Flower or St. Thérèse of the Child Jesus, she was a Carmelite nun and mystic. Born Marie Françoise Thérèse Martin in Alençon, Normandy, France, she was the daughter of Louis Martin, a pious Catholic

St. Thérèse of Lisieux

watchmaker, and Zélie Guérin. Drawn to the religious life, she entered the Carmelite convent of Lisieux in Normandy in 1888, overcoming resistance because of her young age. She would survive only nine more years, enduring severe personal struggles in her prayer life while maintaining the outward plainness of an ordinary nun. She engaged in daily work, prayer, and devotion, but she suffered terribly from doubts, isolation, and scruples. Nevertheless, she adhered steadfastly to the "little way" — placing her trust completely in God. She died on September 30, 1897, from tuberculosis, a malady that ended her hopes of serving in China.

In 1895, Thérèse had been instructed by her superiors to write an autobiography. Her work, *L'Histoire d'une âme* (*The Story of a Soul*), was found by the Carmelites to be truly remarkable. A heavily revised edition of the work was subsequently distributed to all other Carmelite houses, launching Thérèse to worldwide fame. The autobiography was translated into many languages, becoming wildly successful. Miracles were reported in such numbers that a record of them was added to her book in 1907. Her cause was opened in 1910 at Bayeux, taken up by the Holy See in 1918 with exemption from the fifty-year delay required by canon law. Beatified on April 25, 1923, she was canonized on May 17, 1925, by Pope Pius XI. The following year, a basilica was begun in her honor, and in 1929 Pope Pius named her patroness of foreign missions and works toward Russia. In 1947, she was made a patroness of France with Joan of Arc. One of the most beloved saints of the modern era, Thérèse is recognized as a powerful sign to people of all ages, but especially the young, with the fact being stressed that anyone, even a seemingly ordinary, plain, and apparently insignificant person, can achieve sanctity by the fulfillment of duties out of a perfect love for God, in matters great and small. Her autobiography, initially published in its revised form, was restored to its original state through the use of photostats of the original manuscript in the 1930s. This new edition, translated by Ronald Knox, was first published in 1958 under the title *Autobiography of a Saint*. Feast day: October 1.

Thessalonians, First Epistle to the ●
Letter sent by St. Paul to the young Christian community of Thessalonika. It was written in Corinth around the year 50, a few months after Paul's departure from Thessalonika under a storm of attack by local Jewish religious leaders who resented the Apostle's great success in preaching to the Jews and Gentiles of the city. Paul and his assistant Silas fled to Beroea, from where Paul went to Athens and then Corinth. He was soon joined by Silas and Timothy, but Paul, concerned about the forsaken community, dispatched Timothy to give the Christians there encouragement. Timothy's report to Paul prompted Paul's letter, an exhortation and a very important discussion of the meaning of Christ's death and resurrection, a major

contribution to Christian eschatology that is also the earliest of Paul's surviving writings.

Paul begins his epistle by recounting his ministry among the Thessalonians (4:3-5) and goes on to eschatological matters, presenting a symbolic depiction of the end of time. Paul, however, is hopeful and loving, assuring his readers: "For God has not destined us for wrath, but to obtain salvation through our Lord Jesus Christ, who died for us so that whether we wake or sleep we might live with him" (5:9-10). For Paul, this eschatological awareness should be ever present as a guiding light in the life of the Christian; he thus provides concrete examples for this in his exhortations concerning chastity, charity, and respect for "those who labor among you and are over you in the Lord and admonish you. . ." (5:12).

Thessalonians, Second Epistle to the ●
Second letter sent to the Christian community of Thessalonika by St. Paul. Written after the first, it was apparently intended to give the Thessalonians encouragement during a difficult period of suffering and persecution. Paul's main purpose in the letter is to correct certain misconceptions concerning the "day of the Lord." As in 1 Thessalonians, Paul utilizes remarkable symbolism and imagery to describe an apocalypse, calling upon his readers to stand firm against the "mystery of lawlessness" that "is already at work" (2:7), exhorting them to "stand firm and hold to the traditions which were taught to you by us, either by word of mouth or by letter" (2:15), a second reference to the cause of the erroneous misunderstanding that had apparently developed in the Christian population of Thessalonika. Paul's mention of "a letter allegedly from us" points to a possible forgery and explains in his closing, "I, Paul, write this greeting with my own hand. This is the mark in every letter of mine; it is the way I write. The grace of our Lord Jesus Christ be with you all" (3:17-18).

Thierry of Chartres (c. 1100-c. 1151) ● Also called Theodoric of Chartres and Thierry the Breton. Theologian and Scholastic philosopher, he was the younger brother of Bernard of Chartres, chancellor of the famed school of Chartres, where Thierry became a teacher in 1121. According to Peter Abelard, that same year he attended the Council of Soissons, which condemned Abelard's teachings. Eventually becoming an instructor in Paris, he claimed among his students John of Salisbury. In 1141, he returned to Chartres where he served as archdeacon and chancellor, succeeding Gilbert de la Porrée. In 1148, Thierry took part in the Synod of Reims and the next year participated in the Diet of Frankfurt. Between 1151 and 1156 he retired to a monastery, dying probably in Chartres. A devoted Platonist, he authored commentaries on Boethius's *De Trinitate* and Cicero's *De Inventione*; he also wrote a treatise on the seven liberal arts, the *Heptateuchon*, and the Platonist treatise *De Sex Dierum Operibus*.

Thirty Years' War ● Bloody conflict lasting from 1618-1648. It ultimately involved most European nations but was fought mainly in Germany. The causes of the war were manifold and its conduct was distinguished by complicated political maneuvering by the participants and wholesale carnage and destruction inflicted upon entire parts of Europe. The principal issues precipitating the launching of the war were religious, dynastic, and territorial. The tensions caused by the rise of Protestantism were still very real, having not been abated at all by the Peace of Augsburg of 1555. Further, the Protestant German princes, perceiving the decay of the House of Habsburg, which ruled the Holy Roman Empire, Spain, Austria, Bohemia, Hungary, parts of Italy, and the southern Netherlands, were anxious to free themselves from imperial mastery. To complicate matters even more, France and Sweden were both eager to improve their positions in European affairs; for France, this objective was especially connected with a policy of working for the reduction of power and influence of the Holy Roman Empire.

The event that sparked the war was the rebellion of the Bohemians who had chosen as their king Frederick V of the Palatinate, the so-called Winter King against King (later Emperor) Ferdinand II. Under the imperial general Tilly, Ferdinand's troops, aided by the Catholic League under Duke Maximilian I of Bavaria (1573-1651), smashed the Bohemians at the Battle of White Mountain (1620), defeated Christian of Brunswick and Mansfeld in the Palatinate (1622-1623), and seized the Protestant stronghold of Heidelberg. Catholicism was now restored in these conquered lands.

A new phase in the war soon began, however, when Christian IV, king of Denmark, entered on the side of his fellow Protestants. The campaign that followed, centered in Lower Saxony, ended in Tilly's triumph and was marked by the rise of the talented imperial commander Albrecht von Wallenstein. By the Treaty of Lübeck (1629), Denmark withdrew from the conflict. The peace did not last, as in the same year the emperor took the unfortunate step of enforcing the Peace of Augsburg of 1555 and issuing the Edict of Restitution, which ordered all ecclesiastical lands seized unlawfully by Protestants since 1552 to be restored. The measure aroused severe indignation, and the situation militarily was thrown into confusion by the removal of Wallenstein as general of the imperial armies, replaced by Johann Tilly. At this juncture, Sweden, aided by France, under Cardinal Richelieu, intervened. The brilliant king and general Gustavus Adolphus landed with his Swedish army in Pomerania in 1630. His arrival changed the course of the war because it bolstered the Protestant cause and led to Swedish victories at Breitenfeld (1631), Lechfeld (1630, where Tilly was killed), and

Lützen (1632). Gustavus was also killed at Lützen, but Sweden carried on the war. As negotiations proceeded, a Protestant army under Bernard of Weimar laid waste to Bavaria and seized Ratisbon; Wallenstein was murdered for his failure to resist this disaster. The imperial cause finally recovered that same year when, at the Battle of Nördlingen, the Protestants were crushed. The Peace of Prague (1635) ensued, a compromise treaty with the German states.

Anxious to prevent a victory by the empire, Richelieu took France openly into the war, beginning the long struggle's final and most terrible phase. Fighting soon spread into Italy, the Iberian Peninsula, Scandinavia, the Low Countries, and across Germany. The Swedes and the French, especially under Turenne and Louis II de Condé, proved increasingly successful, but the severe destruction and depopulation of whole parts of Germany brought the combatants to the point of exhaustion. Negotiations began in 1644 between the empire and France at Münster and the empire and Sweden at Osnabrück. The Treaty of Westphalia was signed in 1648. War continued between Spain and France until 1659 and the Peace of the Pyrenees. The war had left Germany in ruins, and the Holy Roman

St. Thomas,
by the Echternach master

Empire was now only an increasingly doomed political entity. France was a major power, and the Protestant states had secured once and for all their right to exist. The Thirty Years' War was also a defeat for the Catholic Church, for the treaty recognized the idea of secularized property, gave Church property as compensation, and ignored the concern of Pope Innocent X who was placed in the unenviable position of denouncing the Peace of Westphalia because of its restrictions on papal involvement in German affairs.

Thomas, St. ● One of the Apostles. He is counted as a member of the Twelve in all four Gospels; in John, he is called Didymus (Greek for "twin"). Known for his doubts, Thomas is mentioned in three remarkable episodes in John: he is willing to die with Christ, saying on the way to Bethany, "Let us also go, that we may die with him" (11:16); he tells Christ "Lord, we do not know where you are going; how can we know the way?" — to which Christ declares, "I am the way, and the truth, and the life; no one comes to the Father, but by me" (14:5-6); and he doubts his fellow Apostles when they tell him of seeing the risen Christ (20:25). When meeting Christ, however, he cries out, "My Lord and my God!" (20:28).

His subsequent life has been subject to much speculation among historians. According to Eusebius of Caesarea in his *Ecclesiastical History*, he preached the Gospel among the Parthians. Subsequent legend tells of his journey to India. There he is still considered the founder of the Malabar Christians, who are also called St. Thomas Christians. The interesting but apocryphal *Acts of Thomas*, composed in Syriac under Gnostic influence in the third century, describes his missionary work in India where he was martyred. Tradition says that he was put to death in Mylapore, near Madras. Other writings attributed to Thomas include *The Book of Thomas the Athlete* and the *Gospel of Thomas*. His relics are supposedly enshrined in Ortona, Italy. Feast day: July 3.

Thomas à Becket ● See **Thomas Becket, St**.

Thomas à Jesu (1564-1627) ● Spanish Discalced Carmelite writer and theologian. Born in Andalusia, Diez Sanchez de Ávila was the son of Don Baltasar de Ávila and Dona Teresa de Herrera. After studying the humanities, he focused on law at the University of Salamanca (1583). While there, he was able to read some of the as yet unpublished writings of St. Teresa of Ávila (1515-1562). So inspired was he by her work, that he entered the Carmelites in 1586 or 1587, subsequently teaching theology at Seville, and serving as prior at Saragossa and provincial of Old Castile. At the end of his time of office, Thomas (as he was now known) withdrew to the desert of Las Batuecas, establishing for himself a strict erimitical life. Becoming prior of the austere community, he helped launch the innovation of the erimitical life in the order, establishing it in several Carmelite monasteries and formalizing the regulation that there should be but one such community in each province and only four permanent ones for the religious. Known for his missionary zeal, he

was summoned to Rome in 1607 by Pope Paul V, who expressed a desire to promote missionary work by the Carmelites. Thomas undertook this program with enthusiasm, founding with papal approval a missionary branch for the order, the Congregation of St. Paul, in 1608. This development was opposed, however, by both Thomas's Spanish and Italian superiors who feared it might cause a rupture in the order. At their advice, the pope withdrew his permission. Thomas's work was not in vain, because his two large treatises on missionary activity, *Stimulus missionum* (1610) and *De procuranda salute omnium Gentium* (1616), gave a complete outline for the organization and functioning of a papal congregation devoted to evangelization. Pope Gregory XV used the extensive program developed by Thomas when he created the Congregation of the Propaganda Fide in 1622. Thomas, meanwhile, was sent by Pope Paul V to the Low Countries where he began Carmelite convents in Brussels, Louvain, Cologne, Antwerp, Lille, Namur, and elsewhere. After holding the post of provincial of Flanders, he was ordered back to Rome in 1621 to be definitor general. His writings were ordered collected by Pope Urban VIII (r. 1623-1644) and were published in Cologne in 1684. Aside from the previously mentioned works, he authored treatises on mystical theology, systematizing into Scholastic terms the Thomistically based teachings of St. Teresa. These included *De contemplatione divina* (1620) and *Divinae Orationis Methodus*.

Thomas à Kempis (c. 1380-1471) ● Known originally as Thomas Hemerken von Kempen. An ascetic writer and probably the author of the *Imitation of Christ*, he was born in Kempen, near Cologne. Thomas studied at the school of the Brethren of the Common Life, coming under the influence of Florentius Radewyns. In 1399, with the urging and commendation of Florentius, he entered the monastery of Agnietenberg, a house of the canons regular, near Zwolle, of which his brother John was prior. He took his vows in 1406 or 1408 and was ordained in 1413, remaining in the monastery for the rest of his life, writing, preaching, copying manuscripts, and serving as a spiritual adviser. His favorite topics for preaching were the mystery of the Redemption and Christ's passion. A portrait at Getruidenberg, considered possibly authentic, bore his motto, "Everywhere I have sought rest and found it nowhere, save in tiny nooks with tiny books." His chief work, the *Imitatio Christi*, was a manual of spiritual perfection, first circulated in 1418 and divided into four parts: Useful Admonitions for a Spiritual Life, Admonitions Concerning Interior Things, Interior Consolation, and the Blessed Sacrament. While the book is traditionally ascribed to Thomas and generally accepted by scholars to have been his work, other possible authors have been suggested over the years, including Pope Innocent III and Jean Gerson. Other works were sermons, hagiographies, and devotional writings.

Thomas à Kempis

Thomas Aquinas, St. (c. 1224- or 1225-1274) ● Dominican theologian and philosopher. Considered one of the greatest intellectual figures in the history of the world and the Church. For his immense contributions to the theology of the faith, he is called *Doctor Angelicus* and *Doctor Communis*, and is honored as the patron of Catholic schools, colleges, and universities.

Life: Born at Roccasecca, Italy, Thomas was the son of Count Landulf of Aquino, a local Italian magnate, and Theodora, countess of Teano. Around the age of five (1230), he was entered as an oblate into the famed Benedictine Abbey of Monte Cassino. He displayed genuine brilliance as a student, but in 1239 he returned home after the monks were ejected by troops of Emperor Frederick II. That same year, he was sent to the University of Naples.

As a student, he focused on philosophy, grammar, rhetoric, and logic, quickly surpassing his own instructors. He also had the opportunity to study for the first time a few tantalizing works by Aristotle that were then gradually coming to exert a profound influence on Western thought. Thomas naturally attracted the attentions of the Dominican friars in the city who observed his many hours of prayer, his intellectual gifts, and his steadfast refusal to involve himself in the vice and corruption of the highly cosmopolitan metropolis of Naples. To their great pleasure, Thomas approached them one day in 1243 and stated his desire to join the Order of Friars Preacher.

His decision was quite at odds with the wishes of his family and, while journeying to Rome with several friars, he was waylaid by his brothers, who carried him back to Roccasecca. He was then imprisoned from 1244-1245 at Monte San Giovanni by his brothers and mother as they tried to convince him to abandon his vocation as a Dominican and return to Monte Cassino where they had planned for him to become an abbot. This he would not do, resisting all efforts to break his will. While a prisoner, he studied Scripture and theology. His family finally gave up in 1245, and he was released. He went to Rome and then Paris where he entered the university.

From 1245-1248, Thomas studied at Paris, coming under the instruction of another of the Church's foremost theologians, Albertus Magnus. Around 1248, he was chosen by Albert to accompany him to Cologne where Thomas served as bachelor in the new *studium generale* that the Dominicans had opened recently in the city. While in Cologne, he was ordained, returning two years later to Paris. There he lectured on theology at the Dominican convent of St. Jacques. While continuing his own studies, he also authored an important commentary on the *Sentences* of Peter Lombard.

Around this time, Thomas and the mendicant friars (the Dominicans and Franciscans) encountered much opposition from members of the university who were of the mind that the friars should not be permitted to teach. On behalf of the orders and against such secular enemies as William of St. Amour, Thomas wrote *Contra impugnantes Dei cultum et religionem*, an apology for the mendicants. Around 1255-1256, he was told to prepare himself for a doctorate in theology. More delays would ensue owing to secular attacks, but on October 23, 1257, he and his Franciscan friend St. Bonaventure received their doctorates. Soon after, he gave his

St. Thomas Aquinas

inaugural lecture, "The Majesty of Christ," based on Psalms (104:13).

In 1259, Thomas was appointed a theological adviser to the papal court, spending time at Anagni and Orvieto, and undertaking at the behest of Pope Urban IV a number of writings, including the Office for the Feast of Corpus Christi, the *Catena Aurea* (*The Golden Chain*), and the *Contra Errores Graecorum* (*Against the Errors of the Greeks*). From 1265-1267, he taught at Rome in the Dominican *studium generale* of Santa Sabina. During his period in Rome, he began work on his greatest labor, the *Summa Theologiae*.

In 1267, Thomas traveled to Viterbo to resume his duties at the papal court, this time for Pope Clement IV. He remained there for two years, tearfully declining the post of archbishop of Naples, which Clement offered to him. Around 1269, he was recalled to Paris where the Dominicans appointed him to their principal chair of theology. His posting came at a decisive moment, for a major controversy had erupted in the school over the teaching of Aristotle. Thomas was forced to combat the extreme Aristotelian ideas of Siger of Brabant and the Averroists (see **Averroism**) and the rigid anti-Aristotelianism of such theologians as John Peckham and Stephen Tempier, bishop of Paris. During this time, he authored the treatises *De unitate intellectus contra Averroistas* (*On the Unity of the Intellect Against the Averroists*) and *De aeternitate mundi contra murmurantes* (*On the Eternity of the World Against the Whisperers*). Through the brilliance of his arguments and the clarity of his theology, Thomas defeated the Averroists and prevented, for the time being at least, the condemnation of Aristotelian thought.

Known and respected throughout Christendom, Thomas was asked in 1272 to organize a *studium generale* by Charles of Anjou, king of Naples. While engaged in the work of lecturing, preaching, and developing the new school, he continued to work on the *Summa*. During the Lenten period in 1273, he gave sermons to huge crowds of the faithful in the city.

Always drawn toward the mystical life — a fact often overlooked because of the value he placed on reason — Thomas grew increasingly distracted, experiencing a series of ecstasies that climaxed on December 6, 1273, with a vision of such extraordinary profundity that he exclaimed to his longtime assistant Reginald of Piperno: "I can do no more. Such secrets have been revealed to me that all that I have written now seems like straw." He would not write again, leaving the *Summa* and many other works unfinished. Exhausted and ill, he set out in January of 1274 for the Council of Lyons at the behest of Pope Gregory X. On the road, he collapsed and died on March 7, 1274, at the Cistercian monastery of Fossanova.

Influence and Writings: Known to his classmates in Paris as the Dumb Ox because he was so heavy and seemingly slow, Thomas amazed his contemporaries by the scale and scope of his thought and writings. In the broadest sense, he sought to reconcile faith and reason and to bring into the Church a Christianized Aristotelianism that could be put to the use and greater glory of the faith. In these efforts he was utterly successful, but in so doing, he revolutionized the very

theology of the Christian Church by rendering theology into a science and systematized to an unprecedented degree the entire body of Christian dogma. He challenged and then reversed the centuries of dominance enjoyed by Augustinianism and conferred on theology a Christianized Aristotelianism whose influence would endure into the modern age. Harmonizing reason and faith, he also called for the precise distinction between them. Reason, he felt, while helpful in discovering the existence of God and such attributes as his eternity and simplicity, was insufficient as a certain guide for human action. Revelation was needed, reached by faith, for the distinguishing between the higher truths discovered by reason and those revealed by divine consent. In no way are reason and faith in contradiction; rather, reason should work in the service of faith and faith should assist in the preservation of reason from error. A demonstration of the cooperation of the two was in the Five Ways (*Quinque Viae*), used to prove the existence of God (see **Quinque Viae**.)

His vast system of thought, called Thomism and considered the crowning moment of Scholasticism, was not immediately accepted, as was seen in 1277 when twelve theses were condemned at the University of Paris, followed by further criticism at Oxford. This situation did not long endure, however, as in 1278 the Dominicans officially imposed Thomas's writings upon the entire order. He was canonized in 1323 by Pope John XXII. In 1567, Pope St. Pius V declared him a Doctor of the Church, and in 1879, Pope Leo XIII issued the encyclical *Aeterni Patris*, commanding the study of St. Thomas upon all priests and students of theology.

The writings of St. Thomas covered virtually the entire body of Church doctrine, including treatises on philosophy and theology and commentaries on Aristotle and Scripture. He supposedly wrote his first work while a prisoner of his family, a treatise on Aristotle or the mistakes commonly made by young students of theology. His earliest known works were a commentary on the *Sentences* of Peter Lombard (1254-1256), and *De ente et essentia* (*On Being and Essence*), around the same time. Biblical commentaries included those on the Gospels of John and Matthew (1269-1272), the letters of St. Paul (n.d., and left incomplete), and the Psalms of David. Other works included: *De regimine principum* (*On Kingship*); *Contra impugnantes religionem* (1256), in defense of the mendicant orders; *De perfectione vitae sprirtualis*, on the spiritual life; *De unitate intellectus contra Averroistas*; commentaries on Aristotle such as his Physics, Nicomachean Ethics, and *De Anima* (*On the Soul*); *Quaestiones Disputatae* and *Quaestiones Quodlibetales*, a collection of debated questions that were examined in the lecture hall; and the writings he did for Pope Urban IV. His two most famous books were the *Summa Contra Gentiles* and the *Summa Theologiae*.

Known in full as the *Summa de veritate catholicae fidei contra gentiles*, the *Summa Contra Gentiles* is a brilliant manual on promoting conversions to the Christian faith. It was written for use by missionaries among the educated Muslims and Jews and was penned for Raymond of Peñafort. It is considered a precursor to the other *Summa*.

The *Summa Theologiae* (or *Theologica*) is the greatest single exposition of the Christian faith. It was intended by Thomas to be a simple manual on doctrine but quickly acquired a reputation for its vastness, erudition, and complexity as well as an official orthodoxy and value that are unquestioned. It was begun in 1266 probably at Rome. While left incomplete, it has three parts. Part I (*Prima Pars*) was finished at Viterbo in 1267. Its central theme was God, divided into three subjects titled "On those things which pertain to the Essence of God," "On the distinctions of Persons in God," and

"On the creation of beings by God and the beings so created." Part II (*Secunda Pars*) was started in Rome and completed at Paris in 1271. There Thomas was concerned with the advance of rational creatures to God; it stands on its own as a genuinely great manual on moral theology and Christian ethics, using as its guiding maxim "On God as He is the End of Man." It has two main sections: on human acts in general and on human acts in detail, in the virtues and vices. Throughout, Thomas displays a deep sensitivity and insight into the human mind and heart. Part III (*Tertia Pars*) was composed at Naples from 1272-1272. He never finished it because of the vision granted to him after which he would write nothing else. Its aim was the presentation of Christ: "On the Incarnation," "On the Sacraments," and "On Eternal Life." Some later editions had a supplement comprised of writings attributed to Thomas; the material was supposedly gathered by Peter of Auvergne, Henry of Gorkum, or Reginald of Piperno. In all, the *Summa* presents 38 treatises, 612 questions, 3,120 articles, and around 10,000 individual objections. Feast day: January 28.

Thomas Becket, St. (1118-1170) ● Also Thomas à Becket. Archbishop of Canterbury, chancellor of England, and martyr. A Norman by descent, Thomas was born in Cheapside, London, studying at Merton Priory and then at Paris, under Robert of Melun. He entered into the service of the sheriffs, working for three years as a clerk until 1141 when he became a member of the household of Archbishop Theobald of Canterbury. A young man with considerable promise, he was sent to study at Bologna and Auxerre. In 1154, he was appointed archdeacon of Canterbury and the next year, having impressed King Henry II of England, he was chosen chancellor. Thomas wielded vast powers in England as a result of his remarkable gifts for administration and ruthless application of Henry's political will, but he also enjoyed the king's total confidence, an expression of their close friendship and similar tastes. During this period, Thomas exhibited a fondness for hunting and luxuries, his worldly interests matched by his brilliant performance as chancellor. Chief among his achievements were the reduction of baronial opposition and the implementation of various royal policies of centralization that were often detrimental to the interests of the Church. As the Church remained a problem for Henry, it seemed a logical decision to appoint his most reliable lieutenant to the post of archbishop of Canterbury when that see fell vacant upon the death of Theobald in 1161. Thomas, however, was exceedingly reluctant to take up the office. At Henry's prompting, he was consecrated an archbishop in 1162.

A remarkable transformation took place once Becket was installed. He renounced his worldly interests and adopted an intensely religious and austere lifestyle. Finding that the interests of the Church were at sharp variance with the demands of his duties as chancellor, he resigned from the latter post and soon collided with Henry on a number of issues. He excommunicated a baron, opposed a tax proposal, and fought the Constitutions of Clarendon (1164); he also rejected Henry's claim that clerics who were charged with crimes (so-called criminous clerks) should be

Martyrdom of St. Thomas Becket

tried by secular courts. The king responded with harsh measures against his former friend; he demanded that Thomas settle accounts from his days as chancellor and then convened a council at Northampton. Thomas was condemned, escaping to France, supposedly in disguise, and under the protection of King Louis VII of France. His exile lasted from 1164-1170. During this period he made appeal to a somewhat suspicious Pope Alexander III and for two years stayed in the Cistercian Abbey at Pontigny; in 1166, he moved to the

Benedictine Abbey of Ste. Colombe, Sens, after Henry threatened to expel all Cistercians from England. Finally in 1170, a reconciliation was negotiated and Thomas returned to England in November. A final break occurred the next month when the archbishop refused to absolve those English bishops who had supported Henry unless they took an oath of obedience to the pope. Henry, already infuriated by the vast public displays of support for Thomas, greeted the new attack with an outburst of anger. While at his court in Normandy, he supposedly cried out to his knights, "Will no one here rid me of this meddlesome priest?" Four Norman knights — William de Tracy, Reginald Fitz-Urse, Hugh de Morville, and Richard le Breton — traveled to Canterbury. On the early evening of December 29, 1170, they entered Canterbury Cathedral where they found Becket in a side chapel. Drawing their swords they murdered him in one of the most famous events in the history of England. Thomas's dying words were, "Willingly I die for the name of Jesus and in defense of the Church."

The death of Becket was met with universal condemnation. Miracles were reported a short time later, and pilgrims began appearing at his shrine, turning Canterbury into one of Christendom's foremost pilgrimage sites. Pope Alexander III canonized Becket on February 21, 1173. On July 24, 1174, Henry went to Canterbury and endured the public humiliation of performing penance before Becket's tomb. Canterbury would remain a great center for pilgrims until the reign of King Henry VIII and the English Reformation. In 1538, the shrine to Thomas was destroyed. Thomas, however, has continued to attract the attention of people all over the world, and is the subject of several notable dramatic works, including Tennyson's *Becket*, T. S. Eliot's *Murder in the Cathedral*, and Anouilh's play *Becket*, the basis of the film *Becket*

starring Richard Burton and Peter O'Toole. Feast day: December 29.

Thomas More, St. ● See **More, Thomas, St.**

Thomas of Bradwardine (c. 1290-1349)
● Archbishop of Canterbury and theologian. Also called Thomas Bredwardym or Bradwardinus, he was born by his own account in Chichester, studying at Merton College, Oxford. Becoming the proctor at the university, he gained prominence as a theologian, receiving the title *Doctor Profundus* (the Profound Doctor). The great writer Geoffrey Chaucer likened him to St. Augustine and Boethius. Summoned to Rome in 1335 by the bishop of Durham, Richard Bury, he was appointed chancellor of St. Paul's Cathedral and chaplain to King Edward III (r. 1327-1377), accompanying the ruler on his campaign against the French after the outbreak of the Hundred Years' War in 1337. Thomas was elected archbishop of Canterbury in 1348; but King Edward, taking offense at the Canterbury chapter's failure to acknowledge *congé d'élire* (i.e., right of appointment), insisted that Pope Clement VI appoint John Ufford. Ufford soon died of the plague, and Thomas was duly elected with Edward's approval. Consecrated on July 19, 1349, in Avignon, Thomas returned home to England, dying from the Black Death on August 26, 1349. His writings include the *Summa Doctoris Profundi*.

Thomas of Celano (d. 1260) ● Franciscan poet and the earliest biographer of St. Francis of Assisi. Born in Celano in the area of Abruzzi, Italy, he was one of the earliest followers of St. Francis, entering the Franciscans in 1215. With Caesar of Speyer, he traveled to Germany in 1221 and helped organize the order in German lands, being named vicar of the German province. Returning to Italy sometime before 1223, he remained with Francis over the next years.

After Francis' canonization in 1228, Thomas authored a life of the saint at the urging of Pope Gregory IX, the *Vita primae*, or *First Life*. This was followed by *Vita secunda* (*Second Life*), written in 1246-1247 at the request of the general of the order. Thomas also wrote *Tractatis de Miraculis S. Francisci* (1250-1253), on the miracles of Francis, at the behest of Bl. John of Parma (1209-1284); the *Legend of St. Clare* (between 1255-1261); two sequences, *Fregit victor virtualis* and *Sanctatis nova signa*; and reputedly the *Dies irae*.

Thomas of Strassburg [Strasbourg] (d. 1357) ● General of the Augustinian order, writer, and preacher. Born possibly in Strasbourg or in Hagenau in Alsace, he entered the Augustinians in his native city, journeying to Paris in 1341 where he became a teacher at the university. Elected general in 1345, he ordered a revision of the constitution of the order and promoted learning on part of the members. Through his efforts, a *studium generale* was founded at Verona in 1351. Chief among his writings was a commentary on the *Sentences* of Peter Lombard (published in 1490).

Thomas of Villanova, St. (1486-1555) ● Archbishop of Valencia. Called Father of the Poor, he was born in Fuentellana, Spain. He entered the University of Alcalá at the age of sixteen, later receiving the chair of philosophy, logic, and arts. In 1516, however, he entered the Augustinians. Ordained in 1518, he taught theology in the Augustinian convent at Salamanca and became a brilliant preacher. After holding a number of positions in the order, Thomas was appointed archbishop of Valencia in 1544 and was consecrated in Valladolid. His time as archbishop was noted for his care of the poor and working people: he founded two colleges, one for young candidates of the priesthood and another for poor students, said Mass every day for the simple workers, rebuilt the

hospital in the city after it was burned, closed any underground prisons, and established a home for orphaned or abandoned infants. Further, Thomas spent large sums to feed the hungry who came to his ever open door and sent out his assistants to give money and aid to any who might need them. Invited to the Council of Trent, he was unable to attend owing to illness, dying on September 8, 1555. Beatified in 1618, he was canonized by Pope Alexander VII on November 1, 1658. Feast day: September 22.

Thomism ● Name given to the extensive body of doctrines that was first systematized by St. Thomas Aquinas (d. 1274). Thomism is considered the synthesis of Church teachings in the years prior to St. Thomas and seeks to harmonize faith and reason. The foundational work of Thomistic thought is, of course, the *Summa Theologiae* (or *Summa Theologica*) of St. Thomas, considered the crowning glory of Catholic theology and the summit of achievement in Scholasticism. Thomism was subsequently developed by a host of theologians and philosophers, especially from Thomas's own Dominican order. Somewhat overshadowed by developments in the Church and Europe in the late Middle Ages and Renaissance, Thomism underwent a considerable revival starting in the late 1800s, coincidental with the flowering of the so-called Neo-Scholastic movement. Pope Leo XIII, in the bull *Aeterni Patris* (1879), made the study of St. Thomas mandatory for all theology students. Already a Doctor of the Church (by Pope St. Pius V in 1567), he was made patron of Catholic universities in 1880. Virtually all the modern popes have reiterated Pope Leo's position on the fundamental importance of Thomistic thought, especially in the area of sound priestly formation and theological instruction. Pope John Paul II, a onetime professor of Scholasticism, has long applied the teachings of St. Thomas to the writings, decrees, and exhortations of his pontificate. Such is the stress placed upon Thomistic thought by the Church that the Code of Canon Law requires its study by students of philosophy and theology (c. 253-254). Among the greatest Thomistic theologians were John Capreolus (d. 1444; called the *Princeps Thomistarum*), Thomas Cajetan (d. 1534), John of St. Thomas (d. 1644), and Jacques Maritain (d. 1973).

Transcendental Thomism is a philosophical movement that originated in the twentieth century in an effort to meet the demands of contemporary thought with Thomism. Particularly influential in spurring the movement was the German philosopher Immanuel Kant (1724-1804), who had advanced a system known as transcendentalism and argued that the human mind is incapable of knowing anything determinate about reality itself. Transcendental Thomists reject much of Kant's system, particularly noting that many of his principles rely upon faulty reasoning, but they also acknowledge a certain indebtedness to him. Taking as their basis the writing of St. Thomas, these Thomists attempt to present such transcendentalism within the frameworks of Thomistic thought. They propose that the transcendence of intellectual knowledge is dependent upon our striving for God; as God is infinite, he is, through the effort to understand him, the means to go beyond the finite into the infinite. The founder of the movement was Joseph Maréchal (1878-1944), a Belgian Jesuit. He was influenced by Maurice Blondel (1861-1949). Other notable Transcendental Thomists were Karl Rahner, Bernard Lonergan, and Emeric Coreth.

Thorn, Conference of ● Meeting held in 1645 at Thorn (modern Torun, Poland) between Catholic, Lutheran, and Calvinist theologians. Convened at the urging of King Wladislaw IV, king of Poland (r. 1632-1648), the conference had as its objective the religious unity of Poland. Discussions began on August 28, 1645, and continued until November with no result. Described as the *colloquium caritativam* (conference of charity) at its beginning, it was deemed *colloquium irritativum* (conference of provocation) by the Lutherans who felt that the Catholic delegates were attempting to drive a wedge between them and the Calvinists.

Three Chapters ● Controversy occurring in the middle of the sixth century over the attempt by Emperor Justinian I (r. 527-565) to condemn three subjects: the writing and person of Theodore of Mopsuestia, some writings of Theodoret of Cyprus, and a letter of Ibas of Edessa to Maris. The writings in question came at an early stage in the conflict to be called the Three Chapters, and thus those who refused to agree to the anathematizing were declared to be attacking the chapters. The controversy had its origins in the desire of Justinian to reconcile the Monophysites to the Church. Much concerned with uniting Christianity, Justinian recognized that these heretics were of the view that the Church was guilty of Nestorianism. When the Monophysites were told that Nestorius had been condemned, they pointed to three other sources of Nestorian error. Those were Theodore of Mopsuestia, who had never been condemned; Theodoret, who had been restored to his see by the Council of Chalcedon (381); and a letter written by Ibas that they felt was in grave error but which was never questioned at Chalcedon. Justinian thus decided that to win favor from the Monophysites, he would anathematize these three subjects; at the end of 543 or early 544 the emperor issued his edict.

The bishops of the East were convinced to give their signatures, but, in the West, opposition grew quickly, as the perception that took hold that Justinian was interfering in Church matters and that the anathematization of the Three Chapters was an oblique but objectionable attack on the Council of Chalcedon and Pope St. Leo I. Pope Vigilius (r. 537-555) thus refused to give his approval to the edict. He was summoned from Rome and subjected to intense pressure from Justinian. After being shown Latin translations from the Greek of the most offending passages, Vigilius issued in 548 the *Iudicatum*, condemning the Three Chapters but clearly upholding the decisions taken by Chalcedon. A wild uproar in the West ensued, and Vigilius withdrew his approval. He agreed, however, to wait for the actions of a council. This council, the fifth general council, met at Constantinople in 553. The Three Chapters were once more condemned. The pope ultimately surrendered, confirmed the council, and was set free after a long and difficult captivity. He died a short time later, and his successor, Pelagius I (r. 556-561), continued his policy, which resulted in a schism in the West, most notably in Aquileia and Milan, that endured until 581. As for Justinian, his hopes of a reconciliation with the Monophysites never were fulfilled.

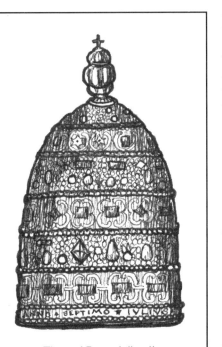

Tiara of Pope Julius II

Thundering Legion ● Name bestowed upon the XII Legion by Emperor Marcus Aurelius (r. 161-180) after Christian members of the legions saved the Roman army through their prayers. According to the tradition associated with the event, the XII Legion took part in a campaign against the Germanic people called the Quadi in 174. At one point, the army and the emperor ran out of water and thus faced imminent disaster from thirst and heat exhaustion. The Christian legionnaires, however, began praying, and a thunderstorm gathered and broke upon the relieved Roman camp. Marcus then declared that henceforth Christians should cease to be persecuted and the XII Legion should be granted the title *legio fulminata*, thundering legion. Pagan Roman historians, such as Julius Capitolinus (*Vita Marci Antonini philosophi*), Claudianus (*In VI Consulatum Honorii*), and Themistius (*Oratio XV*), each mentioned the thunderstorm, albeit under slightly different circumstances in which credit was given to Marcus's prayer to the gods or to the intervention of Jupiter. The earliest Christian reference to the event was made by Tertullian (*Apologeticum* and *Ad Scapulam*); he was quoted by Eusebius in the *Ecclesiastical History*. Later references are found in Orosius' *Historia adversus paganos* and the writings of Jerome and Gregory of Nyssa. While the occurrence of the storm is generally accepted by historians, the story of the prayers of the XII Legion is open to considerable debate, particularly as persecutions of the Christians continued after 174 and, as mentioned by Roman historian Dio Cassius, the *legio fulminata* had existed since the time of Emperor Augustus (r. 27 B.C.-A.D. 14).

Tiara ● Papal crown. Shaped like a beehive with a cross at the highest point and usually decorated with three diadems, it is also called the *triregnum* (triple rule). The tiara is a nonliturgical ornament, meaning that it is not part of the pontiff's liturgical vestments and was thus not worn in liturgical ceremonies. It was used for such ceremonies as the procession to and from Mass or canonizations. In actual liturgical functions, of course, the pope, as any bishop, wears a miter. The tiara is first mentioned in the *Vita* of Pope Constantine (r. 708-715) in the *Liber Pontificalis* where it is known as the *camelaucum*. It is discussed again in the so-called *Constitutum Constantini*, detailing the supposed Donation of Constantine, which was forged most likely in the eighth century. There the pope is given a ceremonial crown or headdress termed the *phrygium*. The early version of the tiara was thus a kind of cap shaped much like a helmet and made of white material. This was subsequently adorned with a royal circlet, but it is unclear at what point in history such a royal ornamentation became attached to the pontifical headdress. It is possible that the tiara developed in the tenth century as part of the differentiation between the tiara and the miter and as a reflection of the growing temporal and supreme spiritual power of the pontiff. In any event, the first use of the word tiara occurs in the *Vita* of Paschal II (r. 1099-1118) in the *Liber Pontificalis*.

The tiara continued to have only one circlet until the reign of Boniface VIII (r. 1294-1303). During this pontiff's reign, a second crown was added to the first, as is made abundantly clear in a number of preserved statues, two of which were ordered created by Boniface himself; for example, there is a statue of Boniface (c. fourteenth century) in the Lateran Basilica, with a double-crowned tiara, the entire work replete with his coat of arms. It is naturally possible that Boniface adapted his second crown to give sumptuous expression to his own policy of double papal authority, in spiritual and temporal affairs. While the earliest notice of a triple-crowned tiara is found in an inventory of papal treasures dated to 1315 or 1316, the first depiction of the innovation is depicted in the effigy of Pope Benedict XII (r. 1334-1342). From that time, with a few exceptions, the popes wore the triple-crowned tiara, its form remaining entirely consistent. It was an important element in the coronation of popes, the famous crown said at various times to represent the pope's position as priest, pastor, and teacher, or to embody the militant, penitent, and triumphant Church. At the time of the accession of Pope Paul VI in 1963, there were four tiaras available for his use, including one given by Napoleon to Pope Pius VII. When given one by his former flock in the archdiocese of Milan, Paul gave it away to be sold for charity, and it eventually ended up in the Basilica of the National Shrine of the Immaculate Conception in Washington, D.C. In 1978, the newly elected John Paul I chose not to use the tiara for his coronation, a precedent followed by his successor, John Paul II. Although unlikely to be used again, the tiara will be available to any future pontiff should he so choose.

Tillemont, Louis-Sébastien (1637-1698)

● In full, Louis-Sébastien le Nain de Tillemont. A French historian, he was born in Paris, studying at Port-Royal under the theologian and controversialist Pierre Nicole (d. 1695). He pursued logic but was attracted early on to history, initiating research at the age of eighteen that would be ongoing for the rest of his life. He left Port-Royal in 1656 and entered the monastery of Beauvais in 1661. Ordained at the age of thirty-nine in 1676, he returned to Port-Royal a short time later, remaining there until 1679 when the institution was dispersed. He retired to his estate in Tillemont, near Paris, living there until his death. His chief work was the remarkable *Mémoires pour servir à l'histoire ecclesiastique des six premieres siècles* (16 vols., 1693-1712), an account of the early history of the Church over its first centuries to the year 513. It relied very heavily upon patristic texts. He also wrote *Histoire des empereurs et autres princes qui ont régné pendant les six premiers siècles de l'Eglise* (6 vols., 1690-1738), a history of the emperors and princes during the same period covered in *L'histoire ecclesiastique*.

Tilly, Johann (1559-1632) ● In full, Johann Tserclaes, count of Tilly and Catholic general who commanded the imperial troops for a long period during the Thirty Years' War (1618-1648). Born in Brabant, he was educated at Cologne by the Jesuits and studied war under General Alexander Farnese. Over the next years, he took part in the numerous wars of the era, including the War of Cologne and the War of the Holy League. From 1600-1608, he fought against the Ottoman Turks and from 1610-1630, he was commander of the army of Bavaria. Receiving the support of Maximilian of Bavaria, Tilly was able to create in the Bavarian forces the core of the Catholic League and the first standing army in the Holy Roman Empire. These troops played an important part in the early phases of the Thirty Years' War, including Tilly's triumph at the Battle of White Mountain (1620), Wimpfen and Höchst (1622), and Lutter am Barenberge (1626). After Albrecht von Wallenstein, commanding general of the army of the Holy Roman Empire, was dismissed, Tilly took over his position and immediately took the offensive against the brilliant Protestant war master Gustavus Adolphus, king of Sweden. Tilly stormed Magdeburg in May 1631, although he did not order or condone the ensuing massacre. At the Battle of Breitenfeld on September 17, 1631, he was nearly destroyed by Adolphus, recovering and returning to the field in March 1632. On April 15, 1632, he once more engaged Adolphus and was once again defeated. During the battle, Tilly was mortally wounded. His death deprived the Catholic cause of one of its most competent soldiers when his skills were most desperately needed.

Timothy, St. (first century) ● Companion of St. Paul on his second missionary journey and the first bishop of Ephesus. Timothy was a native of Lystra, in Asia Minor, the son of a Gentile and a Jewish woman named Eunice. Converted by St. Paul, Timothy was circumcised and then helped Paul in his works (Acts 16:1-4). The circumcision was to appease the Jews to whom they would be preaching, for it was known that Timothy's father was a Greek. Timothy was employed by Paul on a number of missions, including to the Corinthians (1 Cor 4:17) and the Thessalonians (1 Thes 3:2-3), during a time of persecution. The representative of Paul to Ephesus (1 Tm 1:3), he is traditionally considered the first bishop, as noted by Eusebius. According to the fourth century source *Acta s. Timothei*, he was martyred on January 22, 97, by an angry mob of pagans after he opposed the celebration of the feast of Diana. Aside from being included with St. Paul in the salutations of seven epistles in the NT, Timothy was the addressee of two of the three Pastorals (1 Timothy, 2 Timothy, and Titus). Feast day: January 26, in the West; January 22, in the Greek and Syrian Churches.

Timothy, Epistles to ● Two letters from Paul. With the Epistle to Titus they constitute the so-called Pastorals, a term used since the eighteenth century. They are known as Pastorals because Paul addressed them not to the local churches or the universal Church but to individual leaders, Timothy and Titus. Further, the Pastorals are concerned with Church doctrine and its application to life, thereby preserving for future generations considerable detail on the organization and laws of the still formative Church. The elder to whom the two epistles were written was Timothy, the leader of the Christian community in Macedonia. According to Acts (16:1) he was the son of a Greek and a Jewish woman who had been converts. He was chosen by the Apostle to share in his missionary endeavors and was mentioned in several letters from Paul — 1 and 2 Thessalonians, Colossians, Philippians, and 2 Corinthians.

The epistles were accepted as genuinely Pauline from the time of St. Irenaeus in the second century. From the mid-1800s, however, some biblical scholars have questioned whether Paul was indeed the author. Their doubts stem from the language and style used — quite different from the undisputed letters — and the fact that the events described do not conform to the events in Paul's life that are known with certainty. Against this argument, other scholars have pointed out that the Pauline nature of the works are too obvious to be so easily dismissed. They propose, in some cases, that a later compiler gathered together Pauline fragments and put them in coherent form. Questions and discussions continue, with debate present among those who accept composition from fragments, the focus of consideration being on which fragments are genuinely Pauline. If Paul actually wrote the letters, they may be dated to the early 60s; if a later editor wrote or organized them, they were probably written around 90, and the persecution mentioned would refer to that launched under Emperor Domitian.

The First Epistle is much concerned with false teachers, Church organization, and important points of discipline. Paul specifically discusses: false teachers who "promote speculations rather than divine training that is in the faith" (1:4); the proper form of public worship (2:1-7); the role of women (2:8-15); the conduct and selection of bishops and deacons (3:8-16); an affirmation of the goodness of God (4:1-6); the duties of the pastor and Church order (5:1-6:2); exhortations and discussions of other matters (6:3-19); and a conclusion (6:20-21). It was written apparently while Paul was visiting Macedonia on his way to Nicopolis where he was planning to stay for the winter.

The Second Epistle was written most likely while Paul was in prison again in Rome; it was composed perhaps a short time before the Apostle's death (if Paul is indeed the author). The letter places much stress upon the important qualities necessary for a good pastor. Chief among these is endurance, and Paul calls upon him to remember the value of suffering (2:3-6). A renewal of the warning against false teachers is made, true and authentic teaching being known when compared to "godless chatter" (2:16). The preacher must be purified so that "he will be a vessel for noble use, consecrated and useful to the master of the house, ready for any good work" (2:21). Paul then offers himself as an example of steadfastness and one who had been rescued by Christ (3:1-13). He concludes with a poignant farewell (4:6-8).

Timothy Aelurus (d. 477) ● Patriarch of Alexandria and an outspoken Monophysite. He was chosen patriarch after a mob lynched his predecessor. Because of his views, however, the majority of the bishops in the East refused to accept him, leading to Timothy's banishment by Emperor Leo I in 460. While in exile, he wrote extensively in support of Monophysite teachings. Finally recalled by Emperor Basiliscus in 475, he returned to Alexandria but died soon after. His death prevented a second banishment, this time by Emperor Zeno in 477. The name Aelurus (weasel) was bestowed upon him by enemies because of his tiny stature. He is considered a saint in the Coptic Church. Feast day: July 31.

Titus, Epistle to ● Letter from Paul to Titus, a disciple in Crete, and one of the Pastorals (for details, see under **Timothy, Epistles to**). Referred to by Paul as "my true child in a common faith" (1:4), Titus was not mentioned in the Acts of the Apostles but was first met in Galatians (2:1) when Paul writes of going to Jerusalem with Barnabas, taking Titus with him. He was then sent to Corinth (2 Cor 8:6, 16-19, 23), where he was able to restore good relations between the Christian community and its founder Paul. As is clear from the epistle, Titus was left on Crete with the task of organizing the Church on the island. As noted in 2 Timothy (4:10), he was later dispatched to Dalmatia, a region on the Adriatic Sea. Eusebius of Caesarea, in his *Ecclesiastical History*, called Titus the first bishop of Crete. He was buried in Cortyna (Gortyna), Crete, and his head was translated to Venice after the invasion of the isle by the Saracens in 832. It has since been preserved in St. Mark's, Venice. Feast day: January 26.

Paul's Epistle to Titus is concerned with three points: the problem of false teachers, how different groups in the community should live together, and broad ethical instructions. The first part (1:10-16), gives a glimpse of Paul's view of the circumcision party — "they must be silenced, since they are upsetting whole families by teaching for base gain what they have no right to teach" (1:11). In the second part, he talks about older men, older women, younger men, and slaves, writing that "the grace of God has appeared for the salvation of all men, training us to renounce irreligion and worldly passions, and to live sober, upright, and godly lives in the world. . ." (2:11-12). The third part, his ethical system, is a superb summary of the Christian life, especially the passage from 3:4-8.

Toledo, Councils of ● Ecclesiastical councils held in Toledo from the fifth to the sixteenth centuries. There were around thirty *concilia Toletana*, the first being dated to c. 396 and 400. This was aimed at opposing the heresy of Priscillianism. The most famous council was in 589 (the third council) in which King Reccared of the Visigoths in Spain formally abjured Arianism and made a profession of faith according to the Council of Nicaea. Other notable councils were in 650, condemning the Monothelites; 675, formulating disciplinary canons; 1324,

publishing papal constitutions; 1339, commanding a census of all parishes; 1379, establishing that the province would adopt a position of neutrality in the Great Schism; and 1582-1583, promulgating laws for the propagation of the faith. Of special note was the provincial council of 1565-1566, issuing numerous ecclesiastical regulations; its decrees contained many points of Church law that were later adopted into canon law.

Toledo, Francisco de (1532-1596) ● Spanish theologian and philosopher. A native of Córdoba, he studied at Valencia and Salamanca, claiming the great theologian Dominic Soto as an instructor at Salamanca. After ordination, he joined the Society of Jesus in June 1558. Professed at Rome in 1564, he held a variety of posts, including prefect of studies at the Roman College, before being appointed a theologian of the Sacred Penitentiary and preacher to the pope and the Curia, a post he held for twenty-four years. Named a cardinal by Pope Clement VIII in 1593, he retired to a Jesuit house in Rome where he died on September 14, 1596. His extensive writings covered philosophy, theology, and exegesis. Among these were: an introduction to Aristotle, *Introductio in dialecticam Aristotelis* (1561); *De anima* (1574, *On the Soul*); *In Summam theologiae S. Thomae Aquinatis enarratio* (4 vols., published in 1869), an analysis of the theology of Thomas Aquinas; and commentaries on John the Evangelist and the Epistle of St. Paul to the Romans.

Tolentino, Treaty of ● Peace treaty signed by Napoleon Bonaparte and Pope Pius VI on February 19, 1797. The agreement was forced upon Pius by Napoleon, who had invaded the Papal States after the pontiff had remained steadfast in his refusal to withdraw his condemnation of the French Revolution and the Civil Constitution of the Clergy (1790). Aside from enduring the humiliation of being forced to surrender various art treasures and manuscripts, Pius had to pay an indemnity and give up extensive territories belonging to the Papal States. Tolentino, however, was only a foreshadowing of the even harsher steps by the French leading to the entry into Rome on February 15, 1798, of General Louis Berthier and his declaration of a republic and deposition of Pius as the temporal head of state. Pius would die on August 27, 1799, at Valence a prisoner of the French.

Toleration ● See **Toleration Act**, following entry; see also **Relief Acts, Catholic**.

Toleration Act ● Document issued in 1689 by King William and Queen Mary of England, it granted religious toleration to the so-called Nonconformist (or dissenting) Protestants. It also allowed Nonconformists to have their own places of worship and their own preachers, so long as they conformed to the Act of Supremacy and the Oath of Allegiance, although restrictions against Nonconformists continued until 1828. Intended to bring all Protestants in England against the deposed King James II, the Toleration Act was an important step in concretizing the effects of the Glorious Revolution (1688-1689), which had removed James. Significantly, the act in no way applied to Catholics (and Unitarians or Jews), the harsh anti-Catholic laws remaining in full force.

Tome of Damasus ● Set of twenty-four canons approved at a synod in Rome (probably in 382). It derived its name from Pope Damasus I (r. 366-384), who sent it to Paulinus, bishop of Antioch, at the time a central figure in the Melitian Schism. All but one of the canons were concerned with doctrinal orthodoxy, condemning the various heresies that were plaguing the Church in the fourth century. The ninth canon dealt with the illegality of episcopal translations

and was aimed specifically at Melitius, who had been translated from the see of Sebaste and had caused a schism in Antioch. (See **Melitian Schism** for other details.) It is recognized by scholars that St. Ambrose had a hand in the formulation of the Tome.

Tome of Leo ● Important letter (*Epistola*, XXVIII) composed by Pope St. Leo I (r. 440-461), it was sent on June 13, 449, to Flavian, patriarch of Constantinople. While directed specifically against the heresy of Eutyches, the *Tome* established the significant Christological doctrine concerning Christ's two natures in one person. Leo made clear that Christ is one Person, but in him, permanently united, unconfused, and distinct, are two natures, the divine and the human. While each has its own faculties, they are performed entirely within the unity of the Person of Christ. When Emperor Theodosius II (r. 408-450) convened the Council of Ephesus in August 449, Leo expected that the *Tome* would be read by his legates and given approval by the participants. The council failed to do this, restoring instead the monk Eutyches, thereby earning the name Latrocinium, or Robber Council of Ephesus, from the displeased pope. At the Council of Chalcedon (451), however, the orthodox party triumphed. The *Tome* was given full recognition and was declared the Church's formal statement on the Incarnation, as the delegates at Chalcedon proclaimed that "the voice of Peter had spoken through Leo."

Tommasi, Giuseppe (1649-1713) ● Italian cardinal and scholar. The son of the duke of Palma, Tommasi was drawn to the religious life at a young age, choosing in 1664 to surrender his claims as heir to his younger brother so that he might enter the Theatine order. Professed in 1666, he studied at Messina, Rome, and Palermo, receiving holy orders in 1673. Virtually all of his remaining years were devoted to liturgical and biblical studies. He authored a large number of scholarly works, including various important editions of missals, such as the *Missale Gothicum* (or Gallican Sacramentary) and the *Missale Francorum* (an incomplete sacramentary). Many of his writings were published under the pseudonym of J. M. Carus. He was made a cardinal in 1712. Known for his personal sanctity and long practice of austerity, he was beatified in 1803 by Pope Pius VII. Feast day: March 24.

Torquemada, Juan de (1388-1468) ●

Spanish Dominican theologian and cardinal. Known also as Turrecremata, he entered the Dominican order in 1403 and, after years of studies, took part in the Council of Constance in 1417. In 1431, he was appointed master of the sacred palace by Pope Eugenius IV. Two years later, he was named papal theologian for the Council of Basel (1431-1449), playing a useful role in negotiating the reunion of the Latin Church with the Bohemian Hussites and then the Eastern Church. For his work, Torquemada was elevated to the cardinalate in 1439. He was the author of several important works: *Summa de Ecclesiae* (published in 1469), a treatise that defended the spiritual authority and infallibility of the pope, although Torquemada expressed the position that there were limitations of the pontiff's temporal power; and *Commentarii in Decretum Gratiani* (published in 1519), a commentary on canon law. He should not be confused with his fifteenth-century contemporary and nephew Tomás de Torquemada (see following entry).

Torquemada, Tomás de (1420-1498) ●

First grand inquisitor of Spain and a powerful confessor to Ferdinand and Isabella. Born in Valladolid, of Jewish descent, he was the nephew of Juan de Torquemada (see preceding entry). He entered the Dominicans at an early age at Valladolid and was later named prior of the monastery of Santa Cruz in Segovia.

Subsequently appointed by the then Infante Isabella of Castile, he won her complete confidence and wielded considerable influence at her court from 1474, when she came to the throne of Castile. He refused all possible preferments, choosing to remain a simple friar. On February 11, 1482, however, he was given the post of assistant inquisitor. The next year, Pope Sixtus IV (r. 1471-1484) gave him the office of grand inquisitor of Castile and León; this jurisdiction was extended later in the year for Aragon, Catalonia, Majorca, and Valencia.

The most formidable person in the inquisitional court, Torquemada moved quickly to centralize and then expand the Inquisition in Spain. Tribunals were established in Córdoba, Seville, Saragossa, and elsewhere, focusing on heresy, witchcraft, and the recent converts to Christianity from among the Moors and Jews who were suspected of being insincere. To assist his agents, Torquemada authored twenty-eight articles on ferreting out heretics, sinners, and apostates. On November 29, 1484, he convened a general assembly of inquisitors where the articles were presented; additional statutes were added in 1485, 1488, and 1498. Frustrated by the prominence and wealth of the Jews in the now united Spain, Torquemada convinced Ferdinand and Isabella to expel all Jews who would not accept the faith.

Infamous for his cruelty, fanaticism, and the excesses of his administration, Torquemada has long been the subject of hostile treatment by chroniclers and historians. He adapted, as did most institutions during the period, violent and brutal means to extract confessions, permitting torture and intimidation. The number of victims has been, at times, severely exaggerated and probably numbered some two thousand heretics tortured and burned. (See also **Inquisition**.)

Torres, Francesco (1509-1584) ● Also known as Turrianus. A controversialist and scholar, he was a nephew of the bishop of the Canary Islands. He studied at Salamanca and then at Rome where he lived with several cardinals. In 1562, he was sent as a papal theologian to the Council of Trent by Pope Pius IV, and the following year he had published the Apostolic Constitutions, a collection of fourth-century ecclesiastical laws, in their first edition. On January 8, 1567, Torres became a Jesuit, subsequently serving as a professor at the Roman College. During this period, he participated in the revision of the Sistine Vulgate, earning the nickname from his contemporaries of *helluo librorum* (glutton of libraries) for the manner in which he devoured libraries searching for materials. While accused by critics of lacking judgment, he wrote over seventy books, including numerous harsh polemics against Protestants and translations of the Greek Fathers, especially from manuscripts found in libraries or collections. He upheld the authenticity of the Apostolic Canons and the Pseudo-Isidoran decretals (both false) and was a defender of the doctrines of the Immaculate Conception, the authority of the pope over a general council, and the divinely appointed nature of episcopal authority.

Tournon, Charles-Thomas Maillard de (1668-1710) ● Cardinal and papal representative to India and China. Born in Turin to an aristocratic Savoyard family, he studied canon and civil law before going to Rome where, in December 1701, he was appointed by Pope Clement XI to serve as papal legate to India and China. The pope was desirous of having his legate provide him with comprehensive reports on the state of missionary activities in those lands, to coordinate the various missions and to ensure that the papal ban that had been issued concerning the so-called Chinese rites was being followed. Consecrated as a bishop on December 27, 1701, and given the title patriarch of Antioch, Tournon arrived in India in November 1703. One of his most notable acts was to declare that missionaries were forbidden to perform the Malabar rites. Reaching Beijing in December 1705, he was greeted with courtesy by the Chinese emperor but soon earned the imperial court's displeasure by informing the emperor that he had come with the intention of abolishing the Chinese rites. Tournon decreed on January 25, 1707, that missionaries would be excommunicated if they performed the rites. The emperor then imprisoned Tournon at Macao and dispatched Jesuit missionaries to Rome to protest the decree before the pope. Tournon died while in custody on June 8, 1710, after being told that he had been raised to the rank of cardinal.

Tours, Battle of ● More properly, the Battle of Poitiers, it was a famous military engagement fought in 732 between Charles Martel's Franks and a Moorish force under the command of the governor of Córdoba that had invaded southern France. The actual site of the battle is unknown, and scholars have suggested that there were probably several heavy skirmishes after which the Moors withdrew to Spain, never to return. By custom, the Battle of Tours was one of Christianity's greatest victories, sparing Europe from invasion by Islam. Many scholars have noted that it was somewhat overblown and that the Islamic advance was cut short more by internal difficulties among the Muslims, most notably the Berbers in North Africa. Nevertheless, the battle illustrated the prestige and power of Charles Martel, allowing him to claim the title Savior of Christendom. His son, Pepin the Short, became the first Carolingian king of the Franks.

Trappists ● See **Cistercian Order**.

Traversari, Ambrogio (1386-1439) ● Also
Ambrose of Camaldoli, he was an Italian
theologian and humanist. Born near
Florence, he entered the Camaldolese order
in 1400 at the monastery of Sta. Maria degli
Angioli in Florence; in 1431, he was named
general of the order. A gifted scholar and
theologian, he was fluent in both Greek and
Latin, serving as a trusted representative of
Pope Eugenius IV to the Council of Basel
(1431-1439) where he promoted the pope's
position of primacy. At the Council of
Ferrara-Florence (1438-1445) he was an
important figure in negotiating the brief
reunion of the Eastern and Western
Churches, writing the decree of the
union in July 1439. He died soon after, on
October 21, 1439, a much revered
personality in the Church. Traversari was
responsible for the translation of many of the
writings of the Greek Fathers into Latin,
including St. John Chrysostom, St. Basil,
and Pseudo-Dionysius the Areopagite. He
also wrote a treatise on the Eucharist and a
number of saints' lives. While never formally
canonized, he is honored by the Church on
November 20.

Trent, Council of ● Nineteenth
ecumenical council, held between 1545 and
1563. The Council of Trent was one of the
most important general councils in the
history of the Church. The council had as its
aims the refutation of the errors of the
Protestant Reformers (Martin Luther,
Huldrych Zwingli, and John Calvin), the
clarification of Catholic teaching in the wake
of the spread of Protestant teaching, and the
advancing of authentic and genuinely needed
reform for the entire Church. While Pope
Clement VII (r. 1523-1534) had considered
summoning a general council to deal with the
crises of the moment, the pontiff had
ultimately decided against it in order to
prevent any possible outbreak of conciliarism

and owing to the nationalist tendencies in
Germany and the chronic warfare between
Francis I of France and Emperor Charles V.
The decision to convene a general council
came under Pope Paul III (r. 1534-1549), part
of his ambitious program to reform the
Church. He declared in June 1536 that it
should be held in Mantua, but Duke Federigo
of Mantua refused to allow his city to be the
site and, citing the war between Francis and
Charles, he placed so many restrictions and
demands on the pope that Paul moved the
site in October 1537 to Vicenza. Further
obstacles were thrown before the pope by the
Protestant princes who refused to send
delegates. Paul thus adjourned the council
on May 22, 1539. Exactly three years later,
he summoned the council at Trent. This was
now unacceptable to Francis, as the town
was in the empire (now Italy). Only with the
Peace of Crepy of 1544, ending the conflict
between Francis and Charles, did the
monarch agree (in a secret clause) to the
Council of Trent.

Paul issued the bull *Laetare Jerusalem*
(1544), formally summoning the council. It
opened on December 13, 1545. While not
ended until 1563, the council was to be
plagued by constant delays and
interruptions, a testament to the unsettled
political state of affairs in Europe. The work
was not continuous but took place in three
periods: 1545-1547, 1551-1552, and
1562-1563. In all, there would be twenty-five
sessions in the three respective periods:
Sessions I-VIII, Sessions IX-XIV, and
Sessions XV-XXV.

The first session was attended by thirty
Council Fathers, with three papal legates,
Reginald Pole, Marcello Cervini, and Giovanni
del Monte. It established the system by which
the numerous doctrinal decrees would be
promulgated in the form of treatises
comprised of chapters and followed by a set
of canons. Attached to the chapters, the
canons were aimed specifically at refuting
and condemning the errors of the Protestant

Reformers. The first period wound down with the decision of some of the members to move to Bologna, ostensibly because of an outbreak of spotted fever in Trent but also to cut short any efforts by Emperor Charles to influence the proceedings. They were opposed by both Paul III and a minority of Spanish and other imperial cardinals. Paul struggled to bring the cardinals back to Trent, finally winning a compromise that no decrees should be issued by them. Active deliberations ended in February 1548. In November 1549, Paul suspended the council, dying on November 10, 1549.

The second period, 1551-1552, was begun by Pope Julius III (r. 1550-1555) on November 14, 1550. Officially opened on May 1, 1551, it was under the presidency of Sebastiano Pighino and Luigi Lippomani and with the legate Marcello Crescenzio. It was handicapped by the absence of French bishops who acquiesced to the wishes of King Henry II of France. Present at the council were representatives of the Protestant princes who negotiated unsuccessfully with the Council Fathers and departed in 1552 when fighting erupted afresh in Germany between Protestant princes and Emperor Charles V. Pope Julius suspended the proceedings on April 28, 1552.

Eight years would pass before the council could reconvene at the behest of Pope Pius IV (r. 1559-1565). The impetus for his call in November 1560 for the council to reconvene its work was the sudden rise of Calvinism in France. Both the new emperor, Ferdinand I, and King Charles IX of France opposed the pope's decision to continue the council, preferring to have him open a new one, since their Protestant leaders adamantly refused to acknowledge the first two periods of the council at Trent. The council — which opened on January 18, 1562, under the presence of the papal legates Stanislaus Hosius, Girolamo Seripando, Giacomo Simonetta, and Ercole Gonzaga — was clear in its recognition that the reconciliation with the Protestants was impossible. It was also much influenced by the Jesuits, whose theologians enjoyed a prominent place in the deliberations.

The council was closed solemnly on December 4, 1563, after the twenty-fifth session. The decrees were signed by the Council Fathers, including six cardinals, three patriarchs, twenty-five archbishops, and one hundred sixty-nine bishops. These were given confirmation by Pope Pius IV on January 26, 1564, in the bull *Benedictus Deus*. The pope also published his famous creed, the *Professio Fidei Tridentina* (the Profession of the Tridentine Faith).

Of the twenty-five sessions of Trent, seventeen were concerned specifically with doctrine and reform. Among the important decrees promulgated by the council were: the two primary sources for revelation are the Scriptures and Tradition; justification is achieved by man's free cooperation with God's grace through faith, hope, charity, and good works; grace is granted to all and is not lost by mortal sin, although it is forced out by infidelity; there are seven sacraments, which produce their effect independent of faith and the virtue of the minister; the Eucharist is a true sacrament and Christ is present whole and entire under both species, bread and wine, and in each part of both species; the bread and wine are changed entirely into the substance of Christ's body and blood, with only the appearance of bread and wine remaining; and Mass is a true sacrifice. Among the disciplinary decrees were: the pope has the choice of bishops and cardinals; bishops, cardinals, archbishops, and patriarchs should reside in their dioceses; bishops are to visit parishes and take an interest in the welfare of all the souls of the faithful; pastors should be appointed only after consideration of qualifications and with the approval of the bishop; seminaries should be established in every diocese or region; secret marriages are prohibited; the Index of Forbidden Books should be revised;

and members of religious orders should reside in their houses and follow their rules and vows.

The Council of Trent had a major impact upon the Church. It reaffirmed the teachings of the Catholic faith, bolstering and reviving Catholicism after serious crises and doubts had spread among the faithful as a result of the Reformation and its destructive wars. The Church also underwent a marked reform and renewal through discipline, the Roman Catechism of 1566, and the reformed missal of 1570. While the council failed in reconciling the Protestants, it left the Church significantly stronger in the years and even centuries to come when dealing with Protestantism and the social, political, and intellectual movements that would emerge across Europe. (See also **Reformation, Catholic [and Protestant]**.)

Trinitarians ● Popular name for the Order of the Most Holy Trinity for the Redemption of Captives, or O.SS.T., the abbreviation of its Latin name. This religious order was founded in 1198 by St. John of Matha (d. 1213) and St. Felix of Valois (d. 1212) at Cerfroid, France. Its purpose was principally to ransom Christian slaves from Muslim captors in Africa, Moorish Spain, and the Near East. Almost two thirds of the order's revenues went toward this endeavor, and it has been estimated by scholars that perhaps nearly one hundred fifty thousand captives were freed. The members, also called Mathurins after the founder, adhered to an austere form of the Augustinian Rule. After its foundation, the order spread swiftly and owned eight hundred houses by the fifteenth century. Decline set in during the sixteenth century, leading to attempted reforms, most notably the one launched in 1596-1597 by Jean Bautista of the Immaculate Conception known as the Discalced (Barefooted) Trinitarians. The Discalced Trinitarians separated from the order in later years and were joined in 1612 by the Discalced Sisters.

The Trinitarians are today dedicated to educational work and nursing, numbering some six hundred seventy members worldwide.

Tritheism ● Heresy concerning the Trinity. It denies that the Three Persons are united in substance. There are several heretical groups that adopted tritheistic opinions, the first being a branch of Monophysites in the sixth century who were probably organized by one John Ascunages of Antioch. Their principal spokesman was the noted Aristotelian scholar John Philoponus, who speculated that there were three separate substances (i.e., deities) in the Blessed Trinity. A second tritheistic tendency emerged in the Middle Ages as a result of the nominalism of Roscellinus (d. 1125). Both he and Gilbert de la Porrée (d. 1154) were charged with tritheistic teachings. Roscellinus was condemned at the Council of Soissons (1092) and refuted by St. Anselm, while Gilbert was condemned by the Council of Reims (1148). In the late 1600s, the writer Pierre Faydit (d. 1709) was accused of tritheism in his *Eclaircissements sur la doctrine et l'histoire ecclésiastique des deux premiers siècles* (1696), an analysis of the doctrine and history of the early Church; critics noted that Faydit claimed that the earliest of the Church Fathers were tritheists.

Trithemius, Johannes (1462-1516) ● Benedictine abbot and scholar. Born in Trittenheim on the Moselle (from which his name was derived), he was cruelly treated by his stepfather and did not learn to read or write until he was fifteen. As his life at home did not improve, however, he ran away, finally reaching Würzburg. There he studied under the humanist Jacob Wimpheling until 1482 when, while visiting the monastery of Sponheim, he was convinced to join the Benedictines, taking his first vows at the community in December of 1482. While the youngest member of the monastery and not yet ordained, Trithemius was elected abbot the following year. After improving the discipline among the monks and making conditions materially better in the monastery, the abbot of Sponheim promoted scientific study. Under his energetic leadership, the monastery acquired a large number of manuscripts and books that made it one of the foremost centers of learning in Christendom. After twenty-three years, Trithemius resigned when a group of dissenting monks complained that his demands on discipline were excessive. Declining extensive honors from Emperor Maximilian, Trithemius became abbot of the Scottish monastery of St. Jacob, Würzburg. He authored more than eighty books on history, the religious life, and natural science.

Truce of God ● See under **Peace of God**.

True Cross ● Famous relic traditionally held to be the wood of the Cross on which Christ was crucified. According to Christian lore, it was found around 326 by St. Helena (d. 330), mother of Emperor Constantine the Great, during a pilgrimage to Jerusalem. Although he made no mention of the finding of the True Cross, St. Cyril of Jerusalem (d. 386) first discussed its veneration in his catechetical sermons (348-350). A generally disputed letter was supposedly sent by Cyril to Emperor Constantius II in 351, detailing the finding of the Cross sometime during the reign of Constantine (306-337). Although scholars consider the letter to be of highly questionable authenticity, it does indicate that the story of the True Cross was circulating by the mid-fourth century.

Subsequent accounts of the relics added details to its history and mystical attributes. Revered as a truly important relic, the Cross was the stated object of at least two military campaigns, that of Byzantine Emperor Heraclius (622-628) and the Fourth Crusade (1204). John Calvin attacked the relics by declaring that all of the supposed remnants of the Cross could be used to fill a very large ship, a remark refuted by Catholic theologians with the argument that its special value — by virtue of the blood of Christ — allowed it to be divided forever without being in any way reduced. The Feast of the Finding of the True Cross was celebrated by the Church until 1960.

Trullo, Council of ● Synod convened by the Eastern bishops under the auspices of Emperor Justinian II. Its aim was to finish the work of the Second and Third Councils of Constantinople (the fifth and sixth general councils) of 553 and 680-681 respectively. Called the Quinisext (or the Fifth-Sixth) Council, the council had as its purpose the issuing of needed disciplinary canons, as the two previous assemblies had been concerned only with matters of dogma. Its name was derived from the place where the delegates gathered, the dome chamber (*trullus*) in the palace of the emperor in Constantinople. The more than one hundred canons promulgated by the council were generally accepted by the Eastern Church and covered such topics as clerical marriage and proper ecclesiastical dress. Rejected by Pope St. Sergius I (r. 687-701) on the basis that acceptance would have meant recognition that the see of Constantinople was on an equal footing with that of Rome, the canons pointed to the widening gap between the Churches of Eastern and Western Christendom. Approval was finally given with reservations and provisions by Pope John VIII (r. 872-882) in 878, accepting only those canons that were "not opposed to other canons of the pontiffs or, of course, to proper morals." In his codification of the Eastern canon law on marriage, Pope Pius XII (r. 1939-1958) used the canons of the Trullo Council. (See also **Constantinople, Councils of**.)

Truth Society, Catholic ● Society formally established on November 5, 1884, in England to promote the truths about the

Catholic Church and its teachings among Protestant faiths. Its aims have not changed fundamentally from its inception: to make available to Catholics small, inexpensive devotional publications; to assist uneducated Catholics in better understanding their own religion; to spread true information on Catholicism among Protestants; and to contribute to the publication of Catholic literature. The idea of the organization originated with then Rev. Herbert Vaughan (1832-1903) who, while rector of St. Joseph's Missionary College, began publishing penny booklets and leaflets on the faith for the average reader. When he became bishop of Salford in 1872, however, the efforts of the society virtually ceased; but before long, a group of clergy and laypeople launched their own effort, receiving much encouragement from Vaughan, who suggested that they take over the Catholic Truth Society that had long lain dormant. Later appointed archbishop of Westminster (1892) and cardinal (1893), Vaughan remained president of the society until his death, by which time branches had been founded in Ireland (1899) and the United States (1900). In the United States the society is known as the International Catholic Truth Society.

Tunstall, Cuthbert (1474-1559) ● Bishop of London and Durham. Born in Hackforth in Yorkshire, England, he studied at Oxford and Cambridge before graduating from Padua University. A highly respected scholar, he was appointed chancellor to the archbishop of Warsham in 1511, becoming a canon in 1514, and archdeacon of Chester in 1515. A short time later, he was sent as an ambassador to Brussels, subsequently developing an intimate friendship with both St. Thomas More (d. 1535) and Desiderius Erasmus (d. 1536). To no one's surprise, in 1522 he was appointed bishop of London and in 1523 the keeper of the privy seal to King Henry VIII. Continuing to be used in various ambassadorial missions, Tunstall traveled

extensively and became convinced of the very real danger posed to the Church by Luther and the Reformers. In the controversy over Henry's desire to divorce his wife Catherine of Aragon, Tunstall served as one of the advisers, counseling against the appeal to the pope. He was translated to the see of Durham in 1529-1530. In the years that followed, Tunstall proved frequently vacillating in the face of Henry's increasingly harsh measures against the Church. Alarmed at the course of reform, he finally stood firm against the king and was incarcerated in his house in London. Moved to the Tower of London at the end of 1551, he was removed from his see by a royal commission the next year. Upon the accession of Mary Tudor in 1553, he was released and reinstalled as bishop of Durham, the see having been restored after its suppression by Henry. Not active during Mary's reign because of his age, Tunstall remained firm in his faith after Mary's death and the accession of Elizabeth I in 1558. Refusing to take the oath under the Act of Supremacy, the octogenarian bishop was summoned to London and removed from his see on September 28, 1559. Confined to Lambeth Palace, he died there on November 18, 1559, one of the eleven confessor-bishops to die in prison or incarceration. Aside from letters and sermons, he authored a number of treatises, the most notable being *De veritate Corporis et Sanguinis Domini in Eucharistia*, a defense of the doctrines of the Eucharist, written during his confinement in 1551 and published at Paris in 1554.

Turin, Shroud of ● Also called the Holy Shroud (Italian: *Santa Sindone*), it is a linen cloth that has been said to depict the body of the crucified Christ and to have been used as a burial garment when he was laid in the tomb. The shroud measures 14 feet 3 inches in length and 3 feet 7 inches in width. Upon the linen is imprinted the image of a man, with long hair and a beard, who bears the clear marks of crucifixion; all of the wounds described in the NT account of Jesus' passion are present in the hazy brown pigmenting, including the stigmata, the marks from the thorns on the head, bruises on the shoulders, and severe cuts or lacerations on the back where the flogging would have occurred.

The shroud was first seen in France in 1354 when it was reportedly in the possession of the knight Geoffroi de Charnay. At the time of its actual presentation, the cloth was denounced by theologians and Church officials as being a hoax because there is no mention in the detailed accounts of the NT or in any other writings concerning the presence of an image on the cloth. Antipope Clement VII (r. 1378-1394) proclaimed that it could be used as an object of veneration so long as it was considered only a representation of the original shroud. Nevertheless, its authenticity was so widely accepted that it became a prized possession of the House of Savoy when its members were given the Shroud of Turin by Marguerite de Charnay, granddaughter of Geoffroi, in 1453. Kept first at Chambéry, it was damaged by a fire in 1532 and subsequently moved to Turin where it has remained ever since.

Efforts to determine the date and genuineness of the shroud have been made since the late 1800s, propelled by the fascinating results of the first photographs taken in 1898 in which the negative revealed a positive image and the discovery in 1899 of a document purportedly written around 1389, in which the bishop of Troyes proclaimed it a fraud after an artist confessed to painting it. The issue, however, was complicated by the findings in the 1970s of scientists that there is no conclusive evidence to indicate that the image was painted or scorched by natural means upon the cloth. In 1988, meanwhile, radiocarbon dating of the cloth proved that it dates to between 1260 and 1390, a period consistent with the claims made in the document found in 1899. No specific analysis has been done of the portion imprinted with the image of Christ. The Church, which has never formally declared the Shroud of Turin to be genuine, accepted the findings; its position has been that it is still acceptable as an object of veneration.

Turkey ● Modern-day republic occupying Asia Minor and part of the Balkans. The territory occupied by Turkey was long held by the Roman and Byzantine Empires and then by various Islamic states, culminating with the Ottoman Empire. The conversion of much of Asia Minor was undertaken in the first century during apostolic times. The work of St. Paul and others is recorded in much of the NT — the Acts of the Apostles, Letters by Paul, and the Book of Revelation. A strong region for the Church, it boasted such cities as Ephesus, Pergamum, Smyrna, and Miletus, and came to be a center for heightened ecclesiastical development. Throughout the fourth century, the dioceses of Asia Minor played a major role in the heresies that confronted the Church, chiefly Arianism, and a number of very important councils were convened in cities throughout Asia Minor (Nicaea, Constantinople, Chalcedon, and Ephesus). With the division of the Roman Empire into Eastern and Western spheres, the region became an important part of the East and was especially vital in supplying soldiers for the empire. Save for a brief period (1204-1261) under the Latin Empire of Constantinople, which had overthrown the Byzantine Empire, Asia Minor's dioceses acknowledged the patriarch of Constantinople and sided with the Byzantines against the Western Church.

Owing to its position relative to the Middle East, Asia Minor was a constant battlefield. It was overrun in the eleventh and twelfth centuries by the Seljuk Turks, contributing to the call of Emperor Alexius I Comnenus to the West for a crusade. More fighting would follow over the next centuries, culminating with the seizure of the entire area by the Ottoman Turks, a mere prelude to their drive to the very walls of Constantinople in the fifteenth century. Constantinople fell on May 29, 1453, and the onetime Byzantine Empire passed to the Turks, remaining an Ottoman possession until 1920-1923, when the republic of Turkey was declared. Throughout the long history of the Ottoman Empire,

Sultan Mehmet II the Conqueror

the empire did not long survive World War I. The last sultan was overthrown in 1922 by Ataturk. In 1920, interestingly, the Turks erected a statue in honor of Pope Benedict XV (r. 1914-1922) for his efforts at peace during the war; it described him as "the benefactor of all people, irrespective of nationality or religion." Today, Turkey is almost entirely Muslim with an Orthodox population. There are around fifteen thousand Catholics.

there were several efforts by Christendom to defeat it. Several crusades ended in disastrous defeats for Christian armies, and Turkish power in the Balkans and Mediterranean seemed unstoppable in the 1500s. Under the guidance and inspiration of the papacy, a Turkish fleet was routed at the Battle of Lepanto (1571), a mortal blow to Turkish ambitions. Popes continued to promote campaigns against the Turks — such as Clement IX (1667-1669), Clement X (1670-1676), and Innocent XI (1667-1689), who used his enormous diplomatic skill to convince John Sobieski, king of Poland, to rescue Vienna from a Turkish siege in 1683, a triumph that signaled the irretrievable decline of the Ottoman Empire.

Christians were frequently persecuted in the later years of the empire, with the most infamous pogrom undertaken against the Armenians, a genocide that slaughtered millions. Long called the Sick Man of Europe,

Typos ● Decree issued in 847 or 848 by Byzantine Emperor Constans II (r. 642-668). It superseded the decree *Ecthesis* that had been promulgated by Emperor Heraclius (r. 610-641) in 638. While the *Ecthesis* had forbidden the use of the term energies, either one or two, in the Person of Christ — demanding that his two natures were united by one will — the *Typos* placed a ban on all discussions concerning the number of wills and operations in Christ, insisting that the Church should teach only what had been defined by the five general (or ecumenical) councils. Intended to resolve the often bitter theological struggle over the nature of Christ between the Orthodox Church and the Monophysites, the *Typos* was quickly opposed by the papacy, most notably Pope St. Martin I (r. 649-655), who convened a synod in October 649 at the Lateran in Rome condemning Monothelitism and the *Typos* while affirming the belief in the two wills of Christ. Constans was assassinated in Sicily in 668, and his successor, Constantine IV (r. 668-685), owed his rise to the throne in part to the solid support of Pope St. Vitalian (r. 657-672). The new emperor was thus much less energetic in upholding the *Typos*, thereby allowing Vitalian to promote orthodox teaching on the two wills.

Tyrrell, George (1861-1909) ● Priest, theologian, and a leading figure in the Modernist movement. Born in Dublin, Tyrrell was raised as an Evangelical. Studying at Trinity College, he was drawn to the Catholic faith, entering the Church in 1879. The following year, he was accepted into the Jesuits, being ordained in 1891. From 1894-1896, he taught moral theology at Stonyhurst College, Lancashire. In 1896, he was transferred to Farm Street, a Jesuit church in London. While there, he began establishing himself as a writer and developing influential associations with prominent adherents of Modernism such as Baron Friedrich von Hügel, the philosopher-theologian who introduced Tyrrell to the writings of Alfred Loisy, Maurice Blondel, and Lucien Laberthonnière. Among Tyrrell's first major works were collections of meditative writings, *Nova et Vetera* (1897) and *Hard Sayings* (1898), and lectures, *On Eternal Religion* (1899). His

relations with the society were becoming increasingly difficult, particularly after heavy censoring in 1899 of his article "A Perverted Devotion" (on the subject of hell), which was published in the *Weekly Register*. The article led to his removal from Farm Street, and the final break came with the publication in 1906 of extracts, in Italian, from his "Letter to a Professor of Anthropology." This work, appearing in England under the title "A Much Abused Letter," presented an important theme in Tyrrell's writings, that of a dead or moribund theology compared to a vibrant or living faith, and resulted in his expulsion from the Jesuits. An outspoken critic of organized Catholicism, especially theology, Tyrrell wrote against Pope St. Pius X's encyclical *Pascendi dominici gregis* condemning Modernism, his letter to the *Times* in September-October 1907 earning him excommunication. Other books of this period included *Through Scylla and Charybdis* (1907); *Medievalism* (1908), a vicious attack upon the Church and Cardinal Désiré Mercier; and the posthumous *Christianity at the Cross-Roads* (1909), in which he extolled the freedom of faith against the chains of theology and expressed a hope that Christianity was not the culminating creed of humanity but merely the basis of universal faith. He died at Storrington in Sussex, an utterly unrepentant Modernist still clinging to his determination to call himself a Catholic.

U

Ubertino of Casale (1259-c. 1330) ●
Leader of the Spiritual Franciscans. From
Casale, Vercelli, Italy, he entered the
Franciscans in 1273 in Genoa. Sent to Paris
to study, he returned to Italy around 1282
and came under the influence of John of
Parma and Pierre-Jean Olivi, both prominent
among the Spiritual Franciscans. After
teaching for a time, he gave up his position
and began preaching, emerging as one of the
chief spokesmen for the Spirituals of
Tuscany. His harsh criticism of the popes
and his own order concerning their refusal to
adopt the most extreme rules of poverty and
austerity led to his being summoned before
Bl. Pope Benedict XI (r. 1303-1304); the
pontiff forbade him from preaching in Perugia
and banished him to the convent at La
Verna. During this period of exile he wrote
his chief work, *Arbor vitae crucifixiae Jesu
Christi*, a collection of invective allegorical
thoughts and political ideas aimed against
society, the Church, and the Franciscans,
devoting special attention and bitterness to
the Franciscans, and to Popes Boniface VIII
and Benedict XI. In 1307, Ubertino was made
a chaplain to Cardinal Napoleone Orsini,
nephew of Pope Nicholas III (r. 1277-1280),
the papal legate to the area of central Italy.
Summoned to Avignon around 1310,
Ubertino took part in the discussions being
held by Pope Clement V (r. 1305-1314) over
the Spirituals. He defended vociferously the
demands of the Spirituals that the
Franciscans adhere completely to the
demands of poverty as enunciated by
Francis, attacking the popes for declarations
against such austerity. When he failed to win

approval for separate houses and provisions
for the Spirituals, he requested and received
permission to move to the Benedictine Abbey
of Gembloux at Liège. In 1322, Pope John
XXII (r. 1316-1334) invited him to give an
opinion on the question of theological
poverty, that is, the dispute over the poverty
of Christ and the Apostles that was being
debated by the Franciscans and Dominicans.
Working in the Curia and a favorite of
Cardinal Orsini, Ubertino continued to write
on various matters, but in 1325 he departed
Avignon, most likely because of charges of
heresy. Seeking safety with Louis the
Bavarian, he probably accompanied the ruler
in 1328 on a trip to Rome. He may have
preached against Pope John XXII in 1329,
and some stories reported that he joined the
Carthusians in 1332, a possibility discounted
by historians. There is no reliable information
on his death.

Ukraine ● See **Eastern Catholic
Churches**; see also **Russia**.

Ulenberg, Kaspar (1549-1617) ●
Theological writer and biblical translator.
Born in Lippstadt in Westphalia, he was
raised by Lutherans and was intended by
them to be a Lutheran minister. He studied
at Lippstadt, Brunswick, and Wittenberg. As
his studies advanced into Lutheran doctrine,
Ulenburg began having serious doubts,
misgivings only heightened by the rise of
Calvinism and the resultant breakup of
Protestant theological unity. Sent to Cologne
to convince a friend of the family to return to
Lutheranism from Catholicism, he stayed on

in Cologne and in 1572 entered the Church. Ordained in 1575, he held various parish posts until 1593 when he was named regent of the Laurentian school in Cologne, a post he held for twenty-two years. His writings included controversial, ascetical, and polemical treatises, but his chief work was the German translation of the Bible, begun in 1614 at the request of Ferdinand, duke of Bavaria, and the archbishop and elector of Cologne. Finished just before his death, it was published in 1630, enjoying numerous editions during the seventeenth and eighteenth centuries.

Ullathorne, William Bernard

(1806-1889) ● English Benedictine and bishop of Birmingham. A direct descendant of Thomas More, he was born in Peckington, Yorkshire, and spent over three years serving on ships that sailed in the Mediterranean and Baltic. After attending a Mass in Memel, a Baltic port, he returned to England and entered the Benedictine monastery in Downside, near Bath in 1823. Ordained in 1831, he volunteered for the Australian mission in response to a plea from the Benedictine vicar apostolic of Mauritius. Accepted, he was given full authority to serve as a vicar-general, landing in Australia in February 1833. For several years he labored to improve and organize the Church in Australia, devoting special care to the convicts of Norfolk Island. In 1837, he authored *The Catholic Mission in Australia*, an important early condemnation of the English penal system written at the request of the government. Ullathorne also testified before Parliament and was summoned to Rome to give a report on the state of the Australian mission. Leaving Australia for the last time in 1840, he returned to England and was named head of a mission in Coventry, overseeing the construction of a beautiful church. In 1846, he was appointed vicar apostolic for the Western District of England; two years later, he was moved to

the Central District. Journeying to Rome in 1848, he took part in negotiations that led to the return of the English hierarchy. Upon the formal declaration of Pope Pius IX in 1850, Ullathorne was made bishop of Birmingham, enjoying a close friendship with both Cardinal Wiseman and John Henry Newman. Initially approved as successor to Wiseman in 1865 as archbishop of Westminster, Ullathorne was forced to remain in Birmingham after Pius IX nullified the choice of the Congregation of Propaganda and pushed Henry Manning instead. Bishop for thirty-seven years, he took part in the Westminster synods and in Vatican Council I (1869-1870); at the council he was a member of the commission for ecclesiastical discipline. He resigned his see in 1888 but was given the titular rank of archbishop. His writings included *Groundwork of Christian Virtues* (1882), *History of the Restoration of the English Hierarchy* (1871), *The Immaculate Conception* (1855), *Christian Patience* (1886), and sermons.

Ulfilas (c. 311-c. 382)

● Also called Wulfila and Ulphilas. So-called Apostle of the Goths, he was the son of a Christian Cappadocian who had been captured by the Goths. Raised among the Gothic people, he was fluent in their language and familiar with their customs. Thus, after being educated at Constantinople, he was consecrated a bishop in 341 by Eusebius and sent to work as a missionary among the Goths. His missionary labors first took him beyond the borders of the Roman Empire, but he eventually returned to the Goths along the Danube among whom he spent most of his life until he died in Constantinople. An Arian, Ulfilas was responsible for converting the Goths to Arianism, the heresy to which the tribesmen would remain devoted for several centuries; Ulfilas consequently had a major influence upon subsequent history, especially as the Goths would later conquer Italy. He also translated the Bible into Gothic, initiating German literature.

Ulrich, St. (d. 973) ● Bishop of Augsburg from 923, he was the leading supporter of Church reforms sponsored by Emperor Otto I (r. 936-973). Appointed to his post through Henry I the Fowler (r. 919-936), Ulrich helped save the city from destruction by fortifying the walls and improving its defenses. Augsburg thereby survived the Magyar siege. That year the Magyars were crushed by Otto I at the Battle of Lechfeld, and in celebration Ulrich was granted the right to coin money. He is notable for being the first person canonized formally by the pope. In January 993, Pope John XV (r. 985-996) proclaimed him a saint in response to a report on Ulrich's holy life and miracles that was submitted during a council in Rome. Ulrich's name appeared on a letter in the eleventh century in which he supposedly wrote about clerical celibacy. This was later determined to be a forgery. Feast day: July 4.

Ultramontanism ● Movement within the Church that was characterized by its zealous — at times even fanatical — devotion to the Holy See. The name was derived from the Latin phrase meaning "over the mountains" or "on the other side of the mountain," an oblique reference to the Alps and the fact that beyond them lay Rome, the seat of power in the Church. Ultramontanism was used to describe rabid fidelity to the pope as early as the eleventh century, finding expression in such political entities as the Guelphs during the Middle Ages. By the 1600s, however, Ultramontanism had become a focused movement among Catholics who were eager to unite and resist nationalist tendencies in local churches that led to thinking and actions independent from the rightful authority of the Holy See. The movement was especially opposed to Gallicanism in France, which was supported by many elements in the French Church; it was also against Febronianism and Josephinism in the 1700s.

In the nineteenth century, as Europe and the Church struggled to recover from the devastation (both physical and intellectual) caused by the French Revolution, Ultramontanism attracted a wide variety of Catholics who were convinced of the need to support the papacy against dangerous trends of nationalism in the Churches of the European countries and liberalism in the areas of doctrine. The cause of the Ultramontanes was aided by the revival of the Society of Jesus in 1814 by Pope Pius VII (r. 1800-1823), the reestablishing of the hierarchy in England in 1850, the publication of the encyclical *Quanta cura*, with the *Syllabus of Errors*, in 1864, by Pope Pius IX (r. 1846-1879), and the remarkable work done by spokesmen in England, France, and Germany. Chief among the French Ultramontanes was Louis Veuillot, editor and writer, whose newspaper *L'Univers* emerged as the most vociferous and influential adherent of papal rights and power. Hated by liberals and finally suppressed in 1874, the paper was a potent voice for those who believed the Holy See to be under attack in matters of theology, authority, and daily life.

While some scholars point to the work of Vatican Council I as the final triumph of Ultramontanism, it is more accurate to say that the movement played a significant role in rallying Catholics to support a process that had been unfolding for some time and had come to fruition in the council's deliberations and decrees in 1869-1870. The greatest of these, of course, was that concerning papal infallibility. Many Ultramontanist radicals found even that declaration unsatisfactory, preferring a broader administrative infallibility. Nevertheless, the Ultramontanist element at the council was clearly in the majority and reflected consistently the will of the Holy See and the Catholic Church at large. In a wider historical context, Ultramontanism was a major buttress for the papacy at a time when the reunification of Italy had stripped the pope of the Papal States. By steadfastly promoting the Holy See's prerogatives and central authority in the universal Church, the movement assisted Pope Pius IX in making the transition from a political and religious leader to a purely spiritual head of the Church at a time when the liquidation of one posed very real dangers for the irrecoverable decline of the other.

Umbanda ● Cult in Brazil that is an amalgamation of Roman Catholic, African, native Indian, and primitive spiritual beliefs. First emerging in the 1920s, Umbanda today claims membership of more than twelve million and is one of the most pervasive attempts to unite Church ceremonial with native belief cults and religious practices. According to Umbandism, the highest possible officeholder is the *pai de santo*, who oversees the mediumistic offices below him. Actual ceremonies bring together a curious and highly unorthodox practice of mediums performing rituals of consultation with certain West African deities who are identified with the saints of the Catholic Church. The mediums performing the ceremony enter into trances and establish communication with the "saints," giving advice and suggestions for the curing of evils or illness. Umbandism extends into the celebration of Church ritual with its alteration of proper Catholic ceremony, causing severe misunderstandings among worshipers concerning proper beliefs and the warping of the legitimate place of faith in the lives of millions of Brazilians. Owing to its allure of magic, superstition, and long-standing cultural acceptance, Umbanda presents severe problems for the Church's pastoral missions in Brazil, where the faith is already challenged by indifferentism, evangelical Protestantism, and the acute dangers of liberation theology.

Unam Sanctam ● Important bull promulgated on November 18, 1302, by Pope Boniface VIII (r. 1294-1303) during his often bitter struggle with King Philip IV the Fair of France. The name is derived from its opening words ("One Holy") and was possibly written by Aegidus Colonna, archbishop of Bourges, who was a member of a council summoned in Rome in late October 1302 from which was issued the bull. Relying upon extensive passages from the writings and teachings of St. Thomas Aquinas, St. Bernard of Clairvaux, Hugh of St. Victor, and others, *Unam Sanctam* declared that there is but "one Holy Catholic and Apostolic Church," outside of which there can be no salvation, but with one head; that the head of the Church is Jesus Christ and his chosen representative, the Roman pope; and that those who refuse the power and care of Peter cease to be members of the Church; and that there are two swords (or powers), the spiritual and the temporal, which govern the world. The Church has the duty and the right to wield the spiritual sword while the king has jurisdiction over the temporal one, with the understanding that the king does so under the guidance and direction of the Church (*ad nutum et patientiam sacerdotis*). This subordination is considered natural, as the spiritual power must possess precedence for great and divine origins and by virtue of the fact that the temporal power (or sword) is itself judged by a higher power, which is itself judged by God. Thus, whoever opposes the spiritual sword of the Church opposes divine authority granted to Peter and passed to the popes. The bull concludes with: "We declare, state, define, and pronounce that for salvation, it is altogether necessary that every human creature be subject to the authority of the Roman pontiff" (*"Porro subesse Romano Pontifici omni humane creaturae declaramus, dicimus, definimus, et pronuntiamus omnino esse de necessitate salvatis"*).

While *Unam Sanctam* was said to have

done nothing to change the relationship between the Church and the rulers of Christendom, it marked an important moment in the sociopolitical claims of the papacy in the medieval world. The declaration of the necessity of subjection to the Roman pontiff by all people for salvation was also the source of historical and theological debate.

Uniate Churches ● Also spelled Uniat. The Uniate Churches are those Eastern Christians who are in communion with Rome and thus recognize the legitimate authority of the pope; at the same time, such communities have retained their own rites, liturgical languages, and versions of canon law. The term Uniate (derived from the Latin *Unio* and adapted into the Polish *unia*) was first applied by the enemies of the Union of Brest-Litovsk (1595) to those Eastern Christians who had entered into communion with the Western Church; it is taken to be pejorative, since it implies a total surrender to the Latin Church by the Eastern (or Oriental) Catholics. They were looked upon as Latin, or Western, in spirit and thought, retaining only a veneer of their originally rich Eastern rites and customs. Members of the Eastern Catholic Churches naturally reject the appellation Uniate and point to the fact that their rites are today flourishing and expanding in membership, as seen very clearly in the lands once held under the oppressive rule of Communism such as Ukraine where millions have flocked to the faith. Further, any tendencies toward Latinization were sharply reduced by the decree of Vatican Council II *Orientalium Ecclesiarum* ("Decree on Eastern Catholic Churches"), and through the work of Pope John Paul II in promoting recognition of the important contributions made to the Catholic Church by those in the Eastern rites who acknowledge his primacy. (See also **Eastern Catholic Churches**.)

Uniformity, Acts of ● Series of statutes implemented with the aim of establishing uniformity of religious worship in England following the break with Rome under King Henry VIII (r. 1509-1547). The acts were much opposed by English Catholics and Nonconformist Protestants who saw them as deadly threats to the practice of their religion. The first of the Uniformity Acts was passed in January 1549 under sickly King Edward VI (r. 1547-1553) and imposed on all people the use of the Book of Common Prayer in the Mass and all public services. Further, services were to be held in English save for private worship and in universities where Latin, Greek, and Hebrew could be adopted for educational purposes in the services except for the Mass. As the original Book of Common Prayer was a failure, a second act had to be passed. Promulgated in March-April 1552, the second act ordered use of the revised book and made attendance at public service mandatory with various censures and punishments possible for absence. A new Uniformity Act was promulgated under Queen Elizabeth I (r. 1558-1603) in 1559. This oppressive law was especially hard on Catholics who could not, in good conscience, accept its requirements and were then ruthlessly treated and punished for the crime of recusancy. Its terrible efficiency was made manifest by the fact that revision was not necessary until 1662, under King Charles II (r. 1660-1685), an act of little interest to Catholics, since it maintained harsh regulations against Catholicism. While the Uniformity Acts remain technically in effect, revisions in the law in the 1800s rendered them essentially applicable only to the Church of England.

Unigenitus ● Apostolic constitution published on September 8, 1713, by Pope Clement XI (r. 1700-1721) that condemned one hundred one propositions contained in the *Refléxions morales sur le Nouveau Testament* by Pasquier Quesnel (1634-1719).

The propositions were based on and contained Jansenist doctrines from the previously condemned writings of Cornelius Jansen (or Jansenius; 1585-1638) and Michel Baius (1513-1589), or were harsh denunciations of contemporary Catholicism. While Quesnel's work had revived the controversy in France over Jansenism, it was quickly apparent to the pope and King Louis XIV of France that immediate steps would have to be taken to curb its dangerous influence. Quesnel, for example, reiterated Jansenist teachings that without grace humans are incapable of any good actions, that all acts of a sinner, including prayer and attending Mass, are sins, and that grace is unobtainable outside the Church.

An initial bull, *Vineam Domini*, was published in 1703 at the urging of King Louis, but this decree only exacerbated the crisis, as many French Catholics rallied to the support of Jansenism, seeing the bull as interference in French affairs and a means of expressing dissatisfaction with the government. Among the Church leaders who refused to sign the bull were Cardinal de Noailles, archbishop of Paris. King Louis became agitated with the situation, insisting that Clement move more decisively. The result was *Unigenitus*, which was opposed by de Noailles and other Church leaders and was not accepted by Quesnel. There followed a third bull, *Pastoralis Offici*, excommunicating any who might dispute *Unigenitus*. It was endorsed by the regent, the duke of Orléans, who was now running the government after the death of Louis in 1715. (See also **Jansenism**.)

Unitatis Redintegratio ● The "Decree on Ecumenism," as it is known in English, was promulgated by the Second Vatican Council on November 21, 1964. It elaborated the principles guiding Catholic participation in ecumenism and clarifying the Catholic view concerning the status and position of other faiths separate from the Roman Catholic Church. Considered one of the most important documents related to the Church's role in ecumenism, the decree was additionally clarified and supported by *Lumen Gentium* ("Dogmatic Constitution on the Church"), *Gaudium et Spes* ("Pastoral Constitution on the Church in the Modern World"), and *Orientalium Ecclesiarum* ("Decree on Eastern Catholic Churches").

Unitatis Redintegratio (Nos. 1, 3) from the outset makes clear that the Catholic Church as "established by Christ the Lord is, indeed, one and unique," although "From her very beginnings there arose in this one and only Church of God certain rifts." However, the decree goes on to point out, the fault for the schism that separated many from the Church in the Reformation of the sixteenth century lies not merely with the Protestants but with Catholics as well. Nor should those born in these communities be condemned. Rather, they should be given "respect and affection as brothers," for they too were brought up in the Christian faith. While granting the often misunderstood recognition that the gifts of the Holy Spirit (e.g., the life of grace and the theological virtues) are obtainable to those Christians not of the Catholic faith, *Unitatis Redintegratio* makes the vital distinction that "it is through Christ's Catholic Church alone, which is the all-embracing means of salvation, that the fullness of the means of salvation can be obtained" (No. 3). The decree then calls on all Christians to pray and labor toward the unity of the Church, but it makes the important point that this reconciliation, or reunion, is possible only by placing hope entirely in Christ.

United States of America ● Country in North America where the Catholic faith first came with the arrival of explorers from European countries and then with the many groups and powers who sought to establish colonies in the pristine territories of the New World. Three main divisions are recognized in the earliest landing of Catholics: the Spanish, French, and English.

The Spanish, first spreading out through Central America in the early sixteenth century, reached Florida and the Gulf Coast, and then also Texas, New Mexico, and California from their various bases — ecclesiastical and military — in Mexico and the Caribbean. Subsequently, the Church flourished wherever the Spanish Empire was able to gain ascendancy. Spanish missionaries (Dominicans, Franciscans, and Jesuits) founded missions and made converts from among native populations in Florida, California, and the Southwest. The most remarkable of these missionaries included Luis Cancer de Barbastro (1500-1549), Magin Catalan (1761-1830), Eusebio Kino (1645-1711), Juan de Padilla (d. 1542), Bl. Junípero Serra (1713-1784), and the so-called Twelve Apostles of Mexico of the 1500s.

Meanwhile, the French created their first temporary mission in North America in 1604 on an island in Passamaquoddy Bay; this was followed in 1608 by the permanent settlement at Quebec begun under Samuel de Champlain. In 1615, four Recollect Franciscans arrived; they were joined in 1625 by Jesuits, including St. Jean de Brébeuf. The Jesuits, known as the Black Robes to the Indians, spearheaded the French missions to the native peoples, finding converts among the Mohawks, the most famous being Bl. Kateri Tekakwitha. Missionaries were later sent to the five tribes of the Iroquois nation, but new fighting began in the middle of the seventeenth century, with the connivance of the English. By the 1680s, the Jesuit presence had been all but destroyed in New York. The French also sponsored missions to the areas of modern Michigan, Illinois, Wisconsin, and along the Mississippi. Fruitful work was carried out in Louisiana by the Jesuits, Carmelites, and Capuchins.

The French missions, however, did not last, declining as France lost its territories in America. Supported as they were by the French crown and with French money, the missions could not long survive the defeat of France in the French and Indian War in 1763. The suppression of the Jesuits by France also had calamitous consequences for the Church in the Middle West. In 1763, Louisiana was ceded to Spain, bringing it under Spanish jurisdiction. Despite the ultimate decline of the French Church in America, its missionaries had spread Catholicism across much of the Continent.

The English colonies would prove the most harsh environment for the Church in the New World, but the stage would be set through the colonial era for the rise of a strong, independent Church in the new country of the United States. The basis of the New England colonies was, in many ways, predicated upon anti-Catholicism; English colonists had left their homeland to escape what they considered to be lingering Romanism in the Church of England. There was thus a pervasive intolerance and even persecution of Catholics in the colonies. A sizable population of Catholics was found only in Maryland, Pennsylvania, and New York.

There was no formal Catholic hierarchy in North America during the colonial period, in large measure because there was none in England. Priests worked as missionaries in a hostile land, receiving their faculties directly from Rome through the vicars apostolic based in London. Most of the religious were Jesuits, and their difficult circumstances were made more so by the suppression of the society in 1773.

The American Revolution would have momentous consequences for the faith. Interestingly, the Quebec Act of 1774, granting the right to practice Catholicism in Canada, spurred on anti-English fervor in America. Once the Revolution commenced, Catholic loyalties were divided, with some joining the Tory forces. A great many others sided with the Continental Congress, such as the prominent Maryland family of the Carrolls, which would produce Charles Carroll and John Carroll.

Much of the feeling against Catholics was alleviated by the desperately needed assistance provided to the Americans by France and Spain. By the end of the war, it was generally agreed that the time had come to grant full religious freedom. This development necessitated serious examination as to administrative needs and jurisdiction. It was no longer feasible to be under an English vicar apostolic. The creation of an independent American jurisdiction had, in fact, already been proposed as early as 1756 by Bishop Richard Challoner, vicar apostolic of London. It became reality in 1784 when Father John Carroll was named superior of American missions. On November 6, 1789, Pope Pius VI (r. 1775-1799) made him the country's first bishop, with his see in Baltimore. (See **Carroll, John**.)

Carroll set to work laying down an organization for the Church. He was assisted by American Catholics and a host of European priests. A seminary was begun at Baltimore in 1791 under four Sulpicians from France. Native-born clergy soon increased. Also in 1791, Georgetown College was opened, the first Catholic college. The next years would witness rapid expansion of the faith, so much so that strains developed in administration. This was resolved by the important decision of Pope Pius VII in 1808 to elevate the see of Baltimore to an archdiocese and to decree four new dioceses: New York, Boston, Philadelphia, and Bardstown, Kentucky. More dioceses would follow, along with schools, seminaries, and religious houses. In 1829, a council was assembled at Baltimore to discuss the best ways to meet the needs and challenges confronting the Catholic Church in America (see **Baltimore, Councils of**).

Throughout the first half of the nineteenth century, the Church was increased through extensive immigration from Europe. The largest groups came from Ireland and Germany. The Irish were driven from their homeland by English oppression and the potato famine and, moving to the United States, lived in tightly knit and frequently impoverished communities. The Germans did not congregate in the eastern cities but became farmers in Pennsylvania, Michigan, Wisconsin, Illinois, Indiana, Ohio, and elsewhere. Such large-scale immigration did not come without a price as a Nativist movement sprung up, rooted in fear of foreigners and traditional anti-Catholicism. The chief manifestation of this sentiment were the Native American Party, the American Protestant Association, and the Know-Nothings (see **Know-Nothing Movement**).

The American Civil War (1861-1865) did not bitterly divide the Church in the U.S., but individual Catholics and clergy remained loyal to their own states, be they part of the Union or the Confederacy. On the question of the slave trade, the Church opposed the practice, but many Southern bishops accepted the political reality of the institution, struggling nevertheless to protect the basic rights of the slaves. Catholics fought and died on both sides. There were chaplains in both armies, and Catholic nuns from some twenty religious congregations worked in hospitals to tend the wounded. Once the fighting stopped, Catholics were once more generally united.

In 1866, another Baltimore council was held (the Second Plenary Council) to address the new needs of the Church and to plan for the future. The main issue facing American Catholics was immigration. Immigrants were coming from Poland, Hungary, Austria, and Italy. They did not learn English or adapt to American life quickly, so the hierarchy had to take steps to meet the situation: native clergy were brought in, native language-oriented parishes created, and Catholic social groups launched to ease their assimilation. Such a process was not without difficulties within the Church, much as the immigration situation troubled the country itself. With this proliferation of foreign Catholics, the Church fell under renewed attack. To the nationalist feeling were added anger over Catholic opposition to public schools, the deep-seated fear of popery — Catholic pressure and influence upon the government directed from Rome — and the dislike of other Catholic immigrants such as the Irish. As earlier times had seen, anti-Catholics banded together in organizations such as the American Protective Association. This opposition would endure into the twentieth century in the South and elsewhere with the Ku Klux Klan.

Many bishops and Church leaders became outspoken in their support of the labor movement, promoting the rights of workers. Most conspicuous in this period were the Knights of Labor, which had many Catholic members. Some bishops looked upon the movement as a secret society in the mold of the Freemasons and requested condemnation of it by the Holy See. This came in 1884, but in 1887 Cardinal James Gibbons intervened to prevent a wider condemnation. Bishops subsequently were to stand in close affiliation with labor for the betterment of conditions for working people. The encyclical *Rerum novarum* (1891) of Pope Leo XIII (r. 1878-1903) was hailed by many Catholics as vindication of their backing of the labor movement.

As the 1800s drew to a close, the Church was increasingly prosperous, but it also was faced with a schism and Americanism. The schism was the founding of the Polish National Church after a breach had developed between the Irish and Polish Catholic communities. Americanism was condemned by Pope Leo in 1899 with the apostolic letter *Testem Benevolentiae* (see **Americanism**).

By 1900, the Catholic population of the United States numbered over twelve million,

served by some eighty-two dioceses. In 1908, Pope St. Pius X issued the apostolic constitution *Sapienti Consilio* formally removing the Church in the U.S. from the mission status. The Church owed its vitality and growth to various factors, including the talent and skill of the Catholic hierarchy, the ongoing phenomenon of immigration, new conversions (among Native Americans, blacks, and other minorities, from assorted faiths and denominations), and the superbly unified Catholic community on a national scale down to the individual parish. An important element in this was the parochial school system, which had a significant role in safeguarding the faith among the young and preparing sound Catholics for the future.

By World War II, the Church was fully a part of American mainstream culture. A landmark was reached in 1928 with the nomination of the Catholic Alfred E. Smith as the Democratic Party nominee for president. He was defeated and there was an anticipated outburst of anti-Catholic pronouncements, but Smith's loss was not attributed singularly to his Catholicism. The final testament of toleration came in 1960 with the election of the Catholic John F. Kennedy as president of the United States.

In the decades after Vatican Council II, the American Church has been confronted with a variety of difficulties. Among these are: the problems of interpreting the decrees of Vatican II in the face of theological innovation and unauthentic liturgical usage; the extensive changes made in the formation of religious; the increasing age of American religious, especially in the Religious Institutes of Women; the decline in vocations; the presence of nominally Catholic organizations that nevertheless work to counter or alter Catholic teaching on such issues as abortion, contraception, papal supremacy, collegiality, women's ordination, clerical celibacy, and homosexuality; the societal decay precipitated by a proliferation of an abortion culture; the weakening of the family structure and the destructive effects of unrestrained materialism and secular humanism; the subtle prevalence of anti-Catholic bias in many media outlets; the spread of religious apathy and indifferentism; the needs of Catholic immigrants; and the lamentable state of American education.

While many observers are pessimistic about the state of the American Church heading into the next century (contrasting it with the pre-Vatican II Church), there are a number of positive developments that give reason for considerable optimism: the progress made in ecumenism; the rise of new religious congregations; the increase in conversions; the marked sophistication of Catholic communications, centered in the United States Catholic Conference and the National Conference of Catholic Bishops; the Church's active role in social issues (human rights, poverty, health care, race relations, abortion, and economic justice); the decisive leadership provided by the American hierarchy in giving positive direction to the faithful; and the greater involvement of the laity — especially women — in the life of the Church. Today, the membership in the U.S. is approximately 22 percent (56 million) of the U.S. population, with 34 archdioceses and 154 dioceses. There are eleven American cardinals.

Univers, L' ● Extremely Ultramontanist French newspaper of the nineteenth century. Edited from 1843 by Louis Veuillot, the paper was one of the leading Catholic voices against liberalism and in organizing opposition to the French government's policy of anticlericalism. *L'Univers* earned its greatest notoriety, however, for its absolute devotion to the cause of the papacy, most notably the question of papal infallibility, which was promulgated at the First Vatican Council (1869-1870) under Pope Pius IX (r. 1846-1878). Suppressed by the French government in 1860 after publishing Pius's encyclical *Nullis certe verbis* (On the Need for Civil Sovereignty; January 19, 1860), the paper was started again in 1867. Continued publishing against the regime, declarations against the French Revolution, and what was perceived as radical Ultramontanism led to its final suppression in 1874.

Universities ● Institutions of learning that first emerged in the Middle Ages. The universities of Europe originated out of the cathedral schools and thus owed their creation to the Church. Universities would play a significant part in the development of the political, social, and intellectual life of Western Christendom. The earliest schools were found in the so-called cathedral schools, known as the *studium generale* (plural: *studia generalia*), centers of education formed in various dioceses. The schools, at first teaching only local students, began to attract other students from surrounding dioceses and ultimately from other countries. The arrival of foreign students marked the beginnings of the university.

The term university was understood in the medieval era to imply the guilds or communes (*universitas*) that had been founded in the cathedral schools to offer protection and assistance to foreign faculty and students. These groups, called nations, at first had little influence but were gradually accepted. Universities themselves early on lacked support from local authorities, both ecclesiastical and secular. There were struggles for control of the schools between authorities and university masters, conflicts that at times led to riots and civil unrest. Some schools were closed and students migrated out of the university city. Oxford University was founded by English scholars who had fled France in 1167. Schoolmasters thus came to wield wide authority as secular officials gave them considerable latitude.

Prestige was acquired by some schools through papal or royal patronage. Frederick I Barbarossa, the Holy Roman Emperor, gave definite privileges to the University of Bologna, while the University of Paris was the recipient of papal approval and emerged as one of the chief centers for theological training. Paris, of course, has long enjoyed a high reputation for scholastic excellence, boasting some of the most respected professors of the time, among them Peter Abelard and Hugh of St. Victor. New influences arrived in the thirteenth century, most notably the mendicant orders, which were forced to strive with university masters for the right to teach and be accepted. When the friars won their place, they brought with them such profound theologians and philosophers as St. Thomas Aquinas, St. Albertus Magnus, St. Bonaventure, and Bl. John Duns Scotus. Through the Scholastic theologians of Paris and elsewhere, Aristotle was brought back to prominence and the summit of theological thought was reached by Thomas Aquinas in

the *Summa Theologiae*. Parisian scholars also had a lasting influence on the dispute of the Great Schism with their conciliar ideas, and scholars in Prague helped spread Hussite ideas that would cause considerable strife in Bohemia throughout much of the 1400s.

By custom, the university had a specialty (such as theology for Paris and law for Bologna), but the large schools usually taught theology, art, medicine, and law. These were places of professional training, and the student was aware that many hardships would have to be endured before finally reaching the doctorate that normally took sixteen years. The student would be forced to travel from school to school, and the competition became very intense as the student populations grew and licenses to teach became essential for advancement. The language of education was Latin, with students following the seven liberal arts, comprised of the *trivium* (grammar, rhetoric,

Hugh of St. Victor teaching

and logic), and the *quadrivium* (astronomy, music, arithmetic, and geometry); greater emphasis was placed on the *trivium*. For the study of theology, the accepted texts were the *Sentences* of Peter Lombard, the Scriptures, and biblical commentaries; over time the *Summa Theologiae* would become the accepted text for theological instruction. (See **Scholasticism**.)

Urban I, St. ● Pope from 222-230. The successor to Pope St. Callistus I (r. 217-222), he spent his entire pontificate during the reign of Emperor Alexander Severus (r. 222-235), which was noted for its absence of harsh persecution of the Church. Also ongoing during this period was the division of the Church in Rome as a result of the presence of the antipope St. Hippolytus (r. 217-235). Little is known of his activities. According to the *Liber Pontificalis*, he was a Roman, the son of Pontianus, although other details are discounted by scholars as unreliable or the result of confusion with other sources. He was buried in the cemetery of St. Callistus where a fragment of a sarcophagus with his name in Greek was discovered by the Italian archaeologist Giovanni de Rossi (1822-1894). Feast day: May 22.

Urban II, Bl. ● Pope from 1088-1099. Best known for preaching the First Crusade, he was born Odo of Lagery in Châtillon-sur-Marne, the son of noble parents. He studied at Reims under St. Bruno the Carthusian. Around 1068 he entered Cluny and was made a cardinal in 1078 by Pope St. Gregory VII (r. 1073-1085). Serving as a papal legate to France and Germany, he was the loyal servant of both the interests and the cause of Pope Gregory, presiding in 1085 over a synod at Quadlingburg in Saxony, where the antipope Clement III was condemned. Elected the successor to Victor III after a considerable delay, he immediately announced his intention to continue the important work of reform that had been conducted for so long and so well by Pope St. Gregory VII. At the Council of Melfi (1089) he issued sixteen canons against simony and lay investiture. Although initially successful in expelling Clement III, with the aid of Countess Matilda of Tuscany, Urban was forced to flee (c. 1090), returning to the Eternal City at the end of 1093. Throughout, he cultivated excellent relations with the Normans of southern Italy and Sicily, finding safety among them during his conflict with Emperor Henry IV (r. 1056-1105). Urban gave King Roger I of Sicily (r. 1072-1101) the right of control over the Church in Sicily, the so-called *Monarchia Sicula* that would remain in effect until 1869. By 1095, his position was much stronger politically and he was able to convene two important councils, at Piacenza and Clermont. At Piacenza (March 1095) he issued various reforms and condemned the teachings of Berengarius of Tours (d. c. 1088). At Clermont (November 1095) he proclaimed the Truce of God (see **Peace of God**) and, at the urgent plea for help from the Byzantine Emperor Alexius I Comnenus, he proclaimed the First Crusade to liberate the Holy Land from Muslim domination and free Jerusalem. His call was answered, inaugurating the crusader era with the now famous cry *"Deus vult!"* ("God wills!") Urban also reorganized papal finances and in a bull of 1089 first used the term *curia Romana* in describing the departments that assisted in papal administration; his reform of the papal government centralized the Church's administrative authority and enhanced the power and prestige of the College of Cardinals. He died on July 19, 1099, exactly two months after the capture of Jerusalem by the crusaders, an event for which he had long prayed and labored.

Urban III ● Pope from 1185-1187. Born Umberto Crivelli, he was a member of a royal family of Milan. Archdeacon of Bourges and

Milan before being made cardinal by Pope Lucius III in 1182, he was appointed archbishop of Milan in January 1185. His election as successor to Lucius was unanimous, taking place on November 25, the same day that Lucius died in Verona. The haste of the cardinals was probably to avoid any possible interference from Emperor Frederick I Barbarossa (r. 1155-1190); Urban's coronation on December 1 was also equally swift. Knowing that the next pope would inherit the conflict between the papacy and the emperor over various issues, the cardinals chose the best possible person to stand firm where Lucius had vacillated. Urban was not to disappoint them, as he was a personal enemy of Frederick, having endured the emperor's sack of Milan in 1162 during which the future pontiff had watched several relatives put to death. His struggle with Frederick would thus dominate his pontificate. He opposed the marriage of Frederick's son, Henry, to Constance, the Norman heiress of Sicily, suffering a crushing blow when the union took place on January 4, 1186, for it signaled a major political gain for the Hohenstaufen Dynasty in Italy. When Urban refused to crown Henry as co-emperor, Frederick compelled the patriarch of Aquileia to do it; Urban then suspended the patriarch, antagonizing the emperor even further by consecrating Folmar to be archbishop of Trier, the rival to Frederick's hand-picked candidate. Trapped in Verona, Urban tried to rally support from the German bishops. Frederick, however, convened the Diet of Gelnhausen, where the German prelates gave their backing to the imperial cause. Accepting a *fait accompli*, Urban backed down, abandoned Folmar as archbishop of Trier, and accepted a new election. Negotiations soon turned ugly, and Urban undertook preparations to excommunicate his intractable foe. The inhabitants and magistrates of Verona would not permit this, however, and Urban departed, dying at Ferrara around October 19, 1187.

Urban IV ● Pope from 1261-1264. A native of Troyes, he was born Jacques Pantaléon, the son of a cobbler. After serving as a canon in Laon and an archdeacon in Liège, he attended the Council of Lyons (1245) where he came to the notice of Pope Innocent IV. The pontiff used his services on a mission to Germany, and he subsequently served as bishop of Verdun (1253) and patriarch of Jerusalem (1255). While on a visit to Viterbo on patriarchal business, Pantaléon took part in a conclave to elect a successor to Alexander VI, who had died on May 25, 1261. One of only eight cardinals because Alexander had neglected to appoint any, Pantaléon was finally elected on August 29, 1261, after months of jealous and difficult deliberations. Urban made the main causes of his pontificate the strengthening of the papacy's political and financial position and opposing the Hohenstaufen Dynasty, which had long been in conflict with the popes. He named fourteen new cardinals, improved papal government, and although never able to reside in Rome because of civil strife (he lived at Viterbo), he was able to regain mastery over the Papal States and have a favorable local government in the Eternal City. His efforts to reduce Hohenstaufen and Ghibelline ambitions in Italy included an alliance with Charles of Anjou, brother of King Louis IX of France, to whom Urban offered the crown of Sicily in 1263. Urban thus found an ally who would prove a formidable enemy of the Hohenstaufen line and help to bring that imperial house to extinction. Urban was disappointed by the fall of the Latin Empire of Constantinople in 1261 to the Byzantines under Emperor Michael VIII Palaeologus, who resurrected the Byzantine Empire that had been overthrown in 1204 by the Fourth Crusade. The pope also ordered the celebration of the Feast of Corpus Christi for the entire Church. He commissioned St. Thomas Aquinas to compose the Office for the feast.

Urban V ● Pope from 1362-1370. Born Guillaume de Grimoard at Grisac in Languedoc, he was from a noble family, receiving his education at Montpellier and Toulouse. He entered the Benedictines at the priory of Chirac, near Grisac, making his profession at the Abbey of St. Victor in Marseilles. Forever after a devoted Benedictine, he would continue to wear the habit of the order even after his election to the papacy. Receiving a doctorate in 1342 after his ordination, he became one of the foremost canonists in the Church. After holding several posts, including vicar-general of Clermont and Uzés, he was named abbot of St. Germain, Auxerre, in 1352 by Pope Clement VI (r. 1342-1352). Over the next years he undertook a variety of missions as a papal legate to Italy for the Avignon Pope Innocent VI (r. 1352-1362). After Innocent's death, the conclave first chose a brother of Clement VI, but, since he declined, the cardinals chose Grimoard unanimously. He was at the time on a mission to Naples and was elected for his learning and through the deep respect of the cardinals, even though he was not a cardinal himself. He arrived in Marseilles on October 28 and was crowned on November 6, taking the name Urban because all the popes of that name had been saintly.

A deeply religious pontiff, he maintained his Benedictine lifestyle during his

Pope Urban V

pontificate, always finding time for prayer and promoting peace and reform. While never completely comfortable with some members of the Sacred College, Urban proved adroit at curtailing extravagance and wasteful luxury. He was much concerned about the relations with the Byzantines and had a strong desire to return to Rome. He felt the two were connected, as it was to his advantage to reside in the more traditional setting of the Eternal City while negotiating with Constantinople. After improving the social and political conditions in Rome and its environs — most notably the liquidation of bandits and marauding gangs by the gifted Cardinal Gil de Albornoz — Urban entered the city on October 16, 1367. Urban would remain there for three years, residing in the Vatican, as the Lateran was in such poor condition. While the court was in Rome, however, the papal administration continued at Avignon; further, Urban continued to name French cardinals, six in 1368, a clear sign that he continued to have French sympathies. While in Rome, the pontiff met with Byzantine Emperor John V Palaeologus (r. 1354-1391) in June 1369, but no progress was made on a possible reunion of the Churches. In October 1368, he also enjoyed greeting Emperor Charles IV whose empress he crowned while Charles acted as deacon during the Mass.

Despite these diplomatic triumphs, Urban felt increasingly insecure in Rome, especially after the death of Cardinal Albornoz in

August 1367. The Hundred Years' War had begun again in earnest in 1369 and the pope was eager to work for a peaceful solution, an ambition he could not fulfill from Rome. Ignoring the pleas of Petrarch, St. Bridget of Sweden, and especially the Romans (who had prospered since his return), Urban returned to France in September 1370. He entered Avignon on September 27 and soon fell ill as St. Bridget had warned. He died on December 19. Pope Pius IX beatified him in 1870. Feast day: December 19.

Urban VI ● Pope from 1378-1389. His election and pontificate helped cause the Great Schism (1378-1417). Born in Naples, Bartolomeo Prignano was a noted expert on canon law, being consecrated archbishop of Acerenza in 1364. Transferred to the archiepiscopal see of Bari in 1377, he had already been serving as the head of the papal chancery, distinguishing himself for his skills in business and finance. Thus, upon the death of Gregory XI on March 27, 1378, his name was immediately fielded as a possible successor. The conclave, however, was to prove a near disaster. The first held in Rome since 1303, it caused the Roman mobs to storm the palace to threaten the cardinals with dire consequences should a Roman, or at least an Italian, not be elected and thereby keep the papacy in Rome. On April 8, 1378, the cardinals chose Prignano, who was summoned to the Vatican. In the meantime, the crowd, which feared the choice of a Frenchman — specifically the much hated Jean de Bar — was appeased by being presented with aged Cardinal Tebaldeschi as their new pontiff. Once the angry Romans dispersed, Prignano was confirmed as pope, being enthroned on April 18 as Urban VI.

Urban quickly began causing alarm among the cardinals by a violently intemperate personality that caused him to abuse the cardinals while proclaiming his intention to bring reform to the Curia. His harsh treatment of powerful laymen such as Otto of

Brunswick, husband of Queen Joanna of Naples, only heightened the sense of disappointment, a feeling crystallized into action among the French cardinals when Urban promised to create enough Italian cardinals to dash any hopes of French domination of the College of Cardinals. The French prelates withdrew to Anagni and, after deliberations, published a declaration on August 2, 1378, stating that in their view the election of Urban was invalid because they had voted out of fear. They then moved to Fondi where protection was granted by Queen Joanna. They were joined by several cardinals who supported the proclamation that Urban had been deposed most likely in the hopes that they might be elected the next pope. On September 20, the cardinals elected Robert of Geneva as antipope. He took the name Clement VII and was crowned on October 31, thus launching the Great Schism.

Christendom was now split between two papal claimants, Urban (peculiarly but canonically elected) and Clement (the first antipope of the Great Schism). England, Germany, most of Italy, and Central Europe stood by Urban, while Burgundy, Scotland, Savoy, Naples, and France were for Clement; Spain stayed for the moment strictly neutral. Urban solidified his hold on Rome by capturing Castel Sant' Angelo, and Clement retreated to Naples and then Avignon. Urban created a new Curia (as the first one favored Clement) and named twenty-nine new cardinals in September 1378. Obstinate and unwilling to work for a solution to the crisis, Urban continued to demonstrate a highly unstable nature, at one point imprisoning and torturing six cardinals whom he suspected of conspiring against him. After an abortive campaign to capture the kingdom of Naples, he retired to Rome, after his troops began deserting owing to lack of pay, in October 1388. Once back in the Eternal City he offended the Romans with his uncontrollable rages. He died on October 15, 1389, probably from poison, leaving the

Church in chaos, and the Papal States in a state of uproar. Inheriting a deeply wounded Church from the Avignon era, Urban had proven incapable of healing the damage or setting a course for the Church in succeeding years. Instead, the faith was to endure decades of strife. His immediate successor was Boniface IX (r. 1389-1404).

Urban VII ● Pope from September 15-27, 1590. Born Giambattista Castagna in 1521, he was a native of Rome, the son of a nobleman from Genoa; his mother, Costanza Ricci, was a Roman and a sister of Cardinal Jacovazzi. After studying at Perugia and Padua, he graduated with a doctorate of law from Bologna. He then accompanied his uncle, Cardinal Girolamo Verallo, papal legate, on a trip to France in 1551, serving as his datary, or secretary. After returning to Rome, he was appointed an official of the *Signatura di Giustizia*, the Supreme Tribunal of the Church, by Pope Julius III (r. 1550-1555). That same pontiff named him bishop of Rossano in 1553. Governor of Perugia and Umbria under Pope Paul IV (r. 1555-1559), he took part in the final session of the Council of Trent (1562-1563). In 1565, he accompanied Cardinal Buoncampagni (the future Pope Gregory XIII) on a mission to Spain, serving for the next seven years as a nuncio to the court of King Philip II of Spain. In 1573, Pope Gregory sent him to Venice as nuncio, making him governor of Bologna in 1577. Gregory then appointed him consultor to the

Pope Urban VIII, by Bernini

Holy Office and made him cardinal in 1583. Under Pope Sixtus V (r. 1585-1590) he wielded much influence and was given the post of inquisitor-general of the Holy Office. He was elected to succeed Sixtus on September 15, 1590, and his elevation was greeted with widespread jubilation. He took the name Urban, interpreting the Latin meaning, "kindness," as a constant reminder to be kind to his subjects. His immediate moves to care for the poor of Rome, and to declare that no relatives would profit from his papal reign, seemed to point to a pontificate of great promise. He contracted malaria on the night after his election and died within twelve days, before his coronation.

Urban VIII ● Pope from 1623-1644. An active and intellectual pontiff, his reign was overshadowed by his lavish spending and the continuing Thirty Years' War (1618-1648). Maffeo Barberini was born in Florence, a member of the powerful Barberini family of the city. He was educated by the Jesuits there, later studying at Rome and Pisa. After securing a doctorate in law in 1589, he was granted a position in the Curia. Distinguishing himself in papal service, he was twice sent to France and the court of King Henry IV (r. 1589-1610); the second time as nuncio, having been made a titular archbishop by Pope Clement VIII in 1604. Named a cardinal by Pope Paul V in 1606, he was appointed bishop of Spoleto (1608), legate to Bologna, and prefect of the Signatura (1617). He was elected to succeed

Gregory XV (r. 1621-1623) on August 6, 1623, receiving fifty of the fifty-five votes.

On the very day of election, he issued bulls of canonization for Philip Neri, Ignatius Loyola, and Francis Xavier that had been advanced by his predecessor. He himself would canonize or beatify Elizabeth of Portugal, Francis Borgia, Cajetan, Mary Magdalene de' Pazzi, and many others, signaling his sincere desire to continue the Catholic Reformation and promote real change. His revisions of the process of canonization in 1625, which were confirmed in 1634, are still used as the basis of canon law. He also introduced reforms to the breviary (1632), revised the missal and pontifical (1631), writing many hymns himself, and issued the bull *In Coena Domini*, which stipulated excommunication for various heretics and other offenders, and decreed that it be read on every Maundy Thursday. Galileo Galilei, a friend to whom Urban had given advice years before in dealing with the theologians of the Curia, was condemned for a second time in 1633 by a reluctant order and compelled to abjure his theories on the Copernican system. Urban's nephew, Cardinal Francesco Barberini, abstained from accepting the sentence, and his uncle took steps to keep Galileo away from torture, allowing him to live his remaining years in comfort. More severe was Urban's bull *In eminenti* (1642), censuring Cornelius Jansen's *Augustinus*, the cornerstone of Jansenism. Urban also gave his approval to new religious orders, the Lazarists of St. Vincent de Paul (1632) and the Visitation order (1626).

A patron of foreign missions, he gave both encouragement and, when possible, money. Increasing the authority of the Congregation of Propaganda, he founded in 1627 the Collegium Urbanum for the training of missionaries. He hoped to increase missionary activity in Japan and China by opening them to all orders in 1633, thus ending the exclusive privileges granted to the Jesuits by Pope Gregory XIII in 1585. Urban issued a bull in 1639 that prohibited slavery among Indians of the West Indies, Brazil, and Paraguay. In England, meanwhile, improved relations with the court proved possible through Queen Henrietta Marie, the Catholic wife of King Charles I. The pontiff sent several emissaries, notably Gregorio Panzani and George Conn, but his hopes of reviving the Church in England proved impractical, especially with the outbreak of the Civil War (1642-1649) and its bloody conclusion.

Confronted by the ongoing Thirty Years' War, Urban tried to prevent the alliance between France and Sweden in 1631, but his fear of Spanish Habsburg supremacy in Italy drew him increasingly toward France. He gave Cardinal Richelieu surprisingly wide latitude in operations against the empire, aiding the French cause by holding back subsidies promised to the Holy League, all the while declaring his neutrality. This policy weakened the empire at the crisis point of Gustavus Adolphus's brilliant campaigns and effectively wrecked any recovery for Catholicism in Germany.

A poet, classical scholar, and patron of the arts, Urban spent heavily continuing the aggrandizement of Rome. He consecrated the completed St. Peter's Basilica on November 18, 1626, and his family coat of arms can still be seen throughout the city, most notably on the Baldacchino in St. Peter's. Unfortunately, he was also an inveterate nepotist, naming a brother and two nephews cardinals and promoting other family members with appalling frequency. He allowed the Barberini to amass such riches that he became suddenly alarmed in his final years, making an attempt at reforming himself and papal finances. Unfortunately, by then, he had already been led into a disastrous defeat in war against the duke of Parma from 1642-1644 launched at the behest of his nephews. The conflict had drained the treasury and caused such ruin to parts of the Papal States that Urban's death on July 29, 1644, was greeted by the Romans with joy. His successor was the somber Innocent X.

Urbi et Orbi ● Latin meaning "for the city and the world," used for the solemn blessing given by the pope from the balconies of the great basilicas of Rome at certain times of the year or as part of a major event. By custom, the blessing is given from St. Peter's at Christmas and Easter, normally preceded by a papal address that is a message to the world. Greetings for the occasion are usually given in a variety of languages; Pope John Paul II has long amazed those in attendance with the dozens of languages in which his greetings are made. In earlier pontificates the blessing was given at St. Peter's on Holy Thursday, Easter, and the Feast of Sts. Peter and Paul, at St. John Lateran on the Feast of the Ascension, and at Santa Maria Maggiore on the Feast of the Assumption. Solemn blessings were also given on special occasions, such as by Pope Innocent X in 1640 and Pope Pius IX until 1870, from the balcony of the Quirinal Palace. The most dramatic blessing comes after the election of a new pontiff, when the next successor to Peter presents himself to the world and gives his blessing *Urbi et Orbi*. A blessing is also given at the coronation (or installation) and during jubilee years.

Urbs Beata Jerusalem ● Hymn probably composed in the sixth or seventh century celebrating the Heavenly City of Jerusalem as described in the Book of Revelation (see ch. 21). It was comprised of eight stanzas (with a doxology) and was usually sung in the Office for the dedication of a church; the first four stanzas were usually used in Vespers and Matins, the last four for Lauds. Under Pope Urban VIII and the revision of the breviary, the unqualitative accentual, trochaic rhythm was changed into qualitative iambic meter with the beginning of the line *Coelestis Urbs Jerusalem*. Hymnologists long

criticized the revision as having lost much of its beauty and the original version was restored for breviaries in 1971.

Ursula, St. ● Essentially legendary virgin martyr who, with her company, called the Eleven Thousand Virgins, was put to death in Cologne by the Huns around the fourth century. The legend of Ursula and the Eleven Thousand Virgins was based on an inscription found in Cologne and dated to the fourth or fifth century. The inscription states that a certain Clematius had restored an ancient basilica on the site where holy virgins were put to death. The martyrs are again mentioned in the eighth or ninth century in a sermon honoring several thousand virgins killed under the Emperor Maximian. Over time, a version of the story attached the named Ursula to the leader of the virgins. According to this later legend, Ursula was a British princess who journeyed to Rome with a retinue of virgins (some accounts say eleven, others eleven thousand). On their return, they were massacred by the Huns at Cologne, near the Church of St. Ursula, which reputedly contained the relics of the martyrs. Owing to the serious question about the history of the martyrs, their feast day on October 21 is only kept locally. St. Ursula is the patron saint of the Order of St. Ursula and the Ursulines.

Ursulines ● Religious order of women founded by St. Angela Merici in 1535 at Brescia, Italy. It is remarkable for being the first such institute devoted exclusively to education. The Ursulines took their name from and placed themselves under the care of St. Ursula. The society of virgins began as a loose organization, since members lived with their families; they were engaged in numerous programs of charitable work, but their main endeavor was to promote Christian education. Initially approved by Pope Paul III in 1544, the Ursulines quickly spread from Italy to France. In 1572, at the urging of Charles Borromeo, Pope Gregory XIII imposed a simple rule and the beginning of a community life. The Ursulines of Paris in 1612 were allowed by Pope Paul V to adopt solemn vows and to reside in strict cloister. Convents following this pattern increased, with new communities in France and Canada. The Ursuline house in Quebec was founded in 1634 by Marie Gruyard (Marie of the Incarnation), making the Ursulines the first congregation of women to be formally organized in North America. While receiving a setback in their numbers during the French Revolution (1789-1815), the Ursulines prospered once more in the 1800s. In 1900, Pope Leo XIII promoted a Roman union at a congress in Rome that united all the Ursuline convents around the world. Similar unions were made in Belgium (1832), Canada (1953), Germany (1957), and Ireland (1973).

Usuard, Martyrology of ● Martyrology compiled by Usuard (d. c. 875), a Benedictine monk of the Abbey of St.-Germain-des-Prés, Paris. It was the basis of the Roman Martyrology and was the most famous of all martyrologies read throughout the Middle Ages. Written at the request of Charles the Bald, king of the West Franks (r. 843-877), the Martyrology of Usuard was probably completed just before Usuard's death. It was based on the Martyrology of Ado of Vienne, a slightly earlier compilation. He also most likely used the Lyonese recension of the Venerable Bede's augmented Martyrology, generally attributed to the archdeacon Florus. An important edition was edited by Dom Jacques Bouillart (1718), from a manuscript that was certainly contemporary with Usuard, if not the autograph of the author himself. (See also **Martyrology**.)

Usury ● See GLOSSARY.

Utica, Martyrs of ● Also Martyrs of Massa Candida. Group of martyrs traditionally put to death on August 24, 258, in the African city of Utica at a place known as Massa Candida (meaning the White Farm). They were mentioned by St. Augustine in a sermon (306) preached on their anniversary. According to Augustine, there were one hundred fifty-three martyrs, a number derived from a passage in the Gospel of John (21:11). He put the site of their deaths as Utica while the Roman Martyrology and Prudentius (in his *Peristephanon*) placed the number at three hundred; the Roman Martyrology also had them martyred in Carthage, around thirty-five miles from Utica. Feast day: August 24.

Utraquism ● Hussite doctrine first advanced in 1414 by Jacob of Mies, a professor of philosophy at the University of Prague. It declared the necessity of receiving Communion in both forms for the attainment of salvation. According to Utraquist teachings, salvation can only be attained by receiving Communion *sub utraque specie* (i.e., under the forms of bread and wine) because of the precept of Christ: "Truly, truly, I say to you, unless you eat the flesh of the Son of man and drink his blood, you have no life in you; he who eats my flesh and drinks my blood has eternal life, and I will raise him up at the last day" (Jn 6:53-54). This doctrine was rejected by the Council of Constance (1414-1418), the same assembly that condemned the founder of the Hussite movement, Jan Hus. Refusing to accept the council's declaration, the Hussites took up arms, and there followed the Hussite Wars. After years of fighting, the Council of Basel (1431-1449) accepted the compromise of Communion under both forms but with the stipulation that the Hussites (or Calixtines, from the call for the chalice — Latin *calix*) recognize that the body and blood of Jesus Christ were present entirely and completely under both forms and that they cease proclaiming that Communion under both forms is necessary for salvation. The compromise was an important element in the

Compactata of Prague (1435). The Compactata was accepted by the majority of the moderate Hussites. The radical Hussites, the Taborites, refused to adopt any compromise. They were finally defeated in 1453 after which time the cause of Utraquism ceased to have any serious adherents. Although Pope Pius II revoked the use of Communion in both forms in 1462, the practice was continued in Bohemia until 1567 and became part of the Anglican Church's eucharistic celebration.

Utrecht, Declaration of ● Doctrinal foundation of the Old Catholic Church. It was accepted by the assembly of Old Catholic bishops at Utrecht on September 24, 1889. Accepting only the decrees of the ecumenical councils to the year 1000 (the first eight councils), the bishops rejected the actions of Vatican Council I, the *Syllabus of Errors* of 1864, the dogma of the Immaculate Conception, and the encyclicals *Unigenitus* (1713) and *Auctorem fidei* (1794). (See **Old Catholics** for details.)

Valdés, Alfonso de (d. 1532) ● Spanish humanist and Latin secretary to Emperor Charles V. Born in Cuenca, Castile, Spain, he rose quickly in the imperial service and by 1520 accompanied Charles from Spain to Aachen for his coronation. The next year he went with Charles to the Diet of Worms. Appointed secretary in 1522, he was responsible for drafting the letter to Pope Clement VII (r. 1523-1534) in which the pontiff is treated harshly and an appeal is made to a general council. After the sack of Rome in 1527 by imperial troops, Valdés wrote the dialogue *Lactantius* (*Diálogo de Lactancio y un arcediano o de las cosas occuridas en Roma*, published in 1529), a defense of the incident and a vicious attack on the pope as the instigator of the war and a perfidious deceiver, and the portrayal of the Papal States as the worst governed realm in Christendom. Denounced to the Inquisition by Baldassare Castiglione, papal nuncio to Spain, Valdés was protected from all harm by his formidable patron. In 1530, he took part in the Diet of Augsburg and met with various Reformers, including Philipp Melanchthon. He had no particular sympathy for the Protestant cause, as is clear from his letter of congratulations to the Swiss Catholics of their defeat of Zwingli in 1531. A devoted humanist and a special adherent of Desiderius Erasmus, Valdés's chief work, *Diálogo de Mercurio y Caron* (1539; *Dialogue Between Mercurio and Charon*), decries the lamentable state of religion and extols the ideas of Erasmus, most notably the concept of the pure Christianity of the NT, in sharp contrast to the Church of which Clement VII was pontiff. His brother was Juan de Valdés (d. 1541), a Spanish religious writer and author of *Diálogo de la lengua* (1535; published 1737), an important work on the Spanish language, and *Diálogo de doctrina christiana* (1529), on Christian doctrine; the latter book encountered difficulties from the Inquisition.

Valens (d. 378) ● In full, Flavius Julius Valens. Emperor of the Eastern Roman Empire from 364-378. The second son of Gratianus the Elder, founder of the imperial house of Valentinian, he was the brother of Valentinian I (r. 364-375) whom he could never equal in ability. Given the post of co-emperor (or Augustus) by his brother, Valens ruled the East; he was described by the historian Ammianus Marcellinus as cruel, greedy, and unjust. These characteristics were certainly displayed in his treatment of Orthodox Christians. A pagan at the time of his elevation in 364, Valens was baptized an Arian Christian in 367 by Eudoxius, Arian patriarch of Constantinople, and thereafter persecuted Orthodox Christians. Some were put to death, others exiled. The orthodox bishops restored to their sees by Emperor Julian the Apostate (r. 361-363) were once more banished. His unhappy reign came to an end in 378. On August 9, 378, he engaged an army of Goths at Adrianople; his army was crushed and he died in battle. Theodosius I the Great (r. 379-392 in the East and 394-395 over the entire empire) succeeded him.

Valentine ● Pope from August to September 827. A Roman by birth, he was reportedly the son of Leontius who resided in the Via Lata district of the city. Owing to what the *Liber Pontificalis* describes as his piety and purity of morals, he was entered into papal service by Pope Paschal I (r. 817-824), who made him a subdeacon, deacon, then archdeacon and head of the Roman diaconate. Elected unanimously to succeed Pope Eugenius II (r. 824-827), he died after only forty days (according to the *Liber Pontificalis*) or less than a month (according to the *Annales* attributed to Einhard). No details have been preserved of his reign.

Valentinus ● Second-century Gnostic theologian and founder of the heretical sect of Valentinians. According to Epiphanius, St. Irenaeus, and other sources, he was a native of Egypt, born probably on the coast. After studying in Alexandria, he journeyed to Rome where he resided from around 136-165, arriving during the reign of Pope Hyginus (r. 136-140) and departing during that of Anicetus (r. 155-166). He was initially associated with the Orthodox Christians of Rome and, as written by Tertullian (*Adversus Valentinianos*), he had aspirations of being elected Bishop of Rome, *"quia et ingenio poterat et eloquio"* ("because of his intellectual ability and eloquence"). Disappointed in this ambition, he shifted away from orthodoxy and established himself as a heretical theologian. Most likely excommunicated, he traveled to Cyprus where he died. Few of his writings are extant, but he is the reputed author of *Evangelium Veritatis* (*Gospel of Truth*), a curious fusion of NT writings with Gnostic doctrines, a Coptic version of which was discovered in 1946 at Nag Hammadi. His original theology was highly influential in shaping subsequent Gnostic thought, especially as it was elaborated by his disciples, the Valentinians, including Bardesanes, Heracleon, and Theodatus.

Valentinus held that all things begin as emanations from the *Bythos*, or Primal Being. The first beings, called the *aeons*, numbered thirty, comprised of fifteen pairs, the *syzygies*. As the result of the sin of Sophia, one of the youngest *aeons*, the visible (i.e., the lower) world came into being. Her child was Demiurge, at times considered the God of the OT. Humankind was the highest being of the lower world, and redemption brought a freedom of the spiritual (higher) nature from servitude to the material world. The mission of Christ and the Holy Spirit was to bring that redemption. Christologically, Valentinus believed that the *aeon* Christ united himself with the man Jesus so that mankind might learn of its great destiny, that knowledge called *gnosis*. Such *gnosis*, however, was attainable only by the *pneumatics*, or men of the spirit, identified with the Valentinians; Christians and some pagans were classified as *psychics* and were able by good deeds to reach a middle kingdom ruled by Demiurge; all the others, deemed *hylics* (engrossed in matter) were doomed to eternal damnation. A complex theological system relying upon Christian, Pythagorean, and Platonic concepts, Valentinianism became divided into Western and Eastern (Oriental) branches. Its influence has been noted by scholars not only in broad Gnosticism but also in many heretical Christian ideas such as Pelagianism.

Valerian (d. 260) ● In full, Publius Licinius Valerianus, he was Roman emperor from 253-260, a harsh persecutor of Christians. Probably a consul during the reign of Emperor Alexander Severus (222-235), Valerian was rapidly promoted by Emperor Trajanus Decius (r. 249-251), most likely because of their mutual hatred of Christianity. A general in charge of the legions on the Rhine by 253, he was proclaimed emperor by his troops, overcoming Emperor Aemilian, who was murdered by his own soldiers to avoid a civil war. His reign was dominated by wars and a relentless persecution of the Church. Under Valerian, many Christians were put to death, including St. Cyprian of Carthage and Pope St. Sixtus II (r. 257-258). His wars necessitated the appointment of his son Gallienus as ruler of the Western Empire while he campaigned against the Goths in the East. In 260, he was defeated in battle by the Persians, captured, humiliated, and murdered, his body stuffed and put on display as a trophy in a Persian temple.

Valla, Lorenzo (1406-1457) ● Italian humanist and philosopher. Born in Rome, he studied both Latin and Greek and was ordained in 1431. That same year, he accepted a chair of eloquence at the University of Pavia. While there he wrote the first of his important works, *De Voluptate* (1431), a dialogue between spokesmen for Christian, Stoic, and Epicurean schools of thought; a revised edition of the treatise appeared under the title *De vero bono*. In 1433, Valla had to flee the city after making an attack upon the jurist Bartolo and fellow jurists of Pavia. Journeying at first to Milan and then to Genoa, Valla attempted to receive an appointment in the papal administration, finally becoming a secretary in Naples to King Alfonso I. In Naples he authored *De libero arbitrio*, *Dialectae disputationes*, *De professione religiosorum*, and the *Declamatio*, or *Declamazione contro la donazione di Constantino* (1440), an attempt to prove the spurious nature of the Donation of Constantine. In his writings he advanced the idea that Scholasticism confused Aristotelian thought and denied the apostolic origins of the Apostles' Creed. Tried for heresy in Naples, he was saved from any possible condemnation by King Alfonso. After years of hoping for a position in Rome, Valla finally was named scriptor in 1448 by Pope Nicholas

V. Later, he served as apostolic secretary and was granted a canonry by Pope Callistus III. Aside from the *Calattio Novi Testamenti* (1444), a critical comparison of the Greek and Vulgate New Testaments, he also wrote *De elegantia linguae latinae* (1442), a highly influential study of the Latin language that was to become the standard work on the subject in the Renaissance. The first exponent of historical criticism, Valla had a lasting influence on Renaissance thought and was also much read for his humanist writings by the Reformers of the sixteenth century.

Vallarsi, Domenico (1702-1771) ● Italian patristic scholar. A native of Verona, he was educated by the Jesuits and became a priest. He acquired considerable notoriety for his archaeological knowledge and study of patristic writings. His chief work is an edition of St. Jerome (11 vols., 1734-1742, enlarged and revised in 1766-1772). It is considered one of the best if not the finest editions of St. Jerome and was a considerable improvement over the Maurist edition by Martinay and Pouget (1693-1706).

Vallombrosian Order ● Religious order of Benedictines that derived its name from the motherhouse of Vallombrosa, on Mt. Secchieta, near Florence. The Vallombrosians were founded around 1036 as an order of monks by St. John Gualbert (d. 1073, canonized 1193). According to tradition, he set out one day to avenge the murder of a relative, meeting the murderer in a narrow lane. About to kill him, St. John suddenly had a change of heart when the murderer threw himself on the ground with his arms outstretched in the shape of a cross. Overcome with love for Christ, John spared the man's life and went to church to pray. There the crucifix bowed its head in recognition of his charity. After entering the Benedictine order, he found himself drawn to the cenobitic lifestyle, and, after spending some time with the monks at Camaldoli, he found his way to Vallombrosa where he established a monastery. Adopting the Rule of St. Benedict, St. John added to it requirements of great severity and penance, receiving formal approval from

Vatican Apostolic Palace

Pope Victor II in 1055 or 1056. The order quickly spread after the founder's death, with houses in Italy, Sardinia, and France. Reforms were undertaken in the fifteenth century by Cassinese Benedictines and in the early 1600s by St. John Leonardi. The monastery of Vallombrosa was burned in 1527 by troops of Emperor Charles V. Rebuilt in 1637, it was sacked in 1808 by the soldiers of Napoleon, and the monastery was deserted until 1815 and the final defeat of the emperor. It was finally suppressed in 1866 by the Italian government. The loss of the motherhouse began the order's decline and the number of houses was reduced over the next years. The Vallombrosian order of nuns was initially attached to the monastery of Vallombrosa and consisted of lay sisters under the care of a lay brother. The foundress is considered to be Bl. Bertha Bardi (d. 1163), but the real person responsible is St. Umilta (or Humilitas, d. 1310), who established a monastery for nuns just outside Faenza and served as its abbess; she founded a second convent in Florence in 1282.

Valor Ecclesiasticus ● Official tabulation made of revenues from ecclesiastical and monastic institutions that was undertaken in 1535, the result of the steps taken by King Henry VIII (r. 1509-1547) to remove the Church of England from the control and authority of the papacy. By the terms of the laws promulgated under Henry, those amounts that were to be given to the pope, plus one tenth of all annual income, were to be forfeited to the crown, thereby depriving the Church of its rightful monies from the English Church. The accounting is of interest to historians not only for its providing of details on the state of reform in England but also for preserving a clear picture of the Church of England at the time, in a way considered similar to that of the survey during the reign of King William I the Conqueror (r. 1066-1087) that resulted in the Domesday Book.

Vatican ● Current chief residence of the pope (see also **Vatican City, State of**). The Vatican is located in Rome, on the Vatican Hill (*Mons Vaticanus*) and occupies the site originally used for the Circus Nero. It has been the principal home of the popes since 1377. The first papal residence was probably built under Pope St. Symmachus (r. 498-514) to provide quarters near the Basilica of St. Peter. From that beginning, the popes gradually acquired through gifts and purchases the entire Vatican Hill, building and replacing the residence from time to time. This was not the chief home of the popes, however, as they chose to live in the Lateran Palace, near the Lateran Basilica. A new palace was erected by Pope Innocent III (r. 1198-1216) around 1200. Additions were made by Pope Nicholas III (r. 1277-1280), but the palace was soon virtually abandoned when the papacy moved to Avignon in 1308. The so-called Avignon Papacy would last until 1377, during which time the palace fell into disrepair, although Pope Gregory XI (r. 1370-1378) found it in better shape than the Lateran Palace when he entered the city. He thus chose to remain there from 1377, and the first conclave was held in the Vatican the next year, electing Pope Urban VI (r. 1378-1389), one of the key figures in causing the Great Schism.

Extensive rebuilding took place over the next years. Pope Nicholas V (r. 1447-1455) added housing for members of the Sacred College and space for the growing papal bureaucracy. Even more construction was undertaken by subsequent Renaissance pontiffs: Sixtus IV (r. 1471-1484), who built the Sistine Chapel; Innocent VIII (r. 1484-1492); Julius II (r. 1503-1513); and Paul III (r. 1534-1549). Pope Clement VIII (r. 1592-1605) completed the current apostolic palace. Included or attached to the palace are the Sistine Chapel, the Vatican Library, the Vatican Archives, the Vatican Gardens, the Vatican Museums, and the offices and departments of most of the Roman Curia. The term is often used colloquially to mean the City State of the Vatican or the entire central administration of the Church. (See also **Holy See** and **St. Peter's Basilica**.)

Vatican Bank ● Common name given to the more properly titled Instituto per le Opere di Religione (Italian for Institute for Works of Religion), or IOR. It is the institution charged with handling the banking needs of the "population" of the Vatican, the workers, diplomats, certain clients, heads of religious orders, and for those connected in various capacities with the Vatican City State; its other tasks include financial and investment advice and the administration of funds intended for works of religion. The Vatican Bank is one of the elements of the finances of the Holy See, with the Prefecture for the Economic Affairs of the Holy See (begun in 1967 under Pope Paul VI and redefined under Pope John Paul II in 1988), the Administration of the Patrimony of the Apostolic See, the Apostolic Chamber (Apostolic Camera), and the Council of Cardinals for the Study of Organizational and Economic Problems of the Holy See, established in 1981 by John Paul II.

The IOR has its origins in the Administration of Religious Works founded in 1887 by Pope Leo XIII to oversee the distribution of funds intended for religious purposes. This office was replaced in 1942 by Pope Pius XII with the IOR, which had a modified mission from the Administration of Religious Works. It was to administer the funds of the religious orders that might be moved through the Vatican and to oversee the monies, in both cash and bonds, as well as "properties transferred or entrusted to the institute itself by fiscal or legal persons for the purpose of religious works of Christian piety." Its practical purpose was to keep safe the funds of the Vatican through the international connection at a time when the State of Vatican City was in danger of being overrun by Nazi Germany. In the postwar years, the IOR was a major player in the financial stability of the Holy See. The involvement of the bank in the now well-known scandal of the 1970s and early 1980s was the source of considerable and highly sensationalized reports and books that quite often misinterpreted or misrepresented the facts of the case and often relied upon dubious evidence or sources. The errors and misjudgments of the officials of the bank, which were the cause of speculation as to the supposed impending insolvency of the Holy See, have been corrected in the last years, as evidenced by the profit shown by the Vatican in 1994. The IOR itself was substantially reorganized on March 1, 1990, by Pope John Paul II. (See also **Lateran Treaty**.)

Vatican Council I ● Twentieth ecumenical (or general) council in the history of the Church. Convened by Pope Pius IX (r. 1846-1878), it was held between December 8, 1869, and September 1, 1870. Owing to the seizure of Rome by the troops of King Victor Emmanuel II, the council was adjourned by the pope indefinitely; it was never officially ended and never reconvened. The council was best known for two achievements: the dogmatic constitutions *Dei Filius* and *Pastor Aeternus*, the latter giving definition to papal infallibility.

Pope Pius recognized the desirability of holding a council. There had not been one since Trent (1545-1563), and the world had changed immeasurably in the intervening years. Further, the Church was confronted with the rise of liberalism, rationalism, and wide regard for sciences that many felt were dangers to the faith by their promotion of rationalist criticism of Catholic doctrine and Scripture, religious indifference, hostility to many Christian tenets, and the questioning of the place of the Church in the modern world. A council was also desired to strengthen the authority and prestige of the papacy in the wake of the demise of the Papal States in 1860 by the Italians under Victor Emmanuel and the virtual extirpation of the centuries-old temporal power of the Holy See.

Pope Pius IX

The announcement was made by Pius to the cardinals of the Curia of his intentions to summon a council on December 4, 1864, two days before the publication of the *Syllabus of Errors*. In March 1865, Pius appointed a preparatory commission. The formal announcement of a council was made on June 29, 1867, and exactly one year later the pope issued the bull *Aeterni Patris*, which convoked the council. The opening at St. Peter's Basilica had about seven hundred prelates, assorted officials, and dignitaries; interestingly, this was the first council that did not send invitations to ambassadors and princes.

The first of the council's assemblies (called general congregations) was convened on December 10, 1869. Later that month, deliberations commenced on the dogmatic constitution on the faith. After spirited discussions and revisions, it was approved by final vote on April 24, 1870. *Dei Filius* was a profound reaffirmation of the teachings of the Church. Its chapters were concerned with: God as Creator; revelation; faith; and faith and reason — with attached canons to clarify important points and to condemn those who denied certain aspects of the faith (fideists, rationalists, naturalists, etc.). It vindicated human reason as sufficient to know God without revelation, stressed the reasonableness of faith, and elucidated the presence of the two kinds of knowledge, faith and reason.

While the question of infallibility was not specifically on Pius's planned list of topics to be discussed, it was uppermost in the minds of many Fathers owing to the aspirations of the Ultramontanists to have it advanced and the concern of liberal Catholics that it should not be defined. In the period prior to the council, the matter had been the source of often bitter debate. The question was formally raised in January 1870 with a series of petitions supported by some five hundred Council Fathers in favor of giving papal infallibility definition. The debate continued for several months, ending on July 4. Finally, on July 18, the fourth session gave solemn definition of the primacy and infallible authority of the Roman pontiff in the *Constitutio Dogmatica Prima de Ecclesia Christi* (First Dogmatic Constitution on the Church of Christ). (See **Infallibility** for other details.)

The majority of the Council Fathers departed the hot city of Rome for the summer, reassembling in late August. The last (eighty-ninth) general congregation was convened on September 1. One week later, Italian troops pushed across the papal frontier and moved against Rome, which fell on September 20. The papal lands had been left virtually defenseless when French protecting troops had departed the Eternal City with the start of the Franco-Prussian War. Pius suspended the council and it did not reassemble. When Pope John XXIII (r. 1958-1963) considered calling his own council, it was suggested to him that he simply reconvene the First Vatican Council; he chose to start a new one.

Vatican Council II ● Twenty-first ecumenical (or general) council. Held in Rome between 1962 and 1965, it was one of the most important councils in the history of the Church. Vatican II was only the second such assembly since the Council of Trent (1545-1563), the other being Vatican Council I (1869-1870). While a council had been considered by Pope Pius XII (r. 1939-1958), it had not come to any kind of fruition beyond the recognition of many in the Church that a council might be desirable to address the

challenges confronting the faith in the radically changed world following the global conflict of World War II (see **Pius XII**). It was Pius's successor, John XXIII (r. 1958-1963), who is given singular credit for deciding to summon another ecumenical gathering. That pontiff claimed the idea to have been an inspiration by the Holy Spirit. At first discouraged in the undertaking by members of the Curia, he persisted and, despite probably knowing that his health might not permit him to see its end, John gave the order for preparations to go ahead.

On May 16, 1959, Cardinal Domenico Tardini was appointed the head of the first preparatory commission with the task of consulting with the prelates of the Church throughout the globe and the esteemed theologians of the Catholic universities. On June 29, Pope John issued the encyclical *Ad Petri cathedram* in which he gave formal explanation of the purpose of the council. The next year, he wrote the *motu proprio Superno Dei nutu* (June 5, 1960), by which he announced the appointment of a preparatory commission and other ancillary and subordinate commissions and secretariats. John himself headed the central commission and appointed curial cardinals to preside over the others; the one exception was the Secretariat on Communications Media, under Archbishop Martin O'Connor, rector of the North American College (1946-1964; later nuncio to Malta, 1965-1969, and head of the Pontifical Commission for Social Communication, 1964-1969).

These commissions initiated their work in November 1960 and were finished in June 1962. The previous year, on Christmas Day, John published the apostolic constitution *Humanae salutis*, instructing the council to begin in 1962. By the *motu proprio Concilium* (February 2, 1962), he placed the opening of the proceedings at October 2, 1962. After commending the assembly to the protection of St. Joseph, on July 1, 1962, he asked all Catholics to do penance in anticipation of the work of the Council Fathers through the encyclical *Paenitentiam agere.*

John had as his stated goals the renewal of the Church, its modernization to facilitate the accomplishment of its mission in the modern world, and thereby to foster the unity of all Christians. He used the term *aggiornamento* (updating) to describe the aim of his program and hopes. At the opening session (October 11), attended by 2,540 prelates, the pope stressed the distinctly positive nature of his call.

The council was given its organization by the *motu proprio Appropinquante concilio* (August 2, 1962). There were to be three types of meetings: commissions of twenty-four members; general congregations where first votes and discussions would be held; and public sessions, headed by the pope, at which final votes on the assorted documents would be taken. The commissions and secretariats were: Doctrinal Commission for the Faith and Morals; Commission for the Eastern Churches; Commission for the Discipline of the Sacraments; Commission for the Discipline of the Clergy and Christian People; Commission for Religious; Commission for the Missions; Commission for the Liturgy; Commission for Seminaries, Studies, and Catholic Schools; Commission for the Apostolate of the Laity, Press, and Entertainment; and Secretariat for the Promotion of Christian Unity.

The work of the council was carried out in four sessions: Session I (October 11-December 8, 1962), Session II (September 29-December 4, 1963), Session III (September 14-November 21, 1964), and Session IV (September 14-December 8, 1965). At the first congregation of December 13, 1962, in Session I, two cardinals, Joseph Frings of Cologne and Achille Liénart of Lille, requested that the Council Fathers should adjourn until December 16 so as to familiarize themselves with possible candidates for the commissions and be granted the right to choose their own commission members instead of the ones picked by the Curia. This move, approved by John, significantly altered the atmosphere, proceedings, and direction of the commissions and the council itself.

After the close of the first session, the remaining deliberations would be presided over by a new pontiff. Increasingly ill, John had attended the last meeting of the session with difficulty. His health deteriorated over the early part of 1963, and he died on June 3.

In the resulting conclave, the cardinals chose Cardinal Giovanni Montini, archbishop of Milan, on June 21, 1963, Pope Paul VI. Montini had been a clear favorite on entering the conclave and had been used extensively by John in the preparation for the council. Besides being considered the chosen successor of John, Montini also clearly desired to continue the council in the Johannine tradition (although he later confessed that he would not have summoned a council on his own). His eulogy of Pope John — declaring that the council must continue on the path chosen by John — and his own statements of approval were said by many observers to have been critical to his election.

Work resumed on September 29, 1963, and the sessions went on for two years. The result was embodied in the sixteen documents promulgated by the council, two dogmatic and two pastoral constitutions (the heart of the reforms), nine decrees, and three declarations (see TABLE 13; see also under individual documents). Pope Paul solemnly closed the council on December 8, 1965. Since that time, the Church has been faced with the major challenge in implementing the reforms and processes of modernization while maintaining Tradition and interpreting in an authentic way both the specific commands and the spirit of the council. Toward that end, both Popes Paul VI and John Paul II have issued hundreds of decrees and statements on the proper interpretation of its acts and decrees. John Paul II has been a determined champion of the authentic meaning of Vatican II and has warned against interpretations that fail to consider the continuity of Tradition or to de-emphasize or even denigrate the preconciliar Church.

Vatican Library ● Official library of the popes and one of the greatest libraries in the entire world. The history of the Vatican Library is complicated by the fact that there were actually several libraries owing to the destruction of early and subsequent collections through the chronic changes of papal residences and the fires and strife that beset Rome over the centuries. Clearly, as early as the fourth century the papal administration contained assorted archives and libraries. Such is visible in the remains of the library in the Lateran Palace and the library of Pope Agapetus (r. 535-536). Knowledge of the library holdings during the Middle Ages is available only in any detail from the thirteenth century. A third library was organized at Avignon in the fourteenth century, reaching its fullest size under Pope Clement VI (r. 1342-1352). Unfortunately, not many of the manuscripts from Avignon found their way to the Vatican when the papacy returned in 1377. While the groundwork was laid by Pope Martin V (1417-1431) and Eugenius IV (1431-1447), the founder of the Vatican Library (counted as the fourth library), was the remarkable humanist Pope Nicholas V (1447-1455) who, among other contributions, acquired the remains of the great imperial library of Constantinople after the capture of that city by the Turks in 1453. Halls to house the library were built under Pope Sixtus IV (1471-1484), who appointed the humanist Bartolomeo Platina prefect of the apostolic library on June 15, 1475.

Known as the *Libreria Palatina*, it grew under succeeding pontiffs. In 1548, Cardinal Marcello Cervini (later Pope Marcellus II) was named the first cardinal librarian and protector; the post has remained in the hands of a cardinal ever since, although the immediate director is the prefect, assisted by the vice-prefect. Under Sixtus V (1585-1590) special buildings were constructed to house the library and the resulting Salone Sistino della Libreria Vaticana gave the Vatican Library its name. Numerous collections and sumptuous, important manuscripts were added, making the library a tempting target for plunder by the French under Napoleon Bonaparte. In 1797, the heart of the collection was carried off, returned almost intact in 1815. The nineteenth century also witnessed the addition of more manuscripts and collections, including the Borghese manuscripts (with three hundred codices from the old Avignon library), the Barberini Library, and the *Codices Reginae*, *Capponiani, Ottoboniani*, and *Urbinates*. Pope Leo XIII (r. 1878-1903) opened the papal holdings to scholars from all over, citing as his reason that "the Church has no secrets."

Under Pope Pius XI (r. 1922-1939), himself onetime prefect of the library, extensive improvements and additions were made, with modern cataloging and a massive, ultimately seven-mile-long shelving system made of steel. A crucial role was played in this endeavor by Cardinal Eugene Tisserant, who became pro-prefect in 1930. During World War II, the library served as a sanctuary for some of the finest collections in Italy, thereby preventing their irreplaceable destruction, including the National Library, the Frascati Library, and the manuscripts of Monte Cassino. In 1984, Pope John Paul II officially opened a new vault stretching beneath the library courtyard where the most valuable manuscripts in the Vatican's possession are now kept. Aside from the staff of workers who catalog the manuscripts and printed books, there are sections for book repairing, bookbinding, and publishing.

Vatican Museums ● Enormous collection of art gathered and preserved by the Holy

See. Renowned throughout the world, the Vatican Museums are visited by millions of visitors each year and are the repositories of some of the rarest and most significant art pieces to be found anywhere. The museums are the longtime result of the patronage of the popes in art, their private donations, and the fact that the Vatican became the gathering place of the very best of artists and artisans.

Popes had been collecting art for centuries, but the actual organizing of a museum was not undertaken until the pontificate of Pope Benedict XIV (1740-1758), who began the Museum of Christian Antiquities (or Sacred Museums), with a magnificent collection of ivory, bronze, glass, and textiles mostly found in the catacombs. The origins of the museums are traced to two acts of papal goodwill. The first was in 1471 when Sixtus IV (r. 1471-1484), a member of the wealthy Della Rovere family, gathered part of his private collection of sculpture and placed it on display in the Capitoline Palace for the enjoyment of the Romans. The second was under Sixtus's nephew, Julius II (r. 1503-1513), patron of Michelangelo and Bramante. He created a sculpture exhibit in the courtyard of the Belvedere Palace that included the famed Apollo Belvedere and the Laocoön group. While ostensibly open to the Roman populace, the exhibit was rather selective, as shown with the sign at the entrance: *"Procul este prophani"* ("The profane, keep away").

From the time of Benedict XIV, succeeding popes added new museums or expanded old ones. The chief contributors were Clement XIII (1758-1769), Clement XIV (1769-1774), Pius VI (1775-1799), Gregory XVI (1831-1846), Pius IX (1846-1878), Leo XIII (1878-1903), Pius XI (1922-1939), and Paul VI (1963-1978). The museums are under the jurisdiction of the general Administration of the Pontifical Monuments, Museums, and Galleries, part of the Pontifical Commission for the Vatican City State. The buildings housing the collection were originally papal palaces built for several Renaissance popes such as Julius II and Innocent VIII, making the settings of the art as interesting and historically significant as the collections they house.

Vatican Observatory ● Formally, Specola Vaticana (Italian for Vatican Observatory), the organization devoted to the study of astronomy. The formal interest of the popes in matters of astronomy dates to the reign of Pope Gregory XIII (1572-1585), who desired a research institute to assist in the reform of the calendar — and for a proper reform to take place, precise and excellent calculations were essential. To house his new unit, Gregory built in 1576 the Tower of the Winds. This became the home of the Specola Vaticana in 1579. Work gradually moved to the Roman College Observatory, which made contributions to observation during the 1800s, especially through the Jesuit Pietro Angelo Secchi. In 1870, however, the Italian government seized the observatory in the takeover of Rome. Pope Leo XIII (r. 1878-1903) reopened the Specola Vaticana in 1895 in the Tower of the Winds. It would remain in the Vatican until 1930 when Eugenio Pacelli (the future Pope Pius XII), cardinal secretary of state, ordered the observatory moved to Castel Gandolfo. Located at the Palazzo Pontificio in Castel Gandolfo, it had new telescopes from the Zeiss optical company, with an astrophysical laboratory. In the early part of his pontificate, Pope Paul VI was a regular visitor to the Jesuits who run the observatory.

Vatican City, State of ● In Italian, Stato della Città del Vaticano. Also Vatican State, Vatican City State, or Papal State, it is the independent state created in Rome by the terms of the Lateran Treaty (February 11, 1929) signed between the Holy See and the kingdom of Italy. According to the agreement, the pope is recognized as absolute owner and sovereign of Vatican City. The Lateran Treaty ended the difficult situation that had existed between the papacy and the Italian government since 1870, when Rome was seized, the last temporal holdings of the popes were liquidated, and the problematic Roman Question came into being. Interestingly, the existence of the sovereign state of Vatican City is recognized by understanding the spiritual sovereignty of the pope, finding justification not in the reality of its existence but through its relation to the Holy See, to which it is utterly subservient. Despite its spiritual basis, the Vatican State is a true state with a government, territorial limits, and a population. Government is in the hands of the pontiff, who possesses full rights in the executive, judicial, and legislative sense. Overall administrative duties are carried out by the Pontifical Commission for the Vatican State. The size of the state is 108.7 acres, although there are also so-called extraterritorial possessions that are accorded full status as sovereign territories of the State of Vatican City. These include assorted office buildings, basilicas, and Castel Gandolfo. Normally, the population is around one thousand, comprised of several hundred laypersons with the remainder being priests and religious. The laws governing justice are based on canon law. (See also **Holy See**.)

Vaughan, Herbert (1832-1903) ●

Archbishop of Westminster from 1892 and cardinal from 1893. Born in Gloucester, England, he was a member of a long-time Catholic family that had suffered much in previous years for its devout adherence to the faith. The son of Colonel John Vaughan and Eliza Rolls, a convert, Herbert studied at the Jesuit colleges of Stonyhurst in England and Brugelette, Belgium. After attending the Roman College, he was ordained at Lucca, Italy, in 1854. Appointed by Cardinal Nicholas Wiseman to the post of vice-president of the seminary of St.

Edmund's College, Ware, at the time the leading seminary in England, he was disappointed in his time there, in large part because of the dispute that arose between Wiseman and the Oblates of St. Charles of which Vaughan had become a member. Anxious to establish a college in England that might train missionaries (St. Peter Claver was a model for his life), Vaughan departed St. Edmund's and worked from 1863-1865 in South America to raise money for the project. In March 1866, Vaughan founded St. Joseph's College, Mill Hill, near London, and in 1871 the St. Joseph's Missionary Society began work among what they termed the colored people of United States. To improve his understanding of the needs of the society, Vaughan toured the American South, visiting St. Louis, New Orleans, Memphis, and elsewhere. Returning to England, Vaughan added to his interests by purchasing the newspaper *The Tablet* in 1868. The paper proved a leading source of support for the papacy, particularly during the controversies attendant to Vatican Council I and the doctrine of papal infallibility. For his devotion, Vaughan received the thanks of Pope Pius IX (r. 1846-1878) and in 1872 was appointed bishop of Salford. Consecrated in October 1872, Vaughan focused many of his efforts on improving the educational opportunities of the diocese and the training of priests. He also concerned himself with the terrible conditions faced by Catholic (and other) children in workhouses, creating and promoting rescue and protection societies to save children from the streets and premature death from brutal working conditions. On March 29, 1892, Vaughan was made archbishop of Westminster, over his own protests, receiving the red hat the next year. His time as archbishop proved quite active. He secured the right from Church officials in Rome to reverse the policy of discouraging Catholics from attending such renowned universities as Oxford and Cambridge, took part in the ultimately unsuccessful discussions on the Anglican Orders, and launched the building of the great Cathedral of Westminster in 1895. One of Vaughan's last triumphs was seeing the passage of the Education Bill of 1902.

Vázquez, Gabriel (d. 1604) ● Also spelled Vásquez, he was a Spanish theologian known as Bellomontanus, from the place of his birth, Belmonte. After studying in his native town and at Alcalá, Vázquez entered the Society of Jesus in April 1569 and subsequently taught moral theology at Ocana, Madrid, and Alcalá. He was summoned to Rome around 1585, teaching at the Roman College for the next six years and then returning to Alcalá, where he remained a lecturer in theology until his death. Called by Pope Benedict XIV a luminary of theology, Vázquez was one of the most respected theologians of his era. He opposed his renowned contemporary Francisco Suárez on such matters as grace and points of Scholastic, especially Thomistic, thought. In matters of his work, he was criticized for his obstinate defense of opinions often held by contemporary theologians to be erroneous or obtuse and the waste of his considerable talent on matters of little use or value. Chief among his writings was the *Commentariorum ac Disputationum,* on the *Summa* of Thomas Aquinas (8 vols., 1598-1615); he also wrote the *Metaphysicae disputationes,* on philosophical questions (1618).

Venerable Bede ● See **Bede the Venerable, St**.

Venice ● Or Venezia (the Italian name). A onetime powerful maritime republic situated on one hundred eighteen islets in a lagoon in the Gulf of Venice toward the northern end of the Adriatic Sea, it was originally settled in the fifth century by refugees who hoped to find safety from the numerous barbarian invaders then pouring into Italy and along the Adriatic. At first under the control of the Byzantines, specifically the exarch of Ravenna, the Venetians came to desire independence and achieved the rule of the first doge (duke) as early as 697, under Paulutius Anafestus. Some scholars speculate that he was actually a Byzantine governor, but by the early ninth century the doge and Venice were given certification of their independence in a treaty between Emperor Nikephoros I and Emperor Charlemagne in 810. From around 1000, the republic blossomed into a maritime power in the Mediterranean, earning the title "Queen of the Seas" and coming to control Dalmatia, Crete, Cyprus, and a number of Greek islands. Desirous of reducing the mercantile influence of the Byzantines, the Venetians connived to win the contract for transporting the crusader forces embarking for the Fourth Crusade. When, however, the crusaders were unable to pay, the doge Enrico Dandolo convinced them to overthrow the Byzantine Empire by capturing Constantinople (1204). The Venetians profited enormously in plunder, new territories, and international prestige.

Decline set in during the late 1400s, as the Venetians could not stem the advance of the Ottoman Turks in the Balkans and Mediterranean. The discovery of a new route to the East in 1498 by the Portuguese would also have long-term implications for Venetian prosperity. Most of its Greek possessions were lost by 1715, and the republic soon became a pawn in the territorial games between France and Austria. The republic was formally ended in 1797 by Napoleon Bonaparte, who seized it without a shot. It was then given to Austria. In 1866, both Venice and the surrounding area of Venetia were united with the kingdom of Italy.

Throughout its long history, Venice regularly opposed the territorial expansion of the Papal States in the Italian peninsula and the efforts of the popes to enforce their authority over the Italian states. In the early seventeenth century, for example, the Venetians challenged the claims of Pope Paul V (r. 1605-1621) and brought two clerics to trial. Paul protested and in 1606 excommunicated the Venetian senate, placing the city under interdict. The Venetians rejected the decree and gave sanctuary and encouragement to the antipapal theologian Paolo Sarpi (1552-1623). A negotiated settlement was reached in 1607 with French assistance, but the Venetians had won a moral victory against the papacy by retaining the law of exclusion toward the Jesuits and proving that papal decrees were increasingly powerless when issued in a medieval fashion.

The see of Venice was founded in 774 as the diocese of Olivolo, later known as Costello. It was placed under the patriarchate of Grado. Its most famous bishop was Angelo Correr, who served as bishop from 1380-1390. He later became Latin patriarch of Constantinople and in 1406 was elected pope as Gregory XII (r. 1406-1415) during the Great Schism. Throughout the history of the see, the bishops were in constant dispute with the patriarch of Grado. A final solution was reached in 1451 with the suppression of both sees. In their place was established the patriarchate of Venice. The first patriarch was St. Lawrence Giustiniani. The twentieth century has witnessed three patriarchs of Venice become pope: Giuseppe Sarto as St. Pius X (1903-1914), Angelo Roncalli as John XXIII (1958-1963), and Albino Luciani as John Paul I, the "September Pope" (August 26-September 28, 1978). Venice is noted for its unique canal-oriented lifestyle and its magnificent churches and villas. Chief among the churches is St. Mark's, the chapel of the doges and now the cathedral church of the patriarch. (See also **Italy, Mechitarists,** and **Patriarch.**)

Venturino of Bergamo (1304-1346) ● Dominican preacher. A native of Bergamo, he entered the Dominican order in 1319 and by 1328 was a well-known preacher. From 1328-1335, he preached extensively in Italy, drawing large crowds. In 1335, he announced his plans to go on a pilgrimage to Rome with tens of thousands of converts. This pilgrimage was misunderstood, however, by Pope Benedict XII in Avignon; the pope feared that Venturino was planning to crown himself pope in Rome. Consequently, the pope sent messages to officials in Rome imploring them to stop the pilgrims, and the Dominicans decreed at the Chapter of London (1335) that such pilgrimages were to be forbidden. Venturino reached Rome in March 1335 without being aware of the papal ban, but within days he had left Rome. Going to Avignon in June of that year, he was arrested by Benedict and imprisoned until 1343. Restored by Clement VI (r. 1342-1352), Venturino preached a crusade against the Turks.

Veronica, St. ● Legendary woman of Jerusalem who, struck with pity for Christ on the way to Calvary, wiped his face with a cloth (on which the image of his face was imprinted). While there is no reliable historical evidence for this event, the story became widespread in Christian lore, appearing in a variety of forms. In a later version of the apocryphal *Acts of Pilate*, she was identified with the woman mentioned in Matthew (9:20-22) who suffered from an issue of blood. She supposedly cured the emperor Tiberius with the sacred relic. The Veil of Veronica (or Veronica's Veil) was purportedly seen in Rome from the eighth century, being translated to St. Peter's by Pope Boniface VIII in 1297. The name Veronica probably originated, as reported by Giraldus Cambrensis (c. 1147-1223), from the term *veronica*, derived from the title *vera icon* (true image). This was used to distinguish it from other relics found in other cities (such as Milan) where the head cloth was supposedly kept. Despite the presence of several veils, the relic was extremely popular during the Middle Ages; it continues to be kept in St. Peter's. The Stations of the Cross include St. Veronica and the incident of the cloth. St. Veronica is honored with a feast, even though she is not included in the Roman Martyrology. Feast day: July 12.

Vianney, John, St. (1786-1859) ● In full, Jean-Batiste Marie Vianney. Called the Curé d'Ars, he was the patron of parish priests and a great preacher and confessor. He was born in Dardilly, near Lyons, and was the son of a farmer, intended for the priesthood. His training began in 1806 but was soon interrupted by his being conscripted into the French army during the Napoleonic Wars. He deserted and spent fourteen months in hiding avoiding military service. When he returned to priestly studies, his progress was much hindered by his total inability to learn Latin; he was finally ordained in 1815, largely because of his personal devoutness and goodness. Sent in February 1818 to serve as a humble priest in the village of Ars-en-Dombes, he settled in and amazed his flock with his preaching and skills as a confessor. Word began to spread to neighboring areas about his gifts, especially his ability to know the sins of those who came to him for confession. People flocked to Ars to hear him preach, but most importantly to confess their sins and seek his advice. As time passed and his fame continued to spread, people arrived from other countries. St. John Vianney was eventually to spend up to eighteen hours a day in the confessional listening to the sins of tens of thousands of people. He naturally

St. John Vianney

earned the enmity of fellow priests who, dismissing him as ignorant, refused to accept the authenticity of his mission. When some complained that he was insane or mentally unstable, the local bishop replied that he wished all his priests had a touch of the same insanity. The demands of his work were hard on John, however, and he tried several times to leave the parish and find peace in a monastery. Each time he was brought back, dying while still listening to a repentant sinner. Beatified in 1905, he was canonized in 1925 by Pope Pius XI. In 1929, he was named patron of parish priests. Feast day: August 4.

Vicar of Christ ● Title (in Latin, *Vicarius Christi*) borne by the Roman pontiff to designate his primacy over the entire, universal Church of Christ. Based upon Christ's words to Peter in John (21:15-17) to "Feed my lambs. . . . Tend my sheep. . . . Feed my sheep," the pope is considered the successor to St. Peter, the Prince of the Apostles and guardian of Our Lord's entire flock. The pope bears Peter's rights as supreme head of the Church on earth by virtue of the commission of Christ, with vicarial powers derived from him. The pontiff is the inheritor in the fulfillment of Christ's promise to Peter in Matthew (16:18-19).

The title "Vicar of Christ" was first used at the Synod of Rome (495) for Pope St. Gelasius I (r. 492-496), a pontiff who had himself adopted the phrase "Vicar of the Apostolic See." It was not the explicit title of the pope, however, and down to the ninth century it was utilized by other bishops outside of Rome, although its application was probably of an informal nature. Its adoption into curial usage (meaning use by the Roman Curia) came during the pontificate of Pope Eugenius III (1145-1153). Further clarification of the powers delineated by the title came under Pope Innocent III (r. 1198-1216), a pontiff who helped to establish many of the medieval characteristics of the papacy. He appealed to his power as vicar to depose or remove bishops, further proclaiming that the powers of the vicar were granted by Christ only to his vicar, Peter, and Peter's successors; the Roman pontiff is, as Innocent stated, "the successor of Peter and Vicar of Jesus Christ." It superseded completely the title "Vicar of Peter" that was, in any event, rejected as unsatisfactory and limiting by the formidable Innocent. The Council of Florence in its Decrees for the Greeks (1439) defined the pontiff as the "true Vicar of Christ," a definition adopted in toto by Vatican Council I (in *Pastor Aeternis*, 1870). Vatican Council II (in *Lumen Gentium*, No. 27) extended the title to all bishops, calling them "vicars and ambassadors of Christ," thereby making the point that bishops are Vicars of Christ for their own dioceses or local churches while the pope is the Vicar of Christ for the entire Church.

Vicar of Peter ● Title meaning "one who takes the place of Peter." In informal usage for many centuries, it was finally and formally rejected by Pope Innocent III (r. 1198-1216) and replaced by the much clearer "Vicar of Christ." The inadequacy of the term "Vicar of Peter" stems from several sources. First, "Vicar" is not always interpreted to mean successor, thereby permitting the office of the Roman pontiff to be interpreted as not proceeding in succession from Peter and hence not bestowed directly by Christ. Further, it would apparently indicate that the pope is holder of his office at the will of Peter rather than in succession to Peter, a limiting position open to questions of legitimacy. Finally, it would seem to contradict the

broader and more important title "Vicar of Christ" because it tends to show that the office of pontiff has its origin in a human rather than divine source. It is no longer used in any capacity.

Victor I, St. ● Pope from 189-198. Described by the *Liber Pontificalis* as an African, he was the first Latin pontiff, his father named Felix, and through his steady and remarkable leadership the Church in Rome was moved decisively into the cultural sphere of the Latins, as compared to the Greek or Oriental influences that had previously dominated. His efforts to advance the authority of Rome was clear in his imposition of the Roman date of Easter. Succeeding St. Eleutherius (r. c. 175-189), Victor's program was challenged by the churches of the East that desired to retain the so-called Quartodeciman custom (observing Easter — the Christian Passover — according to Jewish practices on the fourteenth day of the month of Nisan, regardless of the day, and not exclusively on a Sunday). Victor was firm in his desire to bring complete uniformity, going so far as to excommunicate Polycrates, bishop of Ephesus, after the prelate refused to comply with the papal order. It would appear that Victor retracted his sentence, but his action is considered the first such extension of papal authority over the churches of Asia Minor and an important event in the acceptance of papal supremacy. Victor did excommunicate the leather-seller Theodotus of Byzantium, leader of a group of Adoptionists (or Monarchianists); he also deposed the priest Florinus for Gnostic writings. Through his policies, Latin replaced Greek as the accepted language of the Church, and Victor himself wrote in Latin. St. Jerome (in *De Viri Illustribus*) noted that Victor was the first ecclesiastical Latin writer, although his works were published in both Latin and Greek. He was also the first pontiff to establish relations with the imperial household, securing the release of Christian prisoners from the terrible mines of Sardinia through Marcia, the Christian mistress of Emperor Commodus (r. 180-192). Stories that Victor was a martyr are generally discounted because his death came before the persecutions of Emperor Septimius Severus (r. 193-211). Under Victor, the Church made much progress in Rome and by his labors the papacy had begun the long road to supremacy over the entire Church.

Victor II ● Pope from 1055-1057. Born Gebhard Dollnstein-Hirschberg, to a noble family, he was the son of Count Hartwig and Countess Baliza; sources vary as to his birthplace, papal records indicating Bavaria, German sources preferring Swabia. Through the influence of his uncle Bishop Gebhard III of Ratisbon, he was appointed bishop of Eichstätt in 1042 by Emperor Henry III, despite the fact that Gebhard was only twenty-four. He proved a remarkably able prelate, emerging as one of the chief advisers to the emperor. In 1053, for example, he convinced Henry to recall an army on its way to assist Pope St. Leo IX in his campaign against the Normans, an action he regretted once he was himself pope. Upon the death of Pope St. Leo on April 19, 1054, legates from Rome under the leadership of Hildebrand (the future Pope St. Gregory VII, r. 1073-1085) arrived at the imperial court to ask the emperor to take Gebhard as his candidate for the papacy. Gebhard hesitated for a number of months, finally accepting at Regensburg in March 1055 but only on condition that those lands taken from the Holy See be restored to it. Enthroned on April 13, 1055, he took the name Victor II and soon continued Leo's work of Church reform, especially against simony and clerical concubinage. On June 4, 1055, he convened a synod in Florence, where decrees against simony and other abuses were confirmed and several bishops deposed for offenses. Hildebrand was sent back to France to take

up once more the process of reform. In 1056, Hildebrand would preside over synods in France as Victor's legate. That same year, Victor was summoned to the imperial court in Germany, where Henry died on October 5. The pope then became guardian for the child Henry IV, acquiring enormous power and influence, which he wielded evenly on the young ruler's behalf. He secured Henry's succession at Aachen, appointed his mother regent, and in December, at Aachen, negotiated peace between the imperial court and the formidable noblemen Godfrey of Lorraine and Baldwin, count of Flanders. On April 18, 1057, Victor organized a synod at the Lateran and on June 14 consecrated Frederick, brother of Godfrey of Lorraine, a cardinal, appointing him abbot of Monte Cassino. Victor was much concerned with the Normans of southern Italy whose expansionist tendencies threatened the Papal States. Falling ill at Arezzo on July 23, he died on July 28. His successor was the briefly reigning Stephen IX (X).

Victor III ● Pope from 1086-1087. Born Daufari (or Daufer) at Benevento, he was of Lombard descent. Living for a time as a hermit, he entered the Benedictine monastery of Benevento, taking the name Desiderius. After assisting Pope St. Leo IX as a negotiator with the Normans of southern Italy, he joined the Benedictines of Monte Cassino (1055) and was elected abbot in April 1058. His time as abbot earned a well-deserved title as the greatest of the abbots of Monte Cassino, described by the historian Gregorovius as imperishable fame. He rebuilt most of the abbey and the church, established schools of the arts, improved and enlarged the library, and reinvigorated monastic discipline. Made a cardinal in March 1059 by Pope Nicholas II, he was also appointed papal vicar for southern Italy, a post that came with the special power of naming bishops and abbots as he saw fit. During this time he negotiated the alliance between the Normans and the papacy. By 1080, not only had he reconciled Pope St. Gregory VII (r. 1073-1085) with the Norman Robert Guiscard, duke of Apulia (c. 1015-1085), but he had secured Robert's promise of troops for Gregory's use against Emperor Henry IV (r. 1056-1106). In 1082, however, Desiderius earned the very serious displeasure of Gregory after attempting to mediate between the pope and the emperor, although Gregory sought refuge in Monte Cassino in 1084 when fleeing from Rome, and Desiderius was conspicuously at his deathbed on May 25, 1085. Almost a year would pass before a successor to Gregory could be elected. The cardinals chose Desiderius against his will. He took the name Victor (III) in honor of Victor II (r. 1055-1057), who had been the guardian of Henry IV, but he set aside his elevation on May 24, 1086, after a few days, out of frustration with those cardinals not enthusiastic about his election and the incessant social disorder in Rome. At the urging of the Norman prince Jordan of Capua, he finally accepted consecration in St. Peter's on May 9, 1087. As Rome was largely in the possession of the antipope Clement III (r. 1080; 1084-1100), Victor went back to Monte Cassino, returning to the Eternal City in July. At Benevento in late August, he apparently reaffirmed the prohibition of Gregory VII against lay investiture and anathematized both Clement III and the fanatical followers of Gregory who disagreed with Victor's conciliatory attitude toward Henry. During the synod, his health failed, and he died on September 16, 1087. His successor was Bl. Urban II (r. 1088-1099). Victor was declared blessed by Pope Leo XIII (r. 1878-1903) in 1887. Feast day: September 16.

Victor IV ● Name of two antipopes. The first reigned from March-May 1138. Originally Gregory Conti, he was a cardinal at the time of his election as antipope by a

faction opposed to Pope Innocent II (r. 1130-1143). He was convinced to be reconciled with the pope by St. Bernard of Clairvaux, submitting on May 29.

The second ruled during the years 1159-1164. Originally Octavian of Monticelli, he is sometimes styled Victor V in recognition of the previous antipope of this name whom he refused to recognize. He was the first of four antipopes named by Emperor Frederick I Barbarossa in his struggle with Pope Alexander (r. 1159-1181). Originally a cardinal, he was elected by a minority of cardinals while Alexander was chosen by a majority. Unwilling to accept defeat, he used supporters to enthrone himself, causing a schism that Frederick attempted to resolve by calling a synod in Pavia in 1160; his aim was to win support and recognition for Victor. The antipope was never widely acknowledged, however, dying in April 1164. He was succeeded by antipope Paschal III.

Victorines ● Name given to the canons regular of the onetime Abbey of St. Victor in Pavia, founded by William of Champeaux (d. 1121). The Victorines acquired a great reputation for their learning, including mystics, theologians, and scholars among their ranks. Notable Victorines were Hugh of St. Victor (d. 1142), Adam of St. Victor (d. c. 1177 or 1192), Richard of St. Victor (d. 1173), and Walter of St. Victor (d. c. 1180).

Victorinus, St. (d. c. 303) ● Bishop of Pattau, ecclesiastical writer, and martyr. Confused until the seventeenth century with Victorinus Afer, he is now considered one of the earliest Latin exegetes, although Jerome, the principal source for details on his life and writings, noted that because he was born on the border of the Eastern and Western Empires, he wrote better Greek than Latin. Jerome states that he composed commentaries on various biblical books, including Genesis, Exodus, Leviticus, Isaiah, Ezekiel, Habakkuk, Ecclesiastes, the Canticle of Canticles (or Song of Solomon), Matthew, and Revelation; he also wrote treatises on the heresies of the time. Virtually all of his writings are lost except for some extracts on Revelation and perhaps a treatise. The fragment on Revelation, preserved in a fifteenth-century Vatican manuscript, is clearly altered by Jerome, and the treatise *De Fabrica Mundi*, while attributable to Victorinus, was not, as long believed, part of his commentary on Genesis. Scholars theorize that his works did not survive because of certain millenarianist tendencies that led to their condemnation as apocryphal by Pope Gelasius in the *Decretalium Gelasianum*. He was probably martyred during the persecutions of Emperor Diocletian in the early fourth century. Feast day: November 2.

Victorinus Afer (fourth century) ● Also Caius Marius Victorinus or Marius Fabius Victorinus. Rhetorician, grammarian, and theologian. Born in Africa, he settled in Rome where he taught rhetoric and acquired such notoriety that a statue was erected in his honor in 353 in the Forum Romanum or the Forum Traianum. He is known today principally through the writings of St. Augustine and St. Jerome. He was at first reluctant to become a Christian, but around the mid-fourth century he entered the Church, an event greeted with great joy by the Christians of Rome. He did not give up teaching, however, continuing until the accession of Emperor Julian the Apostate (r. 361-363), who decreed that Christians could no longer teach. His preconversion writings include *Liber de Definitionibus*, a treatise on *De inventione* by Cicero, and a treatise on grammar; other works are not extant, including commentaries on Aristotle. Most of his work in the years following his conversion are lost; these covered such topics as theology, philosophy, and exegesis. Among surviving works are: commentaries on St. Paul's Epistles to the Galatians, Ephesians,

and the Philippians; three hymns, *"De Trinitate"*; and an anti-Arian treatise.

Vienne, Council of ● The fifteenth ecumenical (or general) council, held in Vienne, France, from 1311-1312, under Pope Clement V (r. 1305-1314). The council was summoned by the bull *Regnans in coelis* (1308) with the declared purpose of "making provision in regard to the Order of Knights Templar, both the individual members and its leaders, and in regard to other things in reference to the Catholic faith, the Holy Land, and the improvement of the Church and of ecclesiastical persons." The Templars were specifically commended to provide *defensores* and for the grand master (Jacques de Molay) to appear with all suitable officials from the order. Owing to the matter of the appeal of King Philip IV the Fair of France (r. 1285-1314) concerning his treatment of Pope Boniface VIII (r. 1294-1303), Clement postponed convening the council until October 16, 1311, when the first session was opened in the Cathedral of Vienne. At the opening, Clement restated his agenda: the controversy of the Templars (who were being accused of various crimes, especially by Philip, who coveted their wealth), aid to the Holy Land, and Church reform.

The commission charged with examining the case against the knights reached the conclusion that the Templars could not be condemned on the basis of the evidence and should thus be allowed to defend themselves. This was, of course, unsatisfactory to King Philip, who applied pressure on Clement, a pontiff residing at Avignon. To demonstrate his resolve, Philip appeared before the gate of Vienne in February 1312 to demand the suppression of the Templars. Clement yielded, issuing the bull of suppression *Vox clamantis* (March 22, 1312), which was promulgated at the second session, held on April 5. At the third session, convened on May 6, a letter from Philip was read in which he promised to go on a crusade within six years. A tithe was to be laid for the undertaking; in France, the money went to Philip, who used it for his war against Flanders. As it was, he never set sail and no crusade was ever launched. The council also issued a large number of decrees on the administration of the Inquisition, the question of Franciscan poverty, the Beguines, the observance of ecclesiastical hours, and various topics related to the clergy. These decrees were gathered together by Pope John XXII and issued on October 25, 1317; with the decrees not promulgated by Clement owing to his death in 1314, they were published in the *Clementiniae.*

Vigilius ● Pope from 537-555. A Roman by birth, he belonged to a noble family, the son of a consul. Becoming a deacon, he was designated by Pope Boniface II (r. 530-532) in 531 as his successor, but after the pope's death Vigilius was forced to withdraw from any consideration as successor in the face of loud calls of protest that the naming of him by Boniface was uncanonical. Sent to Constantinople as *apocrisiarius* (nuncio) by Pope Agapetus I (r. 535-536), he enjoyed the full confidence of Empress Theodora. He took part in the unsuccessful mission to the court of Emperor Justinian I (r. 527-565) to convince him not to invade and reconquer Italy. Agapetus died at Constantinople in April 536, and Theodora apparently hatched a secret deal with Vigilius in which he was promised the papacy in return for reinstating the patriarch Anthimus (who had been deposed at Agapetus's urging for Monophysite leanings) and repudiating the Council of Chalcedon (451). To Vigilius's disappointment, however, by the time he reached Rome, St. Silverius (r. 536-537) had already been installed. That pontiff was soon deposed, and Vigilius was elected as his replacement through Justinian's influence. The complicity of Vigilius in the subsequent brutal exile and treatment of Silverius cannot

be disputed and was a sad beginning to a troubled and tumultuous pontificate.

Aside from working to restore the buildings and churches of Rome, which had been devastated by the recent war between the Goths and Byzantines, Vigilius was probably preoccupied with the major theological crises of the time, most notably that of the Three Chapters. In a decree issued by Justinian in 544, the writings (or chapters) of three Churchmen — Theodore of Mopsuestia, Theodoret of Cyrrhus, and Ibas of Edessa — were condemned for heretical teachings. Justinian had hoped that, by anathematizing the three theologians, he might win over the Monophysites of the empire who had looked upon them as heretical Nestorians for their adherence to the two natures of Christ. As the three had not been condemned by the Council of Chalcedon and had died in good standing with the Church, the edict had been greeted with an uproar in the West, placing Vigilius, with his conflicting interests, in a difficult position. Vacillating, Vigilius was seized by Byzantine troops and taken to Constantinople in January 547. At first firm in opposing the decree, he was finally convinced by pressure to change his position. On April 11, 548, the pontiff issued the *Iudicatum* (verdict) censuring the Three Chapters but making reservation for Chalcedon. This move was the cause of a severe counterreaction in the West.

Vigilius was excommunicated by a synod of African bishops in 550, and the pope faced bitter denunciation from his own entourage. Justinian and the pope realized that a council would be necessary. Justinian, though, chose not to wait, renewing his declarations against the Three Chapters. Vigilius responded by withdrawing to a place of sanctuary and issuing censures of ecclesiastical allies of the emperor. He did not attend the council that confirmed the edict. Having rescinded the *Iudicatum,* Vigilius published the first *Constitutum,* an effort at compromise that was rejected by Justinian. Wearying of the increasingly harsh treatment and humiliations to which he was now subjected, Vigilius canceled the first *Constitutum* and issued a second, on February 23, 554, fully endorsing the acts of the council. Given his freedom, he set out for Rome in early 555, dying on June 7 in Sicily from years of abuse. His policies had caused a schism that would last for one hundred fifty years. Pelagius I succeeded him.

St. Vincent de Paul

Vincent de Paul, St. (c. 1580-1660) ●
Remarkable priest and founder of the Lazarist Fathers and the Sisters of Charity. Born in Ranquine, Gascony, France, he was the son of a peasant farmer. After studying under Franciscans at Dax, he was ordained in 1600, subsequently attending the University of Toulouse. In 1605, he was traveling by sea when his ship was captured by Barbary pirates. Taken into slavery, Vincent spent two hard years as a slave, finally escaping in 1607 to France. Journeying first to Rome, he reached Paris in 1609, coming under the spiritual guidance of Cardinal Pierre de Bérulle, under whose influence Vincent devoted his life to charitable works and was appointed a parish priest in Clichy, France. Named in 1613 to the household of the count of Gondi, Vincent spent time on the galleys, of which the count was commanding general, attempting to reduce the terrible lot of the rowers. Back in Paris, he established confraternities of men and women working to bring charity to the poor and to care for the vast numbers of sick in the city. His chief source of charitable

donations and concerns came from wealthy noblewomen who provided funds for the creation of hospitals and homes for orphaned and foundling children. Behind this movement, the ever-present Vincent stood as the conscience of the nation. A practical man, he also recognized that his work went unnoticed by the wealthy who chose to ignore the problems of the time, and unappreciated by the poor themselves, whom he called hard taskmasters.

To advance his efforts even further, Vincent founded in Paris in 1625 the Congregation of the Missions, called the Lazarists or Vincentians, a society of priests with the express task of missionary labor and the training of clergy. They were particularly charged with preaching among the people in the country. In 1633, with the remarkable St. Louise de Marillac (1591-1660; feast day: April 28), he also established the Sisters (or Daughters) of Charity, the first congregation of women caring for the sick poor outside the confines of the convent. Appointed in 1643 to the Council of the Conscience by Queen Anne of Austria, regent for King Louis XIV, Vincent organized relief efforts for the many unfortunate victims injured and wounded during the Wars of the Fronde that plagued France from 1648-1653. Vincent was also a bitter opponent of Jansenism. He died in Paris on September 27, 1600, and was canonized by Pope Clement XII in 1737. Feast day: September 27.

The Vincentians (Congregation of the Mission, C.M.) spread quickly during Vincent's lifetime, eventually opening seminaries throughout France and in Italy, Spain, and Poland. They arrived in the United States in 1818, and today number some thirty-five hundred worldwide. The Daughters of Charity of St. Vincent de Paul (D.C.) also moved throughout the world. St. Elizabeth Seton opened a house at Emmitsburg, Maryland, in 1809. There are several other congregations, including the Sisters of Charity of St. Vincent de Paul (S.V.Z.; founded in 1845 in Croatia), Sisters of Charity of St. Vincent de Paul (S.C.H.; founded in 1856 in Halifax, Nova Scotia), and the Sisters of Charity of St. Vincent de Paul of New York (S.C.; founded in 1817). The Society of St. Vincent de Paul, a lay organization devoted to the care of the poor, was begun in 1833 by Antoine Frédéric Ozanam (1813-1853) in Paris. The first branch or conference of the society was started in the United States at St. Louis in 1845. Today, the society is involved in a wide variety of programs, including food centers, shelters, workshops, rehabilitation centers, and distribution programs for food and money.

Vincent Ferrer, St. (c. 1350-1419) ●

Famed Spanish Dominican preacher, he contributed to bringing an end to the Great Schism (1378-1417). Born in Valencia, he entered

St. Vincent Ferrer

the Dominicans there in 1367 and was sent the next year to study at Barcelona. After teaching at Lerida, he returned to Barcelona and, during a famine, foretold the arrival of the desperately needed grain ships.

In 1379, he came to the attention of Cardinal Pedro de Luna, at the time legate to the court of Aragon. From 1385-1390, Vincent taught at the Cathedral of Valencia and was thereafter part of the retinue of de Luna, who was elected in 1394 as antipope under the name Benedict XIII. Summoned to Avignon, Vincent was appointed by Benedict to serve as confessor and apostolic penitentiary, refusing, however, all honors that the antipope should decide to bestow upon him, including the cardinalate. During a siege of Avignon by French troops, Vincent fell ill and nearly died, recovering miraculously after beholding a vision of Christ, St. Francis, and St. Dominic in which he was told to go forth and preach. At first resisted by Benedict, his undertaking was finally permitted in November 1399. His preaching took him across Western Europe, including Savoy, Lombardy, Lyons, Flanders, and northern France. He attracted huge crowds everywhere he went. Held in great esteem in Spain, he was appointed as one of the nine judges to decide the succession to the crown of Aragon; they elected Ferdinand I. Much concerned by the damage done to the faith by the Great Schism, Vincent took the important step of calling publicly for Benedict XIII to step down, despite his personal view that he was, in fact, the legitimate pontiff. His continued work in trying to end the crisis contributed to its final resolution, although he did not attend the Council of Constance. The last years of his life were spent preaching in northern France; King Henry V of England invited him to deliver a sermon before his court at Caen in 1418. He died in Vannes, Brittany, on April 5, 1419. Pope Callistus canonized him in 1455. Feast day: April 5.

Vincent of Beauvais (c. 1190-1264) ● French Dominican encyclopedist, author of the *Speculum majus*, arguably the greatest encyclopedia of the Middle Ages. Born perhaps in Beauvais, he entered the Dominicans around 1220 at Paris, subsequently receiving holy orders and appointment as chaplain to the royal court of King St. Louis IX (r. 1226-1270) in 1250. While there, he authored the treatise *De eruditione filiorum nobilium* (1260-1261; *On the Education of Noble Sons*). His chief work, the *Speculum majus* (*Great Mirror*) was written between 1247 and 1259. It consisted of three parts, a fourth being added in the fourteenth century by an anonymous author under the title *Speculum morales* (*Mirror of Morals*). Vincent relied on over two thousand sources and four hundred fifty authors to create the massive compendium in eighty books of virtually the sum of human knowledge to his own era, covering the sciences, economics, law, alchemy, astronomy, and a host of other topics.

Vincent of Lérins, St. (d. c. 450) ● Theologian and ecclesiastical writer in southern Gaul (France). Few details of his life are known outside those preserved in Gennadius's *De viris illustribus*. Perhaps

born in Toul, France, he may have been a soldier before entering (c. 425) the monastery of Lérins, on an island just off the French coast. Ordained a priest, he remained in Lérins, dying sometime before 450. His chief work was the *Commonitorium* (434), written under the pseudonym Peregrinus (meaning "Pilgrim"). Intended to provide a survey and reply to the numerous heresies that were current at the time, the *Commonitorium* was an expression of Vincent's Semi-Pelagianism and an indirect attack on St. Augustine, whom the Semi-Pelagians viewed as being in error. Vincent opposed Augustine's teaching on grace, citing the principle "What all men have at all times and everywhere believed must be regarded as true." He is probably the writer refuted by St. Augustine's friend Prosper of Aquitaine in the *Responsiones ad capitula objectionum Vincentianarum* (*Answer to the Attacks of Vincent*). Vincent's other works are largely lost; those that are extant were preserved in Migne's *Patrologia Latina*. Feast day: May 24.

Vineam Domini ● Apostolic constitution issued by Pope Clement XI (r. 1700-1721) on July 16, 1705, against the Jansenists. Known in full as the *Vineam Domini Sabaoth*, it was published in answer to a renewal of the Jansenist controversy in France and the failure of Clement's brief *Cum nuper* (February 12, 1703) to stem it. The constitution began with a confirmation of three earlier bulls, *Cum occasione* (1653), *Ad Sacram* (1656), and *Regiminis Apostolici* (1664), against Jansenism. Clement then defended Clement IX (r. 1667-1669) and Innocent XII (r. 1691-1700) against the misinformation that had been put forth about them by the Jansenists. He stressed the authority of the pope in matters of both fact and doctrine, adding that all people should accept the decision of the pontiff with their heart and not, as many Jansenists did, with mere respectful silence (*obsequioso illo silento nequaquam satisfieri*). Accepted by the

Assembly of French Clergy with some reservations in August 1705, it was made state law later that month. Most of the French bishops accepted it as well. The nuns of Port-Royal would not submit, however, and King Louis XIV, who had tired of the entire controversy, received permission from the pope to suppress that institution.

Visigoths ● Germanic people, called also the West Goths, they established a large kingdom in the fifth century throughout southern Gaul and northern Spain. Originally part of the large Gothic nation, the Visigoths split from the Ostrogoths (East Goths) in the fourth century, eventually entering the Danube region and coming into conflict with the Roman Empire. During this time they were converted to Arian Christianity by Ulfilas, the Apostle of the Goths (d. c. 382). Pushed by the Huns into Roman lands, the Visigoths were soon forced into war, defeating Emperor Valens in 378 at the Battle of Adrianople. In 410, under their king, Alaric, they swept into Italy and sacked Rome, one of the most shocking events in the history of the empire and a calamity from which the Western Empire never recovered. Searching for a home, the Visigoths finally settled in southern Gaul (France) and northern Hispania (Spain) in 412. The Visigoth kingdom reached its peak under Euric (d. c. 484), entering into decline soon after. Crushed in 507 by the Franks, they retreated completely into Spain. The kingdom survived until 711, when the Moors destroyed it. Long an Arian realm, the Visigoth kingdom generally treated Catholics or Orthodox Christians with toleration, especially after the fall of Gaul to the Franks and Arian numbers declined as the Catholic population increased. Finally, King Reccared (r. 586-601) converted to orthodoxy and the rest of the Visigoths followed him into the Church. Thereafter, the Visigoth and Roman elements became amalgamated.

Visitation Order ● Also called the Visitandines or the Salesian Sisters, it is a contemplative order of nuns founded by St. Francis de Sales and St. Jane Frances de Chantal at Annecy, in the duchy of Savoy. The purpose of the order was to offer the religious life for those women who, for reasons including physical or mental weakness, were unable to endure the severe austerity demanded by contemporary religious orders. St. Francis placed as his objective the attainment of God through interior modification and the performing of every act in accordance with the divine will. Initially, the Visitandines were intended to be a congregation with simple vows, and only novices were to reside in a cloister. After their profession, the nuns were permitted to leave the convent and to go out among the sick, thereby gaining their name as visitors of the ill and performers of mercy. This effort was begun on June 6, 1610, but in 1615 they encountered opposition from Archbishop D. S. de Marquemont of Lyons, who disagreed with their work and refused to permit the nuns into the diocese unless they adopted more common practices for religious life. After initially resisting, St. Francis acquiesced and in 1616 compiled the *Constitutions pour les religieuses de la Visitation de Sainte-Marie.* On April 23, 1618, Pope Paul V formally constituted the *Ordo Visitationis BMV*, which received official approval in 1626 from Pope Urban VIII. The constitutions were a version of the Rule of St. Augustine. St. Francis insisted that the severe demands of the cloister not be placed upon the members but that private mortifications to foster the interior life be followed, especially chastity, poverty, and obedience. Of these, the most difficult was said to be the common life, for the nuns were said to be permitted to have absolutely no property and even their crosses and holy pictures were to be changed every year so as to discourage any sense of ownership. By the 1700s, the order had spread throughout

Europe. The first American house was established in Georgetown in 1799. There are currently two federations of Visitation nuns (V.H.M.) in the United States.

Vision Concerning Piers Plowman, The

● One of the foremost Middle English alliterative poems, attributed to William Langland and dated to the fourteenth century. An allegory describing a profound spiritual journey and praising devoted Christianity, it was written in unrhymed alliterative verse probably in three periods (1362, 1376-1377, and 1392-1399). It tells the story of the dreams of a poet who beholds a field of folk located between the Tower of Truth and the Dale of Death. A number of allegorical figures enter into the vision, including Lady Holychurch, who offers an interpretation of what he sees. The apparently unsophisticated character, Piers Plowman (or Piers the Plowman), offers to assist the folk in reaching the Tower of Truth if they will help him plow his field. The poem attacks the failings of the clergy.

Vitalian, St.

● Pope from 657-672. According to the *Liber Pontificalis*, he was a native of Segni, Campania, the son of one Anastasius. Elected successor to Pope St. Eugenius I, he was enthroned on July 30, 657. From the first, he endeavored to improve relations between the West and the Byzantine Empire, which had soured over recent years owing to the controversy of Monothelitism and the issue of the *Typos* (a decree forbidding discussion of the matter) by Emperor Constans II in 648. Vitalian reopened the route of communication with the East by making friendly overtures to both Constans and the patriarch of Constantinople, Peter, who had shown Monothelite tendencies. Both responded favorably, and Constans even visited Rome where he was warmly received. When the emperor was assassinated in 668 in Sicily, Vitalian supported his son Constantine IV

Pogonatos. He subsequently declined to enforce the *Typos*, and Vitalian made a clear statement of orthodoxy, anticipating the defeat of Monothelitism at the sixth ecumenical council in 681. Vitalian consecrated Theodore of Tarsus as archbishop of Canterbury on March 26, 668, thereby launching a continuation of what proved to be a brilliant process of evangelization in England.

Vitoria, Francisco de (c. 1480-1546) ●

Spanish Dominican theologian. Born in Vitoria, Old Castile, Spain, he studied in his native city and entered the Dominican order around 1502. After studying at the Dominican convent of San Pablo in Burgos, he attended the famed house of St. Jacques, affiliated with the University of Paris, from 1506-1512. During this time he was ordained. He taught at Paris for a number of years, becoming a doctor of theology in 1523 and probably claiming as one of his students the renowned Dominican theologian Dominic Soto. Returning to Spain, he secured a position at the Dominican College of St. Gregory in Valladolid. Around 1526, he was appointed to the principal chair of theology at the University of Salamanca. This post he held with great distinction until 1544, making an enormous contribution to the revitalization of Scholasticism, which by the sixteenth century had lost much of its prestige and was perceived to be in a state of decline. Vitoria launched a thoroughgoing reform of the entire method of Scholastic training, promoting the use of the *Summa Theologiae* by St. Thomas Aquinas in place of the decidedly medieval *Sentences* of Peter Lombard as the main textbook for theological study. His programs, relying upon the *Summa* as well as other writings of the Church Fathers and Scripture, anticipated the Salmanticenses and was quickly adopted by most of the leading universities of Spain. It was then carried on brilliantly in the form of a renewed and vigorous Scholasticism by his chief pupils, Melchior Cano, Bartholomew Medina, Soto, and others, and by the great Carmelite theologians of the period. Vitoria is also respected for his contributions to international law, influencing the Dutch legalist and theologian Hugo Grotius (1583-1645), the so-called Father of International Law. He expounded extensively on the idea of a just war, declaring that should a conflict bring terrible damage or evil it should not be permissible. His writings included a large number of unpublished works, most notably a *Commentaria in universam Summam S. Thomae.*

Vitus, St. (d. c. 300) ● Martyr venerated since at least the fifth century. While it is accepted that he was almost certainly historical, the main source of information on him is legend. The earliest mention of him occurs in the *Martyrologium Hieronymianum* where he is listed with Modestus and Crescentia (*In Sicilia, Viti, Modesti et Crescentiae*), referring to their martyrdom in Sicily. In the same martyrology, listed under the same day, it states Vitus's name at the head of a group of nine martyrs, "in Lucania," or southern Italy. A much detailed but highly dubious narrative of the deaths of Vitus, Modestus, and Crescentia appeared in the sixth and seventh centuries, based entirely on legends and decorated with fantastic tales of miracles. According to this unreliable account, Vitus was born a pagan but was raised a Christian in secret by his tutor Modestia and his wife, Crescentia. The three were put to death, supposedly during the time of the persecution under Diocletian (r. 284-305). Vitus was venerated early on in Sicily and in Rome where Pope Gelasius (r. 492-496) noted a shrine dedicated to him. He is invoked against such diseases as epilepsy and the illness long known as St. Vitus's Dance, severe disorders of the nervous system. He is one of the Auxiliary Saints and his symbol is a dog or a cock. Feast day: June 15.

Vladimir, St. (d. 1015) ● Grand prince of Kiev and the first Christian ruler of Russia whose deeds were recorded in the Kiev Cycle. The son of Prince Svyatoslov of Kiev, he was forced into exile by his brother Yarapolk after the death of their father. Securing help from his Norse relatives (the founder of the dynasty being Varangians, or Vikings), Vladimir returned, crushed his brother, and thereby consolidated his rule over both Kiev and Novgorod. He converted to Christianity around 987 as a central part of his important treaty with the Byzantine Empire, marrying Anne, sister of Emperor Basil II, to cement the pact. By his decree, the subjects of his realm were forcibly converted to the Christian faith, but they were to embrace the Byzantine rite in the Old Slavonic tongue. This decision had long-term ramifications, for it moved Russia decisively away from the religious influence of the West, severely curtailed the progress of the Latin Church in Russian lands, and established the Russian religious character for centuries to come. Feast day: July 15.

Voltaire (1694-1778) ● One of the foremost writers of the 1700s. Born François Marie Arouet and raised in a middle-class family, he was educated by the Jesuits at the College of Louis-le-Grand in Paris, coming away with utter detestation of the Catholic Church. After studying law, he decided instead to become a writer, first coming to public notice through his tragedies. His work, which poked cruel fun at the regency and contemporary religion, provoked a sharp reaction; he was imprisoned for a time in the Bastille and was exiled to London from 1726-1729. Returning to France, he wrote plays, histories, and *Lettres philosophiques* (also *Lettres sur les Anglais*) in 1734, describing his experiences in England, in which he praised such English authors as John Locke and Isaac Newton. In the appendix he attacked Blaise Pascal. Owing to a public outcry against the work, Voltaire fled to Cirey, Lorraine, where he dedicated himself to scientific research and religious study. While there, he authored *Traité de métaphysique* (1734) and the vicious epic *La Pucelle* (1739), on Joan of Arc. In 1750, he visited the court of Frederick II of Prussia and in 1754 settled in Switzerland. He lived there until just before his death in Paris, on May 30, 1778. His most famous work was the satire *Candide* (1759), a biting indictment of philosophical optimism, especially directed toward Gottfried Leibniz (1646-1716). Highly opposed to the Church, which he viewed as corrupt, harsh, and full of superstition, Voltaire was nevertheless firmly convinced of moral values, adhering to Deism. He was thus often in disagreement in his later years with the younger philosophers who had become atheists.

Von Aberle, Maritz (1819-1875) ●

Catholic theologian who served as professor of moral theology and NT studies at the University of Tübingen from 1850. Aside from his extensive (and rather controversial) writings on the Gospels and the Acts of the Apostles, von Aberle labored to ensure religious and ecclesiastical freedom in Würtemberg, using articles in newspapers to convince the local government.

Von Balthasar, Hans Urs (1905-1988) ●

Swiss theologian and founder of the journal *Communio*. He was born in Lucerne, Switzerland, studying with the Benedictines and then the Jesuits. In 1923, he entered the University of Zurich, focusing on philosophy and German literature. After making a retreat through the principles of the *Spiritual Exercises* of St. Ignatius Loyola, he joined the Society of Jesus shortly after earning his doctorate in 1928. He then studied at Berchmanskollege, Munich, and at Lyons, France. In 1936, he was ordained, taking up a post on a Jesuit journal in Munich. Four years later, he became chaplain to students in Basel, Switzerland. While there, he became spiritual director to Adrienne von Speyr. She was converted to the faith and emerged as a mystic and gifted writer. In 1950, he left the Jesuits as a result of differences with his superiors over his activities. He founded a short time later the Community of St. John in Basel, devoting his remaining years to adding to his vast body of works. Shortly before his death, he was named a cardinal by Pope John Paul II in recognition of his immense theological contributions. He died on June 26, 1988, before he could participate in a consistory.

Hans Urs von Balthasar was the author of an enormous corpus of writings that included theology, patristics, translations, and ecumenical thought. His translations ranged from Catholic literature to poetry to drama (such as Paul Claudel). His patristic studies were concerned with such figures as Origen, St. Gregory of Nyssa, and St. Maximus the Confessor. He wrote dialogues with many of the Eastern Fathers, St. Thomas Aquinas, St. Bonaventure, St. Ignatius Loyola, and such literary figures as Dante. His contact with Karl Barth (1886-1968), the brilliant Protestant theologian, was the source of very fruitful discussions, and Balthasar authored a highly respected study, *The Theology of Karl Barth* (1951). He also had cordial and productive relations with the Jewish religious thinker Martin Buber (1878-1965).

It was in his theology that Von Balthasar earned a lasting position in modern theology. His theological outlook was guided by a number of abiding principles: the need to present the faith in terms comprehensible to the modern world; the incomparable glory of God; the decisive place of Christ, the Incarnate Word, as the Way, the Truth, and the Life; the powerful images of the Church as the Body of Christ and the Bride of Christ; the Real Presence in the Eucharist; the role of Mary in the Church; and the vital place of contemplative prayer in the life of the Christian. To organize his entire body of thought, Von Balthasar conceived of an ambitious, multivolume masterwork. Begun in the 1960s, it was largely completed in the 1980s and was divided into three parts, reflecting the traditional scholastic organization of observing the characteristics of beauty, goodness, and truth. The first part, called *The Glory of the Lord: A Theological Aesthetics*, examines theology from the perspective of aesthetics. The second part, focusing on the good, uses the concept of Christian ethics as played out in the drama of salvation, described as Theodrama, or theological dramatics. The third part, devoted to the truth of God's appearance in history, is based in Theologic, or theological logic. Among his other works were *Prayer*, *Christian Meditation*, *The Threefold Garland*, *A Theology of History*, and *Razing the Bastions*.

Vulgate ● See **Bible**; see also GLOSSARY.

Wadding, Luke (1588-1657) ● Franciscan historian and theologian. Born in Waterford, Ireland, he was the eleventh of fourteen children. Receiving an excellent education at home, he entered a seminary in Lisbon, Portugal, around 1608, leaving after six months to become a Franciscan in the convent of the Immaculate Conception at Matozinhos, Oporto. Ordained in 1613, he was ordered to begin preaching, mastering both Portuguese and Castillian Spanish; he also compiled a much respected collection of excerpts from the Church Fathers, Scriptures, lives of the saints, and other material. After impressing his superiors, he was appointed to a chair of theology (1617) at the Irish College of Salamanca University. The following year, he was picked by King Philip III of Spain as a theologian in the embassy sent to Pope Paul V to promote the doctrine of the Immaculate Conception. Studying in the libraries of Naples, Assisi, and Rome, Wadding authored *Legatio Philippi III et IV pro definienda controversia Immaculatae Conceptionis* (1624).

Throughout this period he was involved in numerous writing projects and publishing efforts, including the creation of a printing-press with Hebrew type (paid for by Pope Paul V), which contributed to biblical study; an edition of the writings of St. Francis; a number of commentaries on the Gospels of St. Mark and St. Luke; and a concordance of St. Antony of Padua. While in Rome, he also established an Irish College for Franciscans from his native land in 1625, followed by the Ludovican College for Irish priests in 1627. The popes subsequently employed him on a number of important commissions, most notably to reform the breviary and the missal. He then assisted in organizing the Church in Ireland and was named by Pope Innocent X in 1652 to the board charged with examining Jansenism. Aside from the previous works mentioned, he was the author of an edition of John Duns Scotus (16 vols., 1639); the *Scriptores Ordinis Minorum* (1650), an alphabetical collection of all of the writers of the Franciscan order with a syllabus of their writings; and the *Annales Ordinis Minorum*, his *magnum opus* (8 vols., 1625-1654), a vast history of the Franciscans from its foundation to 1540.

Walafrid Strabo (c. 808-849) ● Benedictine abbot, poet, and theologian. Called Strabo (or Squinter), he was born in Swabia and was educated at Reichenau and later at Fulda; while there he came under the influence of Rabanus Maurus, abbot of Fulda (d. 856). In 838, he became abbot of Reichenau but probably the next year was forced to flee to Speyer after supporting Lothair I against his brother Charles the Bald, being exiled by Louis the German. He eventually returned in 842. Walafrid was a remarkable poet, composing *Visio Wettini* (c. 826; *The Vision of Wettin*), the panegyric *Versus de imagine Tetrici* (*Verse on the Statue of Theodoric*), and *De cultura hortorum* (*The Art of Gardening*). His theological writings included *De exordis et incrementis quarundum in observationibus ecclesiasticus rerum* (841; *On the Origin and Development of Matters in Church Practice*). He also wrote hagiographies and a revision of Einhard's *Life of Charlemagne.*

Waldenses ● Also Waldensians or Valdesii. A heretical sect that first developed in the twelfth century and survived into the twentieth century, the Waldenses took their name from Peter Waldo (or Valdes) of Lyons (d. 1217), who became known as the Poor Man of Lyons. Waldo was originally a merchant of Lyons who underwent a conversion and entered into the life of a mendicant. He began preaching and distributing his wealth to the poor, soon attracting followers. Early communities of Waldenses appeared in France, spreading quickly into Italy and Spain. Waldenses preached aggressively against wealth and the failings of the clergy. As many committed errors in doctrine, censure from Church officials became inevitable, and they were soon prohibited from speaking publicly. Despite prohibitions placed upon them by the Third Lateran Council (1179), the Waldenses continued to preach and were eventually excommunicated by Pope Lucius III at the Council of Verona (1184). Divorced from the Church, the Waldenses organized themselves into a separate body, creating their own clergy. Their numbers increased and efforts were made, in 1191 and 1207, to bring about some kind of reunion. Action during this period against the Albigensians inevitably came to involve the Waldenses, and often severe persecutions in Germany, Spain, Piedmont, and Lombardy reduced their numbers dramatically. Survivors remained, however, especially in the areas of Piedmont and Bohemia. The Bohemian Waldenses ultimately joined the Hussites, with a number of doctrinal differences. With the onset of the Protestant Reformation, many Waldenses joined the cause of the Reformers. They were largely found in Piedmont, suffering religious persecution in the 1600s but receiving religious freedom in 1848 under Victor Emmanuel. (See also **Heresy**.)

Wales ● Western part of the United Kingdom long dominated by England but traditionally independent and determined to maintain its ancient customs and language. The Christian faith first penetrated into Welsh regions during the late period of the Roman occupation of Britain. The main source for any information on the early Church is the history of the Celts' *De Excidio et Conquestu Britanniae ac flebili Castigatione in Reges, Principes et Sacerdotes* by St. Gildas, although information on the Church is limited. Clearly, Celtic missionaries helped spread the faith, reaching a period of supposed rich Christian culture in the sixth century called the Age of Saints. This period saw the flourishing of monasteries and the lasting work of such figures as St. Teilo, St, Dubricius, and St. David, patron saint of Wales (see also **Kentigern, St.**). Among the foremost of the Welsh monasteries were Bangor, St. David's, Llandaff, and St. Asaph.

From the sixth century, the Welsh Church came under increasing pressure from the English Church, which sought to place the monasteries and bishoprics under the jurisdiction of Canterbury and to replace Celtic custom with the Roman. After the Synod of Whitby (664), the Welsh adopted the Roman date for Easter and other usages, but they continued to resist the claims of Canterbury and maintained the practice of having ecclesiastical authority rest in the hands of the territorial bishoprics that had emerged out of the great monastic centers. Nevertheless, the faith continued to spread in the eighth through tenth centuries, even in the face of the constant threat of raids by the Norsemen.

In the 1100s, the English under the Normans invaded Wales. Despite bitter and hard-fought resistance, the region was largely overrun, marking English supremacy. The invasion permitted Church authorities from England to introduce wider contact with the Roman Church and heightened influence from the Continent. Largely through St.

Anselm of Canterbury (d. 1109) much progress was made in attaching the Welsh bishoprics to the jurisdiction of Canterbury. Attendant upon this success was the organization of more set dioceses. The long-held practice of hereditary clergy died out, replaced by a more stable and traditional ecclesiastical structure. Religious orders also arrived, first through the Benedictines and then the Cistercians and others.

Resentment began to spread among the Welsh clergy toward the English throughout the fourteenth century owing to the favored position of English clerics, the abuses of power, and the often unsatisfactory distributions of financial resources. Thus, many Welsh priests and bishops took part in the revolt of Owen Glendower (Owain Glyn Dwr) against King Henry IV in the first years of the fifteenth century. The defeat of the Welsh served only to increase the authority of the English bishops. The Welsh Church was also divided over the question of the Great Schism.

The Reformation was not overly successful in finding converts from among the Welsh, but King Henry VIII was able to use the general popularity of the House of Tudor (of Welsh descent) to implement his religious policies. These were hard on the Church and, after a brief return to Rome under Mary Tudor (r. 1553-1558), further eradication of Catholicism took place under Queen Elizabeth I (r. 1558-1603). The country moved more toward Protestantism, and many Catholic recusants were put to death. The Church continued in relative obscurity as Methodism, first preached by Howard Harris (1714-1773), took root in the eighteenth century. Catholicism revived during the 1800s through the immigration of Irish workers. Toleration was granted in 1829 and the hierarchy was restored in 1850 by Pope Pius IX (r. 1846-1878) as part of the wider restoration of the English ecclesiastical leadership. Currently, Catholics comprise barely five percent of the Welsh population. (See **England**; see also **Celtic Church; David, St.; Deiniol, St.; Easter Controversy; Gildas, St.; Giraldus Cambrensis**; and **Whitby, Synod of**.

Wallenstein, Albrecht von (1583-1634) ●
In full, Albrecht Eusebius Wenzel von Wallenstein, Catholic imperial general during the Thirty Years' War (1618-1648). A member of a Czech noble family in Bohemia, he was not raised a Catholic, studying at the Lutheran University of Altdorf. After traveling in Italy and France, however, he entered the Church, probably in Olmütz. He then married an enormously wealthy widow, inheriting her fortune in 1614. Entering the armed forces of the Holy Roman Empire, he rose rapidly in power and influence through his victories, receiving in 1625 from Emperor Ferdinand II (r. 1619-1637) the title of duke of Friedland, which had been carved out of the vast territories that he had confiscated from various Bohemian princes. As a result of his sincere desire to defend the Church and the Habsburg Dynasty of the Emperors in the war and a willingness to raise an army of twenty thousand men, Wallenstein was named supreme commander of all imperial forces in April 1625. Two years later, he was made duke of Mecklenburg. Failure in new campaigns led to his inability to capture the strategically important city of Stralsund in 1628, thereby permitting his enemies at the imperial court to have him replaced in 1630 by Johann Tilly (1559-1632). Recalled in 1632 in the hopes of reversing declining imperial fortunes in the face of the victories by Gustavus Adolphus, king of Sweden, Wallenstein engaged the Swedes at the Battle of Lützen (November 16, 1632). A stalemate resulted, but imperial losses were so severe that Wallenstein was forced to suspend all operations. Desultory negotiations followed with the Protestants, and Wallenstein's activities were greeted with alarm by the emperor, who suspected him of treason. On

February 25, 1634, the general was murdered at Egers, perhaps with Ferdinand's complicity, by several of his own officers. As a general, he was criticized for being too hesitant in committing himself to battles of a decisive nature and for being too ready and devious in his diplomacy and negotiations. At a time of severe religious strife, he also distinguished himself for having many Protestant soldiers and officers in his army, two of whom were members of the group that assassinated him.

Walsingham, Thomas (d. c. 1422) ●

English Benedictine chronicler and monk of St. Alban's. It is perhaps likely that he was originally from Walsingham, Norfolk, receiving his education at St. Alban's where he was a monk for most of his life save for the period 1394-1409 when he served as superior at the priory of Wymondham. He is chiefly known through extensive writings that are an important source on English history during the Middle Ages. These include: *Historia Anglicana*, a continuation of the *Chronica majora* of Matthew Paris covering the years 1272-1422; *Chronicon Angliae*, from 1328-1388; *Gesta Abbatum*, a continuation of the earlier work by Matthew Paris that presents a history of the abbots of St. Alban's; and the St. Alban's *Chronicle*, compiled around 1393 and covering the years 1272-1395, which extended the history of the abbey that had been begun by Matthew Paris. He also wrote the *Y podigma Neustriae* for King Henry V of England (r. 1413-1422), which traced the history of the ruler's ancestors, the dukes of Normandy.

Walter, Hubert (d. 1205) ●

Archbishop of Canterbury and statesman. Born to a Norman family of Lancashire and Norfolk, Hubert led a somewhat obscure childhood, coming to notice as a chaplain to Ranulf de Glanville. In 1186, he was proposed as a candidate for the archbishopric of York, but he was rejected with four other proposed individuals by King Henry II. By 1189, however, he was considered suitable for the see of Salisbury and was consecrated on October 22. The following year, he set out on the Third Crusade with Richard the Lionhearted (d. 1199), becoming chief chaplain for the crusader army upon the death of Baldwin, archbishop of Canterbury. His role in the events of the crusade was considerable, for he negotiated a truce with Saladin, the great Islamic general, which led to the opening of the sacred sites of the Holy Land once more to pilgrims; he also was conspicuous in his compassion and care of the suffering. On his way home he visited King Richard at Durenstein where the monarch was imprisoned. Once back in England, he helped raise money for Richard's release. In 1193, he was made justiciar and archbishop of Canterbury, serving as virtual ruler of the country while the king was away on his endless campaigns. He introduced heavy taxation to pay for Richard's military ventures and was sorely troubled by a rebellion whose suppression cost him public favor and a disagreement with the monks of Christ Church, Canterbury, who were supported by Pope Innocent III. Walter resigned as justiciar in 1198 but returned to the post the next year to help the unhappy King John (r. 1199-1216). The king utilized him on ultimately unsuccessful missions to King Philip II of France. He died on his way to Boxley trying to end a dispute between the monks of Rochester and their bishop.

Walter of St. Victor ●

Twelfth-century philosopher and theologian. Nothing is known of him beyond his service as prior of the monastery at St. Victor, Paris, around the time of the Third Lateran Council (1179), authoring the famous treatise *Contra quattuor labyrinthos Franciae* (*Against the Four Labyrinths of France*). The "four labyrinths" he attacked were Peter Abelard, Peter Lombard, Gilbert de la Porrée, and Peter of Poitiers. Walter disagreed sharply with the dialectical method then in use in theology, especially condemning the use of logic in the study of the mysteries of the faith. He failed completely in his hope of defeating the dialectical method, for it became the accepted practice in theological training, and both Peter of Poitiers and Peter Lombard were given places of high honor. Walter died sometime after 1180.

Walter the Penniless (d. 1097) ● French knight. Called Walter Sans Avoir (the Penniless), he helped organize, with Peter the Hermit, the People's Crusade to the Holy Land. (See People's Crusade under **Crusades** for other details.)

Ward, William George (1812-1882) ● English theologian and leader of the Oxford movement. Born in London, he was educated at Christ Church, Oxford, becoming a fellow of Balliol College, Oxford, in 1834. He remained there until 1845, having been ordained an Anglican Church priest in 1840. During this period, however, he came under the powerful influence of John Henry Newman, the Tractarian figure and later cardinal. Ward soon joined the Oxford movement, earning criticism from Anglicans at Balliol College. He was suspended for giving his endorsement to Newman in several pamphlets and was then stripped of his degrees and condemned at Oxford for his 1844 work *The Ideal of a Christian Church* in which he called upon the Anglican Church to beg humbly for pardon from Rome and for full restoration to the Catholic Church. Ward joined the Church in 1845, followed shortly thereafter by Newman and many others in the Oxford movement. After teaching moral theology at St. Edmund's College, Ware, from 1851-1858, he was granted a doctorate in theology by Pope Pius IX in 1854. He later served as an editor (1863-1878) of the prominent Catholic quarterly *Dublin Review*. His son, Wilfrid Ward, (1856-1916) became an important biographer, authoring works on his father and biographies of Cardinals Wiseman and Newman.

Wenceslaus, St. (d. 929) ● Also Wenceslas. Patron saint of Bohemia and duke of Bohemia from 924-929, he was born near Prague and was raised a Christian by his grandmother, St. Ludmilla, until her murder by Wenceslaus's own mother, Drahomira, a pagan. Drahomira became regent around 920 after the death of her husband, embarking upon a rule in Wenceslaus's name that was harsh and violent. Urged on by his own oppressed subjects because the rule was becoming intolerable, Wenceslaus claimed power for himself in 924 (or 925). Pious and devoted to spreading the Christian faith, he promoted the work of German missionaries and possibly took a vow of poverty. These policies antagonized the non-Christian members of the nobility who were driven to conspire against him when the duke submitted to the German king Henry the Fowler, who invaded Bohemia in 929. On his way to Mass on September 28, 929, he was murdered by a group of knights led by his brother Boleslav on the doorstep of a church. Revered almost immediately as a saint and martyr, Wenceslaus was moved from his tomb (where miracles had been reported) to the Church of St. Vitus in Prague, which became a major pilgrimage site during the Middle Ages. He is commemorated in the Christmas carol "Good King Wenceslaus." His feast was celebrated in Bohemia from at least 985. Feast day: September 28.

West Indies ● The archipelago situated between North and South America; it includes the Greater Antilles (Cuba, Jamaica, Puerto Rico, and Hispaniola), the Lesser Antilles (Barbados, Trinidad, Tobago, the Windward Islands, and the Leeward Islands) and the Bahamas, Dominican Republic, Virgin Islands, and Haiti. The Church came to the region at the close of the fifteenth century with the Spanish vessels of exploration starting with the second voyage of Columbus. As with the other possessions of the Spanish Empire in the New World, those islands of the West Indies under Spanish control were the object of intense missionary activity. Their initial hopes, however, of converting the indigenous population were left largely unfulfilled, as the natives were virtually wiped out in the early years of the conquest of the islands. The Indian population was essentially replaced by slaves from Africa who had little incentive to become Catholic given the often brutal treatment to which they were subjected by their Spanish masters. Nevertheless, the faith was planted quite successfully and a patriarch of the West Indies was later appointed. This office, one of the few titular patriarchates of the Western Church, fell vacant in 1963. Specifically, the islands of the West Indies and the origins of the Church there are:

Bahamas: The island group was the site of the first Mass in the Americas, celebrated after the arrival of Columbus in October 1492.

Cuba: See **Cuba**.

Dominican Republic: The neighbor of Haiti on the island of Hispaniola, it was the recipient of the earliest Church organization anywhere in the Americas and was subsequently an important strategic possession of Spain.

Haiti: One of the most strife-ridden places in the Western hemisphere, Haiti was an early possession of Spain until ceded in part in 1697 and then completely in 1795 to France. Independence was declared in 1804 through the rebellion of Toussaint L'Ouverture. The island's history is filled with poverty and severely oppressive regimes.

Jamaica: The island discovered by Columbus in 1494 and settled by Diego Columbus in 1509. In 1967, it received its own archbishop.

Virgin Islands: A group of islands currently under the U.S. and Great Britain, first discovered by Columbus in 1493 and named after St. Ursula and her virgin companions. The American portion of the islands was under the jurisdiction of the see of Baltimore from 1804 to 1820.

Western Schism ● See **Schism, Great**.

Westphalia, Peace of (1648) ● General series of agreements that brought an end to the destructive Thirty Years' War (1618-1648). The Peace of Westphalia was actually comprised of two settlements signed on October 24, 1648. The first was at Münster, between the Holy Roman Empire and France. By its terms, France obtained most of the region of Alsace and a number of border fortresses. The second was at Osnabrück, between the empire and the allied Protestant states and Sweden. Sweden received West Pomerania and the bishoprics of Verden and Bremen. Additionally, full independence was granted to the United Provinces of the Netherlands and Switzerland. In religious affairs, the peace accord established as its settlement the Augsburg Formula of *cuius regio eius religio*, in which the accepted religion of the land depended on that of its prince or ruler. Further, to promote stability, the faith of a prince should not change once the agreement was formalized and there should be no intrusion on the part of the Holy See in the affairs of Germany. Aside from reducing the power and influence of the Habsburgs, the peace agreement rendered the Holy Roman Empire a loose confederation of states. Bringing as it did the essential recognition of the Protestants, it was considered a major defeat for the Church in general and the papacy in particular. Pope Innocent X (r. 1644-1655) had tried through his nuncio Fabio Chigi (the future Pope Alexander VII) to minimize the concessions being made to the Protestants, most notably in matters of religion, but the powers involved, exhausted by a war that had depopulated whole parts of

Germany, were no longer prepared to follow the pope's commands. In a fruitless gesture, Innocent issued the bull *Zelo Domus Dei* (November 26, 1648), declaring the agreements to be null and void. It had no influence in Germany, and Emperor Ferdinand III (r. 1637-1657) refused to allow its publication in his territories. For Innocent, of course, the bull was merely a mandatory gesture, for he recognized that peace was inevitable and desirable, hoping only to reduce the damage to the Church's position in European life and politics.

Whitby, Synod of ● Council held at Whitby, England, in 664. At the assembly, it was decided that the date for Easter should be celebrated in the Roman custom, thereby ending the long association of the English Church with the old Irish or Celtic Church in the isles. The controversy over Easter had caused considerable division among Christians in England; the Irish custom was supported by Sts. Colman and Chad, given political backing from King Oswiu of Northumbria, while the Roman cause was championed by St. Wilfrid. King Oswiu decided to settle the matter by calling a synod at which both sides were to be represented. Oswiu there decided to follow Peter and the Council of Nicaea, embracing Rome by declaring that he could no longer contradict the decrees of the keeper of the keys of heaven, lest Peter should refuse him admission. More significantly, Whitby signaled the open association of the English Church with Rome, bringing England into the Western, rather than Irish, Church. The principal source on the synod is the Venerable Bede.

White Fathers ● Properly the Missionaries of Our Lady of Africa of Algeria, the White Fathers are a missionary society founded in 1868 at Algiers by Charles Lavigerie (1825-1892), archbishop of Algeria and later cardinal. Known as the *Pères Blancs* (White Fathers) from their white tunic and mantle, they were established to work for conversion among Muslims and native Africans in the area of Central Africa. The occasion of the society's foundation was the recognition by Lavigerie that a large number of Arab children had been left orphans by a terrible famine in 1867 and that they needed a home and decent education. Beginning in Tunisia and Algeria, the White Fathers soon sent missionaries into the Sudan and the rest of East and Central Africa; early work was always dangerous and the first missionaries to the Sudan were murdered by their guides.

Cardinal Charles Lavigerie, founder of the White Fathers

Aside from their white tunic and mantle, they customarily wore a rosary and cross around their neck. The society received approval of its constitution in 1885 and confirmation in 1908. The White Fathers are not, technically, a religious order. Its members are missionary priests and coadjutor brothers. They are bound by an oath to work for the conversion of Africa and to remain steadfastly obedient to the regulations of the society. Members are permitted to own their own property, but such possessions must be used at the direction of superiors in the order. Converts to the faith under the instruction of the Fathers are expected to undergo a complete four-year program leading to baptism. Aside from making conversions, the order helped give instruction in various skills to converts and encouraged Catholics to enter the priesthood if so called. The White Fathers were particularly active in resisting and then working for the abolition of the pernicious slave trade in Africa. In 1984, the White Fathers changed their name to the Missionaries of Africa (M.Afr.) and today number some twenty-five hundred members. The White Fathers should not be confused with the Society of African Missions (S.M.A.) founded in 1836 at Lyons by Bishop Melchior de Marion Brésillac, which today has over twelve hundred members.

In 1869, Lavigerie founded the Congregation of Missionary Sisters of Our Lady of Africa (M.S.O.L.A.) to assist the White Fathers. Called the White Sisters, they were given formal recognition in 1909 by Pope St. Pius X (r. 1903-1914). They are devoted to educational, medical, and social work in Africa, and members take a simple perpetual vow. They arrived in the United States in 1929.

White Friars ● Name given to the Carmelite Fathers, taken from their white cloaks and scapulars.

White Sisters ● See under **White Fathers**.

Wilfrid of York, St. (634-709) ● Bishop of York. Largely responsible for the triumph of the Roman influence over the Celtic Church at the Synod of Whitby (664), Wilfrid was the son of a Northumbrian noble, receiving an education at Lindisfarne and Canterbury. In 654, he journeyed to Rome with Benedict Biscop and was a student of Boniface, archdeacon to the pope. Returning to England, he became abbot of Ripon, working to introduce the Benedictine Rule to England and promoting Roman custom in the face of continuing adherence to Celtic custom and practice by many in the English Church. The controversy that ensued was finally settled at Whitby, where King Oswiu of Northumbria decided in favor of Rome. The decision was almost entirely through the eloquence and driving will of Wilfrid. Soon after the synod, he was named bishop of York, being consecrated in Compiègne by Frankish bishops because he considered the Celtic bishops in northern England to be schismatic. Upon reaching his see at York in 666, he found it occupied by St. Chad and retired to Ripon. In 669, however, St. Theodore of Canterbury was finally able to install him. Over the next years, Wilfrid vigorously enforced the Roman usage and founded a number of Benedictine monasteries. In 678, Theodore chose to divide the diocese of York into three separate sees under the suffragan bishops of Whiteherne, Hexham, and Lindisfarne. Wilfrid naturally opposed this, appealing to Rome and departing immediately for the Eternal City. On his way, he spent a year preaching in Frisia. A synod in Rome under Pope Agatho found in Wilfrid's favor, but upon reaching home he was imprisoned for a time, the sentence changed to exile from the kingdom of Northumbria. Wilfrid went to Sussex, engaging in notable missionary work among the Saxons from 681-686. Finally reconciled with Theodore, he was reinstalled as bishop of York. Soon, further difficulties began with King Aldfrith, culminating with another trip to Rome in 704. Again vindicated by the Holy See, Wilfrid reached a compromise with his fellow prelates, accepting the see of Hexham and allowing St. John of Beverly to become bishop of York. Wilfrid spent his last years at Ripon. He was notable for having been one of the greatest champions in the seventh century of the rights and authority of the Holy See and for advancing its cause in England. His biography was written by Eddius Stephanus of Ripon. Feast day: October 12.

Willehad, St. (d. 789) ● Bishop of Bremen. A native of Northumbria, England, he probably studied at York under St. Egbert and was a friend of Alcuin. After receiving holy orders, he was granted permission by King Aelhred of Northumbria to embark upon missionary activities in Frisia sometime between 765-774. He preached at Dockum, where St. Boniface had been martyred, and was able to bring many Frisians into the faith. Charlemagne sent him in 780 to Wigmodia near the North Sea to preach among the pagan Saxons. He was able to build many churches there, but his numerous accomplishments were ruined by the bloody Saxon uprising of 782, when his churches were destroyed and many of his friends were murdered. Willehad escaped to Rome where he met with Pope Adrian I (r. 772-795) and then retired to the Abbey of Echternach. After the suppression of the Saxons by Charlemagne (r. 768-814), he was invited back by the ruler to Wigmodia. In July 787 he was consecrated bishop at Worms, taking residence in Bremen where he built a cathedral, dedicated in November 789. He died a short time later from a fever. A life was written by a cleric at Bremen around 840 and an account of his miracles was authored by St. Anskar. Feast day: November 8.

William I (c. 1028-1087) ● Called the "Conqueror," he was the first Norman king of England (r. 1066-1087). The natural son of Robert I, duke of Normandy, he succeeded to the duchy in 1042, suppressing rebellious barons and proving himself willing to use considerable force to secure his position. On a visit to England in 1051, he was possibly designated heir to King Edward the Confessor, strengthening the claim in 1064 by releasing a potential rival, Harold Godwinson, earl of Wessex, after that Saxon magnate had been shipwrecked on the Normandy coast, and most likely after extracting a recognition of William's status as successor. In 1066, however, upon the death of Edward, Harold took the crown of England, giving William full justification to invade. Obtaining the blessing of Pope Alexander II, William sailed across the English Channel, defeated Harold at the Battle of Hastings on October 14, 1066, and had himself crowned in London.

As king, William ruthlessly subjected Saxon England, using fortresses to spread and solidify Norman feudalism throughout the land. He deliberately fostered the sociopolitical custom of obedience more to the king than to any subordinate lord in the feudal chain of power. To make this clear, William ordered a massive survey of the realm in 1085-1086 that resulted in the Domesday Book, a detailed accounting of every piece of land in England that made clear the royal contention that everything was his to govern and to dispose of as he saw fit. Domesday provides, however, a clear picture of the English Church at the outset of the Norman era.

William generally enjoyed excellent relations with the Church, using them to wield enormous influence over the prelates and clergy within his kingdom and to strengthen himself politically. Through investiture, he was able to appoint numerous Norman bishops, deposing many Saxon bishops and abbots in various ways. Personally upright, he was remarkably circumspect in his appointments, and was an avid supporter of the reforms of the Church under Pope Gregory VII (r. 1073-1085). He thus worked with Lanfranc, archbishop of Canterbury, to enforce papal legislation on simony and other important matters; the king himself presided over councils devoted to reform. Around 1072, he issued a writ by which certain pleas were removed from the jurisdiction of secular courts and placed entirely under the jurisdiction of ecclesiastical law. (See also **Domesday Book** and **England**.)

William of Auvergne (c. 1180-1249) ● Also William of Paris. Bishop of Paris, philosopher, and theologian. Born in Aurillac, Auvergne, he studied at Paris, subsequently becoming a member of the faculty of the university. In 1228, he was named bishop of Paris. As a philosopher, William was one of the early Scholastic adherents to the adoption of Aristotelian philosophy in the study of Christian dogma, working to prepare the groundwork for far more comprehensive developments under the Schoolmen (such as St. Thomas Aquinas, St. Albert the Great, Alexander of Hales, etc.) who were to follow. His work was, of course, limited to some degree by the scarcity of reliable and available texts of Aristotle's writings, but he was able to devote himself to freeing Aristotelian thought from what he saw as the baleful influence of Islamic translations and philosophers, most notably Avicebron and Avicenna. His writings included numerous theological treatises including *De Trinitate, De Fide et Legibus, De Anima,* and *De Sacramentis,* compiled into one vast encyclopedia, *Magisterium divinale (Divine Teaching),* composed between 1223 and 1240. He was a much respected figure in the court of King St. Louis IX.

William of Auxerre (d. 1231) ● French scholastic theologian and philosopher, he taught at the University of Paris. A student of Richard of St. Victor, he was an archdeacon of Beauvais before teaching at Paris. In 1231, he was appointed by Pope Gregory IX as a member of a commission charged with examining and amending the physical and metaphysical treatises of Aristotle, which had been forbidden by the university in 1210 owing to the errors contained in the translations and commentaries of Arabic philosophers. His chief work was the *Summa Aurea,* an important *summa* that, while heavily influenced by the *Sentences* of Peter Lombard, was notable for its use of the writings of Aristotle that had only recently

been discovered, making William one of the earliest Schoolmen to utilize Aristotle's works in a creation of genuine originality.

William of Champeaux (d. 1121) ● French Scholastic philosopher and theologian. A native of Champeaux, he was a student under Anselm of Laon, subsequently teaching (from 1103) at the cathedral school of Paris. An adherent of extreme realism, he was so severely criticized by Peter Abelard that in 1108 he retired to the Abbey of St. Victor. While there he lectured extensively, probably modifying his views on realism and having a considerable influence upon the so-called Victorine School. In 1113, he became bishop of Châlons-sur-Marne. Among his surviving writings are portions of *De origine animae (On the Origins of the Soul),* a dialogue, and a *Liber sententiarum.*

William of Conches (d. c. 1154) ● French Scholastic philosopher and theologian, he was a member of the famed school of Chartres. A student of Bernard of Chartres, he was much influenced by Platonism and humanism, and his writings often concerned cosmological questions. He taught at both Chartres and Paris and was the tutor of the future King Henry II of England (r. 1154-1189). William was one of the earliest Christian philosophers of the West to study extensively the philosophical and scientific works of the Arabs, particularly through the translations made by Constantine the African. He was the author of numerous treatises and commentaries including glosses on Plato's *Timaeus,* the dialogue *Dragmaticon* (one of his most popular creations), the treatise *Magna de naturis philosophia, Philosophia Mundi,* and a commentary on *De Consolatione philosophiae* by Boethius.

William of Jumièges (d. c. 1090) ● Benedictine historian. Little is known of him beyond his authorship of the *Historia Normanorum.* Probably a Norman by birth, he spent most of his life at the Abbey of Jumièges, Normandy. His *Historia Normanorum* (or *Normannorum*), in eight books, covered the history of the Normans from 851-1137. William wrote with his own hand the first seven books to 1087; the eighth book, added by an anonymous writer, continued the account to 1137. It was a major source for the work of Ordericus Vitalis.

William of Malmesbury (c. 1090-c. 1143) ● English monk and historian. Educated at Malmesbury, he entered the Benedictine monastery and subsequently devoted his life to historical writing, compiling by 1125 his two main works, the *Gesta Regum Anglorum* (1120) and the *Gesta Pontificum Anglorum* (1125), covering the secular and ecclesiastical history of England. Around 1140, he revised these histories. William also authored an abridgment of the *De Ecclesiasticis Officiis* of Amalarius of Metz, as well as theological and biographical works. The *Gesta Pontificum* is one of the chief sources for details on the early history of the Church in England.

William of Moerbeke (d. 1286) ● Flemish Dominican philosopher and translator. Born in Brabant, Belgium, he entered the Dominicans at Ghent, studying at Paris and then Cologne. While at Cologne, he probably came to know St. Albertus Magnus. Appointed subsequently by Pope Clement IV (r. 1265-1268) to serve as chaplain and translator, he remained in the post until 1278. He participated in the Council of Lyons (1274) at the request of Pope Gregory X (r. 1271-1276) with the task of advising the pontiff on the negotiations aimed at bringing a reunion of the Greek and Latin Churches. In 1278, William was named archbishop of Corinth by Pope Nicholas III (r. 1279-1280). William's principal achievement was to undertake at the behest of his contemporaries Latin translations of the writings of Aristotle. He was particularly encouraged in this by St. Thomas Aquinas, whom he had known in Viterbo and Orvieto. Among the Aristotelian works translated by William were *De caelo* (*On the Heavens*), *Metaphyisica*, *Historia animalium*, *Politics*, and *Poetica*. He also translated commentaries on Aristotle and the works of such Neoplatonists as Proclus. Moreover, William made important contributions to learning, making available to the scholars of the time reliable translations of books and treatises that would accelerate Scholasticism and the brilliance of Thomas Aquinas.

William of Newburgh (1136-c. 1198) ● English Augustinian and chronicler. A native of Bridlington, Yorkshire, he entered the Augustinian Priory of Newburgh at a young age and apparently remained there for most of his life, if not all of it. He was known mainly for his *Historia rerum Anglicarum*, a history of England from the Norman conquest in 1066 to 1198. Written probably in the years just before his death (c. 1196-1198) at the request of the abbot of Rievaulx, the *Historia* is a leading source on English medieval history. William is considered a member of the northern school of English historians, with his remarkable contemporary Roger of Hovedon. He used as sources such excellent writers as Henry of Huntingdon and Symeon of Durham.

William of Norwich, St. (1132-1144) ● A tanner's son, he became famous for being the supposed victim of ritual murder. William was apparently murdered on Holy Saturday, March 25, 1144, in Thorpe Wood, near Norwich. As he had been seen frequenting the homes of Jews in the area, it was immediately assumed that they had crucified the boy and put him to death during Passover. The Jews were soon accused of murdering him, but, as they enjoyed the protection of the sheriff, no charges were ever formally made. Five years later, however, a

Jew named Eleazar was murdered by several followers of Sir Simon de Novers. When the Jews demanded justice, Bishop Turbe of Norwich, acting on behalf of the accused, brought up William's murder. Much uproar followed as William became increasingly revered as a martyr. Through the efforts of Bishop Turbe, the chronicler Thomas of Monmouth (the only source on the entire incident), and others, a cultus developed, customarily dated from the translation of William's remains from the chapter house of the local monks to the cathedral in 1151. The event was accompanied by reports of miracles and an eruption both of religious fervor and highly unfortunate anti-Semitism. The case of William was the first of many so-called blood accusations against the Jews that became common throughout the Middle Ages and that were entirely without foundation.

William of Occam (d. 1349) ● Also William of Ockham. A controversial English Scholastic philosopher, he was born in or near the village of Ockham (Occam), Surrey, England, studied at Merton College, Oxford, and entered the Franciscan order. Among his teachers was John Duns Scotus. He became a lecturer at Oxford, focusing on the *Sentences* of Peter Lombard, but he ultimately departed from the university without his master's degree owing to the stern opposition he faced from several members of the faculty led by the chancellor John Lutterell concerning his teaching.

Lutterell continued his campaign against Occam, denouncing him before the papal court at Avignon. Occam was called there to answer questions in 1324 about the possibly heretical nature of his writings. Pope John XXII (r. 1316-1334) established a commission of six theologians to investigate the matter. While no formal condemnation was made, the commission did censure fifty-one propositions. While in Avignon in 1327, he did participate in the Franciscan controversy over poverty, expressing his support for the so-called Spiritual Franciscans, the advocates of strict poverty for all members. At the command of the pope, he made a study on the papal view of the question, deciding finally against the pontiffs. He soon found it expedient to depart Avignon, fleeing in 1328 to the safety of the court of Emperor Louis IV the Bavarian, who had been excommunicated by John XXII in 1324. Occam was himself excommunicated in 1328 and in 1331 was expelled from the Franciscans. He shared his exile with the controversial thinkers Marsilius of Padua and John of Jandun. He died in Munich in 1349, apparently having taken steps to be reconciled with the Church, although he purportedly did not make peace with the papacy.

Occam has been called the *Princeps Nominalium* (Prince of the Nominalists) for his major contributions to promoting nominalism. He denied the universal in the reality of the world, arguing that real things are known by intuition and not by abstraction. His views, while considered by modern scholars to be a modified nominalism or conceptualism, presented the universal as a mental substitute for real things, earning him the nickname the Terminist to distinguish him from his fellow conceptualists and nominalists. While he rejected any term related to God that limited God's omnipotence, Occam questioned the ability to prove conclusively the existence of God through philosophy. He thus rejected Thomas Aquinas's major contention that there was a harmony between reason and faith. In ecclesiastical affairs he advocated the idea of separation of the Church and secular affairs, holding that an unsatisfactory pope could be deposed by the Holy Roman Emperor, but the pope did not possess the right of similar deposition. These concepts were to have an influence on conciliarism in the fourteenth century. The famous principle of "Occam's razor" — *"Entia non sunt multiplicanda sine necessitate*" ("Beings should not multiply without necessity") — epitomized his own efforts in Scholasticism. He sought to simplify contemporary Scholastic thought, a desire that was validated to some degree by the complex and frequently highly obtuse system that had developed among Schoolmen. His method and the ultimate end to his theories, however, were found unacceptable by theologians who felt the current problems with Scholasticism to be centered in method and expression rather than in theological content.

William of Rubriquis (d. c. 1293) ● Also called William of Rubruck, a Franciscan traveler. Born not far from Rubruck (or Rubrouck) near St. Omer, France, he entered the Franciscans and later was in the Holy Land during the crusade of King St. Louis IX of France. In 1253, the monarch chose William to set out on a journey to find the khan of the Mongol Empire. William began his mission in Constantinople in May 1253, arriving at the camp of Batu Khan, the local Mongol ruler of the area of the Volga in Russia, where he received permission to continue on to the court of the Great Khan. He then traveled north of the Caspian Sea, finally reaching Karakorum and the camp of the Great Khan around late 1253. William remained there until May 1254 when he began his return trip, arriving at Tripoli in August 1255. For King Louis, the friar authored a comprehensive account of his adventures, a work that was much used by his contemporary Roger Bacon but was overshadowed by the fame of Marco Polo. Bacon mentioned William frequently in his *Opus majus*.

William of St. Thierry (c. 1085-1148) ● Scholastic philosopher, theologian, and mystic. Born in Liège, William was of noble descent, studying at Laon under Anselm of Laon. In 1113, he entered the Benedictine

Abbey of St. Nicasius in Reims and was elected abbot around 1119; his brother Simon, also a Benedictine, became abbot of St. Nicholas-aux-Bois. Despite his personal inclination toward the contemplative life, William accepted election, remaining in office largely through the influence of his good friend St. Bernard of Clairvaux, who exhorted him to continue as abbot; William was particularly desirous of retiring to Clairvaux with Bernard. In 1135, he finally resigned from the abbacy, but, fearing Bernard's disapproval, he went to the monastery of Signy in the Ardennes, devoting himself to study and prayer. He died around the time of the convoking of the Synod of Reims by Pope Bl. Eugenius II (r. 1145-1153).

Although a mystic, William was much concerned with theological matters. He was the first theologian to confront the serious errors in the works of Peter Abelard, calling them to Bernard's attention and authoring several treatises against him: *Disputatio adversus Petrum Abelardum* (*The Dispute Against Peter Abelard*); and *Disputatio catholicorum Patrum adversus dogmata Petri Abelardi* (*Disputation of the Fathers Against the Dogma of Peter Abelard*), in reply to Abelard's apology. William also wrote numerous theological and mystical treatises, *De vita solitaria* (*On the Solitary Life*); *De Deo contemplando* (*On the Contemplation of God*); *Aenigma fidei* (*The Enigma of the Faith*); *De sacramento altaris liber* (*On the Sacrament of the Altar*); *Speculum fidei* (*Mirror of Faith*); a commentary on the Epistle of St. Paul to the Romans; a commentary on the Canticle of Canticles (Song of Solomon); and a life of St. Bernard of Clairvaux (the first chapters). These works were noted for their considerable spiritual and theological depth, their knowledge of Greek and Latin, and their familiarity with both the Church Fathers and the Scriptures.

William of Tyre (d. 1185) ● Archbishop of Tyre and noted chronicler. Born in Syria to a

French or Italian family of the merchant class, he studied at Bologna and Paris, where he mastered Greek, Latin, and Arabic. Returning to Palestine in 1160, he became a priest and in 1167 was named archdeacon. After serving on several important diplomatic missions to Constantinople and Rome, he became in 1170 tutor to Baldwin (IV), son of King Amalric of Jerusalem. A trusted councillor to Baldwin, he was promoted to chancellor of the kingdom of Jerusalem and archbishop of Tyre in 1174. As a result of the victories of the Islamic general Saladin against the Crusader States, William was dispatched to Europe to organize a new crusade in 1178. He attended the Lateran Council of 1179 and returned to the Holy Land by way of Constantinople where he performed a diplomatic task for Pope Alexander III. In 1180, he failed to secure election as patriarch of Jerusalem, retiring to Rome in 1183. His remaining years are obscure. William authored two histories: *Historia de principibus orientalibus* (now lost), on the Arabs from the time of Muhammad, preserved in fragmentary form in the *Historia Orientalis* by Jacques de Vitry; and the surviving *Historia rerum in partibus transmarinis Gestarum* (*History of the Deeds Across the Sea*; also *Historia Hierosolymitana*), begun between 1169 and 1175, detailing the history of Palestine from 614-1184. The first sixteen books were written using such sources as Fulcher of Chartres and Albert of Aix; Books XVII to XXIII were more personal, relying upon William's own account of events. Because of this and his familiarity with the events in the kingdom of Jerusalem, he is a major source for information of the doomed Christian realm.

William of York, St. (d. 1154) ●

Archbishop of York. Born William Fitzherbert, he was a member of a noble family. After serving as a chaplain to King Stephen of England and canon and treasurer of York Minster, he was elected archbishop in 1142. Accused of simony, however, by Cistercian monks, he was refused consecration by Theobald, archbishop of Canterbury. An appeal was made to Pope Innocent II, who decided in William's favor so long as he was willing to take an oath of his innocence. Finally consecrated, William was still unable to receive the pallium from Cardinal Hincmar of Reims, which had been sent for William by Pope Lucius II in 1145. He was thus compelled to go to Rome to clear his name before Pope Bl. Eugenius III. Owing to the rash decision by his family in attacking the Abbey of Fountains under William's rival, Abbot Henry Murdac, William was deposed by the Council of Reims (1147), taking refuge with his friend Henry of Blois, bishop of Winchester, until 1153, by which time Eugenius was dead. Pope Anastasius IV restored him to his see and gave him the pallium, and William promised to provide restitution to Fountains Abbey. His death a short time after finally returning to York was possibly by murder. He died a much beloved figure and was considered a martyr. Miracles were reported at his tomb, and in 1227 Pope Honorius III canonized him. Feast day: June 8.

Willibrord, St. (658-739) ●

Also called Wilbrod, Apostle of the Frisians and bishop of Utrecht. Born in Northumbria, England, he studied at the Abbey of Ripon under St. Wilfrid before entering the Benedictine order. Around 678 he journeyed to Ireland, spending twelve years there at the Abbey of Rathmelsigi (perhaps Mellifont, in County Louth) and receiving holy orders. In 690, Willibrord and eleven companions embarked on a mission to Frisia. He went to Rome in 692, receiving papal approbation for his endeavors; on a second trip to Rome, he was consecrated bishop of the Frisians by Pope St. Sergius I (r. 687-701), on November 21, 695. Upon returning to Frisia, Willibrord established a monastery at Utrecht, where he also erected a cathedral. In 716, however, the region came under the control of Duke Radbod, who drove out the bishop, ruined most of his churches, replaced them with pagan temples, and put to death many of Willibrord's priests and missionaries. Willibrord returned in 719 after Radbod's death, receiving much assistance from St. Boniface in recovering the position of the Church in Frisia. He died on November 7, 739, at the monastery of Echternach. Feast day: November 7.

Winchelsea, Robert of (d. 1313) ● Also Robert Winchelsey, archbishop of Canterbury. After studying at the University of Paris, he became rector of the school in 1267. It is possible that he was able to hear some of the great lectures by St. Thomas Aquinas in Paris. Returning to England around 1283, he served as canon of St. Paul's and archdeacon of Essex before attending Oxford. By 1288, Winchelsea was chancellor of Oxford University, being elected in 1293 as archbishop of Canterbury. He soon emerged as one of the great champions of ecclesiastical rights, opposing King Edward I (r. 1272-1307) and Edward II (r. 1307-1327). Against the wishes of Edward I, he published Pope Boniface VIII's bull *Clericis Laicos* (1296), which prohibited the clergy from paying taxes to secular rulers. When Winchelsea refused to contribute money for Edward's war, the king seized Winchelsea's property and outlawed the English clergy. While winning the admiration of Pope Boniface, Winchelsea was finally released from the obligation by the pope, who agreed in 1297 to permit taxation in cases where they were needed for the defense of the realm. The next years were spent in considerable hostility with Edward, culminating in 1305 with the election of Bertrand de Got, a vassal of Edward's, as Pope Clement V. At Edward's prodding, Winchelsea was suspended, allowing the king to banish him in 1306. The following year,

however, Edward II recalled him. He soon joined the baronial opposition, using the threat of excommunication against their opponents, most notably the influential courtier Piers Gaveston. He died considered by many to be a martyr in the tradition of St. Thomas Becket, but nothing came of efforts to secure his canonization.

Wiseman, Nicholas (1802-1865) ● English cardinal and archbishop of Westminster, he played a major role in the formal restoration of the Catholic hierarchy in the country. Born in Seville, Spain, to Irish immigrant parents, he returned home to Ireland in 1805 with his mother following the death of his father. After studying at Waterford and Ushaw College, Durham, he was chosen in 1818 as one of the students to be sent to the newly revived English College in Rome. There he earned his doctorate in 1824 and was ordained in 1825 and appointed professor of Oriental languages at the University of Rome. In 1828, he was made rector of English College. While visiting England in 1835-1836, he earned wide acclaim for his preaching, also establishing the Catholic quarterly *Dublin Review*. In 1840, he ended his tenure as rector, was consecrated a bishop, and appointed coadjutor to the vicar apostolic of the Midland District of England. He became vicar apostolic of the London District in 1847, working tirelessly to revive the Catholic faith in the isles and establishing a lasting association with members of the Oxford movement, many of whom entered the Church, including the future cardinal John Henry Newman. When the hierarchy of England was finally restored in 1850, Wiseman was chosen the first archbishop of Westminster and cardinal. News of Pope Pius IX's decision concerning the reestablishment of the Church's hierarchy was much denounced in England, especially so on Guy Fawkes Day (November 5, 1850) when both the pope and Wiseman were burned in effigy.

Wiseman's pastoral letter of October 7, 1850, sent "from outside the Flaminian Gate" announcing himself, was furiously attacked as papal aggression, but the cardinal was successful in easing public uproar with his "Appeal to the Reason and Good Feeling of the English People on the subject of the Catholic Hierarchy." He followed this with bold public appearances and lectures that helped terminate any virulent anti-Catholic and especially any antipapal activity. His later years were marked by poor health and difficulties within the English Church over the question of Ultramontanism. A devoted Ultramontane, Wiseman was opposed by his own coadjutor, Bishop George Errington. Wiseman was the author of the *Horae Syriacae* (1827; *Syrian Seasons*), a scholarly study of the Syrian version of the OT and the novel *Fabiola, or the Church of the Catacombs* (1854).

Wolfgang, St. (c. 934-994) ● Bishop of Ratisbon. One of the great Church figures in formative Germany, with St. Ulrich and St. Conrad. He was probably from a family of counts from Swabia. He studied at the monastic school of Reichenau, later becoming a teacher in the cathedral school of Trier at the behest of Henry, archbishop of Trier. After Henry's death in 964, Wolfgang entered the Benedictine order at the Abbey of Einsiedeln, Switzerland. He was ordained by St. Ulrich in 968. At this saint's request, Wolfgang journeyed to Pannonia (the Balkan region) in an effort to evangelize the Magyars, laying the groundwork for subsequent missionaries. In 972, Wolfgang was appointed bishop of Ratisbon, succeeding

Cardinal Wolsey

Bishop Michael and receiving his appointment from Emperor Otto I. He was subsequently noted for his enthusiastic efforts at reform, serving also as a tutor to the future Emperor St. Henry II. In June 983, he participated in the Diet of Verona. He was a popular figure in medieval art, most notably in the work of the Tyrolian painter Michael Pacher (1430-1498). Feast day: October 31.

Wolsey, Thomas (c. 1474-1530) English cardinal and archbishop of York. He served as chancellor of England under King Henry VIII (r. 1509-1547). Wolsey was born in Ipswich, the son of a middle-class family; his father was said to be a butcher. He studied at Oxford and, around 1497, he was elected a fellow of Magdalen College. Ordained on March 10, 1498, he was named chaplain to Henry Dean, archbishop of Canterbury, and then court chaplain under King Henry VII (r. 1485-1509). Serving Henry in a variety of diplomatic missions, Wolsey was soon a royal favorite, maintaining the position after the accession of Henry VIII in 1509. His promotions were swift: canon of Windsor and registrar to the Order of the Garter (1511), dean of Hereford (1512), dean of York and St. Stephen's Westminster, and precentor of London (1513), bishop of Tournay (which he never claimed, taking a pension instead), bishop of Lincoln (1514), and archbishop of York; on November 18, 1515, he received the cardinal's red hat in Westminster Abbey. Only a month later, Henry appointed him chancellor of England.

In his position as a secular official, Wolsey devoted his main efforts to the furtherance of England's standing in Europe. He advocated a variety of shifting alliances with France against Spain and the Holy Roman Empire and then with former enemies. He found especially desirable the striking of a suitable middle ground of endeavoring to negotiate a peace between the rivals Emperor Maximilian and King Francis I of France, subsequently adopting neutrality when conflict erupted between Emperor Charles V (Maximilian's successor) and Francis. An eventual alliance with the emperor provided Wolsey with some aspirations for election as pope, but twice Charles declined to put forth his considerable influence to secure Wolsey's election in 1521 (following the death of Leo X) and in 1523 (after the death of Adrian VI). It is a matter of some question as to whether Wolsey desired election as pontiff, although he wrote concerning the elevation of Clement VII, "For my part, as I take God to record, I am more joyous thereof than if it had been fortuned upon my person." The alliance with Charles soon deteriorated, and Henry, under Wolsey's advice, gravitated toward France. The king, meanwhile, was to embark upon his momentous effort to divorce Catherine of Aragon. In this matter Wolsey was to disappoint Henry, failing in several schemes to fulfill his master's all-consuming wishes. Having lost Henry's confidence, Wolsey was further undermined by Anne Boleyn, who sought his political demise for what she felt was an intolerable delay in her marriage to the king. Kept from the court in August and September 1529, the cardinal was stripped of his great seal of England and on November 22 signed a confession of Praemunire. He spent the winter of 1529 in disgrace, receiving a pardon in February 1530 and restoration of the see of York save for York House, which he gave the king. For several months he administered his archdiocese with great diligence. On November 4, however, he was arrested for high treason, dying in Leicester Abbey on November 29, 1530, on the way to London. While a brilliant statesman, Wolsey lamented his own failings as a cleric with the famous statement: "If I had served God as diligently as I have done my king, He would not have given me over in my gray hairs."

Women, Ordination of ● Theological and sacramental question that has been raised most prominently in the last ten years or so by self-styled progressives within the Church who believe that women should be eligible for ordination to the priesthood. They often link the issue with that of celibacy and make predictions of severe consequences for the faith should their views not be adopted. This is, of course, roundly disputed by theologians and Church leaders who point now both to Christian teaching and experience to argue against any such major innovation.

The tradition and teachings of the Church have been quite consistent throughout the centuries with regard to the role of women in the sacrament of holy orders. Accordingly, they should not be ordained because of the special necessity that the representation of Christ at the Eucharist must be male; this maleness — the choosing of Christ to be of the male gender — was not an occurrence of accidence but was specifically chosen as essential to the real and symbolic relationship of Christ as the Bridegroom or Spouse with his bride, the Church, a spiritual communion expressible only with a male priest who presides over the Eucharist. Further, while on earth Christ called only men to be his Apostles, a demonstration of his express desire for the divinely instituted priesthood.

While the Church, especially in modern times, has been eloquent in its praise for women and its recognition of their vital role in the faith and among the people of God, the tradition and teaching remain firm. Questions arose about the issue following the Second Vatican Council, prompting Pope Paul VI to reiterate the doctrine of women's ineligibility in 1975. This was followed the next years by the declaration *Inter Insigniores* by the Congregation for the Doctrine of the

Faith in which it was stated: "In the fact of conferring priestly ordination only on men, it is a question of unbroken tradition throughout the history of the Church, universal in the East and in the West. . . ." Unbroken tradition and teaching have not been enough for some feminists, and Pope John Paul II has repeatedly reaffirmed the doctrinal reasons for the prohibition throughout his pontificate and especially in his visits to the United States. In a letter issued in May 1884, "On Reserving Priestly Ordination to Men Alone," Pope John Paul effectively closed the debate on the subject. He declared that the Church "has no authority whatsoever to confer priestly ordination on women and that this judgement is to be definitively held by all the Church's faithful."

Opponents of the ordination of women are also able to point to the unfortunate result that such a change has inflicted upon the Church of England. Since its implementation in late 1993, the policy has caused the departure of hundreds of priests from the Anglican Church into the Catholic Church, major upheaval among the laity, and even questions concerning the viability of the C of E in the future. Further, it has done nothing to reverse the calamitous decline of church attendance and has forced Church leaders to examine whether the entire policy ever had the support of the clergy and laity that polls had supposedly indicated and that proponents of the change had claimed.

Worms, Concordat of ● Agreement reached in 1122 between Pope Callistus II (r. 1119-1124) and Emperor Henry V that attempted to bring a settlement to the Investiture Controversy. According to the terms of the concordat, abbots and bishops in imperial lands were to be elected by the clergy, the emperor reserving the right to decide all contested elections. After election, the prelate was invested by the emperor with his regalia, doing homage to the crown as a political figure; another investiture was then performed by Church officials, who gave him his *spiritualia*, or ecclesiastical powers. By this practice, the German king agreed to end that part of the investiture that granted spiritual authority to Church officeholders. The concordat is also known as the *Pactum Calixtinum*.

Worms, Diet of ● Series of imperial inquests held at Worms in 1521 to which Martin Luther was summoned by Emperor Charles V to defend his controversial doctrines. The diet was convened on January 27, 1521, at the Bischof of Worms, several days after Luther's excommunication (January 2, 1521) by Pope Leo X, although the papal declaration was not formally received in German lands for a number of months. As Luther was the cause of great controversy in imperial lands but was receiving protection from Frederick III the Wise, elector of Saxony, Emperor Charles sought to have him appear, promising safe-conduct to the diet. The papal legate, Girolamo Alexander (1480-1542), who had arrived in Worms in November 1520, denounced Luther on February 13, 1521, in an Ash Wednesday sermon, calling for his condemnation without trial. Luther arrived on April 16, appearing before the diet the following day. He refused steadfastly to recant his beliefs or to repudiate his writings, declaring, according to tradition, "*Hie stehe ich. Ich kan nicht anders. Gott helf mir. Amen.*" ("Here I stand. I can do no other. God help me. Amen.") As it was Charles's resolution to undertake firmer measures against Luther and his teachings, Luther departed Worms on April 26, seeking refuge at Wartburg Castle, near Eisenach. On May 25, the diet issued the Edict of Worms, in which Luther was pronounced an outlaw and a heretic.

Worms, Disputation of ● Meeting or colloquy assembled at Worms from

1540-1541 that attempted to bring about a reunion of the Catholics and Protestants in Germany. Convened in the hopes of bringing about reunion after the failure of the Conference of Hagenau (June-July 1540), the diet opened on November 25, 1540, attended by theologians from each of the parties. The spokesman for the Catholic side was Johann Eck (1486-1543); for the Protestants it was Philipp Melanchthon. After preliminary discussions, the delegates agreed upon a formula of original sin. Owing, however, to the upcoming meeting of the Reichstag in Ratisbon, the disputation was brought to an end in middle of January 1541.

Worms, Synod of ● Synod convened in 1076 by Emperor Charles IV during his conflict with Pope St. Gregory VII over the Investiture Controversy. It was attended largely by the bishops of Germany, opening on January 24, 1076. A pro-imperial and highly antipapal assembly, the synod's members issued a harsh denunciation of Gregory, additionally accusing the pope of a variety of crimes while calling upon the Romans to overthrow him. Henry, bolstered by the German prelates, sent a vindictive letter to the pontiff, earning excommunication from Gregory.

Wulfstan (d. 1023) ● Bishop of London and Worcester, and archbishop of York. A native of the Danelaw region of England, he was probably a Benedictine monk, although details on his early life are obscure. He became bishop of London in 996, moving to Worcester in 1002, remaining as head of that see until 1016. At the same time, he was archbishop of York (1002-1023). Wulfstan was a noted writer in Old English, authoring treatises and homilies, and making contributions to law. An adviser to both the Saxon king Ethelred and Dane Canute the Great, Wulfstan helped the latter rule over his vanquished subjects with fairness and a Christian manner. He wrote as a result of his

interest in politics the work *Institutes of Polity*, an effort to examine the relationship of Church and State and the duties and responsibilities of all classes of society. For Ethelred and Canute, Wulfstan drafted numerous law codes and pieces of legislation. In matters of the Church, he was much concerned with reform, composing numerous homilies, including the very famous *Sermo Lupi ad Anglos* (*Sermon of the Wolf to the English*), which called in 1014 for the people to repent and described in riveting fashion that disasters and miseries of the time were the result of God's wrath at the sins of the nation's inhabitants. Surviving manuscripts of his writings or works annotated by him indicate the degree of his learning. After his death, an unsuccessful effort was made to promote his cause. He should not be confused with St. Wulfstan (c. 1008-1095), bishop of Worcester from 1062. This Wulfstan is notable for being the last English bishop after the conquest of the isle by the Normans in 1066 under King William I. He was instrumental, with Lanfranc, archbishop of Canterbury, in ending the slave trade that had long flourished between England and Ireland; he also assisted in compiling the Domesday Book. His life was written between 1095 and 1113 by the monk of Worcester Coleman, surviving only in a Latin version by William of Malmesbury. The original Old English work is lost. He was canonized in 1203. Feast day: January 19.

Wycliffe, John (d. 1384) ● Also Wyclif. English reformer, philosopher, and theologian whose controversial writings foreshadowed the Reformation. Born in Yorkshire, he studied at Oxford, becoming a regent of Balliol College, Oxford, in 1360. He resigned from this post in 1361 to serve as vicar of Fillingham (1361-1368), Ludgershall (1368-1384), and Lutterworth (1374-1384); he also received a doctorate in 1372. By this time, Wycliffe was a well-known scholar at Oxford, entering into the service of the powerful government figures John of Gaunt and the Black Prince, Edward. In 1374, he was part of a commission sent to negotiate with Curia members representing Pope Gregory XI (r. 1370-1378) over certain matters of dispute between the pope and King Edward III. With the protection of John of Gaunt, Wycliffe was able to advance his hostile theories concerning the Church. He spoke frequently in London on the abuses of the Church, remaining safe throughout because of his political backing from high figures of state who found him useful at a time when the Church was being wracked by the Great Schism. He called for clergy to practice poverty, declaring that a person's only Lord was Christ — in opposition to the Church, and, most controversially, that the doctrine of transubstantiation was philosophically unsound. This last position proved too much for many authorities. A council of doctors at Oxford in 1381 condemned his teaching on the Blessed Sacrament, followed by a London synod the next year that denounced twenty-four Wycliffite propositions. Wycliffite adherents were soon forced to recant, although Wycliffe himself died unmolested. He was buried at Lutterworth, but the Council of Constance (1414-1418) ordered his writings to be burned and his bones removed from holy ground.

While Wycliffe declined in popularity just after his death because of the Peasants' Revolt of 1381, which had been influenced by his idea of personal lordship through grace, he nevertheless was to have a deep effect upon scholars and theologians, most notably the Lollards and Hussites. Known as the "Morning Star of the Reformation," he was especially revered at Oxford over the next decades and in Bohemia where he was to help give shape to many of the ideas put forth by the Hussites. Among his writings were *De Potestate Papae* (c. 1379), on the papacy; *De Domino Divinio* and *De Civili Dominice*, on the idea that personal lordship was based on grace; and *De Eucharista*, the controversial work on the Holy Eucharist.

Ximénez de Cisneros, Francisco

(1436-1517) ● Spanish cardinal and archbishop of Toledo. Born at Torrelaguna, Castile, he studied at Alcalá and Salamanca before spending several years in Rome (1459-c. 1465). Returning to Spain, he brought with him the promise of Pope Sixtus IV that Ximénez should receive the first available office of prominence. This proved to be the post of archpriest of Uzeda, which the archbishop of Toledo had already promised to another. When Ximénez pressed his claim in 1473, he was imprisoned until 1480, when, upon his release, he was restored to his office. Transferred to the diocese of Siguenza, he served as vicar to the cardinal, who was bishop of the see, resigning in 1481, however, to enter the Franciscan Observantine Congregation of San Juan de los Reyes in Toledo. There he adopted a life of extreme asceticism. In 1492, he accepted, with reluctance, appointment as confessor to Queen Isabella on the enthusiastic endorsement of Cardinal Mendoza, archbishop of Toledo. Three years later, already much relied upon by the queen for his advice in all matters, he was named to succeed Mendoza, accepting the post only after receiving the command of the pope. As archbishop he remained vigorous in his pursuit of the Franciscan lifestyle, devoting large amounts of his time to care for the poor and sick. As his office also carried the high chancellorship of Castile, he was very averse to using the elegant dress, doing so only by compromise: he would show some portion of his Franciscan habit.

In 1499, he accompanied Ferdinand and Isabella to Granada, where he worked to secure the conversion of the recently conquered Muslims.

After the death of Isabella in 1504, he helped ease the succession of Archduke Philip of Burgundy and the retirement of Ferdinand as ruler of Castile. When Philip died in 1506, Ximénez served as viceroy until the return of Ferdinand in 1507 from Italy. That year, Ferdinand secured from Pope Julius II the red hat for Ximénez. In 1509, he led a military expedition against the Moorish city of Oran in Morocco, securing the release of large numbers of Christian slaves. Seven years later, he became regent for the young Charles V upon the passing of Ferdinand (January 23, 1516). The cardinal died on November 8, 1517, at Roa, near Valladolid, while on his way to meet Charles, who had just landed in Spain. It was believed that Ximénez had been poisoned. A remarkable figure in Spain, he left a considerable legacy through his works, most notably the establishing in 1500 of the University of Alcalá, which was to become a major center of learning.

Xystus ● See **Sixtus**.

Ysambert, Nicholas (d. 1642) ● French theologian. Born in Orléans, he studied at the Sorbonne in Paris and eventually taught there with such distinction that in 1616 King Louis XIII himself appointed him to the newly established chair of theology, which was to examine the theological dispute between the Protestants and Catholics. Over the next years, he was involved in a number of controversies, most notably defending the papacy from the Gallican theories of Edmond Richer, another member of the faculty, and securing the condemnation of the treatise *De republica christiana* by the onetime bishop of Spalatre, Marc Antonio de Dominis, for suggesting the liquidation of the hierarchy of the Church.

Yves of Chartres ● See **Ivo of Chartres, St**.

Zabarella, Francisco (1360-1417) ●
Italian cardinal and canonist. A native of
Padua, he studied at Bologna and Florence,
teaching canon law in Florence from
1385-1390 and Padua from 1390-1410. A
recipient of minor orders in 1389, he served
as vicar of the bishop of Florence and pastor
of the Church of Santa Maria in Pruneta,
near Florence. A candidate to succeed to the
see of Florence, he was instead appointed
archpriest of the Cathedral of Padua. There
he was of value to the city government,
representing Padua as a diplomat to the
court of King Charles VI of France to enlist
French aid against Venice (c. 1404). Padua
subsequently became attached to Venice,
and Zabarella served as an adviser to their
delegate to the Council of Pisa in 1409. The
following year, he was appointed bishop of
Florence by antipope John XXIII; on June 6,
1411, he became a cardinal. Zabarella was
henceforth an important figure in the
negotiations to bring about an end to the
Great Schism (1378-1417), supporting John
XXIII at the Council of Rome (1412-1413)
and the Council of Constance from which
John fled in March 1415. Zabarella
continued to take part in the council,
particularly in the proceedings against Pope
Benedict XIII and Jan Hus. He was the
author of a number of important works: *De
schismate* (1402-1408), a collection of
proposals to end the schism, printed in 1545
and placed on the Index of Forbidden Books
because of its conciliar sympathies; and
extensive writings on canon law — *Lectura
super Clementinis* (published in 1471),
Commentarius in libros Decretalum (1502),
and *Consilia* (1581).

Zachary, St. ● Pope from 741-752. Also
called Zacharias. A native of Calabria,
Zachary was Greek by descent, making him
the last of the Greek pontiffs. Having served
as a deacon to Pope Gregory III, he was
elected to succeed him on December 3, 741.
His pontificate was much concerned with
foreign relations, particularly with the
Lombards, the Byzantines, and the Franks.
He ended the hostility of the papacy with the
Lombards by meeting with King Liutprand
and negotiating a truce with him. New
political conditions made it possible for
Zachary to convince Liutprand not to attack
the exarchate of Ravenna, thereby acquiring
the appreciation of the Byzantines under
Emperor Constantine V (r. 741-755).
Meanwhile, Zachary took the politically
astute step of recognizing the deposition of
the last Merovingian king, Childeric III,
granting his permission for the anointing of
Pepin III the Short. He thus began the
association of the Carolingians with the
papacy that was to be of such long-term
historical importance. Zachary also held two
synods in Rome (743, 745) and gave his
support to the work of Boniface, Apostle of
Germany. He authored a Greek translation of
the *Dialogues* of St. Gregory the Great. Feast
day: March 22.

Zacharias, Scholasticus (d. c. 536) ●
Also known as Zacharias of Mitylene and
Zacharias of Gaza. Monophysite writer and
member of the so-called Gaza Triad with

Aeneas of Gaza and Procopius. He authored several notable works: biographies of Severus of Antioch and Peter the Iberian; a dialogue, *De Opificio Mundi*, against the Neoplatonists; and his chief writing, a Church history, in Syriac, that is a valuable source for the second half of the fifth century.

Zephyrinus, St. ● Pope from 199-217. According to the *Liber Pontificalis*, he was a Roman by birth, succeeding Pope St. Victor I. His pontificate is somewhat obscure, although he did clearly rely heavily upon his archdeacon Callistus, who would ultimately succeed him (Pope St. Callistus I). According to the highly critical Hippolytus, Zephyrinus was a weak man who was conspicuous in failing to deal with the heresies of the time. Chief among the controversies was Adoptionism. During his reign, Origen visited Rome. According to an unsupported tradition, he died a martyr. Feast day: August 26.

Pope St. Zephyrinus

Zonaras, Johannes ● Twelfth-century Byzantine historian. A member of the government in Constantinople, Zonaras resigned his position and retired to the island of Niandro where he entered into monastic life. Among his writings were a hymn to the Virgin Mary, a commentary on the poems of St. Gregory of Nazianzus, a commentary on Greek canon law, and, most importantly, a universal history, in eighteen volumes, that is a major source for details on Zonaras's own era.

Zosimus, St. ● Pope from 417-418. A Greek, he was elected on March 18, 417, to succeed Pope St. Innocent I. Much respected at the time of his election, he presided over a pontificate filled with controversy and errors of judgment. His first blunder was in Gaul (France), where he appointed the bishop of Arles, Patraclus, metropolitan in his region, thereby antagonizing the other sees. His plan to make Arles a papal vicariate would be reversed by Pope St. Boniface I, who would restore the abrogated metropolitan rights to the sees of Vienne, Marseilles, and Narbonnes. Twice Zosimus interfered with the African Church, and both times the African bishops compelled him to back down. The first incident concerned his favorable disposition toward Pelagius; the Africans, led by St. Augustine, convinced Zosimus to anathematize the Pelagians. The second concerned an illegal appeal made to the pontiff by an African priest, Apiarius; Zosimus attempted to reverse Apiarius's excommunication, a step vigorously opposed by the African bishops. He died while in the process of excommunicating several members of the clergy of Ravenna who were apparently conspiring against him, and his passing on December 26, 418, was greeted with joy in some circles in Rome. Feast day: December 26.

Zwingli, Huldrych (1484-1531) ● Also Huldreich (or Ulrich) Zwingli. A Swiss Protestant reformer, he was born in Wildhaus in the canton of St. Gall, studying at Berne, Vienna, and Basel before receiving holy orders in 1506. A devoted humanist, he was much influenced by Erasmus. Coming to the view that sole religious authority and teaching should come from the Bible, Zwingli began to separate from the Church, particularly from 1519, the date accepted as the start of the Reformation in Switzerland. The reforming treatises *Von Erkiesen und Fryheit der Spysen* (his first reforming tract, on the controversy of fasting) and *Archeteles* (in which he presented the Bible to be the sole source of faith) were published in 1522. The following year, he defended sixty-seven reforming theses in a disputation with Johannes Faber in Zurich. Supported by the Zurich city council, Zwingli implemented a radical policy for the city: images a d pictures were removed, the papacy viciously attacked, and the Mass suppressed. His theory that the Eucharistic celebration was merely a commemorative feast was much opposed by Luther and caused the Marburg Colloquy (1529) to fail, thereby terminating any possible union of Protestant forces. He was killed on October 11, 1531, in a battle with the Catholic cantons of Switzerland.

APPENDIX 1

Popes

The following list of the supreme pontiffs of the Church includes (when available) their places of birth, length of their reigns, their original names, and the dates of their coronations or installations. Some explanatory notes are included. Source for dates: *Annuario Pontificio.*

Peter, St. (Simon Bar Jona): Bethsaida in Galilee; d. c. 64 or 67.

Linus, St.: Tuscany; 67-76.

Anacletus, St. (Cletus): Rome; 76-88.

Clement, St.: Rome; 88-97.

Evaristus, St.: Greece; 97-105.

Alexander I, St.: Rome; 105-115.

Sixtus I, St.: Rome; 115-125.

Telesphorus, St.: Greece; 125-136.

Hyginus, St.: Greece; 136-140.

Pius I, St.: Aquileia; 140-155.

Anicetus, St.: Syria; 155-166.

Soter, St.: Campania; 166-175.

Eleutherius, St.: Nicopolis in Epirus; 175-189.

Victor I, St.: Africa; 189-199.

Zephyrinus, St.: Rome; 199-217.

Callistus, St.: Rome; 217-222.

Urban I, St.: Rome; 222-230.

Pontian, St.: Rome; July 21, 230, to September 28, 235.

Anterus, St.: Greece; November 21, 235, to January 3, 236.

Fabian, St.: Rome; January 10, 236, to January 20, 250.

Cornelius, St.: Rome; March 251 to June 253.

Lucius I, St.: Rome; June 25, 253, to March 5, 254.

Stephen I, St.: Rome; May 12, 254, to August 2, 257.

Sixtus II, St.: Greece; August 30, 257, to August 6, 258.

Dionysius, St.: Birthplace unknown; July 22, 259, to December 26, 268.

Felix I, St.: Rome; January 5, 269, to December 30, 274.

Eutychian, St.: Luni; January 4, 275, to December 7, 283.

Caius, St.: Dalmatia; December 17, 283, to April 22, 296.

Marcellinus, St.: Rome; June 30, 296, to October 25, 304.

Marcellus I, St.: Rome; May 27 (June 26), 308, to January 26, 309.

Eusebius, St.: Greece; April 18, 309, to August 17, 309 (310).

Melchiades, St.: Africa; July 11, 311, to January 11, 314.

Sylvester I, St.: Rome; January 31, 314, to December 31, 335.

Marcus, St.: Rome; January 18, 336, to October 7, 336.

Julius I, St.: Rome; February 6, 337, to April 12, 352.

Liberius: Rome; May 17, 352, to September 24, 366.

Damasus I, St.: Spain; October 1, 366, to December 11, 384.

Siricius, St.: Rome, December 15 (22 or 29), 384, to November 26, 399.

Anastasius I, St.: Rome; November 27, 399, to December 19, 401.

Innocent I, St.: Albano; December 22, 401, to March 12, 417.

Zozimus, St.: Greece; March 18, 417, to December 26, 418.

Boniface I, St.: Rome; December 28 (29), 418, to September 22, 422.

Celestine, St.: Campania; September 10, 422, to July 27, 432.

Sixtus III, St.: Rome; July 31, 432, to August 19, 440.

Leo I the Great, St.: Tuscany; September 29, 440, to November 10, 461.

Hilary, St.: Sardinia; November 19, 461, to February 29, 468.

Simplicius, St.: Tivoli; March 3, 468, to March 10, 483.

Felix III (II), St.: Rome; March 13, 483, to March 1, 492.

Gelasius I, St.: Africa; March 1, 492, to November 21, 496.

Anastasius II: Rome; November 24, 496, to November 19, 498.

Symmachus, St.: Sardinia; November 22, 498, to July 19, 514.

Hormisdas, St.: Frosinone; July 20, 514, to August 6, 523.

John I, St. (martyr): Tuscany; August 13, 523, to May 18, 526.

Felix IV (III), St.: Samnium; July 12, 526, to September 22, 530.

Boniface II: Rome; September 22, 530, to October 17, 532.

John II: Rome; January 2, 533, to May 8, 535. (John II was the first pope to change his name, his given name being Mercury.)

Agapetus I, St.: Rome; May 13, 535, to April 22, 536.

Silverius, St. (martyr): Campania; June 1 (8), 536, to November 11, 537 (d. December 2, 537).

St. Peter

Benedict I: Rome; June 2, 575, to July 30, 579.

Pelagius II: Rome; November 26, 579, to February 7, 590.

Gregory I the Great, St.: Rome; September 3, 590, to May 12, 604.

Sabinian: Blera in Tuscany; September 13, 604, to February 22, 606.

Boniface III: Rome; February 19, 607, to November 12, 607.

Boniface IV, St.: Abruzzi; August 25, 608, to May 8, 615.

Deusdedit (or Adeusdedit), St.: Rome; October 19, 615, to November 8, 618.

Boniface V: Naples; December 23, 619, to October 25, 625.

Honorius I: Campania; October 27, 625, to October 12, 638.

Severinus: Rome; May 28, 640, to August 2, 640.

John IV: Dalmatia; December 24, 640, to October 12, 642.

Theodore I: Greece; November 24, 642, to May 14, 649.

Martin I, St. (martyr): Todi; July 649 to September 16, 655 (in exile from June 17, 653).

Vigilius: Rome; March 29, 537, to June 7, 555.

Pelagius I: Rome; April 16, 556, to March 4, 561.

John III: Rome; July 17, 561, to July 13, 574.

Eugenius I, St.: Rome; August 10, 654, to June 2, 657.

Vitalian, St.: Segni; July 30, 657, to January 27, 672.

Adeodatus II: Rome; April 11, 672, to June 17, 676.

Donus: Rome; November 2, 676, to April 11, 678.

Agatho, St.: Sicily; June 27, 678, to January 10, 681.

Leo II, St.: Sicily; August 17, 682, to July 683.

Benedict II, St.: Rome; June 26, 684, to May 8, 685.

John V: Syria; July 23, 685, to August 2, 686.

Conon: Birthplace unknown; October 21, 686, to September 21, 687.

Sergius I, St.: Syria; December 15, 687, to September 8, 701.

John VI: Greece; October 30, 701, to January 11, 705.

John VII: Greece; March 1, 705, to October 18, 707.

Sisinnius: Syria; January 15, 708, to February 4, 708.

Constantine: Syria; March 25, 708, to April 9, 715.

Gregory II, St.: Rome; May 19, 715, to February 11, 731.

Gregory III, St.: Syria; March 18, 731, to November 741.

Zachary, St.: Greece; December 10, 741, to March 22, 752.

Stephen II (III): Rome; March 26, 752, to April 26, 757.

Paul I, St.: Rome; April (May 29), 757, to June, 28, 767.

Stephen III (IV): Sicily; August 1 (7), 768, to January 24, 772.

Adrian I: Rome; February 1 (9), 772, to December 25, 795.

Leo III, St.: Rome; December 26 (27), 795, to June 12, 816.

Stephen IV (V): Rome; June 22, 816, to January 24, 817.

Paschal I, St.: Rome; January 25, 817, to February 11, 824.

Eugene II: Rome; February (May) 824 to August 827.

Valentine: Rome; August 827 to September 827.

Gregory IV: Rome; 827 to January 844.

Sergius II: Rome; January 844 to January 27, 847.

Leo IV, St.: Rome; January (April 10), 847, to July 17, 855.

Benedict III: Rome; July (September 29), 855, to April 17, 858.

Nicholas I, St. (the Great): Rome; April 24, 858, to November 13, 867.

Adrian II: Rome; December 14, 867, to December 14, 872.

John VIII: Rome; December 14, 872, to December 16, 882.

Marinus I: Gallese: December 16, 882, to May 15, 884.

Adrian III, St.: Rome; May 17, 884, to September 885.

Stephen V (VI): Rome; September 885 to September 14, 891.

Formosus: Portus; October 6, 891, to April 4, 896.

Boniface VI: Rome; April 896.

Stephen VI (VII): Rome; May 896 to August 897.

Romanus: Gallese; August to November 897.

Theodore II: Rome; December 897.

John IX: Tivoli; January 898 to January 900.

Benedict IV: Rome; January (February) 900 to July 903.

Leo V: Ardea; July to September 903.

Sergius III: Rome, January 29, 904, to April 14, 911.

Anastasius III: Rome; April 911 to June 913.

Landus: Sabina; July 913 to February 914.

John X: Tossignano (Imola); March 914 to May 918.

Leo VI: Rome; May to December 928.

Stephen VII (VIII): Rome; December 928 to February 931.

John XI: Rome; February (March) 931 to December 935.

Leo VII: Rome, January 3, 936, to July 13, 939.

Stephen VIII (IX): Rome; July 14, 939, to October 942.

Marinus II: Rome; October 30, 942, to May 946.

Agapetus II: Rome; May, 10, 946, to December 955.

John XII (Octavius): Tusculum; December 16, 963, to May, 14, 964.

Leo VIII: Rome; December 4 (6), 963, to March 1, 965.

Benedict V: Rome; May 22, 964, to July, 4, 966.

John XIII: Rome; October 1, 965, to September 6, 972.

Benedict VI: Rome; January 19, 973, to June 974.

Benedict VII: Rome; October 974 to July 10, 983.

John XIV (John Campenora): Pavia; December 983 to August 20, 984.

John XV: Rome; August 985 to March 996.

Gregory V (Bruno of Carinthia): Saxony; May 996 to February 18, 999.

Sylvester II (Gerbert): Auvergne; April 2, 999, to May 12, 1003.

John XVII (Siccone): Rome; June to December 1003.

John XVIII (Phasianus): Rome; January 1004 to July 1009.

Sergius IV (Peter): Rome; July 31, 1009, to May 12, 1012.

Benedict VIII (Theophylactus): Tusculum; May 18, 1012, to April 9, 1024.

John XIX (Romanus): Tusculum; April (May) 1024 to 1032.

Benedict IX (Theophylactus): Tusculum; 1032 to 1044.

Sylvester III (John): Rome; January 20 to February 10, 1045.

Benedict IX (second time): April 10 to May 1, 1045.

Gregory VI (John Gratian): Rome; May 5, 1045, to December 20, 1046.

Clement II (Suitger, Lord of Morsleben and Hornburg): Saxony; December 24 (25), 1046, to October 9, 1047.

Benedict IX (third time): November 8, 1047, to July 17, 1048 (d. c. 1055.

Damasus II (Poppo): Bavaria; July 17, 1048, to August 9, 1048.

Leo IX, St. (Bruno): Alsace; February 12, 1049, to April 19, 1054.

Victor II (Gebhard): Swabia; April 16, 1055, to July 28, 1057.

Stephen IX (X): (Frederick): Lorraine; August 3, 1057, to March 29, 1058.

Nicholas II (Gerard): Burgundy; January 24, 1059, to July 27, 1061.

Alexander II (Anselmo da Baggio): Milan; October 1, 1061, to April 21, 1073.

Gregory VII, St. (Hildebrand): Tuscany; April 22 (June 30), 1073, to May 25, 1085.

Pope Benedict XV

Victor III, Bl. (Dauferius, Desiderius): Benevento; May 24, 1086, to September 16, 1087.

Urban II, Bl. (Odo di Lagery): France; March 12, 1088, to July 29, 1099.

Paschal II (Raniero): Ravenna; August 13 (14), 1099, to January 21, 1118.

Gelasius II (Giovanni Caetani): Gaeta; January 24 (March 10), 1118, to January 28, 1119.

Callistus II (Guido of Burgundy): Burgundy; February 2 (9), 1119, to December 13, 1124.

Honorius II (Lamberto): Flagnano (Imola);

December 15 (21), 1124, to February 13, 1130.

Innocent II (Gregorio Papareschi): February 14 (23), 1130, to September 24, 1143.

Celestine II (Guido): Città di Castello; September 26 (October 3), 1143, to March 8, 1144.

Lucius II (Gerardo Caccianemici): Bologna; March 12, 1144, to February 15, 1145.

Eugene III, Bl. (Bernardo Paganelli di Montemagno): Pisa; February 15 (18), 1145, to July, 8, 1153.

Anastasius IV (Corrado): Rome; July 12, 1153, to December 3, 1154.

Adrian IV (Nicholas Breakspear): England; December 4 (5), 1154, to September 1, 1159.

Alexander III (Rolando Bandinelli): Siena; September 7 (20), 1159, to August 30, 1181.

Lucius III (Ubaldo Allucingoli): Lucca; September 1 (6), 1181, to September 25, 1185.

Urban III (Uberto Crivelli): Milan; November 25 (December 1), 1185, to October 20, 1187.

Gregory VIII (Alberto de Morra): Benevento; October 21 (25) to December 17, 1187.

Clement III (Paolo Scolari): Rome; December 19 (20), 1187, to March, 1191.

Celestine III (Giacinto Bobone): Rome; March 30 (April 14), 1191, to January 8, 1198.

Innocent III (Lotario dei Conti di Segni): Anagni; January 8 (February 22), 1198, to July 16, 1216.

Honorius III (Cencio Savelli): Rome; July 18 (24), 1216, to March 18, 1227.

Gregory IX (Ugolino, count of Segni): Anagni; March 19 (21), 1227, to August 22, 1241.

Celestine IV (Goffredo Castiglioni): Anagni; December 12 (20) to November 10, 1241.

Innocent IV (Sinibaldo Fieschi): Genoa; June 25 (28), 1243, tDecember 7, 1254.

Alexander IV (Rinaldo, count of Segni): Anagni; December 12 (20), 1254, to May 25, 1261.

Urban IV (Jacques Pantaleon): Troyes; August 29 (September 4), 1261, to October 2, 1264.

Clement IV (Guy Foulques or Guido le Gros): France; February 5 (15), 1265, to November 29, 1268.

Gregory X, Bl. (Teobaldo Visconti): Piacenza; September 1, 1271 (March 2, 1272), to January 10, 1276.

Innocent IV, Bl. (Peter of Tarentaise): Savoy; January 21 (February 22) to June 22, 1276.

Adrian V (Ottobono Fieschi): Genoa; July 11 to August 8, 1276.

John XXI (Petrus Juliani or Petrus Hispanus): Portugal; September 8 (20), 1276, to May 20, 1277.

Nicholas III (Giovanni Gaetano Orsini): Rome; November 25 (December 26), 1277, to August 22, 1280.

Martin IV (Simon de Brie): France; February 22 (March 23), 1281, to March 28, 1285.

Honorius IV (Giacomo Savelli): Rome; April 2 (May 20), 1285, to April 3, 1287.

Nicholas IV (Girolamo Masci): Ascoli; February 22, 1288, to April 4, 1292.

Celestine V, St. (Pietro del Murrone): Isernia; July 5 (August 29) to December 13, 1294 (d. 1296).

Boniface VIII (Benedetto Caetani): Anagni; December 24, 1294 (January 23, 1295), to October 11, 1303.

Benedict XI, Bl. (Niccolo Boccasini): Treviso; October 22 (27), 1303, to July 7, 1304.

Clement V (Bertrand de Got): France; June 5 (November 14), 1305, to April 20, 1314. (First of the Avignon popes.)

John XXII (Jacques d'Euse): Cahors; August 7 (September 5), 1316, to December 4, 1334.

Benedict XII (Jacques Fournier): France;

December 20, 1334 (January 8, 1335), to April 25, 1342.

Clement VI (Pierre Roger): France; May 7 (19) 1342, to December 6, 1352.

Innocent VI (Etienne Aubert): France; December 18 (30), 1352, to September 12, 1362.

Urban V, Bl. (Guillaume de Grimoard): France; September 28 (November 6), 1362, to December 17, 1370.

Gregory XI (Pierre de Beaufort): France; December 30, 1370 (January 5, 1371), to March 26, 1378. (Last of Avignon popes.)

Urban VI (Bartolomeo Prignano): Naples; April 8 (18), 1378, to October 15, 1389.

Boniface IX (Pietro Tomacelli): Naples; November 2 (9), 1389, to October 1, 1404.

Innocent VII (Cosma Migliorati): Sulmona; October 17 (November 11), 1404, to November 6, 1406.

Gregory XII (Angelo Correr): Venice; November 30 (December 19), 1406, to July 4, 1415; he resigned from the papacy to permit the election of his successor. He died on October 18, 1417.

Martin V (Oddone Colonna): Rome; November 11 (21), 1417, to February 23, 1431.

Eugene IV (Gabriele Condulmer): Venice; March 3 (11), 1431, to February 23, 1447.

Nicholas V (Tommaso Parentucelli): Sarzana; March 6 (19), 1447, to March 24, 1455.

Callistus III (Alfonso Borgia): Jativa (Valencia); April 8 (20), 1455, to August 6, 1458.

Pius II (Enea Silvio Piccolomini): Siena; August 19 (September 3), 1458, to August 14, 1464.

Paul II (Pietro Barbo): Venice; August 30 (September 16), 1464, to July 26, 1471.

Sixtus IV (Francesco della Rovere): Savona; August 9 (25), 1471, to August 12, 1484.

Innocent VIII (Giovanni Battista Cibo): Genoa; August 29 (September 12), 1484, to July 25, 1492.

Pope John Paul II

Alexander VI (Rodrigo Borgia): Jativa (Valencia); August 11 (26), 1492, to August 18, 1503.

Pius III (Francesco Todeschini-Piccolomini): Siena; September 22 (October 1 or 8) to October 18, 1503.

Julius II (Giuliano della Rovere): Savona;

October 31 (November 26), 1503, to February 21, 1513.

Leo X (Giovanni de' Medici): Florence; March 9 (19), 1513, to December 1, 1521.

Adrian VI (Adrian Florensz): Utrecht; January 9 (August 31), 1522, to September 14, 1523.

Clement VII (Giulio de' Medici): Florence; November 19 (26), 1523, to September 25, 1534.

Paul III (Alessandro Farnese): Rome; October 13 (November 3), 1534, to November 10, 1549.

Julius III (Giovanni Maria Ciocchi del Monte): Rome; February 7 (22), 1550, to March 23, 1555.

Marcellus II (Marcello Servini): Montepulciano; April 9 (10), 1555, to May 1, 1555.

Paul IV (Gian Pietro Caraffa): Naples; May 23 (26), 1555, to August 18, 1559.

Pius IV (Giovan Angelo de' Medici): Milan; December 25, 1559 (January 6, 1560), to December 9, 1565.

Pius V, St. (Antonio-Michele Ghislieri): Bosco (Alexandria); January 7 (17), 1566, to May 1, 1572.

Gregory XIII (Ugo Buoncampagni): Bologna; May 13 (25), 1572, to April 10, 1585.

Sixtus V (Felice Peretti): Grottamare (Ripatrasone): April 24 (May 1), 1585, to August 27, 1590.

Urban VII (Giovanni Battista Castagna): Rome; September 15 to September 27, 1590.

Gregory XIV (Niccolo Sfondrati): Cremona; December 5 (8), 1590, to October 16, 1591.

Innocent IX (Giovanni Antonio Facchinetti): Bologna; October 29 (November 3) to December 30, 1591.

Clement VIII (Ippolito Aldobrandini): Florence; January 30 (February 9), 1592, to March 3, 1605.

Leo XI (Alessandro de' Medici): Florence; April 1 (10) to April 27, 1605.

Paul V (Camillo Borghese): Rome; May 16 (29), 1605, to January 28, 1621.

Gregory XV (Alessandro Ludovisi): Bologna; February 9 (14), 1621, to July, 8, 1623.

Urban VIII (Maffeo Barberini): Florence; August 6 (September 29), 1623, to July 29, 1644.

Innocent X (Giovanni Battista Pamfili): Rome; September 15 (October 4), 1644, to January 7, 1655.

Alexander VII (Fabio Chigi): Siena; April 7 (18), 1655, to September 22, 1667.

Clement IX (Giulio Rospigliosi): Pistoia; June 20 (26), 1667, to December 9, 1669.

Clement X (Emilio Altieri): Rome; April 29 (May 11), 1670, to July 22, 1676.

Innocent XI, Bl. (Benedetto Odescalci): Como; September 21 (October 4), 1676, to August 12, 1689.

Alexander VIII (Pietro Ottoboni): Venice; October 6 (16), 1689, to February 1, 1691.

Innocent XII (Antonio Pignatelli): Spinazzola; July 12 (15), 1691, to September 27, 1700.

Clement XI (Giovanni Francesco Albani): November 23, 30 (December 8), 1700, to March 19, 1721.

Innocent XIII (Michelangelo dei Conti): Rome; May 8 (18), 1721, to March 7, 1724.

Benedict XIII (Pietro Francesco Vincenzo Maria Orsini): Gravina (Bari); May 29 (June 4), 1724, to February 21, 1730.

Clement XII (Lorenzo Corsini): Florence; July 12 (16), 1730, to February 6, 1740.

Benedict XIV (Prospero Lambertini): Bologna; August 17 (22), 1740, to May 3, 1758.

Clement XIII (Carlo Rezzonico): Venice; July 6 (16), 1758, to February 2, 1769.

Clement XIV (Giovanni Vincenzo Antonio Lorenzo Ganganelli): Rimini; May 19, 28 (June 4), 1769, to September 4, 1774.

Pius VI (Giovanni Angelo Braschi): Cesena; February 15 (22), 1775, to August 29, 1799.

Pius VII (Barnaba Gregorio Chiaramonti): Cesena; March 14 (21), 1800, to August 20, 1823.

Leo XII (Annibale della Genga): Genga (Fabriano); September 28 (October 5), 1823, to February 10, 1829.

Pius VIII (Francesco Saverio Castiglioni): Cingoli; March 31 (April 5), 1829, to November 30, 1830.

Gregory XVI (Bartolomeo Alberto Mauro Cappelari): Belluno; February 2 (6), 1831, to June 1, 1846.

Pius IX (Giovanni M. Mastai-Ferretti): Senigallia; June 16 (21), 1846, to February 7, 1878.

Leo XIII (Gioacchino Pecci): Carpineto (Anagni); February 20 (March 3), 1878, to July 20, 1903.

Pius X, St. (Giuseppe Sarto): Riese (Treviso); August 4 (9), 1903, to August 20, 1914.

Benedict XV (Giacomo della Chiesa): Genoa; September 3 (6), 1914, to January 22, 1922.

Pius XI (Achille Ratti): Desio (Milan); February 6 (12), 1922, to February 10, 1939.

Pius XII (Eugenio Pacelli): Rome; March 2 (12), 1939, to October 9, 1958.

John XXIII (Angelo Giuseppe Roncalli): Sotto il Monte (Bergamo): October 28 (November 4), 1958, to June 3, 1963.

Paul VI (Giovanni Battista Montini): Concessio (Brescia); June 21 (30), 1963, to August 6, 1978.

John Paul I (Albino Luciani): Forno di Canale (Belluno); August 26 (September 3) to September 28, 1978.

John Paul II (Karol Wojtyla): Wadowice, Poland; October 16 (22), 1978.

APPENDIX 2

Roman Curia

The following is a listing of the congregations, tribunals, councils, and commissions that comprise the Roman Curia. For details on the history of the Curia, the reader is encouraged to consult the entry **Curia, Roman**. See also **Cardinals, College of; Holy See;** and **Vatican**. The present Curia is organized as per the apostolic constitution *Pastor Bonus* issued by Pope John Paul II on June 28, 1988 (effective March 1, 1989). This listing has been compiled with material from the *Annuario Pontificio* and Our Sunday Visitor's *Catholic Almanac.*

Secretariat of State

Founded: Evolved out of various offices dating to at least the fifteenth century. Purpose: To assist the pontiff in the care of the universal Church. It has two main divisions:

The Section for General Affairs, which has the responsibility of administering the day-to-day needs of the Holy See.

The Section for Relations with States (formerly the Council for Public Affairs of the Church), which oversees the diplomatic relations of the Holy See. It has attached a council of bishops and cardinals.

Congregations

Congregation for the Doctrine of the Faith ● Founded: Evolved out of the Holy Office of the Inquisition, begun in the 1200s. Its name was changed by Pope St. Pius X (r. 1903-1914) to Congregation of the Holy Office. Pope Paul VI gave it the present title in 1965. Purpose: To safeguard the teachings of the faith, examine all doctrinal questions and writings, promote theological study, and oversee matters related to the Petrine Privilege in marriages. Attached to it are the Theological Commission and the Pontifical Biblical Commission.

Congregation for Oriental Churches ● Founded: January 6, 1862 (Pius IX) and combined with the Congregation of the Propagation of the Faith. Made autonomous on May 1, 1917 (Benedict XV). Purpose: To oversee all relevant matters pertaining to the Eastern Catholic Churches.

Congregation for Bishops ● Founded: January 22, 1588 (Sixtus V). Reorganized on June 28, 1988 (John Paul II). Purpose: To oversee all issues related to bishops. Supervises Commission for Latin America.

Congregation for Divine Worship and the Discipline of the Sacraments ● Founded: 1588 (Sixtus V), as Congregation of Rites. Replaced on June 29, 1908 (St. Pius X), by the Congregation for the Discipline of the Sacraments; joined by Congregation for Divine Worship on May 8, 1969 (Paul VI). United on July 11, 1975. Purpose: Has authority over the regulation and promotion of the sacraments and the liturgy.

Congregation for the Causes of Saints ● Founded: 1588 (Sixtus V) as the Congregation of Rites; renamed by Paul VI in 1969. Purpose: Oversees all matters related to beatifications and canonizations.

Congregation for the Clergy ● Founded: August 2, 1564 (Pius IV), as Congregation of the Cardinals Interpreters of the Council of Trent; renamed Congregation of the Council until renamed on August 15, 1967. Purpose: Has authority over the clergy, including discipline, preaching, and care of the Church's temporal goods.

Congregation for Institutes of Consecrated Life and Societies of Apostolic Life ● Founded: May 27, 1586 (Sixtus V), as Congregation for Consultations of Regulars; attached to Congregation for Consultations of Bishops and other Prelates (1601) and made autonomous in 1908; renamed Congregation for Religious and Secular Institutes in 1967 (Paul VI); renamed again on June 28, 1988 (John Paul II). Purpose: Oversees all aspects of institutes of religious, third orders, secular institutes, and societies of apostolic life.

Congregation for Catholic Education (for Seminaries and Institutes of Study) ● Founded: 1588 (Sixtus V); joined by a new congregation in 1824 (Leo XII); redesignated as Congregation of Seminaries and Universities on November 4, 1915 (Benedict XV); renamed Congregation for Catholic Education in 1967 (Paul VI); new name given in 1988 (John Paul II). Purpose: Has authority over all institutions of Catholic education.

Congregation for the Evangelization of Peoples ● Founded: A council of cardinals was established by St. Pius V and also Gregory XII; given name Congregation of the Propagation of the Faith in 1599 (Clement VIII); reestablished in 1622 (Gregory XV); given redefinition in 1988 (John Paul II). Purpose: Supervises all missionary activity across the globe. Has control over various societies, unions, and councils to assist in the missionary undertaking.

Tribunals

Apostolic Penitentiary ● Has authority over questions of conscience, the granting of absolutions, dispensations, commutations, etc.

Apostolic Signatura ● The Supreme Court of the Church and the State of Vatican City.

Roman Rota ● The court of appeal for those cases in which appeal is made to the Holy See; it is best known for its jurisdiction over marriage.

Councils

Pontifical Council for the Laity ● Oversees the apostolate of the laity.

Pontifical Council for Promoting Christian Unity ● Deals with the Church's relations with the other Christian communities and is especially concerned with Catholic ecumenism.

Pontifical Council for the Family ● Has the task of promoting the pastoral care of families around the world.

Pontifical Council for Justice and Peace ● Promotes justice and peace through the spread and application of the teachings of the faith.

Pontifical Council "Cor Unum" ● Oversees the coordination of Catholic aid services and human development.

Pontifical Council for Pastoral Care of Migrants and Itinerant Peoples ● Cares for the needs of migratory peoples, tourists, and travelers.

Pontifical Council for Pastoral Assistance to Health Care Workers ● Fosters the development and activities of health care providers.

Pontifical Council for the Interpretation of Legislative Texts ● Oversees the authentic interpretation of Church Law.

Pontifical Council for Interreligious Dialogue ● Promotes dialogue between Christians and Non-Christians. Attached is the Commission for Religious Relations with Muslims.

Pontifical Council for Culture ● Handles the relations between the Holy See and the Church and global culture; it also fosters a dialogue with nonbelievers or those who profess no religion. Its sections include faith and culture and dialogue with cultures. (The former Pontifical Council for Dialogue with Non-Believers was merged with this commission in 1993.)

Pontifical Council for Social Communications ● Is charged with the oversight of all forms of social communication so as to facilitate the propagation of the Church's message in the modern world.

Offices

Apostolic Chamber ● Cares for the temporal goods of the Church during a *sede vacante* (i.e., a papal interregnum, or vacancy). The Apostolic Chamber (or Camera) is headed by the chamberlain of the Holy Roman Church, known also as the camerlengo.

Prefecture for the Economic Affairs of the Holy See ● Cares for the temporalities of the Holy See.

Administration of the Patrimony of the Apostolic See (APSA) ● Oversees the estate of the Apostolic See under the direction of papal delegates.

Curial Offices, Commissions, and Committees

Prefecture of the Papal Household.

Office for Liturgical Celebrations of the Supreme Pontiff.

Commission on Latin America (attached to the Congregation for Bishops).

Pontifical Committee on International Eucharistic Congresses.

Central Statistics Office (attached to the Secretariat of State).

Fabric of St. Peter.

Office of Papal Charities.

Disciplinary Commission of the Roman Curia.

Council of Cardinals for the Study of Organization and Economic Problems of the Holy See.

Theological Commission (attached to the Congregation for the Doctrine of the Faith).

Biblical Commission (attached to the Congregation for the Doctrine of the Faith).

Pontifical Commission, "Ecclesia Dei" (for the return of priests, seminarians, and others to the Church from the fraternity of Archbishop Marcel Lefebvre).

Pontifical Commission for the Revision and Emendation of the Vulgate.

Pontifical Commission for the Cultural Patrimony of the Church Commission on Sacred Archaeology.

Pontifical Committee for Historical Sciences.

Vatican II Archives.

Cardinalatial Commission for the Sanctuaries of Pompeii, Loreto, and Bari (under the Congregation for the Clergy).

Commission for Religious Relations with Muslims (attached to the Council for Inter-religious Dialogue).

Commission for the Protection of the Historical and Artistic Monuments of the Holy See.

Commission for the Preservation of the Faith, Erection of New Churches in Rome.

Institute for Religious Works (IOR), the Vatican Bank.

Labor Office of the Apostolic See (ULSA — Ufficio del Lavoro della Sede Apostolica).

Inter-agency Commissions

These commissions were created through the apostolic constitution *Pastor Bonus* (1988); they are each comprised of officials of several agencies or offices of the Curia and exist on a permanent basis. They are:

Interdepartmental Standing Commission for matters concerning appointments to local churches and the setting and alteration of them and their constitution.

Interdepartmental Standing Commission for matters concerning members, individually or as a community, or Institutes of Consecrated Life founded or working in mission territories.

Interdepartmental Standing Commission for matters concerning the formation of candidates for Sacred Orders.

Interdepartmental Permanent Commission as part of the Congregation for Catholic Education entrusted with the task of promoting a more equitable distribution of priests throughout the world.

Permanent Interdepartmental Commission for the Church in Eastern Europe, replacing the Pontifical Commission for Russia, which was terminated.

TABLE 1

Apostles of Places and Peoples

Alps: St. Bernard of Menthon.
Andalusia (Spain): St. John of Ávila.
Antioch: St. Barnabas.
Armenia: St. Gregory the Illuminator; St. Bartholomew.
Austria: St. Severinus.
Bavaria: St. Kilian.
Brazil: Bl. José de Anchieta.
California: Bl. Junípero Serra.
Carinthia (Yugoslavia): St. Virgil.
Colombia: St. Luis Bertrán.
Corsica: St. Alexander Sauli.
Crete: St. Titus.
Cyrpus: St. Barnabas.
Denmark: St. Anskar.
England: St. Augustine of Canterbury; St. Gregory the Great; St. George.
Ethiopia: St. Frumentius.
Finland: St. Henry.
Florence: St. Andrew Corsini.
France: St. Remigius; St. Martin of Tours; St. Denis.
Friesland (Germany): St. Swithbert; St. Willibrord.
Gaul: St. Irenaeus.
Gentiles: St. Paul.
Georgia (Russia): St. Nino.
Germany: St. Boniface; St. Peter Canisius.
Gothland (Sweden): St. Sigfrid.
Guelderland (Holland): St. Plechelm.
Highlanders (Scotland): St. Columba.
Hungarians (Magyars): St. Stephen, King; St. Gerard of Csanad; Bl. Astericus.
India: St. Thomas, Apostle.
Indies: St. Francis Xavier.

Ireland: St. Patrick.
Iroquois: François Picquit.
Italy: St. Bernardine of Siena; St. Francis of Assisi; St. Catherine of Siena.
Japan: St. Francis Xavier.
Malta: St. Paul.
Mexico: The twelve Apostles of Mexico (Franciscans), headed by Fra Martín de Valencia.
Negro Slaves: St. Peter Claver.
Netherlands: St. Wilibrord.
Northumbria (Britain): St. Aidan.
Norway: St. Olaf.
Ottawa Indians: Father Claude-Jean Allouez.
Persia: St. Maruthus.
Poland: St. Hyacinth.
Portugal: St. Christian.
Prussia (Slavs): St. Adalbert of Magdeburg; St. Bruno of Querfurt.
Rome: St. Philip Neri; Sts. Peter and Paul.
Rumania: St. Nicetas of Remesiana.
Ruthenia: St. Bruno.
Sardinia: St. Ephesus.
Saxony: St. Willibald.
Scandinavia (North): St. Anskar.
Scotland: St. Palladius; St. George.
Slavs: Sts. Cyril and Methodius; St. Adalbert.
Spain: St. James; Sts. Euphrasius and Felix.
Sweden: St. Anskar.
Switzerland: St. Andeol.
Tournai (Belgium): St. Eligius, St. Piaton.

TABLE 2

Concordats

Throughout the history of the Church, a number of important concordats have been signed between the papacy and secular governments both in Europe and beyond. The first is generally counted to be the Concordat of Worms (1122), also called the Paxtum Calixtinum. Some historians prefer to count the first as an agreement signed in 1107 in London. The twentieth century has produced two of the most famous of all concordats, that between the Holy See under Pius XI (r. 1922-1939) and the government of Italy under Benito Mussolini (the Lateran Treaty) in 1929 and between the government of Germany headed by Adolf Hitler and the Holy See under Pius XI in 1933. Various agreements were signed with the Communist regimes of Eastern Europe in the years after World War II, but these were routinely broken. New accords have been signed recently between the Holy See and the newly democratic governments that emerged following the collapse of the Soviet Empire. Among the most notable were with Hungary in 1990 and Poland in 1993. A revision of the Lateran Treaty was signed in 1985 between the Italian government and the Holy See under John Paul II. The following are some of the concordats signed by the popes from 1122-1933.

Date	Country or Ruler	Pope
1122	Emperor Henry V	Callistus II
1288	Diniz of Portugal	Nicholas IV
1516	Manuel of Portugal	Leo X
	Francis I of France	Leo X
1630	Emperor Ferdinand	Urban VIII
1727	Victor Amadeus II of Sardinia	Benedict XIII
1736	Augustus III of Poland	Clement XII
1737	Philip V of Spain	Clement XII
1740	Charles Emmanuel II of Sardinia	Benedict XIII
1741	Charles II of Sicily	Benedict XIV
1742	Charles Emmanuel II of Sardinia	Benedict XIV
1750	Charles Emmanuel III of Sardinia	Benedict XIV
1753	Ferdinand VI of Spain	Benedict XIV
1757	Empress Maria Theresa	Benedict XIV
1770	Charles Emmanuel III of Sardinia	Benedict XIV
1778	Portugal	Pius VI
1784	Emperor Joseph II	Pius VI
1801	Napoleon Bonaparte	Pius VII
1817	Louis XVIII of France	Pius VII
	Maximilian Joseph of Bavaria	Pius VII
	Victor Emmanuel I of Sardinia	Pius VII
1821	States of the Upper Rhine	Pius VII
1824	George IV of England (over Hanover)	Leo XII
1827	Belgium	Leo XII
1834	Ferdinand II of Sicily	Gregory XVI
1841	Sardinia	Gregory XVI
1847	Russia	Pius IX

TABLE 3

Doctors of the Church

The Doctors of the Church are certain men and women who are revered by the Church for the special value of their writings and preaching and the sanctity of their lives. They each made important and lasting contributions to the faith and are to be recognized for their great merits. Initially, the Doctors were considered the Fathers Augustine, Ambrose, Jerome, and Gregory I the Great, but the Church added others to the list over the centuries. The first woman Doctor was St. Teresa of Ávila, named by Pope Paul VI in 1970; she was followed by Catherine of Siena that same year.

Name	Year Declared
St. Albertus Magnus (d. 1280)	1931
St. Alphonsus Liguori (1696-1787)	1871
St. Ambrose (d. 397)	Father of the Church
St. Anselm (1033-1109)	1720
St. Antony of Padua (1195-1231)	1946
St. Athanasius (d. 375)	—
St. Augustine (354-430)	Father of the Church
St. Basil the Great (d. 379)	Father of the Church
St. Bede the Venerable (673-735)	—
St. Bernard of Clairvaux (c. 1090-1153)	1830
St. Bonaventure (c. 1217-1274)	1588
St. Catherine of Siena (c. 1347-1380)	1970
St. Cyril of Alexandria (c. 376-444)	1882
St. Cyril of Jerusalem (c. 315-386)	1882
St. Ephraem (c. 306-373)	1920
St. Francis de Sales (1567-1622)	1877
St. Gregory of Nazianzus (d. c. 390)	Father of the Church
St. Gregory I the Great (d. 604)	Father of the Church
St. Hilary of Poitiers (d. 368)	1851
St. Isidore of Seville (d. 636)	1722
St. Jerome (d. 420)	Father of the Church
St. John Chrysostom (d. 407), Greek Father	451
St. John Damascene (d. c. 749)	1890
St. John of the Cross (1542-1591)	1926
St. Lawrence of Brindisi (1559-1619)	1959
St. Leo I the Great (d. 461)	1574
St. Peter Canisius (1521-1597)	1925
St. Peter Chrysologus (d. 450)	1729
St. Peter Damian (1007-1072)	1828
St. Robert Bellarmine (1542-1621)	1931
St. Teresa of Ávila (1515-1582)	1970
St. Thomas Aquinas (1225-1274)	1567

TABLE 4

Ecumenical Councils

In the history of the Church there have been twenty-one ecumenical (or general) councils. They are:

Nicaea I 325
Constantinople I 381
Ephesus 431
Chalcedon 451
Constantinople II 553
Constantinople III 680
Nicaea II 787
Constantinople IV 869-870
Lateran I.. 1123
Lateran II 1139
Lateran III 1179
Lateran IV 1215
Lyons I 1245
Lyons II 1274
Vienne.. 1311-1312
Constance 1414-1418
Florence (or Ferrara-Florence).. 1431-1445
Lateran V 1512-1517
Trent 1545-1563
Vatican Council I... 1869-1870
Vatican Council II.. 1962-1965

TABLE 5

Emblems of the Saints

Apostles

St. Andrew: Saltire (or X-shaped) cross, fish.

St. Bartholomew: Curved knife, flayed skin.

St. James the Greater: Sword, pilgrim's staff, shell, key.

St. James the Less: Halberd, fuller's club, square rule.

St. John the Evangelist: Chalice with poison (from unsuccessful attempt to martyr him), eagle, kettle, armor.

St. Jude: Sword, club.

St. Matthew: Lance, purse, winged man.

St. Matthias: Ax, open Bible.

St. Peter: Inverted cross, keys, boat, cock.

St. Philip: Column, serpent, three loaves of bread.

St. Simon: Saw, book with fish, cross.

St. Thomas: Lance, ax, carpenter's square.

Saints

St. Agatha: Tongs, veil.

St. Agnes: Lamb.

St. Ambrose: Bees, dove, ox, pen.

St. Angela Merici: Ladder, cloak.

St. Anne, Mother of the Blessed Virgin: Door.

St. Antony, Hermit: Bell, hog.

St. Antony of Padua: Infant Jesus, bread, book, lily.

St. Apollonia: Tooth.

St. Augustine of Hippo: Heart, dove, shell, child, pen.

St. Barbara: Cannon, chalice, palm, tower.

St. Barnabas: Ax, lance, stones.

St. Benedict: Bell, broken cup, bush, crozier, raven.

St. Bernard of Clairvaux: Pen, bees, instruments of the Passion.

St. Bernardine of Siena: Tablet or sun inscribed with IHS.

St. Blaise: Iron comb, two crossed candles.

St. Bonaventure: Cardinal's hat, ciborium, Communion.

St. Boniface: Ax, book, fox, fountain, oak, raven, scourge, sword.

St. Bridget of Kildare: Cross, candle, flame over head.

St. Bridget of Sweden: Book, pilgrim's staff.

St. Bruno: Chalice.

St. Catherine of Alexandria: Lamb, sword, wheel.

St. Catherine of Ricci: Crown, crucifix, ring.

St. Catherine of Siena: Cross, lily, ring, stigmata.

St. Cecilia: Organ.

St. Charles Borromeo: Communion, coat of arms with sword.

St. Christopher: Christ Child, giant, torrent, tree.

St. Clare: Monstrance.

St. Colette: Birds, lamb

Sts. Cosmas and Damian: Box of ointment, vial.

St. Cyril of Alexandria: Blessed Virgin holding the Child Jesus, pen.

St. Cyril of Jerusalem: Book, purse.

St. Dominic: Rosary, star.

St. Dorothy: Flowers, fruit.

St. Edmund the Martyr: Arrow, sword.

St. Elizabeth of Hungary: Bread, flowers, pitcher, alms.

St. Eustace: Roman soldier, stag with crucifix between its antlers, oven.

St. Francis of Assisi: Birds, deer, fish, skull, stigmata, wolf.

St. Francis Xavier: Bell, crucifix, ship, flame, lily.

St. Genevieve: Bread, candle, herd, keys.

St. George: Dragon.

St. Gertrude: Crown, lily, taper.

Sts. Gervase and Protase: Club, scourge, sword.

St. Giles: Crozier, hermitage, hind.

St. Gregory I the Great: Crozier, dove, tiara.

St. Helena: Cross.

St. Hilary: Child, pen, stick.

St. Hubert: Stag with the crucifix.

St. Ignatius Loyola: Communion, chasuble, book, apparition of Lord .

St. Isidore: Bees, pen.

St. Jerome: Lion, skull, raven, cardinal's hat.

St. Joan of Arc: Armor, banner of France, fleur-de-lis.

St. John the Baptist: Head on platter, lamb, skin of animal.

St. John of Berchmans: Rule of St. Ignatius, cross, rosary.

St. John Chrysostom: Bees, dove, pen.

St. John Climacus: Ladder.

St. John of God: Alms, crown of thorns, heart.

St. Josaphat: Chalice, crown, winged deacon.

St. Joseph, Spouse of the Virgin Mary: Infant Jesus, lily, rod, plane, carpenter's square.

St. Justin Martyr: Ax, sword.

St. Lawrence: Book of Gospels, cross, gridiron, dalmatic, coins.

St. Leander: Pen.

St. Liberius: Pebbles, peacock.

St. Longinus: Lance.

St. Louis IX of France: Crown of thorns, nails, crusader's cross, fleur-de-lis.

St. Lucy: Cord, eyes, lantern.

St. Luke: Ox, book, brush, palette.

St. Margaret: Dragon, pearl.

St. Mark: Lion, book.

St. Martha: Dragon, holy water jar.

St. Martin of Tours: Cloak shared with beggar, goose.

St. Mary Magdalene: Alabaster box of ointment.

St. Matilda: Alms, purse.

St. Matthias: Lance.

St. Maurus: Crutch, scales, spade.

St. Meinrad: Two ravens.

St. Michael Archangel: Banner, dragon, scales, sword.

St. Monica: Girdle, tears.

St. Nicholas: Anchor, three boys in boat, three purses or balls.

St. Patrick: Shamrock, baptismal font, cross, harp, serpent.

St. Paul: Sword, book, scroll.

St. Philip Neri: Altar, chasuble, vial.

St. Rita: Crucifix, rose, thorn.

St. Roch (Rocco): Angel, bread, dog.

St. Rose of Lima: Anchor, city, crown of thorns.

St. Scholastica: Lily, crucifix, dove at her feet.

St. Sebastian: Arrows, crown.

Sts. Sergius and Bacchus: Military uniform, palm.

St. Simon Stock: Scapular.

St. Stephen: Dalmatic, stones.

St. Teresa of Ávila: Arrow, book, heart.

St. Thérèse of Lisieux: Roses entwining a crucifix.

St. Thomas Aquinas: Chalice, monstrance, dove, ox, person trampled underfoot.

St. Thomas Becket: Altar and long swords.

St. Ursula: Arrow, clock, ship, white banner with red cross.

St. Veronica: Veil with imprint of Christ's face and the crown of thorns.

St. Vincent: Boat, gridiron.

St. Vincent de Paul: Children.

St. Vincent Ferrer: Captives, cardinal's hat, pupil, trumpet.

TABLE 6

Major Encyclicals (1846-1993)

Pius IX (1846-1878)

1846..................*Qui pluribus* (On Faith and Religion)
1849..................*Ubi primum* (On the Immaculate Conception)
1854..................*Neminem vestrum* (On the Persecutions of Armenians)
          Apostolicae Nostrae caritatis (Prayers for Peace)
1859..................*Qui nuper* (On the Papal States)
1860..................*Nullis certe verbis* (On the Need for Civil Sovereignty)
1867..................*Levate* (On the Afflictions of the Church)
1871..................*Ubi Nos* (On the Papal States)

Leo XIII (1878-1903)

1878..................*Inscrutabili Dei consilio* (On the Evils of Society)
1879..................*Aeterni Patris* (On the Restoration of Christian Philosophy)
1880..................*Arcanum* (On Christian Marriage)
1882..................*Etsi Nos* (On Conditions in Italy)
1884..................*Humanum genus* (On Freemasonry)
1888..................*Libertas* (On the Nature of Human Liberty)
          Exeunte iam anno (On the Right Ordering of Christian Life)
1890..................*Sapientiae Christianae* (On Christians as Citizens)
          Catholicae Ecclesiae (On Slavery in the Missions)
1891..................*Rerum novarum* (On Capital and Labor)
1892..................*Inimica vis* (On Freemasonry)
1893..................*Providentissimus Deus* (On the Study of Holy Scripture)
1897..................*Divinum illud manus* (On the Holy Spirit)
1899..................*Annum Sacrum* (On Consecration to the Sacred Heart)
1901..................*Graves de communi re* (On Christian Democracy)
1902..................*Mirae caritatis* (On the Holy Eucharist)

St. Pius X (1903-1914)

1903..................*E supremi* (On the Restoration of All Things in Christ)
1904..................*Ad diem illum laetissimum* (On the Immaculate Conception)
1905..................*Acerbo nimis* (On Teaching Christian Doctrine)
1906..................*Vehementer Nos* (On the French Law of Separation)
1907..................*Une fois encore* (On the Separation of Church and State in France)
          Pascendi dominici gregis (On the Doctrines of the Modernists)
1911..................*Iamdudum* (On the Law of Separation in Portugal)

Benedict XV (1914-1922)

1914..................*Ad beatissimi Apostolorum* (Appeal for Peace)

1917................Humani generis Redemptionem (On Preaching the Word of God)
1920................Pacem, Dei munus pulcherrimum (On Peace and Christian Reconciliation)

Pius XI (1922-1939)

1922................Ubi arcano Dei consilio (On the Peace of Christ in the Kingdom of Christ)
1923................Studiorem Ducem (On St. Thomas Aquinas)
1926................Rerum Ecclesiae (On the Catholic Missions)
              Iniquis afflictisque (On the Persecution of the Church in Mexico)
1928................Rerum Orientalium (On the Promotion of Oriental Studies)
1930................Casti connubii (On Christian Marriage)
1931................Quadragesimo anno (Commemorating the Fortieth Anniversary of
              Rerum novarum; on Reconstruction of the Social Order)
              Non abbiamo bisogno (On Catholic Action in Italy)
1932................Caritate Christi compulsi (On the Sacred Heart)
              Acerba animi (On the Persecutions of the Church in Mexico)
1933................Dilectissima Nobis (On the Persecution of the Church in Spain)
1937................Mit brennender Sorge (On the Church and the German Reich)
              Divini Redemptoris (On Atheistic Communism)

Pius XII (1939-1958)

1939................Summi Pontificatus (On the Unity of Human Society)
1943................Mystici Corporis Christi (On the Mystical Body of Christ)
              Divino afflante Spiritu (On Promoting of Biblical Studies; Commemorating the
              Fiftieth Anniversary of Providentissimus Deus)
1946................Quemadmodum (Plea for the Care of the World's Destitute Children)
1947................Mediator Dei (On the Sacred Liturgy)
1950................Anni Sacri (On Combating Atheistic Propaganda Throughout the World)
1951................Evangelii praecones (On the Promotion of Catholic Missions)
1952................Orientales Ecclesias (On the Persecution of the Eastern Church)
1954................Sacra virginitas (On Consecrated Virginity)
              Ad Sinarum gentem (On the Supranationality of the Church; Addressed to
              the Bishops, Clergy, and People of China)
              Ad Caeli Reginam (Proclaiming the Queenship of Mary)
1955................Musicae sacrae (On Sacred Music)
1956................Haurietis aquas (On the Devotion to the Sacred Heart)
              Laetamur admodum (Renewing Exhortation for Prayers for Peace in Poland,
              Hungary, and the Middle East)
              Datis nuperrime (Lamenting the Sorrowful Events in Hungary and Condemning
              the Ruthless Use of Force)
1957................Miranda prorsus (On the Communications Field: Motion Pictures, Radio,
              Television)
1958................Ad Apostolorum Principis (On Communism and the Church in China)
              Memnisse iuvat (On Prayers for the Persecuted Church)

John XXIII (1958-1963)

1959.................*Ad Petri Cathedram* (On the Truth, Unity, and Peace, in a Spirit of Charity)
1961.................*Mater et Magistra* (On Christianity and Social Progress)
1963.................*Pacem in terris* (On Establishing Universal Peace in Truth, Justice, Charity, and Liberty)

Paul VI (1963-1978)

1964.................*Ecclesiam Suam* (On the Church)
1965.................*Mysterium Fidei* (On the Holy Eucharist)
1967.................*Populorum progressio* (On the Development of Peoples)
1968.................*Humanae vitae* (On the Regulation of Birth)

John Paul II (1978-)

1979.................*Redemptor hominis* (On Redemption and Dignity of the Human Race)
1981.................*Laborem exercens* (On Human Work)
1986.................*Dominum et Vivificantem* (On the Holy Spirit in the Life of the Church and the World)
1987.................*Redemptoris Mater* (On the Role of Mary in the Mystery of Christ and Her Active and Exemplary Presence in the Life of the Church)
            Sollicitudo Rei Socialis (On Social Concerns; Commemorating the Twentieth Anniversary of *Populorum progressio*)
1991.................*Centesimus annus* (Commemorating the Centenary of *Rerum novarum* and Addressing the Social Questions in a Contemporary Perspective)
1993.................*Veritatis Splendor* (Regarding Certain Fundamental Questions of the Church's Moral Teaching)

TABLE 7

Fathers of the Church

Greek Fathers

St. Anastasius Sinaita (d. 700).
St. Andrew of Crete (d. 740).
Aphraates (fourth century).
St. Archelaus (d. 282).
St. Athanasius (d. 373).
Athenagoras (second century).
St. Basil the Great (d. 379).
St. Caesarius of Nazianzus (d. 369).
St. Clement of Alexandria (d. 215).
St. Clement I of Rome, Pope (r. 88-97).
St. Cyril of Alexandria (d. 444).
St. Cyril of Jerusalem (d. 386).
Didymus the Blind (d. c. 398).
Diodore of Tarsus (d. 392).
St. Dionysius the Great (d. c. 264).
St. Epiphanius (d. 403).
Eusebius of Caesarea (d. 340).
St. Eustathius of Antioch (fourth century).
St. Firmillian (d. 268).
Gennadius I of Constantinople (fifth century).
St. Germanus (d. 732).
St. Gregory of Nazianzus (d. 390).
St. Gregory of Nyssa (d. 395).
St. Gregory Thaumaturgus (d. 268).
Hermas (second century).
St. Hippolytus (d. 236).

St. Ignatius of Antioch (d. 107).
St. Isidore of Pelusium (d. c. 450).
St. John Chrysostom (d. 407).
St. John Climacus (d. 649).
St. John Damascene (d. 749), last Father of the East.
St. Julius I, Pope (r. 337-352).
St. Justin Martyr (d. 165).
St. Leontius of Byzantium (sixth century).
St. Macarius (d. c. 390).
St. Maximus the Confessor (d. 662).
St. Melito (d. c. 180).
St. Methodius of Olympus (d. 311?).
St. Nilus the Elder (d. c. 430).
Origen (d. 254).
St. Polycarp (d. c. 155?).
St. Proclus (d. c. 446).
Pseudo-Dionysius the Areopagite (sixth century)
St. Serapion (d. c. 370).
St. Sophronius (d. 638).
Tatian (second century).
Theodore of Mopsuestia (d. 428).
Theodoret of Cyrrhus (d. c. 458).
St. Theophilus of Antioch (second century).

Latin Fathers

St. Ambrose of Milan (d. 397).
Arnobius (d. 330).
St. Augustine of Hippo (d. 430)
St. Benedict of Nursia (d. c. 550).
St. Caesarius of Arles (d. 542).
St. John Cassian (d. 435).
St. Celestine I, Pope (r. 422-432).
St. Cornelius, Pope (r. 251-253).
St. Cyprian of Carthage (d. 258).
St. Damasus I, Pope (r. 366-384).
St. Dionysius, Pope (r. 259-268).
St. Ennodius (d. 521).
St. Eucherius of Lyons (d. c. 450).

St. Fulgentius (d. 533).
St. Gregory of Elvira (d. c. 392).
St. Gregory I the Great, Pope (r. 590-604).
St. Hilary of Poitiers (d. 367).
St. Innocent I, Pope (r. 401-417).
St. Irenaeus of Lyons (d. c. 202).
St. Isidore of Seville (d. 636), last Father of the West.
St. Jerome (d. 420).
Lactantius (d. 323).
St. Leo I the Great (r. 440-461).
Marius Mercator (d. 451).
Marius Victorinus (fourth century).

Minucius Felix (second century).
Novatian (d. c. 257).
St. Optatus (fourth century).
St. Pacian (d. c. 390).
St. Pamphilus (d. 309).
St. Paulinus of Nola (d. 431).
St. Peter Chrysologus (d. 450).

St. Phoebadius of Agen (fourth century).
Rufinus of Aquileia (d. 410).
Salvian (fifth century).
St. Siricius, Pope (r. 384-399).
Tertullian (d. c. 222).
St. Vincent of Lérins (d. c. 450).

TABLE 8

Major Writings of Pope John Paul II (1979-1993)

Encyclicals

1979.................*Redemptor hominis* (On Redemption and Dignity of the Human Race)

1980.................*Dives in misericordia* (On the Mercy of God)

1981.................*Laborem exercens* (On Human Work)

1985.................*Slavorum Apostoli* (Commemorating Sts. Cyril and Methodius)

1986.................*Dominum et Vivificantem* (On the Holy Spirit in the Life of the Church and the World)

1987.................*Redemptor Mater* (On the Role of Mary in the Mystery of Christ and Her Active and Exemplary Presence in the Life of the Church)

Sollicitudo Reis Socialis (On Social Concerns on the Twentieth Anniversary of *Populorum Progressio*)

1991.................*Redemptoris missio* (On the Permanent Validity of the Church's Missionary Mandate)

Centesimus annus (Commemorating the Centenary of *Rerum novarum* and Addressing the Social Question in a Contemporary Perspective)

1993.................*Splendor Veritatis* (Regarding Certain Fundamental Questions of the Church's Moral Teaching)

Other works

Familiaris Consortio (1981; Exhortations on the Family).

Salvifici Doloris (1984; Letter on Suffering).

Redemptionis Donum (1984; Exhortation for the Religious).

Christifideles laici (1989; Exhortation on the Theme of the Synod of Bishops).

Pastores Dabo Vobis (1992; Exhortation on the Formation of Priests).

Crossing the Threshold of Hope (1994; a best-selling work presenting the Holy Father's personal beliefs concerning the faith, human dignity, hope, and eternal life.

TABLE 9

Mystics

The following are the most notable mystics in the history of the Church. They have contributed enormously to the life of the Church. Readers are encouraged to consult the individual entries for details on their lives, accomplishments, and writings.

St. Augustine (354-430).
Angelus Silesius (1624-1677).
St. Antony of Egypt (fourth century).
St. Bernard of Clairvaux (1090-1153).
St. Bonaventure (d. 1274).
St. Catherine of Genoa (1447-1510).
St. Catherine of Siena (d. 1380).
St. Clement of Alexandria (d. c. 215).
David of Augsburg (d. 1272).
David of Dinant (thirteenth century).
De Foucauld, Charles (1858-1916).
Denys the Carthusian (1402-1471).
Eckhart, Meister (d. 1327).
St. Francis of Assisi (d. 1226).
St. Gemma Galgani (1878-1903).
St. Gertrude the Great (thirteenth century).
St. Gregory of Nyssa (d. c. 395).
Groote, Gerhard (d. 1384).
St. Hildegard of Bingen (1098-1179).
Hilton, Walter (d. 1396).
Hugh of St. Victor (d. 1142).
John of Ávila (1500-1569).
St. John of the Cross (1542-1591).
John Scotus Erigena (ninth century).

Julian of Norwich (d. c. 1413).
Kempe, Margery (d. c. 1433).
St. Louis de Montfort (1673-1716).
St. Luis of Granada (1504-1588).
St. Maximus the Confessor (d. 662).
St. Mechtild (d. c. 1280).
Merton, Thomas (d. 1968).
Nicholas of Cusa (1401-1464).
St. Paul (d. 67).
Pierre d'Ailly (1350-1420).
Pseudo-Dionysius (sixth century).
Richard of St. Victor (d. 1173).
Richard Rolle (d. c. 1349).
Ruysbroeck, Jan van (1293-1381).
Suso, Henry (d. 1366).
Tauler, Johannes (d. 1361).
St. Teresa of Ávila (1515-1582).
St. Thérèse of Lisieux (1873-1897).
Thomas à Kempis (d. 1471).
St. Thomas Aquinas (d. 1274)
(See also **Common Life, Brethren of the; Free Spirit, Brethren of the; Hesychasm; Monasticism;** and **Quietism**.)

TABLE 10

Patron Saints of Countries

Americas: Our Lady of Guadalupe, St. Rose of Lima.

Argentina: Our Lady of Lujan.

Armenia: St. Gregory the Illuminator.

Australia: Our Lady Help of Christians.

Belgium: St. Joseph .

Borneo: St. Francis Xavier.

Brazil: Nossa Senhora de Aparecida, Immaculate Conception, St. Peter of Alcántara.

Canada: St. Joseph, St. Anne.

Ceylon (Sri Lanka): St. Lawrence.

Chile: St. James, Our Lady of Mt. Carmel.

China: St. Joseph.

Colombian: St. Peter Claver, St. Louis Bertrán.

Corsica: Immaculate Conception.

Denmark: St. Anskar, St. Canute.

Dominican Republic: Our Lady of High Grace, St. Dominic.

East Indies: St. Thomas, Apostle.

Ecuador: Sacred Heart.

England: St. George.

Europe: St. Benedict.

Finland: St. Henry.

France: Our Lady of the Assumption, St. Joan of Arc, St. Thérèse of Lisieux.

Germany: Sts. Boniface and Michael.

Greece: St. Nicholas, St. Andrew.

Holland: St. Willibrord.

Hungary: Blessed Virgin, Great Lady of Hungary, St. Stephen, King.

India: Our Lady of the Assumption.

Ireland: Sts. Patrick, Brigid, and Columba.

Italy: St. Francis of Assisi, St. Catherine of Siena.

Japan: St. Peter, Baptist.

Lithuania: St. Casimir, Bl. Cunegunda.

Malta: St. Paul, Our Lady of the Assumption.

Mexico: Our Lady of Guadalupe.

Monaco: St. Devota.

Moravia: Sts. Cyril and Methodius.

New Zealand: Our Lady Help of Christians.

Norway: St. Olaf.

Paraguay: Our Lady of the Assumption.

Peru: St. Joseph.

Philippines: Sacred Heart of Mary.

Poland: St. Casimir, Bl. Cunegunda, St. Stanislaus of Cracow, Our Lady of Czestochowa.

Portugal: Immaculate Conception, St. Francis Borgia, St. Antony of Padua, St. Vincent, St. George.

Russia: St. Andrew, St. Nicholas of Myra, St. Thérèse of Lisieux.

Scandinavia: St. Anskar.

Scotland: St. Andrew, St. Columba.

Silesia: St. Hedwig.

Slovakia: Our Lady of Sorrows.

South America: St. Rose of Lima.

Spain: St. James, St. Teresa of Ávila.

Sweden: St. Bridget, St. Eric.

United States: Immaculate Conception.

Uruguay: Our Lady of Lujan.

Wales: St. David.

West Indies: Gertrude.

TABLE 11

Pontifical Institutes of Higher Learning

The following are the pontifical universities and institutes situated in Rome. They are considered the most prestigious schools in the Church. There are also designated pontifical universities throughout the world. The laws and norms currently followed by the schools were set by the apostolic constitution *Sapienta Christiana* (1979), issued by Pope John Paul II. The information included here is from the *Annuario Pontificio*. The dates refer to the year of the particular university's founding.

Pontifical Gregorian University (1552), called the *Gregorian*. Associated with it are: Pontifical Biblical Institute (1909) and Pontifical Institute of Oriental Studies (1917).

Pontifical Lateran University (1773), called the *Lateran*. Associated with it is: Pontifical Institute of Studies of Marriage and the Family (1982).

Pontifical Urban University (1627).

Pontifical University of St. Thomas Aquinas (1580), called the *Angelicum*.

Pontifical University Salesianum (1940). Associated with it is: Pontifical Institute of Higher Latin Studies, called the Faculty of Christian and Classical Letters.

Pontifical Athenaeum of St. Anselm (1687).

Pontifical Athenaeum of St. Anthony ("Antonianum") (1933). Associated with it is: School of Biblical Studies in Jerusalem.

Pontifical Institute of Sacred Music (1911; 1931).

Pontifical Institute of Christian Archaeology (1925).

Pontifical Theological Faculty ("St. Bonaventure") (1587).

Pontifical Theological Faculty of Sts. Teresa of Ávila and John of the Cross, Pontifical Institute of Spirituality (1935), called the *Teresianum*.

Pontifical Theological Faculty ("Marianum") (1398), called the *Marianum*.

Pontifical Institute of Arabic and Islamic Studies (1926).

Pontifical Faculty of Educational Science ("Auxilium") (1970).

Pontifical Institute ("Regina Mundi") (1970).

Roman Athenaeum of the Holy Cross (1985), part of the personal prelature of Opus Dei.

TABLE 12

Social Encyclicals

The following are the so-called social encyclicals, espousing important Church teachings on social doctrine. The first such encyclical is generally considered *Rerum novarum* of Pope Leo XIII (1891), although it was preceded by two encyclicals on social or political themes.

Pope	Encyclical
Leo XIII	*Inscrutabili Dei consilio* (1878; On the Evils of Society).
	Quod Apostolici muneris (1878; On Socialism).
	Rerum novarum (1891; On Capital and Labor).
Pius XI	*Quadragesimo anno* (1931; On Reconstruction of the Social Order).
John XXIII	*Mater et Magistra* (1961; Christianity and social progress).
	Pacem in terris (1963; On Establishing Universal Peace in Truth, Justice, Charity, and Liberty).
Paul VI	*Populorum progressio* (1967; On the Development of Peoples).
John Paul II	*Laborem exercens* (1981; On Human Work).
	Sollicitudo Rei Socialis (1987; On Social Concerns).
	Centesimus annus (1991; "The 100th Year").

(See also **Gaudium et Spes**.)

TABLE 13

Documents of Vatican Council II

The following are the sixteen documents promulgated by the Vatican Council. They comprise two dogmatic constitutions, two pastoral constitutions, nine decrees, and three declarations. Included are the Latin title, the English title, and the date of its promulgation.

Lumen Gentium (Dogmatic Constitution on the Church), November 21, 1964.

Dei Verbum (Dogmatic Constitution on Divine Revelation), November 18, 1965.

Sacrosanctum Concilium (Constitution on the Sacred Liturgy), December 4, 1963.

Gaudium et Spes (Pastoral Constitution on the Church in the Modern World), December 7, 1965.

Inter Mirifica (Decree on the Instruments of Social Communication), December 4, 1963.

Unitatis Redintegratio (Decree on Ecumenism), November 21, 1964.

Orientalium Ecclesiarum (Decree on Eastern Catholic Churches), November 21, 1964.

Christus Dominus (Decree on the Bishops' Pastoral Office in the Church), October 28, 1965.

Optatam Totius (Decree on Priestly Formation), October 28, 1965.

Perfectae Caritatis (Decree on the Appropriate Renewal of the Religious Life), October 28, 1965.

Apostolicam Actuositatem (Decree on the Apostolate of the Laity), November 18, 1965.

Presbyterorum Ordinis (Decree on the Ministry and Life of Priests), December 7, 1965.

Ad Gentes (Decree on the Church's Missionary Activity), December 7, 1965.

Gravissimum Educationis (Declaration on Christian Education), October 28, 1965.

Nostra Aetate (Declaration on the Relationship of the Church to Non-Christian Religions), October 28, 1965.

Dignitatis Humanae (Declaration on Religious Freedom), December 7, 1965.

GLOSSARY

Abbess ● Superior, both temporally and spiritually, of a community of nuns. She is the symbolic mother of those religious under her authority. The female counterpart of the abbot, she is entitled to the right of wearing a ring and bearing a crosier, but her jurisdiction is not that of an abbot.

Abbé ● French term first applied to abbots but which came to be used for all clerics. It means "Father." In some cases it can refer to non-ordained clerics who teach.

Abbot ● Superior of a monastery, a community of monks. By custom, the abbot is elected for life by the professed members in a ballot that is supposed to be secret. His authority is both quasi-episcopal and paternal — quasi-episcopal in that it confers certain territorial jurisdiction, and paternal in that he is responsible for the administration of property, maintaining all rules and constitutions, and keeping discipline. The title abbot has been replaced in some orders with the name prior (Dominicans), rector (Jesuits), or guardian (Franciscans).

Abjuration ● Formal renunciation of heresy, apostasy, or schism. Derived from the Latin *abjuratio* (forswearing) or *abjurare* (to forswear), it was once required of all converts before the confession of faith. Today, it is not necessary, the profession being considered sufficient.

Ad Limina ● Shortened form of the Latin phrase *ad limina Apostolorum* (to the threshold of the Apostles), used for quinquennial reports that all bishops and military vicars must make to the Holy See. By custom, bishops from dioceses on continents outside of Europe must make the journey every ten years, although their report must be submitted every five years. The report should be exceedingly well-organized and highly detailed concerning the state of diocesan affairs. It is submitted to the Congregation for Bishops. The *ad limina* visit was instituted by Pope Sixtus V (r. 1585-1590).

Ad Majorem Dei Gloriam ● Latin phrase meaning "For the Greater Glory of God," the motto of the Society of Jesus.

Agnosticism ● Philosophical theory arguing that knowledge or certitude of reality is impossible because of the limits of the human mind or because it is unknowable. It states that man's knowledge can be reduced to emotional (subjective) responses or to sense experience. In terms of religious truths or the question of the existence of God, agnosticism stresses uncertainty, denying that the application of reason can permit the discovery of religious truth or knowledge of God. This runs counter to Catholic teaching, especially the work of St. Thomas Aquinas and the doctrinal proclamation of Vatican Council I.

Anchorite ● Individual who withdraws from the world and adopts the lifestyle of a hermit, devoting his life to prayer and penance. The female equivalent is the anchoress.

Anglicanism ● Church that should not be considered synonymous with the Church of England, rather, the worldwide Churches in communion with the see of Canterbury. It is found in most countries but was the long-established Church in those regions that were part of the British Empire, including Canada, South Africa, and Hong Kong. In England, the Anglican Church remains the state-supported faith and is known as the Church of England. It was begun in 1534 with King Henry VIII's Act of Supremacy, by which he was proclaimed supreme head of the English Church. The final separation with the Catholic faith came with the Thirty-Nine Articles in 1563 under Queen Elizabeth I. Anglican doctrine has been much influenced by the Book of

Common Prayer, which underwent a number of editions. The faith has always been placed under stress from the pulls of Calvinism and the inclinations toward what is termed Anglo-Catholicism. Recent progress toward reunion between the Catholics and Anglicans has been dealt a serious setback by the decision of the Anglicans to ordain women. In the United States, the Church is known as the Episcopalian.

Anglo-Catholics ● Members of the Anglican Church who adhere to the use of the Latin Missal and celebrate such "catholic" ceremonies as the Mass. Anglo-Catholics are said to belong to the High Church (or are High Church), as compared to those Anglicans who are Low Church and practice religion more Presbyterian in outlook.

Anti-Catholicism ● Opposition, often of a well-organized or pervasive nature, to the Roman Catholic Church. Anti-Catholicism in its common usage or understanding had its origins in Europe following the Reformation when opponents of the faith came to power in entire countries or regions (e.g., parts of Germany) and used the authority of office and crown to pass and enforce laws that sought to limit or even extirpate the Church as an effective voice in the life of the people or the nation's affairs.

Antichrist ● Term derived from the Greek *antichristos* (against Christ), used to describe the foremost enemy of Christ. The Antichrist is mentioned in the NT (1 Jn 2:18, 2:22, 4:3; 2 Jn 7) and traditional interpretations include the powerful imagery of the Book of Revelation as referring to the Antichrist. Catholic teaching points to a real person and not a movement; throughout history, he has been identified with Nero and Gaius Caligula. The Antichrist stands as the anticipated enemy of Christ with the final cosmological struggle to occur before the Second Coming of Christ.

Anticlericalism ● Policy implemented by a government, country, or movement ranging from vocal opposition to the clergy to outright persecution. As priests have traditionally been viewed as the main representatives of the Church throughout a nation and most in contact with the populace, they have been singled out by anti-Catholic regimes or are targeted for attack by anticlerical elements.

Anti-Semitism ● Term for prejudice, hatred, or antagonism toward the Jews. It originated as a word in 1879 in a pamphlet attacking Jews as descendants of Shem of the Bible and was henceforth used for the historical phenomenon of anti-Jewish activity. The Church recognizes that anti-Semitism is absolutely in contradiction to Christian charity and love, and numerous popes have spoken out against it.

Apostasy ● Word used for a baptized person who has utterly rejected the Catholic faith; by canon law, apostasy is the repudiation of the faith by someone baptized or received into the Church. It is derived from the Greek *apostasis* (revolt) and the Latin *apostasia* (separation from God).

Apostle ● From the Greek *apostolos* (one sent out). In a broad sense in Scripture, the followers of Jesus who then went out to spread the Gospel he had brought; in a specific sense, the chosen twelve picked by Christ to be with him during his ministry. They were known as Christ's disciples while with him, but after his ascension they were called apostles.

Archbishop ● Title borne by a bishop with authority over an archdiocese. He thus has full jurisdiction over his own diocese, but he may also be a metropolitan over an ecclesiastical province. Some archbishops are also considered *ad personam*, meaning that they hold the title without authority over an archdiocese as an honor bestowed upon them by the pope.

Archconfraternity ● Confederation or association of confraternities or sodalities.

Archdeacon ● Office found in the early Church; customarily he was a deacon appointed by the bishop to give assistance in various matters. The archdeacon was abolished in later years owing to abuses by officeholders. It does not exist in the modern Church, the traditional duties being filled by the vicar-general and vicars forane.

Archdiocese ● Ecclesiastical territory governed by an archbishop. It is the primary see of a province consisting of one or more diocese.

Archpriest ● Title used from the fourth and fifth centuries for a priest chosen to assist the bishop directly or to substitute for him in some form of public worship or civil affair. Today, the title used is dean or vicar. An archpriest can also be a priest who assists a newly ordained priest in his first Mass.

Asceticism ● Greek term (from *asketikos*) used for the effort or program adopted in the pursuit of Christian perfection. It is the practical application of the principles and norms laid down in ascetical theology. It should not be confused with the severe austerity of such practices as fasting.

Atheism ● In a broad sense, the opinion that there is no God, that he does not exist. Atheism was long used for those persons who considered the existence of God to be improbable but came to be applied in a more restricted sense after the emergence of agnosticism. Vatican Council II identified eight different types of atheism and spoke of it in some detail in *Gaudium et Spes* ("Pastoral Constitution on the Church in the Modern World").

Autocephalous ● Term used in the Eastern Churches for a national Church that is able to elect its own patriarch or archbishop who is not subject to a patriarch but who is responsible to a provincial synod or the Holy See. It is from the Greek for "self-heading."

Beatification ● Declaration made by the pope that someone who is found to have lived a holy life and/or endured a martyr's death is thus entitled to the honor of being blessed (living with the elect in heaven). One of the steps in the process of canonization, it is bestowed normally after many years of investigation by local Church authorities and acceptance as complete by the Holy See.

Biglietto ● Official notification sent to a cleric that he has been elevated by the pope to the rank of cardinal.

Biretta ● Square cap worn by clerics of the Latin rite. It is square in shape, with three ridges for most clerics (four for those who have obtained a pontifical doctorate). The color varies depending upon the rank of the cleric: black for priests, purple (with a purple tuft) for bishops, scarlet for cardinals; until 1969, monsignori wore a black biretta with a purple tuft.

Bishop ● Highest order of the ministries of holy orders, a successor to the Apostles. The bishop is a cleric who has attained the fullness of the priesthood and who possesses the power to administer all of the sacraments, including ordination. He has the authority to administer a diocese and is under the direct responsibility of the pope.

Blasphemy ● Grave violation against charity that is defined as words or actions that are contemptuous of God or some action that is of great offense to God. It may include vicious or reprehensible language against the saints or the Church.

Blessed ● Title (abbreviated "Bl.") bestowed upon someone who has been beatified.

Body of the Church ● Organized association or commonwealth of the members of the Church. The Holy Spirit is recognized as the soul of the Church.

Bolshevism ● One of the two (with Menshevism) main branches of Marxist socialism that arose in Russia from 1903-1918. The Bolsheviks came under the leadership of Lenin and overthrew the Kerensky regime in November 1917, thus launching the Communist state in Russia from 1918. The Bolsheviks soon liquidated the Mensheviks and installed a severely anti-Christian, anti-Catholic, and antidemocratic program.

Breviary ● Term used for the book containing the Divine Office.

Brief, Apostolic ● Papal letter that carries less solemnity than a bull. It is signed customarily by the secretary of state and is authenticated with the seal of the Fisherman.

Calvinism ● Body of doctrine first organized by John Calvin (1509-1564). Central to Calvin's teaching was the idea of predestination for salvation or damnation, the consequence of the depravity of the human being who possesses no free will and is utterly dependent upon divine grace. Calvin also accepted only two sacraments, baptism and Eucharist, declaring a kind of spiritual presence of Christ in communion. These tenets were expressed in the Institutes of Religion. Calvinist-based Churches today include the United Church of Christ and the United Presbyterian Church.

Canonization ● Formal declaration by the Church that a person is raised to the full honors of the altar, meaning that he or she is in heaven and is worthy of veneration as a saint. Canonization is the culmination of the long process of investigation into a person's life to determine that individual's saintliness. This inquiry examines his or her writings, life, and works, and requires that the individual is normally beatified as the preparatory step. Known then as a *beatus* (or *beata* for a female), the person must have two attested miracles, prior to canonization as evidence of the individual's heroic virtue. Miracles are not required for martyrs, and the pope may also forgo some of the technical requirements, as in the case of St. Thomas Aquinas. The first officially canonized saint was St. Ulrich of Augsburg by Pope John XV in 993. The actual canonization rite is performed at St. Peter's Basilica.

Canon ● (1) Rule, law, or standard; (2) list of authentic Scriptures; (3) Eucharistic Prayer or anaphora of the Mass; (4) clerical

dignitary, for example, a priest attached to a cathedral.

Canon Regular ● Cleric residing in a community that is under the care and direction of a religious order. Most canons regular follow the Augustinian Rule. Orders with canons regular include the Norbertines or Premonstratensians.

Canons, Chapter of ● Today a community of canons, mostly in England, that performs certain liturgical functions and assists in the affairs of the diocese. They are not present in the United States. During the Middle Ages, the so-called Cathedral Chapter, canons appointed to aid the bishop, amassed vast powers and were extensively mentioned by the Council of Trent (1545-1563) and the 1917 Code of Canon Law. Their place was much reduced by the 1983 Code of Canon Law.

Cardinal ● Member of the Sacred College of Cardinals and a high-ranking, powerful member of the Church hierarchy. He gives assistance to the pope in the government of the Church and has the important task of taking part in the election of a new successor of St. Peter. By canon law, all cardinals must be ordained priests; those who are not bishops at the time of their elevation are consecrated to the episcopacy.

Casuistry ● Method used in moral theology that attempts to apply a set of general principles in specific cases of human conduct. Derived from the Latin *causa* (case), casuistry relies upon knowledge of the law and moral theology in so-called real-world situations in matters determining conscience. While it is not itself complete as a moral system, it nevertheless makes invaluable contributions to the determination of moral discussions.

Catechesis ● Name used for the process of oral instruction, aided by a variety of visual aids and presented material, whereby individuals can be developed into mature members of the faith. It is based on Scripture, Tradition, and the liturgy.

Catechism ● Manual of Christian doctrine, from the Greek *cathechesis* (oral instruction). In the early Church, instruction was almost entirely oral. Over time, the writings of St. Augustus and St. Gregory of Nyssa were used to prepare persons for baptism. An important development was the rise of the printing press, which permitted the creation of relatively inexpensive catechisms. An important precursor to the formal catechism was the *Summa of Christian Doctrine* (1555) by St. Peter Canisius. This was followed by the Roman Catechism (1566), issued by Pope St. Pius V and based on the work of the Council of Trent. Other notable catechisms were the Penny Catechism in England and the U.S. Baltimore Catechism. In 1994, the Holy See issued the new *Catechism of the Catholic Church.*

Catechumen ● Name for a person undergoing the process of catechesis. The individual who enters the catechumenate intends to receive instruction with the purpose of full reception into the Church.

Catholic Church ● From the Greek *katholikos* and the Latin *catholicus* (universal), the name that implies the universality of the Church and that today is intended to denote those Christians who participate in the continuing tradition of faith and worship and remain loyal to the Holy See and the apostolic succession of bishops and priests. "Catholic" was first used by St. Ignatius of Antioch (d. c. 107) in his letter to the Smyrneans (8-2) when he noted that "where Jesus is, there is the Catholic Church." The Catholic Church is thus the "universal" body of the faithful (stressed by Vatican Council II as the people of God), who follow the Catholic faith in the sense of the Vincentian Canon: "everywhere, always, and by all." Catholic Church is also applied in differentiating the Church from the Orthodox Churches, which have been separated from the Church since 1054, the Protestant Churches, and all unorthodox bodies, including heretics and schismatics.

Catholicism ● Term used to denote the system of teachings, doctrine, and practices of the Roman Catholic Church.

Cause ● Extensive investigative process by which it is determined whether an individual is worthy of canonization. The entire undertaking is under the authority of the Congregation for the Causes of Saints.

Cenobite ● Type of hermit or anchorite, distinguished by the fact that he or she resides in a community. From the Latin *cenobium*, the cenobites were the ancestors of the monastic orders, and such religious orders as the Benedictines and Cistercians are considered cenobitic.

Censure, Ecclesiastical ● Penalty placed by the Church upon an obstinate or delinquent individual; the penalty or censure brings deprivation of certain spiritual benefits. Considered medicinal or corrective, a censure is imposed only after a recalcitrant Catholic has been repeatedly warned. The three types of censure are excommunication, interdict, and suspension. It is noted that censures may take automatic effect — as in the embracing of heresy — or are imposed by the Church. The penalties do not have a set time limit but are removed through the reception of absolution.

Chancellor ● Technically, the individual appointed by the bishop of a diocese to maintain the diocesan archives. The chancellor is also often granted other duties and authority, including making certain decisions on behalf of and with the approval of the bishop, The chancellor is thus one of the most important diocesan officials.

Chancery ● Name used in the United States and elsewhere for the central administrative offices of a diocese or archdiocese. The other common term, considered more accurate, is "diocesan curia."

Chapter ● See **Canons, Chapter of.**

Charismatic Movement ● Name used for the revived movement within the Catholic

Church for the Pentecostal movement or Pentecostalism. (See **Charismatic Renewal**, following entry.)

Charismatic Renewal ● In full, Catholic Charismatic Renewal, the Catholic movement paralleling the Protestant Pentecostal movement. Charismatic Renewal is characterized by the renewal of an individual through a baptism in the Holy Spirit, the name charismatic being derived from the Greek for "gifted." The movement first came to prominence in the 1960s, becoming quite popular in the 1970s. Tentative approval was given to Charismatic Renewal in 1976, the caution of the Church authorities rooted in the tendency of Protestant Pentecostalism toward extremism and fundamentalism. A leading supporter of the charismatics was Cardinal Leo Suenens (b. 1904), archbishop of Mechelen-Brussels (1961-1979).

Chirograph ● Type of letter written by the pope with his own hand. It is normally concerned with some important ecclesiastical matter and is sent to heads of state and high Church officials.

Christian Church ● Broad name for the worldwide believers in Christ. It may also be used in a specific sense by denoting the essentially undivided Christian faith in the time prior to the final break with the Eastern Church in 1054; after this time, the Christian Church was split into East and West. The Christian Church can also mean the unified faith in the period before the Protestant Reformation in the 1500s, after which greater emphasis was placed on the term "Roman Catholic Church."

Christian Family Movement ● Movement that emerged out of Catholic Action to spread the important values of the family within society. It was begun in 1950 and was distinguished by the fact that it was organized and led by laypeople. The C.F.M. grew enormously in popularity in the years after its founding. In 1968, it was opened to couples from other Christian denominations.

Christology ● Branch of theology concerned with the person and nature of Jesus Christ, with particular attention paid to his Divine Person and his two natures, human and divine. It should not be confused with soteriology, the branch of theology concerned with Christ's labors of salvation.

Church of England ● In a broad sense, the term used for the Christian Church that has existed in England since the arrival of the faith in the isles during the period of Roman occupation; in a more specific meaning, it is today used for the state-supported C of E that has been in existence since the sixteenth century after the split of the kingdom from communion with Rome. C of E members are considered to be in communion with the see of Canterbury. The faithful of the Anglican Church in England are considered to comprise the Church of England. (See also **Anglicanism** and **Thirty-Nine Articles**.)

Church Militant ● Name for the Church on earth; it implies the fact that it is engaged in the struggle against sin and temptation.

Church Suffering ● Name for the Church comprised of the faithful departed who are being purified in purgatory.

Church Triumphant ● Name for the Church of all those who are among the faithful departed and, having triumphed over the sins and temptations of the world, are blessed by enjoying a share of heaven.

Cloister ● Community (described as cloistered) that is largely cut off from the world, its members committing themselves to the contemplative life. The religious belonging to the cloister are severely limited in their contact with the outside world; likewise, others are restricted in their access to the community. The name can also be used for the actual enclosure, often with high walls, that comprises the residence. As an architectural term, cloister refers to the covered passageway that is around the courtyard (called the garth) located in the center of a monastery.

Communion of Saints ● Spiritual union

that exists among the members of the Church in heaven with those who are in purgatory and on earth. All are united in the Mystical Body of Christ. (See also **Church Militant, Church Suffering,** and **Church Triumphant**.)

Concordat ● Agreement signed between the Holy See and a secular government.

Curate ● Name used, especially in England and Canada, for a priest who holds the position of associate pastor or parochial vicar in a parish.

Cursillo ● Meaning the "little course," a movement for Christian renewal that was launched in 1949 by a group of laymen with Bishop Hervas y Benet on the island of Mallorca, Spain. Customarily, the Cursillo program takes place in three stages over three days: preparation (pre-Cursillo), the actual course (Cursillo), and the follow-up (post-Cursillo). The central aim of the course is to change one's mind according to the mind of Christ and then, with others, to change the world. Those who have taken part are known as Cursillistas; they meet regularly with others in gatherings called ultreyas. The Cursillo is based on the *Spiritual Exercises* of St. Ignatius Loyola.

Deacon ● Ordained minister who is charged with the task of assisting the priest in such ministerial duties as preaching, baptizing, witnessing marriages, distributing Communion, and presiding at funerals (but not saying the funeral Mass). There are two forms of the diaconate in the modern Church, the permanent diaconate (including single and married men) and the transitional diaconate (for those who will eventually be ordained).

Dean ● Cleric appointed by the bishop of a diocese with certain authority over a part of the diocese, normally with the purpose of giving aid to other priests in that area. Also known as the vicar forane, the dean was often used in outlying or rural areas; today, he is also found in large cities and is called the urban vicar. His territory is called a deanery.

Diptych ● Listing of the names of the living and dead that is read by a deacon during the canon of the liturgy. The names are kept on a set of tablets, hinged in the center.

Dulia ● Proper degree of veneration to be given to the angels and saints. It is differentiated from *hyperdulia* and *latria*.

Easter ● Feast of the Resurrection of Christ. It is considered the most important event in the Church calendar. The date of Easter was the cause of much controversy within the Church over the centuries.

Ecclesiology ● Branch of theology concerned with the study of the Church in all its facets, including its founding, nature, mission, and organization.

Ecstasy ● Elevation of the soul above or beyond the senses so that an individual is said to be in a state of being beside oneself. It is considered a rare gift of the Holy Spirit by which a person is granted through prayer an experience of union with God. In an interior sense, the mind is focused entirely on a religious subject through the most advanced forms of contemplative prayer. At the same time, the person is completely unaware of the environment through total suppression of the senses. Ecstasy has been granted to a number of saints.

Eminence ● Proper form of address given to a cardinal.

Eparch ● Office corresponding in the Byzantine rite to that of bishop, especially in the Russian Church. The residential bishop is termed an eparch, with jurisdiction over the ecclesiastical territory called an eparchy. (See also **Exarch**.)

Episcopacy ● From the Greek *episkopos*, the office of bishop, divinely instituted and in succession to the Apostles. (See **Bishop**.)

Episcopalians ● Members of the Episcopalian Church (the former Protestant Episcopalian Church) in the United States, one of the worldwide Churches that comprise the Anglican communion. The origins of the Episcopalians are found in the arrival of Anglicans from England in the sixteenth century. It was subsequently established in the colonies, although it was banned for many years in New England. After the American Revolution, the American Anglicans separated from the jurisdiction of the Church of England. The Protestant Episcopalian Church was formally established in 1789. The Church issued an Americanized edition of the Book of Common Prayer and took as its foundational doctrines the Nicene Creed, Apostles' Creed, and a version of the Thirty-Nine Articles. The contemporary Episcopalian Church is generally considered much more progressive and liberal than its counterpart in England; the American Church ordained women long before it was seriously discussed within the Church of England.

Epistemology ● Branch of philosophy that is devoted to the study and examination of knowledge, including its nature and origins.

Evangelization ● Broad term used to denote the entire process by which the Church propagates the Gospel (the "Good News") of Christ. From the Greek *euangélion* (good news), evangelization involves the spread of conversions through the missionary labors of the Church, the impact of such Christianization upon local communities, and the positive transformation of entire regions and cultures.

Exarch ● Greek for "a guide." This title is today applied to the ecclesiastical officials of the Eastern-rite Churches. It is given to a priest who is not a bishop but who leads a Church territory; the jurisdiction under the care of an exarch is called an exarchate. The exarch was originally a title given to a civil governor in the Later Roman (Byzantine) Empire who controlled a province on the frontier or in a disputed area. The most important exarch was that of Ravenna. The term came to be used in the Byzantine Church for a patriarch, then to an archbishop or bishop or priest serving in the place of a bishop in a territory but who lacks the authority to ordain priests.

Ex Cathedra ● Term that implies a formal declaration by the supreme pontiff within the purview of papal infallibility. Latin for "from the chair," *ex cathedra* means that the pope is speaking infallibly from his throne or chair (the *cathedra*) of supreme authority over the Church. Such a declaration is not dependent upon the consent of the Church and is stated to be completely irreformable.

Excellency ● Proper form of address given to a bishop or archbishop.

Excommunication ● Severe ecclesiastical penalty imposed by the Church that excludes a member of the faithful from the wider community. Excommunication is today covered in its particulars by Canon 1331 of the new Code of Canon Law, promulgated in 1983. It exists in two contemporary forms, *ferendae sententiae* and *latae sententiae*. The former is a penalty imposed after a formal proceeding presided over by at least three judges. The latter is considered an automatic penalty for certain acts, including the procuring of a successful abortion (Canon 1398), the embrace of heresy (Canon 1364), violation of the Seal of Confession (Canon 1388), and the blasphemous and sacrilegious use of the Eucharist (Canon 1367). A person under the ban of excommunication is unable to take part in all ceremonies of public worship, especially the Eucharist, to receive or celebrate the sacraments, and to discharge any ecclesiastical offices, ministries, or functions.

Exegesis ● From the Greek "to bring out," the study and investigation of the Sacred Scripture, utilizing the scholarly application of textual analysis and criticism, archaeology, and history to draw forth the true meaning of biblical text. Exegesis is conducted under the science of hermeneutics.

Exemption ● Type of ecclesiastical

privilege by which a religious institute is removed from the jurisdiction of the local bishop; it is instead under the authority of the Holy See or some other recognized agency. Such an exemption is in the internal affairs of the institute; the conduct of the apostolate is under the jurisdiction of the bishop. The bishop is also empowered to intervene in the affairs of the exempt community under certain extraordinary circumstances. An exempt diocese means that it is not under a metropolitan but subject directly to the Holy See.

Existentialism ● Philosophy first established in the 1800s and developed throughout the twentieth century that places primary emphasis on existence and the concrete rather than on abstract concepts and ideas or speculations. Real experiences are given greater importance than theoretical examination, with particular emphasis upon human existence. Christian existentialism was advanced by Søren Kierkegaard in which he suggested that the suffering of life could be alleviated by transcendent faith in God. Atheistic existentialism, the best known of the various forms, was propounded by Jean Paul Sartre and Martin Heidegger. It denies the existence of God and stresses the absolute freedom of the human to choose, with its concomitant misery and pain. Religious existentialists included Gabriel Marcel and Martin Buber, a Catholic and a Jew respectively. Jacques Maritain proposed an existentialism rooted in Thomistic thought. Karl Rahner advanced supernatural existentialism.

Exorcism ● Practice in which demons, devils, or evil spirits are expelled from an afflicted person. According to the Roman Ritual, an exorcism is today performed by a priest with special permission of a bishop. The exorcist was formerly a member of the minor orders until the suppression of the office in 1972 under the revision of the holy orders. The power to perform the exorcism was established by Christ (Mt 8:32-34; Mk 1:21-27; Lk 4:31-36), who bestowed power over evil spirits to his disciples. The priest chosen by a bishop to be an exorcist should be distinguished by knowledge, piety, and the exemplary nature of his life.

Fabric ● Also Fabbrica, a term used for a church building, all of its material possessions, the fund or endowment that might exist for its upkeep, and the department or office that has the task of overseeing its maintenance. The best known Fabric is that of St. Peter's Basilica, which has been in existence since the reign of Pope Julius II (1503-1513). The Fabric of Peter is part of the Roman Curia.

Fascism ● Type of political absolutism that has varied depending upon the country in which it developed but which had certain universal characteristics. These include totalitarianism, a dominant single political power through one party, a sharp curtailing of personal liberty, a corporate state with real control resting in the hands of an elite, and a unifying cultural program predicated upon racist or nationalistic tendencies. Fascism flourished in Italy from 1922 under Benito Mussolini and in Germany under Adolf Hitler and the National Socialists (or Nazis).

Fisherman's Ring ● Or Ring of the Fisherman, the ring worn by the reigning pope. It is engraved with a depiction of St. Peter in a boat, fishing; the name of the pontiff surrounds the image. It is placed upon the finger of a new pope by the camerlengo and is subsequently used to seal important official documents. The symbol of a pontiff's succession to St. Peter, the ring is defaced and broken at the time of the pope's death and a document is signed testifying to the act. The ring dates at least to the reign of Pope Clement IV (1265-1268).

Gentiles ● Name taken from the Latin *gentiles* (people) that was used in the Vulgate for those persons who were non-Jews. Gentiles was itself a translation of the

Hebrew term *goy* (plural: *goyim*) for those who did not belong to the people of Israel. In the early Church, Gentile was applied to those who had not yet received the Gospels, a demonstration of both the origins of the Christian community within the Jewish nation and the degree of self-identity among the members of the Church.

Gospel ● Word derived from the Anglo-Saxon (Old English) *godspel*, meaning good news or good tidings. It is itself a translation of the Greek *euangélion*. The four Gospels of Matthew, Mark, Luke, and John proclaim the Good News by providing accounts of the life, mission, death, and resurrection of Jesus Christ. The remaining works of the NT enhance and magnify the glorious message of salvation presented in the Gospels.

Hagiography ● Name given to writings that are concerned with saints. Hagiographies (from the Greek *hagios* — holy, and *graphein* — to write) present the lives of saints as well as their works and the specific ways in which they were saintly. This type of work began as an account of the martyrs, growing to cover all of the saints.

Heresy ● In the Catholic Church, the denial by a baptized person of any truths that must be believed, having been divinely revealed, and must be held by all Catholics.

Hermeneutics ● Science of interpreting the Sacred Scriptures and studying their true meaning, relying upon the established principles of exegesis. According to Church teaching, hermeneutics is given direction by the magisterium, which exercises a vital role in its formulation and communication to the Church. It is derived from the Greek *hermeneus*, interpretation.

Hermit ● Individual who chooses to live away from society, alone, so as to devote himself to contemplation of God. The hermits first developed in the Church in the third century, and the eremetical life was to exercise a profound influence on the rise of monasticism (see also **Anchorite** and **Cenobite**). The Christian era foundation of the hermit is based on Elijah in the OT and St. John the Baptist in the NT.

Hyperdulia ● Form of veneration that is properly bestowed upon the Blessed Virgin. It is greater in form than *dulia*, which is given to the saints. It should not be confused with adoration, which is proper only to God (*latria*). (See also **Mariolatry**.)

Hypostatic Union ● Important theological formula that expresses the union of natures, human and divine, within the one Person of Christ. This doctrine, central to Christology, was first expressed by St. Cyril of Alexandria, introduced at the Council of Ephesus (431), and affirmed by the Council of Chalcedon (451).

Icon ● Also eikon or ikon, the name meaning image, used for a religious image or representation, often of Our Lord, the Virgin Mary, or a saint, that is painted upon a flat wooden surface or wall. The icon, which substitutes for statues in the Eastern Church, is deeply revered and can be covered with precious materials, including gold, silver, and pearls.

Iconostasis ● Customarily, the screen (or chancel screen) that is decorated with icons and used to separate the sanctuary of an Eastern Church from the rest of the building. Rows of icons are normally placed upon it.

Idolatry ● In a general sense, the worship of idols, that is, bestowing upon some person or object the worship and devotion that are properly to be given to God alone.

IHS ● Monogram for the name of Our Lord using the first three letters of the word Jesus, derived from the Greek letters *iota*, *eta*, and *sigma*. In the Middle Ages it was translated to mean *"In hoc signo (vinces),"* meaning "By this sign (you will conquer)," or *"Iesus Hominum Salvator"* ("Jesus, Savior of Men"). When written out, IHS should not have periods between the letters.

Imprimatur ● Latin phrase meaning "Let

it be printed" that is bestowed by Church authorities upon certain works to be published. All books of the Sacred Scriptures, including translations, and liturgical books require the formal permission of the Holy See. Other books, such as catechisms, Church history, canon law, theology, and moral instruction that are intended to be used as textbooks must also be approved by a competent ecclesiastical authority. Other works relevant to Church matters but not intended for textbook application are no longer required to secure the imprimatur; nevertheless, they should have the approval of authorities to avoid error and possible scandal. It is to be displayed in the book itself as part of publication.

Indifferentism ● Term with two possible meanings. First, it may refer to the failure or refusal to give worship to God as a result of an unwillingness to recognize one's moral obligation or as a consequence of sloth or acedia (apathy). Second, it may be the increasingly pervasive tendency to regard all religions as relatively true and of the same value.

Indissolubility ● Teaching that Christian marriage is absolutely indissoluble, a bond that cannot be broken by any human power or authority.

Indulgence ● Remission of the temporal punishment for sins and the giving of satisfaction owed to God for one's sins. An indulgence is granted by the Church after the penitent receives absolution through the sacrament of penance or through perfect contrition. Indulgences are of two types, plenary and partial. Plenary indulgences remit all temporal punishments and require that one be free of venial sins; partial indulgences do not. By custom, the indulgence is the remission of punishments that might be imposed upon a person by the early Church in terms of duration of time involved, be it for days, months, years, or the so-called quarantine (a fasting season). It can

be granted by the Church for oneself or the souls in purgatory, never for another living person. The power to grant indulgences is found in the treasure of merits of the saints, Christ himself, and the Virgin Mary. Indulgences were sold from time to time starting from around the late Middle Ages and continuing into the sixteenth century. This was a serious abuse and was the cause of much scandal in the early 1500s. The famous effort of Johann Tetzel to sell indulgences — as part of Pope Julius II's scheme to raise money for the building of St. Peter's — was the occasion of Martin Luther's launching the Reformation. Selling indulgences was forbidden by Pope St. Pius V in 1567.

Institute, Religious ● Title used by the Second Vatican Council, and subsequently in the Revised Code of Canon Law, for any religious order, congregation, or society whose members take a public vow, either perpetual or temporary. In essence, a religious institute is a society of consecrated life that has received the formal approval of Church authorities and whose members take public vows of chastity, poverty, and obedience. Community life is customary for all religious institutes.

Intercommunion ● Reception of the Holy Eucharist by other members of Christian Churches. Specific regulations exist pertaining to the ability of a non-Catholic to receive Communion, as established in the decree of Vatican Council II on ecumenism and the 1972 "Instruction on the Admission of Other Christians to the Eucharist" by Pope Paul VI. As both the Catholic and Orthodox Churches have the same Mass and priesthood by virtue of the apostolic succession, intercommunion among Catholic and Orthodox is permitted by the laws promulgated by Vatican Council II in those cases where there is no church of one's own tradition. Communion is forbidden from other denominations.

Interdict ● Type of ecclesiastical penalty

that prohibits the use of certain sacred privileges, including burial, and certain sacraments. It could be applied to individuals or to the population of a country, region, or parish. It was issued only by the Holy See when it applied to a territory but could be imposed on a parish within a diocese by a bishop. The interdict did not separate those under its jurisdiction from communion with the Church and was not to be confused with excommunication. It was normally imposed for some egregious action against the Church by some of the faithful or an individual, very often a ruler or powerful figure in an area. The interdict was a powerful weapon wielded by the Holy See during the Middle Ages, declining in practical value from the time of the Reformation. In the Revised Code of Canon Law (1983), changes were made in the imposition of interdict so that it applies only to individuals and not to groups or geographical localities. Among the crimes that fall under the incurring of an interdict are assault upon the person of a bishop, the celebration of the Eucharist, and the granting of penance by someone not lawfully a priest.

Katholikon ● Greek name for the principal church used by a monastery of the Byzantine rite. It is the equivalent of the cathedral in the West. The Katholikon also denotes the chief church of the Orthodox patriarch of Jerusalem.

Laicization ● Process by which a cleric is returned by Church authorities to the lay state. The Church notes, however, that while a bishop, priest, or deacon is granted dispensation from his duties as an ordained minister and also his vow of celibacy, he does not lose his sacramental powers and is considered still ordained.

Language of the Church ● Officially recognized liturgical language of the Church. For the Latin or Roman rite, the official language remains Latin. While the vernacular is used throughout the regions following the

Roman rite, Latin is still the language of official pronouncements, important legal documents, and canon law. The Latin Mass, while increasingly hard to find in the United States, is still celebrated and is entirely permissible. The languages of the Eastern Churches are Greek, Arabic, Syriac, Slavonic, and Geez.

Laxism ● Moral system that developed in the seventeenth century. By it, a person is permitted to undertake a particular course of action without concern of incurring sin in those cases where doubts can be raised concerning the morality of an action customarily considered wrong; it thus predisposes action toward liberty. Denounced by Blaise Pascal in the *Lettres Provinciales* (1657), laxism was condemned by Pope Alexander VII in 1665 and 1666 and by Pope Innocent XI in 1679.

Leper Window ● Window found in many churches during the Middle Ages. It was located in the chancel wall and was used by lepers who could hear the Mass from there and also receive alms.

Lutheranism ● Body of doctrines followed by members of the Lutheran Church. First expounded by Martin Luther (d. 1546), Lutheranism was developed over succeeding years and given codification through the Formula of Concord (1577) and especially the Book of Concord (1580). Central to Lutheran teaching is the belief that Scripture is superior to any Church authority, being established as the norm of belief. Accordingly, justification is achieved by faith alone, without the need for good works, this principle based upon Luther's own interpretation of Romans (3:28). While initially intended to reform the Church, Luther's doctrines became one of the most significant elements in the religious division of Europe through the Protestant Reformation. The formation of the Lutheran Church in an organized sense was followed by the establishment of local Lutheran churches as the state religion, most notably in Germany and Scandinavia. Lutheranism then spread around the world. The World Lutheran Federation was founded in 1947. The Lutheran-Catholic Dialogue of the last decades has been a by-product of the ecumenical movement in the years after Vatican II.

Magisterium ● Teaching authority of the Church as invested in the bishops in communion with the supreme pontiff, the successor of St. Peter.

Magnificat ● Canticle of the Blessed Virgin, which begins with the phrase *Magnificat anima mea Dominum* (My soul does magnify the Lord). It was spoken by Mary when she visited Elizabeth after the Annunciation, an event recorded in Luke (1:46-55).

Mariolatry ● Improper veneration of Mary, more akin to the worship that is reserved to God alone (*latria*). The Church promotes *hyperdulia*, the proper veneration of Mary that is greater than *dulia* (the veneration given to the saints).

Mariology ● Branch of theology that focuses on the Blessed Virgin. It examines her life, virtues, and important role in the economy of salvation. Mariology dates in a formal sense from the 1500s, broadening in the succeeding centuries so that it came to include other Marian topics such as the Immaculate Conception. It was the focus of part of the Second Vatican Council document *Lumen Gentium* ("Dogmatic Constitution on the Church").

Marxism ● Social philosophy developed by Karl Marx (1818-1883), in collaboration with Friedrich Engels (1820-1895); it formed the basis of Communism and relies upon such central concepts as dialectical materialism, economic determinism, the collapse of the capitalist system, the rise of the worker, and the formation of a classless society. It is antithetical in many ways to Catholic teaching and has been condemned repeatedly by the Church.

Metropolitan ● Archbishop who possesses jurisdiction over an ecclesiastical province. He is known as a metropolitan archbishop and is head of a metropolitan archdiocese. He has certain rights over the suffragan bishops of the province and is permitted to wear the pallium at liturgical services within the province.

Middle Ages ● Period in history that is said to have lasted from approximately 476 and the fall of the Roman Empire in the West until the discovery of the New World by Christopher Columbus. The inception date varies, as some prefer to begin the epoch in 378 and the Battle of Adrianople or even earlier.

Miracle ● Event that can be witnessed by the senses but is in apparent contradiction to the laws of nature. The Church recognizes authentic miracles as a clear, visible sign of God's glory, a divine intervention in the sensible world. According to the Church process of canonization, two miracles must be authenticated for beatification, and two more for canonization.

Missiology ● Study and application of the doctrine of the faith in the missionary field. Missiology helps prepare the missionary (missioner) for the difficult and often dangerous task of serving in the Catholic missions around the world. Among the current trends in missiology are the study of language, history, and anthropology, aside from extensive preparation in systematic and pastoral theology, regulations and customs in the missionary field, and the history of the Church's missionary endeavors.

Missionary ● Individual who is charged by the Church with carrying out mission activity, that is, the promotion of the faith in regions where the Gospel needs to be preached. Also termed a missioner, the missionary may be a religious or layperson; each has received a special call to propagate the faith in keeping with the mission given by Christ to his disciples (cf. Mt 28:19, Lk 24:47). Vatican Council II in the document

Ad Gentes ("Decree on the Church's Missionary Activity") emphasized the need for all potential or future missionaries to be fully and properly trained and to be devoted to missiological studies.

Monastery ● Residence of a community of religious, normally applying to either men or women who dwell together in a contemplative environment, sharing in the recitation of the Divine Office. Customarily, the monastery is comprised of a church, cloister, chapter house, refectory, cells, and areas set aside for manual labor or other work. All monasteries must be established with canonical approval, meaning that formal permission was secured for its erection.

Monsignor ● Title given to certain clerics who hold the position of honorary prelates to His Holiness, or protonotary apostolic. By custom, the monsignori (plural) are permitted to wear violet with their cassock, similar to a bishop to indicate their elevated status. Their vestments vary according to the liturgical function and their specific rank. They are addressed as Monsignor or Father while their full title is Reverend Monsignor. It is derived from the Italian for "My Lord."

Motu Proprio ● Latin term meaning "by one's own motion" that is used for certain types of papal documents. A *motu proprio* is written by the personal initiative of the pontiff and is characterized by the term *motu proprio et certa scientia*. It is concerned with some administrative matter or possibly a note of papal favor.

Mystical Body ● Truth of the Church that its head is Christ and its members are its body. This implies a communion with Christ through baptism and a profession of faith, a communion that is mystical in that it is brought about by sanctifying grace, is not visible to the normal perception of the senses, and is bodily because it is physically comprised of members.

National Church ● Collective name given to a church in a specific country (i.e., the French Church or American Church). A National Church can also refer to establishment or certain puppet or so-called "patriotic" churches that have been established in Communist countries (China, for example).

Nationalism ● Cultural and/or political devotion to one's own country; it may manifest itself in heightened appreciation or even rabid loyalty to the cultural, political, linguistic, artistic, or intellectual traditions of a native land. Differentiated from patriotism, nationalism may be characterized by animosity, racism, and hatred toward other peoples. Often, nationalist sentiment may be directed against one people in particular, such as occurred in Nazi Germany against the Jews.

Natural Theology ● Field of study that attempts to delineate that knowledge of God which may be obtained by human reason without the assistance of revelation.

Necromancy ● Practice of attempting to communicate with the dead through various means, often with the ultimate aim of foretelling the future. It was especially proscribed in Jewish law. In modern times, necromancy has been known under the name of spiritism (or spiritualism), a field filled with fraud and deceit that was popular in the nineteenth century.

Neoplatonism ● Broad philosophical system first developed by Plotinus (c. A.D. 205-270) and his successors; it is considered the last of the great Greco-Roman philosophies. Inspired by Platonism from which it derived its name, the Neoplatonists attempted to develop the philosophical basis for a moral life, relying upon a pervasive sense of the religious while rejecting the teachings of the Stoics and Epicureans. Their teachings stressed the mystical and the antimaterialistic, advocating the idea of the transcendent One, or Unity, from whom all things in the universe proceeded through a series of emanations. The Neoplatonists first organized themselves in Alexandria; their system gradually spread across the Roman Empire, coming to Rome where Plotinus himself taught for a number of years. The foremost Neoplatonists were Iamblichus, Porphyry, Proclus, and Hypatia. The school virtually disappeared after the closing of the pagan academies by Emperor Justinian I in 529. Many Neoplatonists were ardent opponents of Christianity, but the widespread influence of the school on the Roman world made possible its impact on Christian thought, an influence visible in the works of St. Augustine and Pseudo-Dionysius.

Nominalism ● Theory of knowledge in philosophy that denies the existence of universals; it is in sharp disagreement with realism. It was first advanced in early form by Roscellinus and then in a modified form by Peter Abelard. This nominalism was largely aimed against the Platonists, who held that universals were real and had a separate existence. A new type of nominalism was proposed by William of Occam in the 1300s. He argued that universals existed only in the mind. In the development of this concept, nominalism came to reduce the attributes of God and to limit severely the application of reason in the demonstration of the existence of God, including the proof of the First Cause. Nominalism found increasing popularity among philosophers in the late Middle Ages and was a leading element in the decline of Scholasticism and the rise of Renaissance philosophy.

Novice ● Individual undergoing the novitiate, meaning a period of training for one preparing to enter a religious order.

Nun ● In a general sense, a member of a religious institute of women living under the vows of chastity, poverty, and obedience. Properly, a nun is a woman religious who has taken solemn vows, residing in a cloistered community. It is commonly used for any kind of religious woman, called a sister.

Nunciature ● Official residence and offices of a nuncio, pro-nuncio, or internuncio. It is analogous to an embassy.

Oblate ● From the Latin *oblatus* (offered), which originally designated those children who were sent to a monastery with the intention of remaining there to study and be raised by the monks. In modern usage, it can refer to a layperson who is not a full religious but who is united to a religious order by simple vows.

Occultism ● Derived from the Latin meaning "concealed" (or "hidden"). It is the study of esoteric or hidden subjects and the performance of associated practices for the purposes of acquiring supernatural, preternatural, or divine knowledge, foreknowledge, or personal power. Among the fields of study included in the broad definition of occultism are astrology, tarot, palmistry, ouija boards, rune casting, and a host of other divinatory techniques. There are also highly developed systems of thought devoted to the study of esoteric knowledge, such as Theosophy, Rosicrucianism, Wicca, Satanism, Voodoo, Witchcraft (of both the Left and Right Hand Paths), and other New Age amalgamations of Buddhism, Hinduism, Tantrism, and pantheistic philosophy. Occultism is enjoying one of its most popular periods, considered by experts to be the result of the diminution of traditional religions and values in contemporary materialistic society. All such practices are condemned by the Church, while acknowledging the possibility of diabolical or supernatural activity in this world.

Office ● Properly the Divine Office, the official daily prayers of the Church. The Office is now called the Liturgy of the Hours. It can also refer to any portion of the Divine Office that might be recited. (See also **Breviary**.)

Ontologism ● Philosophy stating that the human mind is capable of intuitively knowing the Infinite Being; it thus postulates that it is possible to deduce the existence of

God through natural reasoning. The philosophical position first arose in France during the nineteenth century in the efforts of philosophers to produce an alternative to the ideas of Immanuel Kant (1724-1804). The Holy Office in 1861 condemned a set of seven errors pertaining to ontologism.

Ordinariate ● Ecclesiastical jurisdiction that has, like a diocese, spiritual authority over a group of people; unlike a diocese, however, the jurisdiction is personal and is normally not subject to territorial limitations. An example is the military ordinariate.

Ordinary ● Term in Church law that denotes a person who exercises ordinary jurisdiction in the external (and internal) forum over a specified territory. Such ordinaries are the pope (who has unlimited jurisdiction), diocesan bishops, vicars prefect and apostolic, apostolic administrators, prelates nullius, superior generals, abbots, and provincial abbots.

Ordinal ● Guidebook or manual used during the Middle Ages by a priest to familiarize himself with the Divine Office.

Ordination ● Act of consecrating a man to one of the sacred ministries for divine worship and service. It must be conferred by a properly empowered minister. The ordination of a priest to the episcopate is also called consecration.

Our Lady ● One of the honorific titles given to the Virgin Mary. It is often the first part of a longer title such as Our Lady of Fátima or Our Lady of Guadalupe.

Pacifism ● Doctrine stating that all forms of warfare are inherently contrary to the teachings of the Gospels and are thus forbidden. Traditional Church teaching, based heavily in St. Augustine, stipulates that while war is absolutely undesirable, it is permissible and at times necessary to engage in a just war.

Paganism ● Name used for the practice of idol worship or, in a more restricted sense, the worship of deities, as distinguished from monotheism. In a broad definition, paganism may be used for any creed other than Christianity, Islam, and Judaism, although it is more proper today to describe these faiths as non-Abrahamic religions. The official state religion of the Roman Empire was a type of paganism until its effective liquidation by Christianity in the fourth and fifth centuries. A pagan can also be an individual who has abandoned any religious belief.

Palimpsest ● Type of parchment or even a skin or hide of a sheep or goat that has been used to hold writing. A palimpsest, however, is distinguished by the fact that the parchment or hide had upon it previous writing that was scraped off for purposes of economy or practicality. To experts in paleography, the palimpsest can be of enormous value, since very often the earlier writing has not been entirely erased or obliterated and can be read beneath the new characters. In some cases, the earlier messages may predate the second material by centuries.

Pallium ● Band of white wool worn over the shoulders by all metropolitan archbishops and the pope. The pallium is decorated with six black crosses and is made from the wool of two lambs blessed in the Church of St. Agnes in Rome. It is a symbol of union with the Holy See. Pope John Paul I was invested with the pallium at his installation in 1978, and John Paul II adopted the custom.

Pantheism ● Belief that God is in all things and all things are in God. Thus, God and the universe are the same.

Parish ● Territorial division of a diocese with its own church and pastor.

Parousia ● Greek term meaning "arrival" or "presence" that is used to refer to the second coming of Christ. It is explained also as the fulfillment of salvation of man by the revealing of Christ the Savior in all of his glory.

Patristic Theology ● Study of the theological writings and expounding of the

Christian faith by the Fathers of the Church.

Patron Saint ● Saint chosen as a special protector or intercessor for a place, person, church, diocese, ethnic group, organization, or country.

Pectoral Cross ● Cross worn around the neck by the pope, cardinals, archbishops, bishops, and abbots and is customarily suspended by a golden chain or a silken chord. The cross can be made of gold and adorned with precious stones, although there is a wide latitude shown in style, especially for the crosses worn while in a cassock.

Penalty, Ecclesiastical ● See **Censure, Ecclesiastical**.

People of God ● Originally a biblical term that is used to describe the Church. It was popularized by Vatican Council II and can be taken to mean that the Church is comprised of a body of people, with Christ at their head.

Personal Prelature ● Ecclesiastical body established by the Holy See. It has as its purpose the fulfilling of some missionary or pastoral task in a variety of settings and walks of life. Opus Dei is a personal prelature, a sign of deep approval on the part of the pope (John Paul II).

Platonism ● Philosophical system established by Plato (427-347 B.C.). Platonism exercised a profound influence upon Christian thought, especially its concepts of the Idea of the Good, the use of the dialectic, the call for order in society, and especially its promotion of the ability of the human mind to find absolute truth. St. Augustine was heavily influenced by Platonic thought, and many elements of Platonism held sway in theology until the 1200s and the time of St. Thomas Aquinas.

Pontificals ● Special insignia worn by a bishop during a liturgical ceremony, such as the miter, pectoral cross, and crosier. A bishop may not use the pontificals in another diocese without the permission of the local bishop.

Positivism ● School of philosophy rejecting metaphysics and proposing that knowledge is based entirely upon sensory experience and especially the experimental method of modern science. It was first developed by the French philosopher Auguste Comte (1798-1857), who postulated that intellectual inquiry should be restricted to observable facts. Similar ideas were fostered by Frederic Harrison (1831-1923) and Herbert Spencer (1820-1903). A broader understanding of positivism was given form by the so-called Vienna Circle around 1922, receiving the name logical positivism. Much influence was exercised upon its proponents by Ludwig Wittgenstein (1889-1951), but its foremost elucidation was undertaken by the Englishman A. J. Ayer (1910-1989). Positivism argues that reality is ultimately reducible to only those things that can be studied through scientific methods. On this basis, moral norms and even ideas about God are not considered worthy of consideration and are even viewed with disdain. Catholic philosophers accept that positive knowledge is an important, even necessary, part of human knowledge, but attention must be paid to vital transcending questions about existence and reality that a positivist outlook cannot answer.

Pragmatism ● System in philosophy in which it is held that the truth of a proposition is measured by its practical consequences. To the pragmatist, truth is not achievable through pure reason or deduction but is merely the justification of itself through its practical results. Attempts have been made to reconcile pragmatism with Catholic thought, most notably by Maurice Blondel (1861-1949) in his major work *L'Action* (1893). Pragmatism was first developed by C. S. Peirce and advanced by William James, Henri Bergson, and others.

Prebend ● Old name given to a cathedral benefice; its holder was called a prebendary. The name was derived from the custom found in the Middle Ages of dividing up the revenues or endowment of the cathedral among its various chapter members. The name was from the Latin *praebere*, to furnish.

Precept ● Command given to an individual by his or her ecclesiastical superior. It may be a decree by which a person is ordered to do some action or refrain from it.

Prelate ● Name used to denote a cleric with ordinary jurisdiction. Prelates of this kind are, by reason of their office, the pope, cardinals, and bishops; vicars apostolic, abbots nullius, apostolic administrators, and prelates nullius are also prelates, but they retain that dignity only for the duration of holding their particular office if they are not bishops. A prelate may also be of an honorary kind, such as a titular bishop who is a member of the Roman Curia. Other honorary prelates are protonotaries apostolic, honorary prelates of His Holiness, and chaplains of His Holiness. They are addressed as Monsignor or Reverend Monsignor.

Prie-dieu ● Kneeling bench that resembles a kind of desk with a shelf for the arms and a resting place for the knees, often with a cushion. Dating from the seventeenth century, it is intended to assist in private meditations.

Priest ● Member of one of the three orders of ordained ministers in the Church, the priest is a person on whom, through ordination, has been conferred the priesthood.

Prior ● Title for the head of some monastic communities. The prior can also be the assistant to an abbot. The female prior is called a prioress.

Priory ● Monastic house governed by a prior. Such a community may be autonomous (called conventual priory) or dependent upon an abbey or motherhouse (called an obedientiary priory).

Promoter of the Faith ● From the Latin *adjutor fidei*, the title given to a cleric who represents the Church in a case affecting a diocese. He has the task of organizing objections to the case against the Church.

The promoter of the faith is also used for the person who conducts an investigation into the cause of a possible saint; he is also called advocate of God or the "devil's advocate."

Proportionalism ● Position in moral theology that holds to the idea that the moral quality of an action is determined by the amount of evil caused when compared with the amount of good caused by the same act.

Protestantism ● Religious movement originating with the Reformation in the sixteenth century. In a broad sense, it is applied to those Christians who do not recognize the supremacy of the Roman Catholic Church and thus are not members. The major denominations of Protestantism include Baptists, Calvinists, Methodists, Lutherans, Presbyterians, Congregationalists, Episcopalians, and Quakers.

Purgatory ● Condition or place wherein the souls of those who are not yet ready to be admitted to heaven are forced to endure a process of purification from the guilt of their venial sins. The suffering, a temporary and partial alienation from God, is considered proportional to the degree of sinfulness on the part of the individual. The Church teaches that the prayers of the living for those in purgatory may be efficacious.

Pythagoreanism ● Philosophical school established by Pythagoras (c. 582-c. 507 B.C.). The Pythagoreans believed that the essence of all things was rooted in numbers and that everything could be expressed numerically. Deeply mystical and secretive, they were persecuted in Magne Graecia, but many elements of their mystical doctrines were revived in the second century B.C. The chief proponent of Neo-Pythagoreanism was Apollonius of Tyana.

Quadrivium ● One of the divisions, with the *trivium*, of the liberal arts as taught during the Middle Ages. The *quadrivium* consisted of arithmetic, geometry, music, and astronomy.

Rationalism ● Any philosophical system that gives a preeminent place to the application of reason in the attainment of knowledge; it is customarily applied to the philosophers of the 1700s who advocated the idea that human reason was sufficiently capable of discovering truth without the need for divine revelation.

Recension ● Term used in biblical study that means the revision of a text based upon a critical examination of the sources. The recension is undertaken only after considerable study and with a clear, substantial reason for doing so, beyond such reasons as alterations of style or language.

Realism ● In philosophy, the recognition of the objective of God and the world, independent of human knowledge; further, it stipulates that these things are knowable in and of themselves.

Rector ● Term with several meanings: for example, the title of a person in charge of a seminary or college; the head of a church that is neither a parish church nor one used by a religious community and who is restricted in his activities by canon law.

Relativism ● Philosophy denying that there are any absolute truths or norms and that all apparently universal norms are in fact merely programmed responses. Truth according to relativism is entirely dependent upon a variety of factors, including circumstances, time, place, and the person or persons involved in the decision-making process. It is a topic especially discussed in the field of moral theology.

Requiem ● Name long given to the Mass offered for the repose of the faithful departed. It is normally today called a Funeral Mass, Mass for the Dead, or Mass of Christian Burial. The name was derived from the *Introit* (entrance chant) at the Mass for the Dead: *"Requiem aeternam dona eis, Domine"* ("Eternal rest grant unto them, O Lord").

Revelation ● Disclosure by God to humanity of himself, his will, and his purposes. It is accomplished by communication and is recognized by the Church in two forms as delineated by the Council of Trent. There is revelation in written books and revelation in Tradition without writing, traditions "received from the mouth of Christ Himself and from the apostles under dictation of the Holy Spirit."

Rigorism ● Moral system stating that the law must be followed unless a contrary position is morally certain and thus frees one from it. Rigorism was condemned as too harsh.

Rogito ● Official documents certifying the death and formal burial of the pope. The *rogito* include various reports, documents, certifications, and testaments; they are stored in the Vatican Archives.

Roman Catholic ● Name of the Church that was established by Christ and that is carried by all members of the Roman rite. It signifies that the Church and its members are in communion with the Bishop of Rome and recognize that he derives his authority from the primacy of Peter as Vicar of Christ. It came into common usage during the 1500s and the Reformation.

Sacred Writers ● Name given to those persons who authored the books of Holy Scripture. They are considered to have written under the inspiration of the Holy Spirit.

Sacrilege ● Willful, conscious, and deliberate violation of those things and persons that are sacred. Sacrilege is a sin against the virtue of religion and is frequently characterized by violent and brutal destruction, mistreatment or disrespect for those places, objects, and persons declared by the Church to be sacred.

Saints ● Name used by St. Paul for Christians in a general sense (Col 1:2) but which was soon understood to mean those individuals who were notable for their holiness and demonstration of heroic virtue. Such individuals are declared saints through the process of canonization, permitting public veneration and invocation. Their lives and very often their heroic deaths as martyrs are considered witnesses and examples of the Christian faith, which should be honored and emulated by the faithful everywhere.

Scapular ● Garment worn over the head and shoulders consisting of two strips of cloth that can reach to the floor or be of shorter length depending upon the circumstances of its use. It is a symbol of devotion and the yoke of Christ. The scapular is commonly part of a religious habit, but an abbreviated version is worn by laypeople. The most common scapulars are the brown (worn by the Carmelite order), red (the Passion), white (the Holy Trinity), black (the Seven Dolors), and blue (the Immaculate Conception); other scapulars are also worn. In recent years, the scapular medal has become quite popular. It is considered to have the same value as a regular scapular.

Scholastic ● Of or pertaining to Scholasticism. It is also used to refer to a student of Scholasticism.

Schoolmen ● Nickname given to the members of the Scholastic movement who taught in the schools of the Middle Ages. Among the greatest of the Schoolmen were Thomas Aquinas, Bonaventure, John Duns Scotus, and Albertus Magnus.

Scotism ● Name given to the system of theological thought established by John Duns Scotus (1265-1308). It is frequently used in comparison with Thomism.

Scruple ● Fears and dread that sin may have been committed when, in fact, no such transgression occurred. Also known as scrupulosity, it is caused by improper training in moral decision-making, exposure to overly rigorous ascetical practices, and, very often, a certain emotional immaturity or psychological dysfunction.

Secret Societies ● Any of numerous organizations whose members hide the facts of their membership, activities, and practices and whose rites, purposes, and customs are revealed only to the initiated. The Church has banned membership in secret societies throughout its history owing to the reality that such groups are most often involved in programs injurious to both the state and the faith. Among the societies long forbidden to members were the Freemasons, Odd Fellows, and the Knights of Pythias.

Secularism ● Philosophical position that advocates the idea that human existence and our world, space, and time are sufficient of themselves for discussion without need for reference to things eternal, in particular notions of God. It developed in England during the 1800s and was the source of a social movement that has been quite pervasive in modern times. In social action, secularism advocates a total absorption in the easing of material needs and the denial of any concern for the afterlife, or eternity.

Sede Vacante ● Latin phrase meaning "the see is vacant" that is used to describe the interregnum between the death of a pontiff and the election of his successor.

See ● Term used to denote the seat of power, papal or episcopal, possessed by the Bishop of Rome for the entire Church or by a bishop for a particular diocese. The boundaries of an episcopal see are determined by the Holy See.

Seminary ● Ecclesiastical institution of higher learning whose sole purpose is to train young men for the priesthood, the reception of holy orders.

Septuagint ● Translation of the Hebrew OT into Greek.

Soteriology ● Branch of theology that has as its focus the salvific work of Christ. (See also **Christology**.)

Stations of the Cross ● Devotion by which one meditates upon the passion of Christ before fourteen stations, each representing an event in Christ's suffering and death. The stations are also called the Way of the Cross.

Subdeacon ● Onetime major order with priests and deacons that existed in the Church from around the third century until

1972 when the rank was suppressed by order of Pope Paul VI. In some regions the acolyte, who assumed many of the duties of the subdeacon, may be referred to by that title.

Suburbicarian Dioceses ● Seven dioceses surrounding Rome whose titular heads are all cardinal bishops. Today, aside from its titular head, each diocese is administered by an actual bishop. The suburbicarian dioceses are Ostia, Palestrina, Porto-Santa Rufina, Velletri-Segni, Frascati, Albano, and Sabina-Poggio Mireto.

Suffragan Bishop ● Bishop who administers a diocese in a province other than the metropolitan.

Tertiary ● Members of a so-called Third Order, individuals who "lead an apostolic life and strive for Christian perfection while living in the world and who share the spirit of some religious institute under the higher direction of that same institute" (Canon 303). Secular tertiaries do not reside in a community nor wear a habit.

Theism ● Belief in a personal God, as distinguished from atheism. The forms of theism include monotheism, polytheism, and henotheism.

Theologian ● Individual who has received training in the field of theology. The term refers especially to a person who has studied all of theology but who has also specialized in one of the branches of theological expertise: moral theology, mystical theology, pastoral theology, ascetical theology, and dogmatic theology.

Theology ● Greek-based term meaning "the science of God." Of classical origin, it was adopted by Christians and came to be understood by St. Augustine as "reasoning or discourse about the Divinity." It has also been described by the Latin phrase *"fides quaerens intellectum"* ("faith seeking understanding"), eloquently expressed by St. Thomas Aquinas. There are many divisions of Catholic theology, including moral theology,

ecclesiology, dogmatic theology, mystical theology, ascetical theology, and pastoral theology.

Third Orders ● See **Tertiary**.

Thirty-Nine Articles ● Collection of theological positions that were used to form the basis of Anglican dogma. The articles were first issued in 1563, but they had their origins in earlier foundational collections of tenets such as the Ten Articles (1536), the Bishops' Book (1537), and the King's Book (1545), which sought to give order to the position of the Anglican Church. Among the issues discussed were transubstantiation, Holy Scripture, and predestination, but the articles were composed in such a masterfully ambiguous fashion that a wide latitude was possible in interpretation.

Tithe ● Portion of one's money or income that is given by an individual to support the Church. It is based on the Jewish law as established in Leviticus (27:30) requiring a tithe of all animals, plants, and produce to be given to God.

Titular See ● See now existing in name only that is given to those bishops who do not occupy what is called a residential see. Titular sees are taken from those dioceses that existed at one time and were lost or destroyed over the centuries, such as those of Asia Minor and North Africa, which were ended by the Islamic conquests. Auxiliary bishops, coadjutors, vicars apostolic, and members of the Curia raised to episcopal dignity are all given titular sees.

Toleratus ● See **Vitandus**.

Tonsure ● Practice of shaving the head or part of the hair to signify the entrance of an individual into the clerical state. It was not part of the rite of holy orders but was considered a preparatory act to it. Originating in the fourth and fifth centuries, the custom of tonsure varied from the snipping of the hair in portions on the sides, front and back, to the leaving of a ring of hair or even shaving off all of the hair.

Traducianism ● Heretical teaching

propagated in the fifth century. It held that the souls of offspring were somehow generated or derived from the souls of their parents. Traducianism was condemned by Pope St. Anastasius II (r. 496-498).

Triptych ● Three panels painted and joined together by several hinges. The middle panel, normally the largest, was depicted a major event in the life of Christ, Our Lady, or some saint. During the Middle Ages, the triptych was hung above the high altar. (See also **Diptych**.)

Ubiquitarianism ● Teaching held by Martin Luther that Christ in his human nature is present everywhere. This idea was defended in his writings on the Eucharist and to uphold his view on the Real Presence of Christ.

Usury ● Sin that involves the charging of excessive interest on the loan of money. It was initially forbidden and was understood to mean the taking of interest on any loan, a prohibition of Jewish origin that was retained by the early Church. The Councils of Carthage (348) and Aix (789) placed restrictions upon even laymen profiting from a loan, and later councils repeated this teaching, although Jews were allowed to charge interest. This practice made them important sources for banking and commercial enterprise, but it also added to the sentiment of anti-Semitism in Europe. With the rise of modern banking and commerce, the charging of interest was tolerated, so long as it was not exorbitant (usurious).

Venerable ● Rank bestowed upon those proved to the satisfaction of Church authorities to have lived the cardinal and theological virtues to a heroic degree. Martyrs are also honored with the title "Venerable" (abbreviated "Ven.").

Veneration of Saints ● Devotion paid to the saints of the Church. In theology, there is a clear distinction made between the veneration paid to saints (called *dulia*), and the worship and adoration given to God (*latria*). See also **Hyperdulia** and **Icon**.

Vespers ● Evening prayer, considered, with Lauds, one of the most important hours of the Divine Office. It is now customarily known as Evening Prayers.

Vicar ● Title borne by a cleric who takes the place of another in the fulfillment of some duty or the exercise of authority as stipulated by canon law. There are various types of vicars, including vicars apostolic, vicars-general, and vicars parochial.

Vicariate, Apostolic ● Term for a territory that, for whatever reason, does not possess full diocesan status. Customarily, the vicariate is established in mission territories out of the apostolic prefecture, the early status for mission organization.

Virginity ● Evangelical counsel that entails the maintaining of sexual abstinence or integrity. This may be of a physical or moral nature and is considered to be of intent or fact. The practice of virginity is rooted in love, love of God alone. It was practiced from the earliest times of the Church, and great honor was paid to those men and especially those women who chose to remain in a virginal state for the love of Christ.

Vitandus ● One of the two states of excommunication as delineated by the 1917 Code of Canon Law. The person who was *vitandus* was not to be associated with in any way by other members of the Church, as compared to a person who was *toleratus*. In the revised Code of 1983, there was no distinction made between excommunicants and the state of *vitandus* was no longer mentioned.

Vocation ● Term used for the call received by an individual to the religious life. In a broad sense, the vocation implies the universal call of the Church to holiness.

Voluntarism ● Doctrine that teaches the primacy of the will. This can be used to advance the idea of the precedence of God's will over his intellect, implying, according to Bl. John Duns Scotus, that goodness and truth are such because of an active decision on the part of God. It also implies that the human will has precedence over human reason and is what makes a person distinctly human. To Kant, voluntarism meant that the will made the determination for an individual of what was morally right and wrong.

Vulgate ● Name given to the Latin translation of the Bible. The chief work of the translation was undertaken by St. Jerome at the request of Pope Damasus I in 382. The term is derived from the Latin *vulgata* (meaning "common" or "popular").

Index

Dominic Loricatus 324
Dominic Savio 468
Dominican Order 41, 42, 57, 92, 131, 156, 161, 258, 271, 341, 414, 430, 445, 494, 706, 801, 840, 848, 890, 901
Dominici, Giovanni 273
Dominus Ac Redemptor 210, 273, 456
Domitian 205, 215, 273, 367, 461, 719, 727, 810, 845
Domitilla, Flavia 139, 173, 273, 367, 441, 727
Donatello 42
Donation of **Constantine** 273, 620, 805, 843, 880; **Pepin** 274, 327, 442, 620, 795
Donatism 35, 81, 90, 249, 274, 398, 600, 616, 644
Dorothy 274, 948
Douai-Reims Bible 128, 275, 539
Drexel, Katherine 275
Dreyfus Affair 496
Dryden, John 490
Du Cange, Charles 276
Dubois, Jean-Antoine 276
Dubois, Guillaume 432, 815
Ducaeus, Fronto 276
Duchesne, Louis 277, 433, 563
Duke of Wellington 294, 581, 715, 788
Dulia 969, 972, 975, 984
Dunstan 54, 277, 283, 290, 367
Dupanloup, Felix 277, 278
Duperron, Jacques 278, 574
Durandus of Troarn 278

E

Easter 29, 66, 200, 210, 246, 251, 261, 289, 290, 305, 462, 465, 501, 587, 624, 642-644, 683, 713, 765, 785, 815, 875, 892, 906, 911, 969
Easter Controversy 279, 762, 907
Eastern Catholic Churches 152, 190, 279, 280, 282, 283, 536, 604, 739, 858, 862, 863, 939, 960
Eastern Schism 151, 152, 280, 607, 626, 756
Ebbo 258, 280
Ecclesiam Suam 280, 633, 952
Ecclesiastical Penalty 970, 973
Ecclesiology 969, 983
Eck, Johann 281, 309, 705, 710-712, 923
Eckhart, Meister 258, 281, 371, 696, 801, 813, 956
Ecstasy 178, 541, 659, 798, 969
Ecumenical Council(s) 78, 189, 214, 218, 220, 225, 228, 233, 282, 296, 308, 467, 501, 523, 586, 593, 596, 598, 665, 666, 809, 812, 850, 877, 901, 947
Ecumenism 65, 282, 283, 477, 478, 553, 633, 863, 867, 940, 960, 973
Edict of **Beaulieu** 716; **Milan** 226, 264, 457, 540, 550, 558, 728; **Nantes** 39, 140, 317, 323, 328, 329, 416, 431, 494, 579, 712, 716; **Restitution** 318, 718, 831; **Toleration** 326, 550; **Worms** 922
Edmund of Abingdon 283
Edmund Rich 283
Edmund the Martyr 948

Edward the **Confessor** 34, 290, 913; **Martyr** 277, 283
Egbert 188, 913
Egbert (archbishop) 283, 299, 300
Ehrle, Franz 258
Einhard 191, 284, 879, 906
El Castillo Interior 818
El Greco 709
Eleutherius 128, 265, 284, 438, 892, 931
Elias of Cortona 285, 334, 391, 790
Elizabeth I 53, 77, 138, 141, 275, 285, 287, 292, 294, 390, 391, 397, 436, 533, 541, 668, 690, 695, 707, 748, 800, 811, 854, 862, 907, 963
Elizabeth of Hungary 155, 223, 287, 948
Elizabethan Settlement 286, 287, 292
Elmo 287, 651
Emser, Hieronymius 288
Emser Punktation 287, 612
Encyclical(s) 21, 24, 34, 76, 114, 128, 130, 179, 185, 217, 222, 230, 264, 267, 268, 280, 288, 295, 302, 330, 351, 352, 360, 361, 364, 374, 416, 417, 458, 460, 467, 477, 478, 492, 493, 496, 498, 508, 511, 512, 515, 528, 534, 544, 552, 556, 563, 564, 570, 578, 582, 608, 612, 620, 622, 633, 672, 674-677, 685-687, 695, 697, 698, 717, 718, 733, 741, 752, 783, 784, 788, 804, 812, 836, 857, 860, 866, 867, 877, 884, 885, 950, 955, 959
Encyclopedists 256, 288, 289
Enlightenment 37, 116, 256, 288, 293-295, 339, 341, 360, 399, 456, 569, 582, 788
Ennodius 295, 778, 953
Ephraem 128, 296, 297, 414, 424, 946
Episcopalians 969, 970, 980
Epistemology 970
Epistle(s) of **James** 125, 446, 579; **John** 461; **Jude** 125; **Peter** 481
Epistle(s) to **Philemon** 657; **Timothy** 844, 845; **Titus** 844, 846
Epistle to the **Ephesians** 215; **Galatians** 91, 344; **Hebrews** 125, 392; **Philippians** 683; **Romans** 742, 786
Erasmus 94, 651
Erasmus, Desiderius 217, 297, 298, 321, 483, 520, 574, 682, 708, 710, 854, 878, 929
Erastianism 298, 479
Erastus 298
Eskil of Lund 298
Estates General 299, 658, 722, 791
Etchegaray, Roger 331
Ethelbert 89, 163, 164, 299
Ethelbert of York 299, 300
Ethelburga 638
Ethelhard 300
Ethelwold 34
Etheria 20, 664
Ethiopian Church 301, 343
Eucharist 36, 65, 78, 119, 120, 132, 161, 205, 218, 221, 234, 257, 261, 262, 266, 278, 301, 302, 318, 383, 448, 470, 477, 478, 499, 523, 531, 623, 624, 637, 643, 680, 691, 698,

705, 706, 712, 716, 724, 740, 742, 810, 829, 850, 851, 854, 903, 921, 924, 950, 952, 966, 970, 973, 974, 984
Eudes II 202, 302, 470, 602, 741
Eudists 124, 302, 470, 471
Eugenius I 302, 901, 932
Eugenius II 303, 879, 917
Eugenius III 83, 121, 203, 303, 356, 403, 703, 892, 918
Eugenius IV 40, 42, 58, 63, 72, 108, 148, 157, 188, 218, 303, 316, 318, 336, 355, 473, 495, 510, 589, 590, 666, 690, 848, 850, 886
Eunomianism 35, 66, 67, 304
Eunomius 304, 383, 660
Eusebians 304, 306
Eusebius 304, 305
Eusebius of **Caesarea** 22, 27, 200, 266, 305-307, 410, 441, 446, 451, 480, 493, 524, 545, 577, 587, 616, 647, 660, 687, 736, 784, 785, 812, 815, 816, 825, 833, 846, 953; **Dorylaeum** 305, 307; **Emesa** 305; **Nicomedia** 79, 226, 304, 306, 518, 524, 587; **Samosata** 306; **Vercelli** 306
Eustace 94, 948
Eustathius of **Antioch** 79, 307, 953; **Sebaste** 307
Eustochium 311, 451, 637
Eustochium, Julia 307
Eutyches 189, 266, 305, 307, 322, 323, 354, 504, 570, 650, 847
Eutychianism 230, 266, 307, 606, 825
Eutychianus 155, 307, 308
Evagrius Ponticus 308, 615
Evangelization 27, 135, 136, 143, 147, 151, 185, 195, 199, 216, 289, 326, 356, 377, 484, 558, 583, 760, 796, 801, 808, 833, 901, 940, 970
Evaristus 46, 308, 931
Eve — See Adam
Evodius, Stephen 537
Ex **Cathedra** 427, 970; **Quo Singulare** 116
Excommunication 23, 61, 75, 104, 137, 147, 148, 158, 183, 230, 240, 281, 287, 292, 298, 304, 306, 308, 316, 322, 323, 340, 341, 378, 396, 412, 429, 432, 477, 499, 538, 550, 590, 631, 642, 711, 715, 733, 756, 776, 796, 806, 811, 822, 826, 857, 874, 919, 922, 923, 928, 967, 970, 974, 984
Exegesis 22, 91, 157, 158, 232, 415, 417, 564, 721, 846, 895, 970, 972
Exemption 109, 308, 425, 728, 830, 970, 971
Existentialism 702, 971
Exorcism 308, 402, 971
Exsecrabilis 218, 308
Exsurge Domine 156, 281, 309, 522, 711

F

Faber, Frederick 310, 611
Faber, Johannes 310, 929
Faber, Peter 41, 454
Fabian 232, 253, 310, 595, 684, 931
Fabiola 310, 311, 414, 616, 920
Facundus 311

Otto of **Brunswick** 339, 872; **Freising** 610, 611, 652, 691, 733
Ottoman Empire 855, 856
Our Lady of **Africa** 911; **the Angels** 687; **the Assumption** 957; **Banneux** 100; **Bethlehem** 124; **Charity** 470, 471; **the Conception** 474; **Czestochowa** 957; **Fátima** 313, 978; **Gethsemane** 553; **Guadalupe** 386, 555, 957, 978; **High Grace** 957; **La Salette** 500; **Loreto** 517; **Lourdes** 231; **Lujan** 957; **Mercy** 552; **Montjoie** 560; **Mt. Carmel** 167, 957; **the Poor, the Sick, and the Indifferent** 100; **the Rosary** 313; **the Rotunda** 136; **the Snows** 749; **Sorrows** 957; **Victory** 668
Oxford Movement 53, 65, 66, 142, 257, 294, 529, 585, 586, 611, 909, 919
Ozanam, Antoine 611, 898

P
Pacca, Bartolomeo 612
Pacelli, Marcantonio 675
Pacem in Terris 264, 467, 608, 612, 952, 959
Pacheco, Alphonsus 242
Pacifism 978
Padilla, Juan de 864
Padre Pio 664, 798
Paganism 38, 57, 69, 135, 177, 184, 245, 256, 321, 421, 458, 484, 698, 826, 828, 978
Pagi, Antoine 613
Pagninus, Santes 613
Paine, Thomas 341
Palamas, Gregory 400, 613
Palatine Guard 387, 614, 618
Palestine 106, 138, 141, 151, 167, 183, 184, 210, 216, 237, 238, 240, 241, 305, 306, 311, 333, 384, 394, 401, 441, 451, 452, 517, 524, 525, 560, 605, 606, 615, 636, 687, 765, 786, 822, 828, 918
Palladius 181, 435, 615, 627, 943
Pallavicino, Pietro 615, 751
Pallium 283, 298, 300, 316, 392, 475, 510, 526, 537, 616, 617, 626, 725, 766, 807, 821, 918, 975, 978
Pammachius 616
Panormitanus 591
Pantheism 281, 478, 672, 735, 790, 804, 978
Papacy 19, 23-25, 28, 30-33, 42, 47, 60, 66, 70, 71, 83, 93, 95, 97, 107, 113, 114, 119, 134, 136-138, 145, 146, 148, 151, 156, 157, 159, 161, 176, 179, 180, 182, 187, 191, 192, 196, 206-209, 218, 219, 225, 229, 234, 236, 241, 243, 262, 264, 267, 269, 273, 284, 285, 287, 290-292, 314, 315, 318, 328, 330, 338-340, 347-350, 353, 357, 358, 360, 369, 375, 376, 377, 380, 386, 387, 391, 395, 407-409, 412, 418, 426, 428, 430, 432, 434, 441-443, 454, 455, 458, 459, 462, 464, 470, 472, 483, 484, 500, 504, 505, 507, 508, 510, 522, 526, 539, 542, 544, 547, 551, 560, 565, 581, 582, 585, 589, 590, 608, 610, 614, 616-618, 621, 622,

628, 629, 631, 642, 658, 662, 664, 665, 670-672, 675, 677, 683-685, 689, 690, 695, 703, 708-710, 713, 724, 725, 731, 732, 738, 746, 751-753, 757, 764, 767, 772, 773, 777, 779, 780, 788, 794-796, 805, 806, 822, 856, 860-862, 867, 870-872, 881-883, 886, 888, 890, 892, 893, 894, 896, 910, 916, 924, 926, 927, 929, 936, 944
Papal **Coronation** 232, 236, 475, 616, 685; **Crown** 842; **Decorations** 198, 254, 617, 618; **Elections** 23, 166, 375, 381, 416, 463, 464, 501, 588, 616, 618, 633, 795; **Flag** 618; **Knights** 618; **Legate** 23, 27, 30, 32, 40, 42, 44, 47, 63, 69, 76, 109, 137, 156, 240, 246, 271, 283, 298, 404, 413, 431, 437, 484, 499, 526, 555, 575, 589, 590, 594, 618, 619, 630, 667, 680, 682, 690, 694, 708, 723, 768, 770, 784, 801, 821, 849, 858, 869, 871, 873, 922; **Letters** 147, 148, 233, 254, 311, 619, 620; **States** 45, 71, 85, 111, 116, 137, 151, 208, 209, 215, 224, 225, 267, 269, 274, 327, 329, 340, 380-382, 387, 407, 409, 429, 430, 432, 442, 443, 483, 497, 500, 501, 507, 539, 581, 589, 608, 612, 617, 619-621, 623, 627, 628, 655, 667, 669, 671, 672, 720, 723, 724, 731, 732, 735, 763, 782, 791, 794, 795, 846, 847, 861, 870, 873, 874, 878, 888, 889, 893, 950
Paris 19, 20, 25, 28, 29, 37, 39, 42, 43, 47, 49, 56, 57, 60, 63, 66, 68, 78, 82, 83, 95, 97, 100, 103, 120, 128, 133-135, 140, 141, 145-147, 149, 158, 160, 164, 176, 190, 193, 201, 213, 218, 223, 224, 233, 236, 251, 252, 253, 258, 259, 261, 265, 271-273, 276-278, 281, 283, 297, 299, 312, 317, 319, 323-326, 328, 330-332, 334, 335, 347, 348, 350, 353, 354, 356, 357, 362, 364, 366-370, 372, 379, 383, 385, 388, 390, 391, 397, 400, 404, 412, 415, 416, 423, 429, 433, 444, 448, 450, 452, 454, 465, 467, 468, 470, 472, 473, 478, 492-496, 498, 499, 508, 509, 515, 518, 527, 530, 533, 534, 538, 543, 545, 553, 557, 570, 572, 574, 575, 580, 581, 590, 591, 594, 595, 598, 599, 604, 610, 622, 624, 640, 645, 650-653, 656, 662, 665, 666, 670, 688, 696, 698, 699, 703, 704, 716-718, 721, 725, 726, 728, 736, 743, 744, 772, 774-778, 785, 791, 797, 799, 800, 810, 811, 813, 815, 831, 835-837, 840, 843, 854, 858, 863, 868, 876, 897-899, 901-903, 914, 915, 918, 919, 926
Paris, Matthew 124, 200, 568, 908
Parker, Matthew 285, 292
Parousia 978
Parsons, Roger 77
Pascal, Blaise 329, 449, 456, 553, 591, 621, 622, 693, 747, 902, 974
Pascendi Dominici Gregis 498, 564, 622, 674, 857, 950
Paschal I 181, 280, 303, 622, 879, 933

Paschal II 156, 353, 379, 395, 411, 559, 566, 623, 771, 806, 843, 934
Paschal III (antipope) 71, 157, 339, 703, 894
Paschal Baylon 623
Paschal Controversy 279, 587
Paschal Vigil 813
Paschasius Radbertus 120, 478, 623, 702, 705, 778
Passion Plays 624, 625, 678
Passionists 624, 637
Pastor Aeternus 427, 883
Patriarch of Constantinople 22, 23, 32, 33, 36, 50, 61, 87, 99, 136, 148, 181, 189, 228, 302, 307, 316, 318, 322, 373, 383, 402, 411-413, 418, 428, 429, 463, 526, 534, 550, 556, 570, 583, 587, 588, 597, 607, 626, 652, 661, 756, 767, 780, 796, 812, 822, 827, 847, 855, 878, 890, 901
Patriarchate of Jerusalem 453, 626
Patrick 81, 143, 145, 356, 367, 435, 615, 626, 627, 943, 949, 957
Patrimonium Petri; *also* Patrimony of St. Peter 30, 376, 378, 620, 627
Patriotic Association of Chinese Catholics 180, 196, 627
Patristic Theology 978
Paul I 628, 933
Paul II 21, 33, 130, 154, 355, 531, 628, 677, 779, 781, 822, 936
Paul III 63, 229, 254, 321, 364, 380, 399, 423, 433, 443, 454, 484, 496, 557, 575, 628-630, 667, 682, 709, 712, 713, 732, 742, 745, 778, 783, 850, 851, 875, 882, 937
Paul IV 155, 161, 297, 380, 385, 413, 425, 443, 458, 575, 614, 629, 630, 667, 668, 683, 709, 736, 742, 782, 820, 873, 937
Paul IV (patriarch) 812
Paul V 112, 171, 331, 379, 381, 423, 488, 511, 602, 630, 725, 745, 746, 751, 798, 833, 873, 876, 890, 900, 905, 937
Paul VI 21, 30, 65, 67, 130, 159, 160, 163, 166, 172, 179, 211, 218, 219, 222, 230, 243, 280, 282, 313, 326, 416, 425, 427, 433, 467, 471, 475-477, 491, 492, 503, 512, 521, 562, 571, 585, 603, 607, 608, 614, 617, 618, 626, 631, 649, 656, 668, 677, 679, 684-686, 712, 738, 741, 757, 769, 770, 784, 808, 812, 816, 818, 843, 882, 885, 887, 921, 938, 939, 940, 946, 952, 959, 973, 983
Paul of **Samosata** 384, 587, 634, 637; **Tarsus** 634, 728, 752; **the Cross** 443, 624, 637
Paul the **Deacon** 46, 638; **Hermit** 637
Paula 307, 311, 451, 637
Paulianists 634
Paulicians 422, 637
Paulinus of **Aquileia** 320, 638; **Nola** 61, 93, 236, 326, 638, 800, 954; **York** 638
Paulists 59, 819
Paulus Diaconos 638
Peace of **Alais** 416, 722; **Augsburg** 88, 89, 192, 242, 359, 631, 639, 711, 712, 831; **Catabellotta** 771; **the**